ISC Exams 2026

AF819604

All in One®

Physics

Class 12

Simplified Theory

Topic & Chapter Exercises

Exam Pattern Questions

Specimen & Sample Papers

Author

Keshav Mohan (M.Sc.)

arihant

SUCCESS AND NOTHING LESS

arihant
SUCCESS AND NOTHING LESS

ARIHANT PRAKASHAN
(School Division Series)

卐 ADMINISTRATIVE & PRODUCTION OFFICES

Regd. Office

'Ramchhaya' 4577/15, Agarwal Road, Darya Ganj, New Delhi -110002
Tele: 011- 47630600, 43518550; Fax: 011 23200316

卐 Head Office

Kalindi, TP Nagar, Meerut (UP) - 250002, Tel: 0121-7156203, 7156204

卐 SALES & SUPPORT OFFICES

Agra, Ahmedabad, Bengaluru, Bareilly, Chennai, Delhi, Guwahati, Hyderabad, Jaipur, Jhansi, Kolkata, Lucknow, Nagpur & Pune.

PO No : TXT-XX-XXXXXXX-X-XX

Published By Arihant Publications (India) Ltd.

For further information about the books published by Arihant, log on to www.arihantbooks.com or e-mail at info@arihantbooks.com

Follow us on

卐 PRICE ₹590.00

PRODUCTION TEAM

Publishing Managers: Mahendra Singh Rawat & Keshav Mohan
Cover Designer: Salman Shaikh
Inner Designer: Ankit Tyagi
Project Head: Yojna Sharma
Page Layouting: Subhash Chaprana
Proof Reader: Manshi, Amit

Index *cum* Study Planner

One Book- Endless Features

to Help you Succeed

In this Chapter

At the start of each chapter, all the topics of the chapter have been listed, so that students may know what they are going to study.

CHAPTER

02

Electrostatic Potential and Capacitance

The degree of electrification of a body is represented by the electrostatic potential of the charged body. The direction of flow of charge between two charged bodies placed in contact with each other is determined by electrostatic potential.

- Electrostatic Potential, Electrostatic Potential Difference and Electrostatic Potential Energy
- Dielectric and Capacitance

Example 1 Potential at a point P in space is given as 3×10^5 V. Find the work done in bringing a charge of 2×10^{-6} C from infinity to the point P. Does the answer depend on the path along which the charge is brought?

Sol. Given,

Potential at the point P,

$$V = 3 \times 10^5 \text{ V},$$

charge, $q_0 = 2 \times 10^{-6}$ C

Work done in bringing the charge from infinity to the point P is

Complete Theory in Each Chapter

Each chapter has Complete, Easy to Understand and Simplified theory covering latest syllabus and latest NCERT Textbook. Theory is developed in such a way that it is Suitable for all typer of learners.

Solved Examples

To explain the application of concept, Solved Examples have been given in between the theory. These examples have been solved in Step-by-Step manner, so that students can learn the problem solving process completely.

TOPIC 01 **Electrostatic Potential, Electrostatic Potential Difference and Electrostatic Potential Energy**

The electrostatic potential at any point in the region of electric field is equal to the amount of work done in bringing a unit positive test charge (without acceleration) from infinity to that point.

$$\therefore \quad \text{Electrostatic potential } (V) = \frac{\text{Work done } (W)}{\text{Charge } (q_0)}$$

It is a scalar quantity. Its SI unit is volt (V) and 1V = 1 J/C and its dimensional formula is $[ML^2T^{-3}A^{-1}]$.

Work done ($[W_\infty]_{ext}$) by an external force in bringing (without acceleration) a unit positive charge from infinity to a point is equal to the potential (V) at that point,

Topic Practice 1

Multiple Choice Questions

(1 Mark)

1. In figure, shown the work done on a test charge q by the electrostatic field due to any given charge configuration is depends

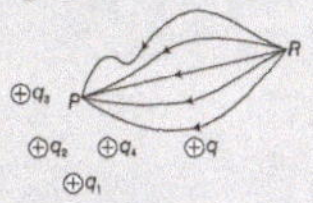

(a) on the path followed
(b) on its final and initial positions
(c) Both (a) and (b)
(d) Neither (a) nor (b)

Topical Exercises

To make students understand the chapter in a smooth part-by-part manner, Topical Exercises have been given in each chapter. These Exercises help students to assess the understanding of related concepts at regular interval.

One Book- Endless Features

to Help you Succeed

Chapter Practice

The students can check their understanding of the chapter through Chapter Practice given at the end of each chapter.

Chapter Practice

Very Short Answer Type Questions
(2 Marks)

1 Check whether the relation R, defined in the set {1, 2, 3, 4, 5, 6} as $R = \{(a, b) : b = a + 1\}$, is reflexive, symmetric or transitive. [NCERT]

2 Let N be the set of natural numbers and relation R on N be defined by $R = \{(x, y) : x, y \in N, x + y = 10\}$. Then, check whether R is reflexive, symmetric and transitive.

3 Show that the function $f : R \to R$, $f(x) = x^4$ is many-one and into.

4 Show that the function $f : Z \to Z$ defined by $f(x) = x^2 + x$, is a many-one function.

Short Answer Type Questions
(4 Marks)

11 If $A = \{1, 2, 3, 4\}$, define relations on A which have properties of being
(i) reflexive, transitive but not symmetric.
(ii) symmetric but neither reflexive nor transitive. [NCERT Exemplar]

12 Show that relation R in the set of real numbers, defined as $R = \{(a, b) : a \le b^2\}$ is neither reflexive nor symmetric nor transitive. [NCERT]

13 Check whether the relation R defined in the set A of human beings in a city at particular time as $R = \{(x, y) : x$ is wife of $y\}$, is reflexive, symmetric and transitive. [NCERT]

ISC EXAMINATION PAPER 2025

PHYSICS (Fully Solved)

Time : 3 hours | Max. Marks : 70

General Instructions
1. This paper is divided into four **Sections- A, B, C** and **D**. Answer all questions.
2. **Section A** consists of one question having Fourteen sub-parts of one mark each.
3. **Section B** consists of seven questions of two marks each.
4. **Section C** consists of nine questions of three marks each.
5. **Section D** consists of three questions of five marks each.
6. Internal choices have been provided in two questions each in Section B, Section C and Section D.

Section-A [14 Marks]

1. (A) In questions (i) to (vii) given below, choose the correct alternative (a), (b), (c) or (d).

(i) When a battery is connected between the terminals P and Q, as shown in figure below, it is found that no current flows through 5 Ω resistor. Then, the value of resistor X is [1]

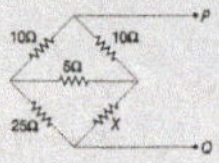

(a) 10 Ω (b) 20 Ω
(c) 25 Ω (d) 45 Ω

(ii) The relative permeability of substance X is slightly less than one and that of substance 'Y' is slightly more than one. Then, [1]
(a) X is paramagnetic and Y is ferromagnetic.
(b) X is diamagnetic and Y is ferromagnetic.
(c) X is paramagnetic and Y is diamagnetic.
(d) X is diamagnetic and Y is paramagnetic.

(iii) If kinetic energy of moving electrons is made four times, then their de-Broglie wavelength becomes [1]
(a) eight times
(b) four times
(c) two times
(d) half

Sample Question Papers & Latest ISC Specimen Paper

Chapterwise study is not the only feature of this book, after the Chapterwise Study it has a supplement of **3 Sample Question Papers** and **Latest ISC Specimen Paper.**

SAMPLE QUESTION PAPER 1

A Highly Simulated Sample Question Paper for ISC Class XII

PHYSICS (Fully Solved)

Time : 3 hours | Max. Marks : 70

General Instructions
1. This paper is divided into four **Sections-A, B, C** and **D.** Answer all questions.
2. **Section A** consists of one question having Fourteen sub-parts of one mark each.
3. **Section B** consists of seven questions of two marks each.
4. **Section C** consists of nine questions of three marks each.
5. **Section D** consists of three questions of five marks each.
6. Internal choices have been provided in two questions each in Section B, Section C and Section D.

ISC SPECIMEN PAPER 2025

PHYSICS (Fully Solved)

Time : 3 hours | Max. Marks : 70

General Instructions
1. This paper is divided into four **Sections- A, B, C** and **D.** Answer all questions.
2. **Section A** consists of one question having Fourteen sub-parts of one mark each.
3. **Section B** consists of seven questions of two marks each.
4. **Section C** consists of nine questions of three marks each.
5. **Section D** consists of three questions of five marks each.
6. Internal choices have been provided in two questions each in Section B, Section C and Section D.

Previous Year Paper

For complete practice, there is Solved Paper 2025 also given at the end of the book.

Latest Course Structure

There will be two papers in the subject.

Paper I	Theory : 3 Hours	70 Marks
Paper II	Practical : 3 Hours	15 Marks
	Project Work	10 Marks
	Practical File	5 Marks

PAPER I THEORY 70 Marks

There is no overall choice

S. No.	UNIT	TOTAL WEIGHTAGE
1.	Electrostatics	14 Marks
2.	Current Electricity	
3.	Magnetic Effects of Current and Magnetism	16 Marks
4.	Electromagnetic Induction and Alternating Currents	
5.	Electromagnetic Waves	2 Marks
6.	Optics	18 Marks
7.	Dual Nature of Radiation and Matter	7 Marks
8.	Atoms and Nuclei	6 Marks
9.	Electronic Devices	7 Marks
	Total	70 Marks

Note

(i) Unless otherwise specified, only S. I. Units are to be used while teaching and learning, as well as for answering questions.

(ii) All physical quantities to be defined as and when they are introduced along with their units and dimensions.

(iii) Numerical problems are included from all topics except where they are specifically excluded or where only qualitative treatment is required.

1. ELECTROSTATICS

(i) **Electric Charges and Fields** Electric charges; conservation and quantisation of charge, Coulomb's law; superposition principle and continuous charge distribution. Electric field, electric field due to a point charge, electric field lines, electric dipole, electric field due to a dipole, torque on a dipole in uniform electric field.

Electric flux, Gauss's theorem in electrostatics and its applications to find field due to infinitely long straight wire, uniformly charged infinite plane sheet and uniformly charged thin spherical shell.

(a) Coulomb's law, SI unit of charge; permittivity of free space and of dielectric medium. Frictional electricity, electric charges (two types); repulsion and attraction; simple atomic structure-electrons and ions; conductors and insulators; quantization and conservation of electric charge; Coulomb's law in vector form; (position coordinates r_1, r_2 not necessary). Comparison with Newton's law of gravitation; Superposition principle ($\mathbf{F}_1 = \mathbf{F}_{12} + \mathbf{F}_{13} + \mathbf{F}_{14} + \dots$).

(b) Concept of electric field and its intensity; examples of different fields; gravitational, electric and magnetic; Electric field due to a point charge $\mathbf{E} = \mathbf{F}/q_0$ (q_0 is a test charge); $\mathbf{E}$ for a group of charges (superposition principle); a point charge q in an electric field $\mathbf{E}$ experiences an electric force $\mathbf{F}_E = q\mathbf{E}$. Intensity due to a continuous distribution of charge i.e. linear, surface and volume.

(c) Electric lines of force: A convenient way to visualize the electric field; properties of lines of force; examples of the lines of force due to (i) an isolated point charge (+ve and –ve); (ii) dipole; (iii) two similar charges at a small distance;(iv) uniform field between two oppositely charged parallel plates.

(d) Electric dipole and dipole moment; derivation of the $\mathbf{E}$ at a point, (1) on the axis (end on position) (2) on the perpendicular bisector (equatorial i.e. broad side on position) of a dipole, also for $r >> 2l$ (short dipole); dipole in a uniform electric field; net force zero, torque on an electric dipole: $\tau = \mathbf{p} \times \mathbf{E}$ and its derivation.

(e) Gauss's theorem: the flux of a vector field; $Q = vA$ for velocity vector $\mathbf{v} || \mathbf{A}$, $\mathbf{A}$ is area vector. Similarly, for electric field $\mathbf{E}$, electric flux $\phi_E = EA$ for $\mathbf{E}||\mathbf{A}$ and $\phi_E = \mathbf{E} \cdot \mathbf{A}$ for uniform $\mathbf{E}$. For non-uniform field $\phi_E = \int d\phi = \int \mathbf{E} \cdot d\mathbf{A}$. Special cases for $\theta = 0°, 90°$ and $180°$. Gauss's theorem, statement: $\phi_E = q/\varepsilon_0$ or $\phi_E = \oint \mathbf{E} \cdot d\mathbf{A} = q/\varepsilon_0$ where ϕ_E is for a closed surface; q is the net charge enclosed, ε_0 is the permittivity of free space. Essential properties of a Gaussian surface.

Applications: Obtain expression for $\mathbf{E}$ due to 1. an infinite line of charge, 2. a uniformly charged infinite plane thin sheet, 3. a thin hollow spherical shell (inside, on the surface and outside). Graphical variation of E vs r for a thin spherical shell.

(ii) **Electrostatic Potential, Potential Energy and Capacitance** Electric potential, potential difference, electric potential due to a point charge, a dipole and system of charges; equipotential surfaces, electrical potential energy of a system of two point charges and of electric dipole in an electrostatic field.

Conductors and insulators, free charges and bound charges inside a conductor. Dielectrics and electric polarisation, capacitors and capacitance, combination of capacitors in series and in parallel. Capacitance of a parallel plate capacitor, energy stored in a capacitor.

(a) Concept of potential, potential difference and potential energy. Equipotential surface and its properties. Obtain an expression for electric potential at a point due to a point charge; graphical variation of E and V versus r, $V_P = W/q_0$; hence $V_A - V_B = W_{BA/q_0}$ (taking q_0 from B to A) $= (q/4\pi\varepsilon_0)(^1/r_A - 1/r_B)$; derive this equation; also $V_A = q/4\pi\varepsilon_0 \cdot 1/r_A$; for $q > 0, V_A > 0$ and for $q < 0, V_A < 0$. For a collection of charges V = algebraic sum of the potentials due to each charge; potential due to a dipole on its axial line and equatorial line; also at any point for $r >> 2l$ (short dipole). Potential energy of a point charge (q) in an electric field $\mathbf{E}$, placed at a point P where potential is

V, is given by $U = qV$ and $\Delta U = q(V_A - V_B)$. The electrostatic potential energy of a system of two charges = work done $W_{21} = W_{12}$ in assembling the system; U_{12} or $U_{21} = (1/4\pi\varepsilon_0) q_1 q_2 / r_{12}$. For a system of 3 charges $U_{123} = U_{12} + U_{13} + U_{23} = \frac{1}{4\pi\varepsilon_0}\left(\frac{q_1 q_2}{r_{12}} + \frac{q_1 q_3}{r_{13}} + \frac{q_2 q_3}{r_{23}}\right)$.

For a dipole in a uniform electric field, derive an expression of the electric potential energy $U_E = -\mathbf{p}\cdot\mathbf{E}$, *special cases for* $\phi = 0°, 90°$ *and* $180°$.

(b) *Capacitance of a conductor* $C = Q/V$; *obtain the capacitance of a parallel plate capacitor* $(C = \varepsilon_0 A/d)$ *and equivalent capacitance for capacitors in series and parallel combinations. Obtain an expression for energy stored* $\left(U = \frac{1}{2}CV^2 = \frac{1}{2}QV = \frac{1}{2}\frac{Q^2}{C}\right)$ *and energy density.*

(c) *Dielectric constant* $K = C'/C$; *this is also called relative permittivity* $K = \varepsilon_r = \varepsilon/\varepsilon_0$; *elementary ideas of polarization of matter in a uniform electric field qualitative discussion; induced surface charges weaken the original field; results in reduction in* $\mathbf{E}$ *and hence, in potential difference (V); for charge remaining the same* $Q = CV = C'V' = K\cdot CV'$; $V' = V/K$; *and* $E' = E/K$; *if the capacitor is kept connected with the source of emf, V is kept constant* $V = Q/C = Q'/C'$; $Q' = C'V = K\cdot CV = K\cdot Q$ *increases; For a parallel plate capacitor with a dielectric in between,* $C' = KC = K\cdot\varepsilon_0\cdot A/d = \varepsilon_r\cdot\varepsilon_0\cdot A/d$.
Then $C' = \frac{\varepsilon_0 A}{(d/\varepsilon_r)}$; *for a capacitor partially filled dielectric, capacitance,* $C' = \varepsilon_0 A/(d - t + t/\varepsilon_r)$.

2. CURRENT ELECTRICITY

Mechanism of flow of current in conductors. Mobility, drift velocity and its relation with electric current; Ohm's law and its proof, resistance and resistivity and their relation to drift velocity of electrons; *V-I* characteristics (linear and non-linear), electrical energy and power, electrical resistivity and conductivity.

temperature dependence of resistance and resistivity.

Internal resistance of a cell, potential difference and emf of a cell, combination of cells in series and in parallel, Kirchhoff's laws and simple applications, Wheatstone bridge, metre bridge. Potentiometer-principle and its applications to measure potential difference, to compare emf of two cells; to measure internal resistance of a cell.

(a) *Free electron theory of conduction; acceleration of free electrons, relaxation time* τ; *electric current* $I = Q/t$; *concept of drift velocity and electron mobility. Ohm's law, current density* $J = I/A$; *experimental verification, graphs and slope, ohmic and non-ohmic conductors; obtain the relation* $I = v_d enA$. *Derive* $\sigma = ne^2\tau/m$ *and* $\rho = m/ne^2\tau$; *effect of temperature on resistivity and resistance of conductors and semiconductors and graphs. Resistance* $R = V/I$; *resistivity* ρ, *given by* $R = \rho\cdot l/A$; *conductivity and conductance; Ohm's law as* $\mathbf{J} = \sigma\mathbf{E}$;.

(b) *Electrical energy consumed in time t is* $E = Pt = VIt$; *using Ohm's law* $E = \left(\frac{V^2}{R}\right)t = I^2Rt$. *Potential difference* $V = P/I$; $P = VI$; *Electric power consumed* $P = VI = V^2/R = I^2R$; *commercial units; electricity consumption and billing.*

(c) *The source of energy of a seat of emf (such as a cell) may be electrical, mechanical, thermal or radiant energy. The emf of a source is defined as the work done per unit charge to force them to go to the higher point of potential (from – ve terminal to + ve terminal inside the cell) so,* $\varepsilon = dW/dq$; *but* $dq = Idt$; $dW = \varepsilon dq = \varepsilon Idt$. *Equating total work done to the work done across the external resistor R plus the work done across the internal resistance r;* $\varepsilon Idt = I^2R\,dt + I^2r\,dt$; $\varepsilon = I(R + r)$; $I = \varepsilon/(R + r)$; *also* $IR + Ir = \varepsilon$ *or* $V = \varepsilon - Ir$ *where Ir is called the back emf as it acts against the emf* ε; *V is the terminal potential difference. Derivation of formulae for combination for identical cells in series, parallel and mixed grouping. Parallel combination of two cells of unequal emf. Series combination of n cells of unequal emf.*

(d) *Statement and explanation of Kirchhoff's laws with simple examples. The first is a conservation law for charge and the 2nd is law of conservation of energy. Note change in potential across a resistor* $\Delta V = IR < 0$ *when we go 'down' with the current (compare with flow of water down a river), and* $\Delta V = IR > 0$ *if we go up against the current across the resistor. When we go through a cell, the – ve terminal is at a lower level and the + ve terminal at a higher level, so going from – ve to + ve through the cell, we are going up and* $\Delta V = +\varepsilon$ *and going from + ve to – ve terminal through the cell, we are going down, so* $\Delta V = -\varepsilon$. *Application to simple circuits. Wheatstone bridge; right in the beginning take* $I_g = 0$ *as we consider a balanced bridge, derivation of* $R_1/R_2 = R_3/R_4$ *[Kirchhoff's law not necessary]. Metre bridge is a modified form of Wheatstone bridge, its use to measure unknown resistance. Here* $R_3 = l_1\rho$ *and* $R_4 = l_2\rho$; $R_3/R_4 = l_1/l_2$. *Principle of Potentiometer: fall in potential* $\Delta V \propto \Delta l$; *auxiliary emf* ε_1 *is balanced against the fall in potential* V_1 *across length* l_1. $\varepsilon_1 = V_1 = Kl_1$; $\varepsilon_1/\varepsilon_2 = l_1/l_2$; *potentiometer as a voltmeter. Potential gradient and sensitivity of potentiometer. Use of potentiometer: to compare emfs of two cells, to determine internal resistance of a cell.*

3. MAGNETIC EFFECTS OF CURRENT AND MAGNETISM

(i) **Moving Charges and Magnetism**

Concept of magnetic field, Oersted's experiment. Biot-Savart law and its application. Ampere's Circuital law and its applications to infinitely long straight wire, straight solenoids (only qualitative treatment). Force on a moving charge in uniform magnetic and electric fields. Force on a current carrying conductor in a uniform magnetic field, force between two parallel current-carrying conductors-definition of ampere, torque experienced by a current loop in uniform magnetic field; moving coil galvanometer - its sensitivity. Conversion of galvanometer into an ammeter and a voltmeter.

(ii) **Magnetism and Matter**

A current loop as a magnetic dipole, its magnetic dipole moment, magnetic dipole moment of a revolving electron, magnetic field intensity due to a magnetic dipole (bar magnet) on the axial line and equatorial line, torque on a magnetic dipole (bar magnet) in a uniform magnetic field; bar magnet as an equivalent solenoid, Diamagnetic, paramagnetic and ferromagnetic substances, with examples. Electromagnets and factors affecting their strengths, permanent magnets.

(a) *Only historical introduction through Oersted's experiment. [Ampere's swimming rule not included]. Biot-Savart law and its vector form; application; derive the expression for B (i) at the centre of a circular loop carrying current; (ii) at any point on its axis. Current carrying loop as a magnetic dipole. Ampere's circuital law: statement and brief explanation. Apply it to obtain* $\mathbf{B}$ *near a long wire carrying current and for a solenoid (straight as well as toroidal). Only formula of* $\mathbf{B}$ *due to a finitely long conductor.*

(b) *Force on a moving charged particle in magnetic field* $\mathbf{F}_B = q(\mathbf{v}\times\mathbf{B})$; *special cases, modify this equation substituting* $d\mathbf{l}/dt$ *for v and I for q/dt to yield* $\mathbf{F} = Id\mathbf{l}\times\mathbf{B}$ *for the force acting on a current carrying conductor placed in a magnetic field. Derive the expression for force between two long and parallel wires carrying current, hence, define ampere (the base SI unit of current) and hence, coulomb; from* $Q = It$. *Lorentz force,.*

(c) *Derive the expression for torque on a current carrying loop placed in a uniform* $\mathbf{B}$, *using* $\mathbf{F} = I\mathbf{l}\times\mathbf{B}$ *and* $\tau = \mathbf{r}\times\mathbf{F}$; $\tau = NIAB\sin\phi$ *for N turns* $\tau = \mathbf{m}\times\mathbf{B}$, *where the dipole moment* $\mathbf{m} = NI\mathbf{A}$, *unit:* A-m^2.

A current carrying loop is a magnetic dipole; directions of current and **B** *and* **m** *using right hand rule only; no other rule necessary. Mention orbital magnetic moment of an electron in Bohr model of H-atom. Concept of radial magnetic field. Moving coil galvanometer; construction, principle, working, theory $I = k\phi$, current and voltage sensitivity. Shunt. Conversion of galvanometer into ammeter and voltmeter of given range.*

(d) *Magnetic field represented by the symbol* **B** *is now defined by the equation $\mathbf{F} = q_0(\mathbf{v} \times \mathbf{B})$; **B** is not to be defined in terms of force acting on a unit pole, etc.; note the distinction of* **B** *from* **E** *is that* **B** *forms closed loops as there are no magnetic monopoles, whereas* **E** *lines start from + ve charge and end on − ve charge. Magnetic field lines due to a magnetic dipole (bar magnet). Magnetic field in end-on and broadside-on positions (No derivations). Magnetic flux $\phi = \mathbf{B} \cdot \mathbf{A} = BA$ for B uniform and $\mathbf{B} \| \mathbf{A}$; i.e. area held perpendicular to for $BA(\mathbf{B} \| \mathbf{A})$, $B = \phi/A$ is the flux density [SI unit of flux is weber (Wb)]; but note that this is not correct as a defining equation as* **B** *is vector and ϕ and ϕ/A are scalars, unit of B is tesla (T) equal to 10^{-4} gauss. For non-uniform* **B** *field, $\phi = \int d\phi = \int \mathbf{B} \cdot d\mathbf{A}$.*

(e) *Properties of diamagnetic, paramagnetic and ferromagnetic substances; their susceptibility and relative permeability. It is better to explain the main distinction, the cause of magnetisation (M) is due to magnetic dipole moment (m) of atoms, ions or molecules being 0 for dia, > 0 but very small for para and > 0 and large for ferromagnetic materials; few examples; placed in external* **B***, very small (induced) magnetisation in a direction opposite to* **B** *in dia, small magnetisation parallel to* **B** *for para, and large magnetisation parallel to* **B** *for ferromagnetic materials; this leads to lines of* **B** *becoming less dense, more dense and much more dense in dia, para and ferro, respectively; hence, a weak repulsion for dia, weak attraction for para and strong attraction for ferro magnetic material. Also, a small bar suspended in the horizontal plane becomes perpendicular to the* **B** *field for dia and parallel to* **B** *for para and ferro. Defining equation $H = (B/\mu_0) - M$; the magnetic properties, susceptibility $\chi_m = (M/H) < 0$ for dia (as M is opposite H) and > 0 for para, both very small, but very large for ferro; hence relative permeability $\mu_r = (1 + \chi_m) < 1$ for dia, > 1 for para and >> 1 (very large) for ferro; further, $\chi_m \propto 1/T$ (Curie's law) for para, independent of temperature (T) for dia and depends on T in a complicated manner for ferro; on heating ferro becomes para at Curie temperature. Electromagnet: its definition, properties and factors affecting the strength of electromagnet; selection of magnetic material for temporary and permanent magnets and core of the transformer on the basis of retentivity and coercive force (B-H loop and its significance, retentivity and coercive force not to be evaluated).*

4. ELECTROMAGNETIC INDUCTION AND ALTERNATING CURRENTS

(i) **Electromagnetic Induction** Faraday's laws, induced emf and current; Lenz's Law, eddy currents. Self-induction and mutual induction. Transformer.

(ii) **Alternating Current** Peak value, mean value and RMS value of alternating current/voltage; their relation in sinusoidal case; reactance and impedance; *L-C* oscillations (qualitative treatment only), *L-C-R* series circuit, resonance; power in AC circuits, wattless current. AC generator.

(a) *Electromagnetic induction, magnetic flux, change in flux, rate of change of flux and induced emf; Faraday's laws. Lenz's law, conservation of energy; motional emf $\varepsilon = Blv$, and power $P = (Blv)^2/R$; eddy currents (qualitative);*

(b) *Self-Induction, coefficient of self-inductance, $\phi = LI$ and $L = \dfrac{\varepsilon}{dI/dt}$; henry = volt. Second/ampere, expression for coefficient of self-inductance of a solenoid $L = \dfrac{\mu_0 N^2 A}{l} = \mu_0 n^2 A \times l$.*

Mutual induction and mutual inductance (M), flux linked $\phi_2 = MI_1$; induced emf $\varepsilon_2 = \dfrac{d\phi_2}{dt} = M\dfrac{dI_1}{dt}$. Definition of M as $M = \dfrac{\varepsilon_2}{dI_1/dt}$ or $M = \dfrac{\phi_2}{I_1}$. SI unit henry. Expression for coefficient of mutual inductance of two coaxial solenoids. $M = \dfrac{\mu_0 N_1 N_2 A}{l} = \mu_0 n_1 N_2 A$

Induced emf opposes changes, back emf is set up, eddy currents. Transformer (ideal coupling): principle, working and uses; step up and step down; efficiency and applications including transmission of power, energy losses and their minimisation.

(c) *Sinusoidal variation of V and I with time, for the output from an AC generator; time period, frequency and phase changes; obtain mean values of current and voltage, obtain relation between RMS value of V and I with peak values in sinusoidal cases only.*

(d) *Variation of voltage and current in AC circuits consisting of only a resistor, only an inductor and only a capacitor (phasor representation), phase lag and phase lead. May apply Kirchhoff's law and obtain simple differential equation (SHM type), $V = V_0 \sin\omega t$, solution $I = I_0 \sin\omega t$, $I_0 \sin(\omega t + \pi/2)$ and $I_0 \sin(\omega t - \pi/2)$ for pure R, C and L circuits respectively. Draw phase (or phasor) diagrams showing voltage and current and phase lag or lead, also showing resistance R, inductive reactance X_L; $(X_L = \omega L)$ and capacitive reactance X_C, $(X_C = 1/\omega C)$. Graph of X_L and X_C versus f.*

(e) *The L-C-R series circuit: Use phasor diagram method to obtain expression for I and V, the potential difference across R, L and C; and the net phase lag/lead; use the results of 4(e), V lags I by $\pi/2$ in a capacitor, V leads I by $\pi/2$ in an inductor, V and I are in phase in a resistor, I is the same in all three; hence draw phase diagram, combine V_L and V_C (in opposite phase; phasors add like vectors) to give $V = V_R + V_L + V_C$ (phasor addition) and the max. values are related by $V^2{}_m = V^2_{Rm} + (V_{Lm} - V_{Cm})^2$ when $V_L > V_C$ Substituting potential difference = current × resistance or reactance, we get $Z^2 = R^2 + (X_L - X_C)^2$ and $\tan\phi = (V_{Lm} - V_{Cm})/V_{Rm}$ $= (X_L - X_C)/R$ giving $I = I_m \sin(\omega t - \phi)$, where $I_m = V_m/Z$. Special cases for R-L and R-C circuits. [May use Kirchhoff's law and obtain the differential equation] Graph of Z versus f and I versus f.*

(f) *Power P associated with L-C-R circuit $= \dfrac{1}{2}V_0 I_0 \cos\phi = V_{rms} I_{rms} \cos\phi = I^2_{rms} R$; power absorbed and power dissipated; electrical resonance; bandwidth of signals and Q factor (no derivation); oscillations in an LC circuit $(\omega_0 = 1/\sqrt{LC})$. Average power consumed averaged over a full cycle $\mathbf{P} = (1/2) V_0 I_0 \cos\phi$, power factor $\cos\phi = R/Z$. Special case for pure R, L and C; choke coil (analytical only), X_L controls current but $\cos\phi = 0$, hence $\mathbf{P} = 0$, wattless current; LC circuit; at resonance with $X_L = X_C$, $Z = Z_{min} = R$, power delivered to circuit by the source is maximum, resonant frequency $f_0 = \dfrac{1}{2\pi\sqrt{LC}}$.*

(g) *Simple AC generators: Principle, description, theory, working and use. Variation in current and voltage with time for AC and DC Basic differences between AC and DC.*

5. ELECTROMAGNETIC WAVES

Basic idea of displacement current. Electromagnetic waves, their characteristics, their transverse nature (qualitative ideas only). Complete electromagnetic spectrum starting from radiowaves to gamma rays: elementary facts of electromagnetic waves and their uses.

Concept of displacement current, qualitative descriptions only of electromagnetic spectrum; common features of all regions of em spectrum including transverse nature (**E** and **B** perpendicular to **c**); special features of the common classification (gamma rays, X-rays, UV rays, visible light, IR, microwaves, radio and TV waves) in their production (source), detection and other properties; uses; approximate range of λ or f or at least proper order of increasing f or λ.

6. OPTICS

(i) **Ray Optics and Optical Instruments** Ray Optics: Reflection of light by spherical mirrors, mirror formula, refraction of light at plane surfaces, total internal reflection and its applications, optical fibres, refraction at spherical surfaces, lenses, thin lens formula, lens maker's formula, magnification, power of a lens, combination of thin lenses in contact, combination of a lens and a mirror, refraction and dispersion of light through a prism.

Optical instruments: Microscopes and astronomical telescopes (reflecting and refracting) and their magnifying powers.

(a) *Reflection of light by spherical mirrors. Mirror formula: its derivation; $R = 2f$ for spherical mirrors. Magnification.*

(b) *Refraction of light at a plane interface, Snell's law; total internal reflection and critical angle; total reflecting prisms and optical fibres. Total reflecting prisms: application to triangular prisms with angle of the prism 30°, 45°, 60° and 90° respectively; ray diagrams for refraction through a combination of media, ${}_1n_2 \times {}_2n_3 \times {}_3n_1 = 1$, real depth and apparent depth. Simple applications.*

(c) *Refraction through a prism, minimum deviation and derivation of relation between n, A and δ_{min}. Include explanation of i - δ graph, $i_1 = i_2 = i$ (say) for δ_m; from symmetry $r_1 = r_2$; refracted ray inside the prism is parallel to the base of the equilateral prism. Thin prism. Dispersion; Angular dispersion; dispersive power, rainbow-ray diagram (no derivation). Simple explanation.*

(d) *Refraction at a single spherical surface; detailed discussion of one case only-convex towards rarer medium, for spherical surface and real image. Derive the relation between n_1, n_2, u, v and R. Refraction through thin lenses: derive lens maker's formula and lens formula; derivation of combined focal length of two thin lenses in contact. Combination of lenses and mirrors (silvering of lens excluded) and magnification for lens, derivation for biconvex lens only; extend the results to biconcave lens, plano convex lens and lens immersed in a liquid; power of a lens $P = 1/f$ with SI unit dioptre. For lenses in contact $1/F = 1/f_1 + 1/f_2$ and $P = P_1 + P_2$. Lens formula, formation of image with combination of thin lenses and mirrors.*

[Any one sign convention may be used in solving numericals].

(e) *Ray diagram and derivation of magnifying power of a simple microscope with image at D (least distance of distinct vision) and infinity; Ray diagram and derivation of magnifying power of a compound microscope with image at D. Only expression for magnifying power of compound microscope for final image at infinity.*

Ray diagrams of refracting telescope with image at infinity as well as at D; simple explanation; derivation of magnifying power; Ray diagram of reflecting telescope with image at infinity. Advantages, disadvantages and uses. Resolving power of compound microscope.

(ii) **Wave Optics** Wavefront and Huygen's principle. Proof of laws of reflection and refraction using Huygen's principle. Interference, Young's double slit experiment and expression for fringe width(β), coherent sources and sustained interference of light, Fraunhofer diffraction due to a single slit, width of central maximum;

(a) *Huygen's principle: wavefronts-different types/shapes of wavefronts; proof of laws of reflection and refraction using Huygen's theory. [Refraction through a prism and lens on the basis of Huygen's theory not required].*

(b) *Interference of light, interference of monochromatic light by double slit. Phase of wave motion; superposition of identical waves at a point, path difference and phase difference; coherent and incoherent sources; interference: constructive and destructive, conditions for sustained interference of light waves [mathematical deduction of interference from the equations of two progressive waves with a phase difference is not required]. Young's double slit experiment: set up, diagram, geometrical deduction of path difference $\Delta x = d\sin\theta$, between waves from the two slits; using $\Delta x = n\lambda$ for bright fringe and $\Delta x = (n + \frac{1}{2})\lambda$ for dark fringe and $\sin\theta = \tan\theta = y_n/D$ as y and θ are small, obtain $y_n = (D/d)n\lambda$ and fringe width $\beta = (D/d)\lambda$. Graph of distribution of intensity with angular distance.*

(c) *Single slit Fraunhofer diffraction (elementary explanation qualitative treatment only). Diffraction at a single slit: experimental setup, diagram, diffraction pattern, obtain expression for position of minima, $a\sin\theta_n = n\lambda$, where n = 1, 2, 3... and conditions for secondary maxima, $a\sin\theta_n = (n + \frac{1}{2})\lambda$; distribution of intensity with angular distance; angular width of central bright fringe*

7. DUAL NATURE OF RADIATION AND MATTER

Wave particle duality; photoelectric effect, Hertz and Lenard's observations; Einstein's photoelectric equation-particle nature of light. Matter waves-wave nature of particles, de-Broglie relation; conclusion from Davisson-Germer experiment (Qualitative only).

(a) Photoelectric effect, quantisation of radiation; Einstein's equation $E_{max} = h\nu - W_0$; threshold frequency; work function; experimental facts of Hertz and Lenard and their conclusions; Einstein used Planck's ideas and extended it to apply for radiation (light); photoelectric effect can be explained only assuming quantum (particle) nature of radiation. Determination of Planck's constant (from the graph of stopping potential V_s versus frequency f of the incident light).

Momentum of photon $p = E/c = h\nu/c = h/\lambda$.

(b) de-Broglie hypothesis, phenomenon of electron diffraction (qualitative only). Wave nature of radiation is exhibited in interference, diffraction and polarisation; particle nature is exhibited in photoelectric effect. Dual nature of matter: particle nature common in that it possesses momentum p and kinetic energy KE. The wave nature of matter was proposed by Louis de-Broglie, $\lambda = h/p = h/mv$. Davisson and Germer experiment; qualitative description of the experiment and conclusion.

8. ATOMS AND NUCLEI

(i) **Atoms** Alpha-particle scattering experiment; Rutherford's atomic model; Bohr's atomic model, energy levels, hydrogen spectrum.

Rutherford's nuclear model of atom (mathematical theory of scattering excluded), based on Geiger-Marsden experiment on α-scattering; nuclear radius r in terms of closest approach of α-particle to the nucleus, obtained by equating $\Delta K = \frac{1}{2}mv^2$ of the α-particle to the change in electrostatic potential energy ΔU of the system $U = \frac{2e \times Ze}{4\pi\varepsilon_0 r_0} = r_0 \sim 10^{-15}$ m = 1 Fermi; atomic structure; only general qualitative ideas, including atomic number Z, neutron number N and mass number A. A brief account of historical background leading to Bohr's theory of hydrogen spectrum; formulae for wavelength in Lyman, Balmer, Paschen, Brackett and Pfund series. Rydberg constant. Bohr's model of H-atom, postulates ($Z = 1$); expressions for orbital velocity, kinetic energy, potential energy, radius of orbit and total energy of electron. Energy level diagram, calculation of ΔE, frequency and wavelength of different lines of emission spectra; agreement with experimentally observed values. [Use nm and not Å for unit of λ].

(ii) **Nuclei** Composition and size of nucleus, Mass-energy relation, mass defect; binding energy per nucleon and its variation with mass number; Nuclear reactions, nuclear fission and nuclear fusion.

(a) *Atomic masses and nuclear density; Isotopes, Isobars and Isotones – definitions with examples of each. Unified atomic mass unit, symbol* u, 1u = 1/12 *of the mass of* ^{12}C *atom* = 1.66×10^{-27} *kg). Composition of nucleus; mass defect and binding energy, BE* = $(\Delta m)\, c^2$. *Graph of BE/nucleon versus mass number A, special features-less BE/nucleon for light as well as heavy elements. Middle order more stable [see fission and fusion] Einstein's equation* $E = mc^2$. *Calculations related to this equation; mass defect/binding energy, mutual annihilation and pair production as examples.*

(b) ***Nuclear Energy*** *Theoretical (qualitative) prediction of exothermic (with release of energy) nuclear reaction, in fusing together two light nuclei to form a heavier nucleus and in splitting heavy nucleus to form middle order (lower mass number) nuclei, is evident from the shape of BE per nucleon versus mass number graph. Also calculate the disintegration energy Q for a heavy nucleus (A* = 240) *with BE/A* ~ 7.6 *MeV per nucleon split into two equal halves with A* = 120 *each and BE/A* ~ 8.5 *MeV/nucleon; Q* ~ 200 *MeV. Nuclear fission: Any one equation of fission reaction. Chain reaction- controlled and uncontrolled; nuclear reactor and nuclear bomb. Main parts of a nuclear reactor including their functions - fuel elements, moderator, control rods, coolant, casing; criticality; utilization of energy output - all qualitative only. Fusion, simple example of* $^4\text{H} \rightarrow {}^4$ He *and its nuclear reaction equation; requires very high temperature* ~ 10^6 *degrees; difficult to achieve; hydrogen bomb; thermonuclear energy production in the sun and stars. [Details of chain reaction not required].*

9. ELECTRONIC DEVICES

(i) Semiconductor Electronics: Materials, Devices and Simple Circuits. Energy bands in conductors, semiconductors and insulators (qualitative ideas only). Intrinsic and extrinsic semiconductors. *p and n type, p-n junction*

(ii) Semiconductor diode: *I-V* characteristics in forward and reverse bias, diode as a rectifier; special types of junction diodes: LED, photodiode, solar cell and Zener diode and its characteristics, zener diode as a voltage regulator.

(a) *Energy bands in solids; energy band diagrams for distinction between conductors, insulators and semiconductors-intrinsic and extrinsic; electrons and holes in semiconductors.*
Elementary ideas about electrical conduction in metals [crystal structure not included]. Energy levels (as for hydrogen atom), 1s, 2s, 2p, 3s, etc. of an isolated atom such as that of copper; these split, eventually forming bands of energy levels, as we consider solid copper made up of a large number of isolated atoms, brought together to form a lattice; definition of energy bands-groups of closely spaced energy levels separated by band gaps called forbidden bands. An idealised representation of the energy bands for a conductor, insulator and semiconductor; characteristics, differences; distinction between conductors, insulators and semiconductors on the basis of energy bands, with examples; qualitative discussion only; energy gaps (eV) in typical substances (carbon, Ge, Si); some electrical properties of semiconductors. Majority and minority charge carriers-electrons and holes; intrinsic and extrinsic, doping, p-type, n-type; donor and acceptor impurities.

(b) *Junction diode and its symbol; depletion region and potential barrier; forward and reverse biasing, V-I characteristics and numericals; half wave and a full wave rectifier. Simple circuit diagrams and graphs, function of each component in the electric circuits, qualitative only. [Bridge rectifier of 4 diodes not included]; elementary ideas on solar cell, photodiode and light emitting diode (LED) as semi conducting diodes. Importance of LED's as they save energy without causing atmospheric pollution and global warming. Zener diode, V-I characteristics, circuit diagram and working of zener diode as a voltage regulator.*

CHAPTER 01

Electric Charges and Fields

Electrostatics is a branch of Physics that studies with the electric charges at rest. This chapter gives the idea of the development of charge and the evolution of electrostatic field and its effect.

- Electric Charges
- Coulomb's Law and Electrostatic Field
- Electric Dipole
- Electric Flux

TOPIC 01 Electric Charges

According to William Gilbert, charge is something possessed by material objects that makes it possible for them to exert electrical force and respond to the electrical force. Electric charge is a scalar quantity.

When two unlike objects like amber and wool are rubbed against each other, two types of charges namely positive charge and negative charge are produced, called **frictional electricity**. Transfer of electrons is the cause of frictional electricity.

An object can attain positive charge by loosing electrons, this result in a decrease in mass of object, while other can attain negative charge by gaining electrons, this result in an increase in mass of object. Charges with same sign, i.e. like charges repel each other while charges with opposite sign, i.e. unlike charges attract each other.

Charge on a body is independent of frame of reference, i.e. charge on a body does not change whatever be its speed.

Charges always reside on the surface of the charged conducting object. An object can be charged by different methods like friction, conduction and induction.

Gold leaf electroscope is an instrument which detects the electric charges by means of electrostatic forces.

Atomic Structure

According to the atomic model, every atom has an extremely small portion in its centre called **nucleus.** Nucleus consists of particles proton and neutron; proton is a positively charged particle, while neutron is chargeless. The electron revolves around the nucleus and consists of negative charge.

In an atom, the number of electrons is equal to the number of protons in the nucleus. As a whole, atom is electrically neutral, this is why, there is no electrical attraction or repulsion in ordinary bodies.

If an atom loses electron, it becomes **positively charged ion.** Similarly, if it gains electron, becomes **negatively charged ion.**

Conductors and Insulators

Conductors are those substances which can be used to carry or conduct electric charge/electron from one point to other. They allow electricity to pass through them easily. Metals, human body, earth, mercury and electrolytes are conductors of electricity.

In metals, the outer electrons of atom leave the atom and become 'free' to move throughout the volume of metal is called **free electron.**

Insulators are those substances which cannot conduct electricity. They are also called **dielectrics.** They offer high resistance to the passage of electricity through them, e.g. Glass, rubber, plastic, ebonite, mica, etc.

Basic Properties of Electric Charge

Some basic properties of the electric charge are discussed below:

(i) Electric charge is additive in nature. In general, if a system consists of n charges $q_1, q_2, q_3, \ldots, q_n$, then the total charge of the system will be $q_1 + q_2 + q_3 + \ldots + q_n$.

(ii) During any process, the net electric charge of an isolated system remains constant (i.e. conserved). In simple words, charge can neither be created nor be destroyed. In any physical process, the charge may get transferred from one part of the system to another, but the net charge will always remain the same.

Quantisation of Electric Charge

The charge on any body can be expressed as an integral multiple of basic unit of charge, i.e. charge on one electron. This phenomena is called quantisation of electric charge.

It can be written as $\boxed{q = \pm ne}$

where, $n = 1, 2, 3, \ldots$ is any integer, positive or negative and e is the basic unit of charge. It is called elementary charge.

Charge of electron $= -e$

Charge of proton $= +e$

The SI unit of charge is called coulomb and denoted by C and its value is $e = 1.602192 \times 10^{-19}$ C or 1.6×10^{-19} C.

The stat-coulomb (stat-C) is the CGS unit of charge. It is also called electrostatic unit (esu) of charge.

$$1\text{C} = 3 \times 10^9 \text{ stat-C}$$

Example 2 A polythene piece rubbed with wool is found to have a negative charge of 3×10^{-7} C.

(i) Estimate the number of electrons transferred from which to which?

(ii) Is there a transfer of mass from wool to polythene?

NCERT

Sol. (i) Here, $q = -3 \times 10^{-7}$ C

Charge on one electron,

$$e = -1.6 \times 10^{-19} \text{ C}$$

$\therefore$ Number of electrons transferred from wool to polythene piece,

$$n = \frac{q}{e} = \frac{-3 \times 10^{-7} \text{ C}}{-1.6 \times 10^{-19} \text{ C}}$$

$$= 1.875 \times 10^{12}$$

(ii) Yes, there is a transfer of mass from wool to polythene piece.

As, mass of each electron, $m_e = 9 \times 10^{-31}$ kg

$\therefore$ Mass transferred from wool to polythene,

$$m = n \times m_e = 1.875 \times 10^{12} \times 9 \times 10^{-31} \text{ kg}$$

$$= 1.687 \times 10^{-18} \text{ kg}$$

Example 3 A copper slab of mass 2 g contains 2×10^{22} atoms. The charge on the nucleus of each atom is 29 e. What fraction of the electrons must be removed from the sphere to give it a charge of +2 μC ?

Sol. Total number of electrons in the slab $= 29 \times 2 \times 10^{22}$

Number of electrons removed $= \dfrac{q}{e} = \dfrac{2 \times 10^{-6}}{1.6 \times 10^{-19}}$

$$= 1.25 \times 10^{13}$$

$\therefore$ Fraction of electrons removed $= \dfrac{1.25 \times 10^{13}}{29 \times 2 \times 10^{22}}$

$$= 2.16 \times 10^{-11}$$

Topic Practice 1

Multiple Choice Questions

1 Mark

1. When a body is connected to Earth, electrons from the Earth flow into the body. This means the body is ...*A*... . Here, *A* refers to
(a) uncharged (b) charged positively
(c) charged negatively (d) as insulator

2. Two bodies are rubbed and one of them is negatively charged. For this body, if m_i = initial mass, m_f = mass after charging, then
(a) $m_i = m_f$ (b) $m_i < m_f$
(c) $m_i > m_f$ (d) $m_i + m_f = 2m_f$

3. Every object has billions of electrons, but no repulsion is found between any two objects, because
(a) force of electrons is very less
(b) gravitation present is large, so force of electrons is not observed
(c) every object also contains equal number of protons
(d) no explanation is found till date

4. If a body gives out 10^9 electrons per second, how much time is required to get a total charge of 1 C from it?
(a) Around 200 min (b) Around 200 h
(c) Around 200 days (d) Around 200 yr

5. A body has a positive charge of 8×10^{-19}C. It has **ISC 2012**
(a) an excess of 5 electrons
(b) a deficiency of 5 electrons
(c) an excess of 8 electrons
(d) a deficiency of 8 electrons

Very Short Answer Type Questions

1 Mark

6. A glass rod when rubbed with silk cloth acquires a charge 1.6×10^{-13} C. What is the charge on the silk cloth?

7. Consider three charged bodies *A*, *B* and *C*. If *A* and *B* repel each other and *A* attracts *C*, then what is nature of the force between *B* and *C*?

8. 'An object becomes positively charged through the removal of negatively charged electrons rather than through the addition of positively charged protons'. Explain, why?

9. A glass object is charged to +3 nC by rubbing it with a silk cloth. In this rubbing process, have protons been added to the object or have electrons been removed from it?

10. What does $q_1 + q_2 = 0$ signify in electrostatics?

11. Which property of dielectrics make them different from conductors?

12. Two insulated charged copper spheres *A* and *B* of identical size have charges q_A and q_B, respectively. A third sphere *C* of the same size but uncharged is brought in contact with the first and then in contact with the second and finally removed from both. What are the new charges on *A* and *B*?

13. What is the basic cause of quantisation of charge? **ISC 2015, 13**

14. What is meant by 'elementary charge'? What is its value?

15. Can 8.6×10^{-19} C of charge be given to a conductor? Explain. **ISC 2024, 06**

16. Which is bigger, a coulomb of charge or a charge on an electron?

17. If a negative charge is given to a soap bubble, then what effects occur on its size?

Short Answer Type I Questions

2 Marks

18. In filling the gasoline tank of an aeroplane, the metal nozzle of hose from the gasoline truck is always carefully connected to the metal body of the aeroplane by a wire, before the nozzle is inserted in the tank. Explain, why?

19. Automobile ignition failure occurs in damp weather. Explain, why?

20. An ebonite rod held in hand can be charged by rubbing with flannel but a copper rod cannot be charged like this, why?

21. Ordinary rubber is an insulator. But the special rubber tyres of aircrafts are made slightly conducting. Why is this necessary?

22. Can two balls having same kind of charge on them attract each other? Explain.

23. Can ever the whole excess charge of a body P be transferred to the other body Q? If yes, how and if not, why?

24. When a glass rod is rubbed with a silk cloth, charges appear on both. A similar phenomenon is observed with many other pairs of bodies. Explain, how this observation is consistent with the law of conservation of charge? **NCERT**

25. Give any two points of difference between charge and mass.

Short Answer Type II Question

3 Marks

26. (i) Explain the meaning of the statement 'electric charge of a body is quantised'.
   (ii) Why can one ignore quantisation of electric charge, when dealing with macroscopic, i.e. large scale charges? **NCERT**

Numerical Problems

27. What is the total charge of a system containing five charges +1, +2, −3, +4 and −5 in some arbitrary unit? **(1 M)**

28. How many electrons are there in one coulomb of negative charge? **(1 M)**

29. A metal sphere has a charge of $-6\,\mu$C. When 5×10^{12} electrons are removed from the sphere, what would be net charge on it? **(2 M)**

30. A sphere of lead of mass 10 g has net charge -2.5×10^{-9} C.
   (i) Find the number of excess electrons on the sphere.
   (ii) How many excess electrons are per lead atom? Atomic number of lead is 82 and its atomic mass is 207 g/mol. **(3 M)**

31. A polythene piece rubbed with wool is found to have a negative charge of 3×10^{-7} C. Estimate the number of electrons transferred from which to which? **(2 M)**

32. The charge on a conductor is − 1.6 C. How many electrons are in excess on it than normal state? **(2 M)**

Hints & Solutions

1. (*b*) If a body is positively charged, electrons from Earth are attracted to it.

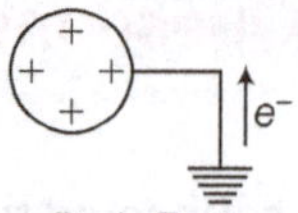

Electrons from Earth come to body to neutralise the positive charge of body. Earth is conductor and has lot of positive and negative charges inside due to metals, ions, etc.

2. (*b*) A negatively charged body acquires some electrons, so its mass is more than its neutral mass.

3. (*c*) Due to an equal number of protons object is electrically neutral. Atom of matter has equal number of electrons and protons. So, matter in general is overall neutral, so no two objects repel each other.

4. (*d*) 1 C of charge is made of $n = \frac{q}{e} = \frac{1\text{ C}}{1.6\times10^{-19}\text{ C}}$
$= 6.25\times10^{18}$ electrons

$\therefore$ Time required $= \frac{6.25\times10^{18}}{10^9}$ s $= 6.25\times10^9$ s ≈ 200 yr

($\because 1$ yr $= 3.17\times10^7$ s)

5. (*b*) $\therefore\ n = \frac{q}{e} = \frac{8\times10^{-19}}{1.6\times10^{-19}} = 5$

Since, body has a positive charge, so it has a deficiency of 5 electrons.

6. Silk cloth will also acquire a charge 1.6×10^{-13} C. However, it will be negative in nature.

7. It is also attractive in nature.

8. In ordinary matter, a positive charge is much less mobile than a negative charge. For this reason, an object becomes positively charged through the removal of negatively charged electrons rather than through the addition of positively charged protons.

9. Electrons have been removed from the object.

10. The charges q_1 and q_2 are equal and opposite in nature.

11. Dielectrics do not have free electrons at all. They offer high resistance to passage of electricity through them. e.g. Glass, rubber, plastic, etc.

12. When sphere C is brought in contact with A, then charge on sphere C,

$$q_C = \frac{q_A + 0}{2} = \frac{q_A}{2}$$

and new charge on sphere A, $q'_A = \frac{q_A}{2}$

When sphere C is brought in contact with B, then charge on sphere C,

$$q'_C = \frac{q_C + q_B}{2} = \frac{\frac{q_A}{2} + q_B}{2} = \frac{q_A + 2q_B}{4}$$

$\therefore$ New charge on sphere B, $q'_B = \frac{q_A + 2q_B}{4}$

13. The basic cause of quantisation of charge is only the integral number of electrons which is transferred from one body to another, i.e. $\pm ne$.

14. The elementary charge is the electric charge carried by a single electron or proton. It's value is e $(1.6 \times 10^{-19}$ C).

15. No, because 8.6×10^{-19} C is not an integral multiple of quantum of charge which is 1.6×10^{-19} C.

16. We know that, $q = ne$

$\Rightarrow \quad 1 = n \times 1.6 \times 10^{-19} \quad$ [given, $q = 1$C]

i.e. $\quad n = \frac{1}{1.6 \times 10^{-19}} \simeq 6 \times 10^{18}$

$\therefore$ 1C is the charge of 6×10^{18} electrons.

So, a coulomb of charge is bigger than the charge on an electron.

17. When a negative charge is given to a soap bubble, this means that some electrons are added to it, therefore its size increases.

18. Since, the aeroplane and the gasoline truck usually have wheels with rubber tyres, they are insulated from the ground. Further, the service ramps are usually made of concrete and are not necessarily good conductors to the earth. Therefore, inspite of grounding metallic ropes, the aeroplane and the truck could remain charged. (1+1)

19. The insulating porcelain of the spark plugs accumulates a film of dirt. The surface dirt is hygroscopic and picks up moisture from the air. Therefore, in humid weather, the insulating porcelain of the plugs becomes quasi-conductor. This allows an appreciable proportion of the spark to leak across the surface of the plug instead of discharging across the gap. (1+1)

20. Both the human body and the copper rod conduct electricity. When it is attempted to charge a copper rod by rubbing, the charge flows from the rod to the earth through the hand. However, when ebonite rod is charged by rubbing, the charges so produced stay on the ebonite rod as it is a bad conductor of electricity. (2)

21. During landing or take off, the tyres of aircrafts get charged due to the friction between tyres and ground. In case, the tyres are slightly conducting, the charge developed on the tyres will not stay on them and it finds its way to the earth. (1+1)

22. Yes, two balls having same kind of charge can attract each other. If any one of them has more charge as compared to the other, then due to the induction, they induce opposite kind of charges on the faces of each other when they are brought nearer. Therefore, they behave as oppositely charged balls and hence they attract each other. (1+1)

23. Yes, the whole charge of a body P can be transferred to a conducting body Q, when P is enclosed by Q and is connected to it. This is because the charge always resides on the outer surface of the conductor. (1+1)

24. When a glass rod is rubbed with a silk cloth, charges appear on both, these charges are equal in magnitude and opposite in sign, so that algebraic sum of the charges produced on both is zero. The net charge on the two bodies was zero even before rubbing them. Thus, we find that charges can be created only in equal and unlike pairs. This is consistent with the law of conservation of charge. (1+1)

25.

Charge	Mass
Electric charge can be positive, negative or zero. Charge is quantised.	Mass of a body is always a positive quantity. The quantisation of mass is yet to be established.
Force between charges can be attractive or repulsive, accordingly as charge are unlike or like charges.	The gravitational force between two masses is always attractive.

26. (i) Refer to text on page 1 (Electric charges). (1)

(ii) In practice, the charge on a charged body is very large. On the other hand, the charge on an electron is very small. When electrons are added to a body or removed from a body, the change taking place in the total charge on the body is so small that the charge seems to be varying in a continuous manner. Therefore, quantisation of electric charge can be ignored, when dealing with a large scale charged body. (2)

27. As charges are additive in nature, i.e. the total charge of a system is the algebraic sum of all the individual charges located at different points inside the system, i.e.

$$q_{\text{net}} = q_1 + q_2 + q_3 + q_4 + q_5$$

$\therefore$ Total charge $= +1 + 2 - 3 + 4 - 5 = -1$ in the same unit.

28. The negative charge is due to the presence of excess electrons. Because an electron has a charge whose magnitude is $e = 1.6 \times 10^{-19}$ C, the number of electrons is equal to the charge q divided by the charge e on each electron.

Therefore, the number of electrons is

$$n = \frac{q}{e} = \frac{1.0}{1.6 \times 10^{-19}}$$

$$= 6.25 \times 10^{18} \text{ electrons}$$

29. Here, $q_1 = -6\,\mu$C

and $\quad q_2 = ne = 5 \times 10^{12} \times (1.6 \times 10^{-19})$

$= 8.0 \times 10^{-7}$ C $= 0.8 \times 10^{-6}$ C

$= 0.8\mu$C (1)

Since, electrons are removed from the sphere, q_2 is positive.

Therefore, net charge on the sphere,

$$q = q_1 + q_2 = (-6.0 + 0.8)\,\mu C$$

$$= -5.2\,\mu C \quad (1)$$

30. (i) The charge of an electron $= -1.6 \times 10^{-19}$ C

Net charge on sphere $= -2.5 \times 10^{-9}$ C

So, the number of excess electrons

$$= \frac{-2.5 \times 10^{-9}\,C}{-1.6 \times 10^{-19}\,C}$$

$$= 1.5 \times 10^{10} \text{ electrons} \quad (1\tfrac{1}{2})$$

(ii) Atomic number of lead is 82.

Atomic mass of lead is 207 g/mol.

∴ 10 g of lead will have

$$\frac{10\text{ g}}{207\text{ g / mol}} \times 6.02 \times 10^{23} \text{ atoms/mol}$$

$$= 2.91 \times 10^{22} \text{ atoms}$$

∴ The number of excess electrons per atom

$$= \frac{1.56 \times 10^{10}}{2.91 \times 10^{22}}$$

$$= 5.36 \times 10^{-13} \text{ electrons} \quad (1\tfrac{1}{2})$$

31. Given, negative charge on polythene piece, $q = 3 \times 10^{-7}$ C.

Since, charge is negative, therefore electrons are transferred from wool to polythene. (1/2)

So, number of electrons, $n = \frac{q}{e} = \frac{3 \times 10^{-7}}{1.6 \times 10^{-19}}$

$$= 1.875 \times 10^{12} \quad (1)$$

Hence, 1.875×10^{12} electrons have been transferred from wool to polythene. (1/2)

32. Given, negative charge on a conductor, $q = 1.6$ C.

Since, conductor is negative charged, therefore it has excess of electron. (1)

So, number of excess electron, $n = \frac{q}{e}$

$$= \frac{1.6}{1.6 \times 10^{-19}}$$

$$= 10^{19} \quad (1)$$

TOPIC 02 Coulomb's Law and Electrostatic Field

Coulomb's Law

The force of interaction (attraction or repulsion) between two stationary point charges in vacuum is directly proportional to the product of the charges and inversely proportional to the square of distance between them.

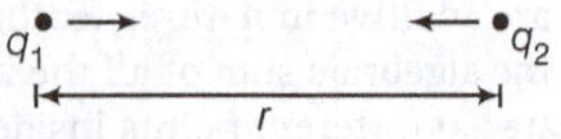

Mathematically, electrostatic force between two stationary charges is given by

$$\boxed{F = \frac{k|q_1 q_2|}{r^2}}$$

where, k is a proportionality constant.

In SI unit, k is given by

$$k = \frac{1}{4\pi\varepsilon_0}$$

$$= 9 \times 10^9 \text{ N-m}^2\text{C}^{-2}$$

where, $\varepsilon_0 = 8.85 \times 10^{-12}\ C^2N^{-1}m^{-2}$ and is called the **permittivity of free space.**

i.e. $$F = 9 \times 10^9 \frac{|q_1 q_2|}{r^2}$$

The Coulomb force acts along the straight line connecting the points of location of the charges. It is central and spherically symmetric.

If $q_1 = q_2 = 1$ C and $r = 1$ m

Then, $$F = 9 \times 10^9 \frac{1 \times 1}{(1)^2}$$

$$\boxed{F = 9 \times 10^9 \text{ N}}$$

i.e. **One coulomb** is the charge, that when placed at distance of 1m from another charge of same magnitude in vacuum, experiences an electric force of repulsion of magnitude 9×10^9 N. Coulomb is a bigger unit, in practice we use smaller units like mC or μC.

Absolute Permittivity of Medium (Dielectric Constant)

The force between two charges q_1 and q_2 located at a distance r apart in a medium may be expressed as,

$$F_{\text{medium}} = \frac{1}{4\pi\varepsilon} \frac{|q_1 q_2|}{r^2}$$

where, ε is **absolute permittivity** of the medium.

Now, $$\frac{F_{\text{vacuum}}}{F_{\text{medium}}} = \frac{\dfrac{1}{4\pi\varepsilon_0}\dfrac{|q_1q_2|}{r^2}}{\dfrac{1}{4\pi\varepsilon}\dfrac{|q_1q_2|}{r^2}} = \frac{\varepsilon}{\varepsilon_0}$$

The ratio $\frac{\varepsilon}{\varepsilon_0}$ is denoted by ε_r, which is called **relative permittivity** of the medium with respect to vacuum. It is also denoted by K called **dielectric constant** of the medium. It has no unit being a ratio.

$$\therefore \quad K \,(\text{or } \varepsilon_r) = \frac{\varepsilon}{\varepsilon_0} = \frac{F_{\text{vacuum}}}{F_{\text{medium}}}$$

$$\Rightarrow \quad \varepsilon = K\varepsilon_0$$

$$\therefore \quad \boxed{F_{\text{medium}} = \frac{1}{4\pi\varepsilon_0}\frac{|q_1q_2|}{Kr^2} = \frac{F_{\text{vacuum}}}{K}}$$

Note Some important facts,

- For water, $K = 81$
- For vacuum, $K = 1$
- For metal, $K = \infty$
- There is no medium with $K < 1$

Coulomb's Law in Vector Form

Consider two like charges q_1 and q_2 present at points A and B respectively in vacuum at a distance r apart.

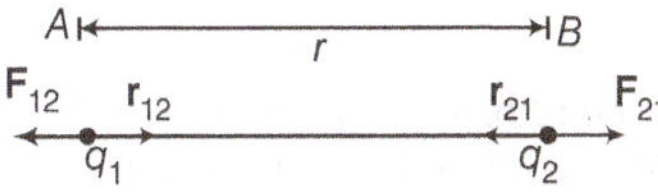

Coulomb force between two charges

According to Coulomb's law, the magnitude of force on charge q_1 due to q_2 (or on charge q_2 due to q_1) is given by

$$F_{12} = F_{21} = \frac{1}{4\pi\varepsilon_0}\cdot\frac{q_1q_2}{r^2} \quad \ldots\text{(i)}$$

Let $\mathbf{r}_{12}$ be the unit vector pointing from charge q_1 to q_2.

$$\mathbf{F}_{12} = \frac{1}{4\pi\varepsilon_0}\cdot\frac{q_1q_2}{r^2}\,\hat{\mathbf{r}}_{21} \quad \ldots\text{(ii)}$$

[$\because$ $\mathbf{F}_{12}$ is along the direction of unit vector $\mathbf{r}_{21}$]

Also, $\mathbf{r}_{21}$ be the unit vector pointing from charge q_2 to q_1.

$$\therefore \quad \mathbf{F}_{21} = \frac{1}{4\pi\varepsilon_0}\cdot\frac{q_1q_2}{r^2}\,\hat{\mathbf{r}}_{12} \quad \ldots\text{(iii)}$$

[$\because$ $\mathbf{F}_{21}$ is along the direction of unit vector $\mathbf{r}_{12}$]

$$\therefore \quad \hat{\mathbf{r}}_{21} = -\hat{\mathbf{r}}_{12}$$

Eq. (ii) becomes,

$$\mathbf{F}_{12} = \frac{-1}{4\pi\varepsilon_0}\cdot\frac{q_1q_2}{r^2}\,\hat{\mathbf{r}}_{12} \quad \ldots\text{(iv)}$$

On comparing Eq. (iii) with Eq. (iv), we get

$$\mathbf{F}_{12} = -\mathbf{F}_{21}$$

i.e. Coulomb's law agrees with Newton's third law.

Comparison of Coulomb's Law with Gravitational Law

Both the Coulomb's and Newton's law follow inverse square law. According to Newton's universal law of gravitation, "every body in the universe attracts every other body with a force which is directly proportional to the product of the masses of two bodies and inversely proportional to the square of distance between them."

i.e. $$F = \frac{Gm_1m_2}{r^2}$$

As discussed earlier, according to Coulomb's law

$$F = \frac{kq_1q_2}{r^2}$$

The electric force is much stronger than the gravitational force between two electrons.

i.e. $$F_E = 10^{43} F_G$$

Note

- Electric force may be attractive or repulsive, while gravitational force are always attractive in nature.
- Electrostatic force between two charged particles is much stronger than gravitational force.
- Electric force depends on the nature of medium between the charges while gravitational force does not.

Example 1 What is the force between two small charged spheres having charges of 2×10^{-7} C and 3×10^{-7} C placed 30 cm apart in air? **NCERT**

Sol. Given, $q_1 = 2 \times 10^{-7}$ C

$q_2 = 3 \times 10^{-7}$ C

$r = 30$ cm $= 30 \times 10^{-2}$ m $= 0.3$ m

$k = 9 \times 10^9$ N-m^{2}C^{-2}

$F = ?$

We have, $$F = \frac{1}{4\pi\varepsilon_0}\frac{|q_1q_2|}{r^2} = \frac{k|q_1q_2|}{r^2} \quad \left[\because \frac{1}{4\pi\varepsilon_0} = k\right] \ldots\text{(i)}$$

Substituting the given values in Eq. (i), we get

$$F = \frac{(9\times10^9\,\text{N-m}^2\text{C}^{-2})(2\times10^{-7}\,\text{C})\times(3\times10^{-7}\,\text{C})}{(0.3\,\text{m})^2}$$

$$\therefore \quad F = 6\times10^{-3}\,\text{N}$$

This force is repulsive, since the spheres have same charges.

Example 2 The sum of two point charges is 7μC. They repel each other with a force of 1 N when kept 30 cm apart in free space. Calculate the value of each charge.

Sol. Let one of two charges be $x\mu C$. Therefore, other charge will be $(7-x)\mu C$.

By Coulomb's law,

$$F = \frac{1}{4\pi\varepsilon_0} \cdot \frac{q_1 q_2}{r^2}$$

$$\Rightarrow \quad 1 = 9\times 10^9 \times \frac{(x\times 10^{-6})(7-x)\times 10^{-6}}{(0.3)^2}$$

$$\Rightarrow \quad 9\times 10^{-2} = 9\times 10^{9-12} x(7-x)$$

$$\Rightarrow \quad 10 = x(7-x)$$

$$\Rightarrow \quad x^2 - 7x + 10 = 0$$

$$\Rightarrow \quad (x-2)(x-5) = 0$$

$$\therefore \quad x = 2\,\mu C \quad \text{or} \quad 5\mu C$$

Therefore, charges are 2μC and 5μC.

Forces between Multiple Charges: Superposition Principle

According to the superposition principle, forces on any charge due to number of other charges is the vector sum of all the forces on that charge due to other charges, taken one at a time. The individual forces are unaffected due to the presence of other charges.

Consider a system of n point charges $q_1, q_2, q_3, \ldots, q_n$ be distributed in space in a discrete manner. The charges are interacting with each other. Let the charges be $q_2, q_3, \ldots, q_n$ exert forces $\mathbf{F}_{12}, \mathbf{F}_{13}, \ldots, \mathbf{F}_{1n}$, respectively on charge q_1.

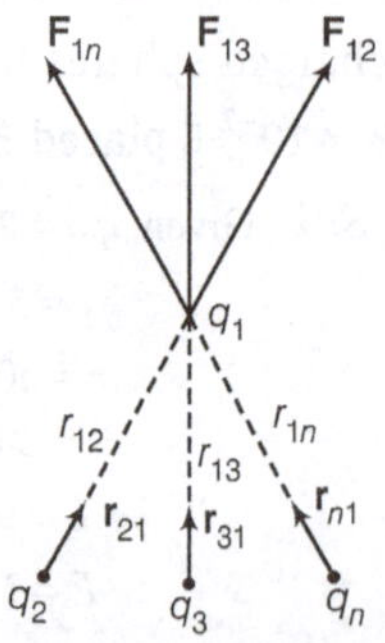

Then, according to the principle of superposition, the total force on charge q_1 is given by

$$\mathbf{F}_1 = \mathbf{F}_{12} + \mathbf{F}_{13} + \ldots + \mathbf{F}_{1n} \quad \ldots\text{(i)}$$

If the distance between the charges q_1 and q_2 is denoted as r_{12} and $\hat{\mathbf{r}}_{21}$ is unit vector from charge q_2 to q_1, then

$$\mathbf{F}_{12} = \frac{1}{4\pi\varepsilon_0} \cdot \frac{q_1 q_2}{r_{21}^2} \hat{\mathbf{r}}_{21}$$

Similarly, the force on charge q_1 due to other charges is given by

$$\mathbf{F}_{13} = \frac{1}{4\pi\varepsilon_0} \cdot \frac{q_1 q_3}{r_{31}^2} \hat{\mathbf{r}}_{31}, \quad \mathbf{F}_{1n} = \frac{1}{4\pi\varepsilon_0} \cdot \frac{q_1 q_n}{r_{n1}^2} \hat{\mathbf{r}}_{n1}$$

Substituting these values in Eq.(i), we get

$$\mathbf{F}_1 = \frac{1}{4\pi\varepsilon_0}\left(\frac{q_1 q_2}{r_{21}^2}\hat{\mathbf{r}}_{21} + \frac{q_1 q_3}{r_{31}^2}\hat{\mathbf{r}}_{31} + \cdots + \frac{q_1 q_n}{r_{n1}^2}\hat{\mathbf{r}}_{n1}\right)$$

$$\Rightarrow \quad \mathbf{F}_{1i} = \frac{q_1}{4\pi\varepsilon_0}\sum_{i=2}^{n}\frac{q_i}{r_{i1}^2}\hat{\mathbf{r}}_{i1}$$

Note This force is on the charge which is to be studied due to other charges.

Example 3 Two charges each of $+q$ Coulomb are placed along a line. A third charge $-q$ is placed between them. At what position will the system be in equilibrium?

Sol.

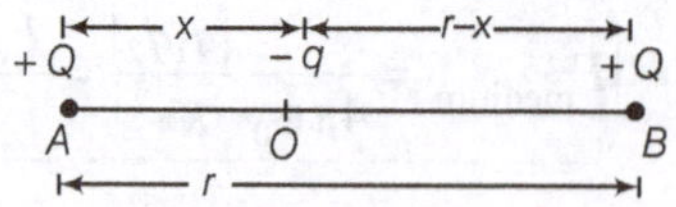

For charge $-q$ to be in equilibrium, force on the charge $-q$ at point O due to the charge $+Q$ at point A should be equal and opposite to that due to the charge $+Q$ at the point B, i.e. $\dfrac{1}{4\pi\varepsilon_0}\dfrac{Qq}{x^2} = \dfrac{1}{4\pi\varepsilon_0}\dfrac{Qq}{(r-x)^2}$

$$\Rightarrow \quad x^2 = (r-x)^2 \quad \text{or} \quad x = r - x$$

$$\therefore \quad x = \frac{r}{2}$$

Hence, for equilibrium the charge $-q$ should be kept at the middle of the line joining the points A and B.

Example 4 Find the magnitude of the resultant force on a charge of 1 μC held at P due to two charges of $+2\times 10^{-8}$ C and -10^{-8} C at A and B, respectively. Given, $AP = 10$ cm, $BP = 5$ cm and $\angle APB = 90°$,

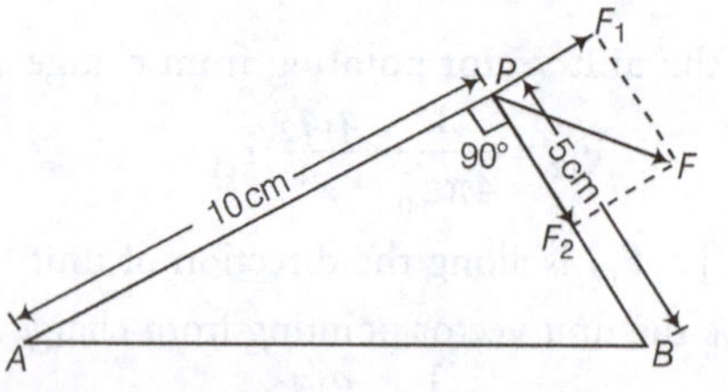

Sol. Here, charge at P, $q = 1\,\mu C = 10^{-6}$ C

Charge at A, $q_1 = 2\times 10^{-8}$ C

Charge at B, $q_2 = -10^{-8}$ C

$AP = 10\,\text{cm} = 0.1\,\text{m}$, $BP = 5$ cm $= 0.05$ m,

$\angle APB = 90°, F = ?$

Force at P due to q_1 charge at A,

$$F_1 = \frac{1}{4\pi\varepsilon_0}\frac{q_1 q}{AP^2}, \text{ along } AP \text{ produced}$$

$$= \frac{9\times 10^9 \times 2\times 10^{-8}\times 10^{-6}}{(0.1)^2} = 18\times 10^{-3}\,\text{N}$$

Force at P due to q_2 charge at B,

$$F_2 = \frac{1}{4\pi\,\varepsilon_0}\frac{q_2 q}{BP^2}, \text{ along } PB \text{ produced}$$

$$= \frac{9\times 10^9 \times -10^{-8} \times 10^{-6}}{(0.05)^2} = -36\times 10^{-3}\,\text{N}$$

As, angle between $\mathbf{F}_1$ and $\mathbf{F}_2$ is 90°.

∴ Resultant force,

$$F = \sqrt{F_1^2 + F_2^2} = \sqrt{(18\times 10^{-3})^2 + (-36\times 10^{-3})^2}$$

$$= \sqrt{(324+1296)\times 10^{-6}} = \sqrt{1620\times 10^{-6}}$$

$$= 40.2\times 10^{-3} = 4.0\times 10^{-2}\,\text{N}$$

Example 5 Two equal positive charges, each of $2\mu C$ interact with a third positive charge of $3\mu C$ situated as shown in figure. Calculate the magnitude and direction of the force on the $3\mu C$ charge. **NCERT**

Sol. In the figure, $OA = OB = 3\,\text{m}$, $OP = 4\,\text{m}$

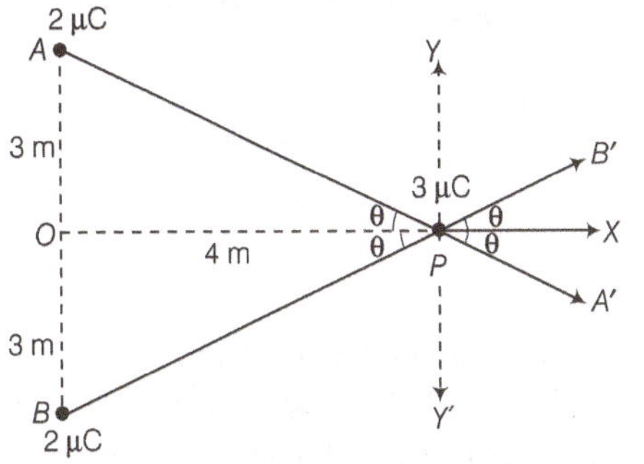

∴ $$AP = BP = \sqrt{3^2 + 4^2} = 5\,\text{m}$$

According to Coulomb's law,

force on charge at P due to charge at A,

$$F_1 = \frac{1}{4\pi\varepsilon_0}\frac{q_1 q_2}{AP^2} = \frac{9\times 10^9 \times (2\times 10^{-6})\times(3\times 10^{-6})}{5^2}$$

$$= \frac{54}{25}\times 10^{-3} = 2.16\times 10^{-3}\ \text{N, along } PA'.$$

It has two rectangular components $F_1 \cos\theta$ along PX and $F_1 \sin\theta$ along PY'.

Similarly, force on charge at P due to charge at B, $F_2 = F_1$ (in magnitude). It is along PB'. It also has two rectangular component $F_2 \cos\theta$ along PX and $F_2 \sin\theta$ along PY.

The components along PY and PY' cancel. The components along PX add up.

∴ Total force on $3\,\mu C$ charge is $F = 2F_1 \cos\theta$

$$= 2\times 2.16\times 10^{-3} \times 4/5$$

$$= 3.5\times 10^{-3}\ \text{N, along } PX.$$

Electric Field

The electric field due to a charge Q at a point in space may be defined as the force that a unit positive charge would experience if placed at that point.

The charge Q which produces the electric field is called **source charge** and the charge q which experiences the effect of source charge is called **test charge.**

Electric Field Intensity

The electric field intensity at any point due to source charge is defined as the force experienced per unit positive test charge placed at that point without disturbing the source charge.

It is expressed as, $\mathbf{E} = \dfrac{\mathbf{F}}{q_0}$

where, $\mathbf{E}$ = electric field intensity

and $\mathbf{F}$ = force experienced by the test charge q_0.

It is a vector quantity.

Its SI unit is NC^{-1} and dimension is $[\text{MLT}^{-3}\text{A}^{-1}]$.

The figure (a) is representing the electric field due to charge $+q$. In this, it can be seen that for a positive charge, the electric field vector is directed radially outwards, i.e. away from **positive charge.**

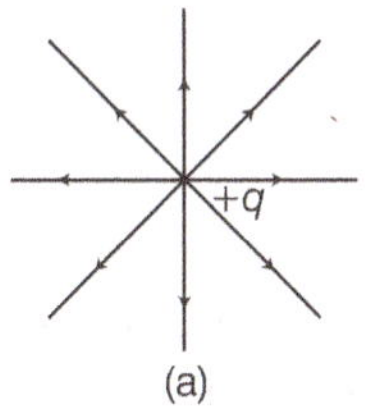

(a)

The figure (b) is representing the electric field due to charge $-q$. In this, it can be seen that for a negative charge, the electric field vector is directed radially inwards, i.e. towards **negative charge.**

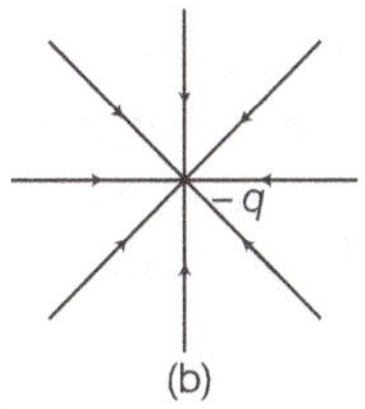

(b)

Note

- Electric field intensity is also called electric field.
- Positive charges move along the direction of electric field, while negative charges move in opposite direction of electric field.

Example of Different Field

Magnetic Field

The area around a magnet within which magnetic force is exerted is called a magnetic field. It is produced by moving electric charges. The presence and strength of a magnetic field is denoted by "magnetic flux lines". The direction of the magnetic field is also indicated by these lines.

Electric Field

A moving charge always has both a magnetic and an electric field. They are two different fields with nearly the same characteristics. Therefore, they are inter-reated in a field called the electromagnetic field.

Gravitational Field

It is the force field that exists in the space around every mass or group of masses. This field extends out in all directions, but the magnitude of the gravitational force decreases as the distance from the object increases.

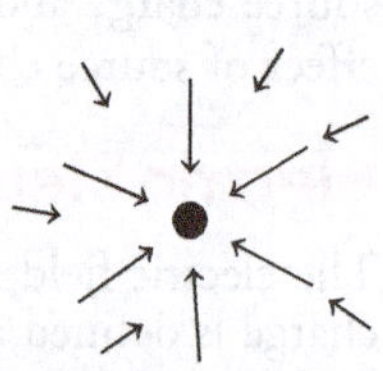

A gravitaional field is a type of force field and is analogous to electric and magnetic fields for electrically charged particles and magnets, respectively.

Electric Field due to a Point Charge

We have to find the electric field at a point P due to a point charge $+q$ placed at the origin such that OP = r.

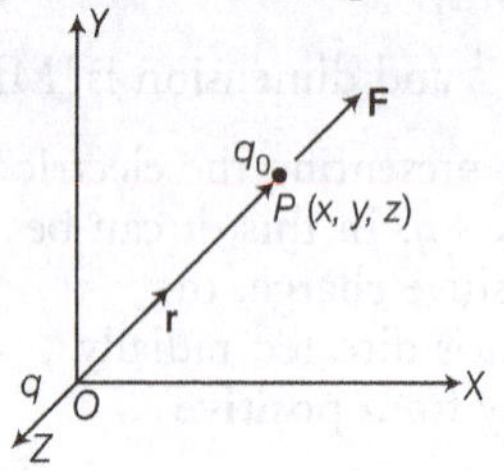

Electric field due to a point charge in coordinate frame

To find the electric field at point P, we have to find the electric force on a test charge q_0 placed at point P, due to source charge q.

According to Coulomb's law, force on the test charge q_0 due to charge q is given by

$$\mathbf{F} = \frac{1}{4\pi\varepsilon_0}\frac{qq_0}{r^2}\hat{\mathbf{r}}$$

If **E** is the electric field at a point P, then

$$\mathbf{E} = \lim_{q_0 \to 0}\frac{\mathbf{F}}{q_0} = \lim_{q_0 \to 0}\left(\frac{1}{q_0}\cdot\frac{1}{4\pi\varepsilon_0}\frac{qq_0}{r^2}\hat{\mathbf{r}}\right)$$

$$\Rightarrow \quad \mathbf{E} = \frac{1}{4\pi\varepsilon_0}\cdot\frac{q}{r^2}\hat{\mathbf{r}} \quad \ldots(\text{i})$$

The magnitude of the electric field at a point P is given by

$$E = \frac{1}{4\pi\varepsilon_0}\cdot\frac{q}{r^2}$$

From the above formula, it is clear that electric field at any point in space due to a charge depends only on the distance. That means, the magnitude of electric field due to point charge is same at all the points of sphere, i.e. it has spherical symmetry.

If $q > 0$, the electric field vector points radially outwards from the point. If $q < 0$, the electric field vector points radially inwards towards the point.

Example 6 A conducting sphere of radius 10 cm has an unknown charge. If the electric field 20 cm from the centre of the sphere is 1.5×10^3 N/C and points radially inwards, then what is the net charge on the sphere?

NCERT

Sol. Let the value of unknown charge be q.

Electric field at 20 cm away, $E = 1.5 \times 10^3$ N/C

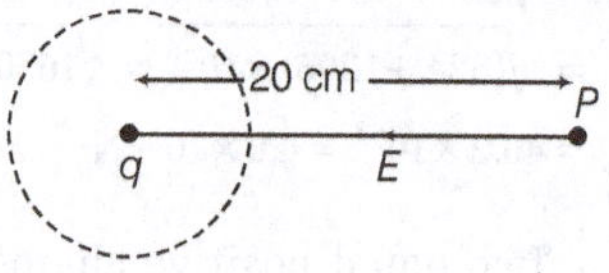

From the formula, electric field, $E = \frac{1}{4\pi\varepsilon_0}\cdot\frac{q}{r^2}$

$$\Rightarrow 1.5 \times 10^3 = \frac{9 \times 10^9 \times q}{(20 \times 10^{-2})^2}$$

$$\therefore \quad q = \frac{1.5 \times 10^3 \times 20 \times 20 \times 10^{-4}}{9 \times 10^9} = 6.67 \times 10^{-9}\,\text{C}$$

As the electric field is radially inwards which shows that the nature of unknown charge q is negative.

Electric Field due to System of Charges

Consider that n point charges $q_1, q_2, q_3, \ldots, q_n$ exert forces $\mathbf{F}_1, \mathbf{F}_2, \mathbf{F}_3, \ldots, \mathbf{F}_n$ on a test charge q_0 placed at origin O. Let $\mathbf{F}_i$ be the force due to ith charge q_i on q_0, then

$$\mathbf{F}_i = \frac{1}{4\pi\varepsilon_0}\frac{q_i q_0}{r_i^2}\hat{\mathbf{r}}_i$$

where, r_i is the distance of the test charge q_0 from q_i.

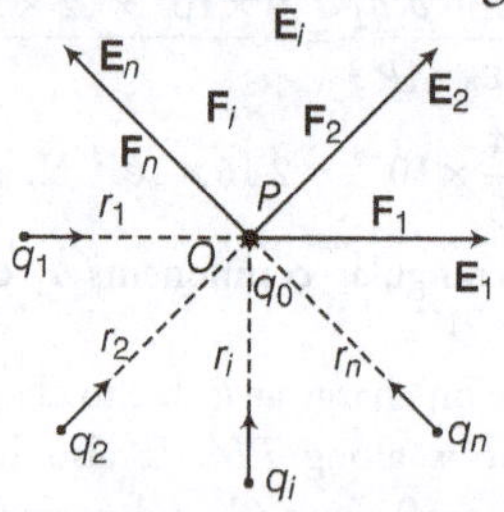

The electric field at the observation point P is given by

$$\mathbf{E}_i = \lim_{q_0 \to 0}\frac{\mathbf{F}_i}{q_0} = \lim_{q_0 \to 0}\left[\frac{1}{q_0}\left(\frac{1}{4\pi\varepsilon_0}\cdot\frac{q_i q_0}{r_i^2}\hat{\mathbf{r}}_i\right)\right]$$

$$\mathbf{E}_i = \frac{1}{4\pi\varepsilon_0}\cdot\frac{q_i}{r_i^2}\hat{\mathbf{r}}_i \quad \ldots(\text{i})$$

If **E** is electric field at point P due to the system of charges, then by principle of superposition of electric fields, $\mathbf{E} = \mathbf{E}_1 + \mathbf{E}_2 + \mathbf{E}_3 + \cdots + \mathbf{E}_n = \sum_{i=1}^{n}\mathbf{E}_i$

Using Eq. (i), we get

$$\mathbf{E} = \sum_{i=1}^{n} \frac{1}{4\pi\varepsilon_0} \cdot \frac{q_i}{r_i^2} \hat{\mathbf{r}}_i$$

or $$\boxed{\mathbf{E} = \frac{1}{4\pi\varepsilon_0} \sum_{i=1}^{n} \frac{q_i}{r_i^2} \hat{\mathbf{r}}_i}$$

∴ E is a vector quantity.

Example 7 Two charges $+Q$ and $-Q$ are kept at points $(-x_2, 0)$ and $(x_1, 0)$ respectively, in the XY-plane. Find the magnitude and direction of the net electric field at the origin $(0, 0)$.

> **Key Point** To find the electric field intensity at a point due to two charges, first of all find the individual electric field due to both charges and then find the resultant field by using vector addition.

Sol.

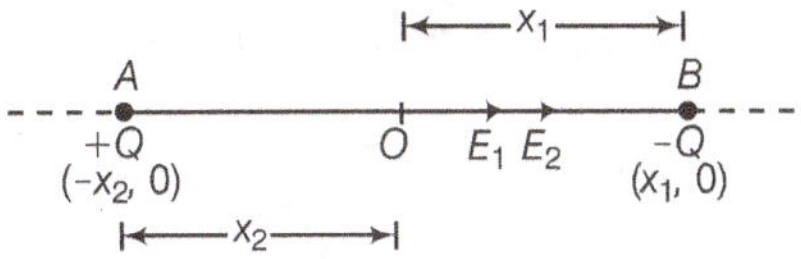

Electric field intensity at point O due to $+Q$ charge,

$$E_1 = \frac{1}{4\pi\varepsilon_0} \times \frac{Q}{(x_2)^2} \text{ (towards } B) \quad \ldots\text{(i)}$$

Electric field intensity at point O due to $-Q$ charge,

$$E_2 = \frac{1}{4\pi\varepsilon_0} \times \frac{Q}{(x_1)^2} \text{ (towards } B) \quad \ldots\text{(ii)}$$

∵ E_1 and E_2 act along the same direction.

∴ Net electric field intensity at point O is given by

$$E = E_1 + E_2 = \frac{1}{4\pi\varepsilon_0} \times \frac{Q}{(x_2)^2} + \frac{1}{4\pi\varepsilon_0} \times \frac{Q}{(x_1)^2} \text{ (towards } B)$$

$$= \frac{Q}{4\pi\varepsilon_0}\left[\frac{1}{x_2^2} + \frac{1}{x_1^2}\right]$$

Example 8 Two point charges $+Q$ and $+4Q$ are separated by a distance of $6a$. Find the point on the line joining the two charges, where the electric field is zero.

Sol. The electric field is zero at point P only, if the field due to charge $+Q$ balances the field due to charge $+4Q$.

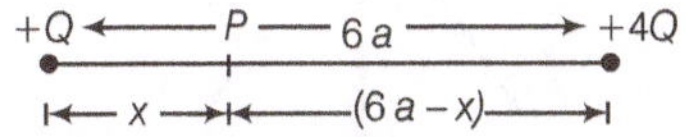

$$\therefore \frac{1}{4\pi\varepsilon_0} \cdot \frac{Q}{x^2} = \frac{1}{4\pi\varepsilon_0} \cdot \frac{4Q}{(6a - x)^2} \Rightarrow \frac{1}{x^2} = \frac{4}{(6a - x)^2}$$

$$\Rightarrow \frac{1}{x} = \frac{2}{(6a - x)} \Rightarrow 2x = 6a - x \Rightarrow x = 2a$$

∴ The required point is at a distance of $2a$ from $+Q$.

Physical Significance of Electric Field

The physical significance of electric field is that we can readily calculate the magnitude and direction of force experienced by any charge q_0 placed at a point by knowing the electric field intensity at that point.

Intensity of electric field due to Continuous Charge Distribution

The region in which charges are closely spaced is said to have continuous distribution of charge. Continuous charge distribution is of three types; linear charge distribution (one dimensional), surface charge distribution (two dimensional) and volume charge distribution (three dimensional).

Linear Charge Distribution

If charge is distributed continuously along a line, i.e. straight or curve is called linear charge distribution.

Charge on an infinitesimally small length element dl will be

$dq = \lambda dl$, where λ is the **linear charge density.**

i.e. $$\lambda = \frac{dq}{dl}$$

Its SI unit is coulomb/metre.

Electric force at a point due to a linear charge distribution is given by $$\mathbf{F} = \frac{q_0}{4\pi\varepsilon_0} \int_l \frac{\lambda dl}{r_0^2} \hat{\mathbf{r}}_0$$

Intensity of electric field, $$\mathbf{E} = \frac{\mathbf{F}}{q_0} = \frac{1}{4\pi\varepsilon_0} \int_l \frac{\lambda dl}{r_0^2} \hat{\mathbf{r}}_0$$

where, $\mathbf{r}_0 = \mathbf{r} - \mathbf{r}'$, $\mathbf{r}'$ is the position vector of length element dl with respect to origin and $\mathbf{r}$ is the position vector of charge q_0 with respect to origin.

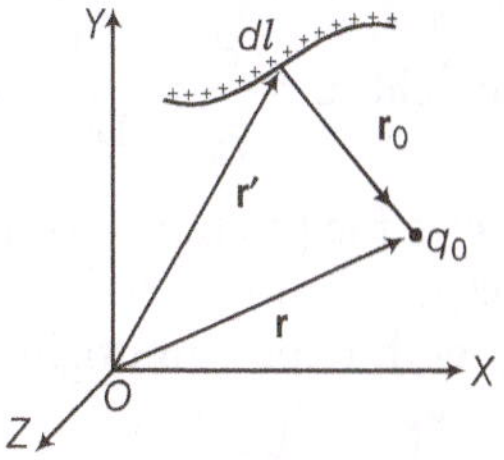

Surface Charge Distribution

If charge is distributed continuously over a surface is called surface charge distribution.

Charge on an infinitesimally small surface element dS will be, $dq = \sigma dS$, where σ is the **surface charge density.**

i.e. $\sigma = \dfrac{dq}{dS}$

Its SI unit is coulomb/metre^2.

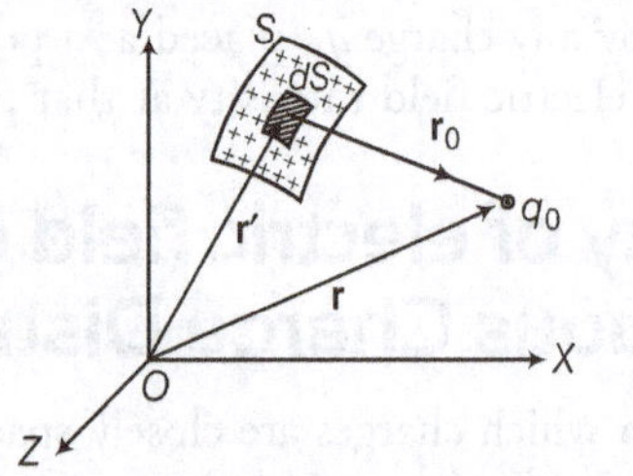

Electric force at a point due to a surface charge distribution is given by

$$\mathbf{F} = \frac{q_0}{4\pi\varepsilon_0} \int_S \frac{\sigma\, dS}{r_0^2} \hat{\mathbf{r}}_0$$

Intensity of electric field,

$$\mathbf{E} = \frac{\mathbf{F}}{q_0} = \frac{1}{4\pi\varepsilon_0} \int_S \frac{\sigma dS}{r_0^2} \hat{\mathbf{r}}_0$$

where, $\mathbf{r}_0 = \mathbf{r} - \mathbf{r}'$, $\mathbf{r}'$ is the position vector of surface element dS with respect to origin and $\mathbf{r}$ is the position vector of charge q_0 with respect to origin.

Volume Charge Distribution

If charge is distributed continuously over the volume is called volume charge distribution.

Charge on an infinitesimally small element of volume dV will be, $dq = \delta dV$, where δ is the **volume charge density**.

i.e. $\delta = \dfrac{dq}{dV}$

Its SI unit is coulomb/metre^3.

Electric force at a point due to volume charge distribution is given by $\mathbf{F} = \dfrac{q_0}{4\pi\varepsilon_0} \displaystyle\int_V \frac{\rho dV}{r_0^2} \hat{\mathbf{r}}_0$

Intensity of electric field, $\mathbf{E} = \dfrac{\mathbf{F}}{q_0} = \dfrac{1}{4\pi\varepsilon_0} \displaystyle\int_V \frac{\rho dV}{r_0^2} \hat{\mathbf{r}}_0$

where, $\mathbf{r}_0 = \mathbf{r} - \mathbf{r}'$, $\mathbf{r}'$ is the position vector of volume element dV with respect to origin and $\mathbf{r}$ is the position vector of charge q_0 with respect to origin.

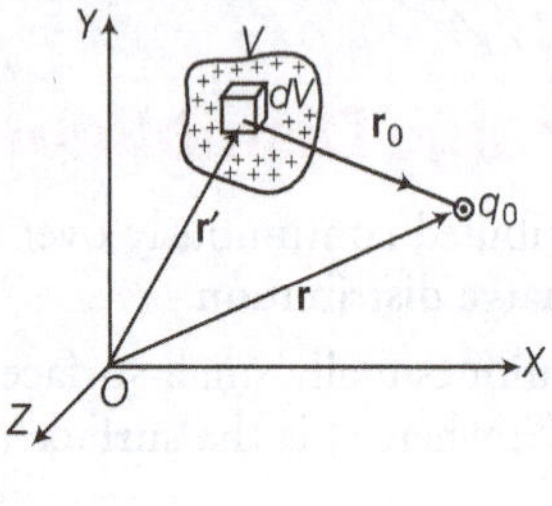

Example 9 What charge would be required to electrify a sphere of radius 25 cm, so as to get a surface charge density of $\frac{3}{\pi}$ Cm^{-2}?

Sol. Here, $r = 25$ cm $= 0.25$ m, $\sigma = \dfrac{3}{\pi}$ Cm^{-2}

As, $\sigma = \dfrac{q}{4\pi r^2}$

$\therefore$ $q = 4\pi r^2 \sigma = 4\pi \times (0.25)^2 \times \dfrac{3}{\pi}$ C

$= 0.75$ C

Example 10 The radius of gold nucleus ($Z = 79$) is about 7.0×10^{-15} m. Assuming that the positive charge is distributed uniformly throughout the nuclear volume, find the volume charge density.

Sol. The total positive charge in the nucleus is given by

$$q = +Ze = 79 \times 1.6 \times 10^{-19} \text{C}$$

$\therefore$ Volume charge density, $\delta = \dfrac{q}{\frac{4}{3}\pi R^3}$

$$= \frac{79 \times 1.6 \times 10^{-19}}{4/3 \times 3.14 \times (7.0 \times 10^{-15})^3}$$

$= 0.088 \times 10^{26}$

$= 8.8 \times 10^{24}$ Cm^{-3}

Electric Field Lines

An electric field line in general is a curve drawn in such a way that the tangent to it at each point is in the direction of the electric field at that point. A field line is a space curve, i.e. a curve in three dimensions. Electric field lines are thus used to pictorially map the electric field around a charge or a configuration of charges.

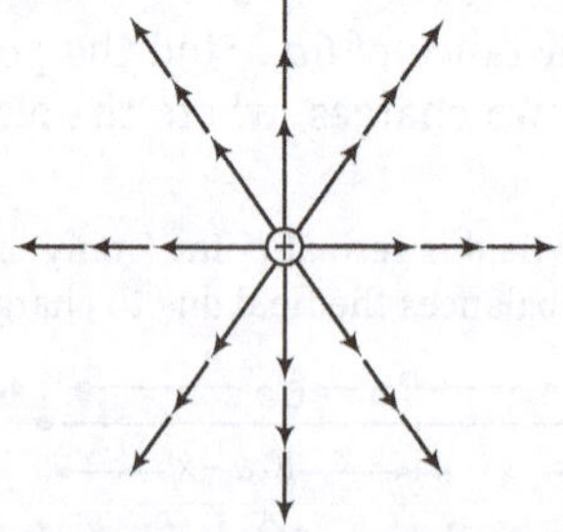

Field lines showing electric field of a point charge

The density of field lines is more near the charge. Away from the charge, the field is weak, so the density of field lines is less.

Properties of Electric Field Lines

Electric field lines follow some important properties which are discussed below

(i) Electric field lines start from positive charges and end at negative charges. In the case of a single charge, they may start or end at infinity.

(ii) Tangent to any point on electric field lines shows the direction of electric field at that point.

(iii) Two field lines can never intersect each other because if they intersect, then two tangents drawn at that point will represent two directions of field at that point, which is not possible.

(iv) In a charge free region, electric field lines can be taken to be continuous curves without any breaks.

(v) Electric field lines do not form closed loops (because of conservative nature of electric field).

(vi) Electric field lines are perpendicular to the surface of a charged conductor.

(vii) Electric field lines contract lengthwise to represent attraction between two unlike charges.

(viii) Electric field lines exert sideways pressure to represent repulsion between two like charges.

Representations of Electric Field

For different types of electric field, lines are represented as shown below

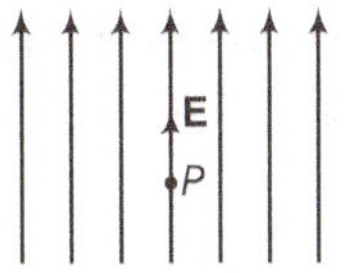

Electric field lines for a uniform field

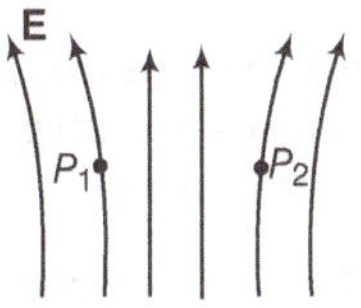

Electric field lines for a non-uniform field

The electric field lines start from positive charges and end at negative charges.

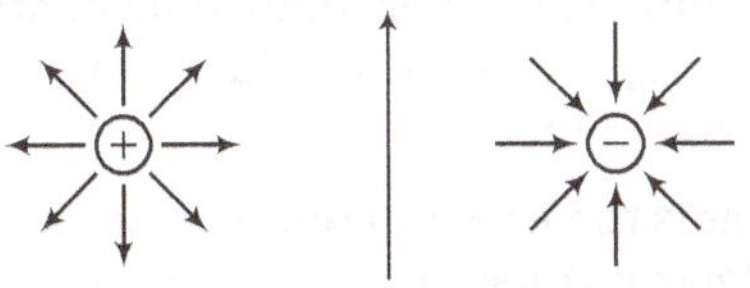

Direction is away from the positive charge

Direction is towards the negative charge

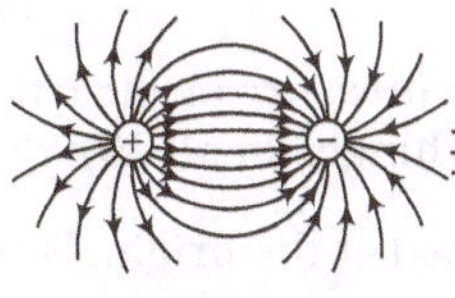

(a) Electric dipole

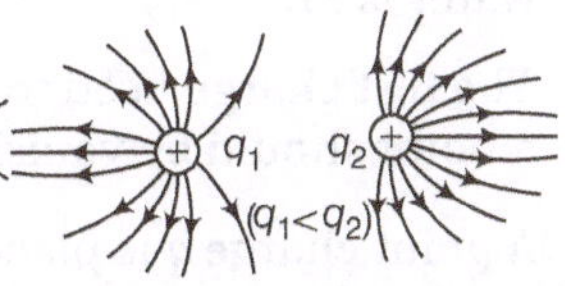

(b) Two similar charge at a small distance

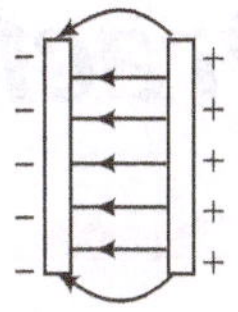

(c) Two opposite charged parallel plate

It is a common misconception that the path traced by a positive charge is a field line. The path traced by a unit positive test charge represents a field line only when it moves along a straight line.

Example 11 Explain, why the following curves cannot possibly represent electrostatic field lines? **NCERT**

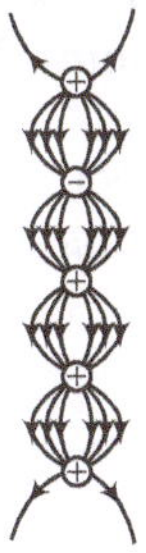

(a)

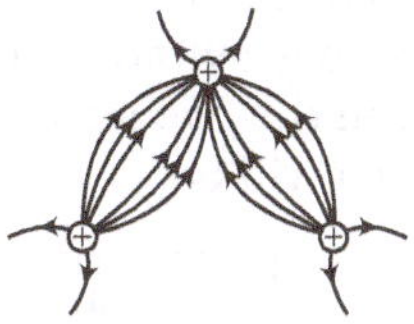

(b)

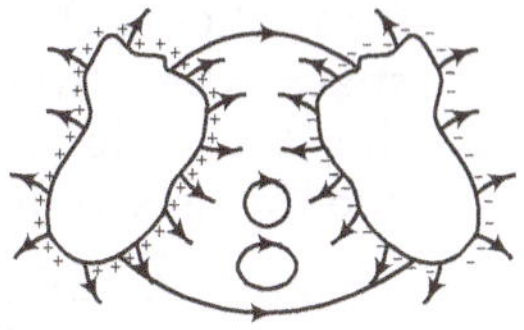

(c)

Sol. (a) Electrostatic field lines cannot start from a negative charge.

(b) Electrostatic field lines cannot end at positive charge.

(c) Electrostatic field lines cannot form closed loops.

Conductors in an Electrostatic Field

(i) Electric field lines do not pass through a conductor. Hence, the interior of the conductor is free from the influence of the electric field.

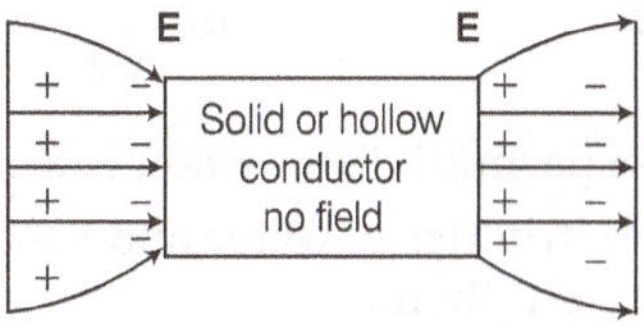

Electrostatic shielding

(ii) Total charge of a charged conductor lies at the outer surface of the conductor.

(iii) The magnitude of field strength at any point on the surface of the conductor is proportional to surface charge density at that point.

Topic Practice 2

Multiple Choice Questions

1 Mark

1. Two charges are at a distance d apart. If a copper plate (conducting medium) of thickness $\frac{d}{2}$ is placed between them, the effective force will be
(a) $2F$
(b) $F/2$
(c) $4F$
(d) $\sqrt{2}\,F$ (F = force without copper plate)

2. Two small spheres each having the charge $+Q$ are suspended by insulating threads of length L from a hook. This arrangement is taken in space, where there is no gravitational effect, then the angle between the two suspensions and the tension in each will be
(a) $180°, \frac{1}{4\pi\varepsilon_0}\frac{Q^2}{(2L)^2}$
(b) $90°, \frac{1}{4\pi\varepsilon_0}\frac{Q^2}{L^2}$
(c) $180°, \frac{1}{4\pi\varepsilon_0}\frac{Q^2}{2L^2}$
(d) $180°, \frac{1}{4\pi\varepsilon_0}\frac{Q^2}{L^2}$

3. The ratio of the forces between two small spheres with constant charge (i) in air (ii) in a medium of dielectric constant K is
(a) $1:K$
(b) $K:1$
(c) $1:K^2$
(d) $K^2:1$

4. For charges q_1 and q_2, if force between them for some separation in air is F, then force between them in a medium of permittivity ε will be
(a) $\frac{\varepsilon_0}{\varepsilon}F$
(b) $\frac{\varepsilon}{\varepsilon_0}F$
(c) $\varepsilon\varepsilon_0 F$
(d) $\frac{F}{\varepsilon_0\varepsilon}$

5. Relative permittivity of water is 81. If ε_w and ε_0 are permittivities of water and vacuum respectively, then **ISC 2013**
(a) $\varepsilon_0 = 9\varepsilon_w$
(b) $\varepsilon_0 = 81\varepsilon_w$
(c) $\varepsilon_w = 9\varepsilon_0$
(d) $\varepsilon_w = 81\varepsilon_0$

6. Field due to multiple charges at a point is found by using
I. superposition principle.
II. Coulomb's law.
III. law of conservation of charges.
IV. law of parallelogram of forces.
(a) I and II
(b) II and III
(c) III and IV
(d) I and IV

7. Consider an arbitrary electrostatic field configuration. A small test charge is placed at a null point (i.e. where E = 0) of the configuration. Then, the equilibrium of test charge is
(a) stable
(b) unstable
(c) can be stable or unstable
(d) no equilibrium is possible

8. Unit of volume charge density is
(a) C/m
(b) C/m^3
(c) C/m^2
(d) None of these

9. The SI unit of electric field is
(a) NC^{-1}
(b) NC
(c) CN^{-1}
(d) NC^2

10. Two field lines can never crosses each other, because
(a) field lines are closed curves
(b) field lines repels each other
(c) field lines crowded only near the charge
(d) field has a unique direction at each point

Very Short Answer Type Questions

1 Mark

11. Write Coulomb's law in vector form. **ISC 2008**

12. Does the Coulomb force that one charge exerts on another charge changes, if other charge is brought nearby?

13. In Coulomb's law, $F = \frac{k_e q_1 q_2}{r^2}$, what are the factors on which the proportionality constant k_e depends?

14. If the distance between two equal point charges is doubled and their individual charges are also doubled, then what would happen to the force between them?

15. What is the effect of temperature on the dielectric constant K of a dielectric?

16. Explain the statement, relative permittivity of water is 81. **ISC 2009**

17. The test charge used to measure electric field at a point should be vanishingly small. Why?

18. A point charge q is placed at the origin. How does the electric field due to the charge vary with the distance r from the origin?

19. Force experienced by an electron in an electric field is F newton. What will be the force experienced by a proton in the same field? Take, mass of a proton is 1836 times the mass of an electron.

20. Two point charges of $+3\,\mu C$ each are 100 cm apart. At what point on the line joining the charges will the electric field intensity be zero?

21. A proton is placed in a uniform electric field directed along a positive X-axis. In which direction will it tend to move?

22. A metallic spherical shell has an inner radius R_1 and outer radius R_2. A charge Q is placed at the centre of the spherical cavity. What will be surface charge density on (i) the inner surface and (ii) the outer surface? **NCERT Exemplar**

23. Why electrostatic field be normal to the surface at every point of a charged conductor?

24. An electrostatic field line is continuous curve, i.e. a field line cannot have sudden breaks. Why not?

25. Why should electrostatic field be zero inside a conductor?

26. Why do the electric field lines not form closed loops?

Short Answer Type I Questions

2 Marks

27. In the given statement, point out the correct or incorrect word or phrase with a proper explanation.
'The mutual forces between two charges do not get affected by the presence of other charges.'

28. Plot a graph showing the variation of Coulomb's force (F) *versus* $1/r^2$, where r is the distance between the two charges of each pair of charges ($1\,\mu C$, $2\,\mu C$) and ($1\,\mu C$, $-3\,\mu C$). Interpret the graphs obtained.

29. A charge q is placed at the centre of the line joining two equal charges (Q). Show that the system of three charges will be in equilibrium, if $q = -\dfrac{Q}{4}$.

30. An uncharged metallic ball is suspended in the region between two vertical metal plates. If the two plates are charged, one positively and one negatively, then describe the motion of the ball after it is brought into contact with one of the plates.

31. Sketch the electric field lines for a uniformly charged hollow cylinder as shown in the figure. **NCERT Exemplar**

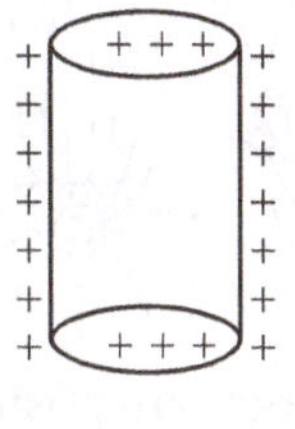

Short Answer Type II Questions

3 Marks

32. Check that the ratio ke^2/Gm_em_p is dimensionless. Look up a table of physical constants and determine the value of this ratio. What does the ratio signify? **NCERT**

33. Consider three charges Q_1, Q_2, Q_3 each equal to Q at the vertices of an equilateral triangle of side a. What is the force on a charge q (with the same sign as q) placed at the centroid of the triangle? **NCERT**

34. An oil drop of 12 excess electrons is held stationary under a constant electric field of 2.55×10^4 N/C in Millikan's oil drop experiment. The density of the oil is $1.26\ \text{g/cm}^3$. Estimate the radius of the drop.
(Take, $g = 9.81\ \text{m/s}^2$, $e = 1.6 \times 10^{-19}$C). **NCERT**

35. Five charges, q each are placed at the corners of regular pentagon of side a as shown in the figure.

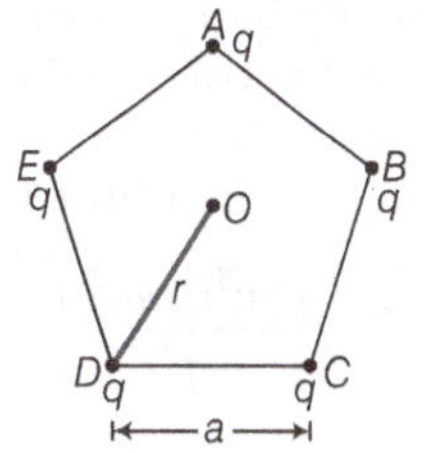

(i) (a) What will be the electric field at O, the centre of the pentagon?
(b) What will be the electric field at O, if the charge from one of the corners (say A) is removed?
(c) What will be the electric field at O, if the charge q at A is replaced by $-q$?

(ii) How would your answer be affected, if pentagon is replaced by n-sided regular polygon with charge q at each of its corners? **NCERT Exemplar**

36. Figure shows the electric field lines around three point charges A, B and C.

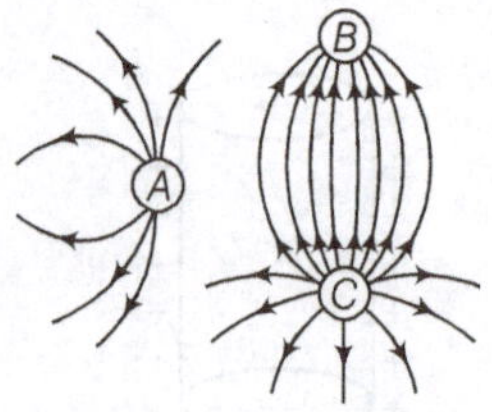

(i) Which charges are positive?

(ii) Which charge has the largest magnitude? Why?

(iii) In which region or regions of the picture could the electric field be zero? Justify your answer. **NCERT Exemplar**

(a) Near A (b) Near B

(c) Near C (d) Nowhere

Long Answer Type Questions

5 Marks

37. Total charge $-Q$ is uniformly spread along length of a ring of radius R. A small test charge $+q$ of mass m is kept at the centre of the ring and is given a gentle push along the axis of the ring. Show that the particle executes a simple harmonic oscillation and obtain its time period. **NCERT Exemplar**

38. Two charges $-q$ each are fixed separated by distance $2d$. A third charge q of mass m placed at the mid-point is displaced slightly by $x(x << d)$ perpendicular to the line joining the two fixed charged as shown in figure. Show that q will perform simple harmonic oscillation of time period.

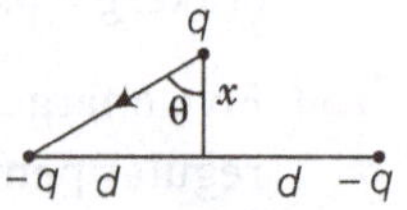

$$T = \left[\frac{8\pi^3\varepsilon_0 md^3}{q^2}\right]^{1/2}$$

NCERT

Numerical Problems

39. A charged oil drop weighing 1.6×10^{-15} N is found to remain suspended in a uniform electric field of intensity 2×10^3 NC^{-1}. Find the charge on the drop. **ISC 2016 (1 M)**

40. Two point charges $Q_1 = 400\ \mu$C and $Q_2 = 100\ \mu$C are kept fixed, 60 cm apart in vacuum. Find the intensity of the electric field at mid-point of the line joining Q_1 and Q_2. **ISC 2016 (1 M)**

41. A point charge of 5×10^{-6} C experiences a force of 2×10^{-3} N when kept in a uniform electric field of intensity E. Then, find the value of E. **ISC 2012 (1 M)**

42. The dielectric constant of water is 80. What is its permittivity? **(1 M)**

43. Two equal balls having equal positive charge q coulombs are suspended by two insulating strings of equal length. What would be the effect on the force when a plastic sheet is inserted between the two? **(1 M)**

44. Two point charges having equal charges separated by 1 m distance experience a force of 8 N. What will be the force experienced by them, if they are held in water, at the same distance? (Given, $K_{water} = 80$) **(1M)**

45. A charge $q = 1\ \mu$C is placed at point (1 m, 2 m, 4 m). Find the electric field at point P (0 m, $-$4 m, 3 m). **(2 M)**

46. An infinite number of charges each equal to q are placed along X-axis at $x = 1, x = 2, x = 4, x = 8$ and so on. Find the electric field at the point $x = 0$ due to this set up of charges. **(2 M)**

47. The opposite corners of a square carry Q charge each and the other two opposite corners of the same square carry q charge each. If the resultant force on q is zero, how are Q and q related? **(3 M)**

48. (i) Two insulated charged copper spheres A and B have their centres separated by a distance of 50 cm. What is the mutual force of electrostatic repulsion, if the charge on each is 6.5×10^{-7} C and the radii of A and B are negligible compared to the distance of separation?

(ii) What is the force of repulsion, if each sphere is charged double the above amount and the distance between them is halved? **NCERT (3 M)**

49. Suppose the spheres A and B in Q. 48 have identical sizes. A third sphere of the same size but uncharged is brought in contact with the first, then brought in contact with the second and finally removed from both. What is the new force of repulsion between A and B? **NCERT (3 M)**

50. Figure represents a crystal unit of caesium chloride CsCl. The caesium atoms, represented by open circles are situated at the corners of a cube of side 0.40 nm, whereas a Cl atom is situated at the centre of the cube. The Cs atoms are deficient in one electron while the Cl atom carries an excess electron.

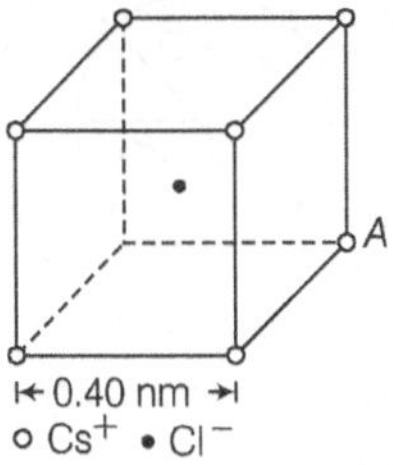

(i) What is the net electric field on the Cl atom due to eight Cs atoms?

(ii) Suppose that the Cs atom at the corner A is missing. What is the net force now on the Cl atom due to seven remaining Cs atoms? **NCERT Exemplar (3 M)**

51. In the figure below, the electric field lines on the left have twice the separation of those on the right.

(i) If the magnitude of the field of A is 40 N/C, then what force acts on a proton at A?

(ii) What is the magnitude of the field at B? **(3 M)**

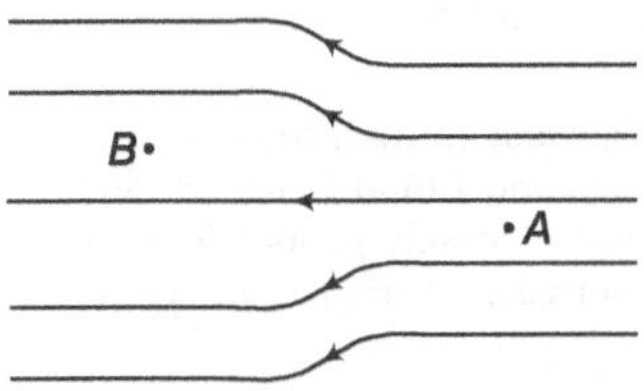

Hints & Solutions

1. (c) Due to copper plate, effective distance is $d/2$,

i.e. $\left(d - \frac{d}{2}\right) = d/2$

$\therefore \quad F' = \frac{kq_1 q_2}{(d/2)^2} = 4F$

Copper plate is conductor, its presence act as reduction of distance between charges, so $F' > F$.

2. (a) In space, there is no gravitational force, so

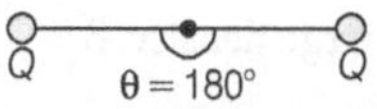

Tension in each thread, i.e. $F = \frac{kQQ}{(2L)^2}$

$$= \frac{1}{4\pi\varepsilon_0} \cdot \frac{Q^2}{(2L)^2}$$

3. (b) Relative permittivity ε_r is also called dielectric constant.

$$F_{\text{air}} = \frac{1}{4\pi\varepsilon_0} \frac{q_1 q_2}{r^2} \qquad [\because \text{for air, } K = 1]$$

$$F_m = \frac{1}{4\pi\varepsilon_0 K} \frac{q_1 q_2}{r^2}$$

$$\frac{F_{\text{air}}}{F_m} = \frac{\frac{1}{4\pi\varepsilon_0} \frac{q_1 q_2}{r^2}}{\frac{1}{4\pi\varepsilon_0 K} \frac{q_1 q_2}{r^2}} = \frac{K}{1}$$

4. (a) Force in air, i.e. $F = \frac{1}{4\pi\varepsilon_0} \frac{q_1 q_2}{r^2}$

and force in medium, i.e. $F_m = \frac{1}{4\pi\varepsilon_0 \varepsilon_r} \frac{q_1 q_2}{r^2} \left(\because \frac{\varepsilon}{\varepsilon_0} = \varepsilon_r\right)$

$$= \frac{1}{4\pi\varepsilon} \frac{q_1 q_2}{r^2} = \frac{\varepsilon_0}{\varepsilon} \cdot \frac{1}{4\pi\varepsilon_0} \frac{q_1 q_2}{r^2}$$

$$\Rightarrow \quad F_m = \frac{\varepsilon_0}{\varepsilon} F$$

5. (d) We know that, relative permittivity,

$$\varepsilon_r = \frac{\varepsilon_w}{\varepsilon_0}$$

$\Rightarrow \varepsilon_w$ = absolute permittivity of water

$= (\varepsilon_r)(\varepsilon_0) = (81)(\varepsilon_0) = 81\varepsilon_0$

For water, relative permittivity, $\varepsilon_r = 81$

6. (a) Consider a system of charges $q_1, q_2, \ldots, q_n$ with position vectors $\mathbf{r}_1, \mathbf{r}_2, \ldots, \mathbf{r}_n$ relative to some origin O. Like the field due to a single charge, electric field at a point in space due to the system of charges is defined to be the force experienced by a unit test charge placed at that point, without disturbing the original positions of charges $q_1, q_2, \ldots, q_n$. We can use Coulomb's law and the superposition principle to determine this field.

7. (b) Let us prove it by contradiction. Suppose the equilibrium is stable. Then, the test charge displaced slightly in any direction will experience a restoring force towards the null point.

So, all field lines near the null point should be directed inwards towards the null-point, i.e. there is a net inward flux of electric field through a closed surface around the null-point. But by Gauss's law, the flux of electric field through a surface, not enclosing any charge, must be zero. Hence, the equilibrium cannot be stable.

8. (*b*) Volume of charge density, $\delta = \dfrac{\text{Charge in volume}}{\text{Volume of wire}}$

$$\delta = \frac{\Delta Q}{\Delta V} = \frac{\text{Charge}}{\text{Volume of wire}} = \frac{\text{C}}{\text{m}^3} = \text{C/m}^3$$

9. (*a*) As we know, electric field, i.e. $\mathbf{E} = \dfrac{\mathbf{F}}{q} = \dfrac{\text{N}}{\text{C}}$. As force F measured in newton (N), charge q measured in coulomb (C). So, unit of E become N/C.

10. (*d*) Field has a direction and magnitude, because it is vector. At a point in space fixed line means fixed direction,two lines mean two directions which is not possible for vector.

11. Vector form of Coulomb's law,

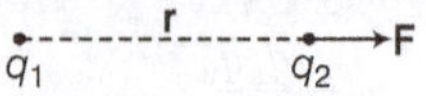

$$\mathbf{F} = \frac{1}{4\pi\varepsilon_0} \cdot \frac{q_1 q_2}{|r|^3} \mathbf{r}$$

or $$|F| = \frac{1}{4\pi\varepsilon_0} \cdot \frac{q_1 q_2}{|r|^2}$$

where, q_1 and q_2 are two charges separated by a distance r which is the displacement vector. It shows direction of force between two charges.

12. Yes, it changes as the distance becomes less.

13. Here, K_e is also called dielectric constant, whose value depends essentially on the type of substance and on the external conditions like temperature, pressure and so on.

14. We know that by Coulomb's law,

$$F = k\frac{q_1 q_2}{r^2}$$

According to question, $q_1' = 2q_1$, $q_2' = 2q_2$, $r' = 2r$

$$\therefore \quad F' = \frac{k(2q_1)(2q_2)}{(2r)^2} = \frac{kq_1 q_2}{r^2} = F$$

Hence, force between these charges remains same.

15. Dielectric constant K decreases with rise in temperature.

16. Relative permittivity (ε_r) of water is the ratio of absolute permittivity (ε) and permittivity of free space (ε_0).

i.e. $\varepsilon_r = \dfrac{\varepsilon}{\varepsilon_0}$

It means that permittivity of water is 81 times that of free space.

17. In case, test charge is not vanishingly small, it will produce its own electric field and the measured value of electric field will be different from the actual value of an electric field at that point.

18. The electric field varies inversely as the square of the distance from the point charge.

19. The proton will experience the same force F newton, but in the opposite direction.

20. At the centre, since the electric field due to two charges is equal and opposite at this point.

21. Proton will tend to move along the positive X-axis in the direction of a uniform electric field.

22. When a charge $+Q$ is placed at the centre of spherical cavity as shown in the figure, then charge induced on the inner surface of a shell is $-Q$ and charge induced on the outer surface of a shell is $+Q$.

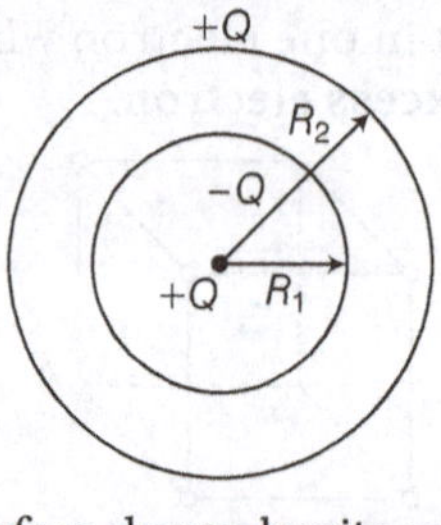

Therefore, surface charge density on inner surface of shell is $\dfrac{-Q}{4\pi R_1^2}$ and on outer surface of shell is $\dfrac{+Q}{4\pi R_2^2}$.

23. For the condition of electrostatics, the electric field lines must be normal to the surface of the conductor, otherwise there would be a non-zero component of electric field along the surface of conductor and charges could not be at rest.

24. An electrostatic field line cannot be a discontinuous curve, i.e. it cannot have breaks.If it has breaks, then it will indicate absence of electric field at the break points. But the electric field vanishes only at infinity.

25. Electric field lines do not pass through a conductor. Hence, the interior of the conductor is free from the influence of the electric field.

26. Electric field lines do not form closed loops because they are always directed from positive charge to negative charge.

27. Correct, because mutual force acting between two point charges is proportional to the product of magnitude of charges and inversely proportional to the square of the distance between them, i.e. independent of the other charges. (2)

28. According to Coulomb's law, the magnitude of force acting between two stationary point charges is given by

$$F = \left(\frac{q_1 q_2}{4\pi\varepsilon_0}\right)\left(\frac{1}{r^2}\right)$$

For given $q_1 q_2$, $F \propto \left(\dfrac{1}{r^2}\right)$

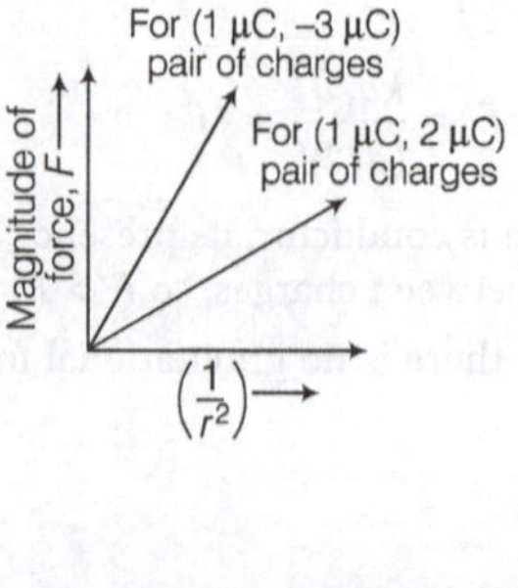

The slope of $F - \frac{1}{r^2}$, graph depends on q_1 and q_2.

Magnitude of $q_1 q_2$ is higher for second pair. (1)

$\therefore$ Slope of $F - \frac{1}{r^2}$ graph, corresponding to second pair (1 μC, −3 μC) is greater. Higher the magnitude of product of charges q_1 and q_2, higher will be the slope. (1)

29. Suppose the three charges be placed as shown in the figure.

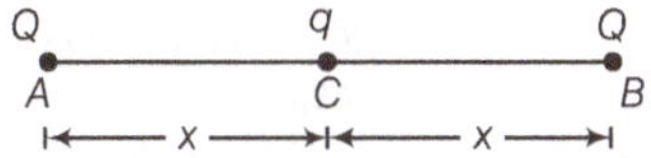

As the net force on q is zero, so it is already in equilibrium. For equilibrium of other two charges, the net force on each charge must be zero. (1)

Total force on charge Q at B is

$$\frac{1}{4\pi\varepsilon_0}\cdot\frac{Qq}{x^2} + \frac{1}{4\pi\varepsilon_0}\cdot\frac{Q\cdot Q}{(2x)^2} = 0$$

$$\Rightarrow \quad \frac{1}{4\pi\varepsilon_0}\cdot\frac{Qq}{x^2} = -\frac{1}{4\pi\varepsilon_0}\cdot\frac{Q^2}{4x^2}$$

$$\therefore \quad q = -\frac{Q}{4}$$ (1)

30. The two charged plates create a region with a uniform electric field between them, directed from the positive towards the negative plate.

Once the ball is disturbed so as to touch one plate (say, the negative one), some negative charge will be transferred to the ball and an electric force will act on the ball, that will accelerate it to the positive plate.

Once the ball touches the positive plate, it will release its negative charge, acquire a positive charge and accelerate back to the negative plate. The metallic ball will continue to move back and forth between the plates until it has transferred all their net charges, thereby making both the plates neutral. (2)

31. Here, the hollow cylinder is positively charged.

We know that, the electric field lines appear to come out from the conductor. Thus, the field lines for a uniformly positive charged hollow cylinder is shown in the figure.

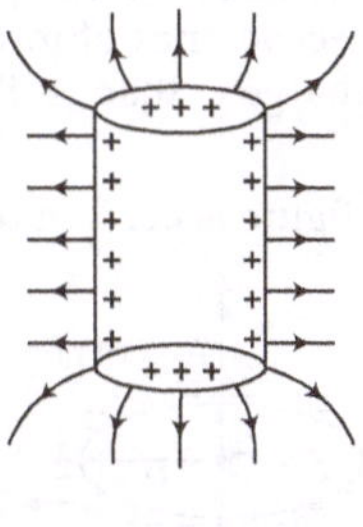

(2)

32. In the ratio $\frac{ke^2}{Gm_e m_p}$, $k = 4\pi\varepsilon_0$ (constant)

where, G = gravitational constant,

m_e = mass of an electron and m = mass of a proton.

From Coulomb's law, $F = k\frac{q_1 q_2}{r^2}$

$$\Rightarrow \quad k = \frac{Fr^2}{q_1 q_2} \text{ or } k = \frac{Fr^2}{q^2}$$

The dimension of $k = \left(\frac{1}{4\pi\varepsilon_0}\right) = \frac{[MLT^{-2}][L^2]}{[AT]\,[AT]}$

$= [ML^3T^{-4}A^{-2}]$ (1)

The dimension of e (electronic charge) = [AT]

The dimension of G (universal gravitational constant)

$$= \frac{[MLT^{-2}]\,[L^2]}{[M^2]} = [M^{-1}L^3T^{-2}]$$

The dimension of m_e or m_p (mass of electron or mass of proton) = [M]

The dimension of $\frac{ke^2}{Gm_e m_p} = \frac{[ML^3T^{-4}A^{-2}]\,[A^2T^2]}{[M^{-1}L^3T^{-2}]\,[M^2]}$

$= [M^0L^0T^0A^0]$ (1)

Thus, the given ratio is dimensionless.

The value of $k = \left(\frac{1}{4\pi\varepsilon_0}\right) = 9\times 10^9$ N-m^2/C^2

The value of e (charge of an electron) $= 1.6\times 10^{-19}$ C

The value of G (universal gravitational constant)

$= 6.67\times 10^{-11}$ N-m^2/kg^2

The value of m_e (mass of electron) $= 9.1\times 10^{-31}$ kg

The value of m_p (mass of proton) $= 1.67\times 10^{-27}$ kg

The value of $\frac{ke^2}{Gm_e m_p}$

$$= \frac{9\times 10^9\times(1.6\times 10^{-19})^2}{6.67\times 10^{-11}\times 9.1\times 10^{-31}\times 1.67\times 10^{-27}}$$

$= 2.29\times 10^{39}$

The ratio signifies that the ratio of electrostatic force to the gravitational force is 2.29×10^{39}. This means the electrostatic force between an electron and a proton is 2.29×10^{39} times the gravitational force between an electron and a proton. (1)

33. As shown in the figure, draw $AD \perp BC$.

$\therefore \quad AD = AB\cos 30° = \frac{a\sqrt{3}}{2}$ $\left[\because \cos 30° = \frac{\sqrt{3}}{2}\right]$

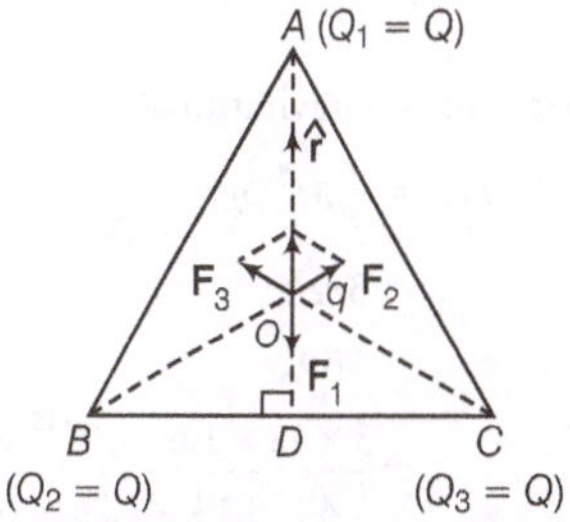

Distance AO of the centroid O from A

$$= \frac{2}{3}AD = \frac{2}{3}\cdot\frac{a\sqrt{3}}{2} = \frac{a}{\sqrt{3}}$$

$\therefore$ Force F_1 on q at O due to charge $(Q_1 = Q)$ at A,

$$F_1 = \frac{1}{4\pi\varepsilon_0}\cdot\frac{Qq}{\left(\frac{a}{\sqrt{3}}\right)^2}$$

$$= \frac{3Qq}{4\pi\varepsilon_0 a^2}, \text{ along } AO \quad (1)$$

Similarly, force F_2 on q due to charge $(Q_2 = Q)$ at B,

$$F_2 = \frac{3Qq}{4\pi\varepsilon_0 a^2}, \text{ along } BO$$

Force F_3 on q due to charge $(Q_3 = Q)$ at C,

$$F_3 = \frac{3Qq}{4\pi\varepsilon_0 a^2}, \text{ along } CO \quad (1)$$

The resultant of forces F_2 and F_3 is $\left(\frac{3}{4\pi\varepsilon_0}Q\frac{q}{a^2}\right)$, along OA by the parallelogram law.

Therefore, the total force on

$$q = \frac{3}{4\pi\varepsilon_0}Q\frac{q}{a^2}(\hat{\mathbf{r}} - \hat{\mathbf{r}}) = 0$$

where, $\hat{\mathbf{r}}$ is the unit vector along OA. It is also clear by symmetry that the sum of three forces will zero. (1)

34. **Key Point:** Here, oil drop is held stationary under electric field that means the weight of the drop is balanced by the electrostatic force applied on it.

Given, the number of excess electrons, $n = 12$

Electric field, $E = 2.55 \times 10^4$ N/C

Density of oil, $\rho = 1.26$ g/cm^3

$= 1.26 \times 10^3$ kg/m^3

Electronic charge, $e = 1.6 \times 10^{-19}$ C

$\Rightarrow \quad g = 9.81$ m/s^2

Let the radius of drop be r.

The electrostatic force on drop $= qE = neE$ $\quad [\because q = ne]$

The gravitational force on the drop $= mg$

[where, m = mass of the drop]

$= \text{Volume} \times \text{Density} \times g$ $\quad [\because \text{mass} = \text{volume} \times \text{density}]$

$$= \frac{4}{3}\pi r^3 \times \rho \times g \quad (1)$$

As the drop is held stationary. So, the net force on the drop is zero.

$\therefore$ Electrostatic force = Gravitational force

$$\Rightarrow \quad neE = \frac{4}{3}\pi r^3 \rho g$$

$$\Rightarrow \quad r^3 = \frac{3neE}{4\pi\rho g}$$

$$= \frac{3 \times 12 \times 1.6 \times 10^{-19} \times 2.55 \times 10^4}{4 \times 3.14 \times 1.26 \times 10^3 \times 9.81}$$

$$\Rightarrow \quad r^3 = 0.94 \times 10^{-18}$$

$$\Rightarrow \quad r = (0.94 \times 10^{-18})^{1/3} = 9.81 \times 10^{-7}$$

Thus, the radius of the drop is 9.81×10^{-7} m. (2)

35. (i) (a) The point O is equidistant from all the charges at the end points of pentagon. Thus, due to symmetry, the forces due to all the charges are cancelled out. As a result, electric field at O is zero. (1)

(b) When charge q is removed from A, electric field at O would become

$$E = \frac{q \times 1}{4\pi\varepsilon_0 r^2}(\text{along } OA) \quad (1/2)$$

(c) If charge q at A is replaced by $-q$, then it is equivalent to adding charge $-2q$. Thus, the electric field at O would become

$$E = \frac{2q}{4\pi\varepsilon_0 r^2}(\text{along } OA) \quad (1/2)$$

(ii) When pentagon is replaced by n-sided regular polygon with charge q at each of its corners, the electric field at O would continue to be zero as symmetricity of the charges is due to the regularity of the polygon. It does not depend on the number of sides or the number of charges. (1)

36. Electric field lines always start from a positive charge and end at a negative charge. In case of a single charge, electric lines of force start from positive charge and end at infinity.

The magnitude of a charge depends on the number of lines of force emanating from a charge, i.e. higher the number of lines of force, higher the magnitude of charge and *vice-versa*.

(i) In the given figure, the electric lines of force emanate from A and C. Therefore, charges A and C must be positive. (1/2)

(ii) The number of electric lines of force emanating is maximum from charge C here, so C must have the largest magnitude. (1)

(iii) Point between two like charges, where electrostatic force is zero, is called neutral point. So, the neutral point lies between A and C only.

Now, the position of neutral point depends on the strength of the forces of charges. Here, more number of electric lines of force show higher strength of charge C than A. So, neutral point lies near A. (1½)

37. Let us draw the figure according to question,

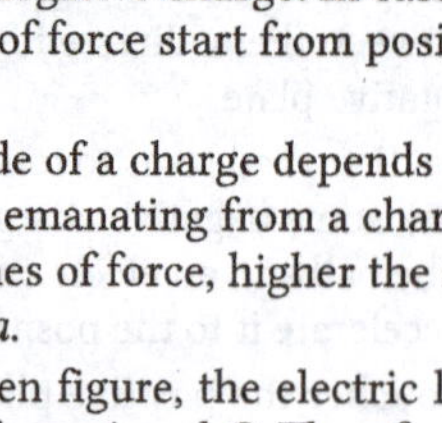

A gentle push on q along the axis of the ring gives rise to the situation shown in the figure below.

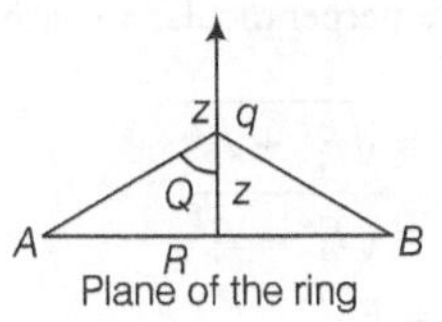

Taking line elements of charge at A and B, having unit length, then charge on each elements.

$$dF = 2\left(-\frac{Q}{2\pi R}\right)q \times \frac{1}{4\pi\varepsilon_0}\frac{1}{r^2}\cos\theta \quad (2)$$

Total force on the charge q, due to entire ring

$$F = -\frac{Qq}{\pi R}(\pi R)\cdot\frac{1}{4\pi\varepsilon_0}\frac{1}{r^2}\cdot\frac{2}{r}$$

$$F = -\frac{Qqz}{4\pi\varepsilon_0 (Z^2 + R^2)^{3/2}}$$

Here, $Z << R$, $F = -\dfrac{Qqz}{4\pi\varepsilon_0 R^3} = -Kz$

where $\dfrac{Qq}{4\pi\varepsilon_0 R^3} = \text{constant}$

$$\Rightarrow \quad F \propto -Z \quad (2)$$

Clearly, force on q is proportional to negative of its displacement. Therefore, motion of q is simple harmonic.

$$\omega = \sqrt{\frac{K}{m}}$$

and $T = \dfrac{2\pi}{\omega} = 2\pi\sqrt{\dfrac{m}{K}}$

$$T = 2\pi\sqrt{\frac{m\,4\pi\varepsilon_0 R^3}{Qq}}$$

$$\Rightarrow \quad T = 2\pi\sqrt{\frac{4\pi\varepsilon_0\, m\, R^3}{Qq}} \quad (1)$$

38. Let us elaborate the figure first.

Given, two charge $-q$ at A and B

$$AB = AO + OB = 2d$$

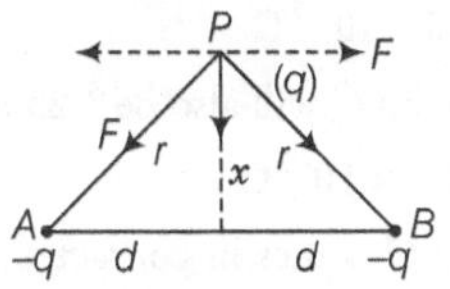

(1)

x = small distance perpendicular to O.

i.e. $x < d$ mass of charge q is. So, force of attraction at P towards A and B are each $F = \dfrac{q\,(q)}{4\pi\varepsilon_0 r^2}$,

where, $AP = BP = r$

Horizontal components of these forces F_n are cancel out. Vertical components along PO add.

If $\angle APO = O$, the net force on q along PO is

$F' = 2F\cos Q$

$$= \frac{2q^2}{4\pi\varepsilon_0 r^2}\left(\frac{x}{r}\right)$$

$$= \frac{2q^2 x}{4\pi\varepsilon_0 (d^2 + x^2)^{3/2}} \quad (2)$$

When $x << d$, $F' = \dfrac{2q^2 x}{4\pi\varepsilon_0 d^3} = Kx$

where, $K = \dfrac{2q^2}{4\pi\varepsilon_0 d^3}$

$$\Rightarrow \quad F \propto x$$

i.e. force on charge q is proportional to its displacement from the centre O and it is directed towards O.

Hence, motion of charge q would be simple harmonic, where

$$\omega = \sqrt{\frac{K}{m}}$$

and $T = \dfrac{2\pi}{\omega} = 2\pi\sqrt{\dfrac{m}{K}}$

$$= 2\pi\sqrt{\frac{m.4\pi\varepsilon_0 d^3}{2q^2}} = \left[\frac{8\pi^3\varepsilon_0\, m\, d^3}{q^2}\right]^{1/2} \quad (2)$$

39. Given, force, $F = 1.6 \times 10^{-15}$ N

Electric field intensity, $E = 2 \times 10^3\ \text{NC}^{-1}$

$\because$ Force, $F = \dfrac{q}{E}$

$\Rightarrow \quad q = F \times E = 1.6 \times 10^{-15} \times 2 \times 10^3$

$\Rightarrow \quad q = 3.2 \times 10^{-12}$ C

40. According to the question,

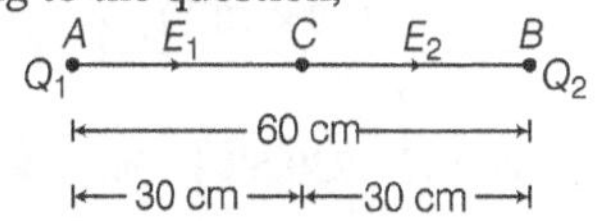

So, net electric field at point C,

$$E = E_1 - E_2 = \frac{kQ_1}{r^2} - \frac{kQ_2}{r^2} = \frac{k}{r^2}(Q_1 - Q_2)$$

$$= \frac{9 \times 10^9}{(30 \times 10^{-2})^2}(400 \times 10^{-6} - 100 \times 10^{-6})$$

$$= \frac{9 \times 10^9 \times 300 \times 10^{-6}}{900 \times 10^{-4}} = 3 \times 10^7\ \text{N/C}$$

41. Given, $F = 2 \times 10^{-3}$ N, $q = 5 \times 10^{-6}$ C

$\therefore$ Electric field, $E = \dfrac{F}{q} = \dfrac{2 \times 10^{-3}\ \text{N}}{5 \times 10^{-6}\ \text{C}} = 400$ N/C

42. Given, $K = 80$

We have, $K = \dfrac{\varepsilon_m}{\varepsilon_0}$

$\therefore \quad \varepsilon_m = K\varepsilon_0 \quad [\because \varepsilon_0 = 8.85 \times 10^{-12}\ \text{C}^2\text{N}^{-1}\text{m}^{-2}]$

$= 80 \times 8.85 \times 10^{-12}$
$= 708 \times 10^{-12}$
$= 7.08 \times 10^{-10} C^2 N^{-1} m^{-2}$

43. From Coulomb's law, electric force between the two charged bodies, in a medium,

$$F = \frac{1}{4\pi\varepsilon_0 K} \frac{|q_1 q_2|}{r^2}$$

where, K = dielectric constant of the medium.
For vacuum, $K = 1$
For plastic, $K > 1$
Therefore, after insertion of plastic sheet, the force between the two balls will reduce.

44. Two point charges system is taken from air to water keeping other variables (e.g. distance, magnitude of charge) unchanged. So, the only factor which may affect the interacting force is dielectric constant of medium.
Force acting between two point charges,

$$F = \frac{1}{4\pi\varepsilon_0 K} \frac{q_1 q_2}{r^2} \text{ or } F \propto \frac{1}{K} \Rightarrow \frac{F_{\text{air}}}{F_{\text{medium}}} = K$$

$$\Rightarrow \frac{8}{F_{\text{water}}} = 80 \Rightarrow F_{\text{water}} = \frac{8}{80} = \frac{1}{10} \text{ N}$$

45. Here, $\mathbf{r}_q = \hat{\mathbf{i}} + 2\hat{\mathbf{j}} + 4\hat{\mathbf{k}}$ and $\mathbf{r}_p = -4\hat{\mathbf{j}} + 3\hat{\mathbf{k}}$

$\therefore \quad \mathbf{r}_p - \mathbf{r}_q = -\hat{\mathbf{i}} - 6\hat{\mathbf{j}} - \hat{\mathbf{k}}$

or $|\mathbf{r}_p - \mathbf{r}_q| = \sqrt{(-1)^2 + (-6)^2 + (-1)^2} = \sqrt{38}$ m

Now, electric field, $\mathbf{E} = \frac{1}{4\pi\varepsilon_0} \cdot \frac{q}{|\mathbf{r}_p - \mathbf{r}_q|^3} (\mathbf{r}_p - \mathbf{r}_q)$

Substituting the values, we get

$$\mathbf{E} = \frac{(9.0 \times 10^9)(1.0 \times 10^{-6})}{(38)^{3/2}} (-\hat{\mathbf{i}} - 6\hat{\mathbf{j}} - \hat{\mathbf{k}})$$

$$= (-38.42\,\hat{\mathbf{i}} - 230.52\,\hat{\mathbf{j}} - 38.42\,\hat{\mathbf{k}}) \text{N/C}$$ **(2)**

46. At the point $x = 0$, the electric field due to all the charges are in the same negative x-direction and hence get added up, i.e.

$$E = \frac{1}{4\pi\varepsilon_0} \left[\frac{q}{1^2} + \frac{q}{2^2} + \frac{q}{4^2} + \frac{q}{8^2} + \dots \right]$$

$$= \frac{q}{4\pi\varepsilon_0} \left[1 + \frac{1}{4} + \frac{1}{16} + \frac{1}{64} + \dots \right]$$

$$= \frac{q}{4\pi\varepsilon_0} \frac{1}{[1 - 1/4]} = \frac{q}{3\pi\varepsilon_0}$$

This electric field is along negative X-axis. **(2)**

47. Let each side of square be x.

Diagonal $= \sqrt{x^2 + x^2} = x\sqrt{2}$

$$F_1 = F_2 = \frac{Qq}{4\pi\varepsilon_0 x^2}$$

and $F_3 = \frac{qq}{4\pi\varepsilon_0 (x\sqrt{2})^2} = \frac{q^2}{2 \times 4\pi\varepsilon_0 x^2}$ **(1)**

As, F_1 and F_2 are perpendicular to each other, their resultant force,

$$F = \sqrt{F_1^2 + F_2^2}$$
$$= \sqrt{F_1^2 + F_1^2}$$
$$\Rightarrow \quad F = F_1\sqrt{2}$$ **(1)**

As, net force on q is zero, therefore

$$F_1\sqrt{2} = -F_3$$

$$\Rightarrow \quad \frac{Qq\sqrt{2}}{4\pi\varepsilon_0 x^2} = \frac{-q^2}{2 \times 4\pi\varepsilon_0 x^2}$$

$$\Rightarrow \quad q = -2\sqrt{2}\,Q$$ **(1)**

48. (i) Here, $q_1 = q_2 = 6.5 \times 10^{-7} C$, $r = 50$ cm $= 0.5$ m

Electrostatic force of repulsion,

$$F = \frac{1}{4\pi\varepsilon_0} \frac{q_1 q_2}{r^2} = \frac{9 \times 10^9 \times (6.5 \times 10^{-7})^2}{(0.5)^2}$$

$$= 1.521 \times 10^{-2} \text{N}$$ **(1½)**

(ii) Now, q_1, q_2 both are doubled and r is halved in $F = \frac{1}{4\pi\varepsilon_0} \frac{q_1 q_2}{r^2}$, then

F becomes 16 times, i.e. $F' = 16$ F.

$F' = 16 \times 1.521 \times 10^{-2}$ N or $F' = 0.24$ N **(1½)**

49.

> **Key Point:** It is based on the distribution of charges when the two identical bodies come into contact, charge is distributed equally on identical bodies.

In initially,

$q_A = 6.5 \times 10^{-7}$C $\quad q_B = 6.5 \times 10^{-7}$C $\quad$ Initially, $q_C = 0$

Now, the sphere C comes in contact with A, the charges will be divided equally on both spheres as they have same mass and size. Now, charge on A is

$$q'_A = \frac{q_A + q_C}{2} = \frac{6.5 \times 10^{-7} + 0}{2}$$

$$= 3.25 \times 10^{-7} \text{C}$$ **(1/2)**

Now, the charge on C will also be 3.25×10^{-7} C.

$\therefore \quad q'_C = 3.25 \times 10^{-7}$ C **(1/2)**

Now, the sphere C comes in contact with B, the charges are shared again.

Then, charge on B is

$$q'_B = \frac{q_B + q'_C}{2} = \frac{6.5 \times 10^{-7} + 3.25 \times 10^{-7}}{2}$$

$$= 4.875 \times 10^{-7} \text{C}$$ **(1/2)**

Finally, the charge on C is $q'_C = 4.875 \times 10^{-7}$ C

Finally, the charge on A is $q'_A = 3.25 \times 10^{-7}$ C

The charge on B is $q'_B = 4.875 \times 10^{-7}$ C

From the Coulomb's law, the force between two spheres,

$$F = \frac{1}{4\pi\varepsilon_0} \cdot \frac{q'_A \cdot q'_B}{r^2} \quad \textbf{(1/2)}$$

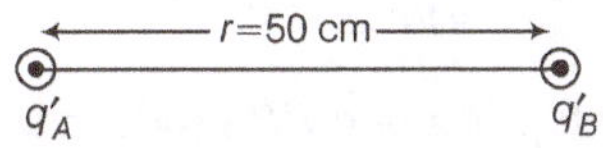

$$= \frac{9 \times 10^9 \times 3.25 \times 10^{-7} \times 4.875 \times 10^{-7}}{(50 \times 10^{-2})^2}$$

$$= \frac{9 \times 3.25 \times 4.875 \times 10^{-5}}{50 \times 50 \times 10^{-4}} = 5.7 \times 10^{-3} \text{ N}$$

This force will be repulsive in nature because both spheres have like charges. **(1)**

50. **Key Point:** Net force on a charge due to two equal and opposite charges will be zero. Also, electric field on a charge is given by

$$E = \frac{F}{q}$$

where, E = electric field, F = force on charge q due to electric field and q = magnitude of charge.
If a Cs atom is removed from the corner A, then a singly charged negative Cs ion at A will appear.

(i) From the given figure, we can analyse that the chlorine atom is at the centre of the cube, i.e. at equal distance from all the eight corners of cube, where caesium atoms are placed.

Thus, due to symmetry, the force due to all Cs atoms, on Cl atom will cancel out.

Hence, $E = \frac{F}{q'}$

where, $F = 0$

$\therefore$ $E = 0$ **(1)**

(ii) Thus, net force on Cl atom at A would be given by

$$F = \frac{e^2}{4\pi\varepsilon_0 r^2}$$

where, r = distance between Cl ion and Cs ion.
Applying Pythagoras theorem, we get

$$r = \sqrt{(0.20)^2 + (0.20)^2 + (0.20)^2} \times 10^{-9} \text{ m} = 0.346 \times 10^{-9} \text{ m}$$

$$\therefore \quad F = \frac{q^2}{4\pi\varepsilon_0 r^2} = \frac{e^2}{4\pi\varepsilon_0 r^2} = \frac{9 \times 10^9 (1.6 \times 10^{-19})^2}{(0.346 \times 10^{-9})^2}$$

$$= 1.92 \times 10^{-9} \text{ N} \quad \textbf{(2)}$$

51. (i) Charge of proton, $q = 1.6 \times 10^{-19}$ C

Force on proton at A is $F = qE_A$

$= (1.6 \times 10^{-19} \text{ C})(40 \text{ N/C}) = 6.4 \times 10^{-18}$ N **(1½)**

(ii) Since, electric field,

$$E \propto \frac{\text{Number of electric field lines}}{\text{Area}}$$

Hence, $E_B = \frac{1}{2} E_A$

$$= \frac{1}{2}(40 \text{ N/C}) = 20 \text{ N/C} \quad \textbf{(1½)}$$

TOPIC 03 Electric Dipole

An electric dipole is a pair of point charges with equal magnitude and opposite in sign separated by a very small distance. The mid-point of locations of $-q$ and q is called the **centre of the dipole.**

Dipole Moment of an Electric Dipole

The strength of an electric dipole is measured by a vector quantity known as **electric dipole moment** (**p**) which is the product of the charge (q) and separation between the charges ($2l$).

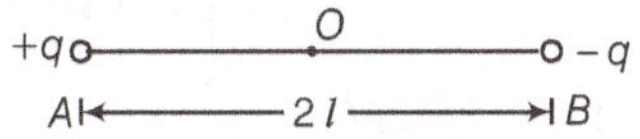

Electric dipole

i.e. $p = q \times 2l$

or $|\mathbf{p}| = q(2l)$

It is a vector quantity and its direction is always from negative charge to positive charge. The SI unit of dipole moment is coulomb-metre (C-m).

If charge q gets larger and the distance $2l$ gets smaller and smaller, keeping the product $|\mathbf{p}| = q \times 2l$ = constant, we get what is called an **ideal dipole** or **point dipole**. Thus, an ideal dipole is the smallest dipole having almost no size.

Example 1 A system has two charges $q_A = 2.5 \times 10^{-7}$ C and $q_B = -2.5 \times 10^{-7}$ C located at points $A(0, 0, -15 \text{ cm})$ and $B(0, 0, +15 \text{ cm})$, respectively. What are the total charge and electric dipole moment of the system? **NCERT**

Sol. Two charges q_A and q_B are located at points $A(0, 0, -15\text{cm})$ and $B(0, 0, 15\text{cm})$ on Z-axis.

They form an electric dipole.

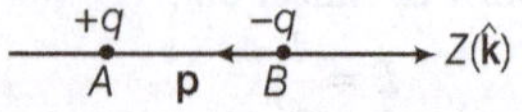

Total charge, $q = q_A + q_B = 2.5\times10^{-7} - 2.5\times10^{-7}$

$\Rightarrow \quad q = 0$

Also, $\quad AB = 15 + 15 = 30$ cm or $AB = 30\times10^{-2}$ m

Electric dipole moment, p = Either charge × BA

$$= 2.5\times10^{-7}\times(30\times10^{-2})(-\hat{k})$$

$$= -7.5\times10^{-8}\,\hat{k}\text{ C-m}$$

Electric Field Intensity Due to an Electric Dipole

Electric field of an electric dipole is the space around the dipole in which the electric effect of the dipole can be experienced. An electric dipole consists of two charges $+q$ and $-q$, therefore according to the superposition principle, the electric field due to an electric dipole at a point will be equal to the vector sum of the electric fields due to the two individual charges.

At a Point on the Axial Line

We have to calculate the field intensity (E) at a point P on the axial line of the dipole and at a distance $OP = x$ from the centre O of the dipole.

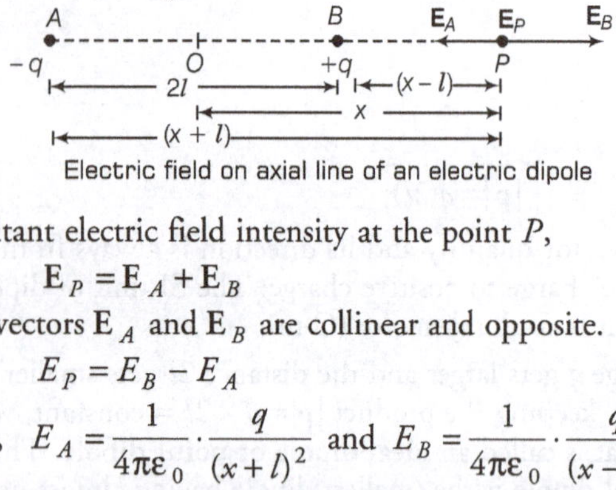

Electric field on axial line of an electric dipole

Resultant electric field intensity at the point P,

$$\mathbf{E}_P = \mathbf{E}_A + \mathbf{E}_B$$

The vectors $\mathbf{E}_A$ and $\mathbf{E}_B$ are collinear and opposite.

$\therefore \quad E_P = E_B\ E_A$

Here, $E_A = \dfrac{1}{4\pi\varepsilon_0}\cdot\dfrac{q}{(x+l)^2}$ and $E_B = \dfrac{1}{4\pi\varepsilon_0}\cdot\dfrac{q}{(x-l)^2}$

$$\therefore \quad E_P = \frac{1}{4\pi\varepsilon_0}\left[\frac{q}{(x-l)^2} - \frac{q}{(x+l)^2}\right]$$

$$= \frac{1}{4\pi\varepsilon_0}\cdot\frac{4qlx}{(x^2-l^2)^2}$$

Hence, $E_P = \dfrac{1}{4\pi\varepsilon_0}\cdot\dfrac{2px}{(x^2-l^2)^2}$ $\quad [\because p = q\times 2l]$

In vector form, $\mathbf{E}_P = \dfrac{1}{4\pi\varepsilon_0}\cdot\dfrac{2\mathbf{p}x}{(x^2-l^2)^2}$

If dipole is short, i.e. $2l << x$, then

$$E_P = \frac{2|\mathbf{p}|}{4\pi\varepsilon_0 x^3} \quad \text{...(i)}$$

The direction of $\mathbf{E}_P$ is along BP produced.

Clearly, $\quad E_P \propto \dfrac{1}{x^3}$

At a Point on the Equatorial Line

Consider an electric dipole consisting of two point charges $+q$ and $-q$ separated by a small distance $AB = 2l$ with centre at O and dipole moment, $p = q(2l)$ as shown in the figure.

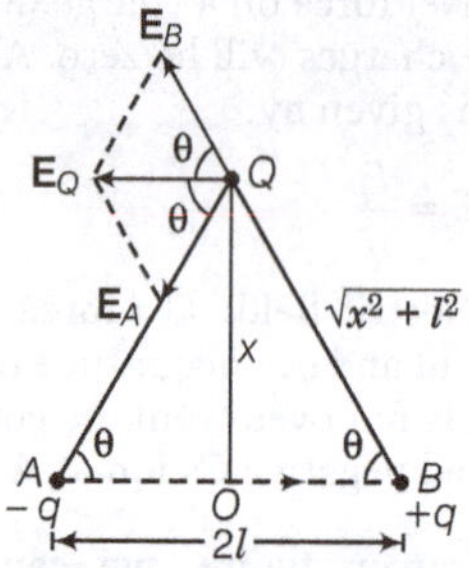

Resultant electric field intensity at the point Q,

$$\mathbf{E}_Q = \mathbf{E}_A + \mathbf{E}_B$$

The vectors $\mathbf{E}_A$ and $\mathbf{E}_B$ are acting at an angle 2θ.

Here, $\quad E_A = \dfrac{1}{4\pi\varepsilon_0}\cdot\dfrac{q}{(x^2+l^2)}$

and $\quad E_B = \dfrac{1}{4\pi\varepsilon_0}\cdot\dfrac{q}{(x^2+l^2)}$

On resolving $\mathbf{E}_A$ and $\mathbf{E}_B$ into two rectangular components, the vectors $E_A\sin\theta$ and $E_B\sin\theta$ are equal in magnitude and opposite to each other and hence cancel out.

The vectors $E_A\cos\theta$ and $E_B\cos\theta$ are acting along the same direction and hence add up.

$$\therefore \quad E_Q = E_A\cos\theta + E_B\cos\theta$$

$$= 2E_A\cos\theta \quad [\because E_A = E_B]$$

$$= \frac{2}{4\pi\varepsilon_0}\cdot\frac{q}{(x^2+l^2)}\cdot\frac{l}{(x^2+l^2)^{1/2}}$$

$$\left[\because \cos\theta = \frac{l}{(x^2+l^2)^{1/2}}\right]$$

$$= \frac{1}{4\pi\varepsilon_0}\cdot\frac{2ql}{(x^2+l^2)^{3/2}}$$

But $q\times 2l = |\mathbf{p}|$, the dipole moment

$$E_Q = \frac{1}{4\pi\varepsilon_0} \cdot \frac{|\mathbf{p}|}{(x^2 + l^2)^{3/2}}$$

The direction of **E** is along **QE** || **BA**, i.e. opposite to **AB**.

In vector form, we can rewrite as $\mathbf{E}_Q = \dfrac{-\mathbf{p}}{4\pi\varepsilon_0 (x^2 + l^2)^{3/2}}$

Obviously, $\mathbf{E}_Q$ is in a direction opposite to the direction of **p**. If the dipole is short, i.e. $2l << x$, then

$$\therefore \quad \boxed{E_Q = \frac{1}{4\pi\varepsilon_0} \cdot \frac{|\mathbf{p}|}{x^3}} \quad \text{...(ii)}$$

Clearly, $E_Q \propto \dfrac{1}{x^3}$

From Eqs. (i) and (ii), we get

$$\frac{E_{\text{axial}}}{E_{\text{equatorial}}} = 2$$

Both the magnitude and the direction of dipole field depend not only on the distance *x*, but also on the angle between the position vector **x** and dipole moment **p**.

The electric field due to a dipole falls off at large distances, at a much faster rate $\left(\propto \dfrac{1}{x^3}\right)$ than the electric field due to a single charge $\left(\propto \dfrac{1}{x^2}\right)$.

Example 2 Two charges $\pm 5\ \mu C$ are placed 5 mm apart. Determine the electric field at

(i) a point *X* on the axis of dipole 10 cm away from its centre *O* on the side of the positive charge as shown in Fig. (a).

(ii) a point *Y*, 10 cm away from centre *O* on a line passing through *O* and normal to the axis of the dipole as shown in Fig. (b).

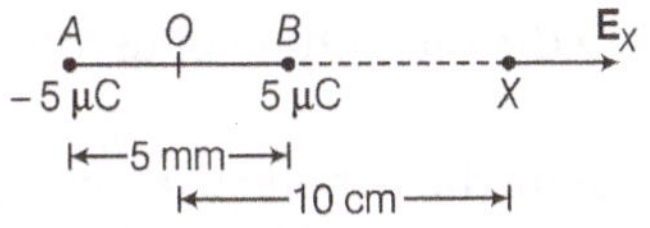

(a)

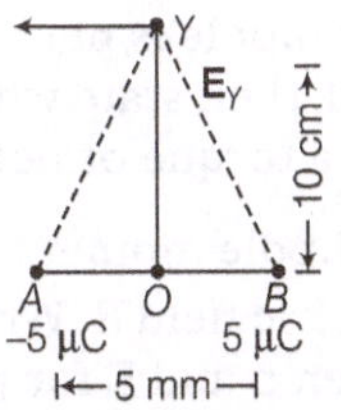

(b)

Sol. Given, $q = \pm 5\ \mu C = \pm 5 \times 10^{-6}$ C,

$2l = 5\text{mm} = 5 \times 10^{-3}$ m

$x = OX = OY = 10$ cm $= 10 \times 10^{-2}$ m

$E_X = ?$ and $E_Y = ?$

Dipole moment, $\mathbf{p} = q \times 2l$

$= 5 \times 10^{-6} \text{C} \times 5 \times 10^{-3}$ m

$= 25 \times 10^{-9}$ C-m

(i) Now, find out the electric field at point *X* on the axial line of dipole.

$$\mathbf{E}_X = \frac{2\mathbf{p}x}{4\pi\varepsilon_0 (x^2 - l^2)^2}, \text{ along } BX \text{ produced}$$

Since $l << x$, therefore

$$\mathbf{E}_X = \frac{2\mathbf{p}}{4\pi\varepsilon_0 x^3} = \frac{2 \times 25 \times 10^{-9} \times 9 \times 10^9}{(10 \times 10^{-2})^3}$$

$= 4.5 \times 10^5$ NC^{-1}, along *BX* produced.

(ii) Now, find out the electric field at point *Y* on equatorial line of dipole.

$$\mathbf{E}_Y = \frac{\mathbf{p}}{4\pi\varepsilon_0 (x^2 + l^2)^{3/2}}, \text{ along a line parallel to } BA$$

Since, $l << x$, therefore $\mathbf{E}_Y = \dfrac{\mathbf{p}}{4\pi\varepsilon_0 x^3}$

$$\therefore \quad \mathbf{E}_Y = \frac{25 \times 10^{-9} \times 9 \times 10^9}{(10 \times 10^{-2})^3}$$

$= 2.25 \times 10^5$ NC^{-1}, along a line parallel to *BA*.

Electric Field Intensity at any Point due to a Short Electric Dipole

Due to a short electric dipole at a point, the electric field intensity is

$$E = \frac{1}{4\pi\varepsilon_0} \frac{p}{r^3} \sqrt{3\cos^2\theta + 1}$$

where, θ = Angle between dipole moment and direction of electric field.

Dipole in a Uniform External Field

Torque on an Electric Dipole in a Uniform Electric Field

Consider an electric dipole consisting of two charges $-q$ and $+q$ placed in a uniform external electric field of intensity **E**.

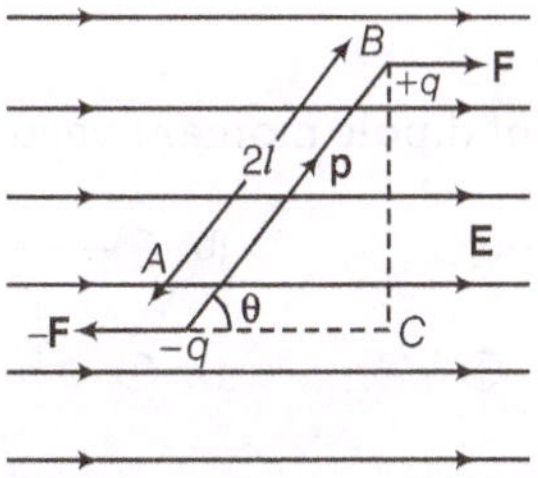

The length of the electric dipole is $2l$. The dipole moment **p** makes an angle θ with the direction of the electric field. Two forces **F** and $-$**F** which are equal in magnitude and opposite in directions act on the dipole.

$$|F| = |-F| = qE$$

The net force is zero. Since, the two forces are equal in magnitude and opposite in direction and act at different points, therefore they constitute a couple. A net torque τ acts on the dipole about an axis passing through the mid-point of the dipole.

Now, τ = Either force × Perpendicular distance BC between the parallel forces $= qE(2l\sin\theta)$

$$\tau = (q \times 2l)E\sin\theta$$

or $\boxed{\tau = pE\sin\theta}$

In vector notation, $\boxed{\tau = \mathbf{p} \times \mathbf{E}}$

SI unit of torque is newton-metre (N-m) and its dimensional formula is $[ML^2T^{-2}]$.

Case I If $\theta = 0°$, then $\tau = 0$

The dipole is in stable equilibrium.

Case II If $\theta = 90°$, then $\tau = pE$ (maximum value)

The torque acting on dipole will be maximum.

Case III If $\theta = 180°$, then $\tau = 0$

The dipole is in unstable equilibrium.

Example 3 An electric dipole consists of two charges of 0.1 μC separated by a distance of 2.0 cm. The dipole is placed in an external field of 10^5 N/C. What maximum torque does the field exert on the dipole?

Sol. Here, $q = 0.1\ \mu C = 10^{-7}$ C, $2l = 2.0$ cm $= 2 \times 10^{-2}$ m,

$$E = 10^5 \text{ N/C} \Rightarrow \tau = pE\sin\theta = q \times 2l \times E\sin\theta$$

$$\therefore \tau_{max} = 10^{-7} \times 2 \times 10^{-2} \times 10^5 \times 1 \quad [\because \sin 90° = 1]$$

$$= 2 \times 10^{-4} \text{ N-m}$$

Topic Practice 3

Multiple Choice Questions

1 Mark

1. Direction of dipole moment vector is best shown by

2. What is the angle between the electric dipole moment and the electric field strength due to it on the equatorial line? **ISC 2005**
   (a) 0° (b) 90°
   (c) 180° (d) None of these

3. Two electric dipoles of moment p and $64p$ are placed in opposite direction on a line at a distance of 25 cm. The electric field will be zero at point between the dipoles whose distance from the dipole of moment p is
   (a) 5 cm (b) $\frac{25}{9}$ cm
   (c) 10 cm (d) $\frac{4}{13}$ cm

4. The ratio of electric fields on the axis and at equator of an electric dipole will be
   (a) 1 : 1 (b) 2 : 1
   (c) 4 : 1 (d) None of these

5. Intensity of an electric field E due to a dipole, depends on distance r as
   (a) $E \propto \frac{1}{r^4}$ (b) $E \propto \frac{1}{r^3}$ (c) $E \propto \frac{1}{r^2}$ (d) $E \propto \frac{1}{r}$

Very Short Answer Type Questions

1 Mark

6. Is it correct to write the unit of electric dipole moment as mC?

7. What do you mean by an 'ideal electric dipole'?

8. What is the angle between the directions of electric field at any
   (i) axial point and
   (ii) equatorial point due to an electric dipole?

9. At what points dipole field intensity is parallel to the line joining the charges?

10. Three electric charges q, q and $-2q$ are placed at the corners of an equilateral triangle of side L. Calculate the magnitude of dipole moment of the system.

11. What will be the net electric force acting on an electric dipole placed in a uniform electric field? **ISC 2007**

12. If an electric dipole is placed in a uniform electric field, then state whether it always experiences a torque or not?

13. A dipole of dipole moment **p** is present in a uniform electric field **E**. Write the value of the angle between **p** and **E** for which the torque, experienced by the dipole is minimum.

Short Answer Type I Questions

2 Marks

14. What is meant by the statement, "the electric field of a point charge has spherical symmetry, whereas that of an electric dipole is cylindrically symmetric"?

15. Three charges are placed as shown. Find dipole moment of the arrangements.

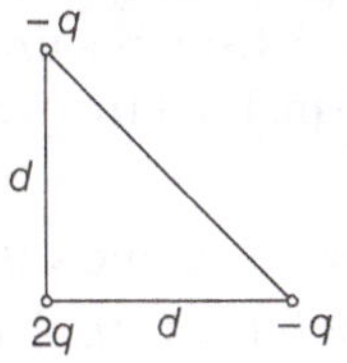

16. Two small identical dipoles AB and CD, each of dipole moment **p** are kept at an angle of 120° as shown in the figure.

What is the resultant dipole moment of this combination? If this system is subjected to electric field (**E**) directed along positive x-direction, what will be the magnitude and direction of the torque acting on this?

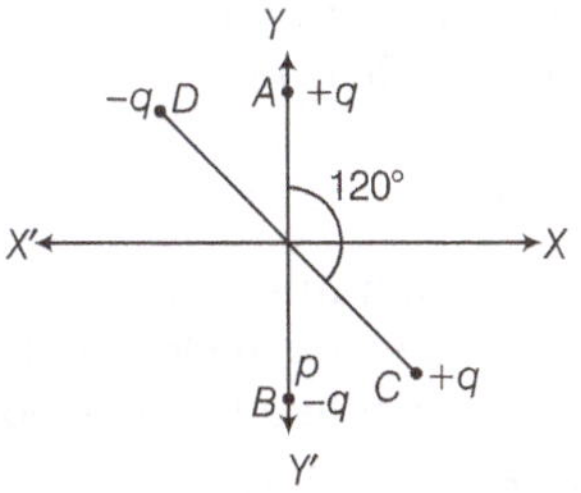

Short Answer Type II Questions

3 Marks

17. Show that intensity of electric field at a point in broadside position of an electric dipole is given by **[3]**

$$E = \left(\frac{1}{4\pi\varepsilon_0}\right)\frac{p}{(r^2 + l^2)^{3/2}}$$

where the terms have their usual meaning. **ISC 2023, 20**

18. Obtain an expression for intensity of electric field at a point in end on position, i.e. axial position of an electric dipole. **ISC 2018**

19. An electric dipole is held at any angle θ in a uniform electric field E. Will there be any
    (i) net translating force and
    (ii) torque acting on it?

    Explain, what happens to dipole on being released?

20. An electric dipole of dipole moment **p** is placed in a uniform electric field **E** with its axis inclined to the field. Write an expression for the torque τ experienced by the dipole in vector form.

    Show diagramatically, show the dipole should be kept in the electric field, so that the torque acting on it is
    (i) maximum
    (ii) zero **ISC 2014**

21. (i) Write an expression (derivation not required) for intensity of electric field in
    (a) axial position.
    (b) broadside position of an electric dipole, in terms of its length ($2a$) dipole moment (p) and distance (r).
    (ii) What is the ratio of these two intensities, i.e. $E_1 : E_2$, for a short electric dipole? **ISC 2013**

22. An electric dipole is placed in a uniform external electric field **E**. Show that the torque acting on the dipole is given by τ = **p** × **E**, where **p** is the dipole moment. **ISC 2005**

Long Answer Type Questions

5 Marks

23. Define electric dipole moment. Is it a scalar or a vector? Derive the expression for the electric field of a dipole at a point on the equatorial plane of the dipole.

    For a short dipole, what is the ratio of electric field intensities at two equidistant points from the centre of the dipole? One along the axial line and other on the equatorial line.

24. Deduce the expression for the torque acting on a dipole of dipole moment **p** in the presence of a uniform electric field E.

25. (i) Derive the expression for the electric field E due to a dipole of length $2l$ at a point distant r from the centre of the dipole on the axial line.
    (ii) Draw a graph of E versus r for $r >> a$.
    (iii) If this dipole is kept in a uniform external electric field E_0, diagrammatically represent

the position of the dipole in stable and unstable equilibrium and write the expressions for the torque acting on the dipole in both the cases.

26. Derive an expression for intensity of electric field at a point in broadside position or on an equatorial line of an electric dipole. **ISC 2015**

Numerical Problems

27. Find the electric dipole moment electron and a proton which distance is 4.3 nm apart. **(1 M)**

28. Two charges of $+25\times10^{-9}$ C and -25×10^{-9} C are placed 6 m apart. Find the electric field at a point 4 m from the centre of the electric dipole (i) on axial line (ii) on equatorial line. **(2 M)**

29. A system has two charges $q_A = 3.5\times10^{-7}$ C and $q_B = -3.5\times10^{-7}$ C located at points $A(0, 0, -10\text{cm})$ and $B\ (0, 0, +10\ \text{cm})$, respectively. What are the total charge and electric dipole moment of the system? **(2 M)**

30. Two charges q_1 and q_2 of 0.1 μμC and − 0.1 μμC respectively are 10Å apart. What is the electric field at a point on the line joining them at a distance of 10 cm from their mid-point? **(3 M)**

31. Two charges $\pm 10\,\mu$C are placed 5 mm apart. Determine the electric field at

(i) a point P on the axis of dipole 15 cm away from its centre O on the side of the positive charge

(ii) a point Q, 15 cm away from centre O on a line passing through centre O and normal to axis of the dipole as **NCERT (3 M)**

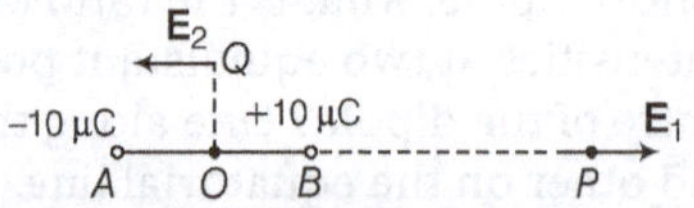

32. The electric field at a point on the axial line at a distance of 10 cm from the centre of an electric dipole is 3.75×10^5 N/C in air, while at a distance of 20 cm, the electric field is 3×10^4 N/C. Calculate the length of an electric dipole. **(5 M)**

33. A two point charges q_1 and q_2 of magnitude 10^{-7} C and -10^{-7} C, respectively are placed 0.2 m apart. Calculate the electric fields at points A, B and C as shown in the figure. **NCERT (5 M)**

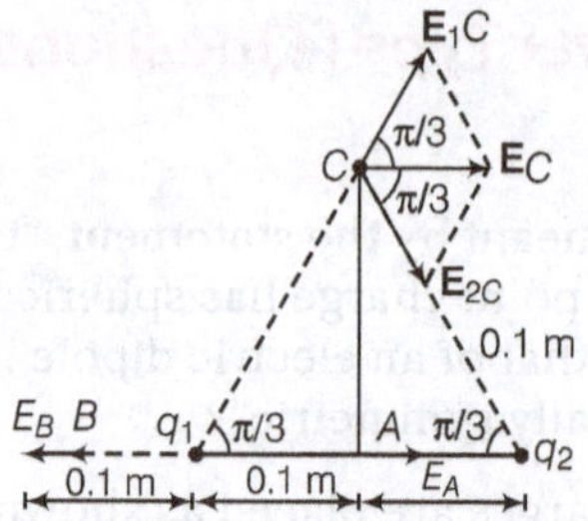

34. Maximum torque acting on an electric dipole of moment 3×10^{-29} C-m in a uniform electric field E is 6×10^{-25} N-m. Find the value of E. **ISC 2017 (1 M)**

35. Two charges of − 9 μC and + 9 μC are placed at the points $P(1, 0, 4)$ and $Q(2, -1, 5)$ located in an electric field $E = 0.20\,\hat{i}$ V/cm. Calculate the torque acting on the dipole. **(1 M)**

36. An electric dipole with dipole moment 4×10^{-9}C-m is aligned at 30° with the direction of a uniform electric field of magnitude 5×10^4 N/C. Calculate the magnitude of the torque acting on the dipole. **(2 M)**

37. An electric dipole consists of two opposite charges each of magnitude 1.0×10^{-6} C separated by 2 cm. The dipole is placed in an external uniform field of 1×10^5 N/C. Find the maximum torque exerted by the field on the dipole. **(1 M)**

38. Calculate the maximum torque experienced by a water molecule whose electric dipole moment is 6.2×10^{-30} C-m, when it is placed in an electric field of intensity 10^6 N/C. **(1 M)**

39. In a certain region of space, electric field is along the z-direction throughout. The magnitude of electric field is, however not constant but increases uniformly along the positive z-direction, at the rate of 10^5 N $C^{-1}m^{-1}$. What are the force and torque experienced by a system having a total dipole moment equal to 10^{-7} C-m in the negative z-direction? **NCERT (5M)**

Hints & Solutions

1. (a) Direction of dipole moment vector **p** is from $-q$ to $+q$ by convention.

Observing in small distance between charges **E** is opposite to **p** but outside this distance **E** and **p** are in same direction, on axis of dipole.

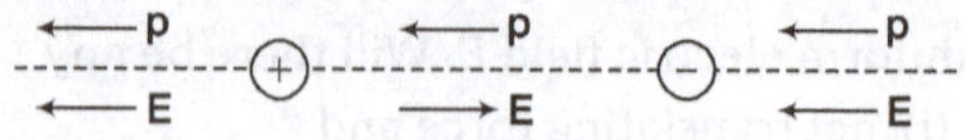

2. (*c*)

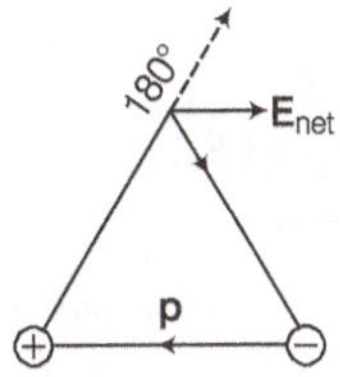

Observing $\mathbf{E}_{net}$ and $\mathbf{p}$ are in opposite directions, so angle between them is 180°.

3. (*a*) Suppose neutral point N lies at a distance x from dipole of moment p or at a distance x_2 from dipole of 64 **p**.

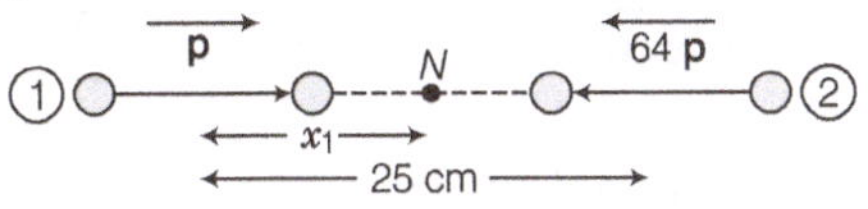

At N, | Electric field due to dipole (1) |

= | electric field due to dipole (2) |

$$\Rightarrow \quad \frac{1}{4\pi\varepsilon_0}\cdot\frac{2p}{x^3} = \frac{1}{4\pi\varepsilon_0}\cdot\frac{2(64p)}{(25-x)^3}$$

$$\Rightarrow \quad \frac{1}{x^3} = \frac{64}{(25-x)^3}$$

$$\Rightarrow \quad x = 5 \text{ cm}$$

4. (*b*) As we know, $\dfrac{E_{\text{axis}}}{E_{\text{equator}}} = \dfrac{2p/4\pi\varepsilon_0 r^3}{p/4\pi\varepsilon_0 r^3}$

$$= \frac{2}{1}$$

Here, E_{axis} = electric field at axis at distance and E_{equator} = electric field at equator at distance r is measured from centre of dipole.

5. (*b*) For a dipole, $E \propto \dfrac{1}{r^3}$

As, $\quad E_{\text{axis}} = \dfrac{2p}{4\pi\varepsilon_0 r^3} \propto \dfrac{1}{r^3}$

Also, $E_{\text{equatorial}} = \dfrac{p}{4\pi\varepsilon_0 r^3} \propto \dfrac{1}{r^3}$

6. No, it is not correct to write the unit of electric dipole moment as mC. The symbol mC represents milli-coulomb, i.e. unit of electric charge. In SI system, unit symbols are written in alphabetical order.

∴ Unit of dipole moment is C-m.

7. If charge q gets larger and distance $2l$ gets smaller; and smaller keeping the product $|p| = q \times 2l$ = constant. The dipole is called an ideal electric dipole.

8. At axial point, field is along the axis and at an equatorial point, field is perpendicular to equatorial line.
So, angle between (i) and (ii) is 180°.

9. At any point on axial line or equatorial line of dipole.

10. We have two dipoles at 60° to each other. On solving, we get equivalent magnitude of dipole moment of the system = $\sqrt{3}p$

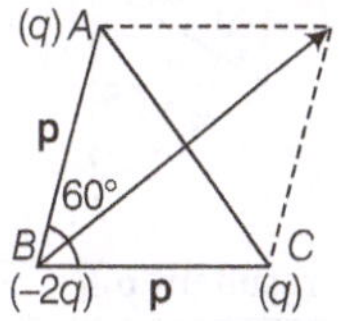

11. Consider the diagram. Total force on the dipole placed in a uniform electric field **E** is

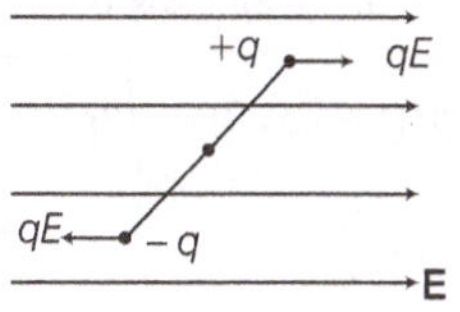

$$|\mathbf{F}| = \mathbf{E}(qE - qE) = 0$$

12. No, it does not experience a torque, when it is placed along the direction of electric field.

13. $\tau = pE\sin\theta$, τ is minimum when $\theta = 0°$.

14. The electric field due to a point charge q at a distance r is given by $E = q/4\pi\varepsilon_0 r^2$. Clearly, the magnitude of field **E** will be the at all points on the surface of a sphere of radius r drawn around the point charge and does not depend on the direction **r**. Hence, the field line due to a point charge is spherically symmetric. Electric field at distance r on the equatorial line of a dipole moment p is given by $E = \dfrac{1}{4\pi\varepsilon_0}\dfrac{p}{(r^2+a^2)^{3/2}}$.

The electric field E is same at all points which lie on a cylinder of radius r with its axis on the dipole axis and the field pattern looks same in all planes passing through the dipole axis. We say that the electric field of an electric dipole is cylindrical symmetric. (2)

15. Here, two dipoles are formed. These are shown in diagram below.

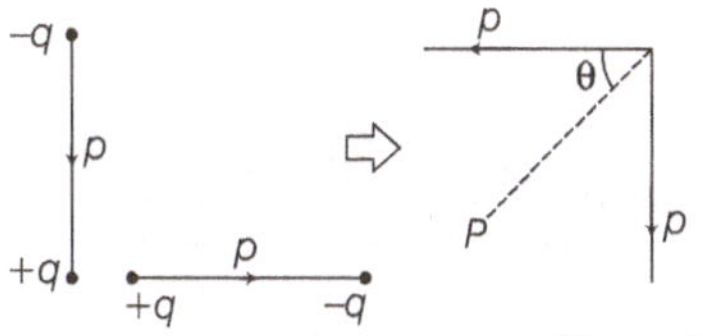

Resultant dipole moment, $P = \sqrt{2}p = \sqrt{2}qd$, $\theta = 45°$ (2)

16. Consider the figure, $|\mathbf{p}_A| = \mathbf{p}_C = p$

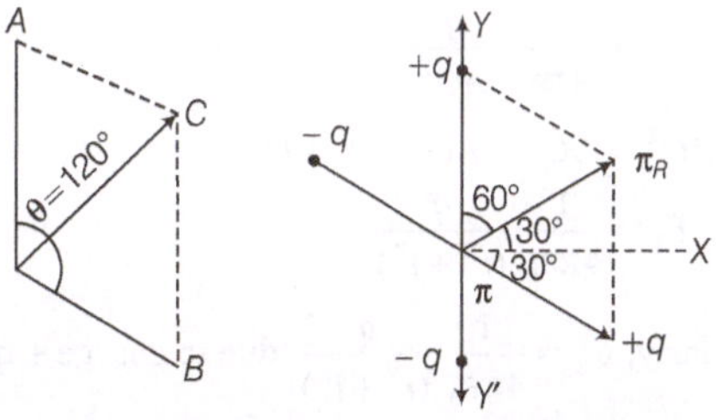

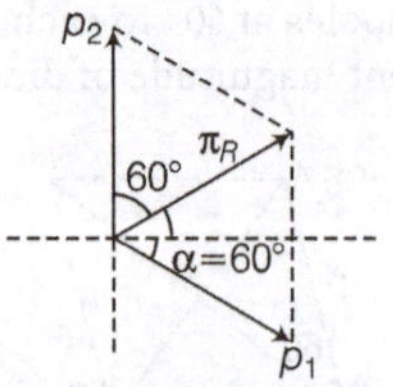

The magnitude of resultant p_R,

$$p_R = \sqrt{p_1^2 + p_2^2 + 2p_1p_2 \cos\theta}$$

$$= \sqrt{p^2 + p^2 + 2p^2 \cos\theta}$$

$$= \sqrt{2p^2(1+\cos\theta)} = \sqrt{2p^2 \times 2\cos^2\frac{\theta}{2}}$$

$$= 2p \cos\frac{\theta}{2}$$ (1)

$$\tan\alpha = \frac{p_2 \sin\theta}{p_1 + p_2 \cos\theta} = \frac{p \sin 120^\circ}{p + p\cos 120^\circ} = \frac{p\sqrt{3}/2}{p - \frac{p}{2}} = \sqrt{3}$$

$$\Rightarrow \; |p_R| = 2p\cos\frac{\theta}{2} = 2p\cos\frac{120^\circ}{2} = 2p \times \frac{1}{2} = p$$

p_R will subtend an angle of 30° with X-axis.

Now, torque acting on the system,

$$\tau = p_R \times E = p_R E \sin\theta = \frac{1}{2}pE$$

Torque will work to align the dipole in the direction of electric field **E**. (1)

17. Consider an electric dipole, consisting of two point charges $-q$ and $+q$, separated by a small distance $AB = 2l$, with centre at O.

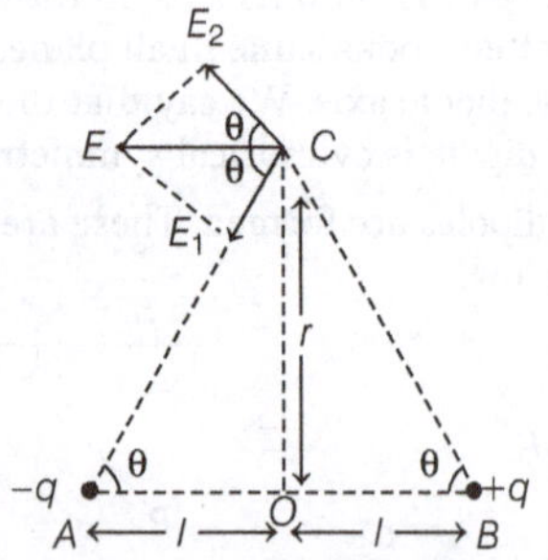

So, dipole moment, $\mathbf{p} = q(2l)$

Let $OC = r$

Here, E_1 = Electric intensity at C due to charge $-q$ at A.

$$\therefore \quad E_1 = \frac{1}{4\pi\varepsilon_0}\frac{q}{AC^2}$$

$$\because \quad AC^2 = OC^2 + AO^2 = r^2 + l^2$$

$$\Rightarrow \quad E_1 = \frac{1}{4\pi\varepsilon_0}\frac{q}{(r^2+l^2)}$$

Similarly, $E_2 = \dfrac{1}{4\pi\varepsilon_0}\dfrac{q}{(r^2+l^2)}$ (due to charge $+q$ at B)

$\because$ For equatorial point C,

$\angle CAB = \angle CBA = \theta$

Hence, the equivalent of E_1 and E_2,

$$\mathbf{E} = [(\hat{\mathbf{i}}E_1\cos\theta + \hat{\mathbf{j}}\,E_1\sin\theta) + (-)\,\hat{\mathbf{i}}\,E_2\cos\theta - \hat{\mathbf{j}}\,E_2\sin\theta]$$

$$\Rightarrow |\mathbf{E}| = E_1\cos\theta + E_2\cos\theta$$

$$\Rightarrow \quad E = 2E_1\cos\theta \qquad (\because E_1 = E_2)$$

$$= \frac{2}{4\pi\varepsilon_0}\frac{q}{(r^2+l^2)}\cos\theta \qquad \left(\because \cos\theta = \frac{l}{\sqrt{r^2+l^2}}\right)$$

$$= \frac{2ql}{4\pi\varepsilon_0(r^2+l^2)^{3/2}} = \frac{p}{4\pi\varepsilon_0(r^2+l^2)^{3/2}}$$

$$\therefore \quad E = \frac{1}{4\pi\varepsilon_0}\frac{p}{(r^2+l^2)^{3/2}}$$

18. Refer to text on page 24 (At a point on the axial line).

19. Refer to text on pages 25 and 26 (Torque on an electric dipole in a uniform electric field).

20. Torque on an electric dipole placed in the uniform electric field (**E**)

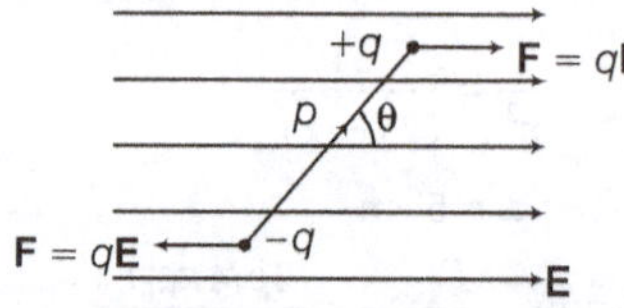

Torque, $\tau = \mathbf{p} \times \mathbf{E} \Rightarrow |\tau| = pE\sin\theta$

$\tau = pE\sin\theta$

(i) For maximum torque, $\sin\theta = 1$ or $\theta = 90^\circ$

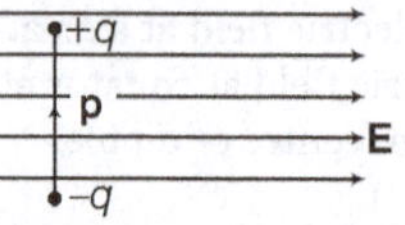

So, dipole should be kept perpendicular to the electric field. (1½)

(ii) **Minimum torque** experienced by electric dipole in electric field, when $\theta = 0^\circ$ or π (180°)

$$\tau = \tau_{min} = 0$$

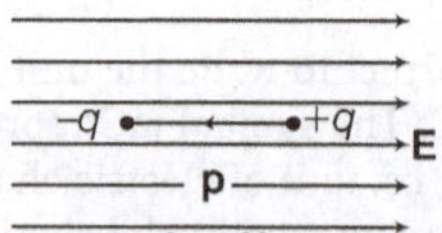

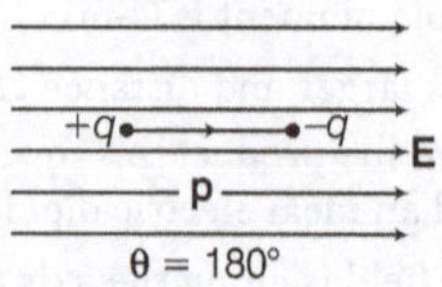

(1½)

21. (i) Electric field at a general point $P(r, \theta)$ due to dipole is given by

$$E = \frac{1}{4\pi\varepsilon_0}\frac{p}{r^3}\sqrt{3\cos^2\theta + 1}$$

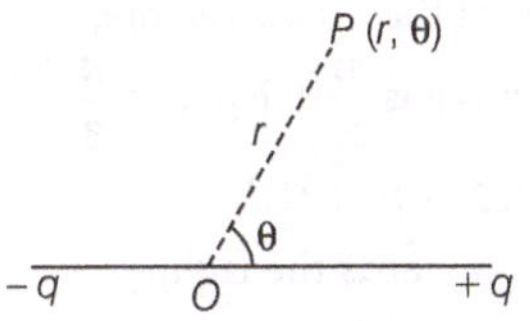

(a) For axial position $\theta = 0°$ and $p = P$,

$$E_a = \frac{1}{4\pi\varepsilon_0}\frac{P}{r^3} \times 2 = \frac{1}{4\pi\varepsilon_0}\frac{2P}{r^3}$$

(b) For broadside on position $\theta = 90°$ and $p = P$,

$$E_b = \frac{1}{4\pi\varepsilon_0}\frac{P}{r^3} \times 1 = \frac{1}{4\pi\varepsilon_0}\frac{P}{r^3}$$ (2)

(ii) The ratio of **E** at axial and broad on positions is given by

$$\frac{E_a}{E_b} = \frac{\frac{1}{4\pi\varepsilon_0}\left(\frac{2P}{r^3}\right)}{\frac{1}{4\pi\varepsilon_0}\left(\frac{P}{r^3}\right)} = \frac{2}{1}$$

$\Rightarrow \quad E_a : E_b = 2:1$ (1)

22. We can find torque by multiplying magnitude of either force by perpendicular distance between the forces.

The dipole shown in the diagram is placed in a uniform electric field **E**. The direction of electric dipole moment **p** makes an angle θ with electric field. The forces in a pair are acting on the dipole as shown in the figure.

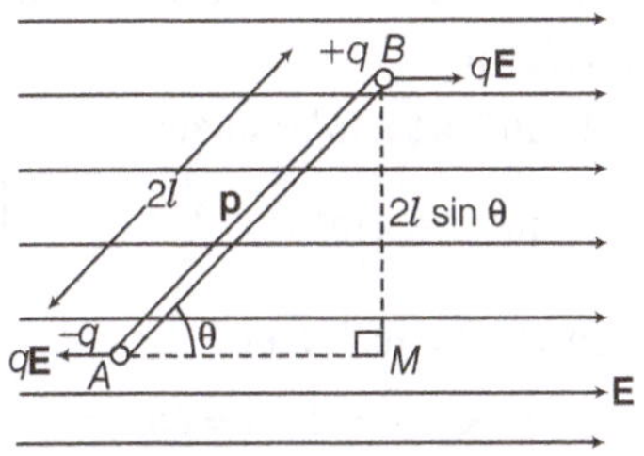

(1½)

By definition,

Torque (τ) = Magnitude of either force × Perpendicular distance between the forces

$= qE \times BM = qE \times 2l\sin\theta$

$= 2qlE\sin\theta = PE\sin\theta$

$\Rightarrow \quad \tau = \mathbf{p} \times \mathbf{E}$ (1½)

23. Refer to text on pages 24 and 25 (Electric dipole).

24. Refer to text on pages 25 and 26 (Torque on an electric dipole in a uniform electric field).

25. (i) Refer to text on page 24 (Electric field intensity due to an electric dipole). (2)

(ii) $E \propto \frac{1}{r^3}$. As r will increase, E will sharply decreases.

The shape of the graph will be as given in the figure. (1)

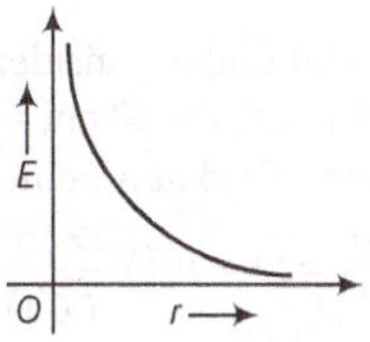

(iii) When the dipole were kept in a uniform electric field E_0. The torque acting on dipole, $\tau = p \times E$ (1)

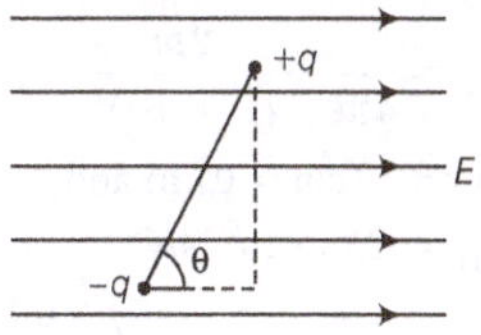

(a) If $\theta = 0°$, then $\tau = 0$, $\mathbf{p} \parallel \mathbf{E}$

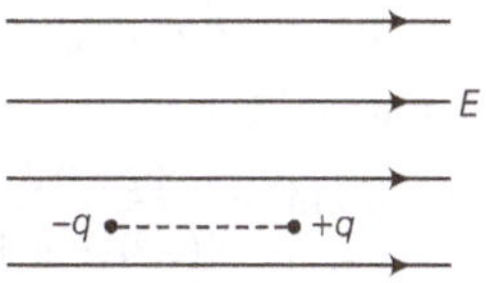

The dipole is in stable equilibrium.

(b) If $\theta = 180°$, then $\tau = 0$, $\mathbf{p} \parallel -\mathbf{E}$

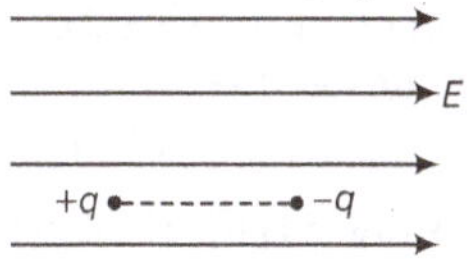

The dipole is in unstable equilibrium. (1)

26. Refer to text on pages 24 and 25 (At a point on the equatorial line).

27. Dipole moment,

$$p = q \times r = 1.6 \times 10^{-19} \times 4.3 \times 10^{-9} = 6.8 \times 10^{-28} \text{ C-m}$$

28. Here, $q = 25 \times 10^{-9}$C, $2a = 6$ m, $r = 4$ m,

$$p = q(2a) = 25 \times 10^{-9} \times 6 = 1.5 \times 10^{-7} \text{ C-m}$$

(i) Now, $E_{\text{axial}} = \frac{1}{4\pi\varepsilon_0} \cdot \frac{2pr}{(r^2 - a^2)^2}$

$$= \frac{9 \times 10^9 \times 2 \times 1.5 \times 10^{-7} \times 4}{(4^2 - 3^2)^2} = \frac{2700 \times 4}{49}$$

$= 220.4 \text{ NC}^{-1}$ (1)

(ii) $\therefore \; E_{\text{equatorial}} = \frac{1}{4\pi\,\varepsilon_0} \cdot \frac{p}{(r^2 + a^2)^{3/2}}$

$$= \frac{9 \times 10^9 \times 1.5 \times 10^{-7}}{(4^2 + 3^2)^{3/2}} = \frac{1350}{125} = 10.8 \text{ N C}^{-1}$$ (1)

29. Refer to example 1 on pages 23 and 24.

30. Here, $q_1 = q_2 = q = 0.1\mu\mu\text{C} = 10^{-13}$ C [in magnitude]

Length of the electric dipole formed by these charges,

$$2a = 10\text{Å} = 10^{-9} \text{ m}$$

Thus, electric dipole moment,

$$p = 2aq = 10^{-13} \times 10^{-9} = 10^{-22} \text{ C-m}$$ (1)

Distance of the point under consideration on the axial line from the mid-point, $r = 10$ cm $= 0.1$ m

Since, $a << r$, electric field at a point on the axial line,

$$E = k_c \frac{2p}{r^3} = (9\times10^9)\frac{2\times10^{-22}}{(0.1)^3} = 18\times10^{-10} \text{ N/C}$$ (2)

31. Refer to example 2 on page 25.

32. We know that,

$$E_{axial} = \frac{1}{4\pi\varepsilon_0}\cdot\frac{2pr}{(r^2-a^2)^2}$$

***Case* I** When $r = 10$ cm $= 0.1$ m and

$$E_{axial} = 3.75\times10^5 \text{ N/C}$$

$$\Rightarrow \quad 3.75\times10^5 = 9\times10^9\times\frac{2p\times0.1}{[(0.1)^2-a^2]^2} \quad ...(i)$$ (1½)

***Case* II** When $r = 20$ cm $= 0.2$ m and

$$E_{axial} = 3\times10^4 \text{ N/C}$$

$$\Rightarrow \quad 3\times10^4 = 9\times10^9\times\frac{2p\times0.2}{[(0.2)^2-a^2]^2} \quad ...(ii)$$ (1½)

Solving the Eqs. (i) and (ii), we get

$$a = 0.05 \text{ m}$$

Therefore, length of the dipole is $2a$.

So, $\quad 2a = 2\times0.05 = 0.1$ m (2)

33. The electric field vector $\mathbf{E}_{1A}$ at A due to the positive charge q_1 points towards the right. Its magnitude,

$$E_{1A} = \frac{(9\times10^9\text{N-m}^2\text{C}^{-2})(10^{-7}\text{C})}{(0.1\text{ m})^2} = 9\times10^4\text{N C}^{-1}$$ (1)

The electric field vector $\mathbf{E}_{2A}$ due to q_2 points to the right and has the same magnitude.

Hence, the magnitude of total electric field $\mathbf{E}_A$ at A,

$$E_A = E_{1A} + E_{2A} = 18\times10^4\text{NC}^{-1}$$ (1)

i.e. $\mathbf{E}_A$ is directed towards right.

The electric field $\mathbf{E}_{1B}$ at B due to q_1 points towards the left and has a magnitude,

$$E_{1B} = \frac{(9\times10^9\text{N-m}^2\text{C}^{-2})(10^{-7}\text{C})}{(0.1\text{ m})^2} = 9\times10^4\text{NC}^{-1}$$

The electric field $\mathbf{E}_{2B}$ at B due to the negative charge q_2 points towards the right and has a magnitude

$$E_{2B} = \frac{(9\times10^9\text{ N-m}^2\text{C}^{-2})(10^{-7}\text{C})}{(0.3\text{ m})^2} = 1\times10^4\text{NC}^{-1}$$

The magnitude of the total electric field at B,

$$E_B = E_{1B} - E_{2B} = 8\times10^4\text{NC}^{-1}$$ (1)

i.e. $\mathbf{E}_B$ is directed towards the left.

The magnitude of each electric field vector at point C due to charge q_1 and q_2,

$$E_{1C} = E_{2C}$$

$$= \frac{(9\times10^9\text{N-m}^2\text{C}^{-2})(10^{-7}\text{C})}{(0.2\text{ m})^2}$$

$$= 2.25\times10^4\text{ NC}^{-1}$$

The resultant of these two vectors,

$$E_C = E_{1C}\cos\frac{\pi}{3} + E_{2C}\cos\frac{\pi}{3}$$

$$= 2.25\times10^4\text{NC}^{-1}$$

i.e. $\mathbf{E}_C$ points towards the right. (2)

34. Torque, $\tau = 3\times10^{-29}$C-m

$$p = 6\times10^{-25}\text{N-m}$$

$$\tau = \mathbf{p}\times\mathbf{E} = pE\sin\theta$$

For maximum value, $\theta = 90°$

$$\tau = pE$$ (1/2)

$$\Rightarrow 3\times10^{-29} = 6\times10^{-25}\times E$$

$$\Rightarrow E = \frac{3\times10^{-29}}{6\times10^{-25}} = 0.5\times10^{-29+25}$$

$$= 0.5\times10^{-4}\text{ N/C}$$ (1/2)

35. As, $P(1, 0, 4)$ and $Q(2, -1, 5)$

$\therefore \quad 2l = \text{PQ} = [(2-1)\hat{i} + (-1-0)\hat{j} + (5-4)\hat{k}] = (\hat{i}-\hat{j}+\hat{k})$

and $q = \pm 9\times10^{-6}$ C, $E = 0.20\,\hat{i}$ V/cm, $\tau = ?$

Since, $\tau = p\times E = q(2l)\times E$

$\therefore \quad \tau = 9\times10^{-6}(\hat{i}-\hat{j}+\hat{k})\times0.20\hat{i} = 18\times10^{-7}(\hat{k}-\hat{j})$ (1/2)

$\therefore$ Magnitude of torque,

$$\tau = 18\times10^{-7}[\sqrt{(1)^2+(1)^2}]$$

$$= 25.45\times10^{-7}\text{N-m}$$ (1/2)

36. Given, $p = 4\times10^{-9}$ C-m, $E = 5\times10^4$, $\theta = 30°$

$$\therefore \quad \tau = pE\sin\theta$$

$$= 4\times10^{-9}\times5\times10^4\times\sin30°$$

$$= 4\times10^{-9}\times5\times10^4\times\frac{1}{2} \quad \left[\because \sin30° = \frac{1}{2}\right]$$

$$= 10\times10^{-5} = 10^{-4}\text{N-m}$$ (2)

37. Here, $q = 1\times10^{-6}$ C, $2a = 2$ cm $= 0.02$ m

$\therefore p = q\times2a = (1\times10^{-6})\times0.02 = 2\times10^{-8}$cm

Intensity of the external electric field, $E = 1.0\times10^5$ N/C

Then, maximum torque,

$$\tau_{max} = pE = (2\times10^{-8})(1.0\times10^5) = 2\times10^{-3}\text{N-m}$$ (1)

38. Here, $p = 6.2\times10^{-30}$ C-m and $E = 10^6$ N/C

$\therefore \quad \tau = pE\sin\theta \quad$ [for maximum value $\theta = 90°$]

$$= pE\sin90° = 6.2\times10^{-30}\times10^6\times1$$

$$= 6.2\times10^{-24}\text{ N-m}$$ (1)

39. Consider an electric dipole with charge $-q$ at A and charge $+q$ at B, placed along Z-axis, such that its dipole moment is in negative z-direction, i.e. $p_Z = -10^{-7}$ C-m, as shown in the figure.

The electric field is along positive direction of Z-axis, such that $\frac{dE}{dZ} = 10^5\text{NC}^{-1}\text{m}^{-1}$. (2)

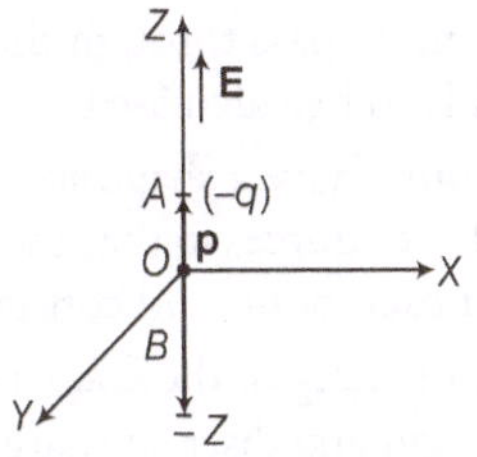

(1)

Using, $F = qdE = q \times \frac{dE}{dZ} \times dZ$

$$= (q \times dZ) \times \frac{dE}{dZ} = p\frac{dE}{dZ}$$

$$= 10^{-7} \times 10^{5}$$

$$= -10^{-2} \text{ N}$$ (1)

Thus, the force on the dipole is along negative direction of Z-axis.

As, $\theta = 180°$

∴ Torque on dipole,

$$\tau = pE \sin 180° = 0$$ (1)

TOPIC 04 Electric Flux

Area Vector

The vector associated with every area element of a closed surface is taken to be in the direction of the outward normal. Thus, the area element vector $\Delta \mathbf{S}$ at a point on a closed surface is equal to $\Delta S\, \hat{\mathbf{n}}$, where ΔS is the magnitude of the area element and $\hat{\mathbf{n}}$ is a unit vector in the direction of outward normal at the point.

$$\Delta \mathbf{S} = \hat{\mathbf{n}}(\Delta S)$$

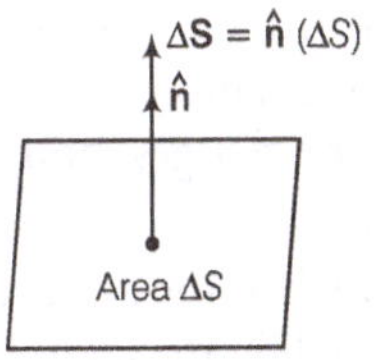

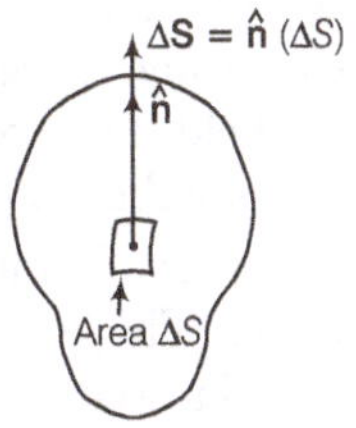

Electric Flux

Electric flux linked with any surface is defined as the total number of electric field lines that normally pass through that surface.

If the electric field is uniform, the electric flux ϕ through a surface S due to an electric field E at an angle θ with S is, $\phi = \mathbf{E} \cdot \mathbf{S} = ES \cos\theta$

If the electric field is non-uniform, the electric flux $d\phi$ through a small area element $d\mathbf{S}$ due to an electric field E at an angle θ with $d\mathbf{S}$ is

$$d\phi = \mathbf{E} \cdot d\mathbf{S} = E\, dS \cos\theta$$

which is proportional to the number of field lines cutting the area element. Total electric flux ϕ over the whole surface S due to an electric field E,

$$\phi = \oint_S \mathbf{E} \cdot d\mathbf{S} = \oint_S E\, dS \cos\theta$$

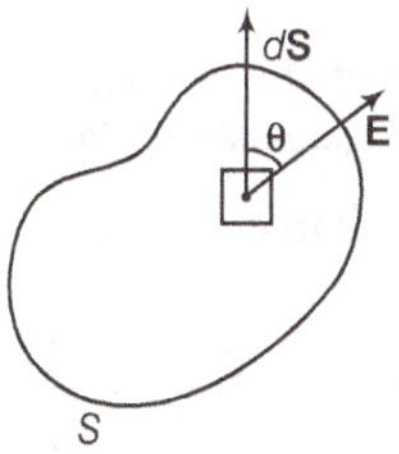

Special Cases

If the plane surface is normal to the electric field E, i.e. $(\theta = 0°)$, then

$$\phi = \mathbf{E} \cdot \mathbf{A} \cos 0° = EA$$

If the plane surface is parallel to the electric field $(\theta = 90°)$, then

$$\phi = \mathbf{E} \cdot \mathbf{A} \cos 90° = 0$$

If the electric field lines entering the plane surface normally $(\theta = 180°)$, then

$$\phi = \mathbf{E} \cdot \mathbf{A} \cos 180° = -EA$$

Electric flux is a scalar quantity. But it is a property of vector field.

SI unit of electric flux is N-m^{2}C^{-1}

and dimensional formula of electric flux is expressed as

$$\phi = [MLT^{-2}][L^2][AT]^{-1}$$

$$= [ML^3T^{-3}A^{-1}]$$

If $\oint \mathbf{E} \cdot d\mathbf{S}$ over a closed surface is negative, then the surface encloses a net negative charge.

Analogy Between Electric Flux And Liquid Flux

It should be known that electric flux is analogous to flux of a liquid flowing across a plane, which is equal to $\mathbf{v} \cdot \Delta \mathbf{S}$, where $\mathbf{v}$ is the velocity of flow of liquid. In electric flux, there is no flow of a physically observable quantity like liquid.

Example 1 A box encloses an electrical dipole consisting of charge $5\ \mu C$ and $-5\ \mu C$ and of length 10 cm. What is the total electric flux through the box?

Sol. Since, an electric dipole consists of two equal and opposite charges, the net charge on the dipole is zero.
Hence, the net electric flux coming out of the closed surface of the box or through the box is zero.

Gauss' Theorem

Statement

The surface integral of the electric field intensity over any closed surface (called Gaussian surface) in free space is equal to $\frac{1}{\varepsilon_0}$ times the net charge enclosed within the surface.

$$\phi_E = \oint_S \mathbf{E} \cdot d\mathbf{S} = \frac{1}{\varepsilon_0} \sum_{i=1}^{n} q_i = \frac{q}{\varepsilon_0}$$

where, $q = \sum_{i=1}^{n} q_i$ is the algebraic sum of all the charges inside the closed surface and ε_0 is the permittivity of free space.

Hence, total electric flux over a closed surface in vacuum is $\frac{1}{\varepsilon_0}$ times the total charge within the surface, regardless of how the charges may be distributed.

Gaussian Surface

Any hypothetical closed surface enclosing a charge is called the Gaussian surface of that charge. It is chosen to evaluate the surface integral of the electric field produced by the charge enclosed by it, which in turn gives the total flux through the surface.

The Essential Properties of a Gaussian Surface

(i) It should be a closed surface, so that a clear distinction can be made between points that are inside the surface, on the surface and outside the surface.

(ii) This surface must pass through the point, where electric field is to be calculated.

(iii) The surface must have a shape according to the symmetry of the source, so that the field is normal to the surface at each point and constant in magnitude.

(iv) For a system of charges, the Gaussian surface should not pass through any discrete charge. It is because electric field at the location of any charge is not well defined. However, the Gaussian surface can pass through a continuous charge distribution.

(v) Electric flux through a small portion of the closed surface is affected by the charges present outside the surface. However, the total electric flux through a closed surface is not affected by the charge present outside the closed surface.

(vi) Electric flux through a small portion of the closed surface may change, if the charges inside the closed surface are moved to the new position. However, the total electric flux through a closed surface is not affected, if the charges inside the closed surface are moved to the new positions.

Some Features of Gauss's Law

(i) Gauss' law is true for any closed surface, no matter what its shape or size be.

(ii) In the situation, when the surface is so chosen that there are some charges inside and some outside, the electric field is due to all the charges, both inside and outside the closed surface.

(iii) Gauss' law is often useful when the system has some symmetry. This is facilitated by the choice of a suitable Gaussian surface.

Example 2 A charge q is placed at the centre of a cube of side l. What is the electric flux passing through each face of the cube?

Sol. By Gauss' theorem, total electric flux linked with a closed surface is given by

$$\phi = \frac{q}{\varepsilon_0}$$

where, q is the total charge enclosed by the closed surface.

$\therefore$ Total electric flux linked with cube,

$$\phi = \frac{q}{\varepsilon_0}.$$

As charge is at centre, therefore electric flux is symmetrically distributed through all 6 faces.

$\therefore$ Flux linked with each face $= \frac{1}{6}\phi = \frac{1}{6} \times \frac{q}{\varepsilon_0} = \frac{q}{6\varepsilon_0}$

Example 3 Figure shows three point charges, $+2q$, $-q$ and $+3q$. Two charges $+2q$ and $-q$ are enclosed within a surface S. What is the electric flux due to this configuration through the surface S?

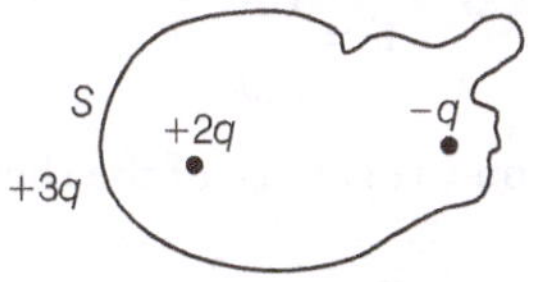

Sol. Electric flux through the closed surface S is

$$\phi_S = \frac{\Sigma q}{\varepsilon_0} = \frac{+2q - q}{\varepsilon_0} = \frac{q}{\varepsilon_0}$$

Charge $+3q$ is outside the closed surface S, therefore it would not be taken into consideration in applying Gauss' theorem.

Example 4 A point charge causes an electric flux -3×10^{-14} N-m^2/C to pass through a spherical Gaussian surface.

(i) Calculate the value of the point charge.

(ii) If the radius of the Gaussian surface is doubled, how much flux would pass through the surface?

Sol. (i) By Gauss' theorem, total electric flux through closed Gaussian surface is given by

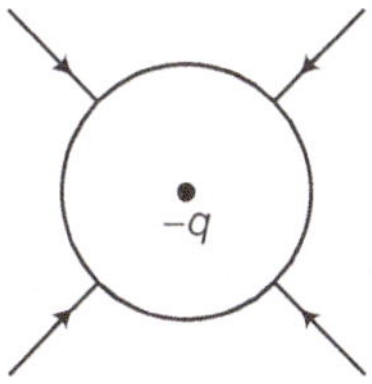

$$\phi = \frac{q}{\varepsilon_0}$$

$$\therefore \quad q = \phi\varepsilon_0$$

But electric flux passing through the surface,

$$\phi = -3\times 10^{-14} \text{ N-m}^2/\text{C}$$

$$\therefore \quad q = (-3\times 10^{-14})\times 8.85\times 10^{-12} = -26.55\times 10^{-26} \text{ C}$$

$$= -2.655\times 10^{-25} \text{ C}$$

(ii) Electric flux passing through the surface remains unchanged because it depends only on charge enclosed by the surface and is independent of its size.

Applications of Gauss' Theorem

The electric field due to some symmetric charge configurations can be obtained using Gauss' law.

Field due to an Infinitely Long Thin Straight Charged Wire

Consider an infinitely long thin straight wire with uniform linear charge density (λ).

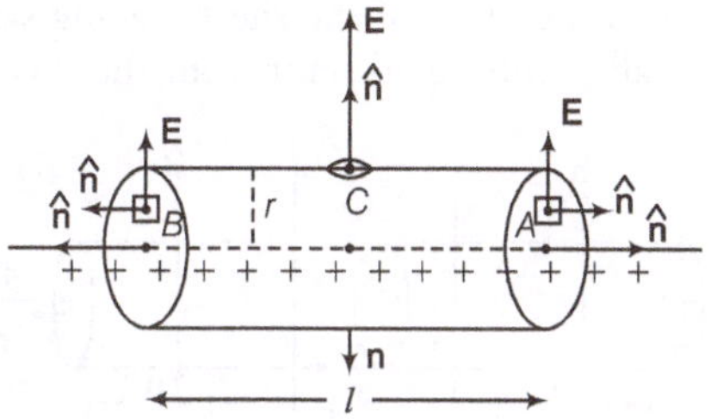

From symmetry, the electric field is everywhere radial in the plane cutting the wire normally and its magnitude only depends on the radial distance (r).

From Gauss' law, $\phi_E = \oint_S \mathbf{E}\cdot d\mathbf{S} = \dfrac{q}{\varepsilon_0}$

Now, $$\phi_E = \oint_S \mathbf{E}\cdot d\mathbf{S} = \oint_S \mathbf{E}\cdot\hat{\mathbf{n}}\, dS$$

$$= \oint_A \mathbf{E}\cdot\hat{\mathbf{n}}\, dS + \oint_B \mathbf{E}\cdot\hat{\mathbf{n}}\, dS + \oint_C \mathbf{E}\cdot\hat{\mathbf{n}}\, dS$$

$$\therefore \quad \oint_S \mathbf{E}\cdot d\mathbf{S} = \oint_A E\, dS\cos 90^\circ + \oint_B E\, dS\cos 90^\circ + \oint_C E\, dS\cos 0^\circ$$

$$= \oint_C E\, dS = E(2\pi r l)$$

Charge enclosed in the cylinder, $q = \lambda l$

$$\therefore \quad E(2\pi r l) = \frac{\lambda l}{\varepsilon_0}$$

or $$\boxed{E = \frac{\lambda}{2\pi\varepsilon_0 r}}$$

Vectorially, $\mathbf{E} = \dfrac{\lambda}{2\pi\varepsilon_0 r}\hat{\mathbf{r}}$

The direction of the electric field is radially outward from the positive line charge. For negative line charge, it will be radially inward.

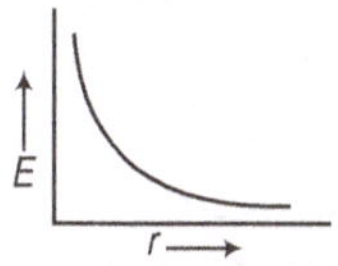

Thus, electric field (E) due to the linear charge is inversely proportional to the distance (r) from the linear charge. The variation of electric field (E) with distance (r) is shown in figure.

Field due to a Thin Infinite Plane Sheet of Charge

Let σ be the surface charge density of the sheet. From symmetry, $\mathbf{E}$ on either side of the sheet must be perpendicular to the plane of the sheet, having same magnitude at all points equidistant from the sheet.

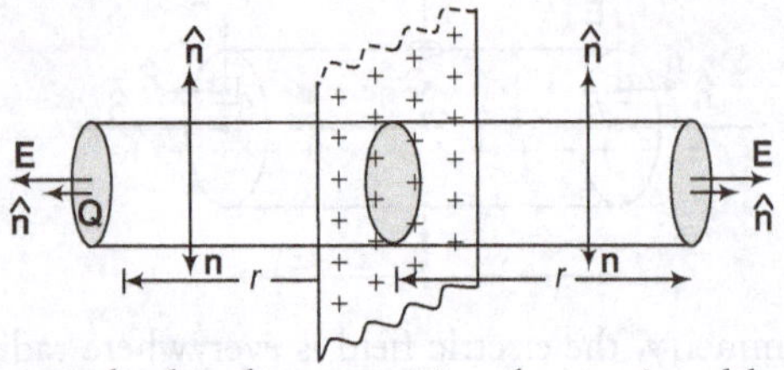

We take a cylindrical cross-sectional area A and length $2r$ as the Gaussian surface. On the curved surface of the cylinder, **E** and **n̂** are perpendicular to each other. Therefore, flux through curved surface = 0.

Flux through the flat surfaces $= EA + EA = 2EA$

$\therefore$ Total electric flux over the entire surface of cylinder,

$$\phi_E = 2EA$$

Total charge enclosed by the cylinder, $q = \sigma A$

According to Gauss' law, $\phi_E = \dfrac{q}{\varepsilon_0}$

$$\therefore \quad 2EA = \frac{\sigma A}{\varepsilon_0}$$

or

$$\boxed{E = \frac{\sigma}{2\varepsilon_0}}$$

E is independent of r, the distance of the point from the plane charged sheet.

Field due to a Uniformly Charged Thin Spherical Shell

Let σ be the uniform surface charge density of a thin spherical shell of radius (R). The Gaussian surface will be a spherical surface centered at the centre of shell.

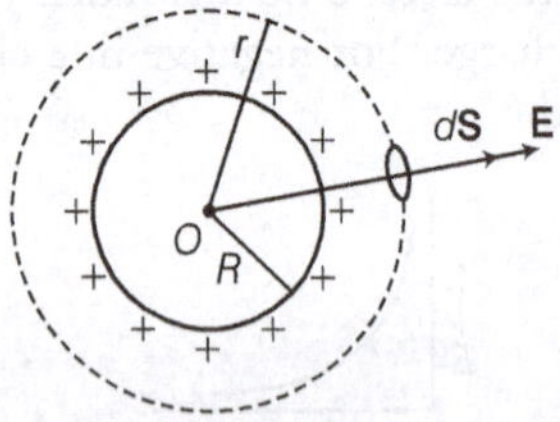

(i) **At a point outside the shell ($r > R$)**

Since, **E** and d**S** are in the same direction.

$$\therefore \quad \phi_E = \oint_S \mathbf{E} \cdot d\mathbf{S} = \frac{q}{\varepsilon_0} \text{ or } E(4\pi r^2) = \frac{q}{\varepsilon_0}$$

$$\therefore \quad \boxed{E = \frac{q}{4\pi\varepsilon_0 r^2}}$$

Since, $\quad q = \sigma \times 4\pi R^2$

$$\therefore \quad E = \frac{\sigma R^2}{\varepsilon_0 r^2}$$

Vectorially, $\quad \mathbf{E} = \dfrac{\sigma R^2}{\varepsilon_0 r^2}\hat{\mathbf{r}}$

(ii) **At a point on the surface of the shell ($r = R$)**

$$\boxed{E = \frac{q}{4\pi\varepsilon_0 R^2}}$$

and $\quad E = \dfrac{\sigma}{\varepsilon_0}$

(iii) **At a point inside the shell ($r < R$)**

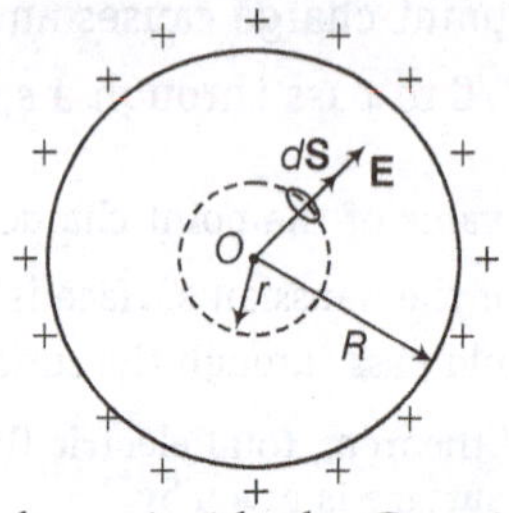

Here, the charge inside the Gaussian surface shell.

$$q = 0$$

$$\therefore \quad E(4\pi r^2) = 0$$

$$\therefore \quad E = 0$$

This important result is a direct consequence of Gauss' law which follows from Coulomb's law. The experimental verification of this result confirms $1/r^2$ dependence in Coulomb's law.The variation of electric field intensity (E) with distance from the centre of a uniformly charged spherical shell is shown in figure.

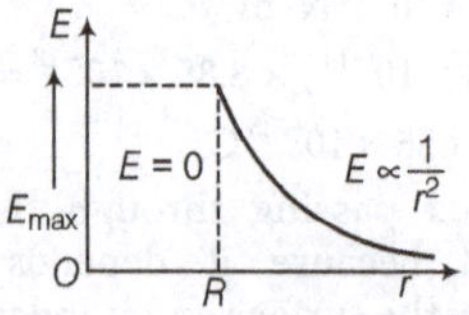

Example 5 **A hollow charged conductor has a tiny hole cut into its surface. Show that the electric field in the hole is $\left(\dfrac{\sigma}{2\varepsilon_0}\right)\hat{\mathbf{n}}$, where n̂ is the unit vector in the outward normal direction and σ is the surface charge density near the hole.** **NCERT**

Sol. Surface charge density near the hole $= \sigma$

Unit vector $= \hat{n}$ (normal directed outwards)

Let P be the point on the hole. The electric field at point P closed to the surface to conductor, according to Gauss' theorem,

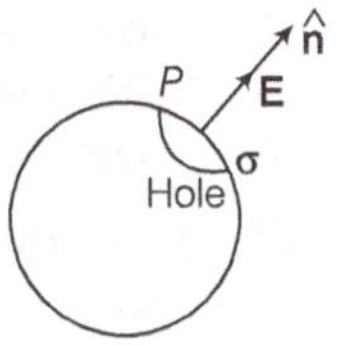

$$\oint \mathbf{E} \cdot d\mathbf{S} = \frac{q}{\varepsilon_0}$$

where, q is the charge near the hole.

$$EdS \cos\theta = \frac{\sigma dS}{\varepsilon_0}$$

$[\because \sigma = q / dS \Rightarrow q = \sigma dS$, where dS = area$]$

$\therefore$ Angle between electric field and area vector is $0°$.

$$\therefore \quad E\, dS = \frac{\sigma\, dS}{\varepsilon_0} \qquad [\because \cos 0° = 1]$$

$$\Rightarrow \quad E = \frac{\sigma}{\varepsilon_0} \Rightarrow \mathbf{E} = \frac{\sigma}{\varepsilon_0}\hat{n}$$

This electric field is due to the filled up hole and the field due to the rest of the charged conductor. The two fields inside the conductor are equal and opposite.

So, there is no electric field inside the conductor. Outside the conductor, the electric fields are equal in the same direction.

So, the electric field at point P due to each part

$$= \frac{1}{2}\mathbf{E} = \frac{\sigma}{2\varepsilon_0}\hat{n}$$

Topic Practice 4

Multiple Choice Questions

1 Mark

1. For a given surface, the $\oint E \cdot dS = 0$. From this we can conclude that
   (a) E is necessarily zero on the surface
   (b) E is perpendicular to the surface at every point
   (c) the total flux through the surface is zero
   (d) the flux is only going out of the surface

2. A hollow sphere of radius R has a point charge Q at its centre. Electric flux emanating from it is ϕ. If both the charge and the radius of the sphere be doubled, electric flux emanating from the sphere will **ISC 2023**
   (a) remain the same
   (b) become 2ϕ
   (c) become 4ϕ
   (d) become 8ϕ

3. A closed surface in vacuum encloses charges $-q$ and $+3q$. The total electric flux emerging out of the surface is **ISC 2019**
   (a) zero (b) $\frac{2q}{\varepsilon_0}$ (c) $\frac{3q}{\varepsilon_0}$ (d) $\frac{4q}{\varepsilon_0}$

4. A point charge $+q$ is placed at the centre of a cube of side L. The electric flux emerging from the cube is
   (a) $\frac{q}{\varepsilon_0}$ (b) zero (c) $\frac{6qL^2}{\varepsilon_0}$ (d) $\frac{q}{6L^2\varepsilon_0}$

5. Consider the charge configuration and spherical Gaussian surface as shown in the figure. When calculating the flux of the electric field over the spherical surface the electric field will be due to

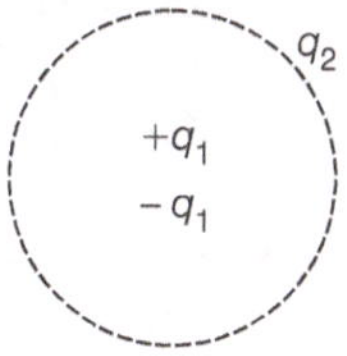

   (a) q_2
   (b) only the positive charges
   (c) all the charges
   (d) $+q_1$ and $-q_1$

6. A short electric dipole which consists of two point charges $-q$ and $+q$, is placed at the centre O and inside a large cube ($ABCDEFGH$) of length L as shown in the figure. The electric flux emanating through the cube is **ISC 2015**

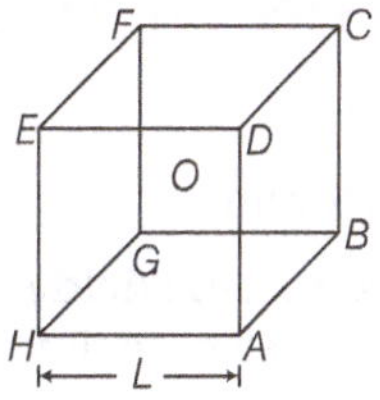

   (a) $q/4\pi\varepsilon_0 L$ (b) zero
   (c) $q/2\pi\varepsilon_0 L$ (d) $q/3\pi\varepsilon_0 L$

7. Two point charges $(+e)$ and $(-e)$ are kept inside a large metallic cube without touching its sides. Electric flux emerging out of the cube is **ISC 2011**
   (a) $\frac{e}{\varepsilon_0}$ (b) $\frac{-e}{\varepsilon_0}$ (c) zero (d) $\frac{2e}{\varepsilon_0}$

8. Electric field intensity E at a point P at a perpendicular distance r from an infinitely long line charge $X'X$ having linear charge density λ is given by **ISC 2010**

(a) $E=\left(\frac{1}{4\pi\varepsilon_0}\right)\frac{2\lambda}{r^2}$ (b) $E=\left(\frac{1}{4\pi\varepsilon_0}\right)\frac{2\lambda}{r}$

(c) $E=\left(\frac{1}{4\pi\varepsilon_0}\right)\frac{\lambda}{r^2}$ (d) $E=\left(\frac{1}{4\pi\varepsilon_0}\right)\frac{\lambda}{r}$

9. Intensity of electric field at a point at a perpendicular distance r from an infinite line charge, having linear charge density λ is given by **ISC 2014**

(a) $E=\left(\frac{1}{4\pi\varepsilon_0}\right)\frac{\lambda}{r}$ (b) $E=\left(\frac{1}{4\pi\varepsilon_0}\right)\frac{2\lambda}{r}$

(c) $E=\left(\frac{1}{4\pi\varepsilon_0}\right)\frac{\lambda}{r^2}$ (d) $E=\left(\frac{1}{4\pi\varepsilon_0}\right)\frac{2\lambda}{r^2}$

10. Two infinite plane parallel sheets separated by a distance d have equal and opposite uniform charge densities σ. Electric field at a point between the sheets is

(a) zero

(b) $\frac{\sigma}{\varepsilon_0}$

(c) $\frac{\sigma}{2\varepsilon_0}$

(d) depends upon the location of the point

Very Short Answer Type Questions

1 Mark

11. State Gauss' theorem. **ISC 2020, 16, 07**

12. The unit of electrostatic field E is volt/metre. Obtain the unit of electric flux.

13. An arbitrary surface encloses a dipole. What is the electric flux through this surface? **NCERT Exemplar**

14. A square surface of side l metres in the plane of paper is placed in a uniform electric field E acting along the same plane at an angle θ with the horizontal side of square as shown in the figure. What is the electric flux linked to the surface?

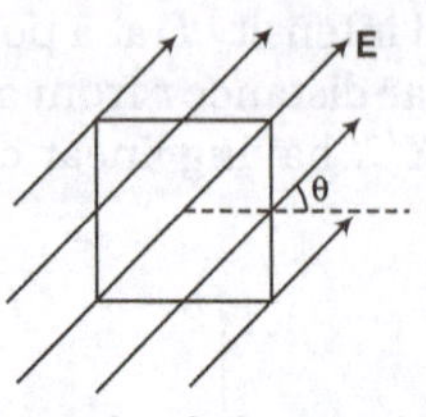

15. Does the strength of electric field due to an infinite long line charge depend upon the distance of the observation point from the line charge?

16. How does electric field at a point charge vary with distance r from an infinitely long charged wire?

17. Does the strength of electric field due to an infinite plane sheet of charge depend upon the distance of the observation point from the sheet of charge?

18. How does the electric flux due to a point charge enclosed by a spherical Gaussian surface get affected when its radius is increased?

19. Two charges of magnitudes $-2Q$ and $+Q$ are located at points $(a, 0)$ and $(4a, 0)$, respectively. What is the electric flux due to these charges through a sphere of radius $3a$ with its centre at the origin?

20. What is the electric flux through a cube of side 1 cm which encloses an electric dipole?

21. (i) A charge q is placed at the centre of a cube. What is the electric flux passing through each face of cube?

(ii) If radius of Gaussian surface enclosing some charge q is halved, then how does electric flux through Gaussian surface change?

Short Answer Type I Questions

2 Marks

22. If the total charge enclosed by a surface is zero, does it imply that the electric field everywhere on the surface is zero, conversely, if the electric field everywhere on the surface is zero? Does it imply the net charge inside is zero? **NCERT Exemplar**

23. A hollow sphere of radius R has a point charge q at its centre. Electric flux emanating from the sphere is X. How will the electric flux change, if at all, when **ISC 2024**

(i) radius of the sphere is doubled?

(ii) charge q is replaced by an electric dipole?

24. Rank the Gaussian surfaces as shown in the figure. In order of increasing electric flux, starting with the most negative.

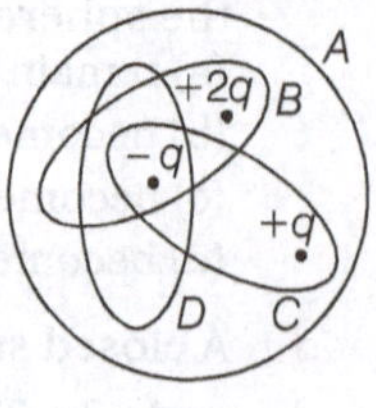

25. Consider the charge configuration and a spherical Gaussian surface as shown in the figure.

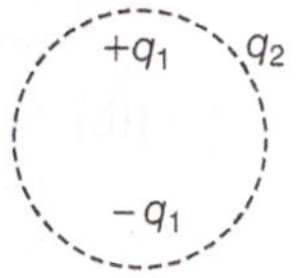

Which one of the three charges will be the cause of electric field while calculating the flux of the field over the spherical surface?

26. Deduce Coulomb's law from Gauss' law.

27. What will be the electric field intensity at the centre of a uniformly charged circular wire of linear charge density?

28. A thin straight infinitely long conducting wire having charge density λ is enclosed by a cylindrical surface of radius r and length l, its axis coinciding with the length of the wire. Find the expression for the electric flux through the surface of the cylinder.

29. In case of an infinite line charge, how does intensity of electric field at a point change, if at all, when **ISC 2024**
   (i) charge on it is doubled?
   (ii) distance of the point is halved?

30. Consider two hollow concentric spheres S_1 and S_2 enclosing charges $2Q$ and $4Q$ respectively, as shown in the figure.

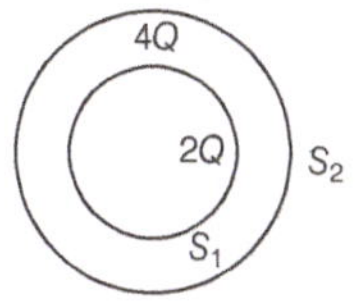

   (i) Find out the ratio of the electric flux through them.
   (ii) How will the electric flux through the sphere S_1 change, if a medium of dielectric constant ε_r is introduced in the space inside S_1 in place of air? Deduce the necessary expression.

Short Answer Type II Questions

3 Marks

31. State Gauss' law in electrostatics. A cube with each side a is kept in an electric field given by $\mathbf{E} = Cx\hat{\mathbf{i}}$ as shown in the figure, where C is a positive dimensionless constant.

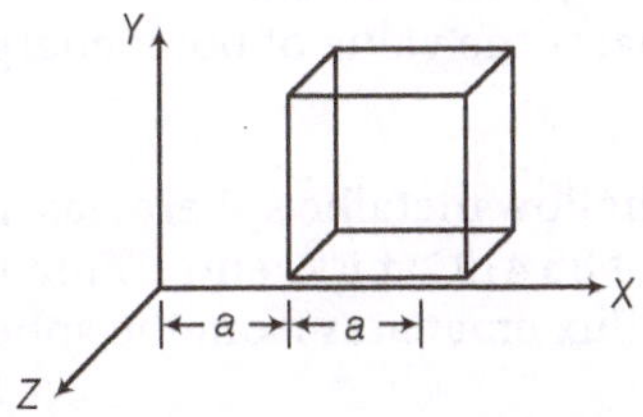

Find out
   (i) the electric flux through the cube and
   (ii) the net charge inside the cube. **NCERT**

32. Use Gauss' law to derive the expression for the electric field between two uniformly charge parallel, sheets with surface charge densities σ and $-\sigma$, respectively.

33. (i) Using Gauss' law, prove that the electric field at a point due to a uniformly charged infinite plane sheet is independent of the distance from it.
   (ii) How is the field directed, if the sheet is positively charged?

Long Answer Type Questions

5 Marks

34. (i) Define electric flux. Write its SI unit. Gauss' law in electrostatics is true for any closed surface, no matter what its shape or size is. Justify this statement with the help of a suitable example.
   (ii) Use Gauss' law to prove that the electric field inside a uniformly charged spherical shell is zero.

35. State Gauss' theorem and derive an expression for Gauss' theorem.

36. (i) Use Gauss's theorem to find the electric field due to a uniformly charged infinitely large plane thin sheet with surface charge density σ.
   (ii) An infinitely large thin plane sheet has a uniform surface charge density $+\sigma$. Obtain the expression for the amount of work done in bringing a point charge q from infinity to a point, distant r, in front of the charged plane sheet.

37. (i) An electric dipole of dipole moment $\mathbf{p}$ consists of point charges $+q$ and $-q$ separated by a distance $2a$ apart. Deduce an expression for the electric field $\mathbf{E}$ due to the dipole at a distance x from the centre of the dipole on its axial line in terms of the dipole moment $\mathbf{p}$. Hence, show that in the limit
   $x >> a$, $\mathbf{E} \longrightarrow 2\,\mathbf{p}/(4\pi\varepsilon_0 x^3)$.

(ii) Given the electric field in the region $\mathbf{E} = 2x\hat{\mathbf{i}}$, find the net electric flux through the cube and the charge enclosed by it.

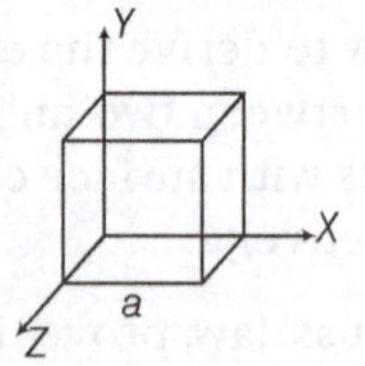

Numerical Problems

38. Consider a uniform electric field $\mathbf{E} = 3 \times 10^3 \hat{\mathbf{i}}$ N/C.

(i) What is the flux of this field through a square of 10 cm on a side whose plane is parallel to the YZ-plane?

(ii) What is the flux through the same square, if the normal to its plane makes an angle 60° with the X-axis? **NCERT, (2M)**

39. Given a uniform electric field $\mathbf{E} = 5 \times 10^3 \mathbf{i}$ N/C, find the flux of this field through a square of 10 cm on a side whose plane is parallel to the YZ-plane. What would be the flux through the same square, if the plane makes an angle of 30° with the X-axis? **(2 M)**

40. A hollow cylindrical box of length 1 m and area of cross-section 25 cm^2 is placed in a three dimensional coordinate system as shown in the figure. The electric field in the region is given by $\mathbf{E} = 50x\hat{\mathbf{i}}$, where E is in NC^{-1} and x is in metre.

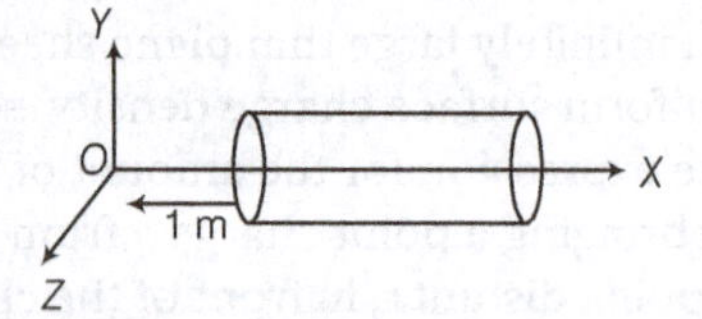

Find

(i) net flux through the cylinder and

(ii) charge enclosed by the cylinder. **(3M)**

41. A uniform electric field is given as $\mathbf{E} = 100\hat{\mathbf{i}}$ N/C for $x > 0$ and $\mathbf{E} = 100\hat{\mathbf{i}}$ N/C for $x < 0$. A right circular cylinder of length 20 cm and radius 5 cm has its centre at the origin and its axis along the X-axis, so that one face is at $x = +10$ cm and other is at $x = -10$ cm.

(i) What is the net outward flux through each flat face?

(ii) What is the flux through the side of cylinder?

(iii) What is the net outward flux through the cylinder?

(iv) What is the net charge inside the cylinder? **(3 M)**

42. The electric field components in given figure are $E_X = \alpha x^{1/2}$, $E_Y = E_Z = 0$, in which $\alpha = 600\ \text{N/C-m}^{1/2}$.

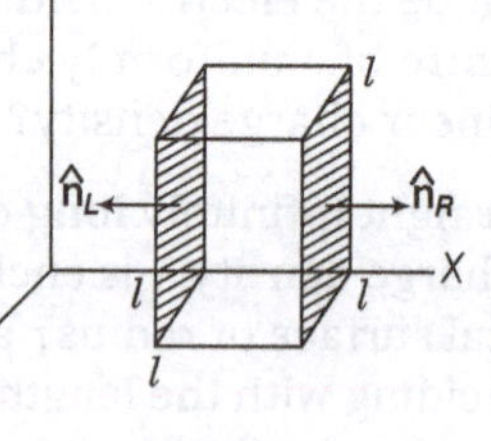

Calculate (i) the flux through the cube and (ii) the charge within the cube. Assume that $l = 0.1$ m. **(5 M)**

43. A point charge $+10\ \mu\text{C}$ is at a distance 5 cm directly above the centre of a square of side 10 cm, as shown in figure. What is the magnitude of the electric flux through the square? **NCERT (2 M)**

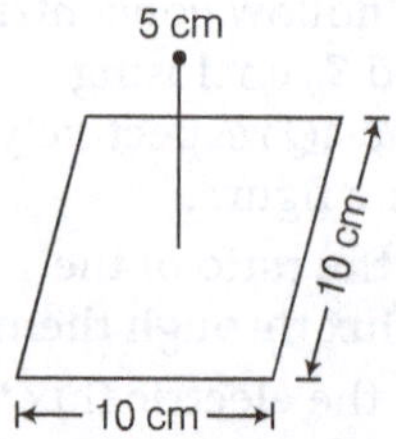

44. A point charge of 2.0 μC is at the centre of a cubic Gaussian surface 9.0 cm on edge. What is the net electric flux through the surface? **NCERT (2 M)**

45. A point charge causes an electric flux of $-1.0 \times 10^3\ \text{N-m}^2/\text{C}$ to pass through a spherical Gaussian surface of 10.0 cm, radius centred on the charge.

(i) If the radius of the Gaussian surface were doubled, how much flux would pass through the surface?

(ii) What is the value of point charge? **NCERT (3 M)**

46. A large hollow metallic sphere has a positive charge of 35.4 μC at its centre. Find how much electric flux emanates from the sphere? **ISC 2013 (1 M)**

47. Careful measurement of the electric field at the surface of a black box indicates that the net outward flux through the surface of the box is $8.0 \times 10^3 \text{N-m}^2\text{C}^{-1}$.

(i) What is the net charge inside the box?

(ii) If the net outward flux through the surface of the box was zero, could you conclude that there were no charges inside the box. Why or why not? **NCERT (3 M)**

48. An infinite line charge produces a field of 9×10^4 N/C at a distance of 2 cm. Calculate the linear charge density. **ISC 2006, NCERT (2 M)**

49. Intensity of electric field at a perpendicular distance of 0.5 m from an infinitely long line charge having linear charge density (λ) is 3.6×10^3 Vm^{-1}. Find the value of λ. **ISC 2017 (2 M)**

50. A uniformly charged conducting sphere of diameter 2.4 m has a surface charge density of $80.0 \, \mu\text{C/m}^2$.

(i) Find the charge on the sphere.

(ii) What is the total electric flux leaving the surface of the sphere? **NCERT (2 M)**

51. Two large thin metal plates are parallel and close to each other. On their inner faces, the plates have surface charge densities of opposite signs and of magnitude $17.0 \times 10^{-22} \text{Cm}^{-2}$. What is E

(i) to the left of the plates,

(ii) to the right of the plates and

(iii) in between the plates? **NCERT (3 M)**

Hints & Solutions

1. (c) This means total charge and so total flux is zero.

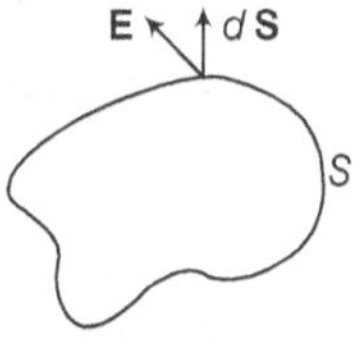

$\oint \mathbf{E} \cdot d\mathbf{S}$ = Total flux through the surface.

Given, total flux through surface

$$= \oint \mathbf{E} \cdot d\mathbf{S} = 0 \quad \text{...(i)}$$

By Gauss's law (total flux through) $= \dfrac{1}{\varepsilon_0}$ (net charge enclosed in S) ...(ii)

From Eqs. (i) and (ii), we get

Net charge inside $S = 0$

Total flux through the surface S is zero.

2. (b) From Gauss theorem, $\phi = \dfrac{Q_{\text{enclose}}}{\varepsilon_0}$

$\therefore \quad \phi \propto Q_{\text{enclose}}$

Thus, if the radius as well as the charge becomes double than the electric flux emanating from the sphere will be also doubled.

$$\phi' = 2\phi$$

3. (b) The total electric flux through the closed surface,

$$\phi = \frac{1}{\varepsilon_0}[-q + 3q] \Rightarrow \phi = \frac{2q}{\varepsilon_0}$$

4. (a) Electric flux emerging out from the surface is independent of shape of surface. As enclosed charge is q. Net flux emerging out from surface, using Gauss's law, is $\dfrac{q}{\varepsilon_0}$.

5. (c) As flux $= \dfrac{q_{\text{enclosed}}}{\varepsilon_0}$. So, flux is due to only charges $+q_1$ and $-q_2$ that makes a sum zero. But q_2 produces its own flux and net flux linked with sphere is zero. Electric field will be due to all the charges.

6. (b) The electric flux, emanating through the cube is zero. Since, the number of lines 'poking in' from the left is equal to the number of lines 'poking out' from the right.

7. (c) Refer to solution no. 6.

8. (b) By applying Gauss's law, electric field due to an infinitely long line charge of line as charge density λ is

$$E = \left(\frac{1}{4\pi\varepsilon_0}\right)\frac{2\lambda}{r}$$

where, r is the perpendicular distance from the charged wire.

9. (b) Refer to solution no. 8.

10. (b)

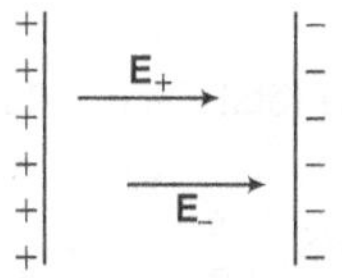

$$E_+ = E_- = \frac{\sigma}{2\varepsilon_0} \Rightarrow E_{\text{net}} = 2\left(\frac{\sigma}{2\varepsilon_0}\right) = \left(\frac{\sigma}{\varepsilon_0}\right)$$

11. Gauss' theorem The total electric flux linked with closed surface S is equal $1/\varepsilon_0$ times the total charge inside the surface.

$$\therefore \quad \phi_E = \oint \mathbf{E} \cdot dS = \frac{q}{\varepsilon_0}$$

where, q is the total charge enclosed by the closed Gaussian (an imaginary) surface.

12. The electric flux through a plane of area of A, normal to an electrostatic field E, is given by

$$\phi_E = EA$$

$\therefore$ Unit of electric flux (ϕ_E)

= Unit of electric field $\times$ Unit of area

= (volt/metre) $\times$ metre^2 = volt-metre

13. If any arbitrary surface encloses a dipole, then the net charge is zero, because the total charge on the dipole is zero (dipole consists of two equal and opposite charges). According to Gauss's law,

total flux $= \frac{1}{\varepsilon_0} \times$ charge enclosed $= \frac{1}{\varepsilon_0} \times (0) = 0 \Rightarrow \phi = 0$

14. Since, E is acting along the same plane at an angle θ as shown in the figure, therefore electric flux,

$\phi = EA \cos\theta$, where θ is angle between E and normal to surface, i.e.

$$\theta = 90°$$

$$\Rightarrow \quad \phi = EA \cos 90° = 0$$

15. Yes, the electric field due to an infinitely long line charge depends upon the distance of the observation point from the line charge.

16. The electric field due to a line charge falls of with distance as $1/r$.

17. No, the electric field due to an infinite plane sheet of charge does not depend upon the distance of the observation point from the plane sheet of charge.

18. According to question, electric flux (ϕ) due to a point charge enclosed by a spherical Gaussian surface is given by

$$\phi = \mathbf{E} \cdot \mathbf{A}$$

$$= \frac{kq}{r^2} \cdot 4\pi r^2 = kq \cdot 4\pi \quad \left[\because E = \frac{kq}{r^2} \text{ and } A = 4\pi r^2\right]$$

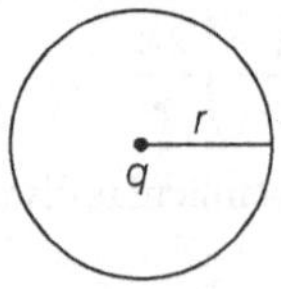

(1/2)

So, there is no effect of change in radius on the electric flux. (1/2)

19. Gauss' theorem states that the total electric flux linked with closed surface S,

$$\phi_E = \mathbf{E} \cdot d\mathbf{S} = \frac{q}{E_0}$$

where, q is the total charge enclosed by the closed Gaussian (imaginary) surface. (1/2)

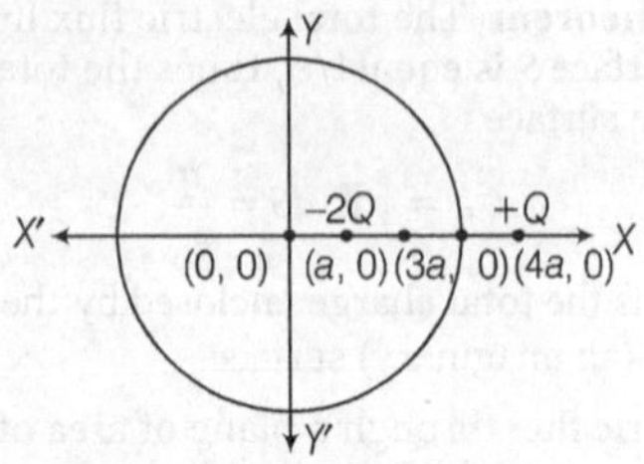

The sphere enclosed charge $= -2Q$

Therefore, $\quad \phi = \frac{2Q}{\varepsilon_0}$ (inwards) (1/2)

20. Since, according to the Gauss' law of electrostatics, electric flux through any closed surface is given by

$$\phi_E = \oint E \cdot dS = \frac{q}{\varepsilon_0} \quad \text{...(i)}$$

where, E = electrostatic field,
q = total charge enclosed by the surface
and ε_0 = absolute electric permittivity of free space.

So, in the given case, cube encloses an electric dipole. Therefore, the total charge enclosed by the cube is zero.

i.e. $\quad q = 0$

Therefore, from Eq. (i), we get $\phi_E = \frac{q}{\varepsilon_0} = 0$

i.e. Electric flux is zero.

21. (i) Flux through each face $= \frac{1}{6}\left(\frac{q}{\varepsilon_0}\right) = \frac{q}{6\varepsilon_0}$ (1/2)

(ii) Electric flux, $\phi = \frac{q}{6\varepsilon_0}$, since q does not change, ϕ will remain same. (1/2)

22. No, since $\oint \mathbf{E} \cdot d\mathbf{S} = \frac{q}{\varepsilon_0} = 0$, therefore the field may be normal to the surface. (1)

However, the reverse is true, i.e. when $E = 0$ everywhere on the surface, the net charge inside is zero. (1)

23. (i) Using Gauss' theorem, we have
Electric flux, $\phi_E = q/\varepsilon_0$
So, making the radius of the sphere double does not change the electric flux emanating the sphere.

(ii) Since, the total charge of on an electric dipole is zero. So, if charge q is replaced by an electric dipole, then electric flux will be zero. (2)

24. Since, surface D enclosed negative charge, hence it has least flux negative.

In parts C and A, there is zero net charge, hence flux is zero, surface B has most flux, which is positive in nature, since it consist positive charge, i.e. $+2q$. (2)

25. Refer to example 3 on page 35.

26. According to Gauss' theorem, $\int_S \mathbf{E} \cdot d\mathbf{S} = \frac{q}{\varepsilon_0}$

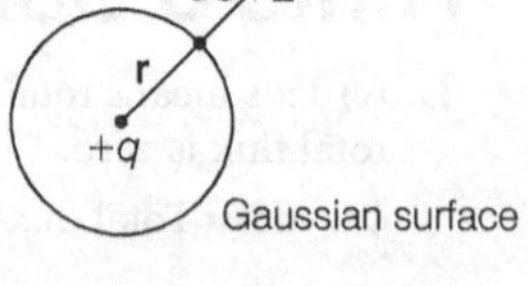

$$\Rightarrow \quad E \cdot 4\pi r^2 = \frac{q}{\varepsilon_0} \quad (1)$$

$$\therefore \quad E = \frac{q}{4\pi\varepsilon_0 r^2}$$

If a charge q_0 is kept on the surface, then

$F = E \times q_0 = \frac{qq_0}{4\pi\varepsilon_0 r^2}$, which is Coulomb's law. (1)

27. A uniformly charged circular wire can be considered to be subdivided into pairs of diametrically opposite elements. The electric field intensity at the centre of wire due to each of the pairs is zero, therefore the electric field intensity due to the entire circular wire will be zero. (1+1)

28. **Key Point:** A thin straight conducting wire will have a uniform linear charge distribution.

Let q charge be enclosed by the cylindrical surface.

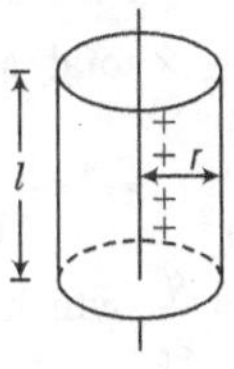

$\therefore$ Linear charge density, $\lambda = \frac{q}{l} \Rightarrow q = \lambda l$ ...(i) (1/2)

By Gauss' theorem,
total electric flux through the surface of cylinder,

$$\phi = \frac{q}{\varepsilon_0}$$ (1)

$$\therefore \quad \phi = \frac{\lambda l}{\varepsilon_0}$$ [from Eq. (i)] (1/2)

29. The intensity of electric field at a point due to infinite line charge is

$$E = \frac{\lambda}{2\pi\varepsilon_0 r}$$

where, λ is the uniform line charge density and r is the magnitude of radial distance.

(a) If charge on line charge conductor is doubled, electric field will remain same as it is independent of charge.

(b) If distance of the point is halved, the electric field will become double. i.e.

$$E' = \frac{\lambda}{2\pi\varepsilon_0 \left(\frac{r}{2}\right)} = 2\left(\frac{\lambda}{2\pi\varepsilon_0 r}\right) = 2E$$

30. (i) According to Gauss' theorem,

$$\phi = \frac{\Sigma q}{\varepsilon_0 \varepsilon_r} \propto \Sigma q$$

$$\therefore \quad \frac{\phi_{S_1}}{\phi_{S_2}} = \frac{2Q}{2Q+4Q} = \frac{2Q}{6Q} = \frac{1}{3}$$ (1)

(ii) If a medium of dielectric constant ε_r is introduced in the space inside S_1 in place of air, then

$$\phi_{S_1} = \frac{\Sigma q}{\varepsilon_0 \varepsilon_r} = \frac{2Q}{\varepsilon_0 \varepsilon_r}$$ (1)

31. Refer to text on page 34 (Gauss' theorem). (1)

(i) Now, the electric field, $\mathbf{E} = Cx\hat{\mathbf{i}}$ is in x-direction only.

So, face with surface normal vector perpendicular to this field would give zero electric flux, i.e. $\phi = E\,dS \cos 90° = 0$, through it.

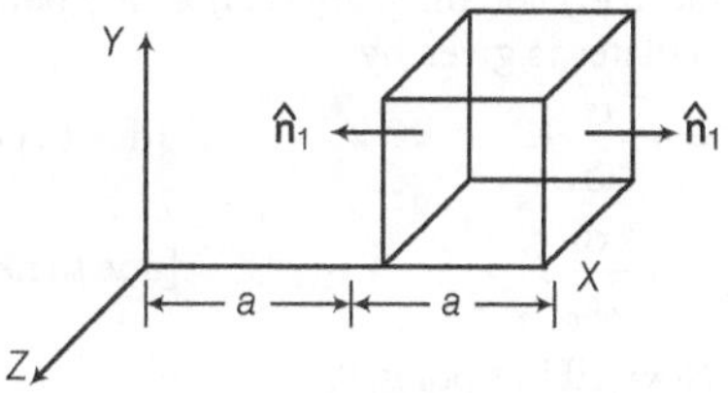

So, flux would be across only two surfaces.
Magnitude of E at left face,

$$E_L = Cx = Ca \qquad [x = a \text{ at left face}]$$

Magnitude of E at right face,

$$E_R = Cx = C\,2a = 2aC \qquad [x = 2a \text{ at right face}]$$

Thus, corresponding fluxes are

$$\phi_L = \mathbf{E}_L \cdot d\mathbf{S} = E_L dS \cos\theta = -aC \times a^2 = -a^3 C \qquad [\because \theta = 180°]$$

and

$$\phi_R = \mathbf{E}_R \cdot d\mathbf{S} = 2aC\,dS\cos\theta \qquad [\because \theta = 0°]$$
$$= 2aCa^2 = 2a^3C$$ (1)

Now, net flux through cube

$$= \phi_L + \phi_R = -a^3C + 2a^3C = a^3C \text{ N-m}^2\text{C}^{-1}$$ (1/2)

(ii) Net charge inside the cube, again we can use Gauss' law to find total charge q inside the cube.

We have, $\phi = \frac{q}{\varepsilon_0}$

or $q = \phi\varepsilon_0$

$\Rightarrow q = a^3 C \varepsilon_0$ (1/2)

32. Let us consider two uniformly charge parallel sheets carrying surface charge densities $+\sigma$ and $-\sigma$ respectively and are separated by a small distance from each other.

By Gauss' law, it can be proved that, electric field intensity due to a uniformly charged infinite plane sheet as nearby is given by, $E = \frac{\sigma}{2\varepsilon_0}$

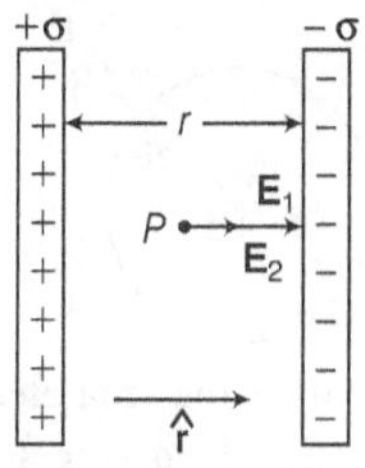

(1)

The electric field is directed normally outward from the plane sheet, if nature of charge on sheet is positive and normally inward, if charge is of negative nature. Let $\hat{r}$ represents unit vector directed from positive plate to negative plate.

Now, Electric Field Intensity (EFI) at any point P between the two plates is given by

(i) $E_1 = +\frac{\sigma}{2\varepsilon_0}\hat{r}$ [due to positive plate]

(ii) $E_2 = +\frac{\sigma}{2\varepsilon_0}\hat{r}$ [due to negative plate]

$\therefore$ New EFI at point P, (1)

$$E = E_1 + E_2 = \frac{\sigma}{2\varepsilon_0}\hat{r} + \frac{\sigma}{2\varepsilon_0}\hat{r} = \frac{\sigma}{\varepsilon_0}\hat{r}$$

Thus, uniform electric field is produced between the two infinite parallel plane sheet of charge which is directed from positive plate to negative plate. (1)

33. (i) and (ii); refer to text on pages 35 and 36 (Field due to a thin infinite plane sheet of charge).

34. (i) Electric flux over an area in an electric field represents the total number of electric field lines crossing the area. The SI unit of electric flux is $N\text{-}m^2C^{-1}$.

According to Gauss' law in electrostatics, the surface integral of electrostatic field **E** produced by any source over any closed surface S enclosing a volume V in vacuum, i.e. total electric flux over the closed surface S in vacuum, is $1/\varepsilon_0$ times the total charge (q) contained inside S, i.e.

$$\phi_E = \oint_S E \cdot dS = \frac{q}{\varepsilon_0}$$

Gauss' law in electrostatics is true for a closed surface, no matter what its shape or size is.

So, in order to justify the above statement, suppose in isolated positive charge q is situated at the centre O of a sphere of radius r.

According to Coulomb's law, electric field intensity at any point P on the surface of the sphere is

$$E = \frac{q}{4\pi\varepsilon_0} \cdot \frac{\hat{r}}{r^2}$$

where, $\hat{r}$ is unit vector directed from O to P.

Consider a small area element dS of the sphere around P. Let it be represented by the vector $dS = \hat{n} \cdot dS$.

where, $\hat{n}$ is unit vector along out drawn normal to the area element.

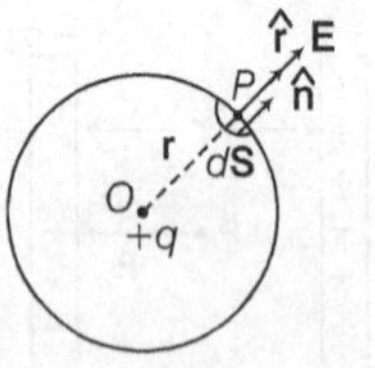

$\therefore$ Electric flux over the area element,

$$d\phi_E = E \cdot dS = \left(\frac{q}{4\pi\varepsilon_0} \cdot \frac{\hat{r}}{r^2}\right) \cdot (\hat{n} \cdot dS)$$

$$E \cdot dS = \frac{q}{4\pi\varepsilon_0} \cdot \frac{dS}{r^2} \cdot \hat{r} \cdot \hat{n}$$

As normal to a surface of every point is along the radius vector at that point, therefore $\hat{r} \cdot \hat{n} = 1$

$$E \cdot dS = \frac{q}{4\pi\varepsilon_0} \cdot \frac{dS}{r^2}$$

Integrating over the closed surface area of the sphere, we get total normal electric flux over the entire sphere,

$$\phi_E = \oint_S E \cdot dS = \frac{q}{4\pi\varepsilon_0 r^2}\oint_S dS$$

$$= \frac{q}{4\pi\varepsilon_0 r^2} \times \text{total area of surface of sphere.}$$

$$= \frac{q}{4\pi\varepsilon_0 r^2}(4\pi r^2) = \frac{q}{\varepsilon_0}$$

Hence, $\oint_S E \cdot dS = \frac{q}{\varepsilon_0}$, which proves Gauss' theorem. (2½)

(ii) **Electric field inside a uniformly charged spherical shell**

Refer to text on page 36. (2½)

35. Refer to text on page 34. (Gauss' Theorem) (2)

Prove Electric flux through a surface element dS is given by

$$d\phi_E = E \cdot dS = \frac{1}{4\pi\varepsilon_0} \cdot \frac{q}{r^2}\hat{r} \cdot (dS\,\hat{n})$$

$$\Rightarrow \quad d\phi_E = \frac{1}{4\pi\varepsilon_0} \cdot \frac{q\,dS}{r^2}\hat{r} \cdot \hat{n}$$

Here, $\hat{r} \cdot \hat{n} = 1 \cdot 1 \cos 0° = 1$

$$\therefore \quad d\phi_E = \frac{1}{4\pi\varepsilon_0} \cdot \frac{q\,dS}{r^2}$$

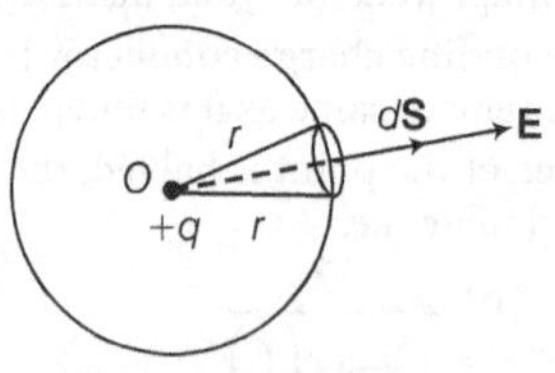

Total electric flux through the spherical surface,

$$\phi_E = \oint_S d\phi_E = \frac{1}{4\pi\varepsilon_0} \cdot \frac{q}{r^2}\oint_S dS$$

$$= \frac{1}{4\pi\varepsilon_0} \cdot \frac{q}{r^2} \cdot 4\pi r^2 = \frac{q}{\varepsilon_0}$$

$$\Rightarrow \quad \phi_E = \frac{q}{\varepsilon_0}$$

If the medium surrounding the charge has a dielectric constant K, then

$$\phi_E = \frac{q}{K\varepsilon_0} = \frac{q\varepsilon_0}{\varepsilon\varepsilon_0} = \frac{q}{\varepsilon}, \text{ where } K = \varepsilon_r = \frac{\varepsilon}{\varepsilon_0}$$

$$\therefore \phi_E = \frac{q}{\varepsilon}$$

If there is no net charge within the closed surface, i.e. when $q = 0$, then $\phi_E = 0$.

$\therefore$ The total electric flux through a closed surface is zero, if no charge is enclosed by the surface.

36. (i) Refer to text on pages 35 and 36 (Field due to a thin infinite plane sheet of charge). (3)

(ii) Surface charge density of the uniform plane sheet which is infinitely large $=+\sigma$. The electric potential (V) due to infinite sheet of a uniform charge density $+\sigma$,

$$V=\frac{-\sigma r}{2\varepsilon_0}$$

The amount of work done in bringing a point charge q from infinite to point, at distance r in front of the charged plane sheet, is

$$W=q'\times V=q'\cdot\frac{-\sigma r}{2\varepsilon_0}=-\frac{\sigma r\cdot q'}{2\varepsilon_0}\text{ joule}$$ (2)

37. (i) Refer to text on page 24 in Topic 3 (At a point on the axial line). (2½)

(ii) Since, the electric field has only x-component, for faces normal to x-direction, the angle between E and ΔS is $\pm\frac{\pi}{2}$. Therefore, the flux is separately zero for each of the cube except the shaded ones.

The magnitude of the electric field at the left face is

$E_L=0$ [as $x=0$ at the left face]

The magnitude of the electric field at the right face is

$E_R=3a$ [as, $x=a$ at the right face] (1)

The corresponding fluxes are

$\phi_L=\mathbf{E}_L\cdot\Delta\mathbf{S}=0$

and $\phi_R=\mathbf{E}_L\cdot\Delta\mathbf{S}=E_R\Delta S\cos\theta=E_R\Delta S$ [$\because\theta=0°$]

$\Rightarrow\ \phi_R=E_Ra^2$

Net flux (ϕ) through the cube

$=\phi_L+\phi_R=0+E_Ra^2=E_Ra^2$

$\Rightarrow\ q=2a\,(a)^2=2a^3$

We can use Gauss' law to find the total charge q inside the cube.

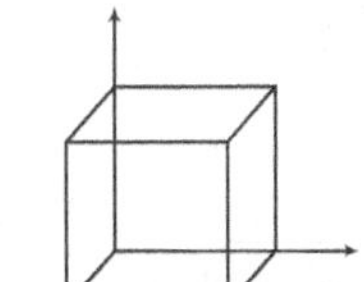

$$\phi=\frac{q}{\varepsilon_0}\ \Rightarrow\ \phi=\frac{2a^3}{\varepsilon_0}$$ (1½)

38. Electric field, $\mathbf{E}=3\times10^3\,\hat{\mathbf{i}}$ N/C, i.e. electric field is directed towards X-axis (due to involvement of $\hat{\mathbf{i}}$).

(i) As the surface is in YZ-plane, so the area vector (normal to the square) is along X-axis.

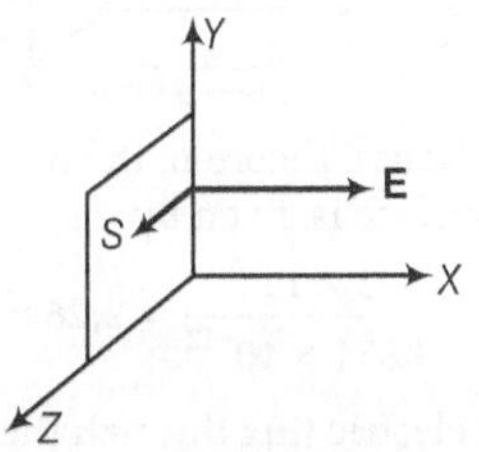

Area, $S=10\times10=100\text{ cm}^2=10^{-2}\text{ m}^2$

Area vector, $\mathbf{S}=10^{-2}\,\hat{\mathbf{i}}\text{ m}^2$

Using the formula of electric flux,

$\phi=\mathbf{E}\cdot\mathbf{S}=ES\cos\theta$

$=ES$ [$\because$ angle between E and S is 0°]

$=3\times10^3\times10^{-2}=30\text{ N-m}^2/\text{C}$ (1)

(ii) Now, the area vector makes an angle of 60° with X-axis.

$\mathbf{E}=3\times10^3\,\hat{\mathbf{i}}$ N/C

$S=100\text{ cm}^2=10^{-2}\text{m}^2,\ \theta=60°$

Using the formula of electric flux, $\phi=\mathbf{E}\cdot\mathbf{S}$

$\Rightarrow\ \phi=ES\cos\theta=3\times10^3\times10^{-2}\cos60°$

$=3\times10\times\frac{1}{2}=15\text{ N-m}^2/\text{C}$ (1)

39. Given, electric field intensity,

$\mathbf{E}=5\times10^3\,\hat{\mathbf{i}}$ N/C

Magnitude of electric field intensity,

$|\mathbf{E}|=5\times10^3$ N/C

Side of square, $S=10$ cm $=0.1$ m

Area of square, $A=(0.1)^2=0.01\text{ m}^2$

The plane of the square is parallel to the yz-plane.

Hence, the angle between the unit vector normal to the plane and electric field is zero, i.e. $\theta=0°$. (1)

$\therefore$ Flux through the plane,

$\phi=|\mathbf{E}|\times A\cos\theta$

$=5\times10^3\times0.01\cos0°=50\text{ N-m}^2/\text{C}$

If the plane makes an angle of 30° with the X-axis, then $\theta=60°$.

$\therefore$ Flux through the plane,

$\phi=|\mathbf{E}|\times A\times\cos60°=5\times10^3\times0.01\times\cos60°$

$=25\text{N-m}^2/\text{C}$ (1)

40. (i)

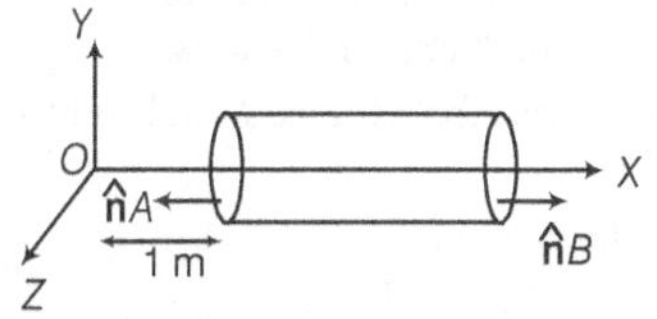

Given, $\mathbf{E}=50x\,\hat{\mathbf{i}}$

and $\Delta S=25\text{ cm}^2$

$=25\times10^{-4}\text{m}^2$

As the electric field is only along the X-axis, so flux will pass only through the cross-section of cylinder.

Magnitude of electric field at cross-section A,

$E_A=50\times1=50\text{ N C}^{-1}$

Magnitude of electric field at cross-section B,

$E_B=50\times2=100\text{ NC}^{-1}$ (1)

The corresponding electric fluxes are

$\phi_A=\mathbf{E}_A\cdot\Delta\mathbf{S}$

$=50\times25\times10^{-4}\times\cos180°$

$=-0.125\text{ N-m}^2\text{ C}^{-1}$

and $\phi_B = E_B \cdot \Delta S$

$= 100 \times 25 \times 10^{-4} \times \cos 0°$

$= 0.25 \text{ N-m}^2\text{C}^{-1}$

So, the net flux through the cylinder,

$\phi = \phi_A + \phi_B = -0.125 + 0.25$

$= 0.125 \text{ N-m}^2 \text{ C}^{-1}$ (1)

(ii) Using Gauss' law,

$$\oint E \cdot dS = \frac{q}{\varepsilon_0} \qquad [\because \oint E \cdot dS = \phi]$$

$$\Rightarrow \quad 0.125 = \frac{q}{8.85 \times 10^{-12}}$$

$$\Rightarrow \quad q = 8.85 \times 0.125 \times 10^{-12}$$

$= 1.1 \times 10^{-12}$ C (1)

41. (i) On the left face, the outward flux,

$\phi_L = E \cdot \Delta S = -100\hat{i} \cdot \Delta S = 100\Delta S,$

since $\hat{i} \cdot \Delta S = -\Delta S$

$= 100 \times \pi(0.05)^2 = 0.785 \text{ N-m}^2\text{C}^{-1}$

On the right face, E and ΔS are parallel and therefore,

$\phi_R = E \cdot \Delta S = 0.785 \text{ N-m}^2\text{C}^{-1}$ (1)

(ii) For any point on the side of the cylinder, $E \perp \Delta S$ and hence $E \cdot \Delta S = 0$

$\therefore$ Flux out of the side of the cylinder = 0 (1/2)

(iii) Net outward flux through the cylinder,

$\phi = 0.785 + 0.785 + 0$

$= 1.57 \text{ N-m}^2\text{C}^{-1}$ (1/2)

(iv) From Gauss' law, the net charge within the cylinder $= 1.57 \times 8.854 \times 10^{-12}\text{C} = 1.39 \times 10^{-11}\text{C}$ (1)

42. Given, $E_X = \alpha x^{1/2}$, $E_Y = 0$, $E_Z = 0$

$\alpha = 600 \text{ N/C-m}^{1/2}$, $l = 0.1$ m, $\phi = ?$, $q = ?$

As the electric field has only x-component, therefore $E \cdot \Delta S = \phi_E = 0$ for each of four faces of cube perpendicular to Y-axis and Z-axis.

Flux is there only for left face L and right face R of the cube.

At the left face, $x = l$

$\therefore \quad E_L = \alpha l^{1/2}$

The flux for left face of cube,

$\phi_L = E_L \cdot \Delta S = \alpha l^{1/2} (l^2) \cos 180° = -\alpha l^{5/2}$ (1½)

Similarly, at right face, $x = l + l = 2l$

The flux for right face of cube,

$E_R = \alpha(2l)^{1/2}$

$\phi_R = E_R \cdot \Delta S$

$= \alpha(2l)^{1/2}(l^2) \cos 0° = \alpha l^{5/2}\sqrt{2}$ (1½)

The net flux through the cube,

$\phi = \phi_R + \phi_L$

$= \alpha l^{5/2}\sqrt{2} - \alpha l^{5/2}$

$= \alpha l^{5/2} (\sqrt{2} - 1)$

$= 600 (0.1)^{5/2} (\sqrt{2} - 1) = 0.785 \text{ N-m}^2 \text{ C}^{-1}$ (1)

Apply Gauss' theorem and the charge within the cube,

$q = \varepsilon_0 \phi = 8.85 \times 10^{-12} \times 0.785 = 6.95 \times 10^{-12}$ C (1)

43. **Key Point:** Think of the square as one face of a cube with edge 10 cm.

Electric flux linked with a surface can be calculated using Gauss' theorem, according to which total electric flux linked with a closed surface is $\frac{q}{\varepsilon_0}$.

Now, we imagine an enclosed cubical surface and the given square be one side of this cubical surface. Let a charge q be placed at the centre of cube.

Now, the figure looks like as shown below.

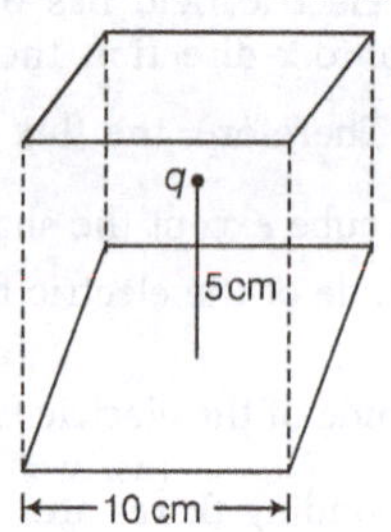

The total flux enclosed through the centre of cube is given by

$$\phi = \frac{q}{\varepsilon_0} \qquad \text{...(i)}$$

[according to Gauss' theorem]

Here, $q = 10\,\mu$C (1)

The flux enclosed by one face, i.e. square is 1/6 of total flux (because the cube has six square shaped faces), so the flux linked with each square,

$$\phi' = \frac{\phi}{6} = \frac{1}{6} \cdot \frac{q}{\varepsilon_0} \qquad \text{[from Eq. (i)]}$$

$$\Rightarrow \quad \phi' = \frac{1}{6} \times \frac{10 \times 10^{-6}}{8.854 \times 10^{-12}} = 1.88 \times 10^5 \text{ N-m}^2/\text{C}$$

Thus, the flux linked with the square is $1.88 \times 10^5 \text{ N-m}^2/\text{C}$. (1)

44. Let us consider a charge q is placed at the centre of a cubic Gaussian surface. As per the question,

$q = 2\,\mu\text{C} = 2 \times 10^{-6}$ C

Length of edge = 9 cm (1)

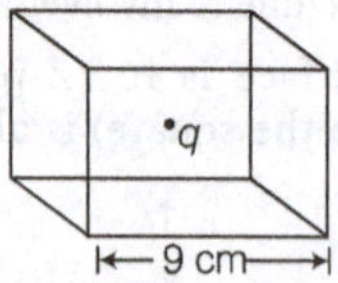

According to Gauss' theorem, the net electric flux (ϕ) through the surface is given by

$$\phi = \frac{q}{\varepsilon_0} = \frac{2 \times 10^{-6}}{8.854 \times 10^{-12}} = 2.26 \times 10^5 \text{ N-m}^2/\text{C}$$

Thus, the net electric flux through the surface is $2.26 \times 10^5 \text{ N-m}^2/\text{C}$. (1)

45. Refer to example 4 on page 35.

46. As from Gauss' law, $\oint d\phi = \oint \mathbf{E}\cdot d\mathbf{S} = q/\varepsilon_0$

Electric flux $(\phi_E) = \dfrac{q}{\varepsilon_0}$

$$= \frac{35.4 \times 10^{-6}}{8.85 \times 10^{-12}} = 4 \times 10^6 \text{ N-m}^2/\text{C} \quad (1)$$

47. Here, $\phi = 8.0 \times 10^3$ N-m^{2}C^{-1}

(i) Suppose that the net charge inside the box is q, then according to Gauss' theorem,

$$\phi = \frac{q}{\varepsilon_0} \text{ or } q = \varepsilon_0 \phi$$

$\because \quad \varepsilon_0 = 8.854 \times 10^{-12}$ C^{2}N^{-1}m^{-2}

$\therefore \quad q = 8.854 \times 10^{-12} \times 8.0 \times 10^3$

$= 70.832 \times 10^{-9}$C (1½)

(ii) If the net outward flux through the surface of the box is zero, then it cannot be concluded that there is no charge inside the box. There may be equal amount of positive and negative charges inside the box. Therefore, if the net outward flux is zero, we cannot conclude that the charge inside the box is zero.

One can only say that the net charge inside the box is zero. (1½)

48. Here, $E = 9 \times 10^4$ N/C, $r = 2$ cm $= 2 \times 10^{-2}$ m

and $\lambda = ?$

As, $E = \dfrac{\lambda}{2\pi\varepsilon_0 r}$ (1/2)

$$\Rightarrow \lambda = 2\pi\varepsilon_0 rE = \frac{1}{2\times 9\times 10^9} \times 2\times 10^{-2} \times 9 \times 10^4 = 10^{-7}\text{Cm}^{-1} \quad (1½)$$

49. By applying Gauss's theorem, electric field due to an infinitely long straight charged wire is

$$E = \frac{1}{2\pi\varepsilon_0}\cdot\frac{\lambda}{r}$$

where, $\dfrac{1}{2\pi\varepsilon_0} = 2\times 9\times 10^9$ mF^{-1} (1)

λ = linear charge density = ?

$r = 0.5$ m

$E = 3.6 \times 10^3$ Vm^{-1}

$$\Rightarrow 3.6 \times 10^3 = \frac{2\times 9 \times 10^9 \times \lambda}{0.5} \quad (1)$$

$$\Rightarrow \lambda = \frac{3.6 \times 10^3 \times 0.5}{2 \times 9 \times 10^9}$$

$= 10^{-7}$Cm^{-1} (1)

50. Given, $R = \dfrac{D}{2} = \dfrac{2.4}{2} = 1.2$ m

and $\sigma = 80.0\ \mu$C/m^2

(i) Charge on sphere, $q = 4\pi R^2 \cdot \sigma$

$= 4 \times 3.14 \times (1.2)^2 \times 80$

$= 1446.912\ \mu$C

$= 1.45 \times 10^{-3}$C (1)

(ii) Electric flux, $\phi = \dfrac{q}{\varepsilon_0}$

$$= \frac{1.45 \times 10^{-3}}{8.854 \times 10^{-12}}$$

$= 0.1637 \times 10^9$

$= 1.637 \times 10^8$ N-m^2/C (1)

51. We know that,

$\sigma = 17.0 \times 10^{-22}$ Cm^{-2}

(i) E on the left of the plates is zero. (1)

(ii) E on the right of the plates is zero. (1)

(iii) In between the plates, $E = \dfrac{\sigma}{\varepsilon_0}$

$$E = \frac{17.0 \times 10^{-22}}{8.85 \times 10^{-12}}$$

$= 1.9 \times 10^{-10}$ NC^{-1} (1)

Summary

- **Electric Charge** It is the intrinsic property of the material which is responsible to exert the electric force.
- **Conductors and Insulators** Conductors are those substances which conduct the electricity, whereas insulators are those substance which cannot conductor electricity.
- **Quantisation of Electric Charge** The charge on any body can be expressed as an integral multiple of basic unit of charge, i.e. charge on one electron. It can be expressed as

  $$q = \pm\, ne, \text{ where } n = 1, 2, \ldots$$

  where, e is also called as 'elementary charge'.
- **Coulomb's Law** The force of interaction (attraction or repulsion) between two stationary point charges in vacuum is directly proportional to the product of the charges and inversely proportional to the square of distances between them, i.e.

  $$F = \frac{kq_1 q_2}{r^2}$$

  where, k is proportionality constant.

  In medium, $F_{\text{medium}} = \dfrac{1}{4\pi\varepsilon_0} \cdot \dfrac{q_1 q_2}{Kr^2}$

  where, K is dielectric constant of medium.
- **Superposition Principle** Force on any charge due to number of charges is the vector sum of all the forces on that charge due to other charges, taken one at a time.
- **Electric Field** It is the space around the given charge in which another charge experiences an electrostatic force of repulsion or attraction.
- **Electric Field Intensity due to Continuous Charge Distribution**

  $\lambda = \dfrac{q}{l}$, where λ is a linear charge density.

  $\sigma = \dfrac{q}{A}$, where σ is a surface charge density.

  $\delta = \dfrac{q}{V}$, where δ is a volume charge density.
- **Electric Field Lines** It is a path traversed by a test charge around the given charge.
- **Properties of Electric Field Lines**

  Electric lines of force start from positive charges and end at negative charges. Two field lines never intersect each other. These are perpendicular to the surface of charged conductor. These do not pass through a conductor.
- **Electric Field Intensity** At a point is the force experienced per unit positive test charge placed at that point without disturbing the source charge, i.e. $E = \left(\dfrac{F}{q_0}\right)$
- **Electric Dipole** It is a pair of point charges with equal magnitude and opposite in sign separated by a very small distance.
- **Dipole Moment** It is the product of the charge and separation between the charges,

  i.e. $p = 2a \cdot q$
- **Electric Field Intensity due to an Electric Dipole**

  At a point on axial line, $E = \dfrac{2kpx}{(x^2 - l^2)^2}$.

  At a point on equatorial line, $E = \dfrac{2kp}{(x^2 + l^2)^{3/2}}$.

  At any point, $|E| = \dfrac{p\sqrt{3\cos^2\theta + 1}}{4\pi\varepsilon_0 r^3}$.
- **Torque on an electric Dipole in a Uniform Electric Field** It is given by, $\tau = pE \sin\theta$
- **Electric Flux** It is defined as the total number of electric lines of force passing normally through the surface.

  For non-uniform electric field, $\phi = \mathbf{E} \cdot \mathbf{S} = \mathbf{ES} \cos\theta$

  For uniform electric field, $\phi = \oint_S \mathbf{E} \cdot d\mathbf{S} = \oint_S \mathbf{E} \cdot d\mathbf{S} \cos\theta$
- **Gauss' Theorem** The surface integral of the electric field intensity over any closed surface in free space is equal to $\dfrac{1}{\varepsilon_0}$ times the net charge enclosed with in the surface.

  $$\phi_E = \oint_S \mathbf{E} \cdot d\mathbf{S} = \frac{q}{\varepsilon_0}$$
- **Gaussian Surface** Any hypothetical closed surface enclosing a charge is called the Gaussian surface of that charge.
- **Applications of Gauss' Theorem**

  Field due to an infinitely long straight charged wire,

  $$E = \frac{\lambda}{2\pi\varepsilon_0 r}$$

  Field due to thin infinite sheet of charge, $E = \dfrac{\sigma}{2\varepsilon_0}$.

  Field due to a uniformly charged thin spherical shell

  Outside the shell, $E = \dfrac{\sigma R^2}{\varepsilon_0 r^2}$

  On the surface of shell, $E = \dfrac{\sigma}{\varepsilon_0}$

  Inside the shell, $E = 0$

For Mind Map

Visit : https://goo.gl/h6f1H2 OR **Scan the Code**

Chapter Practice

Multiple Choice Questions

1 Mark

1 A body is charged to $+3.2\mu C$ by induction, then number of electrons transferred by the body is [Give, charge on one electron $(e) = 1.6\times10^{-19}$ C]
(a) 2×10^{13} (b) 10^{13} (c) 6.4×10^{25} (d) 0

2 Consider a neutral conducting sphere. A positive point charge is placed outside the sphere. The net charge on the sphere is, then
(a) negative and distributed uniformly over the surface of the sphere
(b) negative and appears only at the point on the sphere, closest to the point charge
(c) negative and distributed non-uniformly over the entire surface of the sphere
(d) zero

3 Charge q_2 of mass m revolves around a stationary charge q_1 in a circular orbit of radius r. The orbital periodic time of q_2 would be
(a) $\left(\frac{4\pi^3 mr^2}{kq_1q_2}\right)^{1/2}$ (b) $\left(\frac{kq_1q_2}{4\pi^2 mr^2}\right)^{1/2}$
(c) $\left(\frac{4\pi^2 mr^4}{kq_1q_2}\right)^{1/2}$ (d) $\left(\frac{4\pi^2 mr^3}{kq_1q_2}\right)^{1/2}$

4 A uniform electric field **E** exists between the plates of a charged condenser. A charge particle enters the space between the plates and perpendicular to **E**. The path of the particle between the plates is a
(a) straight line (b) hyperbola
(c) parabola (d) circle

5 The electric flux through the surface

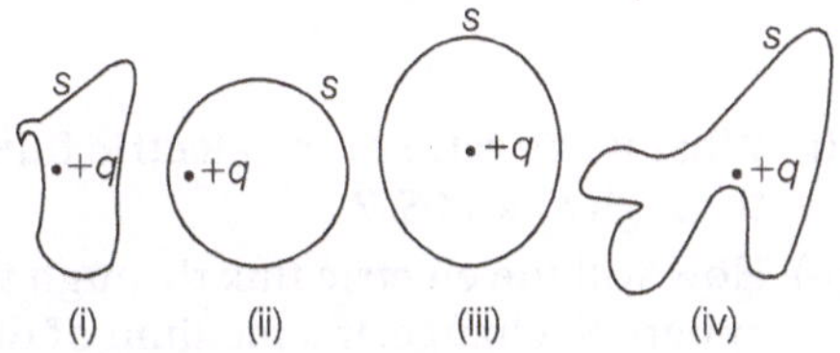

NCERT Exemplar

(a) in Fig. (iv) is the largest
(b) in Fig. (iii) is the least
(c) in Fig. (ii) is same as Fig. (iii), but is smaller than Fig. (iv)
(d) is the same for all the figures

6 A solid sphere of radius R has a charge Q distributed in its volume with a charge density $\rho = kr^a$, where k and a are constants; and r is the distance from its centre. If the electric field at $r = \frac{R}{2}$ is $\frac{1}{8}$ times that at $r = R$, find the value of a.
(a) 2 (b) 3 (c) 2.5 (d) 0.2

Assertion and Reason

Directions (Q. Nos. 7-11) *In the following questions, two statements are given- one labelled Assertion* (A) *and the other labelled Reason* (R). *Select the correct answer to these questions from the codes* (a), (b), (c) *and* (d) *as given below*
(a) Both Assertion and Reason are true and Reason is the correct explanation of Assertion.
(b) Both Assertion and Reason are true but Reason is not the correct explanation of Assertion.
(c) Assertion is true but Reason is false.
(d) Assertion is false but Reason is true.

7. **Assertion (A)** In a non-uniform electric field, a dipole will have translatory as well as rotatory motion.
Reason (R) In a non-uniform electric field, a dipole experiences a force as well as torque.

8. **Assertion (A)** **E** outside vicinity of a conductor depends only on the local charge density σ and it is independent of the other charges present anywhere on the conductor.
Reason (R) **E** in outside vicinity of a conductor is given by $\frac{\sigma}{\varepsilon_0}$.

9. **Assertion (A)** Upon displacement of charges within a closed surface, **E** at any point on the surface does not change.
Reason (R) The flux crossing through a closed surface is independent of the location of charge within the surface.

10. **Assertion (A)** If Gaussian surface does not enclose any charge, then E at any point on the Gaussian surface must be zero.
Reason (R) No net charge is enclosed by Gaussian surface, so net flux passing through the surface is zero.

11. **Assertion (A)** Surface charge density of an irregularly shaped conductor is non-uniform.
Reason (R) Surface charge density is defined as charge per unit area.

Very Short Answer Type Questions

1 Mark

12 Electric charge is additive in nature. Explain.

13 Two identical metallic spheres of exactly equal masses are taken. One is given a positive charge (q) and the other an equal negative charge by friction. Is three masses after charging equal?

14 Give one difference between the conductors and insulators.

15 'Electrostatic forces are much stronger than the gravitational forces'. Give one example to justify this statement.

16 The electric field induced in a dielectric when placed in an external field is 1/10 times the electric field. Calculate relative permittivity of the dielectric.

17 A point charge $+Q$ is placed in the vicinity of a conducting surface. Draw the electric field lines between the surface and the charge.

18 A metallic solid sphere is placed in a uniform electric field as shown below.

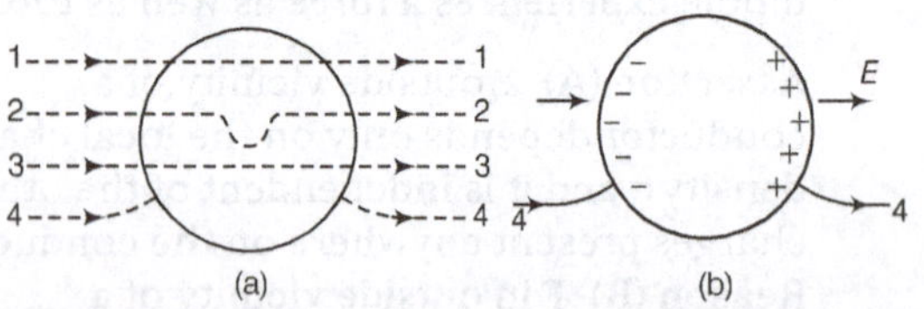

Which path is followed by electric field lines?

Short Answer Type I Questions

2 Marks

19 Two identical metallic spherical shells A and B having charges $+4Q$ and $-10Q$ are kept a certain distance apart.

A third identical uncharged sphere C is first placed in contact with sphere A and then with sphere B, then spheres A and B are brought in contact and then separated.
Find the charge on the spheres A and B.

20 Deduce the expression for the electric field **E** due to a system of two charges q_1 and q_2 with position vectors r_1 and r_2 at a point r with respect to a common origin.

21 Two small identical dipoles AB and CD, each of dipole moment **p** are kept at an angle of 120° as shown in the figure.

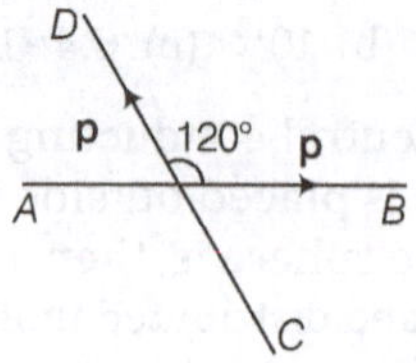

What is the resultant dipole moment of this combination? If this system is subjected to electric field (**E**) directed along positive x-direction, what will be the magnitude and direction of the torque acting on this?

22 What is the use of Gaussian surface? Also, mention the importance of Gauss' theorem.

23 A point charge causes an electric flux of -3.1×10^4 N-m^2/C to pass through a spherical Gaussian surface.
(i) Find the value of the point charge.
(ii) If the radius of the Gaussian surface is doubled, how much flux would pass through the surface?

24 S_1 and S_2 are two parallel concentric spheres enclosing charges Q and $2Q$ as shown in the figure.

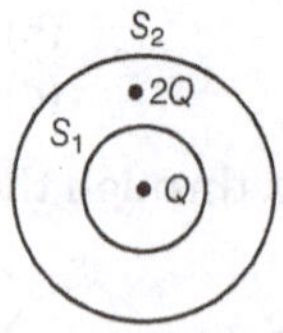

(i) What is the ratio of the electric flux through S_1 and S_2?
(ii) How will the electric flux through the sphere S_1 change, if a medium of dielectric constant $5\varepsilon_0$ is introduced in the space inside S_1 in place of air?

Short Answer Type II Questions

3 Marks

25 A large plane sheet of charge having surface charge density 5×10^{-6} C/m^2 lies in XY-plane. Find the electric flux through a circular area of radius 0.1 m, if the normal to the circular area makes an angle of 60° with Z-axis.
[Take, $\varepsilon_0 = 8.85\times10^{-12}$ C^2/N-m^2]

26 Consider a region bounded by conical surface as shown in the figure.

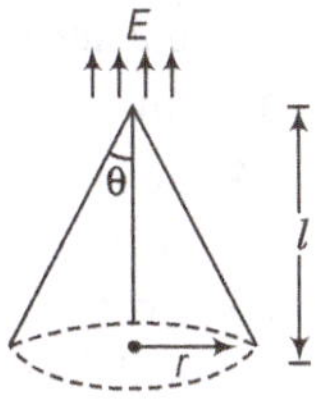

In this region, **E** is in vertical upward direction, then find the electric field when electric flux is passing through curved surface.

27 A spherical conducting shell of inner radius R_1 and outer radius R_2 has a charge Q. A charge q is placed at the centre of the shell.
(i) What is the surface charge density on the
(a) inner surface?
(b) outer surface of the shell?
(ii) Write the expression for the electric field at a point $X > R_2$ from the centre of the shell.

Long Answer Type Questions

5 Marks

28 (i) Derive an expression for electric field due to electric dipole on equatorial position.
(ii) Two point charges $4\,\mu$C and $+1\mu$C are separated by a distance of 2 m in air. Find the point on the line joining charges at which the net electric field of the system is zero.

29 (i) State Gauss' law. Using this law, obtain the expression for the electric field due to an infinitely long straight conductor of linear charge density λ.
(ii) A wire AB of length L has linear charge density $\lambda = kx$, where x is measured from the end A of the wire. This wire is enclosed by a Gaussian hollow surface.
Find an expression for the electric flux through this surface.

Case Based Questions

Directions (Q.No. 30) *This questions is case study based questions. Read the following paragraphs and answer the questions.*

30. The electric field due to a charge at a point in space may be defined as the force that a unit positive charge would experience, if placed at that point. It is vector quantity and its SI unit is N/C.

The magnitude of the electric field at a point is given by $E = \dfrac{1}{4\pi\varepsilon_0}\cdot\dfrac{q}{r^2}$

Electric field lines start from positive charges and end at negative charges. In the case of a single charge, they may start or end at infinity.

Two field lines can never intersect each other because, if they intersect, then two tangents drawn at that point will represent two directions of field at that point, which is not possible. Electric field lines do not pass through a conductor.

(i) Four point charges are placed at the corners of a square of side a cm as shown in figure. Find the magnitude and direction of the electric field at the centre O of the square.

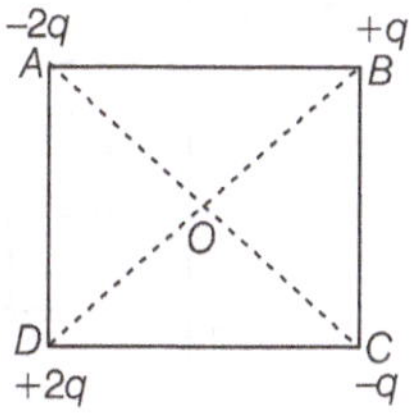

(ii) The dimensions of an atom are of the order of an angstrom, thus there must be large electric fields between the protons and electrons. Why there is the electrostatic field inside a conductor zero?
(iii) A charged particle is free to move in an electric field. Will it always along a line of force? Explain.
(iv) Sketch the electric field lines for a uniformly charged hollow cylinder as shown in the figure.

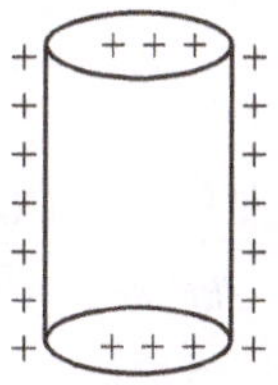

Answers

1 (*d*) When a body is charged by the induction, then no electrons are transferred or gain.

2 (*d*) Charge will be induced, but net charge is zero.

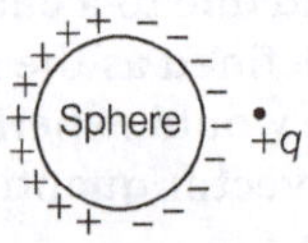

As, there is no contact between sphere and charge is $+q$. Net charge induced on sphere is zero near by charge induced is negative and another charge induced is positive.

3 (*d*) Coulomb's attraction = Centripetal force

$$\therefore \quad \frac{1}{4\pi\varepsilon_0}\frac{q_1q_2}{r^2} = mr\omega^2 = \frac{4\pi^2 mr^2}{T^2} = k\frac{q_1q_2}{r^2} = k\frac{q_1q_2}{r^2}$$

$$T^2 = \frac{4\pi^2 mr^3}{Kq_1q_2}$$

$$\Rightarrow \quad T = \left[\frac{4\pi^2 mr^3}{kq_1q_2}\right]^{1/2}$$

4 (*c*)

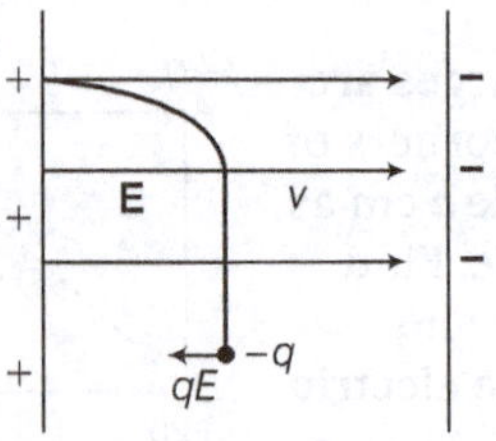

As the speed of particle is perpendicular to the intensity vector and there is no acceleration in the direction perpendicular to **E** but there is an electric force acting on the particle (charge), whenever its motion is in electric field.
Hence, continuously a force exerting on the perpendicular to its velocity or speed. Hence, path of particle must be parabola, as in the projectile motion.

5 (*d*) Electric flux through all surfaces is equal, this is $\frac{q}{\varepsilon_0}$.

As charge enclosed inside each surface is q.

6 (*a*) From Gauss's theorem,

$$E \propto \frac{q}{r^2} \quad \text{(where, } q = \text{charge enclosed)}$$

$$\frac{E_2}{E_1} = \frac{q_2}{q_1} \times \frac{r_1^2}{r_2^2}$$

$$8 = \frac{\int_0^R (4\pi r^2)\, kr^a\, dr}{\int_0^{R/2} (4\pi r^2)\, kr^a\, dr} \times \frac{(R/2)^2}{(R)^2}$$

Solving this equation, we get

$$a = 2$$

7 (*a*)

8 (*d*) **E** in outside vicinity of conductor's surface depends on all the charges present in the space, but expression $E = \frac{\sigma}{\varepsilon_0}$.

9 (*d*) Due to displacement of charge within closed surface, E at any point may change. But net flux crossing the surface will not change.

10 (*d*) **E** at any point on Gaussian surface may be due to outside charges also.

11 (*a*)

12 Refer to text on page 2 (Basic properties of electric charge).

13 No, the sphere which have given a charge of $+q$ that will decrease in mass as positive charge is only the absence of electron, you have taken $+q$ charge equivalent of electrons, and the other sphere will gain the same mass as first sphere lost, as negative charge is excess presence of electrons.

14 Conductors are those substances which can be used to carry or conduct electric charge/electron from one point to other. Insulators are those substances which cannot conduct electricity.

15 This statement can be proved by taking comparison of electric and magnetic forces between two protons.
Let the distance between two protons having charge $+e$ and mass m is placed at a distance r from each other as shown in figure.

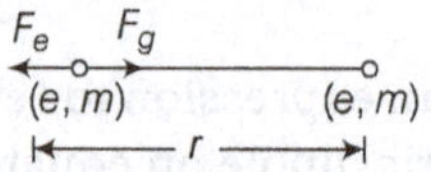

$$\therefore \quad F_e = \frac{1}{4\pi\varepsilon_0}\frac{q_1q_2}{r^2} \quad \text{[Coulomb's law]}$$

$$= \frac{1}{4\pi\,\varepsilon_0}\frac{e \times e}{r^2}$$

$$\Rightarrow \quad F_g = G\frac{m_1m_2}{r^2} \text{ (gravitation law)} = G\frac{m \times m}{r^2}$$

where, F_e and F_g are electric and gravitational force respectively, on putting the values, we get

$$\frac{F_e}{F_g} = \frac{\frac{1}{4\pi\varepsilon_0}\frac{e}{r^2}}{\frac{Gm^2}{r^2}} = \frac{1}{4\pi\varepsilon_0}\frac{e^2}{m^2}\cdot\frac{1}{G}$$

$$= \frac{(9\times10^9)(1.6\times10^{-19})^2}{(1.67\times10^{-27})^2} \times \frac{1}{(6.67\times10^{-11})}$$

$$= 1.2\times10^{36}$$

$$\simeq 10^{36}$$

$\Rightarrow \quad F_e >> F_g$

Hence, the electric force is much stronger than gravitational force.

16 We know that, $E_r = K = \dfrac{\varepsilon_0}{\varepsilon}$

Here, $\varepsilon = \dfrac{1}{10}\varepsilon_0$

$$\therefore \quad \varepsilon_r = \frac{\varepsilon_0}{\frac{1}{10}\varepsilon_0} = 10$$

Hence, relative permittivity of the dielectric becomes 10 times of the original value.

17

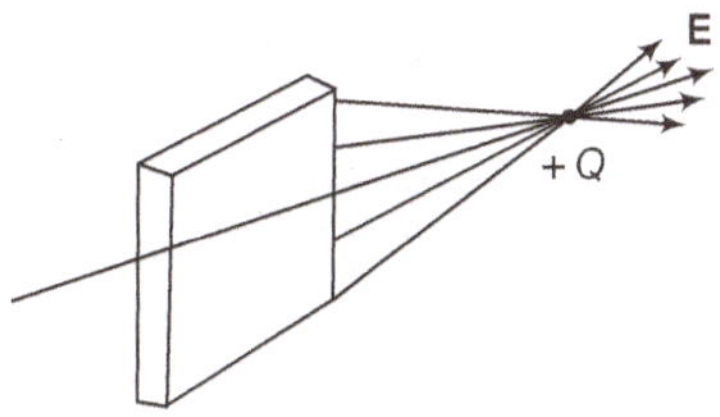

Conducting surface

18 Path 4 is followed by electric field lines. Since, these are no electric field lines with in the metallic sphere and field lines as normal each point on the surface.

19 Refer to Q. 12 on page 3.

20 Refer to text on pages 10 and 11 (Electric field due to system of charges).

21 Refer to Q. 16 on page 27.

22 Refer to text on page 34 (Gaussian surface).

23 (i) Use $\phi = \dfrac{q}{\varepsilon_0}$

(ii) Refer to Q. 23 on page 38.

24 Refer to Q. 30 on page 39.

25 According to Gauss's law, the electric field due to a plane sheet of charge is

$$E = \frac{\sigma}{2\varepsilon_0}$$

Given that, $\sigma = 5 \times 10^{-6}$ C/m^2

$$\text{So,} \quad E = \frac{5 \times 10^{-6}}{2 \times 8.85 \times 10^{-12}} = \frac{5 \times 10^{6}}{17.7}$$

$$= 282.5 \times 10^3 \text{ V/m}$$

$$\therefore \quad d\phi = E \cdot dA$$

$$\Rightarrow \quad \phi = EA\cos\theta$$

$$= 282.5 \times 10^3 \times 3.14 \times 10^{-2} \times \cos 60°$$

$$= 4.44 \text{ kVm}$$

$$= 4.44 \times 10^3 \text{ N-m}^2\text{/C}$$

26 Use Gauss's theorem,

$$\oint \mathbf{E} \cdot d\mathbf{S} = \frac{q}{\varepsilon_0}$$

27 Refer to text on page 36 (Field due to uniformly charged thin spherical shell).

28 (i) Refer to text on pages 24 and 25 (At a point on the equatorial line).

(ii)

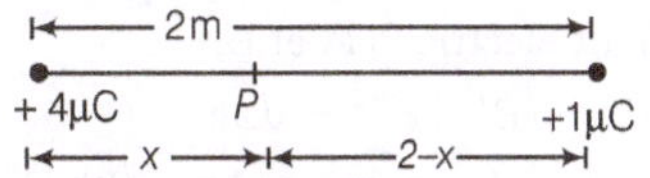

Let the net electric field be zero at point P at a distance x from charge $+4\mu$C, then

$$\frac{1}{4\pi\varepsilon_0}\frac{4 \times 10^{-6}}{x^2} - \frac{1 \times 10^{-6} \times 1}{4\pi\varepsilon_0 \times (2-x)^2} = 0$$

$$\Rightarrow \quad \frac{4}{x^2} = \frac{1}{(2-x)^2},$$

$$\Rightarrow \quad \frac{2}{x} = \frac{1}{2-x}$$

$$\Rightarrow \quad x = 4 - 2x$$

$$\Rightarrow \quad x = \frac{4}{3} \text{ m}$$

29 (i) Refer to text on pages 34 and 35 (Gauss' theorem; Field due to an infinitely long thin straight charged wire).

(ii) Here, $\lambda = \dfrac{dq}{dx} = kx, \sigma = ?$

$\Rightarrow \quad dq = kx\,dx$

Total charge on the wire,

$$q = \int_0^L kx\,dx = \left(\frac{kx^2}{2}\right)_0^L = \frac{kL^2}{2}$$

Electric flux through the Gaussian hollow surface is

$$\sigma = \frac{q}{\varepsilon_0} = \frac{kL^2}{2\varepsilon_0}$$

30 (i)

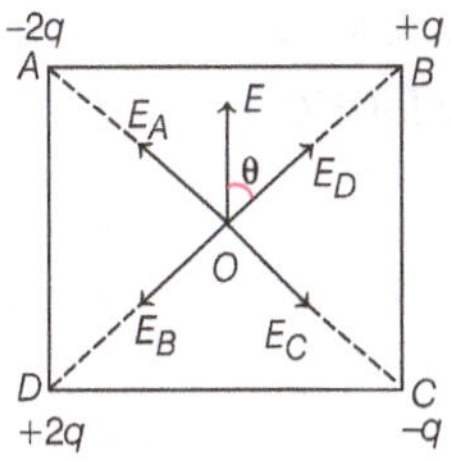

The side of square is a.

Let $OA = OC = OB = OD$, then

$$(2r)^2 = a^2 + a^2$$

$$\text{or} \quad r = \frac{a}{\sqrt{2}}$$

Consider a unit charge placed at O,then

$$E_A = E_D = \frac{1}{4\pi\varepsilon_0} \cdot \frac{2q}{r^2}$$

$$E_B = E_C = \frac{1}{4\pi\varepsilon_0} \cdot \frac{q}{r^2}$$

$$E' = E_A - E_C = \frac{1}{4\pi\varepsilon_0} \cdot \frac{q}{r^2} (O \to A)$$

$$E'' = E_D - E_B = \frac{1}{4\pi\varepsilon_0} \cdot \frac{q}{r^2} (O \to B)$$

Resultant electric field at O,

$$E = \sqrt{E'^2 + E''^2} = \sqrt{2}E'$$

$$= \frac{1}{4\pi\varepsilon_0} \cdot \frac{\sqrt{2}q}{r^2} = \frac{1}{4\pi\varepsilon_0} \cdot \frac{\sqrt{2}q}{a^2/2}$$

$$= \frac{1}{4\pi\varepsilon_0} \cdot \frac{2\sqrt{2}q}{a^2}$$

Direction of field,

$$\theta = \tan^{-1}\frac{E''}{E'} = \tan^{-1}(1) = 45^\circ$$

(ii) The electric fields find the atoms to neutral entity. As it is known that, electrostatic fields are caused by excess charges. However, there is no excess charge on the inner surface of an isolated conductor. Therefore, electrostatic field inside a conductor is zero.

(iii) The electric force on the particle will always act in the direction of a line of force. Hence, if the particle is initially at rest, then it will be accelerated along the line of force. But if it enters with accelerated motion at an angle with the direction of the field, then its path will not be along the line of force.

(iv) Here, the hollow cylinder is positively charged.

We know that, the electric field lines appear to come out from the conductor. Thus, the field lines for a uniformly positive charged hollow cylinder is shown in the figure.

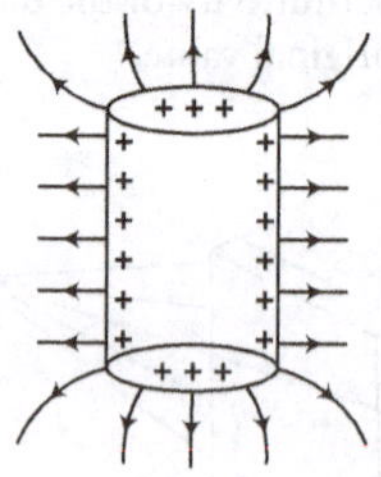

RELATED ONLINE VIDEOS

Visit : www.youtube.com/watch?v=RhNk8meZc2w
OR **Scan the Code**

Visit : https://www.youtube.com/watch?v=q7Js6LLlxLo
OR **Scan the Code**

Visit : https://www.youtube.com/watch?v=hm-c2V_yx8k
OR **Scan the Code**

Visit : https://www.youtube.com/watch?v=i5BVuipVky4
OR **Scan the Code**

Visit : https://www.youtube.com/watch?v=_9Xo-7oMMxw
OR **Scan the Code**

CHAPTER

02

Electrostatic Potential and Capacitance

The degree of electrification of a body is represented by the electrostatic potential of the charged body. The direction of flow of charge between two charged bodies placed in contact with each other is determined by electrostatic potential.

TOPIC 01 Electrostatic Potential, Electrostatic Potential Difference and Electrostatic Potential Energy

The electrostatic potential at any point in the region of electric field is equal to the amount of work done in bringing a unit positive test charge (without acceleration) from infinity to that point.

$$\therefore \quad \text{Electrostatic potential } (V) = \frac{\text{Work done } (W)}{\text{Charge } (q_0)}$$

It is a scalar quantity. Its SI unit is volt (V) and 1V = 1 J/C and its dimensional formula is $[ML^2T^{-3}A^{-1}]$.

Work done ($[W_\infty]_{ext}$) by an external force in bringing (without acceleration) a unit positive charge from infinity to a point is equal to the potential (V) at that point,

i.e. $$V = \frac{[W_\infty]_{ext}}{q_0} = \frac{-[W_\infty]_{elec}}{q_0} \qquad [\because [W_\infty]_{ext} = -[W_\infty]_{elec}]$$

where, $[W_\infty]_{elec}$ is the work done by the electric field on a charged particle as that particle moves from infinity to a point. A potential (V) can be positive, negative or zero depending on the signs and magnitudes of q_0 and W_∞.

Positive charge always flows from a higher potential to lower potential, while negative charge always flows from a lower potential to higher potential until the potentials become equal.

Note Electric potential is state dependent function as electrostatic forces are conservative forces. No work is done in moving a unit positive test charge over a closed path in an electric field.

Example 1 Potential at a point P in space is given as 3×10^5 V. Find the work done in bringing a charge of 2×10^{-6} C from infinity to the point P. Does the answer depend on the path along which the charge is brought?

Sol. Given,

Potential at the point P,

$$V = 3 \times 10^5 \text{ V},$$

charge, $q_0 = 2 \times 10^{-6}$ C

Work done in bringing the charge from infinity to the point P is

$$W_\infty = q_0 V$$

$$= 2 \times 10^{-6} \times 3 \times 10^5$$

$$= 6 \times 10^{-1}$$

$$= 0.6 \text{ J}$$

No, the work done will be path independent.

Electrostatic Potential Difference

In electric field, potential difference between two points P and Q is defined as equal to the amount of work done (by external agent) in moving a unit positive charge from Point P to point Q.

If V_Q and V_P are the electrostatic potentials at points Q and P respectively, then electrostatic potential difference between points Q and P is

$$\Delta V = V_P - V_Q$$

Thus, $$\boxed{\Delta V = \frac{W_{QP}}{q_0}}$$

The dimensional formula for electrostatic potential difference is given by

$$\Delta V = \frac{W_{QP}}{q_0}$$

$$= \frac{[ML^2T^{-2}]}{[AT]} = [ML^2T^{-3}A^{-1}]$$

The SI unit of electrostatic potential difference is **volt**.

$$1 \text{ V} = 1 \text{ JC}^{-1} = 1 \text{ N-m C}^{-1}$$

Note **One electron-volt** (1 eV) is the energy equal to the work required to move a single elementary charge e such as an electron or the proton through a potential difference of exactly one volt (1 V).

$\therefore$ $1 \text{ eV} = e\ (1\text{V}) = (1.60 \times 10^{-19}\text{C})\ (1\text{J/C}) = 1.60 \times 10^{-19}$ J

Example 2 The potential difference between two points is 20 V. How much work will be done in carrying a charge of 400 μC from one point to the another?

Sol. Given, $\Delta V = 20$ V and $q = 400\,\mu\text{C} = 400 \times 10^{-6}$ C

We know that,

$$\text{Electrostatic potential difference} = \frac{\text{Work done}}{\text{Charge}}$$

$$\Rightarrow \quad \Delta V = \frac{W}{q}$$

$$\Rightarrow \quad 20 = \frac{W}{400 \times 10^{-6}}$$

$$\therefore \quad W = 20 \times 400 \times 10^{-6} = 8 \times 10^{-3} \text{ J}$$

Example 3 If 100 J of work must be done to move an electric charge of magnitude 4 C from a place A, where potential is −10 V to another place B where potential is V volt. Find the value of V.

Sol. Given, $W_{AB} = 100$ J, $q = 4$ C, $V_A = -10$ V, $V_B = V = ?$

Since, $W_{AB} = q(V_B - V_A)$

$\Rightarrow \quad 100 = 4(V + 10) \quad \Rightarrow \quad V = 15$ V

Electrostatic Potential due to a Point Charge

Let P be the point at a distance r from the origin O at which the electric potential due to charge $+q$ is required.

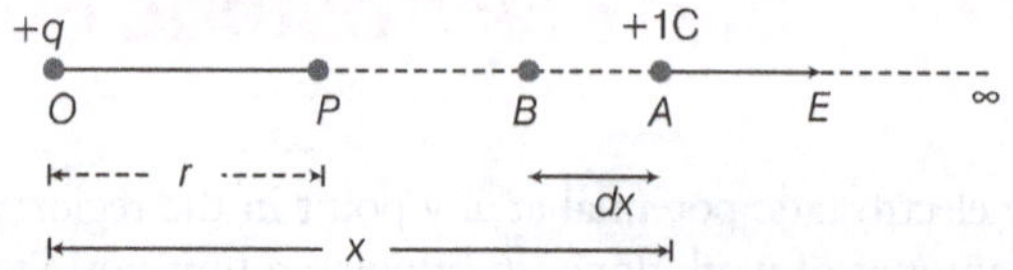

The electric potential at a point P is the amount of work done in carrying a unit positive charge from infinity (∞) to the point P. As, work done is independent of the path, we choose a convenient path along the radial direction from infinity to the point P without acceleration. Let A be an intermediate point on this path where $OA = x$. The electrostatic force on a unit positive charge at A is given by

$$F = \frac{1}{4\pi\varepsilon_0} \cdot \frac{q \times 1}{x^2} \quad [\text{along } OA] \quad \ldots\text{(i)}$$

Small work done in moving the charge through a distance dx from A to B is given by

$$dW = \mathbf{F} \cdot d\mathbf{x}$$

$$= Fdx \cos 180° = -Fdx \quad [\because \cos 180° = -1]$$

$$\Rightarrow \quad dW = -Fdx \quad \ldots\text{(ii)}$$

Total work done in moving a unit positive charge from infinity (∞) to the point P is given by

$$W = \int_{\infty}^{r} -F\,dx = \int_{\infty}^{r} -\frac{1}{4\pi\varepsilon_0}\cdot\frac{q}{x^2}\,dx = -\frac{q}{4\pi\varepsilon_0}\int_{\infty}^{r} x^{-2}dx$$

$$= -\frac{q}{4\pi\varepsilon_0}\left[\frac{-1}{x}\right]_{\infty}^{r} \qquad \left[\because \int x^{-2}\,dx = -\frac{1}{x}\right]$$

$$= \frac{q}{4\pi\varepsilon_0}\left[\frac{1}{r} - \frac{1}{\infty}\right] = \frac{q}{4\pi\varepsilon_0 r} \qquad \text{...(iii)}$$

From the definition of electric potential, this work is equal to the potential at point P.

$$\boxed{V = \frac{q}{4\pi\varepsilon_0 r}} \qquad \text{...(iv)}$$

Potential difference between two points A and B in the electric field will be

$$V_B - V_A = \frac{q}{4\pi\varepsilon_0}\left(\frac{1}{|\mathbf{r}_B|} - \frac{1}{|\mathbf{r}_A|}\right) \qquad \text{...(v)}$$

where, $\mathbf{r}_A$ and $\mathbf{r}_B$ respectively, are the position vectors of A and B.

A positively charged particle ($q > 0$) produces a positive electric potential ($V > 0$). A negatively charged particle ($q < 0$) produces a negative electric potential ($V < 0$).

Eq.(iv) shows that at equal distances from a point charge q, value of V is same.

Hence, electrostatic potential due to a single charge is spherically symmetric.

Variation of Electrostatic Potential and Electric Field with Distance

Figure given below shows the variation of electrostatic potential with distance, i.e. $V \propto \frac{1}{r}$ and also the variation of electrostatic field with distance, i.e. $E \propto \frac{1}{r^2}$.

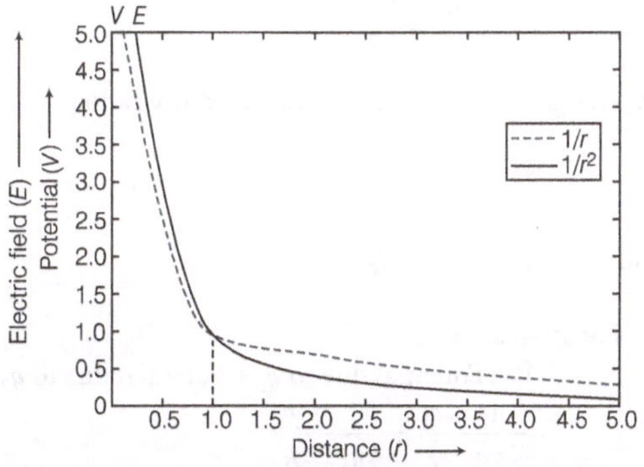

Variation of electrostatic potential V and electric field E with distance r

Example 4 What is the electrostatic potential at the surface of a silver nucleus of diameter 12.4 fermi? Atomic number (Z) for silver is 47.

Sol. Given, $r = \frac{12.4}{2} = 6.2\text{ fermi} = 6.2\times10^{-15}\text{ m}$ and $Z = 47$

∴ Charge of the nucleus, $q = Ze = 47\times1.6\times10^{-19}$ C

$[\because e = 1.6\times10^{-19}\text{ C}]$

∴ Electrostatic potential at the surface,

$$V = \frac{q}{4\pi\varepsilon_0 r} = \frac{9\times10^9\times47\times1.6\times10^{-19}}{6.2\times10^{-15}} = 1.09\times10^7\text{ V}$$

Example 5 A point charge Q is placed at point O as shown in the figure. Is the potential difference $(V_A - V_B)$ positive, negative or zero, if Q is

(i) positive? (ii) negative?

$O\overset{Q}{\bullet}$- - - - - - - -$\overset{A}{\bullet}$- - - - - - - -$\overset{B}{\bullet}$

Sol. Let the distance of points A and B from charge Q be r_A and r_B, respectively.

∴ Potential difference between points A and B,

$$V_A - V_B = \frac{Q}{4\pi\varepsilon_0}\left[\frac{1}{r_A} - \frac{1}{r_B}\right]$$

As, $r_A = OA$, $r_B = OB$ and $r_A < r_B \Rightarrow \frac{1}{r_A} > \frac{1}{r_B}$

Therefore, $\left[\frac{1}{r_A} - \frac{1}{r_B}\right]$ has positive value.

$(V_A - V_B)$ depends on the nature of charge Q, then

(i) $(V_A - V_B)$ is positive when $Q > 0$

(ii) $(V_A - V_B)$ is negative when $Q < 0$.

Electrostatic Potential due to a System of Charges

Let there be a number of point charges $q_1, q_2, q_3, \ldots, q_n$ at distances $r_1, r_2, r_3, \ldots, r_n$ respectively from the point P, where electric potential is to be calculated.

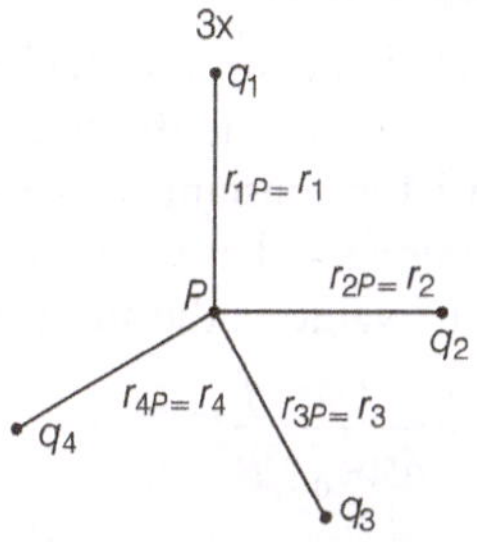

A system of charges

Potential at P due to charge q_1,

$$V_1 = \frac{1}{4\pi\varepsilon_0}\cdot\frac{q_1}{r_{1P}}$$

Similarly, $V_2 = \frac{1}{4\pi\varepsilon_0} \cdot \frac{q_2}{r_{2P}}, \quad V_3 = \frac{1}{4\pi\varepsilon_0} \cdot \frac{q_3}{r_{3P}}, \ldots,$

$$V_n = \frac{1}{4\pi\varepsilon_0} \cdot \frac{q_n}{r_{nP}}$$

Using superposition principle, we obtain resultant potential at point P due to total charge configuration as the algebraic sum of the potentials due to individual charges.

$$\therefore \quad V = V_1 + V_2 + V_3 + \cdots + V_n$$

$$\Rightarrow V = \frac{1}{4\pi\varepsilon_0} \cdot \frac{q_1}{r_{1P}} + \frac{1}{4\pi\varepsilon_0} \cdot \frac{q_2}{r_{2P}} + \frac{1}{4\pi\varepsilon_0} \cdot \frac{q_3}{r_{3P}} + \cdots + \frac{1}{4\pi\varepsilon_0} \cdot \frac{q_n}{r_{nP}}$$

$$\Rightarrow \quad V = \frac{1}{4\pi\varepsilon_0}\left(\frac{q_1}{r_1} + \frac{q_2}{r_2} + \frac{q_3}{r_3} + \cdots + \frac{q_n}{r_n}\right)$$

$$\Rightarrow \quad \boxed{V = \frac{1}{4\pi\varepsilon_0} \sum_{i=1}^{n} \frac{q_i}{r_i}}$$

The net electrostatic potential at a point due to multiple charges is equal to the algebraic sum of the potentials due to individual charges at that particular point.

Mathematically, it is expressed as

$$V_{\text{net}} = \sum_{i=1}^{n} V_i$$

Important Results

For a uniformly charged conducting spherical shell, the electric field outside the shell is as, if the entire charge is concentrated at the centre. Thus, the potential outside the shell is given by

$$V = \frac{1}{4\pi\varepsilon_0} \cdot \frac{q}{r} \qquad [\because r \geq R]$$

where, q is the total charge on the shell and R is its radius. The electric field inside the shell is zero. This implies that potential is constant inside the shell (as no work is done in moving a charge inside the shell) and therefore equal to its value at the surface, which is

$$V = \frac{1}{4\pi\varepsilon_0} \cdot \frac{q}{R}$$

Example 6 Two point charges of 4 μC and −2 μC are separated by a distance of 1 m in air. Find the location of a point on the line joining the two charges, where the electric potential is zero.

Sol. Let the electrostatic potential be zero at point P between the two charges separated by a distance x metre.

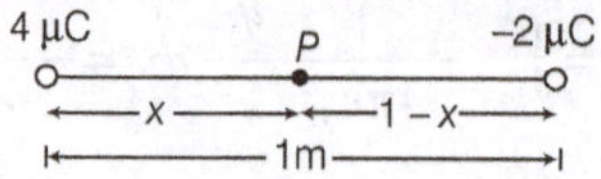

At point P, $\quad V_P = V_1 + V_2 = 0$

$$\Rightarrow \quad \frac{1}{4\pi\varepsilon_0} \cdot \frac{q_1}{r_1} + \frac{1}{4\pi\varepsilon_0} \cdot \frac{q_2}{r_2} = 0$$

$$\Rightarrow \quad \frac{1}{4\pi\varepsilon_0} \cdot \frac{4 \times 10^{-6}}{x} + \frac{1}{4\pi\varepsilon_0} \cdot \frac{(-2 \times 10^{-6})}{(1-x)} = 0$$

$$\Rightarrow \quad \frac{4 \times 10^{-6}}{x} = \frac{2 \times 10^{-6}}{(1-x)}$$

$$\Rightarrow \quad \frac{4}{x} = \frac{2}{(1-x)}$$

$$\Rightarrow \quad 2(1-x) = x$$

$$\Rightarrow \quad 2 = 3x \quad \text{or} \quad x = \frac{2}{3}$$

∴ Electrostatic potential is zero at a distance 2/3 m from charge 4μC between the two charges.

Example 7 A charge Q is distributed over two concentric hollow spheres of radii r and R (>r) such that the surface densities are equal. Find the potential at the common centre.

Sol. Let q_1 and q_2 be the charges on them.

We have, $\sigma_1 = \sigma_2$

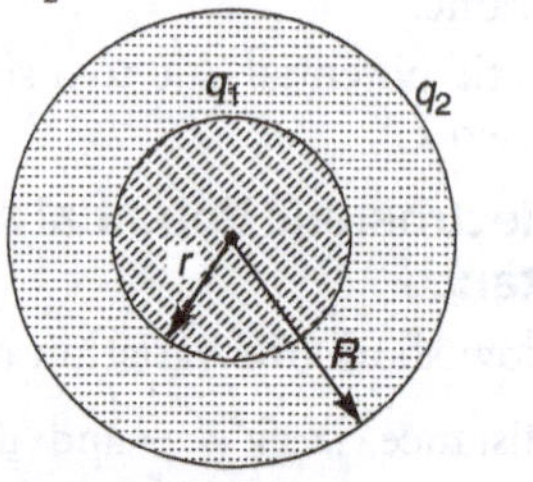

$$\therefore \quad \frac{q_1}{4\pi r^2} = \frac{q_2}{4\pi R^2}$$

$$\therefore \quad \frac{q_1}{q_2} = \frac{r^2}{R^2}$$

i.e. charge on them is distributed in above ratio

or $\quad q_1 = \frac{r^2}{r^2 + R^2} Q$

and $\quad q_2 = \frac{R^2}{r^2 + R^2} Q$

∴ Potential at centre

V = Potential due to q_1 + Potential due to q_2

$$\therefore \quad V = \frac{1}{4\pi\varepsilon_0} \frac{q_1}{r} + \frac{1}{4\pi\varepsilon_0} \frac{q_2}{R}$$

$$= \frac{Q(R + r)}{4\pi\varepsilon_0 (r^2 + R^2)}$$

Example 8 Two spherical metal shells with different radii r and R are far apart and connected by a thin conducting wire. A charge Q is placed on one of them. The charge redistributes so that same is on each sphere. How much charge is on the sphere with radius r?

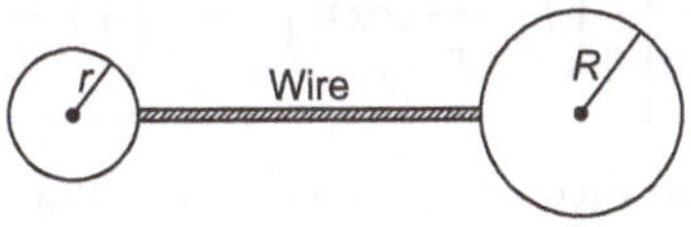

Sol. The electrical potential of a spherical shell with charge q and radius r is kq/r, where $k = 1/(4\pi\varepsilon_0)$.

Since, the shells are joined by a conductor the charge will distribute between them so that they attain the same electrical potential.

Let the charge on the sphere with radius r be q_r and that on the another sphere q_R. Then, equating the potentials gives $q_r/r = q_R/R$.

$\Rightarrow \quad q_r = q_R\,(r/R)$ ...(i)

$\because$ The total charge equals the original charge.

$\therefore \quad Q = q_r + q_R \Rightarrow \quad q_R = Q - q_r$

By Eq. (i), $\quad q_r = (Q - q_r)(r/R)$

Solving for q_r gives $\quad q_r(1 + r/R) = Q(r/R)$

$\Rightarrow \quad q_r = Qr/(R + r)$

which is the required charge.

Note The value of k is not needed, stating proportionally is sufficient.

Electric Potential Due to an Electric Dipole on its Axial Line

AB ia an electric dipole as shown in figure.

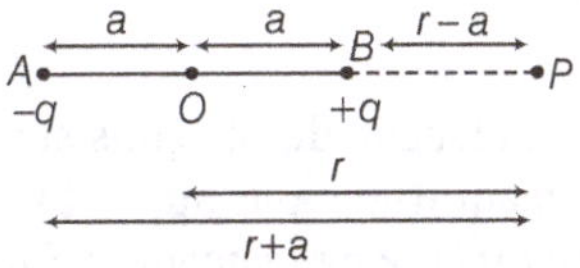

Dipole moment of electric dipole (AB),

$$p = 2qa \quad \text{...(i)}$$

We have to calculate electric potential at point P on axial line at a distance r from mid point O.

Electric potential at point P due to change $(-q)$ at A,

$$V_1 = \frac{1}{4\pi\varepsilon_0} \cdot \frac{(-q)}{(r + a)} \quad \text{...(ii)}$$

Electric potential at point P due to change (q) at B,

$$V_2 = \frac{1}{4\pi\varepsilon_0} \cdot \frac{(q)}{(r - a)} \quad \text{...(iii)}$$

Net electric potential at point P due to electric dipole AB,

$$V = V_1 + V_2$$

$$= \frac{q}{4\pi\varepsilon_0}\left(\frac{1}{r - a} - \frac{1}{r + a}\right)$$

$$= \frac{2qa}{4\pi\varepsilon_0 \cdot (r^2 - a^2)}$$

Since, $r >> a$

$$\therefore \quad V = \frac{2qa}{4\pi\varepsilon_0 \cdot r^2}$$

$$V = \frac{1}{4\pi\varepsilon_0} \cdot \frac{p}{r^2} \quad \text{[from Eq. (i)]}$$

Electric Potential Due to an Electric Dipole on its Equitorial Line

AB is an electric dipole of dipole moment

$$p = 2qa \quad \text{...(i)}$$

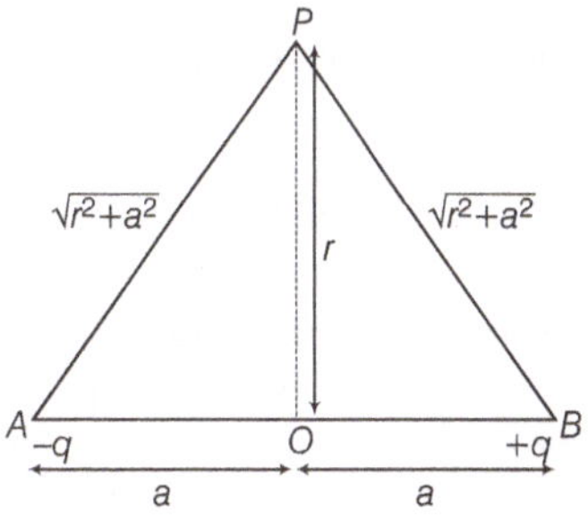

We have to calculate electric potential at point P on equitorial line at a distance r from mid point O.

Electric potential at point P due to change $(-q)$ at A,

$$V_1 = \frac{1}{4\pi\varepsilon_0} \cdot \frac{(-q)}{\sqrt{r^2 + a^2}} \quad \text{...(ii)}$$

Electric potential at point P due to change (q) at B,

$$V_2 = \frac{1}{4\pi\varepsilon_0} \cdot \frac{(q)}{\sqrt{r^2 + a^2}} \quad \text{...(iii)}$$

Net electric potential at point P due to electric dipole AB,

$$V = V_1 + V_2$$

$$\Rightarrow \quad V = \frac{1}{4\pi\varepsilon_0} \cdot \frac{-q}{\sqrt{r^2 + a^2}} + \frac{1}{4\pi\varepsilon_0} \cdot \frac{q}{\sqrt{r^2 + a^2}}$$

$$\Rightarrow \quad V = 0$$

Electrostatic Potential Due to an Electric Dipole

Let us consider an electric dipole consisting of charges $+q$ and $-q$ separated by a distance $2a$.

The dipole moment $|\mathbf{p}| = q \times 2a$

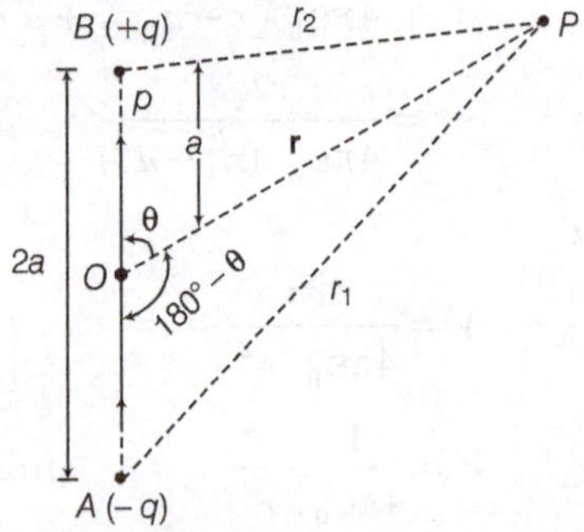

Electric potential at point P due to electric dipole

Let O be the centre of the dipole, P be any point near the electric dipole inclined at an angle θ as shown in the figure.

Let P be the point at which electric potential is required.

Potential at P due to $-q$ charge, $V_1 = \dfrac{-q}{4\pi\varepsilon_0 r_1}$

Potential at P due to $+q$ charge, $V_2 = \dfrac{q}{4\pi\varepsilon_0 r_2}$

As, potential is related to work done by the field, electrostatic potential also follows the superposition principle. Therefore, potential at P due to the dipole,

$$V_P = V_1 + V_2 = \frac{q}{4\pi\varepsilon_0}\left[\frac{1}{r_2} - \frac{1}{r_1}\right] \quad \ldots\text{(i)}$$

Now, by geometry,

$$r_1^2 = r^2 + a^2 + 2ar\cos\theta$$

Similarly, $$r_2^2 = r^2 + a^2 + 2ar\cos(180^\circ - \theta)$$

or $$r_2^2 = r^2 + a^2 - 2ar\cos\theta$$

$$[\because \cos(180^\circ - \theta) = -\cos\theta]$$

and $$r_1^2 = r^2\left(1 + \frac{a^2}{r^2} + \frac{2a}{r}\cos\theta\right)$$

If $r >> a$, $\dfrac{a}{r}$ is small.

Therefore, $\dfrac{a^2}{r^2}$ can be neglected.

$$r_1^2 = r^2\left(1 + \frac{2a}{r}\cos\theta\right) \Rightarrow r_1 = r\left(1 + \frac{2a}{r}\cos\theta\right)^{1/2}$$

or $$\frac{1}{r_1} = \frac{1}{r}\left(1 + \frac{2a}{r}\cos\theta\right)^{-1/2}$$

Similarly, $$\frac{1}{r_2} = \frac{1}{r}\left(1 - \frac{2a}{r}\cos\theta\right)^{-1/2}$$

Putting these values in Eq. (i), we obtain

$$V_P = \frac{q}{4\pi\varepsilon_0}\left[\frac{1}{r}\left(1 - \frac{2a}{r}\cos\theta\right)^{\frac{1}{2}} - \frac{1}{r}\left(1 + \frac{2a}{r}\cos\theta\right)^{\frac{1}{2}}\right]$$

Using Binomial theorem, $[(1+x)^n = 1 + nx, x << 1]$ and retaining terms upto the first order in $\dfrac{a}{r}$, we set

$$V_P = \frac{q}{4\pi\varepsilon_0 r}\left[\left(1 + \frac{a}{r}\cos\theta\right) - \left(1 - \frac{a}{r}\cos\theta\right)\right]$$

$$= \frac{q}{4\pi\varepsilon_0 r}\left[1 + \frac{a}{r}\cos\theta - 1 + \frac{a}{r}\cos\theta\right]$$

$$= \frac{q}{4\pi\varepsilon_0 r}\left(\frac{2a\cos\theta}{r}\right) = \frac{q \times 2a\cos\theta}{4\pi\varepsilon_0 r^2}$$

$$\Rightarrow \boxed{V_P = \frac{p\cos\theta}{4\pi\varepsilon_0 r^2}} \quad [\because p = q \times 2a]$$

Special cases

(i) When point P lies on axial line, then $\theta = 0^\circ$

$$\therefore V_P = \frac{p\cos 0^\circ}{4\pi\varepsilon_0 r^2} = \frac{1}{4\pi\varepsilon_0} \cdot \frac{p}{r^2}$$

(ii) When point P lies on equitorial line, then $\theta = 90^\circ$

$$\therefore V_P = \frac{p\cos 90^\circ}{4\pi\varepsilon_0 r^2} = 0$$

Example 9 An electric dipole consists of two charges of equal magnitude and opposite signs separated by a distance $2a$ as shown in figure. The dipole is along the X-axis and is centred at the origin.

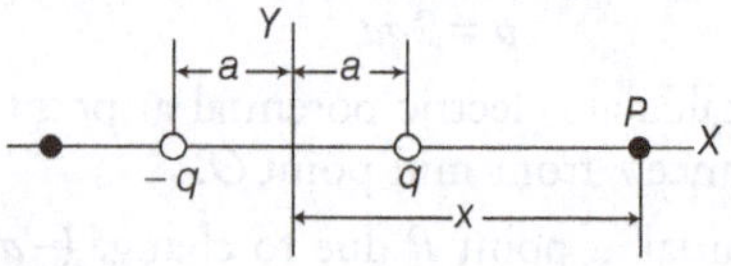

(i) Calculate the electric potential at point P.

(ii) Calculate V at a point far from the dipole.

Sol. (i) For the point P in figure,

$$V = k_e \Sigma \frac{q_i}{r_1} = k_e\left(\frac{q}{x-a} - \frac{q}{x+a}\right) = \frac{2k_e qa}{x^2 - a^2}$$

(ii) If point P is far from the dipole, such that $x >> a$, then a^2 can be neglected in the terms, $x^2 - a^2$ and V becomes

$$V = \frac{2k_e qa}{x^2} \quad [\because x >> a]$$

Equipotential Surfaces

Any surface which has same electrostatic potential at every point, on it is called an equipotential surface.

The shape of equipotential surface due to a

(i) line charge is cylindrical

(ii) point charge is spherical.

Different properties of equipotential surfaces are given as below:

(i) Equipotential surfaces do not intersect each other as it gives two directions of electric field at intersecting point which is not possible.

(ii) Equipotential surfaces are closely spaced in the region of strong electric field and widely spaced in the region of weak electric field.

(iii) For any charge configuration, equipotential surface through a point is normal to the electric field at that point and directed from one equipotential surface at higher potential to the other equipotential surface at lower potential.

(iv) No work is required to move a test charge on an equipotential surface.

(v) For a uniform electric field E, let along X-axis, the equipotential surfaces are normal to the X-axis, i.e. planes parallel to the YZ-plane.

(vi) For a plane equipotential surface, the source charge is situated at infinity.

Equipotential Surfaces in Different Cases

Case I The equipotential surfaces produced by a point charge or a spherically symmetrical charge distribution is a family of concentric spheres as shown below.

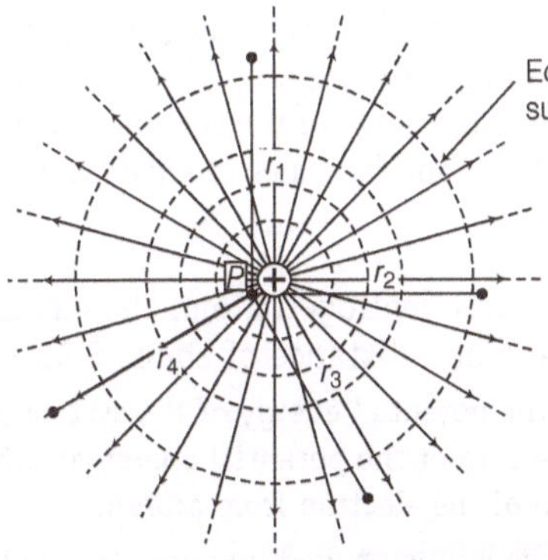

Equipotential surfaces for a point charge

Case II The equipotential surfaces for a uniform electric field are as shown below.

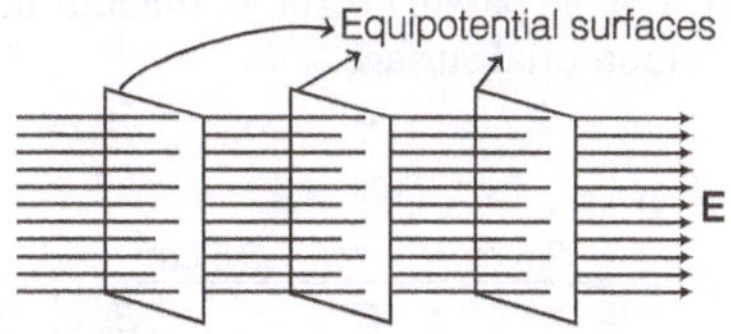

Equipotential surfaces for a uniform electric field

Case III The equipotential surfaces due to two identical positive charges are as shown below.

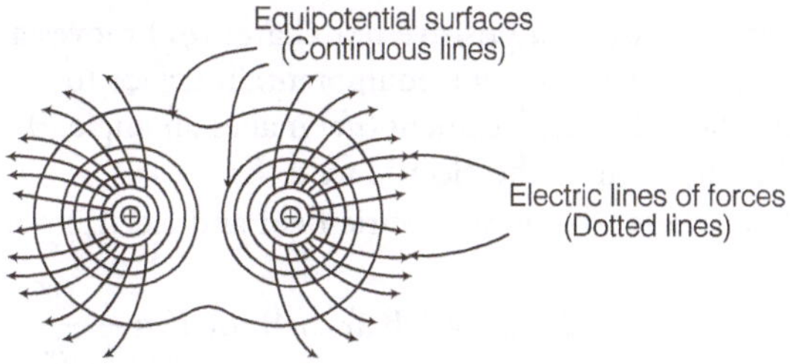

Equipotential surfaces due to two positive charges

Case IV The equipotential surfaces for an electric dipole are as shown below in the figure by dotted lines.

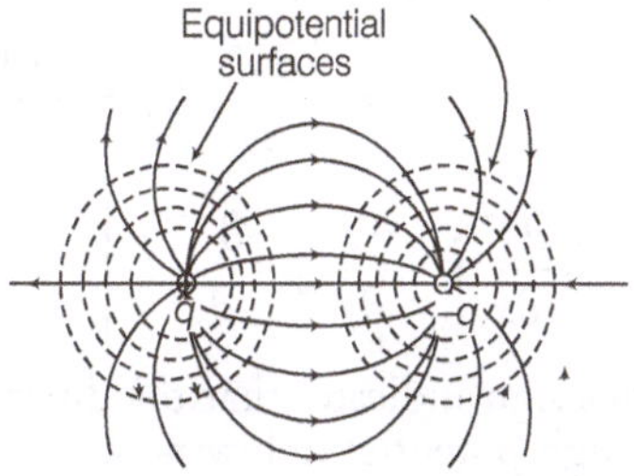

Equipotential surfaces due to an electric dipole

Electric field is always perpendicular to an equipotential surface and as a result, work done in moving a charge between two points on an equipotential surface is zero.

Example 10 Two charges 2μC and – 2 μC are placed at points A and B, 5 cm apart. Depict an equipotential surface of the system.

Sol. Equipotential surface means the surface where potential remains same at each point.

Here, this is the system of two equal and opposite charges.

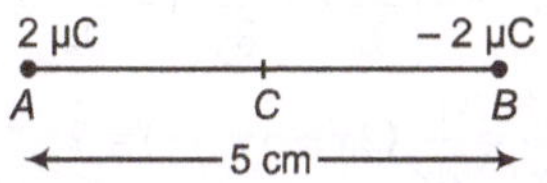

∴ The potential at C (mid-point of AB),

$$V = \frac{1}{4\pi\varepsilon_0}\left(\frac{q_1}{r_1}+\frac{q_2}{r_2}\right) = \frac{1}{4\pi\varepsilon_0}\left[\frac{2\times10^{-6}}{2.5\times10^{-2}}+\frac{(-2\times10^{-6})}{2.5\times10^{-2}}\right] = 0$$

Thus, potential is zero at each point on the line which passes through the mid-point of AB and perpendicular to it. So, a plane passing through the mid-point C of AB is an equipotential surface.

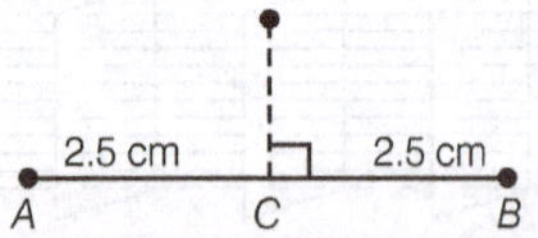

Relation between Electric Field and Electric Potential

Let us consider a positive test charge (q_0) moves a distance (dr) from one equipotential surface to another. The displacement (dr) makes an angle (θ) with the direction of the electric field (E).

The relation between electric field and electric potential is given as

$$dV = -\mathbf{E}\cdot d\mathbf{r} = -E\,dr\cos\theta \quad \text{or} \quad E = -\frac{dV}{dr}$$

If electric field is present in three dimensions, then

$$\mathbf{E} = E_x\hat{\mathbf{i}} + E_y\hat{\mathbf{j}} + E_z\hat{\mathbf{k}}$$

$$E_x = -\frac{\partial V}{\partial x},\ E_y = -\frac{\partial V}{\partial y},\ E_z = -\frac{\partial V}{\partial z}$$

$$\therefore \qquad \mathbf{E} = -\left[\frac{\partial V}{\partial x}\hat{\mathbf{i}} + \frac{\partial V}{\partial y}\hat{\mathbf{j}} + \frac{\partial V}{\partial z}\hat{\mathbf{k}}\right]$$

where, negative sign indicates that the direction of electric field is from high potential to low potential, i.e. in the direction of decreasing potential.

Note

- Electric field is in the direction in which the potential decreases steepest.
- Its magnitude is given by the change in the magnitude of potential per unit displacement normal to the equipotential surface at the point.

Example 11 The electric potential in a region is represented as

$$V = 2x + 3y - z.$$

Obtain expression for electric field strength.

Sol. As, $\mathbf{E} = -\left[\frac{\partial V}{\partial x}\hat{\mathbf{i}} + \frac{\partial V}{\partial y}\hat{\mathbf{j}} + \frac{\partial V}{\partial z}\hat{\mathbf{k}}\right]$

Here, $\frac{\partial V}{\partial x} = \frac{\partial}{\partial x}(2x + 3y - z) = 2$

$\frac{\partial V}{\partial y} = \frac{\partial}{\partial y}(2x + 3y - z) = 3$

and $\frac{\partial V}{\partial z} = \frac{\partial}{\partial z}(2x + 3y - z) = -1$

$\therefore$ Electric field, $\mathbf{E} = -2\hat{\mathbf{i}} - 3\hat{\mathbf{j}} + \hat{\mathbf{k}}$

Electrostatic Potential Energy of a System of Charges

Electrostatic potential energy of a system of point charges is defined as the total amount of work done in bringing the different charges to their respective positions from infinitely large mutual separations.

Electrostatic Potential Energy of a System of Two Point Charges

Consider two point charges q_1 and q_2 lying at points A and B whose locations are $\mathbf{r}_1$ and $\mathbf{r}_2$, respectively.

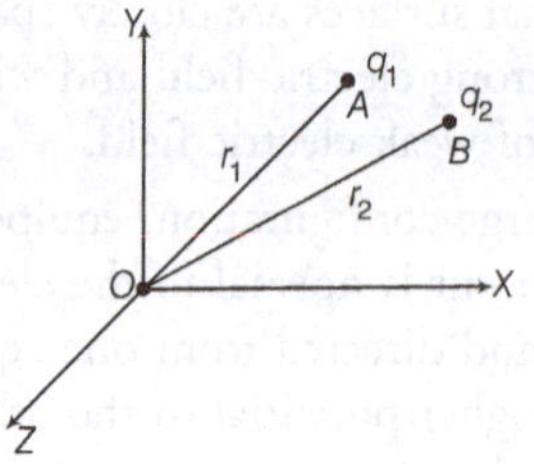

The potential energy is given by the formula

$$U = W = \frac{1}{4\pi\varepsilon_0}\cdot\frac{q_1 q_2}{r_{AB}}$$

Electrostatic potential energy is a scalar quantity. In the above formula, the values of q_1 and q_2 must be with proper signs.

If $q_1, q_2 > 0$, then potential energy is positive. It means that two charges are of same sign, i.e. they repel each other. Then, in bringing closer, work is done against the force of repulsion, so that the electrostatic potential energy of the system increases.

Conversely, in separating them, work is obtained from the system, so the potential energy of the system decreases.

If $q_1 > 0, q_2 < 0$, potential energy is negative. It means that two charges are of opposite sign, i.e. they attract each other. In this case, potential energy of the system decreases in bringing them closer and increases in separating them further.

Example 12 In a hydrogen atom, the electron and proton are bound at a distance of about 0.53 Å.

(i) Estimate the potential energy of the system in eV, taking the zero of the potential energy at infinite separation of the electron from proton.

(ii) What is the minimum work required to free the electron, given that its kinetic energy in the orbit is half the magnitude of potential energy obtained in (i)?

(iii) What are the answers to (i) and (ii) above, if the zero of potential energy is taken at 1.06 Å separation? **NCERT**

> **Key Point:** The potential energy of any object at any point is equal to the difference in its potential energy at infinity and at that point. Work done is equal to the total energy of the system.

Sol. Charge on electron, $q_e = -1.6\times 10^{-19}$ C and charge on proton, $q_p = 1.6\times 10^{-19}$ C

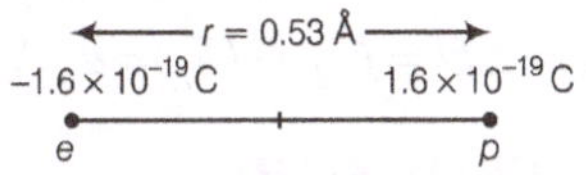

(i) Potential energy of the system

= Potential energy at infinity

− Potential energy at a distance of 0.53 Å

$$= 0 - \frac{1}{4\pi\varepsilon_0}\cdot\frac{q_e q_p}{r}$$

$$= 0 - \frac{9\times10^9 \times (-1.6)\times 10^{-19}\times 1.6\times 10^{-19}}{0.53\times 10^{-10}}$$

$$= -43.47\times 10^{-19}\text{ J} \qquad [\because 1\text{ eV} = 1.6\times 10^{-19}\text{ J}]$$

$$= -\frac{43.47\times 10^{-19}}{1.6\times 10^{-19}} = -27.16\text{ eV}$$

(ii) The kinetic energy $= -\frac{1}{2}\times$ Potential energy

$$= -\frac{1}{2}\times(-27.16) = 13.58\text{ eV}$$

Total energy = KE + PE = 13.58 − 27.16 = −13.58 eV

Thus, the minimum work done required to free the electron is 13.58 eV.

(iii) Potential energy at separation of 1.06 Å

$$= \frac{1}{4\pi\varepsilon_0}\cdot\frac{q_e q_p}{1.06\times 10^{-10}}$$

$$= \frac{9\times10^9\times(-1.6)\times10^{-19}\times1.6\times10^{-19}}{1.06\times10^{-10}}$$

$$= -21.73\times10^{-19}\text{ J} = -\frac{21.73\times10^{-19}}{1.6\times10^{-19}} = -13.58\text{ eV}$$

Thus, the potential energy of the system at 1.06 Å

= PE at distance 1.06 Å − PE at distance 0.53 Å

= − 13.58 − (− 27.16) = 13.58 eV

Thus, on shifting the zero of potential energy, work required to free electron remains same and it is equal to 13.58 eV.

Electrostatic Potential Energy of a System of Three Point Charges

Let there be three charges q_1, q_2 and q_3 placed at the three corners of a triangle, then electrostatics potential energy of a system of three charges is given by

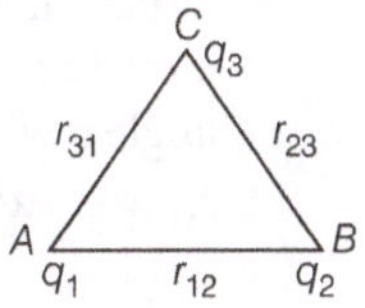

$$U = \frac{1}{4\pi\varepsilon_0}\left[\frac{q_1q_2}{r_{12}} + \frac{q_2q_3}{r_{23}} + \frac{q_3q_1}{r_{31}}\right]$$

In general, if a system has n different charges, then its energy is written as

$$U = \frac{1}{2}\left[\frac{1}{4\pi\varepsilon_0}\sum_{i=1}^{n}\sum_{\substack{j=1\\ j\neq i}}^{n}\frac{q_iq_j}{r_{ij}}\right]$$

The SI unit of electrostatic potential energy is joule (J). Another convenient unit of energy is electron volt (eV).

$$1\text{ eV} = 1.6\times10^{-19}\text{C}\times 1\text{ V} = 1.6\times10^{-19}\text{ J}$$

Example 13 Three charges (all $q = 10$ C) are placed at the edge of an equilateral triangle of side 2 m. Find the net potential energy of the system.

Sol. Given, charge, $q = 10$ C $(q_1 = q_2 = q)$

Each side of equilateral triangle, $r = 2$ m

Potential energy (PE) = ?

Potential energy between two charges is given by

$$\text{PE} = \frac{kq_1q_2}{r} \qquad [\because r = \text{distance between } q_1 \text{ and } q_2]$$

∴ PE of system will be three times the potential energy between the two charges as the equal charge is placed at the vertices of equilateral triangle.

$$\text{So, PE}_{\text{net}} = \frac{3\times kqq}{r} = \frac{3\,kq^2}{r} = \frac{3\times9\times10^9\times10\times10}{2}$$

$$= 135\times10^{10}\text{ J}$$

Example 14 Three point charges q, $2q$ and $8q$ are to be placed on a 9 cm long straight line. Find the positions where the charges should be placed such that the potential energy of this system is minimum. In this situation, what is the electric field at the position of the charge q due to the other two charges ?

Sol. Consider the given situation as shown in figure.

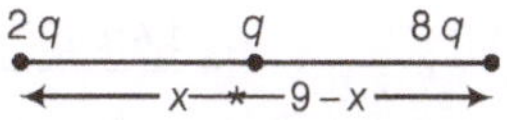

For potential energy to be minimum the bigger charges should be farthest. Let x be the distance of q from $2q$. Then potential energy of the system shown in figure would be

$$U = K\left[\frac{(2q)(q)}{x} + \frac{(8q)(q)}{(9-x)} + \frac{(2q)(8q)}{9}\right]$$

Here, $K = \frac{1}{4\pi\varepsilon_0}$

For U to be minimum $\frac{2}{x} + \frac{8}{9-x}$ should be minimum.

$$\frac{d}{dx}\left[\frac{2}{x} + \frac{8}{9-x}\right] = 0 \Rightarrow \frac{-2}{x^2} + \frac{8}{(9-x)^2} = 0 \Rightarrow \frac{x}{9-x} = \frac{1}{2}$$

or $\qquad x = 3$ cm

i.e. distance of charge q from $2q$ should be 3 cm.

$\therefore$ Electric field at q, $E = \dfrac{K(2q)}{(3\times10^{-2})^2} - \dfrac{K(8q)}{(6\times10^{-2})^2} = 0$

Example 15 If one of the two electrons of H_2 molecule is removed, we get a hydrogen molecular ion H_2^+. In the ground state of an H_2^+, the two protons are separated by roughly 1.5 Å and the electron is roughly 1 Å from each proton. Determine the potential energy of the system. Specify your choice of the zero of potential energy. **NCERT**

Sol. Let there are two protons p_1 and p_2 with an electron e.

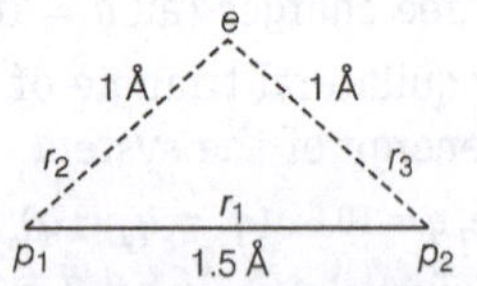

Distance between two protons is given by

$$r_1 = 1.5\ \text{Å} = 1.5\times10^{-10}\ \text{m}$$

Distance between proton p_1 and electron e is given by

$$r_2 = 1\ \text{Å} = 1\times10^{-10}\ \text{m}$$

Distance between proton p_2 and electron e is given by

$$r_3 = 1\ \text{Å} = 1\times10^{-10}\ \text{m}$$

The total potential energy of the system,

$$U = \frac{1}{4\pi\varepsilon_0}\cdot\left[\frac{q_{p_1}q_{p_2}}{r_1} + \frac{q_{p_1}q_e}{r_2} + \frac{q_{p_2}q_e}{r_3}\right] \quad ...(i)$$

Given, $q_{p_1} = q_{p_2} = 1.6\times10^{-19}$C

and $q_e = -1.6\times10^{-19}$ C

Putting these values in Eq. (i), we get

$$U = 9\times10^9\left[\frac{1.6\times10^{-19}\times1.6\times10^{-19}}{1.5\times10^{-10}} + \frac{(1.6\times10^{-19})\times(-1.6\times10^{-19})}{10^{-10}} + \frac{1.6\times10^{-19}\times(-1.6\times10^{-19})}{10^{-10}}\right]$$

$$= \frac{9\times10^9\times1.6\times1.6\times10^{-38}}{10^{-10}}\left[\frac{1}{1.5}-1-1\right]$$

$$= -30.72\times10^{-19}\ \text{J} = \frac{-30.72\times10^{-19}}{1.6\times10^{-19}}\ \text{eV} = -19.2\ \text{eV}$$

Here, we use that potential energy at infinity is zero.

Potential Energy in an External Field

A single charge or a system of charges possess electrostatic potential energy in the presence of an external electric field, these are discussed as follows.

Potential Energy of a Single Charge in External Field

Potential energy of a single charge q at a point with position vector **r** in an external field $= q\cdot V(\mathbf{r})$, where, $V(\mathbf{r})$ is the potential at the point due to external electric field **E**.

Work done against electrostatic field, while going from A to B,

$$\Delta W_{AB} = \Delta U = U_B - U_A = q_0(V_A - V_B)$$

Potential Energy of a Dipole in an External Field

Consider a dipole with charges $+q$ and $-q$ placed in a uniform external electric field as shown in the figure. In a uniform electric field, the dipole experiences no force, but experiences a torque τ given by $\tau = \mathbf{p}\times\mathbf{E}$. This torque will tend to rotate the dipole.

Suppose an external torque τ_{ext} is applied to the dipole so that it rotates from angle θ_1 to θ_2 with respect to the electric field (E).

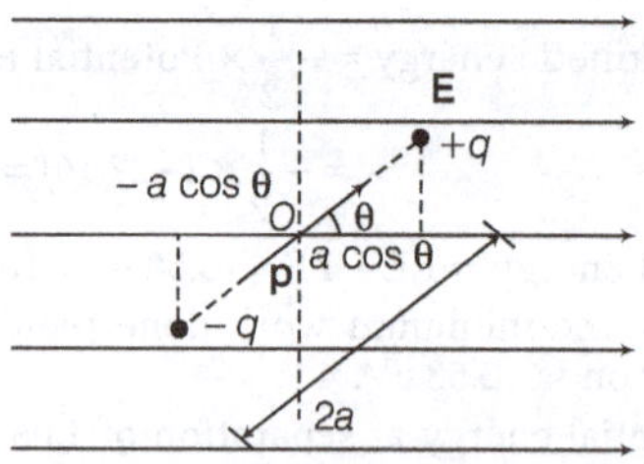

Dipole in a uniform external field

The amount of work done by the external torque is given by

$$W = \int_{\theta_1}^{\theta_2}\tau_{ext}\,\theta\,d\theta = \int_{\theta_1}^{\theta_2} pE\sin\theta\,d\theta$$

$$= pE[-\cos\theta]_{\theta_1}^{\theta_2} = pE(\cos\theta_1 - \cos\theta_2)$$

The work done W is stored as the potential energy of the system. Therefore, the potential energy of the dipole placed in external field **E** is given by

$$U(\theta) = pE(\cos\theta_1 - \cos\theta_2)$$

Particular Cases

(i) When the dipole is initially aligned along the electric field, i.e. $\theta_1 = 0°$ and we have to set it at angle θ with **E**, i.e. $\theta_2 = \theta$.

$$\therefore \quad W = -pE(\cos\theta - \cos 0°)$$
$$= -pE(\cos\theta - 1)$$

This work done is stored in the dipole in the form of potential energy.

(ii) When the dipole is initially at right angle to **E**, i.e. $\theta_1 = 90°$ and we have to set it at angle θ with **E**, i.e. $\theta_2 = \theta$.

$\therefore \quad W = -pE(\cos\theta - \cos 90°) = -pE\cos\theta$

$\therefore$ Potential energy of dipole, $U = W = -pE\cos\theta$

$$U = -\mathbf{p}\cdot\mathbf{E}$$

Special Cases

(i) When $\theta = 90°$, then $U = -pE\cos 90° = 0$
This gives the position of zero potential energy of the dipole.

(ii) When $\theta = 0°$, then $U = -pE\cos 0° = -pE$
In this position, the dipole will be in 'stable' equilibrium.

(iii) When $\theta = 180°$, then $U = -pE\cos 180° = +pE$
In this position, the dipole will be in 'unstable' equilibrium.

Important Results

Some important results related to electric dipole are as given below

(i) Electric potential at any point on the bisector of dipole is zero.

(ii) A dipole experiences a net force in a non-uniform electric field.

(iii) A dipole experiences maximum torque at the position where potential energy is zero.

Example 16 An electric dipole of length 4 cm, when placed with its axis making an angle of 60° with a uniform electric field, experiences a torque of $4\sqrt{3}$ N-m. Calculate the potential energy of the dipole, if it has charge ± 8 nC.

Sol. Given, length, $2a = 4\text{ cm} = 4\times 10^{-2}$ m

Angle, $\theta = 60°$, torque $\tau = 4\sqrt{3}$ N-m

Charge, $Q = 8\times 10^{-9}$ C

We know that, $\tau = Q(2a)E\sin\theta$

$\Rightarrow$ Electric field, $E = \dfrac{\tau}{Q(2a)\sin\theta}$

$$= \frac{4\sqrt{3}}{8\times 10^{-9}\times 4\times 10^{-2}\times \sin 60°}\ \text{N/C}$$

$\therefore$ Potential energy, $U = -pE\cos\theta$

$$= -Q(2a)E\cos\theta$$
$$= -8\times 10^{-9}\times 4\times 10^{-2}\times\left[\frac{4\sqrt{3}\times\cos 60°}{8\times 10^{-9}\times 4\times 10^{-2}\times\sin 60°}\right]$$
$$= \frac{-4\sqrt{3}}{\sqrt{3}} = -4\text{ J}$$

Example 17 A point charge q is fixed at origin. A dipole with a dipole moment **p** is placed along the X-axis far away from the origin with **p** pointing along positive X-axis. Find

(i) the kinetic energy of the dipole when it reaches a distance d from the origin.

(ii) the force experienced by the charge q at this moment.

Sol. (i) Applying energy conservation principle, increase in kinetic energy of the dipole = decrease in electrostatic potential energy of the dipole.

$\therefore$ Kinetic energy of dipole at distance d from origin

$$= U_i - U_f$$
$$= 0 - (-\mathbf{p}\cdot\mathbf{E}) = \mathbf{p}\cdot\mathbf{E}$$
$$= (p\hat{\mathbf{i}})\cdot\left(\frac{1}{4\pi\varepsilon_0}\frac{q}{d^2}\hat{\mathbf{i}}\right)$$
$$= \frac{qp}{4\pi\varepsilon_0 d^2}$$

(ii) Electric field at origin due to the dipole,

$$\mathbf{E} = \frac{1}{4\pi\varepsilon_0}\frac{2p}{d^3}\hat{\mathbf{i}} \qquad [\because \mathbf{E}_{\text{axis}} \uparrow\uparrow \mathbf{p}]$$

$\therefore$ Force on charge q,

$$\mathbf{F} = q\mathbf{E}$$
$$= \frac{pq}{2\pi\varepsilon_0 d^3}\hat{\mathbf{i}}$$

Topic Practice 1

Multiple Choice Questions

1 Mark

1. In figure, shown the work done on a test charge q by the electrostatic field due to any given charge configuration is depends

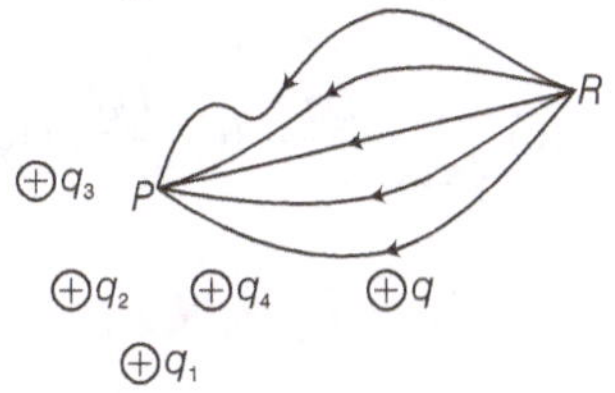

(a) on the path followed
(b) on its final and initial positions
(c) Both (a) and (b)
(d) Neither (a) nor (b)

2. If x joule of work must be done to move electric charge equal to 4C from a place, where potential is -10 V to another place, where potential is 5V, find the value of x.
(a) 100 J (b) 50 J (c) 60 J (d) 30 J

3. Work done (by the external force) per unit positive test charge in bringing it from infinity to the point is negative, for
(a) $Q>0, V<0$ (b) $Q>0, V>0$
(c) $Q<0, V>0$ (d) $Q<0, V<0$

4. A hollow metal sphere of radius 10 cm is charged such that the potential on its surface becomes 80 V. The potential at the centre of the sphere is
(a) 80 V (b) 800 V (c) 8 V (d) zero

5. A point charge q is kept at each of the vertices of an equilateral triangle having each side a. Total electrostatic potential energy of the system is **ISC 2020**
(a) $\left(\frac{1}{4\pi\varepsilon_0}\right)\frac{3q^2}{a^2}$ (b) $\left(\frac{1}{4\pi\varepsilon_0}\right)\frac{3q}{a}$
(c) $\left(\frac{1}{4\pi\varepsilon_0}\right)\frac{3q^2}{a}$ (d) $\left(\frac{1}{4\pi\varepsilon_0}\right)\frac{3q}{a^2}$

6. The electrostatic potential energy of two point charges, 1 μC each, placed 1 m apart in air is **ISC 2017**
(a) 9×10^3 J (b) 9×10^9 J
(c) 9×10^{-3} J (d) 9×10^{-6} eV

7. In the given figure below, a charge Q is fixed. Another charge q is moved along a circular arc MN of radius r around it, from the point M to the point N such that the length of the arc $MN = l$. The work done in this process is

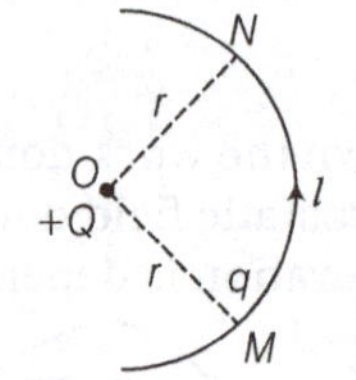

ISC 2016
(a) zero (b) $\frac{1}{4\pi\varepsilon_0}\cdot\frac{Qq}{r^2}l$ (c) $\frac{Qq}{2\varepsilon_0 r^2}l$ (d) $\frac{Qq}{2\pi\varepsilon_0 r^2}$

Very Short Answer Type Questions

1 Mark

8. A point charge $+Q$ is placed at point O as shown in the figure. Is the potential difference $(V_A - V_B)$ positive, negative or zero?

9. Is electrostatic potential necessarily zero at a point, where electric field strength is zero? Illustrate your answer.

10. In an electric dipole, at which point is the electric potential zero? **ISC 2024, 16**

11. A charge q is moved from a point A above a dipole of dipole moment p to a point B below the dipole in equatorial plane without acceleration. Find the work done in this process.

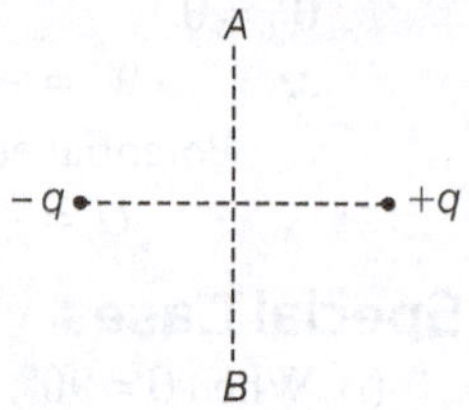

12. Why are electric field lines perpendicular at a point on an equipotential surface of a conductor?

13. How much work is done in taking an electron around a nucleus in a circular path? **ISC 2011**

14. Define the term potential energy for charge q at a distance r in an external field.

Short Answer Type I Questions

2 Marks

15. Calculate electric potential at a point P which is at a distance of 9 cm from a point charge of 50μC. **ISC 2023**

16. What is the geometrical shape of equipotential surface due to a single isolated charge?

17. Can two equipotential surface intersect each other? Justify your answer.

18. Two point charges 3μC and −3μC are placed at points A and B, 5 cm apart.
(i) Draw the equipotential surfaces of the system.
(ii) Why do equipotential surfaces get close to each other near the point charge?

19. Two uniformly large parallel thin plates having charge densities $+\sigma$ and $-\sigma$ are kept in the XZ-plane at a distance d apart. Sketch an equipotential surface due to electric field between the plates. If a particle of mass m and charge $-q$ remains stationary between the plates. What is the magnitude and direction of this field?

20. What will be the equipotential surfaces corresponding to (i) a constant electric field in the z-direction, (ii) a field that uniformly increases in magnitude but its direction remains unchanged along the Z-axis and (iii) a single positive charge at the origin?

21. Find out the expression for the potential energy of a system of three charges q_1, q_2 and q_3 located at r_1, r_2 and r_3 with respect to the common origin O.

22. A dipole with its charges, $-q$ and $+q$, located at the points $(0, -b, 0)$ and $(0, +b, 0)$ is present in a uniform electric field **E**. The equipotential surfaces of this field are planes parallel to the YZ-planes.
   (i) What is the direction of the electric field **E**?
   (ii) How much torque would the dipole experience in this field?

Short Answer Type II Questions

(3 Marks)

23. Obtain an expression for the electric potential at a point which is at a distance r from the point charge Q. **ISC 2008**

24. A cube of side b has a charge q at each of its vertices. Determine the potential and electric field due to this charge array at the centre of the cube. **NCERT**

25. Obtain an expression for electric potential V at a point in an end-on position, i.e. axial position of an electric dipole. **ISC 2019**

26. Given figure shows a charge array known as an electric quadrupole. For a point on the axis of the quadrupole, obtain the dependence of potential on r for $r/a >> 1$ and contrast your results with that due to an electric dipole and an electric monopole (i.e. a single charge).

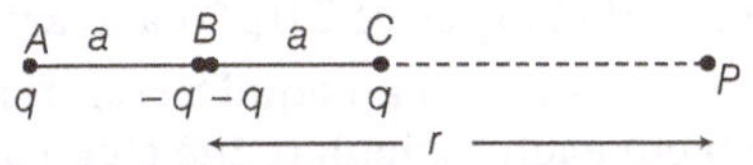

NCERT

27. Define an equipotential surface. Draw equipotential surfaces
   (i) in case of a single point charge.
   (ii) in a constant electric field in Z-direction. Why the equipotential surfaces about a single charge are not equidistant?
   (iii) Can electric field exist tangential to an equipotential surface? Give reason.

28. Three charges $-q$, $+Q$ and $-q$ are placed at equal distance on straight line. If the potential energy of the system of the three charges is zero, then what is the ratio of $Q : q$?

Long Answer Type Questions

(5 Marks)

29. Show that electric potential at a point P, at a distance r from a fixed point charge Q is given by
$$V = \left(\frac{1}{4\pi\varepsilon_0}\right)\frac{Q}{r}$$
ISC 2017

30. Three concentric metal shells A, B and C of radius a, b and c $(a < b < c)$ have surface charge densities $+\sigma$, $-\sigma$ and $+\sigma$, respectively.
   (i) Find the potential of three shells at A, B and C.
   (ii) If the shells A and C are at the same potential, obtain the relation between the radii a, b and c.

31. Two metal spheres, one of radius R and the other of radius $2R$, both have same surface charge density σ. They are brought in contact and separated. What will be new surface charge densities on them? **NCERT Exemplar**

Numerical Problems

32. A charge of 5 C is placed at the centre of a circle of radius 10 cm as shown in the figure below. Calculate the work done in moving a charge of 2 C from point A to B on the circumference of the circle.

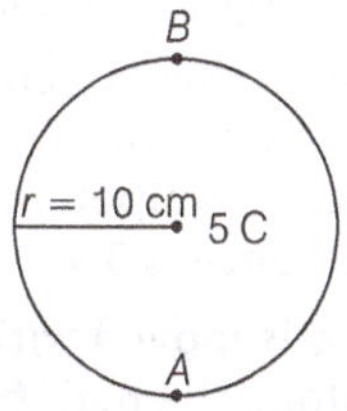

ISC 2005 (1 M)

33. What is the work done in moving a $2\,\mu$C point charge from corner A to corner B of a square $ABCD$, when a $10\,\mu$C charge exists at the centre of the square? **(2 M)**

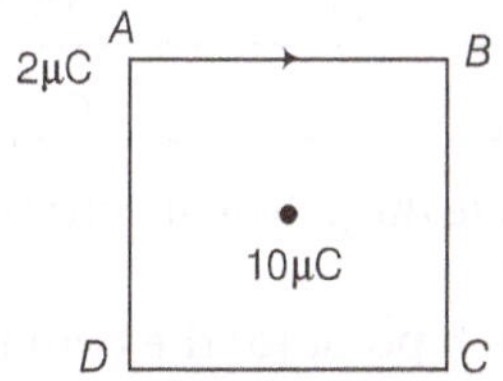

34. A charge of 8 mC is located at the origin. Calculate the work done in taking a small charge of -2×10^{-9} C from a point $P(0, 0, 3)$ (in cm) to a point Q (0, 4, 0) (in cm), *via* a point R (0, 6, 9) (in cm). **NCERT (3 M)**

35. The electric potential at 0.1 m from a point charge is + 50 V. What is the magnitude and sign of the charge? **(2 M)**

36. The circular arc is shown in the figure given below, has a uniform charge per unit length of 1×10^{-8} C/m. Find the potential at the centre O of the arc. **(2 M)**

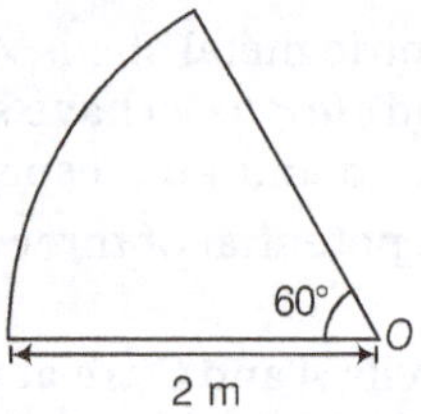

37. Two charges 5×10^{-8} C and -3×10^{-8} C are located 16 cm apart. At what point (s) on the line joining the two charges is the electric potential zero? Take the potential at infinity to be zero. **NCERT (2 M)**

38. A regular hexagon of side 10 cm has a charge 5 μC at each of its vertices. Calculate the potential at the centre of the hexagon. **NCERT (2 M)**

39. A small particle carrying a negative charge of 1.6×10^{-19} C is suspended in equilibrium between the horizontal metal plates 10 cm apart, having a potential difference of 4000 V across them, find the mass of the particle. **(2 M)**

40. An infinite plane sheet of charge density 10^{-8} C/m^2 is held in air. In this situation, how far apart are two equipotential surfaces whose potential difference is 5 V? **(2 M)**

41. A test charge q is moved without acceleration from A to C along the path from A to B and then from B to C in electric field E as shown in the figure.

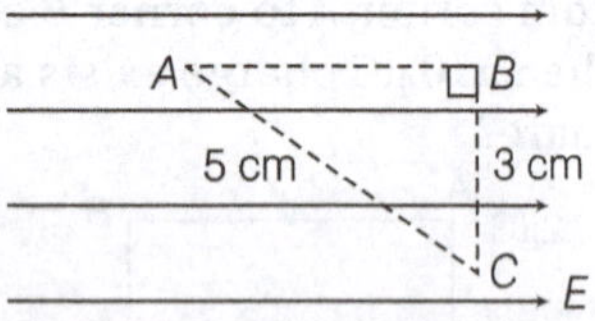

(i) Calculate the potential difference between A and C.

(ii) At which point (of the two) is the electric potential more and why? **(2 M)**

42. Two identical plane metallic surfaces A and B are kept parallel to each other in air, separated by a distance of 1 cm, surface A is given a positive potential of 10 V and the outer surface of B is earthed.

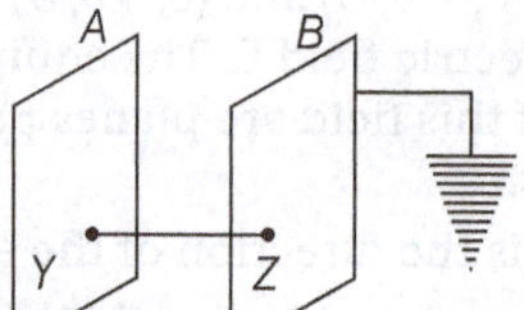

(i) What is the magnitude and direction of the electric field between the points Y and Z?

(ii) What is the work done in moving a charge of 20 μC from point Y to point Z? **(2 M)**

43. Two point charges of 10 C each, are kept at a distance of 3 m in vacuum. Calculate their electrostatic potential energy. **ISC 2015 (1 M)**

44. How much kinetic energy is gained by an electron, initially at rest, when it moves through a potential difference of 1000 V? Give your answer in joule. **ISC 2008 (1 M)**

45. An electron revolves around the nucleus of hydrogen atom in a circular orbit of radius 5×10^{-11} m. Calculate

(i) intensity of electric field of the nucleus at the position of the electron.

(ii) electrostatic potential energy of the hydrogen nucleus and electron system. **ISC 2010 (2 M)**

46. Three equal charges of 5.0 μC each are placed at the three vertices of an equilateral triangle of side 5.0 cm each. Calculate the electrostatic potential energy of the system of charges. **ISC 2007 (3 M)**

47. Three point charges $Q_1 = 25$ μC, $Q_2 = 50$ μC and $Q_3 = 100$ μC are kept at the corners A, B and C respectively of an equilateral ΔABC having each side equal to 7.5 m. Calculate the total electrostatic potential energy of the system. **ISC 2012 (5 M)**

Hints & Solutions

1. (*b*)

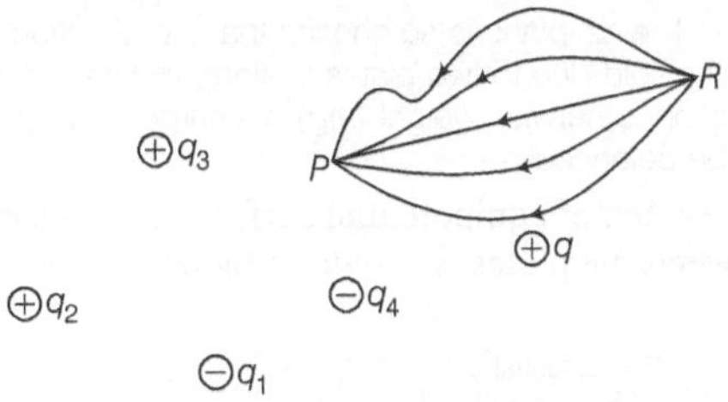

Work done on a test charge q by the electrostatic field due to any given charge configuration is independent of the path, and depends only on its initial and final positions.

2. (*c*) As, $W_{A \to B} = q(V_B - V_A) = 4[5 - (-10)] = 60$ J

$\therefore \quad x = 60$ J

3. (*d*) For $Q < 0$, $V < 0$, i.e. work done (by the external force) per unit positive test charge in bringing it from infinity to the point is negative. This is equivalent to saying that work done by the electrostatic force in bringing the unit positive charge from infinity to the point P is positive. [This is as it should be, since for $Q < 0$, the force on a unit positive test charge is attractive, so that the electrostatic force and the displacement (from infinity to P) are in the same direction.] Finally, we note that equation $V(r) = \dfrac{Q}{4\pi\varepsilon_0 r}$ is consistent with the choice that potential at infinity be zero.

4. (*a*) The potential at the centre of the sphere is 80 V because it is remains same at each point under the metallic hollow sphere.

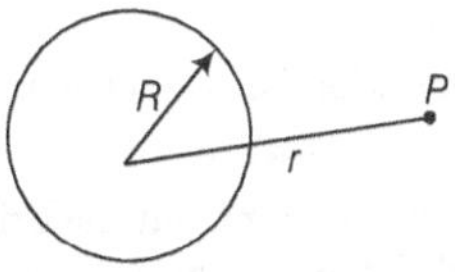

$$V(r) = \begin{cases} \dfrac{Q}{4\pi\varepsilon_0 r}; & r > R \\ \dfrac{Q}{4\pi\varepsilon_0 R}; & r \le R \end{cases}$$

5. (*c*) Given, charge, $q_A = q_B = q_C = q$

Each side of equilateral triangle $= a$

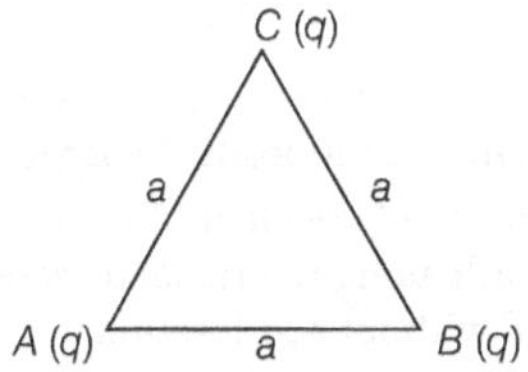

Potential energy,

$$U = \frac{1}{4\pi\varepsilon_0}\left[\frac{q^2}{a} + \frac{q^2}{a} + \frac{q^2}{a}\right] = \frac{1}{4\pi\varepsilon_0} \cdot \frac{3q^2}{a}$$

6. (*c*) The electric potential energy of two point charges 1 μC each, placed metre apart in air is

$$U = \frac{1}{4\pi\varepsilon_0} \cdot \frac{q_1 q_2}{r_{12}}$$

$$= 9 \times 10^9 \times \frac{10^{-6} \times 10^{-6}}{1}$$

$$= 9 \times 10^9 \times 10^{-12} = 9 \times 10^{-3} \text{ J}$$

7. (*a*)

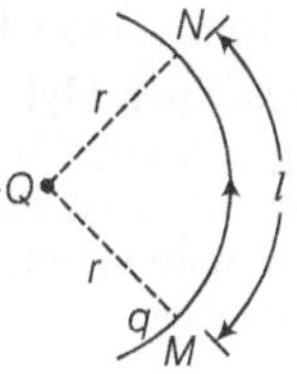

As the potential at points M and N are same and equals to $\dfrac{Kq}{r}$.

So, work done $= (\Delta V)q = 0$

($\because$ surface MN is equipotential, so $\Delta V = 0$)

8. According to question,

$r_2 > r_1$

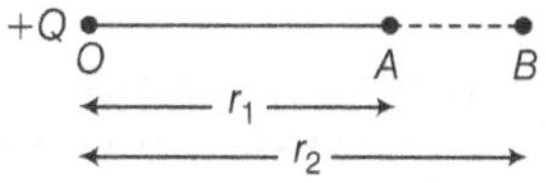

Potential at point A due to charge $+Q$, $(V_A) = \dfrac{kQ}{r_1}$

Potential at point B due to charge $+Q$, $(V_B) = \dfrac{kQ}{r_2}$ (1/2)

As $\quad V_A \propto \dfrac{1}{r_1}$ and $V_B \propto \dfrac{1}{r_2}$ and $r_2 > r_1$

so, $\quad V_A > V_B$

Thus, $(V_A - V_B)$ is positive. (1/2)

9. No, it is not necessary because electric field strength inside a hollow charged spherical shell is zero but potential at the point is same as that on the surface of shell.

10. Electric potential at any point on the equitorial plane of dipole is zero.

11. As, A and B are points on the equitorial plane of dipole $V_A = V_B$

Potential difference between point A and B,

$$V_{AB} = V_B - V_A = V_A - V_A \qquad (V_A = V_B)$$
$$= 0$$

Work done, $W = \dfrac{V_{AB}}{q}$.

As $V_{AB} = 0$, $W = 0$

So, the work done by the process will be zero.

12. Electric field is always normal to the equipotential surface at every point, because no work is done, as

$$W = q_0(V_A - V_B) \Rightarrow V_A - V_B = 0$$

hence $\quad W = 0$.

If the field were not normal to the equipotential surface, it would have a non-zero component along the surface. So, to move a test charge against this component, a work would have to be done.

13. The circular path around the nucleus will act as equipotential surface. Hence, work done in moving the electron around the nucleus $= e\,|\Delta V| = e(0) = 0$

14. The electric potential energy at any point lying at a distance r from the source charge q is equal to the amount of work done in moving unit positive test charge from infinity to that point without any acceleration against electrostatic force.

15. Given, $r = 9\times10^{-2}$ m, $Q = 50\times10^{-6}$ C

$$V = \frac{KQ}{r},\ K = 9\times10^{9}$$

$$V = 9\times10^{9}\times50\times\frac{10^{-6}}{9\times10^{-2}} = 5\times10^{7}$$

Electric potential $= 5\times10^{7}$ V

16. Refer to text on page 61 (Equipotential surfaces in different cases).

17. Equipotential surfaces do not intersect each other as it gives two directions of electric field at intersecting point which is not possible. (2)

18. (i) Equipotential surfaces of the system (dipole),

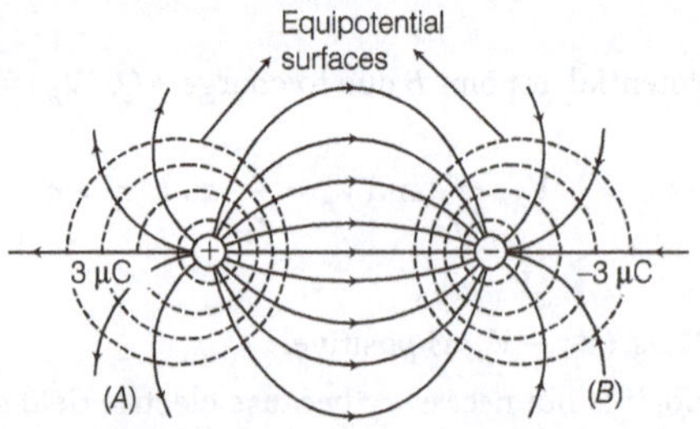

(1)

(ii) Equipotential surfaces get closer to each other near the point charges as strong electric field is produced there.

$$\because\ E = -\frac{\Delta V}{\Delta r}$$

$$\Rightarrow E \propto \frac{1}{\Delta r}\quad \text{[for a given equipotential surface]}$$

where, small Δr represents strong electric field and *vice-versa.* (1)

19. Here, $-q$ charge experiences force in a direction opposite to the direction of electric field.

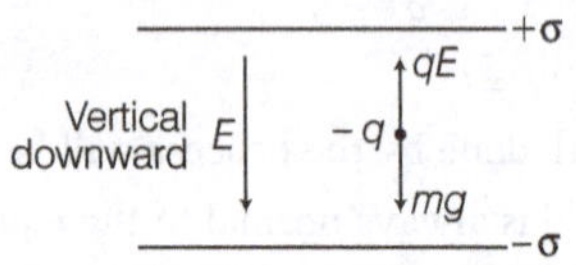

$\therefore$ $-q$ charge balances, when

$$qE = mg \Rightarrow E = \frac{mg}{q}$$

The direction of electric field is along vertically downward direction. (1)

Note: The *XZ*-plane is so chosen that the direction of electric field due to two plates is along vertically downward direction, otherwise weight (*mg*) of charged particle could not be balanced.

The sketch of equipotential surface due to electric field between the plates is shown in figure below.

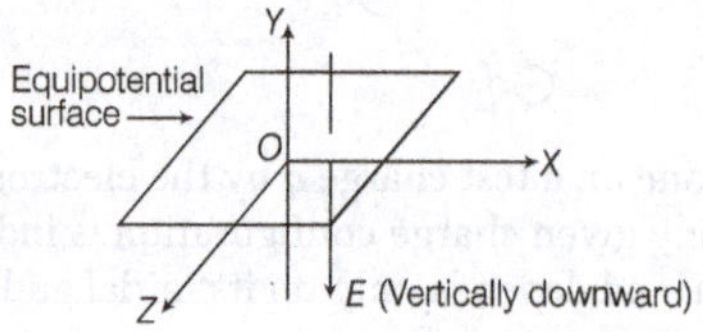

(1)

20. (i) Equidistant planes parallel to the *XY*-plane.

(ii) Again the equipotential surfaces are planes parallel to the *XY*-plane but they became closer together as the field increases.

(iii) Concentric sphere with centre at the origin. (2)

21. Refer to text on page 63 (Electrostatic potential energy of a system of three point charges).

22. (i) The direction of electric field is perpendicular to their equipotential surface. So, the direction of electric field is along *X*-axis as its length should be perpendicular to equipotential surface lying in *YZ*-plane. (1)

(ii) Length of the dipole $= 2b$

As dipole's axis is along the *Y*-axis.

$\therefore$ Electric dipole moment, $\mathbf{p} = q(2b)\hat{\mathbf{j}}$

and electric field, $\mathbf{E} = E\,\hat{\mathbf{i}}$

$$\because\quad \tau = \mathbf{p}\times\mathbf{E} = q(2b)\hat{\mathbf{j}}\times E\,\hat{\mathbf{i}}$$
$$= +\,2qbE\,(\hat{\mathbf{j}}\times\hat{\mathbf{i}}) = 2qbE\,(-\hat{\mathbf{k}})$$

$\therefore$ Torque, $|\tau| = 2qbE$ (1)

23. We have to apply the relation between electric field (**E**) and potential difference dV as $dV = -\mathbf{E}\cdot d\mathbf{r}$

Let P be the point at a distance r from the origin O at which the electric field E due to charge $+q$ is required.

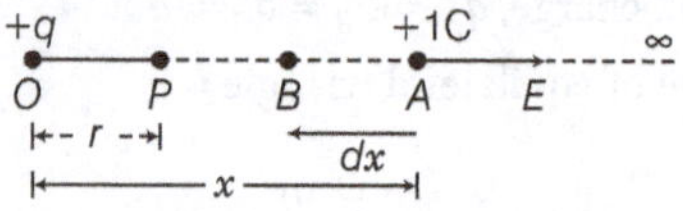

The electric potential at a point P is the amount of work done in carrying a unit positive charge from ∞ to P.

As work done is independent of the path, we choose a convenient path along the radial direction from infinity to the point P without acceleration.

Let A be an intermediate point on this path, where $OA = x$.

The electrostatic force on unit positive charge A is

$$F = \frac{1}{4\pi\varepsilon_0}\frac{q}{x^2},\ \text{along } OA \quad \text{...(i)}$$

Small work done in moving the charge through a distance dx from A to B

$$dW = \mathbf{F}\cdot\mathbf{dx} = F\,dx\cos180^\circ = -Fdx \quad [\because \cos180^\circ = -1]$$

$$dW = -Fdx \quad \text{...(ii)} \quad (1\tfrac{1}{2})$$

Total work done in moving unit positive charge from ∞ to the point P is

$$W = \int_{\infty}^{r} -Fdx = \int_{\infty}^{r} -\frac{1}{4\pi\varepsilon_0}\frac{q}{x^2}dx$$

$$= -\frac{q}{4\pi\varepsilon_0}\int_{\infty}^{r} x^{-2}\,dx = -\frac{q}{4\pi\varepsilon_0}\left[\frac{-1}{x}\right]_{\infty}^{r}$$

$$= \frac{q}{4\pi\varepsilon_0}\left[\frac{1}{r} - \frac{1}{\infty}\right] \qquad \left[\because \int x^{-2}dx = -\frac{1}{x}\right]$$

$$W = \frac{q}{4\pi\varepsilon_{0r}} \quad \text{...(iii)}$$

From the definition of electric potential, this work is equal to the potential at point P.

$$V = \frac{q}{4\pi\varepsilon_0 r} \quad \text{... (iv)}$$

(1½)

24. Consider a cube of side b and its centre be O. The charge q is placed at each of the corners.

Side of the cube $= b$

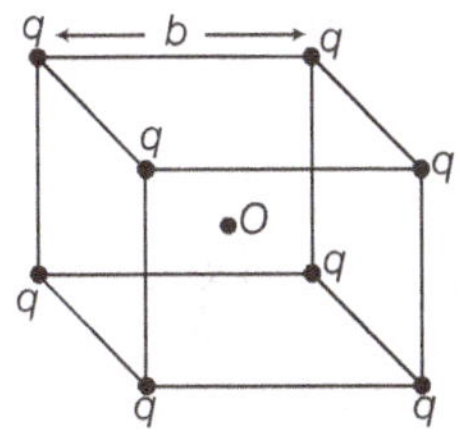

Length of the main diagonal of the cube

$$= \sqrt{b^2 + b^2 + b^2} = \sqrt{3}\,b \quad (1/2)$$

Distance of centre O from each of the vertices is

$$r = \frac{b\sqrt{3}}{2} \quad \text{...(i)} \quad (1)$$

Potential at point O due to one charge,

$$V = \frac{1}{4\pi\varepsilon_0}\cdot\frac{q}{r}$$

Potential at point O due to all charges placed at the vertices of the cube,

$$V' = 8V = \frac{8 \times 1 \times q}{4\pi\varepsilon_0 r}$$

$$= \frac{8q \times 2}{4\pi\varepsilon_0 \cdot b\sqrt{3}} \quad \text{[from Eq. (i)]}$$

$$= \frac{4q}{\sqrt{3}\pi\varepsilon_0 b} \quad (1)$$

The electric field due to one vertex is balanced by the electric field due to the opposite vertex because all charges are positive in nature. Thus, the resultant electric field at the centre O of the cube is zero. (1/2)

25. Electrostatic potential at axial point of an electric dipole Let the electric dipole AB is placed in a medium of K dielectric constant. The electric dipole has $+q$ and $-q$ charge separated by the distance d.

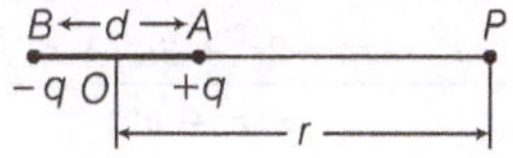

We have to determine the electric potential at point P, situated at distance r from the centre of the electric dipole.

The distance of point P from centre of electric dipole from $+q$ is charge $\left(r - \frac{d}{2}\right)$ and from charge $-q$, $\left(r + \frac{d}{2}\right)$, then potential due to $+q$ charge at point P,

$$V_1 = \frac{1}{4\pi\varepsilon_0 K}\left[\frac{q}{r - (d/2)}\right] \quad \text{...(i)}$$

Potential due to $-q$ charge at point P,

$$V_2 = \frac{1}{4\pi\varepsilon_0 K}\left[\frac{-q}{r + (d/2)}\right] \quad \text{...(ii)}$$

$\therefore$ Resultant potential at point P, $V = V_1 + V_2$

$$V = \frac{q}{4\pi\varepsilon_0 K}\left[\frac{1}{r - (d/2)} - \frac{1}{r + (d/2)}\right]$$

$$= \frac{1}{4\pi\varepsilon_0 K}\left[\frac{q \times d}{r^2 - (d/2)^2}\right]$$

If the dipole moment is p, then $p = q \times d$

$$V = \frac{1}{4\pi\varepsilon_0 K}\left[\frac{p}{r^2 - (d/2)^2}\right]$$

If $\frac{d}{2} << r$, then neglecting $\left(\frac{d}{2}\right)^2$ in comparison to r^2,

$$V = \frac{1}{4\pi\varepsilon_0 K}\cdot\left(\frac{p}{r^2}\right)$$

If the electric dipole is situated in air or vacuum, then $K = 1$,

$$V = \frac{1}{4\pi\varepsilon_0}\left[\frac{p}{r^2}\right]$$

(ii) Refer to text on page 61 (Equipotential surfaces in different cases, case IV).

26. Given, $AC = 2a$, $BP = r$

$AP = r + a$ and $PC = r - a$

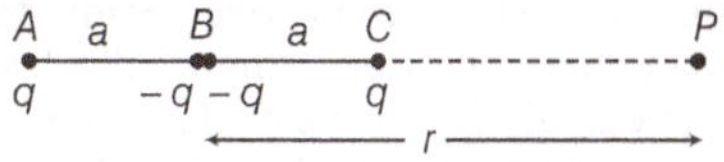

The potential at P is V.

$\therefore$ $V =$ Potential at P due to A + Potential at P due to B + Potential at P due to C

$$= \frac{1}{4\pi\varepsilon_0}\left[\frac{q}{AP} - \frac{2q}{BP} + \frac{q}{CP}\right]$$

$$= \frac{1}{4\pi\varepsilon_0}\cdot q\left[\frac{1}{(r+a)} - \frac{2}{r} + \frac{1}{(r-a)}\right]$$

$$= \frac{q}{4\pi\varepsilon_0}\left[\frac{r(r-a)-2(r+a)(r-a)+r(r+a)}{r(r+a)(r-a)}\right]$$

$$= \frac{q}{4\pi\varepsilon_0}\left[\frac{r^2-ra-2r^2+2a^2+r^2+ra}{r(r^2-a^2)}\right]$$

$$= \frac{q\cdot 2a^2}{4\pi\varepsilon_0\, r(r^2-a^2)} = \frac{q\cdot 2a^2}{4\pi\varepsilon_0\cdot r\cdot r^2\left(1-\frac{a^2}{r^2}\right)} \quad (1)$$

According to the question,

If $\frac{r}{a} >> 1, a << r.$

Therefore, $V = \frac{q\cdot 2a^2}{4\pi\varepsilon_0\cdot r^3}$

$$V \propto \frac{1}{r^3} \quad (1)$$

As, we know that electric potential at a point on axial line due to an electric dipole is

$$V \propto \frac{1}{r^2}$$

In case of electric monopole, $V \propto \frac{1}{r}$.

Then, we conclude that for larger r, the electric potential due to a quadrupole is inversely proportional to the cube of the distance r, while due to an electric dipole, it is inversely proportional to the square of r and inversely proportional to the distance r for a monopole. (1)

27. (i) Refer to text on page 61 (Equipotential surfaces in different cases, case I). (1)

(ii) Equipotential surfaces when the electric field is in Z-direction.

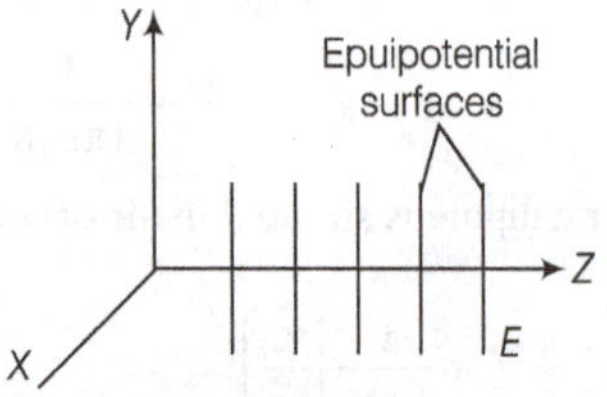

The equipotential surfaces due to a single point charge is represented by concentric spherical shells of increasing radius, so they are not equidistant. (1)

(iii) No, the electric field does not exist tangentially to an equipotential surface because no work done in moving a charge from one point to other on equipotential surface. This indicates that the component of electric field along the equipotential surface is zero. Hence, the equipotential surface is perpendicular to field lines. (1)

28. Let the three charges be located as shown in the figure.

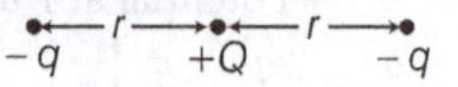

The potential energy of the system be

$$U = \frac{1}{4\pi\varepsilon_0}\cdot\frac{(-q)Q}{r} + \frac{1}{4\pi\varepsilon_0}\cdot\frac{Q(-q)}{r} + \frac{1}{4\pi\varepsilon_0}\cdot\frac{(-q)(-q)}{2r} \quad (1)$$

As, $\frac{1}{4\pi\varepsilon_0}\left(\frac{-qQ}{r} - \frac{qQ}{r} + \frac{q^2}{2r}\right) = 0$ (1)

$$\Rightarrow \frac{2qQ}{r} = \frac{q^2}{2r} \Rightarrow \frac{Q}{q} = \frac{1}{4} = 1:4 \quad (1)$$

29. Refer to Solution of Q. No. 23 on page 70.

30. (i) Potential of three shells

At shell A

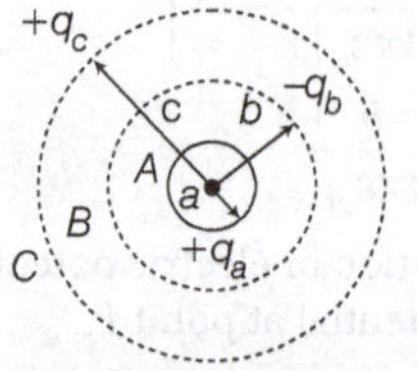

(1/2)

$$\text{Potential, } V_A = \frac{1}{4\pi\varepsilon_0}\left(\frac{q_a}{a} - \frac{q_b}{b} + \frac{q_c}{c}\right)$$

$$= \frac{1}{4\pi\varepsilon_0}\left(\frac{4\pi a^2\sigma}{a} - \frac{4\pi b^2\sigma}{b} + \frac{4\pi c^2\sigma}{c}\right)\left[\because \sigma = \frac{q}{4\pi r^2}\right]$$

$$= \frac{\sigma}{\varepsilon_0}(a-b+c) \quad (1)$$

At shell B

$$\text{Potential, } V_B = \frac{1}{4\pi\varepsilon_0}\left(\frac{q_a}{b} - \frac{q_b}{b} + \frac{q_c}{c}\right)$$

$$= \frac{1}{4\pi\varepsilon_0}\left(\frac{4\pi a^2\sigma}{b} - \frac{4\pi b^2\sigma}{b} + \frac{4\pi c^2\sigma}{c}\right)\left[\because \sigma = \frac{q}{4\pi r^2}\right]$$

$$= \frac{\sigma}{\varepsilon_0}\left(\frac{a^2-b^2}{b} + c\right) \quad (1)$$

At shell C

$$\text{Potential, } V_C = \frac{1}{4\pi\varepsilon_0}\left(\frac{q_a}{c} - \frac{q_b}{c} + \frac{q_c}{c}\right)$$

$$= \frac{1}{4\pi\varepsilon_0}\left(\frac{4\pi a^2\sigma}{c} - \frac{4\pi b^2\sigma}{c} + \frac{4\pi c^2\sigma}{c}\right)\left[\because \sigma = \frac{q}{4\pi r^2}\right]$$

$$= \frac{\sigma}{\varepsilon_0}\left(\frac{a^2-b^2+c^2}{c}\right) \quad (1)$$

(ii) Relation between the radii

Now, $V_A = V_C$ (given)

$$\frac{\sigma}{\varepsilon_0}(a-b+c) = \frac{\sigma}{\varepsilon_0}\frac{(a^2-b^2+c^2)}{c}$$

$$a-b+c = \frac{a^2-b^2+c^2}{c}$$

$$= \frac{a^2-b^2}{c} + c$$

$$c(a-b) = a^2-b^2$$

$$\Rightarrow c = a+b \quad [\because (a^2-b^2) = (a-b)(a+b)] \quad (1\tfrac{1}{2})$$

31. Radius of sphere, $A = R$

Surface charge density on sphere, $A = \sigma$

Radius of sphere, $B = 2R$

Surface charge density on sphere, $B = \sigma$

Before contact, the charge on sphere A is

$Q_1 =$ Surface charge density × Surface area

$\Rightarrow \quad Q_1 = \sigma \cdot 4\pi R^2 \qquad \text{...(i)} \quad (1/2)$

Before contact, the charge on sphere B is

$Q_2 =$ Surface charge density × Surface area

$Q_2 = \sigma \cdot 4\pi (2R)^2 = \sigma \cdot 16\pi R^2 \qquad \text{...(ii)} \quad (1/2)$

Let after the contact, the charge on A be Q_1' and the charge on B be Q_2'.

According to the conservation of charge, the charge before contact is equal to charge after contact. (1/2)

$$Q_1' + Q_2' = Q_1 + Q_2$$

Now, from Eqs. (i) and (ii), we get

$$Q_1' + Q_2' = 4\pi R^2\sigma + 16\pi R^2\sigma$$

$$= 20\pi R^2\sigma \qquad \text{...(iii)} \quad (1/2)$$

As they are in contact. So, they have same potential.

Potential on sphere A is $V_A = \frac{1}{4\pi\varepsilon_0} \cdot \frac{Q_1'}{R}$

Potential on sphere B is $V_B = \frac{1}{4\pi\varepsilon_0} \cdot \frac{Q_2'}{2R}$

So, $\quad V_A = V_B$

$$\Rightarrow \quad \frac{1}{4\pi\varepsilon_0} \cdot \frac{Q_1'}{R} = \frac{1}{4\pi\varepsilon_0} \cdot \frac{Q_2'}{2R}$$

$$\Rightarrow \quad \frac{Q_1'}{R} = \frac{Q_2'}{2R} \qquad (1)$$

$$\Rightarrow \quad 2Q_1' = Q_2' \qquad \text{...(iv)}$$

Putting the value of Q_2' in Eq. (iii), we get

$$Q_1' + 2Q_1' = 20\pi R^2\sigma$$

$$\Rightarrow \quad 3Q_1' = 20\pi R^2\sigma$$

$$\Rightarrow \quad Q_1' = \frac{20}{3}\pi R^2\sigma$$

and $\quad Q_2' = \frac{40}{3}\pi R^2\sigma \qquad$ [from Eq. (iv)] (1)

Let the new charge densities be σ_1 and σ_2.

$$\sigma_1 = \frac{Q_1'}{4\pi R^2} = \frac{20\,\pi\, R^2\sigma}{3 \times 4\pi R^2} = \frac{5}{3}\sigma$$

$$\sigma_2 = \frac{Q_2'}{4\pi(2R)^2}$$

$$= \frac{40\pi R^2\sigma}{3 \times 4\pi \times 4 R^2} = \frac{40\sigma}{16 \times 3}$$

$$\sigma_2 = \frac{10\sigma}{4 \times 3} = \frac{5}{6}\sigma$$

Thus, the surface charge densities on spheres after contact are $\frac{5}{3}\sigma$ and $\frac{5}{6}\sigma$. (1)

32. This circular surface acts as equipotential surface. Hence, work done in moving the 2 C charge from A to B,

$$W_{A \to B} = (2\text{C})(V_{AB})$$

$$= (2\text{C})(V_B - V_A) = 0 \qquad [\because V_B = V_A]$$

33. Work done, $W = q \times \Delta V$

But $\Delta V = 0$ as the two diagonally opposite points are at the same potential due to 10μC charge. (1)

$\therefore \quad W = 2\mu\text{C} \times 0 = 0$

Work done, $W = 0$ (1)

34. Charge q_O at origin $O = 8\text{ mC} = 8 \times 10^{-3}\text{C}$

Charge q_P at point $P = -2 \times 10^{-9}$ C

Distance $\quad OP = r_P = 3\text{ cm} = 0.03\text{ m}$

Distance, $OQ = r_Q = 4\text{ cm} = 0.04\text{ m}$

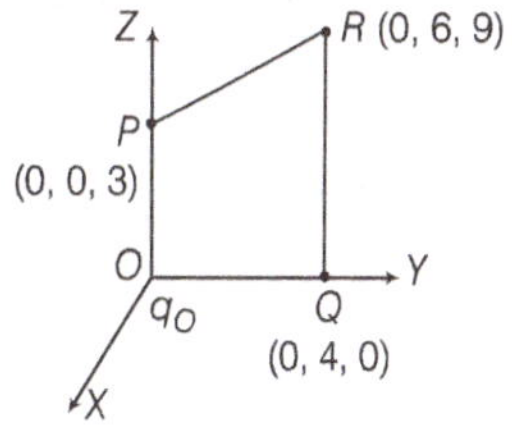

(1/2)

Work done in bringing the charge q_P from P to Q

$= q \times$ potential difference between Q and P

$W_{PQ} = q\,(V_Q - V_P)$ (1)

$$= -2 \times 10^{-9}\left(\frac{1}{4\pi\varepsilon_0} \cdot \frac{q_O}{OQ} - \frac{1}{4\pi\varepsilon_0} \cdot \frac{q_O}{OP}\right)$$

$$= -2 \times 10^{-9}\left(\frac{9\times 10^9 \times 8\times10^{-3}}{0.04} - \frac{9\times 10^9 \times 8\times 10^{-3}}{0.03}\right)$$

$$= \frac{18 \times 8 \times 10^{-3} \times 0.01}{0.0012} = 1.2\text{ J}$$

Thus, the work done in bringing the charge of -2×10^{-9}C from P to Q is 1.2 J. (1½)

35. Given, $\quad r = 0.1\text{ m}, V = +50\text{ V}$ and $q = ?$

As, $\quad V = \frac{1}{4\pi\varepsilon_0} \cdot \frac{q}{r}$ (1/2)

$$\Rightarrow \quad 50 = 9\times 10^9 \times \frac{q}{01}$$

$$\therefore \quad q = \frac{50 \times 01}{9 \times 10^9} = 5.6\times10^{-10}\text{C} \qquad (1)$$

As, V is positive, therefore, q must be positive. (1/2)

36. Potential at the centre,

$$V = \frac{1}{4\pi\varepsilon_0}\left(\frac{q}{r}\right) = 9\times10^9 \times 10^{-8} \times \frac{60}{360} \times 2\pi r \qquad (1)$$

$$= 9 \times 10 \times \frac{2 \times 3.14 \times 2}{6} = 188.4\text{ V} \qquad (1)$$

37. Refer to Example 6 on page 58.

Ans. At 6 cm from charge -3×10^{-8} C.

38. *ABCDEF* is a regular hexagon of side 10 cm each. At each corner, the charge $q = 5\,\mu C$ is placed. *O* is the centre of the hexagon as shown.

Given, $AB = BC = CD = DE = EF = FA = 10$ cm

As, the hexagon has six equilateral triangles, so the distance of centre *O* from every vertex is 10 cm.

i.e. $OA = OB = OC = OD = OE = OF = 10$ cm

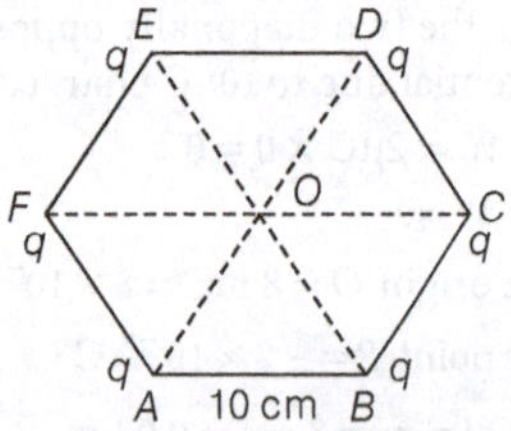

∴ Potential at point O = Sum of potentials at centre O due to individual point charge

i.e. $V_O = V_A + V_B + V_C + V_D + V_E + V_F$ (1/2)

$$= \frac{1}{4\pi\varepsilon_0}\cdot\left[\frac{q}{OA}+\frac{q}{OB}+\frac{q}{OC}+\frac{q}{OD}+\frac{q}{OE}+\frac{q}{OF}\right]$$

$$\left[\because V = \frac{1}{4\pi\varepsilon_0}\cdot\frac{q}{r}\right] \quad (1)$$

Putting the values, we get

$$V_O = 9\times10^9\left[\frac{5\times10^{-6}}{10\times10^{-2}}+\frac{5\times10^{-6}}{10\times10^{-2}}+\frac{5\times10^{-6}}{10\times10^{-2}}+\frac{5\times10^{-6}}{10\times10^{-2}}+\frac{5\times10^{-6}}{10\times10^{-2}}+\frac{5\times10^{-6}}{10\times10^{-2}}\right]$$

$$= 9\times10^9\times\frac{6\times10^{-6}\times5}{10\times10^{-2}} = 27\times10^5 = 2.7\times10^6 \text{ V}$$ (1/2)

39. Given, charge on particle, $q = 1.6\times10^{-19}$ C

Distance between the plates, $d = 10\text{cm} = 0.1$ m

Potential difference, $V = 4000$V

Electric field, $E = \frac{V}{d} = \frac{4000}{0.1} = 40000$ V/m

Since, charge particle is suspended in equilibrium between the plates, therefore

$$mg = qE$$

$$m = \frac{qE}{g} = \frac{1.6\times10^{-19}\times40000}{9.8}$$

$$= 6.5\times10^{-16} \text{ kg}$$

40. Surface charge density, $\sigma = 10^{-8}$ C/m^2

Potential difference of two equipotential surface,

$$dV = 5 \text{ V}$$

Let the separation between two equipotential surfaces be *dr*. Electric field intensity E due to infinite plane sheet is given by

$$E = \frac{\sigma}{\varepsilon_0}$$ (1/2)

The relation between E and V is given by

$$E = \frac{dV}{dr} \Rightarrow \frac{dV}{dr} = \frac{\sigma}{2\varepsilon_0}$$ (1/2)

$$\Rightarrow dr = \frac{2\varepsilon_0\cdot dV}{\sigma} = \frac{2\times(8.85\times10^{-12})\times5}{10^{-8}}$$

$$= 8.85\times10^{-3} \text{ m}$$ (1)

41. (i) ∵ Electric field intensity and potential difference are related as,

$$E = -\frac{\Delta V}{\Delta r} \Rightarrow \Delta V = -E\,\Delta r$$

By Pythagoras law, $AC^2 = AB^2 + BC^2$

$\Rightarrow \quad 5^2 - 3^2 = AB^2$

$\Rightarrow \quad AB = \Delta r = 4$

$\Rightarrow \quad V_A - V_C = -4E \Rightarrow V_C - V_A = 4E$ (1)

(ii) As, $V_C - V_A = 4E$, is positive.

∴ $V_C > V_A$

Potential is greater at point C than at point A, as potential decreases along the direction of electric field. (1)

42. (i) Electric field between the plates is given by

$$E = \frac{\Delta V}{\Delta x} = -\frac{(V_B - V_A)}{1\times10^{-2}} = \frac{-(0-10)}{10^{-2}} = 10^3 \text{ V/m}$$

It is directed from A to B. (1)

(ii) Work done in moving a charge from Y to Z is

$$W_{Y\text{-}Z} = q(\Delta V) = 20\times10^{-6}(V_Z - V_Y)$$

$$= 20\times10^{-6}(0-10) = -20\times10^{-5} \text{ J}$$ (1)

43. Given, $q_1 = 10$ C, $q_2 = 10$ C,

distance between charge $(a) = 3$ m

Electrostatic potential energy is given by

$$U = \frac{1}{4\pi\varepsilon_0}\times\frac{q_1q_2}{a} \quad ...(i)$$

Here, $\frac{1}{4\pi\varepsilon_0} = 9\times10^9$ (1/2)

Substituting the all values in Eq. (i), we get

$$U = 9\times10^9\times\frac{10\times10}{3} \Rightarrow U = 3\times10^{11} \text{ J}$$ (1/2)

44. From conservation of mechanical energy

Change in PE = Gain in KE

$$\Delta U = \Delta K \Rightarrow eV = \frac{1}{2}mv^2$$

where, *V* is potential difference and *e* is electronic charge, *m* is the mass and *v* is the speed of electron. (1/2)

∴ $\Delta K = eV = 1.6\times10^{-19}\times1000 = 1.6\times10^{-16}$ J (1/2)

45. Given, radius of the orbit,

$$r = 5\times10^{-11} \text{ m}$$

Charge $= +e = 1.6\times10^{-19}$ C

(i) Intensity of electric field,

$$E = \frac{1}{4\pi\,\varepsilon_0}\frac{q}{r^2}$$

$$= 9\times10^9 \times \frac{1.6\times10^{-19}}{(5\times10^{-11})^2} = 5.76\times10^{10}\ \text{NC}^{-1}$$ (1)

(ii) Electrostatic potential energy of the system

$$U = \frac{1}{4\pi\varepsilon_0}\frac{q_1q_2}{r}$$

$$= \frac{9\times10^9\times1.6\times10^{-19}\times(-)1.6\times10^{-19}}{5\times10^{-11}}$$

$$= -4.608\times10^{-18}\ \text{J}$$ (1)

46. Potential energy (PE) of a system of two charges q_1 and q_2 separated by r is $U = \frac{1}{4\pi\,\varepsilon_0}\cdot\frac{q_1q_2}{r}$ (1/2)

For a system of three charges q_1, q_2 and q_3 the total potential energy U is

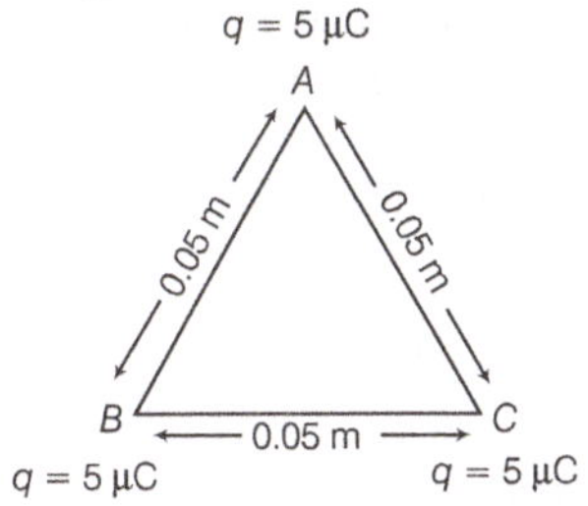

(1/2)

$$U = U_{AB} + U_{BC} + U_{CA}$$

$$= \frac{1}{4\pi\,\varepsilon_0}\left(\frac{q_1q_2}{r_{12}} + \frac{q_2q_3}{r_{23}} + \frac{q_1q_3}{r_{13}}\right) = \frac{1}{4\pi\,\varepsilon_0}\cdot3\frac{q^2}{r}$$

$[\because r_{12} = r_{23} = r_{13} = r$ and $q_1 = q_2 = q_3 = q]$

$$= 9\times10^9\times\frac{5\times10^{-6}\times5\times10^{-6}}{5\times10^{-2}}\times3 = 13.5\ \text{J}$$ (2)

47. We have to find electrostatic potential energy corresponding to each pair of charge. Consider the diagram, total electrostatic potential energy of the system,

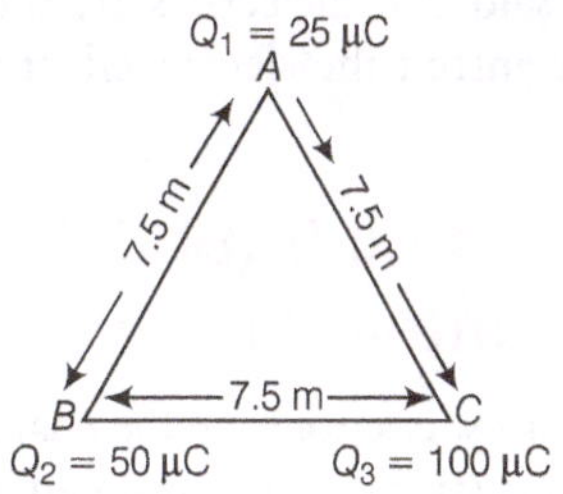

(2)

$$U = U_{AB} + U_{BC} + U_{CA}$$

$$= \frac{1}{4\pi\varepsilon_0}\frac{Q_1Q_2}{AB} + \frac{1}{4\pi\varepsilon_0}\frac{Q_2Q_3}{BC} + \frac{1}{4\pi\varepsilon_0}\frac{Q_3Q_1}{CA}$$

$$= \frac{1}{4\pi\varepsilon_0}\left(\frac{Q_1Q_2}{AB} + \frac{Q_2Q_3}{BC} + \frac{Q_3Q_1}{CA}\right)$$ (1)

$$= 9\times10^9\left(\frac{25\times50\times10^{-12}}{7.5} + \frac{50\times100\times10^{-12}}{7.5} + \frac{100\times25\times10^{-12}}{7.5}\right)$$

$$= \frac{9\times10^9\times10^{-12}}{7.5}\times25\times50[1+4+2]$$

$$= \frac{9\times2}{15}\times25\times5\times7\times10^{-2} = \frac{21\times5}{10} = 10.5\ \text{J}$$ (2)

TOPIC 02 Dielectric and Capacitance

In this topic, we are going to learn about characteristic properties of conductors and insulators. Also we will go through the concepts of capacitors and their combinations.

Conductors and Insulators

Electrically, most of the materials can be placed in one of the two classes: Conductors and insulators.

Conductors

Conductors are the materials through which electric charge can flow easily. Most of the metals are conductors of electric charge. Silver is the best conductor of electric charge. Under electrostatic conditions, the conductors have following properties

(i) Inside a conductor, electrostatic field is zero.

(ii) At the surface of a charged conductor, electrostatic field must be normal to the surface at every point.

(iii) The interior of the conductor can have no excess charge in the static situation.

(iv) Electrostatic potential is constant throughout the volume of the conductor and has the same value (as inside) on its surface.

(v) Surface charge density of a conductor could be different at different points.

Insulators

Insulators are the materials through which electric charge cannot flow e.g. glass, rubber, wood, etc. Insulators are also called dielectrics, when an electric field is applied, induced charges appear on the surface of the dielectric. Hence, it can be said that dielectrics are the insulating materials which transmit the electric effect without conducting.

Free Charges and Bound Charges Inside the Conductor

In metallic conductors, electrons are the charge carriers. In a metal, the outer (valence) electrons part away from their atoms and are free to move, these electrons are called **free electrons** or **conduction electrons**. The electrical conductivity of a material depends upon the number of free electrons present in it. Materials which have high number of free electrons are good conductors and which have less number of free electrons are bad conductors. When an electron leaves an atom, atom becomes positively charged ion. The positively charged ions and bound electrons remain held in their fixed positions and are called **bound charges**.

Dielectrics

Dielectrics (or insulators) are non-conducting substances. In contrast to conductors, they have no (or negligible number of) free charges or charge carriers.

Dielectric Constant (K)

The ratio of the strength of the applied electric field to the strength of the reduced value of the electric field on placing the dielectric between the two plates is called the dielectric constant of the dielectric medium.

It is also known as **relative permittivity** or **specific inductive capacity** and is denoted by K(or ε_r). Therefore, dielectric constant of a dielectric medium is given by

$$\boxed{K = \frac{E_0}{E}}$$

Note The value of K is always greater than 1.

Polarisation (P)

The induced dipole moment developed per unit volume in a dielectric slab on placing it in an electric field is called polarisation. It is denoted by P. If p is induced dipole moment acquired by an atom of the dielectric and N is the number of atoms per unit volume, then polarisation is given by $\boxed{P = Np}$

The induced dipole moment (p) acquired by the atom is found to be directly proportional to the reduced value of electric field (E) and is given by

$$\boxed{p = \alpha \varepsilon_0 E}$$

where, α is constant of proportionality and is called **atomic polarisability.**

SI unit of polarisation P is Cm^{-2}.

Its dimensional formula is $[L^{-2}T^1A^1]$.

Dielectrics in Electric Field

In a dielectric under the effect of an external field, a net dipole moment is induced in the dielectric. Due to molecular dipole moments, a net charge appears on the surface of the dielectric.

These induced charges (of densities $-\sigma_p$ and and $+\sigma_p$) produce a field opposing the external field. Induced field is lesser in magnitude than the external field. So, field inside the dielectric gets reduced.

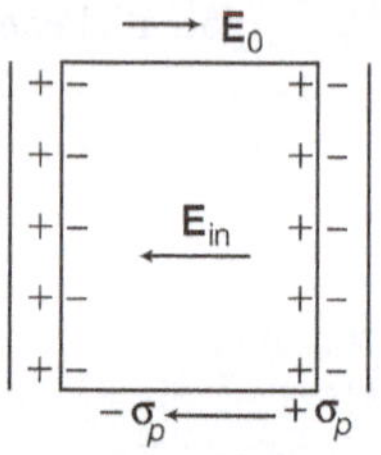

Polarised dielectric slab

$$E = |E_0| - |E_{in}|$$

where, E = resultant electric field in the dielectric,

E_0 = external electric field between two plates

and E_{in} = electric field inside the dielectric.

The reduction in electric field from E_0 to E causes a reduction in the potential difference between the plates of capacitor. If V_0 and V be the potential difference without dielectric and with dielectric completely filling the space between the plates, then $\dfrac{E_0}{E} = \dfrac{V_0}{V}$

But $$\frac{E_0}{E} = K$$

$$\therefore \quad \frac{E_0}{E} = \frac{V_0}{V} = K \text{ or } E = \frac{E_0}{K} \text{ and } V = \frac{V_0}{K}$$

Thus, the electric field within the dielectric as well as potential difference across the capacitor plates, are reduced by factor K.

A net dipole moment is developed by an external field in either case, whether a polar or non-polar dielectric.

Dielectric Strength

The maximum electric field that a dielectric can withstand without breakdown (of its insulating property), is called its dielectric strength. For air, it is about 3×10^6 V/m.

Capacitors and Capacitance

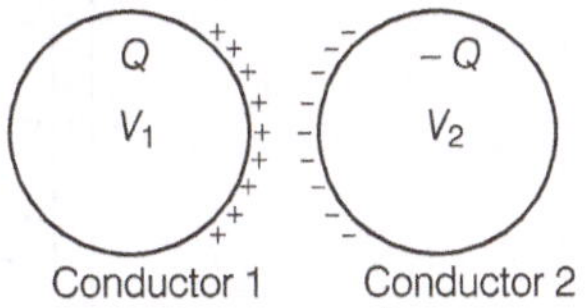

A system of two conductors

A capacitor is a system of two conductors separated by an insulating medium. The conductors have charges Q and $-Q$ with potential difference, $V = V_1 - V_2$ between them. The electric field in the region between the conductors is proportional to the charge Q.

If the potential difference (V) is the work done per unit positive charge in taking a small test charge from the conductor 2 to 1 against the field, then V is proportional to Q and the ratio $\frac{Q}{V}$ is a constant.

$$C = \frac{Q}{V}$$

The constant C is called the capacitance of the capacitor. It depends on shape, size and separation of the system of two conductors. The SI unit of capacitance is farad. Its dimensional formula is $[M^{-1}L^{-2}T^{4}A^{2}]$.

$$1 \text{ farad} = 1 \text{ coulomb/volt}$$

In practice, farad is a very big unit, the most common units are its sub-multiples.

$$1\,\mu F = 10^{-6}\text{ F}, 1\text{ nF} = 10^{-9}\text{ F}, 1\text{ pF} = 10^{-12}\text{ F}$$

Example 1 When 1×10^{12} electrons are transferred from one conductor to another, a potential difference of 10 V appears between the conductors. Find the capacitance of the two conductors.

Sol. Given, number of electrons,

$$n = 1 \times 10^{12}$$

∴ Charge transferred,

$$Q = ne = 1 \times 10^{12} \times 1.6 \times 10^{-19}$$
$$= 1.6 \times 10^{-7}\text{ C} \qquad [\because e = 1.6 \times 10^{-19}\text{ C}]$$

∴ Capacitance between two conductors,

$$C = \frac{Q}{V} = \frac{1.6 \times 10^{-7}}{10}$$
$$= 1.6 \times 10^{-8}\text{ F}$$

Parallel Plate Capacitor

Parallel plate capacitor consists of two thin conducting plates each of area A held parallel to each other at a suitable distance d. One of the plates is insulated and other is earthed. And also there is vacuum between the plates.

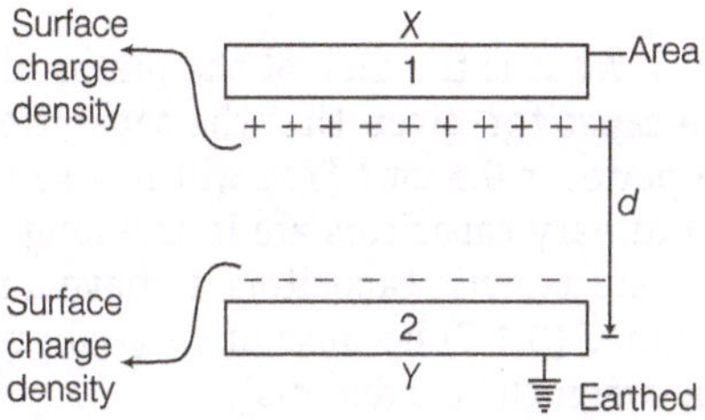

Suppose the plate X is given a charge of $+q$ coulomb. By induction, $-q$ coulomb of charge is produced on the inner surface of the plate Y and $+q$ coulomb on the outer surface. Since, the plate Y is connected to the earth, the $+q$ charge on the outer surface flows to the earth. Thus, the plates X and Y have equal and opposite charges.

Suppose the surface density of charge on each plate is σ. We know that the intensity of electric field at a point between two plane, parallel sheets of equal and opposite charges is σ/ε_0, where ε_0 is the permittivity of free space. The intensity of electric field between the plates will be given by

$$E = \frac{\sigma}{\varepsilon_0}$$

The charge on each plate is q and the area of each plate is A. Thus,

$$\sigma = \frac{q}{A} \text{ and so, } E = \frac{q}{\varepsilon_0 A} \qquad \ldots\text{(i)}$$

Now, let the potential difference between the two plates be V volt. Then, the electric field between the plates is given by

$$E = \frac{V}{d} \text{ or } V = Ed$$

Substituting the value of E from Eq. (i), we get

$$V = \frac{qd}{\varepsilon_0 A}$$

∴ Capacitance of the parallel plate capacitor is given by

$$C = \frac{q}{V} = \frac{q}{qd/\varepsilon_0 A} \text{ or } C = \frac{\varepsilon_0 A}{d}$$

where, $\varepsilon_0 = 8.85 \times 10^{-12}$ F/m

It is clear from this formula that in order to obtain high capacitance.

(i) A should be large, i.e. the plates of large area should be taken.

(ii) d should be small, i.e. the plates should be kept close to each other.

Note Capacity of an isolated spherical conductor is

$$C = 4\pi\varepsilon_0 r$$

where, r = radius of the sphere.

Example 2 What is the area of the plates of a 2F parallel plate capacitor, given that the separation between the plates is 0.5 cm? (You will realise from your answer why ordinary capacitors are in the range of μF or less. However, electrolytic capacitors do have a much larger capacitance (0.1 F) because of very minute separation between the conductors). **NCERT**

Sol. Given, capacitance, $C = 2\text{ F}$

and separation between plates, $d = 0.5\text{ cm} = 0.5 \times 10^{-2}\text{ m}$

Capacitance of a parallel plate capacitor,

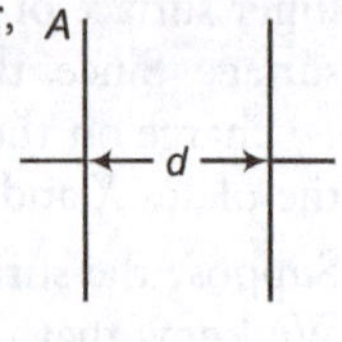

$$C = \frac{\varepsilon_0 A}{d}$$

$$\text{or } A = \frac{Cd}{\varepsilon_0} = \frac{2 \times 0.5 \times 10^{-2}}{8.854 \times 10^{-12}}$$

$$= 1.13 \times 10^{9}\text{ m}^2$$

$$= 1130\text{ km}^2$$

This area is very large, so it is not possible that the capacitance of a capacitor is too large as 2 F.

So, the capacitance of any capacitor should be the range of 2 μF.

Example 3 A parallel plate capacitor has plate area 25 cm^2 and a separation of 2 mm between the plates. The capacitor is connected to a battery of 12 V.

(i) Find the charge on the capacitor.

(ii) If the plate separation is decreased to 1.0 mm, then find the extra charge given by the battery to the positive plate.

Sol. Given, area of plate, $A = 25\text{ cm}^2 = 25 \times 10^{-4}\text{ m}^2$

Distance between the plates, $d = 2\text{ mm} = 2 \times 10^{-3}\text{ m}$

Potential difference, $V = 12\text{ V}$

(i) Charge on the capacitor, $q = CV$

$$= \frac{\varepsilon_0 A}{d} V = \frac{8.85 \times 10^{-12} \times 25 \times 10^{-4} \times 12}{2 \times 10^{-3}}$$

$$= 1.33 \times 10^{-10}\text{ C}$$

(ii) If the plate separation is decreased to half, the capacity becomes twice. Then, charge becomes twice as battery is still connected.

∴ Extra charge given by the battery $= q' - q$

$$= 2q - q = q = 1.33 \times 10^{-10}\text{ C}$$

Effect of Dielectric on Parallel Plate Capacitor

Consider a dielectric is inserted between the plates of a parallel plate capacitor and fully occupying the intervening region as shown in figure. The dielectric is polarised by the field, with surface charge densities σ_P and $-\sigma_P$.

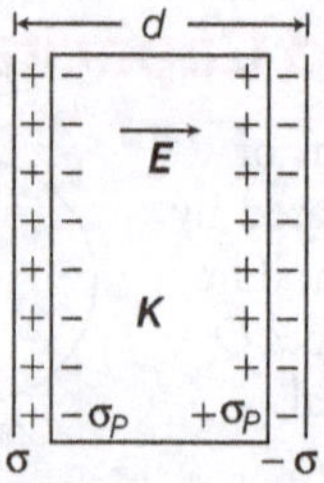

Dielectric between the plates of a capacitor

The electric field in the dielectric then corresponds to the case when the net surface charge density on the plates is $\pm(\sigma - \sigma_P)$.

So, net electric field between the plates, $E = \dfrac{\sigma - \sigma_P}{\varepsilon_0}$

[∵ dielectric is polarised in the opposite direction of external field]

∴ Potential difference between the plates,

$$V = Ed = \frac{\sigma - \sigma_P}{\varepsilon_0} d$$

For linear dielectrics, we expect σ_P to be proportional to E_0 i.e. to σ.

Thus, $(\sigma - \sigma_P)$ is proportional to σ and we can write,

$$\sigma - \sigma_P = \frac{\sigma}{K}$$

where, K is a constant characteristics of the dielectric.

Clearly, $K > 1$ [∵ $\sigma_P < \sigma$]

then, $$V = \frac{\sigma d}{\varepsilon_0 K} = \frac{qd}{A\varepsilon_0 K}$$

∴ The capacitance C with dielectric between the plates is given by

$$C = \frac{q}{V} = \frac{\varepsilon_0 KA}{d}$$

The product $\varepsilon_0 K$ is called the **permittivity of the medium** and is denoted by ε.

$$\varepsilon = \varepsilon_0 K$$

For vacuum, $K = 1$ and $\varepsilon = \varepsilon_0$, where ε_0 is called the **permittivity of the vacuum.**

The dimensionless ratio,

$$K = \frac{\varepsilon}{\varepsilon_0}$$

is called the **dielectric constant** of the substance.

Similarly, $$K = \frac{C}{C_0}$$

Thus, the dielectric constant of a substance is the factor ($K > 1$) by which the capacitance increases from its vacuum value, when the dielectric is inserted fully between the plates of a capacitor.

(i) When a dielectric slab of thickness t is inserted between the plates, then

$$\text{Capacitance, } C = \frac{\varepsilon_0 A}{d - t + \frac{t}{K}}$$

(ii) If several slabs of dielectric constants $K_1, K_2, K_3, \ldots$ and respective thicknesses $t_1, t_2, t_3, \ldots$ are placed in between the plates of a capacitor, then capacitance,

$$C = \frac{\varepsilon_0 A}{d - (t_1 + t_2 + t_3 + \ldots) + \frac{t_1}{K_1} + \frac{t_2}{K_2} + \frac{t_3}{K_3} + \ldots}$$

(iii) If a metallic slab ($K = \infty$) of thickness t is placed between the plates of capacitor, then

$$\text{Capacitance, } C = \frac{\varepsilon_0 A}{d - t}.$$

If metallic slab fills the entire space between the plates (i.e. $d = t$), then capacitance will become infinite.

Example 4 In a parallel plate capacitor with air between the plates, each plate has an area of $6 \times 10^{-3} \text{m}^2$ and the separation between the plates is 3 mm.

(i) Calculate the capacitance of the capacitor.

(ii) If this capacitor is connected to 100 V supply, what would be the charge on each plate?

(iii) How would charge on the plates be affected if a 3 mm thick mica sheet of $K = 6$ is inserted between the plates while the voltage supply remains connected?

Sol. Given, area of each plate, $A = 6 \times 10^{-3} \text{ m}^2$

Distance between the plates,

$$d = 3 \text{ mm} = 3 \times 10^{-3} \text{ m}$$

(i) Capacitance of parallel plate capacitor is given by

$$C = \frac{\varepsilon_0 A}{d} = \frac{8.85 \times 10^{-12} \times 6 \times 10^{-3}}{3 \times 10^{-3}}$$

$$\therefore \quad C = 1.77 \times 10^{-11} \text{F}$$

(ii) Charge on parallel plate capacitor is given by

$$Q = CV = 1.77 \times 10^{-11} \times 100 = 1.77 \times 10^{-9} \text{C}$$

(iii) Given, $K = 6$

Now, $C' = KC \Rightarrow \frac{Q'}{V} = \frac{KQ}{V}$

$$\therefore \quad Q' = KQ = 6 \times 1.77 \times 10^{-9}$$

$$= 10.62 \times 10^{-9} \text{C}$$

Example 5 An air-cored capacitor of plate area A and separation d has a capacity C. Two dielectric slabs are inserted between its plates in two different manners as shown. Calculate the capacitance in it.

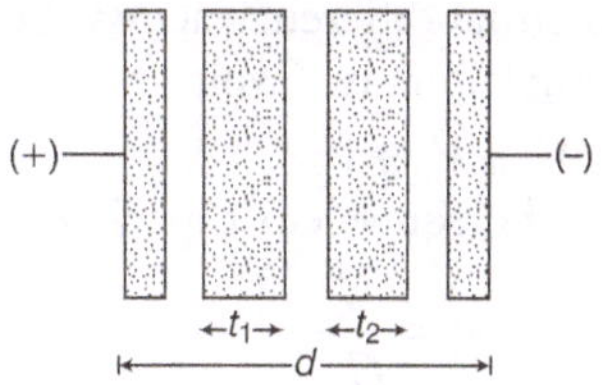

Sol. Let the charges on the plates are Q and $-Q$.

Electric field in free space is $E_0 = \frac{\sigma}{\varepsilon_0} = \frac{Q}{A\varepsilon_0}$.

Electric field in first slab is $E_1 = \frac{E_0}{K_1} = \frac{Q}{A\varepsilon_0 K_1}$.

Electric field in second slab is $E_2 = \frac{E_0}{K_2} = \frac{Q}{A\varepsilon_0 K_2}$.

The potential difference between the plates is

$$V = E_0(d - t_1 - t_2) + E_1 t_1 + E_2 t_2$$

$$\Rightarrow V = E_0\left(d - t_1 - t_2 + \frac{t_1}{K_1} + \frac{t_2}{K_2}\right)$$

$$\left[\because E_1 = \frac{E_0}{K_1} \text{ and } E_2 = \frac{E_0}{K_2}\right]$$

$$\therefore \quad V = \frac{Q}{A\varepsilon_0}\left(d - t_1 - t_2 + \frac{t_1}{K_1} + \frac{t_2}{K_2}\right)$$

$$\therefore \quad C = \frac{\varepsilon_0 A}{d - t_1 - t_2 + \frac{t_1}{K_1} + \frac{t_2}{K_2}}$$

Combination of Capacitors

In many situations, we need to combine two or more capacitors. There are two basic combinations of capacitors which can be replaced by single equivalent capacitor.

Capacitors in Series

When a potential difference (V) is applied across several capacitors connected end to end in such a way that, sum of potential differences across all the capacitors is equal to the applied potential difference V, then these capacitors are said to be connected in series.

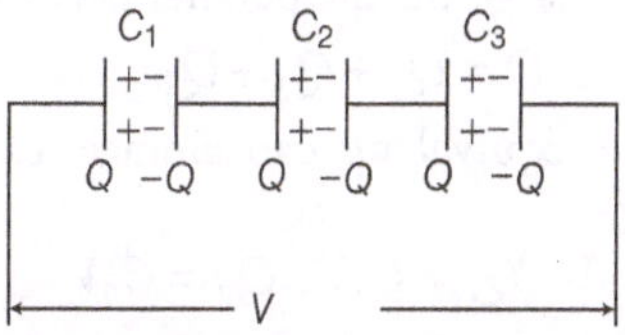

Series combination of capacitors

The potential difference across the separate capacitors are given by

$$V_1 = \frac{Q}{C_1}, V_2 = \frac{Q}{C_2} \text{ and } V_3 = \frac{Q}{C_3}$$

However, the potential difference across the series combination of capacitors is V volt

where, $\quad V = V_1 + V_2 + V_3 \quad \ldots\text{(i)}$

Let C_S represents the equivalent capacitance, then

$$V = \frac{Q}{C_S} \quad \ldots\text{(ii)}$$

Combining Eqs. (i) and (ii), we get

$$\frac{Q}{C_S} = \frac{Q}{C_1} + \frac{Q}{C_2} + \frac{Q}{C_3} \Rightarrow \frac{1}{C_S} = \frac{1}{C_1} + \frac{1}{C_2} + \frac{1}{C_3}$$

The equivalent capacitance of n capacitors connected in series is equal to the sum of the reciprocals of individual capacitances of the capacitors.

Mathematically, it is expressed as,

$$\boxed{\frac{1}{C_{\text{eq}}} = \frac{1}{C_1} + \frac{1}{C_2} + \frac{1}{C_3} + \ldots + \frac{1}{C_n}}$$

All the capacitors connected in series have same amount of charge, but potential differences between their plates are inversely proportional to their capacitances. This combination is used when a high voltage is to be divided on several capacitors. Here, capacitor with minimum capacitance has maximum potential difference between the plates.

Capacitors in Parallel

Capacitors are said to be connected in parallel when a potential difference that is applied across their combination results in the potential differnce same across each capacitor. When a potential difference (V) is applied across several capacitors connected in parallel, then the potential difference (V) exists across each capacitor. The total charge (Q) stored on the capacitor is the sum of the charges stored on all the capacitors.

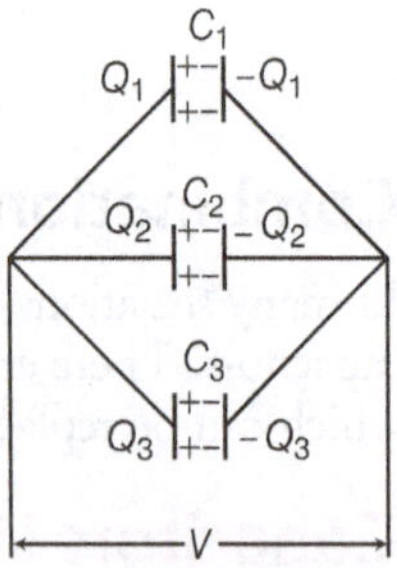

Parallel combination of capacitors

If Q is the total charge on the parallel network, then

$$Q = Q_1 + Q_2 + Q_3 \quad \ldots\text{(i)}$$

Let C_P be the equivalent capacitance of the parallel combination, then

$$Q = C_P V,\ Q_1 = C_1 V,\ Q_2 = C_2 V$$

and $\quad Q_3 = C_3 V \quad \ldots\text{(ii)}$

Combining Eqs. (i) and (ii), we obtain

$$C_P V = C_1 V + C_2 V + C_3 V$$

$$\Rightarrow \quad C_P = C_1 + C_2 + C_3$$

The equivalent capacitance of n number of capacitors in parallel is equal to the algebraic sum of the individual capacitances of the capacitors.

Mathematically, it is expressed as,

$$\boxed{C_{\text{eq}} = C_1 + C_2 + C_3 + \ldots + C_n}$$

All the capacitors connected in parallel have same potential difference between their plates but the charge is distributed proportionally to their capacitances. Capacitors are combined in parallel, when we require a large capacitance at small potential.

Example 6 Three capacitors each of capacitance 9 pF are connected in series.

(i) What is the total capacitance of the combination?

(ii) What is the potential difference across each capacitor, if the combination is connected to a 120 V supply? **NCERT**

Sol. There are three capacitors each of capacitance 9 pF.

$\therefore \quad C_1 = C_2 = C_3 = 9\text{ pF}$

and voltage, $V = 120\text{ V}$

(i) The total capacitance in series combination,

$$\frac{1}{C_S} = \frac{1}{C_1} + \frac{1}{C_2} + \frac{1}{C_3} = \frac{1}{9} + \frac{1}{9} + \frac{1}{9}$$

$$\Rightarrow \quad \frac{1}{C_S} = \frac{3}{9}$$

$$\Rightarrow \quad C_S = 3\text{ pF}$$

(ii) Let the charge across the system be q and potentials across C_1, C_2 and C_3 be V_1, V_2 and V_3, respectively.

Charge, $q = C_S \cdot V = 3 \times 120 = 360\text{ pC}$

Potential difference across C_1,

$$V_1 = \frac{q}{C_1} = \frac{360}{9} = 40\text{ V}$$

Potential difference across C_2,

$$V_2 = \frac{q}{C_2} = \frac{360}{9} = 40\text{ V}$$

Potential difference across C_3,

$$V_3 = \frac{q}{C_3} = \frac{360}{9} = 40\text{ V}$$

Thus, the potential difference across each capacitor is 40 V.

Example 7 It is required to construct a 10 μF capacitor which can be connected across a 200 V battery. Capacitors of capacitance 10 μF are available but they withstand only 50 V. Design a combination which can yield the desired result.

Sol. Capacitor of $10\mu F$ can withstand only 50 V, therefore to be connected across a 200 V battery, four capacitors must be connected in series in a row. Capacitor C_1 of each row of four capacitors is

$$\frac{1}{C_1} = \frac{1}{10} + \frac{1}{10} + \frac{1}{10} + \frac{1}{10} = \frac{4}{10}$$

$$\Rightarrow \quad C_1 = \frac{10}{4} = 2.5\,\mu F$$

For a total capacity of $10\,\mu F$, four such rows of capacitors must be connected in parallel, so that

$$C_P = 4\,C_1 = 4 \times 2.5 = 10\,\mu F$$

Hence, we need 16 capacitors with 4 capacitors in series in each row and 4 such rows in parallel.

Example 8 In the circuit shown in figure, find

(i) the equivalent capacitance and

(ii) the charge stored in each capacitor.

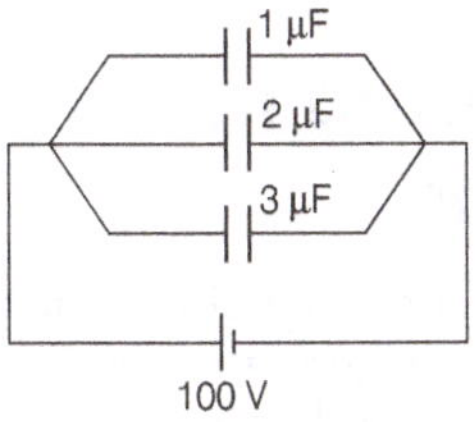

Sol. (i) The capacitors are in parallel. Hence, the equivalent capacitance is

$$C = C_1 + C_2 + C_3 = (1 + 2 + 3) = 6\,\mu F$$

(ii) Total charge drawn from the battery,

$$q = CV = 6 \times 100\,\mu C = 600\,\mu C$$

This charge will be distributed in the ratio of their capacities. Hence,

$$q_1 : q_2 : q_3 = C_1 : C_2 : C_3 = 1 : 2 : 3$$

$$\therefore \quad q_1 = \left(\frac{1}{1+2+3}\right) \times 600 = 100\,\mu C$$

$$q_2 = \left(\frac{2}{1+2+3}\right) \times 600 = 200\,\mu C$$

and $$q_3 = \left(\frac{3}{1+2+3}\right) \times 600 = 300\,\mu C$$

Example 9 Three capacitors of $1\mu F$, $2\mu F$ and $3\mu F$ are joined in series.

(i) How many times will the capacity become when they are joined in parallel ?

(ii) Determine the charge supplied by the battery of 100 V to the maximum resultant capacitor among both the arrangements.

Sol. (i) Given, $C_1 = 1\,\mu F$, $C_2 = 2\mu F$, $C_3 = 3\,\mu F$

The combined capacity (C_S) in series combination is given by

$$\frac{1}{C_S} = \frac{1}{C_1} + \frac{1}{C_2} + \frac{1}{C_3} = \frac{1}{1} + \frac{1}{2} + \frac{1}{3} = \frac{11}{6}$$

$$\Rightarrow \quad C_S = \frac{6}{11}\,\mu F$$

The combined capacity (C_P) in parallel combination is given by

$$C_P = C_1 + C_2 + C_3 = 1 + 2 + 3 = 6\,\mu F$$

$$\Rightarrow \quad C_P = 11 C_S$$

(ii) As, $C_P > C_S$

$\therefore$ The charge supplied by 100 V battery,

$$q_p = C_P V = 6\mu F \times 100 = 6 \times 10^{-6} \times 100$$

$$\Rightarrow \quad q_p = 6 \times 10^{-4} C = 600\,\mu C$$

Example 10 Seven capacitors each of capacitance $2\,\mu F$ are connected in a configuration to obtain an effective capacitance $\frac{10}{11}\mu F$. Which of the following combinations will achieve the desired result?

(i)

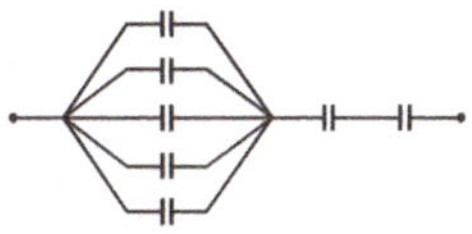

(ii)

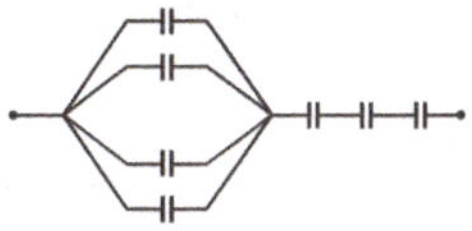

(iii)

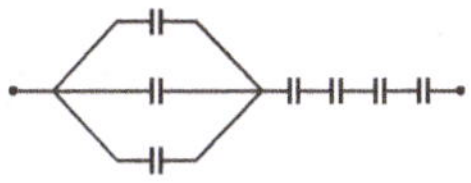

(iv)

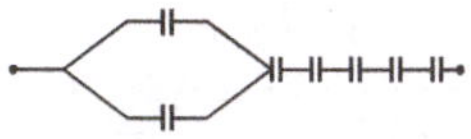

Sol. Consider the first configuration, we have

In series, $C = \dfrac{C_1 C_2}{C_1 + C_2}$

$$\therefore \quad C_{net} = \frac{(10)(1)}{10+1} = \frac{10}{11}\,\mu F$$

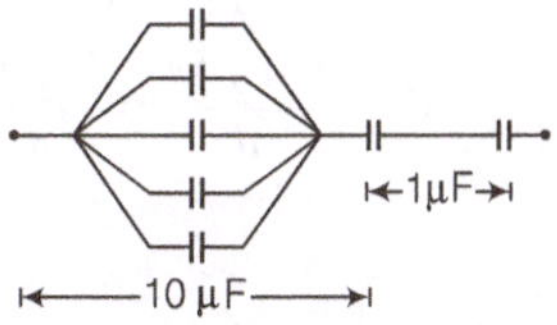

Example 11 A network of six identical capacitors, each of value C is made as shown in the figure. Find the equivalent capacitance between the points A and B.

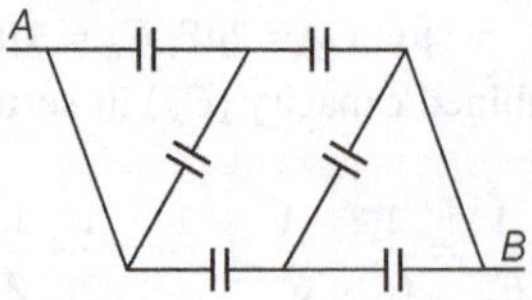

Sol. The equivalent network of the given network is shown below.

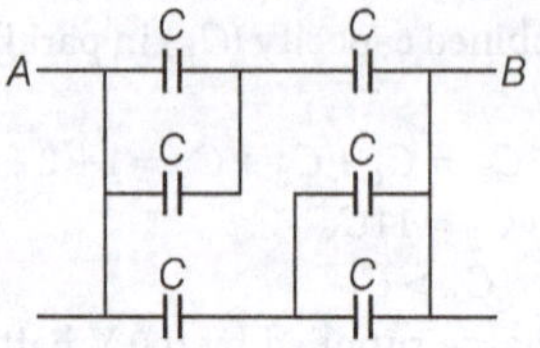

Therefore equivalent capacitance,

$$C_{eq} = [2\ C \text{ series } C] \| [C \text{ series } 2C]$$

$$= 2\left[\frac{2C \times C}{2C + C}\right] = \frac{4C}{3}$$

Example 12 Find the equivalent capacitance between A and B. Given area of each plate $= A$ and separation between plate $= d$.

(i)

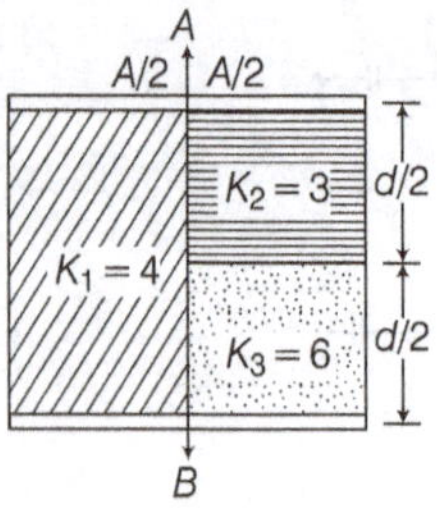

(ii)

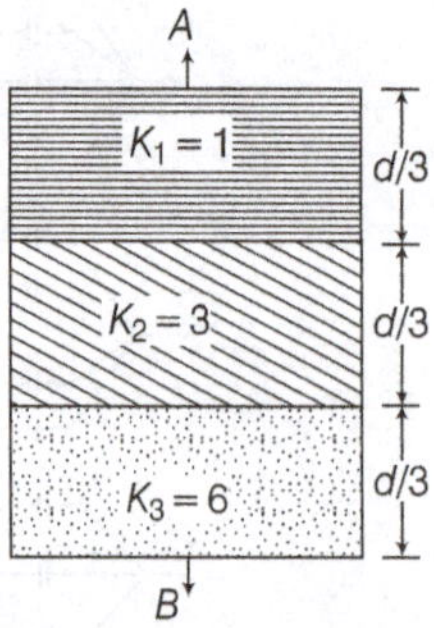

Sol. (i)

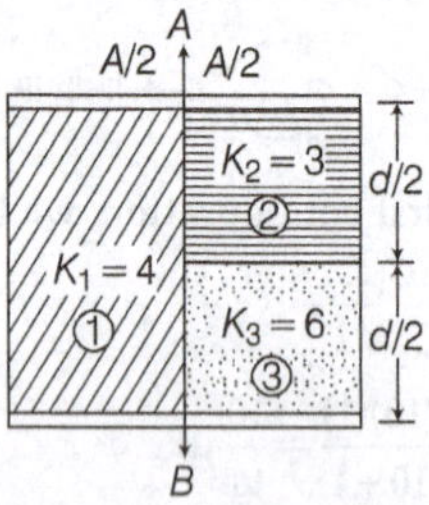

$$\text{Capacitance, } C_1 = \frac{K_1 \frac{A}{2} \varepsilon_0}{d} = \frac{4 \frac{A}{2} \varepsilon_0}{d} = \frac{2A\varepsilon_0}{d}$$

$$\left[\because C = \frac{KA\varepsilon_0}{d}\right]$$

$$\text{Capacitance, } C_2 = \frac{K_2 \frac{A}{2} \varepsilon_0}{\frac{d}{2}} = \frac{3A\varepsilon_0}{d}$$

$$\text{Capacitance, } C_3 = \frac{K_3 \frac{A}{2} \varepsilon_0}{\frac{d}{2}} = \frac{6A\varepsilon_0}{d}$$

$$C_2 \text{ and } C_3 \text{ are in series, } C' = \frac{C_2 C_3}{C_2 + C_3} = \frac{2A\varepsilon_0}{d}$$

$$C' \text{ and } C_1 \text{ are in parallel} = \frac{4A\varepsilon_0}{d}$$

(ii) $$\text{Capacitance, } C_1 = \frac{K_1 A\varepsilon_0}{d/3} = \frac{3A\varepsilon_0}{d},$$

$$C_2 = \frac{K_2 A\varepsilon_0}{d/3} = \frac{9A\varepsilon_0}{d}$$

and $$C_3 = \frac{K_3 A\varepsilon_0}{d/3} = \frac{18A\varepsilon_0}{d}$$

$\because C_1, C_2$ and C_3 are in series,

$$\frac{1}{C_{eq}} = \frac{1}{C_1} + \frac{1}{C_2} + \frac{1}{C_3}$$

$$\therefore \text{Equivalent capacitance, } C_{eq} = \frac{2A\varepsilon_0}{d}$$

Energy Stored in a Capacitor

The energy of a charged capacitor is measured by the total work done in charging the capacitor to a given potential. Let us assume that initially both the plates are uncharged. Now, we have to repeatedly move small positive charges from one plate and transfer them to the other plate.

Now, when an additional small charge (dq) is transferred from one plate to another plate, the small work done is given by $dW = V'dq = \frac{q'}{C} dq$

[$\because$ charge on plate when dq charge is transferred be q']

The total work done in transferring charge Q is given by

$$W = \int_0^Q \frac{q'}{C} dq = \frac{1}{C} \int_0^Q q'\, dq$$

$$= \frac{1}{C}\left[\frac{(q')^2}{2}\right]_0^Q = \frac{Q^2}{2C}$$

This work is stored as electrostatic potential energy U in the capacitor.

$$U = \frac{Q^2}{2C} = \frac{1}{2}QV = \frac{(CV)^2}{2C} = \frac{1}{2}CV^2 \quad [\because Q = CV]$$

The energy stored per unit volume of space in a capacitor is called energy density.

Energy density, $u = \frac{1}{2}\varepsilon_0 E^2$

Total energy stored in series combination or parallel combination of capacitors is equal to the sum of energies stored in individual capacitors.

i.e. $U = U_1 + U_2 + U_3 + \ldots$

Change in Energy on Introducing a Dielectric Slab

(i) When a dielectric slab is inserted between the plates of a charged capacitor, with battery connected to its plates. Then, the capacitance becomes K (dielectric constant) times and energy stored in the capacitor becomes KU_0.

(ii) When a dielectric slab is inserted between the plates of a charged capacitor and battery is disconnected. Then, the charge on the plates remains unchanged and energy stored in the capacitor becomes $\frac{U_0}{K}$, i.e. energy decreases.

Example 13 A capacitor of capacity 10 μF is subjected to charge by a battery of 10 V. Calculate the energy stored in the capacitor.

Sol. Given, capacity, $C = 10\,\mu\text{F} = 10 \times 10^{-6}$ F

Voltage, $V = 10$ V, energy, $E = ?$

$\therefore$ Energy stored in the capacitor, $E = \frac{1}{2}CV^2$

$$= \frac{1}{2} \times 10 \times 10^{-6} \times 10 \times 10 = 5 \times 10^{-4}\,\text{J}$$

Example 14 A parallel plate capacitor has plate area A and separation d. It is charged to a potential difference V_0. This charging battery is disconnected and the plates are pulled apart to three times the initial separation. Calculate the work required to separate the plates.

Sol. $\therefore$ Capacitance, $C = \frac{\varepsilon_0 A}{d}$

Charge on plate, $Q = CV = \frac{\varepsilon_0 A}{d} V_0$

Energy stored, $U = Q^2 / 2C$

As d is increased 3 times, so C decreases 3 times. Battery is disconnected, so Q remains same. The difference in the energy is the work done,

Change in potential energy

$$\Delta U = U_i - U_f$$

$$= \frac{Q^2}{2}\left[\frac{1}{C_i} - \frac{1}{C_f}\right] = \left(\frac{\varepsilon_0 A V_0}{d}\right)^2 \times \frac{1}{2}\left[\frac{1}{C} - \frac{1}{C/3}\right]$$

$$= -\frac{1}{2} \times \left(\frac{\varepsilon_0 A V_0}{d}\right)^2 \times \frac{2}{C} = \left(\frac{\varepsilon_0 A V_0}{d}\right) \times \frac{d}{\varepsilon_0 A V_0}$$

$$= -\frac{\varepsilon_0 A V_0}{d}$$

$\therefore$ Work done, $\Delta W = -\Delta U = \frac{\varepsilon_0 A V_0}{d}$

Example 15 A 2μF capacitor is charged as shown in the figure. Find the percentage of its stored energy dissipated after the switch S is turned to position 2.

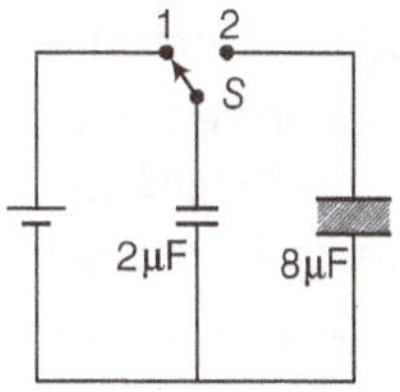

Sol. Initially, charge on the capacitor,

$$q_i = C_i V = 2V = q$$

This charge will remain constant after switch is shifted from position 1 to position 2.

$$U_i = \frac{1}{2}\frac{q^2}{C_i} = \frac{q^2}{2 \times 2} = \frac{q^2}{4}$$

$$U_f = \frac{1}{2}\frac{q^2}{C_f} = \frac{q^2}{2 \times 10} = \frac{q^2}{20}$$

$\therefore$ Energy dissipated $= U_i - U_f = \frac{q^2}{5}$

This energy dissipated $\left(= \frac{q^2}{5}\right)$ is 80% of the initial stored energy $\left(= \frac{q^2}{4}\right)$.

Common Potential

When two capacitors of different potentials are connected by a conducting wire, they share charges, i.e. charge flows from capacitor at higher potential to the capacitor at lower potential. This flow of charge continues till their potentials become equal, this equal potential is called **common potential.**

Common potential, $V = \frac{C_1 V_1 + C_2 V_2}{C_1 + C_2}$

where, C_1 and C_2 are capacities of two capacitors charged to potentials V_1 and V_2, respectively.

i.e. Common potential $= \frac{\text{Total charge}}{\text{Total capacitance}}$

$\therefore$ $C_1 V_1 + C_2 V_2 = C_1 V + C_2 V$

or $C_1 V_1 - C_1 V = C_2 V - C_2 V_2$

i.e. Charge lost by one capacitor
= Charge gained by the other capacitor

Note This is not true for potential, i.e. potential lost by one is not equal to potential gained by the other, as their capacities are different.

During sharing of charges, there is always some loss of energy, given by

$$\Delta U = \frac{C_1C_2(V_1 - V_2)^2}{2(C_1 + C_2)}$$

Example 16 A 600 pF capacitor is charged by a 200 V supply. It is then disconnected from the supply and is connected to another uncharged 600 pF capacitor. How much electrostatic energy is lost in this process? **NCERT**

Sol. Given, $C_1 = C_2 = 600\text{pF} = 600 \times 10^{-12}\text{F} = 6 \times 10^{-10}\text{F}$

$V_1 = 200$ V, $V_2 = 0$

$$\therefore \text{Energy lost} = \frac{C_1C_2(V_1 - V_2)^2}{2(C_1 + C_2)} = \frac{(6 \times 10^{-10})^2(200 - 0)^2}{2 \times 12 \times 10^{-10}}$$

$$= 6 \times 10^{-6}\,\text{J}$$

Topic Practice 2

Multiple Choice Questions

1 Mark

1. What happens when a conductor is placed in an external electric field?
(a) The free charge carriers move and charge distribution in the conductor adjusts itself in such a way that the electric field due to induced charge opposes the external field within the conductor
(b) In the static situation, the two fields cancel each other and the electrostatic field in the conductor is zero
(c) Both (a) and (b)
(d) Neither (a) nor (b)

2. When a dielectric is placed in an electric field, the electric field inside a dielectric
(a) increases (b) decreases
(c) constant (d) zero

3. The maximum electric field that a dielectric medium can withstand without break down (of its insulating property) is called its
(a) polarisation (b) capacitance
(c) dielectric strength (d) None of these

4. The graph, shows the variation of voltage V across the plates of two capacitors A and B *versus* increase of charge Q stored in them. Which of the capacitors has higher capacitance?

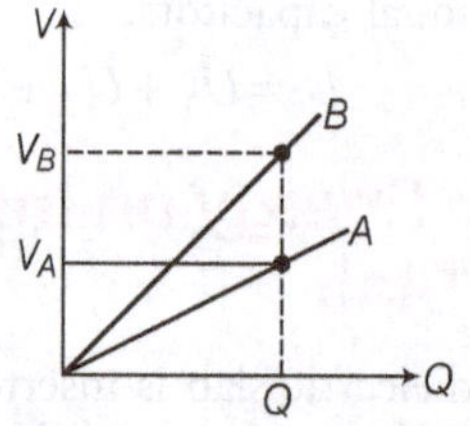

(a) Capacitor A (b) Capacitor B
(c) Both (a) and (b) (d) None of these

5. A series combination of n_1 capacitors, each of value C_1 is charged by a source of potential difference 4V. When another parallel combination of n_2 capacitors, each of value C_2, is charged by a source of potential difference V, it has the same (total) energy stored in it, as the first combination has. The value of C_2, in terms of C_1 is, then

(a) $\frac{2C_1}{n_1n_2}$ (b) $16\frac{n_1}{n_2}$ (c) $2\frac{n_2}{n_1}C_1$ (d) $\frac{16\,C_1}{n_1n_2}$

6. If the energy of a 100 μF capacitor charged to 6 kV could all be used to lift a 50 kg mass, what would be the greatest vertical height through which mass could be raised?
(a) 0.6 mm (b) 3.6 m (c) 1.2 mm (d) 12 m

Very Short Answer Type Questions

1 Mark

7. Distinguish between a dielectric and a conductor.

8. Define the dielectric constant of a medium. What is its unit?

9. The given graph shows the variation of charge q *versus* potential difference V for two capacitors C_1 and C_2. Both the capacitors have same plate separation but plate area of C_2 is greater than that C_1. Which line (A or B) corresponds to C_1 and why?

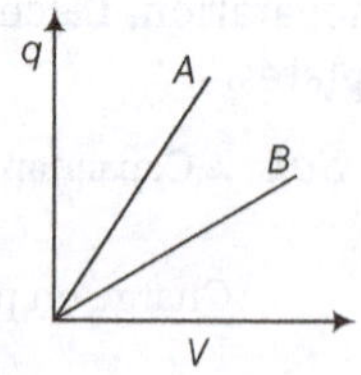

10. A metal plate is introduced between the plates of a charged parallel plate capacitor. What is its effect on the capacitance of the capacitor?

Short Answer Type I Questions

(2 Marks)

11. A slab of material of dielectric constant K has the same area as that of the plates of a parallel plate capacitor, but has the thickness $d/2$, where d is the separation between the plates. Find out the expression for its capacitance when the slab is inserted between the plates of the capacitor.

12. Two identical parallel plate (air) capacitors C_1 and C_2 have capacitance C each. The space between their plates is now filled with dielectrics as shown in the figure. If the two capacitors still have equal capacitance, then obtain the relation between dielectric constants K, K_1 and K_2.

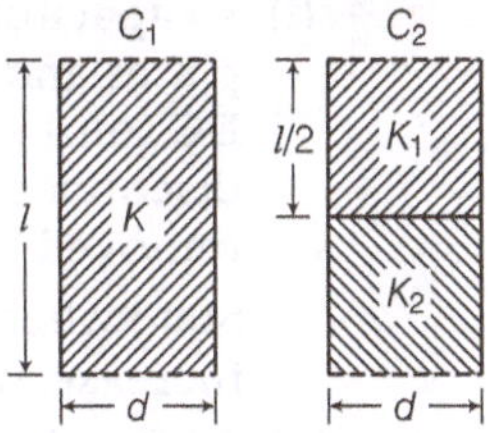

13. Figure shows a sheet of aluminium foil of negligible thickness placed between the plates of a capacitor. How will its capacitance be affected, if

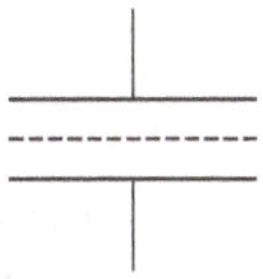

(i) the foil is electrically insulated?

(ii) the foil is connected to the upper plate with a conducting wire?

14. Obtain an expression for equivalent capacitance C when three capacitors having capacitance C_1, C_2 and C_3 are connected in series. **ISC 2024, 16, 12**

15. Three capacitors each of capacitance C are connected in series. Their equivalent capacitance is C_s. The same three capacitors are now connected in parallel. Their equivalent capacitance becomes C_p. Find the ratio (C_p/C_s). **ISC 2011**

16. A parallel plate capacitor of capacitance C is charged to a potential V. It is then connected to another uncharged capacitor having the same capacitance. Find out the ratio of the energy stored in the combined system to that stored initially in the single capacitor.

17. You are given an air filled parallel plate capacitor C_1. The space between its plates is now filled with slabs of dielectric constants K_1 and K_2 as shown in figure. Find the capacitance of the capacitor C_2, if area of the plates is A and distance between the plates is d. **Foreign 2011**

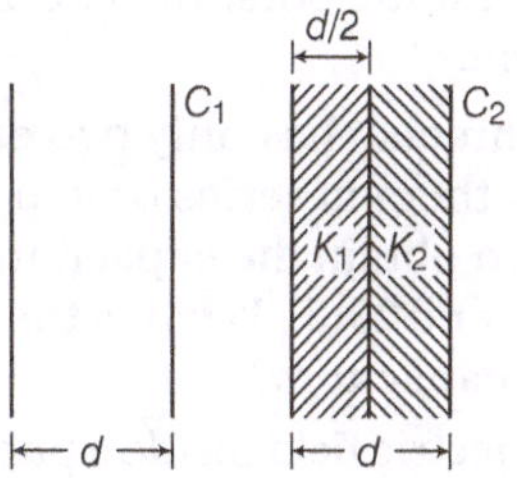

18. Two parallel plate capacitors of capacitances C_1 and C_2 such that $C_1 = 2C_2$ are connected across a battery of V volt as shown in the figure. Initially, the key (k) is kept closed to fully charge the capacitors. The key is now thrown open and a dielectric slab of dielectric constant K is inserted in the two capacitors to completely fill the gap between the plates.

Find the ratio of

(i) the net capacitance and

(ii) the energies stored in the combination before and after the introduction of the dielectric slab.

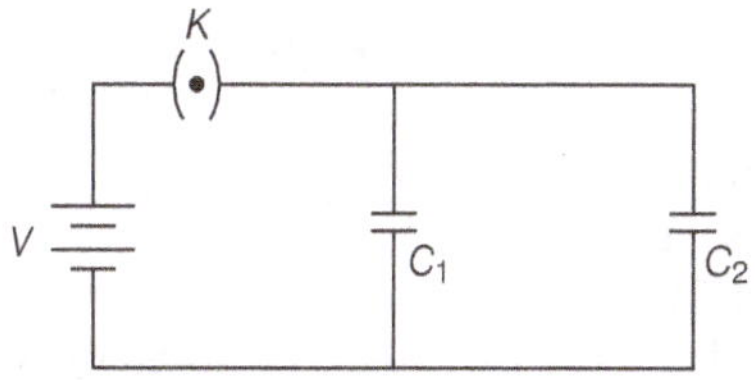

Short Answer Type II Questions

(3 Marks)

19. Deduce an expression for equivalent capacitance C when three capacitors C_1, C_2 and C_3 are connected in parallel. **ISC 2018**

20. Three capacitors of capacitance $C_1 = 3\mu F, C_2 = 6\mu F$ and $C_3 = 10\mu F$ are connected to a 10V battery as shown in the figure given below.

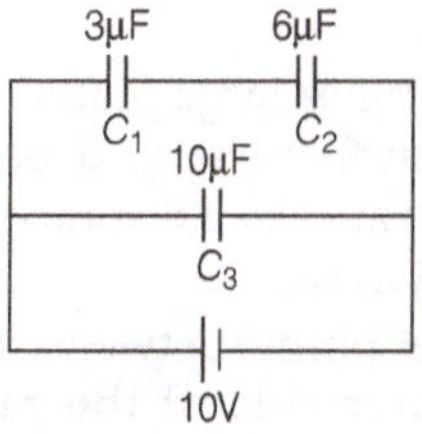

Calculate

(i) equivalent capacitance.

(ii) electrostatic potential energy stored in the system. **ISC 2019**

21. (i) A technician has only two capacitors. By using them in series or in parallel, he is able to obtain the capacitance of 4 μF, 5μF, 20 μF and 25 μF. What is the capacitance of both capacitors?

(ii) The electric field inside a parallel plate capacitor is E. Find the amount of work done in moving a charge q over a closed rectangular loop *abcda*.

22. A parallel plate capacitor is charged by a battery, which is then disconnected. A dielectric slab having dielectric constant (relative permittivity) K, is now introduced between its two plates in order to occupy the space completely.

State, in terms of K, its effect on the following

(i) the capacitance of the capacitor.

(ii) the potential difference between its plates.

(iii) the energy stored in the capacitor. **ISC 2020**

23. Two identical parallel plate capacitors A and B are connected to a battery of V volts with the switch S is closed. The switch is now opened and the free space between the plates of the capacitors is filled with a dielectric of dielectric constant K. Find the ratio of the total electrostatic energy stored in both capacitors before and after the introduction of the dielectric.

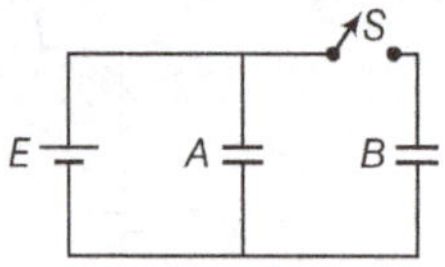

24. Show that the force on each plate of a parallel plate capacitor has a magnitude equal to $1/2QE$, where Q is the charge on the capacitor and E is the magnitude of electric field between the plates. Explain the origin of the factor 1/2. **NCERT**

Long Answer Type Questions

5 Marks

25. (i) If two similar large plates, each of area A having surface charge densities $+\sigma$ and $-\sigma$ are separated by a distance d in air, find the expression for

(a) field at points between the two plates and on outer side of the plates. Specify the direction of the field in each case.

(b) the potential difference between the plates.

(c) the capacitance of the capacitor so formed.

(ii) Two metallic spheres of radii R and $2R$ are charged, so that both of these have same surface charge density σ. If they are connected to each other with a conducting wire, in which direction will the charge flow and why?

26. (i) A capacitor has some dielectric between its plates and the capacitor is connected to a DC source. The battery is now disconnected and then the dielectric is removed.

State whether the capacitance will increase, or decreases and why?

(ii) A fully charged parallel plate capacitor is connected across an uncharged identical capacitor. Show that the energy stored in the combination is less than stored initially in the single capacitor.

Numerical Problems

27. Calculate equivalent capacitance of the circuit shown in figure given below. **ISC 2023 (2M)**

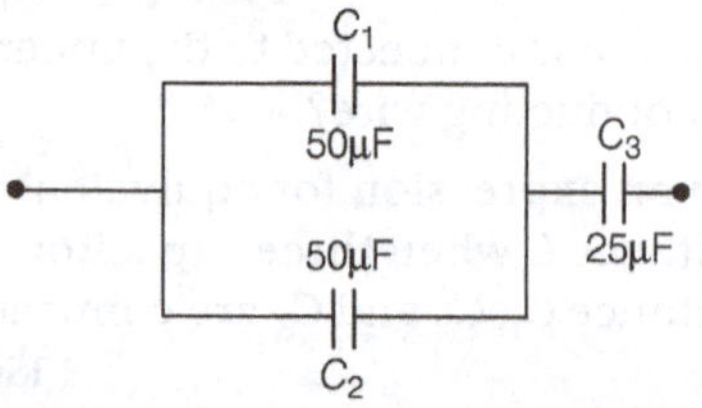

28. A capacitor of unknown capacitance is connected across a battery of V volt. The charge stored in it is 360μC. When potential across the capacitor is reduced by 120 V, the charge stored in it becomes 120 μC.

(i) Calculate the potential V and the unknown capacitance C.

(ii) What will be the charge stored in the capacitor, if the voltage applied had increased by 120 V? **(3 M)**

29. In the circuit shown below, initially K_1 is closed and K_2 is opened, what are the charges on each of the capacitors? Then K_1 was opened and K_2 was closed (order is important), what will be the charge on each capacitor now?

[Given, $C = 1\mu F$] **NCERT Exemplar (3M)**

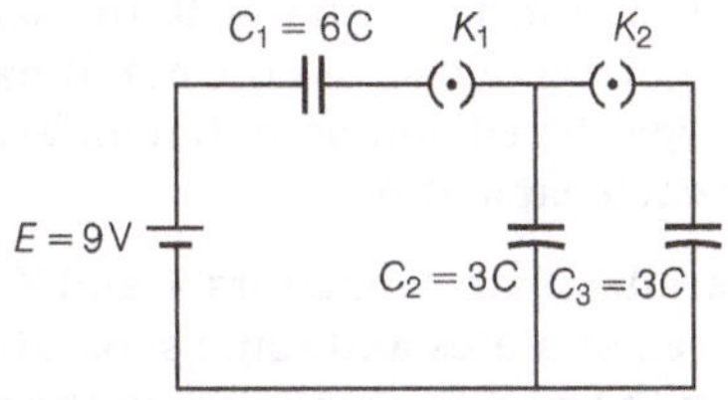

30. A spherical capacitor has an inner sphere of radius 12 cm and an outer sphere of radius 13 cm. The outer sphere is earthed and the inner sphere is given a charge of 2.5 μC. The space between the concentric spheres is filled with a liquid of dielectric constant 32.

(i) Determine the capacitance of the capacitor.

(ii) What is the potential of the inner sphere?

(iii) Compare the capacitance of this capacitor with that of an isolated sphere of radius 12 cm. Explain, why the later is much smaller. **NCERT (3 M)**

31. Figure shows two identical capacitors C_1 and C_2, each of 2μF capacitance, connected to a battery of 5 V. Initially switch S is closed. After sometime, S is left open and dielectric slabs of dielectric constant $K = 5$ are inserted to fill completely the space between the plates of the two capacitors. How will the (i) charge and (ii) potential difference between the plates of the capacitors be affected after the slabs are inserted? **(3 M)**

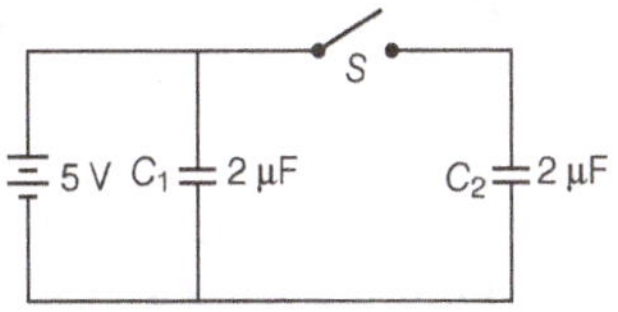

32. An isolated 16 μF parallel plate air capacitor has a potential difference of 1000 V [shown in Fig. (a)]. A dielectric slab having relative permittivity (i.e., dielectric constant) = 5 is introduced to fill the space between the two plates completely [shown in Fig. (b)].

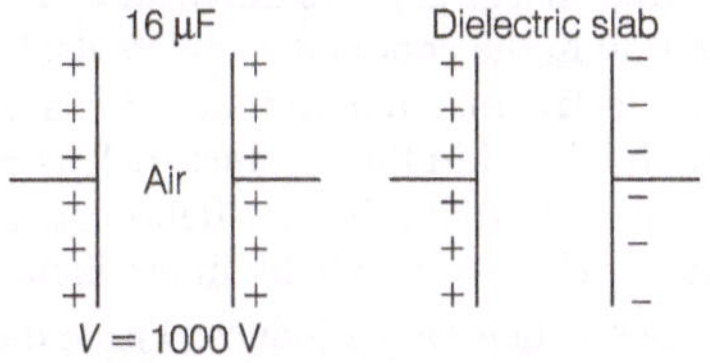

(a) (b)

Calculate

(i) the new capacitance of the capacitor.

(ii) the new potential difference between the two plates of the capacitor. **ISC 2010 (2 M)**

33. A parallel plate air capacitor has a capacitance of 5 μF. It becomes 50 μF when a dielectric medium occupies the entire space between its two plates. What is the dielectric constant of the medium? **ISC 2014 (1 M)**

34. Three capacitors $C_1 = 3\mu F$, $C_2 = 6\mu F$ and $C_3 = 10\mu F$ are connected to a 50 V battery as shown in the figure below.

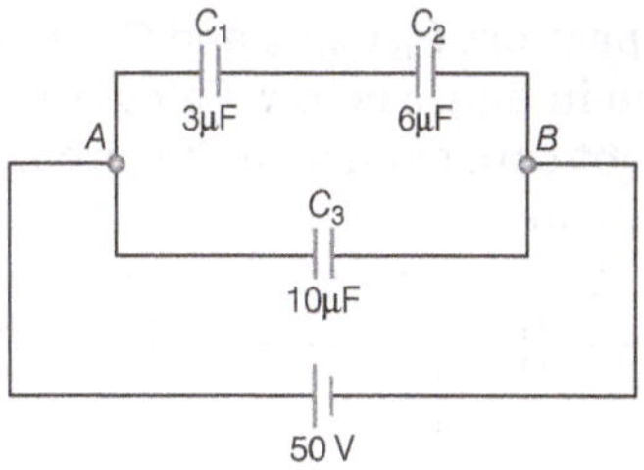

Calculate

(i) the equivalent capacitance of the circuit between points A and B.

(ii) the charge on C_1. **ISC 2017 (2 M)**

35. You are provided with 8μF capacitors. Show with the help of a diagram how you will arrange minimum number of them to get a resultant capacitance of 20 μF. **ISC 2014 (2 M)**

36. Three capacitors $C_1 = 6\mu F$, $C_2 = 12\mu F$ and $C_3 = 20\mu F$ are connected to a 100 V battery as shown in figure below.

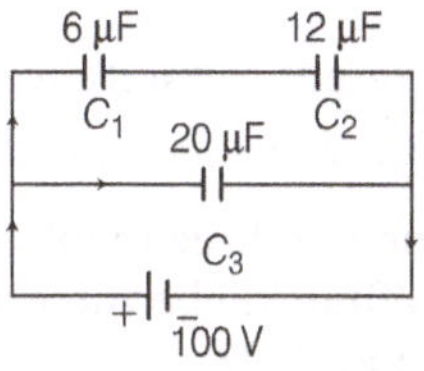

Calculate

(i) charge on each plate of capacitor C_1.

(ii) electrostatic potential energy stored in capacitor C_3. **ISC 2013 (2 M)**

37. Find the electric charge Q_1 on plates of capacitor C_1, shown in figure below.

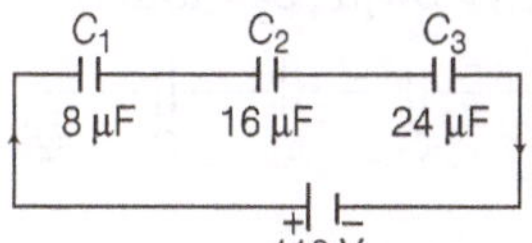

ISC 2009 (2 M)

38. Find the equivalent capacitance of the following circuit between the junctions A and B given $C_1 = C_2 = C_3 = C_4 = 10\,\mu F$ and $C_5 = 5\,\mu F$.

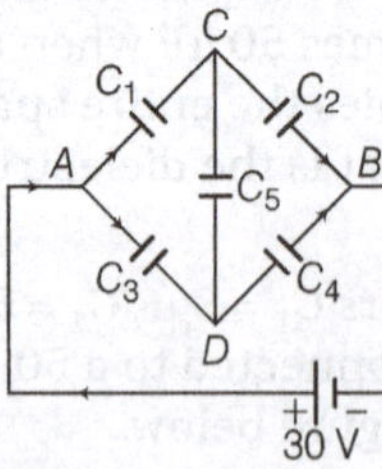

ISC 2008 (2 M)

39. Four capacitors C_1, C_2, C_3 and C_4 are connected as shown in figure below. Calculate the equivalent capacitance of the circuit between points X and Y.

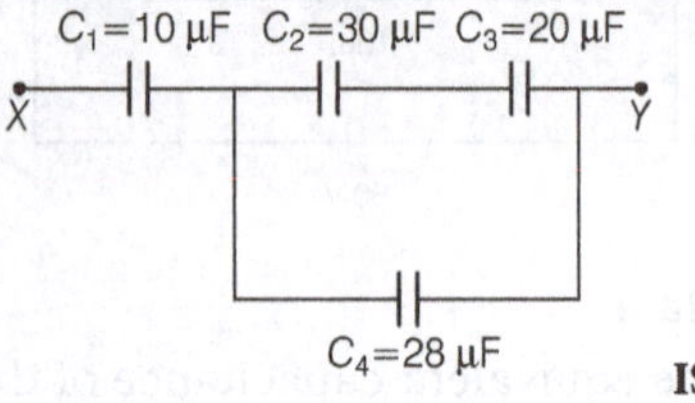

ISC 2007 (2 M)

40. A network of four capacitors each of $12\,\mu F$ capacitance is connected to a 500 V supply as shown in the figure.

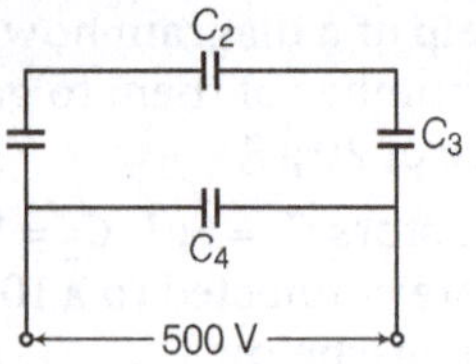

Determine

(i) the equivalent capacitance of the network

(ii) the charge on each capacitor. **(3 M)**

41. Net capacitance of three identical capacitors in series is $1\,\mu F$. What will be their net capacitance, if connected in parallel?

Find the ratio of energy stored in these two configurations, if they are both connected to the same source. **(3 M)**

42. Calculate the potential difference and the energy stored in the capacitor C_2 in the circuit shown in the figure. Given, potential at A is 90 V, $C_1 = 20\,\mu F$, $C_2 = 30\,\mu F$, $C_3 = 15\,\mu F$. **(3 M)**

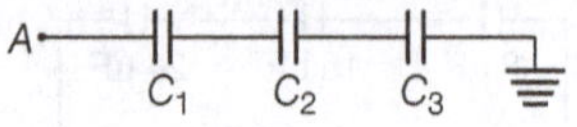

43. A 12 pF capacitor is connected to a 50 V battery. How much electrostatic energy is stored in the capacitor? If another capacitor of 6 pF is connected in series with it with the same battery connected across the combination, find the charge stored and potential difference across each capacitor. **(3 M)**

44. Two parallel plate capacitors X and Y have the same area of plates and same separation between them, X has air between the plates while Y contains a dielectric medium of $\varepsilon_r = 4$.

(i) Calculate the capacitance of each capacitor, if equivalent capacitance of the combination is $4\mu F$.

(ii) Calculate the potential difference between the plates of X and Y.

(iii) Estimate the ratio of electrostatic energy stored in X and Y. **(5 M)**

45. Two capacitors of unknown capacitances C_1 and C_2 are connected first in series and then in parallel across a battery of 100 V. If the energy stored in the two combinations is 0.045 J and 0.25 J respectively, then determine the value of C_1 and C_2. Also, calculate the charge on each capacitor in parallel combination. **(5 M)**

46. In the following arrangement of capacitors, the energy stored in the $6\,\mu F$ capacitor is E. Find the value of the following

(i) energy stored in $12\mu F$ capacitor.

(ii) energy stored in $3\mu F$ capacitor.

(iii) total energy drawn from the battery. **(5 M)**

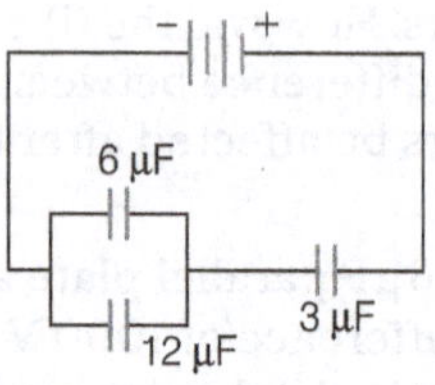

Hints & Solutions

1. (c) The free charge carriers move and charge distribution in the conductor adjusts itself in such a way that the electric field due to induced charges opposes the external field within the conductor. This happens until, in the static situation, the two fields cancel each other and the net electrostatic field in the conductor is zero.
2. (b) An electric field (E_i) is induced inside the dielectric in a direction opposite to the external field (E_0) due to polarisation. On account of this, the net electric field (E) inside the slab is less than the external field as $E = E_0 - E_i$.
3. (c) The maximum electric field that a dielectric medium can withstand without breakdown (of its insulating

property) is called its dielectric strength; for air it is about 3×10^6 Vm^{-1}.

For a separation between conductors of the order of 1 cm or so, this field corresponds to a potential difference of 3×10^4 V between the conductors. Thus, for a capacitor to store a large amount of charge without leaking, its capacitance should be high enough so that the potential difference and hence the electric field do not exceed the breakdown limits. Put differently, there is a limit to the amount of charge can be stored on a given capacitor without significant leaking.

4. (*a*) From the given graphs, find the voltages, V_A and V_B, on capacitors A and B corresponding to charge Q on each of the capacitors. Clearly,

$$V_A = \frac{Q}{C_A} \quad \text{and} \quad V_B = \frac{Q}{C_B}$$

or $$\frac{V_B}{V_A} = \frac{Q/C_B}{Q/C_A} = \frac{C_A}{C_B}$$

Since, $V_B > V_A$, $C_A > C_B$, i.e. the capacitor A has the higher capacitance.

5. (*d*) ***Case* I** When the capacitors are joined in series,

$$U_{\text{series}} = \frac{1}{2}\frac{C_1}{n_1}(4V)^2$$

***Case* II** When the capacitors are joined in parallel,

$$U_{\text{parallel}} = \frac{1}{2}(n_2 C_2)V^2$$

Given, $U_{\text{series}} = U_{\text{parallel}}$

or $$\frac{1}{2}\frac{C_1}{n_1}(4V)^2 = \frac{1}{2}(n_2 C_2)V^2 \Rightarrow C_2 = \frac{16\,C_1}{n_1 n_2}$$

6. (*b*) Energy stored in the capacitor is used in lifting the mass.

$$\therefore \quad mgh = \frac{1}{2}CV^2$$

$$\Rightarrow 50 \times 9.8 \times h = \frac{1}{2} \times 100 \times 10^{-6} \times (6 \times 10^3)^2$$

$$\Rightarrow 50 \times 9.8 \times h = \frac{1}{2} \times 100 \times 10^{-6} \times 36 \times 10^6$$

$$\therefore \quad h = \frac{1800}{50 \times 9.8} = 3.6 \text{ m}$$

7. Dielectrics are non-conductors and do not have free electrons at all. While conductor has free electrons which makes it able to pass the electricity through it.

8. When a dielectric slab is introduced between the plates of charged capacitor or in the region of electric field, an electric field E_p induces inside the dielectric due to induced charge on dielectric in a direction opposite to the direction of applied external electric field. Hence, net electric field inside the dielectric get reduced to $E_0 - E_p$, where E_0 is external electric field. The ratio of applied external electric field and reduced electric field is known as dielectric constant K of dielectric medium,

i.e. $K = \dfrac{E_0}{E_0 - E_p}$ and it is a dimensionless quantity. So, it has no unit.

9. Line B corresponds to C_1, because slope (q/V) of B is less than slope of A.

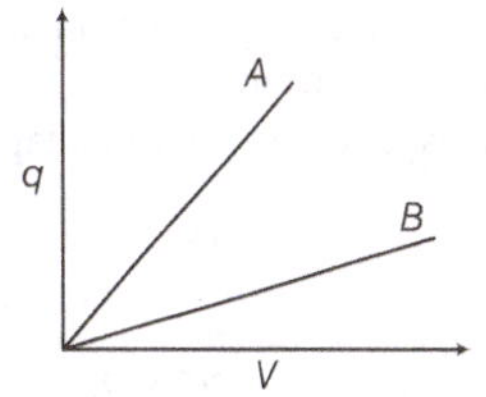

10. If a metal plate is introduced between the plates of a charged parallel plate capacitor, then capacitance of parallel plate capacitor will become infinite.

11. Initially, when there is a vacuum between two plates, the capacitance of the plate is $C_0 = \dfrac{\varepsilon_0 A}{d}$, where A is the area of parallel plates.

Suppose that the capacitor is connected to a battery, an electric field E_0 is produced. Now, if we insert the dielectric slab of thickness $t = d/2$, the electric field reduces to E.

Now, the gap between plates is divided in two parts, for distance t, there is electric field E and for the remaining distance $(d - t)$, the electric field is E_0. (1)

If V be the potential difference between the plates of the capacitor, then $V = Et + E_0(d - t)$

$$V = \frac{Ed}{2} + \frac{E_0 d}{2} = \frac{d}{2}(E + E_0) \qquad \left[\because t = \frac{d}{2}\right]$$

$$\Rightarrow \quad V = \frac{d}{2}\left(\frac{E_0}{K} + E_0\right) = \frac{dE_0}{2K}(K+1) \qquad \left[\text{as, } \frac{E_0}{E} = K\right]$$

Now, $$E_0 = \frac{\sigma}{\varepsilon_0} = \frac{q}{\varepsilon_0 A}$$

$$\Rightarrow \quad V = \frac{d}{2K} \cdot \frac{q}{\varepsilon_0 A}(K+1)$$

We know that, $$C = \frac{q}{V} = \frac{2K\varepsilon_0 A}{d(K+1)}$$ (1)

12. After inserting the dielectric medium, let their capacitances become C_1' and C_2'.

For C_1 $\quad C_1' = KC$ ...(i) (1/2)

For C_2 $\quad C_2' = \dfrac{K_1 \varepsilon_0 (A/2)}{d} + \dfrac{K_2 \varepsilon_0 (A/2)}{d}$

C_2 acts as if two capacitors each of area $A/2$ and separation d are connected in parallel combination,

$$C_2' = \frac{\varepsilon_0 A}{d}\left(\frac{K_1}{2} + \frac{K_2}{2}\right)$$

$$C_2' = C\left(\frac{K_1 + K_2}{2}\right) \qquad \left[\because C = \frac{\varepsilon_0 A}{d}\right] \text{ ...(ii)}$$ (1/2)

According to the problem, $C_1' = C_2'$

$$\Rightarrow \quad KC = C\left(\frac{K_1 + K_2}{2}\right) \Rightarrow K = \frac{K_1 + K_2}{2} \quad (1)$$

13. (i) The system will be equivalent to two identical capacitors connected in series combination in which two plates of each capacitor have separation half of the original separation.

Thus, new capacitance of each capacitor,

$$C' = 2C \qquad \left[\because C \propto \frac{1}{d}\right]$$

$\because$ C and C' are in series.

$$\Rightarrow \quad C_{\text{net}} = \frac{2C \times 2C}{2C + 2C} = C$$

$$C_{\text{net}} = C \qquad \text{[original capacitor]} \quad (1)$$

(ii) System reduces to a capacitor whose separation reduces to half of original one.

$\therefore$ New capacitance, $C' = 2C$ (1)

14. In series combination, charge on each capacitor will be same. The potential will be divided across the individual capacitors.

Let a battery of emf V is connected with the series combination of capacitors and let V_1, V_2 and V_3 are potential difference across each capacitor, then

$$V_1 = \frac{Q}{C_1},\ V_2 = \frac{Q}{C_2} \text{ and } V_3 = \frac{Q}{C_3}$$

But, $\quad V = V_1 + V_2 + V_3$

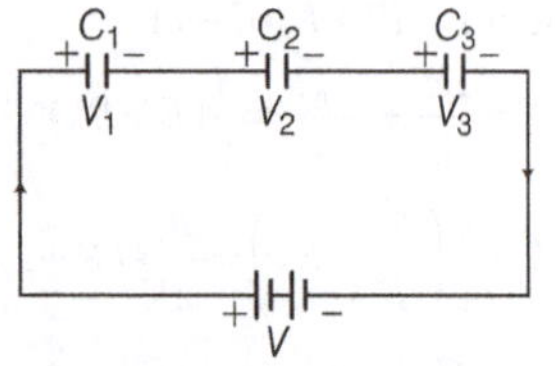

$$\Rightarrow \quad V = \frac{Q}{C_1} + \frac{Q}{C_2} + \frac{Q}{C_3} \Rightarrow V = Q\left(\frac{1}{C_1} + \frac{1}{C_2} + \frac{1}{C_3}\right)$$

But $\quad V = \dfrac{Q}{C_{\text{eq}}}$

where, C_{eq} is equivalent capacitance of the combination.

$$\Rightarrow \quad \frac{1}{C_{\text{eq}}} = \frac{1}{C_1} + \frac{1}{C_2} + \frac{1}{C_3} \quad (2)$$

15. Let n capacitors each of capacitance C are connected in series to a battery of voltage V as shown below.

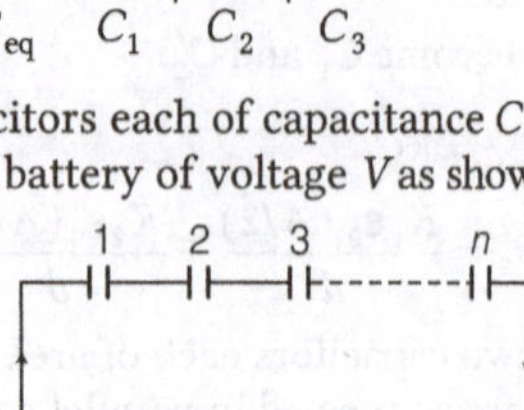

Let C_p and C_s be the equivalent capacitance in parallel and series combination, respectively. The equivalent capacitance of the series combination

$$C_s = C_{\text{eq}^1} = \frac{C}{n} \quad (1)$$

For the parallel combination, $C_p = C_{\text{eq}^2} = nC$

$$\Rightarrow \quad \frac{C_{\text{eq}^2}}{C_{\text{eq}^1}} = \frac{C_p}{C_s} = \frac{nC}{C/n} = n^2 \quad (1/2)$$

According to the question, $n = 3$

$$\Rightarrow \quad \frac{C_p}{C_s} = n^2 = (3)^2 = 9 \quad (1/2)$$

16. Let q be the charge on the charged capacitor.

$\therefore$ Energy stored in it is given by $U = \dfrac{q^2}{2C}$

When another uncharged similar capacitor is connected, then the net capacitance of the system is given by

$$C' = 2C \quad (1)$$

The charge on the system remains constant. So, the energy stored in the system is given by

$$U' = \frac{q^2}{2C'} = \frac{q^2}{4C} \qquad [\because C' = 2C]$$

Thus, the required ratio is given by

$$\frac{U'}{U} = \frac{q^2/4C}{q^2/2C} = \frac{1}{2} \quad (1)$$

17. After introducing the dielectric medium of dielectric constants K_1 and K_2, capacitor acts as if it consists of two capacitors, each having plates of area A and separation $\frac{d}{2}$ connected in series combination for

$$C_1 = \frac{\varepsilon_0 A}{d} \quad \text{...(i)}$$

$$\Rightarrow \quad \frac{1}{C_2} = \frac{1}{\left(\frac{K_1 \varepsilon_0 A}{d/2}\right)} + \frac{1}{\left(\frac{K_2 \varepsilon_0 A}{d/2}\right)}$$

$$\Rightarrow \quad \frac{1}{C_2} = \frac{1}{\left(\frac{\varepsilon_0 A}{d}\right)}\left(\frac{1}{2K_1} + \frac{1}{2K_2}\right)$$

$$\Rightarrow \quad \frac{1}{C_2} = \frac{1}{2C_1}\left(\frac{K_2 + K_1}{K_1 K_2}\right)$$

$$\Rightarrow \quad C_2 = C_1\left(\frac{2K_1 K_2}{K_1 + K_2}\right) \quad (2)$$

18. (i) Given, $\quad C_1 = 2C_2 \quad$ ...(i)

Net capacitance before filling the gap with dielectric slab is given by $C_{\text{initial}} = C_1 + C_2$

$$C_{\text{initial}} = 2C_2 + C_2 \qquad \text{[from Eq. (i)]}$$

$$= 3C_2 \quad \text{...(ii)}$$

Net capacitance after filling the gap with dielectric slab of electric constant K

$$C_{\text{initial}} = KC_1 + KC_2 = K(C_1 + C_2) \qquad \text{[from Eq. (ii)]}$$

$$C_{\text{final}} = 3KC_2 \quad \text{...(iii)}$$

Ratio of net capacitance is given by

$$\frac{C_{\text{initial}}}{C_{\text{final}}}=\frac{3C_2}{3KC_2}=\frac{1}{K}$$ [from Eqs. (ii) and (iii)] (1)

(ii) Energy stored in the combination before introducing the dielectric slab,

$$U_{\text{initial}}=\frac{Q^2}{3C_2} \quad \text{...(iv)}$$

Energy stored in the combination after introducing the dielectric slab,

$$U_{\text{final}}=\frac{Q^2}{3KC_2} \quad \text{... (v)}$$

Ratio of energies stored

$$\frac{U_{\text{initial}}}{U_{\text{final}}}=\frac{K}{1}$$ [from Eqs. (iv) and (v)] (1)

19. Capacitors in parallel Suppose $+Q$ charge is given to the point A by means of an electric source. This charge is distributed on all the three capacitors according to their capacitances.

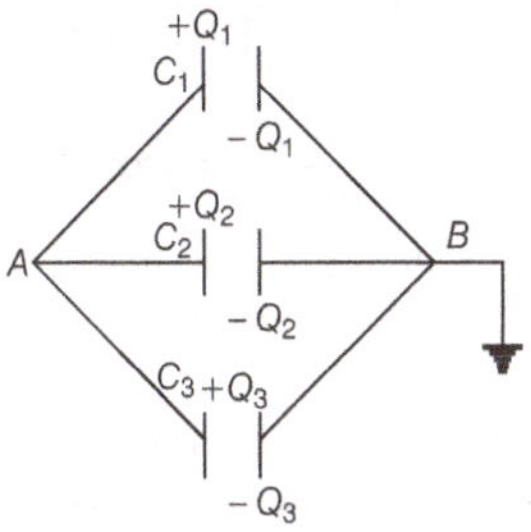

(1)

If the charges on the capacitors C_1, C_2 and C_3 be Q_1, Q_2 and Q_3 respectively, then

$$Q_1=C_1V,\ Q_2=C_2V \text{ and } Q_3=C_3V$$

Total charge on all the three capacitors is

$$Q=Q_1+Q_2+Q_3$$
$$=C_1V+C_2V+C_3V$$
$$=V(C_1+C_2+C_3) \quad \text{...(i)}$$

If the capacitor of this capacitor be C, then

$$Q=CV \quad \text{...(ii)}$$ (1)

Combining Eqs. (i) and (ii), we obtain

$$CV=V(C_1+C_2+C_3)$$
$$C=C_1+C_2+C_3$$

The equivalent capacitance of the capacitors connected in parallel is equal to the sum of their individual capacitance. (1)

20. (i) C_1 and C_2 are in series combination.
Then, equivalent capacitance,

$$C'=\frac{3\times 6}{3+6}=2\mu\text{F}$$

Now C' and C_3 are in parallel combination.
Then, equivalent capacitance,

$$C=C'+C_3=2+10=12\,\mu\text{F}$$

(ii) Total charge,

$$Q=CV=12\times 10=120\,\mu\text{C}$$

Potential energy stored in the system,

$$U=\frac{1}{2}QV$$
$$=\frac{1}{2}\times 120\times 10^{-6}\times 10$$
$$=600\times 10^{-6}=6\times 10^{-4}\text{J}$$

21. (i) Let the two capacitors be C_1 and C_2, capacitance will be maximum when connected in parallel.
i.e. $C_1+C_2=25$
Capacitance will be minimum when connected in series.
i.e. $\frac{C_1C_2}{C_1+C_2}=4$
Since, we are left with only two values 5 μF and 20 μF.
So, the value of capacitances will be 5 μF and 20 μF. (2)

(ii) Due to conservative nature of electric force, the work done in moving a charge in a close path in a uniform electric field is zero. (1)

22. (i) Refer to text on page 76 (Dielectric in electric field).
(ii) Refer to text given on page 78 (Effect of dielectric on parallel plate capacitor).
(iii) Refer to text on page 83 (Change in energy on introducing a dielectric slab).

23. The given figure is shown below.

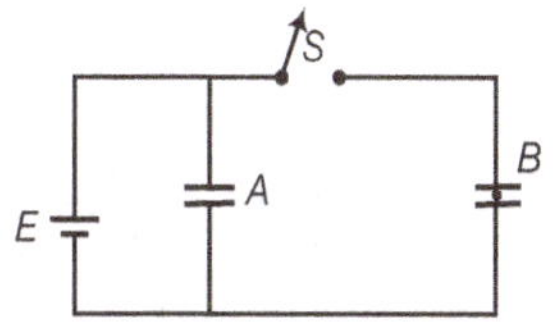

When switch S is closed, the potential difference across capacitors A and B are same

i.e. $$V=\frac{Q_A}{C}=\frac{Q_B}{C}$$

Initial charges on capacitors

$$Q_A=Q_B=CV$$ (1)

When the dielectric is introduced, the new capacitance of either capacitor

$$C'=KC$$

As switch S is opened, the potential difference across capacitor A remains same (V volts).
Let potential difference across capacitor B be V'. When dielectric is introduced with switch S open (i.e. battery disconnected), the charges on capacitor B remains unchanged, so

$$Q_B=CV=C'V'$$
$$\Rightarrow \quad V'=\frac{C}{C'}V=\frac{V}{K}\text{ volt}$$ (1)

Initial energy of both capacitors

$$U_i=\frac{1}{2}CV^2+\frac{1}{2}CV^2=CV^2$$

Final energy of both capacitors

$$U_f=\frac{1}{2}C'V^2+\frac{1}{2}C'V'^2=\frac{1}{2}(KC)V^2+\frac{1}{2}(KC)\left(\frac{V}{K}\right)^2$$

$$= \frac{1}{2}CV^2\left[K + \frac{1}{K}\right] = \frac{1}{2}CV^2\left(\frac{K^2+1}{K}\right)$$

$$\Rightarrow \frac{U_i}{U_f} = \frac{CV^2}{\frac{1}{2}CV^2\left(\frac{K^2+1}{K}\right)} = \frac{2K}{K^2+1}$$ (1)

24. Let the distance between the plates be increased by a very small distance Δx. The force on each plate is F. The amount of work done in increasing the separation by Δx, i.e.

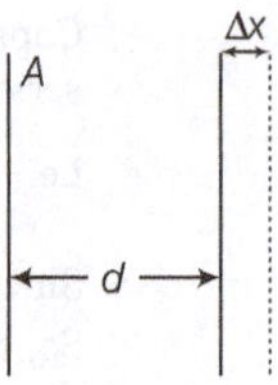

$W = F \cdot \Delta x$ ...(i)

Increase in volume of capacitor

$= \text{Area of plates} \times \text{Increased distance}$ (1)

$= A \cdot \Delta x$

$$u = \text{Energy density} = \frac{\text{Energy}}{\text{Volume}}$$

Increase in energy $= u \times \text{volume} = u \cdot A \cdot \Delta x$ ...(ii) (1)

As, energy = work done (W)

$\Rightarrow F \cdot \Delta x = u \cdot A \cdot \Delta x$ [from Eqs. (i) and (ii)]

$\Rightarrow F = u \cdot A$

$$= \frac{1}{2}\varepsilon_0 E^2 \cdot A \qquad \left[\because u = \frac{1}{2}\varepsilon_0 E^2 \text{ and } E = \frac{V}{d}\right]$$

$$= \frac{1}{2}\varepsilon_0 \cdot \frac{V^2}{d^2} \cdot A = \left(\frac{\varepsilon_0 A}{d} \cdot V\right)\frac{V}{d} \times \frac{1}{2}$$

$$= \frac{1}{2} \cdot E \cdot C \cdot V = \frac{1}{2}QE \qquad \left[\because C = \frac{\varepsilon_0 A}{d}, CV = Q\right]$$ (1)

25. (i) According to the question,

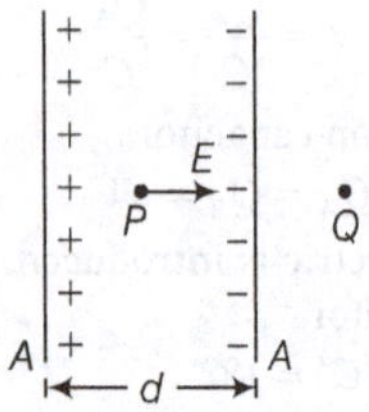

(a) Electric field due to a plate of positive charge at point

$$P = \frac{\sigma}{2\varepsilon_0}$$

Electric field due to other plate $= \frac{\sigma}{2\varepsilon_0}$

Since, they have same direction, so

$$E_{\text{net}} = \frac{\sigma}{2\varepsilon_0} + \frac{\sigma}{2\varepsilon_0} = \frac{\sigma}{\varepsilon_0}$$

Outside the plate, electric field will be zero because of opposite direction. (1)

(b) Potential difference between the plates is given by $V = Ed = \frac{\sigma d}{\varepsilon_0}$ $\left[\because E = \frac{\sigma}{\varepsilon_0}\right]$ (1)

(c) Capacitance of the capacitor is given by

$$C = \frac{Q}{V} = \frac{\sigma A}{\sigma d}\varepsilon_0 = \frac{\varepsilon_0 A}{d}$$ (1)

(ii) According to question,

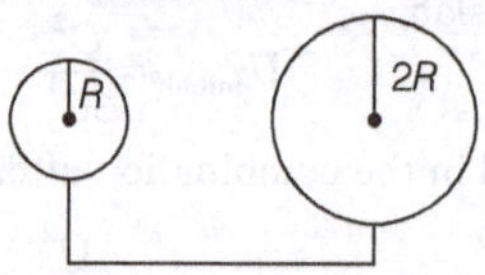

Potential at the surface of radius R,

$$V = \frac{kq}{R} \qquad [\because q = \sigma \times 4R^2]$$

$$= \frac{k\sigma 4\pi R^2}{R}$$

$$= \sigma k 4\pi R = 4k\sigma\pi R$$

Potential at the surface of radius $2R$,

$$V' = \frac{kq}{2R} \qquad [\because q = \sigma \times 4\pi(2R)^2 = 16\sigma\pi R^2]$$

So, $$V' = \frac{k\sigma 16\pi R^2}{2R} = 8k\sigma\pi R$$

Since, the potential of bigger sphere is more. So, charge will flow from sphere of radius $2R$ to sphere of radius R. (2)

26. (i) The capacitance of the parallel plate capacitor, filled with dielectric medium of dielectric constant K is given by, $C = \frac{K\varepsilon_0 A}{d}$

The capacitance of the parallel plate capacitor decreases with the removal of dielectric medium as for air or vacuum $K = 1$. (2½)

(ii) Initially, if we consider a charged capacitor, then its charge would be $Q = CV$

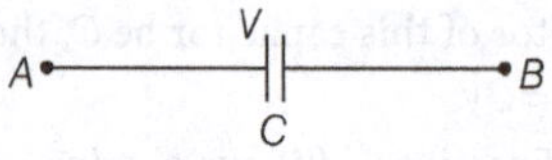

and energy stored, $U_1 = \frac{1}{2}CV^2$ ...(i)

Then, this charged capacitor is connected to uncharged capacitor.

Let the common potential be V_1. The charge flows from first capacitor to the other capacitor unless both the capacitors attain common potential

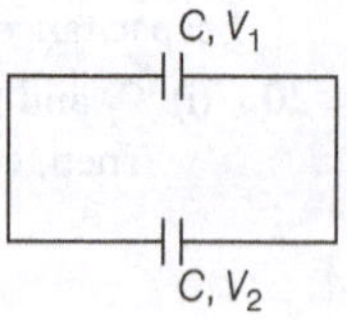

$Q_1 = CV_1$ and $Q = CV_2$

Applying conservation of charge,

$$Q = Q_1 + Q_2$$

$$\Rightarrow CV = CV_1 + CV_2$$

$$\Rightarrow V = V_1 + V_2$$

$$\Rightarrow V_1 = \frac{V}{2}$$

Total energy stored, $U_2 = \frac{1}{2}CV_1^2 + \frac{1}{2}CV_2^2$

$$= \frac{1}{2}C\left(\frac{V}{2}\right)^2 + \frac{1}{2}C\left(\frac{V}{2}\right)^2 \Rightarrow U_2 = \frac{1}{4}CV^2 \quad \text{...(ii)}$$

From Eqs. (i) and (ii), we get

$$U_2 < U_1$$

Hence, energy stored in the combination is less than that stored initially in single capacitor. (2½)

27. From the given circuit C_1 and C_2 are in parallel and C_3 is in series with C_1 and C_2.

C_1 and C_2 are in parallel.

$C_1 + C_2 = 50\mu F + 50\mu F = 100\,\mu F$

Now, $(C_1 + C_2)$ series with C_3

$$\frac{100\mu F \times 25\mu F}{100\mu F + 25\mu F} = \frac{2500\mu F}{125\mu F} = 20\,\mu F$$

28. (i) We have initial voltage, $V_1 = V$ volt

and charge stored, $Q_1 = 360\mu C$

$$Q_1 = CV_1 \quad \text{...(i)}$$

Charged potential, $V_2 = V - 120$

$$Q_2 = 120\,\mu C \quad (1/2)$$

$$\Rightarrow \quad Q_2 = CV_2 \quad \text{...(ii)}$$

By dividing Eq. (ii) from Eq. (i), we get

$$\frac{Q_1}{Q_2} = \frac{CV_1}{CV_2} \Rightarrow \frac{360}{120} = \frac{V}{V-120}$$

$$\Rightarrow \quad V = 180\text{ V} \quad (1/2)$$

$$\therefore \quad C = \frac{Q_1}{V_1} = \frac{360 \times 10^{-6}}{180}$$

$$= 2 \times 10^{-6}\text{ F}$$

$$= 2\,\mu F$$

Hence, the potential, $V = 180$ V and unknown capacitance is $2\,\mu F$. (1)

(ii) If the voltage applied had increased by 120 V, then $V_3 = 180 + 120 = 300$ V

Hence, charge stored in the capacitor,

$Q_3 = CV_3 = 2 \times 10^{-6} \times 300 = 600\,\mu C$ (1)

29. In the circuit, when initially K_1 is closed and K_1 is opened, the capacitor C_1 and C_2 acquire potential difference V_1 and V_2, respectively. So, we have

$$V_1 + V_2 = E$$

and $\quad V_1 + V_2 = 9\text{V}$

Also, in series combination, $V \propto 1/C$ (1)

$$V_1 : V_2 = 1/6 : 1/3$$

On solving,

$\Rightarrow \quad V_1 = 3\text{V}$ and $V_2 = 6\text{V}$

$\therefore \quad Q_1 = C_1V_1 = 6\,\mu C \times 3\text{V}$

$= 18\,\mu C \quad [\because C = 1\,\mu F]$

$\Rightarrow \quad Q_2 = C_2V_2 = 3\,\mu C \times 6\text{V} = 18\,\mu C$

and $\quad Q_3 = 0$ (1)

When K_1 was opened and K_2 was closed, the parallel combination of C_2 and C_3 in series with C_1.

[Charge on C_1 remains unchanged]

i.e. $\quad Q_1' = Q_2 = 18\,\mu C$

Charge on C_2 is shared between C_2 and C_3 in parallel.

As, $\quad C_2 = C_3$

$$\therefore \quad Q_2' = Q_2 = \frac{Q_2}{2} = \frac{18}{2} = 9\,\mu C$$

$[\because Q_2 = 18\,\mu C]$ (1)

30. Radius of inner sphere, $r_1 = 12$ cm

Radius of outer sphere, $r_2 = 13$ cm

and charge on inner sphere, $q = 2.5\,\mu C$

The dielectric constant, $K = 32$

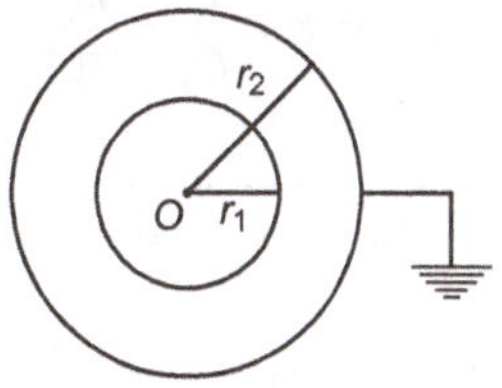

(i) Capacitance of a spherical capacitor,

$$C = \frac{4\pi\varepsilon_0 K r_1 r_2}{r_1 - r_2}$$

$$= \frac{1}{9 \times 10^9} \cdot \frac{32 \times 12 \times 13 \times 10^{-4}}{(13-12) \times 10^{-2}}$$

$$= 5.5 \times 10^{-9}\text{ F} \quad (1)$$

(ii) Electric potential of inner sphere,

$$= 4.5 \times 10^2\text{ V} \quad (1)$$

(iii) Capacitance of an isolated sphere of radius, $r = 12$ cm

$$C = 4\pi\varepsilon_0 r$$

$$= \frac{1}{9 \times 10^9} \times 12 \times 10^{-2}$$

$$= 1.33 \times 10^{-11}\text{ F}$$

The capacitance of an isolated sphere is much smaller as compared to the spherical capacitor because the outer sphere is earthed. The potential difference decreases and hence the capacitance increases. (1)

31. Two identical capacitors C_1 and C_2 get fully charged with 5 V battery initially.

So, the charge and potential difference on both capacitors becomes

$$q = CV = 2 \times 10^{-6} \times 5\text{ V} = 10\,\mu C$$

and $\quad V = 5$ V

On introduction of dielectric medium of $K = 5$. (1)

For C_1 (Continue to be connected with battery)

Potential difference of C_1, $V' = 5$ V

Capacitance, $C_1' = KC = 5 \times 2 = 10\,\mu F$

Charge, $q' = C'V' = 10 \times 5 = 50\,\mu C$ (1)

For C_2 (Disconnected from battery)

Charge, $q' = q = 10\,\mu C$

$$\therefore \quad \text{Potential difference, } V' = \frac{V}{K} = \frac{5}{5} = 1\text{ V} \quad (1)$$

32. Given, $V_0 = 1000$ V, $C_0 = 16\mu F = 1.6 \times 10^{-5}$ F, $K = 5$

(i) We know that, $C_0 = \frac{\varepsilon_0 A}{d}$

The new capacitance,

$$C = KC_0 = 5 \times 1.6 \times 10^{-5} = 8 \times 10^{-5} \text{ F}$$ (1)

(ii) New potential, $V = \frac{V_0}{K} = \frac{1000}{5} = 200$ V (1)

33. Given, capacitance in air, $C_0 = 5\mu F$

Capacitance with dielectric, $C = 50\mu F$

$\therefore$ Dielectric constant, $K = \frac{C}{C_0} = \frac{50\mu F}{5\mu F} = 10$

34. (i)

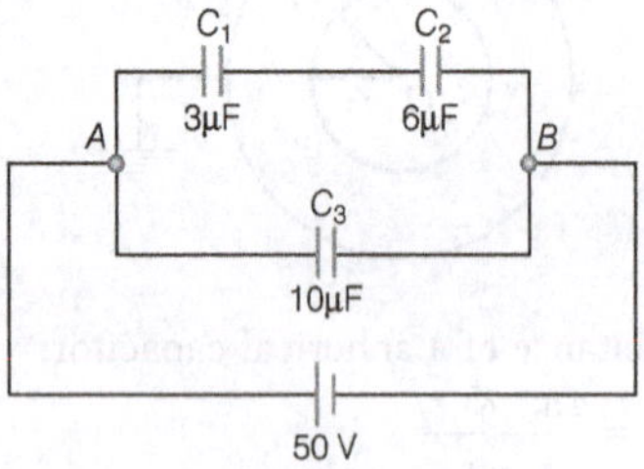

From the above figure, as C_1 and C_2 are connected in series.

Hence, $\frac{1}{C_{eq}} = \frac{1}{C_1} + \frac{1}{C_2} \Rightarrow \frac{1}{C_{eq}} = \frac{1}{3} + \frac{1}{6}$

$\Rightarrow$ $C_{eq} = 2\mu F$

Now, C_{eq} is in parallel with C_3, hence equivalent capacitance of the circuit between points A and B will be $10 + 2 = 12\mu F$ (1)

(ii) Capacitors C_1 and C_2 are in series. Thus, charge on equivalent capacitance of C_1 and C_2 will be same as charge on C_1 and C_2 is dividually.

$\therefore$ Charge on $C_1 = q_1 = (C_{eq})(V)$

$= (2\mu F)(50 V) = 100\,\mu C$ (1)

35. For getting a capacitance of 20 μF, the combination should be as shown in the diagram.

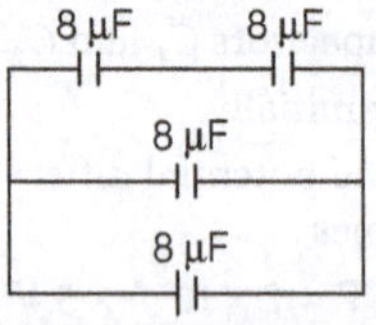

(1/2)

The series combination of 8 μF capacitors will give equivalent capacitance of 4μF.

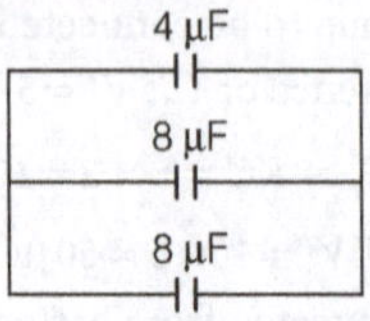

(1/2)

Now, capacitors 4μF, 8μF and 8μF are in parallel.

Hence, $C_{eq} = 4\mu F + 8\mu F + 8\mu F = 20\mu F$ (1)

36. We have to apply the concept of series and parallel combination to find equivalent capacitance.

(i) It is clear from the diagram that C_1 and C_2 are in series.

$$\frac{1}{C_{eq}} = \frac{1}{C_1} + \frac{1}{C_2} = \frac{1}{6} + \frac{1}{12} = \frac{2+1}{12} = \frac{3}{12} = \frac{1}{4}$$

$\therefore$ $C_{eq} = 4\,\mu F$

Charge on 4 μF capacitor,

$$q = CV = 4 \times 10^{-6} \times 100 = 4 \times 10^{-4} \text{ C}$$

Charge on positive plate of C_1 is $+4 \times 10^{-4}$ C.

and on negative plate of C_1 is -4×10^{-4} C.

Note that charge on C_1 and C_2 will be same. (1)

(ii) Electric potential difference across the plate of C_3 capacitor = 100 V

$\therefore$ Electrostatic energy $= \frac{1}{2} CV^2$

$= \frac{1}{2} \times 20 \times 10^{-6} \times 100 \times 100 = 10^{-1} = 0.1$ J (1)

37. According to the diagram, capacitors are in series.

$$\frac{1}{C_{eq}} = \frac{1}{C_1} + \frac{1}{C_2} + \frac{1}{C_3}$$

$$\Rightarrow \frac{1}{C} = \frac{1}{8} + \frac{1}{16} + \frac{1}{24} \Rightarrow \frac{1}{C} = \frac{6+3+2}{48} = \frac{11}{48}$$

$\therefore$ $C = \frac{48}{11}\mu F$ (1)

Charge on each capacitor,

$$Q = CV = \frac{48}{11} \times 110 = 480\,\mu C$$ (1)

38. For a Wheatstone bridge to be balanced, the ratio of capacitances of adjacent arms must be equal.

Clearly, from the given circuit,

$$C_1C_4 = 100\mu F \text{ and } C_3C_2 = 100\mu F$$

$$\Rightarrow C_1C_4 = C_2C_3 \Rightarrow \frac{C_1}{C_2} = \frac{C_3}{C_4}$$

So, it is a balanced Wheatstone bridge.

Now, we can remove C_5 from the given circuit.

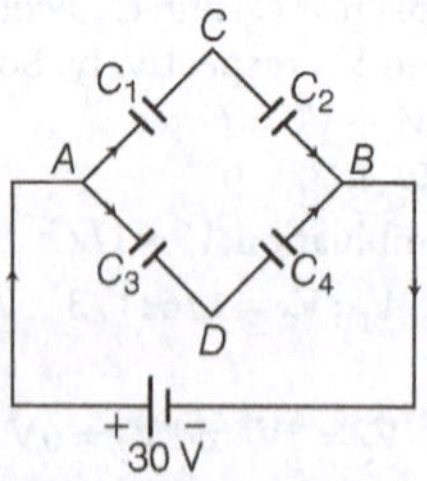

So, C_1 and C_2 are in series,

$$\frac{1}{C'} = \frac{1}{10} + \frac{1}{10} = \frac{1}{5} \Rightarrow C' = 5\,\mu F$$

and C_3 and C_4 are in series, $C'' = 5\,\mu F$

Now, C' and C'' are in parallel.

$\therefore$ Net capacitance,

$$C = C' + C'' = 5 + 5 = 10\mu F$$

Caution The capacitor C_5 is removed, because potential of its terminals is same and hence potential difference is zero across it. (2)

39. Given, $C_1 = 10\mu F$, $C_2 = 30\mu F$, $C_3 = 20\mu F$, $C_4 = 28\mu F$

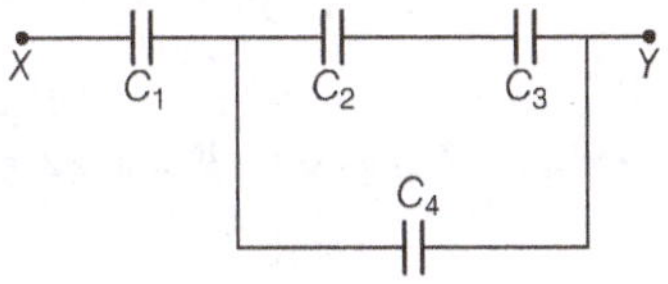

In the figure, C_2 and C_3 are in series, so the equivalent capacitance is given by $\frac{1}{C'} = \frac{1}{C_2} + \frac{1}{C_3}$ (1/2)

Substituting the values of C_2 and C_3, we get

$$\frac{1}{C'} = \frac{1}{30} + \frac{1}{20} = \frac{20+30}{30 \times 20}$$

$$\Rightarrow \quad C' = \frac{30 \times 20}{50} = 12\mu F$$ (1/2)

The resultant C' of C_2 and C_3 is in the parallel with C_4.
So, $C'' = C' + C_4 = 12 + 28 = 40\mu F$

Now, the resultant C'' of C' and C_4 is in the series with C_1.

So, the total equivalent capacitance is given by

$$\frac{1}{C_T} = \frac{1}{C''} + \frac{1}{C_1} = \frac{1}{40} + \frac{1}{10} = \frac{1+4}{40}$$

$$\Rightarrow C_T = \frac{40}{5} = 8\mu F$$ (1)

40. (i) Here, C_1, C_2 and C_3 are in series, therefore their equivalent capacitance

$$\frac{1}{C'} = \frac{1}{C_1} + \frac{1}{C_2} + \frac{1}{C_3}$$

$$\Rightarrow \quad C' = \frac{C}{3} = \frac{12}{3} = 4\ \mu F$$ (1)

Now, C' and C are in parallel combination.

$$\therefore \quad C_{net} = C' + C$$
$$= 4\ \mu F + 12\ \mu F = 16\ \mu F$$ (1)

(ii) Being C' and C are in parallel, 500 V potential difference is applied across them.

$\therefore$ Charge on C'

$$q_1 = C'V = (4\ \mu F) \times 500 = 2000\ \mu C$$

$\therefore$ C_1, C_2 and C_3 capacitors each will have $2000\ \mu C$ charge.

$\therefore$ Charge on C_4, $q_2 = C \times V = 12 \times 500 = 6000\ \mu C$ (1)

41. If n identical capacitors, each of capacitance C are connected in series combination give equivalent capacitance, $C_s = \frac{C}{n}$ and when connected in parallel combination, then equivalent capacitance, $C_p = nC$.

Also, for same voltage, energy stored in the capacitor is given by

$$U = \frac{1}{2}CV^2 \quad \text{[for } V = \text{constant]}$$

$$\Rightarrow \quad U \propto C$$

In series combination, $C_s = \frac{C}{n}$

$$\Rightarrow \quad C_s = 1\ \mu F \quad [\because n = 3]$$

$$\Rightarrow \quad C = nC_s = 3 \times 1\ \mu F = 3\ \mu F$$

In parallel combination,

$$C_p = nC = 3 \times 3 = 9\ \mu F$$ (1)

For same voltage, $U \propto C$

$$\Rightarrow \quad \frac{U_s}{U_p} = \frac{C_s}{C_p} \Rightarrow \frac{U_s}{U_p} = \frac{C/n}{nC} = \frac{1}{n^2}$$

$$\Rightarrow \quad \frac{U_s}{U_p} = \frac{1}{(3)^2} = \frac{1}{9} \quad \text{or} \quad U_s : U_p = 1:9$$ (2)

42. Consider the given figure,

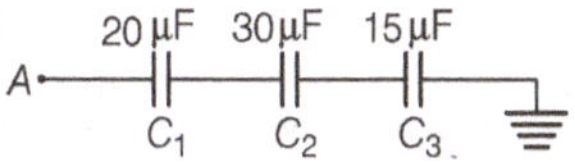

Given, $C_1 = 20\ \mu F$, $C_2 = 30\ \mu F$, $C_3 = 15\ \mu F$

Potential at $A = 90$ V

As, we can see that capacitor C_3 is earthed, therefore, potential across C_3 will be zero.

Since, capacitors C_1, C_2 and C_3 are connected in series, therefore

$$\frac{1}{C_{eq}} = \frac{1}{C_1} + \frac{1}{C_2} + \frac{1}{C_3} = \frac{1}{20} + \frac{1}{30} + \frac{1}{15}$$

$$\Rightarrow \quad \frac{1}{C_{eq}} = \frac{3+2+4}{60} = \frac{9}{60} \Rightarrow C_{eq} = \frac{60}{9} = \frac{20}{3}\ \mu F$$ (1)

Since, charge remains same in series combination.

So, $$Q = C_{eq}V = \frac{20}{3} \times 90$$

$$\Rightarrow \quad Q = 600\ \mu C = 600 \times 10^{-6} C = 6 \times 10^{-4} C$$

$\therefore$ Potential difference across $C_2 = \frac{Q}{V_2}$

$$\Rightarrow \quad V_2 = \frac{Q}{C_2} \Rightarrow V_2 = \frac{6 \times 10^{-4}}{30 \times 10^{-6}} = 20 V$$ (1)

$\therefore$ Energy stored in capacitor C_2 is given by

$$E = \frac{1}{2}C_2V_2^2 = \frac{1}{2} \times 30 \times 10^{-6} \times (20)^2$$

$$= \frac{1}{2} \times 30 \times 400 \times 10^{-6} \quad E = 6 \times 10^{-3} J$$ (1)

43. Energy stored in capacitor $= \frac{1}{2}C_1V^2$

$$= \frac{1}{2} \times 12 \times 10^{-12} \times (50)^2 J = 15 \times 10^{-9} J$$

With other capacitor 6 pF in series.

Total capacitance (C)

$$= \frac{C_1 \times C_2}{C_1 + C_2} = \frac{6 \times 12}{6+12} pF = \frac{12 \times 6}{18} = 4\ pF$$ (1)

Charge stored in each capacitor is same and is given by

$$Q = CV = 4 \times 10^{-12} \times 50 C = 2 \times 10^{-10} C$$

Each of the capacitors will have charge equal to Q

$$= 2\times10^{-10}\text{C}$$ (1)

Potential on capacitors with capacitance 12 pF is

$$= \frac{Q}{C_1} = \frac{2\times10^{-10}}{12\times10^{-12}} \text{ V} = 16.67 \text{ V}$$

Potential on capacitor with capacitance 6 pF is

$$= \frac{2\times10^{-10}}{6\times10^{-12}} \text{ V} = 33.33 \text{ V}$$ (1)

44. According to question, let the capacitance of X be C, so capacitance of $Y = \varepsilon_r\ C = 4C$ $[\because \varepsilon_r = 4]$

(i) Equivalent capacitance $= \dfrac{C\times4C}{C+4C}$

[$\because$ X and Y are in series]

$$= \frac{4C^2}{5C} \Rightarrow \frac{4C}{5} \text{ and it is given that } \frac{4C}{5} = 4\mu\text{F}$$

So, $4C = 20\mu\text{F} =$ capacitance of Y

Capacitance of $X = C = \dfrac{20}{4} = 5\,\mu\text{F}$ (1½)

(ii) Charge flowing through the capacitor is given by

$$q = CV = \frac{4C}{5}\times15 = \frac{4\times5}{5}\times15 = 60\,\mu\text{C}$$

Now, let the potential difference between plates of capacitors X and Y are V_x and V_y, respectively.

So, $V_x = \dfrac{q}{C_x} = \dfrac{60}{5} = 12$ V and $V_y = \dfrac{q}{C_y} = \dfrac{60}{20} = 3$ V (2)

(iii) Electrostatic energy stored in capacitance

$$X(E_x) = \frac{1}{2}CV_x^2 \quad ...(i)$$

Similarly for Y, $E_y = \dfrac{1}{2}4CV_y^2$ ...(ii)

From Eqs. (i) and (ii), we get

$$\text{Ratio} = \frac{E_x}{E_y} = \frac{\frac{1}{2}CV_x^2}{\frac{1}{2}4CV_y^2} = \frac{V_x^2}{4V_y^2} = \frac{12\times12}{4\times3\times3} = 4:1$$ (1½)

45. When the capacitors are connected in parallel, equivalent capacitance, $C_P = C_1 + C_2$.

The energy stored in the combination of the capacitors,

$$E_P = \frac{1}{2}C_PV^2 = \frac{1}{2}(C_1+C_2)(100)^2 = 0.25\text{ J}$$

$$\Rightarrow \quad C_1 + C_2 = 5\times10^{-5} \quad ...(i)$$ (1)

When the capacitors are connected in series, equivalent capacitance, $C_S = \dfrac{C_1C_2}{C_1+C_2}$

The energy stored in the combination of the capacitors,

$$E_S = \frac{1}{2}C_SV^2$$ (1)

$$\Rightarrow \quad E_S = \frac{1}{2}\frac{C_1C_2}{C_1+C_2}(100)^2$$

$$= \frac{1}{2}\times\frac{C_1C_2}{5\times10^{-5}}(100)^2 = 0.45\text{ J}$$

$$\Rightarrow \quad C_1C_2 = 0.045\times10^{-4}\times5\times10^{-5}\times2$$

$$= 4.5\times10^{-10}$$

$$\because \quad (C_1-C_2)^2 = (C_1+C_2)^2 - 4C_1C_2$$

$$\Rightarrow \quad (C_1-C_2)^2 = 25\times10^{-10} - 4\times4.5\times10^{-10}$$

$$= 7\times10^{-10}$$

$$\Rightarrow \quad (C_1-C_2) = \sqrt{7\times10^{-10}} = 2.64\times10^{-5}$$

$$\Rightarrow \quad C_1 - C_2 = 2.64\times10^{-5} \quad ...(ii)$$

On solving Eqs. (i) and (ii), we get

$C_1 = 35\ \mu\text{F}$ and $C_2 = 15\ \mu\text{F}$ (1½)

$$\Rightarrow \quad Q_1 = C_1V = 35\times10^{-6}\times100 = 35\times10^{-4}\text{ C}$$

and $Q_2 = C_2V = 15\times10^{-6}\times100 = 15\times10^{-4}\text{ C}$ (1½)

46. (i) As given in the question, energy of the 6 μF capacitor is E. Let V be the potential difference along the capacitor of capacitance 6 μF.

Now, $\dfrac{1}{2}CV^2 = E$

$$\frac{1}{2}\times6\times10^{-6}\times V^2 = E \Rightarrow V^2 = \frac{E}{3}\times10^6 \quad ...(i)$$

Since, potential is same for parallel connection, the potential through 12 μF capacitor is also V. Hence, energy of 12 μF capacitor is

$$E_{12} = \frac{1}{2}\times12\times10^{-6}\times V^2 \quad \text{[from Eq. (i)]}$$

$$= \frac{1}{2}\times12\times10^{-6}\times\frac{E}{3}\times10^6 = 2E$$ (2)

(ii) Since, charge remains constant in series, the charge on 6μF and 12 μF capacitors combined will be equal to the charge on 3 μF capacitor.

Using the formula, $Q = CV$, we can write

$$\Rightarrow (6+12)\times10^{-6}\times V = 3\times10^{-6}\times V'$$

$$V' = 6V$$

Squaring on both sides, we get

$$V'^2 = 36V^2$$

Putting the value of V^2 from Eq. (i), we get

$$V'^2 = 36\times\frac{E}{3}\times10^6$$

$$\Rightarrow \quad V'^2 = 12E\times10^6$$

$$\therefore \quad E_3 = \frac{1}{2}\times3\times10^{-6}\times12E\times10^6$$

$$= 18E$$ (2)

(iii) Total energy drawn from battery is

$$E_{\text{total}} = E + E_{12} + E_3$$

$$= E + 2E + 18E$$

$$= 21E$$ (1)

SUMMARY

- **Electrostatic Potential** It is the amount of work done (w) in moving a unit positive test charge (q) without acceleration form infinity to that point against the electrostatic force

  $\therefore \quad V = \dfrac{W}{q}$

  Its SI unit is volt (V) and $1\,V = 1\,J/C$.
- **Electrostatic Potential Difference** Electrostatic potential difference between two points P and Q is equal to the work done (W_{QP}) by external force in moving a unit positive charge (q_0) against the electrostatic force from point Q to P along any path between these two points

  $\therefore \quad \Delta V = \dfrac{W_{QP}}{q_0}$

  Its SI unit is volt and $1V = 1\,JC^{-1}$.
- **Electric Potential due to a Point Charge**

  It can be given as, $V = \dfrac{q}{4\pi\varepsilon_0 r}$

  Here, r is distance of the point from the charge.

  Electrostatic potential due to a system of charges at point P,

  $$V = \frac{1}{4\pi\varepsilon_0}\sum_{i=1}^{n}\frac{q_i}{r_{ip}} \text{ or } V_{\text{net}} = \sum_{i=1}^{n} V_i$$
- Electrostatic potential due to a thin charged spherical shell carrying charge q and radius R respectively, at any point P lying

  (i) inside the shell is $V = \dfrac{1}{4\pi\varepsilon_0}\cdot\dfrac{q}{R}$

  (ii) on the surface of shell is $V = \dfrac{1}{4\pi\varepsilon_0}\cdot\dfrac{q}{R}$

  (iii) outside the shell is $V = \dfrac{1}{4\pi\varepsilon_0}\cdot\dfrac{q}{r}$ for $r > R$

  where, r is the distance of point P from the centre of the shell.
- Electrostatic potential due to dipole,

  (i) On its axial line,

  $$V = \pm\frac{p}{4\pi\varepsilon_0 r^2}$$

  (ii) On its equatorial line,

  $$V = 0$$

  (iii) At any point P,

  $$V = \frac{1}{4\pi\varepsilon_0}\cdot\frac{p\cos\theta}{r^2} \text{ or } V = \frac{1}{4\pi\varepsilon_0}\cdot\frac{\mathbf{p}\cdot\hat{\mathbf{r}}}{|r|^2}$$

  where, θ is the angle between $\hat{\mathbf{r}}$ and $\mathbf{p}$.
- **Equipotential Surfaces** Any surface which has same electrostatic potential at every point is called an equipontential surface.
- **Equipotential Surface in Different Cases** The equipotential surface can be obtained for different cases:

  (i) For a point charge, it is spherical surface.

  (ii) For a uniform electric field, it is plane surface.
- **Relation between Electric Field and Electrostatic Potential**

  It can be given as, $E = -\dfrac{\partial V}{\partial r} = -$ (Potential gradient)

  where, negative sign indicates that the direction of electric field is from higher potential to lower potential, i.e. in the direction of decreasing potential.
- **Electrostatic Potential Energy of a System of Charges** It is defined as, the total work done in bringing the different charges to their respective positions from infinitely large mutual separations.
- **Due to System of Two Point Charges** It can be given by,

  $$U = W = \frac{kq_1q_2}{r_{AB}}$$
- **Due to System of Three Point Charges** It can be given by,

  $$U = \left[K\sum_{i=1}^{3}\sum_{\substack{j=1 \\ j \# 1}}^{3}\frac{qq_j}{r_{ij}}\right]$$
- **Potential Energy of a Dipole in an External Field** Potential of a dipole in an external field can be given as,

  $$U = pE(\cos\theta_1 - \cos\theta_2)$$

  Here, θ_1 and θ_2 are initial and final orientations of the dipole. When dipole is initially at right angle θ with E, i.e. $\theta_2 = \theta$, then potential energy of dipole, $U = -\mathbf{p}\cdot\mathbf{E}$
- **Conductors and Insulators**

  Conductors These are those materials through which electric charge can flow easily.

  The process which involves the making of a region free from electric field is known as electrostatic shielding.

  Insulators Insulators are those materials through which electric charge cannot flow.
- **Dielectric and Polarisation**

  Dielectric Constant It is the ratio of the strength of applied electric field to the strength of reduced value of electric field on placing the dielectric between the plates of a capacitor.

  Polarisation The induced dipole moment developed per unit volume in a dielectric slab on placing it in an electric field is called polarisation.

Dielectric Strength The maximum electric field that a dielectric can withstand without breakdown is called its dielectric strength.

- **Capacitors and Capacitance** A capacitor is a system of two conductors separated by an insulating medium.

  The capacitance of the capacitor, $C = \frac{Q}{V}$

  In SI system unit of capacity is farad.

  Parallel Plate Capacitor Capacitance of a parallel plate capacitor can be given by, $C = \frac{\varepsilon_0 A}{d}$

  Effect of Dielectric on Parallel Plate Capacitor On introducing a dielectric between the parallel plates, capacitance can be given by,

  $$C = \frac{\varepsilon_0 KA}{d}, \text{ where } K \text{ is the dielectric constant}$$

- **Combination of Capacitors**

  In parallel combination,

  $$C_{eq} = C_1 + C_2 + \ldots\ldots + C_n$$

  In series combination,

  $$\frac{1}{C_{eq}} = \frac{1}{C_1} + \frac{1}{C_2} + \ldots\ldots + \frac{1}{C_n}$$

  The energy U stored in a capacitor of capacitance C, with charge q and voltage V is,

  $$U = \frac{1}{2}qV = \frac{1}{2}CV^2 = \frac{q^2}{2C}$$

  The electrostatic energy density (energy per unit volume) in a region with electric field E is

  $$U = \frac{1}{2}\varepsilon_0 E^2$$

For Mind Map

Visit : https://goo.gl/NuqVQ4 OR **Scan the Code**

Chapter Practice

Multiple Choice Questions

1 Mark

1 The electric potential at a certain distance from a point charge is 600 V and the electric field is 200 N/C. The distance of the point charge (in metres) is

(a) 2 (b) 3 (c) 1 (d) 0

2 In a Millikan drop experiment, a drop of diameter 10^{-4} cm with a density of 900 kg / m^3 is observed. The capacitor plates are 2 cm apart. A potential of 72 V applied across the plates keeps the drop in balance. How many electronic charges are there on the drop?

(a) 1 (b) 8
(c) 4 (d) 2

3 Two metal spheres A and B of different sizes are charged such that the electric potential is the same at the surface of each sphere A has a radius three times that of sphere B. If E_A and E_B be the electric field magnitudes at the surface of each sphere, then E_B/E_A is

(a) 4 (b) 6
(c) 3 (d) 9

4 Figure shows some equipotential lines distributed in space.

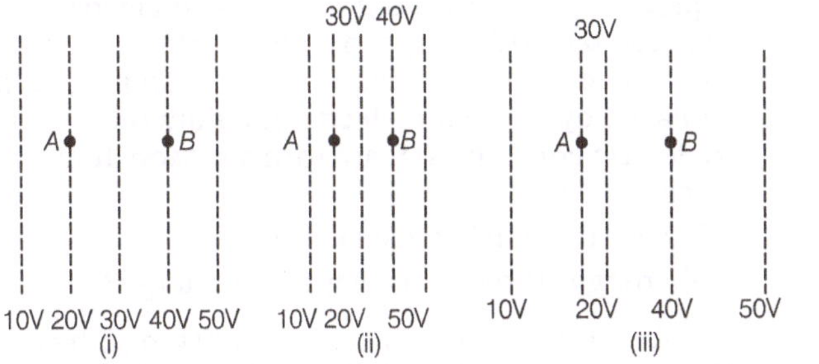

A charged object is moved from point A to point B, then **NCERT Exemplar**

(a) the work done in Fig. (i) is the greatest
(b) the work done in Fig. (ii) is the least
(c) the work done is the same in Fig. (i), Fig (ii) and Fig (iii)
(d) the work done in Fig. (iii) is greater than that in Fig. (ii) but equal to that in Fig. (i)

5 When a series combination of two uncharged capacitors is connected to a 12 V battery, 173 μJ of energy is drawn from the battery. If one of the capacitors has a capacitance of 4μF, the capacitance of the other capacitor (in μF) is

(a) 8 (b) 4 (c) 2 (d) 6

6

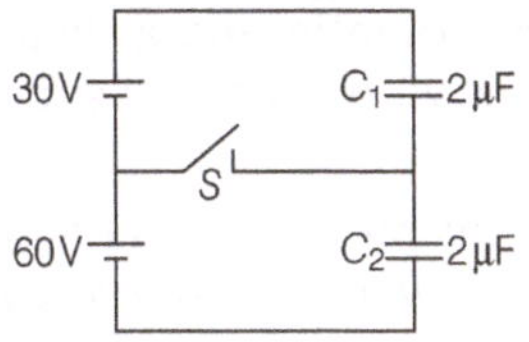

Column I	Column II
A. 108 μC	1. Charge on both the capacitors (S open)
B. 180 μC	2. Charge on both the capacitors (S closed)
C. 60 μC	3. Charge on C_1 (S closed)
D. 240 μC	4. Charge on C_2 (S closed)

Codes

	A	B	C	D
(a)	1	2	3	4
(b)	4	3	2	1
(c)	1	4	3	2
(d)	1	3	2	4

Assertion and Reason

Directions (Q. Nos. 7-11) *In the following questions, two statements are given- one labelled Assertion (A) and the other labelled Reason (R). Select the correct answer to these questions from the codes (a), (b), (c) and (d) as given below*

(a) Both Assertion and Reason are true and Reason is the correct explanation of Assertion.
(b) Both Assertion and Reason are true but Reason is not the correct explanation of Assertion.
(c) Assertion is true but Reason is false.
(d) Assertion is false but Reason is true.

7 **Assertion (A)** There is no potential difference between any two points on the equipotential surface.

Reason (R) No work is required to move a test charge on the equipotential surface from one point to other.

8 **Assertion (A)** The expression of potential energy $U = \frac{1}{4\pi\varepsilon_0} \frac{q_1 q_2}{r_{12}}$, is unaltered whatever way the charges are brought to the specified locations.

Reason (R) Path-independence of work for electrostatic force.

9 **Assertion (A)** An electron has a high potential energy when it is at a location associated with a more negative value of potential, and a low potential energy when at a location associated with a more positive potential.

Reason (R) Electrons move from a higher potential region to lower potential region.

10 **Assertion (A)** In the absence of an external electric field, the dipole moment per unit volume of a polar dielectric is zero.

Reason (R) The dipoles of a polar dielectric are randomly oriented.

11 **Assertion (A)** Polar molecules have permanent dipole moment.

Reason (R) In polar molecules, the centres of positive and negative charges coincide even when there is no external field.

Very Short Answer Type Questions

1 Mark

12 Determine the work done in moving a test charge q through the distance 1 cm along the equatorial axis of an electric dipole.

13 Why there is no work done in moving a charge from one point to another on an equipotential surface?

14 Assume a charge starting at rest on an equipotential surface is moved off that surface and then is eventually returned to the same surface of rest after a round trip. How much work did it take to do this? Explain.

15 Do electrons tend to go to regions of high potential or low potential?

16 A proton is released at rest in a uniform electric field. Does the proton's electric potential energy increase or decrease?

Does the proton move towards a location with a higher or lower electric potential?

17 What is the net charge on a charged capacitor?

18 Two circular metal plates, each of radius 10 cm, are parallel to each other at a distance of 1mm. What kind of capacitor do they make? Mention one application of this capacitor.

19 A metal plate is introduced between the plates of a charged parallel plate capacitor. What is its effect on the capacitance of the capacitor?

Short Answer Type I Questions

2 Marks

20 How capacitance of parallel plate capacitor increase on introducing dielectric material between the plates of it? Explain.

21 Two point charge 5 μC and −5 μC are placed at points A and B, 5 cm apart.

(i) Draw the equipotential surface of the system.

(ii) Why do equipotential surfaces get close to each other near the point charge.

22 The plates in a parallel plate capacitor are separated by a distance d with air as the medium between the plates in order to increase the capacity by 66%. A dielectric slab of dielectric constant 5 is introduced between the plates. What is the thickness of dielectric slab?

23 A parallel plate capacitor with air as dielectric is charged by a DC source to a potential V. Without disconnecting the capacitor from the source, air is replaced by another dielectric medium of dielectric constant K. State with a reason, how does

(i) electric field between the plates?

(ii) energy stored in the capacitor charge?

24 A slab of material of a dielectric constant K has the same area as that of plates of a parallel plate capacitor but has the thickness $2d/3$, where d is separation between the plates.

Find the expression of the capacitance when the slab is inserted between the plates of the capacitor.

Short Answer Type II Questions

(3 Marks)

25 You are given an air filled parallel plate capacitor C_1. The space between its plates is now filled with slabs of dielectric constants K_1 and K_2 as shown in figure.

(i) Find the capacitance of the capacitor C_2 if area of the plates is A and distance between the plates is d.

(ii) What is the value of capacitance if $K_1 = K_2 = K$?

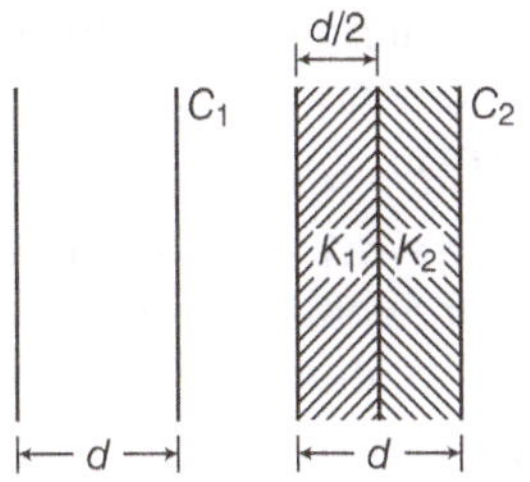

26 Two parallel plate capacitors of capacitances C_1 and C_2 such that $C_1 = C_2/2$ are connected across a battery of V volts as shown in the figure.

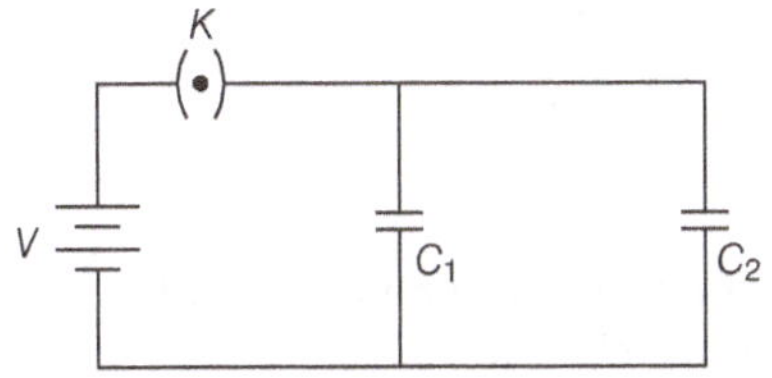

Initially, the key (K) is kept closed to fully charge the capacitors.

The key is now thrown open and a dielectric slab of dielectric K is inserted in the two capacitors to completely fill the gap between the plates. Find the ratio of

(i) the net capacitance and

(ii) the energies stored in the combination before and after the introducing dielectric slab.

27 Choose the statement as wrong or right and justify.

(i) Inside a conductor, electric field is not zero because electrostatic potential is constant.

(ii) On insertion of dielectric, capacitance of capacitor increases.

(iii) When capacitors are connected in parallel, the amount of charge in each capacitor will be same.

Long Answer Type Questions

(5 Marks)

28 (i) Depict the equipotential surfaces for a system of two identical positive point charges placed at distance d apart.

(ii) Deduce the expression for the potential energy of a system of two point charges q_1 and q_2 brought from infinity to the points with positions r_1 and r_2, respectively in presence of external electric field **E**.

29 (i) Obtain the expression for the potential due to an electric dipole of dipole moment p at a point x on the axial line.

(ii) Two identical capacitors of plate dimensions $l \times b$ and plate separation d have dielectric slabs filled in between the space of the plates as shown in figure.

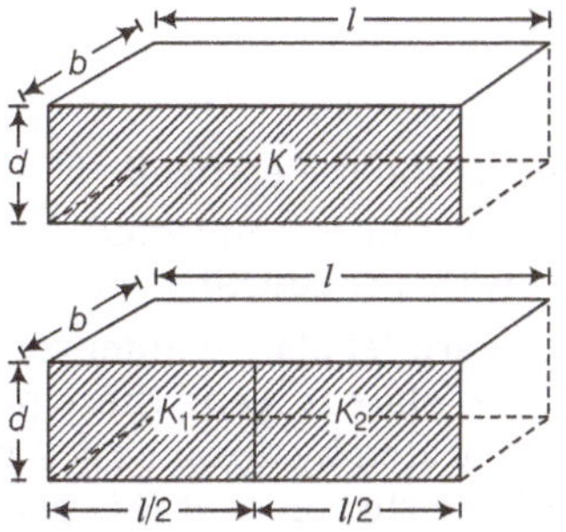

Obtain the relation between dielectric constants K, K_1 and K_2.

Case Based Questions

Directions (Q. No. 30) *These questions are case study based questions. Read the following paragraph and answer the questions.*

30. A capacitor is a system of two conductors separated by an insulating medium.

A capacitor works on a principle, which states that the capacitance of an insulated conductor is considerably increased, when we place on earth connected conductor near it. Parallel plate capacitor consists of two thin conducting plates each of area A held parallel to each other at a suitable distance d. Capacitance of the parallel plate capacitor is given by $C = \frac{\varepsilon_0 A}{d}$

If n capacitors of equal capacity C are connected in series, with supply voltage V, then their equivalent capacitance is $\frac{C}{n}$ and potential difference across each capacitor is $V' = \frac{V}{n}$.

If n identical capacitors are connected in parallel, then equivalent capacitance is $C_{eq} = nC$ and charge on each capacitor is $q' = \frac{q}{n}$.

(i) Describe any two applications of capacitor.

(ii) Figure shows a sheet of aluminium foil of negligible thickness placed between the plates of a capacitor. How will its capacitance be affected, if

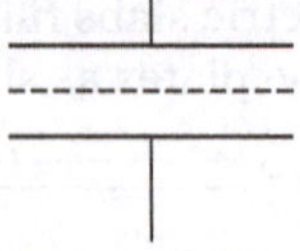

(a) the foil is electrically insulated?

(b) the foil is connected to the upper plate with a conducting wire?

(iii) In parallel plate condenser, the area of each plate is A and these plates are separated by distance d. A plate of dielectric constant K is placed between the parallel plates. If the charge on one of the plate is $+q$ and on another plate is $-q$, then how much charge will be induced on the surface of dielectric slab? Derive an expression for it.

(iv) You are given an air filled parallel plate capacitor C_1. The space between its plates is now filled with slabs of dielectric constants K_1 and K_2 as shown in figure. Find the capacitance of the capacitor C_2, if area of the plates is A and distance between the plates is d

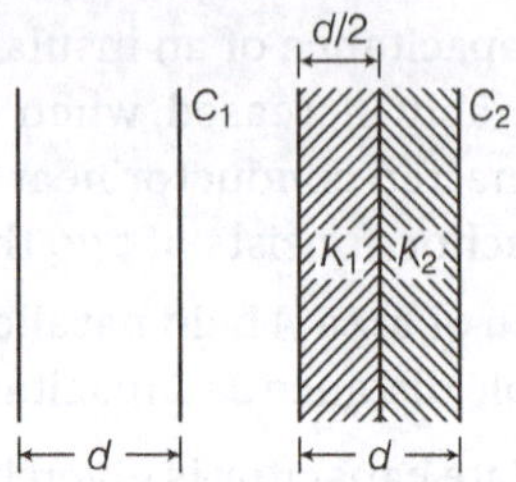

Numerical Problems

31 Calculate the potential at a point P due to a charge of 5×10^{-7} C located 11 cm away. **(1 M)**

32 A hollow metal sphere of radius 7 cm is charged such that potential on its surface is 20 V. What is the potential at the centre of the sphere? **(1 M)**

33 When reaching for door handle often sliding across a car seat on a dry winter day, you get a spark when your finger tip is 5 mm away from the handle.

What was the potential difference between you and the door handle just before the spark? Given that dielectric strength of air $= 3 \times 10^6$ V/m. **(1 M)**

34 Calculate the work done to dissociate the system of three charges placed on the vertices of a triangle as shown in the figure.

Here, $q = 1.6 \times 10^{-10}$C. **(2 M)**

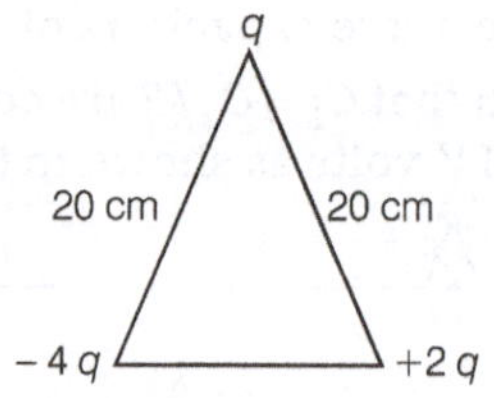

35 Read the following passage and answer the question below it:

Potential difference (ΔV) between two points A and B separated by a distance x, in a uniform electric field **E** is given by $\Delta V = -Ex$, where x is measured parallel to the field lines. If a charge q_0 moves from A to B, the change in potential energy (ΔU) is given as $\Delta U = q_0 \Delta V$. A proton is released from rest in uniform electric field of magnitude 8×10^4 V/m directed along the positive X-axis. The proton undergoes a displacement of 0.50 m in the direction of E.

Mass of a proton $= 1.66 \times 10^{-27}$ kg and charge on a proton $= 1.6 \times 10^{-19}$ C.

With the help of the comprehension given above, choose the most appropriate alternative for each of the following questions.

(i) What will happen to the potential energy of proton, when it moves from A to B?

(ii) What will be the velocity (v_B) of the proton after it has moved 0.50 m starting from rest? **(2 M)**

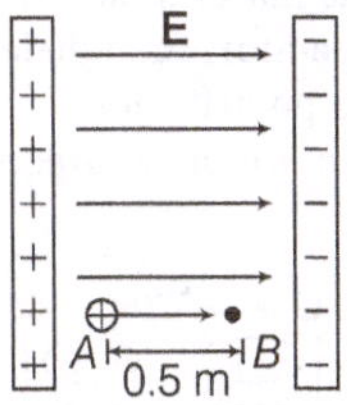

36 What is the area of the plates of a 2 F parallel plate capacitor, given that the separation between the plates is 0.5 cm? (You will realise from your answer why ordinary capacitors are in the range of μF or less. However, electrolytic capacitors do have a much larger capacitance (0.1 F) because of very minimum separation between the conductors). **NCERT, (2 M)**

37 Figure shows two identical capacitors C_1 and C_2, each of 2μF capacitance, connected to a battery of 5 V. Initially switch *S* is closed. After sometime, *S* is left open and dielectric slabs of dielectric constant $K = 5$ are inserted to fill completely the space between the plates of the two capacitors. How will the

(i) charge?

(ii) potential difference between the plates of the capacitors be affected after the slabs are inserted? **(3 M)**

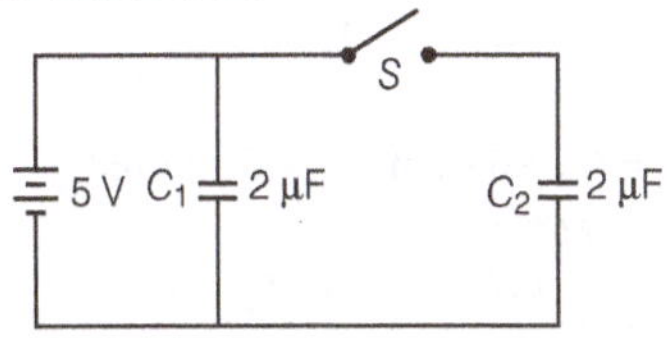

38 A network of four 10μF capacitors is connected to a 500V supply as shown in the figure. Determine the equivalent capacitance of the network along *AD*. **(2 M)**

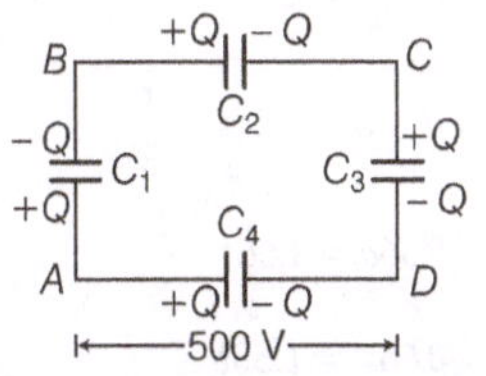

39 If two parallel plate capacitors *A* and *B* are connected in series combination with the same supply voltage, the capacitor *A* has air in between its plates while *B* has dielectric of dielectric constant 4, then

(i) determine the capacitance of each capacitor, if the equivalent capacitance of the combination is 4μF.

(ii) what is the ratio of electrostatic energy stored in *A* and *B* ? **[5 M]**

Answers

1 (*b*) As $E = \dfrac{V}{r}$, $r = \dfrac{V}{E} = \dfrac{600\text{ V}}{200\text{ N/C}} = 3\text{ m}$

2 (*b*)

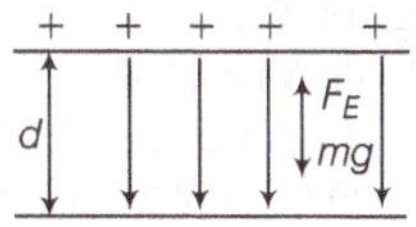

$\because \quad V = Ed \Rightarrow E = V/d$

Force acting on oil-drop

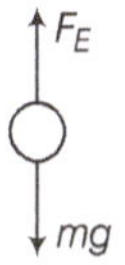

where, F_E = electrostatic force = qE

In equilibrium, $F_E = mg$

$\Rightarrow \quad qE = mg \Rightarrow (ne)E = V \times \rho g$

$(ne)E = \dfrac{4}{3}\pi r^3 \times \rho \times g$

$$\Rightarrow \quad n = \frac{\left(\frac{4}{3}\pi r^3 \rho g\right)}{E \times (e)} = \frac{\left(\frac{4}{3}\pi r^3 \rho g\right)}{(V/d) \times e}$$

$$= \frac{\frac{4}{3} \times (3.14) \times \left(\frac{10^{-6}}{2}\right)^3 \times 900 \times 10}{3600 \times 1.6 \times 10^{-19}} = 8.17 = 8$$

3 (*c*) $V = k_e \dfrac{Q_B}{R_B} = k_e \dfrac{Q_A}{R_A} = k_e = \dfrac{Q_B}{R_A/3}$

$Q_A = 3Q_B$ or $\dfrac{Q_B}{Q_A} = \dfrac{1}{3}$

Further, $\dfrac{E_B}{E_A} = \dfrac{Q_B/R_B^2}{Q_A/R_A^2} = \left(\dfrac{Q_B}{Q_A}\right)\left(\dfrac{R_A}{R_B}\right)^2 = \left(\dfrac{1}{3}\right)(3)^2 = 3$

4 (*c*) Fall in potential (as the charged object moves from point *A* to point *B*) is the same in Figs. (i), (ii) and (iii), since work done = charge × fall in potential, it is also the same in all the three figures.

Work done = $q(V_B - V_A)$ = is same for all three cases

5 (*d*) As, $C_S = \left(\dfrac{4C}{4+C}\right)\mu\text{F}$

(where, *C* is capacitance of other capacitor)

and $\quad \dfrac{1}{2}C_s V^2 = 173\,\mu\text{J}$

$\dfrac{1}{2}\left(\dfrac{4C}{4+C}\right)(12)^2 = 173$

$\Rightarrow \quad \dfrac{4C}{4+C} = \dfrac{2 \times 173}{144} = 2.4$

Hence, $C = 6\,\mu\text{F}$

6 (c) A → 1; B → 4; C → 3; D → 2

(i) When S is open,

$$C_{eq} = \frac{C_1 C_2}{C_1 + C_2} = \frac{(2\mu F)(3\mu F)}{(2\mu F + 3\mu F)} = \frac{6}{5}\mu F$$

Charge (q) on both the capacitors will be the same (as these are in series), i.e.

$$q = C_{eq}\, V = \left(\frac{6}{5}\mu F\right)(30 + 60)\, V = 108\,\mu C$$

(ii) When S is closed, charge on C_1, i.e.

$$q_1 = C_1 V_1 = (2\mu F)(30 V) = 60\,\mu C$$

Charge on C_2, i.e. $q_2 = C_2 V_2 = (3\mu F)(60\ V) = 180\mu C$

Charge on C_1 and $C_2 = 60\mu C + 180\,\mu C = 240\,\mu C$

7 (a) The proof of this statement is simple. There is no potential difference between any two points on the surface and no work is required to move a test charge on the surface because work done = potential difference × charge.

8 (a) The potential energy $U = \frac{1}{4\pi\varepsilon_0}\frac{q_1 q_2}{r_{12}}$, is unaltered whatever way the charges are brought to the specified locations, because of path independence of work for electrostatic force.

9 (c) Electrons move from a lower potential region to higher potential region.

10 (a) There are polar and non-polar dielectric materials. The molecules of a polar dielectric have a permanent dipole moment. However, due to random orientations, net dipole moment is zero. If there is no external electric field, there is no polarisation.

11 (c) The molecules of a substance may be polar or non-polar. In a non-polar molecule, the centre of positive and negative charges coincides. On the other hand, a polar molecule is one is which the centres of positive and negative charges are separated, even when there is no external field. Such molecules have a permanent dipole moment.

12 Electrostatic ptoential at any point is the equatorial plane of dipole is zero.

∴ Work done, $\Delta W = q\Delta V = 0$

13 Change in potential is zero on an equipotential.

14 Work done,

$\Delta W = q\Delta V = q(0) = 0$

15 High potential

16 Proton moves from a location of higher potential to lower potential. Thus, potential energy decreases.

17 Zero

18 Parallel plate capacitor. It is used to store electrostatic energy.

19 Increases

20 When a dielectric material is introduced between the parallel plate capacitor, then dielectric material gets polarised. Due to polarisation, an internal electric field $\mathbf{E}_i$ is developed in opposite direction of external electric field.

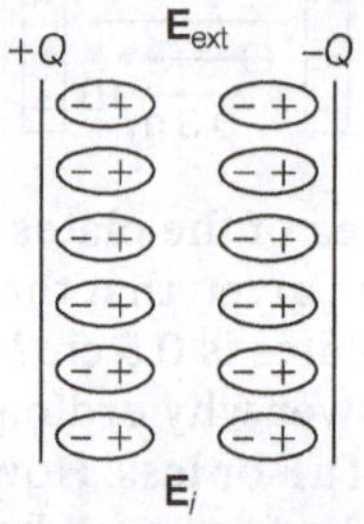

Therefore, net electric field between plates of capacitor decreases

$$\mathbf{E}_{net} = \mathbf{E}_{ext} - \mathbf{E}_i$$

∴ Potential difference decreases due to decreasing electric field.

$$\therefore \text{ Capacitance} \propto \frac{1}{\text{Potential difference}}$$

Hence, capacitance of parallel plate capacitor increases.

21 Refer to text on page 61 (Equipotential surfaces in different cases, case IV).

22 If t be the thickness of dielectric medium, then

$$C' = \frac{\varepsilon_0 A}{(d-t) + t/K} \quad \text{...(i)}$$

$$C_0 = \frac{\varepsilon_0 A}{d} \quad \text{...(ii)}$$

Given, $C' = C_0 + 66\%$ of $C_0 = C_0 + 0.66C_0$

$$C' = 1.66C_0$$

$$\therefore \frac{C'}{C_0} = \frac{\varepsilon_0 A/(d-t) + t/K}{\varepsilon_0 A/d}$$

$$\frac{1.66C_0}{C_0} = \frac{d}{(d-t) + t/K}$$

$$1.66(d-t) + \frac{t}{K} = d$$

$$\Rightarrow \quad 1.66d - d = 1.66t - \frac{t}{K}$$

$$0.66d = 1.66t - \frac{t}{5} \quad \text{[Given, } K = 5]$$

$$0.66d = 1.33t$$

$$\Rightarrow \quad t = \frac{0.66d}{1.33}$$

$$t = \frac{d}{2}$$

23 (i) Refer to text on pages 78 and 79 (Effect of dielectric on parallel plate capacitor).

(ii) Refer to text on page 83 (Change in energy on introducing dielectric slab).

24 Refer to Q. 11 on page 85. $\left[\textbf{Ans. } \left(\frac{3K}{K+2}\right)\cdot\left(\frac{\varepsilon_0 A}{d}\right)\right]$

25 Refer to Q. 12 on page 85.

26 Refer to Q. 18 on page 85.

27 (i) Refer to text on page 61 (Equipotential surfaces).

(ii) Refer to Q. 20 on page 100.

(iii) Refer to text on page 80 (Capacitors in parallel).

28 (i) Refer to text on page 61, case (iii).

(ii) Refer to text on page 62 (Electric potential energy of a system of two point charges).

29 (i) Refer to text on page 59 (Electric potential due to an electric dipole on its axial line).

(ii) Refer to Q. 12 on page 85.

30. (i) Applications of capacitors are given below :

(a) **To store charge** The main purpose or use of capacitor is to collect more charge in electric circuit. If strong current for very short period is required in any electric circuit, then capacitor is used for it. Pulsating electromagnets produce strong magnetic field for very short period. Electric current is obtained from charged capacitors.

(b) **To store energy** Energy is also stored in capacitors. Sufficient energy is stored between the plates of the capacitor in electric field. In synchrocyclotron, large number of capacitors are used as energy collectors. Synchrocyclotron obtains energy from these capacitors according to its need.

(ii) (a) The system will be equivalent to two identical capacitors connected in series combination in which two plates of each capacitor have separation half of the original separation.

Thus, new capacitance of each capacitor,

$$C' = 2C \qquad \left[\because C \propto \frac{1}{d}\right]$$

$\because$ C and C' are in series.

$$\Rightarrow \quad C_{net} = \frac{2C \times 2C}{2C + 2C} = C$$

$$C_{net} = C \quad \text{[original capacitor]}$$

(b) System reduces to a capacitor whose separation reduces to half of original one.

$\therefore$ New capacitance, $C' = 2C$

(iii) The electric field between the plates of the condenser filled with air only, $E_0 = \dfrac{q}{\varepsilon_0 A}$

where, ε_0 = permittivity of vacuum.

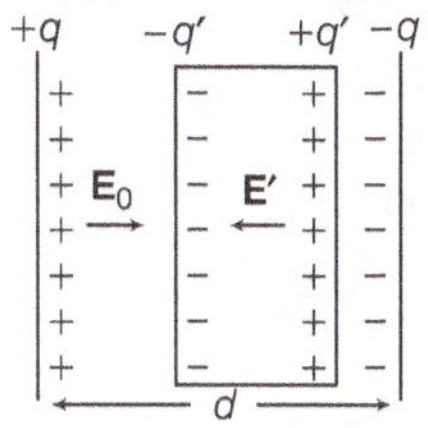

Let the charge induced on the faces of dielectric slab be $-q'$ and $+q'$, respectively. The electric field due to these charges,

$$E' = q'/A\varepsilon_0$$

E' and E_0 are in the same direction, the resultant electric field,

$$E = E_0 - E' = \frac{q}{\varepsilon_0 A} - \frac{q'}{\varepsilon_0 A} = \frac{q - q'}{\varepsilon_0 A} \quad \text{...(i)}$$

Field in the presence of dielectric medium,

$$E = \frac{E_0}{K} = \frac{q}{K\varepsilon_0 A} \quad \text{...(ii)}$$

From Eqs. (i) and (ii), we get

$$\frac{q}{KA\varepsilon_0} = \frac{q - q'}{\varepsilon_0 A} \quad \text{or} \quad \frac{q}{K} = q - q'$$

or

$$q' = q - \frac{q}{K} = q\left(1 - \frac{1}{K}\right)$$

i.e. The induced charge on the faces of dielectric slab will be $-q\left(1 - \frac{1}{K}\right)$ and $+q\left(1 - \frac{1}{K}\right)$.

(iv) After introducing the dielectric medium of dielectric constants K_1 and K_2, capacitor acts as if it consists of two capacitors, each having plates of area A and separation $\frac{d}{2}$ connected in series combination for

$$C_1 = \frac{\varepsilon_0 A}{d} \quad \text{...(i)}$$

$$\Rightarrow \quad \frac{1}{C_2} = \frac{1}{\left(\frac{K_1 \varepsilon_0 A}{d/2}\right)} + \frac{1}{\left(\frac{K_2 \varepsilon_0 A}{d/2}\right)}$$

$$\Rightarrow \quad \frac{1}{C_2} = \frac{1}{\left(\frac{\varepsilon_0 A}{d}\right)}\left(\frac{1}{2K_1} + \frac{1}{2K_2}\right)$$

$$\Rightarrow \quad \frac{1}{C_2} = \frac{1}{2C_1}\left(\frac{K_2 + K_1}{K_1 K_2}\right)$$

$$\Rightarrow \quad C_2 = C_1\left(\frac{2K_1\,K_2}{K_1 + K_2}\right)$$

The capacitors will be in series.

31 Potential, $V = \dfrac{q}{4\pi\varepsilon_0 r} = \dfrac{9\times10^9\times5\times10^{-7}}{11\times10^{-12}} = 40.9\text{ kV}$

32 Potential, $V = 20\text{ V}$

33 As, $\quad E = \dfrac{dV}{dr}$

$$\Rightarrow \quad 3\times10^6 = \frac{\Delta V}{5\times10^{-3}}$$

$$\Rightarrow \quad \Delta V = 15000\text{ V}$$

34 Refer to solution of Q. 46 on page 75.

35 (i) Refer to text on page 62 (Relation between electric field and electric potential).

(ii) Apply

$$\frac{1}{2}mv^2 = eV \Rightarrow v = 2.77\times10^6\text{ m/s}$$

36 Refer to example 2 on page 78. **[Ans.** 1130 km^2**]**

37 Refer to Q. 31 on page 87.

38 $\dfrac{1}{C'} = \dfrac{1}{C_1} + \dfrac{1}{C_2} + \dfrac{1}{C_3}$

$$C_{eq} = C' + C_4 = 13.3\,\mu\text{F}$$

39 Refer to Q. 44 on page 88.

(i) $5\,\mu\text{F}$, $20\,\mu\text{F}$ (ii) 1 : 4

RELATED ONLINE VIDEOS

Visit : https://www.youtube.com/watch?v=-Rb9guSEeVE
OR **Scan the Code**

Visit : https://www.youtube.com/watch?v=KBJl1qiYOgo
OR **Scan the Code**

Visit : https://www.youtube.com/watch?v=lvAnzZgwcFQ
OR **Scan the Code**

Visit : https://www.youtube.com/watch?v=mJxAlNAiTds
OR **Scan the Code**

CHAPTER

03

Current Electricity

In electrostatics, we have studied about the charges at rest. Here, we will study about charges in motion which constitute an electric current. Such electric currents occur naturally in many situations, e.g. in lightning, charges flow from the clouds to the earth through the atmosphere, which sometimes becomes disastrous, as the flow of charges is not steady. However, in our everyday life we see many devices such as a torch, a cell-driven clock, etc. where charges flow in steady manner.

TOPIC 01 Electric Current and Ohm's Law

If we maintain the constant potential difference between two conductors, we get a constant flow of charge in a metallic wire connecting the two conductors. The flow of charge in a metallic wire constitutes **electric current**. The branch of physics which deals with the charges in motion is called **current electricity**.

Electric Current

It is defined as the rate of flow of electric charge through any cross-section of a conductor. It is denoted by I. Electric current can be expressed by

$$I = \frac{\text{Total charge flowing } (q)}{\text{Time taken } (t)}$$

If the charge dq flows through a conductor for small time dt, then $I = \frac{dq}{dt}$.

It means that the current through a conductor at a time is defined as the first derivative of charge passing through a cross-section of the conductor in a particular direction with respect to time.

If n = number of charges, e = electric charge and t = time,

then $$\boxed{I = \frac{q}{t} = \frac{ne}{t}}$$ [here, $q = ne$]

Conventionally, the direction of electric current is along the direction of motion of positive charges and opposite to the direction of motion of negative charges.

Electric current is not always steady and hence more generally, we can define the current as follows

Let Δq be the net charge flowing through a cross-section of the conductor in a particular direction during the time interval Δt [i.e. between times t and $(t+\Delta t)$] . Then, at time t, the current in the conductor is given by

$$dI(t) = \lim_{\Delta t \to 0} \frac{\Delta q}{\Delta t} = \frac{dq}{dt}$$

Current is a scalar quantity. Although it represents the direction of flow of positive charges, it does not follow the laws of vector addition (since the angle between the wires carrying current does not affect the total current). It follows the laws of scalar addition.

Unit of Electric Current

The SI unit of current is ampere and it is represented by A. $1 \text{ ampere (A)} = \frac{1 \text{ coulomb (C)}}{1 \text{ second (s)}} = 1$ coulomb per second or 1 Cs^{-1}.

Current through a wire is said to be **one ampere**, if a charge of one coulomb flows through any cross-section of the wire in one second.

Example 1 How many electrons pass through a lamp in 1 min, if the current is 300 mA? Given, the charge on an electron is 1.6×10^{-19} C.

Sol. Given, current, $I = 300 \text{ mA} = 300 \times 10^{-3}$ A

Charge on one electron, $e = 1.6 \times 10^{-19}$ C

Time, $t = 1 \text{ min} = 60$ s

Charge passing through a lamp in 1 min, $q = I \times t$

$= 300 \times 10^{-3} \times 60$

Let n electrons pass through the lamp in 1 min.

$$\therefore \quad q = ne \Rightarrow n = \frac{q}{e} = \frac{300 \times 10^{-3} \times 60}{1.6 \times 10^{-19}} = 1.125 \times 10^{20} \text{ C}$$

Important Points Related to Flow of Current

As a matter of convention, the direction of flow of positive charge gives the direction of current. This is called **conventional current.** The direction of flow of electrons gives the direction of **electronic current.** Therefore , the direction of electronic current is opposite to that of conventional current.

If the current varies with time, it is represented by differential limit of q, i.e. $I = \frac{dq}{dt}$.

Further, I is same, even when cross-sectional area is different at different points of the conductor.

Through a cross-section of the conductor in a time t, if a positive charge q_1 is flowing from A to B and a negative charge q_2 is flowing from B to A, then total current through the conductor is given by

$$I = \frac{q_1}{t} + \frac{q_2}{t} = \frac{q_1 + q_2}{t}$$

Current Density

The current density at a point in a conductor is the ratio of the current at that point in the conductor to the area of cross-section of the conductor at that point.

If a current I is distributed uniformly over the cross-section A of a conductor, then the current density at that point is

$$J = \frac{I}{A}$$

It is a characteristic property of a point inside the conductor. It is a vector quantity. Its direction at a point is the direction of flow of positive charge at that point.

The SI unit of current density is Am^{-2}.

Example 2 An aluminium wire of diameter 0.24 cm is connected in series to a copper wire of diameter 0.16 cm. The wires carry an electric current of 10 A. Determine the current density in aluminium wire.

Sol. Given, diameter = 0.24 cm,

radius, $r = \frac{0.24 \times 10^{-2}}{2} = 0.12 \times 10^{-2}$ m

and current, $I = 10$ A

$\therefore$ Current density, $J = \frac{I}{A} = \frac{I}{\pi r^2}$

$= \frac{10}{3.14 \times (0.12 \times 10^{-2})^2}$

$= 2.2 \times 10^6 \text{ Am}^{-2}$

Mechanism of Flow of Current in Conductor

All metals are good conductors of electricity. The electric conduction in them can be explained by the electron theory. In an atom of a substance, the electrons in the orbits close to the nucleus are bound to it due to the strong attraction of the positive charge, but the electrons far from the nucleus experience a very weak attractive force.

Hence, the outer electrons can be removed easily from the atom (by rubbing or by heating the substance).

In fact, a few outer electrons leave their atoms and move freely within the substance (in the vacant spaces between the atoms). These electrons called **free electrons** or **conduction electrons.** They carry the charge in the substance from one place to the other. Therefore, the electrical conductivity of a solid substance depends upon the number of free electrons in it.

In metals, this number is quite large ($\approx 10^{29}$ per m^3). Hence, metals are good conductors of electricity. Silver is the best conductor of electricity than copper, gold and aluminium, respectively.

In liquids and gases, electric conduction takes place by the movement of both positive and negative charge carriers unlike in metals, where the electric conduction occurs by the movement of negative charge carriers (electrons) only.

In case of a liquid conductor such as electrolytic solution, there are positive and negative charged ions, which can move on applying electric field and hence generating the electric current. Whereas in case of a solid conductor (i.e. Cu, Fe, Ag, etc.) atoms are tightly bound to each other. They consist of large number of free electrons, which are responsible for the strong current in them when electric field is applied on them.

There are some other materials in which the electrons will be bound and they will not be accelerated, even if the electric field is applied, i.e. no current on applying electric field. Such materials are called **insulators.** e.g. Wood, plastic, rubber, etc.

In our discussions, we will focus only on solid conductors in which the positive ions are at fixed positions and the current is carried by the negatively charged electrons.

Ohm's Law

It states that the current I flowing through a conductor is always directly proportional to the potential difference V across the ends of the conductor, provided that the physical conditions (temperature, mechanical strain, etc.) are kept constant. Mathematically,

$$I \propto V \quad \text{or} \quad V \propto I$$

or $$\boxed{V = IR}$$

where, R is resistance of the conductor.

Its value depends upon the length, shape and the nature of the material of the conductor. It is independent of the values of V and I. Such conductors are said to obey Ohm's law.

For an ohmic conductor, the graph between V and I is a straight line as shown in the figure.

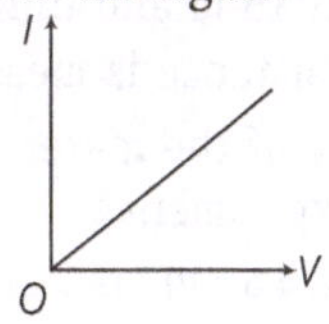

Example 3 A potential difference of 3 V is applied across a conductor through which 5A of current is flowing. Determine the resistance of the conductor.

Sol. Given, potential difference, $V = 3\text{ V}$

Current, $I = 5\text{A}$

According to Ohm's law, $R = \frac{V}{I} \Rightarrow R = \frac{3}{5} = 0.6\,\Omega$

Resistance of a Conductor

It is defined as the ratio of the potential difference applied across the ends of the conductor to the current flowing through it.

Mathematically, $R = \frac{V}{I}$

The SI unit of resistance is ohm and denoted by Ω.

$$1\text{ ohm }(\Omega) = \frac{1\text{ volt (V)}}{1\text{ ampere (A)}} = 1\text{ volt/ampere (or V/A)}$$

The resistance of a conductor is said to be **one ohm**, if one ampere of current flows, when a potential difference of one volt is applied across the ends of the conductor.

Dimensional formula of electrical resistance is $[ML^2T^{-3}A^{-2}]$.

The resistance of the conductor depends upon the following factors

(i) It is directly proportional to the length of the conductor.

i.e. $$R \propto l \quad \text{...(i)}$$

(ii) It is inversely proportional to the area of the cross-section of the conductor.

i.e. $$R \propto \frac{1}{A} \quad \text{...(ii)}$$

From Eqs. (i) and (ii), we get

$$R \propto \frac{l}{A} \quad \text{or} \quad \boxed{R = \rho\frac{l}{A}} \quad \text{...(iii)}$$

where, ρ is the constant of proportionality known as **resistivity** or **specific resistance** of the conductor.

(iii) It depends upon the nature of the material and temperature of the conductor.

Example 4 A negligible small current is passed through a wire length 15 m and uniform cross-section 6×10^{-7} m^2 and its resistance is measured to be 5 Ω. What is the resistivity of the material at the temperature of the experiment? **NCERT**

Sol. Given, $R = 5\Omega$, $A = 6\times10^{-7}\,\text{m}^2$ and $l = 15\text{m}$

Let the resistivity of the material be ρ.

$\therefore$ Resistance of wire, $R = \rho\dfrac{l}{A}$

$$\Rightarrow \quad \rho = \frac{RA}{l} = \frac{5\times6\times10^{-7}}{15} = 2\times10^{-7}\,\Omega\text{-m}$$

Thus, the resistivity of the material at the temperature of the experiment is $2\times10^{-7}\,\Omega$-m .

Example 5 Consider a thin square sheet of side L and thickness t, made of a material of resistivity ρ. The resistance between two opposite faces, shown by the shaded areas in the figure. **(2010)**

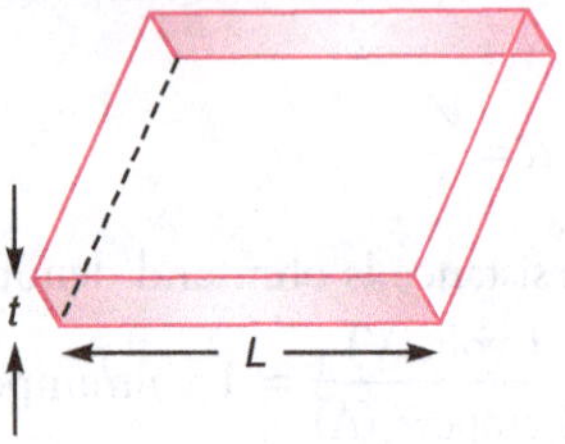

Sol. Resistance between the shaded opposite faces is

$$R = \frac{\rho(L)}{A} = \frac{\rho L}{tL} = \frac{\rho}{t}$$

Note Here, R is independent of L.

Effect of Temperature on Resistance

Resistance of a metallic conductor at temperature t°C is given as

$$R_t = R_0(1+\alpha t+\beta t^2) \quad \ldots\text{(i)}$$

where, R_0 = resistance of conductor at 0°C and α, β are the temperature coefficients of resistance.

If the temperature t°C is not sufficiently large which is so in most of the practical cases, then Eq. (i) can be written as

$$R_t = R_0(1+\alpha t) \quad \text{or} \quad \alpha = \frac{R_t - R_0}{R_0\times t}$$

$$\alpha = \frac{\text{Change in resistance}}{\text{Original resistance}\times\text{Rise of temperature}}$$

Therefore, temperature coefficient of resistance is defined as the increase in resistance per unit original resistance per degree celsius or kelvin rise of temperature.
For metals, the value of α is positive, therefore, resistance of the metal increases with rise in temperature.

For insulators and semiconductors, the value of α is negative, therefore, resistance decreases with rise in temperature.

For alloys, the value of α is very small. The value of α is different at different temperatures. Temperature coefficient of resistance averaged over the temperature range t_1°C to t_2°C is given by

$$\alpha = \frac{R_2 - R_1}{R_1(t_2 - t_1)}$$

where, R_1 and R_2 are the resistances at t_1°C and t_2°C, respectively.

Example 6 A silver wire has a resistance of 2.1 Ω at 27.5 °C and a resistance of 2.7 Ω at 100 °C. Determine the temperature coefficient of resistivity of silver. **NCERT**

Sol. Given, $t_1 = 27.5$°C, $t_2 = 100$°C

$R_1 = R_{27.5} = 2.1\,\Omega$ and $R_2 = R_{100} = 2.7\,\Omega$

$\therefore$ Temperature coefficient of silver is given by

$$\alpha = \frac{R_2 - R_1}{R_1(t_2 - t_1)} = \frac{2.7-2.1}{2.1(100-27.5)}$$
$$= 0.0039\,°\text{C}^{-1}$$

Flow of Electric Charge in a Conductor

When no electric field is applied on a solid conductor, the free electrons in them move like molecules in a gas due to their thermal velocities. There is no preferential direction for the velocities of the electrons. The average thermal random velocity is zero. Due to this, there is no net flow of electric charge in a particular direction inside the conductor and hence no current flows in it.

When an electric field is applied on a solid conductor, at the two ends, an electric field is generated in the conductor from positive terminal towards negative terminal.

All the free electrons move from negative terminal to positive terminal under the effect of electric field with constant speed called drift velocity, thus constitute electric current.

Drift Velocity (Proof of Ohm's Law)

Drift velocity is defined as the average velocity with which the free electrons in a conductor get drifted towards the positive end of the conductor under the influence of an electric field applied across the conductor. It is denoted by v_d. The drift velocity of electron is of the order of $10^{-4}\,\text{ms}^{-1}$.

Let V be the potential difference applied across the ends of a conductor of length l, then the magnitude of electric field is

$$E = \frac{V}{l}$$

The direction of electric field is from positive to negative end of conductor as shown in figure. Since, the charge on an electron is $-e$ and each free electron in the conductor experiences a force F.

$\therefore$ $$\mathbf{F} = -e\mathbf{E}$$

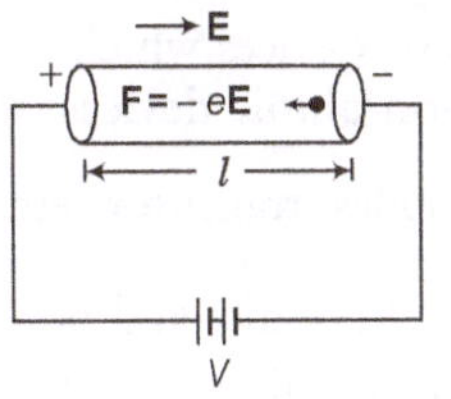

Current in a metallic conductor

Here, negative sign indicates that the direction of force is opposite to that of electric field applied.

Acceleration of each electron is given by

$$\mathbf{a} = -\frac{e\mathbf{E}}{m}$$

$$\left[\text{from Newton's second law, } a = \frac{F}{m}\right]$$

where, m is mass of the electron.

Under the effect of applied electric field, the free electrons accelerate and acquire a velocity component in a direction opposite to the direction of electric field in addition to their thermal velocities.

However, this gain in velocity of electron due to the electric field is very small and it is lost in the next collision with the ion/atom of the conductor.

At any instant of time, the velocity acquired by electron having thermal velocity $\mathbf{u}_1$ is given by

$$\mathbf{v}_1 = \mathbf{u}_1 + \mathbf{a}t_1$$

where, t_1 is the time elapsed as it has suffered its last collision with ion atom of conductor.

Similarly, $\mathbf{v}_2 = \mathbf{u}_2 + \mathbf{a}t_2, \ldots, \mathbf{v}_n = \mathbf{u}_n + \mathbf{a}t_n$

$\therefore$ Average velocity, $$\mathbf{v}_d = \frac{\mathbf{v}_1 + \mathbf{v}_2 + \ldots + \mathbf{v}_n}{n}$$

$$= \frac{(\mathbf{u}_1 + \mathbf{a}t_1) + (\mathbf{u}_2 + \mathbf{a}t_2) + \cdots + (\mathbf{u}_n + \mathbf{a}t_n)}{n}$$

$$= \frac{\mathbf{u}_1 + \mathbf{u}_2 + \ldots + \mathbf{u}_n}{n} + \frac{\mathbf{a}[t_1 + t_2 + \ldots + t_n]}{n}$$

We know that, $\dfrac{\mathbf{u}_1 + \mathbf{u}_2 + \ldots + \mathbf{u}_n}{n} = 0$

and $\dfrac{t_1 + t_2 + \ldots + t_n}{n}$ is called average time elapsed or **average relaxation time** and is denoted by τ. Its value is of the order of 10^{-14} s.

$\therefore$ $\mathbf{v}_d = 0 + \mathbf{a}\tau$ or $\mathbf{v}_d = \mathbf{a}\tau$ or $\mathbf{v}_d = -\dfrac{e\mathbf{E}}{m}\tau$

Negative sign shows that $\mathbf{v}_d$ is opposite to the direction of $\mathbf{E}$.

$\therefore$ $$\boxed{\text{Average drift velocity, } \mathbf{v}_d = \frac{e\mathbf{E}}{m}\tau}$$

Average relaxation time

= Mean free path of electron/Drift speed of electron.

Relation between Drift Velocity and Electric Current

Consider a conductor of length l and A be the uniform area of cross-section.

$\therefore$ Volume of conductor $= Al$

If the conductor contains free electrons n per unit volume.

Then, number of free electrons in the conductor $= nAl$

If e is the charge of an electron, then total charge on all free electrons in the conductor is given by

$$q = nAle \qquad \ldots(\text{i})$$

Time taken by the free electrons to cross the length of the conductor

$$t = \frac{l}{v_d} \qquad \ldots(\text{ii})$$

Since, current is the rate of flow of the charge through conductor.

$$I = \frac{q}{t}$$

Using Eqs. (i) and (ii), we get

$$I = \frac{nAle}{l/v_d} \Rightarrow \boxed{I = neAv_d} \qquad \ldots(\text{iii})$$

Eq. (iii) gives the relation between the current flowing through the conductor and drift velocity of the electron.

Putting the value of $v_d \left(= \dfrac{eE\tau}{m}\right)$ in Eq. (iii), we get

$$\boxed{I = \frac{Ane^2\tau E}{m}}$$

Proof of Ohm's Law

We know that, $I = \dfrac{Ane^2\tau E}{m}$ and $V_d = \dfrac{eE}{m}.\tau = \left(\dfrac{eV}{ml}\tau\right)$

$$\left[\text{as } E = \frac{V}{l}\right]$$

So, $$I = Anev_d = Ane\left(\frac{eV}{ml}\tau\right) = \left(\frac{Ane^2\tau}{ml}\right)V$$

or $$\frac{V}{I} = \frac{ml}{Ane^2\tau} = R = \text{constant}$$

$\therefore \quad \frac{V}{I} = R \Rightarrow \boxed{V = RI}$

This is called Ohm's law.

Example 7 Estimate the average drift speed of conduction electrons in a copper wire of cross-sectional area $1.0 \times 10^{-7}\ m^2$ carrying a current of 1.5 A. Assume the density of conduction electrons to be $9 \times 10^{28}\ m^{-3}$.

Sol. Given, cross-sectional area, $A = 1.0 \times 10^{-7}\ m^2$

Current, $I = 1.5A$, Electron density, $n = 9 \times 10^{28}\ m^{-3}$

Drift velocity, $v_d = ?$

We know that, $I = neAv_d$

$$\Rightarrow \quad v_d = \frac{I}{neA} = \frac{1.5}{9 \times 10^{28} \times 1.6 \times 10^{-19} \times 1.0 \times 10^{-7}}$$

$$= 1.042 \times 10^{-3}\ m/s$$

Mobility

It is defined as the magnitude of drift velocity of charge per unit electric field applied. It is expressed as

$$\mu = \frac{\text{Drift velocity } (v_d)}{\text{Electric field } (E)} = \frac{qE\tau / m}{E} = \frac{q\tau}{m}$$

where, τ is the **average relaxation time** of the charge while drifting towards the opposite electrode and m is the mass of the charged particle.

Mobility of electrons, $\mu_e = \frac{e\tau_e}{m_e}$.

and **mobility of holes,** $\mu_h = \frac{e\tau_h}{m_h}$.

where, τ_e and τ_h are average relaxation time for electrons and holes, respectively. m_e and m_h refer to mass of electrons and holes, respectively. Charge on either is e.

The SI unit of mobility is $m^2s^{-1}V^{-1}$ or $ms^{-1}N^{-1}C$ and it is in the order of 10^4. The practical unit of mobility is $(Cm^2/V\text{-}s)$. Mobility is a positive quantity.

Example 8 Find the current flow through a copper wire of length 0.2 m, area of cross-section 1 mm^2, when connected to a battery of 4 V. Given that, for electron mobility is $4.5 \times 10^{-6} m^2s^{-1}V^{-1}$ and charge on an electron is 1.6×10^{-19}C. The number density of electrons in copper wire is $8.5 \times 10^{28}\ m^{-3}$.

Sol. Given, length of copper wire, $l = 0.2$ m

Cross-sectional area, $A = 1\ mm^2 = 10^{-6}\ m^2$

Potential difference, $V = 4$ V

Electron mobility, $\mu = 4.5 \times 10^{-6}\ m^2s^{-1}V^{-1}$

Charge of an electron, $e = 1.6 \times 10^{-19}$ C

Number density of electrons, $n = 8.5 \times 10^{28}\ m^{-3}$

We know that electric field set up across the conductor,

$$E = \frac{V}{l} = \frac{4}{0.2} = 20\ V/m$$

$\therefore$ Current through the wire, $I = nAe\,v_d = nAe\mu E$ $\quad [\because \mu = v_d/E]$

$$= 8.5 \times 10^{28} \times 10^{-6} \times 1.6 \times 10^{-19} \times 4.5 \times 10^{-6} \times 20$$

$$= 1.22\ A$$

Limitations of Ohm's Law

The devices which do not obey Ohm's law are called **non-ohmic devices**, such as vacuum tubes, semiconductor diodes, transistors etc. The relation $\left(\frac{V}{I} = R\right)$ is valid for both, ohmic and non-ohmic devices.

For ohmic conductors, value of R is constant.

For non-ohmic devices, value of R is not constant, i.e. Ohm's law fails.

The limitations of Ohm's law are given below

(i) Potential difference may vary non-linearly with current.

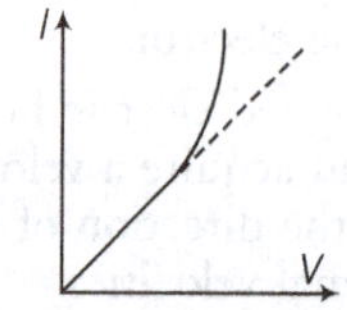

Variation of potential difference with current

(ii) The variation of current with potential difference may depend upon sign of potential difference applied.

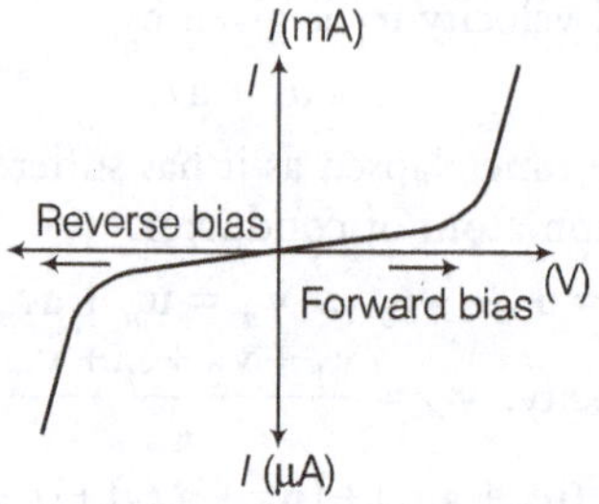

Variation of current according to the sign of potential difference

(iii) The relation between potential difference and current is not unique, i.e. there is more than one value of V for the same current I.

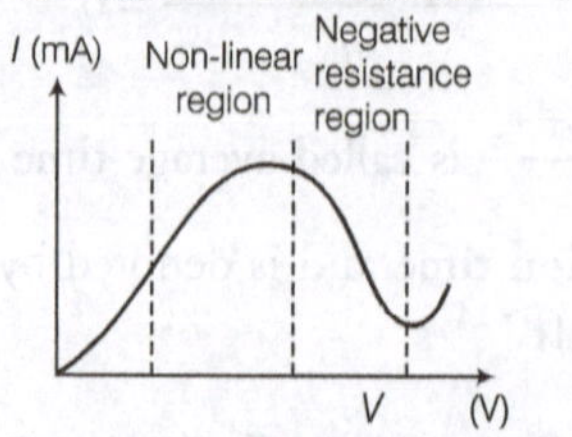

Graph of current *versus* potential difference for GaAs

Resistivity of Various Materials

Specific resistance or resistivity of the material of a conductor is defined as the resistance of a unit length with unit area of cross-section of the material of the conductor, i.e. it is also defined as the resistance of unit cube of a material of the given conductor. The unit of resistivity is ohm-metre or Ω-m and its dimensional formula is $[ML^3T^{-3}A^{-2}]$.

Since, we know that $R = \rho \frac{l}{A} \Rightarrow \rho = \frac{RA}{l}$ ...(i)

Substituting the value of $R = \frac{ml}{ne^2 A\tau}$ in Eq. (i),

we have, $\rho = \left(\frac{ml}{ne^2 A\tau}\right) \cdot \frac{A}{l}$

∴ Resistivity of the material,

$$\boxed{\rho = \frac{m}{ne^2\tau}}$$

From the above formula, it is clear that resistivity of a conductor depends upon the following factors:

(i) $\rho \propto \frac{1}{n}$, i.e. resistivity of a material is inversely proportional to the number density of free electrons (number of free electrons per unit volume).
As the free electron density depends upon the nature of material, so resistivity of a conductor depends on the nature of the material.

(ii) $\rho \propto 1/\tau$, i.e. resistivity of a material is inversely proportional to the average relaxation time τ of free electrons in the conductor.
As value of τ depends on the temperature of conductor, so resistivity of a conductor changes with temperature, as temperature increases, τ decreases, hence ρ increases.

Example 9 Find the time of relaxation between collision and free path of electrons in copper at room temperature.
(Given, resistivity of copper = 1.7×10^{-8} Ω-m, density of electrons in copper = 8.5×10^{28} m^{-3}, charge on an electron = 1.6×10^{-19} C, mass of electron = 9.1×10^{-31} kg and drift velocity of free electrons = 1.6×10^{-4} ms^{-1})

Sol. Given, $\rho = 1.7 \times 10^{-8}$ Ω-m, $n = 8.5 \times 10^{28}$ m^{-3}, $e = 1.6 \times 10^{-19}$ C, $m_e = 9.1 \times 10^{-31}$ kg

and $v_d = 1.6 \times 10^{-4}$ ms^{-1}

We know that, $\rho = \frac{m_e}{ne^2\tau}$

∴ Relaxation time,

$$\tau = \frac{m_e}{e^2 n\rho}$$

$$= \frac{9.1 \times 10^{-31}}{(1.6 \times 10^{-19})^2 \times 8.5 \times 10^{28} \times 1.7 \times 10^{-8}}$$

$$= 2.5 \times 10^{-14} \text{ s}$$

∴ Mean free path of electron (distance covered between two collisions) $= v_d\tau = 1.6 \times 10^{-4} \times 2.5 \times 10^{-14}$

$$= 4 \times 10^{-18} \text{ m}$$

Temperature Dependence of Resistivity

Resistivity of a metal conductor is given by

$$\rho = \rho_0[1 + \alpha(T - T_0)] \quad \text{...(i)}$$

where, ρ = resistivity at temperature T,

and ρ_0 = resistivity at temperature T_0

$$\Rightarrow \quad \alpha = \frac{\rho - \rho_0}{\rho_0(T - T_0)} = \frac{d\rho}{\rho_0} \cdot \frac{1}{dT}$$

Thus, temperature coefficient of electrical resistivity is also defined as the fractional change in electrical resistivity $\frac{d\rho}{\rho_0}$ per unit change in temperature dT.

For metals, the value of α is **positive**, therefore resistivity of metal increases with increase in temperature.

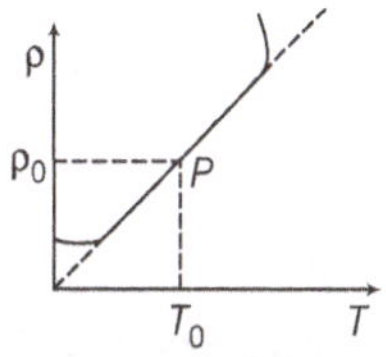

Resistivity as a function of temperature for metals

Eq.(i) implies that a graph of ρ plotted against T would be a straight line. At temperatures much lower than 0 °C, the graph deviates considerably from a straight line. Eq.(i) can be used approximately over a limited range of T around any reference temperature T_0, where the graph can be approximated as a straight line.

For semiconductors, the resistivity decreases with increase in temperature.

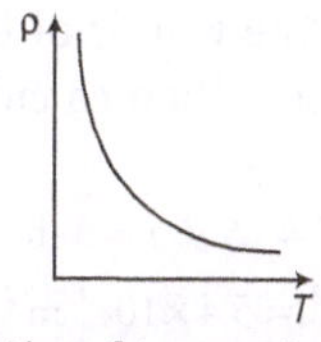

Resistivity as a function of temperature for semiconductors

For alloys, the resistivity is very large, but has weak dependence on temperature.

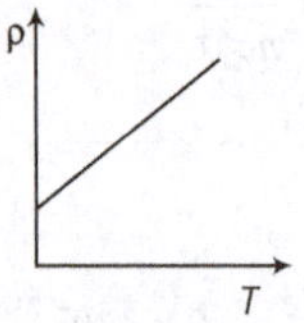

Resistivity as a function of temperature for alloys

Note The resistivity of electrolytes also decreases with rise in temperature.

Electric fuse is made of an alloy of zinc, copper, silver and aluminium. This is because alloys have low melting point and high resistivity. This causes the wire to melt, if a current more than safe current flows through the circuit.

Conductance and Conductivity

Conductance

It is defined as the reciprocal of resistance of a conductor. It is expressed as

$$\boxed{G = \frac{1}{R}}$$

Its SI unit is mho (Ω^{-1}) or siemen (S).

The dimensional formula of conductance is

$$[M^{-1}L^{-2}T^{3}A^{2}].$$

Conductivity

It is defined as the reciprocal of resistivity of a conductor. It is expressed as

$$\boxed{\sigma = \frac{1}{\rho}}$$

Its SI unit is mho per metre ($\Omega^{-1}\,m^{-1}$) or siemen per metre (S/m).

The dimensional formula of conductivity is $[M^{-1}L^{-3}T^{3}A^{2}]$.

Note Relation between conductivity and mobility for semi-conductor is $\sigma = e(n_e\mu_e + n_p\mu_p)$

Example 12 A wire carries a current of 0.5 A, when a potential difference of 1.5 V is applied across it. What is its conductance? If the wire is of length 3m and area of cross-section 5.4 mm^2, then calculate its conductivity.

Sol. Here, $I = 0.5$ A, $V = 1.5$ V, $l = 3$ m,

$$A = 5.4\,mm^2 = 5.4 \times 10^{-6}\,m^2$$

$\therefore$ New resistance, $R = \frac{V}{I} = \frac{1.5}{0.5} = 3\,\Omega$

$\therefore$ Conductance, $G = \frac{1}{R} = \frac{1}{3} = 0.33$ S

and electrical conductivity,

$$\sigma = \frac{1}{\rho} = \frac{l}{RA} = \frac{3}{3 \times 5.4 \times 10^{-6}} = 1.85 \times 10^{5}\,Sm^{-1}$$

Relation between J, σ and E (Microscopic form of Ohm's Law)

Since, the relation between the current flowing through the conductor and drift velocity of electron is given by

$$I = nAe\,v_d$$

$$\therefore \quad I = nAe\left(\frac{eE}{m}\tau\right) = \frac{nAe^2\tau E}{m}$$

$$\Rightarrow \quad \frac{I}{A} = \frac{ne^2\tau E}{m} \Rightarrow J = \frac{ne^2\tau E}{m} \quad \left[\because J = \frac{I}{A}\right]$$

$$\text{or} \quad J = \frac{1}{\rho}E \quad \left[\because \rho = \frac{m}{ne^2\tau}\right]$$

$$\therefore \quad \boxed{J = \sigma E} \quad \left[\because \sigma = \frac{1}{\rho}\right]$$

It is a **microscopic** form of **Ohm's law.**

Classification of Materials in Terms of Conductivity

On the basis of conductivity, the materials can be classified into the following categories

Insulators

These are materials whose electrical conductivity is either very small or nil, e.g. glass, rubber, etc.

Conductors

These are materials whose electrical conductivity is very high, e.g. silver, aluminium, etc.

Semiconductors

These are those materials whose electrical conductivity lies in between that of insulators and conductors, e.g. germanium, silicon, etc.

Note **Thermistor** A thermistor is a heat sensitive device whose resistivity changes very rapidly with change of temperature.

A thermistor can have a resistance in the range of 0.1 Ω to $10^7\,\Omega$, depending upon its composition.

Superconductivity The resistivity of certain metal or alloy drops to zero, when they are cooled below a certain temperature is called superconductivity. It was observed by Prof. Kamerlingh in 1911.

Topic Practice 1

Multiple Choice Questions

1 Mark

1. The amount of charge Q passing at in time t through a cross-section of a wire is $Q = 5t^2 + 3t + 1$. The value of current at time $t = 5$s is
(a) 9 A (b) 49 A
(c) 53 A (d) None of these

2. In current electricity, Ohm's law is obeyed by all **ISC 2011**
(a) solids (b) metals (c) liquids (d) gases

3. If potential difference between the two ends of a metallic wire is doubled, drift speed of free electrons in the wire **ISC 2024**
(a) remains same (b) becomes double
(c) becomes four times (d) becomes half

4. Mobility of charge carrier in conductor is
(a) directly proportional to E, inversely proportional to v_d
(b) inversely proportional to E, directly proportion to v_d
(c) directly proportional to both v_d and E
(d) inversely proportional to both v_d and E

5. Which of the following is correct expression for mobility μ?
(a) $\mu = \frac{e}{m}$ (b) $\mu = \frac{e\tau}{m}$
(c) $\mu = \frac{em}{\tau}$ (d) $\mu = \frac{m\tau}{e}$

Very Short Answer Type Questions

1 Mark

6. What is the order of number of free electrons in any metal?

7. I-V graph for a metallic wire at two different temperatures T_1 and T_2 is as shown in the figure below.

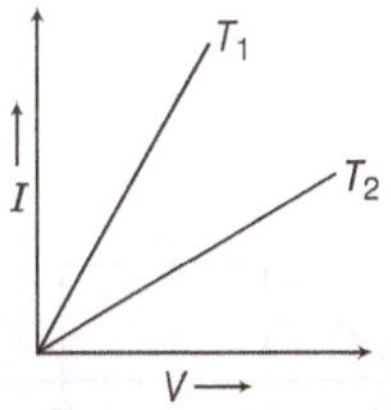

Which of the two temperatures is lower and why?

8. Graph showing the variation of current *versus* voltage for a material GaAs is shown in the figure.

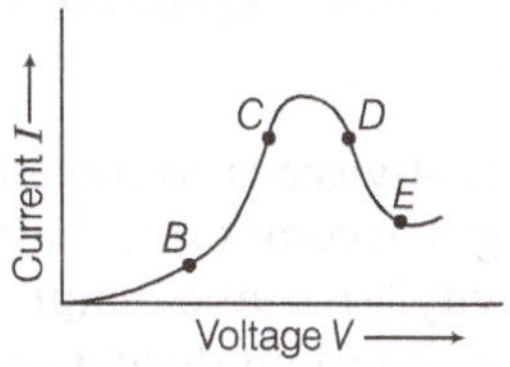

Identify the region of
(i) negative resistance.
(ii) where Ohm's law is obeyed.

9. A given length of conductor of rectangular cross-section has a resistance R. If every linear dimension (length, breadth and height) were halved, what would be the new resistance be?

10. State the physical condition in which Ohm's law is not valid for a conductor. **ISC 2002**

11. If the potential difference applied across a variable resistor is constant, draw a graph between the current in the resistor and the resistance. **ISC 2000**

12. State and explain Ohm's law and hence define one ohm. **ISC 2014**

13. Show graphically how electrical resistance of a piece of silicon or germanium varies when its temperature is varied. **ISC 2008**

14. Define temperature coefficient of resistance of the material of a conductor. **ISC 2014**

15. Explain the statement temperature coefficient of resistance of metal is $4 \times 10^{-3}/°C$. **ISC 2010**

16. When electrons drift in a metal from lower to higher potential, does it mean that all the free electrons of the metal are moving in the same direction?

17. What is meant by drift speed of free electrons? **ISC 2017**

18. A current I flows through a metallic wire of radius r and free electrons in it drift with a velocity v_d. Calculate the drift velocity of the free electrons through the wire of the same material, having double the radius, when same current flows through it. **ISC 2014, 13**

19. Define the term mobility of charge carriers in a conductor. Write its SI unit.

20. Define resistivity. What is its unit?

Short Answer Type I Questions

2 Marks

21. A wire of resistivity ρ is stretched uniformly, so that its length becomes four times. What is its new resistivity? (Assume temperature of the wire remains constant during stretching of the wire.) **ISC 2008**

22. For a metallic conductor, what is the relation between current density (J), conductivity (σ) and electric field intensity (E)? **ISC 2016**

23. A potential difference of V volt is applied across a copper wire of length l and diameter d. How will the drift velocity be affected, if **ISC 2005**
   (i) V is doubled. (ii) l is doubled.

24. Draw a labelled graphs to show how electrical resistance varies with temperature for **ISC 2015**
   (i) a metallic wire. (ii) a piece of carbon.

25. Define current density. Write an expression which connects current density with drift speed. **ISC 2018**

26. A uniform copper wire having a cross-sectional area of 1 mm^2 carries a current of 5A. Calculate the drift speed of free electrons in it.
(Free electron number density of copper $= 2 \times 10^{28}/m^3$) **ISC 2020**

27. With reference to free electron theory of conductivity, explain the terms **ISC 2014**
   (i) drift speed (ii) relaxation time

28. A metal rod of square cross-sectional area A having length l has current I flowing through it when a potential difference of V volt is applied across its ends (Fig. I). Now, the rod is cut parallel to its length into two identical pieces and joined as shown in Fig. II. What potential difference must be maintained across the length of $2l$, so that the current in the rod is still I?

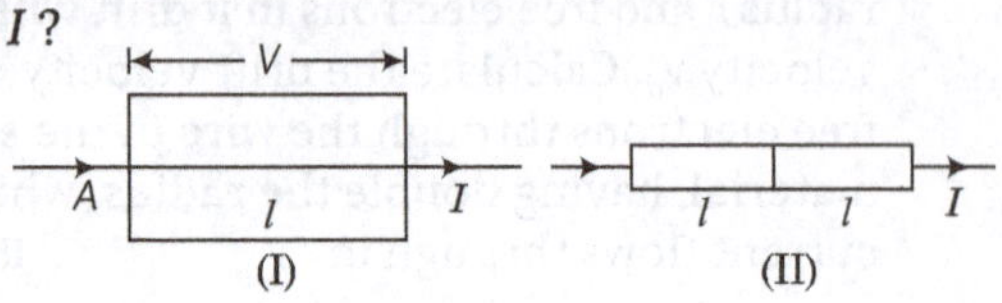

29. A conductor of length l is connected to a DC source of potential V. If the length of the conductor is tripled by gradually stretching it, keeping V constant, how will
   (i) drift speed of electrons and
   (ii) resistance of the conductor be affected? Justify your answer.

30. Using the concept of drift velocity of charge carriers in a conductor, deduce the relationship between current density and resistivity of the conductor.

31. (i) A wire of resistivity ρ is stretched to three times its length. What will be its new resistivity?
   (ii) In what manner do the relaxation time in the good conductor change when its temperature increases?

32. Name one material whose resistivity decreases with rise in temperature. Explain briefly on the basis of free electron theory why the resistivity decreases. **ISC 2000**

33. What is current density? Write the vector equation connecting current density J with electric field intensity E, for an ohmic conductor. **ISC 2010**

Short Answer Type II Questions

3 Marks

34. A wire of resistivity ρ_1 is plated with a material of resistivity ρ_2, so that its radius changes from r to $2r$. If l is the length of wire, prove that the new wire has a resistance $R = \dfrac{\rho_1\rho_2 l}{\pi r^2(3\rho_1 + \rho_2)}$.

35. (i) Deduce the relation between current I flowing through a conductor and drift velocity v_d of the electrons.
   (ii) Figure shows a plot of current I flowing through the cross-section of a wire *versus* the time t. Use the plot to find the charge flowing in t_2 second through the wire.

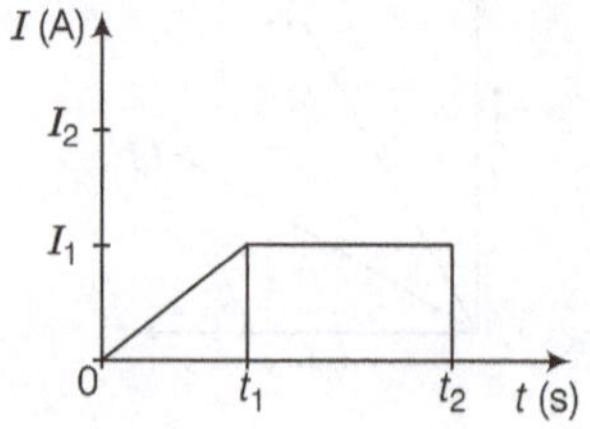

36. (i) What is meant by
(a) drift velocity (b) relaxation time?
(ii) A metallic plug AB is carrying a current I (see figure below). State how the drift velocity of free electrons varies from end A to B. **ISC 2009**

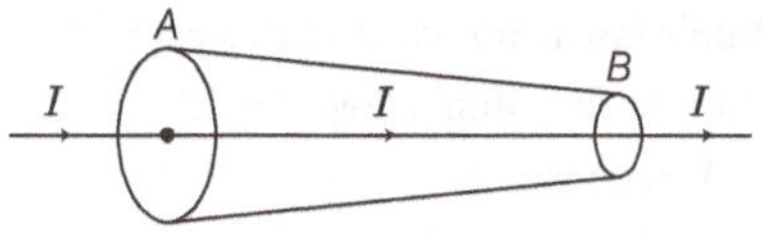

37. Write down a simple relationship to show the variation of resistance with temperature. Define temperature coefficient of resistance. In what way, the temperature coefficient of carbon is different from that of the common conductors? **ISC 2001**

38. Define relaxation time of the free electrons drifting in a conductor. How it is related to the drift velocity of free electrons? Use this relation to deduce the expression for the electrical resistivity of the material.

Long Answer Type Questions

5 Marks

39. (i) Derive an expression for drift velocity of electrons in a conductor. Hence, deduce Ohm's law.
(ii) A wire whose cross-sectional area is increasing linearly from its one end to the others, is connected across a battery of V volts. Which of the following quantities remain constant in the wire?
(a) Drift speed (b) Current density
(c) Electric current (d) Electric field
Justify your answer.

40. The current flowing through a conductor is given by $I = neAv_d$.
(i) Identify each term in the equation.
(ii) Obtain an expression for v_d, if the current flowing through the conductor of length l has its ends maintained at a potential difference V volt. **ISC 2006**

Numerical Problems

41. In hydrogen atom, the electron moves in an orbit of radius 0.5 Å with speed 2.2×10^6 m/s. Find the equivalent current. **(2 M)**

42. A metallic wire has a resistance of 3.0Ω at 0°C and 4.8 Ω at 150°C. Find the temperature coefficient of resistance of its material. **ISC 2016 (2 M)**

43. Resistance of a cylindrical wire of length 27 cm and area of cross-section 1 cm^2 is 2 Ω. This cylinder is recast in a solid cube. Find the resistance of this cube along any two parallel faces. **(2 M)**

44. When a potential difference of 3 V is applied between the two ends of a 60 cm long metallic wire, current density in it is found to be 1×10^{-7} Am^{-2}. Find conductivity of the material of the wire in SI system. **ISC 2012 (2 M)**

45. A 3.0 m long copper wire is carrying current of 3.0 A. How long does it take for an electron to drift from one end to the wire to the other? The cross-sectional area of the wire is $2 \times 10^{-6} m^2$ and number of free electrons in the wire is 8.5×10^{28} per m^3. **(2 M)**

46. In a wire of copper of resistivity 1.7×10^{-8} Ω-m, when there is a potential difference 10 V across 10 m of wire, what is the current density in ampere per square metre? **(2 M)**

47. A heating element using nichrome connected to a 230 V supply draws an initial current of 3.2 A which settles after a few seconds to a steady value of 2.8 A. What is the steady temperature of the heating element, if the room temperature is 27°C? Temperature coefficient of resistance of nichrome averaged over the temperature range involved is 1.70×10^{-4} °C^{-1}. **NCERT (3 M)**

Hints & Solutions

1. (c) Current, $i = \frac{dQ}{dt} = \frac{d}{dt}(5t^2 + 3t + 1)$

$= 10t + 3$

$t = 5\text{ s}$

$i = 10 \times 5 + 3$

$= 53\text{ A}$

2. (b) Ohm's law is obeyed by all metals, provided temperature remains unchanged.
Hence, option (b) is correct.

3. (b) Drift speed is given as $v_d = \frac{eE}{m}\tau$ ... (i)

and $E = \frac{V}{l}$

Put value of E in Eq. (i),

$v_d = \frac{eV}{ml}\tau \Rightarrow v_d \propto V$

So, if potential difference is doubled, then v_d also becomes double.
Hence, option (b) is correct.

4. (c) Mobility, $\mu = \frac{v_d}{E}$

μ is directly proportional to v_d and
μ is inversely proportional to E.

5. (b) Drift velocity, $v_d = \frac{e\tau E}{m}$

Hence, $\mu = \frac{v_d}{E} = \frac{e\tau}{m}$

where, τ is the average collision time for electrons. It is average time between two collisions of an electron. It is also called relaxation time.

6. 10^{29} per cubic metre.

7. Since, slope of 1> slope of 2
$\therefore$ $R_1 < R_2$ (1/2)
Also, we know that resistance is directly proportional to the temperature.
Therefore, $T_2 > T_1$. (1/2)

8. (i) DE is the region, of negative resistance because the slope of curve in this part is negative. (1/2)
(ii) BC is the region, where Ohm's law is obeyed because in this part, the current varies linearly with the voltage. (1/2)

9. We know that,

Resistance, $R = \frac{\rho l}{A} = \frac{\rho l}{b \times h}$ $[\because A = b \times h]$

Given, $l_1' = l/2$, $A' = A/2$

New resistance, $R' = \frac{l'}{A'} = \frac{l/2}{b/2 \times h/2} = \frac{4l}{2 \cdot b \times h} = \frac{2l}{A}$

$\Rightarrow$ $R' = 2R$

Hence, the resistance of the conductor would be doubled.

10. We know that, Ohm's law is

$V = RI$

where, R is resistance of the conductor which is constant at a given temperature

$\Rightarrow$ $V \propto I$

But when temperature changes, R changes, so potential difference (V) will not be proportional to the current (I), thus Ohm's law is not valid in this case.

11. According to the Ohm's law, $V = IR$
Now, if V = constant

So, $I \propto \frac{1}{R}$

where, I = current, R = variable resistance
The variation is shown in the diagram.

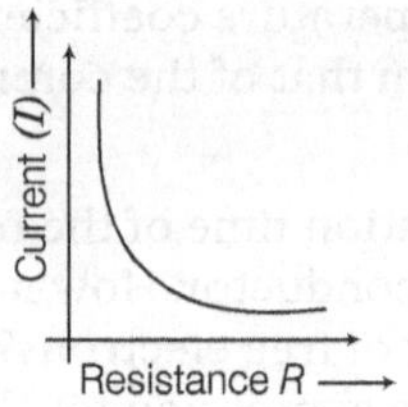

12. At constant temperature and other physical conditions (like mechanical strain, etc. remaining same), the potential difference V across the ends of a given metallic wire (conductor) in a circuit (electric) is directly proportional to the current flowing through it.

$V \propto I$

$V = IR \Rightarrow R = \frac{V}{I}$

where, R = resistance of the conductor.
Ohm is the unit of resistance. It is defined as the volt per ampere. If the current in any resistor is 1 A due to 1 V of emf, there are resistance of that resistance is 1 Ω.

13. While temperature increases, resistance of semiconductor decreases as shown below.

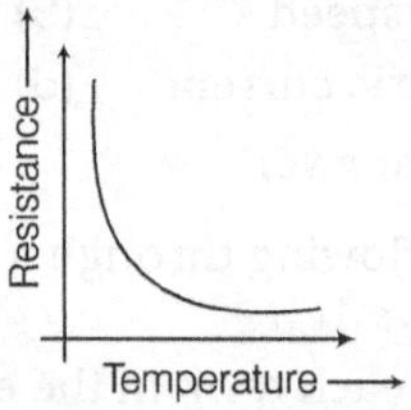

14. Change in resistance per unit original resistance per unit rise in temperature is called temperature coefficient of resistance.

i.e. $\alpha = \frac{R_2 - R_1}{R_1(t_2 - t_1)}$

R_1, R_2 are resistances at t_1 °C, t_2 °C.

15. As given temperature coefficient of resistance of a metal is 4×10^{-3}/°C, it represents the increase in resistance by 4×10^{-3} Ω for rise of temperature by unit degree celsius. (1°C)

16. Yes, all the free electrons drift in the same direction.

17. **Drift velocity** It is defined as the average velocity with which the free electrons in a conductor get drifted towards the positive end of the conductor under the influence of an electric field applied across the conductor. It is denoted by v_d. The drift velocity of an electron is of the order of $10^{-4}\ \text{ms}^{-1}$.

Average drift velocity, $v_d = \frac{eE}{m}\tau$

where, $v_d = \tau$ = average relaxation time,
E = electric field
and e = charge on electron.

18. We know that,

$$J = nev_d \Rightarrow \frac{I}{A} = nev_d \Rightarrow v_d = \frac{I}{neA} \quad \text{...(i)}$$

As radius is doubled $A' = 4A$ $\left[\begin{array}{l}\text{as } A = \pi r^2 \\ A' = \pi(2r)^2\end{array}\right]$

As $$v'_d = \frac{1}{ne4A} \quad \text{...(ii)}$$

So, from Eqs. (i) and (ii),

$$\frac{v'_d}{v_d} = \frac{A}{A'} = \frac{A}{4A}$$

$$\Rightarrow \quad v'_d = \frac{1}{4}v_d$$

19. Mobility of charge carriers inside conductor is defined as the magnitude of drift velocity of charge per unit electric field applied.
SI unit of mobility is $\text{m}^2\text{s}^{-1}\text{V}^{-1}$ or $\text{ms}^{-1}\text{N}^{-1}\text{C}$.

20. We know that resistance $R = \frac{\rho l}{A}$, where ρ is specific resistance or resistivity of the conductor.

$$\rho = \frac{RA}{l}$$

If cross-section area, $A = 1$ and length $l = 1$, then (1)

$$\rho = R$$

Unit of specific resistance or resistivity,

$$\rho = \frac{RA}{l} = \frac{\Omega \times \text{m}^3}{\text{m}} = \Omega \times \text{m} \quad (1)$$

21. Resistivity, $\rho = \frac{m}{ne^2\tau}$

where, n = number of electrons = constant
e = electron charge = constant
τ = relaxation time = constant
m = mass of electron = constant

$\Rightarrow$ ρ is independent of dimension (1)

So, resistivity remains unchanged when the wire is stretched. (1)

22. For a metallic conductor, the relation between current density (J), conductivity (σ) and electric field intensity (E) can be given as $\mathbf{J} = \sigma \mathbf{E}$. (2)

23. We know that, drift velocity,

$$v_d = \frac{eV}{ml} \times \tau$$

where, V = potential difference,
m = mass of the electron,
l = length of the wire
and τ = relaxation time.

(i) If V is doubled, then drift velocity will also be double. (1)

(ii) If l is doubled, then drift velocity will be half. (1)

24. (i) The resistance of metal increases exponentially with temperature as shown in the graph.

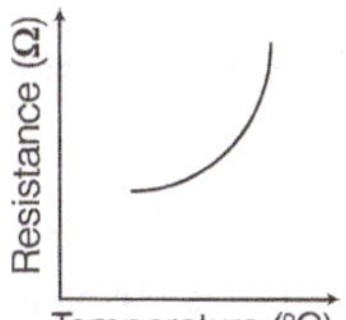

Graph for metallic wire (1)

(ii) The resistance of carbon decreases exponentially with temperature as shown in the graph.

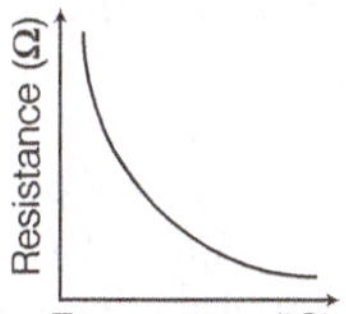

Graph for a piece of carbon (1)

25. The ratio of current flowing at any point in a conductor to the area of cross-section at that place is defined as current density.

$$J = \frac{I}{A} \quad (1)$$

The current density at any point of conductor,

$$J = nev_d$$

where, v_d = drift velocity. (1)

26. Given, cross-sectional area of a copper wire,

$$A = 1\ \text{mm}^2 = 1 \times 10^{-6}\ \text{m}^2,$$

Current, $I = 5\text{A}$

Free electron number density, $n = 2 \times 10^{28}/\text{m}^3$

Drift velocity, $v_d = ?$

As we know that, $I = nAev_d$

$$\Rightarrow \quad v_d = \frac{I}{neA} = \frac{5}{2 \times 10^{28} \times 1.6 \times 10^{-19} \times 1 \times 10^{-6}}$$

$$= 1.56 \times 10^{-3}\ \text{ms}^{-1}$$

27. (i) Refer to text on pages 110 and 111. (Drift velocity). (1)

(ii) Relaxation time is the average time interval between two successive collisions of a free electron with the positive ions in the metal. (1)

28. From Ohm's law, we have $V = IR$

$\Rightarrow \quad V = I\rho\dfrac{l}{A} \quad \left[\because R = \rho\dfrac{l}{A}\right] \ldots(i)$ (1)

When the rod is cut parallel and rejoined by length, the length of the conductor becomes $2l$, whereas the area decrease to $\dfrac{A}{2}$. If the current remains the same, then the potential changes as

$$V = I\rho\frac{2l}{A/2} = 4 \times I\rho\frac{l}{A} = 4V \quad \text{[using Eq. (i)]}$$

The new potential applied across the metal rod will be four times the original potential (V). (1)

29. The potential, V = constant, $l' = 3l$

(i) Drift speed of electrons, $v_d = \dfrac{V}{nel\rho}$

$$v_d \propto \frac{1}{l} \quad [\because \text{other factors are constant}]$$

So, when length is tripled, drift velocity gets one-third. (1)

(ii) Resistance of conductor is $R = \rho\dfrac{l}{A}$.

Here, wire is stretched to triple its length, that means the mass of the wire remains same in both conditions.

Before stretching mass = After stretching mass

$$M_1 = M_2$$

$\Rightarrow \quad V_1\rho_1 = V_2\rho_2 \quad [\because \rho_1 = \rho_2]$

or $\quad A_1l_1 = A_2l_2$

Since, length is tripled after stretching.

$\therefore \quad A_1l = A_2(3l)$ or $A_2 = \dfrac{A_1}{3}$

Hence, $R' = \rho\dfrac{l'}{A'} = \rho\dfrac{3l}{A/3} = \dfrac{9\rho l}{A}$

$\Rightarrow \quad R' = 9R$

Thus, new resistance is 9 times of its original value. (1)

30. Refer to text on page 114 (Relation between J, σ and E).

31. (i) Resistivity is a property of the material, it does not depend on the dimensions of the wire. Thus, when the wire is stretched, then its resistivity remains same. (1)

(ii) We know that, $R = \dfrac{ml}{ne^2\tau A}$

or relaxation time, $\tau = \dfrac{ml}{ne^2RA}$

If temperature increases, the resistance (R) of a good conductor increases and hence relaxation time decreases. (1)

32. Resistivity in semiconductors like germanium or silicon decreases with rise in temperature i.e., their temperature coefficient of resistance is negative.

The reason is that, for such substance e.g., silicon, the value of n (the number of free electrons in unit volume) is very small compared to the metals; but with rise in temperature the number of free electrons i.e., the value of n goes on increasing in the conduction band.

Therefore, the resistance $R = \left(\dfrac{ml}{\tau e^2 nA}\right)$ goes on decreasing. Although in these substances also the relaxation time τ decreases with rise in temperature but the increase in the value of n is large compared to the decrease in τ. Hence, the net effect of rise in temperature is that the resistance decreases. (2)

33. The ratio of current flowing at any point in a conductor to the area of cross-section at that place is defined as current density. (1)

$$|\mathbf{J}| = \frac{I}{|\mathbf{A}|}$$

In vector form, current density $\mathbf{J} = \sigma \mathbf{E}$

where, σ = conductivity

and $\quad E$ = electric field across the conductor. (1)

34. Let resistance of wire be R_1; and R_2 be the resistance of plated part of wire.

Then, $\quad R_1 = \dfrac{\rho_1 l}{\pi r^2} \quad \ldots(i)$

and $\quad R_2 = \dfrac{\rho_1 l}{\pi[(2r)^2 - r^2]} \quad \left[\because R = \dfrac{\rho l}{A}\right] \ldots(ii)$ (1)

Also, R_1 and R_2 are connected in parallel.

Equivalent resistance, $R = \dfrac{R_1R_2}{R_1 + R_2} \quad \ldots(iii)$

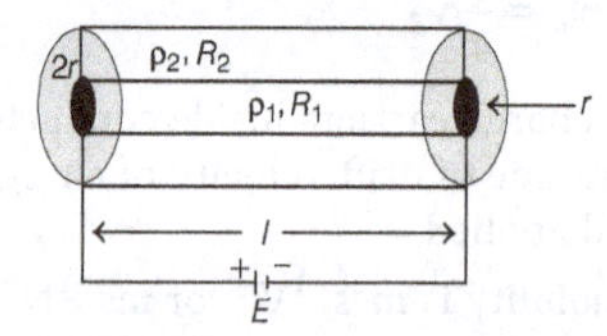

(1)

Put the value of R_1 and R_2 from Eqs. (i) and (ii), we get

$$R = \frac{\left(\dfrac{\rho_1 l}{\pi r^2}\right)\left(\dfrac{\rho_2 l}{3\pi r^2}\right)}{\left(\dfrac{\rho_1 l}{\pi r^2}\right) + \left(\dfrac{\rho_2 l}{3\pi r^2}\right)} = \frac{\rho_1\rho_2 l^2}{3\pi^2 r^4} \times \frac{3\pi r^2}{3\rho_1 l + \rho_2 l}$$

$$R = \frac{\rho_1\rho_2 l}{\pi r^2(3\rho_1 + \rho_2)}$$ (1)

35. (i) Refer to text on page 111 (Relation between drift velocity and electric current). (1½)

(ii) Area under I-t curve on t-axis is charge flowing through the conductor.

$$Q = \frac{1}{2} \times t_1 \times I_1 + (t_2 - t_1) \times I_1$$ (1½)

36. (i) (a) Refer to text on pages 110 and 111 (Drift velocity).

(b) Refer to solution of Q. 27 (ii) on page 119. (1½)

(ii) We know that,

$$J = nev_d \Rightarrow \frac{I}{A} = nev_d \Rightarrow v_d \propto \frac{1}{A}$$

$[\because n, e, I$ and v_d are constants$]$

where, n = no. of free electrons, e = electron charge v_d = drift speed and A = area of cross-section.

So, drift velocity (v_d) at A is smaller than at B. Because area of cross-section A is larger than B. (1½)

37. The variation of resistance with temperature is given by the relation $R_t = R_0 (1 + \alpha t)$ ...(i)

where, R_t and R_0 are the resistance of the conductor at t °C and 0°C respectively and α is the temperature coefficient of the resistance.

Using Eq. (i), we get $\alpha = \dfrac{R_t - R_0}{R_0 t}$ (1)

then temperature coefficient of resistances is defined as the change in resistance per unit original resistance for each degree rise in temperature. (1)

The temperature coefficient of carbon (a semiconductor) is negative whereas for metals, it is positive. Thus, the resistance of carbon falls when its temperature increases. (1)

38. Refer to text on pages 110 and 111 (Drift velocity).

39. (i) Refer to text on pages 110 and 111 (Drift velocity). (1)

(ii) The setup is shown in the figure. Here, electric current remains constant throughout the length of the wire. Electric field also remains constant which is equal to $\dfrac{V}{l}$.

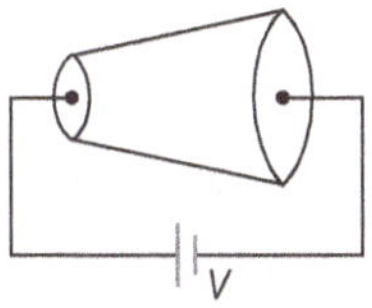

Current density and hence drift speed changes. (2)

40. Drifting occurs due to application of external electric field. When no external field is applied there is no drift of electrons in the conductor.

(i) The given expression is

$$I = neAv_d$$

where, I = current flowing through the conductor,
n = number of free electrons per unit volume,
e = charge of an electron,
A = area of cross-section
and v_d = drift velocity. (1)

(ii) When a conductor of length l is subjected to the potential difference of V, each electron experiences a force

$$F = -e\frac{V}{l}$$

and free electron acquires an acceleration

$$a = \frac{F}{m} = -\frac{eE}{m} = \frac{-eV}{ml} \quad \left[\text{as, } E = \frac{V}{l}\right] \quad \text{...(i)}$$

where, m = mass of electron, e = electronic charge and E = electric field. Free electrons starts accelerating in the conductor.

The average time difference between two consecutive collisions is known as relaxation time of electron and

$$\bar{\tau} = \frac{\tau_1 + \tau_2 + \cdots + \tau_n}{n} \quad \text{...(ii)}$$

where, $\tau_1, \tau_2, \cdots, \tau_n$ are the average time differences between 1st, 2nd, ..., n th collisions.

$\therefore v_1, v_2, \ldots, v_n$ are velocities gained by electron in 1st, 2nd, ..., nth collisions with initial thermal velocities $u_1, u_2, \ldots, u_n$ respectively.

$$\therefore \quad v_1 = u_1 + a\tau_1$$
$$v_2 = u_2 + a\tau_2$$
$$\vdots \quad \vdots \quad \vdots$$
$$v_n = u_n + a\tau_n$$

The drift speed v_d may be defined as

$$v_d = \frac{v_1 + v_2 + \cdots + v_n}{n}$$

$$v_d = \frac{(u_1 + u_2 + \cdots + u_n) + a(\tau_1 + \tau_2 + \cdots + \tau_n)}{n}$$

$$v_d = \frac{(u_1 + u_2 + \cdots + u_n)}{n} + \frac{a(\tau_1 + \tau_2 + \cdots + \tau_n)}{n}$$

$$v_d = 0 + a\tau \quad [\because \text{average thermal velocity} = 0]$$

$$v_d = -\left(\frac{eV}{ml}\right)\tau \quad [\text{from Eq. (i)}]$$

This is the required expression of drift speed of free electrons.

$$\Rightarrow \quad |v_d| = \frac{eV}{lm}\tau \quad \left[\because E = \frac{V}{l}\right] \quad (2)$$

41. Current, $i = \dfrac{q}{t} = \dfrac{e}{2\pi r/v} = \dfrac{e \cdot v}{2\pi r}; \left[\text{as, } v = \dfrac{2\pi r}{t}\right]$ (1)

Given, speed, $v = 2.2 \times 10^6$ m/s

Radius, $r = 0.5$ Å $= 0.5 \times 10^{-10}$ m

$$= \frac{1.6 \times 10^{-19} \times 2.2 \times 10^6}{2 \times 3.14 \times 0.5 \times 10^{-10}} = 1.12 \times 10^{-3} \text{ A} \quad (1)$$

42. At temperature t_0 (0°C), resistance $R_0 = 3\Omega$

At temperature t (150 °C), resistance $R_t = 4.8\,\Omega$

$\because$ Temperature coefficient of resistance,

$$\alpha = \frac{R_t - R_0}{R_0 \times \Delta t} \quad (1)$$

$$\alpha = \frac{4.8 - 3.0}{3 \times 150} \quad [\because \Delta t = 150 - 0]$$

$$\alpha = \frac{1.8}{3 \times 150}$$

$$= \frac{0.6}{150} = \frac{6}{1500} = \frac{2}{500}$$

$$\alpha = 0.004 \text{ °C}^{-1} \quad (1)$$

43. Given, $l = 27$ cm, $A = 1$ cm^2, $R = 2\Omega$

So, specific resistance of the material,

$$\rho = \frac{R \times A}{l} = \frac{2 \times 1}{27} = \frac{2}{27}\ \Omega\text{-cm} \quad \left[\because R = \frac{\rho l}{A}\right] \quad (1/2)$$

Since, volume is constant, $A \times l = x^3$

where, x is the edge of the cube.

$$27 \times 1 = x^3$$

or $\quad x = 3$ cm

Area of any surface of cube,

$$x^2 = 3 \times 3 = 9 \text{ cm} \quad (1/2)$$

Now, resistance of cube between any two parallel faces,

$$R = \frac{\rho \cdot l}{A} = \frac{2 \times 3}{27 \times 9} = 0.024 \Omega \quad (1)$$

44. We have to apply Ohm's law for current density

$$\mathbf{J} = \sigma \mathbf{E}$$

Given, potential difference $V = 3$ V,

Length, $l = 60$ cm $= 0.6$ m,

Current density, $J = 1 \times 10^{-7}$ Am^{-2} (1)

We know that,

Conductivity,

$$\sigma = \frac{J}{E} = \frac{J \cdot l}{V} = \frac{1 \times 10^{-7} \times 0.6}{3} \quad \left[\text{as, } E = \frac{V}{l}\right] \quad (1)$$

$$= 2 \times 10^{-8} \ (\Omega\text{-m})^{-1} \quad (1)$$

45. Given, $i = 3$ A, $A = 2 \times 10^{-6}$ m^2, $n = 8.5 \times 10^{28}$ / m^3

Drift velocity of electrons,

$$v_d = \frac{i}{nAe} = \frac{3}{8.5 \times 10^{28} \times 2 \times 10^{-6} \times 1.6 \times 10^{-19}}$$

$$= 1.1 \times 10^{-4} \text{ m/s} \quad (1)$$

Time taken by free electrons in moving across the wire,

$$T = \frac{\text{distance}}{\text{velocity}} = \frac{d}{v}$$

$$= \frac{3}{1.1 \times 10^{-4}} \quad [\because d = 3 \text{m}]$$

$$= 2.73 \times 10^4 \text{s} = 7.5 \text{ h (approx.)} \quad (1)$$

46. Current density, $j = \frac{i}{A} = \frac{iR}{\rho l}$ $\quad \left[\because R = \frac{\rho l}{A}\right]$ (1)

$$j = \frac{V}{\rho l} = \frac{10}{1.7 \times 10^{-8} \times 10} = 5.8 \times 10^7 \text{ A/m}^2 \quad (1)$$

47. Given, potential difference = 230 V

Initial current at 27 °C = $I_{27°C} = 3.2$ A

Final current at t °C = $I_{t°C} = 2.8$ A

Room temperature = 27 °C

Temperature coefficient of resistance, $\alpha = 1.70 \times 10^{-4}$ °C^{-1}

Resistance at 27 °C,

$$R_{27°C} = \frac{V}{I_{27°C}} = \frac{230}{3.2} = \frac{2300}{32} \Omega$$

Resistance at t °C, $R_{t°C} = \frac{V}{I_{t°C}} = \frac{230}{2.8} = \frac{2300}{28} \Omega$ (1)

Temperature coefficient of resistance

$$\alpha = \frac{R_t - R_{27}}{R_{27}(t - 27)}$$

$$\Rightarrow \quad 1.70 \times 10^{-4} = \frac{\frac{2300}{28} - \frac{2300}{32}}{\frac{2300}{32}(t - 27)}$$

or $\quad t - 27 = \frac{82.143 - 71.875}{71.875 \times 1.70 \times 10^{-4}} = 840.347$

or $\quad t = 840.3 + 27 = 867.3$ °C

Thus, the steady temperature of heating element is 867.3 °C. (2)

TOPIC 02 Electrical Energy

Electrical Energy and Power

Electrical Energy

It is defined as the total work done W by the source of emf V in maintaining the electric current I in the given circuit for a specified time t.

According to Ohm's law, we have

$$V = IR$$

Total charge that crosses the resistor is given by $q = It$

Energy gained is given by

$$E = W = Vq$$

$$= V(It) = VIt$$

$$= [IR] It = I^2 Rt \quad [\because V = IR]$$

$$= \left[\frac{V}{R}\right]^2 Rt = \frac{V^2 t}{R} \quad \left[\because I = \frac{V}{R}\right]$$

$$\therefore \quad \boxed{E = VIt = I^2 Rt = \frac{V^2}{R} t}$$

The SI unit of electrical energy is joule (J),

where, 1 joule = 1 volt × 1 ampere × 1 second

= 1 watt × 1 sec

Commercial Unit of Electrical Energy

1 kilowatt hour (kWh) = 3.6×10^6 joule (J)

1 Megawatt-hour (MWh) = 1000 Kilowatt-hour

= 10^6 watt-hour

Example 1 A resistance coil is made by joining in parallel of two resistances each of 10 Ω. An emf of 1V is applied between the two ends of coil for 5 min. Calculate the heat produced in calories.

Sol. Given, resistance, $R_1 = 10\Omega$, $R_2 = 10\Omega$

Voltage, $V = 1\text{V}$

and time, $t = 5 \text{ min} = 5\times 60 \text{ s} = 300 \text{ s}$

Since, effective resistance in parallel combination will be

$$R_p = \frac{R_1R_2}{R_1+R_2} = \frac{10\times 10}{10+10} = 5\Omega$$

$$\therefore \text{ Heat produced} = \frac{V^2t}{R_p} = \frac{1^2}{5}\times 5\times 60$$

$$= \frac{60}{4.2}\text{ cal} = 14.3 \text{ cal}$$

Electrical Power

It is defined as the rate of electrical energy supplied per unit time to maintain the flow of electric current through a conductor.

Mathematically, $$P = VI = I^2R = \frac{V^2}{R}$$

The SI unit of power is watt (W).

where, 1 watt = 1 volt × 1 ampere = 1 ampere-volt.

Power of an electric circuit is said to be **one watt**, if one ampere current flows in it against a potential difference of one volt. The bigger units of electrical power are kilowatt (kW) and megawatt (MW).

where, 1kW = 1000 W and 1 MW = 10^6 W

Commercial unit of electrical power is horse power (HP), where, 1HP = 746 W.

Example 2 A heating element is marked 210 V, 630 W. What is the value of the current drawn by the element when connected to a 210 V DC source?

Sol. Given, $P = 630\text{W}$ and $V = 210\text{V}$

Since, $P = VI$

Therefore, $I = \frac{P}{V} = \frac{630}{210} = 3\text{A}$

Topic Practice 2

Multiple Choice Questions

1 Mark

1. An electric current (I) flowing through a metallic wire is gradually increased. The graph of heating power (P) developed in it *versus* the current (I) is

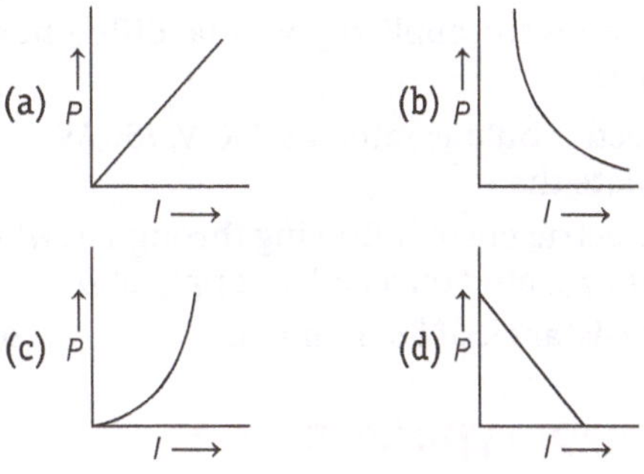

ISC 2023

Very Short Answer Type Questions

1 Mark

2. Two identical slabs, of a given metal, are joined together, in two different ways, as shown in figures (a) and (b).

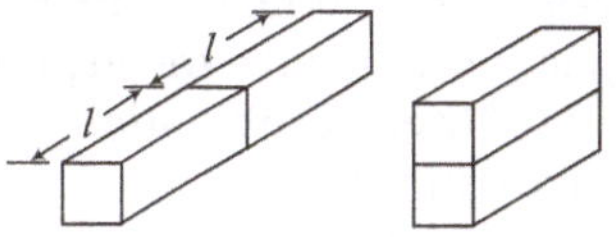

(a) (b)

What is the ratio of the resistances of these two combinations?

3. How should a group of resistances be connected, so that same current flows through all of them?
4. Name the unit of electric energy used for domestic purpose.
5. What is the commercial unit of electrical energy and how is it related to joules?
6. Two electric bulbs are marked 60 W, 220 V and 100 W, 220 V, respectively. Which bulb will glow more, if connected in series to a DC supply?
7. Two electric bulbs have same power and same operating potential, but their filaments are made of tungsten and carbon, respectively. Which bulb after a passage of time of switching ON in parallel will glow more?
8. Three bulbs B_1 (230V, 40W), B_2 (230V, 60W) and B_3(230V, 100W) are connected in series to a 230V supply. Which bulb glows the brightest?

ISC 2024

Short Answer Type I Questions

2 Marks

9. The potential difference applied across a given resistor is altered, so that the heat produced per second increases by a factor of 9. By what

factor does the applied potential difference change?

10. An electric bulb is rated as 250 V, 750 W. Calculate the [2]

(i) electric current flowing through it, when it is operated on a 250 V supply and

(ii) resistance of its filament. **ISC 2020**

Long Answer Type Questions

5 Marks

11. (i) Obtain the formula for the power loss (i.e. power dissipated) in a conductor of resistance R, carrying a current.

(ii) Two heating elements of resistances R_1 and R_2 when operated at a constant supply of voltage V, consume powers P_1 and P_2, respectively. Deduce the expressions for the power of their combination when they are in turn, connected in

(a) series and

(b) parallel across their same voltage supply.

Numerical Problems

12. A voltmeter of resistance 100 Ω is connected in parallel to 400 Ω resistor and this arrangement is connected to a 200 Ω resistance and a 6 V battery in series. Calculate the reading of the voltmeter. **(3 M)**

13. In the given figure, calculate the current in the circuit and the heat produced in 1.5 Ω resistor.

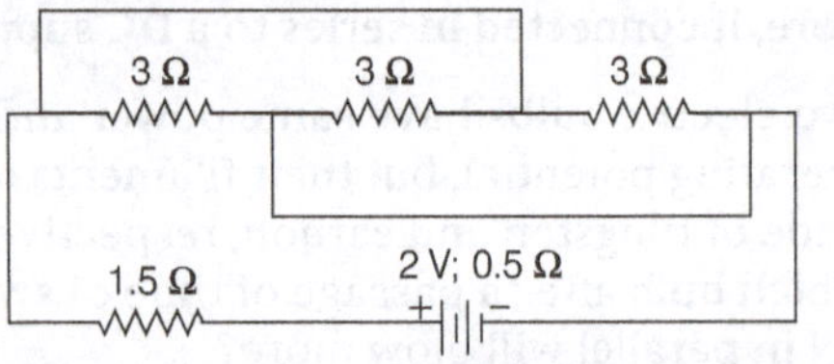

(2 M)

14. Two resistors $R_1 = 60\,\Omega$ and $R_2 = 90\,\Omega$ are connected in parallel. If electric power consumed by the resistor R_1 is 15 Ω, calculate the power consumed by the resistor R_2. **(2 M)**

15. An electric bulb is marked 200 V, 100 W. Calculate electric resistance of its filament. If five such bulbs are connected in series to a 200 V supply, how much current will flow through them? **(3 M)**

16. Given that the resistance of the voltmeter is 400 Ω, find the voltmeter's reading. **(3 M)**

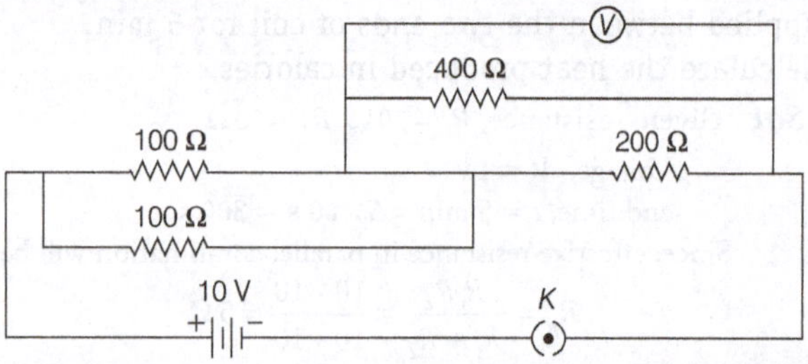

17. Two bars of radius r and $2r$ are kept in contact as shown in the figure. An electric current I is passed through the bars. Find the ratio of heat produced in bars AB and BC.

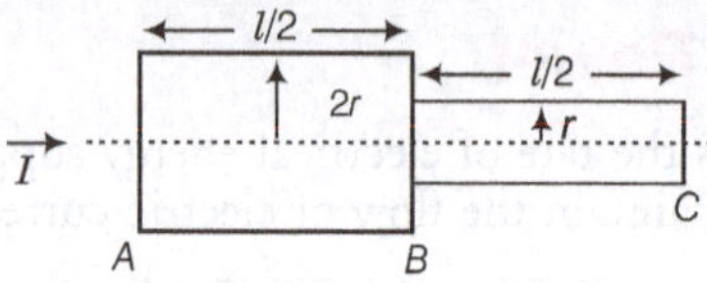

(3 M)

18. Determine the current drawn from a 12 V supply with internal resistance 0.5 Ω by the infinite network shown in given figure. Each resistor has 1 Ω resistance. **NCERT (3 M)**

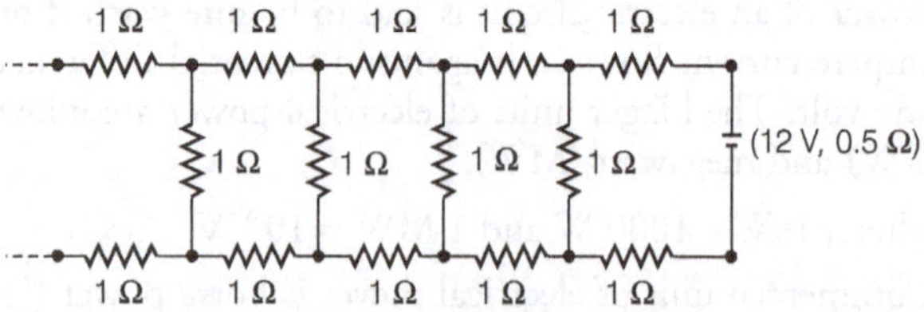

19. In an aluminium (Al) bar of square cross section, a square hole is drilled and is filled with iron (Fe) as shown in the figure. The electrical resistivities of Al and Fe are $2.7 \times 10^{-8}\,\Omega$-m and $1.0 \times 10^{-7}\,\Omega$-m, respectively.

Calculate the electrical resistance between the two faces P and Q of the composite bar. **(3 M)**

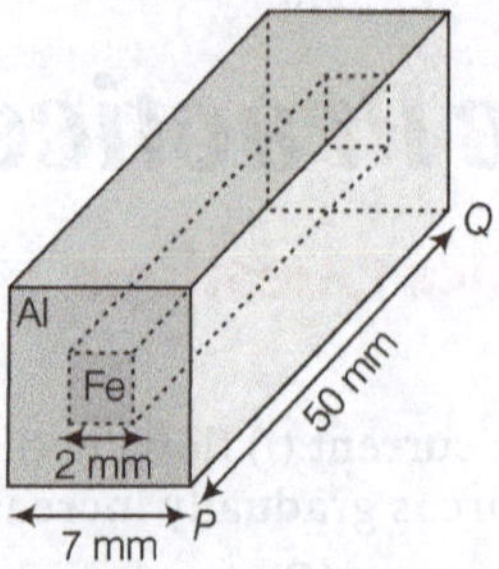

20. A room has AC run for 5 hour a day at a voltage of 220 V. The wiring of the room consists of Cu of 1 mm radius and a length of 10 m. Power consumption per day is 10 commercial units. What fraction of it goes in the joule heating in wires? What would happen, if the wiring is made of aluminium of the same dimensions? [Given, $\rho_{Cu} = 1.7 \times 10^{-8}\ \Omega\text{-m}$, $\rho_{Al} = 2.7 \times 10^{-8}\ \Omega\text{-m}$]
NCERT Exemplar (5 M)

21. A 100 W, 220 V bulb is connected to a 110 V DC source. Calculate the power consumed by the bulb. **(2 M)**

22. Two bulbs B_1 and B_2 are connected in series with an AC source of emf 200 V as shown in the figure. The labels on the bulbs read 200 V, 60 W and 220 V, 100 W, respectively. Calculate the ratio of

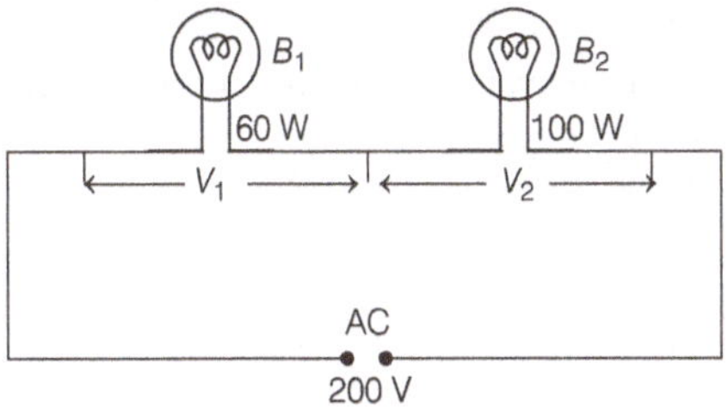

(i) the resistances of the bulbs R_1/R_2.
(ii) the power being consumed when connected in series P_1/P_2.
(iii) the potential difference across the bulbs V_1/V_2. **(3 M)**

23. What is the highest voltage you can safely put across a 98 Ω-0.5 W resistor? **(1 M)**

24. The maximum power dissipated in a 10000 Ω resistor is 10 W. What is the maximum current? **(1 M)**

25. How much charge flows through a 250 V, 1000 W heater in 1 min? **(1 M)**

26. Two resistors $R_1 = 400\,\Omega$ and $R_2 = 20\,\Omega$ are connected in parallel to a battery. If heating power developed in R_1 is 25 W, find the heating power developed in R_2. **(1 M)**

Hints & Solutions

1. (c) Heating power (P) is directly proportional to I^2.
As, $H = VIt$
Applying Ohm's law, $H = I^2Rt$. From this equation, we can conclude that the heat produced is directly proportional to the square of electric current.

2. Let the resistance of each slab is R.
***Case* I** According to Fig. (a), the resistances are connected in series combination, so equivalent resistance of slab, $R_1 = R + R = 2R$.
***Case* II** According to Fig. (b), the resistances are connected in parallel combination, so equivalent resistance,

$$\frac{1}{R_2} = \frac{1}{R} + \frac{1}{R} \Rightarrow \frac{1}{R_2} = \frac{2}{R} \Rightarrow R_2 = \frac{R}{2}$$ (1/2)

Ratio of the equivalent resistance in two combinations is

$$\frac{R_1}{R_2} = \frac{2R}{(R/2)} = 4 \Rightarrow \frac{R_1}{R_2} = 4$$ (1/2)

3. Same current flows through all the resistances when they are connected in series.

4. The unit of electric energy used for domestic purpose is kilowatt hour (kWh). It is also called commercial unit of electric energy.

5. The commercial unit of electrical energy is kilowatt hour (kWh).

$$1\text{kWh} = 3.6 \times 10^6\text{J}$$

6. Since, $P = \frac{V^2}{R}$; at constant $V = 220$ V, $P \propto \frac{1}{R}$.
Therefore, the resistance of the 60 W bulb would be more. In series, where current is constant and $P \propto R$, power of 60 W bulb would be more than 100 W bulb and it will glow more.

7. Resistances of the bulbs are same (initially). After sometime due to the heating of the filament, resistance of tungsten bulb will increase, while the resistance of the carbon bulb will decrease. Since, in parallel $P \propto \frac{1}{R}$, carbon bulb will increase in power and glow more.

8. In series combination, the same current flows through each bulb. A resistance, $R = \frac{V^2}{P}$ or $R \propto \frac{1}{P}$.
Therefore, the resistance of 40 W bulb is highest for the given three bulbs.
Heat produced, $H = I^2Rt$ or $H \propto R$, so maximum heat is produced in 40 W bulb.
As a result of it, 40 W bulb will glow more brightly than the other two bulbs.

9. Heat produced per second

$$= I^2R = \frac{V^2}{R}.$$

So, when voltage is made three times, then heat produced increase nine times for same R. (2)

10. (i) Given, voltage, $V = 250$ V

and power, $P = 750$ W

Power, $P = VI$

$$750 = 250 \times I$$

$$\Rightarrow \text{C urrent, } I = \frac{750}{250} = 3 \text{ A}$$

(ii) Now, from Ohm's law $V = IR$

$$\Rightarrow \quad R = \frac{V}{I} = \frac{250}{3} = 83.33\,\Omega$$

Hence, resistance of filament = 83.33Ω

11. (i) Refer to text on page 123 (Electrical power). (2)

(ii) To deduce the expression for the power of the combination, first find the equivalent resistance of the combination in the given conditions.

$$\because \quad P_1 = \frac{V^2}{R_1}$$

$$\Rightarrow \quad R_1 = \frac{V^2}{P_1} \quad (1/2)$$

$$\text{and} \quad P_2 = \frac{V^2}{R_2} \Rightarrow R_2 = \frac{V^2}{P_2} \quad (1/2)$$

(a) In series combination,

$$R_s = R_1 + R_2 = \frac{V^2}{P_1} + \frac{V^2}{P_2}$$

$$\Rightarrow \quad R_s = V^2\left(\frac{1}{P_1} + \frac{1}{P_2}\right) = V^2\left(\frac{P_1 + P_2}{P_1 P_2}\right)$$

Now, let the power of heating element in series combination be P_s.

$$\therefore \quad P_s = \frac{V^2}{R_1 + R_2} = \frac{V^2}{V^2\left(\frac{P_1 + P_2}{P_1 P_2}\right)} = \frac{P_1 P_2}{P_1 + P_2} \quad (1)$$

(b) In parallel combination,

$$\frac{1}{R_p} = \frac{1}{R_1} + \frac{1}{R_2} = \frac{1}{\frac{V^2}{P_1}} + \frac{1}{\frac{V^2}{P_2}}$$

$$= \frac{P_1}{V^2} + \frac{P_2}{V^2}$$

$$\Rightarrow \frac{1}{R_p} = \frac{1}{V^2}(P_1 + P_2)$$

Now, power consumption in parallel combination,

$$P_p = \frac{V^2}{R_p} = V^2\left(\frac{1}{R_p}\right)$$

$$\Rightarrow \quad P_p = V^2\left[\frac{1}{V^2}(P_1 + P_2)\right]$$

$$\therefore \quad P_p = P_1 + P_2 \quad (1)$$

12. 400 Ω resistance and 100 Ω voltmeter are in parallel.

$$\text{Therefore, } \frac{1}{R} = \frac{1}{400} + \frac{1}{100} = \frac{5}{400}$$

$$\Rightarrow \quad R = \frac{400}{5} = 80\Omega \quad (1)$$

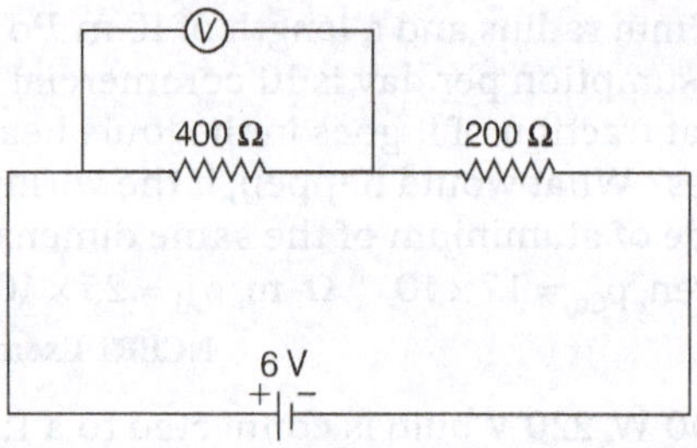

This is in series to 200 Ω, $R = 200 + 80 = 280\Omega$

$$\text{Current from cell, } i = \frac{V}{R} = \frac{6}{280} \text{ A} \quad (1)$$

Hence, potential difference across voltmeter,

$$V = iR = \frac{6}{280} \times 80 = \frac{48}{28} = 1.71 \text{ V} \quad (1)$$

13. Here all three resistors of resistance 3 Ω each are connected in parallel.

Hence, the equivalent resistance of three resistors,

$$\frac{1}{R_1} = \frac{1}{3} + \frac{1}{3} + \frac{1}{3} = \frac{3}{3} \text{ or } R_1 = 1\Omega \quad (1/2)$$

Total resistance of the circuit, $R = 1 + 1.5 + 0.5 = 3\Omega$ (1/2)

$$\text{Current in the circuit, } i = \frac{V}{R} = \frac{2}{3} = 0.67 \text{ A} \quad (1/2)$$

Heat produced in 1.5 Ω resistor,

$$Q = i^2 R = (0.67)^2 \times 1.5 = 0.67 \text{ J/s} \quad (1/2)$$

14. In parallel, $P = \dfrac{V^2}{R}$ (1/2)

$$\text{Therefore, } \frac{P_1}{P_2} = \frac{R_2}{R_1}; \; \frac{15}{P_2} = \frac{90}{60} \quad (1)$$

$$\Rightarrow P_2 = \frac{15 \times 60}{90} = 10 \text{ W} \quad (1/2)$$

15. The resistance of the filament of the bulb,

$$R = \frac{V^2}{P} = \frac{200 \times 200}{100} = 400\Omega \quad (1)$$

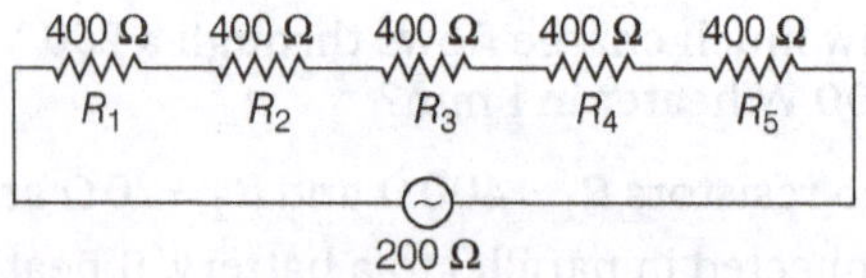

If five bulbs are connected in series, then total resistance of the circuit,

$$R_1 + R_2 + R_3 + R_4 + R_5 = 400 \times 5 = 2000\Omega \quad (1)$$

$$\text{Current, } I = \frac{V}{R} = \frac{200}{2000} = \frac{1}{10} = 0.1 \text{ A} \quad (1)$$

16. The 400 Ω resistor and voltmeter are connected in parallel.

$$\therefore \quad \frac{1}{R} = \frac{1}{400} + \frac{1}{400} = \frac{2}{400}; \text{ or } R = 200\Omega$$

Now, the equivalent circuit is

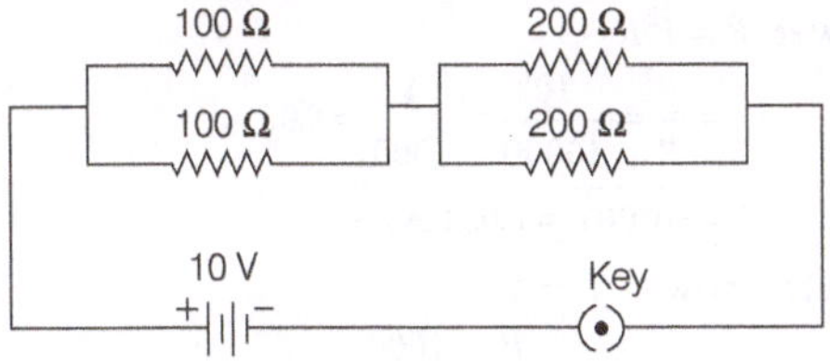

or

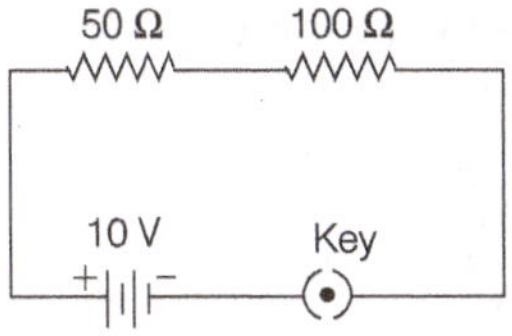

(1)

Total resistance, $R = 50 + 100 = 150\Omega$

Current, $i = \frac{E}{R} = \frac{10}{150} = \frac{1}{15}$ A

Current in each 200 Ω resistor $= \frac{1}{2} \times \frac{1}{15} = \frac{1}{30}$ A (1)

Voltmeter and 400 Ω resistor are again in parallel.

Current in voltmeter $= \frac{1}{2} \times \frac{1}{30} = \frac{1}{60}$ A

Hence, the reading of voltmeter $= iR = \frac{1}{60} \times 400 = 6.67$ V (1)

17. Current flowing through both the bars is equal.

Now, the heat produced is given by

$$E = I^2Rt$$ (1)

$\because$ $E \propto R$

$\therefore$ $$\frac{E_{AB}}{E_{BC}} = \frac{R_{AB}}{R_{BC}} = \frac{(1/2r)^2}{(1/r)^2} \quad \left[\because R \propto \frac{1}{A} \propto \frac{1}{r^2}\right]$$

$$= \frac{1}{4}$$ (2)

18. Let the effective resistance of the network be x. If one part of the network has resistance (1 Ω, 1 Ω, 1 Ω) and is separated as shown in the figure, the effective resistance remains x (as it is an infinite network). Here, x and 1 Ω are in parallel.

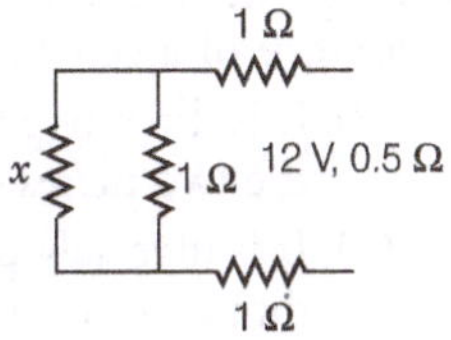

$\therefore$ $\frac{1}{R_p} = \frac{1}{x} + \frac{1}{1} = \frac{1+x}{x} \Rightarrow R_p = \frac{x}{1+x}$ (1)

Now, resistances R_p, 1 Ω and 1 Ω are in series. So, the resultant resistance,

$$R = R_p + 1 + 1 = \frac{x}{1+x} + 1 + 1 = \frac{x}{1+x} + 2 \quad \ldots(i)$$

In case of infinite resistances, the value of R remains x.

$\therefore$ $$x = \frac{x}{1+x} + 2$$

$\Rightarrow$ $x(x+1) = x + 2 + 2x$

$\Rightarrow$ $x^2 - 2x - 2 = 0$

$\Rightarrow$ $$x = \frac{-(-2) \pm \sqrt{4+8}}{2}$$

$$= \frac{2 \pm \sqrt{12}}{2} = 1 \pm \sqrt{3}$$ (1)

The value of resistance cannot be negative. So, the resistance of network

$$x = 1 + \sqrt{3} = 1 + 1.732$$
$$= 2.732\ \Omega$$

Total resistance of the circuit $= 2.732 + 0.5 = 3.232\ \Omega$

$\therefore$ Current drawn from the supply,

$$I = \frac{V}{3.232} = \frac{12}{3.232} = 3.72 \text{ A}$$ (1)

19. Resistance between the two faces P and Q of the composite bar is given by

$$\frac{1}{R} = \frac{1}{R_{Al}} + \frac{1}{R_{Fe}} = \left(\frac{A_{Al}}{\rho_{Al}} + \frac{A_{Fe}}{\rho_{Fe}}\right)\frac{1}{l}$$ (1½)

$\Rightarrow$ $$\frac{1}{R} = \left[\frac{(7^2 - 2^2)}{2.7} + \frac{2^2}{10}\right]\frac{10^{-6}}{10^{-8}} \times \frac{1}{50 \times 10^{-3}}$$

$\therefore$ $$R = \frac{1875}{64} \times 10^{-6}\ \Omega = \frac{1875}{64}\ \mu\Omega$$ (1½)

20. Power consumption in a day, i.e. in 5 h = 10 units

or power consumption per hour = 2 units

or power consumption = 2 units = 2 kW = 2000 J/s (1)

Also, we know that, power consumption in resistor,

$$P = V \times I \Rightarrow 2000 \text{ W} = 220 \text{ V} \times I$$

or $$I \approx 9 \text{ A}$$ (1)

Now, the resistance of wire is given by $R = \rho \frac{l}{A}$

where, A is cross-sectional area of conductor.

Power consumption in first current carrying wire is given by $P = I^2R$

$$= \rho \frac{l}{A} I^2 = 1.7 \times 10^{-8} \times \frac{10}{\pi \times 10^{-6}} \times 81 \text{ J/s} \approx 4 \text{ J/s}$$ (1)

The fractional loss due to the joule heating in first wire

$$= \frac{4}{2000} \times 100 = 0.2\%$$

Power loss in aluminium wire $= 4 \frac{\rho_{Al}}{\rho_{Cu}}$

$$= 1.6 \times 4 = 6.4 \text{ J/s}$$ (1)

The fractional loss due to the joule heating in second wire

$$= \frac{6.4}{2000} \times 100 = 0.32\ \%$$ (1)

21. Given, $P_1 = 100$ W, $V_1 = 220$ V, $V_2 = 110$ V

Power, $P = \frac{V^2}{R}$. As resistance of the bulb is R. (1/2)

Therefore, $\frac{P_1}{P_2} = \left(\frac{V_1}{V_2}\right)^2$ (1/2)

$\Rightarrow \quad \dfrac{100}{P_2} = \left(\dfrac{220}{110}\right)^2 \Rightarrow P_2 = \dfrac{100}{4} = 25\text{ W}$ (1)

22. (i) We know that, electric power,

$P = \dfrac{V^2}{R}$ or $P \propto \dfrac{1}{R}$

As, $V = 200$ V for each bulb or constant

$\therefore \dfrac{R_1}{R_2} = \dfrac{P_2}{P_1} = \dfrac{100}{60} = \dfrac{5}{3} \quad [\because P_1 = 100\text{ W}, P_2 = 100\text{ W}]$ (1)

(ii) In series, $P = i^2R$ or $\dfrac{R_1}{R_2} = \dfrac{P_1}{P_2} = \dfrac{5}{3}$

As, i = constant. (1)

(iii) In series, $\dfrac{V_1}{V_2} = \dfrac{R_1}{R_2} = \dfrac{5}{3}$

As, current, i = constant. (1)

23. Electric power, $P = \dfrac{V^2}{R}$

or $V^2 = PR = 0.5 \times 98 = 49$

or $V = \sqrt{49} = 7$ V (1)

24. Power, $P = i^2R$

$\Rightarrow \quad i^2 = \dfrac{P}{R} = \dfrac{10}{10000} = \dfrac{1}{1000} = 0.001$

or $\quad i = \sqrt{0.001} = 0.031$ A (1)

25. Electric power, $P = Vi$

or $\quad i = \dfrac{P}{V} = \dfrac{1000}{250} = 4$ A

Now, $q = it = 4 \times 60 = 240$ C (1)

26. $\therefore$ Power, $P = \dfrac{V^2}{R}$

$\Rightarrow \quad \dfrac{P_1}{P_2} = \dfrac{R_2}{R_1}$

$\Rightarrow \quad \dfrac{25}{P_2} = \dfrac{20}{400}$

or $\quad P_2 = 25 \times 20 = 500$ W (1)

TOPIC 03 Cells, EMF and Internal Resistance

Cells

An electric cell is a source of energy that maintains a continuous flow of charge in a circuit. Electric cell changes chemical energy into electrical energy. In an ordinary cell, the source of electrical energy is chemical. However, the energy source may also be mechanical (as a generator), thermal (as in a thermopile) or radiant (as in a solar cell).

Note Cell consists of two rods in different metals, which are called electrodes. These are immersed in a liquid called electrolyte.

Electromotive Force (EMF) of a Cell (E)

Electric cell has to do some work in maintaining the current through a circuit. The work done by the cell in moving unit positive charge through the whole circuit (including the cell) is called the **electromotive force** (emf) of the cell. If during the flow of q coulomb of charge in an electric circuit, the work done by the cell is W, then

emf of the cell, $\boxed{E = \dfrac{W}{q}}$

Its unit is joule/coulomb or volt.

If $W = 1$ joule and $q = 1$ coulomb, then $E = 1$ volt, i.e. if in the flow of 1 coulomb of charge, the work done by the cell is 1 joule, then the emf of the cell is 1 volt.

Internal Resistance (r)

Internal resistance of a cell is defined as the resistance offered by the electrolyte of the cell to the flow of current through it. It is denoted by r. Its unit is ohm. Internal resistance of a cell depends on the following factors

(i) It is directly proportional to the separation between the two plates of the cell.

(ii) It is inversely proportional to the area of plate dipped into the electrolyte.

(iii) It depends on the nature, concentration and temperature of the electrolyte and increases with increase in concentration.

Terminal Potential Difference (V)

Terminal potential difference of a cell is defined as the potential difference between the two terminals of the cell in a closed circuit (i.e. when current is drawn from the cell). It is represented by V and its unit is volt. Terminal potential difference of a cell is always less than the emf of the cell.

Relation between Terminal Potential Difference, emf of a Cell and Internal Resistance of a Cell

(i) If no current is drawn from the cell, i.e. the cell is in open circuit, so emf of the cell will be equal to the terminal potential difference of the cell.

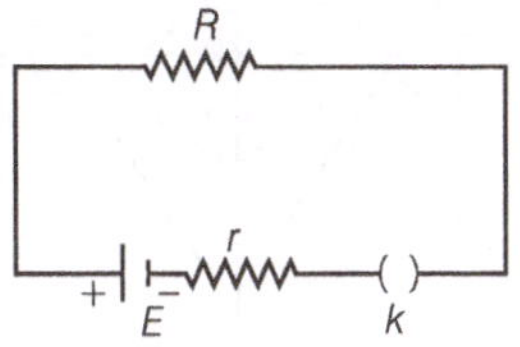

$$I = 0 \quad \text{or} \quad V = E$$

The emf of the cell is directed from the negative electrode to the positive electrode inside the cell.

(ii) Consider a cell of emf E and internal resistance r is connected across an external resistance R.

Current drawn from the cell, $I = \dfrac{E}{R+r}$ ...(i)

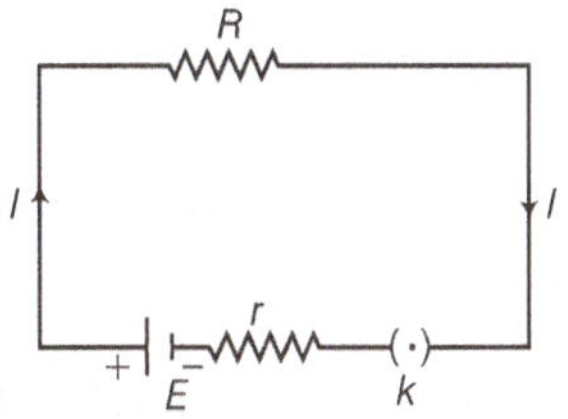

where, E = emf of the cell,

R = external resistance

and r = internal resistance of a cell.

Here, $(R+r)$ is the total (external + internal) resistance of the circuit.

Now, from Ohm's law,

$$V = IR \Rightarrow I = \frac{V}{R} \quad \text{...(ii)}$$

From Eqs. (i) and (ii), we get

$$\frac{V}{R} = \frac{E}{R+r}$$

$$\Rightarrow \quad \boxed{r = \left(\frac{E}{V} - 1\right)R}$$

From definition of terminal potential difference,

$$\boxed{V = E - Ir}$$

$$\therefore \quad V < E$$

When current is drawn from a cell, its terminal potential difference is less than the emf. Since, $V = E - Ir$, the Ir factor is also called **back emf** of the cell.

Example 1 The reading on a high resistance voltmeter, when a cell is connected across it, is 2.2 V. When the terminals of the cell are connected to a resistance of 5 Ω as shown in figure given below, the voltmeter reading drops to 1.8 V. Find the internal resistance of the cell.

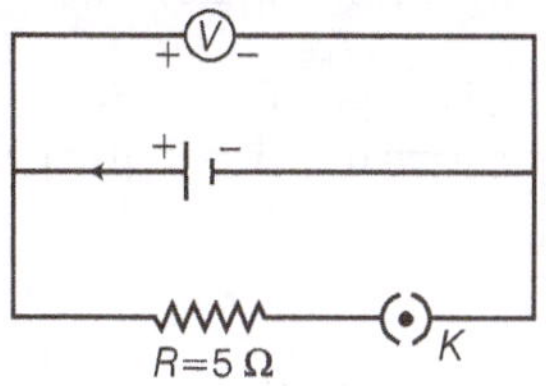

Sol. Given, emf, $E = 2.2\ V$

Terminal potential difference, $V = 1.8$ V

External resistance, $R = 5\Omega$

$\therefore$ Internal resistance, $r = \left(\dfrac{E-V}{V}\right)R$

$$= \left(\frac{2.2-1.8}{1.8}\right) \times 5 = \frac{10}{9}\ \Omega$$

Example 2 A cell of emf E and internal resistance r gives a current of 0.5 A with an external resistance of 12 Ω and a current of 0.25 A with an external resistance of 25 Ω. Calculate the

(i) internal resistance of the cell (ii) emf of the cell.

Sol. Let R be external resistance in series with the cell of emf E and internal resistance r. The current in circuit is

$$I = \frac{E}{R+r}$$

Case I $I = 0.5\text{A}, R = 12\ \Omega$, then

$$0.5 = \frac{E}{12+r}$$

$$\Rightarrow \quad E = 0.5\,(12+r)$$

$$\Rightarrow \quad E = 6.0 + 0.5r \quad \text{...(i)}$$

Case II $I = 0.25\text{A}, R = 25\Omega$, then

$$0.25 = \frac{E}{25+r}$$

$$\Rightarrow \quad E = 0.25\,(25+r)$$

$$\Rightarrow \quad E = 6.25 + 0.25r \quad \text{...(ii)}$$

From Eqs. (i) and (ii), we get

$$6.0 + 0.5\ r = 6.25 + 0.25\ r$$

$$\Rightarrow \quad r = 1\Omega$$

From Eq. (i), we get

$$E = 6.0 + 0.5 \times (1) = 6.5\text{V}$$

Hence, (i) internal resistance of the cell is 1 Ω.

(ii) emf of the cell is 6.5 V.

Cells in Series and Parallel

Cells in Series

In this combination, n identical cells each of emf E and internal resistance r are connected in series to the external resistance R as shown in the figure.

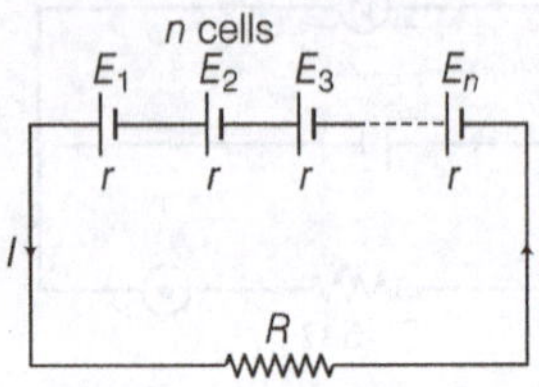

Points to remember for series combination of cells

(i) The equivalent emf of a series combination of n cells is equal to the sum of their individual emfs.

(ii) The equivalent internal resistance of a series combination of n cells is equal to sum of their individual internal resistances.

Equivalent emf of n cells in series,

$E_{eq} = E_1 + E_2 + ... +$ upto n terms $= nE$

Equivalent internal resistance of n cells in series,

$r_{eq} = r_1 + r_2 + ... +$ upto n terms $= nr$

Total resistance of the circuit $= nr + R$

$\therefore$ Current in the resistance R is given by

$$\boxed{I = \frac{nE}{R + nr}}$$

where, n = number of cells,
r = internal resistance,
R = external resistance,
E = emf of cell
and I = current flowing.

Case I When $R << nr$, then

$$I = \frac{E}{r} = \text{current due to a single cell}$$

Case II When $R >> nr$, then

$$I = \frac{nE}{R}$$
$= n$ times the current due to a single cell

Case III When cells are of different emfs and different internal resistances, then

$$I = \frac{E_1 + E_2 + ... + E_n}{R + (r_1 + r_2 + ... + r_n)}$$

Note The maximum current can be drawn from the series combination of cells, if the value of external resistance is very high as compared to the total internal resistance of the cells.

Cells in Parallel

In this combination, m cells each of emf E and internal resistance r are connected in parallel the external resistance R as shown in the figure.

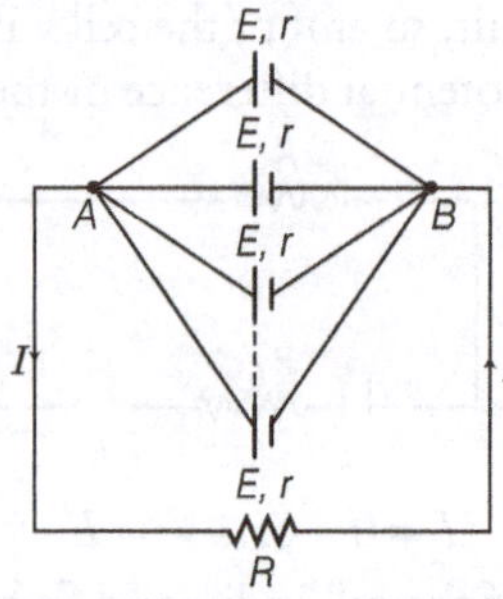

Points to remember for parallel combination of cells

(i) The equivalent emf of parallel combination of cells of same emfs is equal to emf of one cell.

(ii) The reciprocal of equivalent internal resistance of parallel combination of cells is equal to the sum of the reciprocals of the internal resistance of each cell.

$\therefore \frac{1}{r_p} = \frac{1}{r_1} + \frac{1}{r_2} + ...$ upto m terms $= \frac{m}{r}$ or $r_p = \frac{r}{m}$

As, R and r_p are in series, so total resistance in the circuit $= R + \frac{r}{m}$

In parallel combination of identical cells, the effective emf in the circuit is equal to the emf due to a single cell, because in this combination, only the size of the electrodes increases but not emf.

$\therefore$ Current in the resistance R is given by

$$\boxed{I = \frac{E}{R + \frac{r}{m}}}$$

Case I When $R >> \frac{r}{m}$, then

$$I = \frac{E}{R} = \text{current due to a single cell}$$

Case II When $R << \frac{r}{m}$, then $I = \frac{E}{r/m}$

$$= \frac{mE}{r} = m \text{ times current due to a single cell}$$

Case III When cells are of same emf and different internal resistances, then

$$I = \frac{E}{R + r'} \quad [\because E_1 = E_2 = ... E_n = E]$$

where, $\frac{1}{r'} = \frac{1}{r_1} + \frac{1}{r_2} + \frac{1}{r_3} + ... + \frac{1}{r_n}$ and E is emf of each cell.

Note The maximum current can be drawn from the parallel combination of cells, if the external resistance is very low as compared to the total internal resistance of the cells.

Example 3 Two identical cells, when joined together in series or in parallel give the same current, when connected to external resistance of 2 Ω. Find the internal resistance of each cell.

Sol. Let E, r be the emf and internal resistance of each cell.

External resistance, $R = 2\Omega$

If two cells are connected in series, then

Total emf of cells $= E + E = 2E$

Total resistance of circuit $= R + r + r = 2 + 2r$

Current in the circuit, $I_1 = \dfrac{2E}{2+2r}$

If two cells are connected in parallel, effective emf of two cells = emf of single cell = E

Total internal resistance of two cells $= \dfrac{r \times r}{r + r} = \dfrac{r}{2}$

Total resistance of the circuit $= R + \dfrac{r}{2} = 2 + \dfrac{r}{2}$

Current in the circuit, $I_2 = \dfrac{E}{2+\dfrac{r}{2}} = \dfrac{2E}{4+r}$

As per question, $I_1 = I_2$

$$\Rightarrow \quad \frac{2E}{2+2r} = \frac{2E}{4+r}$$

$$\Rightarrow \quad 2 + 2r = 4 + r$$

$$\therefore \quad r = 2\Omega$$

Example 4 When 14 cells in series, are connected to the ends of a resistance of 82.6 Ω, then the current is found to be 0.25A. When same cells after being connected in parallel are joined to the ends of a resistance of 0.053Ω, then the current is 25A. Calculate the internal resistance and the emf of each cell.

Sol. Let E and r be the emf and internal resistance of each cell.

***Case* I** When the cells are in series.

Total emf of cells $= 14E$

Total resistance of circuit $= 82.6 + 14r$

∴ Current in the circuit is given by

$$\frac{14\,E}{82.6+14r} = 0.25\,\text{A} \quad \text{...(i)}$$

***Case* II** When the cells are in parallel.

Total emf of cells $= E$

Total resistance of circuit $= 0.053 + \dfrac{r}{14}$

∴ Current in the circuit is given by

$$\frac{E}{0.053+\dfrac{r}{14}} = 25\,\text{A} \quad \text{...(ii)}$$

Dividing Eq. (i) by Eq. (ii), we get

$$\frac{14\left(0.053+\dfrac{r}{14}\right)}{(82.6+14r)} = 10^{-2}$$

$$\Rightarrow \quad 14 \times \frac{14 \times 0.053 + r}{14} \times 10^2 = 82.6 + 14r$$

$$\Rightarrow \quad 5.3 \times 14 + 100r = 82.6 + 14r$$

Solving, we get

$$r = 0.097\,\Omega \approx 0.1\,\Omega$$

Substituting the value of r in Eq. (i), we get

$$E = 1.5\,\text{V}$$

Mixed Combination of Cells

In this combination, some cells are connected in series and some cells are connected in parallel as shown in the figure. Let there be n cells in series in one row and m rows of cells are in parallel.

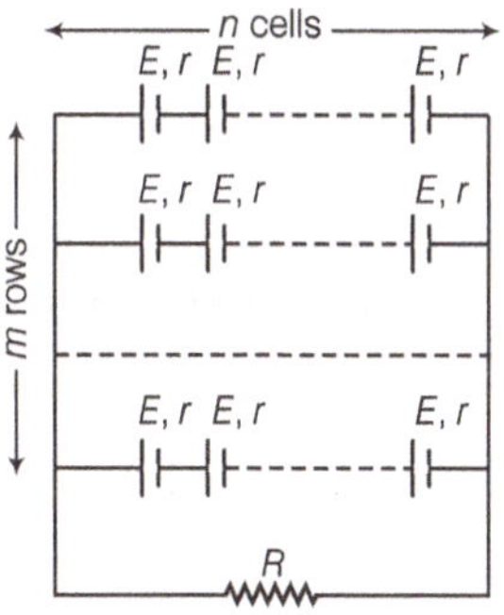

Suppose all the cells are identical. Let each cell be of emf and internal resistance r.

Equivalent emf of each row $= nE$

Equivalent internal resistance of each row $= nr$

Total emf of combination $= nE$

Total internal resistance of combination,

$$\frac{1}{r'} = \frac{1}{nr} + \frac{1}{nr} + \ldots \text{ upto } m \text{ times}$$

$$\frac{1}{r'} = \frac{m}{nr}$$

or

$$r' = \frac{nr}{m}$$

Total resistance of the circuit $= r' + R = \dfrac{nr}{m} + R$

Current in the resistance R is given by

$$I = \frac{nE}{\dfrac{nr}{m} + R}$$

Thus, we get the maximum current in mixed grouping of cells, if the value of external resistance is equal to the total internal resistance of all the cells, i.e. external resistance

= total internal resistance of all the cells $\left(R = \dfrac{nr}{m}\right)$.

Example 5 36 cells, each of internal resistance 0.5 Ω and emf 1.5 V each are used to send current through an external circuit of 2 Ω resistance. Find the best mode of grouping them and the current through the external circuit.

Sol. Here, $E = 1.5\text{ V}, r = 0.5\,\Omega, R = 2\,\Omega$

Total number of cells, $mn = 36$ ...(i)

For maximum current in the mixed grouping,

$$\frac{nr}{m} = R$$

$$\Rightarrow \quad \frac{n \times 0.5}{m} = 2 \quad \text{... (ii)}$$

Multiplying Eqs. (i) and (ii), we get

$$0.5n^2 = 72$$

$$\Rightarrow \quad n^2 = 144$$

$$\therefore \quad n = 12$$

and $$m = \frac{36}{12} = 3$$

Thus, for maximum current, there should be three rows in parallel, each containing 12 cells in series.

$$\therefore \text{Maximum current} = \frac{mnE}{mR + nr}$$

$$= \frac{36 \times 1.5}{3 \times 2 + 12 \times 0.5} = 4.5\text{ A}$$

Example 6 12 cells, each of emf 1.5 V and internal resistance of 0.5 Ω, are arranged in m rows each containing n cells connected in series, as shown in the figure. Calculate the values of n and m for which this combination would send maximum current through an external resistance of 1.5 Ω.

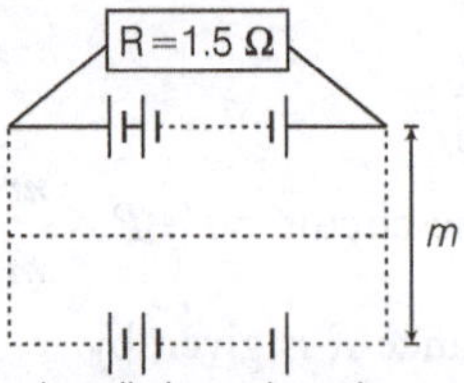

Sol. For maximum current through the external resistance, external resistance = total internal resistance of cells

or $$R = \frac{nr}{m}$$

$$\therefore \quad 1.5 = \frac{n \times 0.5}{\frac{12}{n}} \quad [\because mn = 12]$$

or $$36 = n^2$$

$$\therefore \quad n = 6 \text{ and } m = 2$$

☑ Topic Practice 3

Multiple Choice Questions

1 Mark

1. A simple device to maintain a steady current in an electric circuit is the
(a) electrolytic cell
(b) resistor
(c) electrode
(d) None of the above

2. Inside cell, the electrolyte through which a current flows has a finite resistance r, this r is called the
(a) chemical resistance
(b) resistivity
(c) conductivity
(d) internal resistance of cell

3. The internal resistance of dry cells is ...A..., than the internal resistance of common electrolytic cell. Here, A refers to
(a) much lower (b) much higher
(c) slightly lower (d) slightly higher

4. Is it possible that any battery has some constant non-zero value of emf, but the potential difference between the plates is zero?
(a) Not possible
(b) Yes, if another identical battery is joined in series
(c) Yes, if another identical battery is joined in opposition
(d) Yes, possible, if another similar battery is joined in parallel

5. Which of the following are true, when the cells are connected in series?
(a) Current capacity decreases
(b) Current capacity increases
(c) The emf decreases
(d) The emf increases

6. Figure below shows five DC sources (cells). Their emfs are shown in the figure.

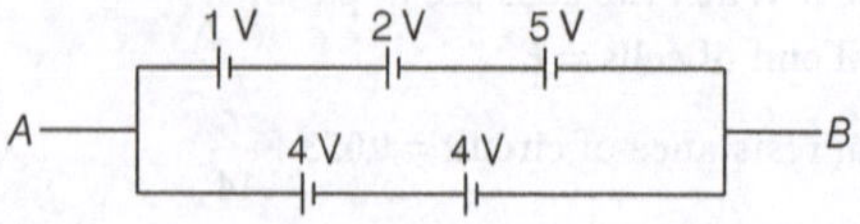

Emf of the battery AB is **ISC 2012**
(a) 8 V (b) 16 V (c) 4 V (d) 2 V

Very Short Answer Type Questions

1 Mark

7. The emf of a cell is always greater than its terminal voltage. Why?

8. A resistor R is connected to a cell of emf e and internal resistance r. Potential difference across the resistor R is found to be V. State the relation between e, V, R and r. **ISC 2015**

9. A cell of emf E and internal resistance r is connected across an external resistance R. Plot a graph showing the variation of potential difference across R *versus* R. **NCERT Exemplar**

10. Write any two factors on which internal resistance of a cell depends.

11. Calculate the net emf across A and B shown in the figure below

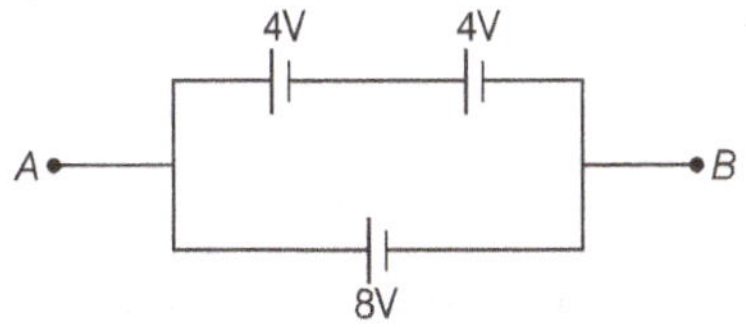

ISC 2019

12. A cell of emf E and internal resistance r is connected across a variable resistor R. Plot a graph showing variation of terminal voltage V of the cell *versus* the current I. Using the plot, show how the emf of the cell and its internal resistance can be determined.

13. Three identical cells each of emf e are connected in parallel to form a battery. What is the emf of the battery? **ISC 2024**

14. You are given a primary and a secondary cell of same emf. Which cell you will prefer for larger current? Why?

15. State one important property of a standard cell.

Short Answer Type I Questions

2 Marks

16. Write the relation between emf and potential difference for a cell. What are their respective units?

17. What is the difference between the values of potential difference across the two terminals of a cell in an open circuit and closed circuit?

18. A low voltage supply from which one needs high currents must have very low internal resistance. Why?

Short Answer Type II Questions

3 Marks

19. What do you mean by terminal potential difference of a cell? Under what conditions will the terminal potential difference of a cell be greater than its emf?

20. Which type of combination of cells is used in the following three cases.
    (i) If the external resistance is much larger than the total internal resistance?
    (ii) If the external resistance is much smaller than the total internal resistance?
    (iii) If the external resistance is equal to the total internal resistance?

21. n cells, each of emf e and internal resistance r are joined in the series to form a row. m such rows are connected in parallel to form a battery of $N = mn$ cells. This battery is connected to an external resistance R.
    (i) What is the emf of this battery and how much is its internal resistance?
    (ii) Show that current I flowing through the external resistance R is given by

$$I = \frac{Ne}{mR + nr}$$

ISC 2013

22. Eight identical cells, each of emf 2 V and internal resistance 3 Ω, are connected in series to form a row. Six such rows are connected in parallel to form a battery. This battery is now connected to an external resistor R of resistance 6 Ω. Calculate **ISC 2023**
    (a) emf of the battery,
    (b) internal resistance of the battery and
    (c) current flowing through R

Long Answer Type Questions

5 Marks

23. (i) The emf of a cell is always greater than its terminal voltage. Why? Give reason.
    (ii) Plot a graph showing the variation of terminal potential difference across a cell of emf E and internal resistance r with current drawn from it. Using this graph, how does one determine the emf of the cell?
    (iii) Three cells of emf E, $2E$ and $5E$ having internal resistances r, $2r$ and $3r$, variable

resistance R as shown in the figure. Find the expression for the current. Plot a graph for variation of current with R.

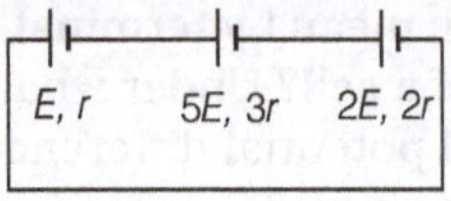

24. Two cells of same emf E, but different internal resistances r_1 and r_2 are connected to an external resistance R as shown in the figure. The voltmeter V reads zero. Obtain an expression for R in terms of r_1 and r_2. Calculate the voltage across the cell of internal resistance r_2. (Assume that the voltmeter V is of infinite resistance). **ISC 2005**

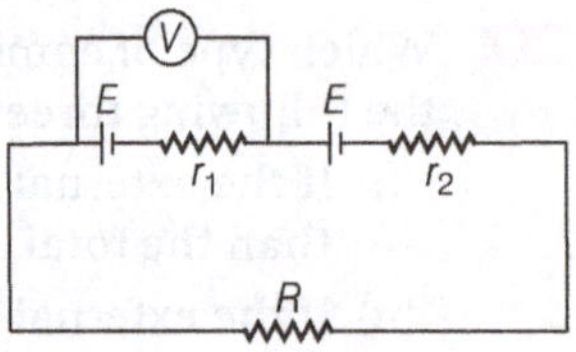

25. Define the emf of a cell in terms of the work done in moving a charge through the cell. Using Joule's law obtain the equation, emf = $I(R + r)$. (The symbols have their usual meaning). **ISC 2007**

Numerical Problems

26. A 2 V battery with internal resistance of 0.1 Ω is charged with a current of 5 A. Calculate the potential difference between the terminals of the battery. **ISC 2005 (1 M)**

27. Calculate the electric current density in a uniform wire connected to a battery of emf 3.5 V and negligible internal resistance. The resistance of the wire is 2.0 Ω and its area of cross-section is 0.70×10^{-6} m^2. **ISC 2007 (2 M)**

28. Three identical cells each of emf 2 V and internal resistance 1Ω are connected in series to form a battery. The battery is then connected to a parallel combination of two identical resistors, each of resistance 6Ω. Find the current delivered by the battery. **ISC 2015 (2 M)**

29. Find the emf of the battery shown in the figure.

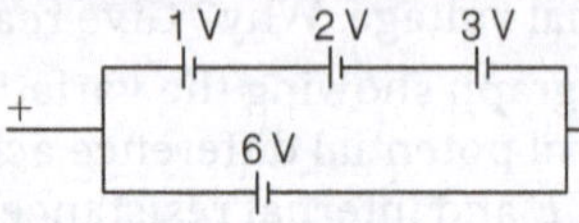

ISC 2014 (2 M)

30. A battery of emf 10 V and internal resistance 3 Ω is connected to a resistor. If the current in the circuit is 0.5 A, what is the resistance of resistor? What is the terminal voltage of the battery when the circuit is closed? **NCERT (3 M)**

31. The reading on a high resistance voltmeter, when a cell is connected across it, is 2.2 V. When the terminals of the cell are also connected to a resistance of 5 Ω as shown in the circuit, the voltmeter reading drops to 1.8 V. Find the internal resistance of the cell. **(3 M)**

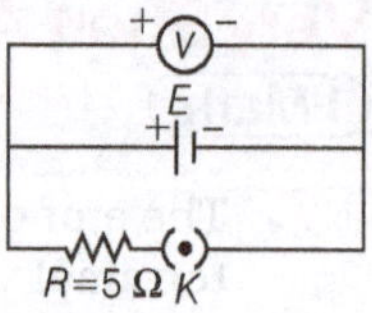

32. In the figure shown, an ammeter A and a resistor of 4 Ω are connected to the terminals of the source. The emf of the source is 12 V having an internal resistance of 2 Ω. Calculate the voltmeter and ammeter readings.

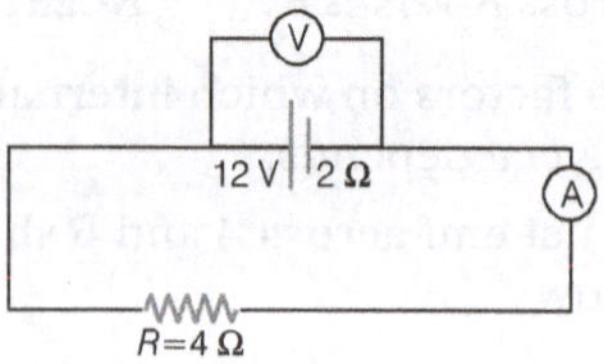

(3 M)

33. A battery of emf 12 V and internal resistance 2 Ω is connected to a 4 Ω resistor as shown in the figure.

(i) Show that a voltmeter when placed across the cell and across the resistor, in turn, gives the same reading.

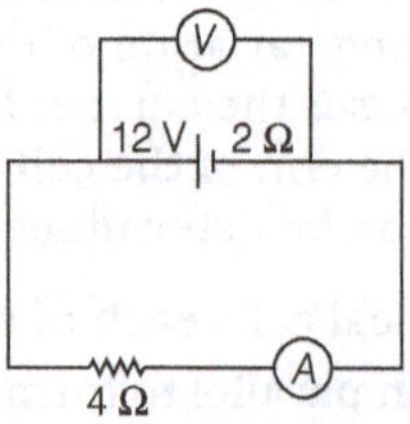

(ii) To record the voltage and the current in the circuit, why is voltmeter placed in parallel and ammeter in series in the circuit? **(3 M)**

34. A 10 V battery of negligible internal resistance is connected across a 200 V battery and a resistance of 38 Ω as shown in the figure. Find the value of the current in the circuit. **(3 M)**

35. (i) Six lead-acid type of secondary cells each of emf 2 V and internal resistance 0.015 Ω are joined in series to provide a supply to a resistance of 8.5 Ω. What are the current drawn from the supply and its terminal voltage?

(ii) A secondary cell after long use has an emf of 1.9 V and a large internal resistance of 380 Ω. What maximum current can be drawn from the cell? Could the cell drive the starting motor of a car? **NCERT (3 M)**

36. Calculate the current in given figure of the circuit shown below. What is the terminal potential of each cell?

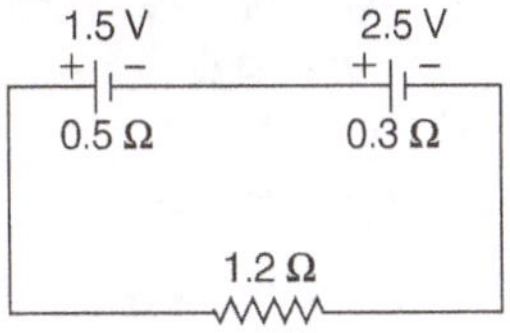

(3 M)

Hints & Solutions

1. (*a*) A simple device to maintain a steady current in an electric circuit is the electrolyte cell.
2. (*d*) The electrolyte through which a current flows has a finite resistance *r*, called the internal resistance. This is due to collision among ions.
3. (*b*) The internal resistance of dry cells, is much higher than the common electrolytic cells.
4. (*c*) If an identical battery is connected in opposition net emf $= E - E = 0$ and the current through circuit will be zero, although each one of them has constant emf.
5. (*d*) When cells are in series, emf of the combination of cells increases. As the equivalent emf is given by equation $\varepsilon_{eq} = \varepsilon_1 + \varepsilon_2 + \ldots + \varepsilon_n$.
6. (*a*) Consider the diagram

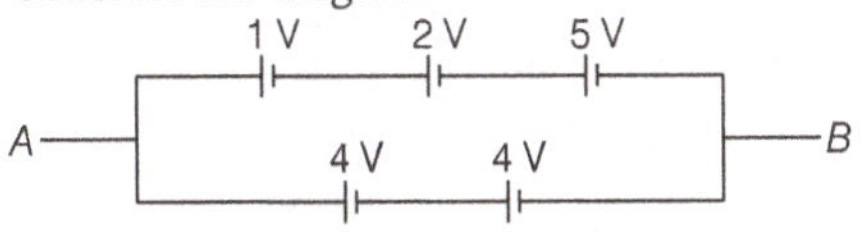

The cells connected in series will be added up for the calculation of equivalent emf.

Now, the two cells are in parallel.

So, the equivalent emf will be V_e = emf of each cell = 8 V.

The correct option is (a).

7. The emf of a cell is greater than its terminal voltage because there is some potential drop across the cell due to its small internal resistance.
8. The relation between *e*, *V*, *R* and *r* is that

$$e = IR + Ir = V + Ir$$

where, *e* = emf of cell,

$V = IR$ = potential drop across external resistance *R*

and Ir = potential drop across internal resistance *r*.

9. The graphical relationship between voltage across *R* and the resistance *R* is given below

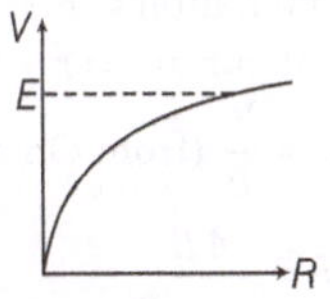

$$\left[\because V = \frac{E}{1 + r/R}\right]$$

10. The internal resistance of a cell depends on
    (i) the concentration of electrolyte and
    (ii) distance between the two electrodes. (1)
11. 4 V and 4V cells are in series so their combined emf, $E_1 = 4 + 4 = 8$ V. Now, E_1 and 8 V cells are in parallel, so the combined emf of the battery is 8 V.
12. We know that, $V = E - Ir$

The plot between *V* and *I* is a straight line of positive intercept and negative slope as shown below

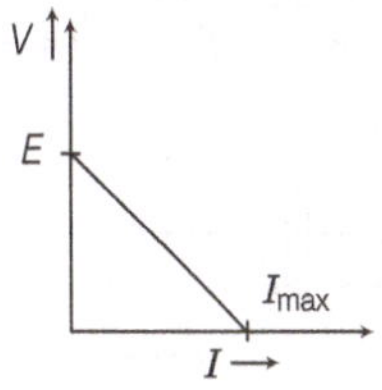

(i) The value of potential difference corresponding to zero current gives emf of the cell. (1/2)

(ii) Maximum current is drawn, when terminal voltage is zero, so

$$V = E - Ir \Rightarrow 0 = E - I_{max}r \Rightarrow r = \frac{E}{I_{max}}$$ (1/2)

13. Refer to text on page 130 (Cells in parallel).
14. Secondary cell, because its internal resistance is less.
15. Its emf is always constant.
16. For a cell of emf *E*, potential difference *V* and internal resistance *r*, $V = E - Ir$, where *I* is the current flowing through the circuit. The SI unit of both emf and potential difference of a cell is volt (V). (2)
17. The potential difference across the terminals of a cell is given by $V = E - Ir$.

In an open circuit, there is no current, i.e. $I = 0$

$\therefore V = E$, i.e. potential difference across the terminals of a cell = emf

In a closed circuit, $V < E$.

The difference between the two values of potential difference $= Ir$, which is called the lost voltage. (2)

18. We know that, $V = E - Ir$

$\therefore$ Current in the circuit, $I = \dfrac{E - V}{r}$ (1)

If the value of *V* is small, for high value of current *I*, then the internal resistance *r* should be small as $I \propto \dfrac{1}{r}$. (1)

19. Refer to text on page 128 (Terminal potential difference). (1½)

The terminal potential difference of the cell becomes greater than the emf of the cell during charging of the cell. In this process, current flows from positive electrode to negative electrode of the cell.

Hence, $V = E + Ir$. (1½)

20. (i) Series combination of cells. (1)
    (ii) Parallel combination of cells. (1)
    (iii) Mixed combination of cells. (1)

21. In mixed grouping of cells the equivalent emf can be calculated by first calculating emf for the series combination and then find equivalent emf for the parallel combination. Let $E_1, E_2, \ldots, E_n$ are emf's and $r_1, r_2, \ldots, r_n$ are the internal resistances of n cells.

(i) For I cell, $E_1 = V_1 + ir_1 \Rightarrow V_1 = E_1 - ir_1$

For II cell, $V_2 = E_2 - ir_2$

For nth cell, $V_n = E_n - ir_n$

Total voltage difference

$V = V_1 + V_2 + V_3 + \cdots + V_n$

$V = (E_1 + E_2 + \cdots + E_n) - i(r_1 + r_2 + \cdots + r_n)$

$V = E_{eq} - ir_{eq}$

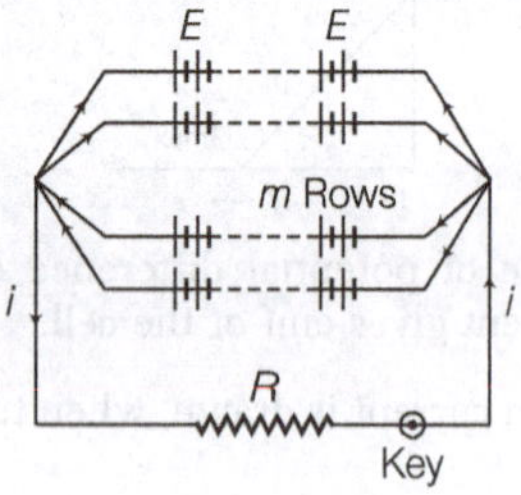

where, $E_{eq} = E_1 + E_2 + \cdots + E_n$

$r_{eq} = r_1 + r_2 + \cdots + r_n$

If $E_1 = E_2 = \cdots = E_n = E$

and $r_1 = r_2 = \cdots = r_n = r$

Then, $E_{eq} = nE \Rightarrow r_{eq} = nr$

If m rows of series of n cells are connected in parallel, then

Total emf of battery i.e., equivalent emf $= nE$

Total internal resistance $= \dfrac{nr}{m}$ (1½)

(ii) The electric current flow in the circuit

$$I = \frac{\text{Total emf}}{\text{Total resistance}}$$

$$I = \frac{nE}{\frac{nr}{m} + R} = \frac{mnE}{nr + mR}$$

According to the question, $E = e$

$$I = \frac{mne}{mR + nr} = \frac{Ne}{mR + nr} \quad [\because N = mn]$$ (1½)

22. (a) Emf of each cell = 2 V

8 such cells are connected in series.

Therefore, the emf of the battery is $2\text{V} \times 8 = 16\text{V}$

(b) 6 of such rows are connected in parallel

∴ A series connection,

Let R_s be total internal resistance of series connection

$R_s = R_1 + R_2 + \ldots + R_n$

Here, $n = 8$

Therefore,

$R_s = 3 + 3 + 3 \ldots 8\text{times}$

$R_s = 3 \times 8 = 24\,\Omega$

Let R_p be the total internal resistance of parallel connection.

$$\frac{1}{R_p} = \frac{1}{R_1} + \frac{1}{R_2} + \ldots + \frac{1}{R_n}$$

$R = 24\,\Omega$

$$\therefore \quad \frac{1}{R_p} = \frac{1}{24} + \frac{1}{24} + \ldots 6\text{times.}$$

$$\frac{1}{R_p} = \frac{6}{24} = 4\,\Omega$$

Total internal resistance of the battery is $4\,\Omega$.

(c) To calculate the current flowing through the external resistance R.

External resistance = $6\,\Omega$

Internal resistance = $4\,\Omega$

∴ For a series connection,

$R_s = R_1 + R_2 + \ldots + R_n$

$R_s = 6\,\Omega + 4\,\Omega = 10\,\Omega$

From, Ohm's law, $I = V/R$

where, V = emf of battery = 16 V

R = total resistance = $10\,\Omega$

$I = 16\text{V}/10\,\Omega$

$I = 1.6\text{ A}$

The current flowing through the external resistor R is 1.6 A.

23. (i) The emf of a cell is greater than its terminal voltage because there is some potential drop across the cell due to its small internal resistance. (1)

(ii) $\because \quad V = \left(\dfrac{E}{R + r}\right)R = \dfrac{E}{1 + r/R}$ (1/2)

i.e. with the increase of R, V increases

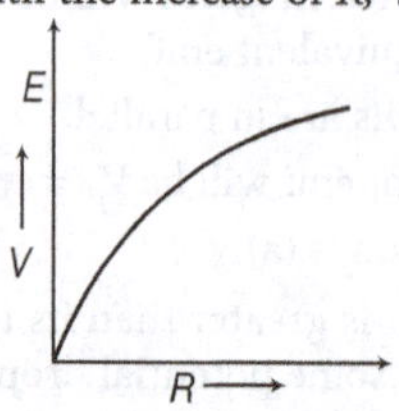

One can determine the emf of cell by finding terminal potential difference when current I becomes zero. (1/2)

(iii) In these type of questions, we have to look out the connections of different cells, if the opposite terminals of all the cells are connected, then they support each other, i.e. these individual emf's are added up. If the same terminals of the cells are connected, then the equivalent emf is obtained by taking the difference of emf's. (1)

Net emf of combination $= E - 2E + 5E = 4E$

Net resistance of current $= r + 2r + 3r + R = 6r + R$

$\therefore$ Current, $I = \dfrac{V}{R}$ (from Ohm's law)

$$\Rightarrow \quad I = \frac{4E}{6r + R}$$

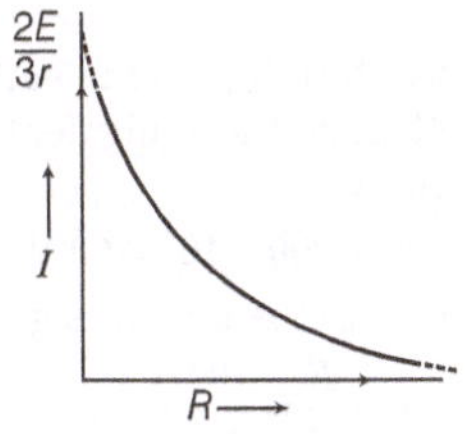

(2)

24. Find effective emf of the series combination of the cell. Then, current through the circuit can be calculated using $i = \frac{E_{net}}{r_{net}}$. (1)

As the two cells are in series, the effective emf is $2E$ and the total resistance is $r_1 + r_2 + R$. (1/2)

Therefore, the current in the circuit is

$$i = \frac{2E}{r_1 + r_2 + R} \quad \text{...(i)}$$ (1)

The voltage across the cell of internal resistance r_1 is

$$V = E - ir_1 = 0 \quad [\because \text{voltmeter } V \text{ reads zero}]$$

$$i = \frac{E}{r_1} \quad \text{...(ii)}$$ (1)

From Eqs. (i) and (ii), we get

$$\frac{E}{r_1} = \frac{2E}{r_1 + r_2 + R} \Rightarrow R = r_1 - r_2$$ (1)

This is required relation.

The voltage across the cell of internal resistance r_2 is $V' = E - ir_2$ (1/2)

25. Work done by a battery of emf E, when charge dq passes through the battery is $(d_q E)$. Work done in carrying a unit positive charge in a circuit is defined as emf of a cell. (1)

Suppose, when a steady current I is established in a circuit containing a cell of emf E, internal resistance r and an external resistance R, a charge dq flows in the circuit in time dt. By the definition of emf and according to Joule's law, the work done by the cell is given by

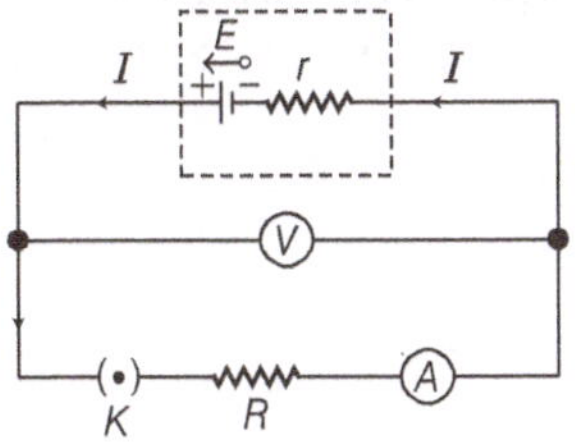

$$dW = E\,dq = EI\,dt \quad [\because dq = I\,dt]$$ (2)

If $V = IR$ be the potential difference across R, then the external work done by the cell is given by

$$dW_{ext} = V\,dq = VI\,dt = I^2R\,dt \quad \text{[by Joule's law]}$$

If $V = Ir$ be the potential drop across the internal resistance r, the internal work done by the cell is given by

$$dW_{int} = VIdt = I^2rdt \quad \text{[by Joule's law]}$$

By the law of conservation of energy,

$$dW = dW_{ext} + dW_{int}$$

$$EI\,dt = I^2R\,dt + I^2r\,dt$$

$$E = I(R + r)$$ (2)

26. Given, $E = 2\text{V}$, $i = 5\text{A}$, $r = 0.1\,\Omega$

Terminal voltage when a cell is charging is

$$V = E + ir = 2 + 5 \times 0.1 = 2 + 0.5 = 2.5\text{ V}$$ (1)

27. We know, electric current is given by

$$i = \frac{E}{R + r} = \frac{3.5}{2 + 0} = 1.75\text{ A}$$ (1)

Current density, $J = \frac{i}{A} = \frac{1.75}{0.70 \times 10^{-6}} = 2.50 \times 10^6\text{ A/m}^2$ (1)

28. According to the figure, all $1\,\Omega$ resistors are in the series combination and $6\,\Omega$ resistors are in parallel combination. So, the equivalent resistance of the circuit,

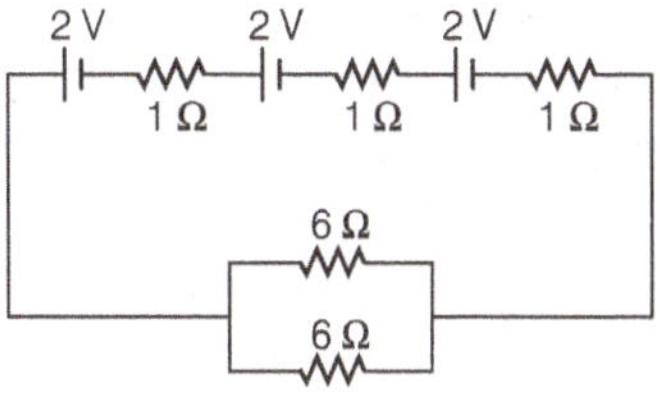

$$R_T = 1 + 1 + 1 + \frac{6 \times 6}{6 + 6} \Rightarrow R_T = 3 + \frac{36}{12} \Rightarrow R_T = 6\,\Omega$$ (1)

Total voltage of the circuit,

$$V_T = 2 + 2 + 2 = 6\text{ V}$$

Now current in the circuit, $I = \frac{V_T}{R_T} = \frac{6}{6} = 1\text{ A}$ (1)

29. Consider the circuit. Let the emf of the battery is E_{eq}. It is clear from the figure that the cells E_1, E_2 and E_3 are in series.

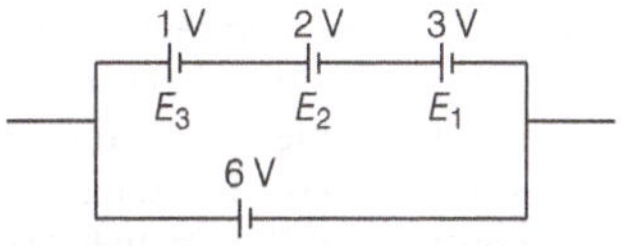

So, equivalent emf $E_4 = E_1 + E_2 + E_3$

$$= 3\text{V} + 2\text{V} + 1\text{V} = 6\text{V}$$ (1)

As the two cells are in parallel

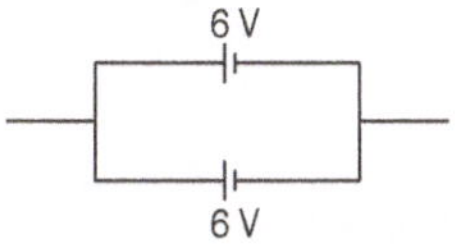

So, equivalent emf

$$E_{eq} = \text{emf of single cell} = 6\text{ V}$$ (1)

30. Given, $E = 10\text{ V}$, $r = 3\,\Omega$, $I = 0.5\text{A}$

As, $I = \frac{E}{R + r}$ (1)

$$\Rightarrow R = \frac{E}{I} - r = \frac{10}{0.5} - 3 = 17\,\Omega$$ (1)

and terminal voltage, $V = IR = 0.5 \times 17 = 8.5\text{ V}$ (1)

31. The emf of cell, $E = 2.2$ V

The terminal voltage across cell, when 5 Ω resistance R is connected across it, $V = 1.8$ V (1)

Let internal resistance $= r$

$\therefore$ Internal resistance, $r = R\left(\frac{E}{V} - 1\right)$ (1)

$$= 5\left(\frac{2.2}{1.8} - 1\right)$$

$$= 5 \times \frac{0.4}{1.8} = \frac{2}{1.8} = \frac{10}{9}\ \Omega$$ (1)

32. Current in the circuit, $I = \frac{E}{R+r} = \frac{12}{4+2} = 2$ A (1)

Also, terminal voltage across the cell,

$$V = E - Ir = 12 - 2 \times 2 = 8 \text{ V}$$ (1)

So, ammeter reading = 2 A

and voltmeter reading = 8 V (1)

33. According to question,

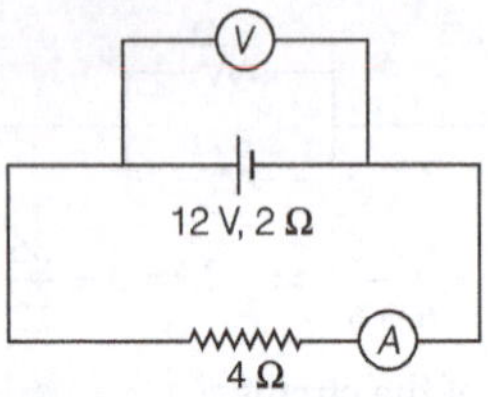

(i) Net current in the circuit $= \frac{12}{6} = 2$A

Voltage across the battery,

$$V_b = 12 - 2 \times 2 = 8\text{V}$$

Voltage across the resistance,

$$V_r = IR = 2 \times 4 = 8\text{V}$$ (1½)

(ii) In order to measure the device's voltage from a voltmeter, it must be connected in parallel to that device. This is necessary because device in parallel experiences the same potential difference. An ammeter is connected in series with the circuit because the purpose of the ammeter is to measure the current through the circuit. Since, the ammeter is a low impedance device. Connecting in parallel with the circuit would cause a short circuit, damaging the ammeter of the circuit. (1½)

34. Since, the positive terminal of the batteries are connected together, so the equivalent emf of the batteries is given by

$$E = 200 - 10 = 190 \text{ V}$$ (1½)

Hence, the current in the circuit is given by

$$I = \frac{E}{R} = \frac{190}{38} = 5 \text{ A}$$ (1½)

35. (i) Six cells are joined in series.

emf of each cell, $E = 2$ V

Number of cells, $n = 6$

Total emf of circuit $= n \times E = 6 \times 2 = 12$ V

Internal resistance of each cell, $r = 0.015\ \Omega$

Total internal resistance $= n \times r = 6 \times 0.015 = 0.09\ \Omega$

External load, $R = 8.5\ \Omega$

Current in the circuit, $I = \frac{nE}{nr + R} = \frac{12}{0.09 + 8.5} = 1.4$ A

$\therefore$ The terminal voltage of battery,

$$V = IR = 1.4 \times 8.5 = 11.9 \text{ V}$$ (1½)

(ii) emf of cell, $E = 1.9$ V

Internal resistance of cell, $r = 380\ \Omega$

Maximum current can be drawn from the cell, if there is zero external resistance. Therefore,

$$I_{max} = \frac{E}{r} = \frac{1.9}{380} = 0.005 \text{ A}$$ (1)

Now, we see that the maximum current drawn from the cell is very low, thus the cell cannot be used to drive the starting motor of a car as the current required for this purpose is approximately 100 A for few records. (1/2)

36. Current in the circuit $= \frac{\text{Total emf}}{\text{Total resistance}}$

$$= \frac{1.5 + 2.5}{0.5 + 0.3 + 1.2} = 2.0 \text{ A}$$ (1)

Terminal potential of the first cell,

$$V = E - ir = 1.5 - 2 \times 0.5 = 0.5 \text{ V}$$ (1)

Terminal potential of the second cell,

$$V = E - ir = 2.5 - 2 \times 0.3 = 1.9 \text{ V}$$ (1)

TOPIC 04 Kirchhoff 's Laws and its Applications

Kirchhoff's Rules or Laws

In 1842, Kirchhoff gave the following two rules to solve the complicated electrical circuits. These rules are basically the expressions of conservation of electric charge and energy.

These laws were stated as follows

First Law (Junction Rule)

This law states that the algebraic sum of the currents meeting at a point in an electrical circuit is always zero. It is also known as junction rule.

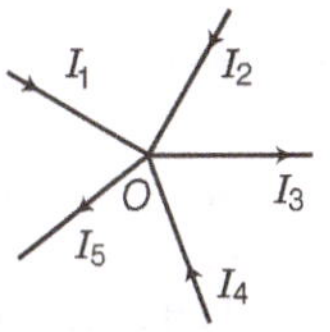

Electric junction

Consider a point O in an electrical circuit at which currents I_1, I_2, I_3, I_4 and I_5 flowing through the different conductors meet, as shown in the figure.

According to Kirchhoff 's first law, we have

$$I_1 + I_2 + (-I_3) + I_4 + (-I_5) = 0$$

$$\Rightarrow \quad I_1 + I_2 - I_3 + I_4 - I_5 = 0$$

$$\therefore \quad I_1 + I_2 + I_4 = I_3 + I_5$$

So, junction rule can also be stated as the sum of currents entering the junction is equal to the sum of currents leaving the junction.

Sign Convention for Kirchhoff's First Law

The current flowing towards the junction of conductors is considered as positive and the current flowing away from the junction is taken as negative.

Second Law (Kirchhoff's Voltage Rule)

This law states that the algebraic sum of changes in potential around any closed loop involving resistors and cells in the loop is zero. It means that in any closed part of an electrical circuit, the algebraic sum of the emfs is equal to the algebraic sum of the products of the resistances and currents flowing through them. It is also known as **loop rule.**

Consider a closed electrical circuit $ABCDA$ containing two cells E_1 and E_2 and five resistances R_1, R_2, R_3, R_4 and R_5.

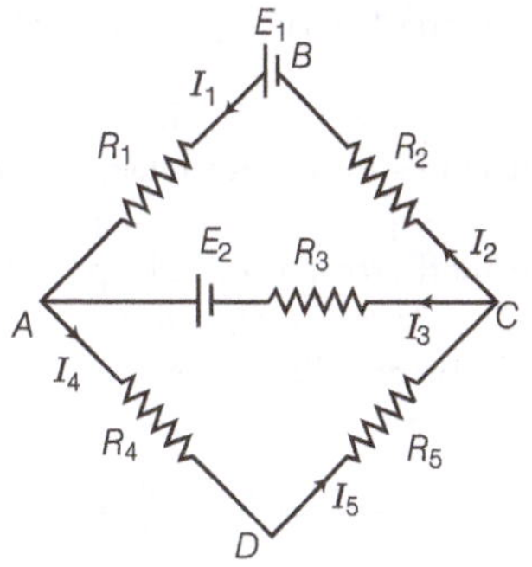

Consider the closed loop $ABCA$. E_1 will send current in anti-clockwise and E_2 will send current in clockwise direction.

$\therefore$ Total emf of closed loop

$$ABCA = E_1 + (-E_2) = E_1 - E_2$$

But currents (I_1 and I_2) flow in anti-clockwise direction while current I_3 flows in clockwise direction.

The algebraic sum of products of resistances and current

$$= I_1R_1 + I_2R_2 + (-I_3)R_3$$

$$= I_1R_1 + I_2R_2 - I_3R_3$$

$\therefore$ According to second law, for closed part $ABCA$,

$$E_1 - E_2 = I_1R_1 + I_2R_2 - I_3R_3$$

Similarly, for closed part $ACDA$,

$$E_2 = I_3R_3 + I_4R_4 + I_5R_5$$

Sign Convention for Kirchhoff 's Second Law

The product of resistance and current in an arm of the loop is taken as negative, if the direction of current in that arm is in the same sense as one moves and is taken as positive, if the direction of current in an arm is opposite to the sense as one moves.

Example 1 Find currents in different branches of the electric circuit shown in figure.

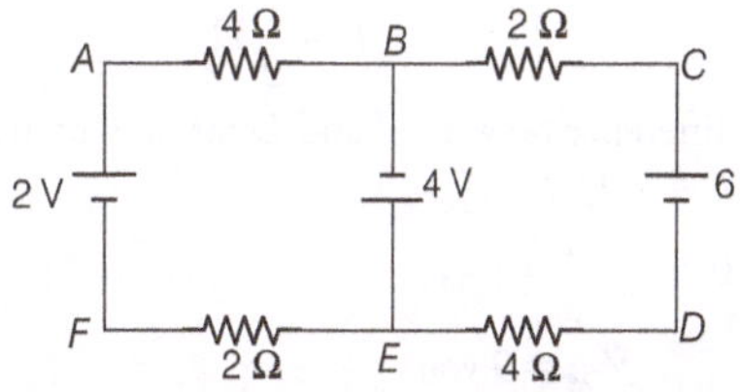

Sol.

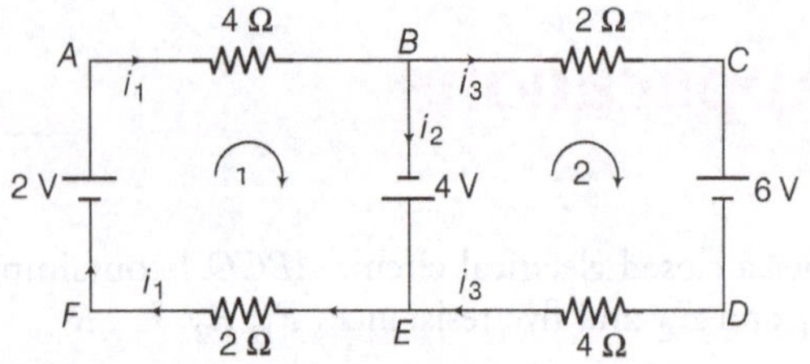

Applying Kirchhoff's first law (junction law) at junction B,

$$i_1 = i_2 + i_3 \quad \ldots\text{(i)}$$

Applying Kirchhoff's second law in loop 1 ($ABEFA$),

$$-4i_1 + 4 - 2i_1 + 2 = 0 \quad \ldots\text{(ii)}$$

Applying Kirchhoff's second law in loop 2 ($BCDEB$),

$$-2i_3 - 6 - 4i_3 - 4 = 0 \quad \ldots\text{(iii)}$$

Solving Eqs. (i), (ii) and (iii), we get

$$i_1 = 1\text{ A}$$

$$\Rightarrow \quad i_2 = \frac{8}{3}\text{ A} \Rightarrow i_3 = -\frac{5}{3}\text{ A}$$

Here, negative sign of i_3 implies that current i_3 is in opposite direction of what we have assumed.

Example 2 Use Kirchhoff's rules to determine the potential difference between the points A and D. When no current flows in the arm BE of the electric network shown in the figure below.

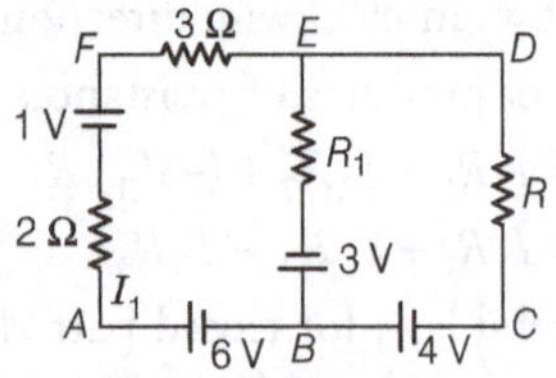

Sol. Applying Kirchhoff's loop rule for loop $ABEFA$,

$$-6 - 3 + R_1 \times 0 + 3I_1 - 1 + 2I_1 = 0$$

or

$$10 - 5I_1 = 0 \text{ or } I_1 = 2\text{A}$$

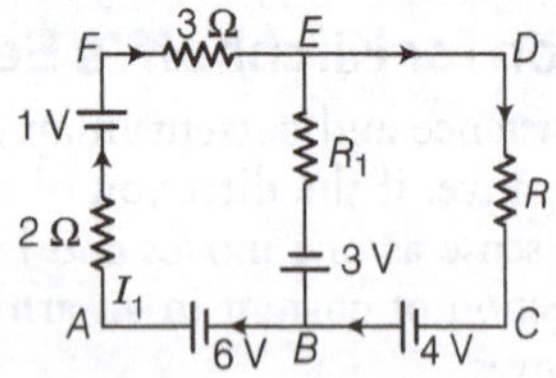

For loop $BCDEB$,

$$-4 + I_1 \cdot R + R_1 \times 0 + 3 = 0$$

or

$$-1 + 2R = 0$$

$$\therefore \quad R = \frac{1}{2}\,\Omega$$

Potential difference between A and D through path $ABCD$ is

$$-6 - 4 + I_1 R = V_{DA}$$

$$\Rightarrow \quad -10 + 2 \times \frac{1}{2} = V_{DA}$$

$$\therefore \quad V_{DA} = 9 \text{ volt}$$

Example 3 In the circuit shown in figure E, F, G, H are cells of emf 2, 1, 3 and 1 V respectively, and their internal resistances are 2, 1, 3 and 1 Ω, respectively. Calculate

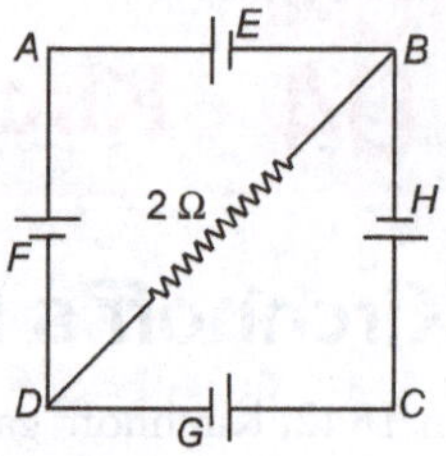

(i) the potential difference between B and D and

(ii) the potential difference across the terminals of each cells G and H.

Sol.

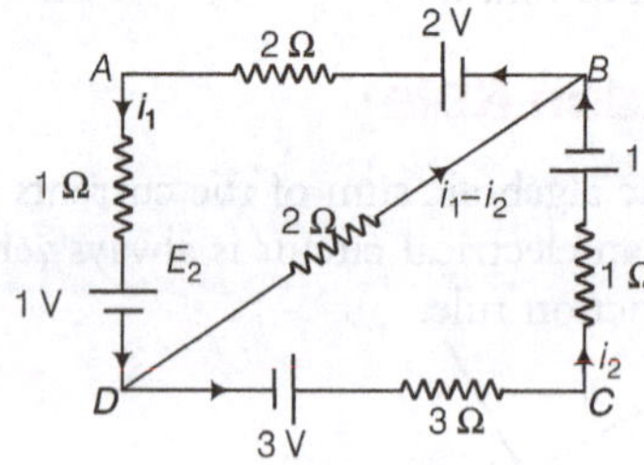

Applying Kirchhoff's second law in loop $BADB$,

$$2 - 2i_1 - i_1 - 1 - 2(i_1 - i_2) = 0 \quad \ldots\text{(i)}$$

Similarly, applying Kirchhoff's second law in loop $BDCB$,

$$2(i_1 - i_2) + 3 - 3i_2 - i_2 - 1 = 0 \quad \ldots\text{(ii)}$$

Solving Eqs. (i) and (ii), we get

$$i_1 = \frac{5}{13}, i_2 = \frac{6}{13} \text{ and } i_1 - i_2 = -\frac{1}{13}$$

(i) Potential difference between B and D,.

$$V_B + 2(i_1 - i_2) = V_D$$

$$\therefore \quad V_B - V_D = -2(i_1 - i_2) = \frac{2}{13}\text{V}$$

(ii) $V_G = E_G - i_2 r_G = 3 - \frac{6}{13} \times 3 = \frac{21}{13}$ V

$$V_H = E_H + i_2 r_H = 1 + \frac{6}{13} \times 1 = \frac{19}{13}\text{V}$$

Wheatstone Bridge

It is an arrangement of four resistances used to measure one of them in terms of the other three.

Consider four resistances P, Q, R and S are connected in the four arms of a quadrilateral. The galvanometer G and a tapping key K_2 are connected between points B and D. The cell of emf E and 1-way key K_1 are connected between points A and C as shown in the figure. Resistances P and Q are called ratio arms, resistance R is a variable resistance and S is unknown resistance.

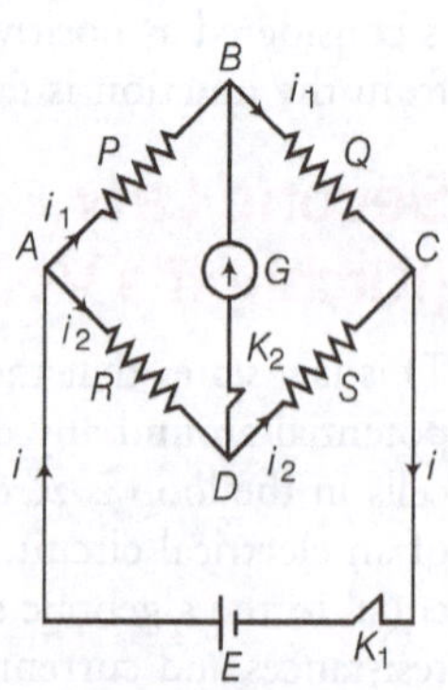

Wheatstone bridge

The bridge is said to be balanced, when the galvanometer gives zero deflection.

Thus, we have balance condition as

$$\frac{P}{Q} = \frac{R}{S}$$

It is clear from this formula that if the ratio of the resistances P and Q and resistance R are known, then the unknown resistance S can be calculated. This is why, the arms AB and BC are called **ratio arms,** arm AD **known arm** and arm CD **unknown arm.**

When the bridge is balanced, then on interchanging the positions of the galvanometer and the cell there is no effect on the balance condition of the bridge. Hence, the arms BD and AC are called **conjugate arms** of the bridge. (In balanced state, no current flows in the galvanometer arm, hence while computing the equivalent resistance between A and C, the resistance connected between B and D may be neglected.) The sensitivity of the bridge depends upon the values of the resistance. The bridge is maximum sensitive, when all the four resistances are of the same order.

Note The Wheatstone bridge is most sensitive, when the resistance of all the four arms of the bridge is of same order (or same), i.e. null point is obtained at the middle of bridge wire.

The advantage of null point method /zero deflection in a Wheatstone bridge is that the resistance of galvanometer does not affect the balance point, there is no need to determine current in resistances and internal resistance of a galvanometer.

Example 4 In a Wheatstone bridge circuit, $P = 7\,\Omega$, $Q = 8\,\Omega$, $R = 12\,\Omega$ and $S = 7\,\Omega$. Find the additional resistance to be used in series with S, so that the bridge is balanced.

Sol. Let the bridge be balanced when additional resistance x is put in series with S.

Then, $(S + x) = \frac{Q}{P} R$

or $x = \frac{Q}{P} R - S$

$= \frac{8}{7} \times 12 - 7$

$= 6.72\,\Omega$

Example 5 The Wheatstone bridge circuit have the resistances in various arms as shown in figure. Calculate the current through the galvanometer.

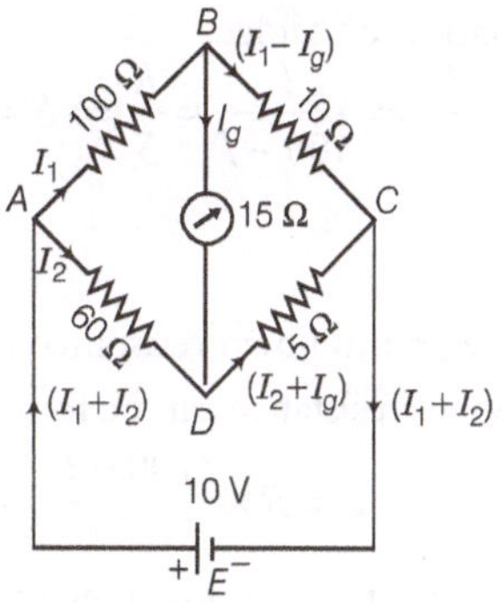

Sol. In the closed loop $ABDA$,

$$-100\,I_1 - 15\,I_g + 60\,I_2 = 0$$

$$\Rightarrow \quad 20\,I_1 + 3\,I_g - 12\,I_2 = 0 \quad \text{...(i)}$$

In the closed loop $BCDB$,

$$-10(I_1 - I_g) + 5\,(I_2 + I_g) + 15 I_g = 0$$

$$\Rightarrow \quad 10 I_1 - 30\,I_g - 5\,I_2 = 0$$

$$\Rightarrow \quad 2 I_1 - 6\,I_g - I_2 = 0 \quad \text{...(ii)}$$

In the closed loop $ADCEA$,

$$-60\,I_2 - 5\,(I_2 + I_g) + 10 = 0$$

$$\Rightarrow \quad 65\,I_2 + 5\,I_g = 10$$

$$\Rightarrow \quad 13 I_2 + I_g = 2 \quad \text{...(iii)}$$

On solving Eqs. (i), (ii) and (iii), we get

$$I_g = 4.87 \text{ mA}$$

Meter Bridge

A meter bridge is also known as **slide wire bridge.** It is a modified form of Wheatstone bridge.

Principle

It is constructed on the principle of balanced Wheatstone bridge, i.e. when a Wheatstone bridge is balanced, $\frac{P}{Q} = \frac{R}{S}$, where the initials have usual meanings.

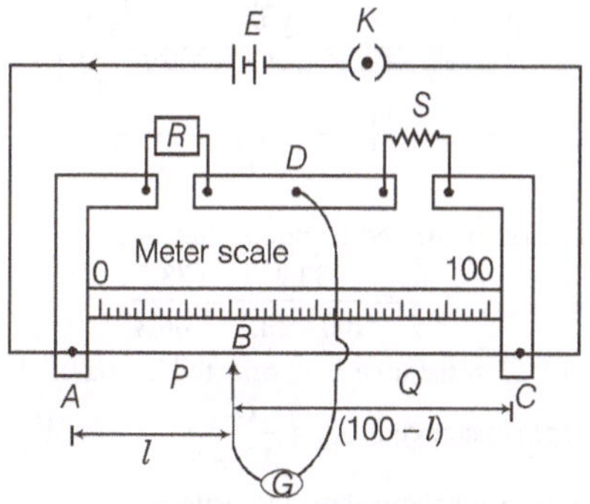

A meter bridge

At balancing situation of bridge,

$$\frac{P}{Q}=\frac{R}{S} \Rightarrow \frac{l}{100-l}=\frac{R}{S} \Rightarrow S=\frac{100-l}{l}\times R$$

Applications

(i) To measure an unknown resistance.

The unknown resistance can be found by

$$S=R\times\frac{(100-l)}{l}$$

(ii) To compare the two unknown resistances,

$$\frac{R}{S}=\frac{l}{100-l}$$

The meter bridge cannot be used to measure very low or very high resistances.

The end error in meter bridge arises due to the following reasons:

(a) The zero mark of the scale provided along the bridge wire may not start from the position where the bridge wire leaves the copper strip and 100 cm mark of the scale may not be at position, where the bridge wire just touches the other copper strip.

(b) The resistances of connecting wire and copper strips of meter bridge have not been taken into account. It can be removed by repeating the experiment by interchanging the known and unknown resistances and by taking the mean of resistances determined.

Example 6 **In a meter bridge, the null point is found at a distance of 33.7 cm from A. If a resistance of 12 Ω is connected in parallel with S, the null point occurs at 51.9 cm. Determine the values of R and S.**

NCERT Exemplar

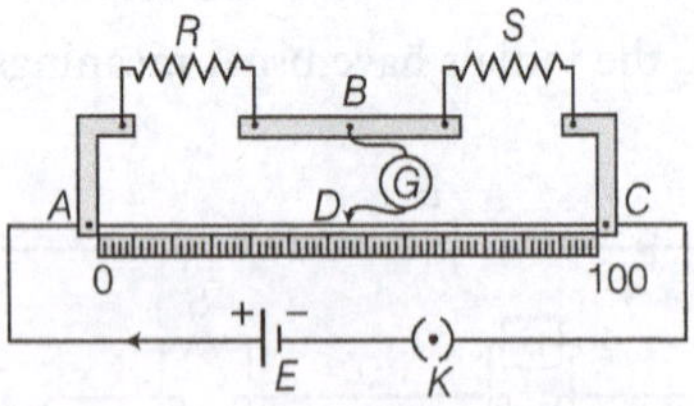

Sol. For the first balanced bridge situation,

$$\frac{R}{S}=\frac{33.7}{100-33.7}=\frac{33.7}{66.3} \quad \text{...(i)}$$

When 12 Ω resistance is connected in parallel with S, the equivalent resistance is $S_{eq}=\frac{12S}{12+S}$

For the second balanced bridge situation,

$$\frac{R}{S_{eq}}=\frac{51.9}{100-51.9}=\frac{51.9}{48.1}$$

or $$\frac{R(12+S)}{12S}=\frac{51.9}{48.1} \quad \text{...(ii)}$$

Putting the value of $\frac{R}{S}$ from Eq. (i) in Eq. (ii), we have

$$\frac{(12+S)}{12}\times\frac{33.7}{66.3}=\frac{51.9}{48.1}$$

On solving, we get $S=13.5\,\Omega$

From Eq. (i), we get

$$R=\frac{33.7}{66.3}S=\frac{33.7}{66.3}\times 13.5=6.86\,\Omega$$

Example 7 **When two resistance wires are in the two gaps of a meter bridge, the balance point was found to be 1/3 m from the zero end. When a 6 Ω coil is connected in series with the smaller of the two resistances, the balance point is shifted to 2/3 m from the same end. Find the resistance of the two wires.**

Sol. Refer to meter bridge circuit, let the resistance of wire in left gap be R_1 and resistance of wire in right gap be R_2.

Then, $R=R_1$, $S=R_2$, $l=\frac{1}{3}$ m and $(100-l)=1-\frac{1}{3}=\frac{2}{3}$ m

$$\therefore \quad \frac{R_1}{R_2}=\frac{l}{(100-l)}=\frac{1/3}{2/3}=\frac{1}{2}$$

or $R_2=2R_1$

So, $R_1<R_2$

As 6 Ω coil is connected in series with the smaller resistance R_1, so resistance of the left gap becomes, $R_1'=R_1+6$. Resistance of right gap is R_2.

Now, $l'=\frac{2}{3}$ m

and $(100-l')=1-\frac{2}{3}=\frac{1}{3}$ m

$$\therefore \quad \frac{R_1'}{R_2}=\frac{l'}{(100-l')}$$

or $$\frac{R_1+6}{R_2}=\frac{2/3}{1/3}=2$$

or $$R_1+6=2R_2=2\times 2R_1=4R_1$$

and $$R_2=2R_1=2\times 2=4\,\Omega$$

$$R_1=2\,\Omega$$

Potentiometer

Potentiometer is an apparatus used to compare emfs of two cells or to measure internal resistance of a cell.

Working Principle

It is based on the fact that the fall of potential across any portion of the wire is directly proportional to the length of that portion provided the wire is of uniform area of cross-section and a constant current is flowing through it.

Construction

It consists of a number of segments of wire having uniform cross-sectional area stretched over a wooden board between two thick copper strips. Each segment of wire (constantan or manganin) having length of 1 m. A meter rod is fixed parallel to its length. A battery is connected across the two end terminals which sends current through the wire, which is kept constant by using a rheostat.

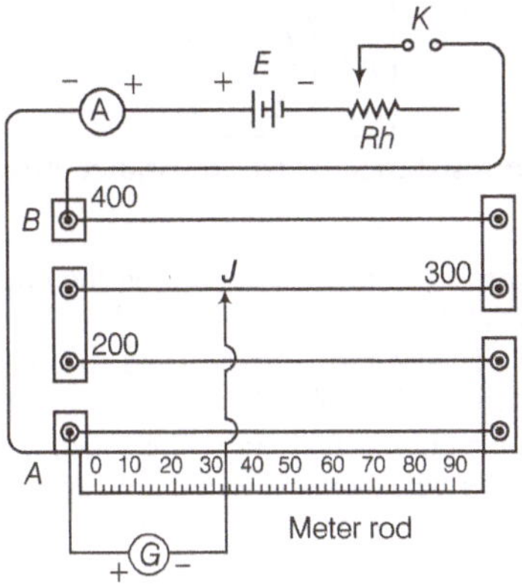

Potentiometer

Theory

Let V be the potential difference across the wire having resistance R. If the current I is flowing through the wire, then we have

$$V = IR$$

But we know that, $R = \frac{\rho l}{A}$

where, ρ, l and A have their usual meaning.

$$\therefore \quad V = I\rho\frac{l}{A}$$

If a constant current is passed through the wire of uniform area of cross-section, then I and A are constants. But for the given wire, ρ is also constant.

$$\therefore \quad V = \text{constant} \times l$$

$$V \propto l$$

Hence, the potential drop along the wire is directly proportional to the length of wire.

Here, $\frac{V}{l} = K$ is called **potential gradient**, i.e. the fall of potential per unit length of potentiometer wire.

Applications

To Compare the Emf's of Two Cells

Consider two cells of emf's E_1 and E_2 which are to be compared. The positive poles of both the cells are connected to terminal A of potentiometer and the negative pole of both cells are connected to terminals 1 and 2 of a 2-way key, while its common terminal is connected to a jockey J through a galvanometer G. A battery E, ammeter A, rheostat Rh and 1-way key K are connected between the terminals A and B of the potentiometer.

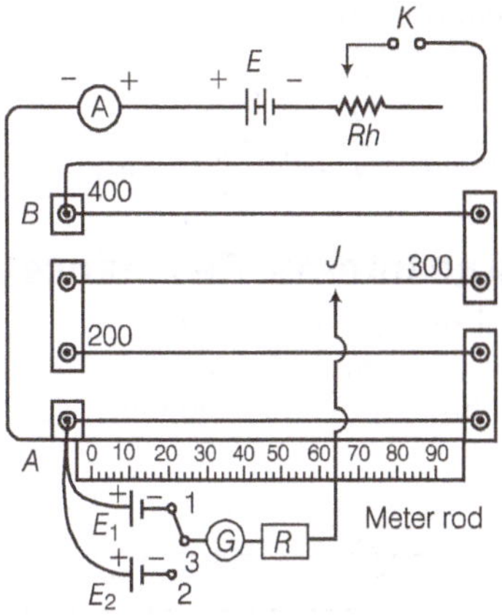

Circuit for comparing emf's of two cells

Now, to compare emf's of two cells having a constant current passing through the wire between terminals A and B, the current is kept constant by using rheostat. If the plug is put in the gap between terminals 1 and 3 of 2-way key, then the emf E_1 of the cell is given by

$$E_1 = (xl_1)\, I \qquad \text{...(i)}$$

where, x = resistance per unit length of potentiometer wire [$\because$ l_1 = balancing length]

Now, when the key is put in the gap between terminals, 2 and 3 after removing it from the gap between 1 and 3, the emf E_2 is given by

$$E_2 = (xl_2)I \qquad \text{...(ii)}$$

[$\because$ l_2 = balancing length]

From Eqs. (i) and (ii), we have

$$\boxed{\frac{E_1}{E_2} = \frac{l_1}{l_2}}$$

Example 8 In a potentiometer arrangement, a cell of emf 2.25 V gives a balance point at 30 cm length of the wire. If the cell is replaced by another cell and the balance point shifts to 60 cm, what is the emf of the second cell?

Sol. Given, $E_1 = 2.25$ V, $l_1 = 30$ cm, $l_2 = 60$ cm, $E_2 = ?$

As, we know that in case of potentiometer, the potential gradient remains constant.

So, $E \propto l$

$$\therefore \quad \frac{E_1}{E_2} = \frac{l_1}{l_2} \quad \ldots\text{(i)}$$

Substituting the given values in Eq.(i), we get

$$\frac{2.25}{E_2} = \frac{30}{60}$$

$$\therefore \quad E_2 = \frac{2.25 \times 60}{30} = 4.5 \text{ V}$$

To Measure Internal Resistance of a Cell

Now, to find the internal resistance r of a cell of emf E let E' be emf of the battery. A constant current I is maintained through the potentiometer wire with the help of rheostat.

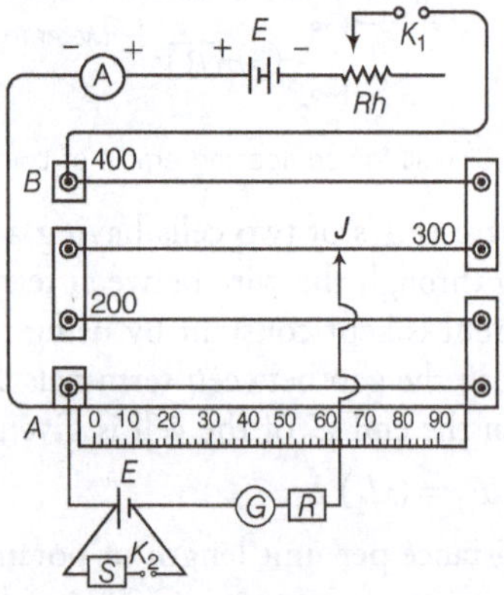

Circuit for determining internal resistance of cell

The plug key K_2 is kept out and the jockey J is moved on the potentiometer wire to balance the emf E of the cell, whose internal resistance r is to be determined.

Suppose l_1 be the balancing length of the potentiometer wire between point A and jockey J. If x is resistance per unit length of wire, then emf of cell is given by

$$E = xl_1I \quad \ldots\text{(i)}$$

Now we introduce some resistance, say S from the resistance box S and now put in the plug key K_2. The potential difference V between the two poles of the cell is given by

$$V = xl_2I \quad \ldots\text{(ii)}$$

[$\because l_2$ = balancing length]

Dividing the Eq. (i) by Eq. (ii), we have

$$\frac{E}{V} = \frac{l_1}{l_2}$$

The internal resistance of the cell is given by

$$r = \left(\frac{E}{V} - 1\right) S$$

Now, substituting the value of $\frac{E}{V}$ in above equation,

we get
$$r = \left(\frac{l_1}{l_2} - 1\right) S$$

where, S is the resistance of the resistance box.

Note

- The sensitiveness of potentiometer means the smallest potential difference that can be measured with its help.
  - A potentiometer can also be used to compare unknown resistances and to calibrate a voltmeter or an ammeter.
- A balance point is obtained on the potentiometer wire, if the fall of potential along the potentiometer wire due to driving cell is greater than the emf of the cell to be balanced.

Example 9 A cell can be balanced against 110 cm and 100 cm of potentiometer wire respectively, when in open circuit and when short circuited through a resistance of 10 Ω. Find the internal resistance of the cell.

Sol. Given, $l_1 = 110$ cm, $l_2 = 100$ cm

$R = 10\ \Omega$ and $r = ?$

$$\therefore \quad r = \left(\frac{l_1 - l_2}{l_2}\right)R = \frac{110 - 100}{100} \times 10 = 1\ \Omega$$

Topic Practice 4

Multiple Choice Questions

1 Mark

1. Five conductors are meeting at a point x as shown in the figure. What is the value of current in fifth conductor?

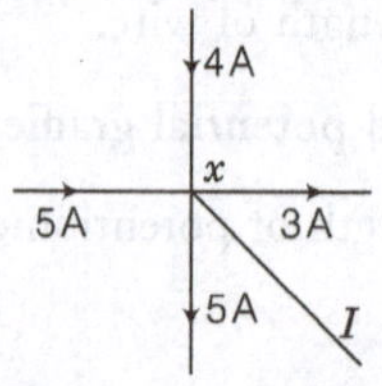

(a) 3A away from x
(b) 1A away from x
(c) 4A away from x
(d) 1A towards x

2. Five resistors are connected as shown in the figure.

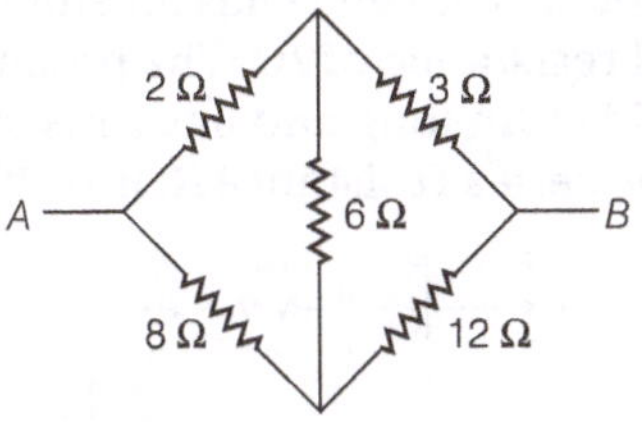

The effective resistance, i.e. equivalent resistance between the points A and B is **ISC 2013**

(a) 4 Ω (b) 5 Ω (c) 15 Ω (d) 20 Ω

3. The Wheatstone bridge and its balance condition provide a practical method for determination of a/an

(a) known resistance (b) unknown resistance
(c) both (a) and (b) (d) None of these

4. A meter bridge is balanced with a known resistance (R) in the left hand gap and an unknown resistance (S) in the right hand gap. Balance point is found to be at a distance of l cm from the left hand side. When the battery and the galvanometer are interchanged, balance point will **ISC 2024**

(a) shift towards left
(b) shift towards right
(c) remain same
(d) shift towards left or right depending on the values of R and S

5. Potentiometer measures the potential difference more accurately than a voltmeter, because

(a) it has a wire of high resistance
(b) it has a wire of low resistance
(c) it does not draw current from external circuit
(d) it draws a heavy current from external circuit

6. In a potentiometer arrangement, a cell of emf 1.25 V gives a balance point at 35.0 cm length of the wire. If the cell is replaced by another cell and the balance point shifts to 63.0 cm, what is the emf of the second cell?

(a) 2.25 V (b) 3.25 V (c) 4.5 V (d) 6 V

Very Short Answer Type Questions

1 Mark

7. Name the two conservation laws implied in Kirchhoff's laws for electric circuits. **ISC 2017, 07, 02**

8. Which conservation principle is involved in Kirchhoff's first law of electric circuits? **2012**

9. When a Wheatstone bridge is most sensitive?

10. Write one reason for end error in a meter bridge.

11. What is the advantage of using thick metallic strips to join wires in a potentiometer? **NCERT Exemplar**

12. Why is a potentiometer preferred over a voltmeter in measuring the emf of a cell? **ISC 2007**

Short Answer Type I Questions

2 Marks

13. In the meter bridge experiment, balance point was observed at J with $AJ = l$.

(i) The values of R and X were doubled and then interchanged. What would be the new position of balance point?

(ii) If the galvanometer and battery are interchanged at the balanced position, how will the balance point get affected?

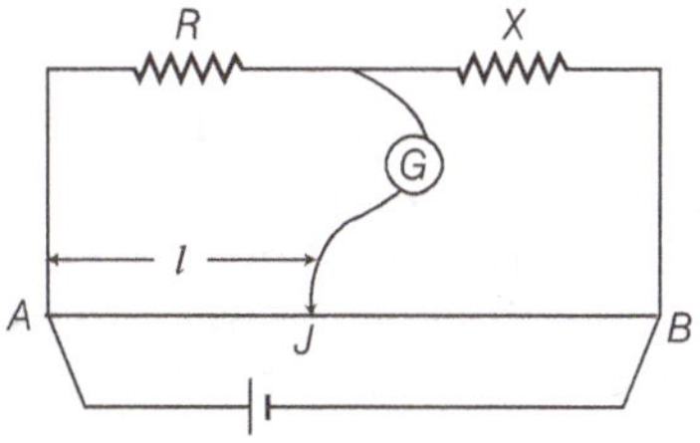

14. In a potentiometer experiment, the balancing length with a resistance of 2Ω is found to be 100 cm, while that of an unknown resistance is 500 cm. Calculate the value of the unknown resistance. **ISC 2019**

15. Draw a circuit diagram for the determination of the internal resistance of a cell using a potentiometer. Derive the formula to be used. **ISC 2002**

16. Two students X and Y perform an experiment on potentiometer separately using the circuit given below

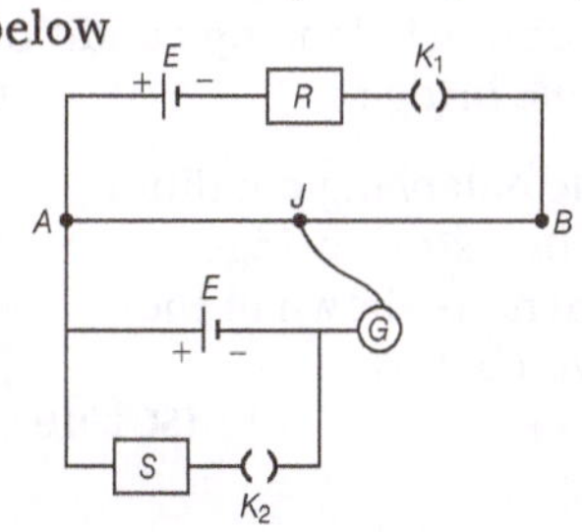

Keeping other parameters unchanged, how will the position of the null point be affected, if

(i) X increases the value of resistance R in the set up by keeping the key K_1 closed and the key K_2 open?

(ii) Y decreases the value of resistance S in the set up, while the key K_2 remains open and then K_1 closed? Justify your answer.

Short Answer Type II Questions

3 Marks

17. Figure below shows two batteries E_1 and E_2 having emfs of 18V and 10V and internal resistances of 1Ω and 2Ω respectively. W_1, W_2 and W_3 are uniform metallic wires AC, FD and BE having resistance of 8Ω, 6Ω and 10Ω respectively. B and E are mid-points of the wires W_1 and W_2. Using Kirchhoff's laws of electrical circuits, calculate the current flowing in the wire W_3. **ISC 2024**

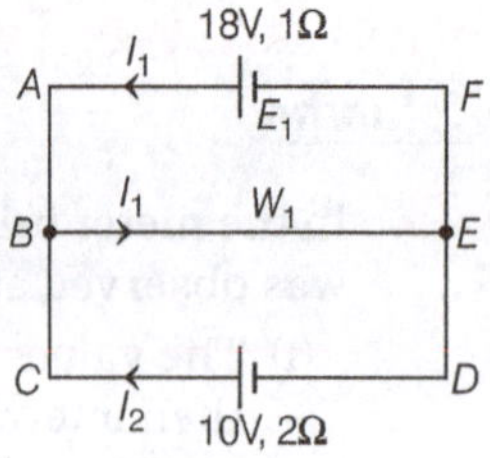

18. In the circuit shown in figure below, E_1 and E_2 are batteries having emfs of 25 V and 26 V. They have an internal resistance of 1 Ω and 5 Ω respectively. Applying Kirchhoff's s laws of electrical networks, calculate the currents I_1 and I_2. **ISC 2023**

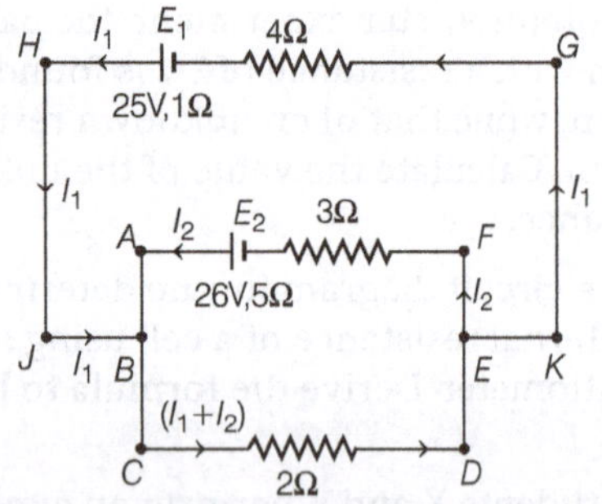

19. With the help of a neatly drawn and labelled diagram, obtain balancing condition of a Wheatstone bridge. **ISC 2015, 12, 02**

20. Obtain the balancing condition for the Wheatstone bridge arrangement as shown in the figure given below. **ISC 2019**

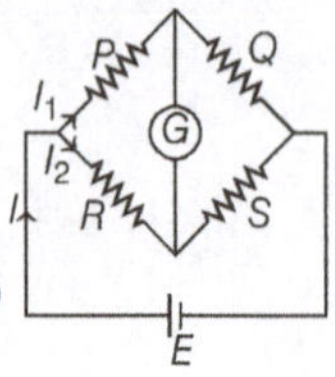

21. Figure below shows a potentiometer circuit in which the driver cell D has an emf of 6 V and internal resistance of 2Ω. The potentiometer wire AB is 10m long and has a resistance of 28Ω. The series resistance R, is of 20 Ω.

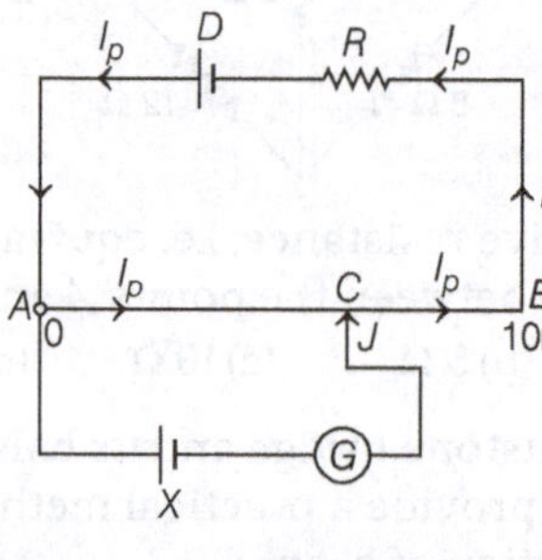

Calculate

(a) The current I_p flowing in the potentiometer wire AB when the jockey (J) does not touch the wire AB.

(b) emf of the cell X, if the balancing length AC is 4.5 m. **ISC 2024**

22. Draw a labelled circuit diagram of a potentiometer to measure the internal resistance r of a cell. Write the working formula (derivation is not required). **ISC 2019**

23. Draw a labelled circuit diagram of a potentiometer to measure internal resistance of a cell. Write the working formula. (Derivation not required). **ISC 2016**

Long Answer Type Questions

5 Marks

24. State and explain Kirchhoff's law for electric circuits. What are the conservation laws implied in each law? State the sign convention for current and emf. Use the figure given alongside for your explanation. **ISC 2000**

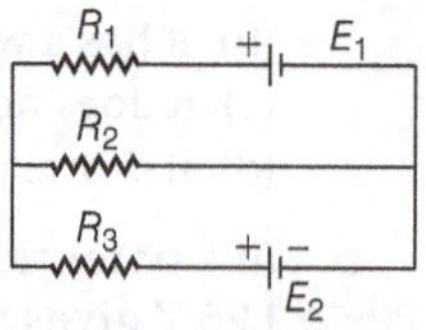

25. (i) State with the help of a circuit diagram, the working principle of a meter bridge. Obtain the expression used for determining the unknown resistance.

(ii) What happens, if the galvanometer and cell are interchanged at the balance point of the bridge?

(iii) Why is it considered important to obtain the balance point near the mid-point of the wire?

26. (i) State the working principle of a potentiometer. With the help of the circuit diagram, explain how a potentiometer is used to compare the emf's of two primary cells. Obtain the required expression used for comparing the emfs.

(ii) Write two possible causes for one sided deflection in a potentiometer experiment.

(iii) Why is potentiometer preferred over a voltmeter for comparison of emf of cells ?

(iv) Draw a circuit diagram to determine internal resistance of a cell in the laboratory.

27. (i) State the working principle of a potentiometer. Draw a circuit diagram to compare emf of two primary cells. Derive the formula used.

(ii) Which material is used for potentiometer wire and why?

(iii) How can the sensitivity of a potentiometer be increased ?

Numerical Problems

28. A part of an electric circuit is shown below.

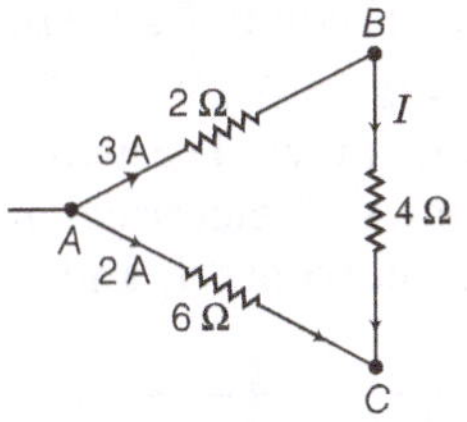

Using Kirchhoff's second law, find the current I flowing through the 4Ω resistor. **ISC 2010 (1 M)**

29. Find the value of resistance X in the circuit below, so that the junctions M and N are at the same potential.

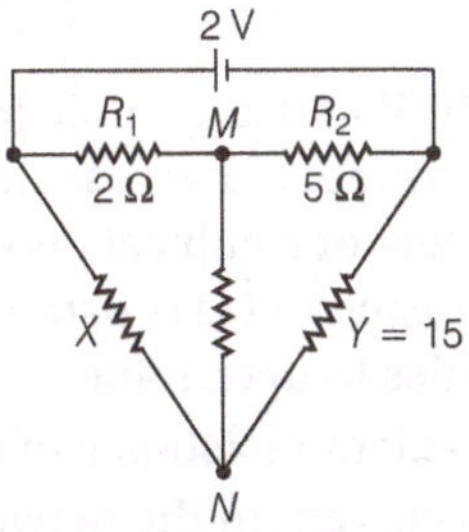

ISC 2009 (1 M)

30. In the circuit (given figure below), the length of the wire $AB = 400$ cm. Where should the jockey J be placed, so that the galvanometer shows a zero deflection?

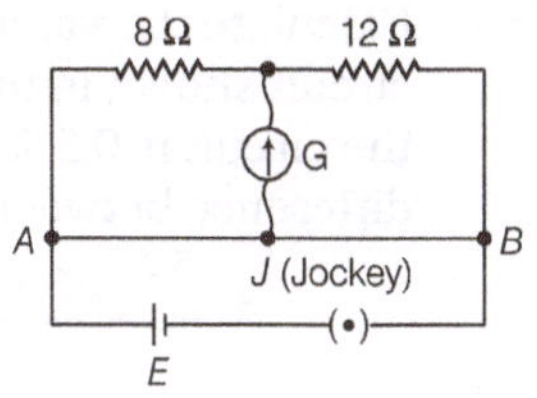

ISC 2006 (1 M)

31. In figure given below, find the value of resistance X for which points A and B are at the same potential. **ISC 2016 (1 M)**

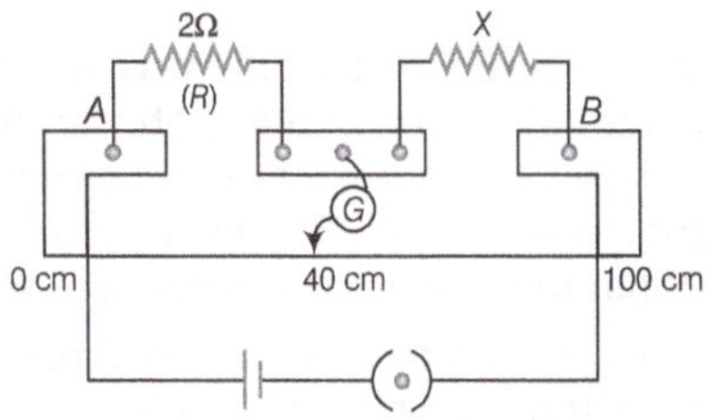

32. A 10 m long potentiometer wire carries a steady current. A standard cell of emf 1.018 V is balanced against a length of 254.5 cm of the wire. What is the potential gradient across the potentiometer wire? **ISC 2011 (1 M)**

33. In the figure given below, find the value of resistance X for which points A and B are the same potential.

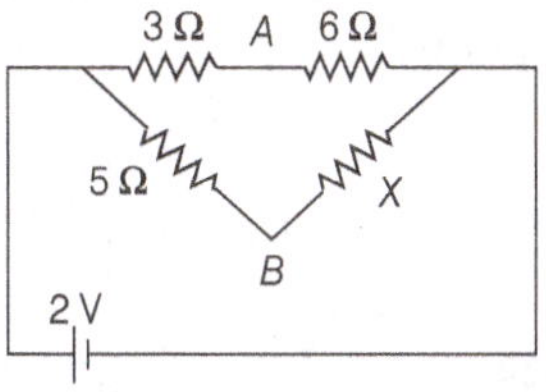

2016 (1 M)

34. In a potentiometer experiment, balancing length is found to be 120 cm for a cell ε_1 of emf 2 V. What will be the balancing length for another cell ε_2 of emf 1.5 V? No other changes are made in the experiment. **ISC 2018 (1 M)**

35. Using Kirchhoff's rules in the given circuit, determine

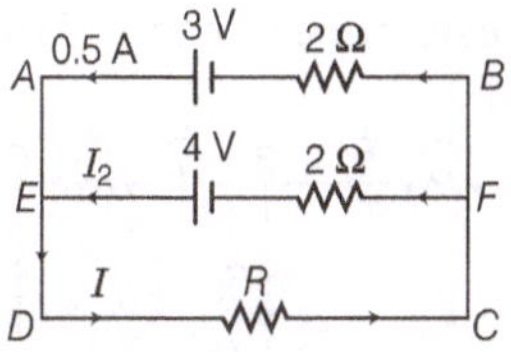

(i) the voltage drop across the unknown resistor R.

(ii) the current I in the arm EF. **(2 M)**

36. Calculate the value of the resistance R in the circuit shown in the figure, so that the current in the circuit is 0.2 A. What would be the potential difference between points A and B? **(3 M)**

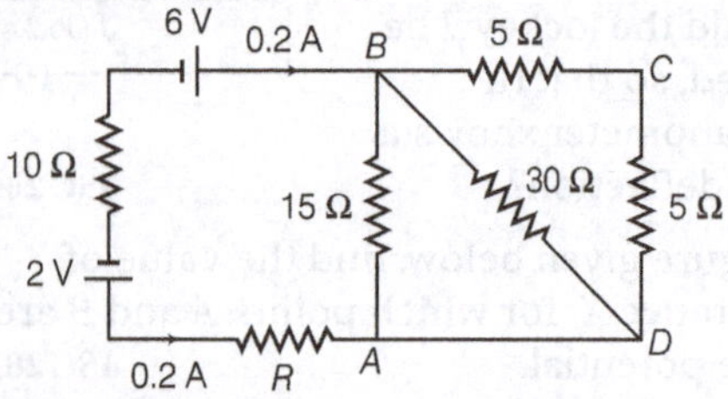

37. A 10 m long uniform metallic wire having a resistance of 20 Ω is used as potentiometer wire. This wire is connected in series with another resistance of 480 Ω and a battery of emf 5V having negligible internal resistance. If an unknown emf e is balanced across 6 m of the potentiometer wire, calculate

(i) the potential gradient across the potentiometer wire.

(ii) the value of the unknown emf e.

ISC 2015 (3 M)

38. In the circuit given below, E_1 and E_2 are two cells of emfs 4 V and 6 V respectively, having negligible internal resistances. Applying Kirchhoff's laws of electrical networks, find the values of I_1 and I_2.

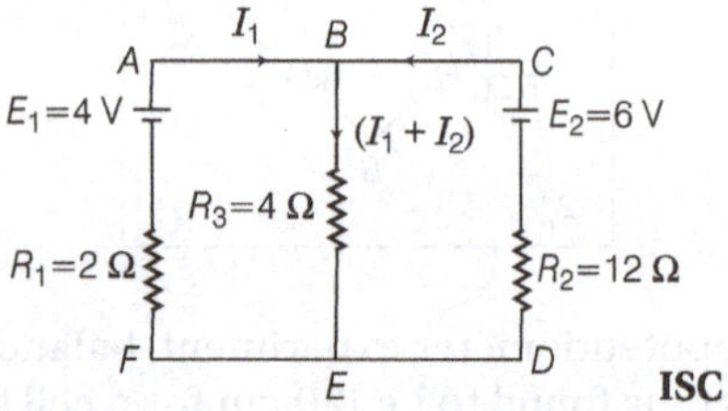

ISC 2008 (3 M)

39. In the circuit shown in figure, $E_1 = 17\text{ V}, E_2 = 21\text{ V}, R_1 = 2\ \Omega, R_2 = 3\ \Omega$ and $R_3 = 5\ \Omega$. Using Kirchhoff's laws, find the currents flowing through the resistors R_1, R_2 and R_3.

(Internal resistance of each of the batteries is negligible.)

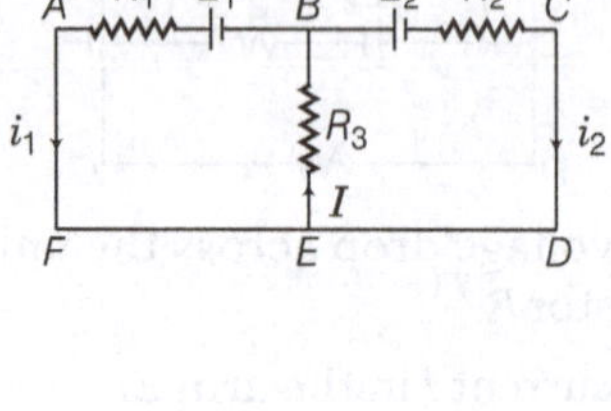

ISC 2013 (4 M)

40. Figure shows two circuits each having a galvanometer and a battery of 3 V.

When the galvanometer in each arrangement do not show any deflection, obtain the ratio R_1/R_2.

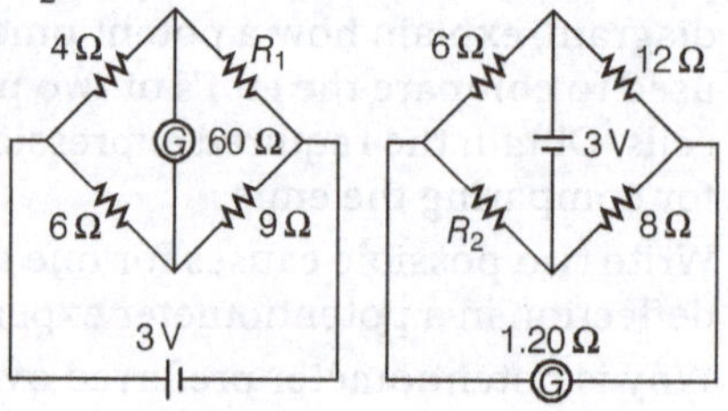

(2 M)

41. In the circuit shown in figure, E_1 and E_2 are batteries having emfs 4.0 V and 3.5 V respectively and internal resistances 1 Ω and 2 Ω, respectively. Using Kirchhoff's laws, calculate currents I_1, I_2 and I_3.

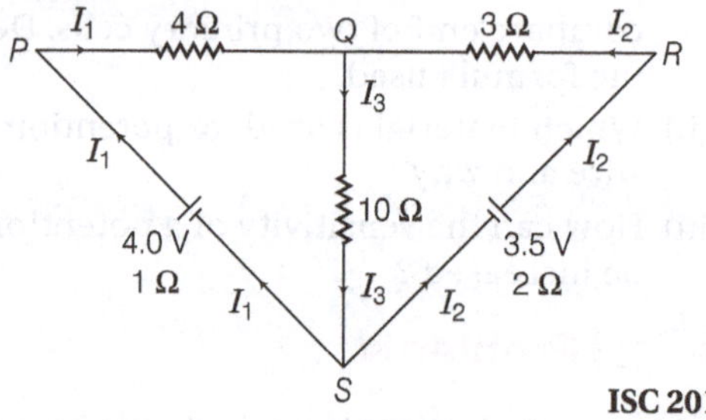

ISC 2011 (4 M)

42. In the circuit shown in figure below, E_1 and E_2 are cells having emfs 2V and 3V respectively and negligible internal resistances. Applying Kirchhoff's laws of electrical networks, find the values of currents I_1 and I_2.

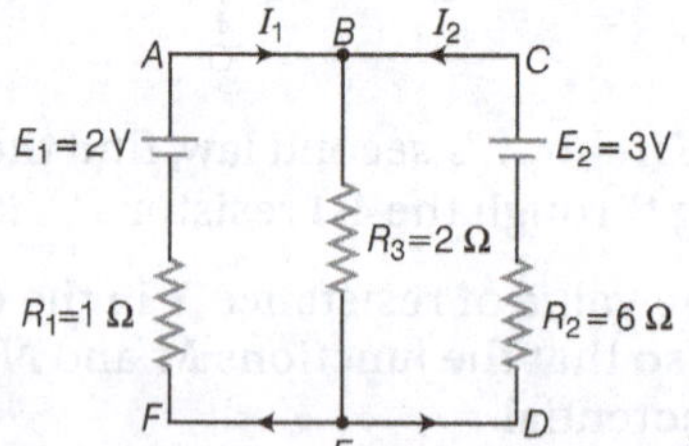

ISC 2016 (3 M)

43. A battery of 10 V and negligible internal resistance is connected across the diagonally opposite corners of a cubical network consisting of 12 resistors each of 1 Ω resistance. Use Kirchhoff's rules to determine

(i) the equivalent resistance of the network.

(ii) the total current in the network. **(4 M)**

44. Calculate the current drawn from the battery in the given network. **(4 M)**

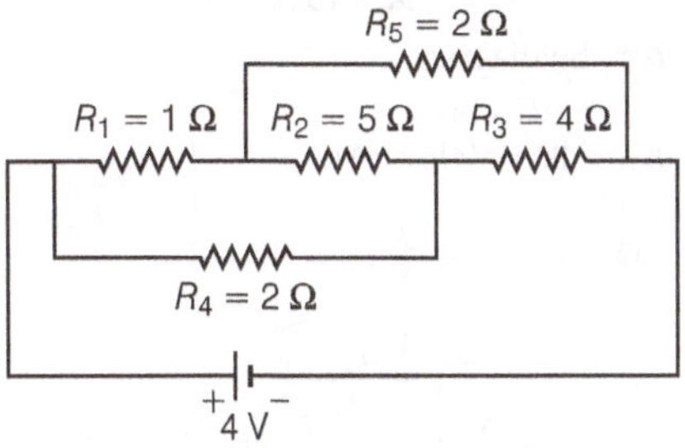

45. In a meter bridge circuit, resistance in the left hand gap is 2 Ω and an unknown resistance X is in the right hand gap as shown in figure below. The null point is found to be 40 cm from the left end of the wire. What resistance should be connected to X, so that the new null point is 50 cm from the left end of the wire?

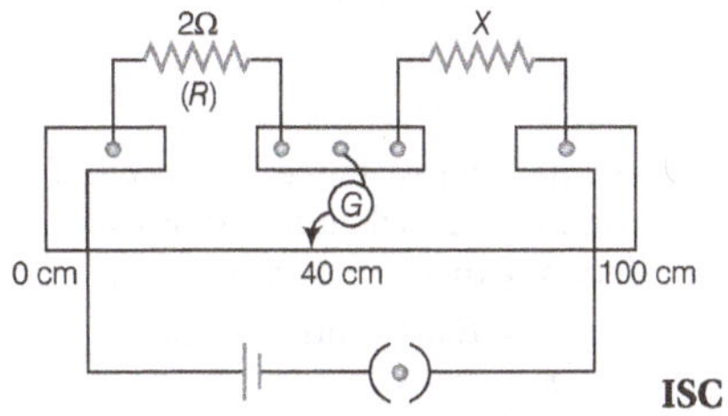

ISC 2017 (4 M)

46. In the circuit shown below, PQ is a uniform metallic wire of length 4 m and resistance 20 Ω. Battery B has an emf of 10 V and internal resistance of 1 Ω. J is a jockey or slide contact. Resistance of the ammeter A and connecting wires is negligible.

(i) When the jockey J does not touch the wire PQ, what is the reading of ammeter A?

(ii) Where should the jockey J be pressed on the wire PQ, so that the galvanometer G shows no deflection?

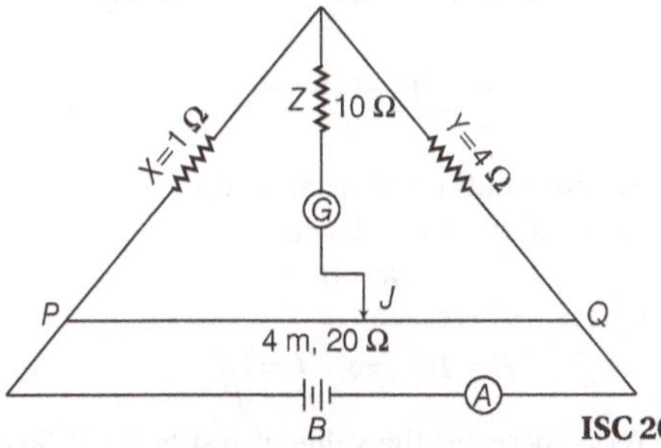

ISC 2010 (4 M)

47. The figure below shows a uniform manganin wire XY of length 100 cm and resistance 9 Ω, connected to an accumulator D of emf 4 V and internal resistance 1 Ω through a variable resistance R. E is a cell of emf 1.8 V connected to the wire XY *via* jockey J and a galvanometer G. It is found that the galvanometer shows no deflection when $XJ = 80$ cm. Find the value of R.

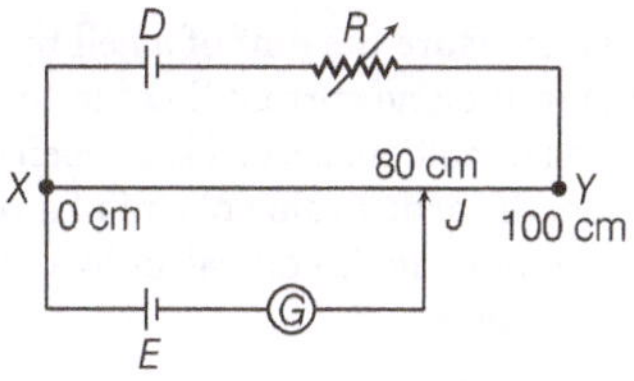

ISC 2009 (4 M)

Hints & Solutions

1. (*b*) According to Kirchhoff's first law,

$(5\text{A}) + (4\text{A}) + (-3\text{A}) + (-5\text{A}) + I = 0$

$\Rightarrow \qquad I = -1\text{A}$

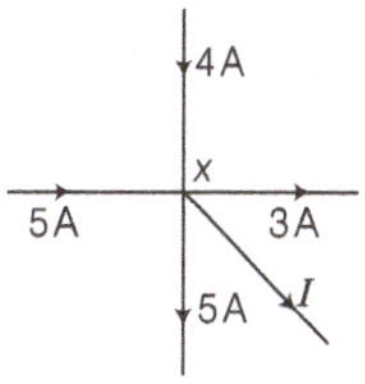

2. (*a*) The given combination will act as balanced Wheatstone bridge. The resistance of the middle branch can be removed.

Clearly,

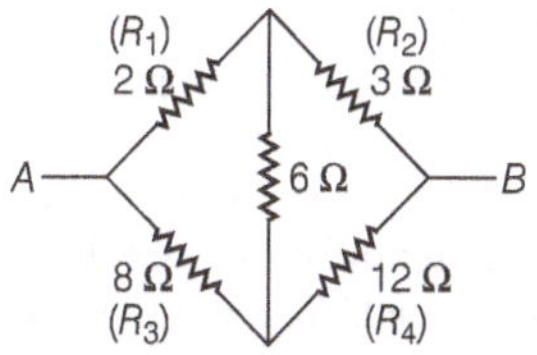

Here, $\frac{P}{Q} = \frac{R}{S}$ or $\frac{2}{3} = \frac{8}{12}$

Hence, bridge is balanced

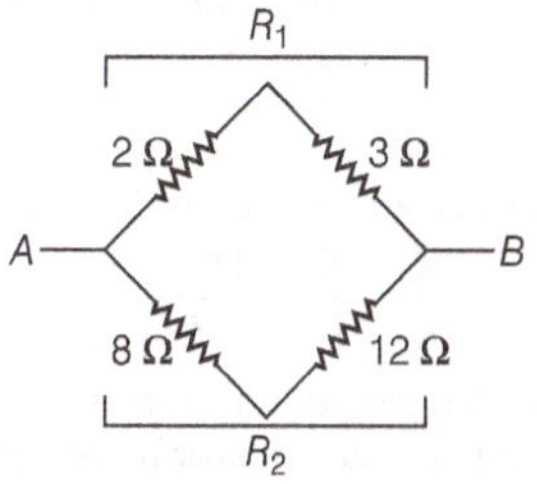

$R_1 = 5\,\Omega,\ R_2 = 20\,\Omega$

$\therefore \qquad R_{eq} = \frac{R_1 R_2}{R_1 + R_2} = \frac{5 \times 20}{25}$

$= \frac{100}{25} = 4\,\Omega$

Hence, option (a) is correct.

3. (*b*) In meter bridge, balanced Wheatstone bridge is used to determine unknown resistance.

4. (*c*) If the galvanometer and battery are interchanged, the position of balance point remains unchanged. Hence, the galvanometer will show no current. Interchanging the resistors R and S can change the balance point.

5. (*c*) When we measure the emf of a cell by the potentiometer, then no current flows in the circuit in zero deflection condition, i.e. cell is in open circuit. Thus, in this condition, the actual value of emf of a cell is found. In this way, potentiometer is equivalent to an ideal voltmeter of infinite resistance.

6. (*a*) As we know that, in case of potentiometer, the potential gradient remains constant.

i.e. $E \propto l$

$$\therefore \quad \frac{E_1}{E_2} = \frac{l_1}{l_2} \Rightarrow \frac{1.25}{E} = \frac{35}{63}$$

$$\text{or} \quad E = \frac{1.25 \times 63}{35} = 2.25 \text{ V}$$

7. Kirchhoff's first law is based on conservation of charge and second law is based on conservation of energy.

8. Conservation of electric charge.

9. The Wheatstone bridge is most sensitive, when the resistance of all the four arms of the bridge are equal.

10. Reason behind the end error in a meter bridge is due to the avoidance of resistance of connecting wire and resistance of copper strip.

11. Resistance of thick metallic strips is extremely small and hence negligible.

12. Potentiometer works on the principle of null deflection and it does not draw any current from the cell whose actual emf is to be measured whereas voltmeter measures the potential difference, because it draws some current from the cell. So, potentiometer is preferred over voltmeter.

13. (i) The balancing condition states that

$$\frac{R}{X} = \frac{l}{(100 - l)}$$

$$\Rightarrow \quad \frac{X}{R} = \frac{100 - l}{l}$$

When both X and R are doubled, then

$$\frac{2X}{2R} = \frac{X}{R} = \frac{100 - l}{l}$$

Balancing length would be at $(100 - l)$ cm. (1)

(ii) On changing the position of galvanometer and battery, the meter bridge continue to be balanced and hence no change occur in the balance point. (1)

14. If l_1 and l_2 are the balancing length corresponding to resistance R and X respectively,

$$\frac{X}{R} = \frac{l_2}{l_1}$$

Unknown resistance, $X = \frac{l_2}{l_1} R = \frac{500}{100} \times 2$

$$X = 10\Omega$$

15. Consider the diagram

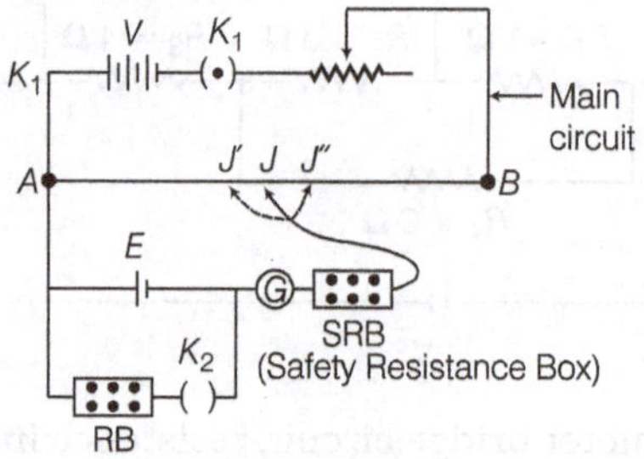

Let E is potential difference across l_1.

As ($E \propto l_1$). So, $E = kl_1$ ...(i)

V is potential difference across l_2.

So, $\quad V = Kl_2$ ...(ii)

On dividing Eq. (i) by Eq. (ii), we get

$$\frac{E}{V} = \frac{kl_1}{kl_2} \Rightarrow \frac{E}{V} = \frac{l_1}{l_2}$$ (1)

Let r be the internal resistance of the cell. If current I flows through the cell when it is shunted with resistance R from safety box then from Ohm's law,

$$E = I(R + r) \text{ and } V = IR$$

$$\frac{E}{V} = \frac{R + V}{R}$$

$$r = R\left(\frac{l_1}{l_2} - 1\right)$$ (1)

16. When K_1 is closed and K_2 is open, then only the cell connected in upper part branch will work. When K_2 is closed and K_1 is open, then only the cell connected in lower branch will work.

(i) $K_1 \to$ closed, $K_2 \to$ open

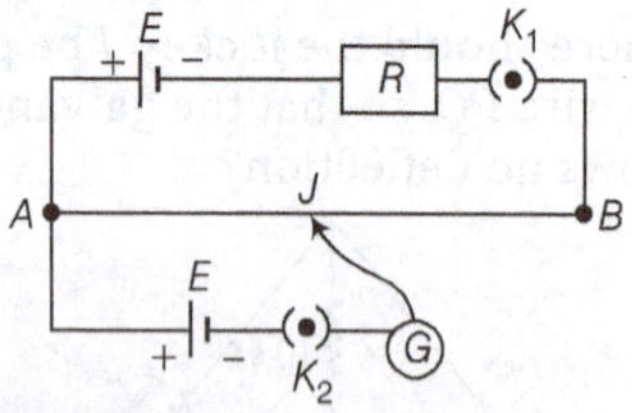

Suppose null point occurs at J.

Apply KVL in smaller loop,

$$E - IR = 0 \quad \text{...(i)}$$

where, R = resistance

$$\therefore \quad E = IR \Rightarrow I = \frac{E}{R}$$

As X increases the value of resistance R. So, current in the circuit (wire) decreases. Hence, R will be increased. Then, I will decrease. We can say, as X increases the value of R, null point decreases. (1)

(ii) $K_2 \to$ open and $K_1 \to$ closed.

Then, the circuit will be same as shown earlier.
We see that resistance S is not involved in the circuit because K_2 is open.

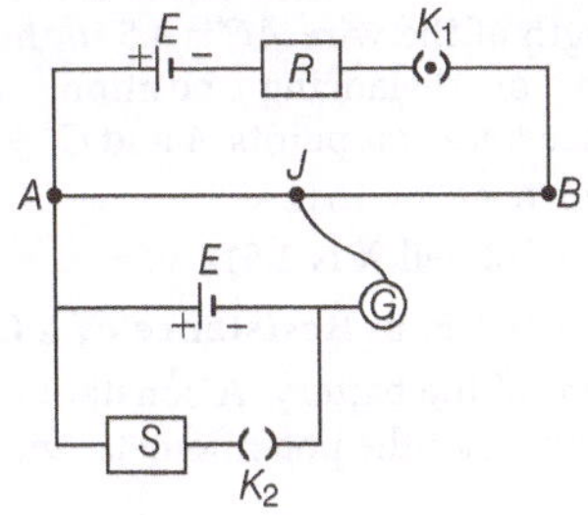

So, from Eq. (i), we get

$$E = RI$$

$$\because \quad I = \frac{E}{R}$$

Here, set up does not depend on the value of resistance S. So, null point is not affected by decreasing the value of resistance S. (1)

17.

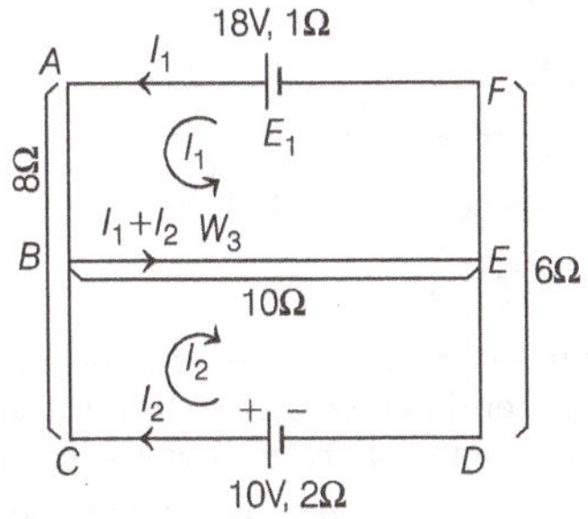

Loop equation, Loop $AFEB$

$$3I_1 + 4I_1 + 1I_1 + 10(I_1 + I_2) = 18 \quad \text{...(i)}$$

$$3I_2 + 2I_2 + 4I_2 + 10(I_1 + I_2) = 10 \quad \text{...(ii)}$$

Loop $BCDE$,

from Eqs. (i) and (ii),

$$18I_1 + 10I_2 = 18 \quad \text{...(iii)}$$

$$10I_1 + 19I_2 = 10 \quad \text{...(iv)}$$

From Eq. (iv) thus, $I_1 = \dfrac{10 - 19I_2}{10}$

Substitute in Eq. (iii)

Here, $\dfrac{18}{10}(10 - 19I_2) + 10I_2 = 18$

$$\Rightarrow \quad \frac{180}{10} - \frac{342}{10}I_2 + 10I_2 = 18$$

$$\Rightarrow \quad \frac{(-342 + 100)}{10}I_2 = 18 - \frac{180}{10}$$

$$I_2 = 0$$

from I_1, $\dfrac{10 - 19I_2}{10} = \dfrac{10}{10} = 1\text{A}$

18.

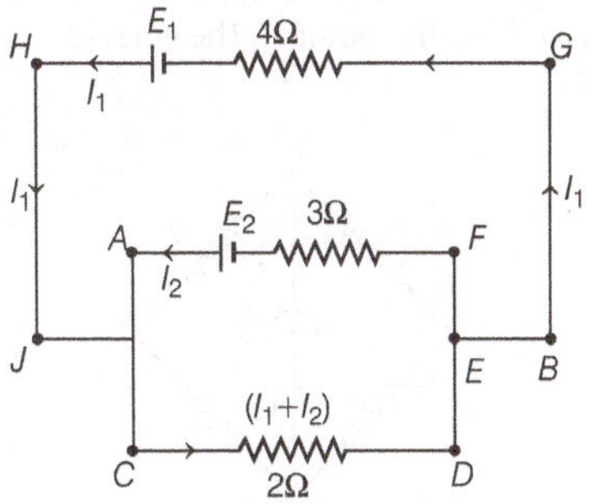

Applying KVL in loop $HJAFEBGH$

$$\Rightarrow \quad 25 = 7I_1 + 2I_2 \quad \text{... (i)}$$

Applying KVL in loop $ACDFA$

$$\Rightarrow \quad 26 = 6I_2 + 2I_1 \quad \text{... (ii)}$$

From Eqs. (i) and (ii), $I_2 = \dfrac{132}{38} = 3.47\text{ A}$

Putting the value of I_2 in Eq. (ii), $I_1 = 2.59\text{A}$.

19. In case of balanced Wheatstone bridge, the current through the galvanometer is zero. The labelled diagram of Wheatstone bridge is given

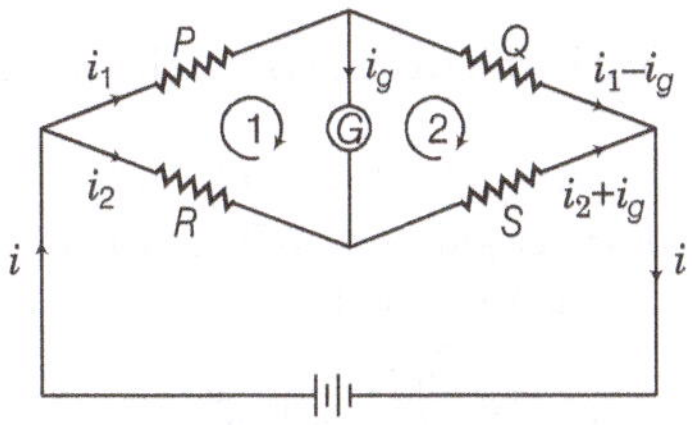

P, Q, R and S are the arm resistances of Wheatstone bridge. (1)

Proof By Kirchhoff's law

In loop 1,

$$-i_1P - i_gG + i_2R = 0 \quad \text{...(i)}$$

In loop 2,

$$-(i_1 - i_g)Q + (i_2 + i_g)S + i_g G = 0 \quad \text{...(ii)}$$

If there is no current in galvanometer, i.e. $i_g = 0$, then Wheatstone bridge will be balance, then Eqs. (i) and (ii) gives

$$i_1P - i_2R = 0$$

$$i_1P = i_2R \quad \text{...(iii)}$$

$$i_1Q - i_2S = 0$$

$$i_1Q = i_2S \quad \text{...(iv)}$$

On dividing Eq. (iii) by Eq. (iv), we get

$$\frac{P}{Q} = \frac{R}{S}$$

$$\Rightarrow \quad PS = QR$$

i.e. Product of resistances of opposite arms are equal. (2)

20. In figure, four resistances P, Q, R and S are connected in the four arms of a parallelogram $ABCD$. Between B and D there is a sensitive galvanometer and a cell is connected between A and C. K_1 and K_2 are two keys.

By pressing the key K_1, a current i is allowed to flow from the cell. At the point A, the current i is divided into two parts.

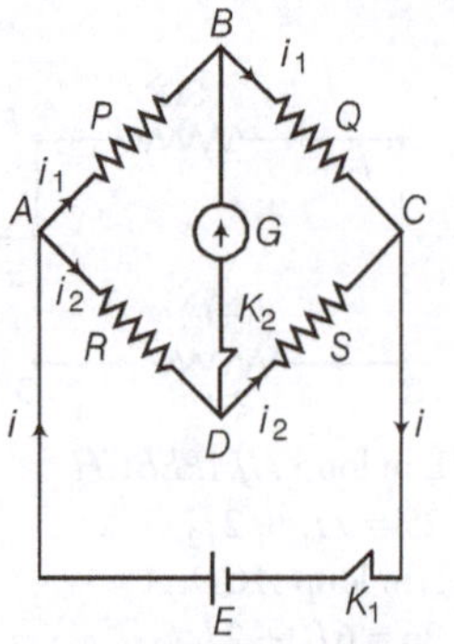

One part i_1 flows in the arm AB and the other part i_2 flows in the arm AD. The resistances P, Q, R and S are so adjusted that on pressing the key K_2 there is no deflection in the galvanometer G. That is, there is no current in the diagonal BD. Thus, the same current i_1 will flow in the arm BC as in the arm AB and the same i_2 will flow in the arm DC as in the arm AD.

Applying Kirchhoff 's second law for the closed loop $BADB$, we have

$$-i_1P + i_2R = 0 \Rightarrow Pi_1 = Ri_2 \quad \text{...(i)}$$

Similarly, for the closed loop $CBDC$, we have

$$-i_1Q + i_2S = 0$$

$$\Rightarrow \quad Qi_1 = Si_2 \quad \text{...(ii)}$$

Dividing Eq. (i) by Eq. (ii), we have

$$\frac{i_1P}{i_1Q} = \frac{i_2R}{i_2S} \quad \text{or} \quad \frac{P}{Q} = \frac{R}{S}$$

21.

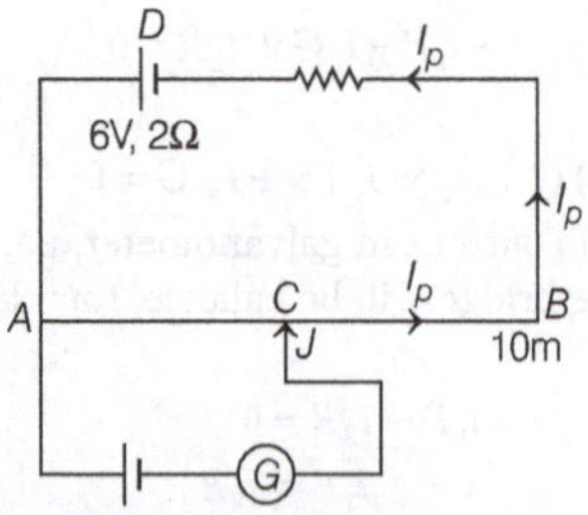

(a) The current I_p flowing in the potentiometer wire AB when the jockey (J) does not touch the wire AB, is

$$I_p = \frac{V}{R_{net}} = \frac{6\text{V}}{R_{AB} + R_s + r}$$

$$= \frac{6}{28 + 20 + 2} = \frac{6}{50} = 0.12 \text{ A}$$

(b) When the jockey is moved to point B, potential drop will be

$$V_{AB} = 28 \times 0.12 = 3.36 \text{ V}$$

Length of the wire AB is 10 m, so potential gradient,

$$K = \frac{V_{AB}}{L} = \frac{3.36}{10} = 0.36 \ \Omega / \text{m}$$

The length of the wire AC is 4.5 in the null deflection position or balancing position, then potential difference between points A and C,

$$V_{AC} = 0.336 \times 4.5 = 1.512 \text{ V}$$

$\therefore$ The emf of cell X is 1.512 V.

22. To Measure Internal Resistance of a Cell

Let E' be emf of the battery. A constant current i is maintained through the potentiometer wire with the help of rheostat.

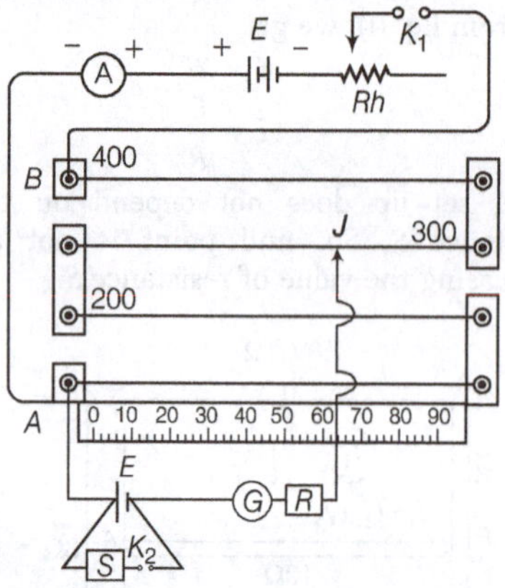

The plug key K_2 is kept out and the jockey J is moved on the potentiometer wire to balance the emf E of the cell, whose internal resistance r is to be determined. Suppose l_1 be the balancing length of the potentiometer wire between point A and jockey J. If x is resistance per unit length of wire, then emf of cell is given by

$$E = xl_1 i \quad \text{...(i)}$$

Introduce some resistance, say S from the resistance box S and now put in the plug key K_2. The potential difference V between the two poles of the cell is given by

$$V = xl_2 i \quad \text{...(ii)}$$

[$\because l_2$ = balancing length]

Dividing the Eq. (i) by Eq. (ii), we have

$$\frac{E}{V} = \frac{l_1}{l_2}$$

The internal resistance of the cell is given by

$$r = \left(\frac{E}{V} - 1\right)S$$

Now, substituting the value of $\frac{E}{V}$ in above equation, we get

$$r = \left(\frac{l_1}{l_2} - 1\right)S$$

where, S is the resistance of the resistance box.

23. 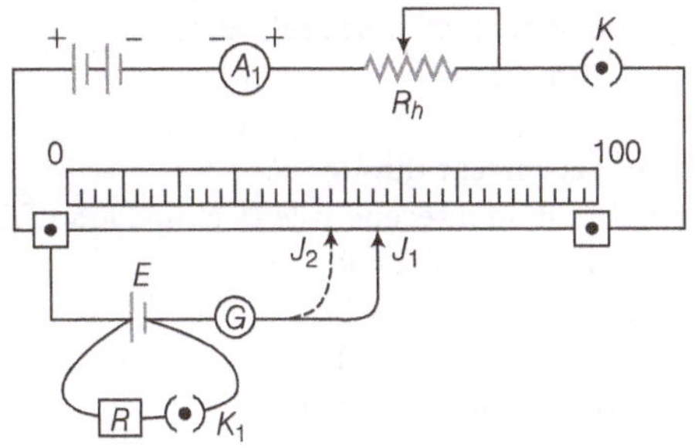

The working formula is $r = \left(\frac{l_1}{l_2} - 1\right) R$.

Thus, knowing the values of l_1, l_2 and R, the internal resistance r of the cell can be determined. (3)

24. Kirchhoff had given two rules based on conservation of electric charge and of energy, these are known as **Kirchhoff's laws.** (1)

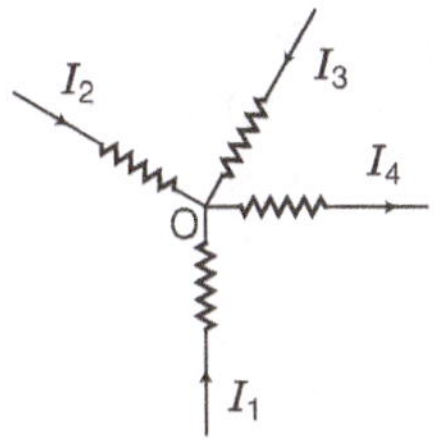

Kirchhoff's first law or junction rule The algebraic sum of electric currents at any junction of electric circuit is equal to zero, i.e. the sum of current entering into a junction is equal to the sum of current leaving the junction,

i.e. $\Sigma I = 0,\ I_4 = I_1 + I_2 + I_3$

Junction law supports law of conservation of charge, because this is a point in circuit which cannot act as a source or sink of charge(s). (1)

Kirchhoff's second law or voltage rule In any closed mesh of electrical circuit, the algebraic sums of emf of cell and the product of currents and resistance is always equal to zero, i.e.

$$\Sigma E + \Sigma IR = 0$$

Kirchhoff's second law supports the law of conservation of energy. Because the net change in the energy of a charge, after the charge complete a closed path must be zero. (1)

Note Sign convention for Kirchhoff's second law

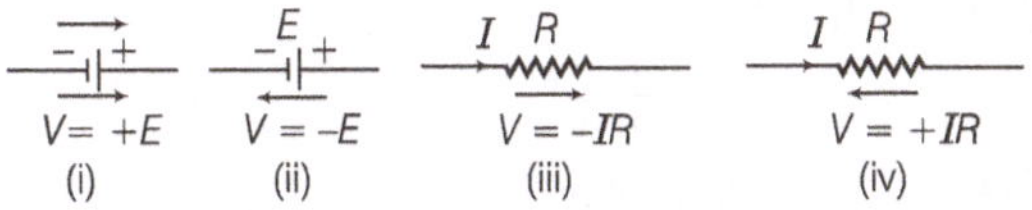

Consider the circuit diagram shown above. The second law can be expressed as, $\Sigma E + \Sigma IR = 0$

As given in the diagram, applying this law for mesh (1)

For mesh or loop (1),

$$-I_1 R_1 - (I_1 + I_2) R_2 + E_1 = 0$$

$\therefore$ $$I_1 R_1 + (I_1 + I_2) R_2 = E_1$$

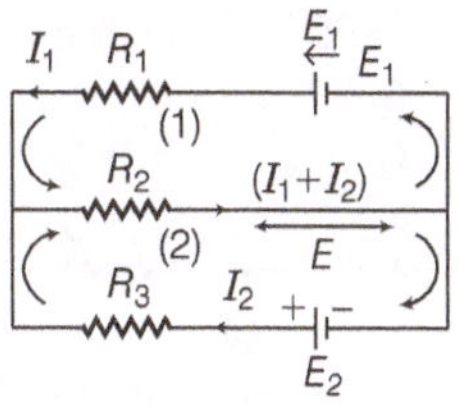

For mesh (2),

$$-I_2 R_3 - (I_1 + I_2) R_2 + E_2 = 0$$

$\therefore$ $$I_2 R_3 + (I_1 + I_2) R_2 = E_2$$ (2)

25. (i) Refer to text on pages 141 and 142 (Meter bridge).

(ii) Refer to solution of Q.13 part ii on page 150.

(iii) Th error in the measured value of unknown resistance S using bridge wire will be minimum when the null point is obtained at the middle of bridge wire.

In this situation, the end error of the bridge will be ineffective.

26. (i) Refer to text on pages 142 and 143 (Potentiometer). (1)

(ii) (a) The emf of the cell connected in main circuit may not be more than the emf of the primary cells whose emfs are to be compared.

(b) The positive ends of all cells are not connected to the same end of the wire. (1½)

(iii) Potentiometer is preferred over a voltmeter for comparison of emf of cells because at null point, it does not draw any current from the cell and thus there is no potential drop due to the internal resistance of the cell. It measures the potential difference in an open circuit which is equal to the actual emf of the cell. (1)

(iv) Refer to text on page 144 (To measure internal resistance of a cell). (1½)

27. (i) Refer to text on pages 142 and 143 (Potentiometer). (3)

(ii) Constantan or manganin (alloy) is used for potentiometer, as they have low temperature coefficient of resistance. (1)

(iii) The sensitivity of potentiometer can be increased by increasing the number of wires of potentiometer and hence, decreasing the value of potential gradient. (1)

28. Applying Kirchhoff's second law in the given loop $ABCA$, i.e. net voltage across this loop must be equals to zero. (1/2)

$$-3 \times 2 - I \times 4 + 6 \times 2 = 0$$

$\Rightarrow$ $$-6 - 4I + 12 = 0 \Rightarrow 4I = 6$$

$\therefore$ $$I = \frac{6}{4} = 1.5\text{ A}$$ (1/2)

29. For balanced condition of Wheatstone bridge,

$$\frac{P}{Q} = \frac{R}{S} \Rightarrow \frac{R_1}{R_2} = \frac{X}{Y}$$ (1/2)

$\Rightarrow$ $$\frac{2}{5} = \frac{X}{15} \Rightarrow X = 6\,\Omega$$

where, P, Q, R and S are arm resistances of the Wheatstone bridge. (1/2)

30. By Wheatstone's bridge principle,
Resistance (R) $\propto$ Length (l)

$$\Rightarrow \frac{R_1}{R_2} = \frac{l_1}{l_2}$$

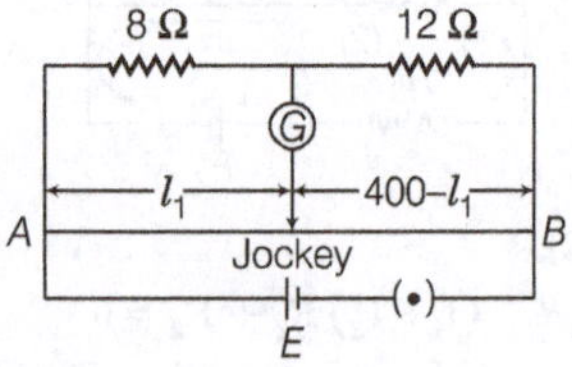

(1/2)

According to the figure,

$$\frac{8}{12} = \frac{l_1}{400 - l_1}$$

$$\Rightarrow 3200 - 8l_1 = 12\, l_1$$

$$\therefore \quad l_1 = \frac{3200}{20} = 160 \text{ cm from end } A$$ (1/2)

31. Applying the Wheatstone bridge condition (balanced),

$$\frac{R}{X} = \frac{l}{100 - l}$$

$$R = 2\Omega,\ X = ?,\ l = 40 \text{ cm}$$ (1/2)

$$\frac{2}{X} = \frac{40}{100 - 40}$$

$$\Rightarrow \frac{2}{X} = \frac{40}{60}$$

$$\Rightarrow X = \frac{2 \times 60}{40} = 3\Omega$$ (1/2)

32. Given, $l = 254.5$ cm, $E = 1.018$ V
where, $E =$ emf of the cell
and $l =$ balancing length.
Potential gradient, $k = E/l$ (1/2)

$$= \frac{1.018}{254.5} = 0.004 \text{ V / cm}$$ (1/2)

33. For the potential of A and B to be equal, the condition of balanced Wheatstone bridge is required. (1/2)

So, $\frac{3}{6} = \frac{5}{X}$ or $X = 10\Omega$ (1/2)

34. If l_1 and l_2 are the balancing length corresponding to emfs ε_1 and ε_2, then

$$\frac{\varepsilon_1}{\varepsilon_2} = \frac{l_1}{l_2} \Rightarrow \frac{2}{1.5} = \frac{120}{l_2}$$ (1/2)

$$\therefore \text{ Balancing length, } l_2 = \frac{120 \times 1.5}{2} = 90 \text{ cm}$$ (1/2)

35. (i) Applying Kirchhoff's second rule in the closed loop $ABFEA$,

$$V_B - 0.5 \times 2 + 3 = V_A$$

$$\Rightarrow V_B - V_A = -2$$

$$V = V_A - V_B = +2 \text{ V}$$

Potential drop across R is 2 V as R, EF and upper row are in parallel. (1)

(ii) Applying Kirchhoff's first rule at E,

$$0.5 + I_2 = I$$

where, I is current through R.
Now, Kirchhoff's second rule in closed loop $FEABF$,

$$-2I_2 + 4 - 3 + 0.5 \times 2 = 0$$

$$2I_2 - 2 = 0$$

or $I_2 = 1$ A

The current in arm EF = 1 A (1)

36. For loop BCD, equivalent resistance,

$$R_1 = 5\,\Omega + 5\,\Omega = 10\,\Omega$$ (1)

Across BA, equivalent resistance R_2,

$$\frac{1}{R_2} = \frac{1}{10} + \frac{1}{30} + \frac{1}{15} = \frac{3 + 1 + 2}{30} = \frac{6}{30} = \frac{1}{5}$$

$$\Rightarrow R_2 = 5\,\Omega$$ (1)

$\therefore$ Potential difference,

$$V_{BA} = I \times R_2 = 0.2 \times 5 = 1\text{V}$$

$$\Rightarrow V_{AB} = -1\text{ V}$$ (1)

37. Given, $l_1 = 10$ m, $R = 20\Omega$, $R_1 = 480\Omega$,
$E_1 = 5$V, balancing length $l_2 = 6$ m

(i) The potential gradient across the potentiometer wire is given by

$$K = \frac{V}{l} = \frac{5}{6} = 0.83 \text{ V/m}$$ (1½)

(ii) We know that, $\frac{E_1}{E_2} = \frac{l_1}{l_2}$

Substituting the all values,

$$\frac{5}{E_2} = \frac{10}{6}$$

$$\Rightarrow E_2 = \frac{6 \times 5}{10} = 3\text{V}$$ (1½)

38. Currents and emfs are shown in the given circuit. Now, applying Kirchhoff's second law, in closed loop $ABEFA$,

$$4 = (I_1 + I_2)4 + I_1 \times 2$$

$$\Rightarrow 4 = 4I_1 + 4I_2 + 2I_1$$

$$\Rightarrow 4 = 6I_1 + 4I_2 \quad \text{...(i)}$$ (1)

Similarly, in closed loop $BCDEB$,

$$6 = 4\,(I_1 + I_2) + 12I_2$$

$$6 = 4I_1 + 16I_2 \quad \text{...(ii)}$$ (1)

On solving Eqs. (i) and (ii), we get

$$6I_1 + 4I_2 = 4$$

and $$I_1 + 4I_2 = 3/2$$

$$5I_1 = \frac{5}{2}$$

$$\Rightarrow I_1 = 0.5 \text{ A}$$

Substituting $I_1 = 0.5$ A in Eq. (i), we get

$$\therefore \quad I_2 = 0.25 \text{ A}$$ (1)

39. Apply Kirchhoff's current and voltage rule for each loop.
Given, according to the figure,

$$E_1 = 17 \text{ V},\ E_2 = 21 \text{ V}$$

$R_1 = 2\,\Omega$, $R_2 = 3\,\Omega$ and $R_3 = 5\,\Omega$

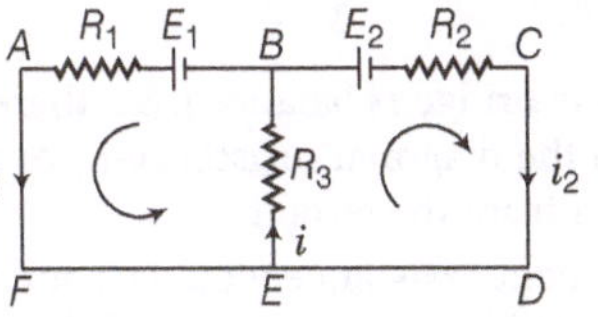

(1)

In loop *AFEBA*,

$$E_1 - i_1R_1 - iR_3 = 0$$

$$\Rightarrow \quad 17 = 2i_1 + 5i \quad \text{...(i)}$$

In loop *BCDEB*,

$$E_2 - i_2R_2 - iR_3 = 0$$

$$\Rightarrow \quad E_2 = i_2R_2 + iR_3$$

$$21 = 3i_2 + 5i \quad \text{...(ii)} \quad (1)$$

By Kirchhoff's first law,

$$i_1 + i_2 = i \quad \text{...(iii)}$$

From Eqs. (i) and (ii), we get

$$17 = 2i_1 + 5(i_1 + i_2) = 2i_1 + 5i_1 + 5i_2$$

$$17 = 7i_1 + 5i_2 \quad \text{...(iv)} \quad (1/2)$$

From Eqs. (ii) and (iii), we get

$$21 = 3i_2 + 5(i_1 + i_2) = 3i_2 + 5i_1 + 5i_2$$

$$21 = 5i_1 + 8i_2 \quad \text{...(v)} \quad (1/2)$$

On solving Eqs. (iv) and (v), we get

$$i_1 = 1\text{A}, \; i_2 = 2\text{A}$$

$$i = i_1 + i_2$$

$$= 1 + 2 = 3\text{ A} \quad (1)$$

40.

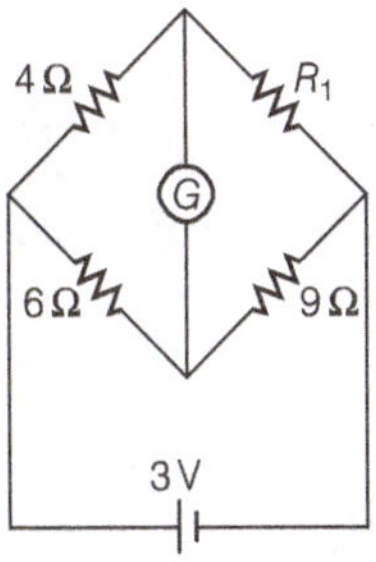

For balanced Wheatstone bridge, there will be no deflection in the galvanometer.

$$\frac{4}{R_1} = \frac{6}{9}$$

$$\Rightarrow \quad R_1 = \frac{4 \times 9}{6} = 6\Omega \quad (1)$$

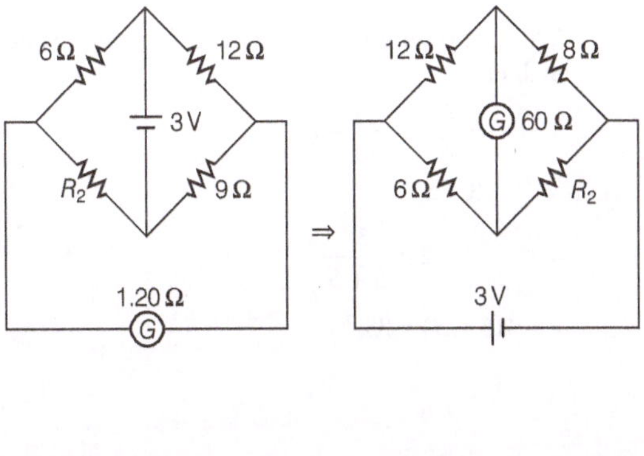

For the equivalent circuit, when the Wheatstone bridge is balanced, there will be no deflection in the galvanometer.

$$\therefore \quad \frac{12}{8} = \frac{6}{R_2}$$

$$\Rightarrow \quad R_2 = \frac{6 \times 8}{12} = 4\Omega$$

$$\therefore \quad \frac{R_1}{R_2} = \frac{6}{4} = \frac{3}{2} \quad (1)$$

41. To solve this problem, we have to apply Kirchhoff's first law for current division and Kirchhoff's second law for potential differences in each loop. Applying Kirchhoff's second law for closed mesh *PQSP*,

$$1I_1 + 4I_1 + 10(I_1 + I_2) = 4$$

As, $\quad I_3 = I_1 + I_2$

[by applying Kirchhoff's first law at point Q] (1½)

$$\therefore \quad 15\,I_1 + 10\,I_2 = 4 \quad \text{...(i)}$$

Similarly, for closed loop *RQSR*,

$$2I_2 + 3\,I_2 + 10(I_1 + I_2) = 3.5$$

$$10\,I_1 + 15\,I_2 = 3.5 \quad \text{...(ii)} \quad (1)$$

On solving Eqs. (i) and (ii), we get

$$I_1 = 0.2\text{ A and } I_2 = 0.1\text{ A}$$

$$I_3 = I_1 + I_2 = 0.3\text{ A}$$

Currents I_1, I_2 and I_3 are shown in the circuit diagram.

Caution *We should not confuse with signs, while applying Kirchhoff's laws, specially about signs, of incoming and outgoing currents.* (1½)

42. Consider the figure given in the question,

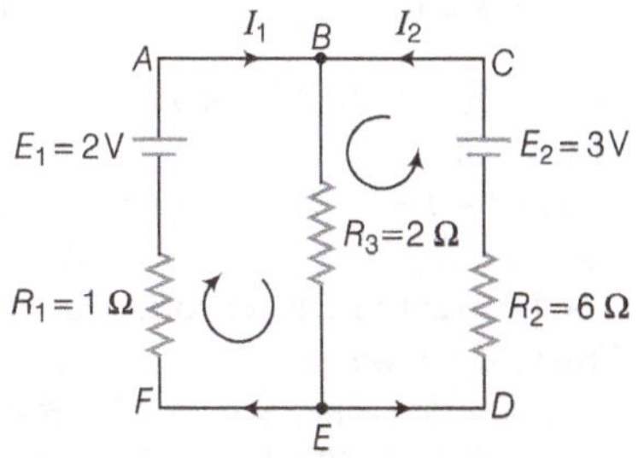

Consider the loop *ABEFA* and apply Kirchhoff's second law to it,

$$2(I_1 + I_2) + I_1 \times 1 = 2$$

$$\Rightarrow \quad 2I_1 + 2I_2 + I_1 = 2$$

$$\Rightarrow \quad 3I_1 + 2I_2 = 2 \quad \text{...(i)}$$

Consider the loop *BCDEB* and apply Kirchhoff's second law to it,

$$2(I_1 + I_2) + 6I_2 = 3$$

$$\Rightarrow \quad 2I_1 + 2I_2 + 6I_2 = 3$$

$$\Rightarrow \quad 2I_1 + 8I_2 = 3 \quad \text{...(ii)}$$

On multiplying Eq. (i) by 4, we get

$$12I_1 + 8I_2 = 8 \quad \text{...(iii)} \quad (1½)$$

On solving Eqs. (ii) and (iii), we get

$$\begin{aligned} 12I_1 + 8I_2 &= 8 \\ 2I_1 + 8I_2 &= 3 \\ - \quad - \quad & \quad - \\ \hline 10I_1 &= 5 \end{aligned}$$

$\Rightarrow \quad I_1 = \dfrac{5}{10} = 0.5$ A

On substituting the value of I_1 in Eq. (i), we get $I_2 = 0.25$ A.

$\therefore \quad I_1 = 0.5$ A $\Rightarrow I_2 = 0.25$ A (1½)

43. Let $6I$ current be drawn from the cell. Since, the paths AA', AD and AB are symmetrical, current through them is same.

As per Kirchhoff's junction rule, the current distribution is shown in the figure.

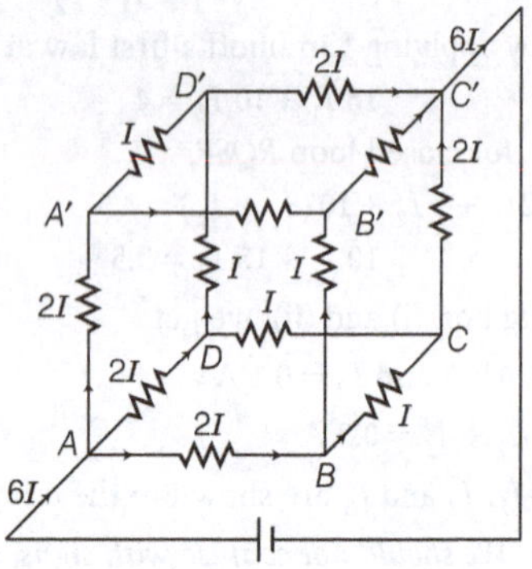

(1)

(i) Let the equivalent resistance across the combination be R.

$\therefore \quad E = V_A - V_B = (6I)\, R$

$\Rightarrow \quad 6IR = 10$ [$\because E = 10$ V]...(i) (1)

(ii) Applying Kirchhoff 's second rule in loop $AA'B'C'A$,

$-2I \times 1 - I \times 1 - 2I \times 1 + 10 = 0 \Rightarrow 5I = 10$

$\Rightarrow \quad I = 2$ A (1)

Total current in the network $= 6I = 6 \times 2 = 12$ A

From Eq. (i), we get

$6IR = 10 \quad \Rightarrow \quad 6 \times 2 \times R = 10$

$\Rightarrow \quad R = \dfrac{10}{12} = \dfrac{5}{6}\ \Omega$ (1)

44. The given circuit can be redrawn as given below

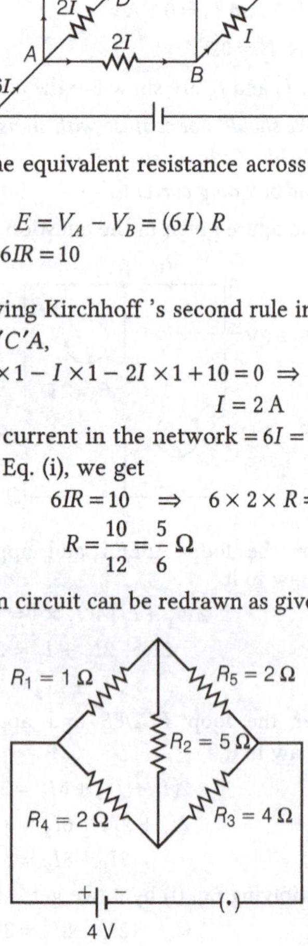

Here, $\dfrac{R_1}{R_5} = \dfrac{R_4}{R_3}$ or $\dfrac{1}{2} = \dfrac{2}{4}$

Wheatstone bridge is balanced. So, there will be no current in the diagonal resistance R_2 or it can be withdrawn from the circuit. (2)

The equivalent resistance would be equivalent to a parallel combination of two rows, which consists of series combination of R_1 and R_5 and R_4 and R_3, respectively.

$$\frac{1}{R} = \frac{1}{1+2} + \frac{1}{2+4} = \frac{1}{3} + \frac{1}{6} \Rightarrow R = \frac{18}{9} = 2\ \Omega$$

$\therefore \quad I = \dfrac{V}{R} = \dfrac{4}{2} = 2$ A (2)

45.

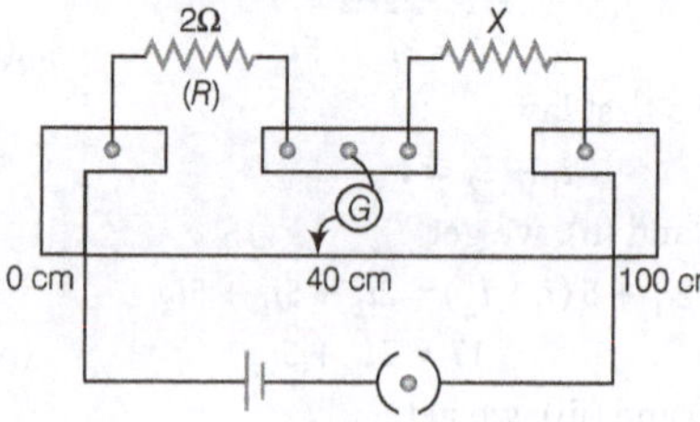

Applying the condition of balanced Wheatstone bridge,

$$\frac{R}{X} = \frac{l}{100 - l}$$ (1)

According to the question, $R = 2\Omega$, $X = ?$

$l = 40$ cm

$$\frac{2}{X} = \frac{40}{100 - 40}$$

$$\frac{2}{X} = \frac{40}{60} \Rightarrow X = \frac{2 \times 60}{40} = 3\ \Omega$$ (1)

The equivalent resistance of 3 Ω and 5 Ω in parallel is $\dfrac{3S}{3+S}\ \Omega$

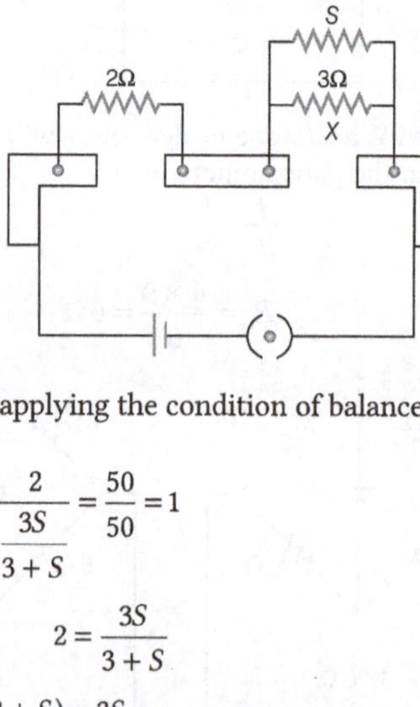

(1)

Again, applying the condition of balanced Wheatstone bridge,

$$\frac{2}{\dfrac{3S}{3+S}} = \frac{50}{50} = 1$$

$$\Rightarrow \quad 2 = \frac{3S}{3+S}$$

$\Rightarrow \quad 2(3 + S) = 3S$

$\Rightarrow \quad 6 + 2S = 3S$

$\Rightarrow \quad 3S - 2S = 6$

$\Rightarrow \quad S = 6\,\Omega$ (1)

46. For no deflection in the galvanometer the bridge should be balanced.

(i) When jockey does not touch the wire PQ, 10 Ω is not connected.

In upper arm of PQ,

Resistances $X + Y = 1 + 4 = 5\,\Omega$

[for series combination]

20 Ω and 5 Ω are in parallel.

$\therefore \; R_{total} = \frac{20 \times 5}{20 + 5} = \frac{100}{25} = 4\,\Omega$

$\therefore$ Current in circuit, $I = \frac{E}{r + R_{total}}$

$= \frac{10}{1 + 4} = 2\text{A}$ (2)

(ii) Let the distance of the jockey (J) be x.

Then, by Wheatstone bridge under balanced condition,

$$\frac{X}{Y} = \frac{x}{4 - x}$$

$$\Rightarrow \quad \frac{1}{4} = \frac{x}{4 - x}$$

$$4 - x = 4x \quad \Rightarrow \quad 4 = 5x$$

$\therefore \quad x = 0.8$ m (2)

47. For no deflection in the galvanometer balanced condition should be achieved that a null point is obtained by the jockey (J).

Given, the cell E is balanced at $l = 80$ cm.

Let K is potential gradient.

$E = Kl \;\Rightarrow\; 1.8 = K \times 0.80$

$\therefore \; K = 2.25\ \text{Vm}^{-1}$ (1)

Potential gradient along the wire XY,

$K = \frac{V}{l}$ [$\because l$ = length of the wire = 100 cm = 1m]

$\therefore \quad 2.25 = \frac{V}{1}$

$\Rightarrow \quad V = 2.25\ \text{V}$ (1)

Current in the potentiometer wire XY is

$I = \frac{4}{1 + R + 9}$ (1/2)

Now, $\quad V = I \times$ Resistance of wire

$$2.25 = \frac{4}{1 + R + 9} \times 9$$

$$\Rightarrow \quad 2.25 = \frac{36}{10 + R}$$

$$\Rightarrow \quad 10 + R = \frac{36}{2.25} = 16$$

$\therefore \quad R = 16 - 10 = 6\,\Omega$ (1½)

SUMMARY

- **Electric Current** It is defined as the rate of flow of electric charge through any cross-section of a conductor, i.e.

$$I = (dq / dt)$$

- The directed rate of flow of electric charge through any cross-section of a conductor is known as **electric current**.

$$I = \frac{q}{t} = \frac{ne}{t} \qquad [\because q = ne]$$

where, n = number of charged particles constitute the current

- **Current Density** It is the ratio of the current at a point in conductor to the area of cross-section of the conductor at that point, i.e. $J = (I / A)$.

  where, I is current and A is cross-section area of the conductor.

- **Ohm's Law** At constant temperature, the potential difference V across the ends of a given metallic wire (conductor) in a circuit (electric) is directly proportional to the current flowing through it.

  i.e. $V \propto I$

  or $V = IR$

  where, R = resistance of conductor.

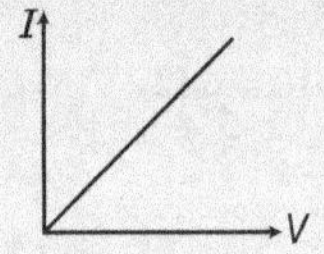

The variation of current w.r.t. applied potential difference is shown with the help of given graph.

- **Flow of Electric Charges in Metallic Conductors** In case of solid conductor, large number of free electrons causes the strong current in them.

  In the case of a liquid conductor, movement of positive and negative charged ions causes the electric current.

- **Resistance of a Conductor** Mathematically, it is the ratio of potential difference applied across the ends of conductor to the current flowing through it.

$$\Rightarrow \quad R = \frac{V}{I}$$

SI unit is ohm (Ω).

Resistance can also be written as, $R = \rho \frac{L}{A}$.

where, L = length of the conductor,

A = area of cross-section

and ρ = constant, known as resistivity of the material.

It depends upon nature of the material.

- **Effect of Temperature on Resistance**

  For metals, resistance increases with rise in temperature.

  For insulators and semiconductors, resistance decreases with rise in temperature.

  For alloys, temperature coefficient of resistance is small.

- **Temperature coefficient** of resistance is given by

$$\alpha = \frac{R_2 - R_1}{R_1 (t_2 - t_1)}$$

where, R_1 and R_2 are the resistances at t_1°C and t_2°C, respectively.

- **Drift Velocity** It is defined as the average velocity with which the free electrons move towards the positive end of a conductor under the influence of an external electric field applied.

$$\Rightarrow \quad \mathbf{v}_d = \frac{e\mathbf{E}}{m}\tau$$

where, τ = relaxation time, $\mathbf{E}$ = electric field,

m = mass and e = electronic charge.

- **Relation between Drift Velocity and Electric Field**

  It is given by, $I = neAv_d$

  where, n = number density of free electrons,

  e = electronic charge,

  A = cross-sectional area

  and v_d = drift velocity of an electron.

- The ratio of drift velocity of electrons and the applied electric field is known as **mobility**.

$$\Rightarrow \quad \mu = \frac{v_d}{E} = \frac{q\tau}{m}$$

$\therefore$ SI unit is $m^2 s^{-1} V^{-1}$.

- **Resistivity** It is the resistance of a unit length with unit area of cross-section of the material of the conductor.

- **Relationship between resistivity and relaxation time**

$$\rho = \frac{m}{ne^2\tau}$$

where, τ = relaxation time.

Specific resistance or resistivity (ρ) depends on the material of conductor and independent from the length and cross-sectional area (A), i.e. geometry of the conductor.

- **Effect of Temperature on Resistivity**

  For metals, resistivity increases with increase in temperature.

  For semiconductor, resistivity decreases with increase in temperature.

  For alloys, resistivity is very large but has a weak dependence on temperature.

- **Classification of Materials in terms of Conductivity**

  For insulators, electrical conductivity is very small or nil.

  For conductors, electrical conductivity is very high.

  For semiconductors, electrical conductivity lies in between that of insulators and conductors.

- **Conductance and Conductivity**

  Conductance is the reciprocal of resistance of conductor,
  $$G = \frac{1}{R}$$
  Its SI unit is mho (Ω^{-1}) or siemen (S).

  Conductivity is the reciprocal of the resistivity of conductor,
  $$\sigma = \frac{1}{\rho}$$
  Its SI unit is mho per metre ($\Omega^{-1}m^{-1}$) or siemen per metre (S/m).

- **Electrical Energy and Power** Electrical energy is the total work done in maintaining the electric current in the given circuit for a specified time,
  $$E = \frac{V^2}{R}t$$
  Its SI unit is joule (J).

  Electrical power is the rate of electrical energy supplied per unit time to maintain flow of electric current through conductor,
  $$P = \frac{V^2}{R}$$
  Its SI unit is watt (W).

- **Internal Resistance and Electromotive Force of a Cell**

  EMF (E) It is the maximum potential difference between two terminals of circuit, when circuit is open.

  Internal Resistance (r) The resistance offered by the electrolyte of the cell, to the flow of current through it.

  Terminal Potential Difference (V) It is the maximum potential difference between two terminals of circuit, when the circuit is closed.

- **The relationship between r, R, E and V is**
  $$r = R\left(\frac{E}{V} - 1\right) \quad \ldots(i)$$
  where, r = internal resistance, R = external resistance, E = emf of cell, V = terminal voltage of cell.

  Also, $V = E - Ir = \left(\frac{E}{R+r}\right)R \quad \ldots(ii)$

  where, E = emf of the cell, R = external resistance and r = internal resistance of a cell.

- **Combination of Cells**

  In series grouping, current is given by, $I = (n\varepsilon / R + nr)$.

  In parallel grouping, current is given by, $I = (m\varepsilon / r + mR)$.

  In mixed grouping, current is given by, $I = \left(\frac{mn\varepsilon}{nr + mR}\right)$.

  where, n = number of cells in series, m = number of rows, r = internal resistance, R = external resistance, E = emf of cell and I = current flowing.

- **Kirchhoff's Laws**

  First Law (Junction Rule) The algebraic sum of the currents meeting at a point in an electrical circuit is always zero.

  Second Law (Loop Rule) The algebraic sum of changes in potential around any closed loop involving resistors and the cells in the loop is zero.

- **Wheatstone Bridge** It is an arrangement of four resistances used to measure one of them in terms of another three. The bridge is said to be balanced when the galvanometer shows zero deflection.

  The balance condition is $\frac{P}{Q} = \frac{R}{S}$.

- **Meter Bridge** It is also known as slide wire bridge. It is a practical form of Wheatstone bridge.

  The unknown resistance is given by
  $$S = R \times \left(\frac{100 - l}{l}\right)$$

- **Potentiometer** It is an apparatus used to compare emf's of two cells or to measure the internal resistance of a cell.

  Comparison of the emfs of two cells.

  i.e. $$\frac{E_1}{E_2} = \frac{l_1}{l_2}$$

  where, l_1 and l_2 are the balancing lengths corresponding to cells of emf E_1 and E_2, respectively.

  Comparison of the internal resistance of a primary cell.

  i.e. $$r = R\left(\frac{l_1}{l_2} - 1\right)$$

  where, l_1 and l_2 are balancing lengths and R is applied resistance.

For Mind Map

Visit : https://goo.gl/2Uuc7X OR **Scan the Code**

Chapter Practice

Multiple Choice Questions

(1 Mark)

1 The SI unit of the current density is
(a) ampere (A)
(b) ampere/metre^2 or (A / m^2)
(c) A- kg^3
(d) has no unit

2 The resistance will be least in a wire with length, cross-section area respectively,
(a) $L/2, 2A$ (b) $2L, A$
(c) L, A (d) $L, 2A$

3 A copper wire of cross-sectional area 2.0 mm^2, resistivity $= 1.7 \times 10^{-8}$ Ω, carries a current of 1 A. The electric field in the copper wire is
(a) 8.5×10^{-5} Vm^{-1} (b) 8.5×10^{-4} Vm^{-1}
(c) 8.5×10^{-3} Vm^{-1} (d) 8.5×10^{-2} Vm^{-1}

4 A potential difference V is applied to a copper wire of length l and diameter d. If V is doubled, then the drift velocity
(a) is doubled (b) is halved
(c) remains same (d) becomes zero

5 What is the safest voltage you can put across a 98 Ω, 0.5 W resistor?
(a) 14 V (b) 9.5 V (c) 7 V (d) 8.5 V

6 Two resistances are joined in parallel whose equivalent resistance is 3/5 Ω. One of the resistance wire is broken and the effective resistance becomes 3Ω. The resistance (in ohm) of the wire that got broken was
(a) 4/3 (b) 2 (c) 6/5 (d) 3/4

Assertion and Reason

Directions (Q. Nos. 7-11) *In the following questions, two statements are given- one labelled Assertion (A) and the other labelled Reason (R). Select the correct answer to these questions from the codes (a), (b), (c) and (d) as given below*

(a) Both Assertion and Reason are true and Reason is the correct explanation of Assertion.
(b) Both Assertion and Reason are true but Reason is not the correct explanation of Assertion.
(c) Assertion is true but Reason is false.
(d) Assertion is false but Reason is true.

7. **Assertion (A)** The average time of collisions τ, decreases with increasing temperature.
Reason (R) With an increase in temperature, average speed of the electrons, which act as the carriers of current, increases, resulting in more frequent collisions.

8. **Assertion (A)** Charge carriers do not move with acceleration, with a steady drift velocity.
Reason (R) Charge carriers under go collisions with ions and atoms during transit.

9. **Assertion (A)** If we bend an insulated conducting wire, the resistance of the wire increases.
Reason (R) The drift velocity of electron in bended wire remains same.

10. **Assertion (A)** The drift velocity of electrons in a metallic wire decreases when temperature of the wire is increases.
Reason (R) On increasing temperature, conductivity of metallic wire decreases.

11. **Assertion (A)** Higher the range, lower is the resistance of an ammeter.
Reason (R) To increase the range of an ammeter, additional shunt is added in series to it.

Very Short Answer Type Questions

(1 Mark)

12 What is the significance of direction of electric current?

13 Describe how the resistivity of the conductor depends upon
(i) number density (n) of free electrons and
(ii) relaxation time (τ).

14 Two conducting wires A and B of the same length but of different materials are joined in series across a battery. If the number density of electrons in A is twice than that in B, find

the ratio of drift velocities of electrons in two wires.

15 Show variation of resistivity of copper as a function of temperature in a graph.

16 On what basic conservation laws, are Kirchhoff's laws based?

17 We prefer a potentiometer with a longer bridge wire. Explain? why?

18 By using a resistance box, how can you make a potentiometer of given wire length more sensitive?

19 Define the conductivity of a conductor. Write its SI unit.

Short Answer Type I Questions

(2 Marks)

20 Figure below shows a plot of current *versus* voltage for two different materials P and Q. Which of the two materials satisfies Ohm's law? Explain.

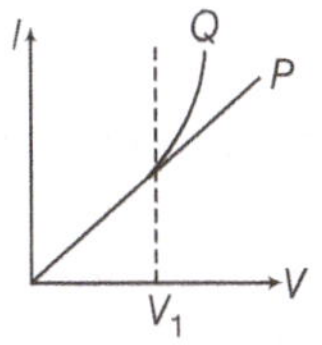

21 Derive the expression for the resistivity of a good conductor in terms of the relaxation time of electrons.

22 Write the expression for the resistivity of a metallic conductor showing its variation over a limited range of temperatures.

23 Car batteries are often rated in unit ampere hours. Does this unit designate the amount of current, energy, power or charge that can be drawn from the battery? Explain.

24 Is there some net field inside the cell, when the circuit is closed and a steady current passes through? Explain.

25 The plot of the variation of potential difference across a combination of three identical cells in series *versus* current is shown in the figure. What is the emf of each cell?

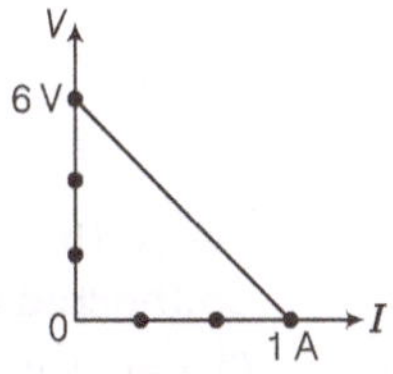

26 R_1, R_2 and R_3 are three different values of resistor R. Such that $R_1 > R_2 > R_3$
A, B and C are the null points obtained corresponding to R_1, R_2 and R_3, respectively. For which resistor, the value of X will be most accurate and why?

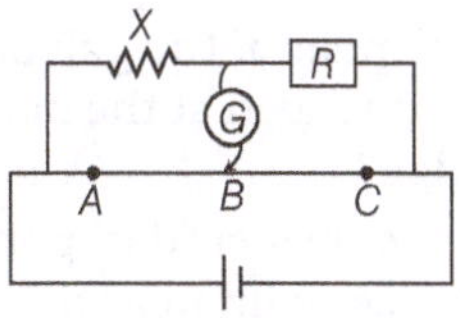

27 The figure shows a plot of terminal voltage V *versus* the current I of a given cell.

Calculate from the graph

(i) emf of the cell.

(ii) internal resistance of the cell.

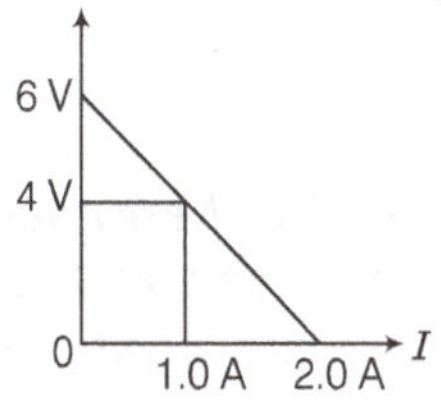

Short Answer Type II Questions

(3 Marks)

28 In a meter bridge, two unknown resistances R and S, when connected in the two gaps, give a null point at a distance x from one end. What is the ratio of R and S?

29 With the help of a suitable diagram, explain in brief about the sensitivity of Wheatstone bridge?

30 Define the term current sensitivity of a galvanometer. In the circuits shown in the figures, the galvanometer shows no deflection in each case. Find the ratio of R_1 and R_2.

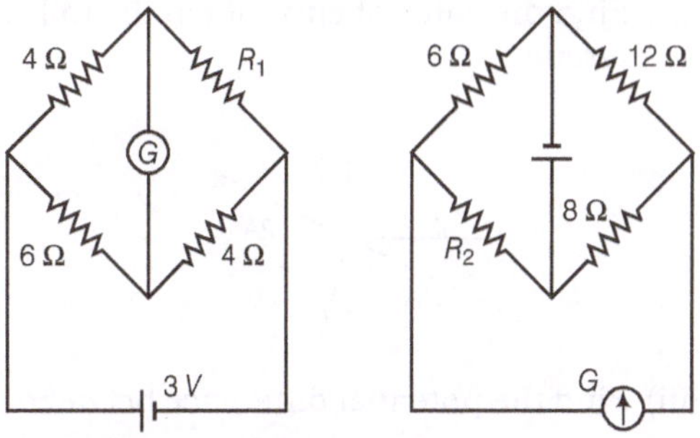

Long Answer Type Questions

5 Marks

31 (i) State with the help of a circuit diagram, the working principle of a meter bridge. Obtain the expression used for determining the unknown resistance.

(ii) What happens, if the galvanometer and cell are interchanged at the balance point of the bridge?

(iii) Why is it considered important to obtain the balance point near the mid-point of the wire?

32 State the principle of potentiometer. Draw a circuit diagram used to measure internal resistance of a cell and derive the expression. How can sensitivity of a potentiometer be increased?

Case Based Questions

Directions (Q. Nos. 33) *These questions are case study based questions. Read the following paragraph and answer the questions.*

33. In 1942, a German physicist Kirchhoff has given two rules to solve complicated electrical circuits. According to Kirchhoff's first rule,the algebraic sum of currents meeting at a junction in a closed electric circuit is zero. The incoming currents towards the junction is taken as positive and the outgoing currents away from the junction is taken as negative. So, Kirchhoff's first rule is on the basis of law of conservation of charge. According to Kirchhoff's second rule, the algebraic sum of potential drop across the resistors and the emfs of the cell in a closed loop is zero. So, Kirchhoff's second rule is based on conservation of energy.

(i) Write the principle on which Kirchhoff's first rule is based.

(ii) Find the value of current I in the following circuit.

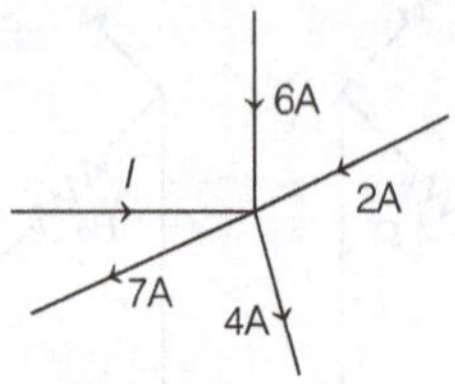

(iii) Find the potential difference between points A and B in the circuit given below.

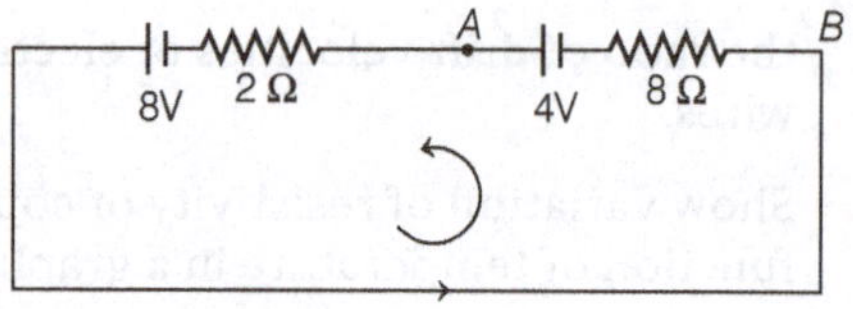

(iv) Write the principle on which Kirchhoff's second rule is based.

Numerical Problems

34 A uniform wire of resistance 20 Ω is cut into two equal parts. These parts are now connected in parallel. What will be the resistance of the combination? **(1 M)**

35 A wire of 20 Ω resistance is gradually stretched to double its original length. It is then cut into two equal parts. These parts are then connected in parallel across a 4.0 V battery. Find the current drawn from the battery. **(2 M)**

36 At 20° C, the carbon resistor in an electric circuit connected to a 5 V battery has a resistance of 200 Ω. What is the current in the circuit when the temperature of the carbon resistor is to 80° C? $[\alpha_{carbon} = -0.5\times10^{-3}\,°C^{-1}]$ **(2 M)**

37 A semiconductor has electron concentration 0.45×10^{12} m^3 and hole concentration 5×10^{20} m^3. Find its conductivity. Given, electron mobility = 0.135 m^2/Vs and hole mobility = 0.048 m^2/ Vs, $e = 1.6\times10^{-19}$C. **(2 M)**

38 The emf of a battery is 2 V and its internal resistance is 2 Ω. Its potential difference is measured by a voltmeter of resistance 998 Ω. Calculate the percentage error in the reading of emf shown by the voltmeter. **(2 M)**

39 Write any two factors on which internal resistance of a cell depends. The reading on a high resistance voltmeter when a cell is connected across it is 2.2 V.

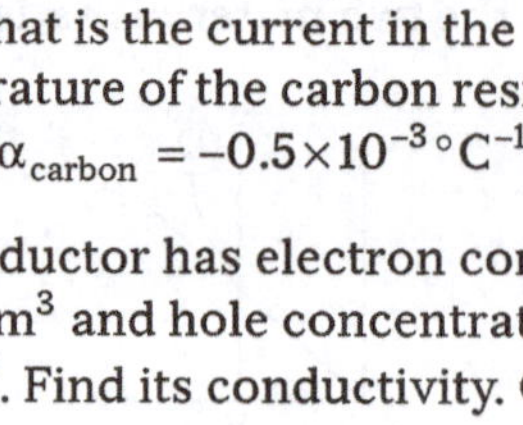

When the terminals of the cell are also connected to a resistance of 5 Ω as shown in the circuit, the voltmeter reading drops to 1.8 V. Find the internal resistance of the cell. **(3 M)**

40 The resistance of a potentiometer wire of length 10 m is 20 Ω. A resistance box and a 2V accumulator are connected in series with it. What resistance should be introduced in the box to have a potential drop of 1 μV/mm of the potentiometer wire? **(3 M)**

41 For what value of unknown resistance *y*, the potential difference between *A* and *B* is zero in the arrangement as shown in figure given below? **(3 M)**

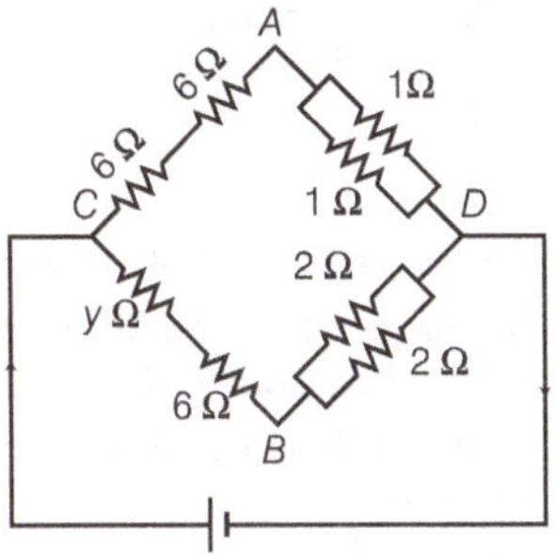

Answers

1 (*b*) The SI unit of current density is A/m^2.

$J = \frac{I}{A}$ (SI unit of current I is ampere, (A) and SI unit of area of cross-section area (A) is m^2)

$\Rightarrow J = \frac{A}{m^2} \Rightarrow J = Am^{-2}$

2 (*a*) $\therefore R = \rho l/A$ or $R \propto l/A$

$\because \quad R_a \propto \frac{L}{4A}, R_b \propto \frac{2L}{A}, R_c \propto \frac{L}{A}.$

Thus, resistance is least in a wire of length $L/2$ and area of cross-section is $2A$.

3 (*c*) $\therefore E = \frac{V}{l} = \frac{iR}{l} = \frac{i\rho l}{Al} = \frac{i\rho}{A}$

$= \frac{1 \times 1.7 \times 10^{-8}}{2 \times 10^{-6}}$

$= 8.5 \times 10^{-3}\ Vm^{-1}$

4 (*a*) $\therefore v_d = \frac{eE}{m}\tau = \frac{e}{m}\tau\left(\frac{V}{l}\right)$

or $\quad v_d \propto V$

Therefore, drift velocity is doubled when V is doubled.

5 (*c*) Let V be the safe voltage applied across the resistance of 98Ω.

Then, $P = \frac{V^2}{R}$

$\Rightarrow \quad V = \sqrt{PR} = \sqrt{0.5 \times 98} = \sqrt{49}$

$\Rightarrow \quad V = 7\ V$

At voltage more than 7 V excessive heat produced may burn the transistor.

6 (*d*) $\therefore R_P = \frac{R_1R_2}{R_1 + R_2} = \frac{3}{5}$ and $R_1 = 3\Omega$, then

$\frac{3 \times R_2}{3 + R_2} = \frac{3}{5} \Rightarrow 15R_2 = 9 + 3R_2 \Rightarrow 12R_2 = 9$

$\therefore \quad R_2 = \frac{3}{4}\Omega$

7 (*a*) With increase in temperature, average speed of the electrons, (which acts as the carriers of current) increases resulting in more frequent collisions. The average time of collisions τ, thus decreases with temperature.

8 (*a*) Charge carriers do not move with acceleration but with a steady drift velocity. This is because of the collisions with ions and atoms during transit.

9 (*d*) Bending will not increase the resistance of the conducting wire. Also, drift velocity of electron is independent of bending of conductor.

10 (*b*) Increasing the temperature of a conductor, the kinetic energy of free electrons increases.
On account of this, they collide more frequently with each other (and with the ions of the conductor) and consequently their drift velocity decreases.

11 (*a*)

12 Electric current is caused by the flow of electrons in a conductor. But the direction of electric current is taken as the opposite direction of movement of electrons.

13 Resistivity of a conductor is given by $\rho = \frac{m}{ne^2\tau}$

(i) Resistivity $\rho \propto \frac{1}{n}$, where n is the number density of free electrons.

(ii) Resistivity $\rho \propto \frac{1}{\tau}$, where τ is the relaxation time.

14 As the wires A and B are joined in series, the current through them is same.

$I_A = I_B$

$(neAv_d)_A = (neAv_d)_B \quad$ [as $I = ne\ Av_d$]

$\Rightarrow \quad n_Av_{d_A} = n_Bv_{d_B}$

$\frac{v_{d_A}}{v_{d_B}} = \frac{n_B}{n_A} = \frac{1}{2}$

15 Graph of resistivity of copper as a function of temperature is given below (resistivity of metals increases with increase in temperature).

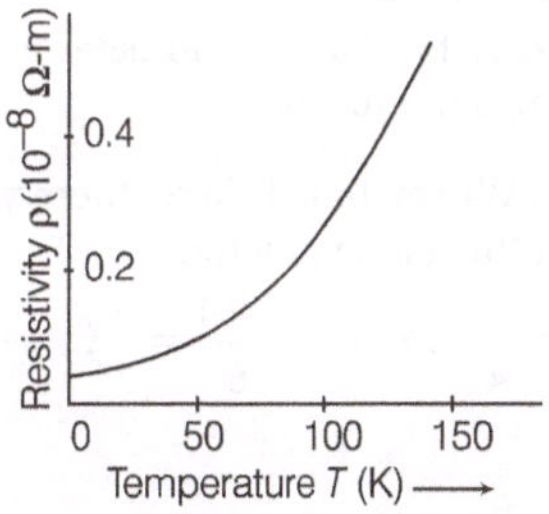

16 Kirchhoff's current law is based on law of conservation of charge and Kirchhoff's voltage law is based on law of conservation of energy.

17 We use a long wire to have a lower value of potential gradient. Hence, the sensitivity of the potentiometer is increased.

18 The sensitivity of the potentiometer can be increased by reducing the current in the circuit. This can be done by increasing the resistance using a resistance box.

19 Refer to text on page 114 (Conductivity).

20 The plot of V *versus* I is a straight line for materials that obey Ohm's law. So, from the figure, material P obeys Ohm's law. (2)

21 Refer the text on page 113 (Resistivity of various materials).

22 Refer to text on page 113 (Temperature dependance of resistivity).

23 Ampere hours is the unit of charge as ampere is the unit of current and hours is the unit of time.
Charge = Current × Time. (2)

24 When the circuit is closed and current flows in the direction of electrostatic field outside and opposite to the direction of electrostatic field inside the cell. This shows that there is net electric field inside the cell.

25 When three identical cells are connected in series, the equivalent emf is given by

$$E_{eq} = E_1 + E_2 + E_3 = 3E$$

From the graph, $3E = 6\text{V}$

$$\Rightarrow \quad E = \frac{6}{3} = 2\text{V}$$

$\therefore$ emf of each cell = 2V (2)

26 The figure given is a potentiometer. The sensitivity of potentiometer can be increased by reducing the current in the circuit. This can be done by increasing the value of R. So, the value of X will be most accurate for R_1. (2)

27 $V = E - ir$

(i) When $i = 0$, then $V = E$.
When $i = 0$, then $V = 6\text{V}$ (from the graph)
$\therefore$ emf of the cell $(E) = 6\text{V}$ (1)

(ii) When $i = 2\text{A}$, then $V = 0$ (from the graph)

$$\therefore E = ir \Rightarrow r = \frac{E}{i} = \frac{6}{2} = 3\Omega$$ (1)

28 Refer to text on pages 141 and 142 (Meter bridge)

29 Refer to text on pages 140 and 141 (Wheatstone bridge).

30 Current sensitivity of a galvanometer is defined as the deflection per unit current. (1)

For balanced Wheatstone bridge, there will be no deflection in the galvanometer.

$$\Rightarrow \quad \frac{4}{R_1} = \frac{6}{4} \Rightarrow R_1 = \frac{4 \times 4}{6} = \frac{8}{3}\,\Omega$$ (1)

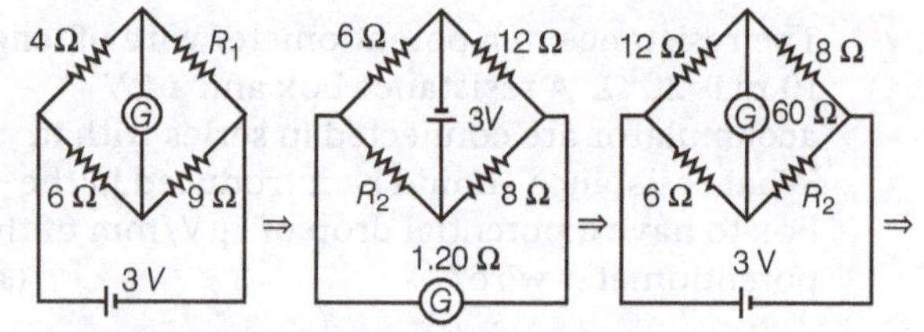

For the equivalent circuit, when the wheatstone bridge is balanced, there will be no deflection in the galvanometer.

$$\therefore \quad \frac{12}{8} = \frac{6}{R_2} \Rightarrow R_2 = \frac{6 \times 8}{12} = 4\Omega$$

$$\therefore \quad \frac{R_1}{R_2} = \frac{8/3}{4} = \frac{2}{3}$$ (1)

31 Refer to text on pages 141 and 142 (Meter bridge).

32 Refer to text on pages 142, 143 and 144 (Potentiometer, To measure internal resistance of a cell).

33 (i) Kirchhoff's first rule is based on the conservation of charge principle.

(ii) The given circuit is

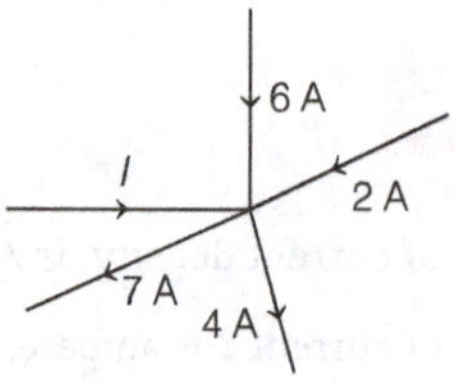

From Kirchhoff's junction rule,

$$\Sigma I_0 = 0$$

$$\Rightarrow \quad I + 6 + 2 - 7 - 4 = 0$$

$$\therefore \quad I = 3\text{A}$$

(iii) The given circuit is

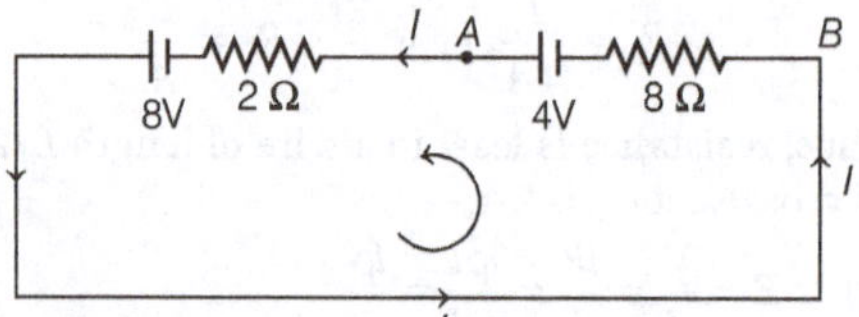

Applying Kirchhoff's second rule,

$$\Sigma \Delta V = 0$$

$$\Rightarrow \quad 8 - 8I - 4 - 2I = 0$$

$$I = 0.4\text{ A}$$

$\therefore$ Potential difference between points A and B is

$$V_{AB} = 4 + 8I = 4 + 8 \times 0.4 = 7.2\text{V}$$

(iv) Kirchhoff's second rule is based on the conservation of energy principle.

34 Resistance of each part = 20 Ω

In parallel combination,

$$R_P = \frac{R_1 \cdot R_2}{R_1 + R_2} = \frac{20 \times 20}{20 + 20} = \frac{400}{40} = 10\,\Omega$$

Hence, resistance of the combination is 10 Ω.

35 When a wire is stretched to double its length, the new resistance is given by

$$R' = (2)^2 R$$

where, R is the original resistance = 20Ω

$$R' = 4 \times 20 = 80\ \Omega$$

When this wire is cut into two parts, each part has a resistance $\frac{80}{2} = 40\ \Omega$.

When these two pieces are connected in parallel, (1)

$$\Rightarrow \quad R_{eq} = \frac{40}{2} = 20\Omega$$

$$\Rightarrow \quad V = 4\text{V}$$

$$\therefore \quad I = \frac{V}{R_{eq}} = \frac{4}{20} = \frac{1}{5}\text{A}$$

(1)

36 At 80°C,

$$I = \frac{\Delta V}{R} = \frac{\Delta V}{R_0[1+\alpha(T-T_0)]}$$

$$= \frac{5}{200[1+(-0.5\times10^{-3})(80-20)]} = 2.6\times10^{-2}\text{A}$$

or $I = 26$ mA

37 Refer to text on page 114 (Conductivity). [**Ans.** 3.84 Sm^{-1}]

38 Given, $E = 2$V

$$r = 2\Omega$$

From the diagram,

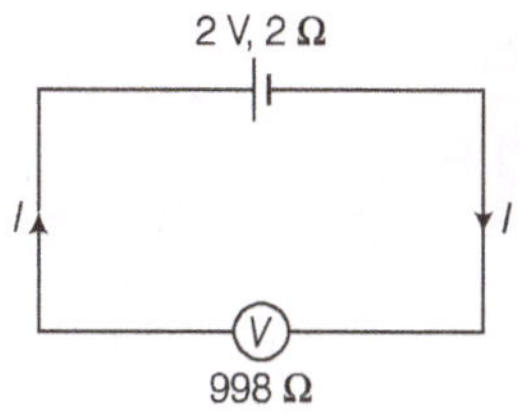

$$I = \frac{2}{2+998} = \frac{2}{1000}\text{A}$$

$$V = E - Ir = 2 - \frac{2}{1000} \times 2$$

$$= 2 - 0.004 = 1.996\text{ V}$$

$$\therefore \% \text{ error} = \frac{0.004}{2} \times 100 = 0.2\%$$

(2)

39 Refer to text on page 128 (Internal resistance) and Q. 31 on page 134. $\left[\textbf{Ans. } \frac{10}{9}\ \Omega\right]$

40 Apply the balancing condition of a potentiometer

Given, $E = 2$ V, $V = 0.01$ V, $R = 2\ \Omega/\text{m}$

Let r is resistance introduced in the box

$$\therefore \quad r = \left(\frac{E}{V} - 1\right)R = \left(\frac{2}{0.01} - 1\right) \times 2$$

or $r = 398\ \Omega$ [**Ans.** 398 Ω] (3)

41 As, $V_A - V_B = 0$

Thus, it is a balanced Wheatstone bridge. [**Ans.** 18 Ω] (3)

RELATED ONLINE VIDEOS

Visit : https://www.youtube.com/watch?v=t6pqrkWSWL8
OR **Scan the Code**

Visit : https://www.youtube.com/watch?v=NfcgA1axPLo
OR **Scan the Code**

Visit : https://www.youtube.com/watch?v=ZDoylghUI44
OR **Scan the Code**

Visit : https://www.youtube.com/watch?v=TS5ihKbOOOs
OR **Scan the Code**

Visit : https://www.youtube.com/watch?v=qebl2kNsDZo
OR **Scan the Code**

CHAPTER

04

Moving Charges and Magnetism

In this chapter, we will be going to study magnetism produced by a moving charge and further we will proceed with Ampere's circuital law and its applications and at last, the chapter will be ended with magnetic force and torque between two parallel conductors. All the topics mentioned above are discussed in detail, so it will be more interesting to understand them very carefully after going through each and every sentence very thoroughly.

- Magnetic Field and Its Applications
- Ampere's Circuital Law and Moving Charges
- Magnetic Force and Torque Experienced by a Current Loop

TOPIC 01 Magnetic Field and Its Applications

The space in the surroundings of a magnet or a current carrying conductor in which its magnetic influence can be experienced is called magnetic field. The SI unit of magnetic field is tesla (T) or weber/metre^2 (Wbm^{-2}) or $NA^{-1}m^{-1}$ and its CGS unit is gauss (G).

$$1 \text{ tesla} = 10^4 \text{ gauss}$$

Oersted's Experiment

Oersted experimentally demonstrated that the current carrying conductor produces magnetic field around it. His experimental arrangement is shown below. A conducting wire AB is connected to the poles of a battery through a key (K). When key K is closed, deflection occurs in compass needle and *vice-versa.*

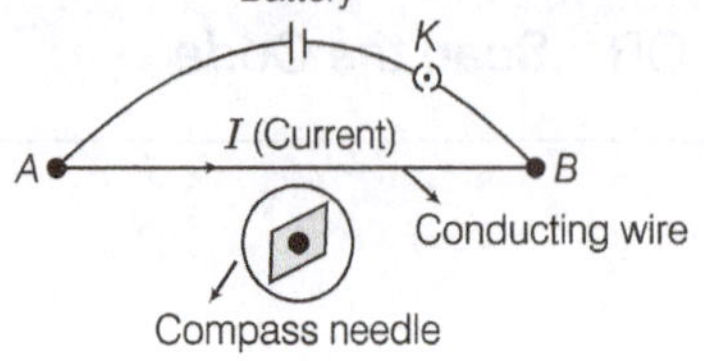

Magnetic Field due to a Current Element : Biot-Savart's Law

Biot-Savart's law is an experimental law predicted by Biot and Savart. This law deals with the magnetic field induction at a point due to a small current element (a part of any conductor, carrying current).

Let XY be current carrying conductor, I be current in the conductor, dl be infinitesimal small element of the conductor, dB be magnetic field at point P at a distance r from the element.

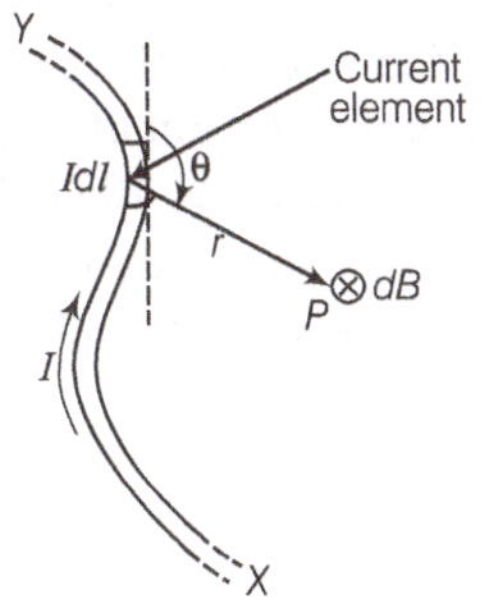

According to Biot-Savart's law, the magnitude of magnetic field induction (dB) at a point P due to a current element depends on the following factors

(i) $dB \propto I$ (i.e. magnetic field is directly proportional to the current flowing through the conductor).

(ii) $dB \propto dl$ (i.e. magnetic field is directly proportional to the length of the element).

(iii) $dB \propto \sin\theta$ (i.e. magnetic field is directly proportional to the sine of angle between the length of element and line joining the element to point (P).

(iv) $dB \propto \dfrac{1}{r^2}$ (i.e. magnetic field is inversely proportional to the square of distance between the element and point P). Combining all the above relations, $dB \propto \dfrac{Idl \sin\theta}{r^2}$

This relation is called **Biot-Savart's law.**

If conductor is placed in air or vacuum, then magnetic field is given by

$$dB = \frac{\mu_0}{4\pi} \cdot \frac{Idl \sin\theta}{r^2}$$

where, $\dfrac{\mu_0}{4\pi}$ is a proportionality constant, μ_0 is the permeability of free space. $\mu_0 = 4\pi \times 10^{-7}$ Tm/A (or Wb/A-m), its dimensions are $[MLT^{-2}A^{-2}]$.

In vector form, Biot-Savart's law can be written as

$$d\mathbf{B} \propto \frac{Id\mathbf{l} \times \mathbf{r}}{r^3} = \frac{\mu_0}{4\pi} \cdot \frac{Id\mathbf{l} \times \mathbf{r}}{r^3} \quad \text{...(i)}$$

From Eq. (i), the direction of $d\mathbf{B}$ would be the direction of the cross-product vector ($d\mathbf{l} \times \mathbf{r}$), which is represented by the right handed screw rule or right hand thumb rule. Here, $d\mathbf{B}$ is perpendicular to the plane containing $d\mathbf{l}$ and $\mathbf{r}$ is directed inwards (since, point P is to the right of the current element).

Magnetic field induction at point P due to current through entire wire is

$$\mathbf{B} = \int \frac{\mu_0}{4\pi} \cdot \frac{Id\mathbf{l} \times \mathbf{r}}{r^3}$$

or

$$B = \int \frac{\mu_0}{4\pi} \cdot \frac{Idl \sin\theta}{r^2}$$

Biot-Savart's law in terms of current density J can be written as

$$d\mathbf{B} = \frac{\mu_0}{4\pi} \cdot \frac{\mathbf{J} \times \mathbf{r}}{r^3} dV \quad \left[\because J = \frac{I}{A} = \frac{Idl}{Adl} = \frac{Idl}{dV}\right]$$

where, J = current density at any point on the current element and dV = volume of the element.

Biot-Savart's law in terms of charge (q) and its velocity (v) can be written as

$$d\mathbf{B} = \frac{\mu_0}{4\pi} \cdot \frac{q(\mathbf{v} \times \mathbf{r})}{r^3} \quad \left[\because Id\mathbf{l} = \frac{q}{dt} d\mathbf{l} = q\frac{d\mathbf{l}}{dt} = q\mathbf{v}\right]$$

Biot-Savart's law in terms of magnetising force or magnetising intensity (H) of the magnetic field is in SI or MKS system,

$$d\mathbf{H} = \frac{d\mathbf{B}}{\mu_0} = \frac{1}{4\pi} \cdot \frac{Id\mathbf{l} \times \mathbf{r}}{r^3} = \frac{1}{4\pi} \cdot \frac{Id\mathbf{l} \times \hat{\mathbf{r}}}{r^2}$$

$$\therefore \quad dH = \frac{1}{4\pi} \cdot \frac{Idl \sin\theta}{r^2}$$

In CGS units, $d\mathbf{H} = \dfrac{Id\mathbf{l} \times \mathbf{r}}{r^3}$ and $dH = \dfrac{Idl \sin\theta}{r^2}$

Permittivity and Permeability

The relation between ε_0 and μ_0 is always a constant, i.e.

$$\mu_0 \varepsilon_0 = (4\pi\varepsilon_0) \times \left(\frac{\mu_0}{4\pi}\right) = \frac{1 \times 10^{-7}}{9 \times 10^9} = \frac{1}{(3 \times 10^8)^2} = \frac{1}{c^2}$$

$$\Rightarrow \quad c = \frac{1}{\sqrt{\mu_0 \varepsilon_0}}$$

where, $\mu_0 = 4\pi \times 10^{-7}$ T/m

and $\varepsilon_0 = 8.86 \times 10^{-12}$ Nm^{2}C^{-2}

Magnetic Field due to a Current Carrying Conductor

Let us consider a straight conductor XY, carrying a current I and P is a point at which the magnetic field is required.

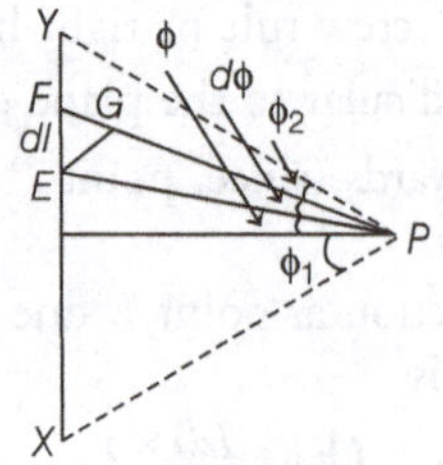

$$B = \frac{\mu_0 I}{4\pi r}(\sin\phi_1 + \sin\phi_2)$$

According to right hand thumb rule, the direction of magnetic field in this case is perpendicular to the plane of paper and directed inwards.

Magnetic field B for infinitely long wire, at any points except end point of wire.

As, $\phi_1 = \phi_2 = \pi/2$

then $\boxed{B_1 = \dfrac{\mu_0 I}{2\pi r}}$

Magnetic field for infinitely long wire, near the end points of wire, $\phi_1 = 0°$ and $\phi_2 = 90°$

$$\boxed{B_2 = \frac{\mu_0}{4\pi}\cdot\frac{I}{r}} \Rightarrow \text{Clearly, } \boxed{B_2 = \frac{B_1}{2}}$$

The direction of the magnetic field associated with a current carrying conductor can be determined by right hand thumb rule or Maxwell's cork screw rule.

Right Hand Thumb Rule

According to this rule, if we imagine a linear wire conductor to be held in the grip of the right hand such that the thumb points in the direction of current, then the curvature of the fingers around the conductor will give the direction of magnetic field lines.

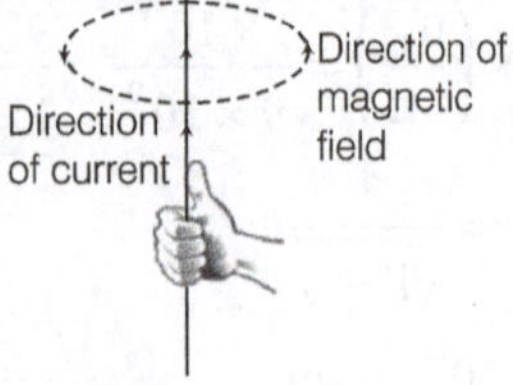

Maxwell's Cork Screw Rule

According to this rule, if we imagine a right handed cork screw placed along the current carrying wire conductor, rotated such that the screw moves in the direction of current, then the direction of rotation of the screw gives the direction of magnetic field lines.

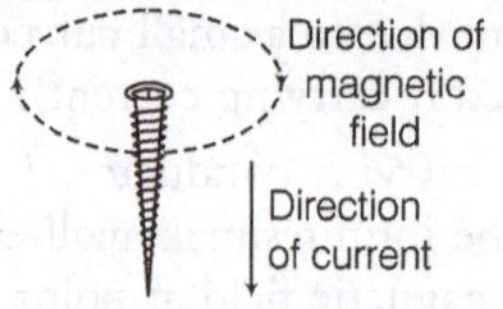

Example 1 A current 10 A is flowing East to West in a long wire kept horizontally in the East-West direction. Find the magnitude and direction of magnetic field in a horizontal plane at a distance of 10 cm North.

Sol. Given, current, $I = 10$ A (East to West)

Distance, $r = 10 \text{ cm} = 10 \times 10^{-2}$ m

Magnetic field, $|\mathbf{B}| = ?$

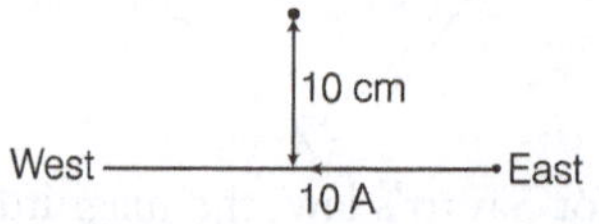

The magnitude of magnetic field $|\mathbf{B}|$ for infinite length of wire $= \dfrac{\mu_0 I}{2\pi r} \Rightarrow |B| = \dfrac{4\pi \times 10^{-7} \times 10}{2 \times \pi \times 10 \times 10^{-2}} = 2 \times 10^{-5}$ T

The direction of magnetic field is given by right hand thumb rule or Maxwell's cork screw rule. So, the direction of magnetic field at point 10 cm North due to flowing current is perpendicularly inwards to the plane of paper.

Example 2 Find an expression for the magnetic field at the centre of a coil bent in the form of square of side $2a$, carrying current I as shown in the figure.

Sol. Given, $\theta_1 = 45°, \theta_2 = 45°$

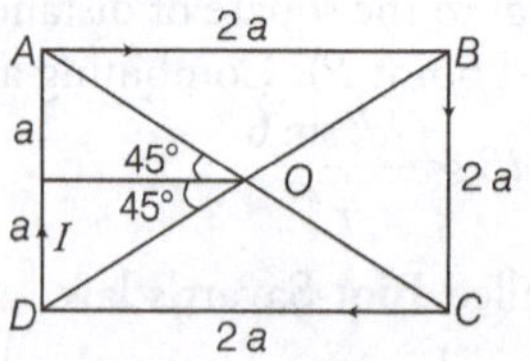

Total magnetic field due to each side at point O is given by

$$B = 4\frac{\mu_0 I}{4\pi a}(\sin\theta_1 + \sin\theta_2)$$

$$= 4\frac{\mu_0 I}{4\pi a}(\sin 45° + \sin 45°)$$

$$= \frac{\mu_0 I}{\pi a}\left(\frac{1}{\sqrt{2}} + \frac{1}{\sqrt{2}}\right) = \frac{\sqrt{2}\mu_0 I}{\pi a}$$

Magnetic Field on the Axis of a Circular Current Carrying Loop

Let us consider a circular loop of radius a with centre C. Let the plane of the coil be perpendicular to the plane of the paper and current I be flowing in the direction shown. Suppose P is any point on the axis of a coil at a distance r from the centre C.

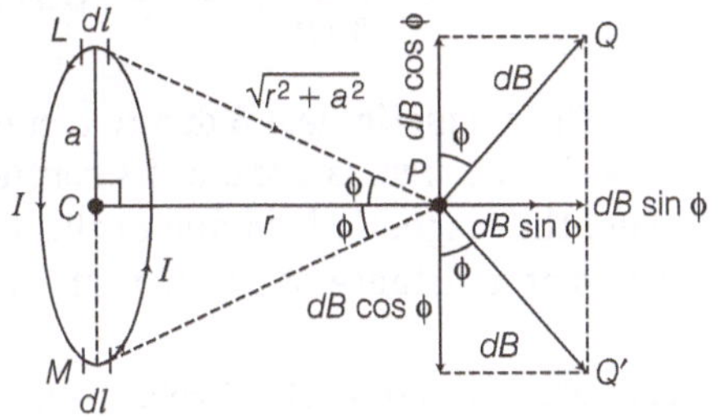

Now, consider a current element Idl on top (L), where current comes out of paper normally, whereas at bottom (M), current enters into the plane paper normally.

$\because \quad LP \perp dl$

Also, $\quad MP \perp dl$

$\therefore \quad LP = MP = \sqrt{r^2 + a^2}$

The magnetic field at point P due to the current element Idl, according to Biot-Savart's law is given by

$$dB = \frac{\mu_0}{4\pi} \cdot \frac{Idl \sin 90°}{(r^2 + a^2)} = \frac{\mu_0}{4\pi} \cdot \frac{Idl}{(r^2 + a^2)}$$

where, a = radius of circular loop

and $\quad r$ = distance of point P from the centre C along the axis.

According to right hand screw rule, the direction of dB is perpendicular to LP and along PQ, where $PQ \perp LP$. Similarly, the same magnitude of magnetic field is obtained due to current element Idl at the bottom and direction is along PQ', where $PQ' \perp MP$.

Now, resolving dB due to current element at L and M. So, $dB \cos \phi$ components balance each other and net magnetic field is given by

$$B = \oint dB \sin \phi = \oint \frac{\mu_0}{4\pi}\left(\frac{Idl}{r^2 + a^2}\right) \cdot \frac{a}{\sqrt{r^2 + a^2}}$$

$$\left[\because \text{In } \Delta PCL, \sin \phi = \frac{a}{\sqrt{r^2 + a^2}}\right]$$

$$= \frac{\mu_0}{4\pi} \frac{Ia}{(r^2 + a^2)^{3/2}} \oint dl$$

$$= \frac{\mu_0}{4\pi} \frac{Ia}{(r^2 + a^2)^{3/2}} (2\pi a)$$

or $$B = \frac{\mu_0 I a^2}{2(r^2 + a^2)^{3/2}} \quad \ldots \text{(ii)}$$

For N turns, the net magnetic field is given by

$$B = \frac{\mu_0 N I a^2}{2\,(r^2 + a^2)^{3/2}}$$

At the centre, $r = 0$

$$B = \frac{\mu_0 N I a^2}{2(0 + a^2)^{3/2}}$$

$$B = \frac{\mu_0 N I}{2a}$$

The direction of B is along the axis and away from the loop, when current in the coil is in anti-clockwise direction.

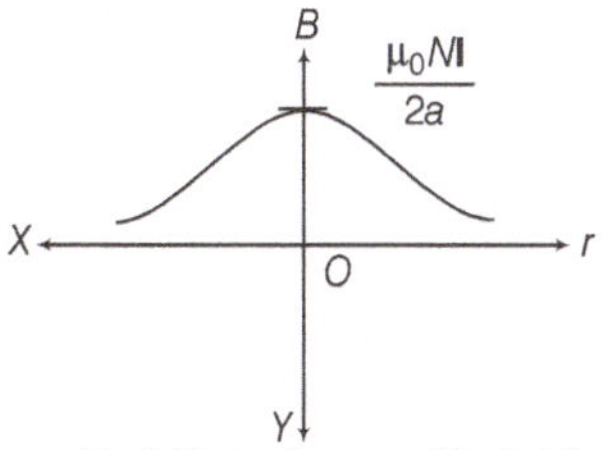

Variation of magnetic field induction (B) with distance r

Example 3 A circular coil of 120 turns has a radius of 18 cm and carries a current of 3 A. What is the magnitude of the magnetic field at a point on the axis of the coil at a distance from the centre equal to the radius of the circular coil?

Sol. Given, number of turns $N = 120$, current $I = 3\text{A}$,

radius of coil, $r = 18 \text{ cm} = 0.18 \text{ m}$ and

distance from the centre to a point on axis, $a = r = 0.18$ m

As, $$B = \frac{\mu_0 N I a^2}{2(a^2 + r^2)^{3/2}}$$

$$= \frac{4\pi \times 10^{-7} \times 120 \times 3 \times (0.18)^2}{2[(0.18)^2 + (0.18)^2]^{3/2}}$$

$$\Rightarrow B = 4.4 \times 10^{-4} \text{ T}$$

Magnetic Field at the Centre of a Current Carrying Circular Loop

Consider a circular loop of radius R carrying current I.

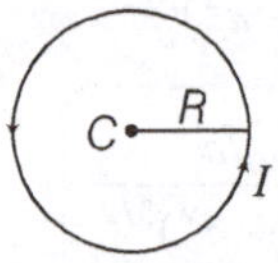

Magnetic field at its centre C is given by

$$B = \frac{\mu_0 I}{2R}$$

is obtained by setting $r = 0$ in previous relation (ii).
If we take a coil having N number of turns, then magnetic field at its centre is

$$\boxed{B = \frac{\mu_0 NI}{2R}}$$

The direction of magnetic field at the centre of circular loop is given by **right hand rule.**
Similarly, magnetic field at the centre of a semi-circular wire of radius R, carrying current I is given by , $B = \frac{\mu_0 I}{4R}$.

Right Hand Rule

According to this rule, if we hold the thumb of right hand mutually perpendicular to the grip of fingers such that the curvature of fingers depicts the direction of current in circular wire loop, then the thumb will point in the direction of magnetic field near the centre of loop.

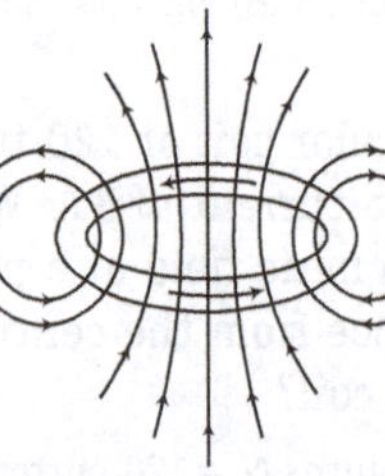

Note As current carrying loop has the magnetic field lines around it thus, it behaves as a magnet with two mutually opposite poles.

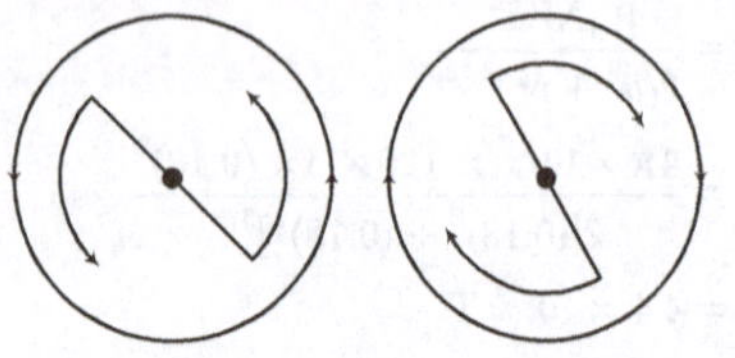

The anti-clockwise flow of current behaves like a North pole, whereas clockwise flow as South pole.

Example 4 A circular coil of wire consisting of 100 turns, each of radius 8.0 cm carries a current of 0.40 A. What is the magnitude of the magnetic field B at the centre of the coil? **NCERT**

Sol. Here, $n = 100$, $r = 8\,\text{cm} = 8 \times 10^{-2}\,\text{m}$ and $I = 0.40\,\text{A}$

$\therefore$ Magnetic field B at the centre,

$$B = \frac{\mu_0}{4\pi} \cdot \frac{2\pi I n}{r} = \frac{10^{-7} \times 2 \times 3.14 \times 0.40 \times 100}{8 \times 10^{-2}} = 3.1 \times 10^{-4}\,\text{T}$$

Example 5 The magnetic field B due to a current carrying circular loop of radius 12cm at its centre is 0.5×10^{-4} T. Find the magnetic field due to this loop at a point on the axis at a distance of 5.0 cm from the centre.

Sol. Magnetic field at the centre of a circular loop,

$$B_1 = \frac{\mu_0 I}{2R}$$

and that at an axial point, $B_2 = \dfrac{\mu_0 IR^2}{2(R^2 + x^2)^{3/2}}$

Thus, $\dfrac{B_2}{B_1} = \dfrac{R^3}{(R^2 + x^2)^{3/2}}$ or $B_2 = B_1 \left[\dfrac{R^3}{(R^2 + x^2)^{3/2}}\right]$

Substituting the values, we have

$$B_2 = (0.5 \times 10^{-4}) \left[\frac{(12)^3}{(144 + 25)^{3/2}}\right] = 3.9 \times 10^{-5}\,\text{T}$$

Example 6 An electric current is flowing in a circular coil of radius a. At what distance from the centre on the axis of the coil will the magnetic field be $\frac{1}{8}$ th of its value at the centre?

Sol. Magnetic field induction at a point on the axis at distance x from the centre of the circular coil carrying current is

$$B_1 = \frac{\mu_0}{4\pi} \cdot \frac{2\pi n I a^2}{(a^2 + x^2)^{3/2}}$$

Magnetic field induction at the centre of the circular coil carrying current is

$$B_2 = \frac{\mu_0}{4\pi} \cdot \frac{2\pi n I}{a}$$

But as per question, $B_1 = \dfrac{B_2}{8}$

$$\Rightarrow \quad \frac{\mu_0}{4\pi} \cdot \frac{2\pi n I a^2}{(a^2 + x^2)^{3/2}} = \frac{\mu_0}{4\pi} \cdot \frac{2\pi n I}{a} \times \frac{1}{8}$$

$$\Rightarrow \quad \frac{a^2}{(a^2 + x^2)^{3/2}} = \frac{1}{8a} \Rightarrow 8a^3 = (a^2 + x^2)^{3/2}$$

$$\Rightarrow \quad 2a = (a^2 + x^2)^{1/2}$$

$$\Rightarrow \quad 4a^2 = a^2 + x^2 \Rightarrow x = \sqrt{3}a$$

Example 7 A long insulated copper wire is closely wound as a spiral of N turns. The spiral has inner radius a and outer radius b. The spiral lies in the XY-plane and a steady current I flows through the wire. Find the Z-component of the magnetic field at the centre of the spiral.

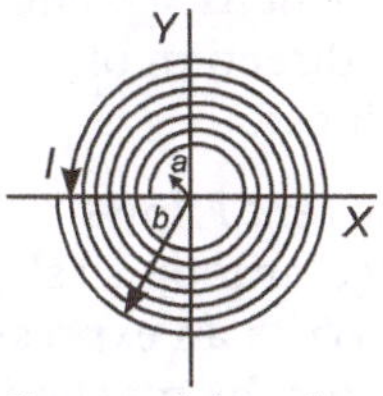

Sol. If we take a small strip of dr at distance r from centre, then number of turns in this strip would be

$$dN = \left(\frac{N}{b-a}\right) dr$$

Magnetic field due to this element at the centre of the coil will be

$$dB = \frac{\mu_0 (dN) I}{2r} = \frac{\mu_0 NI}{2(b-a)} \frac{dr}{r}$$

$$\therefore \quad B = \int_{r=a}^{r=b} dB$$

$$= \frac{\mu_0 NI}{2(b-a)} \ln\left(\frac{b}{a}\right)$$

Topic Practice 1

Multiple Choice Questions

1 Mark

1. Choose the correct option of : The Biot-Savart's law in vector form is **ISC 2013**
   (a) $d\mathbf{B} = \frac{\mu_0}{4\pi} \frac{dl\,(I \times r)}{\mathbf{r}^3}$ (b) $d\mathbf{B} = \frac{\mu_0}{4\pi} \frac{I(dl \times \mathbf{r})}{\mathbf{r}^3}$
   (c) $d\mathbf{B} = \frac{\mu_0}{4\pi} \frac{\mathbf{I}(\mathbf{r} \times dl)}{\mathbf{r}^3}$ (d) $d\mathbf{B} = \frac{\mu_0}{4\pi} \frac{I\,(dl \times \mathbf{r})}{\mathbf{r}^2}$

2. An element $\Delta l = \Delta x\,\hat{i}$ is placed at the origin and carries a current $I = 10$ A.

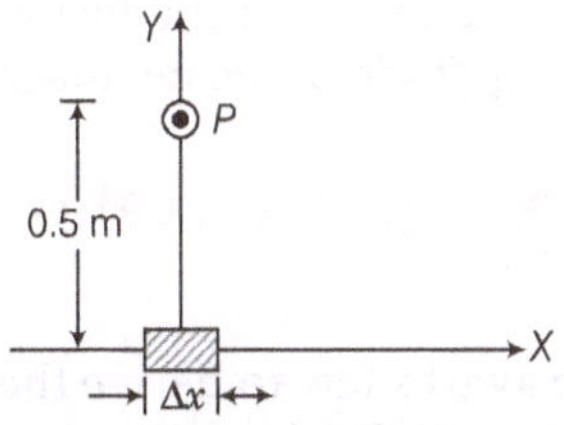

   If $\Delta x = 1$ cm, magnetic field at point P is
   (a) $4 \times 10^{-8}\,\hat{k}$ T (b) $4 \times 10^{-8}\,\hat{i}$ T
   (c) $4 \times 10^{-8}\,\hat{j}$ T (d) $-4 \times 10^{-8}\,\hat{j}$ T

3. A circular coil has radius r, number of turns N and carries a current I, magnetic flux density B at its centre is **ISC 2023**
   (a) $B = \mu_0 NI$ (b) $B = \mu_0 NI / 2r$
   (c) $B = \mu_0 NI / 4\pi r$ (d) $B = \mu_0 NI / 4r$

4. A straight wire carrying a current of 12 A is sent into a semicircular loop of radius 2.0 cm. What will be magnetic field at the centre of the semicircular loop?

   (a) $\mathbf{B} = 1.9 \times 10^{-4}$ T
   (b) $\mathbf{B} = 1.9 \times 10^{4}$ T
   (c) $\mathbf{B} = 1.9 \times 10^{-4}$ T, ⊗
   (d) $\mathbf{B} = 1.9 \times 10^{4}$ T, ⊗

5. An infinitely long conductor PQR is bent to form a right angle as shown. A current I flows through PQR. The magnetic field due to this current at the point M is H_1. Now, another infinitely long straight conductor QS is connected at Q, so that the current is 1/2 in QR as well as in QS. The current in PQ remaining unchanged. The magnetic field at M is now H_2. The ratio H_1/H_2 is given by

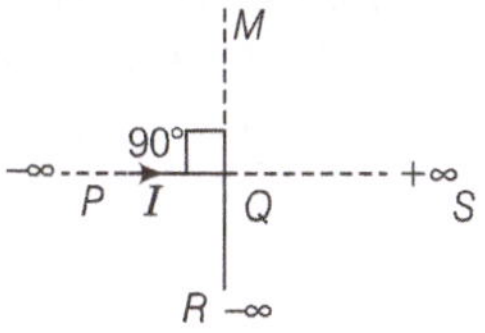

   (a) $\frac{1}{2}$ (b) 1
   (c) $\frac{2}{3}$ (d) 2

Very Short Answer Type Questions

1 Mark

6. In what respect does a wire carrying a current differ from a wire, which carries no current?
7. How can you justify that a current carrying wire produces magnetic field?
8. Give the dependence of magnetic field produced by a current conductor.
9. Write Biot-Savart's law in vector form. **ISC 2020**
10. Among Biot-Savart's law and Coulomb's law, which one is angle dependent?

11. Figure below shows a point P near a long conductor XY carrying a current I. MN is a short current conductor, kept at the point P, parallel to the conductor XY. What is the direction of magnetic flux density B at the point P due to the current flowing through XY?

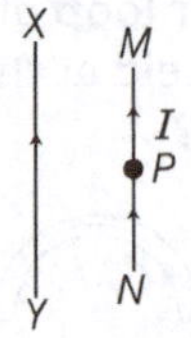

ISC 2012

12. Name the kind of magnetic field produced by an infinitely long current carrying conductor.

13. Draw the magnetic field lines due to a current carrying loop.

14. An electron is revolving around a circular loop as shown in the figure. What will be the direction of magnetic field at the point A?

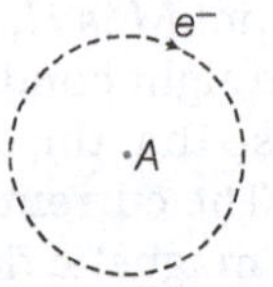

15. There is a circuit given below, where APB and AQB are semi-circles. What will be the magnetic field at the centre C of the circular loop?

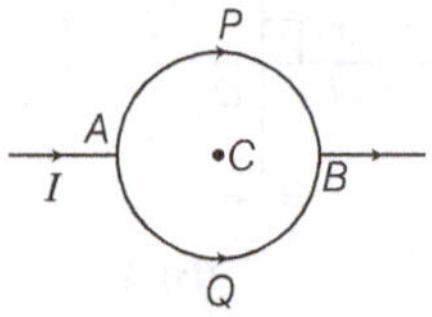

Short Answer Type I Questions

2 Marks

16. State Biot-Savart's law. **ISC 2014, 05, 01**

17. State Biot-Savart's law. A current I flows in a conductor placed perpendicular to the plane of the paper. Indicate the direction of the magnetic field due to a small element dl at a point P situated at a distance r from the element as shown in the figure.

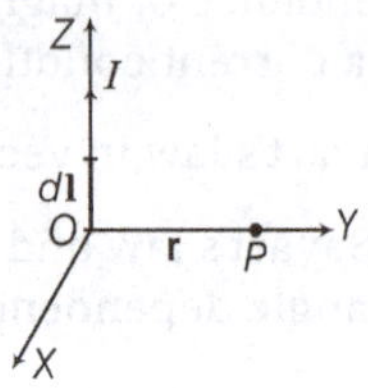

18. An element $\Delta l = \Delta x \hat{\mathbf{i}}$ is placed at the origin (as shown in figure) and carries a current $I = 2$A. Find out the magnetic field at a point P on the Y-axis at a distance of 1.0 m due to the element $\Delta x = w$ cm. Also, give the direction of the field produced.

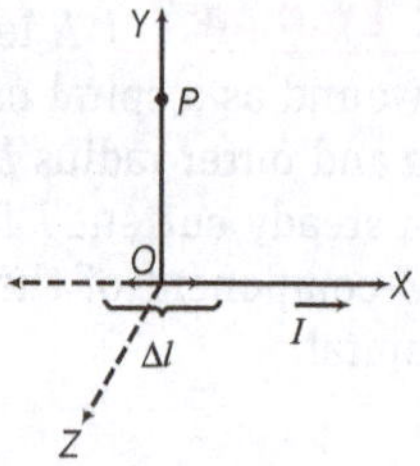

19. An electric current I flows through a circular loop as shown in the figure. Write an expression and direction for the magnetic field at the centre of the loop at point P **ISC 2019**

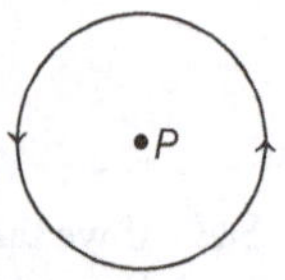

20. A circular coil of closely wound N turns and radius r carries a current I in the clockwise direction. Find
   (i) the direction of magnetic field at its centre.
   (ii) the magnitude of magnetic field at the centre.

21. A straight wire of length L is bent into a semi-circular loop. Use Biot-Savart's law to deduce an expression for the magnetic field at its centre due to the current I passing through it.

22. A wire of length L is bent round in the form of a coil having N turns of same radius. If a steady current I flows through it in clockwise direction, then find the magnitude and direction of the magnetic field produced at its centre.

23. Two identical circular loops P and Q, each of radius r and carrying equal currents are kept in the parallel planes having a common axis passing through O. The direction of current in P is clockwise and in Q is anti-clockwise as seen from O, which is equidistant from the loops P and Q. Find the magnitude of the net magnetic field at O.

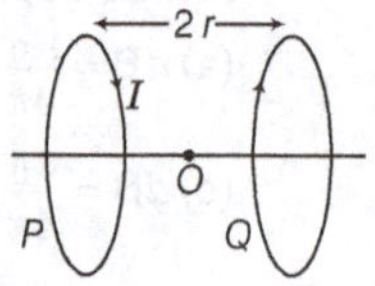

Short Answer Type II Questions

3 Marks

24. Use Biot-Savart's law to derive the expression for the magnetic field on the axis of a current carrying circular loop of radius R. Draw the magnetic field lines due to a circular wire carrying current I.

25. Using Biot-Savart's law, write the expression for the magnetic field **B** due to an element $d\mathbf{l}$ carrying current I at a distance **r** from it in a vector form.
Hence, derive the expression for the magnetic field due to a current carrying loop of radius R at a point P and distance x from its centre along the axis of the loop.

26. Obtain an expression for magnetic flux density B at the centre of a circular coil of radius R having N turns and carrying a current I. **ISC 2015**

Or Using Biot-Savart law, show that magnetic flux density B at the centre of a current carrying circular coil of radius R is given by $B = \frac{\mu_0 I}{2r}$

where, the terms have their usual meanings. **ISC 2024**

27. Obtain an expression for magnetic flux density B at the centre of a circular coil of radius R and having N turns, when a current I is flowing through it. **ISC 2009, 01**

Long Answer Type II Questions

5 Marks

28. State Biot-Savart's law expressing it in the vector form. Use it to obtain the expression for the magnetic field at an axial point distance d from the centre of a circular coil of radius a carrying current I. Also, find the ratio of the magnitudes of the magnetic field of this coil at the centre and at an axial point for which $d = a\sqrt{3}$.

29. Two very small identical circular loops (1) and (2) carrying equal current I are placed vertically (with respect to the plane of the paper) with their geometrical axes perpendicular to each other as shown in the figure. Find the magnitude and direction of the net magnetic field produced at the point O.

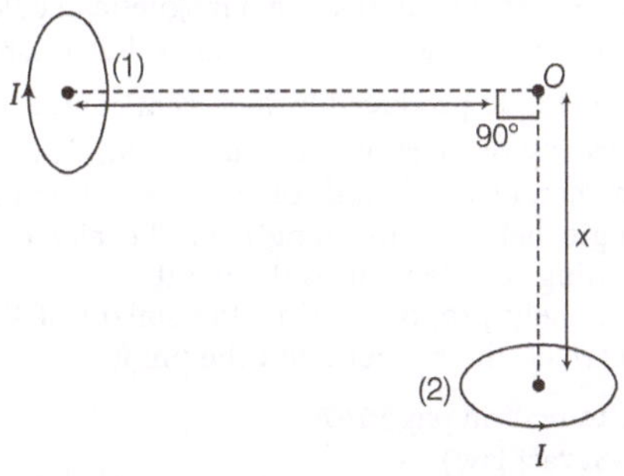

Numerical Problems

30. A current of 5 A is flowing from South to North in a straight wire. Find the magnetic field due to a 1cm piece of wire at a point 1 m North-East from the piece of wire. **(2 M)**

31. An element $dl = dx\,\hat{i}$ (where, $dx = 1$ cm) is placed at the origin and carries a large current $I = 10$ A. What is the magnetic field on the Y-axis at a distance of 0.5 m? **NCERT (2 M)**

32. A long straight wire in the horizontal plane carries a current of 50 A in North to South direction.Give the magnitude and direction of B at a point 2.5 m East of the wire. **NCERT (2 M)**

33. (i) Two infinitely long current carrying conductors X and Y are kept parallel to each other, 24 cm apart in vacuum. They carry currents of 5A and 7A respectively, in the same direction, as shown in figure. Find the position of a neutral point, i.e. a point where resultant magnetic flux density is zero. (Ignore earth's magnetic field).

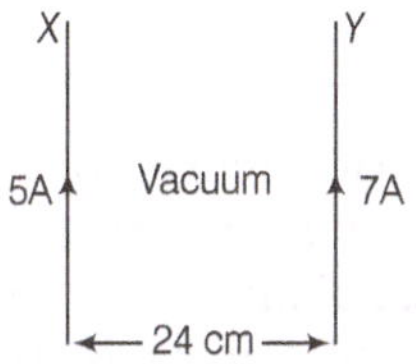

(ii) If current through the conductor Y is reversed in direction, will neutral point lie between X and Y, to the left of X or to the right of Y? **ISC 2016 (2 M)**

34. Two wires A and B have the same length equal to 44 cm and carry a current of 10 A each. Wire A is bent into a circle and wire B is bent into a square.
(i) Obtain the magnitudes of the fields at the centres of the two wires.
(ii) Which wire produces a greater magnetic field at its centre? **(3 M)**

35. Calculate the magnetic field (in SI unit) at the centre of a tangent galvanometer coil of 50 turns and radius 10 cm when a current of 1.0 A passes through it. **ISC 2007 (2 M)**

36. A tightly wound 100 turns coil of radius 10 cm is carrying a current of 1 A. What is the magnitude of the magnetic field at the centre of the coil? **NCERT (2 M)**

37. The wire shown in the figure carries a current of 10 A. Determine the magnitude of magnetic field induction at the centre O. Given the radius of bent coil is 3 cm. **(2 M)**

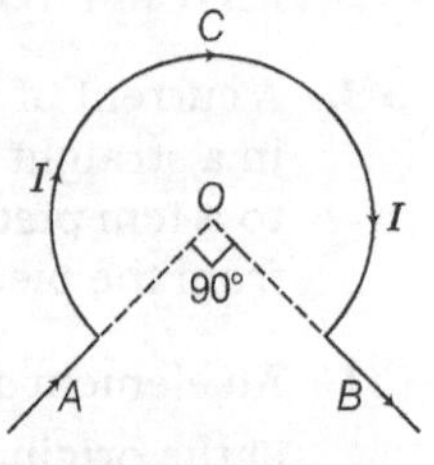

38. Two identical circular coils, P and Q each of radius R, carrying currents 1 A and $\sqrt{3}$ A respectively, are placed concentrically and perpendicular to each other lying in the XY and YZ-planes. Find the magnitude and direction of the net magnetic field at the centre of the coils. **(2 M)**

39. A straight wire carrying a current of 10 A is bent into a semi-circular arc of radius 2.0 cm as shown in the figure. What is the magnetic field at O due to

(i) straight segments?

(ii) the semi-circular arc? **(3 M)**

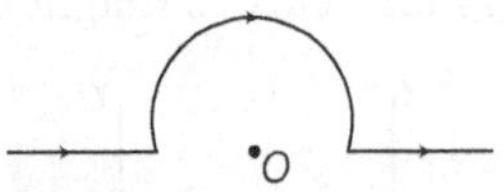

40. Two concentric circular coils x and y of radii 16 cm and 10 cm respectively lie in the same vertical plane containing the North to South direction. Coil x has 20 turns and carries a current of 16 A, coil y has 25 turns and carries a current of 18 A. The sense of the current in x is anti-clockwise and clockwise in y, for an observer looking at the coils facing West. Find the magnitude and direction of the net magnetic field due to the coils at their centre. **NCERT (4 M)**

41. Two identical loops P and Q each of radius 5 cm are lying in perpendicular planes such that they have a common centre as shown in the figure. Find the magnitude and direction of the net magnetic field at the common centre of the two coils, if they carry currents equal to 3 A and 4 A, respectively. **(3 M)**

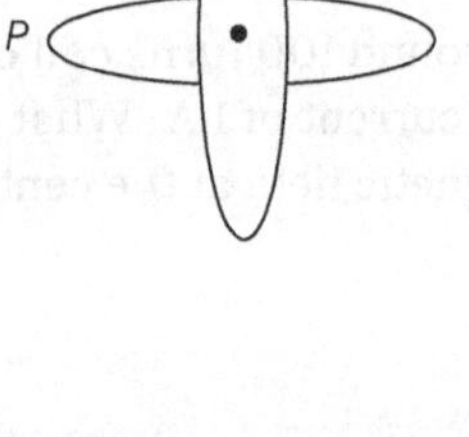

Hints & Solutions

1. (*b*) Biot-Savart's law in vector form is

$$d\mathbf{B} = \frac{\mu_0}{4\pi}\frac{I(dl \times \mathbf{r})}{r^3}$$

Hence, option (b) is correct.

2. (*a*) The magnitude of magnetic field,

$$|d\mathbf{B}| = \frac{\mu_0}{4\pi}\frac{I\, dl \sin\theta}{r^2}$$

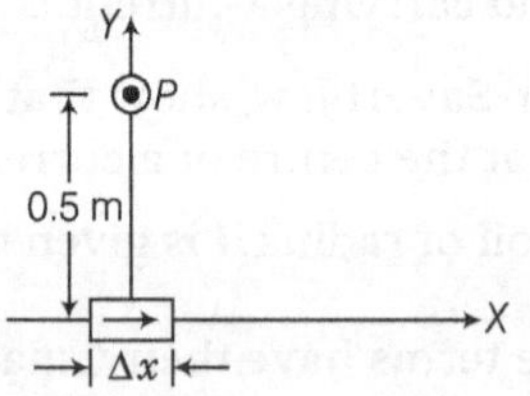

i.e. $|d\mathbf{B}| = \dfrac{10^{-7} \times 10 \times 10^{-2}}{25 \times 10^{-2}} = 4 \times 10^{-8}$ T

As, $dl \times \mathbf{r} = \Delta x\hat{\mathbf{i}} \times y\hat{\mathbf{j}} = y\,\Delta x(\hat{\mathbf{i}} \times \hat{\mathbf{j}}) = y\,\Delta x\hat{\mathbf{k}}$

So, the direction of the field is in the + Z-direction.

3. (*b*) For a circular coil, the magnetic flux density at centre, $B = \dfrac{\mu_0 NI}{2r}$.

4. (*c*) $B = \dfrac{\mu_0}{4\pi}\dfrac{\pi i}{R} = 10^{-7} \times \dfrac{22 \times 12}{7 \times 2 \times 10^{-2}}$

$= 1.9 \times 10^{-4}$ T

Thus, $\mathbf{B}$ is 1.9×10^{-4} T normal to the plane of the paper going into it.

5. (*c*) Magnetic field at any point lying on the current-carrying straight conductor is zero.

Here, H_1 = magnetic field at M due to current in PQ

and H_2 = magnetic field at M due to QR + magnetic field at M due to QS + magnetic field at M due to PQ.

$$= 0 + \frac{H_1}{2} + H_1 = \frac{3}{2}H_1 \Rightarrow \frac{H_1}{H_2} = \frac{2}{3}$$

6. A current carrying wire produces magnetic field but wire which does not carry current has no magnetic field.

7. It can be justified by placing a magnetic needle around current carrying wire, which shows deflection of needle.

8. Magnetic field produced by a current conductor is

(i) Directly proportional to the current flowing through the conductor, length of the element and sine of the angle between the length of the element and line joining the element to the point **(1/2)**

(ii) Inversely proportional to the square of the distance between the element and the point. **(1/2)**

9. Refer to text on page 167. (Biot-Savart law). **(1)**

10. Biot-Savart's law is an angle dependent law. (1)

11. According to Biot-Savart's law, we can say that the direction of magnetic flux density at the point P due to the current flowing through the conductor XY is perpendicular to the plane of the paper directed into the page, as shown in the diagram.

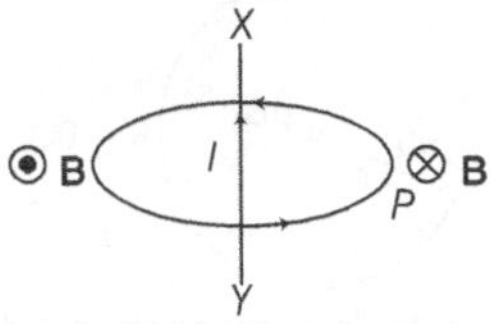

(1)

12. An infinitely long current carrying conductor produces magnetic field in the form of concentric circular loops in a plane of straight conductor. (1)

13. Magnetic field lines due to a current carrying loop is given by

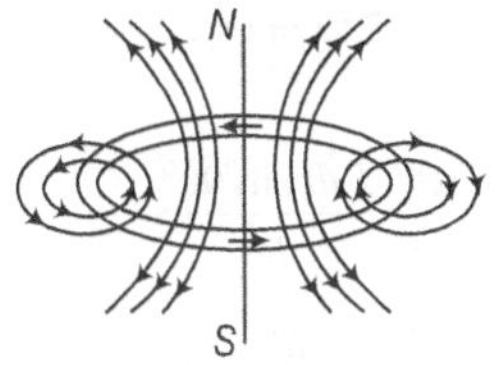

(1)

14. As, electron is revolving clockwise, therefore conventional current due to the motion of electron will be in anti-clockwise direction.

So, according to right hand rule, magnetic field at point A will be in outward direction.

15. Magnetic field due to loop APB at the centre is given by

$$B_1 = \frac{\mu_0 I}{4a} \odot$$

Magnetic field due to loop AQB at the centre is given by

$$B_2 = \frac{\mu_0 I}{4a} \odot \cdot$$

So, net magnetic field at centre $= B_1 + B_2 = 0$ (zero). (1)

16. Refer to text on page 167 (Magnetic field due to a current element : Biot-Savart's law). (2)

17. Refer to text on page 167 (Magnetic field due to a current element : Biot-Savart's law). (2)

18. Biot-Savart's law states that

$$d\mathbf{B} = \frac{\mu_0}{4\pi} \cdot \frac{Id\mathbf{l} \times \hat{\mathbf{r}}}{|\mathbf{r}|^2}$$

(1)

Here $\Delta x = w\,\text{cm}$

$\because$ $\Delta l = \Delta x i$

$\Rightarrow$ $I = 2\text{A}, r = 1 \text{ m}$

$\therefore$ $d\text{B} = \dfrac{\mu_0}{4\pi} \cdot \dfrac{(2w\hat{\text{i}} \times \hat{\text{j}})}{(1)^2}$

$Idl = 2 \times w\hat{\text{i}}$ (1/2)

$\because$ $\hat{\mathbf{r}} = \hat{\mathbf{j}}$

$\Rightarrow$ $|\mathbf{r}| = 1 \text{ m}$

$\therefore$ $d\mathbf{B} = \dfrac{\mu_0 w}{2\pi} \hat{\mathbf{k}} \Rightarrow |d\mathbf{B}| = \dfrac{\mu_0 w}{2\pi}$

and direction along $+Z$-axis. (1/2)

19. The magnitude of the magnetic field at point P,

$$B = \frac{\mu_0 I}{2a}$$

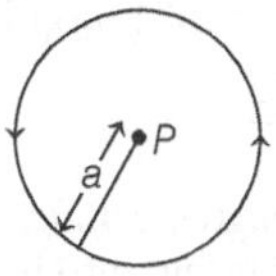

The field $\mathbf{B}$ is perpendicular to the plane of the coil, directed upward. (2)

20. (i) Inward (1)

(ii) Refer to text on page 170 (Magnetic field at the centre of a current carrying circular loop). (1)

21. According to the questions the wire will now look like.

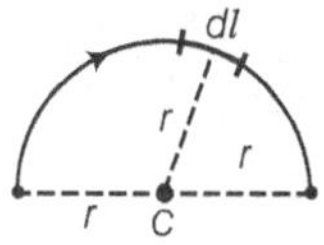

$\because$ Length L is bent into semi-circular loop.

$\therefore$ Length of wire = Circumference of semi-equal circular wire

$\Rightarrow$ $L = \pi r$

$\Rightarrow$ $r = \dfrac{L}{\pi}$ ...(i) (1/2)

Considering a small element dl on current loop. The magnetic field dB due to small current element Idl at centre C. Using Biot-Savart's law, we have

$$dB = \frac{\mu_0}{4\pi} \cdot \frac{Idl \sin 90°}{r^2} \quad [\because Idl \perp \mathbf{r}, \therefore \theta = 90°]$$ (1/2)

$$dB = \frac{\mu_0}{4\pi} \cdot \frac{Idl}{r^2}$$

$\therefore$ Net magnetic field at C due to semi-circular loop,

$$B = \int_{\text{semi-circle}} \frac{\mu_0}{4\pi} \frac{Idl}{r^2} = \frac{\mu_0}{4\pi} \frac{I}{r^2} \int_{\text{semi-circle}} dl$$ (1/2)

$$= \frac{\mu_0}{4\pi} \cdot \frac{I}{r^2} L \quad \left[\text{but } r = \frac{L}{\pi}\right]$$

$$= \frac{\mu_0}{4\pi} \cdot \frac{IL}{(L/\pi)^2} = \frac{\mu_0}{4\pi} \times \frac{IL}{L^2} \times \pi^2$$

$$= \frac{\mu_0 I\pi}{4L}$$

which is the required expression. (1/2)

22. When a straight wire is bent into the form of a circular coil of N turns, then the length of the wire is equal to circumference of the coil multiplied by the number of turns. Let the radius of coil be r.

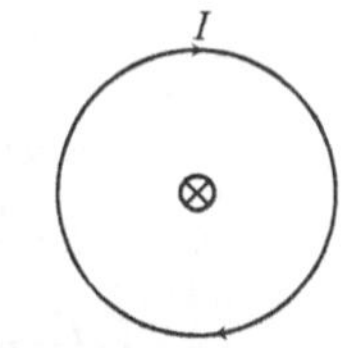

As, the wire is bent round in the form of a coil having N turns.

$\therefore$ $N \times$ circumference of the coil = Length of the wire

$\Rightarrow$ $(2\pi r) \times N = L$

$\Rightarrow$ $r = \dfrac{L}{2\pi N}$ ...(i)

Magnetic field at the centre due to N turns of a coil is given by

$$B = \frac{\mu_0 (NI)}{2r} = \frac{\mu_0 (NI)}{2\left(\frac{L}{2\pi N}\right)} \quad \text{[from Eq. (i)]}$$

$$= \frac{\mu_0 \pi N^2 I}{L} \quad (1½)$$

The direction of magnetic field is perpendicular to the plane of loop and entering into it. (1/2)

23. Magnetic field at O due to two loops will be in same direction ($Q \rightarrow P$, along the axis) and of equal magnitude. (1/2)

$$B = B_1 + B_2 \text{ but } B_2 = B_1$$

$$\Rightarrow \quad B = 2B_1 = 2\left[\frac{\mu_0 I r^2}{2(r^2 + r^2)^{3/2}}\right] \quad (1/2)$$

$$= \frac{\mu_0 I r^2}{(2r^2)^{3/2}} = \frac{\mu_0 I r^2}{2^{3/2} r^3} \quad (1/2)$$

$$= \frac{\mu_0 I}{2^{3/2} r} \quad (1/2)$$

24. Refer to text on page 169 (Magnetic field on the axis of a circular current carrying loop).

For magnetic filed lines, refer to solution 13 on page 175. (3)

25. Refer to text on pages 167 and 169 (Magnetic field due to a current element : Biot-Savart's law and magnetic field on the axis of a circular current carrying loop). (3)

26. Consider a circular coil of radius R and carrying a current I in the direction as shown in figure. Suppose, the entire circular coil is divided into a large number of current elements, each of length dl.

According to Biot-Savart's law, the magnetic field $d\mathbf{B}$ at the centre O of the coil due to the current element Idl is given by

$$\mathbf{B} = \frac{\mu_0}{4\pi} \frac{I(d\,l \times R)}{R^3} \quad (1)$$

The magnitude of $d\mathbf{B}$ at the centre O is

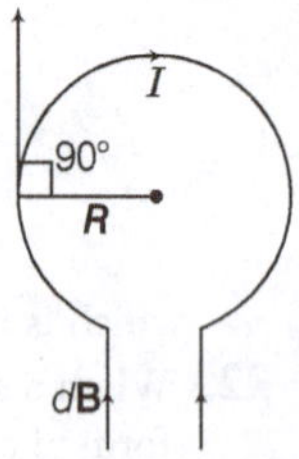

$$dB = \frac{\mu_0}{4\pi} \cdot \frac{Idl \times R\sin\theta}{R^3}$$

$$\Rightarrow \quad dB = \frac{\mu_0}{4\pi} \frac{Idl\sin\theta}{R^2}$$

$$\therefore \quad B = \int dB = \int \frac{\mu_0}{4\pi} \frac{Idl\sin\theta}{R^2}$$

$$\theta = 90° \Rightarrow \sin 90° = 1 \quad (1)$$

$$\therefore \quad B = \frac{\mu_0}{4\pi} \frac{1}{R^2} \int dl$$

$$\int dl = \text{total length of the coil} = 2\pi r$$

$$B = \frac{\mu_0}{4\pi} \frac{1}{R^2}(2\pi R) = \frac{\mu_0 I}{2R}$$

If the coil has N turns.

$$\therefore \quad B = \frac{\mu_0 NI}{2R} \quad (1)$$

27. Take a small current element in the circular coil and find B due to it. After that integrate it for whole length of the loop.

Consider a small element dl on circular coil of radius R carrying current I.

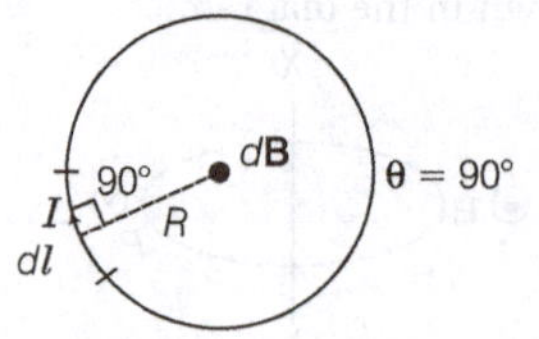

(1)

$\therefore$ By Biot-Savart's law, magnetic field at the centre due to element of coil,

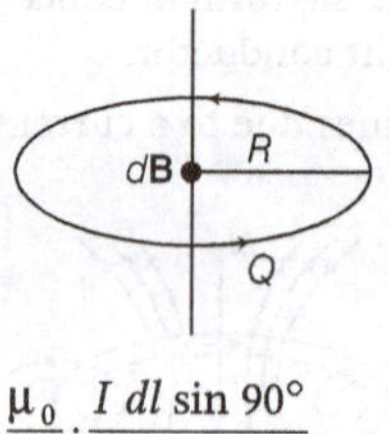

$$dB = \frac{\mu_0}{4\pi} \cdot \frac{I\,dl \sin 90°}{R^2}$$

$$\Rightarrow \quad dB = \frac{\mu_0}{4\pi} \cdot \frac{I}{R^2} dl \quad (1)$$

$$B = \oint \frac{\mu_0}{4\pi} \frac{I}{R^2} dl = \frac{\mu_0}{4\pi} \frac{I}{R^2} \oint dl = \frac{\mu_0}{4\pi} \frac{I}{R^2} \times 2\pi R$$

$$B = \frac{\mu_0 I}{2R} \quad [\because \oint dl = 2\pi R]$$

For N turns of coil $B = \frac{\mu_0 NI}{2R}$. (1)

28. Refer to text on pages 167 and 169 (Magnetic field due to a current element : Biot-Savart's law and magnetic field on the axis of a circular current carrying loop). (2)

Magnetic field at the axial point distance from the centre,

$$B_1 = \frac{\mu_0}{4\pi} \cdot \frac{2\pi a^2 I}{(a^2 + d^2)^{3/2}}$$

In this answer, put $r = d$.

Magnetic field induction at the centre of the circular coil carrying current is

$$B_2 = \frac{\mu_0}{4\pi} \cdot \frac{2\pi I}{a} \Rightarrow \frac{B_1}{B_2} = \frac{a^2 \times a}{(a^2 + d^2)^{3/2}}$$

$$= \frac{a^3}{(a^2 + d^2)^{3/2}} = \frac{a^3}{(a^2 + 3a^2)^{3/2}} \quad [\because d = a\sqrt{3}]$$

$$= \frac{a^3}{(4a^2)^{3/2}} = \frac{a^3}{8a^3} \Rightarrow \frac{B_1}{B_2} = \frac{1}{8} \quad (3)$$

29. The magnetic field at a point due to a circular loop is given by

$$B = \frac{\mu_0}{4\pi} \cdot \frac{2\pi I a^2}{(a^2 + r^2)^{3/2}} \quad (1)$$

where, I = current through the loop,

a = radius of the loop

and r = distance of O from the centre of the loop.

Since I, a and $r = x$ are the same for both the loops, the magnitude of B will be the same and is given by

$$B_1 = B_2 = \frac{\mu_0}{4\pi} \cdot \frac{2\pi I a^2}{(a^2 + x^2)^{3/2}} \quad (1)$$

The direction of magnetic field due to loop (1) will be away from O and that of the magnetic field due to loop (2) will be towards O as shown. The direction of the net magnetic field will be as shown below

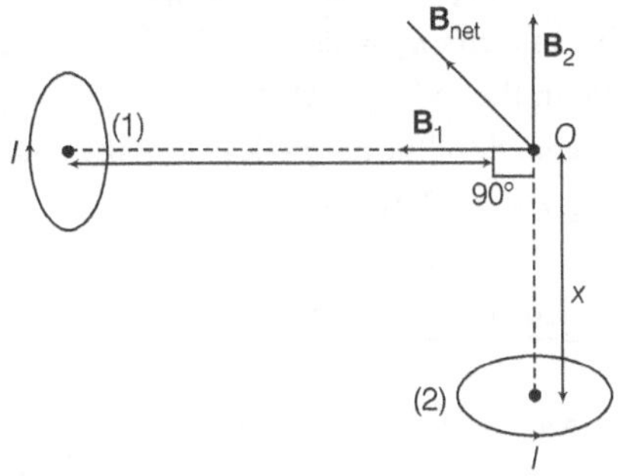

(2)

The magnitude of the net magnetic field is given by

$$B_{net} = \sqrt{B_1^2 + B_2^2} = \frac{\mu_0}{4\pi} \cdot \frac{2\pi \sqrt{2} I a^2}{(a^2 + x^2)^{3/2}} \quad (1)$$

30. Here, $I = 5$ A, $dl = 1$ cm $= 0.01$ m, $r = 1$ m, $\theta = 45°$

[∵ direction is North-East]

$$\therefore \quad dB = \frac{\mu_0}{4\pi} \cdot \frac{Idl \sin\theta}{r^2} = 10^{-7} \times \frac{5 \times 0.01 \times \sin 45°}{(1)^2} \quad (1)$$

$$= 3.54 \times 10^{-9} \text{ T}$$

Its direction is vertically downwards. (1)

31. Here, $dl = dx = 1$ cm $= 10^{-2}$ m

$I = 10$ A, $r = 0.5$ m

Using Biot-Savart's law,

$$d\mathbf{B} = \frac{\mu_0}{4\pi} \cdot \frac{Id\mathbf{l} \times \mathbf{r}}{r^3} \quad (1)$$

$$= \frac{\mu_0}{4\pi} \cdot \frac{Idx}{r^2}(\hat{\mathbf{i}} \times \hat{\mathbf{j}}) = \frac{\mu_0}{4\pi} \cdot \frac{Idx}{r^2}\hat{\mathbf{k}} \quad [\because \hat{\mathbf{i}} \times \hat{\mathbf{j}} = \hat{\mathbf{k}}]$$

$$= \frac{10^{-7} \times 10 \times 10^{-2}}{(0.5)^2}\hat{\mathbf{k}}$$

$$= 4 \times 10^{-8} \hat{\mathbf{k}} \text{ T} \quad (1)$$

32. Refer to example 1 on page 168. **[Ans.** 4×10^{-6} T]

33. (i) According to the question,

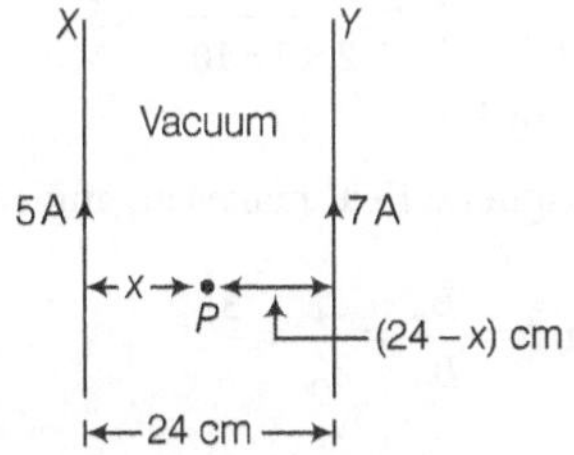

Let at point P, the magnetic flux density be zero.

So, magnetic field due to 5A wire at point P is

$$\frac{\mu_0 5}{2\pi x}(-\hat{\mathbf{k}}) \quad \text{... (i)}$$

Magnetic field due to 7A wire at point P is

$$\frac{\mu_0 7}{2\pi(24 - x)}(+\hat{\mathbf{k}}) \quad \text{... (ii)}$$

We know that, P is a neutral point, so from Eqs. (i) and (ii), we get

$$\frac{5\mu_0}{2\pi x} = \frac{7\mu_0}{2\pi(24 - x)}$$

$$\Rightarrow \quad \frac{5}{x} = \frac{7}{24 - x}$$

$$\Rightarrow \quad 120 - 5x = 7x \Rightarrow 12x = 120$$

$\Rightarrow x = 10$ cm (from current carrying wire X)

Thus, the position of a neutral point is 10 cm. (1½)

(ii) No, on reversing the current in the wire Y, neutral point will not lie between X and Y. It will lie on the left of wire X. (1½)

34. Given, $I = 10$ A, length of each wire = 44 cm

(i) Let r be the radius of wire A when it is bent into a circle.

$$\Rightarrow \quad 2\pi r = 44 \Rightarrow r = \frac{7}{100} \text{ m}$$

Magnetic field at the centre of the circular coil carrying current is given by

$$B = \frac{\mu_0}{4\pi} \cdot \frac{2\pi I}{r} = 10^{-7} \times 2 \times \frac{22}{7} \times 10 \times \frac{100}{7} = 9 \times 10^{-5} \text{ T}$$

When another wire is bent into a square of each side L, then

$$4L = 44 \Rightarrow L = 11 \text{cm} = 0.11 \text{m}$$

Since, magnetic field induction at a point, at perpendicular distance a from the linear conductor carrying current is given by

$$B = \frac{\mu_0 I}{4\pi a}(\sin\theta_1 + \sin\theta_2)$$

$$B = 4 \times \frac{\mu_0 I}{4\pi a}(\sin 45° + \sin 45°)$$

$$= 4 \times 10^{-7} \times \frac{10}{(11/100)}\left(\frac{1}{\sqrt{2}} + \frac{1}{\sqrt{2}}\right)$$

$$= 10.3 \times 10^{-5} \text{ T} \quad (2½)$$

(ii) The magnetic field due to a square will be more than that due to a circle of same perimeter. (1/2)

35. Magnetic field at the centre of tangent galvanometer is given by $B = \frac{\mu_0 NI}{2r}$

Given, $N = 50$, $r = 10$ cm, $I = 1$ A

Also, $\mu_0 = 4\pi \times 10^{-7}$ (1)

$$\text{So,} \quad B = \frac{4 \times 3.14 \times 10^{-7} \times 50 \times 1}{2 \times 0.1}$$

$$= 3.14 \times 10^{-4} \text{ T} \quad (1)$$

36. Refer to example 4 on page 170. **[Ans.** 6.28×10^{-4} T]

37. Here, $I = 10$ A, $r = 3$ cm, $r = 3 \times 10^{-2}$ m

Angle subtended by coil at the centre,

$$\theta = 360° - 90° = 270° = \frac{3\pi}{2} \text{ rad} \quad (1/2)$$

Magnetic field induction at O due to current through circular path ACB is

$$B = \frac{\mu_0}{4\pi} \cdot \frac{I}{r} \theta = 10^{-7} \times \frac{10}{(3 \times 10^{-2})} \times \frac{3\pi}{2} \quad (1½)$$

$$= 1.57 \times 10^{-4} \text{ T}$$

38. Magnetic field due to circular wire P,

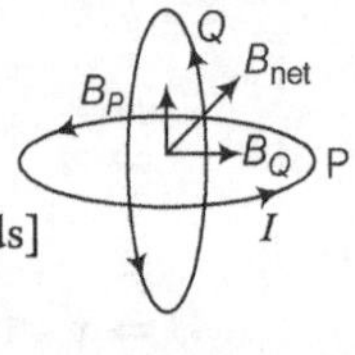

$$B_P = \frac{\mu_0}{4\pi} \times \frac{2\pi I_1}{R}$$

[along vertically upwards]

$$= \frac{\mu_0 I_1}{2R}$$

Magnetic field due to circular wire Q,

$$B_Q = \frac{\mu_0}{4\pi} \times \frac{2\pi I_2}{R} \quad \text{[along horizontal towards left]}$$

$$= \frac{\mu_0 I_2}{2R} \quad (1)$$

Net magnetic field at the common centre of the two coils,

$$B = \sqrt{B_P^2 + B_Q^2}$$

$$= \sqrt{\left(\frac{\mu_0 I_1}{2R}\right)^2 + \left(\frac{\mu_0 I_2}{2R}\right)^2} = \sqrt{\left(\frac{\mu_0}{2R}\right)^2 (I_1^2 + I_2^2)}$$

$$= \frac{\mu_0}{2R}\sqrt{I_1^2 + I_2^2} = \frac{4\pi \times 10^{-7}}{2 \times R}\sqrt{(1)^2 + (\sqrt{3})^2}$$

$$= \frac{4\pi \times 10^{-7}}{R} \text{ T}$$

Resultant magnetic field makes an angle θ with direction of B_Q, which is given by

$$\tan\theta = \frac{B_P}{B_Q} = \frac{1}{\sqrt{3}}$$

$\therefore$ $\theta = 30°$ (1)

39. (i) Magnetic field due to straight segment is

$$\mathbf{B} = \int \frac{\mu_0}{4\pi} \cdot \frac{I \, d\mathbf{l} \times \mathbf{r}}{r^3}$$

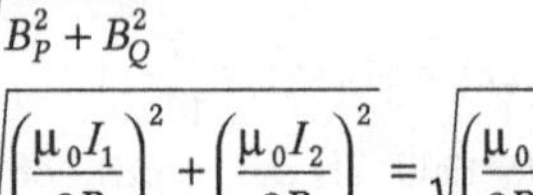

For point O, $d\mathbf{l}$ and $\mathbf{r}$ for each element of straight segments PQ and RS are parallel.

Therefore, $d\mathbf{l} \times \mathbf{r} = 0$.

Thus, magnetic field due to straight segment is zero. (2)

(ii) Magnetic field at centre O due to semi-circular arc

$$= \frac{\text{Magnetic field at centre of circular coil}}{2}$$

$$= \frac{1}{2}\left(\frac{\mu_0 I}{2r}\right) = \frac{\mu_0 I}{4r} = \frac{(4\pi \times 10^{-7}) \times 10}{4 \times 2 \times 10^{-2}}$$

[given, $I = 10$ A and $r = 2.0$ cm $= 2 \times 10^{-2}$ m]

$$= 5\pi \times 10^{-5} \text{ T} \quad (1)$$

40. **For coil x,**

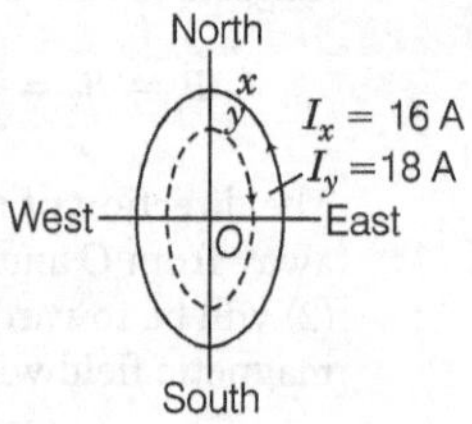

Radius of coil, $r_x = 16$ cm $= 0.16$m

Number of turns, $n_x = 20$

Current in the coil, $I_x = 16$ A (anti-clockwise)

For coil y,

Radius of coil, $r_y = 10$ cm $= 0.1$m

Number of turns, $n_y = 25$

Current in the coil, $I_y = 18$ A (clockwise)

The magnitude of the magnetic field at the centre of coil x,

$$B_x = \frac{\mu_0}{4\pi} \cdot \frac{2I_x \pi n_x}{r_x}$$

$$= \frac{10^{-7} \times 2 \times 16 \times \pi \times 20}{0.16}$$

$$= 4\pi \times 10^{-4} \text{T} \quad (1)$$

The direction of magnetic field due to the coil x at centre O is towards right, i.e. East, according to right hand thumb rule. The magnitude of the magnetic field at the centre of coil y, (1/2)

$$B_y = \frac{\mu_0}{4\pi} \cdot \frac{2\pi I_y n_y}{r_y}$$

$$= \frac{10^{-7} \times 2 \times \pi \times 18 \times 25}{0.1}$$

$$= 9\pi \times 10^{-4} \text{T} \quad (1/2)$$

The direction of magnetic field due to coil y at centre O is towards left, i.e. West, according to right hand thumb rule. Here, the magnitude of B_y is greater than B_x, so the resultant magnetic field will be in the direction of B_y, i.e. left (West). (1)

Net magnetic field at the centre,

$$B = B_y - B_x$$

$$= (9\pi - 4\pi) 10^{-4} \text{T}$$

$$= 5\pi \times 10^{-4} \text{T}$$

[$\because$ B_y and B_x are opposite to each other]

$= 1.6 \times 10^{-3}$ T [towards West] (1)

41. $$B_{net} = \sqrt{B_P^2 + B_Q^2} = \sqrt{\left(\frac{\mu_0 i_P}{2r}\right)^2 + \left(\frac{\mu_0 i_Q}{2r}\right)^2} \quad (1)$$

$$= \frac{\mu_0}{2r}\sqrt{i_P^2 + i_Q^2} = \frac{4\pi \times 10^{-7}}{2 \times 5 \times 10^{-2}} \times 5$$

$$= 2\pi \times 10^{-5} \text{ T} \quad (1)$$

Resultant magnetic field makes an angle θ with B_Q which is given by,

$$\tan\phi = \frac{B_P}{B_Q} = \frac{i_P}{i_Q} = \frac{3}{4} \quad (1)$$

TOPIC 02 Ampere's Circuital Law and Moving Charges

Ampere's Circuital Law

According to this law, the line integral of a magnetic field **B** around any closed path in vacuum is μ_0 times the net current I_{net} enclosed by the curve.

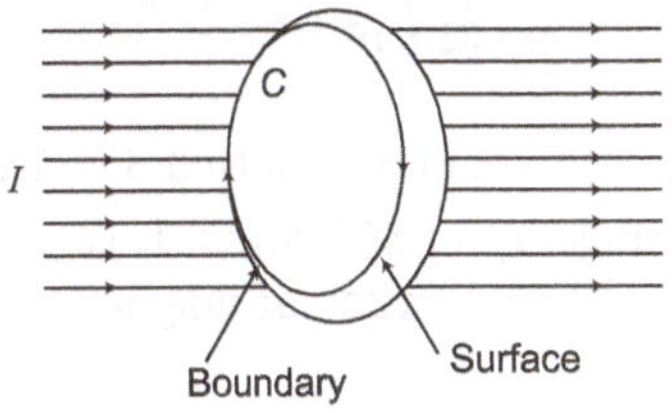

Mathematically, $\oint \mathbf{B} \cdot d\mathbf{l} = \mu_0 I_{net}$

Ampere's law is applicable only for an Amperian loop as the Gauss's law is used for Gaussian surface in electrostatics.

The choice of an Amperian loop has to be such that, at each point of the loop either

(i) **B** is tangential to the loop and is a non-zero constant
(ii) **B** is normal to the loop
(iii) **B** vanishes

Ampere's circuital law has same content as the Biot-Savart's law. Both of these relate magnetic field and current and express the same physical consequences of a steady electrical current. Ampere's circuital law holds for any loop but does not always facilitate. Ampere's circuital law can be conveniently applied in situations of high symmetry. e.g. To find magnetic field of a straight wire, magnetic field of solenoid and toroid as discussed in coming sections.

Magnitude of Magnetic Field of a Infinite Long Straight Wire using Ampere's Circuital Law

Magnetic field due to a straight conductor at a point P at a distance (r) is in the form of a circle of radius (r) which is taken as closed path for Amperian loop. Angle between **B** and $d\mathbf{l}$ is zero, everywhere in this path. Hence, on applying Ampere's law to this closed path, we get

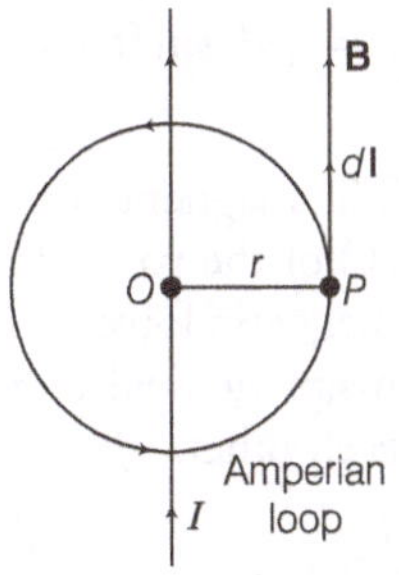

$$\oint \mathbf{B} \cdot d\mathbf{l} = \mu_0 I$$

or $$\oint B\, dl \cos 0° = \mu_0 I$$

$\Rightarrow$ $$B \oint dl = \mu_0 I$$

$\Rightarrow$ $$B \times 2\pi r = \mu_0 I \text{ or } \boxed{B = \frac{\mu_0 I}{2\pi r}}$$

Example 1 A straight wire carries a current of 3 A. Calculate the magnitude of the magnetic field at a point 15 cm away from the wire.

Sol. Here, current, $I = 3$ A, point where magnetic field is to be determined, $a = 15$ cm $= 0.15$ m

$\therefore$ Magnitude of magnetic field, $B = \dfrac{\mu_0 2I}{4\pi a}$

$$= \frac{10^{-7} \times 2 \times 3}{0.15} = 4 \times 10^{-6} \text{ T}$$

Solenoid

A **solenoid** is an insulated long wire closely wound in the form of a helix. Its length is very long as compared to its diameter. Solenoid and toroid are two equipments which are used to produce magnetic fields.

In television, we make use of solenoid to generate magnetic field needed for the deflection of electrons in picture tube.

Magnetic Field of a Solenoid

A long coil of wire consisting of closely packed loops is called solenoid, whose magnetic field resembles that of a bar magnet of south(S) and north(N) poles as shown in the figure given below.

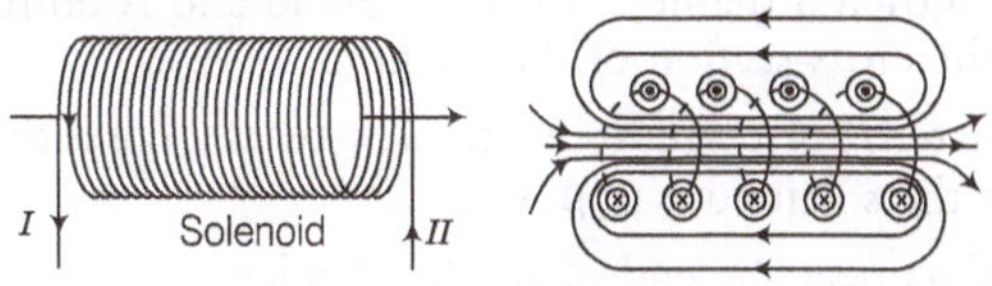

Magnetic field of a solenoid

Inside the solenoid, magnetic field is uniform and parallel to the solenoid axis. Outside the solenoid, magnetic field is assumed to be zero.

Consider an air cored solenoid having closely packed coils in which I is current, n is number of turns per unit length and B is magnetic field inside the solenoid.

Applying Ampere's circuital law to determine magnetic field (**B**) inside the solenoid, we choose rectangular closed path *PQRS*, where $PQ = L$ and the line integral of **B** over closed path *PQRS* is

$$\oint_{PQRS} \mathbf{B}\cdot d\mathbf{l} = \int_P^Q \mathbf{B}\cdot d\mathbf{l} + \int_Q^R \mathbf{B}\cdot d\mathbf{l} + \int_R^S \mathbf{B}\cdot d\mathbf{l} + \int_S^P \mathbf{B}\cdot d\mathbf{l}$$

Now, $\int_Q^R \mathbf{B}\cdot d\mathbf{l} = \int_S^P \mathbf{B}\cdot d\mathbf{l} = 0$

[because along *QR* and *PS*, the field *B* is at right angles to dl, so that $\mathbf{B}\cdot d\mathbf{l} = Bdl\cos 90° = 0$]

$\int_R^S \mathbf{B}\cdot d\mathbf{l} = 0$ [$\because$ **B** is zero at points outside the solenoid]

$$\therefore \oint_{PQRS} \mathbf{B}\cdot d\mathbf{l} = \int_P^Q \mathbf{B}\cdot d\mathbf{l} = \int_P^Q B\,dl\cos 0° = \int_P^Q B\,dl = BL$$

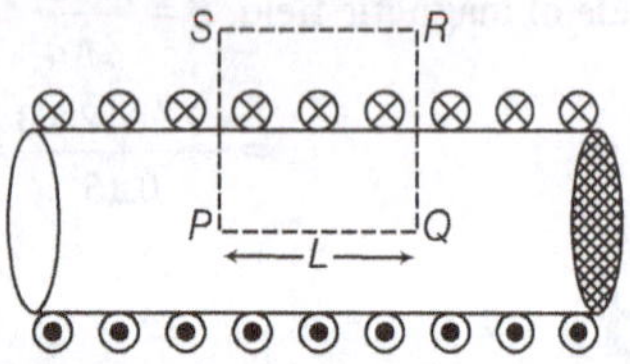

Hence, from Ampere's law,

$$\oint_{PQRS} \mathbf{B}\cdot d\mathbf{l} = \mu_0 \times (\text{current enclosed by } PQRS)$$

Here, number of turns per unit length is *n*, the number of turns in length *L* is *nL*. The current in each turn is *I*, so net current enclosed by the loop is *nLI*.

Total current, $I_{net} = nLI$

$$\therefore \oint_{PQRS} \mathbf{B}\cdot d\mathbf{l} = \mu_0 \times nIL$$

$$\Rightarrow BL = \mu_0 nIL$$

$$\Rightarrow \boxed{B = \mu_0 nI}$$

From the expression, it is clear that *B* is independent of the length and diameter of the solenoid and is uniform over the cross-section of the solenoid.

If a material of permeability μ_r is used as a core, then *B* inside the solenoid is $\mu_0\mu_r n I$.

At points near the end of air closed solenoid,

$$\boxed{B = \frac{1}{2}\mu_0 nI}$$

Note The formula for magnetic field $B = \mu_0 nI$ is only valid when length of the solenoid (l) is much larger than its radius(r), i.e. $l >> r$.

Example 2 The length of a solenoid is 0.2 m and it has 120 turns. Find the magnetic field in its interior, if a current of 2.5 A is flowing through it.

Sol. Here, $l = 0.2$ m, $N = 120$, $I = 2.5$A

Magnetic field in the interior of the solenoid,

$$B = \mu_0 nI = \mu_0 \frac{N}{l} I$$

$$= 4\pi \times 10^{-7} \times \frac{120}{0.2} \times 2.5$$

$$= 1.85 \times 10^{-3} \text{ T}$$

Example 3 A solenoid of length 0.5 m has a radius of 1 cm and is made up of 500 turns. It carries a current of 5 A. What is the magnitude of magnetic field inside the solenoid? **NCERT**

Sol. Given, total number of turns, $N = 500$

Length of solenoid, $l = 0.5$ m

Current, $I = 5$ A

and radius $r = 1 \text{ cm} = 10^{-2}$ m

Here, $\frac{l}{r} = \frac{0.5}{10^{-2}} = 50 \Rightarrow l >> r$

$$\therefore B = \mu_0 nI = \frac{\mu_0 NI}{l} = 4\pi \times 10^{-7} \times \frac{500}{0.5} \times 5$$

$$= 6.28 \times 10^{-3} \text{T}$$

Force on a Moving Charge in a Uniform Magnetic Field

When a charged particle (q) moves with velocity (**v**) inside a uniform magnetic field **B**, then force acting on it is $\mathbf{F} = q(\mathbf{v} \times \mathbf{B})$

Force due to magnetic field depends on q, **v**, **B**. The magnetic force will be zero, if the particle is at rest. The reason is that for the charged particle at rest $|\mathbf{v}| = 0$, which will turn the expression for magnetic force, $q(\mathbf{v} \times \mathbf{B})$, into zero. Only moving charges feel the magnetic force.The magnetic force is at its maximum value, when **v** and **B** are perpendicular to each other because in this case the angle $\theta = 90°$, in the expression $F = qvB\sin\theta$ and the maximum force will be

$$F_{max} = qvB\sin 90° = qvB \qquad [\because \sin 90° = 1]$$

The magnetic force includes the cross product of velocity (**v**) of the particle and magnetic field (**B**). Thus, the magnetic force will be zero, if the velocity vector and magnetic field vector are either parallel or anti-parallel to each other.

The force ($F_{magnetic}$) acting on a charged particle moving with velocity (**v**) through a magnetic field (**B**) is always perpendicular to **v** and **B**.

From right hand thumb rule, the force F is perpendicular to velocity (v) and magnetic field (**B**). Hence, it changes its path continuously.

Motion of a Charge in Magnetic Field

In case of motion of a charge in a magnetic field, the magnetic force is perpendicular to the velocity of the particle. So, no work is done and no change in the magnitude of the velocity is produced.

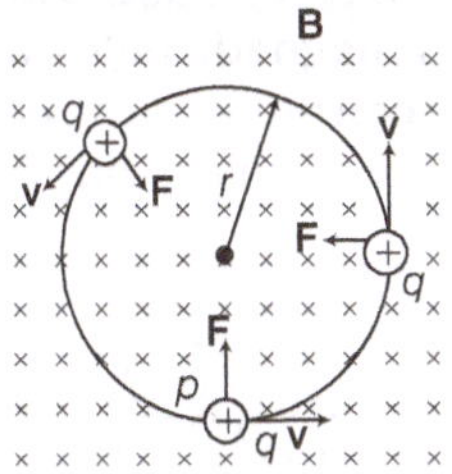

Circular motion

Magnetic force acts as a centripetal force and produces a circular motion perpendicular to the magnetic field. If **v** and **B** are perpendicular to each other, then particle will describe a circle.

As, centripetal force required for circular motion is provided by magnetic force, so

$$\frac{mv_{\perp}^2}{r} = qBv_{\perp} \text{ or } \boxed{r = \frac{mv_{\perp}}{qB} = \frac{p}{qB}} \quad \text{...(i)}$$

where, m = mass of charged particle

and r = radius of circular path.

where, $\mathbf{v}_{\perp}$ and $\mathbf{v}_{\parallel}$ are perpendicular and parallel components of the velocity **v**.

Radius of the path of the charged particle is proportional to the momentum ($p = mv$) of the particle and inversely proportional to the magnitude of charge (q) and magnetic field (B).

In terms of kinetic energy (K), the equation may be expressed as, $\boxed{r = \frac{\sqrt{2mK}}{qB}}$ $\quad [\because p = \sqrt{2mK}]$

Time period (T) of the motion of a charge is given by

$$T = \frac{2\pi r}{v} = \frac{2\pi}{v} \times \frac{mv}{qB}$$

or $$\boxed{T = \frac{2\pi m}{qB}} \quad \text{...(ii)}$$

Angular frequency, $\omega = \frac{2\pi}{T} = \frac{Bq}{m}$

Frequency, $\nu = \frac{Bq}{2\pi m}$ $\quad [\because \omega = 2\pi\nu]$

The angular speed ω of the particle is given by

$$\omega = v/r \text{ or } \omega = (qB)/m$$

Helical Motion

If a charged particle has a velocity not perpendicular to **B**, then component of velocity along **B** remains unchanged as the motion along the magnetic field will not be affected by the magnetic field. Then, the motion of the particle in a plane perpendicular to **B** is as before a circular one, thereby producing a helical motion.

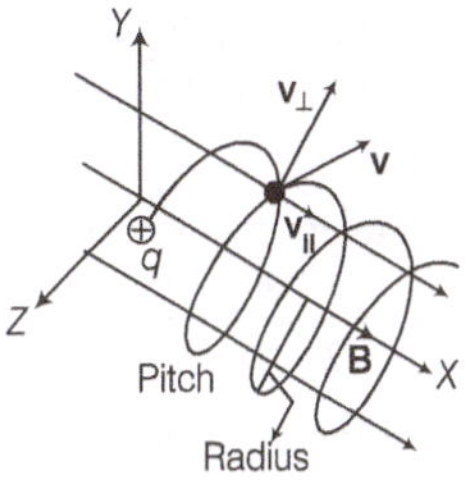

Helical motion

For helical path, the distance moved along the magnetic field in one rotation is called **pitch** (P).

$$\boxed{P = v_{\parallel} T = \frac{2\pi m v_{\parallel}}{qB}}$$

Note One tesla (1 T) is defined as the field which produces a force of one newton (1 N) when a charge of one coulomb (1 C) moves perpendicularly in the region of the magnetic field at a velocity of
1 ms^{-1}

Example 4 **A proton and an α-particle, accelerated through same potential difference, enter in a region of uniform magnetic field with their velocities perpendicular to the field. Compare the radii of circular paths followed by them.**

Sol. Let mass of proton = m, charge of proton = e

Now, mass of α-particle = 4 m, charge of α-particle = $2e$

When a charge q is accelerated by V volts, it acquires a kinetic energy $E_K = qV$

$\therefore$ Momentum is given by $mv = \sqrt{2mE_K} = \sqrt{2mqV}$

Radius, $r = \frac{mv}{qB}$ or $r = \frac{\sqrt{2mqV}}{qB} = \sqrt{\frac{2mV}{qB^2}}$

Thus, $\frac{r_p}{r_\alpha} = \sqrt{\frac{2mV}{eB^2}} \times \sqrt{\frac{2eB^2}{2(4m)V}} = \frac{1}{\sqrt{2}}$

Example 5 A beam of protons with a velocity of 4×10^5 ms^{-1} enters in a region of uniform magnetic field of 0.3 T. The velocity makes an angle of 60° with the magnetic field. Find the radius of the helical path taken by the proton beam and the pitch of the helix.

Sol. Velocity component along the field

$$v_{\|} = 4 \times 10^5 \times \cos 60°$$
$$= 2 \times 10^5 \text{ ms}^{-1}$$

and velocity component perpendicular to the field.

$$v_{\perp} = (4 \times 10^5) \sin 60°$$
$$= 2\sqrt{3} \times 10^5 \text{ ms}^{-1}$$

Proton will describe a circle in plane perpendicular to magnetic field with radius,

$$r = \frac{mv_{\perp}}{qB} = \frac{(1.67 \times 10^{-27} \text{ kg}) \times (2\sqrt{3} \times 10^5 \text{ ms}^{-1})}{(1.6 \times 10^{-19} \text{C}) \times (0.3 \text{ T})}$$
$$= 1.2 \text{ cm}$$

Time taken to complete one revolution is

$$T = \frac{2\pi r}{v_{\perp}} = \frac{2 \times 3.14 \times 0.012}{2\sqrt{3} \times 10^5} \text{ s}$$

Because of $v_{\|}$ protons will also move in the direction of magnetic field.

$\therefore$ Pitch of helix $= v_{\|} \times T$

$$= \frac{2 \times 10^5 \times 2 \times 3.14 \times 0.012}{2\sqrt{3} \times 10^5} \text{ m}$$
$$= 0.044 \text{ m}$$
$$= 4.4 \text{ cm}$$

Force on a Moving Charge in a Uniform Magnetic and Electric Field (Lorentz Force)

Suppose a point charge (q) is moving in the presence of both electric and magnetic fields. Let q be the magnitude of the charge, v be velocity of the point charge, B be the magnetic field and E be the electric field. We have studied two kinds of forces that can be exerted on an electrically charged particle.The electric force is given by $\mathbf{F} = q\mathbf{E}$ and the magnetic force is $\mathbf{F} = q(\mathbf{v} \times \mathbf{B})$.

The sum of these forces represents the net force that can be exerted on a particle due to its electric charge (q), this sum is called the Lorentz force and is given by

$$\mathbf{F}_{\text{Lorentz}} = \mathbf{F}_{\text{electric}} + \mathbf{F}_{\text{magnetic}}$$
$$= q\mathbf{E} + q(\mathbf{v} \times \mathbf{B})$$
$$= q[\mathbf{E} + (\mathbf{v} \times \mathbf{B})]$$

Force on negative charge is opposite to that of positive charge.

Topic Practice 2

Multiple Choice Questions

1 Mark

1. A moving electron centres a uniform and perpendicular magnetic field. Inside the magnetic field, the electron travels along **ISC 2015**

(a) a straight line (b) a parabola
(c) a circle (d) a hyperbola

2. In the given figure, E and B are magnitudes of electric and magnetic fields which are acting on a moving electron as shown. The direction of velocity of electron is along X-axis.

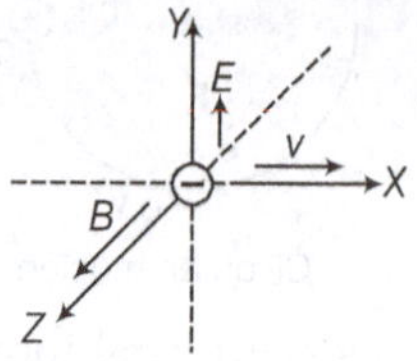

Then, force on electron is given by

(a) $\mathbf{F} = q(E + vB)\,\hat{\mathbf{j}}$ (b) $\mathbf{F} = q(E - vB)\,\hat{\mathbf{j}}$
(c) $\mathbf{F} = q(E + vB)\,\hat{\mathbf{k}}$ (d) $\mathbf{F} = q(E - vB)\,\hat{\mathbf{k}}$

3. An electron moves straight inside a charged parallel plate capacitor. Plates of capacitor have charge density σ. The space between plates is filled with constant magnetic field of induction **B**.

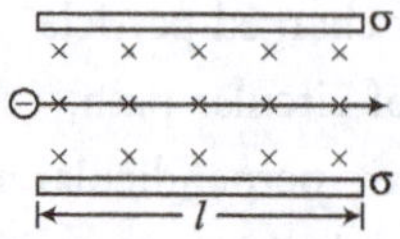

Time taken by electron to pass through the region is

(a) $\frac{e\sigma}{\varepsilon_0 lB}$ (b) $\frac{\varepsilon_0 lB}{\sigma}$ (c) $\frac{\sigma e}{\varepsilon_0 B}$ (d) $\frac{\varepsilon_0 B}{e\sigma}$

4. Lorentz force in vector form is **ISC 2024**

(a) $F = Bqv\sin\theta$ (b) $\mathbf{F} = q(\mathbf{v} \times \mathbf{B})$
(c) $\mathbf{F} = q(\mathbf{B} \times \mathbf{v})$ (d) $\mathbf{F} = \mathbf{v}(q \times \mathbf{B})$

Very Short Answer Type Questions

1 Mark

5. State Ampere's circuital law. **ISC 2005**

6. Magnetic field lines can be entirely confined within the core of toroid, but not within a straight solenoid. Why?

7. A charged particle enters an environment of a strong and non-uniform magnetic field varying from point to point both in magnitude and direction, and comes out of it following a complicated trajectory. Would its final speed equal to the initial speed, if it suffered no collisions with the environment? **NCERT**

8. When does a moving charged particle not experience any force while moving through a uniform magnetic field? **ISC 2014**

9. Write an expression for the Lorentz force **F** in vector form. **ISC 2016**

Short Answer Type I Questions

(2 Marks)

10. An electric current I flows through an infinitely long conductor as shown in the figure. Write an expression and direction for the magnetic field at point P. **ISC 2019**

11. A long solenoid of length L having N turns carries a current I. Deduce the expression for the magnetic field in the interior of the solenoid.

12. Define one tesla using the expression for the magnetic force acting on a particle of charge q moving with velocity v in a magnetic field **B**.

13. A particle of charge q and mass m is moving with velocity v. It is subjected to a uniform magnetic field B directed perpendicular to its velocity. Show that it describes a circular path. Write the expression for its radius.

14. Show that the radius of a charged particle entering perpendicularly in a magnetic field is directly proportional to its momentum. **ISC 2004**

15. A charge q moving along the X-axis with a velocity **v** is subjected to a uniform magnetic field **B** acting along the Z-axis as it crosses the origin O.
    (i) Trace trajectory.
    (ii) Does the charged particle gain kinetic energy as it enters the magnetic field? Justify your answer.

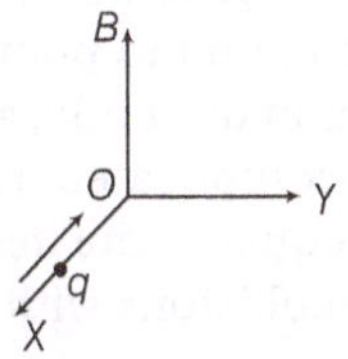

16. Write an expression in the vector form for the Lorentz magnetic force **F** due to a charge moving with velocity **v** in a magnetic field **B**. What is the direction of the magnetic force?

17. Write an expression for Lorentz magnetic force on a particle of charge q moving with velocity v in a magnetic field **B**. Show that no work is done by this force on the charged particle.

18. Find the condition under which the charged particles moving with different speeds in the presence of electric and magnetic field vectors can be used to select charged particles of a particular speed.

19. A point charge is moving with a constant velocity perpendicular to a uniform magnetic field as shown in the figure. What should be magnitude and direction of the electric field so that the particle moves undeviated along the same path?

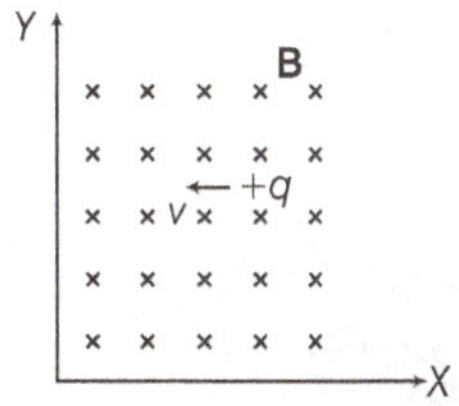

Short Answer Type II Questions

(3 Marks)

20. Using Ampere's circuital law or Biot-Savart's law, show that magnetic flux density B at a point P at a perpendicular distance a from a long current carrying conductor is given by

$$B = \left(\frac{\mu_0}{4\pi}\right)\frac{2I}{a}$$

[Statement of the laws not required] **ISC 2011, 05**

Or Using Ampere's circuital law, obtain an expression for magnetic flux density B at a point near an infinitely long and straight conductor, carrying a current I. **ISC 2023**

21. Explain, how Biot-Savart's law enables one to express the Ampere's circuital law in the integral form, *viz.*

$$\oint \mathbf{B} \cdot d\mathbf{l} = \mu_0 I$$

where, I is the total current passing through the surface.

22. A long straight solid metal wire of radius R carries a current I uniformly distributed over its circular cross-section. Find the magnetic field at a distance r from the axis of wire
(i) inside
(ii) outside the wire.

23. (i) State Ampere's circuital law expressing it in the integral form.
(ii) Two long coaxial insulated solenoids, S_1 and S_2 of equal lengths are wound one over the other as shown in the figure. A steady current I flows through the inner solenoid S_1 to the other end B, which is connected to the outer solenoid S_2 through which the same current I flows in the opposite direction, so as to come out at end A. If n_1 and n_2 are the number of turns per unit length, find the magnitude and direction of the net magnetic field at a point (a) inside on the axis and (b) outside the combined system.

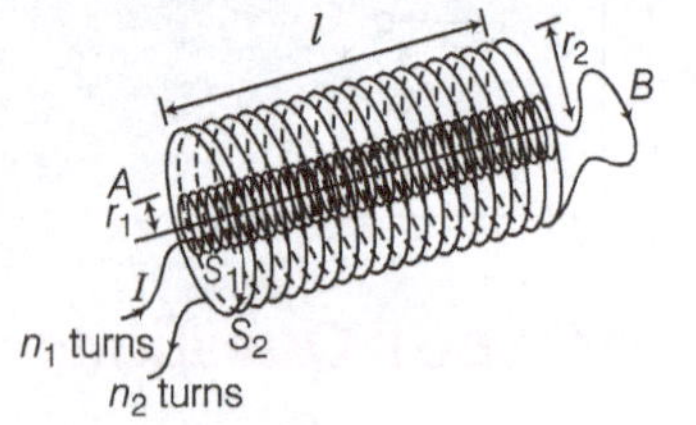

24. (i) Write an expression for the force **F** acting on a particle of mass m and charge q moving with velocity **v** in a magnetic field **B**.
Under what conditions will it move in (a) a circular path (b) a helical path?
(ii) Show that the kinetic energy of the particle moving in magnetic field remains constant.

25. (i) Write an expression for the magnetic force **F** acting on a charged particle q moving with velocity **v** in the presence of magnetic field **B**.
(ii) A neutron, an electron and an alpha particle moving with equal velocities, enter a uniform magnetic field going into the plane of the paper as shown in the figure. Trace their paths in the field and justify your answer.

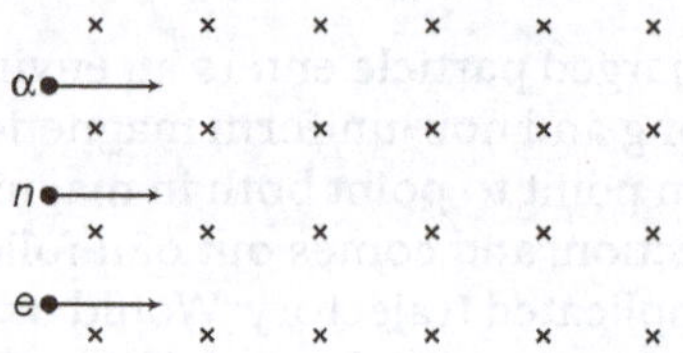

26. A uniform magnetic field **B** is set up along the positive X-axis. A particle of charge q and mass m moving with a velocity v enters the field at the origin in XY-plane such that it has velocity components both along and perpendicular to the magnetic field **B**. Trace, giving reason, the trajectory followed by the particle. Find out the expression for the distance moved by the particle along the magnetic field in one rotation.

Long Answer Type Questions

5 Marks

27. (i) Using Ampere's circuital law, derive the expression for the magnetic field in the vector from at a point on the axis of a solenoid.
(ii) An electron and a proton moving with the same speed enter the same magnetic field region at right angles to the direction of the field. Show the trajectory followed by the two particles in the magnetic field. Find the ratio of the radii of the circular paths which the particles may describe.

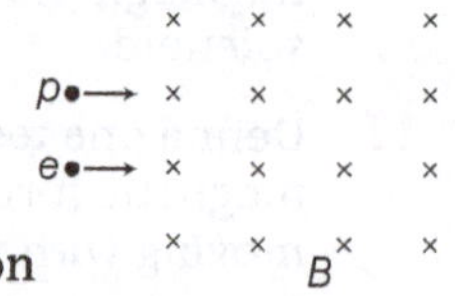

28. Answer the following questions.
(i) A magnetic field that varies in magnitude from point to point but has a constant direction (East to West) is set up in a chamber. A charged particle enters the chamber and travels undeflected along a straight path with constant speed. What can you say about the initial velocity of the particle?
(ii) A charged particle enters an environment of a strong and non-uniform magnetic field varying from point to point both in magnitude and direction, and comes out of it following a complicated trajectory. Would its final speed equal to the initial speed, if it suffered no collisions with the environment?

(iii) An electron travelling West to East enters a chamber having a uniform electrostatic field in North to South direction. Specify the direction in which a uniform magnetic field should be set up to prevent the electron from deflecting its straight line path. **NCERT**

Numerical Problems

29. (i) Using Ampere's circuital law, obtain an expression for the magnetic flux density B at a point X at a perpendicular distance r from a long current carrying conductor. (Statement of the law is not required).

(ii) PQ is a long straight conductor carrying a current of 3A as shown in figure below. An electron moves with a velocity of $2 \times 10^7\ ms^{-1}$ parallel to it. Find the force acting on the electron.

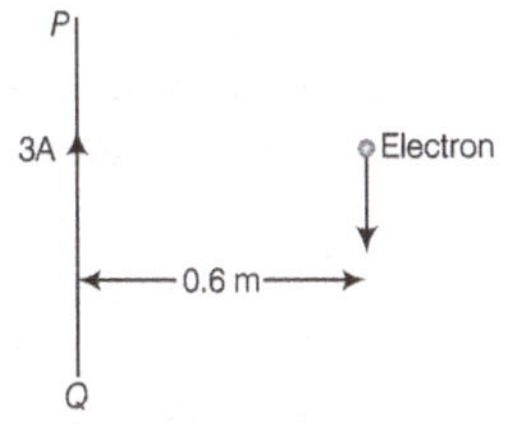

ISC 2017 (3 M)

30. A solenoid of length 50 cm having 100 turns carries a current of 2.5 A. Find the magnetic field (i) in the interior of the solenoid, (ii) at one end of the solenoid. **(2 M)**

31. A solenoid of length 1.0 m and 3.0 cm diameter has 5 layers of windings of 850 turns each and carries a current of 5 A. What is the magnetic field at the centre of solenoid? Also, calculate the magnetic flux from a cross-section of the magnetic flux solenoid at the centre of solenoid. **(2 M)**

32. A magnetic field of 100 G ($1\ G = 10^{-4}$T) is required which is uniform in a region of linear dimension about 10 cm and area of cross-section about $10^{-3}\ m^2$. The maximum current carrying capacity of a given coil of wire is 15 A and the number of turns per unit length that can be wound round a core is at most 1000 turns m^{-1}. Suggest some appropriate design particulars of a solenoid for the required purpose. Assume the core is not ferromagnetic. **NCERT (3 M)**

33. An electron of energy 2000 eV describes a circular path in magnetic field of flux density 0.2 T. What is the radius of path?
Take, $e = 1.6 \times 10^{-19}$ C, $m = 9 \times 10^{-31}$ kg. **(2 M)**

34. An electron beam passes through a region in which a magnetic field of 2×10^{-3} T and an electric field 3.4×10^4 V/m both acting simultaneously at right angles to each other. If the path of the electron remains undeflected, calculate the speed of the electrons. If the electric field is removed, what will be the radius of the circular path of electrons? **ISC 2002 (4 M)**

35. An electron moving with a velocity of $5 \times 10^7\ ms^{-1}$, enters in a magnetic field of $1\ Wb\ m^{-2}$ at an angle of 30°. Calculate the force on the electron. **ISC 2006, 01 (2 M)**

36. An electron is moving vertically upwards in the uniform magnetic field of the Earth. The velocity of the electron is 2.0×10^6 m/s and the horizontal component of the Earth's magnetic field is 0.32×10^{-4} T. Obtain the magnitude and direction of the force on the electron.

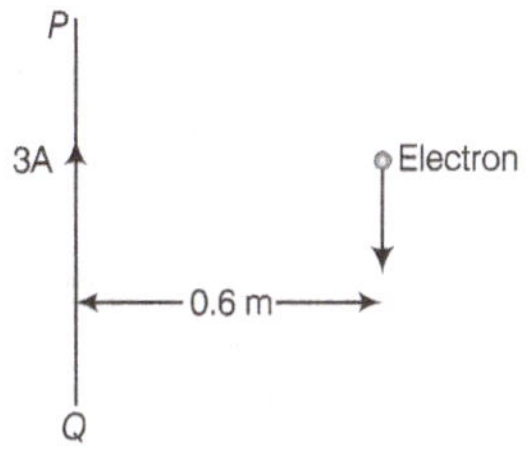

ISC 2000 (2 M)

37. A long straight wire AB carries a current of 5A. P is a proton travelling with a velocity of 2×10^6 m/s, parallel to the wire, 0.2 m from it and in a direction opposite to the current, as shown in figure below. Calculate the force which magnetic field of the current carrying conductor AB exerts on the proton. **ISC 2023**

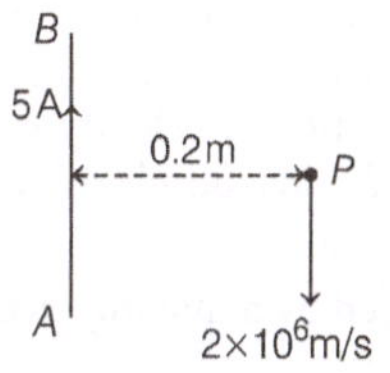

(2 M)

Hints & Solutions

1. (c) According to right hand thumb rule, the electron travels along a circle. Since, the right hand thumb rule states that, when a force is perpendicular to velocity and hence it changes. Its path continuously and this force acts as a centripetal force and produces a circular motion perpendicular to the magnetic field.

2. (b)

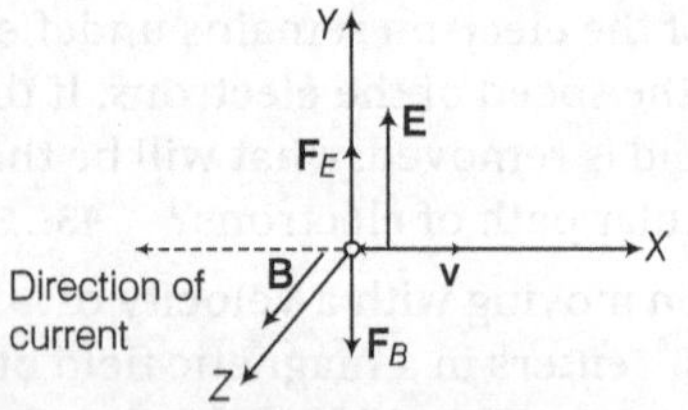

When electric and magnetic fields are perpendicular to each other.

So, $\mathbf{F}_E = q\mathbf{E} = qE\,\hat{\mathbf{j}}$, $\mathbf{F}_B = q\mathbf{v}\times\mathbf{B}$

$$= q(v\hat{\mathbf{i}} \times B\hat{\mathbf{k}}) = -qv\hat{\mathbf{j}} \qquad (\because\ \hat{\mathbf{i}}\times\hat{\mathbf{k}} = -\hat{\mathbf{j}})$$

Therefore, force on electron is given by

$$\mathbf{F} = q(E - vB)\hat{\mathbf{j}}$$

3. (b) Velocity of a particle, $v = \dfrac{E}{B} = \dfrac{\sigma}{\varepsilon_0 B}$

$\therefore$ Time taken by electron to pass through the region,

$$t = \frac{l}{v} = \frac{l\varepsilon_0 B}{\sigma}$$

4. (b) Expression for Lorentz force is given as

$$\mathbf{F} = q(\mathbf{v}\times\mathbf{B})$$

where, q is charge of the particle, **v** is velocity of the particle,

and **B** is the magnetic field in which the particle is moving.

5. Refer to text on page 179 (Ampere's circuital law).

6. The magnetic field lines always form closed loops. As, the turns of the wires in a toroidal solenoid are wound over its core in circular form, the field lines are confined within the core of toroid. In a straight solenoid, the magnetic field lines cannot form closed loops within the solenoid.

7. Yes, the final speed is equal to its initial speed as the magnetic force acting on the charged particle only changes the direction of velocity of charged particle but cannot change the magnitude of velocity of charged particle.

8. Force experienced by a moving charged particle is $|\mathbf{F}| = qvB\sin\theta$

where, θ = angle between **v** and **B**.

$$|\mathbf{F}| = 0 \Rightarrow qvB\sin\theta = 0$$

$$\therefore \qquad \theta = 0 \text{ or } \pi$$

So, for the angle $\theta = 0$ or π force experienced by moving charge is zero.

9. In vector form, expression for Lorentz force can be given as

$$\mathbf{F} = \mathbf{F}_e + \mathbf{F}_m = q\mathbf{E} + q(\mathbf{v}\times\mathbf{B})$$

$$\mathbf{F} = q(\mathbf{E} + \mathbf{v}\times\mathbf{B})$$

10. The magnitude of the magnetic field at a point P,

$$B = \frac{\mu_0 I}{2\pi r}$$

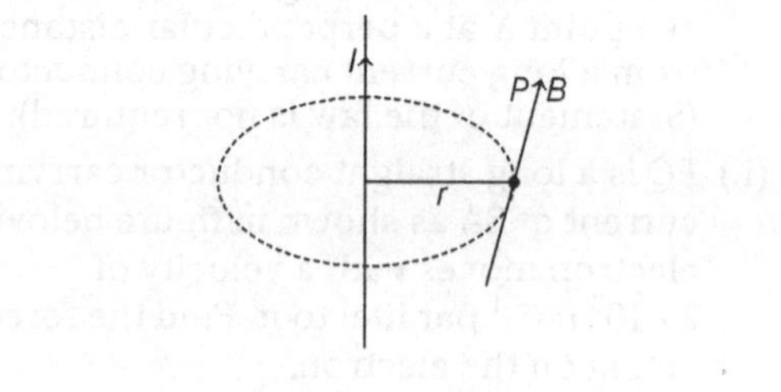

Its direction at point P is along the tangent to a circle of radius r centered on the conductor.

11. Refer to text on pages 179 and 180 (Magnetic field of a solenoid).

12. $\because\ F = qvB \Rightarrow B = \dfrac{F}{qv} \Rightarrow 1\text{T} = \dfrac{1\text{N}}{(1\text{C})(1\text{ms}^{-1})}$

Thus, if a charge of 1 coulomb moving with a velocity of 1 metre per second perpendicular to a uniform magnetic field experiences a force of 1 newton, then the magnitude of the field is 1 tesla. (2)

13. Refer to text on page 181 (Motion of a charge in magnetic field). (1)

14. When a charged particle enters in a uniform magnetic field perpendicularly, central force acts on the particle which provides centripetal force for the circular motion of the particle.

Situation is shown in figure.

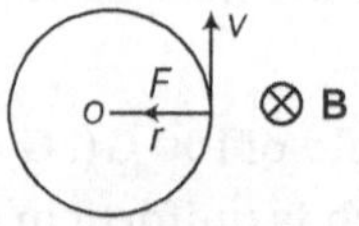

Centripetal force, $F = \dfrac{mv^2}{r}$

As magnetic force will provide the necessary centripetal force to the charged particle.

$$\Rightarrow \quad \frac{mv^2}{r} = qvB \Rightarrow \frac{mv}{r} = qB \quad\Rightarrow\quad p = mv = rqB$$

$$\Rightarrow \qquad r = \frac{p}{qB} \Rightarrow r \propto p$$

where, $p = mv$ = momentum.

15. (i) As, the charged particle is moving perpendicularly to the magnetic field. So, it will perform circular motion in XY-plane. (1)

(ii) No, the charged particle does not gain any KE as Lorentz force acting on it does not perform any work as $\mathbf{F}_m \perp \mathbf{v}$. (1)

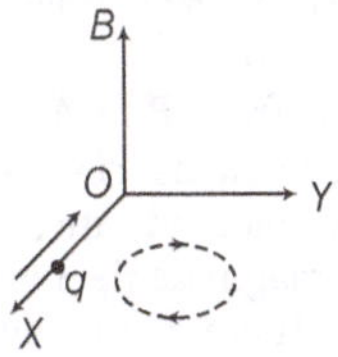

16. The expression in vector form is given by

$$\mathbf{F} = q\,(\mathbf{v} \times \mathbf{B}).$$

The direction of the magnetic force is in the direction of $(\mathbf{v} \times \mathbf{B})$, i.e. perpendicular to the plane containing $\mathbf{v}$ and $\mathbf{B}$ (2)

17. Refer to text on page 182 (Force on a moving charge in a uniform magnetic and electric field (Lorentz force)). (1)

Lorentz magnetic force always acts perpendicular to the direction of motion of the particle. Thus, work done by this force is zero. (1)

18. A diagram in which particle moves in magnetic and electric field is shown below (1)

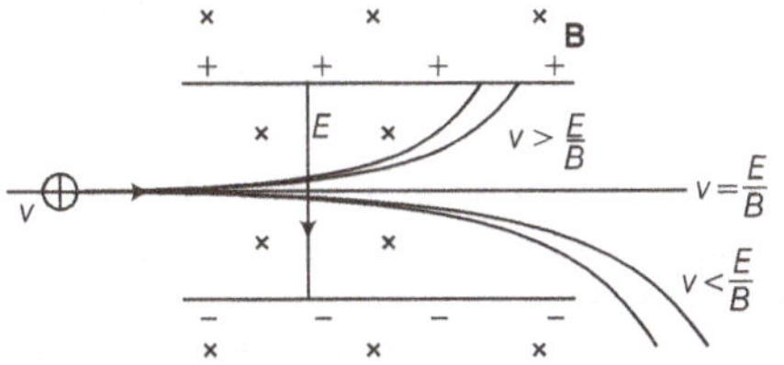

Forces on a charged particle are

F_e = electric force = qE,

F_m = magnetic force = Bqv

For a particle to go straight without any deflection

$$F_e = F_m \Rightarrow qE = Bqv \Rightarrow v = \frac{E}{B}$$

In this way, particles having speed, $v = \frac{E}{B}$ are separated. (1)

19. As, $\mathbf{v} = -v\hat{\mathbf{i}}$ [∵ the particle is moving along X-direction]

$$\mathbf{B} = -B\hat{\mathbf{k}}$$

[∵ the magnetic field is perpendicular to the plane of the paper directed inwards, i.e. negative Z-direction]

∴ Force acting due to magnetic field,

$$\mathbf{F}_m = q\,(\mathbf{v} \times \mathbf{B}) = q\,[-v\hat{\mathbf{i}} \times (-B\hat{\mathbf{k}})],$$

$$\mathbf{F}_m = -qvB\hat{\mathbf{j}} \qquad [\because \hat{\mathbf{i}} \times \hat{\mathbf{k}} = -\hat{\mathbf{j}}] \text{ (1)}$$

⇒ Magnitude of $\mathbf{F}_m = |\mathbf{F}_m| = qvB$

The direction of Fm is along negative Y-direction.For the undeflected motion of particle,

Force due to electric field = Force due to magnetic field,

$$q\mathbf{E} = q(\mathbf{v} \times \mathbf{B})$$

∴ $$\mathbf{E} = \mathbf{v} \times \mathbf{B}$$

Magnitude of electric field, $|E| = |\mathbf{v} \times \mathbf{B}|$ and direction of magnetic field will be perpendicular to both $\mathbf{v}$ and $\mathbf{B}$, i.e. along Y-axis. (1)

20. In such cases, where symmetry exist it is easier to find field by Ampere's circuital law.

To find magnetic field at a point, consider Amperian loop around an infinitely long conducting wire as shown. (1)

In order to determine the magnetic field at point P, which is situated at a distance a from the centre of the circular loop around the conducting wire. The magnetic field ($\mathbf{B}$) is tangential to the circumference of the loop.

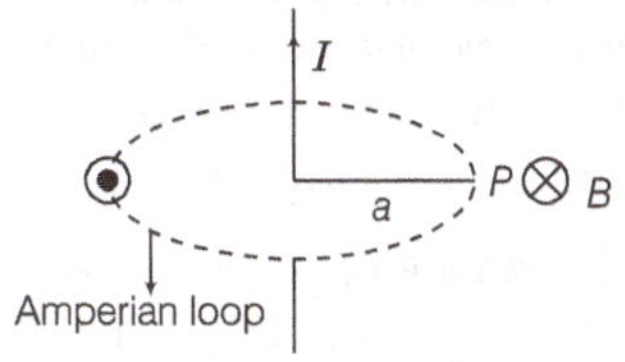

As we know that from Ampere's circuital law,

$$\oint \mathbf{B} \cdot dl = \mu_0 I$$

As $$\oint dl = 2\pi a$$

So, $$\mathbf{B}\, 2\pi a = \mu_0 I$$

$$\mathbf{B} = \frac{\mu_0 I}{2\pi a} \times \frac{2}{2} \Rightarrow \mathbf{B} = \frac{\mu_0}{4\pi}\frac{2I}{a}$$

The direction of magnetic field will be determined by right hand thumb rule. (2)

21.

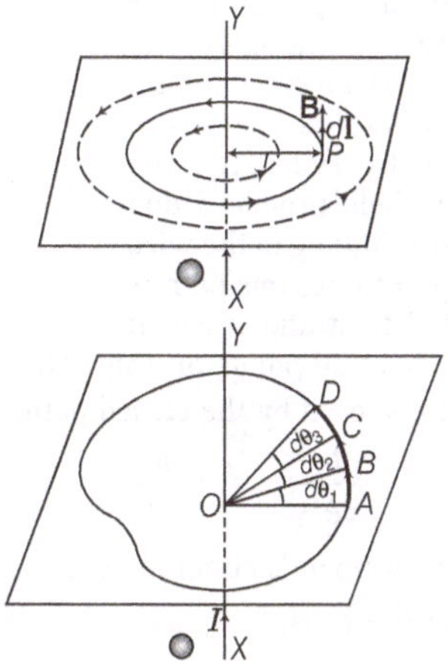

Consider any arbitrary closed path perpendicular to the plane of paper around a long straight conductor XY carrying current from X to Y, lying in the plane of paper.

Let the closed path be made of large number of small elements, where

$$AB = dl_1,\ BC = dl_2,\ CD = dl_3$$

Let $d\theta_1, d\theta_2, d\theta_3$, be the angles subtended by the various elements at point O through which conductor is passing.

Then, $d\theta_1 + d\theta_2 + d\theta_3 + \ldots = 2\pi$

Suppose these small elements $AB, BC, CD, \ldots$ are small circular arcs of radii $r_1, r_2, r_3 \ldots$ respectively.

Then, $d\theta_1 = \frac{dl_1}{r_1}, d\theta_2 = \frac{dl_2}{r_2}, d\theta_3 = \frac{dl_3}{r_3}$ (1)

If $\mathbf{B}_1, \mathbf{B}_2, \mathbf{B}_3$ are the magnetic field inductions at a point along the small elements $dl_1, dl_2, dl_3 \ldots$, then from Biot-Savart's law we know that for the conductor of infinite length, magnetic field is given by

$$B_1 = \frac{\mu_0}{4\pi}\cdot\frac{2I}{r_1}, B_2 = \frac{\mu_0}{4\pi}\cdot\frac{2I}{r_2}, B_3 = \frac{\mu_0}{4\pi}\cdot\frac{2I}{r_3}$$

In case of each element, the magnetic field induction B and current element vector dl are in the same direction. (1)

Line integral of B around closed path is

$$\oint \mathbf{B}\cdot d\mathbf{l} = \mathbf{B}_1\cdot d\mathbf{l}_1 + \mathbf{B}_2\cdot d\mathbf{l}_2 + \mathbf{B}_3\cdot d\mathbf{l}_3 + \ldots$$

$$= B_1(dl_1) + B_2(dl_2) + B_3(dl_3) + \ldots$$

$$= \frac{\mu_0}{4\pi}\cdot\frac{2I}{r_1}dl_1 + \frac{\mu_0}{4\pi}\cdot\frac{2I}{r_2}dl_2 + \frac{\mu_0}{4\pi}\cdot\frac{2I}{r_3}dl_3 + \ldots$$

$$= \frac{\mu_0 2I}{4\pi}\left[\frac{dl_1}{r_1} + \frac{dl_2}{r_2} + \frac{dl_3}{r_3} + \ldots\right]$$

$$= \frac{\mu_0 2I}{4\pi}[d\theta_1 + d\theta_2 + d\theta_3 + \ldots]$$

$$= \frac{\mu_0}{4\pi} 2I \times 2\pi = \mu_0 I$$

which is an expression of Ampere's circuital law. (1)

22. (i) Let the point P be lying inside the wire at a perpendicular distance r from the axis of the wire. Consider a circular path of radius r around the axis of the wire. By symmetry, the magnetic field produced due to current flowing in the wire at any point over this path is tangential to it and equal in magnitude at all points on this path.

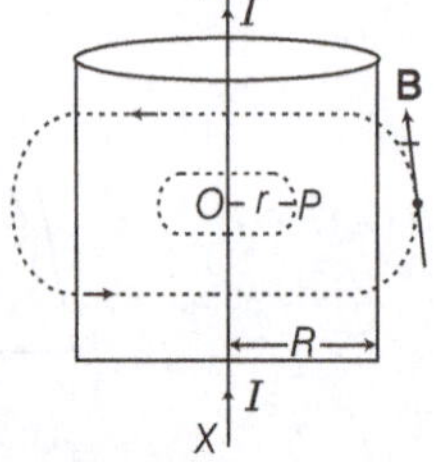

Current enclosed by the closed path,

$$I' = \frac{I}{\pi R^2} \times \pi r^2 = \frac{Ir^2}{R^2}$$

Applying Ampere's circuital law,

$$\oint \mathbf{B}\cdot d\mathbf{l} = \mu_0\mu_r I'$$

$$\Rightarrow B(2\pi r) = \mu_0\mu_r\frac{Ir^2}{R^2}$$

$$\Rightarrow B = \frac{\mu_0\mu_r Ir^2}{2\pi R^2 r} \Rightarrow B = \frac{\mu_0\mu_r Ir}{2\pi R^2}$$ (2)

(ii) When point P is outside the wire, $r > R$, so that the current enclosed by closed path $= I$

Using Ampere's circuital law, $\oint \mathbf{B}\cdot d\mathbf{l} = \mu_0 I$

$$B \times 2\pi r = \mu_0 I \text{ or } B = \frac{\mu_0 I}{2\pi r}$$ (1)

23. (i) Refer to text on page 179 (Ampere's circuital law). (1)

(ii) According to Ampere's circuital law, the net field is given by $B = \mu_0 nI$

(a) The net magnetic field is given by

$$B_{\text{net}} = B_2 - B_1 = \mu_0 n_2 I - \mu_0 n_1 I \quad [\because I_2 = I_1 = I]$$

$$= \mu_0 I(n_2 - n_1)$$

The direction is from B to A. (1)

(b) As the magnetic fields due to S_1 is confined solely inside S_1 as the solenoids are assumed to be very long. So, there is no magnetic field outside S_1 due to current in S_1, similarly, there is no field outside S_2.

$\therefore \quad B_{\text{net}} = 0$ (1)

24. (i) Refer to text on pages 180 and 181 (Force on a moving charge in a uniform magnetic field). (2)

(ii) Since, force always adjusts itself in a direction which becomes perpendicular to velocity, so only direction of velocity changes not the magnitude. Hence, the kinetic energy of the particle always remains constant. (1)

25. (i) Refer to text on pages 180 and 181 (Force on a moving charge in a uniform magnetic field). (1)

(ii) According to question, magnetic force on a charge particle is given by

$$\mathbf{F} = q(\mathbf{v} \times \mathbf{B})$$

The direction of force on the charged particle is given by $(\mathbf{v} \times \mathbf{B})$ with the sign of charged particle, i.e. **for α-particle,** charge is positive and direction of $\mathbf{v}$ is $+\hat{\mathbf{i}}$ and direction of $\mathbf{B}$ is $-\hat{\mathbf{k}}$.

So, direction of force is $+(\hat{\mathbf{i}} \times -\hat{\mathbf{k}})$, i.e. $+\hat{\mathbf{j}}$.

It describes a circle with anti-clockwise motion.

For neutron

It is a neutral particle so, it goes undeviated.

As $\quad \mathbf{F} = q(\mathbf{v} \times \mathbf{B}) = 0$

For electron

Force is given by $\mathbf{F} = -e(\mathbf{v} \times \mathbf{B})$

So, direction $= -(\hat{\mathbf{i}} \times -\hat{\mathbf{k}}) \Rightarrow -\hat{\mathbf{j}}$

e^- describes a circle with clockwise motion

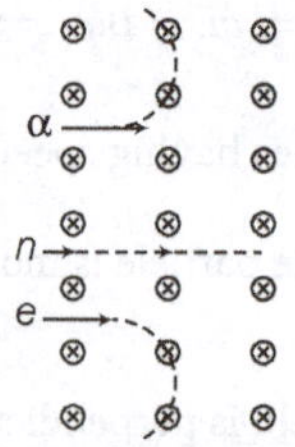

(2)

26.

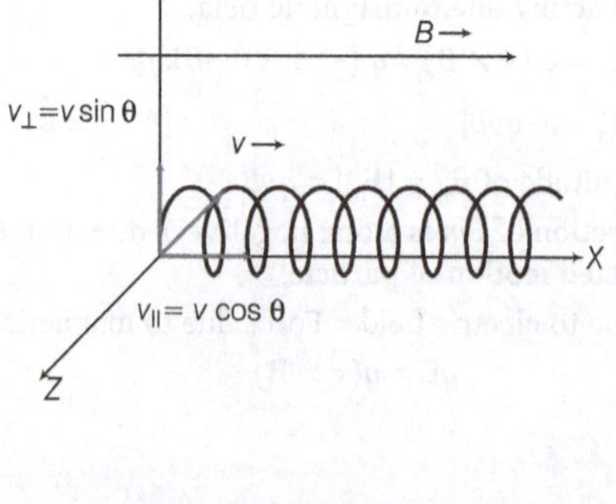

The path of the charged particle will be helix. As, the charge moves linearly in the direction of the magnetic field with velocity $v\cos\theta$ and also describe the circular path due to velocity $v\sin\theta$. (1)

Time taken by the charge to complete one circular

rotation, $$T = \frac{2\pi r}{v_\perp} \quad \text{...(i)}$$

$$\Rightarrow \quad f = qv_\perp B$$

and $$\frac{mv_\perp^2}{r} = qv_\perp B$$

$$\Rightarrow \quad \frac{v_\perp m}{qB} = r \quad \text{...(ii)}$$

From Eqs. (i) and (ii), we get

$$\Rightarrow \quad T = \frac{2\pi v_\perp m}{qB \cdot v_\perp} = \frac{2\pi m}{Bq}$$ (1)

Distance moved by the particle along the magnetic field in one rotation (pitch of the helix path)

$$= v_{\|} \times T \quad [\because v_{\|} = v_{\text{parallel}}]$$

$$= v\cos\theta \times \frac{2\pi m}{Bq}$$

$$P = \frac{2\pi m v\cos\theta}{qB}$$ (1)

27. (i) Refer to text on pages 179 and 180 (Magnetic field of a solenoid). (2)

(ii) When a charged particle enters in the magnetic field at right angle, the particle follows a circular path.

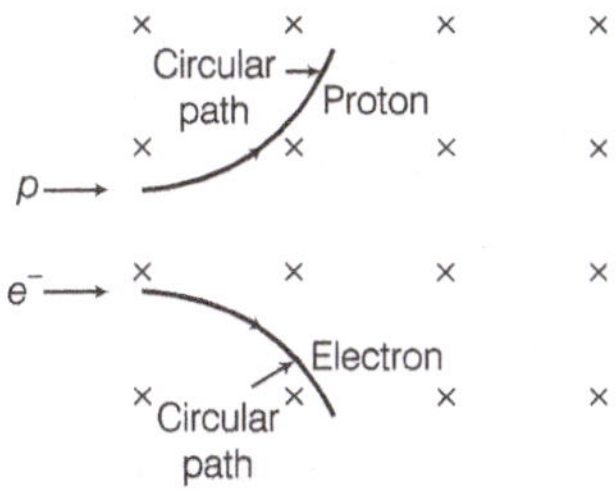

Radius of the circular path, $r = \frac{mv}{qB}$

For same speed v, magnitude of charge and magnetic field $r \propto m$

$$\Rightarrow \quad \frac{r_e}{r_p} = \frac{m_e}{m_p}$$

where, m_e and m_p are masses of electron and proton, respectively.

$\because \quad m_e < m_p$

i.e. Proton is much heavier than electron.

$$\Rightarrow \quad r_e < r_p$$

$$\Rightarrow \quad \frac{r_e}{r_p} < 1$$

The curvature of path of electron is much more than curvature of path of proton.

28. (i) The magnetic field is in constant direction from East to West. According to the question, a charged particle travels undeflecte d along a straight path with constant speed. It is only possible, if the magnetic force experienced by the charged particle is zero.

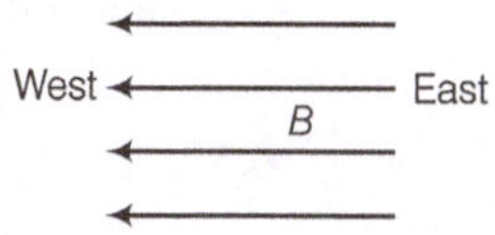

The magnitude of magnetic force on a moving charged particle in a magnetic field is given by $F = qv\, B\sin\theta$ (where θ is the angle between v and B). Here $F = 0$, if and only if $\sin\theta = 0$ (as $v \neq 0$, $q \neq 0$, $B \neq 0$). This indicates the angle between the velocity and magnetic field is 0° or 180°.

Thus, the charged particle moves parallel or anti-parallel to the magnetic field **B**. (2)

(ii) Yes, the final speed be equal to its initial speed as the magnetic force acting on the charged particle only changes the direction of velocity of charged particle but cannot change the magnitude of velocity of charged particle. (1)

(iii) As, the electric field is from North to South, that means the plate in North is positive and in South is negative. Thus, the electrons (negatively charged) attract towards the positive plate that means move towards North. If we want that there should be no deflection in the path of electron, then the magnetic force should be in South direction.

By $\mathbf{F} = -e\,(\mathbf{v} \times \mathbf{B})$, the direction of velocity is West to East, the direction of force is towards South, by using the Fleming's left hand rule, the direction of magnetic field (**B**) is perpendicularly inwards to the plane of paper. (2)

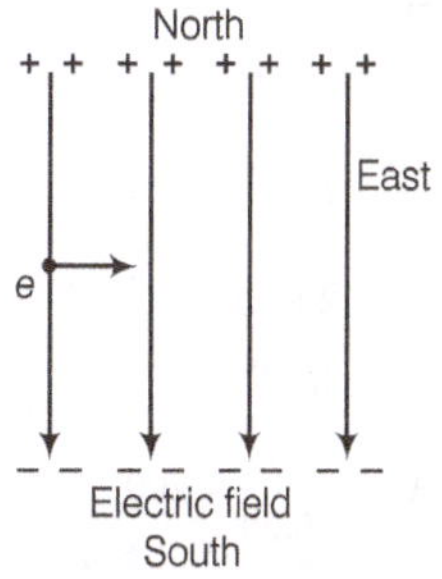

29. To find magnetic field at a point, consider Amperian loop around an infinitely long conducting wire as shown.

(i) In order to determine the magnetic field at point P, which is situated at a distance a from the centre of the circular loop around the conducting wire. The magnetic field (**B**) is tangential to the circumference of the loop.

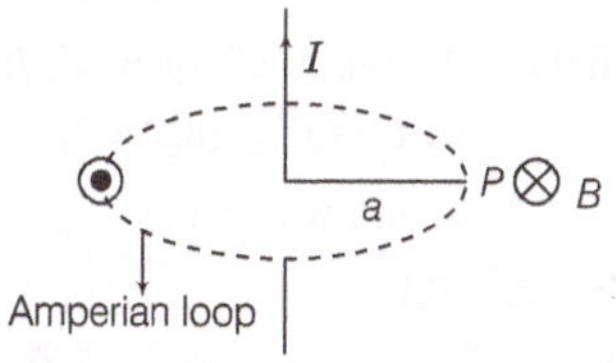

As we know that from Ampere's circuital law,

$$\oint \mathbf{B} \cdot d\mathbf{l} = \mu_0 I$$

As $\oint dl = 2\pi a$

So, $\mathbf{B}\, 2\pi a = \mu_0 I$

$$\mathbf{B} = \frac{\mu_0 I}{2\pi a} \times \frac{2}{2}$$

$$\Rightarrow \quad \mathbf{B} = \frac{\mu_0}{4\pi}\frac{2I}{a}$$

The direction of magnetic field will be determined by right hand thumb rule. (1½)

(ii)

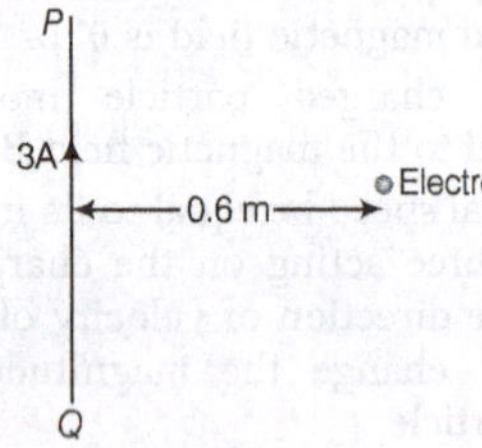

From the given figure, if we have to calculate force on a long straight conductor.

Force acting on the electron,

$$F = qvB$$

Due to wire, the field created is

$$B = \frac{\mu_0 I}{2\pi R} = \frac{\mu_0 \times 3}{2 \times \pi \times 0.6}$$

$$= \frac{4\pi \times 10^{-7} \times 3}{2 \times \pi \times 0.6} = 10^{-6}\ \text{T}$$

Force, $F = Bqv$

Now, $F = 1.6 \times 10^{-19} \times 2 \times 10^{7} \times 10^{-6}$

$$= \frac{16}{10} \times 10^{-19} \times 2 \times 10^{7} \times 10^{-6}$$

$$= 16 \times 2 \times 10^{-19+6-6}$$

$$F = 32 \times 10^{-19}\ \text{N}$$ (1½)

30. Here, $I = 2.5$ A, $n = \frac{100}{0.50} = 200$

(i) $B = \mu_0 nI = 4\pi \times 10^{-7} \times 200 \times 2.5$

$B = 6.28 \times 10^{-4}$ T (1)

(ii) $B = \frac{\mu_0 nI}{2} = \frac{4\pi \times 10^{-7} \times 200 \times 2.5}{2} = 3.14 \times 10^{-4}$ T (1)

31. Number of turns, $N = 850 \times 5$, $l = 1$ m, $I = 5$ A

Area of cross-section, $A = \pi r^2 = \frac{22}{7}\left(\frac{3}{2} \times 10^{-2}\right)^2$ m^2

Magnetic field at the centre of solenoid, $B = \mu_0 NI/l$

$$= 4\pi \times 10^{-7} \times (850 \times 5) \times 5/1$$

$$= 2.671 \times 10^{-2}\ \text{T}$$ (1)

$\therefore$ Magnetic flux $= BA$

$$= 2.671 \times 10^{-2} \times \frac{22}{7} \times \left(\frac{3}{2} \times 10^{-2}\right)^2$$

$$= 1.89 \times 10^{-5}\ \text{Wb}$$ (1)

32. Magnetic field, $B = 100$ G

$$= 100 \times 10^{-4}\ \text{T} = 10^{-2}\ \text{T}$$

To design the solenoid, let us find the product of current and number of turns in the solenoid.

The magnitude of magnetic field, $B = \mu_0 nI$ (1)

or $nI = \frac{B}{\mu_0} = \frac{10^{-2}}{4} \times 3.14 \times 10^{-7}$

$\Rightarrow nI = 7961 \approx 8000$

Here, the product of nI is 8000. (1)

Current, $I = 8$ A and number of turns, $n = 1000$

The other design is $I = 10$ A and $n = 800$/m.

This is the most appropriate design as per the requirement. (1)

33. Here, energy of electron, $E' = 2000$ eV

$$E' = 2000 \times 1.6 \times 10^{-19}\ \text{J} = 3.2 \times 10^{-16}\ \text{J}$$

Now, $B = 0.2$ T, $r = ?$, $E' = \frac{1}{2}mv^2$

$$\Rightarrow \quad v = \sqrt{\frac{2E'}{m}}$$

$$Bev = \frac{mv^2}{r}$$ (1)

$$\therefore \quad r = \frac{mv}{Be} = \frac{m}{Be}\sqrt{\frac{2E'}{m}} = \frac{\sqrt{2E'm}}{Be}$$

$$= \frac{\sqrt{2 \times 3.2 \times 10^{-16} \times 9 \times 10^{-31}}}{0.2 \times 1.6 \times 10^{-19}}$$

$$= 7.5 \times 10^{-4}\ \text{m}$$ (1)

34. As the path of an electron remains undeflected, hence net force on the electron must be zero (balanced).

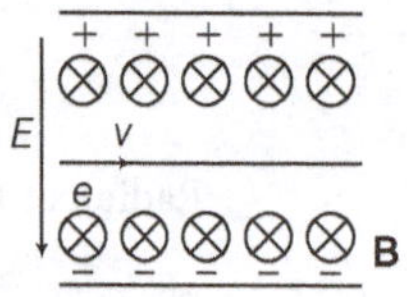

Consider the diagram, where an electron beam enters the region in which magnetic field (B) is perpendicularly inward ⊗ and electric field (E) is downward.

Force on electron due to electric field $= eE$ [upward]

Force on electron due to magnetic field $= evB$ [downward]

[where, v = speed, e = electronic charge] (1)

For no deflection electric force will must be balanced by magnetic force

$$eE = evB$$

$$\Rightarrow \quad v = \frac{E}{B} = \frac{3.4 \times 10^4}{2 \times 10^{-3}} \quad \left[\begin{array}{l}\text{given, } E = 3.4 \times 10^4\ \text{V/m} \\ B = 2 \times 10^{-3}\ \text{T}\end{array}\right]$$

$= 1.7 \times 10^7 \text{ m/s}$ (1)

When electric field is removed, only magnetic field remains, hence path will be circular as shown in the figure.

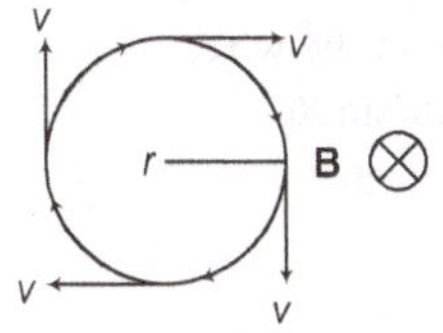

Radius of the circular path (r) is given by $r = \dfrac{mv}{eB}$ (1)

where, m is mass of the electron.

B is magnitude of the magnetic field

$$\Rightarrow \quad r = \frac{mv}{eB} = \frac{9.1 \times 10^{-31} \times 1.7 \times 10^7}{1.6 \times 10^{-19} \times 2 \times 10^{-3}}$$

$$= 4.83 \times 10^{-31+29}$$

$$= 4.83 \times 10^{-2} \text{ m} = 4.83 \text{ cm} \approx 5 \text{ cm}$$ (1)

35. According to the question, $q = 1.6 \times 10^{-19}$ C

$$v = 5 \times 10^7 \text{ m/s}$$

$$\theta = 30°, B = 1 \text{ Wb m}^{-2}$$

$$F = qvB\sin\theta$$

$$= 1.6 \times 10^{-19} \times 5 \times 10^7 \times 1 \times \sin 30°$$

$$= 4 \times 10^{-12} \text{ N}$$ (2)

36. The force on a charged particle moving in a magnetic field **B** with velocity **v** and having charge q is $q(\mathbf{v} \times \mathbf{B})$. The magnitude of force is

$$|\mathbf{F}| = q|\mathbf{v}||\mathbf{B}|\sin\theta$$

where, q = charge,

v = speed of the charged particle,

B = magnitude of the magnetic field

and θ = angle between v and B.

Consider the diagram shown below.

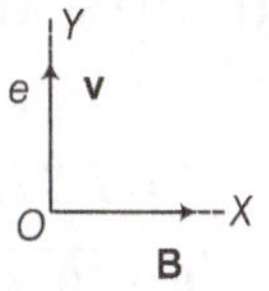

Let the horizontal direction is X and vertical direction is Y.

$$\mathbf{F} = q(\mathbf{v} \times \mathbf{B}) = -e(\mathbf{v} \times \mathbf{B})$$

[along Z-axis which is perpendicular to the plane of paper]

Hence, direction of force will be perpendicularly outward.

$$|\mathbf{F}| = evB \quad [\because \theta = 90°]$$

$$= 1.6 \times 10^{-19} \times 2 \times 10^6 \times 0.32 \times 10^{-4}$$

$$= 1.024 \times 10^{-17} \text{N}$$ **(2)**

37. Given, $I = 5$A

$$v = 2 \times 10^6 \text{m/s}$$

$$r = 0.2 \text{ m}$$

$$B = \frac{\mu_0}{4\pi}\frac{2I}{r} = \frac{10^{-7} \times 2 \times 5}{0.2} = 5 \times 10^{-6} \text{ T}$$

Now, force (F) = $qvB \sin 90°$

$$= (1.6 \times 10^{-19})(2 \times 10^6)(5 \times 10^{-6})$$

$$= 16 \times 10^{-19} \text{ N}$$

TOPIC 03 Magnetic Force and Torque Experienced by a Current Loop

Force on a Current Carrying Conductor in a Uniform Magnetic Field

When a current carrying conductor is placed in a uniform magnetic field, then due to motion of free electrons inside the conductor, a magnetic force acts on it.

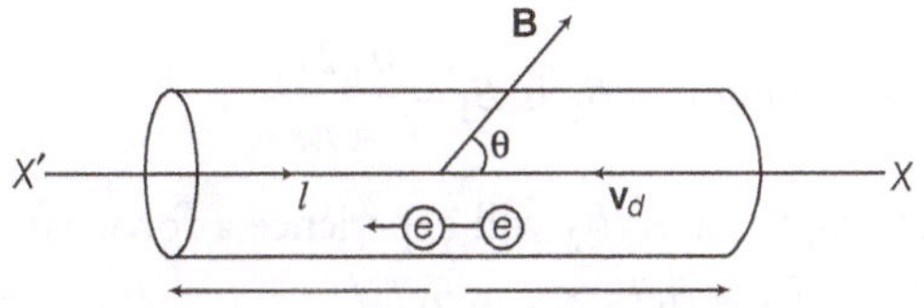

Current carrying conductor in a uniform magnetic field

Let us consider a portion of length l and cross-sectional area A of a straight conductor carrying a current I.

Let the magnetic field **B** be in the plane of the paper directed upwards and making an angle θ with the direction of current.

Each electron of conductor experiences a magnetic Lorentz force, which is given by

$$\mathbf{F} = e(\mathbf{v}_d \times \mathbf{B}) \quad \text{...(i)}$$

If n be the number of free electrons per unit volume in the conductor, then total number of electrons in the conductor is

$$N = n \times \text{volume of conductor}$$

$$N = nAl \quad [A \rightarrow \text{Area of cross section}]$$

∴ Total force on the conductor is

$$\mathbf{F} = N \cdot \mathbf{F}$$
$$= nAl\,[-e\,(\mathbf{v}_d \times \mathbf{B})] = enA\,[-l\,\mathbf{v}_d \times \mathbf{B}]$$
$$= enA\,[v_d \cdot \mathbf{l} \times \mathbf{B}] \qquad [-l\,\mathbf{v}_d = v_d \mathbf{l}]$$
$$= neAv_d\,[\mathbf{l} \times \mathbf{B}] = I\,[\vec{\mathbf{l}} \times \vec{\mathbf{B}}] \qquad [\because I = neAv_d]$$

Magnitude of force is

$$\boxed{F = I\,B\,l\sin\theta}$$

or

$$\boxed{\mathbf{F} = I(\mathbf{l} \times \mathbf{B})}$$

If $\theta = 0°$ or $180°$, then $F = I\,Bl\sin 0° = 0$

$$[\because \sin 0° = 0 \text{ and } \sin 180° = 0]$$

It means a conductor placed parallel to direction of magnetic field, experiences no force due to magnetic field.

If $\theta = 90°$, then force is maximum.

$$F_{\max} = IBl\sin 90° = IBl \qquad [\because \sin 90° = 1]$$

It means a conductor placed perpendicular to direction of magnetic field, experiences maximum force.

Rules to Find Out the Direction of Force

The direction of the force acting on a current carrying conductor in a magnetic field can be found by any of the following two rules.

(i) **Right Hand Palm Rule** If we stretch our right hand palm such that the thumb points in the direction of the current (I) and the stretched fingers in the direction of the magnetic field **B**, then the force **F** on the conductor will be perpendicular to the palm in the direction of pushing by the palm as shown in the Fig. (a).

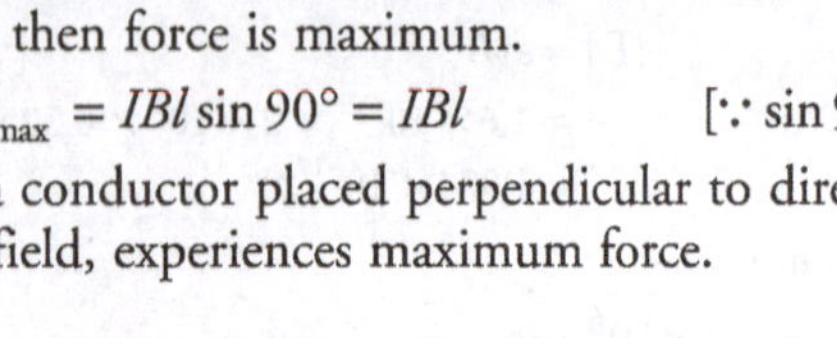

(a) (b)

(ii) **Fleming's Left Hand Rule** If the fore-finger, the middle-finger and the thumb of the left hand are stretched mutually at right angles to one another such that the fore-finger points in the direction of the magnetic field **B** and the middle-finger in the direction of the current I, then the thumb will point in the direction of the force **F** on the conductor as shown in the Fig. (b).

Example 1 A 3.0 cm wire carrying a current of 10 A is placed inside a solenoid perpendicular to its axis. The magnetic field inside the solenoid is given to be 0.27 T. What is the magnetic force on the wire?

Sol. Magnetic force on the wire,

$$F = BIl\sin\theta = BIl\sin 90°$$
$$= 0.27 \times 10 \times 3 \times 10^{-2} \qquad [\because \theta = 90°]$$
$$= 8.1 \times 10^{-2}\,\text{N}$$

Example 2 A straight wire of mass 200 g and length 1.5 m carries a current of 4 A. It is suspended in mid air by a uniform horizontal magnetic field B. What is the magnitude of the magnetic field?

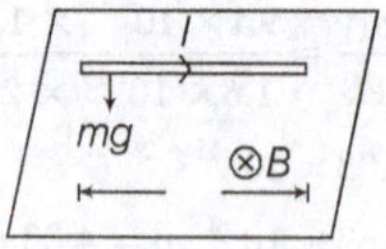

Sol. Applying Fleming's rule, we find that upward force F of magnitude IlB acts. For mid air suspension this must be balanced by the force due to gravity.

$$\therefore \qquad mg = IlB \Rightarrow B = \frac{mg}{Il}$$

Given, $m = 200$ g $= 0.2$ kg, $g = 9.8\ \text{ms}^{-2}$, $I = 4\text{A}$, $l = 1.5$ m

We have, $B = \dfrac{0.2 \times 9.8}{4 \times 1.5} = 0.327$ T

Force between Two Parallel Current Carrying Conductors

To find the force on a current carrying wire due to a second current carrying wire, first find the magnetic field due to second wire at the site of first wire. Then, find the force on the first wire due to that field.

Let us consider A_1B_1 and A_2B_2 are two infinite long straight conductors.

I_1 and I_2 are the currents flowing through them and these are at r distance apart.

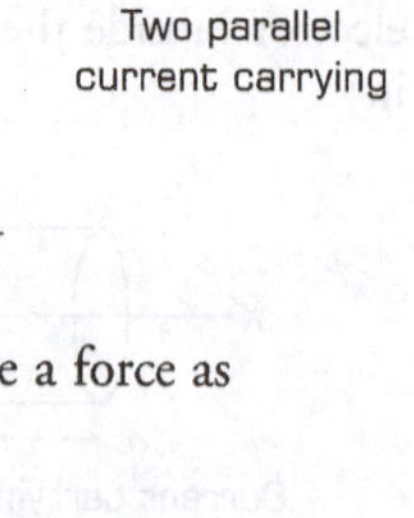

Two parallel current carrying

Magnetic field induction at a point P on conductor A_2B_2 due to current

I_1 passing through A_1B_1 is $B_1 = \dfrac{\mu_0 2I_1}{4\pi r}$

The unit length of A_2B_2 will experience a force as

$$F_2 = B_1 I_2 \times l = B_1 I_2 l$$

or

$$F_2 = \frac{\mu_0}{4\pi} \cdot \frac{2I_1 I_2}{r} \cdot l$$

Conductor A_1B_1 also experiences the same amount of force, directed towards the wire A_2B_2.

Therefore, force between two current carrying parallel conductors per unit length is

$$F = \frac{\mu_0}{4\pi} \cdot \frac{2I_1I_2}{r}$$

Two linear parallel conductors carrying currents in the same direction attract each other while carrying currents in opposite direction they repel each other.

Definition of Ampere (In terms of the force)

One ampere is the current which flows through each of the two parallel uniform long linear conductors, which are placed in free space at a distance of 1 m from each other and which attract or repel each other with a force of 2×10^{-7} N/m of their lengths.

Example 3 Calculate the force per unit length on a long straight wire carrying current of 4 A due to a parallel wire carrying 6 A current, if the distance between the wires is 3 cm.

Sol. Given, $I_1 = 4$ A, $I_2 = 6$ A, $r = 3$ cm $= 0.03$ m

$$F = \frac{\mu_0}{4\pi} \cdot \frac{2I_1I_2}{r} = \frac{10^{-7} \times 2 \times 4 \times 6}{0.03} = 1.6 \times 10^{-4} \text{N/m}$$

Example 4 A short conductor of length 5 cm is placed parallel to a long conductor of length 1.5 m near its centre. The conductors carry currents 4 A and 3 A respectively in the same direction. What is the total force experienced by the long conductor when they are 3 cm apart?

Sol. Force on long conductor is equal and opposite to the force on small conductor $= \frac{\mu_0}{4\pi} \cdot \frac{2I_1I_2l}{r}$

Given, $I_1 = 4$A,

$I_2 = 3$A,

$r = 3 \times 10^{-2}$ m,

$l = 5 \times 10^{-2}$ m

$$\Rightarrow \quad F = \frac{4\pi \times 10^{-7} \times 2 \times 4 \times 3 \times 5 \times 10^{-2}}{4\pi \times 3 \times 10^{-2}} = 4 \times 10^{-6} \text{ N}$$

Torque Experienced by a Current Loop in Uniform Magnetic Field (Magnetic Dipole)

Consider a rectangular loop *ABCD* be suspended in a uniform magnetic field **B**. Let $AB = CD = b$ and $AD = BC = a$. Let I be the current flowing through the loop.

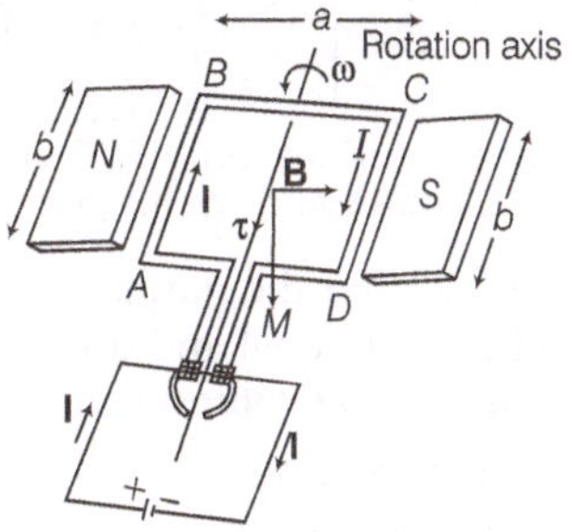

A rectangular current carrying coil in uniform magnetic field

***Case* I** The rectangular loop is placed such that the uniform magnetic field B is in the plane of loop.

No force is exerted by the magnetic field on the arms *AD* and *BC* (∵ they are parallel to the magnetic field).

Magnetic field exerts a force F_1 on arm *AB*,

$$\therefore \quad F_1 = IbB$$

Magnetic field exerts a force F_2 on arm *CD*,

$$F_2 = IbB = F_1$$

F_1 and F_2 are equal and opposite, so net force on the loop is zero. But line of action of F_1 and F_2 are opposite and parallel, so they form a couple.

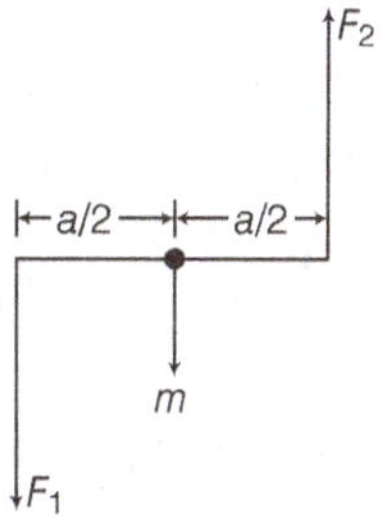

The torque produced due to couple on the loop rotates the loop in anti-clockwise direction.

Torque, $\tau = \mathbf{r} \times \mathbf{F}$

So, $\tau = F_1 \frac{a}{2} + F_2 \frac{a}{2}$ [∵ sin 90° = 1]

(∵ Torque = Force × Perpendicular distance of line of action)

$$\Rightarrow \quad \tau = IbB\frac{a}{2} + IbB\frac{a}{2} = I(ab)B = IAB$$

where, b be breadth of the rectangular coil, a be length of the rectangular coil and $A = ab$ (area of the coil).

Case II The plane of the loop is not along the magnetic field, but makes an angle with it.

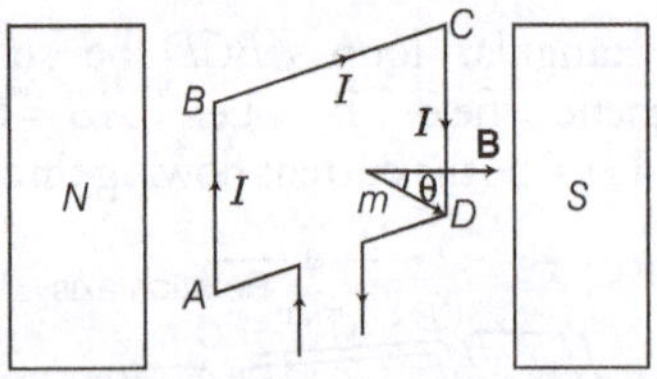

The area vector of the loop *ABCD* makes an arbitrary angle θ with the magnetic field

Angle between the field and the normal to the coil is θ. Forces on *BC* and *DA* are equal and opposite and they cancel each other as they are collinear.

Force on *AB* is F_1 and force on *CD* is F_2.

and $\quad F_1 = F_2 = IbB$

Magnitude of torque on the loop is as shown in figure below:

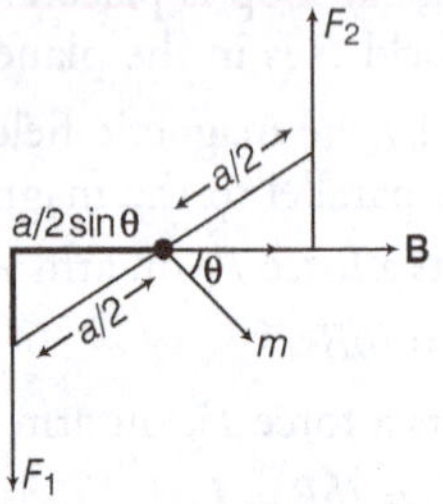

Top view of the loop. The forces F_1 and F_2 acting on the area *AB* and *CD* are indicated

$$\tau = F_1 \frac{a}{2} \sin\theta + F_2 \frac{a}{2} \sin\theta$$

$$\tau = IabB \sin\theta = IAB \sin\theta$$

where, $\quad A = ab$ (area of coil)

The torque on the loop can be expressed as the vector product of the magnetic moment of the coil and the magnetic field

$$\boxed{\tau = MB \sin\theta \hat{n} = \mathbf{M} \times \mathbf{B}}$$

where, $\mathbf{M} = NI\mathbf{A}$ is magnetic moment of the loop, its unit is ampere-metre^2.

This is analogous to the electrostatic case (electric dipole of dipole moment *p* in an electric field *E*)

When **M** and **B** are parallel, then current loop is in stable equilibrium. Any small rotation of the loop produces a torque which brings it back to its original position. When **M** and **B** are anti-parallel, then current loop is in unstable equilibrium.

Magnetic moment of the loop of *N* turns, $M = NIA$

The total torque on the coil is given by

$$\tau = NIAB \sin\theta = (NIA)\, B \sin\theta$$

The presence of this torque is also the reason why a small magnet or any magnetic dipole aligns itself with the external magnetic field.

Example 5 A circular coil of 20 turns and radius 10 cm carries a current of 5 A. It is placed in a uniform magnetic field of 0.10 T. Find the torque acting on the coil, when the magnetic field is applied in the plane of coil.

Sol. Given, total number of turns, $N = 20$

Radius, $r = 10 \text{ cm} = 10 \times 10^{-2}\text{ m}$

Current, $I = 5\text{ A}$; Angle, $\theta = 90^\circ$

External uniform magnetic field $(B) = 0.10\text{ T}$

Torque, $\tau = ?$

As, torque, $\tau = BINA \sin\theta$

$\Rightarrow \quad = 0.10 \times 5 \times 20 \times 0.0314 \times \sin 90^\circ = 0.314\text{ N-m}$

Example 6 Calculate the torque of a 100 turns rectangular coil of length 40 cm and breadth 20 cm, carrying a current of 10 A, when placed making an angle of 60° with a magnetic field of 5 T.

Sol. Given, $I = 10\text{A}$, $N = 100$, $l = 40\text{ cm}$, $b = 20\text{ cm}$

$B = 5\text{ T}, \theta = 60^\circ$

$A = l \times b = 40 \times 20 = 800\text{ cm}^2 = 8 \times 10^{-2}\text{ m}^2$

$\because \quad \tau = NBIA \sin\theta = 100 \times 5 \times 10 \times 8 \times 10^{-2} \times \sin 60^\circ$

$= 346.41\text{ N-m}$

Example 7 Find the magnitude of magnetic moment of the current carrying loop *ABCDEFA*. Each side of the loop is 10 cm long and current in the loop is $I = 2.0$ A.

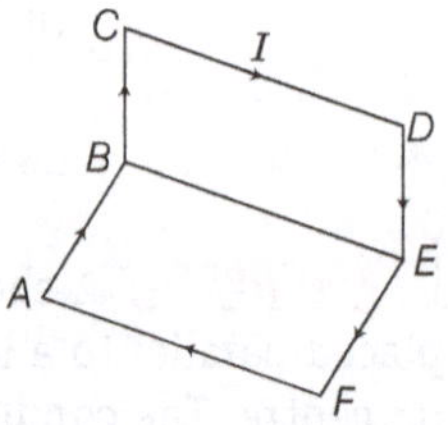

Sol. By assuming two equal and opposite currents in *BE*, two current carrying loops (*ABEFA* and *BCDEB*) are formed. Their magnetic moments are equal in magnitude but perpendicular to each other. Hence,

$$M_{\text{net}} = \sqrt{M^2 + M^2} = \sqrt{2}M$$

$\because \quad M = IA = 2 \times (l \times b) = 2 \times (0.1)\,(0.1) = 0.02\text{ A-m}^2$

$\therefore \quad M_{\text{net}} = (\sqrt{2})\,(0.02) = 0.028\text{ A-m}^2$

Circular Current Loop as a Magnetic Dipole

A current loop behaves as a magnetic dipole. If we look at the upper face, current is anti-clockwise, so it has North polarity. If we look at lower face, current is clockwise, so it has South polarity.

That means current loop behaves as a system of two equal and opposite magnetic poles hence, it acts as a magnetic dipole.

Magnetic dipole moment of loop, $M = NIA$

where, I = current flowing through the loop,

A = area enclosed by the loop

and N = number of turns in the coil.

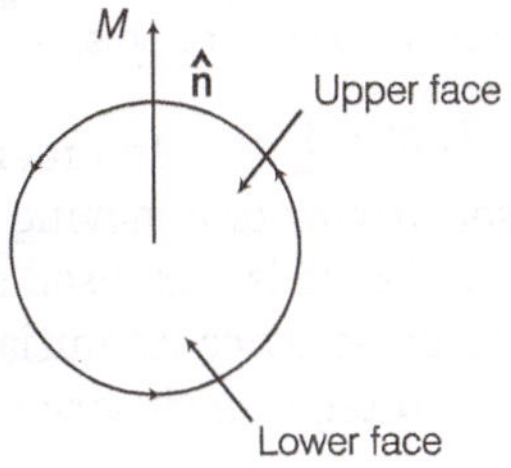

The magnitude of magnetic field on the axis of a circular loop of radius R, carrying steady current I is given by $B = \dfrac{\mu_0 IR^2}{2(x^2 + R^2)^{3/2}}$

For $x >> R$,

$$B = \frac{\mu_0 IR^2}{2x^3} = \frac{\mu_0 IA}{2\pi x^3} \qquad [\because A = \pi R^2]$$

$$\Rightarrow \quad \boxed{B = \frac{\mu_0 M}{2\pi x^3}} \qquad [\because M = IA]$$

Magnetic Dipole Moment of a Revolving Electron

An electron being a charged particle, constitutes a current while moving in its circular orbit around the nucleus ($\because$ Moving charge constitutes a current as well as magnetic field). If T is the time period of revolution, then current constituted by electron is $I = \dfrac{e}{T}$ ... (i)

where, e = charge of electron.

If r is the orbital radius of electron and its orbital speed is v, then

$$T = \frac{2\pi r}{v} \Rightarrow I = \frac{e}{\frac{2\pi r}{v}} = \frac{ev}{2\pi r} \qquad \text{[from Eq. (i)]}$$

Magnetic moment of revolving electron, $M = IA$

$$M = \frac{ev}{2\pi r}\pi r^2 = \frac{evr}{2}$$

The direction of this magnetic moment is into the plane of the paper.

$$M = \frac{e}{2m_e}(m_e vr) = \frac{e}{2m_e}l \text{ or } M = \frac{-el}{2m_e}$$

where, $l = m_e vr$ is angular momentum of the electron.

$\dfrac{M}{l} = \dfrac{e}{2m_e}$ is a constant, called **gyromagnetic ratio**, its value is 8.8×10^{10} C/kg for an electron.

From Bohr's hypothesis, angular momentum can have only some discrete values,

$$l = \frac{nh}{2\pi}$$

where, h = Planck's constant and n is natural number

i.e. $n = 1, 2, 3, \ldots$

$$\Rightarrow \quad M = \frac{e}{2m_e} \cdot \frac{nh}{2\pi} = \frac{e}{4\pi m_e} nh$$

For $n = 1$, M will be minimum.

$$\therefore \quad \boxed{M_{\text{min}} = \frac{eh}{4\pi m_e}}$$

It is Bohr's magneton, which is defined as magnetic moment of revolving electron in its first orbit. Its value is 9.27×10^{-24} A-m^2.

Example 8 An electron in a hydrogen atom is moving with a speed of 2.3×10^6 ms^{-1} in an orbit of radius 0.53 Å. Calculate the magnetic moment of the revolving electron.

Sol. Given, $v = 2.3 \times 10^6$ ms^{-1}, $r = 0.53$ Å $= 0.53 \times 10^{-10}$ **m**

Equivalent current, $I = \dfrac{e}{T} = \dfrac{e}{\frac{2\pi r}{v}} = \dfrac{ev}{2\pi r}$

$$= \frac{1.6 \times 10^{-19} \times 2.3 \times 10^6}{2 \times 3.14 \times 0.53 \times 10^{-10}} = 1.105 \times 10^{-3} \text{ A}$$

$\therefore$ Magnetic moment,

$$M = IA = I(\pi r^2) = 1.105 \times 10^{-3} \times 3.14 \times (0.53 \times 10^{-10})^2$$

$$= 9.75 \times 10^{-24} \text{ A-m}^2$$

Moving Coil Galvanometer

It is an easy and sensitive instrument to defect and measure electric field.

Principle

Its working is based on the fact that when a current carrying coil is placed in a magnetic field, it experiences a torque.

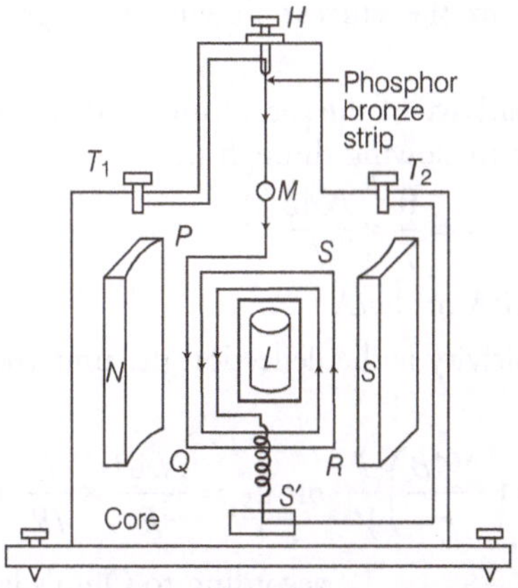

Schematic arrangement of moving coil galvanometer

Construction

The moving coil galvanometer consists of a coil with many turns free to rotate about a fixed axis, in a uniform radial magnetic field. There is a cylindrical soft iron core which not only makes the field radial but also increases the strength of the magnetic field. When a current flows through the coil, a torque acts on it.

Working

Suppose the coil $PQRS$ is suspended freely in the magnetic field. Let l be length PQ or RS of the coil, b be breadth QR or SP of the coil, N be number of turns in the coil and area of each turn of the coil, $A = l \times b$.Let B be strength of the magnetic field in which coil is suspended and I is current passing through the coil in the direction $PQRS$.

Let at any instant, α be the angle, which normal drawn on the plane of the coil makes with the direction of magnetic field. The rectangular coil carrying current when placed in the magnetic field experiences a torque whose magnitude is given by $\tau = NIBA \sin \alpha$.Due to deflecting torque, the coil rotates and suspension wire gets twisted. A restoring torque is set up in the suspension wire.

Let θ be the twist produced in the phosphor bronze strip due to rotation of the coil and k be the restoring torque per unit twist of the phosphor bronze strip. Then,

Total restoring torque produced $= k\theta$

In equilibrium position of the coil, Deflecting torque = Restoring torque

$$NIBA = k\theta \Rightarrow I = \frac{k}{NBA}\theta = G\theta \text{ where, } \frac{k}{NBA} = G$$

It is known as galvanometer constant.

i.e. $\theta \propto I$. It means that the deflection produced is proportional to the current flowing through the galvanometer.

Current sensitivity of the galvanometer is the deflection per unit current flowing through it.

It is given by $I_S = \frac{\theta}{I} = \frac{NAB}{k}$

Its unit is rad/A or div/A.

Voltage sensitivity is the deflection per unit voltage.

It is given by

$$V_S = \frac{\theta}{V} = \left(\frac{NAB}{k}\right)\frac{I}{V} \text{ or } V_S = \frac{NAB}{k} \times \frac{I}{IR} = \frac{NAB}{kR}$$

[$\because$ according to Ohm's law, $V = IR$]

Its unit is rad/V or div/V.

Note Dead beat galvanometer is one in which the coil comes to rest at once after the passage of current through it. The deflection can be noted in no time.

Example 9 In order to increase the current sensitivity of a moving coil galvanometer by 50%, its resistance is increased so that the new resistance becomes twice its initial resistance. By what factor does its voltage sensitivity change?

Sol. Increased current sensitivity, $I'_S = I_S + \frac{50\, I_S}{100} = \frac{150\, I_S}{100}$

$$= \frac{3\, I_S}{2},\ R' = 2R$$

Initial voltage sensitivity, $V_S = \frac{I_S}{R}$ ...(i)

New voltage sensitivity, $V'_S = \frac{I'_S}{R'} = \frac{\frac{3}{2} I_S}{2R}$

$\Rightarrow$ $V'_S = \frac{3}{4} V_S$ [from Eq. (i)]

$\therefore$ % decrease in voltage sensitivity $= \frac{V_S - V'_S}{V_S} \times 100$

$$= \left(1 - \frac{3}{4}\right) \times 100 = 25\%$$

Note This topic has been frequently asked in the previous year exams, i.e. in year 2016, 2015, 2014, 2010, 2009.

Conversion of a Galvanometer into Ammeter

To convert a galvanometer into ammeter, its resistance needs to be lowered, so that maximum current can pass through it and it can give exact reading.

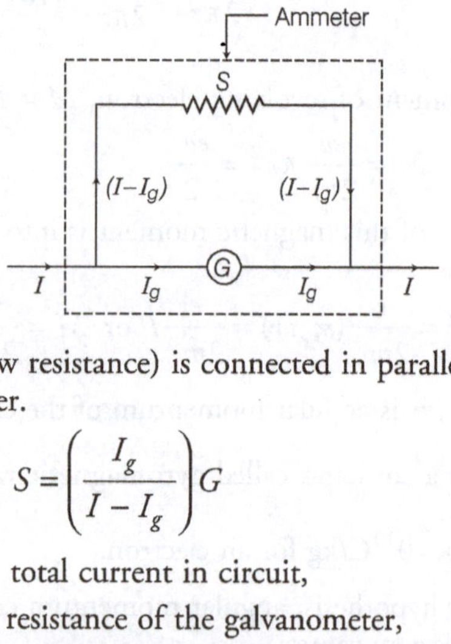

A shunt (low resistance) is connected in parallel with the galvanometer.

$$S = \left(\frac{I_g}{I - I_g}\right)G$$

where, $I =$ total current in circuit,

$G =$ resistance of the galvanometer,

$S =$ resistance of the shunt (low resistance)

and $I_g =$ current through the galvanometer.

Example 10 A galvanometer of resistance 15 Ω gives full scale deflection for a current of 2 mA. Calculate the shunt resistance needed to convert it to an ammeter of range 0 to 5 A.

Sol. Given, $G = 15\ \Omega$, $I_g = 2\text{ mA} = 2\times10^{-3}\text{ A}$, $I = 5\text{ A}$

$\therefore$ Shunt resistance, $S = \dfrac{I_g G}{I - I_g}$

$$= \frac{2\times10^{-3}\times15}{5-2\times10^{-3}} = 0.006\ \Omega$$

This resistance $S = 0.006\ \Omega$ is connected in parallel with the galvanometer. The small resistance is connected in parallel, because we have to decrease the resistance of the galvanometer so that most of the current passes through it and it gives the exact value of the current.

Conversion of a Galvanometer into Voltmeter

To convert a galvanometer into voltmeter, its resistance needs to be increased, so that there is no potential drop across it because with high resistance no current passes through it.

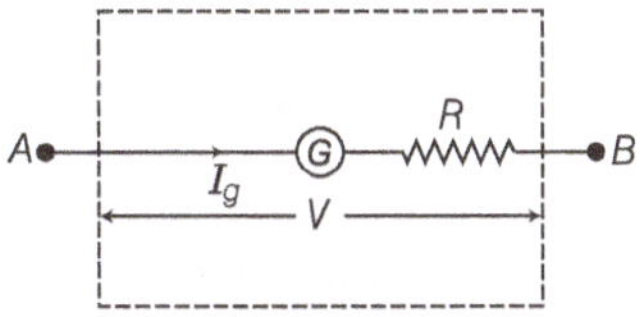

Voltmeter

A high resistance is connected in series with the galvanometer, then the value of R is given by

$$R = \frac{V}{I_g} - G$$

where, V = potential difference across the terminals A and B

I_g = current through the galvanometer (full scale deflection current),

R = high resistance

and G = resistance of the galvanometer.

Example 11 The full scale deflection current of a galvanometer of resistance 1 Ω is 5 mA. How will you convert it into a voltmeter of range 5 V?

Sol. From the relation, $V = I_g (G + R)$, we have

$$R = \frac{V}{I_g} - G = \left(\frac{5}{5\times10^{-3}}\right) - 1 = 999\ \Omega$$

i.e., a resistance of 999 Ω should be connected in series with the galvanometer to convert it into a voltmeter of desired range.

Topic Practice 3

Multiple Choice Questions

1 Mark

1. Two similar coils are placed mutually perpendicular such that their centres coincide. At centre, the ratio of the magnetic field due to one coil and the resultant magnetic field of both coils for same current will be

(a) $1:\sqrt{2}$ (b) $1:2$

(c) $2:1$ (d) $\sqrt{3}:1$

2. Magnetic moment (or magnetic dipole moment) of a current-carrying coil is given by

(a) $\mathbf{m} = IN\mathbf{A}$ (b) $\mathbf{m} = \dfrac{I}{A}$

(c) $\mathbf{m} = N\mathbf{A}$ (d) $\mathbf{m} = \dfrac{NI}{A}$

3. A moving coil galvanometer is an instrument which

(a) is used to measure EMF

(b) is used to measure potential difference

(c) is used to measure resistance

(d) is a deflection instrument which gives a deflection when a current flows through its coil

4. In a moving coil galvanometer of coil of N turns of area A have a spring of stiffness k. If coil is deflected by some angle ϕ due to flow of I current in uniform radial magnetic field B, then

(a) $\phi = \left(\dfrac{NAB}{k}\right)I$ (b) $\phi = \left(\dfrac{k}{BNA}\right)I$

(c) $\phi = \left(\dfrac{kA}{BN}\right)I$ (d) $\phi = \left(\dfrac{BN}{kA}\right)I$

5. **Assertion** When an electric current is passed through a moving coil galvanometer, its coil gets deflected.

Reason A circular coil produces a uniform magnetic field around itself when an electric current is passed through it. **ISC 2024**

(a) Both Assertion and Reason are true and Reason is the correct explanation for Assertion.

(b) Both Assertion and Reason are true but Reason is not the correct explanation for Assertion.

(c) Assertion is true and Reason is false.

(d) Assertion is false and Reason is true.

Very Short Answer Type Questions

1 Mark

6. A coil of N turns and radius R carries a current I. It is unwound and rewound to make another coil of radius $R/2$ having same number of turns N. Keeping the current I same, find the ratio of the magnetic moments of the other new coil and the circular coil.

7. A conducting loop carrying a current I is placed in a uniform magnetic field, pointing into the plane of the paper as shown in the figure, then the loop will have a tendency to expand. Explain.

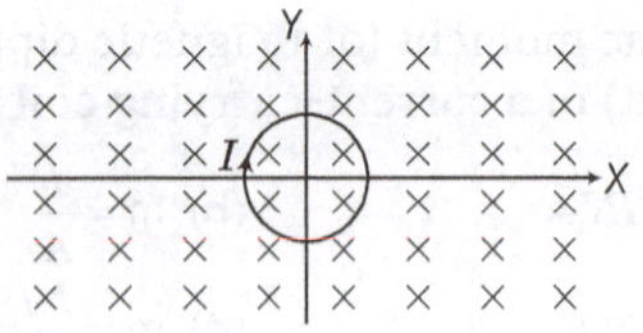

8. Why are the pole pieces of a horseshoe magnet in a moving coil galvanometer made cylindrical in shape? **ISC 2019**

9. Write the underlying principle of a moving coil galvanometer.

10. Why should the spring/suspension wire in a moving coil galvanometer have low torsional constant?

11. Why is a coil wrapped on a conducting frame in a galvanometer?

12. State how a moving coil galvanometer can be converted into an ammeter. **ISC 2016**

13. In a moving coil galvanometer, what is meant by a radial magnetic field? **ISC 2012**

14. State two factors on which the sensitivity of a moving coil galvanometer depends. **ISC 2006**

15. What is the purpose of concave pole pieces in a moving coil galvanometer? **ISC 2001**

16. How can a moving coil galvanometer be converted into a voltmeter? **ISC 2020**

17. A voltmeter, an ammeter and a resistance are connected in series with a lead accumulator. The voltmeter gives some deflection but the deflection of ammeter is zero. Comment.

Short Answer Type I Questions

2 Marks

18. Two long parallel wires carrying a current I, separated by a distance r are exerting a force F on each other. If the distance between them is increased to $2r$ and current in each wire is reduced from I to $I/2$, then what will be the force between them?

19. Two long wires carrying currents I_1 and I_2 are arranged as shown in the figure. One carrying current I_1 is along the X-axis. The other carrying current I_2 is along a line parallel to Y-axis, given by $x = 0$ and $z = d$. Find the force exerted at point O_2 because of the wire along the X-axis.

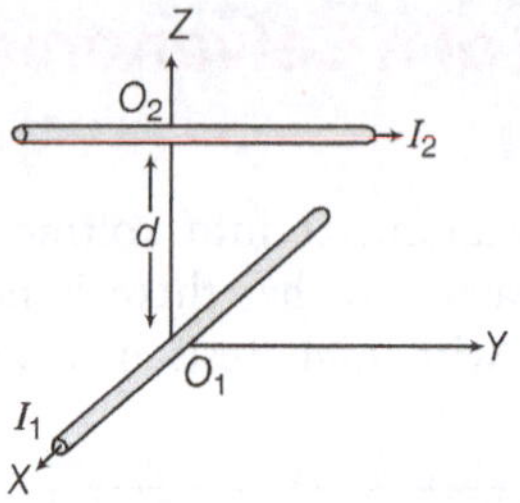

NCERT Exemplar

20. (i) Two long straight parallel conductors a and b carrying steady currents I_a and I_b respectively are separated by a distance d. Write the magnitude and direction, what is the nature and magnitude of the force between the two conductors?

(ii) Show with the help of a diagram, how the force between the two conductors would change when the currents in them flow in the opposite directions.

21. Figure below shows two infinitely long and thin current carrying conductors X and Y kept in vacuum, parallel to each other at a distance a.

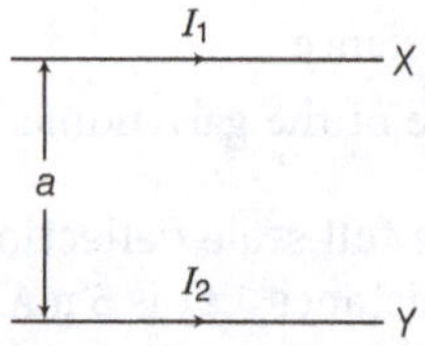

(i) How much force per unit length act on the conductor Y due to the current flowing through X? Write your answer in terms of $\left(\frac{\mu_0}{4\pi}\right)$, I_1, I_2 and a.

[Derivation of formula is not required]

(ii) Define ampere in terms of force between two current carrying conductors.
ISC 2016, 13, 11, 08

22. Write an expression for force per unit length between two long current carrying wires, kept parallel to each other, in vacuum and hence define an ampere, the SI unit of current. **ISC 2020**

23. A rectangular coil of sides l and b carrying a current I is subjected to a uniform magnetic field **B** acting perpendicular to its plane. Obtain the expression for the torque acting on it.

24. Define current sensitivity and voltage sensitivity of galvanometer. Increasing the current sensitivity may not necessarily increase the voltage sensitivity of a galvanometer, justify your answer.

25. How is a moving coil galvanometer converted into a voltmeter? Explain giving the necessary circuit diagram and the required mathematical relation used.

Short Answer Type II Questions

3 Marks

26. Draw a labelled diagram of a moving coil galvanometer and explain its working. What is the function of radial magnetic field inside the coil?

27. A uniform conducting wire of length 12 a and resistance R is wound up as a current carrying coil in the shape of

(i) an equilateral triangle of side a,

(ii) a square of sides a and

(iii) a regular hexagon of side a. The coil is connected to a voltage source V_0. Find the magnetic moment of the coils in each case.
NCERT Exemplar

28. Two very long conductors carrying currents I_1 and I_2 are separated by a distance d as shown in the figure. Give the expressions (do not derive) for the magnetic fields $\mathbf{B}_{12}$ and $\mathbf{B}_{21}$ at P and Q respectively, produced by the electric currents I_2 and I_1. What are the directions of these fields?

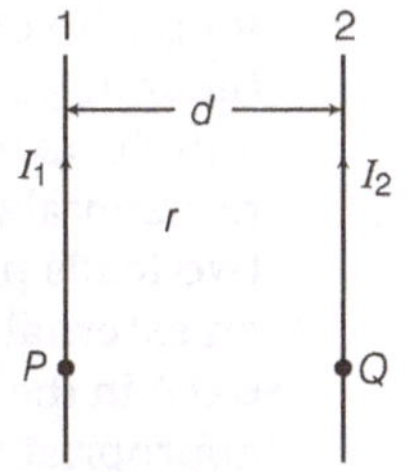

Define the SI unit of currents using the below set up. **ISC 2007**

29. A small magnetic needle NS having magnetic dipole moment $\mathbf{p}_m$ is kept in two uniform and perpendicular magnetic fields $\mathbf{B}_F$ and $\mathbf{B}_H$ as shown below.

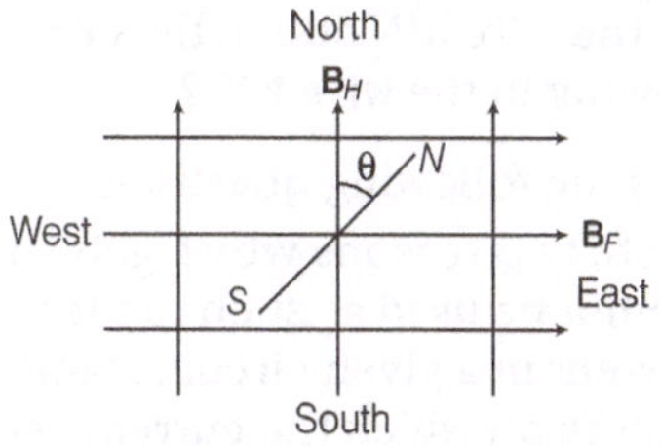

(i) What is the effect of each of the magnetic fields $\mathbf{B}_F$ and $\mathbf{B}_H$ on the needle?

(ii) When the needle is in equilibrium, obtain an expression for angle θ made by the needle with $\mathbf{B}_H$ in terms of $\mathbf{B}_F$ and $\mathbf{B}_H$ only. **ISC 2010**

30. Obtain the formula, $I = k\theta$ for a moving coil galvanometer given the deflecting torque $\tau = \text{M} \times \text{B}$, where M is the magnetic dipole moment of the coil placed in the magnetic field B, I is the current in the galvanometer and θ is the deflection. **ISC 2008**

31. An electron of mass m_e revolves around a nucleus of charge $+Ze$. Show that it behaves like a tiny magnetic dipole. Hence, prove that the magnetic moment associated with it is expressed as $\mu = -\frac{e}{2m_e}\text{L}$, where L is the orbital angular momentum of the electron. Give the significance of negative sign.

32. Figure below shows an infinitely long metallic wire YY' which is carrying a current I'. P is a point at a perpendicular distance r from it.

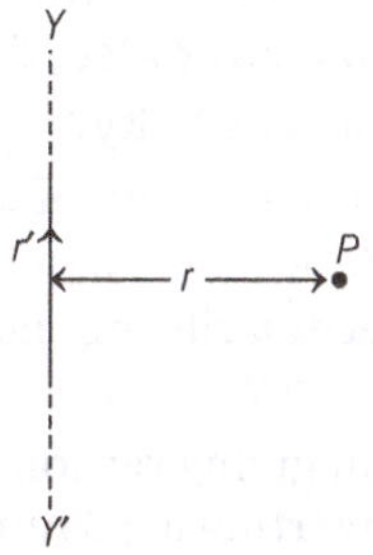

(i) What is the direction of magnetic flux density B of the magnetic field at the point P?

(ii) What is the magnitude of magnetic flux density B of the magnetic field at the point P?

(iii) Another metallic wire MN having length l and carrying a current I is now kept at the point P. If the two wires are in vacuum and parallel to each other, how much force acts on the wire MN due to the current I' flowing in the wire YY'? **ISC 2024**

33. Answers the following questions.
(i) Write two reasons why a galvanometer cannot be used as such to measure the current in a given circuit. Name any two factors on which the current sensitivity of a galvanometer depends.
(ii) Why is it necessary to introduce a cylindrical soft iron core inside the coil of a galvanometer?

34. State the principle of working of a galvanometer. A galvanometer of resistance G is converted into a voltmeter to measure upto V volts by connecting a resistance R_1 in series with the coil. If a resistance R_2 is connected in series with it, then it can measure upto $V/2$ volts. Find the resistance, in terms of R_1 and R_2, required to be connected to convert it into a voltmeter that can read upto 2V. Also, find the resistance G of the galvanometer in terms of R_1 and R_2.

Long Answer Type Questions

5 Marks

35. Explain using a labelled diagram, the principle and working of a moving coil galvanometer. What is the function of
(i) uniform radial magnetic field?
(ii) soft iron core? Also, define the terms.
(iii) current sensitivity?
(iv) voltage sensitivity of a galvanometer?
Why does increasing the current sensitivity not necessarily increase voltage sensitivity?

36. (i) Explain giving reasons, the basic difference in converting a galvanometer into
(a) a voltmeter.
(b) an ammeter.
(ii) Two long straight parallel conductors carrying steady currents I_1 and I_2 are separated by a distance d. Explain briefly, with the help of a suitable diagram, how the magnetic field due to one conductor acts on the other. Hence, deduce the expression for the force acting between the two conductors. Mention the nature of this force.

Numerical Problems

37. What is the magnitude of magnetic force per unit length on a wire carrying a current of 8 A making an angle of 30° with the direction of a uniform magnetic field of 0.15 T? **NCERT (2 M)**

38. A long straight wire carrying current of 25 A rests on a table shown in the figure. Another wire PQ of length 1 m, mass 2.5 g carries the same current but in the opposite direction. The wire PQ is free to slide up and down. To what height will PQ rise? **NCERT Exemplar (3 M)**

39. A 3.0 cm wire carrying a current of 10 A is placed inside a solenoid perpendicular to its axis. The magnetic field inside the solenoid is given to be 0.27 T. What is the magnetic force on the wire? **NCERT (3 M)**

40. A uniform magnetic field of 1.5 T exists in a cylindrical region of radius 10.0 cm, its direction parallel to the axis along East to West. A wire carrying current of 7.0 A in the North to South direction passes through this region. What is the magnitude and direction of the force on the wire, if
(i) the wire intersect the axis?
(ii) the wire is turned from North-South to North East-North West direction?
(iii) the wire in the North-South direction is lowered from the axis by a distance of 6.0 cm? **NCERT (3 M)**

41. A solenoid 60 cm long and of radius 4.0 cm has 3 layers of winding of 300 turns each. A 2.0 cm long wire of mass 2.5 g lies inside the solenoid (near its centre) normal to its axis, both the wire and the axis of the solenoid are in the horizontal plane. The wire is connected through two leads parallel to the axis of the solenoid to an external battery which supplies a current of 6.0 A in the wire. What value of current (with appropriate sense of circulation) in the windings of the solenoid can support the weight of the wire? ($g = 9.8\ m/s^2$) **NCERT (3 M)**

42. A conductor of length 2 m carrying current of 2 A is held parallel to an infinitely long conductor carrying current of 10 A at a distance of 100 mm. Find the force on a small conductor. **(2 M)**

43. Two long and parallel straight wires A and B carrying currents of 8.0 A and 5.0 A in the same direction are separated by a distance of 4.0 cm. Estimate the force on a 10 cm section of wire A. **NCERT (2 M)**

44. A wire AB is carrying a steady current of 12 A and is lying on the table. Another wire CD carrying 5 A is held directly above AB at a height of 1 mm.
Find the mass per unit length of the wire CD, so that it remains suspended at its position, when left free. Give the direction of the current flowing in CD with respect to that in AB. (Take the value of $g = 10\ ms^{-2}$) **(3 M)**

45. A rectangular loop of area $5m^2$, has 50 turns and carries a current of 1 A. It is held in an uniform magnetic field of O.1T, at an angle of 30°. Calculate the torque experienced by the coil. **ISC 2019 (2 M)**

46. A circular coil of N turns and radius R carries a current I. It is unwound and rewound to make another coil of radius $R/2$, current I remaining the same. Calculate the ratio of the magnetic moments of the new coil and the original coil. **ISC 2003 (2 M)**

47. A square coil of side 10 cm consists of 20 turns and carries current of 12 A. The coil is suspended vertically and normal to the plane of the coil makes an angle of 30° with the direction of a uniform horizontal magnetic field of magnitude 0.80 T. What is the magnitude of torque experienced by the coil? **NCERT (2 M)**

48. (i) A circular coil of 30 turns and radius 8.0 cm carrying a current of 6.0 A is suspended vertically in a uniform horizontal magnetic field of magnitude 1.0 T. The field lines make an angle 60° with the normal of the coil. Calculate the magnitude of the counter torque that must be applied to prevent the coil from turning.
(ii) Would your answer change, if the circular coil were replaced by a planar coil of some irregular shape that encloses the same area? All other particulars are also unaltered. **NCERT (3 M)**

49. A circular coil of 20 turns and radius 10 cm is placed in a uniform magnetic field of 0.1 T normal to the plane of the coil. If the current in the coil is 5.0 A, what is the (i) total torque on the coil, (ii) total force on the coil (iii) average force on each electron in the coil due to the magnetic field?
(The coil is made of copper wire of cross-sectional area $10^{-5}\ m^2$ and the free electron density in copper is given to be about $10^{29}/m^3$). **NCERT (3 M)**

50. A moving coil galvanometer of resistance 55 Ω produces a full scale deflection for a current of 250 mA. How will you convert it into an ammeter having a range of 0 to 3 A? **ISC 2023 (2 M)**

51. A rectangular coil of area $2 \times 10^{-4} m^2$ and 40 turns is pivoted about one of its vertical sides. The coil is in a radial horizontal field of 60 G. What is the torsional constant of the hair springs connected to the coil, if a current of 4.0 mA produces an angular deflection of 16°? **(2 M)**

52. Two moving coil meters M_1 and M_2 having the following particulars
$R_1 = 10\ \Omega$, $N_1 = 30$, $A_1 = 3.6 \times 10^{-3} m^2$,
$B_1 = 0.25\ T$
$R_2 = 14\ \Omega$, $N_2 = 42$, $A_2 = 1.8 \times 10^{-3} m^2$,
$B_2 = 0.50\ T$ (The spring constants are identical for the two meters). Determine the ratio of (i) current sensitivity and (ii) voltage sensitivity of M_2 and M_1. **NCERT (3 M)**

53. A galvanometer coil has a resistance of 15 Ω and the meter shows full scale deflection for a current of 4 mA. How will you convert the meter into an ammeter of range 0 to 6 A? **NCERT (2 M)**

54. When a galvanometer having 30 division scale and 100 Ω resistance is connected in series to the battery of emf 3 V through a resistance of 200 Ω, shows full scale deflection. Find the figure of merit of the galvanometer in microampere. **(2 M)**

55. A galvanometer coil has a resistance of 12 Ω and the meter shows full scale deflection for a current of 3 mA. How will you convert the meter into a voltmeter of range 0 to 18 V? **NCERT (2 M)**

Hints & Solutions

1. (*a*)

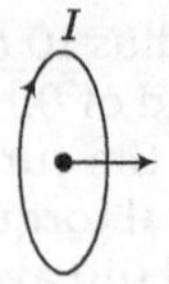

For a single coil, magnetic field, $B_s = \dfrac{\mu_0 I}{2R}$ ...(i)

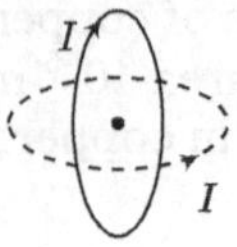

For two coils magnetic field,

$$B_T = \sqrt{B_1^2 + B_2^2} = \sqrt{2}\,\frac{\mu_0 I}{2R} \quad \text{...(ii)}$$

On comparing Eqs. (i) and (ii), we get

$$\frac{B_S}{B_T} = \frac{1}{\sqrt{2}}$$

2. (*a*) Magnetic moment of a current-carrying loop is

$$\mathbf{m} = NI\mathbf{A}$$

where, N is number of turns, I is current flowing on a loop and A is area of cross-section of loop.

3. (*d*) A moving coil galvanometer is a sensitive instrument which is used to measure a deflection when a current flows through its coil.

4. (*a*) When a current flows through the coil, a torque acts on it. This torque is given by $\tau = NIAB$.

where, the symbols have their usual meaning. Since, the field is radial by design, we have taken $\sin\theta = 1$ in the above expression for the torque. The magnetic torque $NIAB$ tends to rotate the coil.

A spring S_P provides a counter torque $k\phi$ that balances the magnetic torque $NIAB$; resulting in a steady angular deflection ϕ. In equilibrium $k\phi = NIAB$.

where, k is the torsional constant of the spring, i.e. the restoring torque per unit twist. The deflection ϕ is indicated on the scale by a pointer attached to the spring. We have

$$\phi = \left(\frac{NAB}{k}\right) I$$

5. (*a*) Both Assertion and Reason are true and Reason is the correct explanation for Assertion.

The moving coil galvanometer consists of a coil with many turns free to rotate about a fixed axis and in this way, coil gets deflected in a uniform radial magnetic field. When a current flows through the coil, a torque acts on it and gets deflected.

6. Ratio of the magnetic moments,

$$\frac{M'}{M} = \frac{\frac{1}{2}\pi NiR^2}{\pi NiR^2} = \frac{1}{2}$$

7. We can see that magnetic field is perpendicular to paper and current in the loop is in clockwise direction. So,by Fleming's left hand rule, force on each element of the loop is radially outwards, so loop will have a tendency to expand.

8. For increasing the strength of the magnetic field, the pole pieces of a horseshoe magnet in a moving coil galvanometer are made cylindrical in shape.

9. The principle of moving coil galvanometer is based on the fact that when a current carrying coil is placed in a magnetic field, it experiences a torque.

10. Low torsional constant facilitates greater deflection θ in coil for given value of current and hence, sensitivity of galvanometer increases.

11. In order to produce electromagnetic damping, i.e. by producing eddy currents in conducting frame which helps in stopping the coil soon.

12. A moving coil galvanometer can be converted into an ammeter by using a low resistance wire in parallel with it.

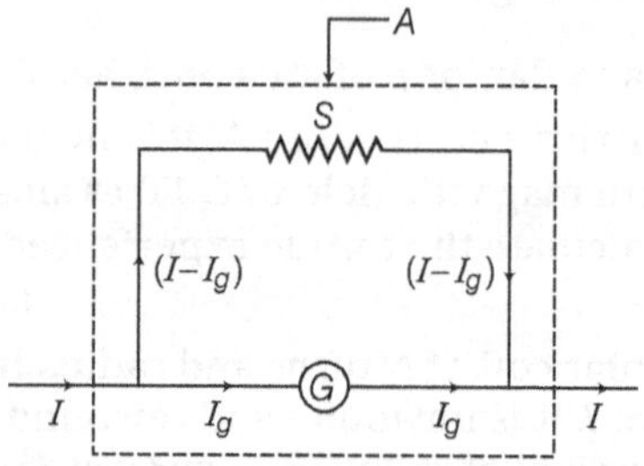

13. **Radial magnetic field** When plane of the coil is parallel to the magnetic field such that the area vector of the coil is perpendicular to the magnetic field, the field is called radial magnetic field.

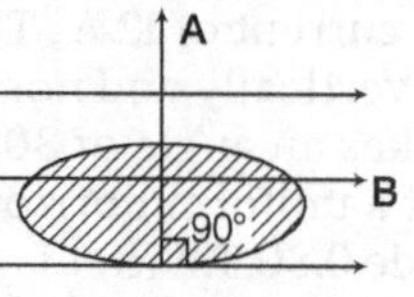

14. The current sensitivity and voltage sensitivity of the galvanometer depend on the number of turns of coil, magnetic field **B**, area A of the coil and torsion constant k of the spring or suspension wire.

15. The purpose of concave pole pieces in a moving coil galvanometer is to ensure that the plane of the coil is always parallel to the magnetic field, such that $\theta = 90°$ and $\tau = NIBA$, where symbols have their usual meanings.

16. Refer to text on page 197.
(Conservation of a galvanometer into voltmeter).

17. Voltmeter and resistance being very high when connected in series, makes the effective resistance of the circuit very high. Due to this, current in the circuit becomes extremely small.

18. Force per unit length is $F = \dfrac{\mu_0 2I^2}{4\pi r}$ $[\because I_1 = I_2 = I]$ (1/2)

If r is increased to $2r$ and I is reduced to $\dfrac{I}{2}$, then new

force per unit length is $F' = \dfrac{\mu_0}{4\pi} \times \dfrac{2(I/2)^2}{2r}$

$$= \frac{1}{8}\left(\frac{\mu_0}{4\pi} \cdot \frac{2I^2}{r}\right)$$

$$\Rightarrow \qquad F' = \frac{F}{8}$$

$\therefore$ Force per unit length between them is $\dfrac{F}{8}$. (1½)

19. Here, first we have to find the direction of magnetic field at point O_2 due to the wire carrying current I_1. Use Maxwell's right hand grip (cork screw) rule, the direction of magnetic field at point O_2 due to current I_1 is along Y-axis.
Here, the wire at point O_2 is placed along Y-axis. Now, by the formula, $\mathbf{F} = I_2 (\mathbf{l} \times \mathbf{B})$
Angle between $\mathbf{l}$ and $\mathbf{B}$ is 0°, both are at Y-axis, i.e.

$$F = IlB \sin 0° = 0$$

So, the force exerted at point O_2 because of wire along X-axis is zero. (2)

20. (i) Refer to text on pages 192 and 193 (Force between two parallel current carrying conductors). (1)

(ii)

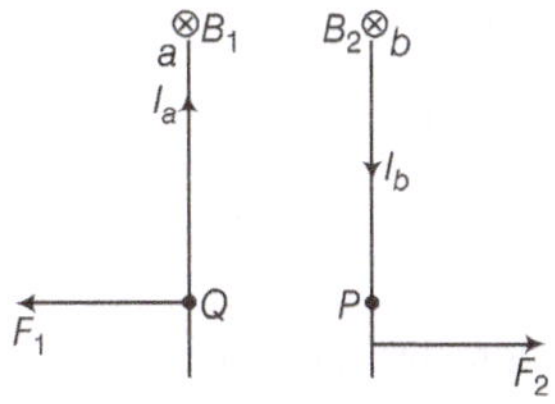

Now, let the direction of current in conductor b be reversed. The magnetic field B_2 at point P due to current I_a flowing through a will be downwards. Similarly, the magnetic field B_1 at point Q due to current I_b passing through b will also be downward as shown. The froce on a will be therefore towards the left. Also, the force on b will be towards the right. Hence, the two conductors will repel each other as shown. (1)

21. First, we have to find force between the wires by assuming that one of the wires is of finite length. Then, force is divided by length to find force per unit length.
(i) Let length of the wire Y be l.

Force on Y, $F_Y = \dfrac{\mu_0 I_1}{2\pi a}(I_2 l)$, towards X.

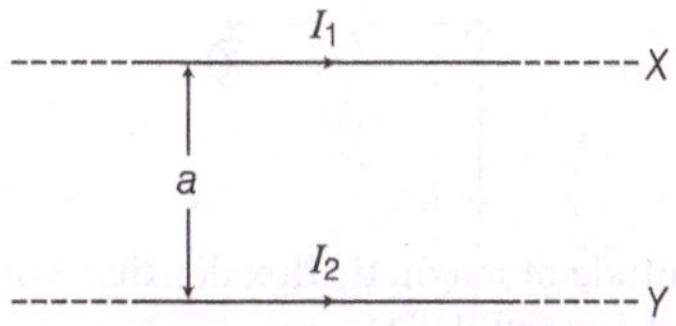

Force per unit length, $\dfrac{F_Y}{l} = \dfrac{\mu_0 I_1 I_2}{2\pi a}$ (1)

(ii) One ampere is that value of steady current which on flowing in each of two parallel infinitely long conductors of negligible cross-section placed in vacuum at a distance of 1m from each other, produces a force of 2×10^{-7} newton per metre between them. (1)

22. Refer to text on pages 192 and 193 (Force between two parallel current carrying conductors).

23. Equivalent magnetic moment of the coil,

$$\mathbf{M} = IA\hat{\mathbf{n}}$$

$$\therefore \qquad \mathbf{M} = Ilb\,\hat{\mathbf{n}}$$

where, $\hat{\mathbf{n}}$ = unit vector $\perp$ to the plane of the coil.

$\therefore$ Torque $= \mathbf{M} \times \mathbf{B} = Ilb(\hat{\mathbf{n}} \times \mathbf{B}) = 0$ (2)

As $\hat{\mathbf{n}}$ and $\mathbf{B}$ are parallel or anti-parallel to each other.

24. Refer to text on pages 195 and 196 (Moving coil galvanometer). (1)

Increasing the current sensitivity may not necessarily increase the voltage sensitivity, because the current sensitivity increases with the increase of number of turns of the coil but the resistance of coil also increases which affect adversely on voltage sensitivity. (1)

25. Refer to text on page 197 (Conversion of galvanometer into voltmeter).

26. Refer to text on pages 195 and 196 (Moving coil galvanometer).

27. We know that magnetic moment of the coil $M = NIA$. Since, the same wire is used in three cases with same potentials, therefore, same current flows in three cases.

> **Key Point:** The different shapes form figures of different area and hence, their magnetic moments vary.

(i) For an equilateral triangle of side a,
$N = 4$, as the total wire of length $= 12a$
Magnetic moment of the coil,

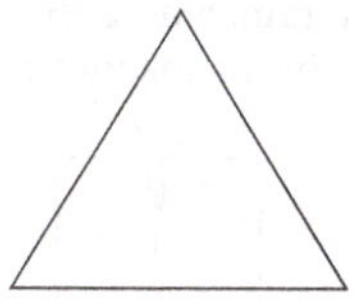

N=4

$$M = NIA = 4I\left(\frac{\sqrt{3}}{4}a^2\right)$$

$$\Rightarrow M = Ia^2\sqrt{3}$$ (1)

(ii) For a square of side a, $A = a^2$
$N = 3$, as the total wire of length $= 12a$
Magnetic moment of the coil,

N=3

$$M = NIA = 3I(a^2) = 3I\,a^2$$ (1)

(iii) For a regular hexagon of sides a,
$N = 2$, as the total wire of length $= 12a$

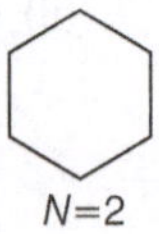

Magnetic moment of the coils,

$$M = NIA = 2\,I\left(\frac{6\sqrt{3}}{4}a^2\right) = 3\sqrt{3}a^2 I$$

$\therefore$ M is in a geometric series. (1)

28. Refer to text on pages 192 and 193 (Force between two parallel current carrying conductors).
The direction of field at P is perpendicular to the plane of the paper and outwards. The direction of field at Q is perpendicularly inwards to the plane of paper.

29. As the magnetic needle is placed in a two mutually perpendicular fields, both the fields will try to rotate the magnet in opposite directions.

(i) We know that, torque on a magnetic dipole placed in a uniform magnetic field **B** is $\tau = \mathbf{M} \times \mathbf{B}$
where, **M** is magnetic dipole moment and **B** is magnetic field.
The diagram (below) shows the situation given in question.

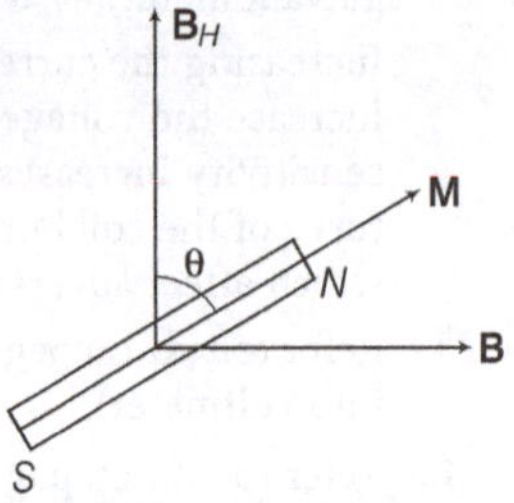

Torque due to $\mathbf{B}_H$ is anti-clockwise and due to $\mathbf{B}_F$ is clockwise. (2)

(ii) In equilibrium, $|\tau_{B_H}| = |\tau_{B_F}|$

$$\Rightarrow MB_H \sin\theta = MB_F \sin(90 - \theta)$$

$$\Rightarrow \tan\theta = \frac{B_F}{B_H} \Rightarrow \theta = \tan^{-1}\left(\frac{B_F}{B_H}\right)$$

Here, **M** represents the magnetic moment. (1)

30. The working of a moving coil galvanometer is based on the fact that when a current carrying coil is placed in a magnetic field, it experiences a net torque.
Consider the diagram, where the coil $PQRS_1$, is suspended freely in the magnetic field.

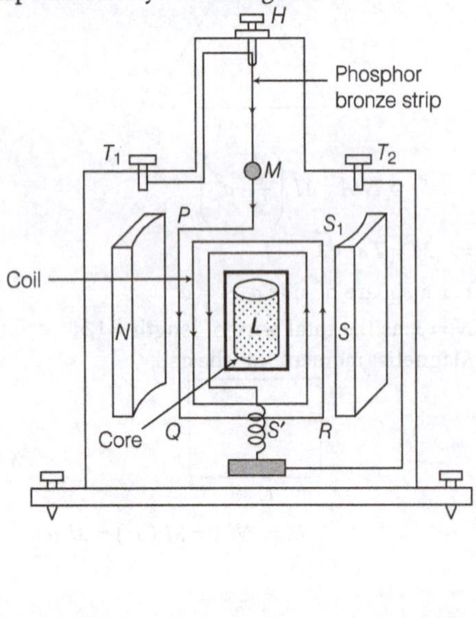

Let l = length PQ or RS of the coil,
b = breadth QR or SP of the coil
and N = number of turns in the coil.
Area of each turn of the coil, $A = l \times b$
Let B = strength of the magnetic field in which coil is suspended
and I = current passing through the coil in the direction of $PQRS$. (1)

Let at any instant of time, α be the angle which the normal drawn to the plane of the coil makes with the direction of magnetic field.
The rectangular current carrying coil when placed in the magnetic field experiences a torque whose magnitude is given by

$$\tau = NIBA \sin\alpha$$

Due to this torque, the coil rotates and suspension wire gets twisted. A restoring torque is set up in the suspension wire.
Let θ be the twist produced in the phosphor bronze strip due to rotation of the coil and k be the restoring torque per unit twist of the phosphor bronze strip.
Then, total restoring torque produced $= k\theta$.
In equilibrium position of the coil,
Deflection torque = Restoring torque

$$\therefore \quad NIBA = k\theta \qquad [\because \alpha = 90°]$$

or

$$I = \frac{k}{NBA}\theta = G\theta$$

where, $\frac{k}{NBA} = G$

It is known as galvanometer constant.

$$\Rightarrow \quad I \propto \theta$$

$\therefore$ Current is directly proportional to the deflection produced in the coil. (2)

31. Refer to text on page 195 (Magnetic dipole moment of a revolving electron). (2)

In vector form, $\mu = \frac{-e\mathbf{L}}{2m_e}$

Here, negative sign indicates that μ directs away from **L**. (1)

32. (i) The direction of magnetic flux density B of the magnetic field at point P is downward and into the paper.

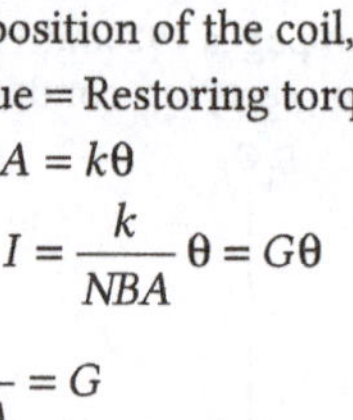

(ii) Magnitude of magnetic flux density B of the magnetic field at the point P is

$$B = \frac{\mu_0 I}{2\pi r}$$

(iii) Force on wire MN having length l and carrying a current I due to long metallic wire YY',

$$F = \frac{\mu_0}{4\pi}\frac{2I'I}{r}l$$

33. (i) The galvanometer cannot be used to measure the current because

(a) all the currents to be measured passes through coil and it gets damaged easily.

(b) its coil has considerable resistance because of length and it may affect original current. (1)

Current sensitivity of galvanometer depends on

(a) the magnetic field

(b) the value of torsional constant. (1)

(ii) It is necessary to introduce a cylindrical soft iron core inside the coil of a galvanometer because magnetic field is increased, so its sensitivity increases and magnetic field becomes radial. So, angle between the plane of coil and magnetic line of force is zero in all orientations of coil. (1)

34. According to the principle of working of a moving coil galvanometer, when a current carrying coil is placed in a magnetic field, it experiences a torque. (1)

A high resistance that is connected in series with the galvanometer to convert into voltmeter. The value of the resistance is given by

$$R = \frac{V}{I_g} - G$$

where, V = potential difference across the terminals of the voltmeter, I_g = current through the galvanometer and G = resistance of the galvanometer.

When resistance R_1 is connected in series with the galvanometer, then

$$R_1 = \frac{V}{I_g} - G. \quad ..\text{(i)}$$

When resistance R_2 is connected in series with the galvanometer, then

$$R_2 = \frac{V}{2I_g} - G \quad ...\text{(ii)}$$

From Eqs. (i) and (ii), we get

$$\frac{V}{2I_g} = R_1 - R_2$$

and $\quad G = R_1 - 2R_2$

The resistance R_3 required to convert the given galvanometer into voltmeter of range 0 to 2 V is given by

$$R_3 = \frac{2V}{I_g} - G$$

$$\Rightarrow \quad R_3 = 4(R_1 - R_2) - (R_1 - 2R_2) = 3R_1 - 2R_2$$

G in terms of R_1 and R_2 is given by $G = R_1 - 2R_2$ (2)

35. For principle and working of galvanometer,

Refer to text on pages 195 and 196 (Moving coil galvanometer). (1)

(i) **Cylindrical soft iron** core which not only makes the field radial but also increases the strength of the magnet.

(ii) **Radial magnetic field** is a field in which coil of the galvanometer always remains parallel to the field even on large deflection. (1)

(iii) and (iv) refer to text on page 196. (1½)

Current sensitivity does not depend upon resistance (R), whereas voltage sensitivity does, as evident from their expression. Current sensitivity can be increased by increasing the number of turns of the coil. However, this increases the resistance of the coil, since voltage sensitivity decreases with increase in the resistance of the coil the effect of increase in number of turns is nullified in the case of voltage sensitivity. (1½)

36. (i) A galvanometer of range I_g and resistance G can be converted into

(a) a voltmeter of range V, by connecting a high resistance R in series with galvanometer whose value is given by

$$R = \frac{V}{I_g} - G \quad (1)$$

(b) an ammeter of range I, by connecting a very low resistance (shunt) in parallel with galvanometer whose value is given by

$$S = \frac{I_g G}{I - I_g} \quad (1)$$

(ii) Refer to text on pages 192 and 193 (Force between parallel current carrying conductors). (2)

Thus, the nature of force is attractive.

When direction of flow of current is in opposite direction, the nature of force becomes repulsive. (1)

37. Here, $I = 8$ A, $\theta = 30°$, $B = 0.15$ T, $F = ?$, $l = 1$ m

We know that, $F = BIl \sin\theta$ (1)

$$\frac{F}{l} = BI\sin\theta$$

$$\frac{F}{l} = 0.15 \times 8 \times \sin 30° = 0.15 \times 8 \times (1/2)$$

$$= 0.6 \text{ N m}^{-1} \quad (1)$$

38. Mass of wire PQ, $m = 2.5$ g $= 2.5 \times 10^{-3}$ kg

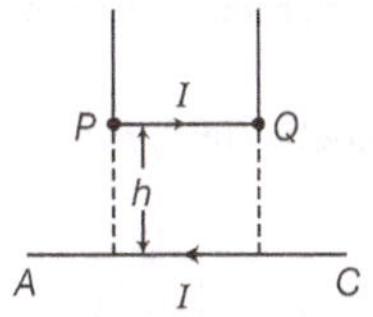

Length of wire PQ, $l = 1$ m

Current in wire PQ and AC, $I = 25$ A

Let the wire PQ rises upto a height h.

The magnetic field on wire PQ due to wire AC is B.

By using the formula of magnetic field due to an infinite length of wire,

$$B = \frac{\mu_0}{4\pi} \cdot \frac{2I}{r} = \frac{\mu_0}{4\pi} \times \frac{2 \times 25}{h}$$

$$= \frac{10^{-7} \times 50}{h} = \frac{50 \times 10^{-7}}{h} \quad \text{...(i)}$$

(1)

The direction of magnetic field B on wire PQ is perpendicularly inwards to the plane of paper (by using Maxwell's right hand rule).

Force on wire PQ, $\mathbf{F} = I\,(\mathbf{l} \times \mathbf{B})$

[$\because$ angle between l and B is 90°]

$$\Rightarrow F = IlB \sin 90° = 25 \times 1 \times \frac{50 \times 10^{-7}}{h} \times 1 \text{ [From Eq.(i)]}$$

$$\Rightarrow F = \frac{1250 \times 10^{-7}}{h} \quad \text{...(ii)}$$

(1)

The wire will lift, if the weight of the wire is balanced by force due to wire AC.

i.e. $F = mg$

$$\Rightarrow \frac{1250 \times 10^{-7}}{h} = 2.5 \times 10^{-3} \times 9.8 \quad \text{[from Eq. (ii)]}$$

$$\therefore \quad h = \frac{1250 \times 10^{-7}}{2.5 \times 9.8 \times 10^{-3}} = 51.02 \times 10^{-4}\,\text{m}$$

$$= 51.02 \times 10^{-2}\,\text{cm} = 0.51\,\text{cm}$$

Thus, the wire PQ will rise upto a height of 0.51 cm. (1)

39. Here, the angle between the magnetic field and the direction of flow of current is 90°. Because the magnetic field due to a solenoid is along the axis of the solenoid and the wire is placed perpendicular to the axis.

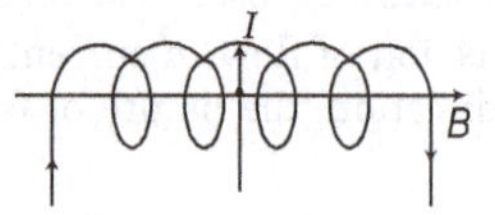

Given, $l = 3\,\text{cm} = 3 \times 10^{-2}\,\text{m}$

$I = 10\,\text{A}, B = 0.27\,\text{T}$

The magnitude of magnetic force on the wire,

$$F = IlB \sin 90°$$

$$= 10 \times 3 \times 10^{-2} \times 0.27 \times \sin 90°$$

$$= 8.1 \times 10^{-2}\,\text{N}$$

(2)

According to right hand palm rule, the direction of magnetic force is perpendicular to plane of paper inwards. (1)

40. (i) Uniform magnetic field, $B = 1.5\,\text{T}$

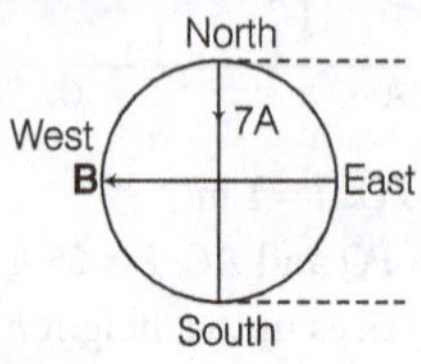

Radius, $r = 10.0\,\text{cm} = 0.1\,\text{m}$

Current in the wire, $I = 7.0\,\text{A}$

The magnitude of force on the wire,

$$\mathbf{F} = I\,(\mathbf{l} \times \mathbf{B}) = IlB \sin 90°$$

[$\because$ angle between l and B is 90° and the length of wire is equal to the diameter of the cylindrical region]

$\therefore$ Force on the wire,

$$F = I \times 2r \times B$$

$$= 7 \times 2 \times 0.1 \times 1.5 = 2.1\,\text{N}$$

According to Fleming's left hand rule, the direction of force is vertically inwards to the plane of paper. (1)

(ii) Now, we take the component of length of wire. The horizontal component experiences no force as B is parallel to length.

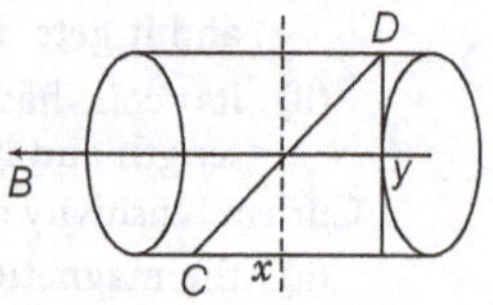

The vertical component,

y = Diameter of the cylinder

So, force $F = IlB \sin 90°$

$$= 7 \times 0.1 \times 1.5 \times 2 \times 1$$

$$= 2.1\,\text{N}$$

According to the Fleming's left hand rule, the direction of force is perpendicularly inwards to the plane of paper. (1)

(iii) Let the wire be shifted by 6 cm and the position of wire is CD.

$$OE = 6\,\text{cm}, OD = 10\,\text{cm}, DE = EC = x$$

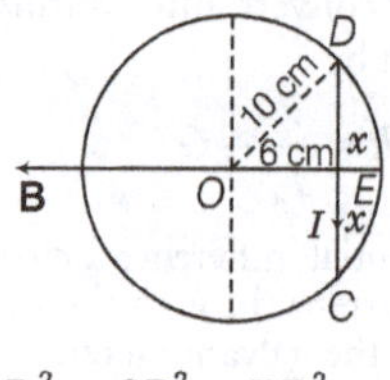

In ΔODE, $OD^2 = OE^2 + DE^2$

$$\Rightarrow \quad 100 = 36 + DE^2$$

$$\Rightarrow \quad DE^2 = 64 \text{ or } DE = 8\,\text{cm}$$

and $\quad l' = CD = 2DE = 16\,\text{cm} = 0.16\,\text{m}$

Magnitude of force,

$$\mathbf{F}' = I\,(\mathbf{l} \times \mathbf{B}) = 7\;(0.16 \times 1.5 \times \sin 90°) = 1.68\,\text{N}$$

According to Fleming's left hand rule, the direction of force is vertically downwards to the plane of the paper. (1)

41. **For solenoid**

Given, length $l = 60\,\text{cm}$,

Radius = 4 cm

Number of layers = 3

Number of turns in each layer = 300

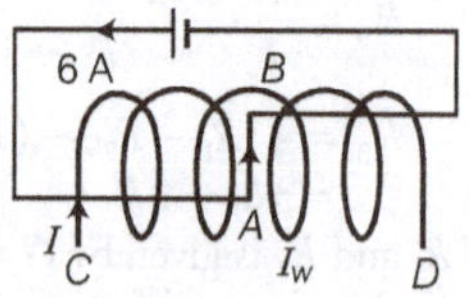

For wire

Given, length, $l_w = 2\,\text{cm}$

Mass, $m = 2.5\,\text{g}$, current $I_w = 6\,\text{A}$

Let I be the current passing through the solenoid, so the magnetic field due to the solenoid.

$$B=\mu_0 nI \qquad \left[\because n=\frac{\text{Number of turns}}{\text{length}}=\frac{300\times 3}{0.6}\right]$$

$$=4\pi\times 10^{-7}\times\frac{300\times 3}{0.6}\times I \qquad \text{...(i)} \quad (1)$$

Force on the wire,

$$F=I_w(l_w\times B)=I_w(l_w B\sin\theta)$$

[$\because$ angle between l_w and B is 90°]

This force balances by the weight of wire = mg

$$\therefore \quad I_w l_w B\sin 90^\circ = mg \qquad (1)$$

$$6\times 0.02\times\frac{4\pi\times 10^{-7}\times 300\times 3}{0.6}I=2.5\times 10^{-3}\times 9.8$$

[from Eq. (i)]

$$\text{Current, } I=\frac{2.5\times 10^{-3}\times 9.8\times 0.6}{108\times 4\pi\times 10^{-7}}=108.36\text{ A} \qquad (1)$$

42. 8×10^{-5} N ; refer to example 4 on page 193.

43. 2×10^{-5} N; refer to example 3 on page 193.

44. Force per unit length between the current carrying wires is given as

$$F=\frac{\mu_0}{4\pi}\cdot\frac{2I_1I_2}{r} \qquad (1)$$

where, I_1 = current in wire AB = 12 A

I_2 = current in wire CD = 5 A

and r = distance between wires = 1 mm = 1×10^{-3} m

$$\therefore \quad \frac{\mu_0}{4\pi}\cdot\frac{2I_1I_2}{r}=mg \qquad (1)$$

where, m = mass per unit length.

$$\Rightarrow \quad 10^{-7}\times\frac{2\times 12\times 5}{1\times 10^{-3}}=m\times 10$$

$$\Rightarrow \quad m=10^{-7}\times\frac{2\times 12\times 5}{1\times 10^{-3}}\times\frac{1}{10}$$

$$m=1.2\times 10^{-3}\text{ kg/m} \qquad (1)$$

Current in CD should be in opposite direction to that in AB.

45. Given, area of rectangular loop, $A=5\text{ m}^2$

Number of turns, $N=50$

Current, $I=1$ A

Magnetic field, $B=0.1$ T

Angle, $\theta=30^\circ$

Torque experienced by the coil,

$$\tau=NIAB\sin(90^\circ-\theta)$$

$$=50\times 1\times 5\times 0.1\times\sin(90^\circ-30^\circ)$$

$$=50\times 1\times 5\times 0.1\times\sin 60^\circ$$

$$=\frac{25\sqrt{3}}{2}=12.5\sqrt{3}\text{ N-m}$$

46. The length of wire will be same in two cases as the same coil is unwound and rewound.

Length of the wire is same.

$$\therefore \quad N_1\times(2\pi R)=N_2\times 2\pi\left(\frac{R}{2}\right)$$

[where, N_1 and N_2 = number of turns in two coils]

$$N_2=2N_1 \qquad (1)$$

Now, the ratio of magnetic moments is given by

$$\frac{M_1}{M_2}=\frac{N_1IA_1}{N_2IA_2}=\frac{N_1\times\pi R_1^2}{N_2\times\pi R_2^2}$$

$$\frac{M_1}{M_2}=\left(\frac{N_1}{2N_1}\right)\times\left(\frac{R}{R/2}\right)^2=\frac{1}{2}\times 4=2$$

$$M_1:M_2=1:2 \qquad (1)$$

47. Given, $N=20$, $I=12$ A, $B=0.80$ T,

$$l=10\text{ cm}=10\times 10^{-2}\text{ m}, \theta=30^\circ$$

$$\because \text{Area, } A=l^2=(10\times 10^{-2})^2=100\times 10^{-4}\text{ m}^2 \qquad (1)$$

As, $\tau=NBIA\sin\theta$

$$\Rightarrow \quad \tau=20\times 0.80\times 12\times 100\times 10^{-4}\times\sin 30^\circ$$

$$=9600\times 10^{-4}$$

$$=0.96\text{ N-m} \qquad (1)$$

48. Here, $N=30$, $R=8.0\text{ cm}=8\times 10^{-2}$ m,

$I=6.0$ A, $\theta=60^\circ$ and $B=1.0$ T

(i) The magnitude of the counter torque

= magnitude of the deflecting torque

= $NAIB\sin\theta$

= $N\cdot(\pi R^2)\,IB\sin\theta$

= $30\times 3.14\times(8\times 10^{-2})^2\times 6.0\times 1.0\times\sin 60^\circ$

= 3.14 N-m (2)

(ii) The answer would not change as area enclosed by the coil as well as all other particulars remain unaltered and the formula, $\tau=NAIB\sin\theta$ is true for planar coil for any shape. (1)

49. Given, number of turns, $N=20$

Radius of circular coil, $r=10$ cm = 0.1 m

Magnitude of magnetic field,

$$B=0.1\text{ T}$$

The angle between the area vector and magnetic field is 0°.

$$\Rightarrow \quad \theta=0^\circ$$

Current in the coil, $I=5.0$ A

(i) Torque on the coil, $\tau=NIAB\sin\theta$

$$=20\times 5\times\pi(0.1)^2\times 0.1\times\sin 0^\circ=0$$

[$\because \sin 0^\circ=0$] (1)

(ii) The forces on the planar loop are in pairs, i.e. the forces on two opposite sides are equal and opposite to each other and on the other two opposite sides, they are same. Thus, the total force on the coil is zero.

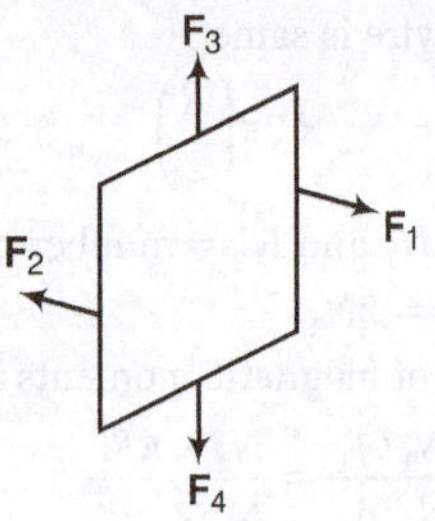

$(\because F_1 = - F_2 \text{ and } F_3 = - F_4)$ (1)

(iii) Number density of electrons, $N = 10^{29}/\text{m}^3$

Area of cross-section of copper wire, $A = 10^{-5}\text{m}^2$

The magnitude of magnetic force, $F = e\,(v_d \times B)$

$\because \quad I = neAv_d$

$\therefore \quad v_d = \dfrac{I}{neA}$

$\Rightarrow \quad F = e \cdot \dfrac{I}{NeA} \cdot B \sin 90°$

$= \dfrac{0.1 \times 5}{10^{-5} \times 10^{29}}$ N $\quad [\because \sin 90° = 1]$

$= 5 \times 10^{-25}$ (1)

50. $I_g = 250 \times 10^{-3}$ A

$R_g = 55\,\Omega$

$I = 3$A

$R_s = \dfrac{I_g R_g}{I - I_g} = \dfrac{250 \times 10^{-3} \times 55}{3 - 250 \times 10^{-3}}$

$= \dfrac{250 \times 10^{-3} \times 55}{2.75} = \dfrac{25 \times 55}{275} = 5 \Rightarrow R_S = 5\,\Omega$ (1)

51. Here, $B = 60$ G, $A = 2 \times 10^{-4}$ m^2, $N = 40$

$I = 4$ mA $= 4 \times 10^{-3}$ A, $\theta = 16°$

$\because \quad I = \dfrac{k}{NBA}\theta$

$\Rightarrow \quad k = \dfrac{NBAI}{\theta}$ (1)

$= \dfrac{40 \times 60 \times 2 \times 10^{-4} \times 4 \times 10^{-3}}{16}$

$= 1.2 \times 10^{-4}$ N-m per degree (1)

52. Given, $R_1 = 10\,\Omega$, $N_1 = 30$, $A_1 = 3.6 \times 10^{-3}\,\text{m}^2$,

$B_1 = 0.25$ T, $R_2 = 14\,\Omega$, $N_2 = 42$,

$A_2 = 1.8 \times 10^{-3}\,\text{m}^2$, $B_2 = 0.50$ T

$k_1 = k_2$ (spring constants are same) ...(i)

(i) Using the formula of current sensitivity, $I = \dfrac{NAB}{k}$

$\therefore \quad \dfrac{I_{S_2}}{I_{S_1}} = \dfrac{N_2 B_2 A_2 k_1}{N_1 B_1 A_1 k_2} = \dfrac{42 \times 0.50 \times 1.8 \times 10^{-3}}{30 \times 0.25 \times 3.6 \times 10^{-3}}$

$= 1.4$ [From Eq. (i)] (1½)

(ii) Using the formula of voltage sensitivity,

$V = \dfrac{NAB}{kR}$

$\therefore \quad \dfrac{V_{S_2}}{V_{S_1}} = \dfrac{N_2 B_2 A_2 k_1 R_1}{k_2 R_2 N_1 B_1 A_1}$

$= \dfrac{42 \times 0.50 \times 1.8 \times 10^{-3} \times 10}{14 \times 30 \times 0.25 \times 3.6 \times 10^{-3}}$

$= 1$ [from Eq. (i)] (1½)

53. Refer to Example 10 on page 197. **[Ans. 0.01 Ω]**

54. Here, $n = 30$, $G = 100\,\Omega$, $E = 3$ V, $R = 200\,\Omega$, $k = ?$

Total resistance $= G + R = 100 + 200 = 300\,\Omega$

$I_g = \dfrac{E}{G + R} = \dfrac{3}{300} = \dfrac{1}{100}$ A (1)

$k = \dfrac{I_g}{n} = \dfrac{1/100}{30}$

$= \dfrac{1}{3} \times 10^{-3}$ A/div

$k = \dfrac{1}{3} \times 10^{-3} \times 10^{6}\,\mu$A/div

Figure of merit (Restoring torque per unit twist)

$k = 333.3\,\mu$A/div (1)

55. Given, resistance of galvanometer coil, $G = 12\,\Omega$

Current in galvanometer,

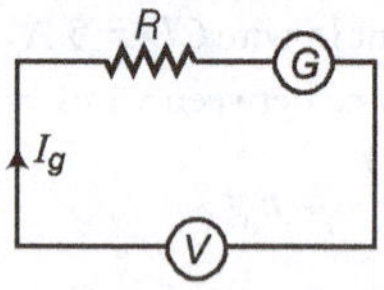

$I_g = 3$ mA $= 3 \times 10^{-3}$ A

and potential difference, $V = 18$ V

We can convert the galvanometer into voltmeter by using a large resistance R in series. The resistance can be calculated using the formula,

$R = \dfrac{V}{I_g} - G$

$R = \dfrac{18}{3 \times 10^{-3}} - 12$

$= 5988\,\Omega$ (1)

This resistance ($R = 5988\,\Omega$) is connected in series with the galvanometer. The resistance is connected in series because we have to increase the resistance of the galvanometer, so that almost no current flows through it and it gives an exact value of potential difference.

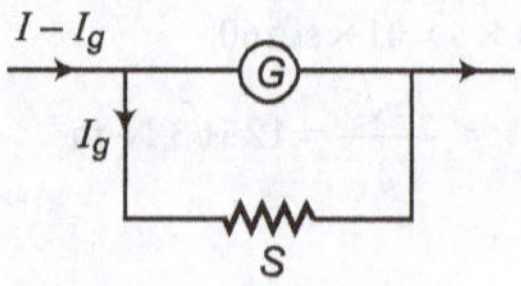

(1)

SUMMARY

- **Magnetic Field** The space in the surroundings of a magnet or a current carrying conductor in which its magnetic influence can be experienced is called magnetic field.
- **Oersted's Experiment** HC Oersted by his experiment observed that a current carrying conductor deflects magnetic compass needle placed near it.
- **Biot-Savart's Law** This law deals with the magnetic field induction at a point due to a small current element, i.e.

$$dB \propto \frac{Idl\sin\theta}{r^2}$$

- **Permittivity and Permeability** Electric permittivity (ε_0), the degree of interaction of electric field with medium.
  Magnetic permeability, the ability of a substance to acquire magnetisation in a magnetic field.
- **Right Hand Thumb Rule** When the thumb of right hand is placed along the direction of current, the fingers curl around the conductor in the direction of magnetic field lines.
- Magnetic field at any point along the **axis of circular current carrying conductor** is $B = \frac{\mu_0 I a^2}{2(r^2 + a^2)^{3/2}}$
- Magnetic field at the **centre of a circular current carrying conductor/ coil**

$$B = \frac{\mu_0 I}{2r}$$

- **Ampere's Circuital Law** According to this law, the line integral of the magnetic field **B** around any closed path in vacuum is equal to μ_0 times the net current enclosed by the curve,
  i.e. $\oint \mathbf{B} \times d\mathbf{l} = \mu_0 I$
- **Magnitude of a Magnetic Field of a Straight Wire** It is given by $B = \frac{\mu_0 I}{2\pi r}$
- **Solenoid** It is an insulated long wire closely wound in the form of a helix.
- **Magnetic Field due to Straight Solenoid** At any point inside the solenoid, $B = \mu_0 nI$
  At points near the end of air closed solenoid, $B = (\mu_0 nI/2)$.
- **Force on Moving Charge in a Uniform Magnetic Field** When a charged particle (q) moves with a velocity (v) inside a uniform magnetic field, then force acting on it is given by $\mathbf{F} = q(\mathbf{v} \times \mathbf{B})$.
- **Magnetic Force On a Charged Particle** It is given by
  $\mathbf{F} = q\,(\mathbf{v} \times \mathbf{B})$.
- When charged particle enters into a magnetic field perpendicularly, then

  (i) $\frac{mv^2}{r} = qvB$ (ii) $r = \frac{mv}{qB}$ (iii) $T = \frac{2\pi m}{qB}$

  (iv) $\nu = \frac{qB}{2\pi m}$ (v) $KE = \frac{q^2B^2r^2}{2m}$

- **Lorentz Force** The sum of the electric force and magnetic force that can be exerted on a charged particle due to its electric charge (q) is called Lorentz force.
  It is $\mathbf{F} = q\,(\mathbf{E} + \mathbf{v} \times \mathbf{B})$
- **Force on a Current Carrying Conductor in a Uniform Magnetic Field** It is given by, $F = IlB\sin\theta$
- **Fleming's Left Hand Rule** If the forefinger, middle finger and the thumb of the left hand are stretched mutually at right angles to one another such that the forefinger points in the direction of magnetic field, middle finger in the direction of current, then thumb will point in the direction of force on the conductor.
- **Force between Two Parallel Current Carrying Conductors**
  It is given by $F = \left[\frac{\mu_0}{4\pi}\frac{2I_1I_2}{r}\right]$
- **Torque Experienced by a Current Loop in a Uniform Magnetic Field** It is given by $\tau = BINA\sin\theta$
- **Circular Current Loop as Magnetic Dipole** The magnitude of the magnetic field on the axis at a distance x from the centre of a circular loop of radius R carrying a steady current I is

$$B = \frac{\mu_0\, IR^2}{2(x^2 + R^2)^{3/2}}$$

  For $x >> R$

$$B = \frac{\mu_0 IA}{2x^3}$$

  or

$$B = \frac{\mu_0 M}{2\pi\, x^3}$$

- **Moving Coil Galvanometer** It is an instrument which is based on the fact that when a current carrying coil is placed in a magnetic field, then it experiences a torque.

For Mind Map

Visit : https://goo.gl/m1mM2z OR **Scan the Code**

Chapter Practice

Multiple Choice Questions

(1 Marks)

1 A long solenoid has 20 turns cm^{-1}. The current necessary to produce a magnetic field of 20 mT inside the solenoid is approximately

(a) 1A (b) 2 A
(c) 4 A (d) 8 A

2 Magnetic field produced by a wire carrying current

(a) is parallel along the axis of wire
(b) is perpendicular to the plane of the wire
(c) forms circular loops along the axis of wire and coplanar to the wire
(d) direction of field is not constant

3 Current sensitivity of a galvanometer is

(a) $\frac{NBA}{k}$ (b) $\frac{k}{NBA}$
(c) $\frac{NBA}{kR}$ (d) $\frac{kR}{NBA}$

Assertion and Reason

Directions (Q. Nos. 4-8) *In the following questions, two statements are given- one labelled Assertion (A) and the other labelled Reason (R). Select the correct answer to these questions from the codes (a), (b), (c) and (d) as given below*

(a) Both Assertion and Reason are true and Reason is the correct explanation of Assertion.
(b) Both Assertion and Reason are true but Reason is not the correct explanation of Assertion.
(c) Assertion is true but Reason is false.
(d) Assertion is false but Reason is true.

4. **Assertion (A)** A proton and an electron, with same momenta, enter in a magnetic field in a direction at right angles to the lines of the force. The radius of the paths followed by them will be same.

Reason (R) Electron has less mass than the proton.

5. **Assertion (A)** When radius of a current carrying loop is doubled, its magnetic moment becomes four times.

Reason (R) The magnetic moment of a current carrying loop is directly proportional to the area of the loop. **(CBSE 2021, Term-1)**

6. **Assertion (A)** On increasing the current sensitivity of a galvanometer by increasing the number of turns, may not necessarily increase its voltage sensitivity.

Reason (R) The resistance of the coil of the galvanometer increases on increasing the number of turns.

7. **Assertion (A)** Higher the range, lower is the resistance of an ammeter.

Reason (R) To increase the range of an ammeter, additional shunt is added in series to it.

8. **Assertion (A)** A galvanometer can be used as an ammeter to measure the current across a given section of the circuit.

Reason (R) For this, it must be connected in series with the circuit.

Very Short Answer Type Questions

(1 Mark)

9 What is the source of magnetic field produced due to flow of current in a wire?

10 What is the value of magnetic field induction at any point on the thin conducting wire carrying current?

11 State the rule that is used to find the direction of magnetic field at a point near a current carrying straight conductor.

12 What will be the magnetic field at the centre of a circular coil carrying current, when the current through the coil is doubled and the radius of the coil is halved?

13 What is the force on a charge moving along the direction of the magnetic field?

14 Name the force which is experienced by a moving charged particle in electric and magnetic field.

15 Under what condition does an electron moving through a magnetic field experience maximum force?

16 A charged particle moves through a magnetic field. Is the momentum of the particle affected?

17 An electron beam projected along $+X$-axis experiences a force due to a magnetic field along the $+Y$-axis. What is the direction of the magnetic field?

18 In a certain arrangement, a proton does not get deflected while passing through a magnetic field region. Under what condition is it possible?

19 Write the expression for the force between parallel current carrying conductors.

Short Answer Type I Questions

2 Marks

20 Two similar coils are placed mutually perpendicular such that their centres coincide. At centre, what will be the ratio of the magnitudes of magnetic fields due to one coil and the resultant magnetic field?

21 In what way, current carrying solenoid behaves like a bar magnet. Find the magnetic field induction at the axis of solenoid due to current flowing through it.

22 What is Lorentz force? Give some important characteristics of this force.

23 Equal currents are flowing through two infinitely long parallel wires in the same direction. What will be the magnetic field at a point mid-way between the two wires?

24 Deduce an expression for the torque on a current carrying loop suspended in a uniform magnetic field.

25 In a moving coil galvanometer having a coil of N turns of area A and carrying current I and is placed in a radial field of strength B. What will be the torque acting on the coil?

26 Is it possible to decrease or increase the range of given voltmeter? Explain.

Short Answer Type II Questions

3 Marks

27 Using Ampere's circuital law, find an expression for the magnetic field at a point situated at a normal distance R from an infinitely long current carrying straight wire.

28 An electron being accelerated through a potential difference of V enters a uniform magnetic field of B perpendicular to the direction of motion. Find the radius of path described by the electron.

29 A wire of length L is bent in the form of a circle of radius R and carries current I. What is its magnetic moment?

Long Answer Type Questions

5 Marks

30 Three wires of equal lengths are bent into the form of three loops. One of the loops is square-shaped, second loop is triangular-shaped and third loop is circular. These are suspended in a uniform magnetic field and the same current is passed through them. Which loop will experience greater torque? Give reasons.

31 A rectangular current carrying loop of length a and breadth b is shown in the figure. Find the magnetic field at the centre of the loop.

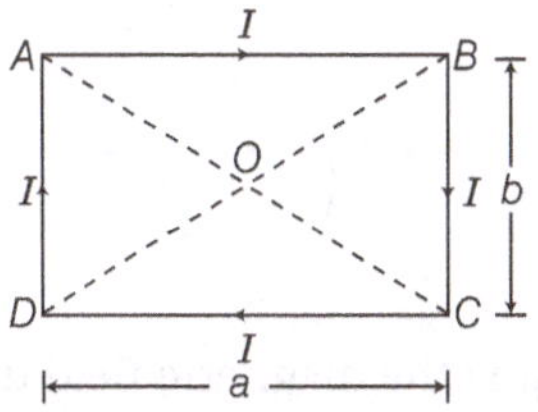

Case Based Questions

Directions (Q. No. 32) *These questions are case study based questions. Read the following paragraph and answer the questions.*

32. A magnetic field can be produced by moving charges or electric current. The basic equation of magnetic field due to a current distribution is governed by Biot-Savart law.

According to this law, the magnetic field at a point due to a current element of length dl carrying current I, at a distance r from the element dl is, $d\mathbf{B}=\frac{\mu_0}{4\pi}\cdot\frac{Id\mathbf{l}\times\mathbf{r}}{r^3}$. This law has certain similarities as well as differences with Coulomb's law of electrostatic. e.g. There is an angle dependence in Biot-Savart law which is absent in electrostatic case.

(i) Write the alternative way to express Biot-Savart law.

(ii) What is the difference between Biot-Savart law and Coulomb's law in electrostatic.

(iii) How magnetic field due to an infinitely long current carrying wire at a distance r on its perpendicular bisector is related with current?

(vi) What is the magnetic field at a point on a long current carrying wire?

Numerical Problems

33 A copper coil of 100 turns, radius 8×10^{-2} m carries a current of 0.40 A. What will be the magnitude of magnetic field at the centre of coil? **(2 M)**

34 A straight wire carrying a current of 12 A is bent into a semi-circular arc of radius 2.0 cm as shown in Fig. (a). Consider the magnetic field **B** at the centre of the arc.

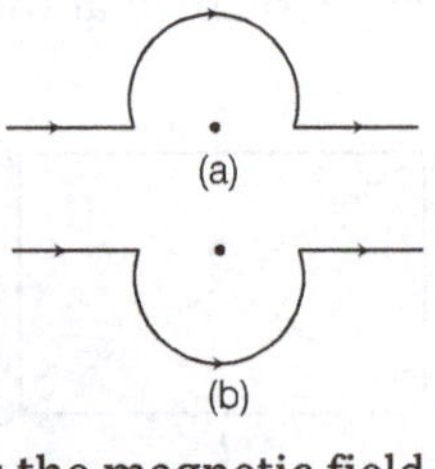

(i) What is the magnetic field due to the straight segments?

(ii) In what way the contribution to **B** from the semi-circle differs from that of a circular loop and in what way does it resemble?

(iii) Would your answer be different, if the wire was bent into a semi-circular arc of the same radius but in the opposite way as shown in Fig. (b)? **(3 M)**

35 A closely wound solenoid 0.80 m long has 5 layers of windings of 400 turns each. The diameter of the solenoid is 1.8×10^{-2}m. If the current carried is 0.8A, what will be the magnitude of field near the centre? **(3 M)**

36 A beam of protons passes undeflected with a horizontal velocity v, through a region of electric and magnetic fields, mutually perpendicular to each other and normal to the direction of beam.

If the magnitudes of electric and magnetic fields are 100 kV/m and 50 mT respectively, calculate the velocity of the beam. **(2 M)**

37 Two concentric circular wire loops of radii 20 cm and 30 cm are located in an XY-plane, each carries a clockwise current of 7 A.

(i) Find the magnitude of the net magnetic dipole moment of the system.

(ii) Repeat for reversed current in the inner loop. **(5 M)**

38 The coil of galvanometer consists of 100 turns and effective area of 1 cm^2. The restoring couple is 10^{-8} N-m/rad. The magnetic field between poles is of 5 T. What will be the current sensitivity of galvanometer? **(3 M)**

39 The current sensitivity of a MCG increases by 20% when its resistance is increased by a factor of 2. Calculate by what factor the voltage sensitivity changes? **(3 M)**

40 A galvanometer with a coil of resistance 12.0 Ω shows full scale deflection for a current of 2.5 mA. How will you convert this meter into

(i) an ammeter of range 0 to 7.5 A?

(ii) a voltmeter of range 0 to 10 V? Determine the net resistance of the meter in each case. When an ammeter is put in a circuit, does it read less or more than the actual current in the original circuit? When a voltmeter is put across a part of the circuit, does it read less or more than the required voltage drop? Explain. **(5 M)**

41 A galvanometer having 30 divisions has a current sensitivity of 20 μA/ div. It has a resistance of 25 Ω.

(i) How will you convert it into an ammeter of range 0-1 A?

(ii) How will you convert this ammeter into a voltmeter of range 0-1 V? **(3 M)**

Answers

1 (*d*) By the formula,

$$B = \mu_0 nI \quad \text{or} \quad 20 \times 10^{-3} = 4\pi \times 10^{-7} \times 2000 \times I$$

or $$I = \frac{20 \times 10^{-3}}{4\pi \times 10^{-7} \times 2000} \Rightarrow I \simeq 8\text{ A}$$

2 (*d*) The Oersted found that the alignment of the magnetic needle is tangential to an imaginary circle which has the straight current-carrying wire, as its centre has its plane perpendicular to the wire as shown in figure.

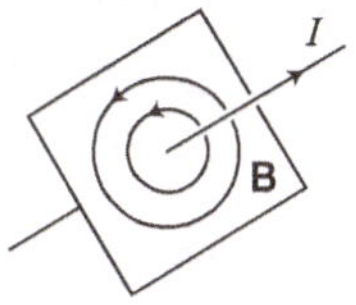

3 (*a*) Current sensitivity of the galvanometer deflection per unit ampere

$$\Rightarrow \quad \frac{\phi}{I} = \frac{NBA}{k}$$

4 (*b*) 5 (*a*) 6 (*a*) 7 (*c*)

8 (*a*)

9 Flow of current refers to moving electrons which are the source of magnetic field.

10 As given that the angle between the length of conducting wire and at the point at which magnetic field is to be determined is zero.

$\therefore \quad B = 0$

11 Right hand thumb rule states that, if we imagine a linear wire conductor to be need in the grip of the right hand such that the thumb points in the direction of current, then the curvature of the fingers around the conductor will give the direction of magnetic field lines.

12 Magnetic field at the centre of the coil is given by

$$B = \frac{\mu_0 I}{2R}$$

$$B' = \frac{\mu_0(2I)}{2(R/2)} = 4B$$

13 Force on a moving charge in magnetic field is given as,

$$F = qvB\sin\theta$$

Here, $\theta = 0° \Rightarrow F = 0$

14 Lorentz force

15 Magnetic forec, $\mathbf{F} = q(\mathbf{v} \times \mathbf{B}) = qvB\sin\theta$

Maximum force, $F_{max} = qvB$

When, $\sin\theta = 1$ or $\theta = 90°$

16 No, its momentum does not get affected.

17 Direction of magnetic field is in Z-axis direction.

18 When it is along the magnetic field.

19 Force between the parallel current carrying conductors is $F = \frac{\mu_0}{4\pi}\frac{2I_1I_2}{r}$.

20 Ratio $= \frac{B_1}{\sqrt{B_1^2 + B_2^2}} = \frac{1}{\sqrt{2}}$

21 Refer to text on pages 179 and 180 (Magnetic field of a solonoid).

22 Refer to text on page 182 (Force on a moving charge in a uniform magnetic and electric field (Lorentz force)).

23 Zero

24 Refer to text on pages 193 and 194 (Torque experienced by a current loop in uniform magnetic field (Magnetic dipole)).

25 Refer to text on pages 195 and 196 (Moving coil galvanometer).

26 Yes, we can increase the range of voltmeter by connecting additional resistance in series with the voltmeter. We can decrease the range of voltmeter by connecting a suitable resistance in parallel with the voltmeter.

27 Refer to text on page 179 (Magnitude of magnetic field of a infinite long straight wire using Ampere's circuital law).

28 $K = \frac{1}{2}mv^2 = eV, \quad r = \frac{mv}{qB} = \frac{mv}{eB} = \sqrt{\frac{2mV}{eB^2}}$

29 As, $L = 2\pi R \Rightarrow R = \frac{L}{2\pi}$

$$\Rightarrow M = IA = I \times \pi R^2$$

$$= I\pi \times \frac{L^2}{4\pi^2} = \frac{IL^2}{4\pi}$$

30 Refer text on pages 193 and 194 (Torque experienced by a current loop in uniform magnetic field (Magnetic dipole)).

Now, apply the formula, $\tau = MB$

Square will experience maximum torque.

31 Refer to example 2 on page 168. $\left[\text{Ans. } B = \frac{2\mu_0 I\sqrt{a^2 + b^2}}{\pi ab}\right]$

32 (i) Biot-Savart law can be expressed alternatively as Ampere's circuital law.

(ii) Biot-Savart law is angle dependence law, whereas Coulomb's law in electrostatic is angle independent law.

(iii) The magnetic field due to an infinitely long current carrying wire,

$$B = \frac{\mu_0 I}{2\pi r}$$

$$\therefore \quad B \propto I$$

(iv) The magnetic field at a point on the long current carrying wire,

$$dB = \frac{\mu_0}{4\pi} \cdot \frac{Idl\sin\theta}{r^2}$$

$$= \frac{\mu_0}{4\pi} \cdot \frac{Idl \sin 0°}{r^2} \qquad [\because \theta = 0°]$$

$$= 0$$

33 Refer to example 4 on page 170.

[**Ans.** $B = \frac{N\mu_0 I}{2r} = 31 \times 10^{-4}$ T]

34 (i) The magnitude of the magnetic field at a point distant r from a current element δl is

$$B = \frac{\mu_0}{4\pi} \cdot \frac{i\delta l \sin\theta}{r^2}$$

Here, for each straight part of the wire, $\theta = 0°$.
Hence, for each straight part of length l, we have

$$B_1 = B_2 = 0$$

(ii) Magnetic field due to a semi-circular wire at its centre is half of magnetic field due to a circular loop.

$$B_{\text{semi-circle}} = \frac{\mu_0 I}{4r} = 1.9 \times 10^{-4} \text{ T}$$

(iii) The magnitude of the magnetic field remains same but the direction will be opposite.

35 Refer to example 2 on page 180.

[**Ans.** $B = \mu_0 \frac{N}{l} I = 2.5 \times 10^{-2}$ T]

36 For undeflected beam,

$$v = \frac{E}{B} = 2 \times 10^6 \text{ m/s}$$

37 (i) $M_1 = N_1 I_1 A_1 \otimes$

$M_2 = N_2 I_2 A_2 \otimes$

$\therefore M = M_1 + M_2 = 2.86$ A-m^2

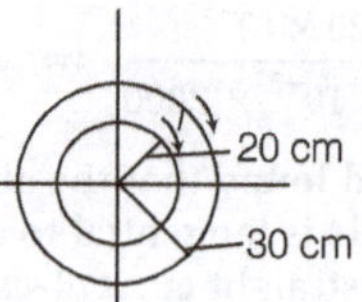

(ii) $M = |M_1 - M_2| = 1.10$ A-m^2

38 Current sensitivity, $I_s = \frac{NAB}{K} = \frac{100 \times 1 \times 10^{-4} \times 5}{10^{-8}}$

$= 5 \times 10^6$ A^{-1}

39 Refer to example 9 on page 196.

[**Ans.** Decreased by a factor 0.4.

40 Refer to example 10 on page 197.

[**Ans.** (i) Resistance of ammeter $4 \times 10^{-3}\ \Omega$

(ii) Resistance of voltmeter = 4000 Ω

41 Refer to example 10 and 11 on page 197.

Ans. (i) Shunt = 0.015Ω

(ii) Resistance in series 0.985Ω

RELATED ONLINE VIDEOS

Visit : https://www.youtube.com/watch?v=1BolH6Quhiw
OR **Scan the Code**

Visit : https://www.youtube.com/watch?v=m2jp0klZHEE
OR **Scan the Code**

Visit : https://www.youtube.com/watch?v=roJO_T0eKDM
OR **Scan the Code**

Visit : https://www.youtube.com/watch?v=09HutPipRGk
OR **Scan the Code**

Visit : https://www.youtube.com/watch?v=a97NpQKlbks
OR **Scan the Code**

CHAPTER

05

Magnetism and Matter

A naturally occurring ore of iron, magnetite attracts small pieces of iron towards it. The phenomenon of attraction of small bits of iron, steel, cobalt, nickel, etc., towards the ore, is called **magnetism**.

TOPIC 01 Bar Magnet and Magnetic Dipole

A **magnet** is a material or an object that produces a magnetic field. The magnetic field is invisible but is responsible for most notable property of a magnet.

Magnets are of two types

(i) **Natural magnets** are generally irregular in shape and weak in strength.

(ii) **Artificial magnets** have desired shape and desired strength. e.g. A bar magnet, a horse shoe magnet, compass needle, etc.

Note It is possible to make magnets out of iron and its alloys. When a piece of a substance, such as soft iron, steel, cobalt, nickel, etc., is placed near a magnet, it acquires magnetism.

The Bar Magnet

The bar magnet has two poles similar to the positive and negative charges of an electric dipole. One pole is designated as **North pole** (N) and the other as **South pole** (S). When a bar magnet is suspended freely, these poles point approximately towards the the geographic North and South poles, respectively. **Like magnetic poles repel** each other and **unlike magnetic poles attract** each other.

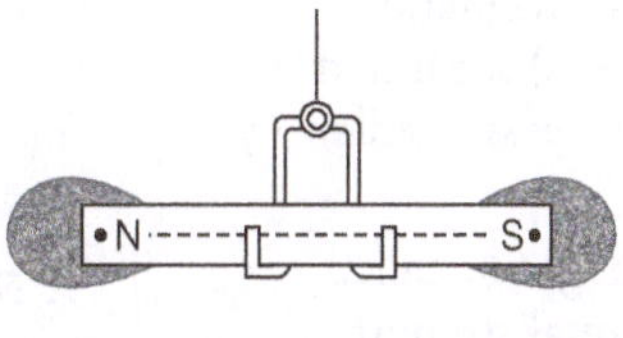

The pattern suggests that attraction is maximum at the two ends of the bar magnet. These ends are called **poles** of the magnet. The poles of a magnet can never be separated. We cannot isolate the North or South pole of a magnet, i.e. magnetic poles exist in pairs.

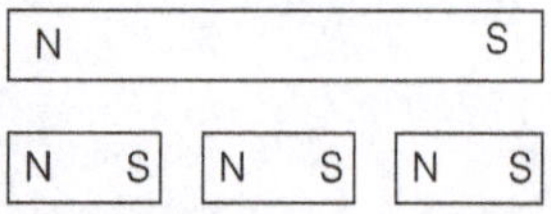

If a bar magnet is broken, each piece behaves as a small magnet

Magnetic Length of a Bar Magnet

The distance between two poles of a bar magnet is known as **magnetic length** of a magnet. Its direction is from S-pole of the magnet to N-pole and is represented by $2l$. It is sometimes also known as effective length (L_e) of the magnet and is less than its geometric length (L_g).

For a bar magnet, $L_e = \left(\frac{5}{6}\right) L_g$.

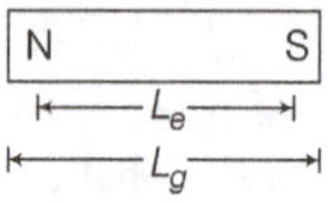

Example 1 Consider a short magnetic dipole of magnetic length 20 cm. Find its geometric length.

Sol. Geometric length of a magnet is $\frac{6}{5}$ times its magnetic length.

$\therefore$ Geometric length $= \frac{6}{5} \times 20 = 24\,\text{cm}$

Example 2 A thin bar magnet of length $4L$ is bent at the mid-point, so that the angle between them is 60°. Find the new length of the bar magnet.

Sol. On bending the bar magnet, the length of the bar magnet,

$$AC = AO + OC$$
$$= 2L\sin\left(\frac{60°}{2}\right) + 2L\sin\left(\frac{60°}{2}\right)$$
$$= 4L\sin 30° = 4L \times \frac{1}{2} = 2L$$

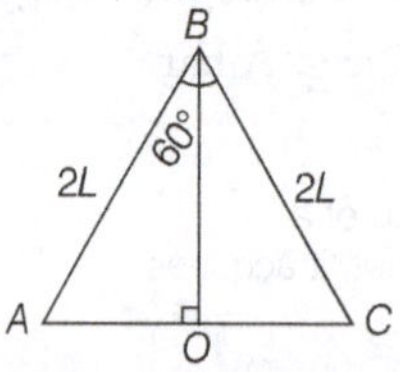

Magnetic Dipole

A **magnetic dipole** is an arrangement of two magnetic poles of equal and opposite strengths ($-m, +m$) separated by a small distance. e.g. A bar magnet, a compass needle, etc., are magnetic dipoles.

The two poles of a magnetic dipole (or a magnet), called North pole and South pole, are always of equal strength and of opposite nature. Further, such two magnetic poles always exist in pair.

Magnetic Dipole Moment

It is the product of the strength of either pole and the magnetic length of the magnet. It is represented by M.

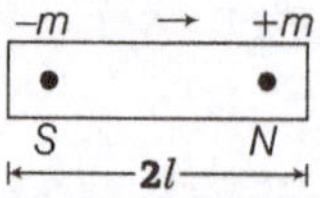

The direction of magnetic dipole moment is same as that of 2l. Therefore,

$$\boxed{\mathbf{M} = m(2\mathbf{l})}$$

SI unit of magnetic dipole moment is ampere-metre^2 (A-m^2)

Note Magnitude of force acting between two magnetic poles is given by

$$F = \frac{\mu_0}{4\pi} \cdot \frac{m_1 m_2}{r^2}$$

where, r is distance between the poles.

Example 3 A magnetic wire of dipole moment 4π A-m^2 is bent in the form of semicircle. Find the new magnetic moment.

Sol. If length of wire is $2l$, then magnetic moment

$$M = m \times 2l = 4\pi \text{ A-m}^2 \quad \text{[given]}$$

As wire is bent in the form of semicircle, effective distance between the ends is $2r$.

So, new dipole moment

$$M' = m \times 2r = m \times 2 \times \frac{2l}{\pi} = \frac{2}{\pi}(m \times 2l) \quad [\because \pi r = 2l]$$
$$= \frac{2}{\pi} M = \frac{2}{\pi} 4\pi = 8 \text{ A-m}^2$$

Example 4 The length of a magnetised steel wire is l and its magnetic moment is M. It is bent into the shape of L with two sides equal. What will be the new magnetic moment?

Sol. If m is strength of each pole, then magnetic moment $M = m \times l$

When the wire is bent into L shape, effective distance between the poles $= \sqrt{\left(\frac{l}{2}\right)^2 + \left(\frac{l}{2}\right)^2} = \frac{l}{\sqrt{2}}$

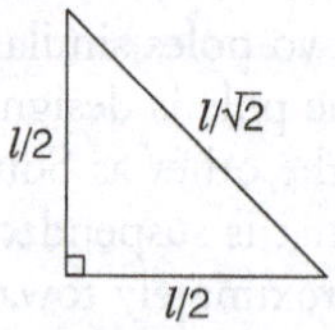

$\therefore$ New magnetic moment,

$$M' = m \times \frac{l}{\sqrt{2}} = \frac{M}{\sqrt{2}} \quad \text{[m will remain unchanged]}$$

Magnetic Field Lines

The magnetic field lines in a magnetic field are those imaginary lines which continuously represent the direction of the magnetic field. The tangent drawn at any point on magnetic field line shows the direction of magnetic field at that point.

Properties of Magnetic Field Lines

Important properties of magnetic field lines are given below

(i) The magnetic field lines of a magnet (or a solenoid) form continuous closed loops. This is unlike the electric dipole, where these field lines begin from a positive charge and end on the negative charge or escape to infinity.

(ii) The tangent to the field line at a given point represents the direction of the net magnetic field **B** at that point.

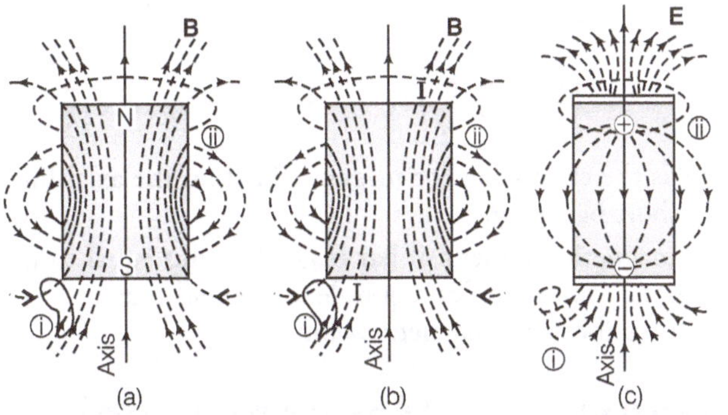

The field lines of (a) a bar magnet, (b) a current carrying finite solenoid and (c) an electric dipole. At large distances, their field lines are very similar. The curves labelled (i) and (ii) are closed to Gaussian surfaces.

(iii) The larger the number of field lines crossing per unit area, the stronger is the magnitude of the magnetic field **B**.

(iv) The magnetic field lines do not intersect, for if they did, the direction of the magnetic field would not be unique at the point of intersection.

Magnetic Field Strength at a Point due to a Bar Magnet

The strength of magnetic field at any point is defined as, the force experienced by a hypothetical unit North pole placed at that point. It is a **vector** quantity. The direction of magnetic field **B** is the direction along which hypothetical unit North pole would tend to move, if free to do so.

We have used the word hypothetical unit North pole in the above discussion because an isolated magnetic pole does not exist.

When Point Lies on Axial Line of a Bar Magnet (End-on-Position)

Let $2l$ be the magnetic length of a bar magnet with centre O. The magnetic dipole moment of the magnet is M, where $M = m \times 2l, OP = d$, is the distance of the point P on the axial line from the centre of the magnet. If m is the strength of each pole, then magnetic field strength at P due to N-pole of magnet is given by

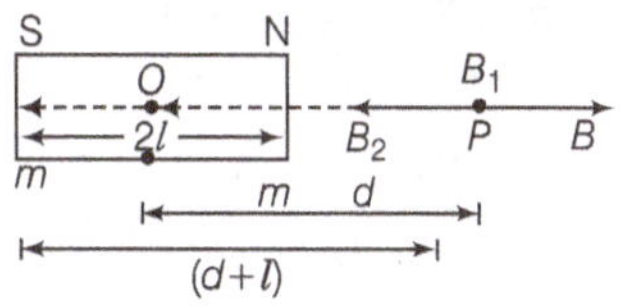

$$B = \frac{\mu_0}{4\pi} \cdot \frac{2Md}{(d^2 - l^2)^2} \qquad [\because M = m \times 2l]$$

When the magnet is short, $l^2 << d^2$, such that l^2 is neglected.

$$\therefore \qquad B = \frac{\mu_0}{4\pi} \cdot \frac{2Md}{d^4}$$

$$\Rightarrow \qquad \boxed{B = \frac{\mu_0}{4\pi} \cdot \frac{2M}{d^3}}$$

The direction of **B** is along NP produced.

Example 5 What is the magnitude of the axial fields due to a bar magnet of length 5 cm at a distance of 50 cm from its mid-point? The magnetic moment of the bar magnet is 0.40 A -m^2.

Sol. Given, magnetic length of bar magnet,

$$2l = 5 \text{ cm}$$

$$\Rightarrow \qquad l = 2.5 \text{ cm} = 2.5 \times 10^{-2} \text{ m}$$

Distance, $d = 50 \text{ cm} = 0.5 \text{ m}$

Magnetic moment, $M = 0.40 \text{ A-m}^2$

$$\therefore \qquad B = \frac{\mu_0}{4\pi} \cdot \frac{2Md}{(d^2 - l^2)^2}$$

$$= \frac{\mu_0}{4\pi} \cdot \frac{2M}{d^3} \quad [\because l << d]$$

$$= \frac{10^{-7} \times 2 \times 0.40}{(0.5)^3}$$

$$= 6.4 \times 10^{-7} \text{ T}$$

When Point Lies on Equatorial Line of a Bar Magnet

In the given figure, the point P is shown on equatorial line of the same bar magnet, where $OP = d$. Magnetic field strength at P due to N-pole of magnet is

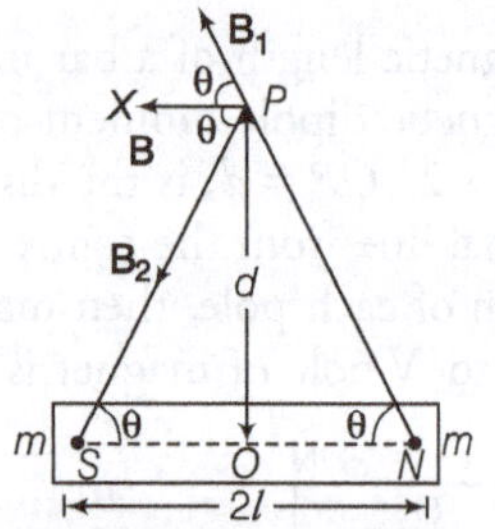

$$\boxed{B = \frac{\mu_0}{4\pi} \cdot \frac{M}{(d^2 + l^2)^{3/2}}}$$

If the magnet is short, $l^2 << d^2$, such that l^2 is neglected.

$$\therefore \quad B = \frac{\mu_0}{4\pi} \cdot \frac{M}{(d^2)^{3/2}}$$

$$= \frac{\mu_0}{4\pi} \cdot \frac{M}{d^3}$$

$$\Rightarrow \quad \boxed{B = \frac{\mu_0}{4\pi} \cdot \frac{M}{d^3}}$$

The direction of B is along PX, a line parallel to NS.

Note From the formulae of magnetic field due to a bar magnet at a point in axial position and at a point in equatorial position, it is clear that magnetic field due to a short bar magnet at any point on the axial line of magnet is twice the magnetic field at a point at the same distance on the equatorial line of the magnet.

Example 6 Determine the magnitude of the equatorial fields due to a bar magnet of length 6 cm at a distance of 60 cm from its mid-point. The magnetic moment of the bar magnet is 0.60 A-m^2.

Sol. Given, magnetic length of bar magnet, $2l = 6$ cm

$\Rightarrow \quad l = 3 \text{ cm} = 3 \times 10^{-2}$ m

Distance, $d = 60 \text{ cm} = 0.6$ m

Magnetic moment, $M = 0.60$ A-m^2

$$\therefore \quad \text{Magnetic field, } B = \frac{\mu_0}{4\pi} \times \frac{M}{(d^2 + l^2)^{3/2}}$$

$$= \frac{\mu_0 M}{4\pi d^3} \qquad [\because l << d]$$

$$= \frac{4\pi \times 10^{-7} \times 0.60}{4\pi \times (0.6)^3}$$

$$= 2.7 \times 10^{-7} \text{ T}$$

Bar Magnet as an Equivalent Solenoid

The magnetic field lines for a bar magnet and a current carrying solenoid resemble very closely. Therefore, a bar magnet can be thought as a large number of circulating currents in analogy with a solenoid.

Cutting a bar magnet in half is like cutting a solenoid. We get two smaller solenoids with weaker magnetic properties. The field lines remain continuous, emerging from one face of the solenoid and entering into other face.

One can test this analogy by moving a small compass needle in the neighbourhood of a bar magnet and a current carrying finite solenoid and noting that the deflections of the needle are similar in both the cases.

If M is the magnetic moment of the solenoid, then

$$M = \text{Total number of turns} \times \text{Current} \times \text{Area of cross-section}$$

$$M = n(2l) \times i \times \pi a^2$$

$$\Rightarrow \quad \boxed{B = \frac{\mu_0}{4\pi} \cdot \frac{2M}{r^3}}$$

This is the expression for magnetic field on the axial line of a short bar magnet.

The magnetic moment of bar magnet is thus equal to the magnetic moment of an equivalent solenoid that produces the same magnetic field.

Torque on a Magnetic Dipole in a Uniform Magnetic Field

When a bar magnet is placed in a uniform magnetic field, torque acts on the magnet. Also, magnetic potential energy is associated with the magnet due to its orientation as discussed below.

In the figure below, a uniform magnetic field **B** is represented by equidistant parallel lines. NS is a bar magnet of length $2l$ and strength of each pole is m.

The magnet is held at $\angle\theta$ with the direction of **B**.

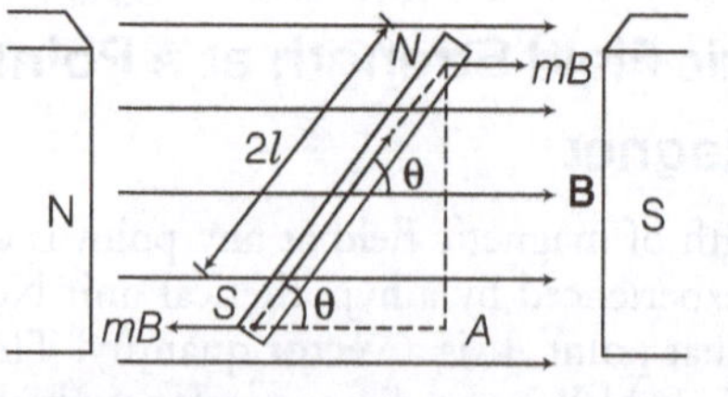

Bar magnet in a uniform magnetic field

Force on N-pole $= mB$, along **B**
Force on S-pole $= mB$, opposite to **B**
where, m = strength of each pole
and B = strength of magnetic field.

These equal and unlike forces form a couple which tend to rotate the magnet clockwise, so as to align it along **B**.

Torque acting on the bar magnet,

$$\tau = \text{Force} \times \text{Perpendicular distance}$$

$$\Rightarrow \quad \tau = mB \times NA$$

In ΔNAS, $\sin\theta = \frac{NA}{NS} = \frac{NA}{2l}$

$$\therefore \quad NA = 2l \sin\theta$$

Now, $\tau = mB \times 2l\sin\theta = B \times (m2l)\sin\theta$

$$\Rightarrow \quad \boxed{\tau = MB\sin\theta}$$

In vector form, $\boxed{\boldsymbol{\tau} = \mathbf{M} \times \mathbf{B}}$

The direction of τ is perpendicular to the plane containing **M** and **B** and is given by right handed screw rule.

When $B = 1$ and $\theta = 90°$,
then $\tau = M \times 1 \sin 90° = M$

Hence, we may define **magnetic dipole moment** as the torque acting on a dipole held perpendicular to a uniform magnetic field of unit strength.

Unit of M is unit of τ divided by unit of B. Therefore, SI unit of **M** is joule per tesla (J T^{-1}).

Note Time period of oscillation of a magnetic dipole in a magnetic field (B) is given by $T = 2\pi\sqrt{\frac{I}{MB}}$
where, I = moment of inertia about the axis of magnet
and M = magnetic moment.

Example 7 A straight solenoid of length 50 cm has 1000 turns per metre and a mean cross-sectional area of 2×10^{-4} m^2. It is placed with its axis at 30°, with a uniform magnetic field of 0.32 T. Find the torque acting on the solenoid when a current of 2 A is passed through it.

Sol. Given, $l = 50$ cm
Number of turns per metre = 1000
$\therefore$ Total number of turns $(N) = 1000 \times \frac{1}{2} = 500$
Area, $A = 2 \times 10^{-4}$ m^2
Current, $I = 2$ A
Magnetic field, $B = 0.32$ T
$\therefore$ Torque, $\tau = MB\sin\theta = (NIA)B\sin\theta$

$$= 500 \times 2 \times (2\times10^{-4}) \times 0.32 \times \frac{1}{2} = 0.032 \text{ N-m}$$

Example 8 A bar magnet when suspended horizontally and perpendicular to the earth's magnetic field experiences a torque of 3×10^{-4} N-m. What is the magnetic moment of the magnet? Horizontal component of earth's magnetic field at that place is 0.4×10^{-4} T.

Sol. Given, $\theta = 90°, \tau = 3\times10^{-4}$ N-m
and $B = 0.4\times10^{-4}$ T
Since, torque $\tau = MB\sin\theta$

$$\therefore \quad M = \frac{\tau}{B\sin\theta} = \frac{3\times10^{-4}}{0.4\times10^{-4}\sin 90°} = 7.5 \text{ JT}^{-1}$$

Example 9 A magnetic needle is free to oscillate in a uniform magnetic field as shown in figure. The magnetic moment of magnetic needle is 7.2 A-m^2 and moment of inertia $I = 6.5 \times 10^{-6}$ kg-m^2. The number of oscillations performed in 5s is 10. Calculate the magnitude of magnetic field.

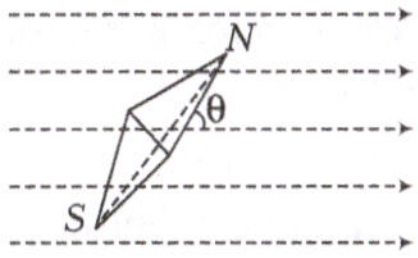

Sol. Here, $T = \frac{\text{Number of revolutions}}{\text{Time taken}} = \frac{5}{10} = 0.5$ s,

$$M = 7.2 \text{ A-m}^2 \text{ and } I = 6.5\times10^{-6} \text{ kg-m}^2$$

As, $T = 2\pi\sqrt{\frac{I}{MB}}$ or $T^2 = 4\pi^2\frac{I}{MB}$

The magnitude of the magnetic field is

$$B = \frac{4\pi^2 I}{MT^2} = \frac{4\times(3.14)^2\times6.5\times10^{-6}}{7.2\times(0.5)^2} = 1.42\times10^{-4} \text{ T}$$

Work Done and Potential Energy of a Magnetic Dipole in a Uniform Magnetic Field

A magnetic dipole is placed in an external magnetic field, then

Total work done in rotating the dipole from $\theta = \theta_0$ to $\theta = \theta$,

$$W = -MB[\cos\theta - \cos\theta_0]$$

$\therefore$ Potential energy of the dipole,

$$U = W = -MB(\cos\theta - \cos\theta_0)$$

Let us assume that, $\theta_0 = 90°$

$$U = W = -MB(\cos\theta - \cos 90°)$$

Therefore, $\boxed{U = -MB\cos\theta}$

In vector notation, we may rewrite this equation as

$$\boxed{U = -\mathbf{M}\cdot\mathbf{B}}$$

Particular Cases

(i) When $\theta = 90°$,

$$U = -MB\cos\theta = -MB\cos 90° = 0$$

i.e. when the dipole is perpendicular to magnetic field, its potential energy is zero.

(ii) When $\theta = 0°$, $U = -MB\cos\theta$

$$= -MB\cos 0° = -MB$$

i.e. when the magnetic dipole is aligned along the magnetic field, it is in **stable equilibrium** having minimum potential energy.

(iii) When $\theta = 180°$, $U = -MB\cos\theta$

$$= -MB\cos 180° = MB$$

which is maximum. This is the position of **unstable equilibrium.**

Example 10 A circular coil of 100 turns and have an effective radius of 5 cm carries a current of 0.1 A. How much work is required to turn it in an external magnetic field of 1.5 Wb/m^2 through 180° about an axis perpendicular to the magnetic field? The plane of the coil is initially perpendicular to the magnetic field.

Sol. Given, number of turns, $N = 100$

Radius, $r = 5\text{ cm} = 0.05\text{ m}$

Current, $I = 0.1\text{ A}$

Magnetic field, $B = 1.5\text{ Wb/m}^2$

$\theta_1 = 0°, \theta_2 = 180°$

Area, $A = \pi r^2 = 3.14(0.05)^2\text{ m}^2$

∴ Required work done,

$$W = -MB(\cos\theta_2 - \cos\theta_1)$$
$$= -(NIA)B(\cos\theta_2 - \cos\theta_1)$$
$$= -100 \times 0.1 \times 3.14\,(0.05)^2 \times 1.5 \times (\cos 180° - \cos 0°)$$
$$= -10 \times 3.14(0.05)^2 \times 1.5(-1-1) = 0.24\text{ J}$$

Topic Practice 1

Multiple Choice Questions

(1 Mark)

1. A thin, long piece of a magnet, suspended freely, points in

(a) North-East direction
(b) East-North direction
(c) East-South direction
(d) North-South direction

2. When two bar magnets are brought close to each other?

(a) Only attractive force exists
(b) Only repulsive forces exists
(c) Depends on the alignment of the two magnets
(d) None of the above

3. Cutting a bar magnet in half is like cutting a solenoid, such that we get two smaller solenoids with

(a) weaker magnetic properties
(b) strong magnetic properties
(c) constant magnetic properties
(d) Both (a) and (b)

4. The areas of cross-section of three magnets of same lengths area A, $2A$ and $6A$, respectively. The ratio of their magnetic moments will be

(a) 6 : 2 : 1 (b) 1 : 2 : 6
(c) 2 : 6 : 1 (d) 1 : 1 : 1

5. Rate of change of torque τ with deflection θ is maximum for a magnet suspended freely in a uniform magnetic field of induction B, when

(a) $\theta = 0°$ (b) $\theta = 45°$ (c) $\theta = 60°$ (d) $\theta = 90°$

Very Short Answer Type Questions

(1 Mark)

6. State the SI unit of magnetic dipole moment. **ISC 2013**

7. State the SI unit of the magnetic moment of a magnet, indicating its direction. **ISC 2006**

8. Define magnetic dipole moment. Also, write its SI unit.

9. A bar magnet is cut into two equal parts as shown in the Fig. (a). One part is now kept over the other such that, the P_2 is above P_1 as shown in the Fig. (b).

If M is the magnetic moment of the original magnet, what would be the magnetic moment of new combination of magnets so formed?

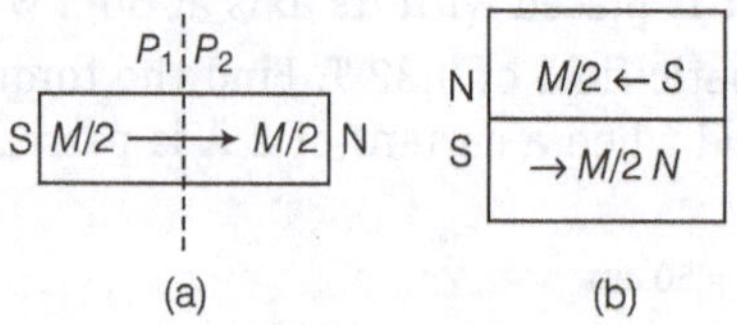

(a) (b)

Short Answer Type I Questions

(2 Marks)

10. What happens to a bar magnet if it is cut into two pieces

(i) transverse to its length?
(ii) along its length?

11. Derive an expression for the magnetic field at a point on the axis located at a distance x from the centre of a magnetic dipole of length $2l$ and magnetic moment M. **ISC 2006**

12. Three identical bar magnets are rivetted together at centre in the same plane as shown in the figure. This system is placed at rest in a slowly varying magnetic field. It is found that the system of magnets does not show any motion. The North-South poles of one magnet is shown in the figure. Determine the poles of the remaining two. **NCERT Exemplar**

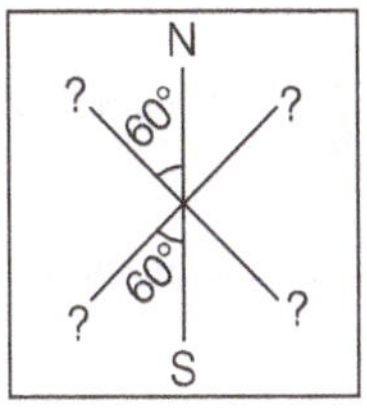

Short Answer Type II Questions

(3 Marks)

13. A short bar magnet placed with its axis making an angle θ with a uniform external field B, experiences a torque τ.
    (i) What is the magnetic moment of the magnet?
    (ii) Write the condition of stable equilibrium.

14. Two bar magnets having same geometry with magnetic moments M and $2M$ are placed in such a way that their similar poles are on the same side, then its time period of oscillation is T_1. Now, if the polarity of one of the magnets is reversed, then time period of oscillation is T_2, then find the relation between T_1 and T_2.

15. An observer to the left of a solenoid of N turns each of cross-section area A observes that a steady current I in it flows in the clockwise direction. Depict the magnetic field lines due to the solenoid specifying its polarity and show that it acts as a bar magnet of magnetic moment $m = NIA$.

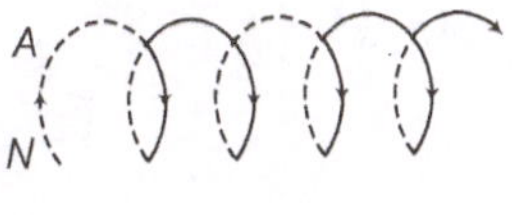

Long Answer Type Questions

(5 Marks)

16. Compare the magnetic fields of a bar magnet and a solenoid.

17. Derive an expression for
    (i) magnetic field at a point lies on axial line of a bar magnet.
    (ii) magnetic field at a point lies on equatorial line of a bar magnet.
    Also, find the ratio of magnetic fields at the axial and equatorial points.

Numerical Problems

18. A short bar magnet has a magnetic moment of 0.48 J/T. Give the direction and magnitude of the magnetic field produced by the magnet at a distance of 10 cm from the centre of the magnet on
    (i) the axis,
    (ii) the equatorial lines (normal bisector) of the magnet. **NCERT (2 M)**

19. A short bar magnet of magnetic moment 5.25×10^{-2} J/T is placed with its axis perpendicular to the earth's field direction. At what distance from the centre of the magnet, the resultant field is inclined at 45° with the earth's field on (i) its normal bisector and (ii) its axis. Magnitude of the earth's field at the place is given to be 0.42 G. Ignore the length of the magnet in comparison to the distances involved. **NCERT (3 M)**

20. A closely wound solenoid of 800 turns and area of cross-section 2.5×10^{-4} m^2 carries a current of 3.0 A. If it can be treated as a bar magnet, then find its magnetic moment. **(2 M)**

21. If the solenoid is treated as a magnet of moment (= 0.6 J/T) is free to turn about the vertical direction and a uniform horizontal magnetic field of 0.25 T is applied, what is the magnitude of torque on the solenoid when its axis makes an angle of 30° with the direction of applied field? **NCERT (2 M)**

22. A closely wound solenoid of 2000 turns and area of cross-section 1.6×10^{-4} m^2, carrying a current of 4 A, is suspended through its centre allowing it to turn in a horizontal plane. If the solenoid is treated as magnet, then
    (i) What is the magnetic moment associated with the solenoid?

(ii) What are the force and torque on the solenoid, if a uniform horizontal magnetic field of 7.5×10^{-2} T is set up at an angle of 30° with the axis of the solenoid?
NCERT (2 M)

23. A short magnet oscillates with a time period 0.1 s at a place, where horizontal magnetic field is 24 μT. A downward current of 18 A is established in a vertical wire 20 cm East of the magnet. What will be the new time period of the oscillator? **(1M)**

24. A circular coil of 16 turns and radius 10 cm carrying a current of 0.75 A, rests with its plane normal to an external field of magnitude 5.0×10^{-2} T. The coil is free to turn about an axis in its plane perpendicular to the field direction. When the coil is turned slightly and released, it oscillates about its stable equilibrium with a frequency of 2.0 s^{-1}. What is the moment of inertia of the coil about its axis of rotation?
NCERT (2M)

25. If two magnets having magnetic moments M and $M\sqrt{3}$ are joined to form a cross (i.e. ×). The combination is suspended freely in a uniform magnetic field. In equilibrium position, the magnet having magnetic moment M makes an angle θ with the field. Calculate the value of θ.
(2 M)

26. A short bar magnet of magnetic moment M= 0.32 J/T is placed in a uniform magnetic field of 0.15 T. If the bar is free to rotate in the plane of the field, which orientation would correspond to its (i) stable and (ii) unstable equilibrium? What is the potential energy of the magnet in each case? **NCERT (2 M)**

27. A bar magnet of magnetic moment 1.5 J/T lies aligned with the direction of a uniform magnetic field of 0.22 T.

(i) What is the amount of work required by an external torque to turn the magnet, so as to align its magnetic moment

(a) normal to the field direction,

(b) opposite to the field direction?

(ii) What is the torque on the magnet in cases (a) and (b)? **NCERT (3 M)**

Hints & Solutions

1. (*d*) When a thin long piece of a magnet is suspended freely it points in North-South direction.

2. (*d*) Attraction or repulsion of a bar magnet depends upon the alignment of the bar magnet when similar poles are aligned together, repulsion occurs when dissimilar poles are aligned together, attraction occurs.

3. (*a*) Cutting a bar magnet in half is like cutting a solenoid,such that we get two smaller solenoids with weaker magnetic properties.

4. (*b*) As magnetic moment ∝ pole strength ∝ area of cross-section, i.e. $m \propto q_m \propto A$

$$m_1 : m_2 : m_3 = 1 : 2 : 6$$

5. (*a*) As we know, torque,

i.e. $\tau = mB \sin\theta$, $\dfrac{d\tau}{d\theta} = mB\cos\theta$ It will be maximum when $\theta = 0$.

6. SI unit of magnetic dipole moment is A-m^2.

7. Refer to solution no. (6).

It is directed along the axis of dipole from South pole to North pole.

8. The magnetic moment of a magnet is a quantity that determines the torque, it will experience in an external magnetic field. Its SI unit is A-m^2.

9. When the bar magnet is cut into two equal parts, as shown in the Fig. (a), P_1 behaves as N and P_2 behaves as S and magnetic moment of each part of magnet becomes $M/2$. When pole P_2 is placed over pole P_1 as shown in Fig. (b), the net magnetic moment of the combination is zero, i.e. $\dfrac{M}{2} - \dfrac{M}{2} = 0$.

10. In both the cases (i) and (ii), we get two magnets, each with a North and South pole. (2)

11. To find magnetic field at an axial point, we have to apply principle of superposition of magnetic field. Consider the situation shown in the diagram. We have to find net magnetic field at point P, on axial point. Find magnetic field at P corresponding to each pole.

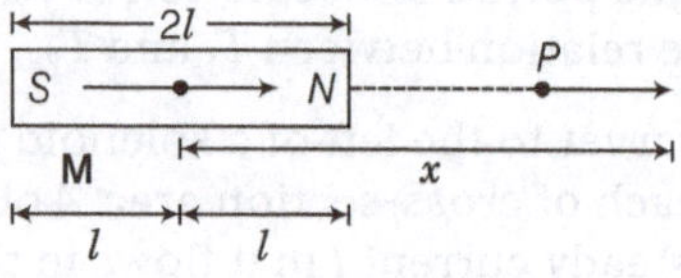

Net magnetic field at P,

$$B = B_N - B_S = \frac{\mu_0}{4\pi} \frac{2Mx}{(x^2 - l^2)^2}$$

$$\approx \frac{\mu_0}{4\pi} \frac{2M}{x^3} \quad \text{[for } l << x\text{]}$$ (2)

12. The system of magnets will be in stable equilibrium, if the net force on the system is zero and net torque on it is also zero. It will be possible, if the poles of the remaining two magnets is as shown in the figure. (2)

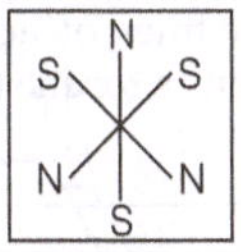

13. (i) Refer to text on pages 218 and 219 (Torque on a magnetic dipole in a uniform magnetic field).

(ii) Refer to text on pages 219 and 220 (Work done and potential energy of a magnetic dipole in a uniform magnetic field).

14. Using the formula for time period for magnetic system

$$T = 2\pi\sqrt{\left(\frac{I}{MH}\right)} \Rightarrow T \propto \frac{1}{\sqrt{M}} \quad \text{...(i)}$$

When similar poles placed at same side, then

$$M_1 = M + 2M = 3M$$

So, from Eq. (i), $T_1 \propto \dfrac{1}{\sqrt{3M}}$ ...(ii) (1)

When the polarity of a magnet is reversed, then

$$M_2 = 2M - M = M$$

So, from Eq . (i),

$$T_2 \propto \frac{1}{\sqrt{M}} \quad \text{...(iii)}$$ (1)

Now, on dividing Eq. (ii) by Eq. (iii), we get

$$\frac{T_1}{T_2} = \frac{\sqrt{M}}{\sqrt{3M}} = \frac{1}{\sqrt{3}}$$

$\Rightarrow$ $T_2 = \sqrt{3}\,T_1$

Hence, $T_1 < T_2$ (1)

15. Since, it is given that the current flows in the clockwise direction for an observer on the left side of the solenoid.

It means that the left face of the solenoid acts as South pole and right face acts as North pole. Inside a bar, the magnetic field lines are directed from South to North. (1½)

Therefore, the magnetic field lines are directed from left to right in the solenoid. (1)

Magnetic moment of a single current carrying loop is given by, $m' = IA$.

So, magnetic moment of the whole solenoid is given by

$$m = Nm' = N(IA)$$ (1/2)

16. Refer to text on page 218 (Bar magnet as an equivalent solenoid).

17. (i) Refer to text on page 217 {When point lies on axial line of a bar magnet (End-on position)}.

(ii) Refer to text on page 218 (When point lies on equatorial line of a bar magnet).

18. (i)

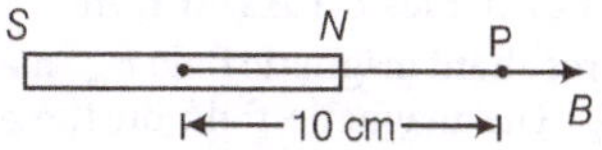

Refer to example 5 on page 217.

The direction of magnetic field is from S to N-pole of magnet. (1)

(ii)

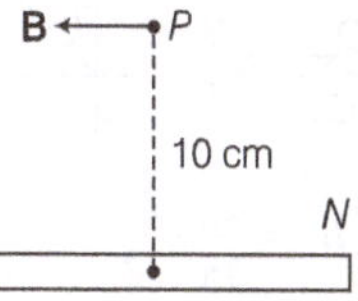

Refer to example 6 on page 218.

The direction of magnetic field is from N to S-pole of magnet. (1)

19. Given, magnetic moment, $m = 5.25 \times 10^{-2}$ J/T

Let the resultant magnetic field be B_{net}.

It makes an angle of 45° with B_e.

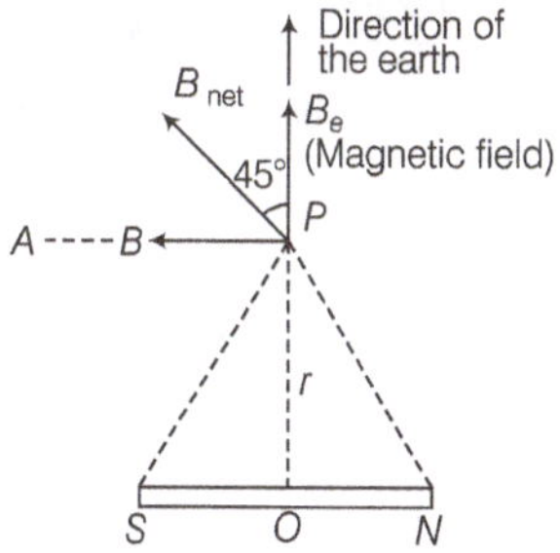

According to the vector analysis,

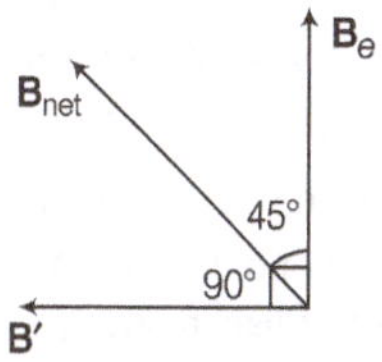

$$\Rightarrow \tan 45° = \frac{B \sin 90°}{B \cos 90° + B_e}$$

$$\Rightarrow \quad 1 = \frac{B}{B_e} \text{ or } B = B_e \quad \text{...(i)}$$ (1/2)

From Eq. (i), we get

$$\Rightarrow 0.42 \times 10^{-4} = \frac{\mu_0}{4\pi} \cdot \frac{m}{r^3}$$

$$0.42 \times 10^{-4} = \frac{10^{-7} \times 5.25 \times 10^{-2}}{r^3}$$

$$r^3 = \frac{5.25 \times 10^{-9}}{0.42 \times 10^{-4}} = 12.5 \times 10^{-5}$$

$$r = 0.05 \text{ m}$$ (1)

(ii) **When Point Lies on Axial Line**

Let the resultant magnetic field B_{net} makes an angle 45° from B_e. The magnetic field on the axial line of the magnet at a distance of r from the centre of magnet.

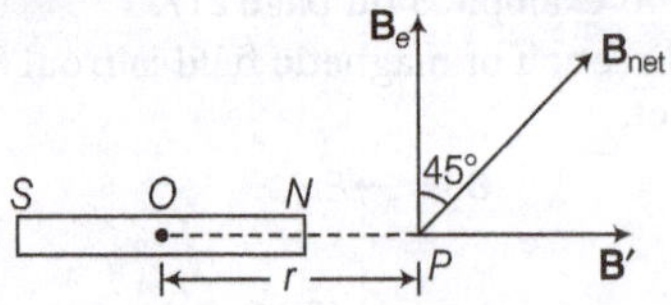

$$B' = \frac{\mu_0}{4\pi}\cdot\frac{2m}{r^3} \quad \text{...(i)}$$

Direction of magnetic field is from S to N.

According to the vector analysis.

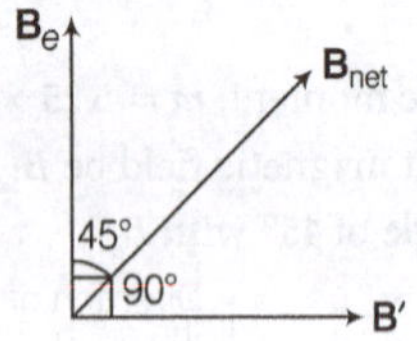

$$\tan 45° = \frac{B' \sin 90°}{B' \cos 90° + B_e} \Rightarrow 1 = \frac{B'}{B_e} \Rightarrow B_e = B' \quad \text{(1/2)}$$

From Eq. (i), we get

$$0.42 \times 10^{-4} = \frac{\mu_0}{4\pi} \times \frac{2m}{r^3}$$

$$\Rightarrow \quad 0.42 \times 10^{-4} = \frac{10^{-7} \times 2 \times 5.25 \times 10^{-2}}{r^3}$$

$$\Rightarrow \quad r^3 = \frac{10^{-9} \times 2 \times 5.25}{0.42 \times 10^{-4}} = 25.0 \times 10^{-5}$$

$$\therefore \quad r = 0.063 \text{ m or } 6.3 \text{ cm} \quad \text{(1)}$$

20. Given, number of turns, $n = 800$

Area of cross-section of solenoid, $A = 2.5 \times 10^{-4}$ m^2

Current through solenoid, $I = 3$ A

Magnetic moment of bar magnet,

$M = nIA = 800 \times 3 \times 2.5 \times 10^{-4}$

$= 0.6$ J/T along the axis of the solenoid. (2)

21. Given, magnetic field, $B = 0.25$ T

Angle between magnetic moment and the magnetic field, $\theta = 30°$

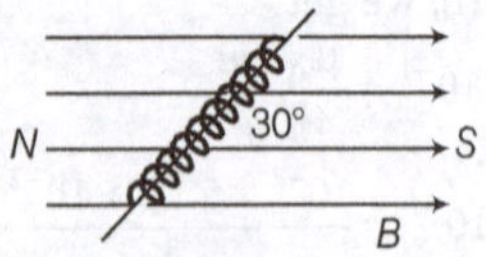

Magnetic moment, $M = 0.6$ J/T

Torque acting on the solenoid, when it is placed at an angle θ with the magnetic field. (1)

$$\tau = MB \sin\theta = 0.6 \times 0.25 \sin 30°$$

$$= 0.6 \times 0.25 \times \frac{1}{2} = 0.075 \text{ N-m}$$

Thus, the magnitude of torque on the solenoid is 0.075 N-m. (1)

22. (i) $M = nIA = 2000 \times 4 \times 1.6 \times 10^{-4}$

$M = 1.28$ J/T; (1/2)

(ii) The force (net) on the solenoid is zero because two equal and opposite forces (on each of its poles) are acting but their lines of action are parallel, so they form a couple thus a torque (not force) is applied on it. (1/2)

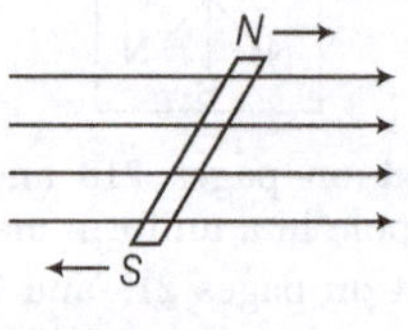

$\tau = 4.8 \times 10^{-2}$ N-m; refer to solution of Q. 21 on page 224. (1)

23. Initially,

$$T = 2\pi\sqrt{\frac{I}{mB'}} \text{ and finally, } T' = 2\pi\sqrt{\frac{I}{m(B+B')}}$$

where, B' = horizontal magnetic field = 24μT

and B = magnetic field due to downward conductor

$$= \frac{\mu_0}{4\pi}\cdot\frac{2i}{a} = 18\mu\text{T} \quad \text{(1/2)}$$

$$\therefore \quad \frac{T'}{T} = \sqrt{\frac{B'}{B+B'}}$$

$$\Rightarrow \quad \frac{T'}{0.1} = \sqrt{\frac{24}{18+24}} \Rightarrow T' = 0.076\text{s} \quad \text{(1/2)}$$

24. Given, number of turns of circular coil, $n = 16$

Radius of circular coil, $r = 10$ cm $= 0.1$ m

Current, $I = 0.75$ A, frequency, $f = 2$ s^{-1}

Magnetic field, $B = 5.0 \times 10^{-2}$ T

Magnetic moment of the coil,

$M = nIA = 16 \times 0.75 \times \pi\,(0.1)^2$

$= 16 \times 0.75 \times 3.14 \times (0.1)^2 = 0.377$ J/T (1/2)

Frequency of oscillation of the coil, $f = \frac{1}{2\pi}\sqrt{\frac{M \times B}{I}}$ (1/2)

where, I = moment of inertia of the coil.

Squaring on both sides, we get

$$f^2 = \frac{1}{4\pi^2}\cdot\frac{MB}{I} \Rightarrow I = \frac{MB}{4\pi^2 f^2}$$

$$= \frac{0.377 \times 5 \times 10^{-2}}{4 \times 3.14 \times 3.14 \times 2 \times 2} = 1.2 \times 10^{-4} \text{ kg-m}^2$$

Thus, the moment of inertia of the coil

$= 1.2 \times 10^{-4}$ kg-m^2 (1)

25. If magnet of magnetic moment M makes an angle θ with the field, then other magnet of magnetic moment $M\sqrt{3}$ makes an angle $(90° - \theta)$ with the field. (1)

In equilibrium, $\tau_1 = \tau_2$

$$\Rightarrow \quad MB\sin\theta = M\sqrt{3}\,B\cos\theta \Rightarrow \frac{\sin\theta}{\cos\theta} = \sqrt{3}$$

$$\Rightarrow \quad \tan\theta = \sqrt{3} \Rightarrow \theta = 60° \quad \text{(1)}$$

26. Given, magnetic moment of magnet, $M = 0.32$ J/T

Magnitude of magnetic field, $B = 0.15$ T

(i) For stable equilibrium, the angle between magnetic moment **M** and magnetic field **B** is $\theta = 0°$.

[$\because$ In this position, it will be in a direction parallel to the magnetic field, thus no torque will act on it.]

$\because$ The potential energy of the magnet,

$$U = -\mathbf{M}\cdot\mathbf{B} = -MB\cos\theta \quad [\because \mathbf{M}\cdot\mathbf{B} = MB\cos\theta]$$
$$= -0.32 \times 0.15 \cos 0°$$
$$= -4.8 \times 10^{-2}\ \text{J}$$

Thus, for the stable equilibrium the potential energy is -4.8×10^{-2} J. (1)

(ii) For unstable equilibrium, the angle between the magnetic moment and magnetic field is 180°.

($\because$ At $\theta = 180°$, although torque is zero but if it is displaced by small angle $d\theta$, then resulting torque would not restore it to the original position).

Potential energy of the magnet,

$$U = -MB\cos 180°$$
$$= -0.32 \times 0.15\,(-1)$$
$$= 4.8 \times 10^{-2}\ \text{J}$$

Thus, for the unstable equilibrium, the potential energy is 4.8×10^{-2} J. (1)

27. Given, magnetic moment of magnet, $M = 1.5$ J/T

Uniform magnetic field, $B = 0.22$ T

(i) (a) Angle, $\theta_1 = 0°$ [$\because$ the magnet lies aligned in the direction of field]

and $\theta_2 = 90°$ [$\because$ the magnet is to be aligned normal to the field direction]

Work done in rotating the magnet from angle θ_1 to θ_2,

$$W = -MB(\cos\theta_2 - \cos\theta_1)$$
$$= -1.5 \times 0.22\,(\cos 90° - \cos 0°) = 0.33\ \text{J}$$

(1)

(b) Angle, $\theta_1 = 0°$ and $\theta_2 = 180°$

[$\because$ Magnet is to be aligned opposite to the direction of field]

$$\text{Work done} = -MB(\cos\theta_2 - \cos\theta_1)$$
$$= -1.5 \times 0.22\,(\cos 180° - \cos 0°)$$
$$= 0.66\ \text{J}$$

(1)

(ii) Using the formula of torque,

$$\tau = MB\sin\theta$$

(a) When magnetic moment is normal to the field, $\theta = 90°$

$\tau = 1.5 \times 0.22 \sin 90° = 0.33$ N-m (1/2)

(b) When magnetic moment is opposite to the field, $\theta = 180°$

$\tau = 1.5 \times 0.22 \sin 180° = 0$ (1/2)

TOPIC 02 Magnetic Properties of Materials

Various Terms Related to Magnetism

Various terms related to the magnetism are given below.

Magnetic Intensity (H)

The capability of magnetic field to magnetise the substance is measured in terms of magnetic intensity of the field. The magnitude of magnetic intensity may be defined as the number of ampere turns flowing round the unit length of toroid to produce the magnetic induction B_0, in the toroid. It is denoted by H.

$$H = \frac{B_0}{\mu_0} \quad \ldots\text{(i)}$$

where, B_0 = magnetic field inside vacuum

and $\mu_0 = 4\pi \times 10^{-7}$ T-m A^{-1}.

Its SI unit is Am^{-1}.

Magnetic intensity is also known as **magnetising force** and **magnetic field strength.**

Intensity of Magnetisation (I)

The intensity of magnetisation of a magnetised substance represents the degree to which the substance is magnetised. It is defined as the net magnetic moment M developed per unit volume V, when a magnetic specimen is subjected to magnetising field. It is denoted by I.

$$I = \frac{M}{V}$$

Its SI unit is Am^{-1}. Its dimension is $[\text{L}^{-1}\text{A}]$ and it is a vector quantity.

Magnetic Induction (B)

It is defined as the number of magnetic lines of induction crossing per unit area normally through the magnetic substance. It is denoted by B. Magnetic induction B is the sum of the magnetic field B_0 and the magnetic field $\mu_0 I$ produced due to the magnetisation of the substance.

Thus, $B = B_0 + \mu_0 I = \mu_0 H + \mu_0 I$

$$B = \mu_0 (H + I) \quad ...(ii)$$

Magnetic induction is also known as **magnetic flux density** or simply magnetic field.

Its SI unit is T or Wbm^{-2}.

The CGS unit of **B** is gauss, where $1\text{G} = 10^{-4}\text{T}$.

Magnetic Susceptibility (χ_m)

It is a measure of how easily a substance is magnetised in a magnetising field. The magnetic susceptibility of a magnetic substance is defined as the ratio of the intensity of magnetisation to the magnetic intensity. It is denoted by χ_m.

$$\chi_m = \frac{I}{H} \quad ...(iii)$$

As units of H and I are same (Am^{-1}), therefore it has no unit.

Magnetic Permeability (μ)

It is a measure of conduction of magnetic field lines through a substance. The magnetic permeability of a magnetic substance is defined as the ratio of the magnetic induction to the magnetic intensity. It is denoted by μ.

$$\mu = \frac{B}{H}$$

Its SI unit is TmA^{-1}.

Relative Magnetic Permeability (μ_r)

It is the ratio of the magnetic permeability μ of the substance to the permeability of free space.

$$\mu_r = \frac{\mu}{\mu_0}$$

It is a dimensionless quantity and is equal to 1 for vacuum.

The **relative magnetic permeability of a substance** is defined as the ratio of magnetic flux density B in that substance and flux density B_0 in vacuum in the same field.

$$\mu_r = \frac{B}{B_0}$$

Relation between Relative Magnetic Permeability (μ_r) and Magnetic Susceptibility (χ_m)

When a substance is placed in a magnetising field, it becomes magnetised. The total magnetic flux density B within the substance is the flux density that would have been produced by the magnetising field in vacuum plus the flux density due to the magnetisation of the substance. If I be the intensity of magnetisation of the substance, then by definition, the magnetic intensity of the magnetising field is given by

$$H = \frac{B}{\mu_0} - I \text{ or } B = \mu_0 (H + I)$$

But $\quad I = \chi_m H$

where, χ_m is the susceptibility of the substance.

$$\therefore \quad B = \mu_0 H (1 + \chi_m)$$

Again $B = \mu H$, where μ is the permeability of the substance.

$$\therefore \quad \mu = \mu_0 (1 + \chi_m) \quad \text{or} \quad \frac{\mu}{\mu_0} = 1 + \chi_m$$

$\frac{\mu}{\mu_0}$ is the relative permeability μ_r.

Thus, $\quad \mu_r = 1 + \chi_m$

The quantity $(1 + \chi_m) = \mu_r$ is the analog of dielectric constant in electrostatics and is known as relative magnetic permeability. It is a dimensionless quantity.

The value of magnetic susceptibility is small and positive for paramagnetic materials and small and negative for diamagnetic materials.

Example 1 The magnetic field B and the magnetic intensity H in a material are found to be 1.6 T and 1000 Am^{-1}, respectively. Determine the relative permeability μ_r and the susceptibility χ_m of the material.

Sol. Magnetic permeability, $\mu = \frac{B}{H} = \frac{1.6}{1000} = 1.6 \times 10^{-3} \text{TmA}^{-1}$

Since, relative magnetic permeability,

$$\mu_r = \frac{\mu}{\mu_0} = \frac{1.6 \times 10^{-3}}{4\pi \times 10^{-7}} = 0.127 \times 10^4$$

Therefore, susceptibility, $\chi_m = \mu_r - 1 = 1.27 \times 10^3 - 1$

$$\Rightarrow \quad \chi_m \approx 1.27 \times 10^3$$

Example 2 A solenoid of 600 turns per metre is carrying a current of 4 A. Its core is made of iron with relative permeability of 5000. Calculate the magnitudes of magnetic intensity, intensity of magnetisation and magnetic field inside the core.

Sol. Given, current, $I = 4\text{ A}$

Number of turns per unit length, $n = 600$

Relative permeability, $\mu_r = 5000$

Since, magnetic intensity, $H = nI = 600 \times 4 = 2400\,\text{Am}^{-1}$

Since, $\mu_r = 1 + \chi_m$

$\Rightarrow \chi_m = \mu_r - 1$

$= 5000 - 1 = 4999 \approx 5000$

Here, χ_m = magnetic susceptibility.

Intensity of magnetisation can be given as

$$I = \chi_m H = 5000 \times 2400$$
$$= 1.2 \times 10^7\,\text{Am}^{-1}$$

Therefore, magnetic field,

$$B = \mu_r \mu_0 H$$
$$= 5000 \times (4\pi \times 10^{-7}) \times 2400$$
$$= 15\,\text{T}$$

Diamagnetism

Diamagnetic substances are those substances which have a tendency to move from stronger to the weaker part of the external magnetic field.

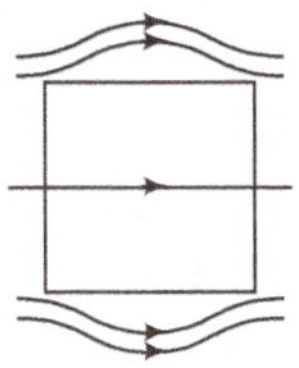

When a bar of diamagnetic material is placed in an external magnetic field, the field lines are repelled or expelled and the field inside the material is reduced.

Explanation of Diamagnetism

Diamagnetic substances are those substances in which resultant magnetic moment in an atom is zero.

When magnetic field is applied, those electrons having orbital magnetic moment in the same direction slow down and those in opposite directions speed up. This happens due to induced current in accordance with Lenz's law. Thus, the substance develops a net magnetic moment in the direction opposite to that of the applied field and hence, repels. e.g. Bismuth, copper, lead, silicon, nitrogen (at STP), water and sodium chloride.

Meissner Effect

Superconductors exhibit perfect diamagnetism. A superconductor repels a magnet and (by Newton's third law) is repelled by the magnet. This phenomenon of perfect diamagnetism in superconductors is called the **Meissner effect**. Superconducting magnets have been used for running magnetically levitated superfast trains.

Paramagnetism

The substances which get weakly magnetised in the direction of external field, when placed in an external magnetic field are called paramagnetic substances. These substances have the tendency to move from a region of weak magnetic field to strong magnetic field, i.e. they get weakly attracted to a magnet.

Explanation of Paramagnetism

The atoms of a paramagnetic material possess a permanent magnetic dipole moment of their own.

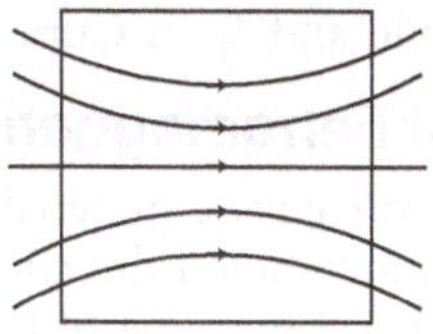

On account of the ceaseless random motion of the atoms, no net magnetisation is seen. But in the presence of an external field B_0, which is strong enough and at low temperatures, the individual atomic dipole moment can be made to align and point in the same direction as B_0.

The field lines get concentrated inside the material and the field inside is enhanced.

When placed in a non-uniform magnetic field, the paramagnetic material tends to move from weaker part of the field to the stronger part.

e.g. Aluminium, sodium, calcium, oxygen (at STP) and a copper chloride.

Curie's Law

Magnetisation of a paramagnetic material is inversely proportional to the absolute temperature (T),

$$I = C\frac{B_0}{T} \quad \text{or equivalently} \quad \chi_m = \frac{C\mu_0}{T}$$

where, C is called Curie's constant.

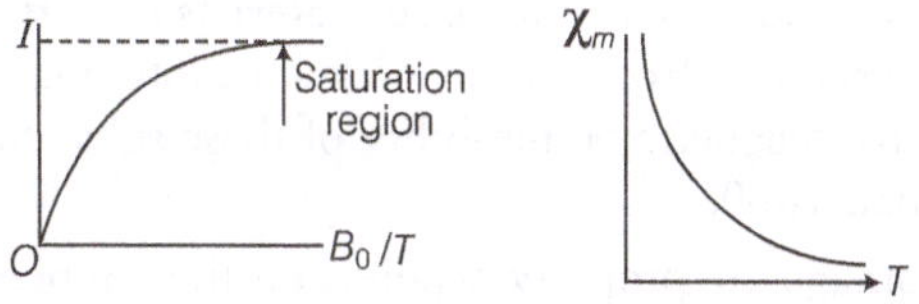

The variation of intensity of magnetisations with B_0/T is shown in the figure. At a particular stage, all the atomic dipoles present in the specimen align in the direction of the external field and this leads to saturation region.

Ferromagnetism

The substances which get strongly magnetised when placed in an external magnetic field are called ferromagnetic substances. They have strong tendency to move from a region of weak magnetic field to strong magnetic field, i.e. they get strongly attracted to a magnet.

Curie-Weiss Law

This describes the magnetic susceptibility χ_m of a ferromagnet in the paramagnetic region above the Curie point. It is expressed as

$$\chi_m = \frac{C}{T - T_C} \quad [\because T > T_C]$$

where, C is called Curie's constant, T is absolute temperature in kelvin and T_C is Curie temperature.

Explanation of Ferromagnetism

The atoms in a ferromagnetic material possess a dipole moment aligned in a common direction over a macroscopic volume called **domain**. Each domain has net magnetisation.

When we apply an external magnetic field B_0, the domains orient themselves in the direction of B_0 and simultaneously the domains grow in size.

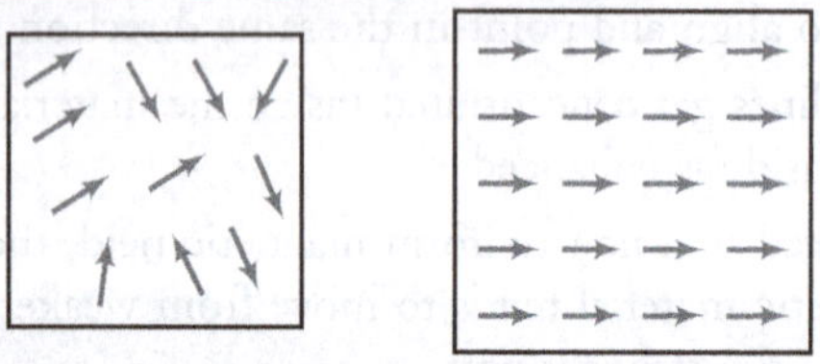

Randomly oriented domains Aligned domains

In some ferromagnetic materials, the magnetisation persists on removal of external magnetic field. Such materials are called **hard magnetic materials or hard ferromagnets**, e.g. alnico (an alloy of iron, aluminium, nickel, cobalt and copper) is one such material which forms permanent magnets to be used among other things as a compass needle. There are some ferromagnetic materials in which the magnetisation disappears on removal of external magnetic field, e.g. soft iron. Such materials are called **soft magnetic materials or soft ferromagnets.** e.g. Iron, cobalt, nickel, gadolinium, etc. The relative magnetic permeability of these substances is greater than 1000.

The ferromagnetic property depends on the temperature. At high temperature, a ferromagnet becomes a paramagnet. The transition of temperature from ferromagnetism to paramagnetism is called the **Curie temperature** (T_C). The susceptibility in the paramagnetic phase is described by

$$\chi_m = \frac{C}{T - T_C} \quad [\because T > T_C]$$

Magnetic Properties of Materials

Materials can be classified as diamagnetic, paramagnetic and ferromagnetic on the basis of susceptibility (χ_m).

Diamagnetic	Paramagnetic	Ferromagnetic
$-1 \le \chi_m < 0$	$0 < \chi_m < \varepsilon$	$\chi_m >> 1$
$0 \le \mu_r < 1$	$1 < \mu_r < 1 + \varepsilon$	$\mu_r >> 1$
$\mu < \mu_0$	$\mu > \mu_0$	$\mu >> \mu_0$

Here, ε is a small positive number introduced to quantify paramagnetic materials.

Example 3 A solenoid having 5000 turns/m carries a current of 2A. An aluminium ring at temperature 300K inside the solenoid provides the core.

(a) If the magnetisation I is 2×10^{-2} A/m, find the susceptibility of aluminium at 300 K.

(b) If temperature of the aluminium ring is 320 K, what will be the magnetisation?

Sol. (a) Here, $H = I = 5000 \times 2 = 10^4$ A/m

and $I = \chi H$

$$\therefore \quad \chi = \frac{I}{H} = \frac{2 \times 10^{-2}}{10^4} = 2 \times 10^{-6}$$

(b) According to Curie law,

$$\chi = \frac{C}{T} \Rightarrow \frac{\chi_2}{\chi_1} = \frac{T_2}{T_1}$$

$$\chi_2 = \frac{T_2}{T_1}\chi_1 = \frac{320}{300} \times 2 \times 10^{-6} = 2.13 \times 10^{-6}$$

$\therefore$ Magnetisation at 320 K,

$$I = \chi_2 H = 2.13 \times 10^{-6} \times 10^4 = 2.13 \times 10^{-2} \text{ A/m}$$

Hysteresis Curve

The hysteresis curve represents the relation between the magnetic induction B or intensity of magnetisation I of a ferromagnetic material with magnetic intensity H. The graph shows the behaviour of the material as we take it through one cycle of magnetisation shown in the figure.

Formation of Hysteresis Curve

An unmagnetised sample is placed in a solenoid and current through the solenoid is increased. The magnetic field B in the material rises and saturates as depicted in the curve Oa. Next, if H is decreased and reduces to zero.

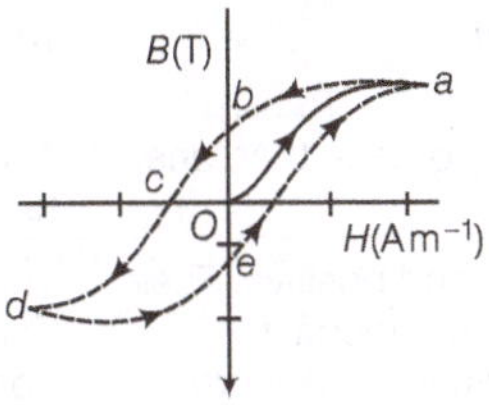

Then, at $H = 0, B \neq 0$ (curve ab)

The value of B at $H = 0$ is called **retentivity**.

Now, the current in the solenoid is reversed and slowly increased, we again obtain saturation in the reverse direction at d. The value of H at c is called **coercivity**.

Now, the current is reduced (curve de), increased, reversed (curve ea) . The cycle repeats itself. For a given value of H, B is not unique, but depends on previous history of the sample. This phenomenon is called **hysteresis.**

It is found that the area of hysteresis loop is proportional to the net energy absorbed per unit volume by the material, as it is taken over a complete cycle of magnetisation. The energy so, absorbed by the specimen appears in the form of heat energy. Hysteresis loop for soft iron is large and narrow, whereas the hysteresis loop for steel is short and wide as shown in the figure.

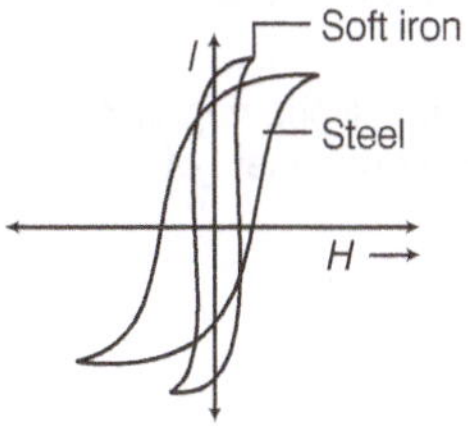

From the hysteresis loops of soft iron and steel, we say

(i) Retentivity of soft iron is greater than that of steel.

(ii) Soft iron is more strongly magnetised than steel.

(iii) Coercivity of soft iron is less than that of steel.

(iv) As area of hysteresis loop for soft iron is smaller than that for steel, therefore, hysteresis loss in case of soft iron is smaller than that in case of steel.

Comparative Study of Magnetic Materials

Diamagnetic Substances	Paramagnetic Substances	Ferromagnetic Substances
These substances when placed in a magnetic field, acquire feeble magnetism opposite to the direction of the magnetic field. 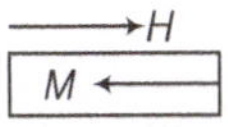	These substances when placed in a magnetic field, acquire feeble magnetism in the direction of the magnetic field. 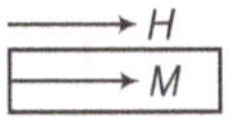	These substances when placed in a magnetic field are strongly magnetised in the direction of the field. 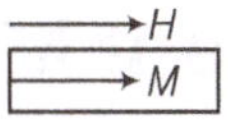
These substances are feebly repelled by a magnet.	These substances are feebly attracted by a magnet.	These substances are strongly attracted by a magnet.
When a diamagnetic solution is poured into a U-tube and one arm is placed between the poles of strong magnet, the level of solution in that arm is lowered. 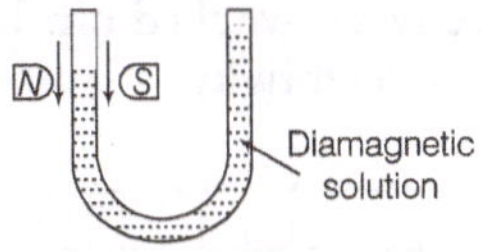	The level of the paramagnetic solution in that arm rises. 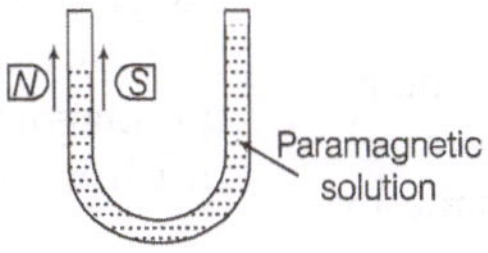	No liquid is ferromagnetic.
If a rod of diamagnetic material is suspended freely between two magnetic poles, its axis becomes perpendicular to the magnetic field. 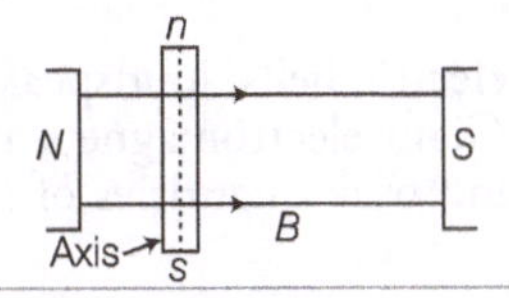	Paramagnetic rod becomes parallel to the magnetic field. 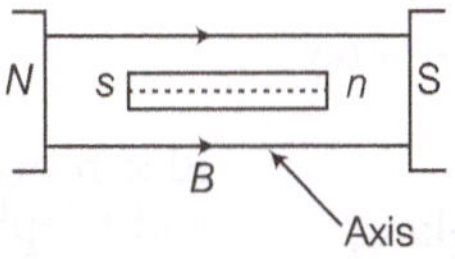	Ferromagnetic rod also becomes parallel to the magnetic field. 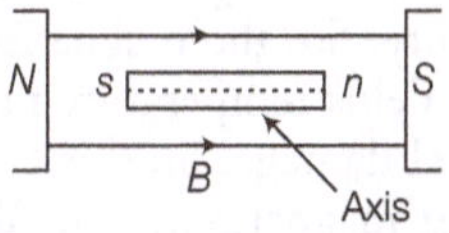

Diamagnetic Substances	Paramagnetic Substances	Ferromagnetic Substances
In non-uniform magnetic field, the diamagnetic substances are attracted towards the weaker fields, i.e. they move from stronger to weaker magnetic field.	In non-uniform magnetic field, paramagnetic substances move from weaker to stronger part of the magnetic field slowly.	In non-uniform magnetic field, ferromagnetic substances move from weaker to stronger magnetic field rapidly.
Their permeability is less than one ($\mu < 1$).	Their permeability is slightly greater than one ($\mu > 1$).	Their permeability is much greater than one ($\mu >> 1$).
Their susceptibility is small and negative. Their susceptibility is independent of temperature.	Their susceptibility is small and positive. Their susceptibility is inversely proportional to absolute temperature, which is Curie's law. i.e. $\chi_m \propto \frac{1}{T}$.	Their susceptibility is large and positive. They follow Curie-Weiss law, when heated above Curie's temperature (T_C). i.e. $\chi_m \propto \frac{1}{T - T_C}$. At Curie temperature, ferromagnetic substances change into paramagnetic substances.
Shape of diamagnetic liquid in a glass crucible and kept over two magnetic poles. 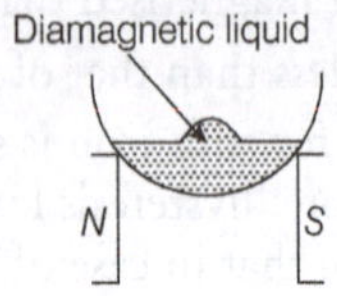	Shape of paramagnetic liquid in a glass crucible and kept over two magnetic poles. 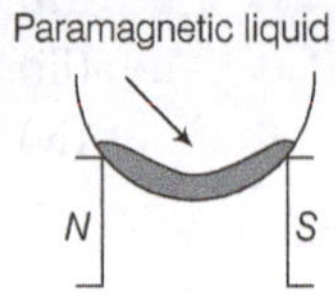	No liquid is ferromagnetic.
In these substances, the magnetic field lines are farther than in air.	In these substances, the magnetic field lines are closer than in air.	In these substances, the magnetic field lines are much closer than in air.
The resultant magnetic moment of these substances is zero.	These substances have a permanent magnetic moment.	These substances also have a permanent magnetic moment.

Permanent Magnets and Electromagnets

On the basis of hysteresis curve, magnets can be categorised as permanent and electromagnets.

Permanent Magnets

The substances which at room temperature retain their ferromagnetic property for a long period of time are called permanent magnets. Permanent magnet can be made by placing a rod of ferromagnetic material in a current carrying solenoid. The magnetic field of the solenoid magnetises the rod. The material used for making permanent magnets should have high retentivity, so that the magnet is strong and have high coercivity and high permeability. So, the magnetisation is not erased by stray magnetic fields/temperature fluctuations or minor mechanical damage. Steel is favoured for making permanent magnet.Some suitable materials for making permanent magnets are alnico, cobalt, steel and ticonal (titanium containing material).

Electromagnets

Electromagnets are usually in the form of iron core solenoids. The core of an electromagnet is made of ferromagnetic materials which have high permeability and low retentivity. Soft iron is suitable material for electromagnets. On placing a soft iron rod in a current carrying solenoid, the magnetism of the solenoid increases by thousands folds.On switching off the solenoid current, the magnetism is effectively switched off. It is because the soft iron core has a low retentivity.

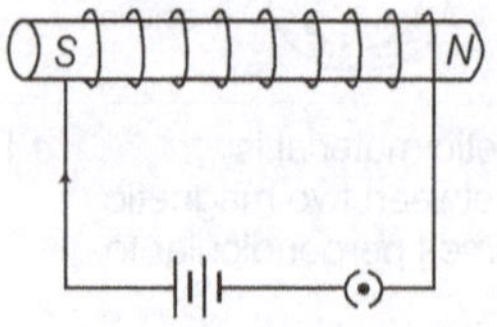

Electromagnets are used in electric bells, loudspeakers and telephone diaphragms. Giant electromagnets are used in cranes to lift machinery and bulk quantities of iron and steel.

Topic Practice 2

Multiple Choice Question

(1 Mark)

1. Those substance which at room temperature retain their ferromagnetic property for a long period of time are called
   (a) permanent magnets (b) electromagnets
   (c) ferromagnets (d) paramagnet

Very Short Answer Type Questions

(1 Mark)

2. In what way, the behaviour of a diamagnetic material is different from that of a paramagnetic, when kept in an external magnetic field?
3. Two substances *A* and *B* have their relative permeabilities slightly greater and slightly less than 1, respectively. What do you conclude about *A* and *B* as far as their magnetic materials are concerned? **ISC 2014**
4. Arrange the three types of magnetic materials, i.e. paramagnetic, diamagnetic and ferromagnetic materials, in decreasing order of their magnetic susceptibility. **ISC 2010, 03**
5. State how the magnetic susceptibility of a ferromagnetic material changes when it is heated. **ISC 2009**
6. State how magnetic susceptibility is different for the three types of magnetic materials, i.e. diamagnetic, paramagnetic and ferromagnetic materials. **ISC 2015**
7. (i) Define Curie temperature.
   (ii) If magnetic susceptibility of a certain magnetic material is 0.0001, find its relative permeability. **ISC 2016**
8. At a certain temperature, a ferromagnetic material becomes paramagnetic. What is the temperature called? **ISC 2014**

Short Answer Type I Questions

(2 Marks)

9. Distinguish between diamagnetic and paramagnetic substances in terms of its relative permeability (μ_r) and magnetic susceptibility (χ). **ISC 2005**
10. From molecular view point, discuss the temperature dependence of susceptibility for diamagnetism, paramagnetism and ferromagnetism. **NCERT Exemplar**
11. Show diagrammatically the behaviour of magnetic field lines in the presence of
    (i) paramagnetic and
    (ii) diamagnetic substances. How does one explain this distinguishing feature?
12. Out of the two magnetic materials, *A* has relative permeability slightly greater than unity while *B* has less than unity. Identify the nature of the materials *A* and *B*. Will their susceptibilities be positive or negative?
13. A ball of superconducting material is dipped in liquid nitrogen and placed near a bar magnet.
    (i) In which direction will it move?
    (ii) What will be the direction of its magnetic moment? **NCERT Exemplar**
14. Explain quantitatively the order of magnitude difference between the diamagnetic susceptibility of N_2 ($\sim 5\times10^{-9}$) (at STP) and Cu ($\sim 10^{-5}$). **NCERT Exemplar**
15. A proton has spin and magnetic moment just like an electron. Why then its effect is neglected in magnetism of materials? **NCERT Exemplar**
16. What is meant by a paramagnetic substance? State Curie's law. **ISC 2011**
17. The susceptibility of a magnetic material is 0.9853. Identify the type of magnetic material. Draw the modification of the field pattern on keeping a piece of this material in a uniform magnetic field.

Short Answer Type II Questions

(3 Marks)

18. Three identical specimens of a magnetic material, nickel, antimony, aluminium are kept in a non-uniform magnetic field. Draw the modification in the field lines in each case. Justify your answer.
19. Answer the following questions:
    (i) Why does a paramagnetic sample display greater magnetisation (for the same magnetising field) when cooled?

(ii) If a toroid uses bismuth for its core, then will the field in the core be (slightly) greater or (slightly) less than when the core is empty?

(iii) Is the permeability of a ferromagnetic material independent of the magnetic field? If not, is it more for lower or higher fields?

(iv) Magnetic field lines are always nearly normal to the surface of a ferromagnet at every point. (This fact is analogous to the static electric field lines being normal to the surface of a conductor at every point.) Why?

(v) Would the maximum possible magnetisation of a paramagnetic sample be of the same order of magnitude as the magnetisation of a ferromagnet? **NCERT**

20. Answer the following questions.

(i) Explain qualitatively on the basis of domain picture the irreversibility in the magnetisation curve of a ferromagnet.

(ii) The hysteresis loop of a soft iron piece has a much smaller area than that of a carbon steel piece. If the material is to go through repeated cycles of magnetisation, which piece will dissipate greater heat energy?

(iii) A system displaying a hysteresis loop such as a ferromagnet, is a device for storing memory. Explain the meaning of this statement.

(iv) What kind of ferromagnetic material is used for coating magnetic tapes in a cassette player or for building 'memory stores' in a modern computer?

(v) A certain region of space is to be shielded from magnetic fields. Suggest a method.

NCERT

Long Answer Type Questions

5 Marks

21. (i) Discuss briefly electron theory of magnetism for diamagnetic and paramagnetic materials.

(ii) Give two methods to destroy the magnetism of a magnet.

22. What are the permanent magnets? What is an efficient way of preparing a permanent magnet? How is an electromagnet designed? What are the uses of electromagnet?

Numerical Problems

23. A Rowland ring of mean radius 15 cm has 3500 turns of wire wound on a ferromagnetic core of relative permeability 800. What is the magnetic field B in the core for a magnetising current of 1.2 A? **NCERT (2 M)**

24. What is the value of magnetic susceptibility of aluminium, if its relative permeability is 1.000022? **ISC 2011 (1 M)**

Hints & Solutions

1. (*a*) Substance which at room temperature retain their ferromagnetic property for a long period of time are called permanent magnet.

2. When paramagnetic materials are placed in external magnetic field, these are feebly magnetised in the direction of the applied external magnetic field, whereas in case of diamagnetic materials, these are feebly magnetised opposite to that of applied external magnetic field.

3. For paramagnetic substances $\mu_r > 1$ and for diamagnetic substances $\mu_r < 1$, where μ_r is relative permeability. Thus, *A* is paramagnetic and *B* is diamagnetic material.

4. For ferromagnetic materials, χ_m is very high.
For paramagnetic materials, χ_m is positive.
For diamagnetic materials, χ_m is negative.
So, decreasing order of magnetic susceptibility is ferromagnetic, paramagnetic and diamagnetic.

5. The magnetic susceptibility (χ) of a ferromagnetic substance varies with temperature as $\chi \propto \frac{1}{T - T_C}$

$[\because T > T_C]$

6. For diamagnetic material, susceptibility is less than zero.
For paramagnetic material, susceptibility is more than zero but less than 1.
Ferromagnetic material has very high value in positive.

7. (i) Curie temperature (T_C) is the temperature at which certain materials lose their ferromagnetic property to become paramagnetic. (1/2)

(ii) Given, magnetic susceptibility of material, $\chi_m = 0.0001$
Since, relative magnetic permeability,

$$\mu_r = 1 + \chi_m \Rightarrow \mu_r = 1 + 0.0001$$
$$\mu_r = 1.0001$$ (1/2)

8. At a temperature known as Curie temperature, ferromagnetic material becomes paramagnetic.

9.

Property	Diamagnetic	Paramagnetic
Relative permeability (μ_r)	$\mu_r < 1$	$\mu_r > 1$
Magnetic susceptibility (χ)	Low and negative	Low and positive

(2)

10. Susceptibility of magnetic material $\chi = \frac{I}{H}$, where I is the intensity of magnetisation induced in the material and H is the magnetising force. (1/2)

Diamagnetism is due to orbital motion of electrons in an atom developing magnetic moments opposite to applied field. Thus, the resultant magnetic moment of the diamagnetic material is zero and hence, the susceptibility χ of diamagnetic material is not much affected by temperature. (1/2)

Paramagnetism and ferromagnetism is due to alignment of atomic magnetic moments in the direction of the applied field. As temperature is raised, the alignment is disturbed, resulting decrease in susceptibility of both with increase in temperature. (1)

11. Refer to pages 229 and 230 (Diamagnetism and paramagnetism) for diagram. (1)

Magnetic permeability of paramagnetic substance is more than air, so it allows more lines to pass through it while permeability of diamagnetic substance is less than air, so it does not allow lines to pass through it. Thus, diamagnetic substances expel magnetic field lines, while paramagnetic substances attract them. (1)

12. The nature of the material A is paramagnetic and its susceptibility χ_m is positive. (1)

The nature of the material B is diamagnetic and its susceptibility χ_m is negative. (1)

13. Both a superconducting material and nitrogen are diamagnetic in nature. When a ball of superconducting material is dipped in liquid nitrogen, it behaves as a diamagnetic material. When placed near a bar magnet, it will be feebly magnetised opposite to the direction of magnetising field. (1)

Because of this, (i) it will be repelled (i.e. move away from magnet) (ii) the direction of magnetic moment will be opposite to the direction of magnetic field of bar magnet. (1)

14. Here, $\chi_{m(N_2)} = 5\times10^{-9}$ and $\chi_{m(Cu)} = 10^{-5}$

$$\therefore \quad \frac{\chi_{m(N_2)}}{\chi_{m(Cu)}} = \frac{5\times10^{-9}}{10^{-5}} = 5\times10^{-4} \quad (1)$$

As, $$\chi_m = \frac{I}{H} = \frac{M/V}{H} = \frac{M}{HV} = \frac{M\rho}{Hm}$$

where, M = magnetic moment,
V = volume, m = mass and ρ = density.

$\therefore \quad \chi_m \propto \rho$, for given value of $\frac{M}{Hm}$

Thus, $$\frac{\chi_{m(N_2)}}{\chi_{m(Cu)}} = \frac{\rho_{N_2}}{\rho_{Cu}} = \frac{28\text{ g}/22400\text{ cc}}{8\text{ g/cc}} = 1.6\times10^{-4} \quad (1)$$

15. As we know that, the magnetic moment of electron or proton is inversely proportional to the mass of electron or proton, respectively.

Magnetic moment of electron, $\mu_e \propto \frac{1}{m_e}$

where, m_e = mass of electron

Magnetic moment of proton, $\mu_p \propto \frac{1}{m_p}$

where, m_p = mass of proton

$$\frac{\mu_e}{\mu_p} = \frac{m_p}{m_e} \quad \ldots\text{(i) (1)}$$

As, we know that, $m_e << m_p$

So, $$\frac{m_p}{m_e} >> 1 \Rightarrow \frac{\mu_e}{\mu_p} >> 1$$

$$\Rightarrow \quad \mu_e >> \mu_p$$

Thus, as the value of magnetic moment of electron is much more as compared to magnetic moment of proton, so the effect of proton is neglected. (1)

16. These substances (paramagnetic) when placed in a magnetic field, acquire feeble magnetism in the direction of the magnetic field. (1)

Curie's law Susceptibility (χ) of a paramagnetic substance varies inversely with absolute temperature of the substance.

i.e. $$\chi \propto \frac{1}{T} \quad (1)$$

17. Given, susceptibility, $\chi_m = 0.9853$

As the susceptibility of material is positive but small.

$\therefore$ The material is paramagnetic in nature. For paramagnetic material, magnetic lines of external magnetic field will pass through the material without much deviation, when it is placed in between magnetic poles.

The modification of the field pattern is shown in the following figure.

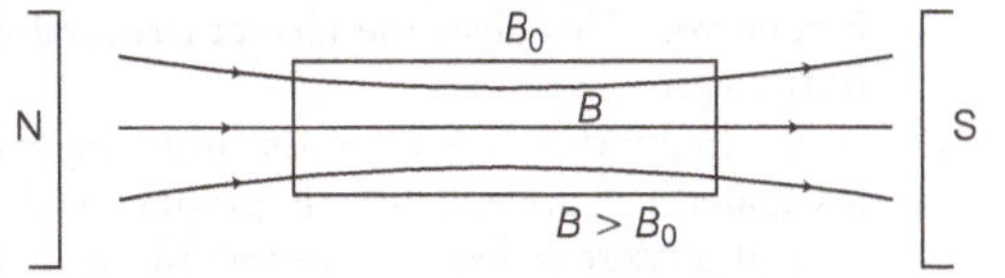

18.

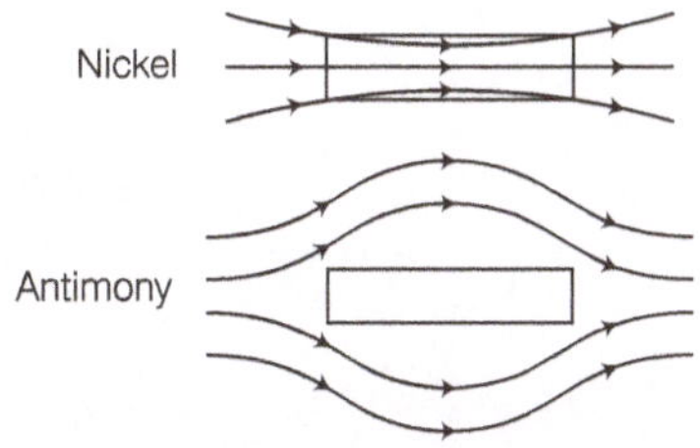

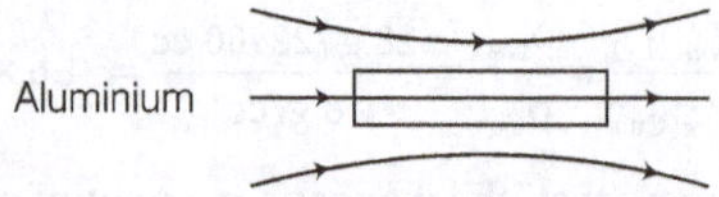

(1½)

The modification in the field lines shown in the figure are as such because

(i) nickel is a ferromagnetic substance.

(ii) antimony is a diamagnetic substance.

(iii) aluminium is a paramagnetic substance.

Refer to text on pages 229 and 230 (Comparative study of magnetic materials). (1½)

19. (i) A paramagnetic sample displays greater magnetisation when cooled because at the lower temperatures, the tendency to disrupt the alignment of magnetic dipoles decreases due to the reduced random thermal motion of atoms or molecules. (1/2)

(ii) Bismuth is a diamagnetic element, so the magnetic field in the core will be slightly less than when the core is empty, because the diamagnetic substances are feebly magnetised in the opposite direction of magnetic field. (1/2)

(iii) No, the permeability of a ferromagnetic material is not independent of the magnetic fields. By observing the hysteresis curve, the value of permeability is greater for lower fields. (1/2)

(iv) The magnetic field lines are always nearly normal to the surface of a ferromagnet at every point because the value of permeability for ferromagnetic substance is always greater than 1 ($\mu >> 1$). It is based on the conditions of B and H at the interface of two media in the hysteresis curve. (1/2)

(v) Yes, the maximum possible magnetisation of a paramagnetic sample will be of the same order of magnitude as the magnetisation of a ferromagnet. Although, the condition of saturation for paramagnets, requires very high magnetising fields which cannot be achieved. (1)

20. (i) To explain qualitatively the domain picture of the irreversibility in the magnetisation curve of a ferromagnet, we draw the hysteresis curve for ferromagnetic substance. We can observe that the magnetisation persists even when the external field is removed. This gives the idea of irreversibility of a ferromagnet. (1)

(ii) As we know that, in hysteresis curve, the energy dissipated per cycle is directly proportional to the area of hysteresis loop. So, as according to the question, the area of hysteresis loop is more for carbon steel, thus carbon steel piece will dissipate greater heat energy. (1/2)

(iii) The magnetisation of a ferromagnet depends not only on the magnetising field, but also on the history of magnetisation (i.e. how many times it was already magnetised in the past). Thus, the value of magnetisation of a specimen is a record of memory of the cycles of magnetisation, it had undergone. The system displaying such a hysteresis loop can thus act as a device for storing memory. (1/2)

(iv) The ferromagnetic materials which are used for coating magnetic tapes in a cassette player or for building memory stores in the modern computer are ferrites. The most commonly ferrites used are $MnFe_2O_4$, $FeFe_2O_4$, $CoFe_2O_4$, $NiFe_2O_4$, etc. (1/2)

(v) To shield any space from magnetic field, surround the space with soft iron ring. As the magnetic field lines will be drawn into the ring, the enclosed region will become free of magnetic field. (1/2)

21. (i) Refer to text on page 227 (Explanation of diamagnetism and explanation of paramagnetism). (3)

(ii) We can destroy the magnetism of a magnet

(a) by heating it.

(b) by applying magnetic field across it in reverse direction. (2)

22. Refer to text on page 230 (Permanent magnets and electromagnets).

23. Given, radius of Rowland ring, $r = 15$ cm $= 0.15$ m

Number of turns, $N = 3500$

Relative permeability of ferromagnetic core, $\mu_r = 800$

Current, $I = 1.2$ A

Magnetic field due to the toroid,

$$B = \mu n I \qquad \left[\because n = \frac{\text{number of turns (N)}}{\text{length}}\right]$$

$$= \mu_0 \mu_r \frac{N}{2\pi r} \cdot I \qquad [\because \text{length of toroid} = 2\pi r]$$

$$= 4 \times 3.14 \times 10^{-7} \times 800 \times \frac{3500 \times 1.2}{2 \times 3.14 \times 0.15} = 4.48 \text{ T}$$ (2)

24. According to the question,

$\mu_r = 1.000022$

$\Rightarrow \chi_m = ?$

We know, $\mu_r = 1 + \chi_m$

$\Rightarrow \chi_m = \mu_r - 1 = 1.000022 - 1 = 0.000022$

SUMMARY

- The phenomenon of attraction of small bits of iron, steel, cobalt, nickel, etc., towards the ore is called magnetism.
- Magnetic materials tend to point in the North-South direction. Like magnetic poles repel and unlike poles attract each other.
- Cutting a bar magnet creates two smaller magnets. Therefore, magnetic poles cannot be separated, i.e. magnetic monopole does not exist.
- **Force between two magnetic poles** is given by, $F = \frac{km_1m_2}{r^2}$

  where k is magnetic force constant and is given by

  $$k = \frac{M_0}{4\pi} = 10^{-7}$$
- **Magnetic Dipole** is defined as two magnetic poles of equal and opposite strengths separated by a small distance, e.g. bar magnet, compass needle, etc.
- The magnetic dipole moment of a magnetic dipole is given by

  $$\mathbf{M} = m \times 2l$$

  where, m is pole strength and $2l$ is dipole length directed from S to N. The SI unit of magnetic dipole moment is A-m^2 or JT^{-1}. It is a vector quantity and its direction is from South pole to North pole.
- **The Magnetic Field Lines** These are the imaginary lines which continuously represent the direction of magnetic field.
- **Magnetic Field Strength at a Point due to Bar Magnet** The force experienced by a hypothetical unit North pole placed at that point.

  (i) **When Point Lies on Axial Line of Bar Magnet** In this case, $B = \frac{\mu_0 2Md}{4\pi(d^2 - l^2)^2}$

  (ii) **When Point Lies on Equatorial Line of a Bar Magnet** In this case, $B = \frac{\mu_0 M}{4\pi(d^2 + l^2)^{3/2}}$
- **Torque** on a bar magnet in a uniform magnetic field is

  $$\tau = MB\sin\theta = \mathbf{M} \times \mathbf{B}$$
- **Oscillation of a Freely Suspended Magnet** The oscillations of a freely suspended magnet (magnetic dipole) in a uniform magnetic field are SHM.

  The time period of oscillation, $T = 2\pi\sqrt{\frac{I}{MB}}$
- **Potential energy** of a magnetic dipole in a magnetic field is given by $U = -MB\cos\theta = -\mathbf{M}\cdot\mathbf{B}$

  where, θ is the angle between **M** and **B**.
- **Magnetic Intensity** i.e. $H = \frac{B_0}{\mu_0}$
- **Intensity of Magnetisation** i.e. $I = \frac{M}{V}$
- **Magnetic Induction** (B) i.e. $B = \mu_0(H + I)$
- **Magnetic Susceptibility** i.e. $\chi_m = I/H$
- **Magnetic Permeability** i.e. $\mu = (B/H)$.
- **Relative Magnetic Permeability** i.e. $\mu_r = (\mu/\mu_0)$
- **Relation between Relative Permeability (μ_r) and Magnetic Susceptibility (χ_m)** It is given by, $\mu_r = 1 + \chi_m$
- Magnetic materials are broadly classified as diamagnetic, paramagnetic and ferromagnetic. For diamagnetic materials, χ is negative and small and for paramagnetic materials, it is positive and small.
- The magnetic susceptibility of a ferromagnetic materials varies as

  $$\chi_m \propto \frac{1}{(T - T_c)}$$

  or

  $$\chi_m = \frac{C}{(T - T_c)}$$

  where, C is a constant. It is known as **Curie-Weiss** law and T_c is called Curie temperature.

For Mind Map

Visit : https://goo.gl/bGqW6v OR **Scan the Code**

Chapter Practice

Multiple Choice Questions

(1 Mark)

1 Two magnets have the same length and the same pole strength. But one of the magnets has a small hole at its centre. Then,

(a) both have equal magnetic moment
(b) one with hole has smaller magnetic moment
(c) one with hole has large magnetic moment
(d) one with hole loses magnetism through the hole

2 If a diamagnetic solution is poured into a U-tube and one arm of this U-tube is placed between poles of a strong magnet, with the meniscus in line with the field, then the level of solution will

(a) rise (b) fall
(c) oscillate slowly (d) remain as such

3 The variation of magnetic susceptibility (χ) with temperature for a diamagnetic substance is best represented by figure.

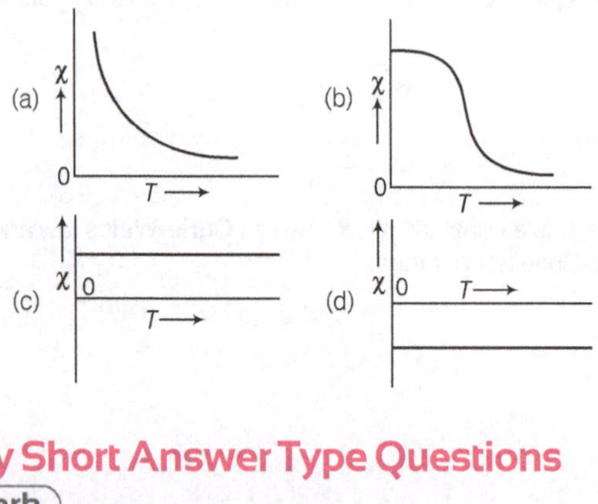

Very Short Answer Type Questions

(1 Mark)

4 What is the basic difference between magnetic and electric field lines?

5 Why is diamagnetism almost independent of temperature?

6 If a toroid uses bismuth for its core, will the field in the core be (slightly) greater or (slightly) less than when the core is empty?

7 One cannot write the proportionality $B = \mu H$ for the ferromagnets. Comment.

8 "Alkali halides are diamagnetic rather than paramagnetic." Explain why?

Short Answer Type I Questions

(2 Marks)

9 What is the net magnetic moment of two identical magnets each of magnetic moment m_0 inclined at 60° with each other?

10 What are the magnetic field lines? State their properties. Why two such lines do not intersect each other?

11 Derive an expression for the torque acting on a bar magnet placed in the uniform magnetic field.

12 Suppose you have two bars of identical dimensions, one made of paramagnetic substance and the another of diamagnetic substance. If you place these bars along a uniform magnetic field, show diagrammatically, what modifications in the field pattern would take place in each case?

Short Answer Type II Questions

(3 Marks)

13 Define magnetic susceptibility of a material. Name two elements, one having positive susceptibility and the other having negative susceptibility. What does negative susceptibility signify?

14 Explain the following:

(i) Diamagnetism is the result of induced magnetic dipole moments.
(ii) Hysteresis associated with a loss in electromagnetic energy.

15 Explain the phenomenon of hysteresis in magnetic materials. Draw a hysteresis loop showing remanence and coercive force.

Long Answer Type Question

(5 Marks)

16 (i) A bar magnet of magnetic moment M is aligned parallel to the direction of a uniform magnetic field B. What is the work done, to turn the magnets, so as to align its magnetic moment

(a) opposite to field direction and

(b) normal to field direction?

(ii) Steel is preferred for making permanent magnets, whereas soft iron is preferred for making electromagnets. Give one reason.

Numerical Problems

17 A bar magnet of length 0.1 m and a pole strength 10^{-4} A-m is placed in a magnetic field of 30 Wb/m ^{2} at an angle 30°. Determine the couple acting on it. (2 M)

Answers

1 (*b*) As we know, magnetic dipole moment $\mathbf{m} = m(2l)$, so hole reduces the effective length of the magnet and hence magnetic moment reduces.

2 (*b*) A diamagnetic liquid moves from stronger parts of magnetic field to weaker parts. Therefore, the meniscus of the level of solution will fall.

3 (*d*) For diamagnetic substances, the magnetic susceptibility is negative, and it is independent of temperature. Therefore, choice (d) is correct in figure.

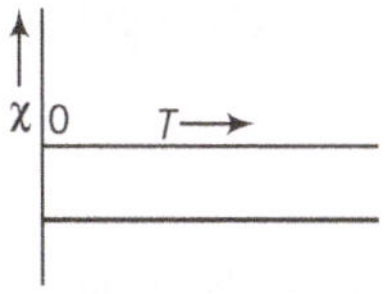

4 The magnetic field lines form continuous closed loops, whereas the electric field lines begin from a positive charge and end on the negative charge or escape to infinity.

5 Diamagnetism is independent of temperature because the value of susceptibility (a measure of relative amount of induced magnetism) is always negative.

6 Bismuth is a diamagnetic material. So, when it is kept in an external magnetic field the field lines are repelled and the field inside the material is reduced.

7 For ferromagnets, we cannot write $B = \mu H$ because the relation between B and H is not linear and it depends on the magnetic history of the sample. This phenomenon is called hysterisis.

8 The alkali halides are all diamagnetic because of the absence of unpaired electrons. So, they do not show paramagnetism.

9 $M = \sqrt{M_1^2 + M_2^2 + 2M_1M_2 \cos\theta}$

10 Refer to text on page 217 (Magnetic field lines).

11 Refer to text on pages 218 and 219 (Torque on a magnetic dipole in a uniform magnetic field).

12 Refer to text on pages 227 and 228 (Diamagnetism and paramagnetism).

13 Refer to text on page 226 (Magnetic susceptibility and relation between relative magnetic permeability (μ_r) and magnetic susceptibility (χ_m)).

14 (i) Refer to text on pags 227 (Explanation of diamagnetism).

(ii) Refer to text on pages 228 and 229 (Hysteresis curve).

15 Refer to text on pages 228 and 229 (Hysteresis curve).

16 (i) $W = -MB(\cos\theta - \cos\theta_0)$

(ii) Refer to text on page 230 (Permanent magnets and electromagnets).

17 Torque, $\tau = MB\sin\theta$

RELATED ONLINE VIDEOS

Visit : https://www.youtube.com/watch?v=DYLQmSuqPjY
OR Scan the Code

Visit : https://www.youtube.com/watch?v=DWQfL5lJTaQ
OR Scan the Code

Visit : https://www.youtube.com/watch?v=JRaAmM5afGw
OR Scan the Code

Visit : https://www.youtube.com/watch?v=dQuPTZgn9rg
OR Scan the Code

CHAPTER

06

Electromagnetic Induction

In the previous chapter, we have seen that a current carrying conductor when kept in a magnetic field, experiences force and torque. Now, in this chapter, we will study that the reverse phenomenon is also possible, i.e. if we rotate the conductor (coil) in a magnetic field, then the current will flow through it.

The phenomenon of generation of current or emf by **changing** the magnetic field is known as **Electromagnetic Induction** (EMI).

Faraday and Henry independently discovered the principle of magnetically induced emfs and found methods to convert mechanical energy into electrical energy. EMI formed the principle of two important electrical devices namely, electric generator and transformer, which have revolutionised the life styles of mankind.

- Faraday's Laws and Motional Electromotive Force
- Self and Mutual Induction

TOPIC 01 Faraday's Laws and Motional Electromotive Force

In this topic, we are going to learn about magnetic flux, Faraday's law and motional emf. Also, we will go through the concept of eddy currents.

Magnetic Flux

The total number of magnetic field lines crossing through any surface normally, when it is placed in a magnetic field is known as the magnetic flux of that surface.

Suppose a loop enclosing an area **A** is placed in a uniform magnetic field **B**.

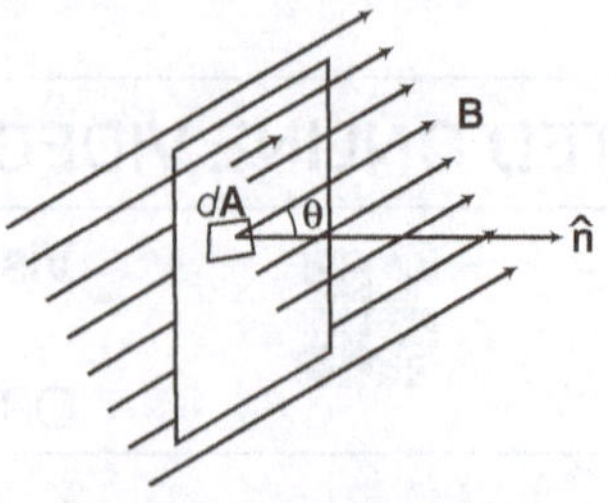

Showing magnetic field lines crossing through surface dA

Then, the magnetic flux through the loop is given by

$$\phi_B = \int \mathbf{B} \cdot d\mathbf{A} \Rightarrow \phi_B = BA\cos\theta$$

If θ is the smaller angle between **B** and **A**.

When the magnetic field is perpendicular to that plane of the loop, i.e. $\theta = 0°$, then magnetic flux will be

$$\phi_B = BA = \text{maximum value}$$

This means that $B = \frac{\phi_B}{A}$, i.e. magnetic field strength B is the magnetic flux per unit area and is called **magnetic flux density** or **magnetic induction**.

If a plane is parallel to the magnetic field, i.e. $\theta = 90°$, then no field line will pass through it and the magnetic flux linked with that plane will be zero.

The SI unit of magnetic flux (ϕ_B) is tesla-metre square, which is also called weber (abbreviated Wb).

$$1 \text{ weber} = 1 \text{ Wb} = 1 \text{ T-m}^2$$

The CGS unit of magnetic flux (ϕ_B) is maxwell (Mx).

where, $1 \text{ weber} = 10^8 \text{ maxwell}$

Magnetic flux is a scalar quantity and its dimensional formula is $[ML^2T^{-2}A^{-1}]$.

Example 1 A long solenoid of radius 4 cm, length 400 cm carries a current of 3 A. The total number of turns is 100. Assuming ideal solenoid, find the flux passing through a circular surface having centre on axis of solenoid of radius 3 cm and is perpendicular to the axis of solenoid (i) inside and (ii) at the end of solenoid.

Sol.

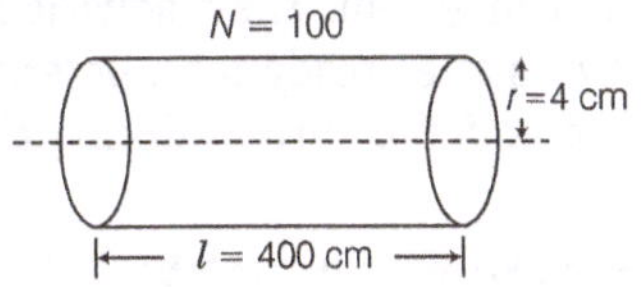

Number of turns per unit length is given by

$$n = \frac{N}{l} = \frac{100}{4} = 25 \text{ turns/m}$$

(i) Magnetic field of a solenoid at a point inside is

$$B = \mu_0 ni$$

Area of cross-section of the solenoid, $A = \pi r_1^2$ and $\theta = 0°$

Magnetic flux,

$$\phi_B = BA\cos\theta = \mu_0 ni \, \pi r_1^2 \cos 0°$$

$$= 4\pi \times 10^{-7} \times 25 \times 3 \times \pi \times (3 \times 10^{-2})^2$$

$$= 0.27 \times 10^{-6} \text{ Wb} = 0.27 \mu \text{ Wb}$$

(ii) At the end, magnetic field of solenoid is

$$B = \frac{1}{2}\mu_0 ni$$

$$\therefore \quad \phi_B = \frac{0.27}{2} = 0.135 \mu \text{ Wb}$$

Experiments of Faraday and Henry

First Experiment (Current Induced by a Magnet)

Whenever there is a relative motion between the coil and the magnet, the galvanometer shows a deflection indicating that current is induced in the coil.

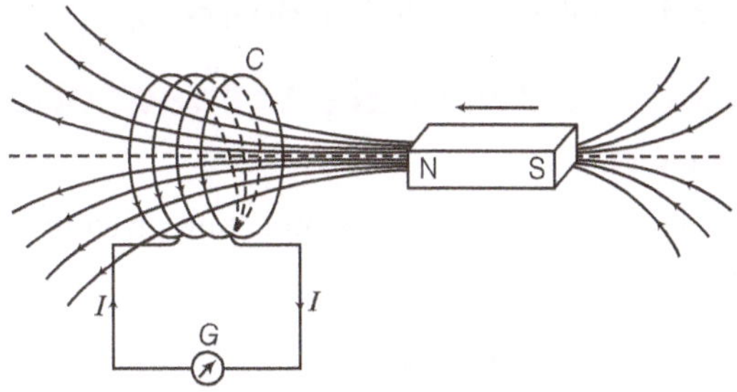

EMI with a stationary coil and moving magnet

Therefore, relative motion between the magnet and the coil generates electric current in the coil. So, the current generated is called **induced current**.

Second Experiment (Current Induced by a Current)

Consider a coil C_2 is connected to a battery, the steady current in coil C_2 produces a steady magnetic field. The galvanometer shows a deflection. This indicates that electric current is induced in the coil C_1.

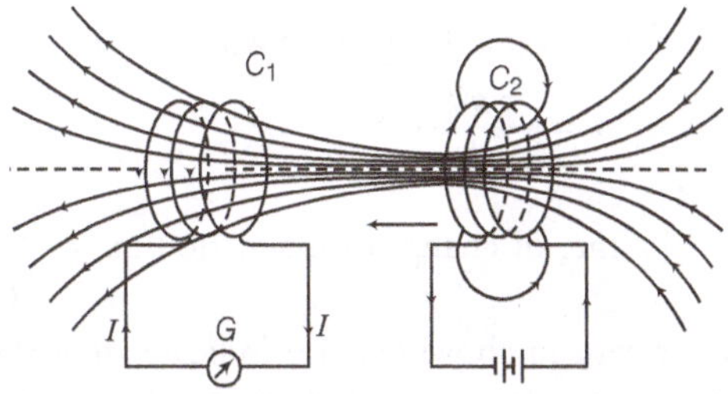

EMI with one coil stationary and another moving

Third Experiment (Current Induced by Changing Current)

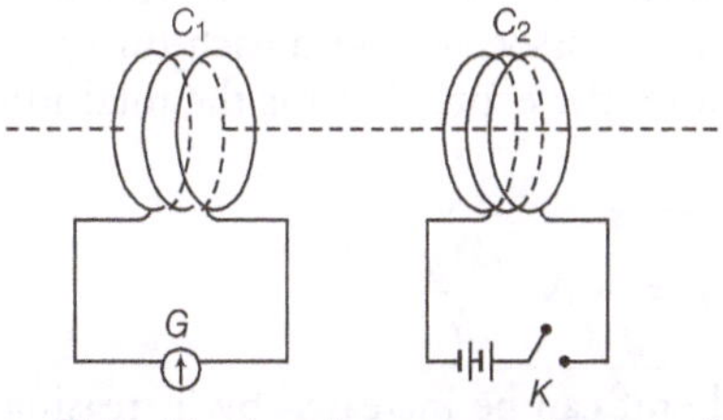

EMI with changing current in one coil

The figure shows two coils C_1 and C_2 held stationary. Coil C_1 is connected to galvanometer G, while the second coil C_2 is connected to a battery through a tapping key K.
It is observed that the galvanometer shows a momentary deflection when the tapping key K is pressed.If the key is pressed continuously, there is no deflection in the galvanometer. When the key is released, a momentary deflection is observed again but in opposite direction. All experimental observations lead us to conclude that induced emf appears in a coil, whenever the amount of magnetic flux linked with the coil changes.

Faraday's Laws of Electromagnetic Induction

The two laws of electromagnetic induction given by Faraday are stated below

Faraday's First Law

Whenever the amount of magnetic flux linked with a circuit changes, an emf is induced in it. The SI unit of this induced emf is volt (V).
The actual number of magnetic field lines passing through the circuit does not depend on the values of the induced emf. Induced current is determined by the rate at which the magnetic flux changes.

Faraday's Second Law

The magnitude of the induced emf in a circuit is equal to the rate of change of magnetic flux through the circuit. Mathematically, Faraday's second law can be expressed as,
Induced emf $\propto$ Rate of change of magnetic flux

i.e. $$e = \frac{-d\phi_B}{dt}$$

$$\left[\because \text{rate of change of magnetic flux} = \frac{\phi_2 - \phi_1}{t_2 - t_1}\right]$$

The negative sign in above relation indicates that the induced emf in the loop due to changing flux always opposes the change in the magnetic flux.
In other words, the direction of induced emf is such that it always opposes the change in magnetic flux linked with the circuit. In the case of a closely wound coil of N turns, the change of flux associated with each turn is same. Therefore, the expression for the total induced emf is given by

$$\boxed{e = -N\frac{d\phi_B}{dt}}$$

The induced emf can be increased by increasing the number of turns N of a closed coil.

Induced Emf and Current

If N is the number of turns and R is the resistance of a coil, and the magnetic flux linked with its each turn changes by $d\phi$ in short time interval dt, then

Induced emf in the coil, $e = -N\dfrac{d\phi_B}{dt}$

Induced current flowing through the coil,

$$I = \frac{e}{R} = -\frac{N}{R}\cdot\frac{d\phi_B}{dt} \qquad \left[\because I = \frac{V}{R}\right]$$

Electric charge flows due to induced current,

$$q = Idt = \frac{N}{R}\,d\phi_B$$

Example 2 **A magnetic field of flux density 10 T acts normally to the coil of 50 turns having 100 cm^2 area. Find emf induced, if the coil is removed from the magnetic field in 0.15 s.**

Sol. Given, $B = 10$ T, $N = 50$ turns,

$$A = 100\text{ cm}^2 = 10^{-2}\text{ m}^2,\ dt = 0.15\text{ s}$$

Magnetic flux linked with the coil initially,

$$\phi_1 = NBA = 50 \times 10 \times 10^{-2} = 5\text{ Wb}$$

But magnetic flux linked with the coil finally, i.e. (when removed from the magnetic field), $\phi_2 = 0$.

$$\therefore \text{ Emf induced, } e = \frac{-d\phi}{dt} = -\left(\frac{\phi_2 - \phi_1}{dt}\right) = -\left(\frac{0-5}{0.15}\right)$$

$$= 33.33\text{ V}$$

Example 3 **A square loop of side 10 cm and resistance 0.5 Ω is placed vertically in the East-West plane. A uniform magnetic field of 0.10 T is set up across the plane in the North-East direction. The magnetic field is decreased to zero in 0.70 s at a steady rate. Determine the magnitudes of induced emf and current during this time interval.**

Sol. Given, $B = 0.10$ T, $A = 100\text{ cm}^2 = 10^{-2}\text{ m}^2, \theta = 45°$ (as the angle made by area vector of the loop with magnetic field is 45°), $R = 0.5\,\Omega$, $dt = 0.70$ s

Initial magnetic flux, $\phi_1 = BA\cos\theta = 0.10 \times 10^{-2} \times \cos 45°$

$$\left(\because \cos 45° = \frac{1}{\sqrt{2}}\right)$$

$$= \frac{10^{-3}}{\sqrt{2}}\text{ Wb}$$

As, final magnetic flux, $\phi_2 = 0$.

$\therefore$ Magnitude of induced emf is

$$e = -\frac{d\phi}{dt} = -\left(\frac{\phi_2 - \phi_1}{dt}\right) = -\left(\frac{0 - \frac{10^{-3}}{\sqrt{2}}}{0.70}\right)$$

$$\approx 10^{-3}\text{ V} = 1.0\text{ mV}$$

$\therefore$ Magnitude of induced current,

$$I = \frac{e}{R} = \frac{10^{-3}\,\text{V}}{0.5\,\Omega}$$

$$= 2\times10^{-3}\,\text{A} = 2\text{ mA}$$

Lenz's Law

According to this law, the polarity of emf induced is such that, it tends to produce a current which opposes the change in magnetic flux that produced it.

Illustration of Lenz's Law

As the magnet is moved towards the loop, a particular amount of current is induced in the loop. The magnetic field is produced by the current, with magnetic dipole moment **m** oriented, so as to oppose the motion of magnet. Thus, the induced current must be counterclockwise as shown in the figure. When the North pole of a magnet moves towards a stationary loop, an induced current I flows in anti-clockwise sense as seen from the above, at which the magnet is located.

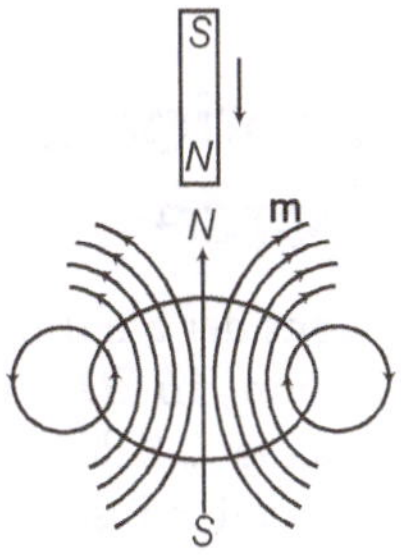

The anti-clockwise sense corresponds to the generation of North pole which opposes the motion of the approaching N-pole of the magnet.

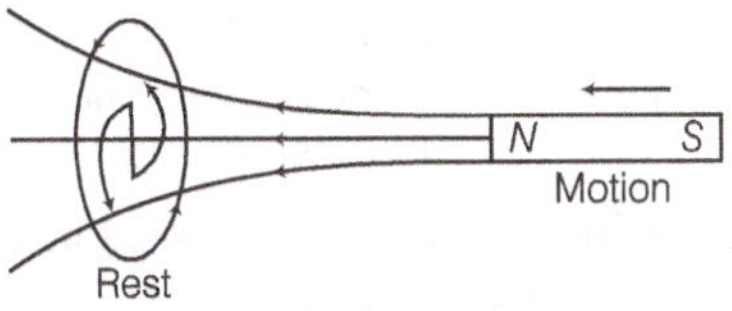

When the North pole of the magnet is moved away from the loop, the current I flows in the clockwise sense, which corresponds to the generation of South pole as shown in figure. The induced South pole opposes the motion of the receding North pole.

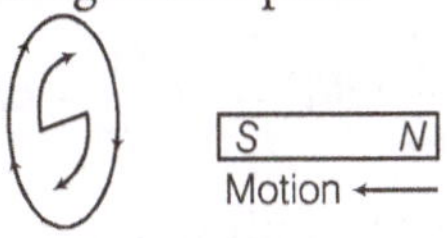

The directions of current induced in all above cases remain same, if instead of the loop, the magnet is kept stationary and loop is moved towards or away from it.

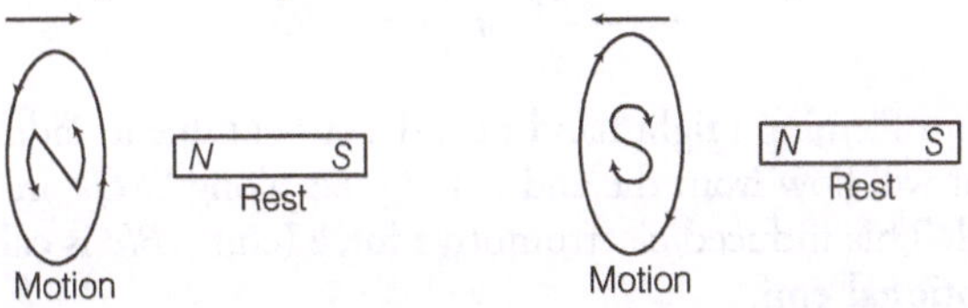

If both the loop and magnet are in relative motion w.r.t. each other, the induced pole on the loop facing magnet is according to Lenz's law.

(i) When $v_1 > v_2$, i.e. the loop is approaching towards N-pole, hence, induced pole in loop is N-pole.

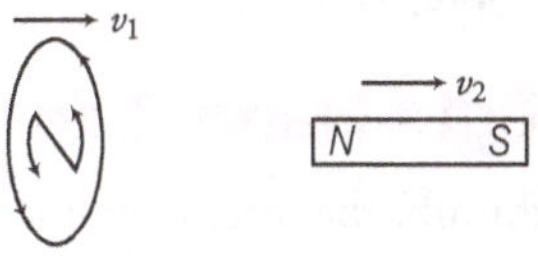

(ii) When $v_1 < v_2$, i.e. the loop is receding away from N-pole, hence induced pole in loop is S-pole.

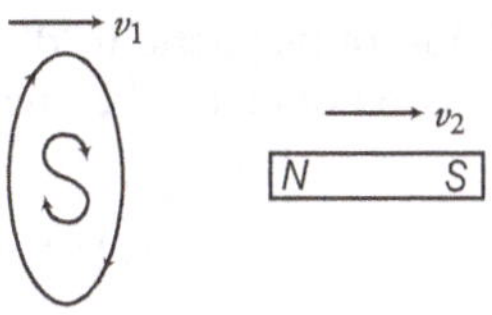

(iii) When loop and magnet having opposite directions of velocities, then loop is approaching towards N-pole, hence, induced pole in loop is N-pole.

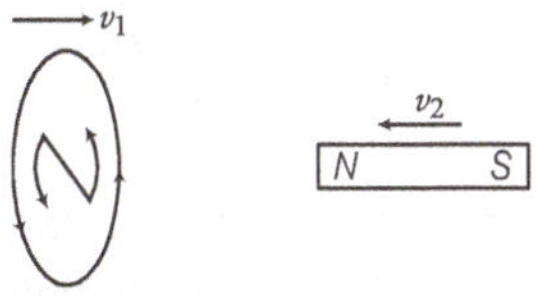

(iv) When loop and magnet having opposite directions of velocities and loop is receding away from N-pole, then induced pole in loop is S-pole.

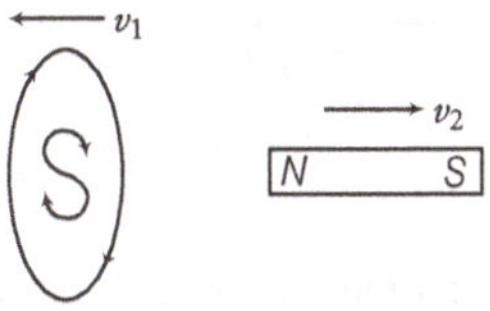

Thus, Lenz's law is used to find the direction of induced current in a closed circuit.

Lenz's Law and Conservation of Energy

Lenz's law is in accordance with the law of conservation of energy.

In the alongside circuit, when N-pole of magnet is moved towards the coil, the front face of the coil acquires North polarity. Thus, work has to be done against the force of repulsion in bringing the magnet closer to the coil.

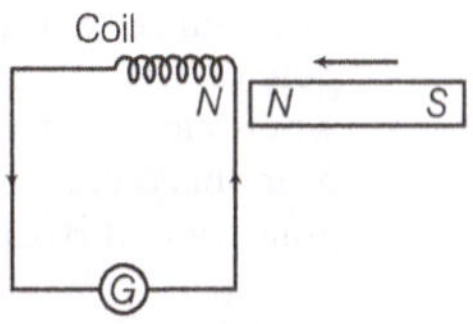

Motion of magnet near a coil

When N-pole of magnet is moved away, South pole develops on the front face of the coil. Therefore, work has to be done against the force of attraction in taking the magnet away from the coil.

This mechanical work in moving the magnet w.r.t. the coil changes into electrical energy producing induced current. Hence, energy transformation takes place. When we do not move the magnet, work done is zero. Therefore, induced current is also zero. Hence, Lenz's law obeys the law of conservation of energy.

Fleming's Right Hand Rule

If we stretch the thumb, the forefinger and the central finger of right hand in such a way that all these three are mutually perpendicular to each other and if thumb represents the direction of motion of the conductor and the forefinger represents the direction of magnetic field, then central finger will represent the direction of induced current as shown below.

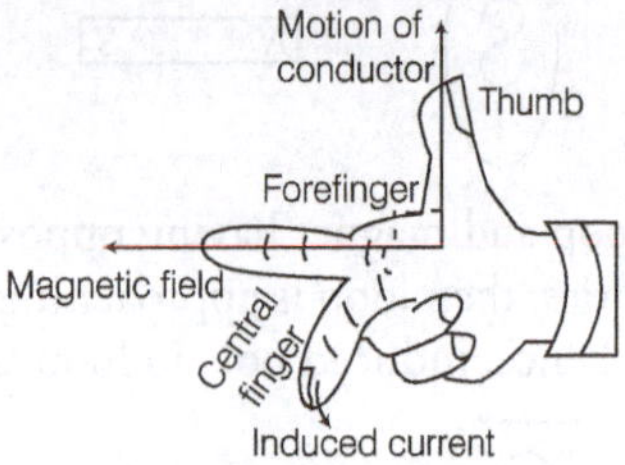

Right hand rule

Example 4 In the given figure, a bar magnet is quickly moved towards a conducting loop having a capacitor. Predict the polarity of the plates A and B of the capacitor.

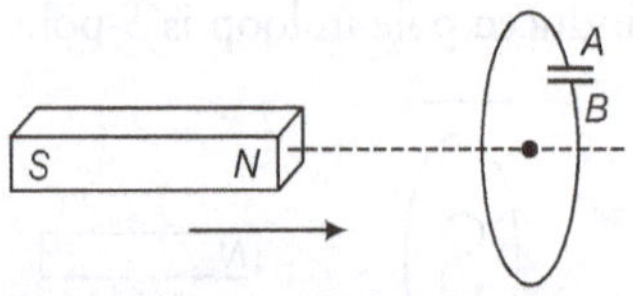

Hints: As, the magnet moves towards the coil, flux linked with the coil, increases, hence according to the Lenz's law, it will oppose the change.

Sol. Here the North pole is approaching towards the magnet, so the induced current in the face of loop viewed from left side will flow in such a way that it will behave like North pole on the other way, South pole is developed in loop when viewed from right hand side of the loop. The flow of induced current is clockwise hence, A acquires positive polarity and B acquires negative polarity.

Example 5 A current carrying straight wire passes inside a triangular coil as shown in figure. The current in the wire is perpendicular to paper inwards. Find the direction of the induced current in the loop, if current in the wire is increased.

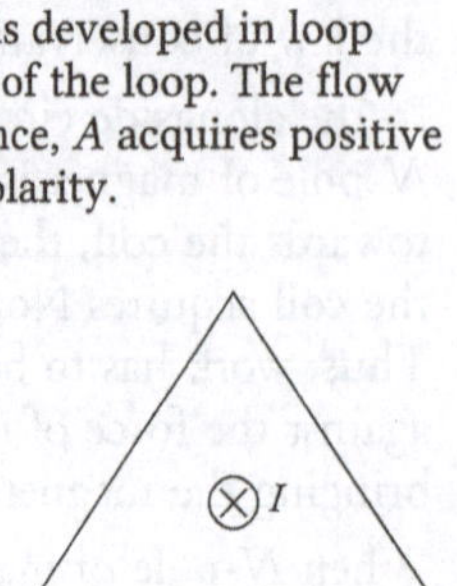

Sol. Magnetic field lines around the current carrying wire are as shown in figure below. Since, the lines are tangential to the loop ($\theta = 90°$), the flux passing through the loop is zero, whether the current is increased or decreased. Hence, change in flux is zero. Therefore, induced current in the loop will be zero.

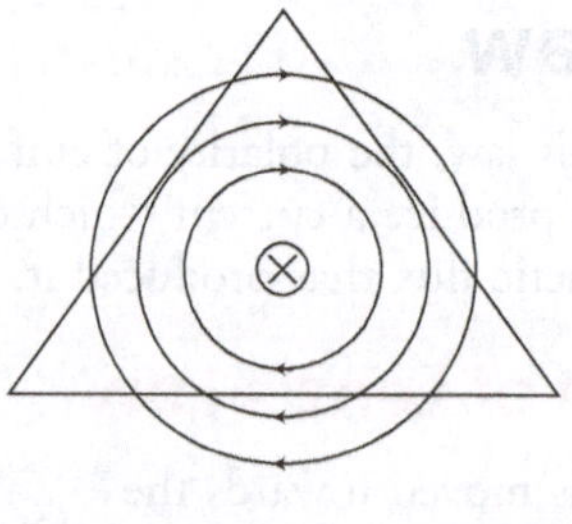

Motional Electromotive Force

Consider a uniform magnetic field **B** confined to the region $ABCD$ and a coil $PQRS$ is placed inside the magnetic field. At any time t, the part $P'Q = S'R = y$ of the coil is inside the magnetic field. Let l be the length of the arm of the coil.

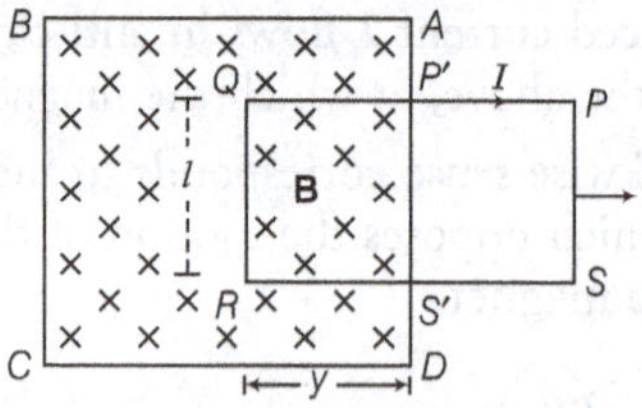

Inducing current by changing the area of the rectangular loop

Area of the coil inside the magnetic field at time t,

$$\Delta S = QR \times RS' = ly$$

Magnetic flux linked with the coil at any time t,

$$\phi = B\Delta S = Bly$$

The rate of change of magnetic flux linked with the coil is given by

$$\frac{d\phi}{dt} = \frac{d}{dt}(Bly) = Bl\frac{dy}{dt} = Blv \qquad \left[\because \frac{dy}{dt} = v\right]$$

where, v is the velocity with which the coil is pulled out of the magnetic field.

If e is the induced emf, then according to Faraday's law,

$$e = -\frac{d\phi}{dt} \text{ or } \boxed{e = -Blv}$$

From Fleming's right hand rule, the current due to induced emf will flow from the end R to Q, i.e. along $SRQP$ in the coil. This induced electromotive force (emf) Blv is called **motional emf.**

Note When a conducting rod of length l fixed at its one end moves on a circular path with angular velocity ω in a uniform magnetic field B normal to it, then induced emf produced in it is $e = \frac{1}{2} B\omega l^2$.

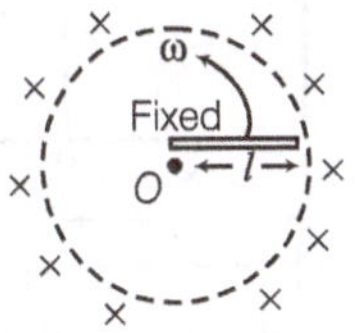

Example 6 A wire of length 0.3 m moves with a speed of 20 m/s perpendicular to the magnetic field of induction 1 Wb/m^2. Calculate the induced emf.

Sol. Given, velocity, $v = 20$ m/s

Length, $l = 0.3$ m, Angle, $\theta = 90°$

Magnetic field, $B = 1$ Wb/m^2

As, induced emf, $e = Blv$

$\therefore \quad e = 1 \times 0.3 \times 20 = 6$V

Example 7 A wheel with 10 metallic spokes each 0.5 m long is rotated with a speed of 120 rev/min in a plane normal to the horizontal component of the earth's magnetic field H_E at a place. If H_E = 0.4 gauss at the place, what is the induced emf between the axle and the rim of the wheel? Take, 1 gauss = 10^{-4} T.

Sol. Induced emf $= \frac{1}{2} B\omega l^2 = (1/2)\,\omega B R^2$

$$\left[\begin{array}{l} \because \omega = 2\pi f = 2\pi \frac{120}{60} = 4\pi \\ \text{and } l = R \end{array}\right]$$

$$= (1/2) \times 4\pi \times 0.4 \times 10^{-4} \times (0.5)^2$$

$$= 6.28 \times 10^{-5} \text{ V}$$

The number of spokes is immaterial because the emf's across the spokes are in parallel.

Note The magnetic flux linked with a loop does not change when

(i) magnet and loop are moving with the same velocity.

(ii) magnet is rotated around its axis without changing its distance from the loop.

(iii) loop is moved in a uniform magnetic field and the whole of the loop remains in the field.

Energy Consideration

(Power Dissipated in Moving a Conductor in Magnetic Field)

Let R be the resistance of movable arm PQ of the irregular conductor. We assume that the remaining arms QR, RS and SP have negligible resistances compared to R.

Thus, overall resistance of the rectangular loop is R and this does not change as PQ is moved.

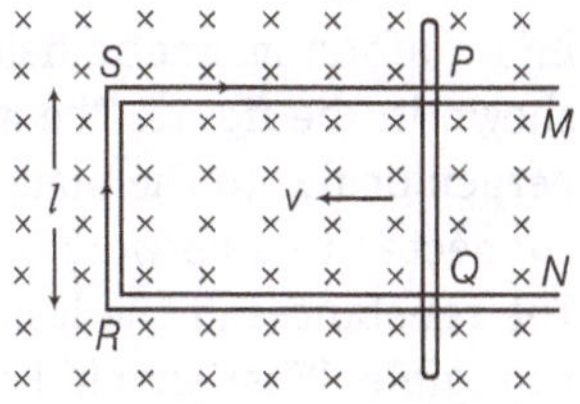

Moving conductor in magnetic field

Current I in the loop is given by

$$I = \frac{e}{R} = \frac{Blv}{R} \quad \dots(i)$$

Due to the presence of the magnetic field, there is a force on the arm PQ. This force is directed outwards in the direction opposite to the velocity of the rod.

The magnitude of this force is given by magnetic force

i.e. $$F = IlB \quad \text{or} \quad F = \frac{B^2 l^2 v}{R}$$

Alternatively, the arm PQ is being pushed with a constant speed v. Power required to do this is given by

$$P = Fv \quad \text{or} \quad P = \frac{B^2 l^2 v^2}{R} \quad \dots(ii)$$

The agent that does this work is mechanical energy.

This mechanical energy is dissipated as joule heat and is given by

$$P_J = I^2 R$$

or $$P_J = \left(\frac{Blv}{R}\right)^2 R$$

or $$P_J = \frac{B^2 l^2 v^2}{R}$$

This is identical to Eq.(ii).

Thus, mechanical energy, which was required to move the arm PQ is converted into electrical energy and then to thermal energy.

Induced Quantities and Their Formulae

S.No.	Name of the quantity	Formula	Circuit open/ closed	Dependence upon resistance	SI unit
1.	Induced emf	$e = -\frac{d\phi}{dt}$	Open or closed	No	volt
2.	Induced current	$I = -\frac{d\phi}{Rdt}$	Closed	Yes	ampere
3.	Charge flown due to induced current	$dq = -\frac{d\phi}{R}$	Closed	Yes	coulomb
4.	Power required to pull a loop out of a magnetic field	$P = \frac{B^2 l^2 v^2}{R}$	Open or closed	Yes	watt

Example 8 A square metal wire loop of side 20 cm and resistance 2 Ω is moved with a constant velocity v_0 in a uniform magnetic field of induction $B = 1 \text{ Wb/m}^2$ as shown in the figure. The magnetic field lines are perpendicular to the plane of the loop. The loop is connected to a network of resistance each of value 5 Ω. The resistances of the lead wires *BF* and *AE* are negligible. What should be the speed of the loop, so as to have a steady current of 2 mA in the loop? Give the direction of current in the loop.

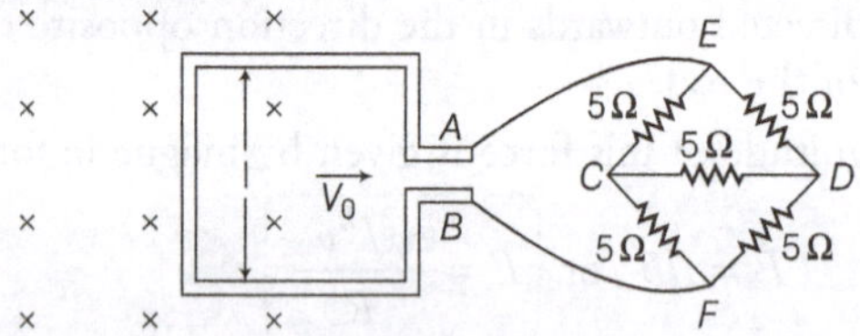

Sol. From the figure, we see that, network *CEDF* is balanced Wheatstone bridge, so no current will flow in branch *CD*.

So, the equivalent resistance of *CEDF* network is

$$R_{eq} = \frac{10 \times 10}{10 + 10} = 5\,\Omega$$

Resistance of loop = 2 Ω

$$R_{total} = 2 + R_{eq} = 2 + 5 = 7\,\Omega$$

We know that, induced emf, $e = Bv_0 l$

and induced current, $I = \dfrac{e}{R_{total}} = \dfrac{Bv_0 l}{7}$

$$\Rightarrow \quad 2 \times 10^{-3} = \frac{1 \times v_0 \times 0.2}{7}$$

$$\Rightarrow \quad v_0 = 7 \times 10^{-2} \text{ m/s} = 7 \text{ cm/s}$$

As flux is decreasing, so induced current *I* will be clockwise.

Example 9 Figure shows a rectangular conducting loop *PQRS* in which arm *RS* of length *l* is movable. The loop is kept in a uniform magnetic field *B* directed downward perpendicular to the plane of the loop. The arm *RS* is moved with a uniform speed *v*.

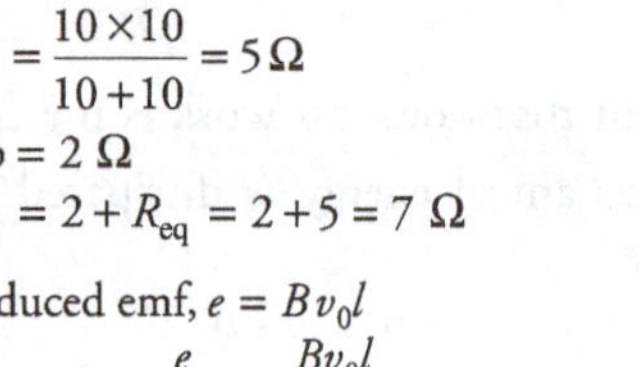

Deduce the expression for

(i) the emf induced across the arm *RS*

(ii) the external force required to move the arm and

(iii) the power dissipated as heat.

Sol. According to the question,

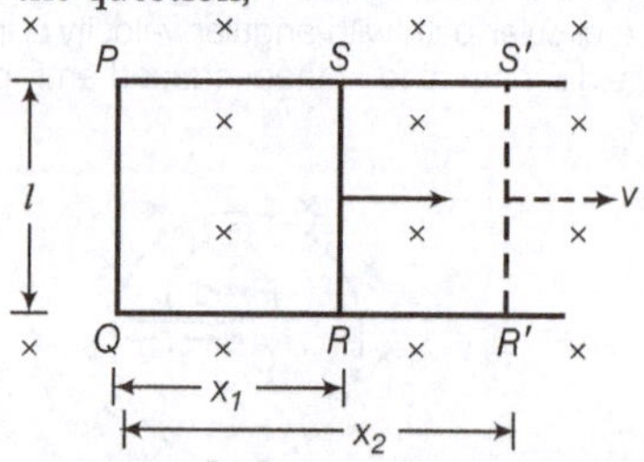

(i) Let *RS* moves with speed *v* rightward and also *RS* is at distances x_1 and x_2 from *PQ* at instants t_1 at t_2, respectively.

∴ At t_1, flux linked with loop 1, i.e. *PQRS*, $\phi_1 = B(lx_1)$

Similarly, at instant t_2, flux linked with loop 2, i.e. *PQR'S'*, $\phi_2 = B(lx_2)$

∴ Change in flux, $\Delta\phi = \phi_2 - \phi_1 = Bl(x_2 - x_1) = Bl\Delta x$

$$\Rightarrow \quad \frac{\Delta\phi}{\Delta t} = Bl\frac{\Delta x}{\Delta t} = Blv \quad \left[\because v = \frac{\Delta x}{\Delta t}\right]$$

By Faraday's law, magnitude of induced emf, $e = vBl$.

(ii) If resistance of loop is *R*, then $I = \dfrac{vBl}{R}$

∴ Magnetic force $= IBl \sin 90° = \left(\dfrac{vBl}{R}\right)Bl = \dfrac{vB^2l^2}{R}$ $\quad [\because \sin 90° = 1]$

∴ External force must be equal to magnetic force and in opposite directions.

∴ External force $= \dfrac{vB^2l^2}{R}$

(iii) As, $P = I^2R = \left(\dfrac{vBl}{R}\right)^2 \times R = \dfrac{v^2B^2l^2}{R^2} \times R$

$$\therefore \quad P = \frac{v^2B^2l^2}{R}$$

Eddy Currents

The currents induced in bulk pieces of conductors, when the magnetic flux linked with it changes, are known as eddy currents. These currents are always produced in a plane, perpendicular to the direction of magnetic field.They shows both heating and magnetic effects.

The magnitude of eddy current is given by

$$I = \frac{\text{Induced emf}}{\text{Resistance}} = \frac{e}{R}$$

According to Faraday's law, $e = -\dfrac{d\phi}{dt}$, then $I = -\dfrac{d\phi/dt}{R}$

The direction of eddy currents can be given by Lenz's law or by Fleming's right hand rule. However, their flow patterns resemble swirling eddies in water. That is why, they are called **eddy currents**. These were discovered by **Foucault** in 1895 and hence, they are also named as **Foucault current**.

Applications of Eddy Currents

Eddy currents are useful in many ways. Some of the important applications of eddy currents are as given below

(i) **Electromagnetic damping** In order to immediately bring the moving coil of a galvanometer to rest, we make the use of electromagnetic damping which uses eddy currents to bring the coil to rest. When the coil oscillates, the eddy currents generated in the core oppose the motion and bring the coil to rest.

(ii) **Induction furnace** In this, high temperature can be produced by using eddy currents. We generally use induction furnace in preparation of alloys by melting the constituents of metal. A coil is wound over the metal which needs to be melted and through the coil, we pass high frequency alternating current.
The eddy current generated in the metal produces high temperature to melt the metal.

(iii) **Electric power meters** Old electric power meters (analog type) had a metallic disc. The disc rotates due to generation of eddy currents which are produced due to sinusoidally varying currents in the coil.

(iv) **Magnetic braking in electronic trains** Some electric powered trains make use of strong electromagnets which are situated above the rails. These electromagnets are used to produce eddy currents in the rails which oppose the motion of the train and thus stop it. In this case, as there is no mechanical linkage, the braking effect is smooth.

Topic Practice 1

Multiple Choice Questions

1 Mark

1. The magnitude of the induced emf in a circuit is equal to the time rate of change of magnetic flux through the circuit, is statement of
(a) Fleming's right hand rule
(b) Fleming's left hand rule
(c) Newton's third law
(d) Faraday's law of electromagnetic induction

2. A rectangular loop and a circular loop are moving out of a uniform magnetic field region in the given figure to a field free region with a constant velocity v. In which loop do you expect the induced emf to be constant during the passage out of the field region?

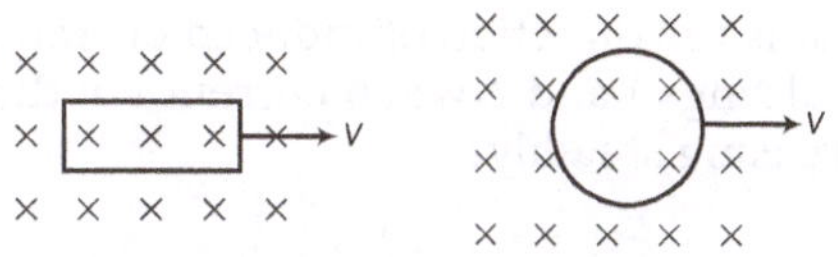

(a) Rectangular loop (b) Circular loop
(c) Both (a) and (b) (d) Neither (a) nor (b)

3. According to Lenz's law of electromagnetic induction,
(a) the induced emf is not in the direction opposing the change in magnetic flux
(b) the relative motion between the coil and magnet produces change in magnetic flux
(c) only the magnet should be moved towards coil
(d) only the coil should be moved towards magnet

4. In a uniform magnetic field of induction B, a wire in the form of semi-circle of radius r rotates about the diameter of the circle with ω. If the total resistance of the circuit is R, then the mean power generated per period of rotation is
(a) $\frac{B\pi r^2\omega}{2R}$ (b) $\frac{(B\pi r^2\omega)^2}{8R}$ (c) $\frac{(B\pi r\omega)^2}{2R}$ (d) $\frac{(B\pi r\omega^2)^2}{8R}$

5. For rails with electromagnets, when electromagnets are activated, ...A... in the rails ...B... the motion of the train. Here, A and B refer to
(a) eddy currents induced, oppose
(b) eddy currents induced, support
(c) springs, cause increase in speed of
(d) springs, increase

Very Short Answer Type Questions

1 Mark

6. Two coils of wire A and B are placed mutually perpendicular. When a current induced is changed in any one coil, will the current induced in another coil?

7. A long straight current carrying wire passes normally through the centre of circular loop. If the current through the wire increases, will there be an induced emf in the loop? Justify.

8. The electric current flowing in a wire in the direction from B to A is decreasing. Find out the direction of the induced current in the metallic loop kept near the wire as shown in the figure below.

9. What is the direction of induced currents in metal rings 1 and 2, when current I in the wire is increasing steadily?

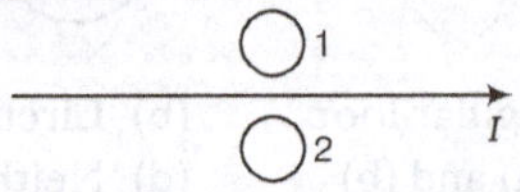

10. In the figure given, mark the polarity of plates A and B of a capacitor when the magnets are quickly moved towards the coil.

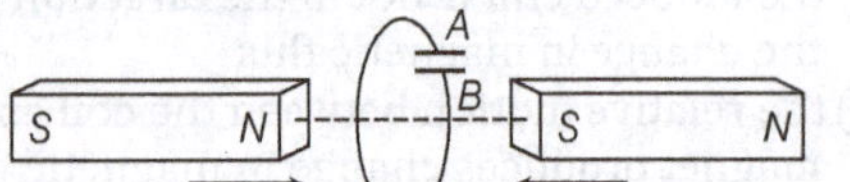

11. The closed loop $PQRS$ of wire is moved inside a uniform magnetic field at right angles to the plane of the paper as shown in the figure. Predict the direction of the induced current in the loop.

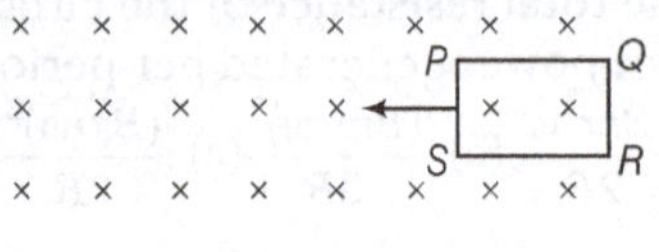

Short Answer Type I Questions

2 Marks

12. A current is induced in coil C_1 due to the motion of current carrying coil C_2.

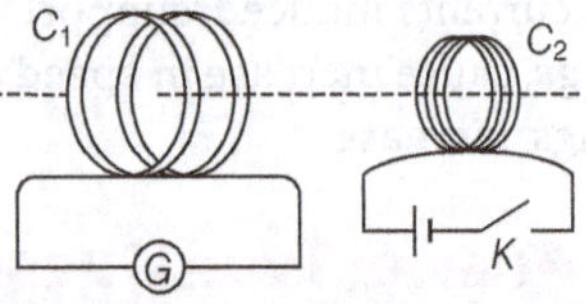

(i) Write any two ways by which a large deflection can be obtained in the galvanometer G.
(ii) Suggest an alternative device to demonstrate the induced current in place of a galvanometer.

13. A coil Q is connected to low voltage bulb B and placed near another coil P as shown in the figure. Give reasons to explain the following observations
(i) The bulb B lights.
(ii) Bulb gets dimmer, if the coil Q is moved towards left.

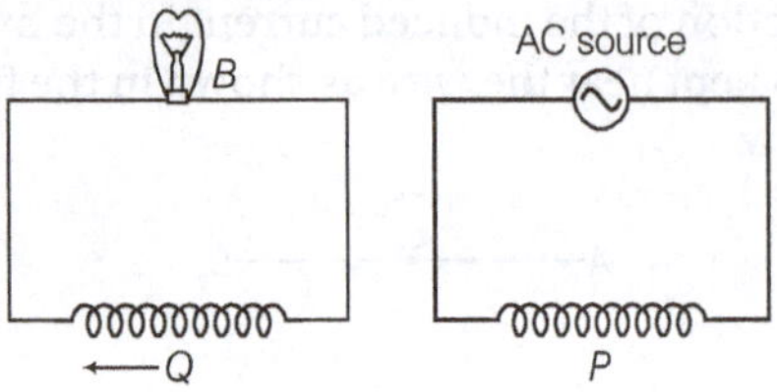

14. Two identical loops, one of copper and the other of aluminium are rotated with the same angular speed in the same magnetic field. Compare
(i) the induced emf and
(ii) the current produced in the two coils.
Justify your answer.

15. State Lenz's law. A metallic rod held horizontally along East-West direction, is allowed to fall under gravity. Will there be an emf induced at its ends? Justify your answer.

16. A rectangular loop of length l and breadth b is placed at distance of x from infinitely long wire carrying current i such that the direction of current is parallel to breadth. If the loop moves away from the current wire in a direction perpendicular to it with a velocity v, what will be the magnitude of emf in the loop?

17. What is motional emf? State any two factors on which it depends? **ISC 2018**

18. A metallic rod of length L is rotated with angular frequency of ω with one end hinged at the centre and the other end at the circumference of a circular metallic ring of radius L, about an axis passing through the centre and perpendicular to the plane of the ring. A constant and a uniform magnetic field B parallel to the axis is present everywhere. Deduce the expression for the emf between the centre and the metallic ring.

19. Mention any two useful applications of eddy currents. **ISC 2009**

Short Answer Type II Questions

3 Marks

20. Use Lenz's law to determine the direction of induced current in the situations described in the figure.
(i) A wire of irregular shape turning into a circular shape.
(ii) A circular loop being deformed into a narrow straight wire. **NCERT**

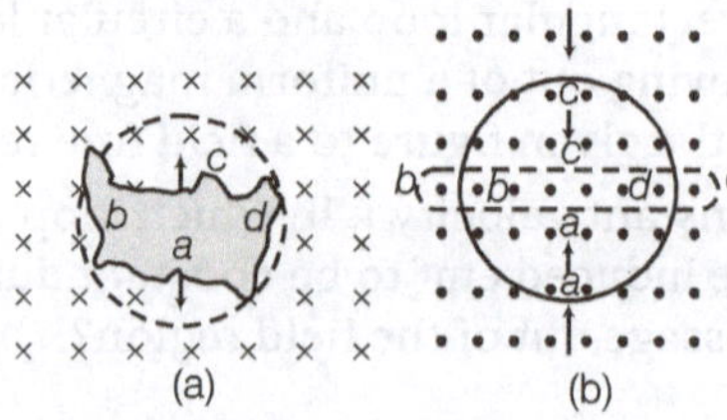

21. With the help of a neatly drawn labelled diagram, prove that the magnitude of motional emf e is given by $e = Blv$, where l is the length of a metallic rod and v is the velocity with which it is pulled in a transverse magnetic field B.
ISC 2010, 03

22. (i) A rod of length l is moved horizontally with a uniform velocity v in a direction perpendicular to its length through a region in which a uniform magnetic field is acting vertically downward. Derive the expression for the emf induced across the ends of the rod.
(ii) How does one understand this motional emf by invoking the Lorentz force acting on the free charge carriers of the conductor? Explain.

23. A metallic rod of length l is rotated with a frequency ν with one end hinged at the centre and the other end at the circumference of a circular metallic ring of radius r, about an axis passing through the centre and perpendicular to the plane of the ring.
A constant uniform magnetic field B parallel to the axis is present everywhere. Using Lorentz force, explain how emf is induced between the centre and the metallic ring and hence obtain the expression for it?

Long Answer Type Questions

(5 Marks)

24. PQ and MN are two parallel conductors at a distance l apart and connected by a resistance R as shown in figure. They are placed in a magnetic field B which is perpendicular to the plane of the conductors.

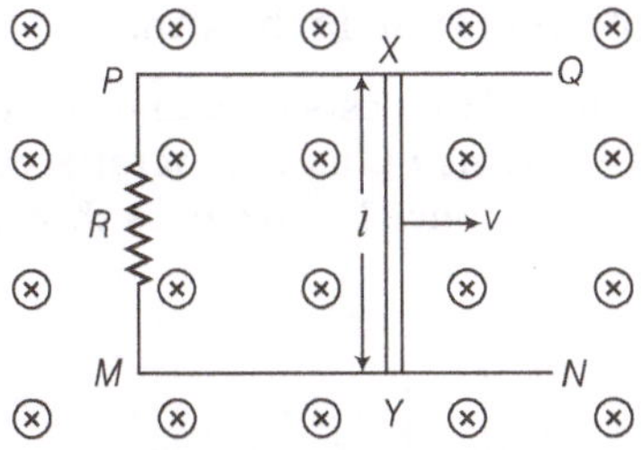

A wire XY is placed over PQ and MN and then made to slide over PQ and MN with a velocity v. Neglecting the resistance of PQ, MN and wire XY, calculate the work done per second to slide the wire XY.
ISC 2006

25. State Faraday's laws of electromagnetic induction.
Figure shows a rectangular conductor $PQRS$ in which the conductor PQ is free to move in a uniform magnetic field B perpendicular to the plane of the paper. The field extends from $x = 0$ to $x = b$ and is zero for $x > b$. Assume that only the arm PQ possesses resistance r. When the arm PQ is pulled outward from $x = 0$ to $x = 2b$ and is then moved backward to $x = 0$ with constant speed v, obtain the expressions for the flux and the induced emf.
Sketch the variation of these quantities with distance $0 \le x \le 2b$.
NCERT

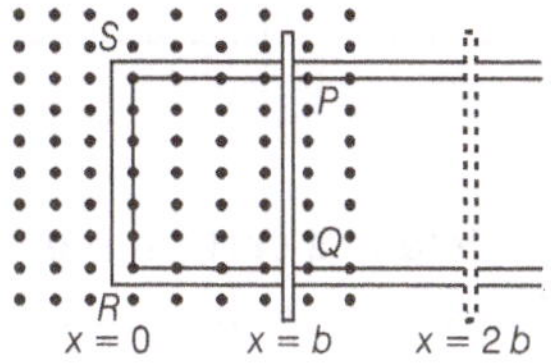

Numerical Problems

26. A rectangular coil of area 50 cm^2 and 100 turns is placed perpendicular to a magnetic field of 10^{-2} Wb / m^2. If the coil is withdrawn from the field in 40 ms, calculate the emf induced.
ISC 2005 (1 M)

27. A rectangular loop of area 20 cm × 30 cm is placed in magnetic field of 0.3 T with its plane
(i) normal to the field,
(ii) inclined 30° to the field and
(iii) parallel to the field.
Find the flux linked with the coil in each case.
(3 M)

28. The magnetic flux through a coil perpendicular to the plane is given by $\phi = 5t^3 + 4t^2 + 2t$.
Calculate induced emf through the coil at $t = 2$s.
(1 M)

29. A circular coil of radius 10 cm, 500 turns and resistance 2 Ω is placed with its plane perpendicular to the horizontal component of the earth's magnetic field. It is rotated about its vertical diameter through 180° in 0.25 s. Estimate the magnitude of the emf and current induced in the coil. Horizontal component of the earth's magnetic field at the place is 3×10^{-5} T.
NCERT Intext (2 M)

30. *AB* and *CD* are two parallel conductors kept 1 m apart and connected by a resistance *R* of 6 Ω, as shown in figure below. They are placed in a magnetic field $B = 3 \times 10^{-2}$ T which is perpendicular to the plane of the conductors and directed into the paper. A wire *MN* is placed over *AB* and *CD* and then made to slide with a velocity 2 ms^{-1}. (Neglect the resistance of *AB*, *CD* and *MN*). Calculate the induced current flowing through the resistor *R*.

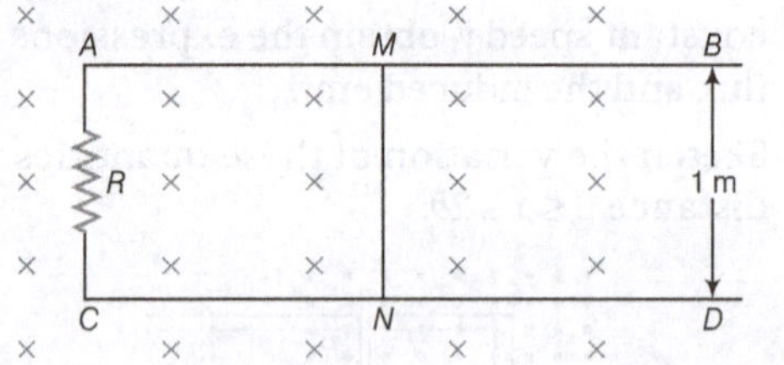

ISC 2017 (2 M)

31. A magnetic field in a certain region is given by $\mathbf{B} = B_0 \cos(\omega t)\hat{\mathbf{k}}$ and a coil of radius *a* with resistance *R*, is placed in the *xy*-plane with its centre at the origin in the magnetic field as shown in the figure.

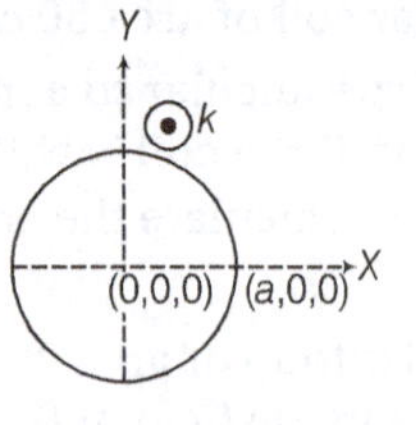

Find the magnitude and the direction of the current at (*a*, 0, 0) at

$t = \frac{\pi}{2\omega}, t = \frac{\pi}{\omega}$ and $t = \frac{3\pi}{2\omega}$. **NCERT Exemplar (2 M)**

32. A wheel with 15 metallic spokes each 60 cm long, is rotated at 360 rev/min in a plane normal to the horizontal component of the earth's magnetic field. The angle of dip at that place is 60°. If the emf induced between rim of the wheel and the axle is 400 mV, calculate the horizontal component of the earth's magnetic field at the place.

How will the induced emf change, if the number of spokes is increased? **(2 M)**

33. A horizontal straight wire 10 m long extending from East to West is falling with a speed of 5.0 m/s, at right angles to the horizontal component of the earth's magnetic field, 0.30×10^{-4} Wb/m^2.

(i) What is the instantaneous value of the emf induced in the wire?

(ii) What is the direction of the emf?

(iii) Which end of the wire is at the higher electrical potential? **NCERT (3 M)**

34. A jet plane is travelling towards West at a speed of 1800 km/h. What is the voltage difference developed between the ends of the wing having a span of 25 m, if the earth's magnetic field at the location has a magnitude of 5×10^{-4} T and the dip angle is 30°? **NCERT (3 M)**

35. A 1 m long conducting rod rotates with an angular frequency of 400 rad/s about an axis normal to the rod passing through its one end. The other end of the rod is in contact with a circular metallic ring. A constant magnetic field of 0.5 T parallel to the axis exists everywhere. Calculate the emf developed between the centre and the ring. **NCERT (3 M)**

36. A rectangular conductor *LMNO* is placed in a uniform magnetic field of 0.5 T. The field is directed perpendicular to the plane of the conductor.

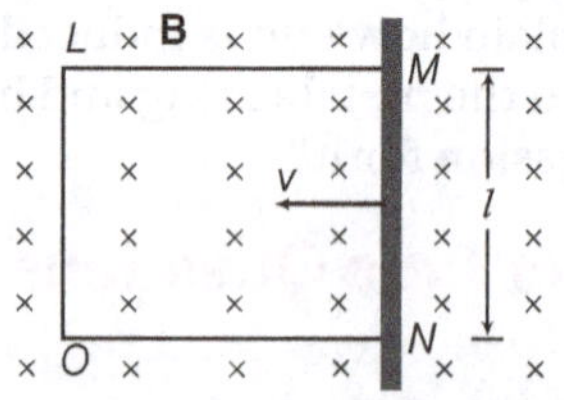

When the arm *MN* of length 20 cm is moved towards left with a velocity of 10 ms^{-1}, calculate the emf induced in the arm. Given, the resistance of the arm to be 5 Ω (assuming that other arms are of negligible resistance), find the value of the current in the arm. **(3 M)**

37. A metallic rod *CD* rests on a thick metallic wire *PQRS* with arms *PQ* and *RS* parallel to each other, at a distance *l* = 40 cm, as shown in figure.

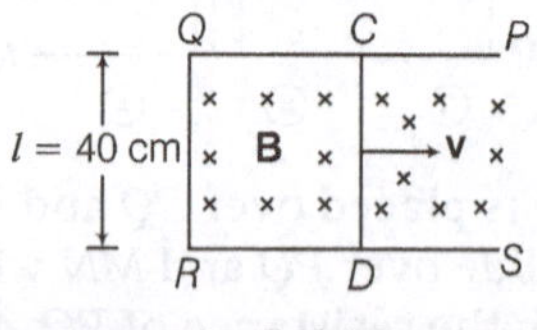

A uniform magnetic field *B* = 0.1T acts perpendicular to the plane of this paper, pointing inwards (i.e. away from the reader).

The rod is now made to slide towards right with a constant velocity of $v = 5.0 \text{ ms}^{-1}$.

(i) How much emf is induced between the two ends of the rod CD?

(ii) What is the direction in which the induced current flows? **ISC 2013 (3 M)**

38. A rectangular loop of sides 8 cm and 2 cm with a small cut is moving out of a region of a uniform magnetic field of magnitude 0.3 T directed normal to the loop. What is the voltage developed across the cut, if velocity of loop is 1 cms^{-1} in a direction normal to the

(i) longer side?

(ii) shorter side of the loop?

For how long does the induced voltage last in each case? **NCERT (3 M)**

39. A square loop of side 20 cm is initially kept 30 cm away from a region of a uniform magnetic field of 0.1 T as shown in the figure.

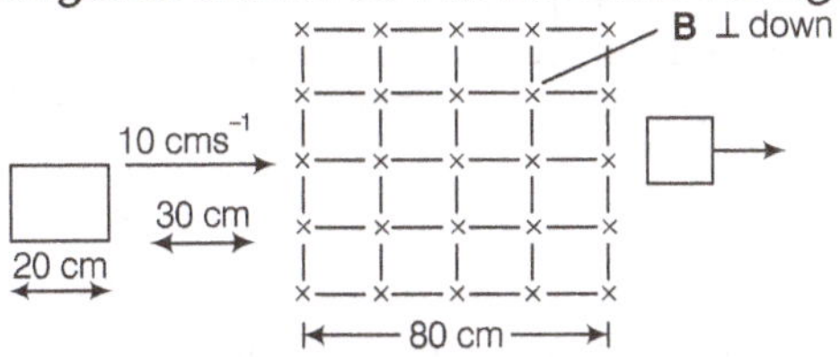

It is then moved towards the right with a velocity of 10 cm s^{-1} till it goes out of the field. Plot a graph showing the variation of

(i) magnetic flux (ϕ) through the loop with time (t).

(ii) induced emf (ε) in the loop with time t.

(iii) induced current in the loop, if it has resistance of 0.1 Ω. **(3 M)**

40. A square loop of side 12 cm with its sides parallel to X and Y-axes is moved with a velocity of 8 cm/s in the positive x-direction in an environment containing a magnetic field in the positive z-direction. The field is neither a uniform in space nor constant in time. It has a gradient of 10^{-3} T/cm along the negative x-direction (i.e. it increases by 10^{-3} T/cm as one moves in the negative x-direction) and it is decreasing in time at the rate of 10^{-3} T/s. Determine the direction and magnitude of the induced current in the loop, if its resistance is 4.50 mΩ. **NCERT (5 M)**

41. A circular coil of radius 8.0 cm and 20 turns rotated about its vertical diameter with an angular speed of 50 rad s^{-1} in a uniform horizontal magnetic field of magnitude 3×10^{-2} T. Obtain the maximum and average emf induced in the coil. If the coil forms a closed loop of resistance 10 Ω, then calculate the maximum value of current in the coil. Calculate the average power loss due to joule heating. Where does this power come from? **NCERT (3 M)**

Hints & Solutions

1. (*d*) The magnitude of the induced emf in a circuit is equal to the time rate of change of magnetic flux through the circuit. Mathematically, the induced emf is given by

$$\varepsilon = -\frac{d\phi_B}{dt}$$

The negative sign indicates the direction of ε and hence the direction of current in a closed loop.

This is statement of Faraday's law of electromagnetic induction. Fleming's rules, Newton's third law deal with forces and their directions.

2. (*a*) The induced emf is expected to be constant only in the case of the rectangular loop. In the case of circular loop, the rate of change of area of the loop during its passage out of the field region is not constant, hence induced emf will vary accordingly.

3. (*b*) According to Lenz's law of electromagnetic induction, the relative motion between the coil and magnet produces change in magnetic flux.

4. (*b*) The flux associated with semi-circular coil of area A and magnetic induction B is

$$\phi = BA\cos\theta \qquad \left(\because A = \frac{1}{2}\pi r^2\right)$$

$$= \frac{1}{2}B\pi r^2 \cos\omega t$$

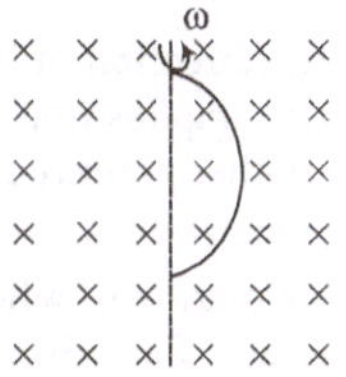

$$\therefore \quad e_{\text{induced}} = -\frac{d\phi}{dt} = -\frac{d}{dt}\cdot\left(\frac{1}{2}B\pi r^2\cos\omega t\right)$$

$$= \frac{1}{2}B\pi r^2\omega\sin\omega t$$

$$\therefore \text{Power, } P = \frac{e^2_{\text{induced}}}{R} = \frac{B^2\pi^2 r^4\omega^2\sin^2\omega t}{4R}$$

$$\text{Hence, } P \text{ mean} = \langle P \rangle = \frac{B^2\pi^2 r^4\omega^2}{4R}\cdot\frac{1}{2} = \frac{(B\pi r^2\omega)^2}{8R}$$

$$(\because \langle \sin^2\omega t \rangle = 1/2)$$

5. (*a*) When the eddy currents induced, the electromagnets are activated in the rails oppose the motion of the train.

6. No, this is because the magnetic field due to the current in coil (A or B) will be parallel to the plane of the other coil (B or A). Hence, the magnetic flux linked with the other coil will be zero and so no current will be induced in it.

7. The flux created by straight current carrying wire is depicted in the figure.

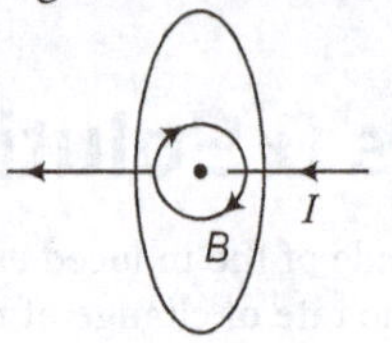

(1/2)

As, induced emf (e) $\propto$ rate of change of magnetic flux (ϕ_B)

and $\phi_B = \mathbf{B} \cdot \mathbf{A} = BA\cos\theta$

Here, $\mathbf{B} \perp \mathbf{A}$

$\Rightarrow$ $\phi_B = BA\cos 90° = 0$

So, induced emf $= 0$

Hence, a change in current of wire will not create any emf in the loop. (1/2)

8. According to Lenz's law, the direction of induced current will oppose the cause of its production. So, the current in the loop will induce in such a way that it will support the current flowing in the wire, i.e. in the same direction. So, the direction of current in the loop will be clockwise.

9. Current in the wire is steadily increasing, so the induced current in rings 1 and 2 will flow in such a way that it opposes the increase of current.
So, it will flow in same direction. Now, from the figure, it is clear that the direction of induced current in
(i) ring 1 is clockwise, (ii) ring 2 is anti-clockwise.

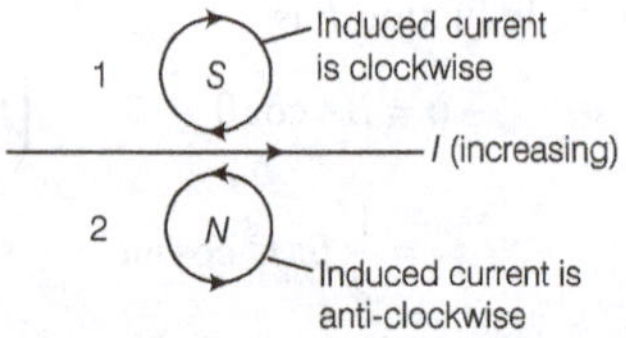

(½+½)

10. From Lenz's law, the direction of induced current is in clockwise sense. This implies that plate A of the capacitor is at the higher potential than plate B, i.e. B will be negative plate, while A will be positive plate.

11. Since, magnetic flux increases, when the loop moves into a uniform magnetic field. So, the induced current should oppose this increase. Thus, the flow will be from $QPSRQ$, i.e. anti-clockwise.

12. (i) Large deflection in the galvanometer can be obtained when change in magnetic flux is fast. So, according to the diagram given in question,
(a) by moving quickly, the coil C_2 towards C_1 or by moving quickly the coil C_2 away from C_1.
(b) by switching off and on the key. (1)
(ii) Alternating device in place of galvanometer can be LED or bulb. (1)

13. (i) Due to varying current in P, the flux linked with P change and hence flux linked with Q also changes, which in turn induces the emf in Q and bulb B lights, where P and Q are coils. (1)
(ii) When Q is moved left or it goes away from P, the lesser flux changes takes place in Q. This leads to decrease the value of rate of change of magnetic flux and hence, lesser emf and bulb B gets dimmer. (1)

14. (i) The induced emf in both the loops will be same as areas of the loop and time periods are same as they are identical and rotated with same angular speed. (1)
(ii) The current induces in Cu coil is more than Al coil as Cu coil has lesser resistance and $I \propto \frac{1}{R}$ (for the same voltage). (1)

15. Lenz's law states that the polarity of induced emf is such that, it tends to produce a current which opposes the change in magnetic flux that produced it. (1)
Yes, emf will be induced in the rod as there is change in magnetic flux. (1)

16. Since, loop is moving away from the wire, so the direction of current in the loop will be as shown in the figure.

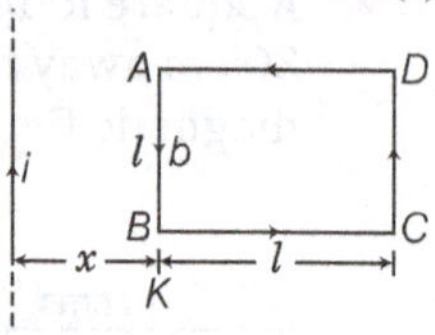

Net magnetic field on the loop due to wire,

$$B = \frac{\mu_0 i}{2\pi}\left[\frac{1}{x} - \frac{1}{l+x}\right] = \frac{\mu_0 il}{2\pi x\,(l+x)}$$

So, the magnitude of the emf in the loop,

$$e = vBb = \frac{\mu_0 il v\, b}{2\pi\, x\,(l+x)}$$

(2)

17. **Motional electromotive force** When a conducting rod is moved through a constant magnetic field, then emf is generated by a conducting rod. This emf is called motional electromotive force, because it arises due to motion of charges through a magnetic field. The expression for motional emf is given by $e = Bvl$.
Therefore, the motional emf depends upon the magnetic field, speed and length of a conductor. (1 + 1)

18. Angular velocity of rod, $\omega = 2\pi/T$, where T = time period
$\therefore$ Charge in flux in one revolution $= BA = B(\pi L^2)$ (1)
According to Faraday's law of EMI, magnitude of induced emf,

$$e = \frac{\Delta\phi}{\Delta T} = \frac{B\pi L^2}{T} = \frac{B\pi L^2}{(2\pi/\omega)} \quad [\because T = 2\pi/\omega]$$

(1/2)

$$\therefore \quad = \frac{1}{2}B\omega L^2$$

which is the required expression. (1/2)

19. Refer to text on page 245 (Applications of eddy currents).

20. (i) Here, the direction of magnetic field is perpendicularly inwards to the plane of paper. If a wire of irregular shape turns into a circular shape then its area increases (therefore the circular loop has greater area than the loop of irregular shape), so that the magnetic flux linked also increases.

Now, the induced current is produced in a direction such that it decreases the magnetic field, i.e. the current will flow in such a direction, so that the wire forming the loop is pulled inward in all directions (to decrease the area), i.e. current is in anti-clockwise direction, i.e. along *adcba*. (1½)

(ii) When a circular loop deforms into a narrow straight wire, the magnetic flux linked with it also decreases. The current induced due to change in flux will flow in such a direction that it will oppose the decrease in magnetic flux, so it will flow anti-clockwise, i.e. along *adcba* due to which the magnetic field produced will be out of the plane of paper. (1½)

21. To calculate the induced emf, the rate of change of flux needs to be calculated first. Here, magnetic field is uniform, so change in flux takes place due to change in area swept by loop. By calculating the rate of change of area, we can calculate the rate of change of flux, i.e. induced emf.

Let the lengths of horizontal arms of circuit be x_1 and x_2 at instants t_1 and t_2, respectively.

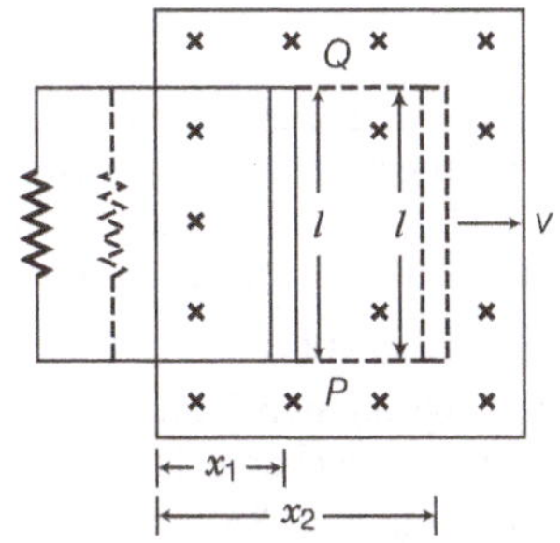

(1½)

$\therefore$ Area of loop inside the magnetic field,

$$A_1 = lx_1,\ A_2 = lx_2$$

$$\therefore \quad \Delta A = A_2 - A_1 = l(x_2 - x_1) = l\Delta x$$

$$\Delta\phi = B\Delta A = Bl\,\Delta x$$

$$\therefore \quad \frac{\Delta\phi}{\Delta t} = Bl\frac{\Delta x}{\Delta t} = Blv \quad (1)$$

By Faraday's law, induced emf,

$$e = \frac{\Delta\phi}{\Delta t} = vBl \quad (1/2)$$

22. (i) Refer to text on page 242 (Motional electromotive force). (1½)

(ii) During motion, free electrons are shifted at one end due to magnetic force. So, due to polarisation of rod electric field is produced which applies electric force on free electrons in an opposite direction.

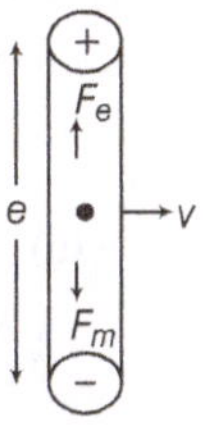

At equilibrium of Lorentz force,

$$F_e + F_m = 0$$

where, F_e = force due to electric field = qE

F_m = force due to magnetic field = $q(v \times B)$

$$\therefore \quad q\mathbf{E} + q(\mathbf{v}\times\mathbf{B}) = 0$$

$$\Rightarrow \quad \mathbf{E} = -\mathbf{v}\times\mathbf{B} = \mathbf{B}\times\mathbf{v}$$

$$\Rightarrow \quad |E| = Bv\sin\theta \quad (1/2)$$

Case I If B, E and v are collinear, then charged particle is moving parallel or anti-parallel. (1/2)

Case II If v, E and B are mutually perpendicular, i.e. $\theta = 90°$, then Lorentz force is zero which means particle will pass through the field without any change. (1/2)

23. Suppose the length of the rod is greater than the radius of the circle and rod rotates anti-clockwise. Suppose the direction of the rod at any instant be along positive y-direction and the direction of the magnetic field is along positive z-direction.

Then, using Lorentz law, we get the following,

$$\mathbf{F} = -e(\mathbf{v}\times\mathbf{B})$$

$$\Rightarrow \quad \mathbf{F} = -e(v\hat{\mathbf{j}}\times B\hat{\mathbf{k}})$$

$$\Rightarrow \quad \mathbf{F} = -evB\hat{\mathbf{i}} \quad [\because \hat{\mathbf{j}}\times\hat{\mathbf{k}} = \hat{\mathbf{i}}] \quad (1)$$

Thus, the direction of force on the electrons is along X-axis. Thus, the electrons will move towards the centre, i.e. the fixed end of the rod.

This movement of electrons will result in current having the direction opposite that of electrons and hence, it will produce emf in the rod between the fixed end and the point touching the ring. Let θ be the angle between the rod and radius of the circle at any time t. (1)

Then, area swept by the rod inside the circle $= \frac{1}{2}\pi r^2\theta$

Now, induced emf $= B \times \frac{d}{dt}\left(\frac{1}{2}\pi r^2\theta\right) = \frac{1}{2}\pi r^2 B\frac{d\theta}{dt}$

$$= \frac{1}{2}\pi r^2 B\omega = \frac{1}{2}\pi r^2 B(2\pi v)$$

$$= \pi^2 r^2 Bv \quad (1)$$

24. When a wire slides in a magnetic field on two conducting wires, an emf is induced in the wire and current flows through the wire, hence a force acts which is opposite to the motion of the wire.

According to the question, we have figure as shown below

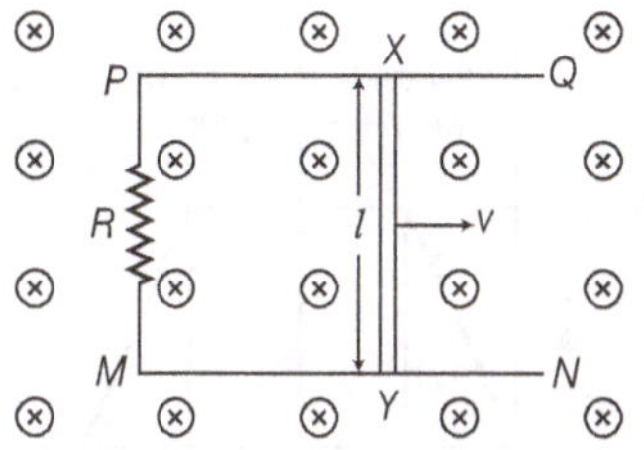

(2)

By Faraday's law of induced emf, $\varepsilon = vBl$

If resistance of loop is R, then $i = vBl/R$

$\therefore$ Magnetic force $= iBl\sin 90°$

$$= (vBl/R)\,Bl = vB^2l^2/R$$

$\therefore$ External force must be equal to magnetic force and in opposite directions.

$\therefore$ External force $= \dfrac{vB^2l^2}{R}$

Now, if under the influence of external force, the rod XY undergoes displacement Δx in the direction of the force in time interval Δt. Then, the work done on the rod will be given by

$$W = \text{External force} \times \Delta x = \frac{vB^2l^2}{R} \cdot \Delta x$$

$$\text{As, } \Delta x = v \times \Delta t = \frac{v^2B^2l^2}{R} \Delta t$$

So, work done per second to slide the wire XY is $\frac{v^2B^2l^2}{R}$. (3)

25. For statement of Faraday's laws of electromagnetic induction. Refer to text on pages 240.

According to the given figure, (1)

Case I When PQ moves forward.

(i) For $0 \leq x < b$

Magnetic field B exists in the region.

$\therefore$ Area of loop $PQRS = lx$

$\therefore$ Magnetic flux linked with loop $PQRS$,

$$\phi = BA = Blx \Rightarrow \phi = Blx \quad \ldots\text{(i)}$$

(ii) For $2b \geq x \geq b \quad (b > x \geq 0)$ (1)

$B = 0$

$\therefore$ Flux linked with loop $PQRS$ is a uniform and given by

$$\phi' = Blb \quad \ldots\text{(ii)}$$

$\Rightarrow \quad x = b$

Forward journey

Thus, for $b > x \geq 0$

Flux, $\phi = Blx \Rightarrow \phi \propto x$

For $\quad 2b \geq x \geq b$

Flux, $\quad \phi = Bbl$ [constant]

Backward journey

For $\quad b \leq x \leq 2b$,

$\quad \phi = \text{constant} = Bbl$

For $\quad 0 \leq x \leq b$,

$\quad \phi = Blx$ [decreasing] (1)

Graphical representation

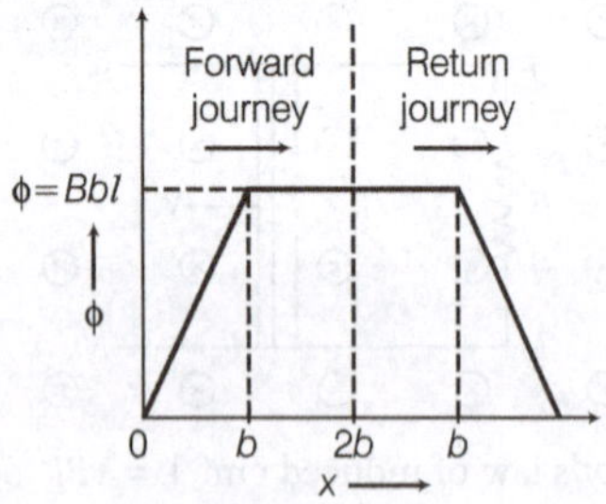

Case II For $\quad b > x \geq 0, \; B = 0$

As, $\quad \phi = Blx$

$$\Rightarrow \quad \frac{d\phi}{dt} = Bl\frac{dx}{dt} = Bvl \quad \left[\because v = \frac{dx}{dt}\right]$$

$$\text{Induced emf,} \quad e = -\frac{d\phi}{dt} = -vBl$$

For $\quad 2b \geq x \geq b$,

As, $\quad \phi' = Bbl \Rightarrow \frac{d\phi'}{dt} = 0 \Rightarrow e = 0$ (1)

Forward journey

For $\quad b > x \geq 0 \Rightarrow e = -vBl$

For $\quad 2b \geq x \geq b \Rightarrow e = 0$

Backward journey

For $\quad b > x \geq 0 \Rightarrow e = vBl$

For $\quad 2b \geq x \geq b, \; e = 0$

Variation of induced emf

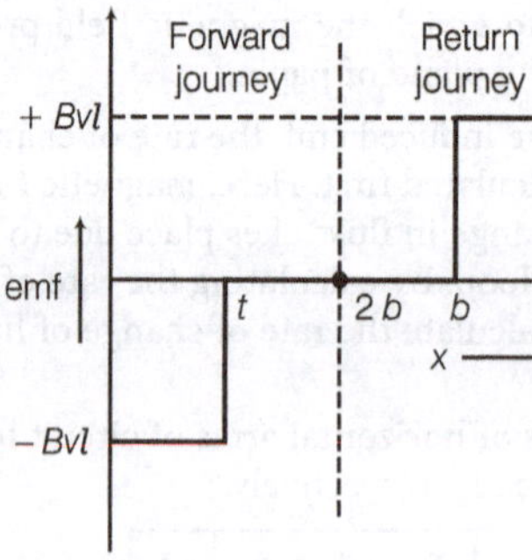

(1)

26. When the coil is withdrawn from the magnetic field, flux linked with the coil reduces to zero. The magnetic flux through each turn of a coil of area A placed perpendicular to a magnetic field B is

$$\phi_B = BA$$

When the coil is withdrawn from the field, the flux with it becomes zero. So, the change in flux is

$$\Delta\phi_B = 0 - \phi_B = -\phi_B = -BA$$
$$= -(10^{-2} \times 50 \times 10^{-4}) = -5 \times 10^{-5} \text{ Wb}$$

Time interval for the change of flux,

$$\Delta t = 40 \text{ ms} = 40 \times 10^{-3} \text{ s}$$

By Faraday's law, the emf induced in the coil is

$$\varepsilon = -N\frac{\Delta\phi_B}{\Delta t} = -100 \times \frac{(-5 \times 10^{-5})}{40 \times 10^{-3}} = 0.125 \text{ V}$$

27. Here, $A = 20 \text{ cm} \times 30 \text{ cm} = 6 \times 10^{-2} \text{ m}^2$

$B = 0.3$ T

Let θ be the angle made by the field B with the normal to the plane of the coil.

(i) Here, $\quad \theta = 90° - 90° = 0°$

So, flux, $\phi = BA \cos\theta$

$$\phi = 0.3 \times 6 \times 10^{-2} \times \cos 0°$$
$$= 1.8 \times 10^{-2} \text{ Wb}$$ (1)

(ii) Here, $\theta = 90° - 30° = 60°$

$$\phi = 0.3 \times 6 \times 10^{-2} \times \cos 60°$$
$$\phi = 0.9 \times 10^{-2} \text{ Wb}$$ (1)

(iii) Here, $\theta = 90°$

$$\phi = 0.3 \times 6 \times 10^{-2} \times \cos 90°$$
$$\phi = 0$$ (1)

28. As we know that, $e = \frac{d\phi}{dt}$

As, $\phi = 5t^3 + 4t^2 + 2t$

So, $e = 15t^2 + 8t + 2$

For $t = 2\text{ s}$, $e = 15 \times 2^2 + 8 \times 2 + 2$

$= 60 + 16 + 2 = 78\text{ V}$

29. Here, radius, $r = 10\text{ cm} = 10^{-1}\text{ m}$, $N = 500$ turns

Resistance, $R = 2\,\Omega$, $\theta_1 = 0°$, $\theta_2 = 180°$

$dt = 0.25\text{ s}$, $e = ?$, $I = ?$, $B = 3 \times 10^{-5}\text{ T}$,

$A = \pi r^2 = 3.14\,(10^{-1})^2 = 3.14 \times 10^{-2}\text{ m}^2$

$$\Rightarrow \quad e = -\frac{N\,(d\phi)}{dt} = -\frac{N\,(\phi_2 - \phi_1)}{dt}$$

$$= -\frac{NBA\,(\cos\theta_2 - \cos\theta_1)}{dt}$$

$$= -\frac{500 \times 3 \times 10^{-5} \times 3.14 \times 10^{-2}(\cos 180° - \cos 0°)}{0.25}$$

$$= \frac{2 \times 500 \times 3 \times 3.14 \times 10^{-7}}{0.25} = 3.8 \times 10^{-3}\text{ V} \quad (1)$$

and $I = \frac{e}{R} = \frac{3.8 \times 10^{-3}}{2} = 1.9 \times 10^{-3}\text{ A}$ (1)

30. Given, $B = 3 \times 10^{-2}\text{ T}$

$MN = BD = 1\text{ m}$ (according to the figure)

$v = 2\text{ ms}^{-1}$

The emf induced in the coil, $e = -\frac{d\phi}{dt}$

$$e = -\frac{d(BA)}{dt} \quad (1/2)$$

A = area of the loop $= l \times x$

$$e = -\frac{d(Bl \times x)}{dt} = -Bl\frac{dx}{dt} = -Blv$$

$$= -3 \times 10^{-2} \times 1 \times 2 = -6 \times 10^{-2}\text{ V} \quad (1)$$

Current, $I = \frac{|e|}{R} = \frac{6 \times 10^{-2}}{6}$

$= 10^{-2} = 0.01\text{ A}$ (1/2)

31. At any instant, flux passing through the ring is given by $\phi = \mathbf{B} \cdot \mathbf{A} = BA\cos\theta = BA$ $[\because \theta = 0]$

or $\phi = B_0(\pi a^2)\cos\omega t$ $[\because B = B_0\cos\omega t]$

By Faraday's law of electromagnetic induction, the magnitude of induced emf is given by

$$e = \frac{d\phi}{dt} = B_0(\pi a^2)\,\omega\sin\omega t$$

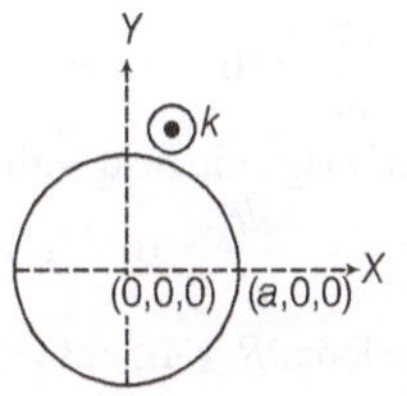

This causes flow of induced current, which is given by

$$I = B_0(\pi a^2)\,\omega\sin\omega t/R \quad (1/2)$$

Now, finding the values of current at different instants. So, we have current at

$$t = \frac{\pi}{2\omega} \Rightarrow I = \frac{B_0(\pi a^2)\,\omega}{R} \text{ along } \hat{j}$$

Because $\sin\omega t = \sin\left(\omega\frac{\pi}{2\omega}\right) = \sin\frac{\pi}{2} = 1$ (1/2)

At $t = \frac{\pi}{\omega} \Rightarrow I = \frac{B_0(\pi a^2)\,\omega}{R} \times \sin\pi = 0$

Because $\sin\omega t = \sin\left(\omega\frac{\pi}{\omega}\right) = \sin\pi = 0$ (1/2)

At $t = \frac{3\pi}{2\omega} \Rightarrow I = \frac{B_0(\pi a^2)\,\omega}{R}$ along $-\hat{j}$

Because $\sin\omega t = \sin\left(\omega\frac{3\pi}{2\omega}\right) = \sin\frac{3\pi}{2} = -1$ (1/2)

32. Refer to example 7 on page 243, $B_H = 58 \times 10^{-3}\text{ T}$

The number of spokes is immaterial because the emf's across the spokes are in parallel.

33. Given, velocity of straight wire, $v = 5\text{ m/s}$

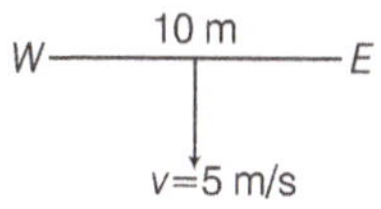

Horizontal component of the earth's magnetic field,

$$B = 0.30 \times 10^{-4}\text{ Wb/m}^2$$

Length of wire, $l = 10\text{ m}$

(i) The emf induced in the wire, $e = Blv\sin\theta$

Here, $\theta = 90°$

$\therefore \sin\theta = 1$ [$\because$ wire is falling at right angle to the earth's horizontal magnetic field component]

$e = 0.30 \times 10^{-4} \times 10 \times 5 = 1.5 \times 10^{-3}\text{ V}$ (1)

(ii) According to the Fleming's right hand rule, if the force is downward, then the direction of induced emf will be from West to East. (1)

(iii) As the direction of induced emf is from West to East, the West end of the wire is at higher potential. (1)

34. Given, speed of jet plane,

$$v = 1800\text{ km/h} = 1800 \times \frac{5}{18}$$

$= 500\text{ m/s}$

and l = distance between the ends of the wings = 25 m

The magnitude of magnetic field,

$$B = 5 \times 10^{-4}\text{ T}$$

Angle of dip, $\delta = 30°$

Use the formula of motional emf,

$e = B_V vl$ or $e = (B\sin\delta)\,vl$

[$\because$ vertical component of the earth's magnetic field, $B_V = B\sin\delta$] (1)

$\Rightarrow e = 5 \times 10^{-4}\sin 30° \times 500 \times 25$

$= 3.1\text{ V}$ (1)

Thus, the voltage difference developed between the ends is 3.1 V. (1)

35. Given, length of rod, $l = 1$ m
Angular frequency, $\omega = 400$ rad s^{-1}, $B = 0.5$ T, $e = ?$
For one end of rod, linear velocity $= 0$
Other end $= \omega l$
Average linear velocity, $v = \frac{0 + \omega l}{2} = \frac{l\omega}{2}$

$$e = Blv \Rightarrow e = Bl\frac{l\omega}{2} = \frac{Bl^2\omega}{2} = \frac{0.5 \times (1)^2 \times 400}{2} = 100 \text{ V}$$

36. Given, $B = 0.5$ T, $l = 20$ cm $= 0.2$ m, $v = 10$ ms^{-1}
emf induced $|e| = |Blv| = |-0.5 \times 0.2 \times 10| = 1$ V (2)
Current in the arm, $I = \frac{e}{R} = \frac{1}{5} = 0.2$ A (1)

37. (i) We know that, motional emf associated with a moving rod in a magnetic field is

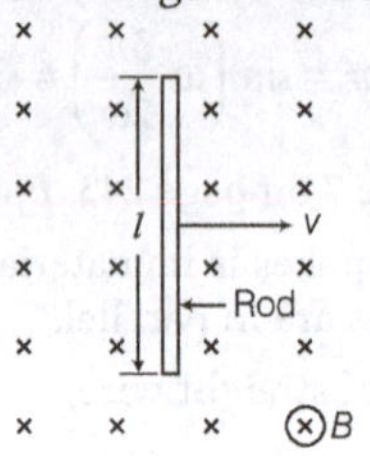

$$\varepsilon = vBl$$

where, ε = emf induced, v = speed of the rod
and l = length of the rod.
Given, $v = 5$ m / s, $l = 40$ cm, $B = 0.1$ T
$\Rightarrow$ $\varepsilon = vBl = 5 \times 0.1 \times 0.4 = 0.2$ V (2)

(ii)

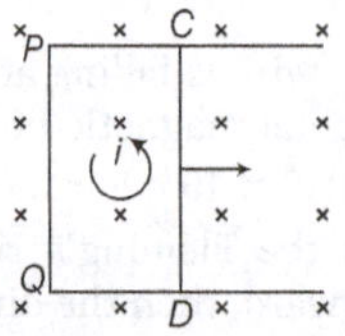

According to Lenz's law, the direction of induced current is from D to C or anti-clockwise. (1)

38. Here, area, $A = 8 \times 2 = 16$ cm^2 $= 16 \times 10^{-4}$ m^2
$B = 0.3$ T, $v = 1$ cm/s $= 10^{-2}$ m/s
Induced emf, $e = ?$
(i) When velocity is normal to longer side,
$l = 8$ cm $= 8 \times 10^{-2}$ m
$$e = Blv = 0.3 \times 8 \times 10^{-2} \times 10^{-2} = 2.4 \times 10^{-4} \text{ V}$$
Induced emf lasts till the loop comes out of the field.
$$\text{Time, } t = \frac{\text{Distance covered by coil in uniform magnetic field}}{\text{Velocity of the coil}}$$
$$= \frac{2 \times 10^{-2}}{10^{-2}}$$
$\Rightarrow$ $t = 2$ s (1½)
(ii) When velocity is normal to shorter side,
$l = 2$ cm $= 2 \times 10^{-2}$ m
$$e = Blv = 0.3 \times 2 \times 10^{-2} \times 10^{-2} = 0.6 \times 10^{-4} \text{ V}$$
$\therefore$ The induced voltage lasts for time,
$$t = \frac{\text{Distance covered by coil in uniform magnetic field}}{\text{Velocity of the coil}}$$
$$= \frac{8 \times 10^{-2}}{10^{-2}} = 8 \text{ s}$$ (1½)

39. Given, $l = 20$ cm $= 0.2$ m,
$B = 0.1$ T, $v = 10$ cms^{-1} $= 0.1$ ms^{-1}
(i) Magnetic flux through loop $\phi = B \cdot A = Blx$
$$\phi_{max} = 0.1 \times 0.2 \times 0.2$$
$$= 0.004 \text{ Wb} = 4 \times 10^{-3} \text{ Wb}$$ (1)

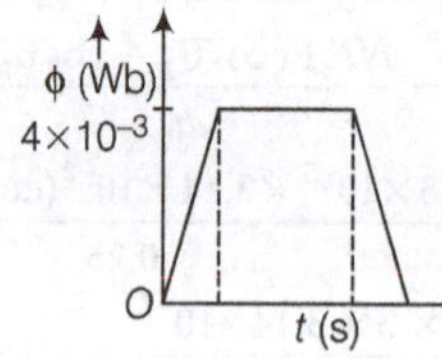

(ii) Induced emf, $\varepsilon = \frac{-d\phi}{dt} = -Blv$
$\therefore$ $|\varepsilon|_{max} = 0.1 \times 0.2 \times 0.1 = 0.002$ V
$= 2 \times 10^{-3}$ V (1)

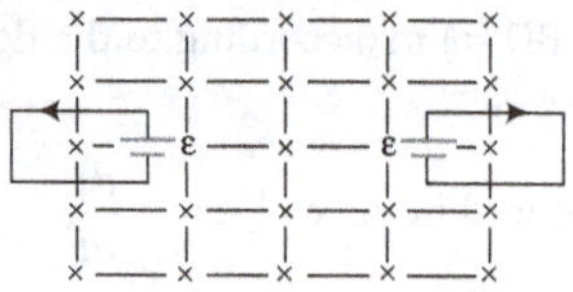

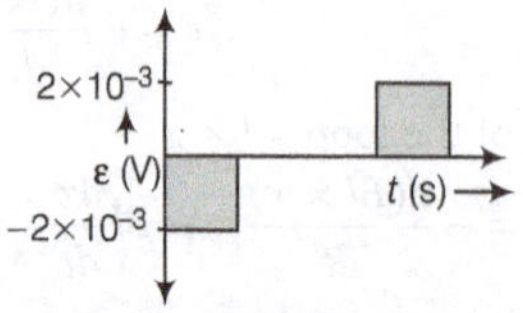

(iii) Induced current, $I = \frac{|\varepsilon|}{R} = \frac{2 \times 10^{-3}}{0.1} = 2 \times 10^{-2}$ A

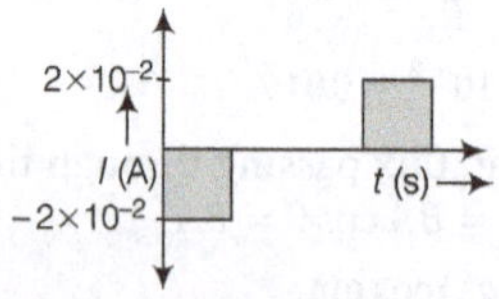

(1)

40. Given, side of loop, $a = 12$ cm
$\therefore$ Area of loop, $A = a^2 = (12)^2 = 144$ cm^2 $= 144 \times 10^{-4}$ m^2
Velocity, $v = 8$ cm/s $= 8 \times 10^{-2}$ m/s [X-axis]
Rate of change of magnetic field with distance,
$$\frac{dB}{dx} = 10^{-3} \text{ T/cm}$$ [negative X-axis]
Rate of change of magnetic field with time,
$$\frac{dB}{dt} = 10^{-3} \text{ T/s}$$
Resistance of the loop, $R = 4.5$ mΩ $= 4.5 \times 10^{-3}$ Ω

Rate of change of magnetic flux with respect to time,

$$\frac{d\phi}{dt} = \frac{d(BA)}{dt} = \left(\frac{dB}{dt}\right)A \qquad [\because \phi = BA]$$

$$= 10^{-3} \times 144 \times 10^{-4} \text{ Wb/s} \qquad (2)$$

Rate of change of magnetic flux due to the motion of loop,

$$\frac{d\phi}{dt} = \frac{dB}{dx} \cdot A \cdot \frac{dx}{dt}$$

$$= 10^{-3} \times 144 \times 10^{-4} \times 8 \qquad \left[\because \frac{dx}{dt} = \text{velocity}\right]$$

$$= 11.52 \times 10^{-5} \text{ Wb/s} \qquad (1)$$

Both of the effects cause a decrease in magnetic flux along the positive *z*-direction.

Total induced emf in the loop,

$$e = 1.44 \times 10^{-5} + 11.52 \times 10^{-5}$$

$$e = 12.96 \times 10^{-5} \text{ V}$$

Induced current in the loop $= \frac{e}{R} = \frac{12.96 \times 10^{-5}}{4.5 \times 10^{-3}}$

$$= 2.88 \times 10^{-2} \text{ A} \qquad (1)$$

The direction of induced current is such as to increase the flux through the loop along positive *z*-direction, i.e. induced current will be anti-clockwise. (1)

41. Given, radius of coil, $r = 8.0\text{cm} = 8 \times 10^{-2}$ m

$N = 20$ turns, $\omega = 50$ rad s^{-1},

$B = 3 \times 10^{-2}$ T, $e_0 = ?$, $e_{av} = ?$

Resistance, $R = 10\ \Omega$, $P = ?$

As, $e_0 = NAB\omega$

$$= N(\pi r^2) B\omega \qquad [\because A = \pi r^2]$$

$$e_0 = 20 \times \frac{22}{7} \times (8 \times 10^{-2})^2 \times 3 \times 10^{-2} \times 50$$

$$e_0 = 0.603 \text{ V} \qquad (1)$$

Average value of emf induced over a full cycle,

$$e_{av} = 0$$

$$I_{max} = \frac{e_0}{R} = \frac{0.603}{10} = 0.0603 \text{ A} \qquad (1)$$

Average power dissipated,

$$P_{av} = \frac{e_0 I_0}{2} = \frac{0.603 \times 0.0603}{2}$$

$$P_{av} = 0.018 \text{ W} \qquad (1/2)$$

The induced current causes a torque opposing the rotation of the coil. An external agent (rotor) must supply torque (and do work) to counter this torque in order to keep the coil rotating uniformly. Thus, the source of power dissipated as heat in the coil is the external rotor. (1/2)

TOPIC 02 Self and Mutual Induction

Inductance

Flux linkage of a closely wound coil is directly proportional to the current I,

i.e. $\qquad \phi_B \propto I$

If the geometry of the coil does not varying with time, then

$$\frac{d\phi_B}{dt} \propto \frac{dI}{dt}$$

For a closely wound coil of N turns, the same magnetic flux is linked with all turns. When flux ϕ_B through the coil changes, each turn contributes to the induced emf. Therefore, flux linked with the coil (flux linkage) is equal to $N\phi_B$.

In this case, total flux, $N\phi_B \propto I$

The constant of proportionality in this relation is called **inductance**. Therefore, inductance is basically a measure of the ratio of the flux to the current.

The SI unit of inductance is the tesla-square metre per ampere (T-m^2/A). We call this as henry (H), named in the honour of American physicist Joseph Henry, who discovered the law of induction, its dimension is $[\text{ML}^2\text{T}^{-2}\text{A}^{-2}]$.

Thus, $\qquad 1 \text{ H} = 1 \text{ T-m}^2/\text{A}$

Inductance is a scalar quantity which plays same role in an electrical circuit as played by inertia in mechanics. It depends only on the geometry of the coil and intrinsic material properties.

Self-Inductance

It is the property of a coil by virtue of which, the coil opposes any change in the strength of current flowing through it by inducing an emf in itself.

This induced emf is also called **back emf.**

Self-induction is also called the **inertia of electricity.**

Coefficient of Self-Induction

Let us consider a coil of N turns carrying a current I. Let ϕ_B be the magnetic flux linked with each turn of the coil. Then, the number of flux linked through the coil will be $N \cdot \phi_B$.

If no magnetic materials (iron, etc.) are present near the coil, then the number of flux linkages with the coil is proportional to the current I, i.e.

$$N\phi_B \propto I \text{ or } N\phi_B = LI$$

where, L is constant called the **coefficient of self-induction** or **self-inductance** of the coil.

By the above equation, we have

$$L = \frac{N\phi_B}{I} \quad \text{...(i)}$$

If $I = 1$, then $L = N\phi_B$.

Hence, **the coefficient of self-induction of a coil is numerically equal to the number of magnetic flux linkages with the coil when unit current is flowing through the coil.**

If on changing the current through the coil, the back emf induced in the coil be e, then by Faraday's law, we have

$$e = -N\frac{\Delta\phi_B}{\Delta t} = -\frac{\Delta(N\phi_B)}{\Delta t}$$

where, $\Delta(N\phi_B)/\Delta t$ is the rate of change of magnetic flux (due to change of current) in the coil. But $N\phi_B = LI$.

$$\therefore \quad e = -\frac{\Delta(LI)}{\Delta t} = -L\frac{\Delta I}{\Delta t}$$

where, $\Delta I/\Delta t$ is the rate of change of current in the coil. The negative sign indicates that the induced emf e is always in such a direction that it opposes the change of current in the coil. From the above formula, we have

$$\boxed{L = -\frac{e}{\Delta I/\Delta t}} \quad \text{...(ii)}$$

If $\Delta I/\Delta t = 1$, then $L = e$ (numerically).

Hence, **the coefficient of self-induction of a coil is numerically equal to the emf induced in the coil when the rate of change of current in the coil is unity.**

The SI unit of the coefficient of self-induction is henry (H) and its dimensions are $[ML^2T^{-2}A^{-2}]$.

Definition of 1 henry The self-inductance of a coil is 1 henry when an induced emf of 1volt is set up in the coil due to a current changing at the rate of 1 ampere per second in the coil, i.e.

$$1 \text{ henry} = \frac{1 \text{ volt}}{1 \text{ ampere/second}}$$

Thus, as before, $1 \text{ H} = 1 \text{ Vs A}^{-1} = 1 \text{Wb A}^{-1}$

But from Eq. (i), 1 henry = 1 weber/ampere.

The smaller units for L are millihenry (mH) and microhenry (μH).

$$1 \text{ mH} = 10^{-3} \text{ H}, \ 1 \,\mu\text{H} = 10^{-6} \text{ H}$$

Note When two coils of coefficient of self-induction L_1 and L_2 are
(i) connected in series, then $L = L_1 + L_2$.
(ii) connected in parallel, then $\frac{1}{L} = \frac{1}{L_1} + \frac{1}{L_2}$.

Self-Inductance of Long Solenoid

A long solenoid is one whose length is very large as compared to its area of cross-section. The magnetic field B at any point inside such a solenoid is practically constant and is given by

$$B = \frac{\mu_0 NI}{l} = \mu_0 nI \quad \left[\because n = \frac{N}{l}\right] \text{...(i)}$$

where, μ_0 = magnetic permeability of free space,
N = total number of turns in the solenoid,
l = length of the solenoid
and n = number of turns per unit length.

$\therefore$ Magnetic flux through each turn of the solenoid,

$$\phi = B \times \text{area of the each turn}$$

$$\phi = \left(\mu_0 \frac{N}{l} I\right) A$$

where, A = area of each turn of the solenoid.

Total magnetic flux linked with the solenoid

= Flux through each turn × Total number of turns

$$N\phi = \mu_0 \frac{N}{l} IA \times N \quad \text{...(ii)}$$

If L is coefficient of self-inductance of the solenoid, then

$$N\phi = LI \quad \text{...(iii)}$$

From Eqs. (ii) and (iii), we get

$$LI = \mu_0 \frac{N}{l} IA \times N$$

or

$$\boxed{L = \frac{\mu_0 N^2 A}{l} = \mu_0 n^2 Al}$$

If a magnetic material of magnetic permeability μ is used as a core of this solenoid, then

$$\mu = \mu_0 \mu_r \quad [\mu_r = \text{relative magnetic permeability}]$$

$$\therefore \quad \boxed{L = \frac{\mu_0 \mu_r N^2 A}{l}}$$

Example 1 Current in a circuit falls steadily from 2.0 A to 0.0 A in 10 ms. If an average emf of 200 V is induced, calculate the self-inductance of the circuit.

Sol. Given, $\Delta I = -2\,A$, $\Delta t = 10 \times 10^{-3}\,s$

$$e = 200\,V, \quad L = ?$$

$\because$ Induced emf, $e = -L\dfrac{\Delta I}{\Delta t} \Rightarrow 200 = -L\left(\dfrac{-2}{10\times 10^{-3}}\right)$

$\Rightarrow \quad 200 = L \times 2 \times 10^{2}$

$\therefore$ Self-induction, $L = 1\,H$

Example 2 What is the self-inductance of a solenoid of length 40 cm, area of cross-section 20 cm^2 and total number of turns is 800?

Sol. Given, $l = 40\text{ cm} = 0.4\,m$

$$A = 20\text{ cm}^2 = 20\times 10^{-4}\,m^2$$

$$N = 800, \; L = ?$$

$$\therefore \quad L = \frac{\mu_0 N^2 A}{l} = \frac{4\pi\times 10^{-7}\times (800)^2 \times 20\times 10^{-4}}{0.4}$$

$$= 4.02\times 10^{-5}\,H$$

Example 3 Two coils having self-inductances, $L_1 = 5\,mH$ and $L_2 = 1\,mH$. The current in the coil is increasing at same constant rate at a certain instant and the power supplied to the coils is also same. Find the ratio of

(i) induced voltages (ii) currents

Sol. Given, $L_1 = 5\,mH$ and $L_2 = 1\,mH$

(i) As we know, induced voltage is given by $e = \dfrac{Ldi}{dt}$

$$\Rightarrow \quad \frac{e_1}{e_2} = \frac{L_1(dI/dt)}{L_2(dI/dt)} = \frac{L_1}{L_2} = \frac{5}{1} = 5:1 \quad \text{...(i)}$$

(ii) Power in the coil is given by

$$P = eI$$

Here, $P_1 = P_2 \Rightarrow e_1 I_1 = e_2 I_2 \Rightarrow \dfrac{I_1}{I_2} = \dfrac{e_2}{e_1}$

Using Eq. (i), we can write as, $\dfrac{i_1}{i_2} = \dfrac{1}{5} = 1:5$

Mutual Inductance

The phenomenon according to which an opposing emf is produced in a coil (i.e. primary coil) as a result of change in current or magnetic flux linked with a neighbouring coil (i.e. secondary coil) is called **mutual induction**.

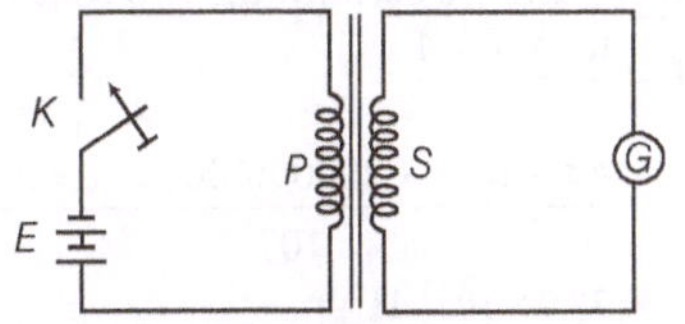

Mutual induction

Coefficient of Mutual Induction

Let a current of I_1 ampere flows in the primary coil (P). Due to this current, the magnetic flux linked with each turn of the secondary coil (S) be ϕ_2. If N_2 is the number of turns in the secondary coil, then the number of flux linkages in the secondary coil will be $N_2\phi_2$. This number of flux linkages is proportional to the current I_1 flowing in the primary coil, i.e.

$$N_2\phi_2 \propto I_1 \quad \text{or} \quad N_2\phi_2 = MI_1$$

where, M is a constant called the **coefficient of mutual induction** or **mutual inductance** of the two coils. From the above equation, we have

$$M = \frac{N_2\phi_2}{I_1}$$

If $I_1 = 1$, then $M = N_2\phi_2$

Hence, the coefficient of mutual induction of two coils is equal to the number of magnetic flux linkages in one coil when a unit current flows in the other.

If on changing the current in the primary coil, the emf induced in the secondary coil is e_2, then according to Faraday's law, we have

$$e_2 = -N_2\frac{\Delta\phi_2}{\Delta t} = -\frac{\Delta(N_2\,\phi_2)}{\Delta t}$$

where, $\Delta\phi_2/\Delta t$ is the rate of change of magnetic flux in the secondary coil (due to change of current in the primary coil). But $N_2\phi_2 = MI_1$.

$$\therefore \quad e_2 = -\frac{\Delta(MI_1)}{\Delta t} = -M\frac{\Delta I_1}{\Delta t}$$

where, $\Delta I_1/\Delta t$ is the rate of change of current in the primary coil. The negative sign indicates that the direction of emf induced in the secondary coil is always such that it opposes any change in current in the primary coil.

From the above expression, we have

$$\boxed{\text{Mutual inductance, } M = -\frac{e_2}{\Delta I_1/\Delta t}}$$

If $\Delta I_1/\Delta t = 1$, then $M = e_2$ (numerically).

Hence, the coefficient of mutual induction of two coils is equal to the numerical value of the induced emf in one coil when the rate of change of current in other coil is unity.

The SI unit of the coefficient of mutual inductance is henry (H). Thus, the mutual inductance of two coils is 1 henry when an induced emf of 1 volt is set up in one of them due to a current changing at the rate of 1 ampere per second in the other.

i.e. $\quad 1 \text{ henry} = \dfrac{1 \text{volt}}{1 \text{ ampere/second}}$

or $\quad 1\text{H} = 1\text{V s A}^{-1} = 1 \text{ Wb A}^{-1}$

The coefficient of mutual induction or mutual inductance of two coils depend on

(i) geometry of two coils, i.e. size of coils, their shape, number of turns, nature of material on which two coils are wound.

(ii) distance between two coils.

(iii) relative placement of two coils (i.e. orientation of the two coils).

Mutual Inductance of Two Long Coaxial Solenoids

Consider two long solenoids S_1 and S_2 of same length l, such that solenoid S_2 surrounds solenoid S_1 completely.

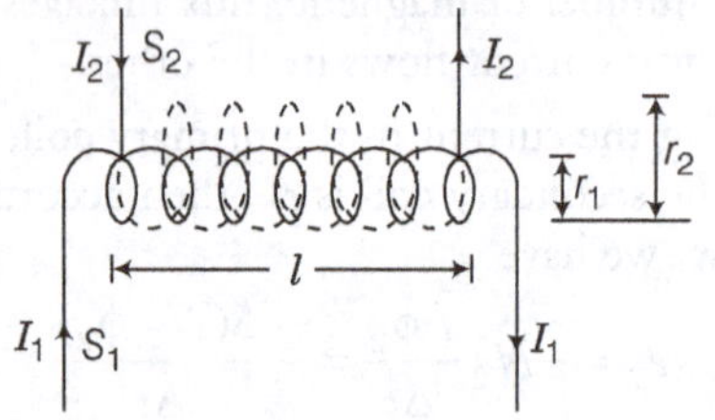

Two long coaxial solenoids of same length l

Let n_1 be the number of turns per unit length of S_1, n_2 be the number of turns per unit length of S_2, I_1 be current passed through solenoid S_1 and ϕ_{21} be flux linked with S_2 due to current flowing through S_1.

$$\phi_{21} \propto I_1 \text{ or } \phi_{21} = M_{21} I_1$$

where, M_{21} is the coefficient of mutual induction of the two solenoids.

When current is passed through solenoid S_1, an emf is induced in solenoid S_2.Magnetic field produced inside solenoid S_1 on passing current through it is.

$$B_1 = \mu_0 n_1 I_1$$

Magnetic flux linked with each turn of solenoid S_2 will be equal to B_1 times the area of cross-section of solenoid S_1.

Magnetic flux linked with each turn of the solenoid $S_2 = B_1 A$.

Therefore, total magnetic flux linked with the solenoid S_2 will be

$$\phi_{21} = B_1 A \times n_2 l = \mu_0 n_1 I_1 \times A \times n_2 l$$

$$\phi_{21} = \mu_0 n_1 n_2 A I_1 l$$

$$M_{21} = \mu_0 n_1 n_2 Al \qquad \text{...(i)}$$

Similarly, the mutual inductance between the two solenoids, when current is passed through solenoid S_2 and induced emf is produced in solenoid S_1 and is given by

$$M_{12} = \mu_0 n_1 n_2 Al$$

$$M_{12} = M_{21} = M \qquad \text{(say)}$$

Hence, coefficient of mutual induction between two long solenoids, $\quad M = \mu_0 n_1 n_2 Al$

We can rewrite Eq. (i) as,

$$M = \mu_0 \left(\frac{N_1}{l}\right)\left(\frac{N_2}{l}\right) \pi r_1^2 \times l$$

$$= \frac{\mu_0 N_1 N_2 A}{l}$$

If core of any other magnetic material μ is placed, then

$$\boxed{M = \frac{\mu_0 \mu_r N_1 N_2 A}{l}}$$

Example 4 **There are two coils, which have mutual inductance of 10 H. When the circuit is closed, current in the primary coil is raised to 3 A within a time range of 1 millisecond. Calculate the emf induced in secondary coil.**

Sol. Given, mutual inductance, $M = 10$ H

Change in current, $dI = 3$ A

Change in time, $dt = 1$ millisecond $= 10^{-3}$ s

emf induced, $e = ?$

emf induced in secondary coil is given by $e = \dfrac{M\,dI}{dt}$

$\therefore$ emf induced $= \dfrac{10 \times 3}{10^{-3}} = 3 \times 10^4$ V

Example 5 **A 1 cm long solenoid with diameter 2 cm and 2000 turns has a secondary coil of 1000 turns wound closely near its mid-point. What will be the mutual inductance between the two coils?**

Sol. Given, $l = 1$ cm, $r = \dfrac{2}{2}$ cm $= 1$ cm $= 10^{-2}$ m

$N_1 = 2000, N_2 = 1000,$

$A = \pi r^2 = \pi (10^{-2})^2 \text{ m}^2$

$= \pi \times 10^{-4} \text{ m}^2, M = ?$

$\therefore$ Mutual inductance between the two coils is given by

$$M = \frac{\mu_0 N_1 N_2 A}{l}$$

$$= \frac{4\pi \times 10^{-7} \times 2000 \times 1000 \times \pi \times 10^{-4}}{10^{-2}}$$

$$= 78.9 \times 10^{-3} \text{ H}$$

Example 6 A circular wire loop of radius R is placed in the XY-plane centred at the origin O. A square loop of side a ($a << R$) having two turns is placed with its centre at $z = \sqrt{3}\,R$ along the axis of the circular wire loop, as shown in figure.

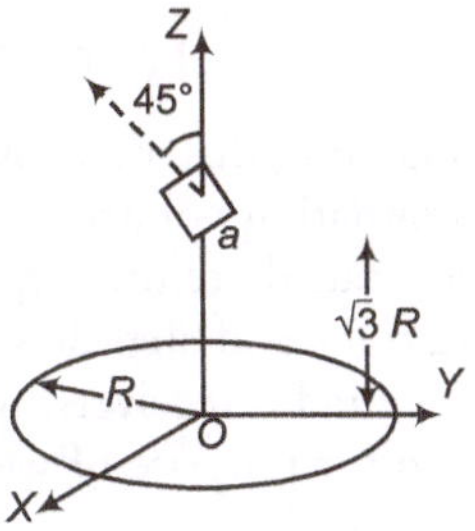

The plane of the square loop makes an angle of 45° with respect to the Z-axis. If the mutual inductance between the loops is given by $\frac{\mu_0 a^2}{2^{p/2} R}$, then find the value of p.

Sol. If I current flows through the circular loop, then magnetic field at the location of square loop is

$$B = \frac{\mu_0 I R^2}{2(R^2 + Z^2)^{3/2}}$$

Substituting the value of $Z = \sqrt{3}R$, we have

$$B = \frac{\mu_0 I}{16R}$$

Now, total flux through the square loop is

$$\phi_T = NBS\cos\theta$$

$$= (2)\left(\frac{\mu_0 I}{16R}\right) a^2 \cos 45° \qquad [\text{here, } S = a^2]$$

$$\left(\frac{\mu_0 I a^2}{2^3 \times 2^{1/2} \times R}\right) = \frac{\mu_0 I a^2}{2^{7/2} R} \qquad \left(\because \cos 45° = \frac{1}{\sqrt{2}}\right)$$

Mutual inductance,

$$M = \frac{\phi_T}{I} = \frac{\mu_0 a^2}{2^{7/2} R}$$

But $$M = \frac{\mu_0 a^2}{2^{p/2} R} \qquad \text{(given)}$$

Hence, on comparing, $p = 7$

Transformer

It is a device which is used for changing the voltage in AC circuits. It is based upon the principle of mutual induction. It works with AC only. It consists of two coils wound on the same core. The alternating current passing through the primary coil creates a continuously changing flux through the core. This changing flux induces an alternating emf in the secondary coil. It cannot change the voltage without changing in the current. There will be a inverse change in current.

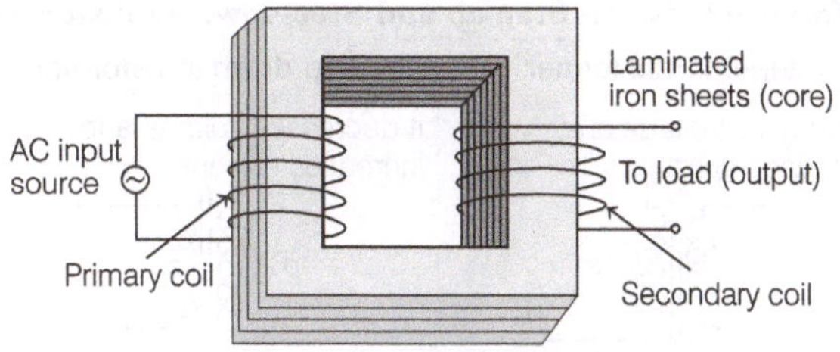

(a) Step-down transformer

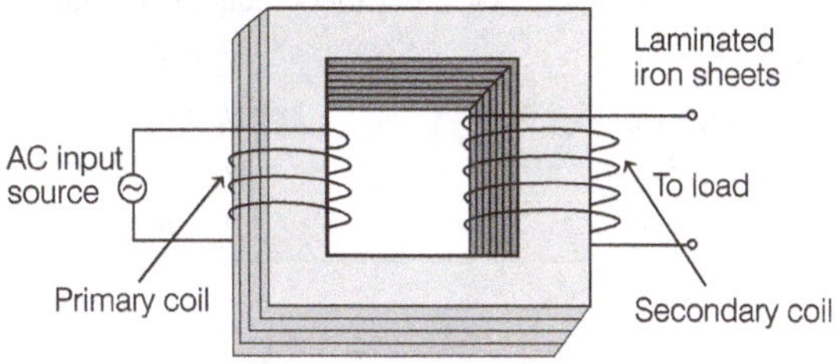

(b) Step-up transformer

For ideal transformer

$$P_{out} = P_{in} \quad \text{or} \quad V_s i_s = V_p i_p \quad \Rightarrow \quad \frac{V_s}{V_p} = \frac{i_p}{i_s}$$

where, V_s = voltage across secondary coil,
V_p = applied (input) voltage to primary coil,
i_p = current in primary coil
and i_s = current in secondary coil.

Same flux links in both primary and secondary coils, so the induced emf per turn is the same in each coil.

Then, $$\frac{d\phi_s}{dt} = \frac{d\phi_p}{dt}$$

For primary coil $$V_p = e_p = N_p \frac{d\phi_p}{dt}$$

For secondary coil $$V_s = e_s = N_s \frac{d\phi_s}{dt}$$

Hence, $$\frac{V_s}{V_p} = \frac{e_s}{e_p} = \frac{N_s}{N_p} = \frac{i_p}{i_s} = K$$

where, K is called **transformer ratio.** If $K > 1$, then it is used for step-up transformer ($N_s > N_p$).

If $K < 1$, then it is used for step-down transformer ($N_s < N_p$).

The symbol of transformer is 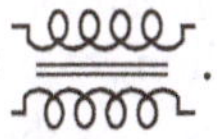.

Difference between Step-up and Step-down Transformer

Step-up transformer	Step-down transformer
It increases voltage and decreases current. 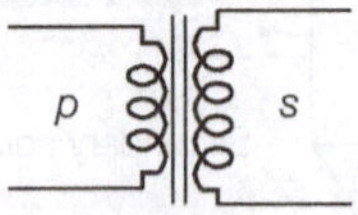	It decreases voltage and increases current. 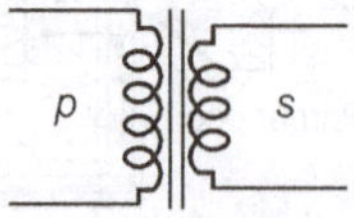
In step-up transformer, smaller number of turns in primary coil.	In step-down transformer, more number of turns in primary coil.
$V_s > V_p$	$V_s < V_p$
$N_s > N_p$	$N_s < N_p$
$i_s < i_p$	$i_s > i_p$
$R_s > R_p$	$R_s < R_p$

Efficiency of Transformer (η)

It is defined as the ratio of output power to the input power. It is expressed as,

$$\eta(\%) = \frac{P_{\text{out}}}{P_{\text{in}}} \times 100 = \frac{V_s i_s}{V_p i_p} \times 100$$

In practice, η can be achieved from 90% to 99%.

Energy Losses in Transformer

In transformer, some power is always lost due to many reasons, which are given below

(i) **Eddy current loss** Eddy current in iron core of transformer facilitate the loss of energy in the form of heat. To minimise this loss, transformer cores are laminated and silicon is added to the core material as it increases the magnetic properties of the materials.

(ii) **Flux leakage** The leakage of magnetic flux occurs due to poor design of core or the air gaps in the core. Therefore, rate of change of magnetic flux linked with each turn of secondary coil is less than the rate of change of magnetic flux linked with each turn of primary coil. It can be reduced by winding the primary and secondary coils over one another.

(iii) **Copper loss** Due to heating, energy loss takes place inside copper wires of primary and secondary coils. These are minimised by using thick wires of low resistance.

(iv) **Hysteresis loss** The energy loss takes place in magnetising and demagnetising the iron core over every cycle. Therefore, the core of transformer is made of soft iron, to minimise the hysteresis loss.

(v) **Humming loss** As the transformer works its core vibrates during each cycle of alternating voltage due to a phenomenon called magnetostriction. This gives rise to humming sound, which is referred as humming loss.

Uses of Transformer

The long distance power transmission takes place at high alternating voltage, so as to minimise losses in the form of heat, therefore step-up transformers are used at power stations and step-down transformers at receiving ends (like radio receivers, telephones, etc). In voltage regulators and for purpose of welding.

Example 7 A step-down transformer converts a voltage of 2200 V into 220 V in the transmission line. Number of turns in primary coil is 5000. Efficiency of transformer is 90% and its output power is 8 kW. Determine

(i) number of turns in the secondary coil.

(ii) input power.

Sol. Given, $E_p = 2200\text{ V}$, $E_s = 220\text{ V}$, $N_p = 5000$

Efficiency, $\eta = 90\%$;

Output power, $P_o = 8\text{ kW}$

Since, efficiency,

$$\eta = \frac{\text{Output power}}{\text{Input power}} = \frac{P_o}{P_i}$$

$$\Rightarrow \quad P_i = \frac{P_o}{\eta} = \frac{8}{90/100} = 8.9\text{ kW}$$

Also, $\dfrac{N_s}{N_p} = \dfrac{E_s}{E_p} \Rightarrow N_s = 500$

Topic Practice 2

Multiple Choice Questions

(1 Mark)

1. An electric current can be induced in a coil by flux change produced by another coil in its vicinity or flux change produced by the same coil. In both cases, the flux through a coil is
(a) proportional to the square of current
(b) inversely proportional to the square of current
(c) proportional to the current
(d) inversely proportional to the current

2. If the number of turns in a coil becomes doubled, then it self-inductance will become
(a) double (b) halved
(c) four times (d) unchanged

3. Two coils are placed close to each other. The mutual inductance of the pair of coils depends upon
(a) the rates at which currents are changing in the two coils

(b) relative position and orientation of the two coils
(c) the materials of the wires of the coils
(d) the currents in the two coils

4. Two concentric circular coils, one of small radius r_1 and the other of large radius r_2, such that $r_1 << r_2$, are placed coaxially with centres coinciding. Obtain the mutual inductance of the arrangement.
(a) $\frac{\mu_0 \pi r_1^2}{2r_2}$ (b) $\frac{\mu_0 \pi r_2^2}{2r_1}$ (c) $\frac{\mu_0 \pi r_2^2}{r_1}$ (d) $\frac{\mu_0 \pi r_1^2}{r_2}$

5. Choose the correct option.
The loss of power in a transformer can be reduced by **ISC 2010**
(a) increasing the number of turns in primary coil
(b) increasing AC voltage applied to primary coil
(c) using a solid core made of steel
(d) using a laminated core of soft iron

Very Short Answer Type Questions

1 Mark

6. The SI unit of coefficient of inductance is henry. Using any defining equation for L or M show that $1\ H = 1\ \Omega\text{-s}$. **ISC 2007, 03**

7. Can a straight wire act as an inductor?

8. Define the term self-inductance of a coil. Write its SI unit.

9. How can the self-inductance of a given coil having N number of turns, area of cross-section A and length l be increased?

10. A plot of magnetic flux (ϕ) *versus* current (I) is shown in the figure for two inductors A and B. Which of the two has larger value of self-inductance?

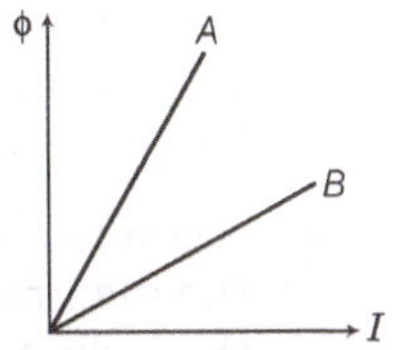

11. Self-induction is called the inertia of electricity. Why?

12. Define mutual inductance. Write its SI unit.

13. How does the mutual inductance of a pair of coils change when
(i) distance between the coils is increased and
(ii) number of turns in the coils is increased?

14. What is an ideal transformer? **ISC 2016**

15. What causes the core of a transformer to get heated up under operation? **ISC 2004**

16. Why is the core of a transformer laminated? **ISC 2018**

Short Answer Type I Questions

2 Marks

17. Define mutual inductance between two long coaxial solenoids. Find out the expression for the mutual inductance of inner solenoid of length l having the radius r_1 and the number of turns n_1 per unit length due to the second outer solenoid of same length and n_2 number of turns per unit length.

Short Answer Type II Questions

3 Marks

18. Define self-inductance. Obtain an expression for the self-inductance of a solenoid, explaining steps with the help of a diagram. **ISC 2000**

19. (i) Define the term 'mutual-inductance' and write its SI unit.
(ii) Obtain the expression for the mutual inductance of two long coaxial solenoids S_1 and S_2 wound one over the other, each of length L and radii r_1 and r_2; and n_1 and n_2 number of turns per unit length, when a current I is set up in the outer solenoid S_2.

20. What are four different types of energy losses in a transformer? State how to reduce/minimise any one of them? **ISC 2012**

Long Answer Type Questions

5 Marks

21. (i) Define mutual inductance and write its SI units.
(ii) Derive the expression for the mutual inductance of two long coaxial solenoids of same length wound one over the other.
(iii) In an experiment, two coils C_1 and C_2 are placed close to each other. Find out the expression for the emf induced in the coil C_1 due to a change in the current through the coil C_2.

22. (i) Explain the meaning of the term mutual inductance. Consider two concentric circular coils, one of the radius r_1 and the other of radius $r_2 (r_1 < r_2)$ placed coaxially with centres coinciding with each other. Obtain the expression for the mutual inductance of the arrangement.

(ii) A rectangular coil of area A, having number of turns N is rotated at f revolutions per second in a uniform magnetic field B, the field being perpendicular to the coil. Prove that the maximum emf induced in the coil is $2\pi f NBA$.

23. (i) Draw a labelled diagram of a step-down transformer. State the principle of its working.

(ii) Express the turn ratio in terms of voltages.

(iii) Find the ratio of primary and secondary currents in terms of turn ratio in an ideal transformer.

24. Draw a schematic diagram of a step-up transformer. Using its working principle, deduce an expression for the secondary to the primary voltage in terms of number of turns in the two coils? In an ideal transformer, how is this ratio related to the currents in the two coils? How is this transformer used in large scale transmission and distribution of electrical energy over large distances?

Numerical Problems

25. When current flowing through one coil changes from 0 A to 15 A in 0.2 s, an emf of 750 V is induced in an adjacent coil. Calculate the coefficient of mutual inductance of the two coils. **ISC 2020**

26. Figure below shows a metallic rod MN of length $l = 80$ cm, kept in a uniform magnetic field of flux density $B = 0.5$ T, on two parallel metallic rails P and Q. Calculate the emf that will be induced between its two ends, when it is moved towards right with a constant velocity v of 36 km/h. **ISC 2020**

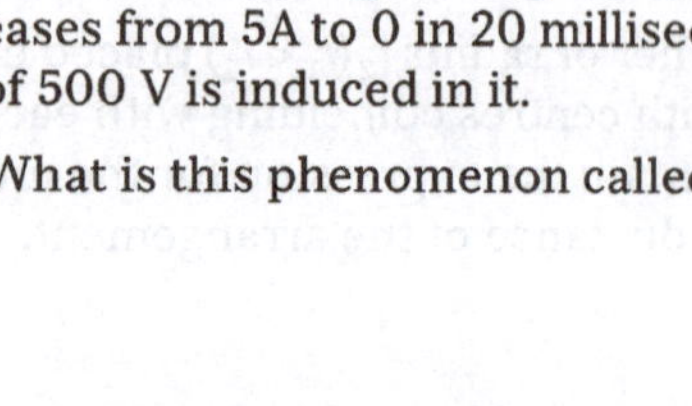

27. When current flowing through a solenoid decreases from 5A to 0 in 20 millisecond, an emf of 500 V is induced in it. **ISC 2024**

(i) What is this phenomenon called?

(ii) Calculate coefficient of self-inductance of the solenoid.

28. A coil has a self-inductance of 0.05 H. Find magnitude of the emf induced in it when the current flowing through it is changing at the rate 100 As^{-1}. **ISC 2016 (1 M)**

29. An emf of 2V is induced in a coil when current in it is changed from 0A to 10 A in 0.40s. Find the coefficient of self-inductance of the coil. **ISC 2011 (1 M)**

30. The number of turns in a coil of a wire of fixed radius is 600 and its self-inductance is 108 mH. Calculate the self-inductance of a coil of 500 turns. **ISC 2016 (1 M)**

31. A 200 turn coil of self-inductance 30 mH carries a current of 5 mA. Find the magnetic flux linked with each turn of the coil. **(2 M)**

32. Self-induction of an air core inductor increases from 0.01 mH to 10 mH on introducing an iron core into it. What is the relative permeability of the core used? **(1 M)**

33. Current in a circuit falls from 5.0 A to 0.0 A in 0.1 s. If an average emf of 200 V is induced, give an estimate of the self-inductance of the circuit. **NCERT (2 M)**

34. If a rate of change of current of 4 As^{-1} induces an emf of 20 mV in a solenoid, what is the self-inductance of the solenoid? **(2 M)**

35. A long solenoid with 15 turns per cm has a small loop of area 2.0 cm^2 placed inside, normal to the axis of solenoid. If the current carried by the solenoid changes steadily from 2 A to 4 A in 0.1 s, what is the induced voltage in the loop, while the current is changing? **NCERT (2 M)**

36. A coil has a self-inductance of 10 mH. What is the maximum magnitude of the induced emf in the inductor, when a current $I = 0.1 \sin 200\, t$ ampere is sent through it. **(2 M)**

37. A solenoid of radius 3 cm and length 1 m has 600 turns per metre. Calculate its self-inductance. **(1 M)**

38. The current flowing in the two coils of self-inductance $L_1 = 16$ mH and $L_2 = 12$ mH are increasing at the same rate. If the power supplied to the two coils are equal, find the ratio of

(i) induced voltages (ii) the currents **(2 M)**

39. A pair of adjacent coils has a mutual inductance of 1.5 H. If the current in one coil changes from 0 to 20 A in 0.5 s, what is the change of flux linkage with the other coil? **(2 M)**

40. When the current flowing through a coil P decreases from 5A to 0 in 0.2 s, an emf of 60 V is induced across the terminals of an adjacent coil Q. Calculate the coefficient of mutual inductance of the two coils P and Q. **ISC 2009 (1 M)**

41. Two coils have mutual inductance of 1.5 H. If current in primary coil is raised to 5 A in one millisecond after closing the circuit, what is the emf induced in the secondary coil? **(1 M)**

42. There are two coils A and B separated by some distance. If a current of 2 A flows through A, a magnetic flux of 10^{-2} Wb passes through B (no current through B). If no current passes through A and a current of 1 A passes through B, what is the flux through A? **NCERT Exemplar (1 M)**

43. The flux linked with a large circular coil of radius R is 0.5×10^{-3} Wb. When a current of 0.5 A flows through a small neighbouring coil of radius r, calculate the coefficient of mutual inductance for the given pair of coils. If the current through the small coil suddenly falls to zero, what would be its effect in the larger coil? **(2 M)**

44. What is the turns ratio, (i.e. transformer ratio, $N_s : N_p$), in an ideal transformer which increases AC voltage from 220 V to 33000 V? **ISC 2014 (1 M)**

45. In an ideal transformer, an output of 66 kV is required when an input voltage of 220 V is available. If the primary has 300 turns, how many turns should the secondary have? **ISC 2017 (1 M)**

46. A transformer has 500 turns in its primary and 1000 turns in its secondary winding. The primary voltage is 200 V and the load in the secondary is 100 Ω. Calculate the current in the primary, assuming it to be an ideal transformer. **ISC 2002 (3 M)**

Hints & Solutions

1. (c) An electric current can be induced in a coil by flux change produced by another coil in its vicinity or flux change produced by the same coil. In both the cases, the flux through a coil is proportional to the current, i.e. $\phi_B \propto I$.

Further, if the geometry of the coil does not vary with time, then

$$\frac{d\phi_B}{dt} \propto \frac{dI}{dt}$$

For a closely wound coil of N turns, the same magnetic flux is linked with all the turns. When the flux ϕ_B through the coil changes, each turn contributes to the induced emf. Therefore, a term called flux linkage is used which is equal to $N\phi_B$ for a closely wound coil and in such a case $N\phi_B \propto I$.

2. (c) From formula for a circular coil, $L = \mu_0 n^2 Al$

$$L \propto n^2$$

So, if n is double, so inductance will be four times.

3. (b) Mutual inductance of the pair of coils depends on distance between two coils and geometry of two coils.

4. (a) Let a current I_2 flow through the outer circular coil. The field at the centre of the coil is $B_2 = \mu I_2 / 2r_2$. Since, the other co-axially placed coil has a very small radius. B_2 may be considered constant over it's cross-sectional area. Hence,

$$\phi = \pi r_1^2 B_2 = \frac{\mu_0 \pi r_1^2}{2r_2} I_2 = M_{12} I_2 \qquad \left(\because B = \frac{\mu_0 I}{2r}\right)$$

Thus, $M_{12} = \dfrac{\mu_0 \pi r_1^2}{2r_2}$

$$\Rightarrow \quad M_{12} = M_{21} = \frac{\mu_0 \pi r_1^2}{2r_2}.$$

5. (d) The loss of power in a transformer can be reduced by using a laminated core of soft iron.

Thus, option (d) is correct.

6. We know that,

$$|\varepsilon| = \frac{-\Delta\phi}{\Delta t} = -M\frac{\Delta i}{\Delta t} = -M\frac{di}{dt}$$

where, $|\varepsilon|$ = magnitude of induced emf,

$\Delta\phi$ = change in magnetic flux,

Δt = duration of change in flux

and M = coefficient of mutual inductance.

So, $M = \dfrac{|\varepsilon|}{\frac{di}{dt}} \Rightarrow 1 \text{ Henry} = \dfrac{\text{Volt}}{\frac{\text{Ampere}}{\text{Second}}}$ [by writting units]

$\Rightarrow$ 1 Henry = 1 Ω-s. [taking all the values as unity]

$$\left[\because \text{ohm} = \frac{\text{volt}}{\text{ampere}}\right]$$

7. A straight wire cannot act as an inductor as the magnetic flux linked with the wire of negligible area of cross-section is zero. The wire has to be in the form of a coil to serve as an inductor.

8. Self-inductance is the property of a coil by virtue of which, the coil opposes any change in the strength of current flowing through it by inducing an emf in itself. Its SI unit is henry (H).

9. The self-inductance can be increased with the help of magnetic fields. It does not depend on the current through circuit but depends upon the permeability of material from which the core is made up.

10. Self-inductance of the inductor, $L = \phi / I$.

The slope of I-ϕ graph gives self-inductance of the coil. Inductor A have greater slope than inductor B, therefore self-inductance of A is greater than self-inductance of B.

11. Self-induction of coil is the property by virtue of which it tends to maintain the magnetic flux linked with it and opposes any change in the flux by inducing current in it. This property of a coil is analogous to mechanical inertia, that's why self-induction is called the inertia of electricity.

12. The phenomenon according to which an opposing emf is produced in a coil as a result of change in current or magnetic flux linked with a neighbouring coil is called mutual induction.

Its SI unit is henry.

13. (i) As $\phi = MI$, with the increase in the distance between the coils, the magnetic flux linked with the secondary coil decreases and hence, the mutual inductance of the two coils will decrease with the increase of separation between them. (1/2)

(ii) Mutual inductance of two coils can be found out by $M = \mu_0 N_1 N_2 Al$, i.e. $M \propto N_1 N_2$, so with the increase in number of turns, mutual inductance increases. (1/2)

14. An ideal transformer is an imaginary transformer which has no copper losses (no winding resistance), no iron loss in core and no flux leakage. In other words, an ideal transformer gives output power exactly equal to the input power.

15. When a metallic wire moves in a uniform magnetic field, due to change in magnetic flux of the wire, emf is induced between two ends of the wire.

The core of a transformer gets heated up due to eddy current and copper losses.

16. The alternating magnetic flux induces eddy currents in iron core of transformer and causes, the loss of energy in the form of heat. To minimise this loss, transformer cores are laminated.

17. Refer to text on page 257 (Mutual inductance).

18. Self-inductance of a solenoid is associated with the geometry of the coil.

Self- inductance of a coil is equal to the total magnetic flux linked with the coil, when unit current passes through it.

Self-inductance of a coil is equal to the emf induced in coil, when rate of change of current in coil is 1 A/s.

The SI unit of self-inductance is henry (H).

$$1 \text{ H} = 1 \text{ V-s/A} \quad (1)$$

Let the radius and length of air cored solenoid be r and l respectively, such that $r << l$ and having n turns per unit length.

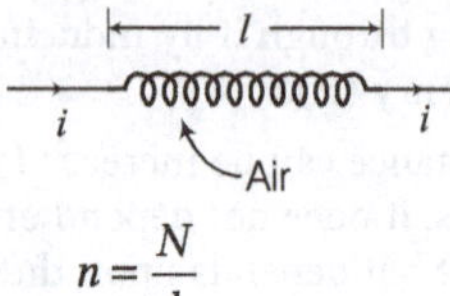

$$\therefore \quad n = \frac{N}{l} \quad \ldots\text{(i)}$$

where, N = total number of turns.

If i current flows through the coil, then magnetic field is given by $B = \mu_0 ni$

where, n = number of turns per unit length.

$\therefore$ Magnetic flux linked with each turn,

$$\phi = BA = \mu_0 niA$$

$\therefore$ Total magnetic flux linked with solenoid,

$$N\phi = (\mu_0 niA)N$$

But $\quad N\phi = Li$

where, L is coefficient of self-induction.

$$(\mu_0 niA) = Li$$

$$\Rightarrow \quad L = \mu_0 nAN = \mu_0 \left(\frac{N}{l}\right) AN = \frac{\mu_0 AN^2}{l}$$

This is the required expression. (2)

19. (i) Refer to text on page 257 (Mutual inductance).

(ii) Refer to text on page 258 (Mutual inductance of two long coaxial solenoids).

20. Refer to text on page 260 (Energy losses in transformer).

21. (i) Refer to text on page 257 (Mutual inductance). (1+1)

(ii) Refer to text on page 258 (Mutual inductance of two long coaxial solenoids)

(iii) Suppose that a current I is flowing through the coil C_2 at any instant. Flux linked with the coil C_1 is given by $\phi \propto I \Rightarrow \phi = MI$

where, M is the coefficient of mutual induction. If e is the induced emf produced in the coil C_1, then

$$e = -\frac{d\phi}{dt} = -\frac{d}{dt}(MI) = -M\frac{dI}{dt} \quad (3)$$

22. (i) Whenever the current passing through a coil or circuit changes, the magnetic flux linked with a neighbouring coil or circuit will also change. Hence, an emf will be induced in the neighbouring coil or circuit. This phenomenon is called 'mutual induction'.

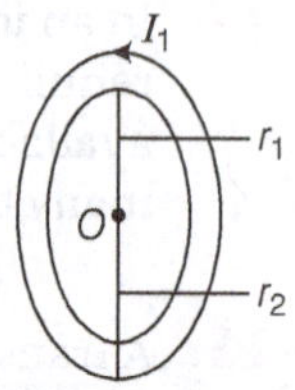

According to question, let the current in big coil of radius r_2 be I_1, so magnetic field at point O due to this coil will be $\frac{\mu_0 I_1}{2r_2}$.

Change in magnetic flux in the coil of radius r_1 is

$$\phi = BA = \frac{\mu_0 I_1}{2r_2} \times \pi r_1^2$$

Mutual inductance,

$$M = \frac{\phi}{I_1} = \frac{\mu_0 I_1 \pi r_1^2}{2r_2 \times I_1} = \frac{\mu_0 \pi r_1^2}{2r_2}$$

This is the required expression. (3)

(ii) According to question, if the coil rotates with an angular velocity of ω and N turns through an angle θ in time t, thus $\theta = \omega t$.

$$\therefore \quad \phi = BA\cos\theta = BA\cos\omega t$$

As the coil rotates, the magnetic flux linked with it changes. An induced emf is set up in the coil which is given by

$$e = \frac{-d\phi}{dt} = \frac{-d}{dt}(BA\cos\omega t)$$
$$= BA\omega \sin\omega t$$

For N number of turns, $e = NBA\omega \sin\omega t$

For maximum value of emf ωt must be equals to 90°.

So, maximum emf induced is = $NBA\omega$.

i.e. $e = NBA2\pi f$ $[\because \omega = 2\pi f]$ (2)

23. Refer to text on pages 259 and 260 (Transformer).

24. Refer to text on pages 259 and 260 (Transformer).

25. We know that, motional emf associated with a moving rod in a magnetic field is $\varepsilon = vBl$ (1)

Given, length of the rod l = 80 cm = 0.8 m

Velocity, v = 36 km/h = 10 m/s and magnetic field,

$B = 0.5$ T

$\Rightarrow$ $\varepsilon = vBl = 10 \times 0.5 \times 0.8 = 4$ V (1)

26. As we know that, $|\varepsilon| = \frac{d\phi}{dt} = M\frac{\Delta i}{\Delta t}$

where, M = coefficient of mutual inductance,

Δi = change in current

and Δt = duration of change of current.

$$\Rightarrow \quad M = -\frac{|\varepsilon|}{\left(\frac{\Delta i}{\Delta t}\right)}$$

According to the question, $|\varepsilon| = 750$ V

$\Delta i = 0 - 15 = -15$ A

and $\Delta t = 0.2$ s

So, $M = \frac{750}{15/0.2} = \frac{750 \times 0.2}{15} = 10$ H (1)

27. (i) Self-inductance of long solenoid.

(ii) Given, $\Delta l = -5$A

$\Delta t = 20 \times 10^{-3}$ s

$e = 500$ V, $L = ?$ (1)

$\therefore$ Induced emf, $e = -L\frac{\Delta l}{\Delta t}$

$$500 = -L\left(\frac{-5}{20 \times 10^{-3}}\right)$$

$L = 2$ H (2)

28. Given, self-inductance, $L = 0.05$H

Rate of change of current, $\frac{di}{dt} = 100$ As^{-1}

Magnitude of induced emf will be given as

$$e = \left|-L \times \frac{di}{dt}\right| = 0.05 \times 100$$

$\Rightarrow$ $e = 5$V

29. Given, $e = 2$ V and change in current, $\frac{di}{dt} = \frac{10}{0.4}$

$\therefore$ Coefficient of self-inductance of coil is given by

$$L = e \times \frac{dt}{di} \Rightarrow L = 2 \times \frac{0.4}{10} = \frac{0.8}{10} = 0.08\text{H}$$

30. Self-inductance of a long solenoid, $L = \mu_0 n^2 lA$

$$\therefore \quad \frac{L_1}{L_2} = \frac{n_1^2}{n_2^2} \Rightarrow L_2 = 108 \times \frac{25}{36} = 75 \text{ mH}$$

31. Let ϕ be the magnetic flux linked with each of the N turns of the coil.

Then, $N\phi \propto I$

$\Rightarrow$ $N\phi = LI$ or $\phi = \frac{LI}{N}$ (1)

$$\Rightarrow \quad \phi = \frac{30 \times 10^{-3} \times 5 \times 10^{-3}}{200} = 7.5 \times 10^{-7} \text{Wb}$$ (1)

32. Here, $L_0 = 0.01$ mH $= 10^{-5}$ H

$L = 10$ mH $= 10^{-2}$ H

$$\mu_r = ?, \mu_r = \frac{L}{L_0} = \frac{10^{-2}}{10^{-5}} = 10^3 \text{ or } \mu_r = 1000$$

33. 4 H; refer to example 1 on page 257.

34. Here, $\frac{dI}{dt} = 4$ As^{-1}

$\Rightarrow$ $|e| = 20$ mV $\Rightarrow |e| = 20 \times 10^{-3}$ V

$\Rightarrow$ $|e| = L\frac{dI}{dt}$

$\therefore$ $L = \frac{|e|}{dI/dt}$ (1)

$\Rightarrow$ $L = \frac{20 \times 10^{-3}}{4} = 5 \times 10^{-3}$ H

$= 5$ mH (1)

35. Here, number of turns per unit length,

$$n = \frac{N}{l} = 15 \text{ turns/cm} = 1500 \text{ turns/m}$$

$A = 2.0$ cm^2 $= 2 \times 10^{-4}$ m^2 (1/2)

$\therefore$ $\frac{dI}{dt} = \frac{4-2}{0.1}$ or $\frac{dI}{dt} = 20$ As^{-1} (1/2)

$\therefore$ $|e| = \frac{d\phi}{dt} = \frac{d}{dt}(BA)$ $\left[\because B = \frac{\mu_0 NI}{l}\right]$

$$= \frac{Ad}{dt}\left(\mu_0 \frac{NI}{l}\right) = A\mu_0\left(\frac{N}{l}\right)\frac{dI}{dt}$$ (1/2)

$= (2 \times 10^{-4}) \times 4\pi \times 10^{-7} \times 1500 \times 20$ V

$= 7.5 \times 10^{-6}$ V (1/2)

36. Here, $L = 10$ mH $= 10^{-2}$ H, $I = 0.1 \sin 200t$

$\therefore$ $\frac{dI}{dt} = 0.1 \times 200 \times \cos 200t = 20\cos 200t$ (1)

$\Rightarrow$ $\left(\frac{dI}{dt}\right)_{max} = 20 \times 1 = 20$As^{-1}

As, $|e| = L(dI/dt)$

$\Rightarrow$ $e_{max} = L(dI/dt)_{max}$

$\Rightarrow$ $e_{max} = 10^{-2} \times 20 = 0.2$ V (1)

37. From the relation of self-inductance, we have

$$L = \frac{\mu_0 N^2 A}{l} = \frac{4\pi \times 10^{-7} \times (600)^2 \times \pi \times (3\times 10^{-2})^2}{1}$$

$$= 4\pi^2 \times 36 \times 10^4 \times 9 \times 10^{-11} = 1.28 \times 10^{-3}\ \text{H}$$

38. Refer to the example 3 on page 257.

(i) $\frac{e_1}{e_2} = \frac{4}{3}$ (1)

(ii) $\frac{I_1}{I_2} = \frac{3}{4}$ (1)

39. emf induced in the secondary coil is given by

$$e = \frac{-MdI}{dt}$$

$\Rightarrow$ $\frac{d\phi}{dt} = \frac{-MdI}{dt}$

$\Rightarrow$ $d\phi = -MdI$

or, $d\phi = -1.5 \times 20 = -30\,\text{Wb}$ (2)

40. We know that, $|\varepsilon| = \frac{d\phi}{dt} = M\frac{\Delta i}{\Delta t}$

where, M = coefficient of mutual inductance,

Δi = change in current

and Δt = duration of change of current.

$\Rightarrow$ $M = \frac{|\varepsilon|}{\left(\frac{\Delta i}{\Delta t}\right)}$

According to the question, $|\varepsilon| = 60$ V

$\Delta I = 5 - 0 = 5\text{A}$

$\Delta t = 0.2$ s

So, $M = \frac{60}{5/0.2} = \frac{60\times 2}{5\times 10} = 2.4$ H

41. Given, $M = 1.5$ H, $\Delta i_1 = 5$A, $\Delta t = 10^{-3}$s

We know that, $M = \left|-\frac{e_2}{\Delta i_1/\Delta t}\right|$

$\Rightarrow$ $e_2 = M \times \frac{\Delta i_1}{\Delta t} = 1.5 \times \frac{5}{10^{-3}} = 7.5\ 10^3$ V

42. Applying the mutual inductance of coil A with respect to coil B,

$$M_{21} = \frac{N_2\phi_2}{I_1}$$

Therefore, we have

Mutual inductance $= \frac{10^{-2}}{2} = 5$ mH

Again, applying this formula for other case,

$N_1\phi_1 = M_{12} I_2 = 5\ \text{mH} \times 1\ \text{A} = 5\ \text{mWb}$

43. Flux linked with larger coil of radius,

$\phi = 0.5 \times 10^{-3}$ Wb and $I = 0.5$ A

current flows through neighbouring coil of radius r.

Total flux (ϕ) linked with one coil = MI

[$\because I$ current flows in neighbour coil]

$\therefore$ $0.5 \times 10^{-3} = M \times 0.5$

$M = 10^{-3}$ H (1)

Mutual inductance of two coils, $M = 10^{-3}$ H.

With the fall of current in small coil to zero, the magnetic flux linked with long coil decreases to zero quickly which in turn produces large induced emf in it. (1)

44. Transformer ratio, K

$$= \frac{\text{Number of turns in secondary coil } (N_s)}{\text{Number of turns in primary coil } (N_p)}$$

$\Rightarrow$ $\frac{N_s}{N_p} = \frac{V_s}{V_p} = \frac{33000\ \text{V}}{220\ \text{V}} = 150$

where, V_s is voltage in secondary coil and V_p is voltage in primary coil.

45. According to the question,

$N_P = 300$ turns (turns of primary)

$N_S = ?$ (turns of secondary)

$V_S > V_P$ because $V_S = 66$ kV

$V_P = 220$ V

Hence, $\frac{V_S}{V_P} = \frac{N_S}{N_P}$

$\Rightarrow$ $\frac{66 \times 1000}{220} = \frac{N_S}{300}$

$\Rightarrow$ $N_S = \frac{66 \times 1000 \times 300}{220}$

$= 9 \times 10^4$ turns = 90000 turns

46. According to the question,

Number of turns in primary coil, $n_p = 500$

Number of turns in secondary coil, $n_s = 1000$

Resistance of secondary coil, $R_s = 100\ \Omega$

emf of primary coil, $E_p = 200$V

We know that, $\frac{E_s}{E_p} = \frac{n_s}{n_p}$

$\Rightarrow$ $\frac{E_s}{200} = \frac{1000}{500}$ $\Rightarrow E_s = 400$ V (1)

Current in secondary coil

$$i_s = \frac{E_s}{R_s} = \frac{400}{100} = 4\ \text{A}$$ (1)

For an ideal transformer, $E_p i_p = E_s i_s$

Current in primary coil,

$$i_p = \frac{E_s i_s}{E_p} = \frac{400 \times 4}{200} = 8\text{A}$$ (1)

SUMMARY

- **Magnetic Flux** The total number of magnetic field lines crossing through any surface normally when it is placed in a magnetic field is known as the magnetic flux through that surface.
- **Faraday's Law of EMI** Faraday gave two laws of EMI
  (i) **First Law** An emf is induced in a circuit when the magnetic flux linked with circuit charges.
  (ii) **Second Law** The magnitude of induced emf in a circuit is equal to the rate of change of magnetic flux through the circuit.
- **Induced emf and Current**
  Induced emf, $e = -N\dfrac{d\phi_B}{dt}$
  Induced current, $I = \dfrac{e}{R} = \dfrac{-N}{R}\dfrac{d\phi_B}{dt}$
  Here, R = resistance of the circuit and N = number of turns of coil.
- **Lenz's Law** According to this law, the polarity of induced emf is such that it tends to produce a current which opposes the change in magnetic flux that produced it.
- **Fleming's Right Hand Rule** If we stretch the thumb, the forefinger, the central finger of our right hand in such a way that all three are mutually perpendicular to each other, then if the thumb represents the direction of force, forefinger represent the direction of magnetic field, then the central finger will represent the direction of induced current.
- **Induced Current in a Circuit** If induced current is produced in a coil rotated in a uniform magnetic field, then $I = I_0 \sin \omega t$.
- **Motional emf and Faraday's Law** If e is the induced emf, then according to Faraday's law,
  $$e = (-d\phi / dt) = -Blv$$
- **Energy Consideration** Power required to move a conductor in a uniform magnetic field perpendicular is, $P = \dfrac{B^2 l^2 v^2}{R}$.
  Here, R = resistance of the circuit through which current is flowing.
  B = a uniform magnetic field, l = length of the conductor, v = speed of the moving conductor.
- **Eddy Currents** The current induced in the bulk pieces of conductors, when the magnetic flux linked with the condutor charges are known as eddy currents.
- **Applications of Eddy Currents**
  (i) Electromagnetic damping
  (ii) Induction furnace
  (iii) Electric power meters
  (iv) Magnetic braking in electronic trains
- **Inductance** It is the ratio of the flux to the current. It depends on the geometry of the coil and intrinsic material properties.
- **Self-inductance** It in the property of a coil by virtue of which it opposes any changes in the strength of current flowing through it by inducing an emf in itself.
- When current in a coil changes, it induces a back emf in the same coil. The self-induced emf is given by, $e = -L\dfrac{dI}{dt}$, where L is the self-inductance of the coil.
- If coil of N turns and area A is rotated with ν revolutions per second in a uniform magnetic field B, then the induced emf is $e = e_0 \sin \omega t = NAB\omega \sin \omega t = NBA\,(2\pi\nu)\sin(2\pi\nu)t$.
- **Self-inductance of a Long Solenoid** Self-inductance of a long solenoid is given by
  $$L = \frac{\mu_0 N^2 A}{l}$$
- **Mutual Inductance** The phenomenon according to which an opposing emf is produced as a result of change in current or magnetic flux linked with a neighbouring coil.
- **Mutual Inductance of Two Long Coaxial Solenoids** Mutual inductance of two long coaxial solenoids is given by
  $$M = \frac{\mu_0 N_1 N_2 A}{l}$$
- **Transformer** is used to increase or decrease the altrenating voltage.
  It is of the two types
  (i) **Step-up Transformer** $N_s > N_p$
  $V_s > V_p$
  $I_s < I_p$
  (ii) **Step-down Transformer** $N_s < N_p$
  $V_s < V_p$
  $I_s > I_p$

For Mind Map

Visit : https://goo.gl/9dHF2n OR **Scan the Code**

Chapter Practice

Multiple Choice Questions

1 Mark

1 Near a circular loop of conducting wire as shown in the figure an electron moves along a straight line. The direction of the induced current, if any in the loop is

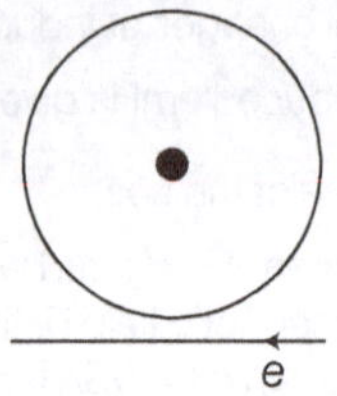

(a) variable (b) clockwise
(c) anti-clockwise (d) zero

2 Two similar circular loops carry equal currents in the same direction, on moving coils further apart, the electric current will
(a) increase in both
(b) decrease in both
(c) remain unaltered
(d) increase in one and decreases in the second

3 Induction furnace is based on the heating effect of
(a) electric field
(b) eddy current
(c) magnetic field
(d) gravitational field

4 A current passing through a coil of self-inductance of 2 mH changes at the rate of 20 mAs^{-1}. The emf induced in the coil is
(a) 10 μV (b) 40 μV
(c) 10 mV (d) 40 mV

5 A solenoid 60 cm long has 50 turns on it and is wound on an iron rod of 7.5 mm radius. Find the flux through the solenoid when the current in it is 3A and the relative permeability of iron is 600.
(a) 1.66 Wb (b) 2.66 Wb
(c) 1.66 mWb (d) 1.66 μWb

Assertion and Reason

Directions (Q. Nos. 6-10) *In the following questions, two statements are given- one labelled Assertion (A) and the other labelled Reason (R). Select the correct answer to these questions from the codes (a), (b), (c) and (d) as given below*
(a) Both Assertion and Reason are true and Reason is the correct explanation of Assertion.
(b) Both Assertion and Reason are true but Reason is not the correct explanation of Assertion.
(c) Assertion is true but Reason is false.
(d) Assertion is false but Reason is true.

6 **Assertion** (A) Faraday's law are consequence of conservation of energy.

Reason (R) The magnitude of the induced emf in a circuit is equal to the rate of change of magnetic flux linked with the circuit.

7 **Assertion** (A) Lenz's law violates the principle of conservation of energy.

Reason (R) Induced emf always opposes the change in magnetic flux responsible for its production.

8 **Assertion** (A) If the inner solenoid was much shorter than (and placed well inside) the outer solenoid, then we could still have calculated the flux linkage $N_1\phi_1$.

Reason (R) The inner solenoid is effectively immersed in a uniform magnetic field due to the outer solenoid.

9 **Assertion** (A) Self-inductance is the electromagnetic analogue of mass in mechanics.

Reason (R) Work needs to be done against the back emf (ε) in establishing the current.

10 **Assertion** (A) The quantity L/R possesses dimensions of time.

Reason (R) To reduce the rate of increase of current through a solenoid, we should increase the time constant (L/R).

Very Short Answer Type Questions

(1 Mark)

11 On what factors does the magnitude of induced emf in a coil depend?

12 If a coil is removed from a magnetic field
(i) slowly and
(ii) rapidly, then in which case, more work will be done?

13 Give any two useful applications of eddy currents.

14 How can self-inductance of a given coil having N number of turns be changed, if N is doubled keeping other factors constant?

15 If two coils are very tightly wound over one another, will their mutual inductance increase or decrease as compared to the case when the coils are placed some distance apart?

16 Why is a core of transformer laminated?

Short Answer Type I Questions

(2 Marks)

17 (i) When primary coil P is moved towards secondary coil S (as shown in the figure below), the galvanometer shows momentary deflection. What can be done to have larger deflection in the galvanometer with the same battery?

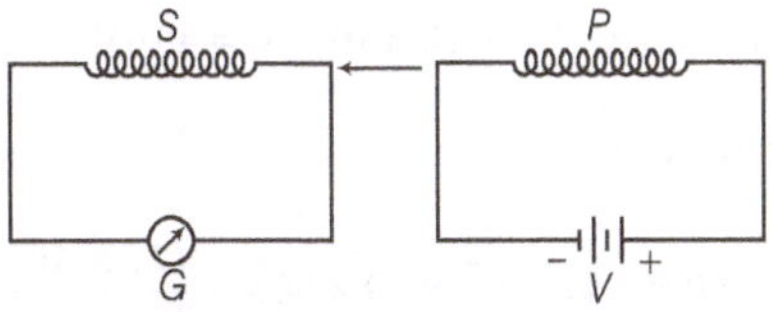

(ii) State the related law.

18 Four shapes made of wires are situated in a magnetic field B, perpendicular to the plane of the paper, directed downwards. If B starts reducing, what will be the directions of the induced currents in these shapes?

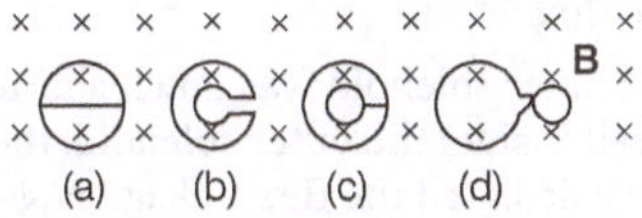

19 A magnet is quickly moved in the direction indicated by an arrow between two coils C_1 and C_2 as shown in the figure.

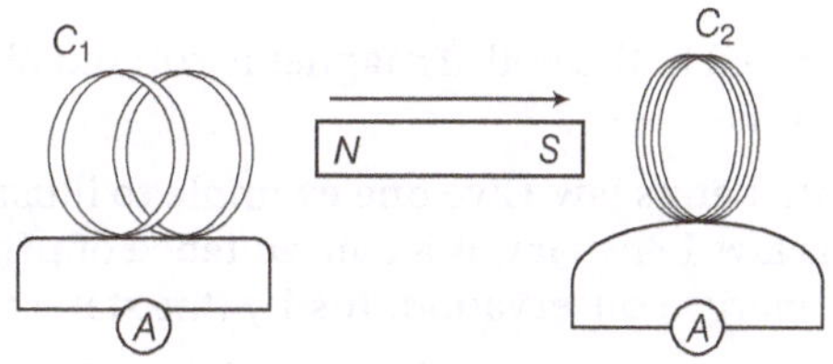

What will be the direction of induced current in each coil as seen from the magnet? Justify your answer.

20 A conducting square loop of side L and resistance R moves in its plane with a uniform velocity v perpendicular to one of its sides. A magnetic induction B, constant in time and space, pointing perpendicular to the plane of the loop exists everywhere. What will be the current induced?

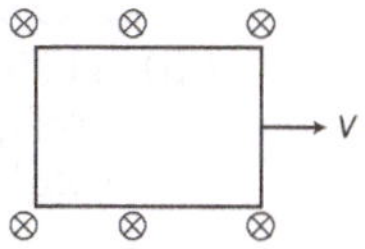

21 Two concentric circular coils C_1 and C_2, radius r_1 and r_2 ($r_1 << r_2$) respectively are kept coaxially. If current is passed through C_2, then find an expression for mutual inductance between the two coils.

Short Answer Type II Questions

(3 Marks)

22 The figure given below shows an arrangement by which current flows through the bulb X connected with coil B, when AC is passed through coil A.
(i) Name the phenomenon involved.
(ii) If a copper sheet is inserted in the gap between the coils, explain how the brightness of the bulb would change?

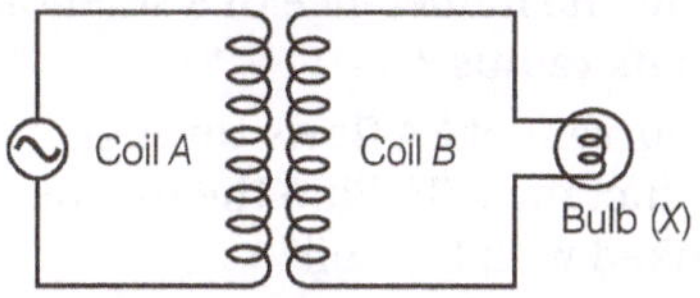

23 State the law that gives the polarity of the induced emf. Give its illustration.

Long Answer Type Questions

(5 Marks)

24 State and explain Faraday's laws of electromagnetic induction.
A cylindrical bar magnet is placed along the axis of a circular coil. Will there be a current

induced in the coil, if magnet is rotated about its axis?

25 State Lenz's law. Give one example to illustrate this law. Lenz's law is a consequence of principle of energy conservation. Justify this statement.

26 How is the mutual inductance of a pair of coils affected, when
(i) separation between the coils is increased?
(ii) the number of turns of each coil is increased?
(iii) a thin iron sheet is placed between the two coils, other factors remaining the same? Explain your answer in each case.

Case Based Questions

Directions (Q. No. 27) *These questions are case study based questions. Read the following paragraph and answer the questions.*

27. Self induction of a coil is a property by virtue of which it opposes any change in the strength of current through it by inducing an emf in the same coil. When a current I flow through the coil, then flux linked with it is given by $\phi = LI$, where L is a constant known as coefficient of self induction of the coil. The emf induced across an inductor carrying a current I is, $e = L\cdot\frac{dI}{dt}$. The Self inductance of a long solenoid is given by $L = \frac{\mu_0 N^2 A}{l}$

(i) Which property of the coil plays the same role as inertia in mechanics ?
(ii) Write the unit of coefficient of self induction in terms of tesla (T).
(iii) How the inductance of a solenoid depends on its radius ?
(iv) A current of 3A flows through a coil of inductance 5H. Find the magnetic flux linked with the coil?

Numerical Problems

28 A jet plane is travelling towards West at a speed of 450 m/s. If the horizontal component of the earth's magnetic field at that place is 4×10^{-4}T and dip angle is 30°, calculate the emf induced between the ends of wings having a span of 30 m. **(3 M)**

29 A long solenoid of 10 turns/cm has a small loop of area 1 cm^2 placed inside with the normal of the loop parallel to the axis. Calculate the voltage across the small loop, if the current in the solenoid is changed from 1 A to 2 A in 0.1 s, during the duration of this charge. **(2 M)**

30 A solenoid of length 80 cm, area of cross-section 1 m^2 with 20 turns per cm completely surrounds another coaxial solenoid of the same length, area of cross-section 25 cm^2 with 20 turns per cm. Calculate the mutual inductance of the system. **(2 M)**

Answers

1 (*a*) Since, electron is moving from right to left, the flux linked with loop will first increase and then decrease as the electron passes by. Therefore, induced current I in the loop will be first clockwise and then will move in anti-clockwise direction as the electron passes by.

2 (*a*) On moving the coils further apart initially the flux linked will reduce. Then, according to Lenz's law, current will increase in both the coils to increase the linked flux.

3 (*b*) Though most of the times eddy currents are undesirable but we find some useful applications such as in induction furnace. Joule's heat causes the melting of a metal piece placed in a rapidly changing magnetic field, inside induction furnance.

4 (*b*) By Faraday's second law, induced emf,

$$e = -\frac{Nd\phi}{dt} \text{ which gives}$$

$$e = -L\frac{dI}{dt}$$

$$\therefore \quad |e| = 2\times10^{-3}\times20\times10^{-3}\text{ V} = 40\,\mu\text{V}$$

5 (*c*) $\phi = \mu_r\mu_0\frac{N^2}{l}AI$

$$= 600\times4\pi\times10^{-7}\times50\times50\pi\times\frac{(7.5\times10^{-3})^2\times3}{6\times10^{-1}}$$

$$= 16.6\times10^{-3}\text{ Wb} = 1.66\text{ m Wb}$$

6 (*b*) According to Faraday's law of the conservation mechanical energy into electrical energy is in accordance with the law of conservation of energy.

7 (*d*) Lenz's law is based on conservation of energy and induced emf always opposes the cause of it, change in magnetic flux.

8 (*a*) If the inner solenoid was much shorter than (and placed well inside) the outer solenoid, then we could still have calculated the flux linkage $N_1\phi_1$ because the inner solenoid is effectively immersed in a uniform magnetic field due to the outer solenoid.

9 (*a*)

10 (*c*) The relation of induced emf is

$$e = \frac{Ldi}{dt} \text{ and current } i \text{ is given by}$$

$$i = \frac{e}{R} = \frac{1}{R}\frac{Ldi}{dt}$$

$$\Rightarrow \quad \frac{di}{dt} = i\frac{R}{L} = \frac{i}{L/R}$$

In order to decrease the rate of increase of current through solenoid we have to increase the time constant $= \frac{L}{R}$.

11 Number of turns in coils, and rate of change of magnetic flux.

12 More work will be done in (ii) Case.

13 In electric power meters and in induction furnace.

14 Doubled.

15 Increases

16 To prevent it from eddy current being produced in the core.

17 Refer to text on pages 239 and 240 (Third experiment).

18 Refer to text on page 241 (Illustration of Lenz's Law).

19 From the figure, it is clear that North Pole of the magnet is moving away from the coil C_1. So the direction of current it the coil C_1 is such that it will oppose the away against movement of North Pole, so it has to act as South Pole. Hence the direction of current will be clockwise.

Again, the South Pole is approaching towards coil C_2 so the current induced in the coil C_2 is such that it opposes the approaching the South Pole. Hence direction of the induced current will be clockwise.

20 Current induced is zero.

21 Refer to Q. 25 on page 262.

22 Mutual induction, increases.

23 Refer to text on page 241 (Lenz's law).

24 Refer to text on page 240 (Faraday's laws of electromagnetic induction).

25 Refer to text on pages 241 and 242 (Lenz's law and conservation of energy).

26 Refer to text on pages 257 and 258 (Coefficient of mutual induction).

27 (i) Self-induction is the property of a coil which plays same role as that of inertia in mechanics.

(ii) The unit of coefficient of self-induction is given by

$$L = \frac{\phi}{I} = \frac{B \cdot A}{I} = \text{T m}^2/\text{A}$$

(iii) The self-inductance of a long solenoid is given by,

$$L = \frac{\mu_0 N^2 A}{l} = \frac{\mu_0 N^2 \pi R^2}{l} \Rightarrow L \propto R^2$$

Hence, the self-inductance of a solenoid is directly proportional to square of its radius.

(iv) Given, $I = 3\text{A}$, $L = 5\text{H}$

The magnetic flux through the coil is

$$\phi = LI = 5 \times 3 = 15 \text{ Wb}$$

28 $e = 3$ kV.

Refer to Q. 34 on page 248.

29 Voltage $= 12.57 \times 10^{-7}$ V

Refer to Q. 35 on page 262.

30 Mutual inductance = 3.92 H

Refer to example 5 on page 258.

RELATED ONLINE VIDEOS

Visit : https://www.youtube.com/watch?v=aee1jb1_vro

OR **Scan the Code**

Visit : https://www.youtube.com/watch?v=s2yBTidfAzI

OR **Scan the Code**

Visit : https://www.youtube.com/watch?v=tC6E9J925pY

OR **Scan the Code**

CHAPTER

07

Alternating Current

Most of the electric power generated and used in the world is in the form of alternating current. This is because

(i) alternating voltages can be easily and efficiently converted from one value to the other by means of transformers.

(ii) the alternating current energy can be transmitted and distributed over long distances economically without much loss of energy.

In this chapter, we will study about some alternating current system that transfers energy efficiently and we will also discuss some of the devices that make use of alternating current.

- Introduction to Alternating Current
- AC Circuits, Chock Coil and Generator

TOPIC 01 Introduction to Alternating Current

Alternating Current (AC)

If the direction of current changes alternatively (periodically) and its magnitude changes continuously with respect to time, then the current is called alternating current.

Alternating current can be defined as the current whose magnitude and direction changes with time and attains the same magnitude and direction after a definite time interval. It changes continuously between zero and a maximum value and flows in one direction in the first half cycle and in the opposite direction in the next half cycle. It is sinusoidal, (i.e. represented by sine or cosine angles) in nature.

The instantaneous value of AC is given by

$$I = I_0 \sin\omega t \qquad \left[\because \omega = \frac{2\pi}{T} = 2\pi\nu\right]$$

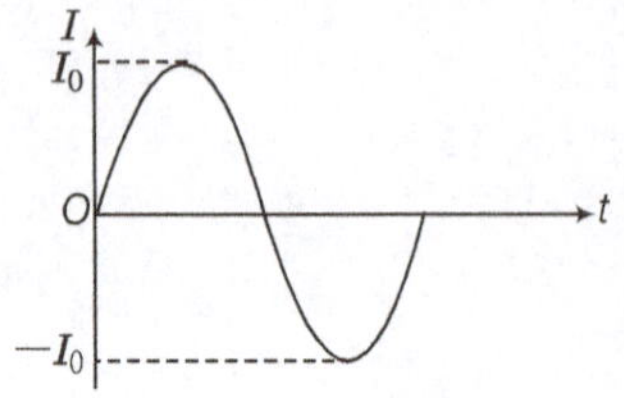

Current *versus* time graph of an AC

where, I = current at any instant t,

I_0 = maximum/peak value of AC,

ν = frequency

and ω = angular frequency.

Alternating emf or Voltage

It can be defined as the voltage whose magnitude and direction changes with time and attains the same magnitude and direction after a definite time interval. It is sinusoidal in nature. The instantaneous value of alternating emf or voltage is given by

$$E = E_0 \sin \omega t$$

where, E = voltage at any time t, E_0 = maximum/peak value of alternating voltage and ω = angular frequency.

Comparison of AC with DC
(Basic Differences between AC and DC)

Alternating current	Direct current
Safe to transfer over longer distances and reduce energy loss.	Voltage of DC cannot travel very far until it begins to loss energy.
The frequency of alternating current is 50 Hz or 60 Hz depending upon the country.	The frequency of direct current is zero.
It reverses its direction, while flowing in a circuit.	It flows in one direction in the circuit.
It is the current of magnitude varying with time.	It is the current of constant magnitude.
Obtained from AC generator through mains.	Obtained from cell or battery.

Mean or Average Value of AC for Half Cycle

It is defined as the value of AC (Alternating Current) which would send same amount of charge through a circuit in half cycle (i.e. $T/2$) that is sent by steady current in the same time. It is denoted by I_m or I_{av}.

Let the instantaneous value of alternating current is represented by

$$I = I_0 \sin \omega t \quad \text{... (i)}$$

The AC changes continuously with time. Suppose current is kept constant for small time (dt). Then, small amount of charge (dq) in small time (dt) is given by

$$dq = Idt = I_0 \sin \omega t \, dt \quad \text{[from Eq. (i)]}$$

To calculate total charge send by AC over half cycle is given by

$$\int dq = \int_0^{T/2} I_0 \sin \omega t \, dt \quad \text{or} \quad q_s = I_0 \int_0^{T/2} \sin \omega t \, dt$$

Here, q_s is steady charge over half cycle.

$$\Rightarrow \quad q_s = I_0 \left[\frac{-\cos \omega t}{\omega}\right]_0^{T/2} = \frac{-I_0}{\omega}[\cos \omega t]_0^{T/2}$$

$$= \frac{-I_0}{\omega}\left[\cos \frac{\omega T}{2} - \cos 0^\circ\right]$$

$$= \frac{-I_0}{\omega}\left[\cos \frac{\omega T}{2} - 1\right] = \frac{-I_0}{\omega}\left[\cos \frac{2\pi}{2} - 1\right]$$

$$\left[\because \omega = \frac{2\pi}{T} \Rightarrow \omega T = 2\pi\right]$$

$$= \frac{-I_0}{\omega}[\cos \pi - 1] = \frac{-I_0}{\omega}[-1-1] [\because \cos \pi = -1]$$

$$\Rightarrow \quad q_s = \frac{2I_0}{\omega}$$

Also, the charge sent by AC in positive half cycle is

$$q_{AC} = I_m \times \frac{T}{2}$$

where, I_m is mean value of AC over half cycle.

According to the definition,

$$q_s = q_{AC} \quad \text{[over any half cycle]}$$

$$\Rightarrow \quad \frac{2I_0}{\omega} = I_m \times \frac{T}{2}$$

$$\Rightarrow \quad I_m = \frac{4I_0}{\omega T} = \frac{4I_0}{2\pi} \quad [\because \omega T = 2\pi]$$

$$\Rightarrow \quad I_m = \frac{2I_0}{\pi} = 0.637 I_0$$

$$\therefore \quad \boxed{I_m = 0.637 I_0}$$

Mean value of AC (I_m) is 63.7% of the peak value of AC (I_0) over positive half cycle. For negative half cycle, the mean value of AC will be $-2I_0/\pi$. Therefore, in a complete cycle, the mean value of AC will be zero.

In the same way, mean value of alternating emf (E_m) is

$$\boxed{E_m = \frac{2E_0}{\pi} = 0.637 E_0}$$

Note Mean or Average value of A.C for full half cycle is zero.

Root Mean Square (RMS) Value of AC

It is defined as that value of alternating current (AC) over a complete cycle which would generate same amount of heat in a given resistor that is generated by steady current in the same resistor and in the same time during a complete cycle.

It is also called **virtual value or effective value of AC.**

It is represented by I_{rms} or I_{eff} or I_V. Suppose I is the current which flows in the resistor having resistance (R) in time (T) produces heat (H).

Instantaneous value of AC, $I = I_0 \sin \omega t$

If dH is small amount of heat produced in time dt in resistor R, then

$$dH = I^2 R\, dt \qquad [\because H = I^2 RT] \ldots\text{(i)}$$

In complete cycle ($0 \to T$), the total heat produced is H.

After integrating Eq. (i), we get

$$\int dH = \int_0^T I^2 R\, dt \Rightarrow H = \int_0^T I^2 R\, dt$$

Put the value of I in the above equation, we get

$$H = \int_0^T (I_0 \sin \omega t)^2 R\, dt$$

$$= I_0^2 R \int_0^T \sin^2 \omega t\, dt = I_0^2 R \int_0^T \left[\frac{1-\cos 2\omega t}{2}\right] dt$$

$$\left[\because \sin^2 \omega t = \frac{1-\cos 2\omega t}{2}\right]$$

$$= \frac{I_0^2 R}{2} \int_0^T (1-\cos 2\omega t)\, dt$$

$$= \frac{I_0^2 R}{2}\left[\int_0^T dt - \int_0^T \cos 2\omega t\, dt\right]$$

$$= \frac{I_0^2 R}{2}\left[|t|_0^T - \left|\frac{\sin 2\omega t}{2\omega}\right|_0^T\right]$$

$$= \frac{I_0^2 R}{2}\left[(T-0) - \frac{1}{2\omega}|\sin 2\omega T - \sin 0°|\right]$$

$$= \frac{I_0^2 R}{2}\left[T - \frac{1}{2\omega}|\sin 2 \times 2\pi - 0|\right] [\because \omega T = 2\pi]$$

$$= \frac{I_0^2 R}{2}\left[T - \frac{1}{2\omega}|0-0|\right] \qquad [\because \sin 4\pi = 0]$$

$$= \frac{I_0^2 RT}{2} \qquad \ldots\text{(ii)}$$

If I_{rms} is rms value of alternating current and H is the heat produced by rms current (I_{rms}), then

$$H = I_{rms}^2 RT \qquad \ldots\text{(iii)}$$

On comparing Eqs. (ii) and (iii), we get

$$I_{rms}^2 RT = \frac{I_0^2 RT}{2} \Rightarrow I_{rms}^2 = \frac{I_0^2}{2}$$

$$\Rightarrow \boxed{I_{rms} = \sqrt{\frac{I_0^2}{2}} = \frac{I_0}{\sqrt{2}} = 0.707 I_0}$$

$$\Rightarrow \boxed{I_{rms} = 70.7\% \text{ of } I_0}$$

From the above equation, we conclude that rms value of current is 70.7% of the peak value of current.

In the same way, the rms value of alternating emf (E_{rms} or E_{eff} or E_V) is

$$\boxed{E_{rms} = \frac{E_0}{\sqrt{2}} = 0.707 E_0 = 70.7\% \text{ of } E_0}$$

The different values I_0, I_{av} and I_{rms} are shown in figure given below.

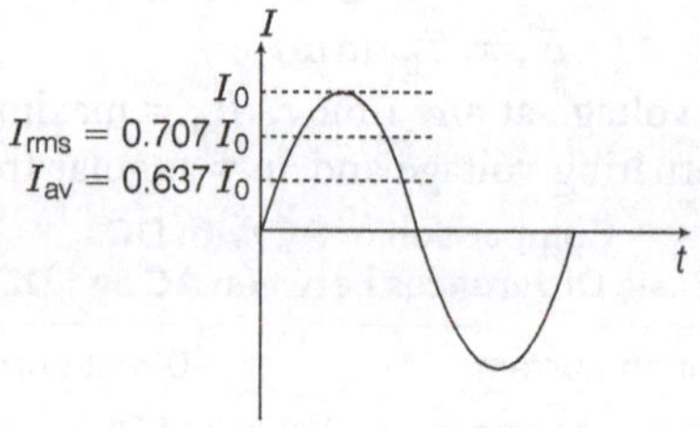

RMS and Average value of current on the same graph

Example 1 The instantaneous current from an AC source is given by $I = 5 \sin 314t$. What is the rms value of the current?

Sol. Given, $I = 5 \sin 314 t$ ...(i)

We know that, $I = I_0 \sin \omega t$ ...(ii)

On comparing Eqs. (i) and (ii), we have

$$I_0 = 5 \text{ A and } \omega = 314$$

$$\therefore \quad I_{rms} = \frac{I_0}{\sqrt{2}} = \frac{5}{\sqrt{2}} = 3.54 \text{ A}$$

Example 2 Calculate the instantaneous voltage for AC supply of 220 V and 50Hz.

Sol. Given, $E_V = 220$ V, $\nu = 50$ Hz and $E = ?$

Since, we know that for calculating the peak value of alternating voltage E_0, we can use the relation

$$E_0 = \sqrt{2} E_V = 1.414 \times 220 = 311 \text{ V}$$

Therefore, instantaneous voltage, $E = E_0 \sin \omega t$

$$E = E_0 \sin(2\pi\nu)t$$
$$= 311 \sin(2\pi \times 50)t = 311 \sin 100\pi t$$

Example 3 In an AC circuit, the rms voltage is $100\sqrt{2}$ V. Determine the peak value of voltage and its mean value during a positive half cycle.

Sol. Given, $E_V = 100\sqrt{2}$ V

Peak value of voltage, $E_0 = ?$

Mean value of voltage, $E_m = ?$

$$\because \quad E_0 = \sqrt{2} E_V = \sqrt{2}(100\sqrt{2}) = 200 \text{ V}$$

$\therefore$ During positive half cycle ($0 \to T/2$),

$$E_m = \frac{2E_0}{\pi} = \frac{2 \times 200}{3.14} = 127.4 \text{ V}$$

Topic Practice 1

Multiple Choice Questions

1 Mark

1. Which of the following graphs, shows I_{rms} *versus* t?

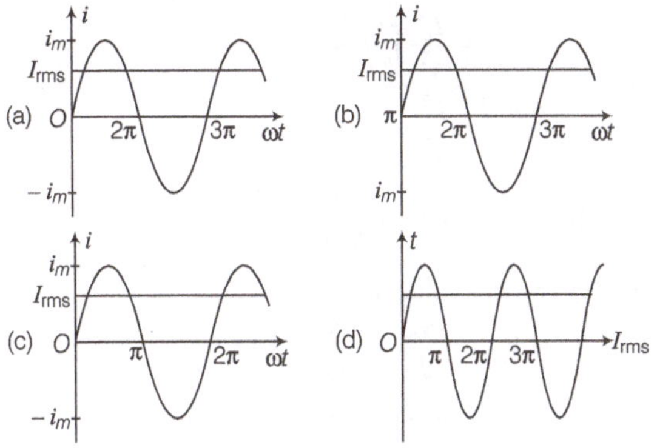

2. The electric mains in the house is marked 220 V, 50 Hz. Write down the equation for instantaneous voltage.
   (a) $3.1 \sin (100\pi) t$ V (b) $31.1 \cos (100\pi) t$ V
   (c) $311.1 \sin (100\pi) t$ V (d) $311.1 \cos (100\pi) t$ V

3. RMS value of AC current is A times its peak value. Here, A refers to
   (a) $0.704\, i_m$ (b) $0.707\, i_m$
   (c) $0.709\, i_m$ (d) $0.7055\, i_m$

4. The electric current in a circuit is given by $I = I_0 (t/\tau)$ for some time. The rms current for the period $t = 0$ to $t = \tau$ is
   (a) $\frac{I_0}{\sqrt{3}}$ (b) $\frac{3I_0}{2}$ (c) $\sqrt{\frac{I_0}{2}}$ (d) $\frac{3}{4}\sqrt{I_0}$

5. The frequency of an alternating voltage is 50 cycles/s and its amplitude is 120 V. Then, the rms value of voltage is
   (a) 101.3 V (b) 84.8 V
   (c) 70.7 V (d) 56.5 V

Very Short Answer Type Questions

1 Mark

6. Define the term rms value of the current. How is it related to the peak value?

7. The peak value of emf in AC is E_0. Write its (i) rms (ii) average value over a complete cycle.

8. An AC current, $I = I_0 \sin \omega t$ produces certain heat H in a resistor R over a time $T = 2\pi/\omega$. Write the value of the DC current that would produce the same heat in the same resistor in the same time.

9. An alternating current is given by $I = I_1 \cos\omega t + I_2 \sin\omega t$. Determine the rms value of current through the circuit.

Short Answer Type I Questions

2 Marks

10. Establish an expression for the average voltage of AC voltage $V = V_0 \sin \omega t$ over the time interval $t = 0$ and $t = \pi/\omega$.

11. (i) RMS value of an alternating current flowing in a circuit is 5A. Calculate its peak value.
    (ii) State any one difference between a direct current (DC) and an alternating current (AC). **ISC 2024**

12. Show that $I_{rms} = \frac{I_0}{\sqrt{2}}$, where I_{rms} is the root mean square value of alternating current and I_0 is the peak value. **ISC 2006**

Numerical Problems

13. An AC generator generates an emf ε, where $\varepsilon = 314 \sin(50\pi t)$ volt. Calculate the frequency of the emf ε. **ISC 2017 (1 M)**

14. Figure below shows emf e generated by an AC generator *versus* time t.

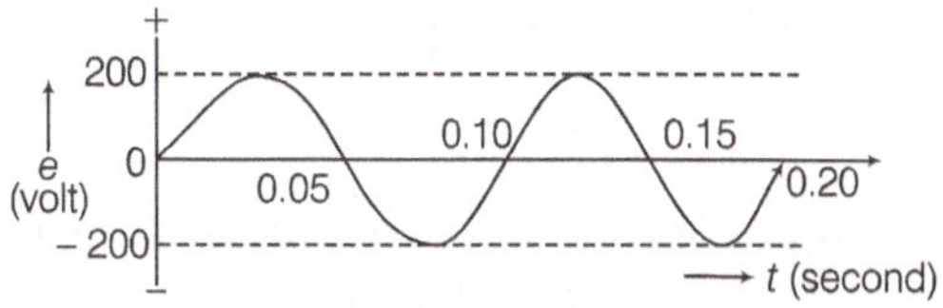

What is the frequency of emf? **ISC 2010 (1 M)**

15. The instantaneous value of current in an AC circuit is $I = 2 \sin (100\pi t + \pi/3)$ A. At what first time, the current will be maximum ? **(1 M)**

16. An alternating current in a circuit is given by $I = 20 \sin(100\pi t + 0.05\pi)$ A. What is the rms value of current? **(1 M)**

17. (i) The peak voltage of an AC supply is 300 V. What is its rms voltage?
(ii) The rms value of current in an AC circuit is 10 A. What is the peak current? **NCERT (2 M)**

18. A light bulb is rated 100 W for 220 V AC supply of 50 Hz. Calculate
(i) resistance of the bulb.
(ii) the rms current through the bulb. **(2 M)**

19. The alternating current in a circuit is described by the graph shown in the figure. Find the rms current in this graph. **NCERT Exemplar (1 M)**

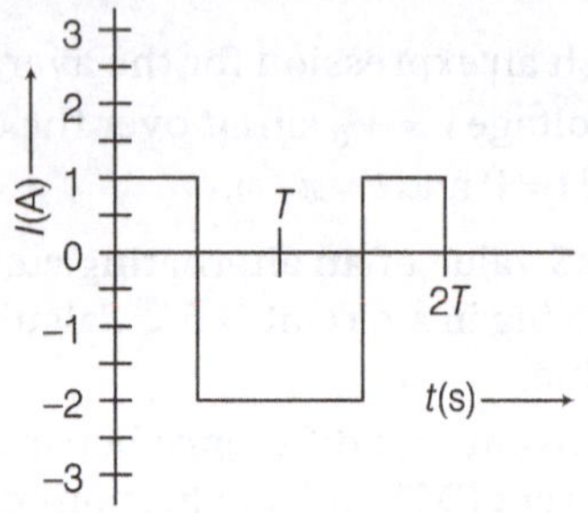

20. An AC generator generates an emf ε given by ε = 311 sin (100 πt) volt. Then, find the rms value of the emf generated by the generator. **ISC 2009 (1 M)**

21. The electric main in a house is marked 220 V-50 Hz. Write down the equation for the instantaneous voltage. The only variable in the equation should be t. **ISC 2005 (1 M)**

Hints & Solutions

1. (c)

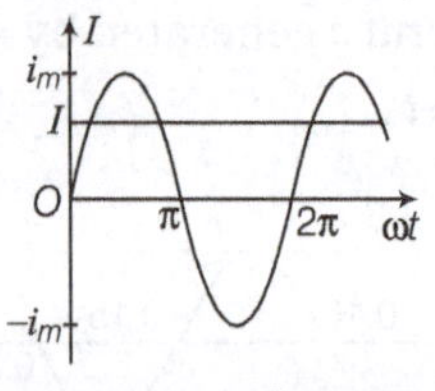

The rms current I is related to the peak current i_m by
$$I = i_m/\sqrt{2} = 0.707\, i_m.$$

2. (c) We are given that,
$$\varepsilon_{rms} = 220 \text{ V}, \nu = 50 \text{ Hz}$$
As, $\varepsilon_{rms} = \frac{\varepsilon_0}{\sqrt{2}}, \varepsilon_0 = \varepsilon_{rms}\sqrt{2}$

(220 V) (1.414) = 311.1 V

Further, $\omega = 2\pi\nu = 2\pi \times 50 = 100\,\pi$ rad/s

Thus, the equation for the instantaneous voltage is given as $\varepsilon = \varepsilon_0 \sin \omega t = 311.1 \text{ V} \sin (100\pi)\, t$

3. (b) The rms current I is related to the peak current i_m by
$$I = \sqrt{\overline{i^2}} = \sqrt{\frac{1}{2} i_m^2}$$
$$= i_m/\sqrt{2} = 0.707\, i_m$$

4. (a) As, $I = I_0\,(t/\tau)$
$$\overline{I^2} = \frac{\int_0^\tau I^2\, dt}{\tau} = \frac{\int_0^\tau I_0^2\,(t/\tau)^2\, dt}{\tau}$$
$$= \frac{I_0^2}{\tau^3}\int_0^\tau t^2 dt$$
$$= \frac{I_0^2}{\tau^3} \times \frac{\tau^3}{3} = \frac{I_0^2}{3}$$
Thus, $I_{rms} = \sqrt{\overline{I^2}} = \sqrt{\frac{I_0^2}{3}} = \frac{I_0}{\sqrt{3}}$

5. (b) The rms value of voltage, i.e.
$$V_{rms} = \frac{V_0}{\sqrt{2}} = \frac{120}{1.414} = 84.8 \text{ V}$$

6. It is defined as the value of Alternating Current (AC) over a complete cycle which would generate same amount of heat in a given resistor that is generated by steady current in the same resistor and in the same time during a complete cycle. It is also called virtual value or effective value of AC.
Let the peak value of the current be I_0.
$$\Rightarrow \quad I_{rms} = \frac{I_0}{\sqrt{2}}$$
where, I_0 = peak value of AC.

7. E_0 = peak value of emf in a complete cycle,
(i) rms value $[E_{rms}] = \frac{E_0}{\sqrt{2}}$ **(1/2)**
(ii) average value $[E]$ = zero **(1/2)**

8. An AC current $I = I_0 \sin \omega t$ produces certain heat H in a resistor R over a time $T = 2\times 3.14/\omega$, is given by $H = \left(\frac{I_0}{\sqrt{2}}\right)^2 RT$ and the same amount of heat produced by DC current in same time is given by $H = I^2RT$.
As, these heats are equal, then $I^2RT = \left(\frac{I_0}{\sqrt{2}}\right)^2 RT$
So, $I = \frac{I_0}{\sqrt{2}}$, where I stands for DC and I_0 is the peak value of AC current.

9. As, $I_{rms_1} = \frac{I_1}{\sqrt{2}}$ and $I_{rms_2} = \frac{I_2}{\sqrt{2}}$
Hence, the resultant of these two currents,
$$I_{rms} = \sqrt{\left(\frac{I_1}{\sqrt{2}}\right)^2 + \left(\frac{I_2}{\sqrt{2}}\right)^2} = \sqrt{\frac{I_1^2 + I_2^2}{2}}$$

10. Average voltage, V_m or $V_{av} = \frac{2V_0}{\pi} = 0.637 V_0$ **(1)**

Refer to the text on page 276 (Mean or average value of AC for half cycle). **(1)**

11. (i) Peak value of current $I_0 = \sqrt{2}\, I_{rms}$

$= \sqrt{2} \times 5 = 7.07$ A **(1)**

(ii) Alternating current (AC) is the current of magnitude varying with time and direct current (DC) is the current of constant magnitude. **(1)**

12. Let the alternating current is $i = i_0 \sin \omega t$.

Mean of square value of current,

$$\overline{i^2} = \frac{1}{T}\int_0^T i^2\, dt \quad [\because \text{for a complete cycle}]$$

$$= \frac{1}{T}\int_0^T i_0^2 \sin^2 \omega t\, dt = \frac{i_0^2}{T}\int_0^T \left(\frac{1-\cos 2\omega t}{2}\right) dt$$

$$= \frac{i_0^2}{2T}\left[t - \frac{\sin 2\omega t}{2\omega}\right]_0^T = \frac{i_0^2}{2T}[T-0] = \frac{i_0^2}{2} \quad \textbf{(1)}$$

Now, by taking roots of mean square value of current,

i.e. $\quad i_{rms} = \sqrt{\overline{i^2}} = \sqrt{i_0^2/2} = \frac{i_0}{\sqrt{2}}$

where, i_{rms} = root of mean square value

and $\quad i_0$ = peak value of current. **(1)**

13. According to the question,

$$\varepsilon = 314 \sin(50\pi t)\text{V}$$

On comparing with,

$$\varepsilon = \varepsilon_0 \sin \omega t$$

Here, ω = angular frequency = 50π **(1/2)**

So, $\quad \omega = 2\pi f$

$$\Rightarrow \quad f = \frac{2\pi}{\omega} = \frac{2\pi}{50\pi} = \frac{1}{25} = 0.04 \quad \textbf{(1/2)}$$

14. From the graph,

Time period, $T = 0.10$ s

Frequency, $f = \frac{1}{T} = \frac{1}{0.10} = 10$ Hz

15. Here, $I = 2 \sin(100\,\pi t + \pi/3)$ A ...(i)

Since, the current will be maximum, when $\sin\theta = 1$

So, $\quad \theta = 100\pi t + \frac{\pi}{3} = \frac{\pi}{2}$

$$\Rightarrow \quad 100\pi t = \frac{\pi}{6}$$

$$\Rightarrow \quad t = \frac{1}{600}\text{ s}$$

16. $I_{rms} = 10\sqrt{2}$ A

Refer to the example 1 on page 274.

17. (i) $E_{rms} = \frac{E_0}{\sqrt{2}} = \frac{300}{\sqrt{2}} = 212.1$ V $\quad [\because E_0 = \text{peak voltage}]$ **(1)**

(ii) $\quad I_{rms} = 10$ A

$\Rightarrow I_{rms} = \frac{I_0}{\sqrt{2}} \quad [\because I_0 = \text{peak current}]$

$\Rightarrow \quad I_0 = \sqrt{2} I_{rms} = 10 \times \sqrt{2} = 14.14$ A **(1)**

18. (i) Power, $P = EI \Rightarrow P = E \times \frac{E}{R} \quad \left[\because I = \frac{E}{R}\right]$

$$\Rightarrow \quad R = \frac{E^2}{P} = \frac{(220)^2}{100}$$

$$= \frac{48400}{100} = 484\ \Omega \quad \textbf{(1)}$$

(ii) The peak voltage of the source is $E_{rms} = \frac{E_0}{\sqrt{2}}$

$$\Rightarrow \quad E_0 = E_{rms} \times \sqrt{2}$$

$$= 220\sqrt{2} = 311.13 \text{ V}$$

$$\therefore \quad I_{rms} = \frac{I_0}{\sqrt{2}} = \frac{E_0}{R\sqrt{2}} = \frac{311.13}{484\sqrt{2}}$$

$$= \frac{311.13}{684.479} = 0.45 \text{ A} \quad \textbf{(1)}$$

19. From the graph, $I_1 = 1$ A, $I_2 = -2$A and $I_3 = 1$A

$$I_{rms} = \sqrt{\frac{I_1^2 + I_2^2 + I_3^2}{3}} = \sqrt{\frac{1^2 + (-2)^2 + 1^2}{3}}$$

$$= \sqrt{\frac{6}{3}} = \sqrt{2} = 1.414 \text{ A}$$

20. According to the question,

Given, $\varepsilon = 311 \sin(100\pi t)$ volt

On comparing with $\varepsilon = \varepsilon_0 \sin \omega t$

Peak emf, $\quad \varepsilon_0 = 311$ V

So, $\quad \varepsilon_{rms} = \frac{\varepsilon_0}{\sqrt{2}} = \frac{311}{\sqrt{2}} = 219.9 \text{ V} \approx 220 \text{ V}$

21. Given, $V_{rms} = 220$ V, $f = 50$ Hz

The equation of an alternating voltage can be written as

$$V = V_0 \sin \omega t$$

where, V_0 = peak voltage

$$= \sqrt{2}\, V_{rms} = \sqrt{2} \times 220 = 311 \text{V} \quad \left(\because V_{rms} = \frac{V_0}{\sqrt{2}}\right)$$

$$\therefore \quad V = 311 \sin 2\pi \times 50t \quad [\because \omega = 2\pi f]$$

$$\Rightarrow \quad V = 311 \sin 100\,\pi t$$

TOPIC 02 AC Circuits, Chock Coil and Generator

Phasor Diagrams

A diagram representing alternating current and alternating emf (of same frequency) as rotating vectors (phasors) with the phase angle between them is called phasor diagram.

The length of the vector represents the maximum or peak value, i.e. I_0 and E_0. The projection of the vector on fixed axis gives the instantaneous value of alternating current and alternating emf. In sine form, ($I = I_0 \sin \omega t$ and $E = E_0 \sin \omega t$), projection is taken on Y-axis. In cosine form, ($I = I_0 \cos \omega t$ and $E = E_0 \cos \omega t$), projection is taken on X-axis.

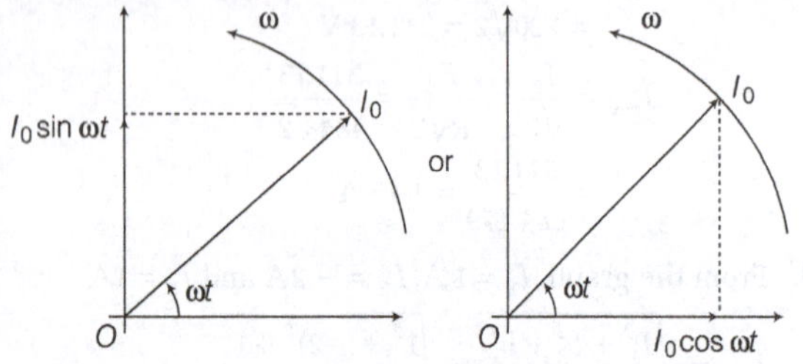

Phasor diagram

Different types of AC Circuit

In this section, we will derive voltage current relations for individual as well as combined circuit elements carrying a sinusoidal current. Here, we will only consider resistors, inductors and capacitors.

AC through Resistor

Suppose a resistor of resistance R is connected to an AC source of emf with instantaneous value (E), which is given by

$$E = E_0 \sin \omega t \quad \ldots(i)$$

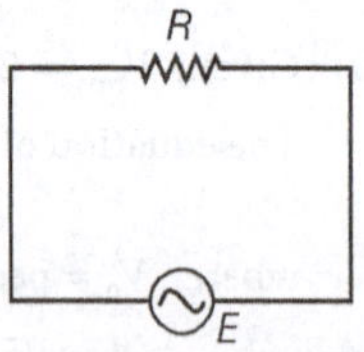

An AC voltage applied to a resistor

Let E be the potential drop across resistance (R), then

$$E = IR \quad \ldots(ii)$$

∵ Instantaneous emf = Instantaneous value of potential drop

From Eqs. (i) and (ii), we have

$$IR = E = E_0 \sin \omega t \Rightarrow I = \frac{E}{R} = \frac{E_0 \sin \omega t}{R}$$

$$\Rightarrow \quad \boxed{I = I_0 \sin \omega t} \quad \left[\because I_0 = \frac{E_0}{R}\right] \quad \ldots(iii)$$

Comparing $I_0 = E_0/R$ with Ohm's law, we find that resistors work equally well for both AC and DC voltages. From Eqs. (i) and (iii), we get that for resistor **there is zero phase difference between instantaneous alternating current and instantaneous alternating emf (i.e. they are in same phase).**

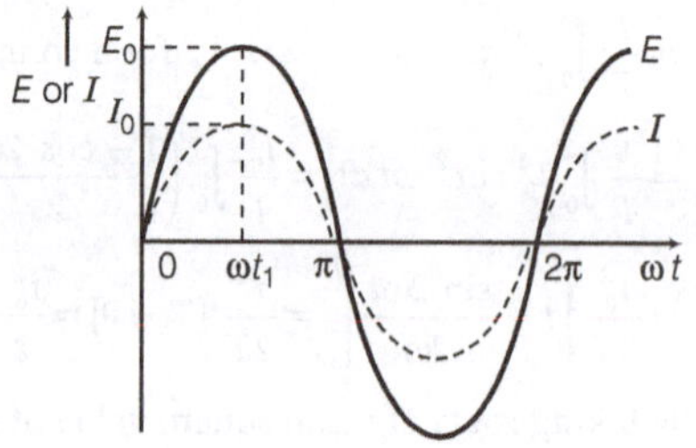

Graph of E and I *versus* ωt

Phasor Diagram

Here, peak values E_0 and I_0 are represented by vectors rotating with angular velocity ω with respect to horizontal reference. Their projections on vertical axis give their instantaneous values.

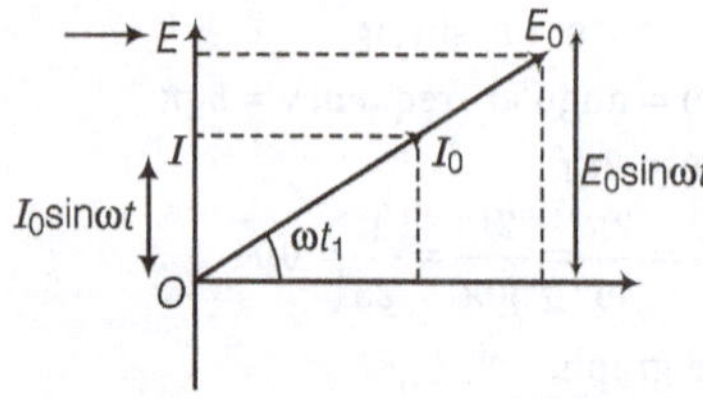

Phasor diagram for a purely resistive circuit

Example 1 A resistance of 20 Ω is connected to a source of alternating current rated 110 V, 50 Hz. Find the

(i) rms current.

(ii) maximum instantaneous current in the resistor.

(iii) time taken by the current to change from its maximum value to the rms value.

Sol. Given, resistance, $R = 20\,\Omega$

The rms value of voltage, $E_{rms} = 110\,V$

Frequency, $\nu = 50$ Hz

(i) $I_{rms} = \dfrac{E_{rms}}{R} = \dfrac{110}{20} = 5.5$ A

(ii) $I_0 = \sqrt{2} I_{rms} = 1.414 \times 5.5 = 7.8$ A

(iii) Let the AC be represented by $I = I_0 \cos \omega t$

At $t = 0, I = I_0 \cos 0 = I_0$(max)

At time $= t$, let $I = I_{rms} = \frac{I_0}{\sqrt{2}} = I_0 \cos \omega t$

$$\because \cos \omega t = \frac{1}{\sqrt{2}} = \cos \frac{\pi}{4} \Rightarrow \omega t = \frac{\pi}{4} \Rightarrow 2\pi \nu t = \frac{\pi}{4}$$

$$\therefore \quad t = \frac{1}{8\nu} = \frac{1}{8 \times 50} = 2.5 \times 10^{-3} \text{ s}$$

AC through Inductor

Suppose an inductor with self-inductance (L) is connected to an AC source with instantaneous emf (E), which is given by

$$E = E_0 \sin \omega t \qquad \ldots \text{(i)}$$

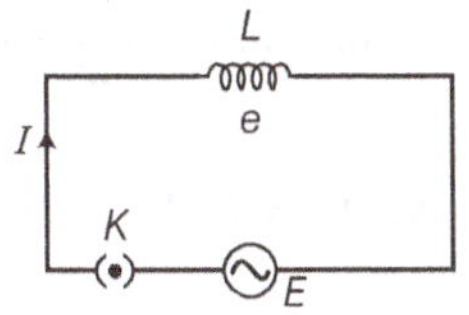

An AC source connected to an inductor

When key K is closed, then current I begins to grow because magnetic flux linked with it changes and induced emf produces which opposes the applied emf.
According to Lenz's law,

$$e = -L\frac{dI}{dt} \qquad \ldots \text{(ii)}$$

where, e is induced emf and $\frac{dI}{dt}$ is the rate of change of current.
To maintain the flow of current in the circuit, applied voltage must be equal and opposite to the induced emf i.e.

$$E = -e$$

$$\therefore \quad E = -\left(-\frac{LdI}{dt}\right) = \frac{LdI}{dt} \quad \text{or} \quad dI = \frac{E}{L}dt \quad \text{[from Eq. (i)]}$$

Integrating the above equation on both sides, we get

$$\int dI = \int \frac{E}{L} dt \Rightarrow I = \int \frac{E_0 \sin \omega t}{L} dt \quad [\because E = E_0 \sin \omega t]$$

$$\Rightarrow \quad I = \frac{E_0}{L}\left[\frac{-\cos \omega t}{\omega}\right]$$

$$\Rightarrow \quad I = -\frac{E_0}{\omega L}\sin(\pi/2 - \omega t) \quad \left[\because \sin\left(\frac{\pi}{2} - \omega t\right) = \cos \omega t\right]$$

$$\Rightarrow \quad I = \frac{E_0}{\omega L}\sin(\omega t - \pi/2)$$

If $\sin(\omega t - \pi/2) = \text{maximum} = 1$, then $I = I_0$

where, peak value of current, $I_0 = \frac{E_0}{\omega L}$

$$\therefore \quad \boxed{I = I_0 \sin(\omega t - \pi/2)} \qquad \ldots \text{(iii)}$$

From Eqs. (i) and (iii), it is clear that in a pure inductor, the current lags behind the voltage by a phase angle of $\pi/2$ radians (90°) or the voltage leads the current by a phase angle of $\pi/2$ radians (90°).

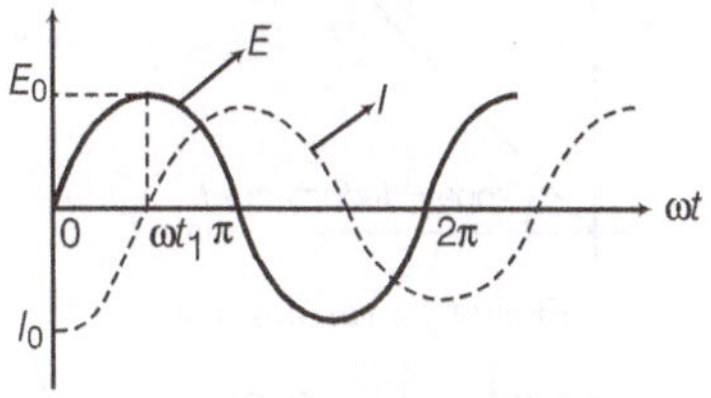

Graph of E and I *versus* ωt

Phasor Diagram

The phasor representing peak emf E_0 makes an angle ωt_1 in anti-clockwise direction from horizontal axis. As current lags behind the voltage by 90°, so the phasor representing I_0 is turned 90° clockwise with the direction of E_0.

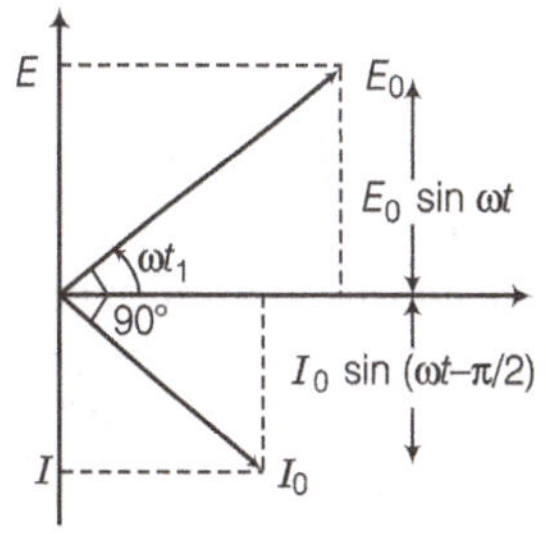

Phasor digram for purely inductive circuit

Inductive Reactance (X_L)

The opposing nature of inductor to the flow of alternating current is called **inductive reactance.**

As, $I = \frac{E_0}{\omega L}\sin(\omega t - \pi/2)$ so, $I_0 = E_0/\omega L$

Comparing the above with Ohm's law, $I_0 = \frac{E_0}{R}$. The quantity ωL is analogous to the resistance and is denoted by X_L.

So, $\boxed{X_L = \omega L}$

where, X_L is called inductive reactance.
If ν is the frequency of AC source, then

$$X_L = \omega L = 2\pi\nu L \qquad \ldots \text{(i)} \qquad \left[\because \omega = \frac{2\pi}{T} = 2\pi\nu\right]$$

The dimension of inductive reactance is the same as that of resistance and its SI unit is ohm (Ω). The inductive reactance limits the current in a purely inductive circuit in the same way as the resistance limits the current in a purely resistive circuit.

It is also directly proportional to the inductance and to the frequency of the AC current. Thus, if the frequency of AC increases, its inductive reactance also increases.

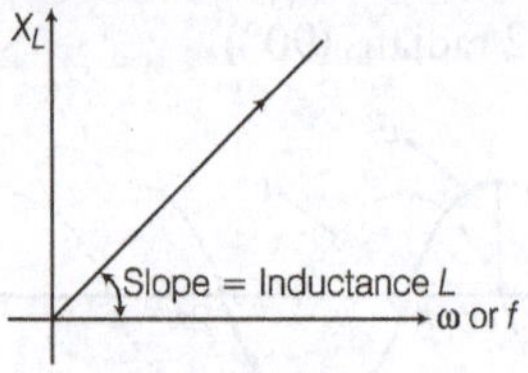

Plot of X_L *versus* ω or f

If inductor is connected to DC source

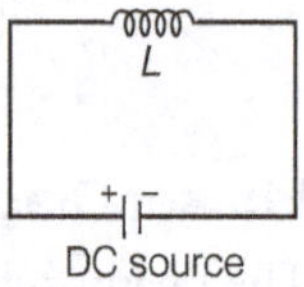

$$\nu = 0 \qquad \left[\because \nu = \frac{1}{T}\right]$$

Here, ν is frequency. So, from Eq. (i)

$X_L = 0$.

Therefore, inductor passes DC and blocks AC of very high frequency.

Note • Current flowing through inductor is called wattless current.

• Average power through inductor is zero.

Example 2 Alternating emf of $E = 220 \sin 100\pi t$ is applied to a circuit containing an inductance of $(1/\pi)$ H. Write equation for instantaneous current through the circuit. What will be the reading of AC galvanometer connected in the circuit?

Sol. Given, $E = 220 \sin 100\pi t$

$$E_0 = 220\text{ V}, \omega = 100\pi, L = (1/\pi)\text{ H}$$

Since, inductive reactance, $X_L = \omega L$

$$X_L = 100\pi \times \frac{1}{\pi} = 100\,\Omega$$

$$\therefore \quad I_0 = \frac{E_0}{X_L} = \frac{220}{100} = 2.2\text{ A}$$

As current lags behind the emf by a phase angle of $\pi/2$.

$\therefore \quad I = I_0 \sin(\omega t - \pi/2) = 2.2 \sin(100\pi t - \pi/2)$

$\therefore$ Reading of AC galvanometer, $I_V = \frac{I_0}{\sqrt{2}} = \frac{2.2}{\sqrt{2}}$

$$= \frac{2.2}{\sqrt{2}} = 1.55\text{ A}$$

AC through Capacitor

Let us consider a capacitor with capacitance C be connected to an AC source with an emf having instantaneous value,

$$E = E_0 \sin \omega t \qquad \ldots\text{(i)}$$

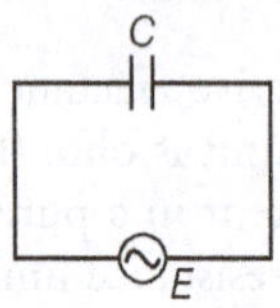

An AC source connected to a capacitor

Due to this emf, charge will be produced and it will charge the plates of capacitor with positive and negative charges. If potential difference across the plates of capacitor is V, then

$$V = \frac{q}{C} \text{ or } q = CV$$

The instantaneous value of current in the circuit,

$$I = \frac{dq}{dt} = \frac{d}{dt}(CE) \qquad [\because V = E]$$

$$= \frac{d}{dt}(CE_0 \sin \omega t) \qquad [\because E = E_0 \sin \omega t]$$

$$= CE_0 \cos \omega t \times \omega = \frac{E_0}{1/\omega C} \cos \omega t$$

$$\Rightarrow \quad I = \frac{E_0}{1/\omega C} \sin(\omega t + \pi/2) \qquad \ldots\text{(ii)}$$

$$[\because \cos \omega t = \sin(\pi/2 + \omega t)]$$

I will be maximum when $\sin(\omega t + \pi/2) = 1$, so that $I = I_0$

where, peak value of current is, $I_0 = \frac{E_0}{1/\omega C}$

$$\therefore \quad \boxed{I = I_0 \sin(\omega t + \pi/2)} \qquad \ldots\text{(iii)}$$

From Eqs. (i) and (iii), it is clear that in a perfect capacitor, the current leads the voltage by a phase angle of $\pi/2$ radians (90°) or the voltage lags behind the current by a phase angle of $\pi/2$ radians (90°).

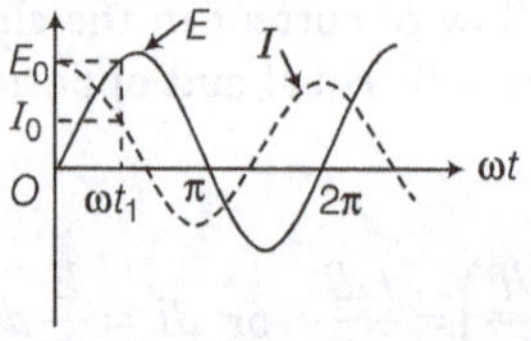

Graph of E and I *versus* ω t

Phasor Diagram

The phasor representing peak emf E_0 makes an angle ωt_1 in anti-clockwise direction with respect to horizontal axis. As current leads the voltage by 90°, the phasor representing I_0 is turned 90° anti-clockwise with the phasor representing E_0. The projections of these phasors on the vertical axis give instantaneous values of E and I.

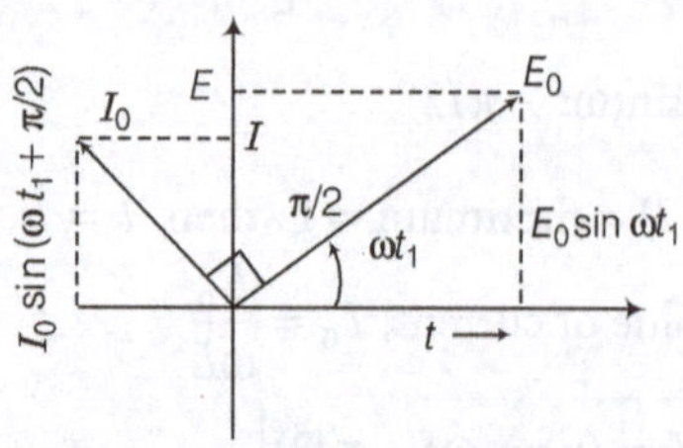

Phasor digram for purely capacitive circuit

Capacitive Reactance (X_C)

The instantaneous value of alternating current through a capacitor is given by

$$I = \frac{E_0}{1/\omega C} \sin(\omega t + \pi/2) = I_0 \sin\left(\omega t + \frac{\pi}{2}\right)$$

Comparing the above with Ohm's law we get,

$$I_0 = \frac{E_0}{1/\omega C} \quad \therefore \quad \boxed{X_C = \frac{1}{\omega C}}$$

where, X_C is called capacitive reactance.

The opposing nature of capacitor to the flow of alternating current is called **capacitive reactance.**

If ν is the frequency of the alternating current, then

$$\boxed{X_C = \frac{1}{2\pi \nu C}} \qquad \left[\because \omega = \frac{2\pi}{T} = 2\pi\nu\right]$$

The dimension of capacitive reactance is same as that of resistance and its SI unit is ohm (Ω). The capacitive reactance limits the amplitude of the current in a purely capacitive circuit in the same way as the resistance limits the current in a purely resistive circuit. It is inversely proportional to the capacitance and frequency of the current.

Thus, if frequency of AC increases, then its capacitive reactance decreases.

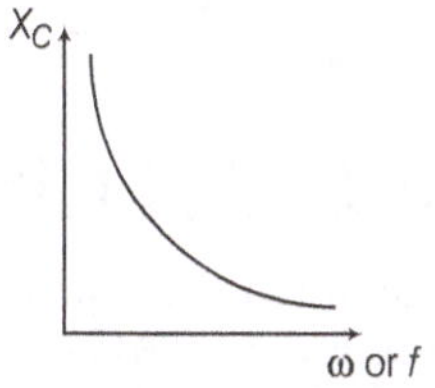

Plot of X_C *versus* ω or f

When capacitor is connected to DC source,

$X_C = 1/\omega C = 1/0 = \infty$ [$\because$ for DC, $\omega = 2\pi\nu = 0$, as $\nu = 0$]

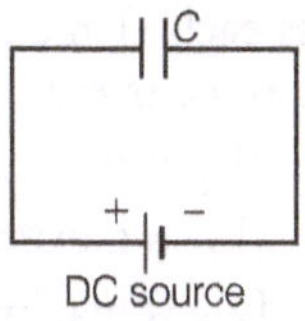

Thus, capacitor blocks DC and acts as open circuit while it passes AC of high frequency.

AC Through *R-L* and *R-C* Circuits

R-L and *R-C* circuits are the circuits containing a combination of only two components of a *L-C-R* circuit. To obtain relation between different quantities of *R-L* and *R-C* circuit we simply put $X_C = 0$ and $X_L = 0$ in *L-C-R* circuit, respectively.

The details are as follows:

Resistive, Inductive Circuit (*R-L* circuit)

$V_L = X_L I$ across the inductance L is ahead of current I in phase by $\pi/2$ and by parallelogram law of vector addition,

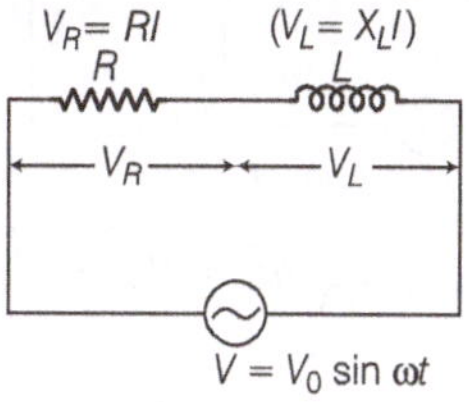

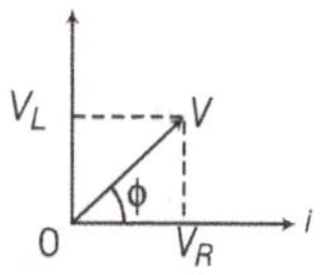

(i) Applied voltage, $V = \sqrt{V_R^2 + V_L^2}$

(ii) Impedance, $Z = \sqrt{R^2 + X_L^2} = \sqrt{R^2 + \omega^2 L^2}$ [$\because X_L = \omega L$]

$$= \sqrt{R^2 + 4\pi^2 f^2 L^2}$$

(iii) Current, $i = i_0 \sin(\omega t - \phi)$

(iv) Peak current, $i_0 = V_0/Z$

$$= \frac{V_0}{\sqrt{R^2 + X_L^2}} = \frac{V_0}{\sqrt{R^2 + 4\pi^2 f^2 L^2}}$$

(v) Phase difference, $\phi = \tan^{-1}\left(\frac{X_L}{R}\right) = \tan^{-1}\left(\frac{\omega L}{R}\right)$

(vi) Power factor, $\cos\phi = \frac{R}{\sqrt{R^2 + X_L^2}}$

(vii) Leading quantity is voltage.

(viii) Graph of Z *versus* f

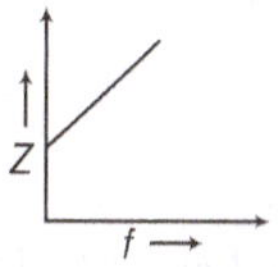

(ix) Graph of E *versus* I

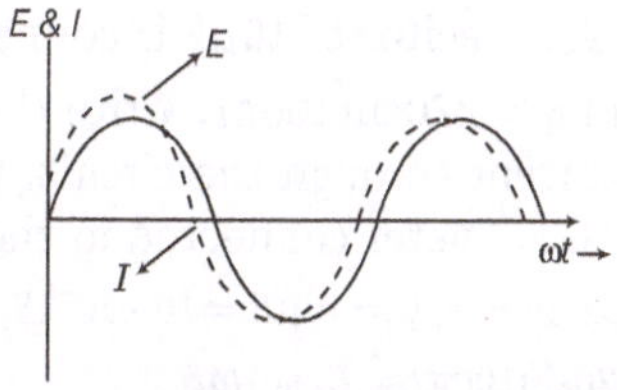

Graph of E and I versus ωt (For R-L circuit)

Resistive, Capacitive Circuit (R-C Circuit)

(i) Applied voltage, $V = \sqrt{V_R^2 + V_C^2}$

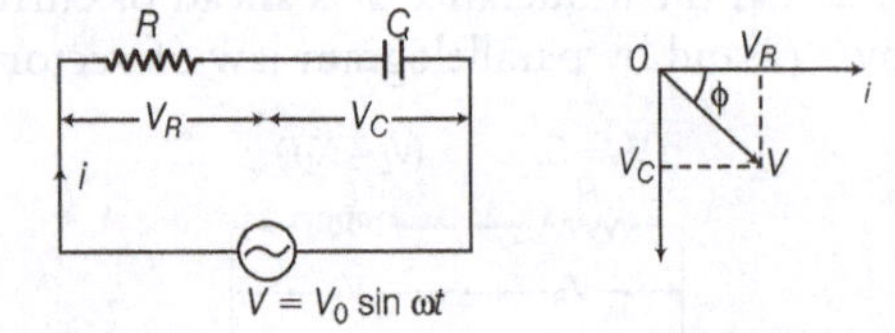

(ii) Impedance, $Z = \sqrt{R^2 + X_C^2} = \sqrt{R^2 + (1/\omega C)^2}$

$$\left[X_C = \frac{1}{\omega C}\right]$$

(iii) Current, $i = i_0 \sin(\omega t + \phi)$

(iv) Peak current, $i_0 = \frac{V_0}{Z} = \frac{V_0}{\sqrt{R^2 + X_C^2}}$

$$= \frac{V_0}{\sqrt{R^2 + \frac{1}{4\pi^2 f^2 C^2}}}$$

(v) Phase difference, $\phi = \tan^{-1}\left(\frac{X_C}{R}\right) = \tan^{-1}\left(\frac{1}{\omega CR}\right)$

(vi) Power factor, $\cos\phi = \frac{R}{\sqrt{R^2 + X_C^2}}$

(vii) Leading quantity is current.

(viii) Graph of Z *versus* f

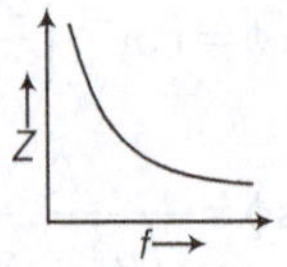

(ix) Graph of E *versus* I

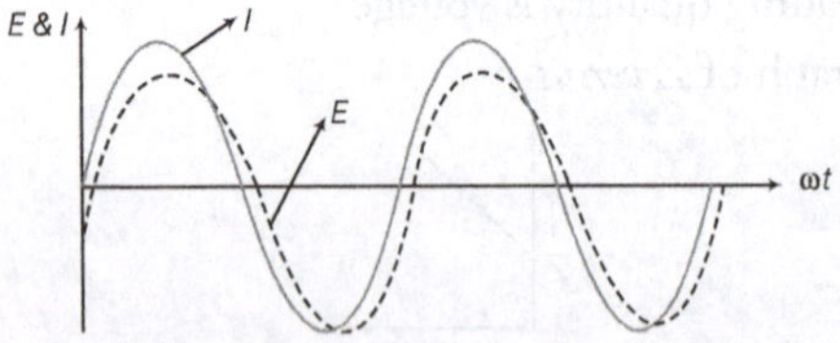

Graph of E and I *versus* ω t (for R-C circuit)

Example 3 A capacitor of 10μF is connected to an AC source of emf $E = 220 \sin 100\pi t$. Write the equation of instantaneous current through the circuit. What will be the reading of AC ammeter connected in the circuit?

Sol. Given, capacitance, $C = 10\mu F = 10 \times 10^{-6}$ F,

emf, $E = 220 \sin 100\pi t = E_0 \sin \omega t$

$\therefore E_0 = 220$ V, $\omega = 2\pi\nu = 100\pi \Rightarrow \nu = 50$ Hz

Since, capacitive reactance,

$$X_C = \frac{1}{\omega C} = \frac{1}{2\pi\nu C} = \frac{1}{2 \times 3.14 \times 50 \times 10^{-5}} = 318.5\,\Omega$$

$$I_0 = \frac{E_0}{X_C} = \frac{220}{318.5} = 0.691 \text{ A}$$

So, reading of AC ammeter, $I_V = \frac{I_0}{\sqrt{2}} = \frac{0.691}{1.414} = 0.489$ A

Example 4 A coil of 0.01H inductance and 1Ω resistance is connected to 200 V, 50 Hz AC supply. Find the impedance of the circuit and time lag between maximum alternating voltage and current. **NCERT Exemplar**

Sol. Given, inductance, $L = 0.01$ H

Resistance, $R = 1\,\Omega$

Voltage, $V = 200$ V

Frequency, $\nu = 50$ Hz

Impedance of the circuit, $Z = \sqrt{R^2 + X_L^2}$

$$= \sqrt{R^2 + (2\pi\nu L)^2} = \sqrt{1^2 + (2 \times 3.14 \times 50 \times 0.01)^2}$$

$$= \sqrt{10.86} = 3.3\,\Omega$$

$$\tan\phi = \frac{\omega L}{R} = \frac{2\pi\nu L}{R} = \frac{2 \times 3.14 \times 50 \times 0.01}{1} = 3.14$$

$$\Rightarrow \phi = \tan^{-1}(3.14) \approx 72°$$

Phase difference, $\phi = \frac{72 \times \pi}{180}$ rad

Time lag between maximum alternating voltage and current, $\Delta t = \frac{\phi}{\omega} = \frac{72\pi}{180 \times 2\pi \times 50} = \frac{1}{250}$ s

AC through L-C-R Circuit

Suppose that an inductor (L), a capacitor (C) and a resistor (R) are connected in series to an AC source. I is the current passing through this circuit. As R, L and C are in series, therefore at any instant through the three elements, AC has the same amplitude and phase. Let it be represented by $I = I_0 \sin \omega t$

However, voltage across each element bears a different phase relationship with the current.

$V_L = I_0 X_L$ [V_L is maximum voltage across L]

$V_C = I_0 X_C$ [V_C is maximum voltage across C]

$V_R = I_0 R$ [V_R is maximum voltage across R]

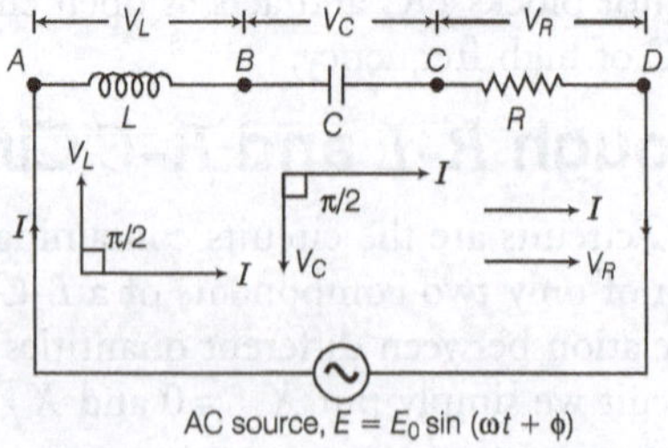

An AC source connected to L-C-R circuit

Inside the above figure for a *L-C-R* circuit, phasor diagrams of each *L*, *C* and *R* are given. To form phasor diagram for series *L-C-R* circuit, combine all these phasor diagrams.

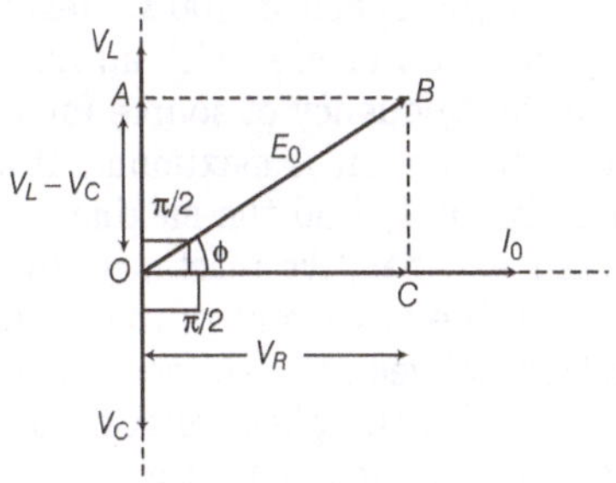

Phasor diagram for a series *L-C-R* circuit

Since, voltage (V_L) is in upward direction and voltage (V_C) in downward direction, so net voltage upto point *A* is $V_L - V_C$ (assuming $V_L > V_C$) and net maximum voltage is V_0.

From phasor diagram,

$$(OB)^2 = (OC)^2 + (CB)^2$$

$$\Rightarrow \quad E_0^2 = V_R^2 + (V_L - V_C)^2$$

$$\Rightarrow \quad E_0 = \sqrt{(I_0 R)^2 + (I_0 X_L - I_0 X_C)^2}$$

$$\Rightarrow \quad E_0 = I_0 \sqrt{R^2 + (X_L - X_C)^2}$$

$$\therefore \quad Z = \frac{E_0}{I_0} = \sqrt{R^2 + (X_L - X_C)^2}$$

Here, *Z* is called **impedance.**

Impedance

It is the total resistance of a circuit applied in the path of alternating current. It is given by

$$Z = \sqrt{R^2 + (X_L - X_C)^2} \quad \ldots\text{(i)}$$

From phasor diagram, it is clear that voltage leads the current by an angle φ.

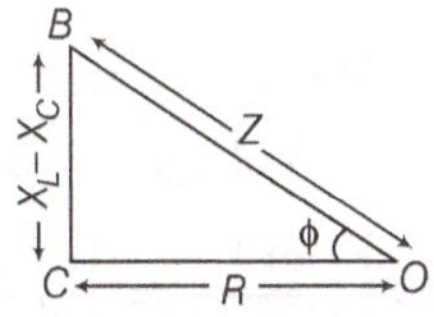

Impedance diagram of *L-C-R* circuit

∴ From ΔOCB,

$$\tan\phi = \frac{CB}{OC} = \frac{V_L - V_C}{V_R} = \frac{I_0 X_L - I_0 X_C}{I_0 R}$$

$$\Rightarrow \quad \tan\phi = \frac{X_L - X_C}{R} \quad \ldots\text{(ii)}$$

So, the alternating emf in the series *L-C-R* circuit would be represented by $E = E_0 \sin(\omega t + \phi)$.

Eqs. (i) and (ii) are graphically shown in the above shown graph. This is called impedance diagram, which is a right angled triangle with *Z* as its hypotenuse.

The amplitude and phase of current for an *L-C-R* series circuit is obtained by using the technique of phasors. But this method of analysing AC circuits have certain disadvantages. Firstly, the phasor diagram does not signify anything about initial condition. One can take any arbitrary value of *t* and draw different phasors which shows the relative angle between different phasors. The solution so obtained is called the steady state solution.

Special Cases

(i) When $X_L = X_C$, then $Z = R$ and $\tan\phi = 0$ $[\because \phi = 0°]$

Hence, voltage and current are in the same phase. Therefore, the AC circuit is non-inductive.

(ii) When $X_L > X_C$, then $\tan\phi$ is positive.

Hence, voltage leads the current by a phase angle φ. Therefore, the AC circuit is inductance dominated circuit.

(iii) When $X_C > X_L$, then $\tan\phi$ is negative.

Hence, voltage lags behind the current by a phase angle φ. Therefore the AC circuit is capacitance dominated circuit.

A graph (given below) is showing variation of *E* and *I* with ω*t* for the case, $X_L > X_C$.

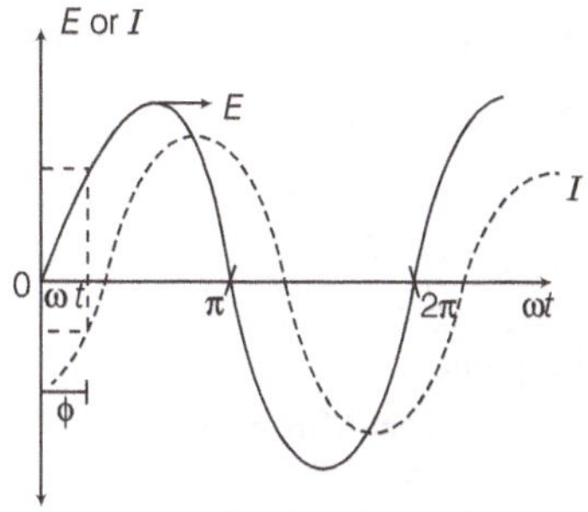

Graph of *E* and *I versus* ω*t* for series *L-C-R* circuit when $X_C < X_L$

Example 5 A capacitor of 100μF and a coil of resistance 50 Ω and inductance 0.5 H are connected in series with a 110 V -50 Hz source. Calculate the rms value of current in the circuit.

Sol. Given, capacitance, $C = 100\,\mu F = 100 \times 10^{-6}\,F = 10^{-4}\,F$

Resistance, $R = 50\,\Omega$

Inductance, $L = 0.5\,H$

Rms value of voltage, $E_V = 110\,V$

Frequency, $\nu = 50\,Hz$

Since, capacitive reactance,

$$X_C = \frac{1}{\omega C} = \frac{1}{2\pi\nu C} = \frac{1}{2 \times 3.14 \times 50 \times 10^{-4}}$$

$$X_C = 31.85\,\Omega$$

and inductive reactance,

$$X_L = \omega L = 2\pi\nu L = 2 \times 3.14 \times 50 \times 0.5 = 157\,\Omega$$

$\because$ Impedance, $Z = \sqrt{R^2 + (X_L - X_C)^2}$

$$= \sqrt{(50)^2 + (157 - 31.85)^2} = 134.77\,\Omega$$

$$\Rightarrow \quad I_V = \frac{E_V}{Z} = \frac{110}{134.77} = 0.816\,A$$

Resonance

In a series *L-C-R* circuit, when phase (ϕ) between current and voltage is zero, then the circuit is said to be a **resonant circuit.**

As applied frequency increases, then

$X_L = \omega L$, X_L increases and $X_C = \frac{1}{\omega C}$, X_C decreases.

At some angular frequency (ω_r), $X_L = X_C$

where, $\quad X_L = \omega_r L$, $X_C = \frac{1}{\omega_r C}$

The frequency at which X_C and X_L become equal, is called **resonant frequency.**

$$\Rightarrow \quad \omega_r L = \frac{1}{\omega_r C} \text{ or } \omega_r^2 = \frac{1}{LC} \text{ or } (2\pi\nu_r)^2 = \frac{1}{LC}$$

[$\because \omega_r = 2\pi\nu_r$, where ν_r is resonating frequency]

$$2\pi\nu_r = \frac{1}{\sqrt{LC}}$$

$$\therefore \quad \boxed{\nu_r = \frac{1}{2\pi\sqrt{LC}}}$$

At resonating frequency,

$$Z = R = \text{Minimum}$$

$$\therefore \quad I = \frac{E}{Z} = \text{Maximum}$$

Since, Z is minimum, therefore I will be maximum.

Phase difference between applied emf and current in the resonant circuit will be zero.

i.e. $\quad \phi = \tan^{-1}\left(\frac{X_L - X_C}{R}\right) = \tan^{-1}(0) = 0°$

So, power delivered to circuit by the source,

$$P_{av} = \frac{E_0}{\sqrt{2}} \cdot \frac{I_0}{\sqrt{2}} \cos 0° = \frac{E_0 I_0}{2} \text{ (maximum)}$$

Example 6 A 2 μF capacitor, 100 Ω resistor and 8 H inductor are connected in series with an AC source. What should be the frequency of source for which the current drawn in the circuit is maximum? If peak value of emf of source is 200 V, find the maximum current, inductive reactance, capacitive reactance, total impedance, peak value of current in the circuit. What is the phase relation between the voltages across inductor and resistor? Also, give the phase relation between voltages across inductor and capacitor.

Sol. Given, capacitance, $C = 2\,\mu F = 2 \times 10^{-6}\,F$

Resistance, $R = 100\,\Omega$

Inductance, $L = 8\,H$

Peak value of voltage, $E_0 = 200\,V$

When frequency of AC source is equal to resonant frequency,

then current drawn in the circuit is maximum.

$$\therefore \quad \nu = \nu_r = \frac{1}{2\pi\sqrt{LC}}$$

$$= \frac{1}{2 \times 3.14 \times \sqrt{8 \times 2 \times 10^{-6}}}$$

$$= \frac{1000}{8 \times 3.14} = 39.8\,Hz$$

Peak value of current, $I_0 = \frac{E_0}{R} = \frac{200}{100} = 2\,A$

$\because \quad X_C = X_L = \omega L = 2\pi\nu L$

$= 2 \times 3.14 \times 39.8 \times 8 = 2000\,\Omega \Rightarrow Z = R = 100\,\Omega$

The voltages across inductor and resistor differ in phase by 90° and the voltages across inductor and capacitor differ in phase by 180°.

Quality Factor (*Q*-Factor)

It is the measure of sharpness of the resonance of an *L-C-R* circuit. It is defined as the ratio of voltage developed across the inductance or capacitance at resonance to the impressed voltage, which is the voltage applied across *R*.

$$Q\text{-factor} = \frac{\text{Voltage across } L \text{ (or } C)}{\text{Voltage across } R}$$

$$Q\text{-factor} = \frac{V_L \text{ or } V_C}{V_R} = \frac{1}{R}\sqrt{\frac{L}{C}}$$

$$\boxed{Q\text{-factor} = \frac{\omega_0 L}{R} = \frac{1}{\omega_0 RC}}$$

Q is just a number having no dimensions, it can also be called **voltage multiplication factor** of the circuit.

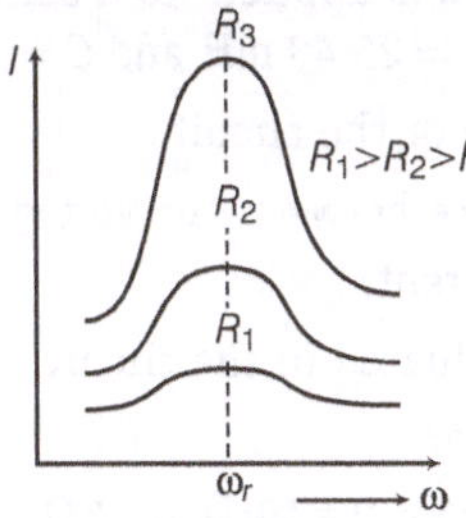

I versus ω graph of an *L-C-R* circuit

The electronic circuit with high Q values would respond to a very narrow range of frequencies and *vice-versa*. Higher the value of Q, the narrower and sharper is the resonance.

Q-factor can also be defined as the ratio of the resonant frequency to the difference in two frequencies taken on both sides of the resonant frequency such that at each frequency, the current amplitude becomes $1/\sqrt{2}$ times the value at resonant frequency.

Mathematically, Q-factor or $Q = \dfrac{\omega_r}{\omega_1 - \omega_2}$

where, ω_1 and ω_2 are frequencies when current decreases to 0.707 $(1/\sqrt{2})$ times the peak value of current.

where, ω_1 and ω_2 are also called as **half power frequencies.**

We can also write,

$$\omega_1 = \omega_r + \Delta\omega$$

$$\Rightarrow \quad \omega_2 = \omega_r - \Delta\omega$$

The difference $\omega_1 - \omega_2 = 2\Delta\omega$ is often called the **bandwidth of the circuit.**

For series resonant circuit, the bandwidth will be

$$\Delta W = \frac{R}{L}$$

Thus, from the above, Q-factor can also be defined as the ratio of resonant angular frequency to bandwidth of the circuit.

The smaller the bandwidth $(\Delta\omega)$, the sharper and narrower is the resonance.

Significance of Q-Factor

(i) Q-factor denotes the sharpness of tuning.

(ii) High Q-factor indicates lower rate of energy loss.

(iii) Higher value of Q-factor indicates sharper peak in the current.

(iv) For $R = 0$, Q-factor = infinity

Average Power Associated in AC Circuit

In AC circuit, both emf and current change continuously with respect to time. So in it we have to calculate average power in complete cycle $(0 \rightarrow T)$.

Instantaneous power, $P = EI$ ...(i)

$[\because E = E_0 \sin \omega t, I = I_0 \sin(\omega t + \phi)]$

Here, E and I are instantaneous voltage and current, respectively. If the instantaneous power remains constant for a small time dt, then small amount of work done in maintaining the current for a small time dt is

$$dW/dt = EI$$

$$\Rightarrow \quad dW = EI\,dt \quad \text{...(ii)}$$

Integrating Eq. (ii) on both sides, we get

$$\int dW = \int_0^T EI\,dt$$

Total work done or energy spent in maintaining current over one full cycle,

$$W = \int_0^T E_0 \sin \omega t \cdot I_0 \sin(\omega t + \phi)\,dt$$

$$= E_0 I_0 \int_0^T \sin \omega t(\sin \omega t \cos\phi + \cos \omega t \sin \phi)\,dt$$

$$= E_0 I_0 \left[\cos\phi \int_0^T \sin^2 \omega t\,dt + \sin\phi \int_0^T \sin \omega t \cos \omega t\,dt\right]$$

$$= E_0 I_0 \left[\cos\phi \int_0^T \left(\frac{1 - \cos 2\omega t}{2}\right) dt + \frac{\sin\phi}{2}\int_0^T 2\sin \omega t \cos \omega t\,dt\right]$$

$$= \frac{E_0 I_0}{2}\left[\cos\phi\left(\int_0^T dt - \int_0^T \cos 2\omega t\,dt\right) + \sin\phi \int_0^T \sin 2\omega t\,dt\right]$$

$$= \frac{E_0 I_0}{2}\left[\left(\cos\phi[t]_0^T - \int_0^T \cos 2\omega t\,dt\right) + \sin\phi \int_0^T \sin 2\omega t\,dt\right]$$

But $\int_0^T \cos 2\omega t\,dt = 0$ or and $\int_0^T \sin 2\omega t\,dt = 0$

$$\therefore \quad W = \frac{E_0 I_0 T}{2} \cos\phi$$

Average power associated in AC circuit,

$$P_{av} = \frac{W}{T} = \frac{E_0 I_0 T \cos\phi}{2T} = \frac{E_0 I_0}{2} \cos\phi$$

$$\boxed{P_{av} = \frac{E_0}{\sqrt{2}} \cdot \frac{I_0}{\sqrt{2}} \cos\phi}$$

or $P_{av} = E_{rms} I_{rms} \cos\phi = E_V I_V \cos\phi$

Here, $\cos\phi$ is power factor, which is defined as the cosine of the angle of lag or lead.

If P_{av} is true power or average power, then power factor is given by,

$$\cos\phi = \frac{P_{av}}{E_{rms} I_{rms}} = \frac{\text{True power}}{\text{Apparent power}} \quad \cos\phi = \frac{R}{Z}$$

Here, ϕ is the phase difference between I_{rms} and E_{rms}.

Special Cases

(i) **AC circuit containing R**

When $\phi = 0°$, then $P_{av} = E_V I_V \cos 0°$

$P_{av} = E_V I_V$

So, average power in R is maximum.

(ii) **AC circuit containing L**

When $\phi = \frac{\pi}{2}$, then $P_{av} = E_V I_V \cos\frac{\pi}{2}$

$$P_{av} = 0$$

So, average power in L is zero.

(iii) **AC circuit containing C**

When $\phi = \frac{\pi}{2}$, then $P_{av} = E_V I_V \cos\frac{\pi}{2}$

$$P_{av} = 0$$

So, average power in C is zero.

(iv) **AC circuit containing L and R**

When $\tan\phi = \frac{\omega L}{R} \Rightarrow \cos\phi = \frac{R}{\sqrt{R^2 + \omega^2 L^2}}$,

then $P_{av} = E_V I_V \cdot \frac{R}{\sqrt{R^2 + \omega^2 L^2}}$

(v) **AC circuit containing C and R**

When $\tan\phi = \frac{1/\omega C}{R} \Rightarrow \cos\phi = \frac{R}{\sqrt{R^2 + 1/\omega^2 C^2}}$

then $P_{av} = E_V I_V \cdot \frac{R}{\sqrt{R^2 + 1/\omega^2 C^2}}$

(vi) **AC circuit containing L, C and R**

When $\tan\phi = \frac{\omega L - 1/\omega L}{R}$

$\Rightarrow \quad \cos\phi = \frac{R}{\sqrt{R^2 + (\omega L - 1/\omega C)^2}}$

then $P_{av} = E_V I_V \cdot \frac{R}{\sqrt{R^2 + \left(\omega L - \frac{1}{\omega C}\right)^2}}$

Example 7 A sinusoidal voltage of peak value 283 V and frequency 50 Hz is applied to a series L-C-R circuit in which $R = 3\,\Omega$, $L = 25.48$ mH and $C = 796\,\mu$F. Find

(i) the impedance of the circuit.

(ii) phase difference between the voltage across the source and current.

(iii) the power dissipated in the circuit.

(iv) the power factor. **NCERT**

Sol. Given, $E_0 = 283\,\text{V}, \nu = 50\,\text{Hz}, R = 3\,\Omega$,

$L = 25.48\,\text{mH} = 25.48 \times 10^{-3}\,\text{H}$

and $C = 796\,\mu\text{F} = 796 \times 10^{-6}\,\text{F}$

(i) Since, inductive reactance, $X_L = \omega L$

$\Rightarrow X_L = 2\pi\nu L$

$= 2 \times 3.14 \times 50 \times 25.48 \times 10^{-3} = 8\,\Omega$

Since, capacitive reactance,

$$X_C = \frac{1}{\omega C} = \frac{1}{2\pi\nu C} = \frac{1}{2 \times 3.14 \times 50 \times 796 \times 10^{-6}}$$

$X_C = 4\,\Omega$

$\therefore$ Impedance, $Z = \sqrt{R^2 + (X_L - X_C)^2}$

$= \sqrt{3^2 + (8-4)^2} = 5\,\Omega$

(ii) Phase difference,

$$\phi = \tan^{-1}\left(\frac{X_L - X_C}{R}\right) = \tan^{-1}\left(\frac{8-4}{3}\right) = 53.1°$$

It means that the current in the circuit lags behind the voltage by 53.1°

(iii) Power dissipated in the circuit, $P = I_V^2 R$

$\because \quad I_V = \frac{I_0}{\sqrt{2}Z} = \frac{283}{1.414 \times 5} = 40\,\text{A}$

$\therefore \quad P = I_V^2 R = (40)^2 \times 3 = 4800\,\text{W}$

(iv) Power factor, $\cos\phi = \cos 53.1° = 0.60°$

Example 8 Suppose the frequency of the source in the above example can be varied.

(i) What is the frequency of the source at which resonance occurs ?

(ii) Calculate the impedance, the current and power dissipated of resonant condition. **NCERT**

Sol. (i) Resonant frequency, $\nu = \frac{1}{2\pi\sqrt{LC}}$

$$= \frac{1}{2 \times 3.14 \times \sqrt{25.48 \times 10^{-3} \times 796 \times 10^{-6}}} = 35.4\,\text{Hz}$$

(ii) At resonance, $Z = R = 3\,\Omega$

$\Rightarrow \quad I_V = \frac{E_V}{Z} = \frac{283}{\sqrt{2} \times 3} = 66.7\,\text{A} \quad \left[\because E_V = \frac{E_0}{\sqrt{2}}\right]$

$\therefore$ Power dissipated, $P = I_V^2 R = (66.7)^2 \times 3 = 13350$ V

Wattless Current

The current which consumes no power for its maintenance in the circuit is called **wattless current** or **idle current.**

or

If the resistance in an AC circuit is zero, although current flows in the circuit, then the average power remains zero, i.e. there is no energy dissipation in the circuit, such a circuit is called **wattless circuit** and the current flowing is called wattless current.

If the circuit contains either inductance or capacitance only, then phase difference between current and voltage is 90°, i.e. $\phi = 90°$. The average power in such a circuit is

$$P_{av} = V_{rms} \times I_{rms} \times \cos\phi = V_{rms} \times I_{rms} \times \cos 90° = 0$$

L-C Oscillations

When a capacitor is supplied with an AC current, it gets charged.

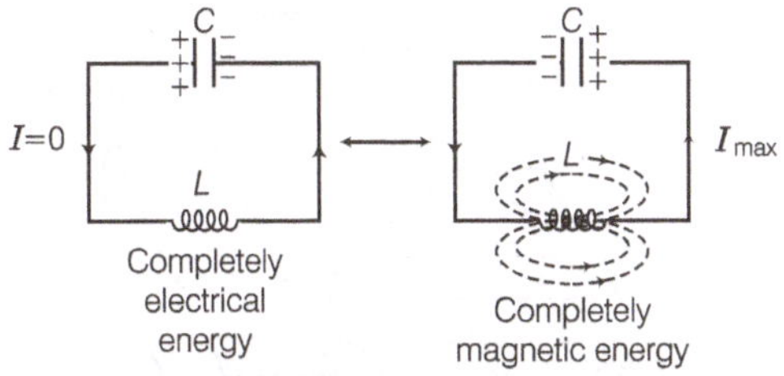

When this charged capacitor is connected with an inductor, current flows through inductor, giving rise to magnetic flux. Hence, induced emf is produced in the circuit. Due to this, the charge (or energy) on the capacitor decreases and an equivalent amount of energy is stored in the inductor in the form of magnetic field. When the discharging of the capacitor completes, current and magnetic flux linked with L starts decreasing.

Therefore, an induced emf is produced which recharges the capacitor in opposite direction. This process of charging and discharging of capacitor is repeated and energy taken once from source keeps on oscillating between C and L.

According to Kirchhoff's loop rule, we have

$$q/C - L dI/dt = 0 \quad \ldots(\text{i})$$

But $\quad I = -\dfrac{dq}{dt} \Rightarrow \dfrac{dI}{dt} = -\dfrac{d^2q}{dt^2}$

Negative sign indicates that as q decreases, I increases.

Putting dI/dt in Eq. (i), we get

$$\frac{d^2q}{dt^2} + \frac{1}{LC}q = 0$$

Compare this equation with equation of simple harmonic oscillator, we get

$$\frac{d^2x}{dt^2} + \omega_0^2 x = 0 \qquad [\text{where, } \omega_0 = 1/\sqrt{LC}]$$

Therefore, the charge oscillates with a frequency,

$$\nu = \frac{\omega}{2\pi} = \frac{1}{2\pi\sqrt{LC}}$$

Note For *L-C* oscillators, the energy oscillates in between the capacitor and inductor as electrostatic energy and magnetic energy. It is given as

$$U = \frac{1}{2}LI^2 = \frac{1}{2}\cdot\frac{q^2}{C}$$

Example 9 A transmitter operates at 1 MHz. The oscillating circuit has a capacitance of 200 pF. What is the inductance and capacitive reactance of the resonant circuit?

Sol. Given, frequency, $\nu = 1\,\text{MHz} = 10^6$ Hz

and capacitance, $C = 200\,\text{pF} = 2 \times 10^{-10}$ F

Since, $\nu = 1/2\pi\sqrt{LC}$

$$\Rightarrow \quad L = \frac{1}{4\pi^2\nu^2 C} = \frac{1}{4 \times 3.14 \times 3.14 \times (10^6)^2 \times 2 \times 10^{-10}}$$

$$= 0.00013\,\text{H}$$

$\therefore$ Capacitive reactance, $X_C = \dfrac{1}{\omega C} = \dfrac{1}{2\pi\nu C}$

$$= \frac{1}{2 \times 3.14 \times 10^6 \times 2 \times 10^{-10}} = 796.2\ \Omega$$

Example 10 A capacitor of 1μF is charged with 0.01C of electricity. How much energy is stored in it?

Sol. Given, capacitance, $C = 1\mu\text{F} = 10^{-6}\text{F}$

and $\qquad$ Charge, $q = 0.01\text{C} = 10^{-2}\text{C}$

$$\therefore \text{Energy stored} = \frac{q^2}{2C} = \frac{(10^{-2})^2}{2 \times 10^{-6}} = 50\,\text{J}$$

Choke Coil

Choke coils (or **ballast**) is a device having high inductance and negligible resistance. It is used to control current in AC circuits and is used in fluorescent tubes. The power loss in a circuit containing choke coil is least. Following are the important points about choke coil.

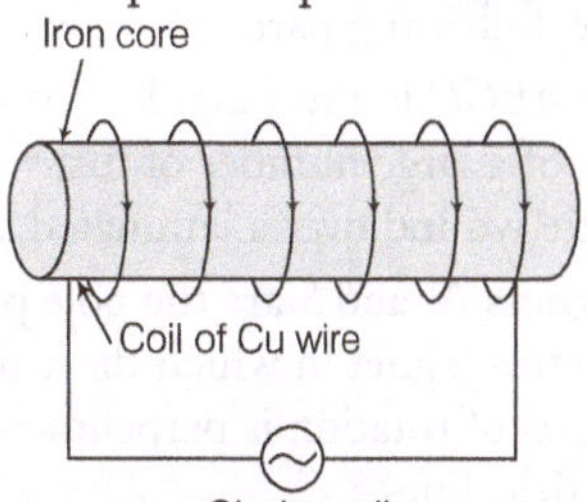

Choke coil

(i) It consists of a copper coil wound over a soft iron laminated core.

(ii) Thick copper wire is used to reduce the resistance (R) of the circuit.

(iii) Soft iron is used to improve inductance (L) of the circuit.

(iv) The inductive reactance or effective opposition of the choke coil is given by $X_L = \omega L = 2\pi f L$.

(v) For an ideal choke coil $R = 0$, no electric energy is wasted, i.e. average power $P = 0$.

(vi) In actual practice, choke coil is equivalent to a R-L circuit.

(vii) Choke coils for different frequencies are made by using different substances in their core.

For low frequency, L should be large, thus iron core choke coil is used. For high frequency AC circuit, L should be small, so air cored choke coil is used.

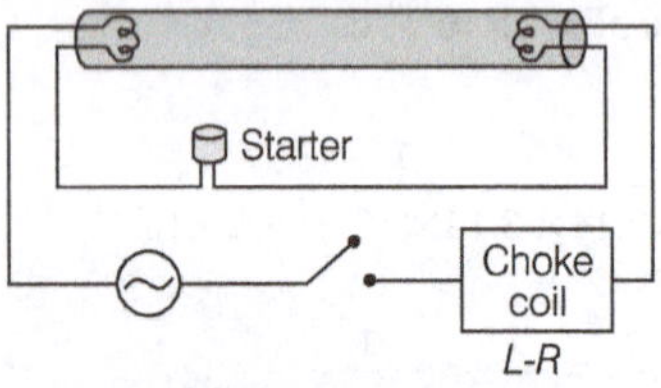

Application of choke coil in fluorescent tube

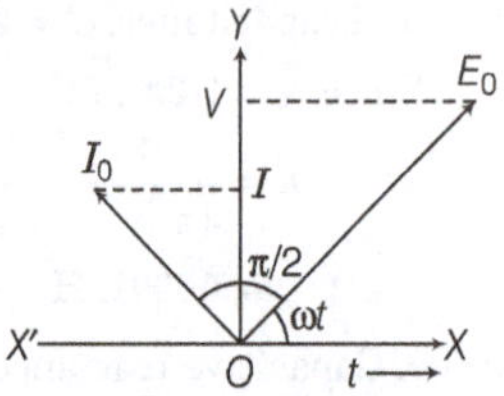

Phasor diagram

AC Generator

A generator produces electrical energy from mechanical work.

Principle

It works on the principle of electromagnetic induction. Whenever, the amount of magnetic flux linked with a coil changes, an emf is induced in the coil. It lasts so long as the change in magnetic flux through the coil continues. The direction of induced current is given by Fleming's right hand rule.

Construction

AC generator has following parts

(i) **Armature** $ABCD$ is a rectangular armature coil consisting of a large number of turns of insulated copper wire wound over a laminated soft iron coil.

(ii) **Field magnets** N and S are the pole pieces of a strong electromagnet in which the armature coil is rotated. Axis of rotation is perpendicular to the magnetic field lines.

(iii) **Slip rings** R_1 and R_2 are two hollow metallic rings which is connected by the two ends of armature coil. These rings rotate with the rotation of the coil.

(iv) **Brushes** B_1 and B_2 are two flexible metal plates. They are fixed and are kept in light contact with R_1 and R_2, respectively. It is used to pass on current from the armature coil to the external load resistance R.

(v) **Source of energy** The armature coil is rotated with the help of turbine or any other device connected to it. The rotational kinetic energy of the turbine is rotational kinetic energy of the turbine is converted into electrical energy by the AC generator.

Working

When a closed armature coil rotates in a uniform magnetic field with its axis perpendicular to the magnetic field, the magnetic flux linked with the loop changes and emf induces in the coil.

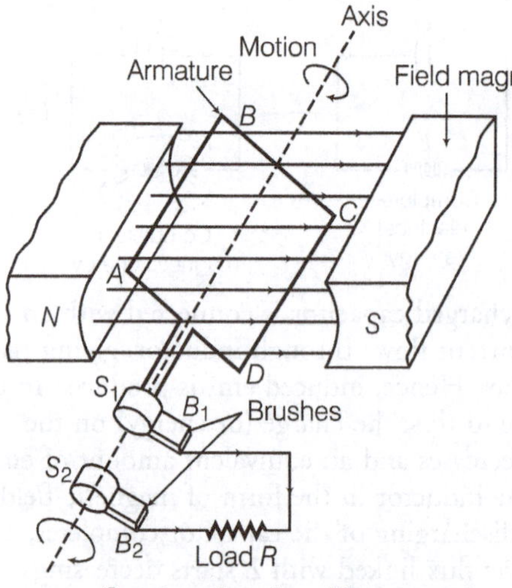

Construction of an AC generator

So, as per the working, the direction of flow of current in resistance R get changed alternatively after every half cycle.

Thus, AC is produced in coil.

If ε is the emf induced in the coil, then

$$\varepsilon = NBA\omega \sin \omega t = \varepsilon_0 \sin \omega t$$

where, N = number of turns in the coil,

B = strength of magnetic field,

A = area of each turn of the coil,

ω = angular velocity of rotation,

and $\varepsilon_0 = NBA\omega$ = peak value of emf

The variation of induced emf (ε) with time (t) is shown in the diagram, which is sinusoidal.

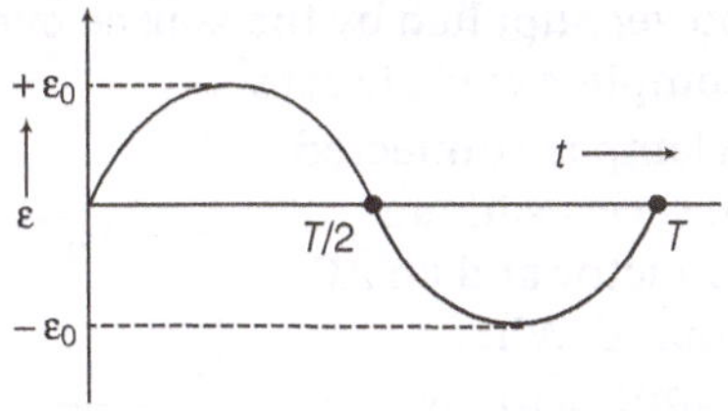

Variation of emf in AC generator

If resistance of the coil is R, then

Current, $i = \frac{\varepsilon_1}{R} = \frac{\varepsilon_0}{R} \sin \omega t$

$\Rightarrow \quad i = i_0 \sin \omega t$

where, $i_0 = \frac{NBA\omega}{R}$ = peak value of current.

The variation of current is also, sinusoidal as shown in figure.

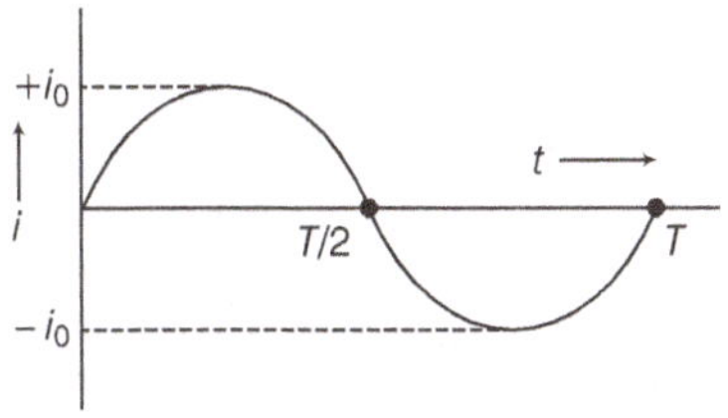

Variation of current in AC generator

Uses

(i) AC generators are used for efficient transmission of power over long distance and in larger amounts.
(ii) AC power can easily be stepped up or stepped down in voltage by using transformers.
(iii) AC can be reduced by using a choke coil without wasting energy.
(iv) AC can be easily converted into DC by using rectifier.
(v) AC machines require less maintenance.

Topic Practice 2

Multiple Choice Questions

1 Mark

1. In a circuit containing an inductance of zero resistance, the emf of the applied AC voltage leads the current by
(a) 90° (b) 45° (c) 30° (d) 0°

2. If the frequency is doubled, what happens to the capacitive reactance and the current?
(a) Capacitive reactance is halved, the current is doubled
(b) Capacitive reactance is doubled, the current is halved
(c) Capacitive reactance and the current are halved
(d) Capacitive reactance and the current are doubled

3. Which one of the following graph in figure represents variation of reactance X_C of a capacitor with frequency f of an AC supply?

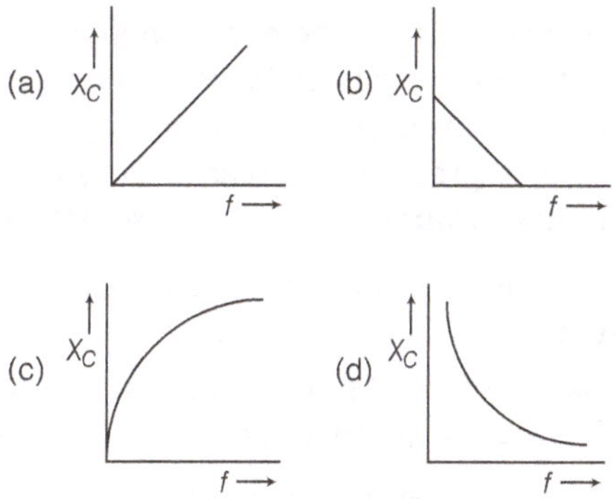

4. Which one of the following diagram, shows the equation $\tan \phi = \frac{X_C - X_L}{R}$ and $Z = \sqrt{R^2 + (X_C - X_L)^2}$?

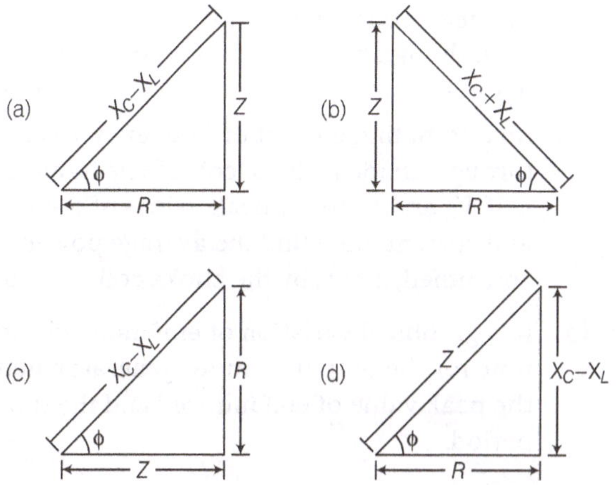

5. A value of ω for which the current amplitude is $1/\sqrt{2}$ times its maximum value. At this value, the power dissipated by the circuit becomes
(a) double (b) one-fourth
(c) one-third (d) half

Very Short Answer Type Questions

1 Mark

6. Alternating current flowing through a certain electrical device leads over the potential difference across it by 90°. State whether this device is a resistor, capacitor or an inductor. **ISC 2013**

7. Explain the statement that a capacitor is a conductor at very high frequencies. Compare this behaviour with that of a capacitor in a DC circuit after the steady state. **NCERT**

8. How does the sign of the phase angle ϕ, by which the supply voltage leads the current in an *L-C-R* series circuit, change as the supply frequency is gradually increased from very low to very high values. **NCERT Exemplar**

9. Define 'quality factor' of resonance in series *L-C-R* circuit. What is its SI unit?

10. What is the value of power factor in a series of *L-C-R* circuit at resonance? **ISC 2009**

11. What is the power factor of a series *L-C-R* circuit? **ISC 2008**

12. What is the value of power factor for a pure resistor connected to an alternating current source? **ISC 2019**

13. An ideal inductor does not consume any power even though both V and I are non-zero. Explain in brief. **ISC 2005, 01**

14. An alternating current of frequency f is flowing through an ideal choke coil of self-inductance L. If V_0 and I_0 be the peak values of the voltage and current, then find the average power consumed, if any, by the choke coil. **ISC 2009**

15. In a graphical variation of emf induced with time for the output of an AC generator, mark the peak value of emf induced and the time period. **ISC 2007**

Short Answer Type I Questions

2 Marks

16. Explain, why the reactance offered by an inductor increases with increasing frequency of an alternating voltage? **NCERT Exemplar**

17. (i) When an AC source is connected to an ideal inductor, show that the average power supplied by the source over a complete cycle is zero.
(ii) A lamp is connected in series with an inductor and an AC source. What happens to the brightness of the lamp when the key is plugged in and an iron rod is inserted inside the inductor? Explain.

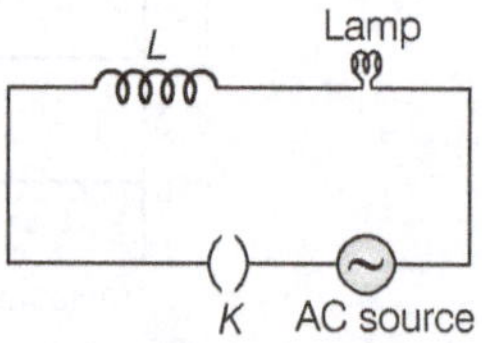

18. (i) The graphs (a) and (b) represent the variation of the opposition offered by the circuit element to the flow of alternating current with frequency of the applied emf. Identify the circuit elements corresponding to each graph.

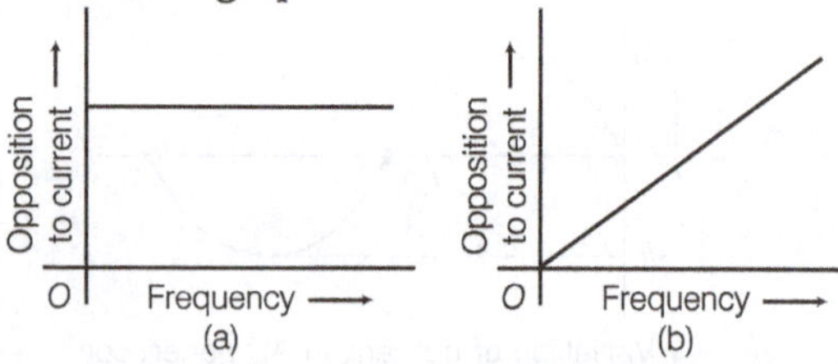

(a) (b)

(ii) Write the expression for the impedance offered by the series combination of the above two elements connected across the AC source. Which will be ahead in phase in this circuit, voltage or current?

19. In a series *L-C-R* circuit, obtain an expression for the resonant frequency. **ISC 2017**

20. (i) Draw a graph showing variation of amplitude of circuit current with changing frequency of applied voltage in a series *L-C-R* circuit for two different values of resistance R_1 and $R_2 (R_1 > R_2)$.
(ii) Define the term sharpness of resonance. Under what condition, does a circuit become more selective?

Short Answer Type II Questions

3 Marks

21. Obtain the relation for the current $I = I_0 \sin(\omega t - \pi/2)$ for a pure inductor across which an alternating emf $\varepsilon = \varepsilon_0 \sin \omega t$ is applied. **ISC 2007**

22. Plot a labelled graph showing variation in impedance Z of a series L-C-R circuit with frequency f of alternating emf applied to it. What is the minimum value of this impedance? **ISC 2010**

23. Obtain an expression for resonant frequency f_0 of a series L-C-R circuit. **ISC 2009**

24. An AC circuit with resistance R, inductance L and capacitance C are connected in series. The value of C is adjusted for resonance. State any three properties of this circuit which hold true for resonance only. (Give the properties in words or equations, relating X_L, X_C, Z, R, ϕ, power, etc.) **ISC 2006**

25. Answer the following questions.
   (i) What is the minimum value of the power factor of a circuit? Under what circumstances can it occur?
   (ii) State the maximum value of the power factor? Under what circumstances can this occur?

26. An AC voltage $V = V_m \sin \omega t$ is applied across an inductor of inductance L. Find the instantaneous power P_i supplied to the inductor. Show graphically the variation of P_i with ωt.

27. (i) Draw a schematic sketch of an AC generator describing its basic elements. State briefly its working principle. Show a plot of variation of
   (a) magnetic flux.
   (b) alternating emf *versus* time generated by a loop of wire rotating in a magnetic field.
   (ii) Why is choke coil needed in the use of fluorescent tubes with AC mains?

Long Answer Type Question

5 Marks

28. (i) Show that a series L-C-R circuit at resonance behaves as a purely resistive circuit. Compare the phase relation between current and voltage in series L-C-R circuit for
   (a) $X_L > X_C$
   (b) $X_L = X_C$ using phasor diagrams.
   (ii) What is an acceptor circuit and where it is used?

Numerical Problems

29. An AC generator generates an emf which is given by $e = 311 \sin(240\pi t$ V. Calculate **ISC 2023**
   (i) frequency of the emf
   (ii) rms value of the emf.

30. When an alternating emf $e = 310 \sin(100\pi t)$ V is applied to a series L-C-R circuit, current flowing through it is $i = 5 \sin(100\pi t + \pi/3)$ A.
   (i) What is the phase difference between the current and the emf?
   (ii) Calculate the average power consumed by the circuit. **ISC 2020**

31. A 60Ω resistor, a 1.0 H inductor and a 4μF capacitor are connected in series to an AC supply generating an emf $e = 300 \sin \quad t$ V. Calculate
   (i) impedance of the circuit
   (ii) peak value of the current flowing through the circuit
   (iii) phase difference between the current and the supply voltage. **ISC 2023**

32. (i) A 220 V, 50 Hz AC source is connected to a coil having coefficient of self-inductance of 1H and a resistance of 400Ω. Calculate
   (a) the reactance of the coil.
   (b) the impedance of the coil.
   (c) the current flowing through the coil.
   (ii) Draw a labelled graph showing variation of impedance (Z) of a series L-C-R circuit *versus* frequency (f) of the AC supply. Mark the resonant frequency as f_o. **ISC 2024**

33. (i) A 400Ω resistor, a 3H inductor and a 5 μF capacitor are connected in series to a 220V, 50 Hz AC source. Calculate the
   (a) impedance of the circuit.
   (b) current flowing through the circuit.
   (ii) Draw a labelled graph showing the variation of impedance (Z) of a series L-C-R circuit *versus* frequency (f) of the AC supply. **ISC 2020**

34. (i) An alternating emf of 200V, 50Hz is applied to an L-R circuit, having a resistance R of 10Ω and an inductance L of 0.05H connected in series. Calculate

(a) impedance.
(b) current flowing in the circuit.

(ii) Draw a labelled graph showing the variation of inductive reactance X_L *versus* frequency f. **ISC 2019**

35. An alternating voltage given by $E = 140 \sin 314t$ is connected across a pure resistor of 50 Ω. Find

(i) the frequency of the source.
(ii) the rms current through the resistor. **(2 M)**

36. When an alternating emf $e = 300 \sin(100\pi t + \pi/6)$ volt is applied to a circuit, the current I through it is $I = 5.0 \sin(100\pi t - \pi/6)$ ampere. Then, find the phase difference between the emf and current. **ISC 2009 (1 M)**

37. A 100 μF capacitor in series with a 40 Ω resistance is connected to a 110 V, 60 Hz supply.

(i) What is the maximum current in the circuit?
(ii) What is the time lag between the current maximum and the voltage maximum? **NCERT (3 M)**

38. A resistor of 400 Ω, an inductor of $5/\pi$ H and a capacitor of $\frac{50}{\pi}$ μF are connected in series across a source of alternating voltage of $140 \sin 100\pi t$ V. Find the voltage (rms) across the resistor, the inductor and the capacitor. Is the algebraic sum of these voltage more than the source voltage? If yes, resolve the paradox. **(5 M)**

39. An alternating emf of 110 V is applied to a circuit containing a resistance R of 80 Ω and an inductor L in series. The current is found to lag behind the supply voltage by an angle $\theta = \tan^{-1}(3/4)$. Then, find the

(i) inductive reactance.
(ii) impedance of the circuit.
(iii) current flowing in the circuit.
(iv) if the inductor has coefficient of self-inductance of 0.1 H, what is the frequency of the applied emf? **ISC 2014 (4 M)**

40. A current of 4 A flows in a coil when connected to a 12 V DC source. If the same coil is connected to a 12 V, 8 Hz AC source, a current 2.4 A flows in the coil. Calculate the coefficient of self-inductance L of the coil. **ISC 2005 (3 M)**

41. An alternating emf of 220 V is applied to a circuit containing a resistor R having resistance of 160 Ω and a capacitor C in series. The current is found to lead the supply voltage by an angle $\theta = \tan^{-1}(3/4)$.

(i) Calculate
(a) the capacitive reactance.
(b) impedance of the R-C circuit.
(c) current flowing in the circuit.

(ii) If the frequency of the applied emf is 50 Hz, what is the value of the capacitance of the capacitor C? **ISC 2018 (5 M)**

42. An alternating emf of frequency 50 Hz is applied to a circuit with a resistor of 20 Ω, an inductor of 100 mH and a capacitor of 30 μF connected in series.

(i) What is the angle by which the current leads or lags the applied emf?
(ii) Represent the voltage and the current in a vector diagram showing the phase angle. **ISC 2006 (3 M)**

43. (i) Figure below shows a series L-C-R circuit connected to an AC source which generates an alternating emf of frequency of 50 Hz. The reading of voltmeters V_1 and V_2 are 80 V and 60 V, respectively.

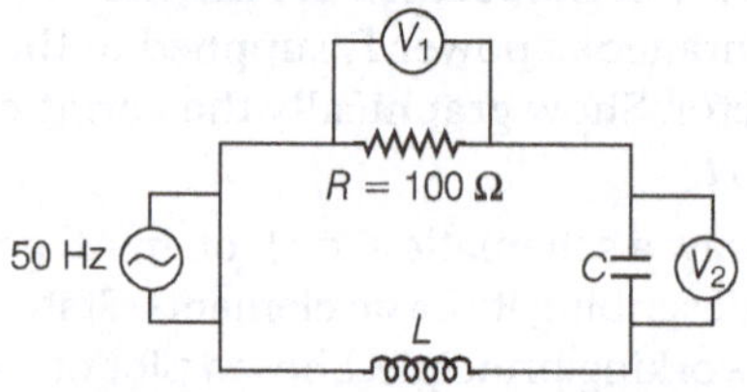

Find
(a) the current in the circuit.
(b) the capacitance C of the capacitor.

(ii) At resonance, what is the relation between impedance of a series L-C-R circuit and its resistance R? **ISC 2013 (4 M)**

44. A 50 μF capacitor, a 30 Ω resistor and a 0.7 H inductor are connected in series to an AC supply which generate an emf e given by $e = 300 \sin(200t)$ V. Calculate peak value of the current flowing through the circuit. **ISC 2012 (4 M)**

45. A 30 μF capacitor, 0.2 H inductor and a 50 Ω resistor are connected in series to an AC source whose emf is given by $E = 310 \sin(314t)$, where E is in volt and t is in second. Calculate

(i) the impedance of the circuit.
(ii) peak value of current in the circuit. **ISC 2008 (4 M)**

46. (i) A coil having self-inductance of 0.7 H and resistance of 165Ω is connected to an AC source of 275 V, 50 Hz. If $\pi = \frac{22}{7}$, then calculate

(a) reactance of the coil.

(b) impedance of the coil.

(c) current flowing through the coil.

(ii) Draw a labelled graph showing variation of impedance of a series *L*-*C*-*R* circuit with frequency of the AC supply. **ISC 2016 (5 M)**

47. (i) Find the value of the phase difference between the current and the voltage in the series *L*-*C*-*R* circuit shown below. Which one leads in phase, current or voltage?

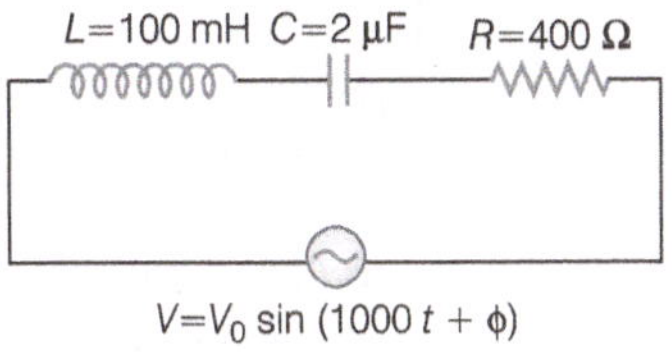

(ii) Without making any other change, find the value of the additional capacitor C', to be connected in parallel with the capacitor C, in order to make the power factor of the circuit unity. **(3 M)**

48. Resonance frequency of a circuit is ν. If the capacitance is made 4 times the initial value, find the change in the resonance frequency. **(1 M)**

49. The figure shows a series *L*-*C*-*R* circuit with $L = 10.0$ H, $C = 40\ \mu$F, $R = 60\ \Omega$ connected to variable frequency 240 V source. Calculate

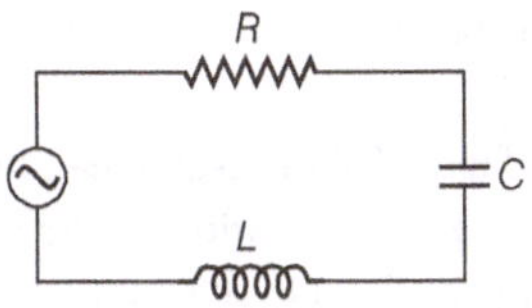

(i) the angular frequency of the source which drives the circuit at resonance.

(ii) the current at the resonating frequency.

(iii) the rms potential drop across the inductor at resonance. **(3 M)**

50. Calculate the quality factor of a series *L*-*C*-*R* circuit with $L = 2.0$ H, $C = 2\ \mu$F and $R = 10\ \Omega$. **(1 M)**

51. Obtain the resonant frequency (ω_r) of a series *L*-*C*-*R* circuit with $L = 2.0$ H, $C = 32\mu$F and $R = 10\ \Omega$. What is the *Q*-value of this circuit? **NCERT (2 M)**

52. An inductor of 200 mH, capacitor of 400 μF and a resistor of 10 Ω are connected in series to AC source of 50V of variable frequency. Calculate

(i) the angular frequency at which maximum power dissipation occurs on the circuit and the corresponding value of effective current.

(ii) the value of *Q*-factor on the circuit. **(3 M)**

53. When emf $e = 300 \sin (100\pi t + \pi/6)$ V is applied to a circuit, the current I through it is $I = 5.0 \sin (100\pi t - \pi/6)$ A. Then, find the average power consumed by the circuit. **ISC 2009 (2 M)**

54. A resistance of 150 Ω and a capacitance of 15 μF are connected in series with an AC source of 220 V. The peak value of the current is 0.20 A. Calculate the average power consumed in the circuit. If the capacitor is removed but the current is kept the same, what is the average power consumed in the resistor alone? **ISC 2007 (3 M)**

55. (i) Figure below shows a capacitor C, an inductor L and a resistor R connected in series to an AC supply of 220 V.

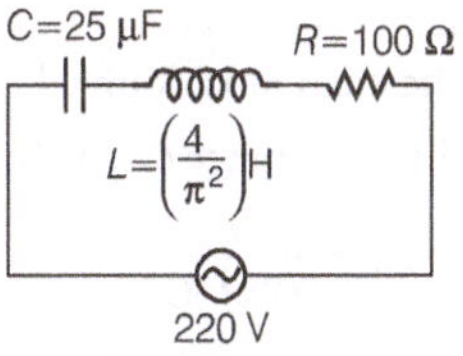

Calculate

(a) the resonant frequency of the given *L*-*C*-*R* circuit.

(b) current flowing through the circuit.

(c) average power consumed by the circuit.

(ii) In a series *L*-*C*-*R* circuit, what is the phase difference between V_L and V_C, where V_L is the potential difference across the inductor and V_C is the potential difference across the capacitor? **ISC 2015 (5 M)**

56. A series *L*-*C*-*R* circuit connected to a variable frequency 230 V source has $L = 5.0$ H, $C = 80\ \mu$F, $R = 40\ \Omega$, as shown in the figure.

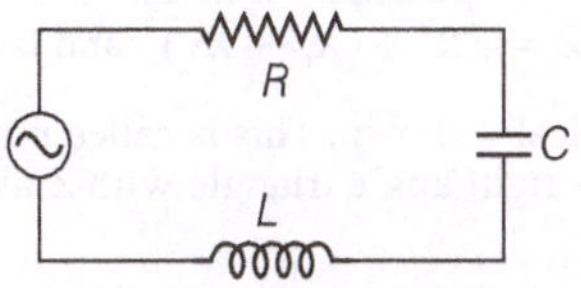

(i) Determine the source frequency which drives the circuit in resonance.

(ii) Obtain the impedance of the circuit and amplitude of current at the resonant frequency.

(iii) Determine the rms potential drop across the three elements of the circuit. Show that the potential drop across the L-C combination is zero at the resonating frequency. **NCERT (3M)**

57. An AC generator generating an emf of $\varepsilon = 300 \sin(100\pi t)$ is connected to a series combination of 16μ capacitor, 1H inductor and $100\,\Omega$ resistor. Calculate

(i) impedance of the circuit at the given frequency.

(ii) resonant frequency f_0.

(iii) power factor at resonant frequency f_0.

ISC 2018 (5 M)

Hints & Solutions

1. (*a*) In a pure inductor (zero resistance), voltage leads the current by 90°, i.e. $\pi/2$.

i.e. $V = V_m \sin\omega t$ and $i = i_m \sin\left(\omega t - \frac{\pi}{2}\right)$

2. (*a*) If the frequency is doubled, the capacitive reactance is halved and the current is doubled.

3. (*d*) We know that, reactance (X_C) of a capacitor is given by $X_C = \frac{1}{\omega C} \Rightarrow X_C = \frac{1}{(2\pi f)C}$

where, C is capacitance and f is frequency.

So, $X_C \propto \frac{1}{f}$ [$\because$ C is constant]

The graph will be rectangular hyperbola as shown below.

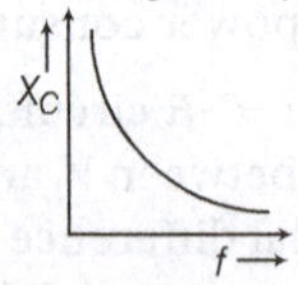

4. (*d*)

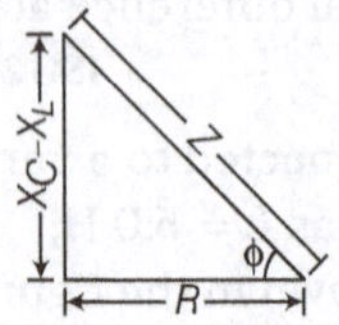

Equation $Z = \sqrt{R^2 + (X_C - X_L)^2}$ and $\tan\phi = \frac{X_C - X_L}{R}$ are graphically shown. This is called impedance diagram which is a right angle triangle with Z as its hypotenuse.

5. (*d*) The amplitude of the current in the series L-C-R circuit is given by

$$i_m = \frac{V_m}{\sqrt{R^2 + \left(\omega L - \frac{1}{\omega C}\right)^2}}$$

and is maximum when $\omega = \omega_0 = 1/\sqrt{LC}$. The maximum value is $i_m^{max} = V_m/R$.

For values of ω other than ω_0, the amplitude of the current is less than the maximum value. Suppose, we choose a value of ω for which the current amplitude is $1/\sqrt{2}$ times its maximum value. At this value, the power dissipated by the circuit become half.

6. As, the current is leading over voltage, hence the device must be capacitor.

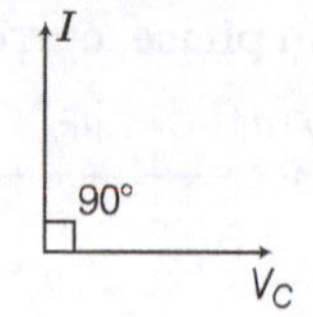

7. By comparison, at very high frequency, the resistance due to capacitor is negligible and hence it works like a pure conductor of negligible capacitive reactance.

In DC circuits, $\omega = 0$ (at steady state)

$\Rightarrow \quad X_C = \frac{1}{\omega C} = \infty$

So, it behaves like an open circuit.

8. The phase angle (ϕ) by which voltage leads the current in L-C-R series circuit is given by

$$\tan\phi = \frac{X_L - X_C}{R} = \frac{2\pi\nu L - \frac{1}{2\pi\nu C}}{R}$$

If $\tan\phi < 0$ (for $\nu < \nu_0$), then circuit is capacitive.

If $\tan\phi > 0$ (for $\nu > \nu_0$), then circuit is inductive.

At resonance, $\tan\phi = 0$ $\left[\text{for } \nu = \nu_0 = \frac{1}{2\pi\sqrt{LC}}\right]$

9. The quality factor (Q) of resonance in series L-C-R circuit is defined as the ratio of voltage drop across inductor (or capacitor) to the applied voltage, **(1/2)**

i.e. $Q = \frac{V_L \text{ or } V_C}{V_R} = \frac{\omega_0 L}{R} = \frac{1}{\omega_0 CR}$

It is an indicator of sharpness of the resonance. Quality factor has no unit. **(1/2)**

10. For a L-C-R series circuit, its defined as cosine of the angle of lag or lead or resistance/impedance.

i.e. power factor, $\cos\phi = \frac{R}{Z} = \frac{R}{\sqrt{(X_C - X_L)^2 + R^2}}$

where, Z = impedance $= \sqrt{(X_C - X_L)^2 + R^2}$

At resonance, $X_C = X_L \Rightarrow \cos\phi = 1$

11. If ϕ is the angle of lag or lead of emf or current in a series L-C-R circuit, then cos ϕ component in the equation of power average is called power factor.

$$\cos\phi = \frac{R}{Z} = \frac{R}{\sqrt{\left(\omega L - \frac{1}{\omega L}\right)^2 + R^2}}$$

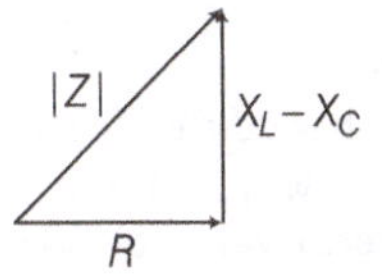

12. For pure resistance, phase difference between alternating current and alternating voltage, $\phi = 0°$.
$\therefore$ Power factor $= \cos\phi = \cos 0° = 1$

13. We know that, power consumed,
$$P_{av} = V_{rms}\, I_{rms} \cos\phi$$
For an ideal inductor, $\phi = 90°$
(i.e. phase difference between V and I is $\frac{\pi}{2}$)
$\Rightarrow \quad \cos\phi = 0$
Power consumed, $P = (V_{rms})(I_{rms})(0) = 0$

14. We know that, average power consumed,
$$P_{av} = I_{rms} V_{rms} \cos\phi$$
For ideal choke coil, phase difference between current (I) and voltage (V) is $\frac{\pi}{2}$.
i.e. $\quad \phi = 90°$
$\Rightarrow \quad \cos\phi = 0$
$$P_{av} = V_{rms} I_{rms} \cos 90° = (V_{rms} I_{rms})(0) = 0$$
Hence, no power consumed by an ideal choke coil.

15. The graphical variation of emf induced with time for the output of an AC generator is shown as below.

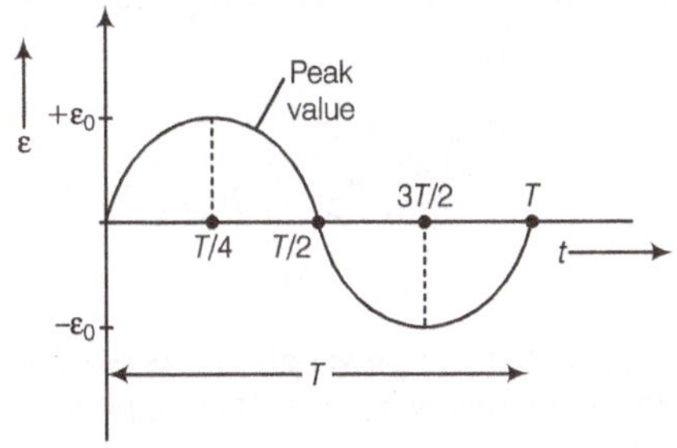

16. Refer to text on pages 279 (Inductive reactance).

17. (i) As $P_{av} = V_{rms} I_{rms} \cos\phi$
In ideal inductor, current I_{rms} lags behind applied voltage V_{rms} by $\pi/2$.
$\therefore \ \phi = \pi/2$
Thus, $P_{av} = V_{rms} I_{rms} \cos\pi/2$
$= V_{rms} I_{rms} \times 0 = 0$ **(1)**

(ii) Brightness of the lamp decreases. It is because when iron rod is inserted inside the inductor, its inductance L increases, thereby increasing its inductive reactance X_L and hence impedance Z of the circuit. As $I_{rms} = \frac{V_{rms}}{Z}$, so this decreases the current I_{rms} in the circuit and hence the brightness of lamp. **(1)**

18. (i) From graph (a), it is clear that resistance (opposition to current) is not changing with frequency, i.e. resistance does not depend on frequency of applied voltage, so the circuit element here is pure resistive (R).
From graph (b), it is clear that resistance increases linearly with frequency, so the circuit element here is inductive in nature.
Inductive resistance, $X_L = 2\pi\nu L \Rightarrow X_L \propto \nu$ **(1)**

(ii) Impedance offered by the series combination of resistance (R) and inductor (L).
$$Z = \sqrt{R^2 + X_L^2} = \sqrt{R^2 + (2\pi\nu L)^2}$$
In L-R circuit, the applied voltage leads the current by phase ϕ, where $\tan\phi = \frac{X_L}{R}$ **(1)**

19. Refer to the text on page 284 (Resonance).

20. (i) Graph showing the variation of amplitude of circuit current with changing frequency is given below.

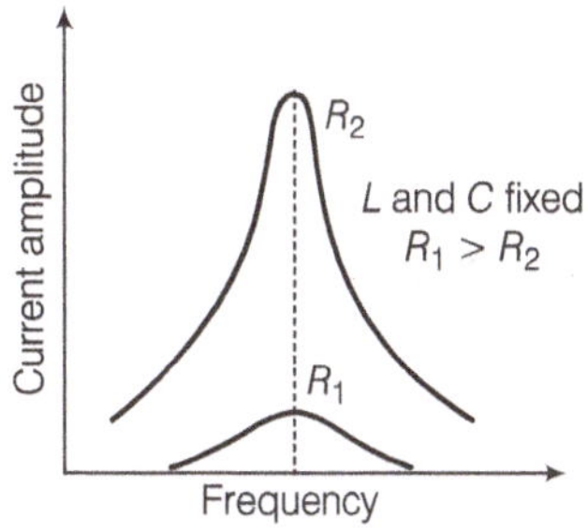

(1)

(ii) **Sharpness of resonance** Refer to the text on page 284 (Resonance).
Circuit become more selective if the resonance is more sharp, maximum current is more, the circuit is close to resonance for smaller range of $(2\Delta\omega)$ of frequencies. Thus, the tuning of the circuit will be good. **(1)**

21. Consider the circuit containing inductor.

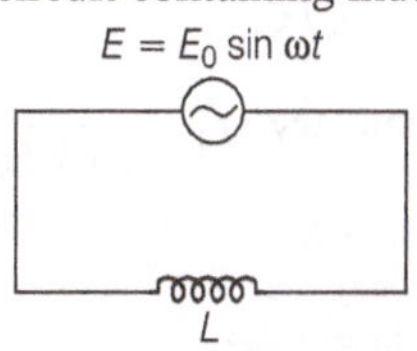

Let the emf $E = E_0 \sin\omega t$ is applied across a pure inductor L.
Since, there is no resistance in the circuit, the net instantaneous emf is zero. **(1)**
Applying KVL across the circuit, we have

$$E_0 \sin \omega t - L\frac{dI}{dt} = 0$$

or $$dI = \frac{E_0}{L} \sin \omega t \, dt$$

Integrating, we have

$$\int dI = \frac{E_0}{L} \int \sin \omega t \, dt$$

$$I = \frac{E_0}{L}\left(\frac{-\cos \omega t}{\omega}\right) = \frac{E_0}{\omega L} \sin\left(\omega t - \frac{\pi}{2}\right)$$

$$\left[\because -\cos \omega t = \sin\left(\omega t - \frac{\pi}{2}\right)\right]$$

or $$I = I_0 \sin\left(\omega t - \frac{\pi}{2}\right)$$

where, $I_0 = \frac{E_0}{\omega L}$ is the maximum value of the current or peak current. **(2)**

22. At $f = f_0$, $Z = R$. This is the minimum value of impedance.

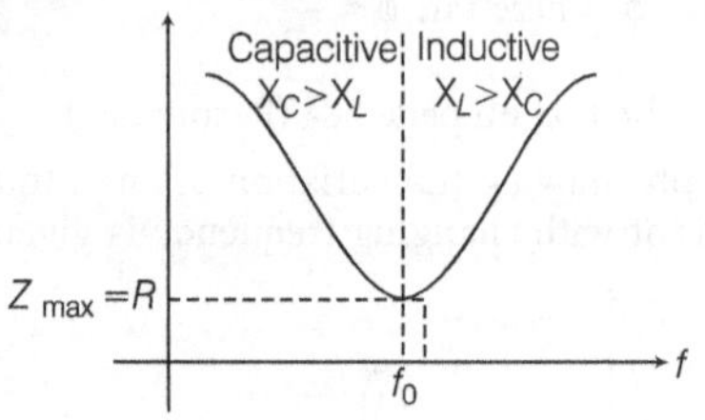

(3)

23. For a series L-C-R circuit at resonance $X_C = X_L$, i.e. reactance of capacitor and inductor must be equal.

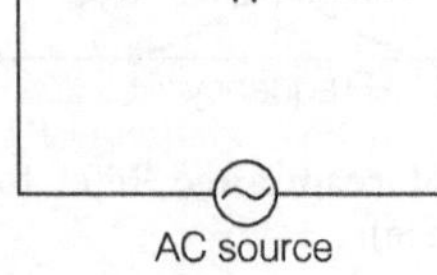

(1)

Now, according to question,

$$\omega_0 L = \frac{1}{\omega_0 C} \Rightarrow \omega_0^2 = \frac{1}{LC}$$

$$\Rightarrow \quad \omega_0 = \frac{1}{\sqrt{LC}} \Rightarrow 2\pi f_0 = \frac{1}{\sqrt{LC}}$$ **(1)**

$\therefore$ Resonant frequency, $$f_0 = \frac{1}{2\pi}\sqrt{\frac{1}{LC}}$$ **(1)**

24. At resonance, $X_L = X_C$

$$\Rightarrow \quad \omega = \frac{1}{\sqrt{LC}}$$

So, the circuit has following characteristics at resonance.

(i) Current in the circuit is maximum ε_0/R or circuit impedance is minimum and purely resistive. **(1)**

(ii) There is no phase difference between current and the applied voltage. **(1)**

(iii) Power utilisation by the circuit is maximum, i.e. $\frac{\varepsilon_{rms}^2}{R}$. **(1)**

25. (i) Power factor = $|\cos \phi|$

Minimum value of power factor is zero (0)

i.e. $\cos \phi = 0$

$\phi = 90°$

[when phase difference between V and I is 90°]

The AC circuit which is free from ohmic resistor has minimum (zero) value of power factor. i.e. power factor is zero for purely inductive circuit and purely capacitive circuit respectively.

(ii) Maximum value of power factor $|\cos \phi| = 1$

i.e. $\phi = 0$

For purely resistive circuit, power factor is maximum (1).

Series L-C-R circuit has also maximum value of power factor only at resonance condition.

26. In an inductor, the current lags the voltage by 90°. If the source voltage is sinusoidal, then the current is also sinusoidal, but shifted in phase. The instantaneous power defined as the product of the instantaneous voltage and current can also be seen to be sinusoidal in time. However, in contrast to the resistive load, the instantaneous power in the inductor goes negative for part of the cycle of the source driving it. **(1)**

As, $V(t) = V_m \sin \omega t$

$\therefore$ $I(t) = -I_m \cos \omega t$

Instantaneous power, $P_i = V(t) \cdot I(t)$

$$= V_m \sin \omega t \times (-I_m \cos \omega t)$$

$$= -\frac{V_m I_m}{2} \times 2 \sin \omega t \cos \omega t$$

$$= -\frac{V_m I_m}{2} [\sin 2\omega t + \sin 0]$$

$$= -\frac{V_m I_m}{2} \sin 2\omega t$$ **(1)**

The variation of P_i with ωt is as given in the figure.

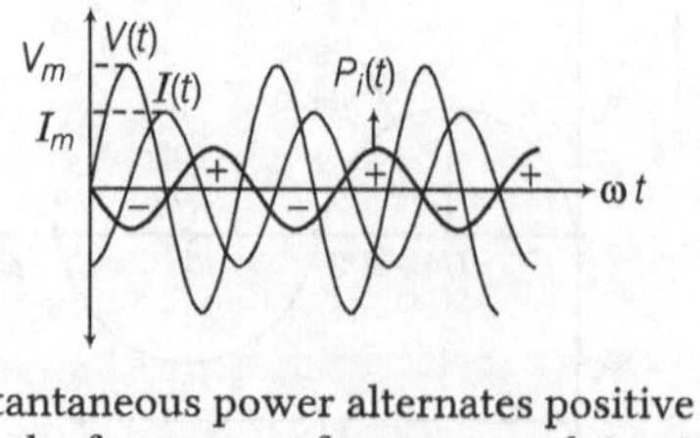

The instantaneous power alternates positive and negative at twice the frequency of source supplying it. **(1)**

27. (i) Refer to text on pages 288 and 289 (AC generator). **(1)**

(a) Variation of magnetic flux with time

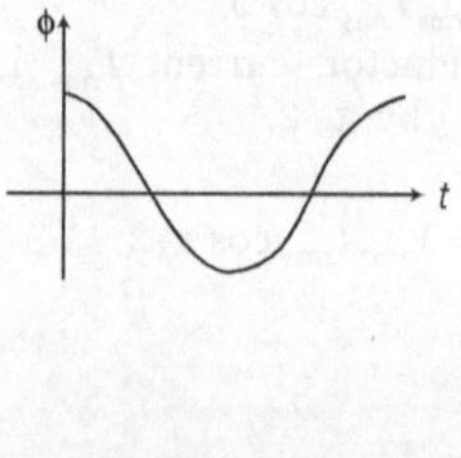

$$\phi = BNA \cos \omega t \quad \textbf{(1/2)}$$

(b) Variation of alternating emf with time

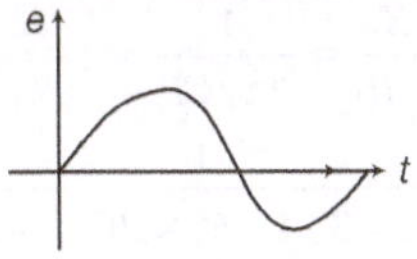

$$e = BNA\,\omega \sin \omega t \quad \textbf{(1/2)}$$

(ii) The choke coil is used to reduce the current. Therefore, it is required in the use of fluorescent tubes with AC mains. **(1)**

28. (i) Refer to text on pages 282 and 283 (AC through *L-C-R* circuit).

(ii) Acceptor circuit is series *L-C-R* circuit.

29. $E = 311 \sin (240\pi t)$ V

(i) $\omega t = 240\pi t$

$2\pi f = 240\pi$

$f = (240/2) = 120$ Hz

(ii) $E_{rms} = 0.707 \times 311 = 219.87$ V

30. Given, $e = 310 \sin(100\pi t)$ V ...(i)

and $I = 5 \sin\left(100\pi t + \frac{\pi}{3}\right)$ A ...(ii)

(i) Comparing Eqs. (i) and (ii) with standard equation, the phase difference between emf (e) and current (I) is

$$\Delta\phi = \phi_1 - \phi_2 = 0 - \frac{\pi}{3} = -\frac{\pi}{3} = 60^\circ$$

(ii) We know that, average power consumed,

$$P_{av} = E_{rms} I_{rms} \cos\theta$$

$$= \frac{E_0}{\sqrt{2}} \times \frac{I_0}{\sqrt{2}} \times \cos\phi$$

E_0 = peak emf = 310 V

I_0 = peak current = 5 A

$\cos\phi$ = power factor = $\cos 60^\circ = \frac{1}{2}$

$$\therefore \quad P_{av} = \frac{310}{\sqrt{2}} \times \frac{5}{\sqrt{2}} \times \frac{1}{2} = \frac{1550}{4} = 387.5 \text{ W}$$

31. (i) $E = 300 \sin (500t)$ V

Total reactance of the circuit is combination of capacitive and inductive reactance.

$$(X_C - X_L) = \left|\frac{1}{\omega C} - \omega L\right|$$

$$= \left|\frac{1}{500 \times 4 \times 10^{-6}} - 500 \times 1\right|$$

$$= \left|\frac{10^6}{2 \times 10^3} - 500\right| = \left|\frac{10 \times 10^{5-3}}{2} - 500\right|$$

$$= \left|5 \times 10^2 - 500\right|$$

$$\therefore \quad (X_C - X_L) = 0$$

$$Z = \sqrt{R^2 + (X_C - X_L)^2} = \sqrt{(60)^2 + 0}$$

$$= \sqrt{3600} = 60\,\Omega$$

(ii) $I_V = \frac{E_V}{Z} = \frac{300\sqrt{2}}{60} = 5\sqrt{2}$ A

(iii) $\tan\phi = \frac{(X_C - X_L)}{R} = \frac{0}{60} = 0^\circ$

32. (i) (a) Reactance, $X_L = \omega L$

$= 2\pi f L$

$= 2\pi \times 50 \times 1$

$= 314\,\Omega$

(b) Impedance, $Z = \sqrt{X_L^2 + R^2}$

$= \sqrt{(314)^2 \times (400)^2}$

$= 508.52\,\Omega$

(c) Current, $I = \frac{V_{rms}}{Z} + \frac{220}{508.52} = 0.433$ A

(ii)

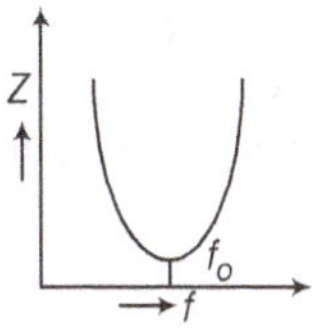

33. (i) It, circuit is a *L-C-R* circuit.

Hence, data given capacitance,

$C = 5\mu F = 5 \times 10^{-6}$ F

Resistance, $R = 400\Omega$

Inductance, $L = 3$HH

V_{rms} value of voltage, $E_V = 220$ V

Frequency, $\nu = 50$ Hz

(a) Since, capacitive reactance,

$$X_C = \frac{1}{\omega C} = \frac{1}{2\pi\nu C}$$

$$= \frac{1}{2 \times 3.14 \times 50 \times 5 \times 10^{-6}}$$

$$X_C = 636.9\,\Omega$$

and inductive reactance

$$X_L = \omega L = 2\pi\nu L$$

$$= 2 \times 3.14 \times 50 \times 3$$

$$= 942\,\Omega$$

$\because$ Impedance, $Z = \sqrt{R^2 + (X_L - X_C)^2}$

$= \sqrt{(400)^2 + (942 - 636.9)^2}$

$= \sqrt{(400)^2 + (305.1)^2} = 503.1\,\Omega$

(b) Current flowing through the circuit, $I = \frac{E}{Z}$

$$= \frac{220}{503.1} = 0.437 \text{ A}$$

(ii)

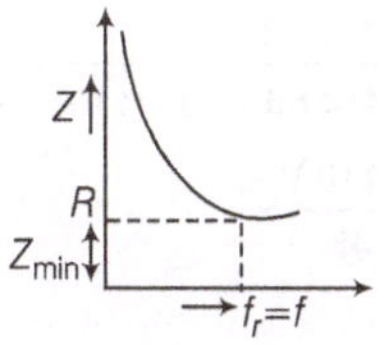

34. (i) Given, $V_{rms} = 200$ V, $L = 0.05$ H, $R = 10\Omega$, $f = 50$ Hz

Angular frequency, $\omega = 2\pi f$

$= 2\pi \times 50$

$= 100\pi$ rad/s

Inductive reactance, $X_L = \omega L$

$= 100\pi \times 0.05$

$= 5\pi\,\Omega$

(a) Impedance, $Z = \sqrt{R^2 + X_L^2}$

$= \sqrt{(10)^2 + (5\pi)^2}$

$= \sqrt{100 + 25\pi^2} = \sqrt{346.74}$

$= 18.614\ \Omega$

(b) Current flowing in the circuit,

$$I = \frac{V_{rms}}{Z} = \frac{200}{18.614}$$

$= 10.744$ A

(ii) Graph showing the radiation of inductive reactance X_L *versus* frequency f.

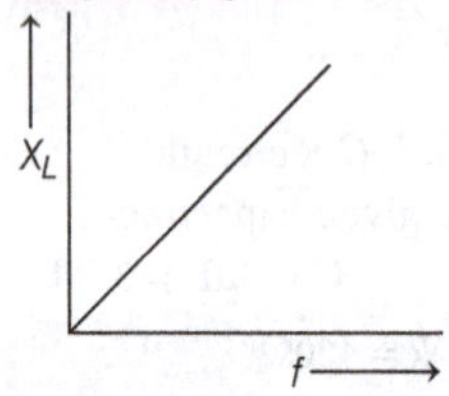

35. (i) As given, $E = 140 \sin 314t$

On comparing with $E = E_0 \sin \omega t$, we have

$\omega = 314$, $E_0 = 140$ V

$\because \quad \omega = 2\pi\nu \Rightarrow \nu = \frac{\omega}{2\pi} = \frac{314}{2 \times 3.14} = 50$ Hz **(1)**

(ii) $E_0 = 140$ V

$$E_{rms} = \frac{E_0}{\sqrt{2}} = \frac{140}{\sqrt{2}} = 99.29 \text{ V}$$

$$\therefore I_{rms} = \frac{E_{rms}}{R} = \frac{99.29}{50} = 1.98 \text{ A}$$ **(1)**

36. Given, $e = 300 \sin(100\pi t + \pi/6)$ V ...(i)

and $I = 5 \sin(100\pi t - \pi/6)$ A ...(ii)

Comparing Eqs. (i) and (ii) with standard equation, the phase difference between emf (e) and current (I) is

$$\Delta\phi = \phi_1 - \phi_2 = \frac{\pi}{6} - \left(-\frac{\pi}{6}\right) = \frac{\pi}{3} \text{ rad} = 60°$$

37. (i) Impedance, $Z = \sqrt{R^2 + X_C^2}$

$$= \sqrt{R^2 + \left(\frac{1}{2\pi\nu C}\right)^2}$$

$$= \sqrt{(40)^2 + \left(\frac{1}{2 \times 3.14 \times 60 \times 100 \times 10^{-6}}\right)^2} = 48\Omega$$

As, $I_V = \frac{E_V}{Z} \Rightarrow I_V = \frac{110 \text{ V}}{48\,\Omega}$

and $I_0 = \sqrt{2}\, I_V = 1.414 \times \frac{110}{48} = 3.24$ A **(1½)**

(ii) As, $\tan\phi = \frac{X_C}{R} = \frac{1}{2\pi\nu CR}$

$$= \frac{1}{2 \times 3.14 \times 60 \times 10^{-4} \times 40} = 0.6628$$

$\Rightarrow \quad \phi = \tan^{-1}(0.6628) = 33.5° = \frac{33.5\pi}{180}$ rad

$\therefore$ Time lag, $t = \frac{\phi}{\omega} = \frac{33.5\pi}{180} \times \frac{1}{2\pi \times 60}$

$= 1.55 \times 10^{-3}$ s **(1½)**

38. Given, applied voltage, $V = 140 \sin 100\pi t$ V

$C = \frac{50}{\pi}\mu\text{F} = \frac{50}{\pi} \times 10^{-6}$ F,

$L = \frac{5}{\pi}$ H, $R = 400\ \Omega$

Comparing with $V = V_0 \sin \omega t$, we get

$V_0 = 140$ V and $\omega = 100\pi$

Inductive reactance, $X_L = \omega L$

$= 100\pi \times \frac{5}{\pi} = 500\ \Omega$

Capacitive reactance, $X_C = \frac{1}{\omega C} = \frac{1}{100\pi \times \frac{50}{\pi} \times 10^{-6}}$

$= 200\ \Omega$

Impedance of the circuit, $Z = \sqrt{R^2 + (X_L - X_C)^2}$

$= \sqrt{(400)^2 + (500 - 200)^2}$

$= \sqrt{1600 + 900}$

$= 500\ \Omega$ **(2)**

Maximum current in the circuit, $I_0 = \frac{V_0}{Z} = \frac{140}{500}$

$$I_{rms} = \frac{I_0}{\sqrt{2}} = \frac{140}{500 \times \sqrt{2}} = 0.2 \text{ A}$$

V_{rms} across resistor, $V_R = I_{rms} R$

$= 0.2 \times 400 = 80$ V **(1)**

V_{rms} across inductor, $V_L = I_{rms} X_L$

$= 0.2 \times 500 = 100$ V **(1)**

V_{rms} across capacitor, $V_C = I_{rms} X_C$

$= 0.2 \times 200 = 40$ V

Now, $V \neq V_R + V_L + V_C$

Because V_C, V_L and V_R are not in same phase, instead

$V = \sqrt{V_R^2 + (V_L - V_C)^2}$

$= \sqrt{80^2 + (100 - 40)^2}$

$= 100$ V

Which is same as that of applied rms voltage. **(1)**

39. We have to apply formula to

$$\tan \phi = \frac{X_L}{R}.$$

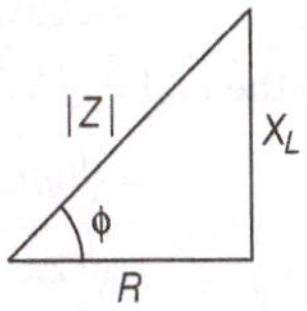

Net impedance can be calculated by

$$Z = \sqrt{X_L^2 + R^2}$$

(i) We can write

$$\tan \phi = \frac{X_L}{R} = \frac{3}{4} \quad \text{[given in the question]}$$

$$\Rightarrow \quad \frac{X_L}{R} = \frac{3}{4}$$

$$\therefore \quad R = 80\Omega \Rightarrow X_L = \frac{3}{4} \times R = \frac{3}{4} \times 80\ \Omega = 60\ \Omega$$ **(1)**

(ii) Impedance, $Z = \sqrt{X_L^2 + R^2} = \sqrt{(60)^2 + (80)^2} = 100\ \Omega$ **(1)**

(iii) Current, $I_{rms} = \frac{V_{rms}}{Z} = \frac{110}{100} = 1.1\ A$ **(1)**

(iv) We know that,

$$X_L = \omega L$$

$$\Rightarrow \quad 60 = (0.1) \times \omega \quad [\because L = 0.1\ H]$$

$$\Rightarrow \quad \omega = 600\ rad/s$$

$$\Rightarrow \quad 2\pi f = 600\ rad/s$$

$$\Rightarrow \quad f = 95.5\ Hz = 96\ Hz$$ **(1)**

40. For DC source, the inductor will act as short circuit and only resistor has to be taken for calculation of current. Now for DC source connected to the circuit,

$$X_L = \omega L = 0 \quad [\because \omega = 0]$$

So, resistance, $R = \frac{E}{I} = \frac{12\ V}{4\ A} = 3\ \Omega$ **(1)**

When the coil is connected to AC source, then

$$i = \frac{E}{\sqrt{R^2 + (\omega L)^2}} \quad [\because Z = \sqrt{R^2 + (\omega L)^2}]$$

$$2.4 = \frac{12}{\sqrt{3^2 + (2\pi f L)^2}}$$

$$\Rightarrow \quad 9 + (2\pi f L)^2 = \left(\frac{12}{2.4}\right)^2 = 25$$

$$(2\pi f L)^2 = 25 - 9 = 16 \Rightarrow 2\pi f L = 4$$

$$\Rightarrow \quad L = \frac{1}{2\pi f} \times 4 = \frac{1}{2\pi \times 8} \times 4 \quad [\because f = 8 Hz]$$

$$\therefore \quad L = \frac{1}{4\pi} H = 0.0795\ H$$ **(2)**

41. We have, $\tan\theta = \frac{X_C}{R}$

$$\because \quad \theta = \tan^{-1}\left(\frac{3}{4}\right) \Rightarrow \tan\theta = \frac{3}{4}$$

$$\therefore \quad \frac{3}{4} = \frac{X_C}{160}$$ **(1)**

(i) (a) Capacitive reactance, $X_C = 160 \times \frac{3}{4} = 120\ \Omega$

(b) Impedance of the *R-C* circuit,

$$Z = \sqrt{R^2 + (X_C)^2} = \sqrt{(160)^2 + (120)^2}$$

$$= \sqrt{40000} = 200\ \Omega$$

(c) We have, $Z = \frac{V}{i}$

Current flowing in the circuit, $i = \frac{V}{Z} = \frac{220}{200} = 1.1\ A$ **(2)**

(ii) $\therefore \quad X_C = \frac{1}{2\pi f C} \Rightarrow 120 = \frac{1}{2\pi \times 50 \times C}$

$$\Rightarrow \quad C = \frac{1}{2\pi \times 50 \times 120}$$

$\therefore$ Capacitance, $C = 2.65 \times 10^{-5}$ F **(2)**

42. According to the question,

Given, $f = 50$ Hz, $R = 20\ \Omega$, $L = 100$ mH $= 100 \times 10^{-3}$ H

$C = 30\ \mu F = 30 \times 10^{-6}$ F

(i) $X_L = 2\pi f L = 2 \times 3.14 \times 50 \times 100 \times 10^{-3} = 31.4\ \Omega$

$$\therefore X_C = \frac{1}{2\pi f C} = \frac{1}{2 \times 3.14 \times 50 \times 30 \times 10^{-6}} = 106.16\ \Omega$$

As we know that, $\tan \phi = \frac{X_C - X_L}{R}$

[where, ϕ = phase difference between current and voltage]

$$= \frac{106.16 - 31.4}{20} = 3.73$$

$$\Rightarrow \quad \phi = 75°$$ **(2)**

(ii) As $X_C > X_L \Rightarrow V_C > V_L$

Hence, current leads the voltage by angle $\phi = 75°$ as shown.

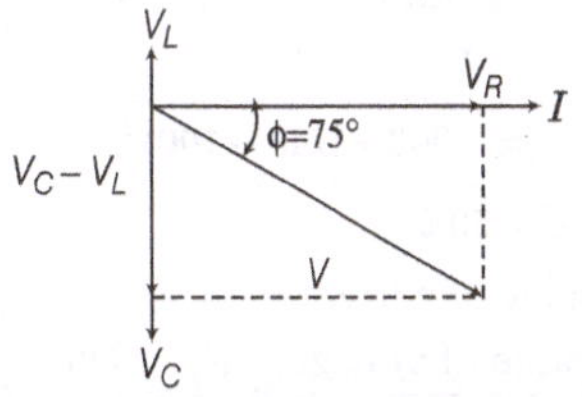

(1)

43. (i) Apply $I = V / R$ to obtain current through the resistor. At resonance, impedance of capacitor and inductor can be equated and cancelled.

Now, according to the question,

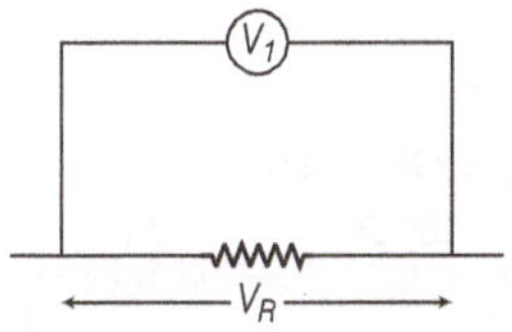

(a) Electric current in the circuit,

$$I = \frac{V_R}{R} = \frac{V_1}{R} = \frac{80}{100} = 0.8\ A$$ **(1)**

(b) Current through the capacitor, I_C is equal to the current through resistor as they are in series

$$I_R = I_C \Rightarrow 0.8 = \frac{V_C}{X_C}$$

$$\Rightarrow \quad V_C = V_L \Rightarrow (0.8) \times X_C = (0.8)\left(\frac{1}{\omega C}\right)$$

$$\Rightarrow \quad \frac{1}{C} = \frac{V_2 \times \omega}{0.8} = \frac{60 \times 2\pi f}{0.8} \qquad [\because V_L = V_C]$$

$$= \frac{600 \times 2\pi \times 50}{8}$$

$$\Rightarrow \quad C = \frac{8}{6 \times 5 \times 2\pi \times 10^3} \Rightarrow C = 42.46\ \mu\text{F}$$ **(1½)**

(ii) At resonance, $X_L = X_C$

$$Z = \sqrt{R^2 + (X_L - X_C)^2} = \sqrt{R^2 + 0} = R$$

At resonance net impedance is equal to resistance (R). **(1½)**

44. According to the question,

$C = 50\mu\text{F}$, $R = 30\ \Omega$, $L = 0.7$ H, $e = 200 \sin (200\,t)$,

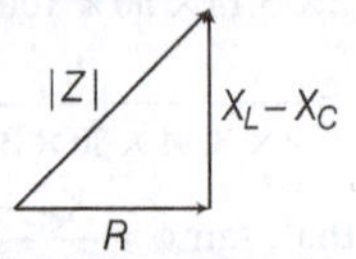

(1)

By comparing with $e = e_0 \sin \omega t$,

$$\omega = 200\ \text{rad/s},\ e_0 = 300\ \text{V}$$ **(1)**

Impedance, $Z = \sqrt{R^2 + (X_L - X_C)^2}$

$$= \sqrt{(30)^2 + \left(\omega L - \frac{1}{\omega C}\right)^2}$$

$$= \sqrt{(30)^2 + \left(200 \times 0.7 - \frac{10^6}{200 \times 50}\right)^2}$$

$$= \sqrt{900 + (140 - 100)^2}$$ **(1)**

$$\Rightarrow \quad Z = 50\ \Omega$$

I_0 = Peak value of current

$$= \frac{\text{Peak value of voltage}}{\text{Impedance}} = \frac{e_0}{Z} = \frac{300}{50} = 6\ \text{A}$$ **(1)**

45. This is a similar question as that of the previous one, hence follow the similar method to calculate impedance and peak current.

(i) $Z = 66.2\ \Omega$

(ii) $I_0 = 4.68$ A **(2 + 2)**

46. (i) According to the question,

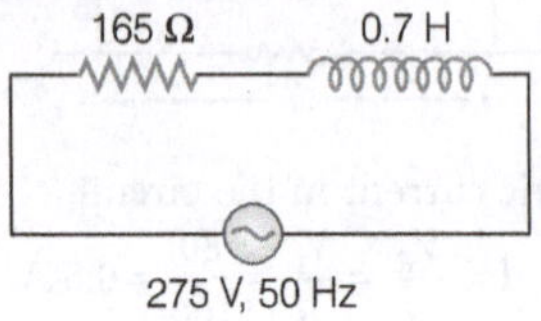

(a) Reactance of the coil is $\omega L = X_L = 2\pi f L$

$$= 2 \times \frac{22}{7} \times 50 \times 0.7$$

$$= 220\Omega$$ **(1)**

(b) Impedance of the coil $= \sqrt{X_L^2 + R^2}$

$$= \sqrt{(\omega L)^2 + R^2}$$

$$= \sqrt{(2\pi \times 50 \times 0.7)^2 + (165)^2}$$

$$= \sqrt{48400 + 27225}$$

$$= \sqrt{75625} = 275$$ **(1)**

(c) Current flowing through the coil, $V = IR$

$$\Rightarrow \quad I = \frac{V}{R}$$

(where, R = resistance of circuit and V = voltage applied)

$$\Rightarrow \quad I = \frac{275}{275} \Rightarrow I = 1\ \text{A}$$

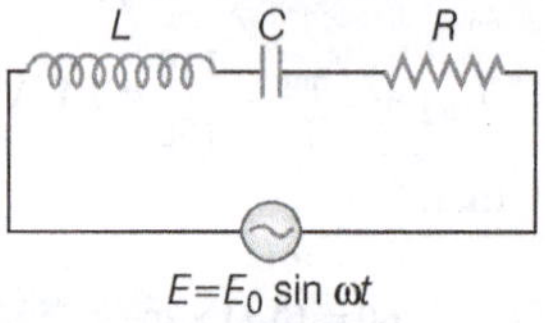

$$\text{Impedance}\,(Z) = \sqrt{(X_L - X_C)^2 + R^2}$$

$$= \sqrt{\left(\omega L - \frac{1}{\omega C}\right)^2 + R^2}$$ **(1)**

(ii) The variation of impedance of a series L-C-R circuit with frequency of AC supply is given below.

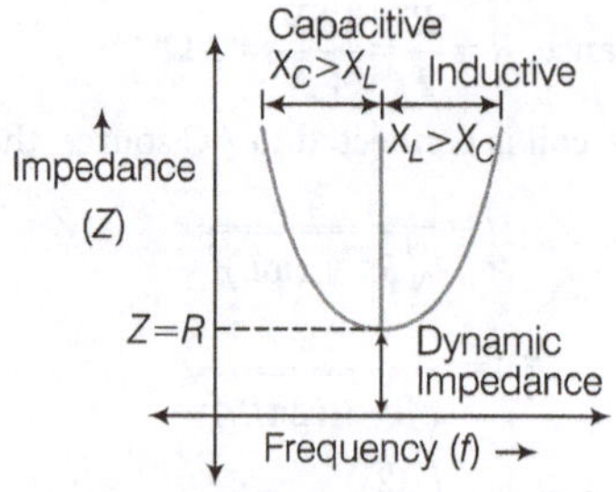

(2)

47. Refer to example 7 on page 286.

$$\phi = 135°$$

Since, $\quad \omega L < \dfrac{1}{\omega C}$ or $X_L < X_C$

Therefore, current is leading in phase by a phase angle 135°. **(1½)**

(ii) For unit power factor, $\cos \phi = 1$

$$\Rightarrow \quad \frac{R}{\sqrt{R^2 + \left(\omega L - \frac{1}{\omega C''}\right)^2}} = 1$$

where, C' is the total capacitance.

$\Rightarrow \quad R^2 + \left(\omega L - \frac{1}{\omega C''}\right)^2 = R^2 \Rightarrow \omega L = \frac{1}{\omega C''}$

$\Rightarrow \quad \omega L = 100 = \frac{1}{\omega C''}$

$\Rightarrow \quad C'' = \frac{1}{10^5} = 10^{-5}\text{ F} = 10\,\mu\text{F}$

Additional capacitance C' required in parallel

$C' = C'' - C = 10\,\mu\text{F} - 2\,\mu\text{F} = 8\,\mu\text{F}$ (1½)

48. As, resonance frequency, $\nu = \frac{1}{2\pi\sqrt{LC}}$

i.e. $\nu \propto \frac{1}{\sqrt{C}}$ (1/2)

$\therefore \quad \nu' \propto \frac{1}{\sqrt{C'}} = \frac{1}{\sqrt{4C}} = \frac{1}{2\sqrt{C}} = \frac{1}{2}\nu$ (1/2)

49. Given, $L = 10$ H, $C = 40\,\mu$F, $R = 60\,\Omega$, $V_{rms} = 240$ V

(i) The angular frequency,

$\omega_r = \frac{1}{\sqrt{LC}} = \frac{1}{\sqrt{10 \times 40 \times 10^{-6}}}$

$\omega_r = 50$ rad/s (1)

(ii) Current at resonating frequency,

$I_{rms} = \frac{V_{rms}}{Z} = \frac{V_{rms}}{R}$ [$\because$ at resonance, $Z = R$]

$= \frac{240}{60} = 4$ A (1)

(iii) Inductive reactance, $X_L = \omega L$

At resonance, $X_L = \omega_r L = 50 \times 10 = 500\,\Omega$

Potential drop across inductor,

$V_{rms} = I_{rms} \times X_L = 4 \times 500 = 2000$ V (1)

50. Given, $L = 2.0$ H, $C = 2\,\mu\text{F} = 2 \times 10^{-6}$ F,

$R = 10\,\Omega$

Now, Q-factor $= \frac{1}{R}\sqrt{\frac{L}{C}} = \frac{1}{10}\sqrt{\frac{2}{2 \times 10^{-6}}} = \frac{1}{10 \times 10^{-3}}$

$= \frac{1}{10^{-2}} = 100$

51. Given, $L = 2.0$ H, $C = 32 \times 10^{-6}$ F and $R = 10\,\Omega$

$\therefore \quad \omega_r = \frac{1}{\sqrt{LC}} = \frac{1}{\sqrt{2.0 \times 32 \times 10^{-6}}} = \frac{10^3}{8} = 125$ rad/s (1)

and $\quad Q = \frac{1}{R}\sqrt{\frac{L}{C}} = \frac{1}{10}\sqrt{\frac{2}{32 \times 10^{-6}}}$

$= \frac{1}{10 \times 4 \times 10^{-3}} = 25$ (1)

52. Refer to Q. 49 and Q. 51 on page 293.
[**Ans.** 0.112×10^3 rad/s, 5A; 2.23]

53. Given, $I = 5\sin\left(100\pi t - \frac{\pi}{6}\right)$

$e = 300\sin\left(100\pi t + \frac{\pi}{6}\right)$

We know that, average power consumed,

$P_{av} = E_{rms} I_{rms} \cos\phi = \frac{E_0}{\sqrt{2}} \times \frac{I_0}{\sqrt{2}} \cos\phi$

where, E_0 = peak emf = 300 V

I_0 = peak current = 5 A

$\cos\phi$ = power factor = $\cos 60° = \frac{1}{2}$ $\left[\because \phi = \phi_1 - \phi_2 = \frac{\pi}{6} + \frac{\pi}{6} = \frac{\pi}{3}\right]$ (1)

$\therefore \quad P_{av} = \frac{300}{\sqrt{2}} \times \frac{50}{\sqrt{2}} \times \frac{1}{2} = 3750$ W (1)

54. Initially, $R = 150\,\Omega$

$C = 15\,\mu$F, peak current, $I_0 = 0.2$ A

Impedance of circuit,

$Z = \frac{V_0}{I_0} = \frac{V_{rms} \times \sqrt{2}}{I_0} = \frac{220 \times \sqrt{2}}{0.20} = \frac{220 \times 100}{20} \times \sqrt{2}$

$= 220 \times 5 \times \sqrt{2} = 1100\sqrt{2}\,\Omega$ (1)

$\therefore$ Average power consumed,

$P_{av} = V_{rms} I_{rms} \cos\phi$ $\left[\because \cos\phi = \frac{R}{Z}\right]$

$P_{av} = 220 \times \frac{0.2}{\sqrt{2}} \times \frac{150}{1100\sqrt{2}} \Rightarrow P_{av} = 3$W (1)

When there is only resistor in the circuit, power consumed is

$P_{av} = I_{rms}^2 R = \left(\frac{I_0}{\sqrt{2}}\right)^2 R = \left(\frac{0.2}{\sqrt{2}}\right)^2 \times 150 = 3$W (1)

55. (i) Given, $E_{rms} = 220$V, $C = 25\mu\text{F} = 25 \times 10^{-6}$ F,

$L = \frac{4}{\pi^2}$ H, $R = 100\Omega$

(a) Resonant frequency is given by

$f_r = \frac{1}{2\pi\sqrt{LC}} = \frac{1}{2 \times 3.14 \times \sqrt{\frac{4}{\pi^2} \times 25 \times 10^{-6}}}$

$= \frac{1}{2 \times 3.14 \times \frac{2}{3.14} \times 5 \times 10^{-3}} = 50$ Hz (1)

(b) Impedance of the circuit is given by

$Z = \sqrt{R^2 + (X_L - X_C)^2}$ ...(i)

We know that, $X_C = \frac{1}{\omega C} = \frac{1}{2\pi f C}$

$= \frac{1}{2 \times 3.14 \times 50 \times 25 \times 10^{-6}} = 127.3\Omega$

$X_L = \omega L = 2\pi f L = 2 \times 3.14 \times \frac{4}{\pi^2} \times 50 = 127.3\Omega$

Substituting the all values in Eq. (i), we get

$Z = \sqrt{(100)^2 + (127.3 - 127.3)^2}$

$= \sqrt{(100)^2} = 100\Omega$

We know that, $I_{rms} = \frac{E_{rms}}{Z} = \frac{220}{100} = 2.2$ A (1)

(c) Average power consumed by the circuit

$$= E_{\text{rms}} \times I_{\text{rms}} \times \frac{R}{\sqrt{R^2 + \left(L\omega - \frac{1}{C\omega}\right)}}$$

$\because \quad Z = R = 100\,\Omega$

So, power $= E_{\text{rms}} \times I_{\text{rms}}$

$= 220 \times 2.2 = 484$ W **(1)**

(ii) Phasor diagram of *L-C-R* circuit is shown below.

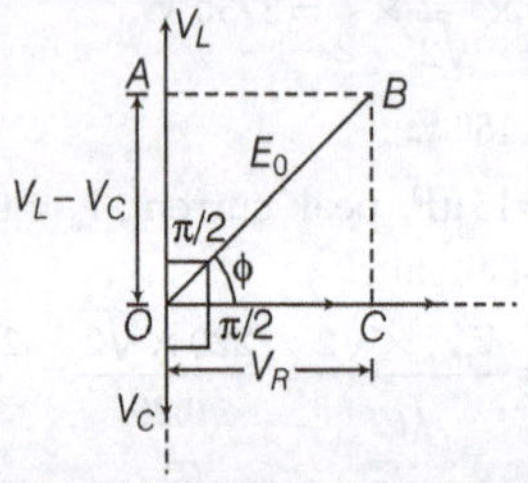

The phase difference across the inductor and phase difference across the capacitor is 180°. **(2)**

56. Given, $L = 5$ H, $C = 80\,\mu\text{F} = 80 \times 10^{-6}$F,

$R = 40\,\Omega$, $V_{\text{rms}} = 230$ V

(i) Resonance angular frequency,

$$\omega_r = \frac{1}{\sqrt{LC}} = \frac{1}{\sqrt{5 \times 80 \times 10^{-6}}} = 50 \text{ rad/s} \quad \textbf{(1)}$$

(ii) Impedance, $Z = \sqrt{R^2 + \left(\omega L - \frac{1}{\omega C}\right)^2}$

At resonance, $\omega L = \frac{1}{\omega C}$

$\therefore \quad Z_r = R = 40\,\Omega$ **(1/2)**

Amplitude of current at resonance frequency,

$$I_0 = \frac{V_0}{Z_r} = \frac{\sqrt{2} \times 230}{40} = 813 \text{ A}$$

$$I_{\text{rms}} = \frac{I_0}{\sqrt{2}} = \frac{8.13}{\sqrt{2}} = 5.75 \text{ A} \quad \textbf{(1/2)}$$

(iii) Potential difference across *L*,

$$V_L = I_{\text{rms}} \times (\omega_r \times L)$$

$= 5.75 \times 50 \times 5$

$= 1437.5$ V

Potential difference across *C*,

$$V_C = I_{\text{rms}} \times \frac{1}{\omega_r C} = \frac{5.75}{50 \times 80 \times 10^{-6}}$$

$= 1437.5$ V

$\therefore$ Potential difference across *L* and *C* combination,

$$V_{LC} = I_{\text{rms}}\left(\omega_r L - \frac{1}{\omega_r C}\right) = 0$$

$\therefore$ Potential difference across *R*,

$$V_R = I_{\text{rms}} R$$

$= 5.75 \times 40$

$= 230$ V **(1)**

57. The equation of emf is given by

$$\varepsilon = 300 \sin(100\pi t) \text{ V}$$

The standard equation of emf,

$$\varepsilon = \varepsilon_0 \sin \omega t$$

$\therefore \quad \omega = 100\pi$

$2\pi f = 100\pi \quad [\because \omega = 2\pi f]$

$f = 50$ Hz

(i) Impedance of the circuit (*L-C-R*),

$$Z = \sqrt{R^2 + (X_L - X_C)^2}$$

$$= \sqrt{R^2 + \left(2\pi f L - \frac{1}{2\pi f C}\right)^2}$$

$$= \sqrt{100^2 + \left(100\pi \times 1 - \frac{1}{100\pi \times 16 \times 10^{-6}}\right)^2}$$

$$= \sqrt{100^2 + (314 - 199)^2}$$

$$= \sqrt{100^2 + 115^2}$$

$= 152.39\,\Omega$ **(2)**

(ii) Resonant frequency,

$$f_0 = \frac{1}{2\pi\sqrt{LC}} = \frac{1}{2\pi\sqrt{1 \times 16 \times 10^{-6}}}$$

$$= \frac{1}{2\pi \times 4 \times 10^{-3}}$$

$= 39.8$ Hz **(2)**

(iii) Power factor, $\cos\theta = \frac{R}{Z}$

At resonant frequency, $R = Z$

$\therefore \quad \cos\theta = 1$ **(1)**

SUMMARY

- **Alternating Current** If the direction of current changes alternatively and its magnitude change continuously with respect to time is called Alternating current. It is sinusoidal in nature.
- The instantaneous value of AC is given by $I = I_0 \sin \omega t$ and instantaneous value of alternating emf is given by $E = E_0 \sin \omega t$.
- Mean value of AC is that value which send same change through a cicruit in half cycle which is sent by steady current in same time.

  $\therefore \qquad I_m = 0.637 I_0$ and $E_m = 0.637 E_0$

  where, I_0 and E_0 are the peak values of current and voltage, respectively.
- **Root mean square** (RMS) value of AC is that value over a complete cycle that generates same amount of heat in the given resistor that is generated by steady current in the same resistor.

  $$\therefore \qquad I_{rms} = \frac{I_0}{\sqrt{2}} \text{ and } E_{rms} = \frac{I_0}{\sqrt{2}}$$
- A diagram representing alternating current and alternating emf (of same frequency) as rotating vectors (phasors) with the phase angle between them is called **phasor diagram.**
- **AC through Resistor Only** In this case, there is zero phase difference between instantaneous alternating current and instantaneous alternating emf. So, they are in same phase.
- **AC through Capacitor Only** In this case, the current leads the voltage by a phase angle of $\frac{\pi}{2}$ or the voltage lags behind the current by the phase angle of $\frac{\pi}{2}$.

  Capacitive reactance, $X_c = \frac{1}{2\pi f C}$
- **AC through Inductor Only** In this case, the current lags behind the voltage by phase angle of $\frac{\pi}{2}$ or the voltage leads the current by phase angle of $\frac{\pi}{2}$.

  Inductive reactance, $X_L = 2\pi f L$.
- **AC through *R-L* and *R-C* Series Circuit**

  ***R-L* Circuit** In this case, impedance

  $$Z = \sqrt{R^2 + X_L^2} \text{ and } \phi = \tan^{-1}\left(\frac{X_L}{R}\right)$$

  ***R-C* Circuit** In this case, impedance,

  $$Z = \sqrt{R^2 + X_C^2} \text{ and } \phi = \tan^{-1}\left(\frac{X_C}{R}\right)$$
- **AC through *L-C-R* Series Circuit** In this case, Impedance

  $$Z = \sqrt{R^2 + (X_L - X_C)^2} \text{ and } \phi = \tan^{-1}\frac{X_L - X_C}{R}$$
- When $X_L > X_C$, then the AC circuit is inductance dominated circuit .
- When $X_C > X_L$, then the AC circuit is capacitance dominated circuit.
- In series *L-C-R* circuit, if phase (ϕ) between current and voltage is zero, then the circuit is said to be **resonant circuit.** Resonating frequency is given by,

  $$\nu_r = \frac{1}{2\pi\sqrt{LC}}$$
- **Quality Factor** (*Q*-Factor) determines the sharpness of the resonance.

  $$Q\text{-factor} = \frac{1}{R}\sqrt{\frac{L}{C}}$$
- **Average Power Associated in AC Circuit,**

  $$P_{av} = I_{rms} E_{rms} \cos\theta$$

  $$\Rightarrow \qquad P_{av} = \frac{E_0}{\sqrt{2}} \cdot \frac{I_0}{\sqrt{2}} \cos\theta$$
- **Wattless Current** is the current which consumes no power for its maintenance in the circuit.
- **For *L-C* Oscillations**, the energy oscillates in between the capacitor and inductor as electrostatic energy and magnetic energy. It is given as,

  $$U = \frac{1}{2} L I^2 = \frac{1}{2}\frac{q^2}{C}$$
- **Choke Coil** is an electrical device which is used for controlling current in AC circuits without wasting electrical energy. It has high inductance and negligible resistance.
- **AC Generator** It is a device which convert mechanical energy into electrical energy. It works on principle of mutual induction.

For Mind Map

Visit : https://goo.gl/LCxcsh OR **Scan the Code**

Chapter Practice

Multiple Choice Questions

1 Mark

1 A generator produces a voltage that is given by $V = 240 \sin 120\, t$, where t is in seconds. The frequency and rms voltage are

(a) 60 Hz and 240 V (b) 19 Hz and 120 V
(c) 19 Hz and 170 V (d) 754 Hz and 70 V

2 An alternating current is given by the equation $i = i_1 \cos \omega t + i_2 \sin \omega t$. The rms current is given by

(a) $\frac{1}{\sqrt{2}}(i_1 + i_2)$ (b) $\frac{1}{\sqrt{2}}(i_1 + i_2)^2$
(c) $\frac{1}{\sqrt{2}}(i_1^2 + i_2^2)^{1/2}$ (d) $\frac{1}{2}(i_1^2 + i_2^2)^{1/2}$

3 The impedance of a R-C circuit is z_1 for frequency f and z_2 for frequency $2f$. Then, z_1/z_2 is

(a) between 1 and 2 (b) 2
(c) between 1/2 and 1 (d) 1/2

4 In a L-C-R circuit, capacitance is changed from C to $16C$. For the resonant frequency to remain unchanged, the inductance should be changed from L to

(a) $4L$ (b) $16L$ (c) $L/16$ (d) $L/4$

5 A choke is preferred to a resistance for limiting current in AC circuit, because

(a) choke is cheap
(b) there is no wastage of power
(c) choke is compact in size
(d) choke is a good absorber of heat

Assertion and Reason

Directions (Q. Nos. 6-10) *In the following questions, two statements are given- one labelled Assertion and the other labelled Reason. Select the correct answer to these questions from the codes (a), (b), (c) and (d) as given below*

(a) Both Assertion and Reason are true and Reason is the correct explanation of Assertion.
(b) Both Assertion and Reason are true but Reason is not the correct explanation of Assertion.
(c) Assertion is true but Reason is false.
(d) Assertion is false but Reason is true.

6. **Assertion (A)** Phasors V and I for the case of a resistor are in the same direction.

Reason (R) The phase angle between the voltage and the current is zero.

7. **Assertion (A)** When the capacitor is connected to an AC source, it limits or regulates the current, but does not completely prevent the flow of charge.

Reason (R) The capacitor is alternately charged and discharged as the current reverses each half-cycle.

8. **Assertion (A)** Capacitor serves as a barrier for DC and offers an easy path to AC.

Reason (R) Capacitor reactance is inversely proportional to frequency.

9. **Assertion (A)** If $X_C > X_L$, ϕ is positive and the circuit is predominantly capacitive. The current in the circuit leads the source voltage.

Reason (R) If $X_C < X_L$, ϕ is negative and the circuit is predominantly inductive, the current in the circuit lags the source voltage.

10. **Assertion (A)** In a series R-L-C circuit, the voltages across resistor, inductor and capacitor are 8V, 16V and 10V, respectively. The resultant emf in the circuit is 10 V.

Reason (R) Resultant emf of the circuit is given by the relation.

$$E = \sqrt{V_R^2 + (V_L - V_C)^2}$$

Very Short Answer Type Questions

1 Mark

11 Draw the graph showing the variation of reactance of (i) a capacitor and (ii) an inductor with the angular frequency of an AC circuit.

12 Distinguish between resistance, reactance and impedance for AC circuit.

13 The total impedance of a circuit decreases, when a capacitor is added in series with L and R. Explain why?

Short Answer Type I Questions

(2 Marks)

14 Prove mathematically that the average value of alternating current over one complete cycle is zero.

15 Show mathematically that an ideal inductor does not consume any power in an AC circuit.

16 A capacitor C, a variable resistance R and a bulb B are connected in series to the AC mains in circuit as shown in the figure. The bulb glows with some brightness.

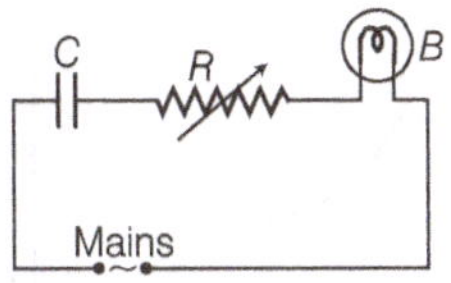

How will the glow of the bulb change, if

(i) a dielectric slab is introduced between the plates of the capacitor, keeping resistance R to be same;

(ii) the resistance R is increased keeping the same capacitance?

17 An inductor L of inductance X_L is connected in series with a bulb B and an AC source. How would brightness of the bulb change when

(i) number of turns in the inductor is reduced?

(ii) a capacitor of reactance $X_C = X_L$ is inserted in series in the circuit? Justify your answer in each case.

18 (i) Mention the significance of quality factor.

(ii) How can you improve the quality factor of a series resonance circuit?

Short Answer Type II Questions

(3 Marks)

19 Draw a circuit diagram showing a series L-C-R circuit and derive an equation for its resonant frequency.

20 Find an expression for the true power and apparent power in an AC circuit. Determine the condition so that current in the circuit may be wattless.

21 An AC source of voltage, $V = V_m \sin \omega t$, is applied across a series L-C-R circuit. Draw the phasor diagram for this circuit when the,

(i) capacitive impedance exceeds the inductive impedance.

(ii) inductive impedance exceeds the capacitive impedance.

22 Answer the following questions.

(i) In any AC circuit, is the applied instantaneous voltage equal to the algebraic sum of instantaneous voltage across the series elements of the circuit? Is the same true for rms voltage?

(ii) A capacitor is used in the primary circuit of an induction coil. Why?

(iii) An applied voltage signal consists of superposition of a DC voltage and an AC voltage of high frequency. The circuit consists of an inductor and a capacitor in series. Show that the DC signal will appear across C and the AC signal across L. **NCERT**

Long Answer Type Questions

(5 Marks)

23 (i) Obtain the expression for the average power consumed in a series L-C-R circuit connected to AC source for which the phase difference between the voltage and the current in the circuit is ϕ.

(ii) Define the quality factor in an AC circuit. Why should the quality factor have high value in receiving circuits? Name the factors on which it depends.

24 (i) What are L-C oscillations? State the reasons, why L-C oscillations are not realistic?

(ii) For circuit used for transporting electric power, a low power factor implies large power loss in transmission. Explain.

Numerical Problems

25 The electric mains in a house are marked 220 V, 50 Hz. Write down the equation for instantaneous voltage. **(1 M)**

26 What is the power dissipation in an AC circuit in which voltage and current are given by $E = 300 \sin(\omega t + \pi/2)$ and $I = 5 \sin \omega t$? **(1 M)**

27 An AC generator consists of a coil of 1000 turns and cross-sectional area of 100 cm^2, rotating at an angular speed of 100 rpm in a uniform magnetic field of 3.6×10^{-2} T. Calculate the maximum emf produced in the coil. **(1 M)**

Answers

1 (c) Frequency of a generator, i.e.

$$\nu = \frac{\omega}{2\pi} = \frac{120 \times 7}{2 \times 22} = 19 \text{ Hz}$$

$$V_{\text{rms}} = \frac{240}{\sqrt{2}} = 120\sqrt{2} \approx 170 \text{ V}$$

2 (c) As we know,

$$i_{\text{rms}} = \sqrt{i_1^2 + i_2^2}\left(\frac{i_1}{\sqrt{i_1^2 + i_2^2}} \cos \omega t + \frac{i_2}{\sqrt{i_1^2 + i_2^2}} \sin \omega t\right)$$

$$I_{\text{rms}} = \frac{I_0}{\sqrt{2}}, \text{ i.e.}$$

$$i_{\text{rms}} = \sqrt{\frac{i_1^2 + i_2^2}{2}} = \frac{1}{\sqrt{2}}(i_1^2 + i_2^2)^{1/2}$$

3 (a) The impedance of R-C circuit for frequency f_1 is

$$Z_1 = \sqrt{R^2 + \frac{1}{4\pi^2 f^2 c^2}}$$

The impedance of R-C circuit for frequency $2f$ is

$$Z_2 = \sqrt{R^2 + \frac{1}{4\pi^2 (2f^2) c^2}}$$

or $$Z_2 = \sqrt{R^2 + \frac{1}{16\pi^2 f^2 c^2}}$$

Then, $$\frac{Z_1^2}{Z_2^2} = \frac{R^2 + \frac{1}{4\pi^2 f^2 c^2}}{R^2 + \frac{1}{16\pi^2 f^2 c^2}} \text{ or } \frac{Z_1^2}{Z_2^2} = \frac{1 + \frac{1}{4\pi^2 f^2 c^2 R^2}}{1 + \frac{1}{16\pi^2 f^2 R^2 c^2}}$$

Hence, the value is greater than 1, then $\frac{Z_1}{Z_2}$ lies between 1 and 2.

4 (c) In the condition of resonance,

$$X_L = X_C \Rightarrow \omega L = \frac{1}{\omega C}$$

Since, resonant frequency remains unchanged,

So, $\sqrt{LC} = \text{constant}$

$\Rightarrow$ $L_1 C_1 = L_2 C_2$

$\Rightarrow$ $L \times C = L_2 \times 16C$

$\therefore$ $L_2 = \frac{L}{16}$

5 (b) In an AC circuit, the coil of high inductance and negligible resistance used to control current, is called the choke coil. The power factor of such a coil is given by

$$\cos \phi = \frac{R}{\sqrt{R^2 + \omega^2 L^2}} = \frac{R}{\omega L} \quad (\because R << \omega L)$$

As $R << \omega L$, $\cos \phi$ is very small. Thus, the power absorbed by the coil is very small. The only loss of energy is due to hysteresis in the iron core, which is much less than the loss of energy in the resistance that can also reduce the current, if placed instead of the choke coil.

6 (a) **7** (a)

8 (a) **9** (b)

10 (a) The resultant emf in the L-C-R circuit is given by

$$E = \sqrt{V_R^2 + (V_L - V_C)^2}$$

$\Rightarrow$ $E = \sqrt{(8)^2 + (16 - 10)^2}$

$\Rightarrow$ $E = \sqrt{64 + 36}$

$\Rightarrow$ $E = 10 \text{ V}$

11 (i) (ii)

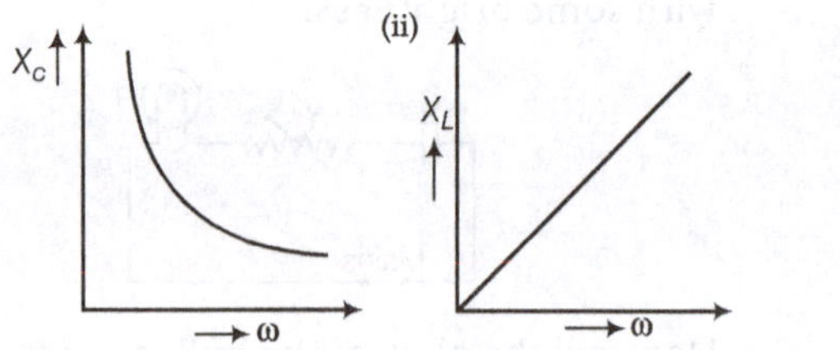

(1/2 + 1/2)

12 The basic function of the three is the same i.e. to oppose the flow of current through the circuit. But the difference lie in their expressions. As,

Resistance, $R = V / I$

Capacitive reactance, $X_C = \frac{1}{\omega C}$

Inductive reactance, $X_L = \omega L$

Impedance, $Z = \sqrt{R^2 + (X_L - X_C)^2}$

13 Impedance of an L-R circuit is,

$$Z = \sqrt{R^2 + X_L{}^2}$$

But with the introduction of a capacitor in series with a L and R, the new impedance will be

$$Z' = \sqrt{R^2 + (X_T - X_C)^2}$$

Hence, the total impedance decreases.

14 Average value of alternating current over one complete cycle

$$I_{\text{avg}} = \frac{1}{T}\int_0^T I_0 \sin \omega t \, dt$$

[$I_0 \rightarrow$ peak value of current]

$$= \frac{1}{T} \cdot I_0 \int_0^T \sin \omega t \, dt$$

$$= \frac{I_0}{T}\left[\frac{-\cos \omega t}{\omega}\right]_0^T$$

$$= \frac{-I_0}{T\omega}[\cos \omega t]_0^T$$

$$= \frac{-I_0}{T\omega}\left[\cos \frac{2\pi}{T} \cdot t\right]_0^T \quad \left[\omega = \frac{2\pi}{T}\right]$$

$$= \frac{-I_0}{T\omega}\left[\cos\frac{2\pi}{T}\cdot T - \cos\frac{2\pi}{T}\cdot 0\right]$$

$$= \frac{-I_0}{T\omega}[\cos 2\pi - \cos 0]$$

$$= \frac{-I_0}{T\omega}[1-1] = 0$$

15 Refer to the text on page 287 (Wattless current).

16 (i) As the dielectric slab is introduced between the plates of the capacitor, its capacitance will increase. Hence, the potential drop across the capacitor will decrease,

i.e. $V = \frac{Q}{C}$.

As a result, the potential drop across the bulb will increase as they are connected in series. Thus, its brightness will increase. **(1)**

(ii) As the resistance R is increased, the potential drop across the resistor will increase. As a result, the potential drop across the bulb will decrease as they are connected in series. Thus, its brightness will decrease. **(1)**

17 (i) We know that, if the number of turns in the inductor decreases, then inductance L decreases. So, the net resistance of the circuit decreases. Hence, the current through the circuit increases, increasing the brightness of the bulb. **(1)**

(iii) If the capacitor of reactance $X_C = X_L$ is connected in series with the circuit, then

$$Z = \sqrt{(X_L - X_C)^2 + R^2}$$

$$\Rightarrow \quad Z = R \qquad [\because X_L = X_C]$$

This is a case of resonance. In this case, the maximum current will flow through the circuit. Hence, the brightness of the bulb will increase. **(1)**

18 (i) Refer to text on page 285 (Significance of *Q*-factor).

(ii) To improve quality factor, ohmic resistance should be made as small as possible.

19 Refer to the text on pages 282, 283 and 284 (AC through *L-C-R* circuit and resonance).

20 Refer to the text on pages 285, 286 and 287 (Average power associated in AC circuit and wattless current).

21 Refer to the text on pages 282 and 283 (AC through *L-C-R* circuit).

22 (i) Yes, it is true for instantaneous voltage.

No, it is not true for rms voltage because voltages across various elements may not be in same phase.

(ii) Because when the circuit is broken, then the large amount of induced voltage is used up in charging the capacitor. Thus, sparking is avoided.

(iii) $X_L = \omega L = 2\pi\nu L$ and $X_C = \frac{1}{\omega C} = \frac{1}{2\pi\nu C}$

***Case* I** For DC, If $\nu = 0$, then $X_C = \infty$

Thus, capacitor blocks DC

***Case* II** For AC of higher frequency, X_L is also higher, thus the inductor blocks the current. Hence, AC signal appears across L.

23 (i) Refer to text on pages 285 and 286 (Average power associated in AC circuit).

(ii) Refer to text on pages 284 and 285 {Quality factor (*Q*-factor)}.

24 (i) Refer to text on page 287 (*L-C* oscillations).

(ii) Refer to text on pages 285 and 286 (Average power associated in AC circuit).

25 Refer to example 2, on page 274.

Ans. $220\sqrt{2}\sin 100\pi t$]

26 720 W, $P_{av} = E_0/\sqrt{2} x I_0/\sqrt{2}\cos\theta$, [here, $\theta = 0°$]

27 Given, $N = 1000$,

$$A = 100\text{ cm}^2 = 10^{-2}\text{ m}^2,$$

$$\nu = 100\text{ rpm} = \frac{100}{60}\text{ rps},$$

$$B = 3.6\times10^{-2}\text{ T}, \; e_0 = ?$$

$\therefore$ Maximum emf produced in the coil is

$$e_0 = NBA\,\omega$$

$$= NBA\,(2\pi\nu)$$

$$= 1000\times3.6\times10^{-2}\times10^{-2}\times2\times\frac{22}{7}\times\frac{100}{60}$$

$$= 3.77\text{ V}$$

RELATED ONLINE VIDEOS

Visit : https://www.youtube.com/watch?v=vN9aR2wKv0U
OR **Scan the Code**

Visit : https://www.youtube.com/watch?v=tibgeKtC7GQ
OR **Scan the Code**

Visit : https://www.youtube.com/watch?v=Mq-PF1vo9QA
OR **Scan the Code**

Visit : https://www.youtube.com/watch?v=Cx4_7IljoBA
OR **Scan the Code**

CHAPTER

08

Electromagnetic Waves

- Displacement Current
- Maxwell's Equations
- Electromagnetic Waves
- Electromagnetic Spectrum

We have learnt that an electric current produces magnetic field and a varying magnetic field gives rise to an electric field. This brought together the phenomena of electricity and magnetism into a coherent and unified theory. After this discovery, Maxwell predicted variation of electric and magnetic field vectors perpendicular to each other leads to electromagnetic disturbance in space. He also concluded that, electromagnetic waves could travel with the speed of light. This led him to conclude that the light itself is an electromagnetic wave.

Displacement Current

It is defined as that current which comes into play in the region in which the electric field and electric flux is changing with time. It is denoted by I_d and expressed as

$$\boxed{I_d = \varepsilon_0 \frac{d\phi_E}{dt}}$$

where, ε_0 = permittivity of free space

and $\frac{d\phi_E}{dt}$ = rate of change of flux through the area between the plates of capacitor.

Basic Idea of Displacement Current

Ampere's circuital law states that, the line integral of magnetic field **B** around any closed path is equal to μ_0 times the total current threading the closed path,

$$\oint \mathbf{B} \cdot d\mathbf{l} = \mu_0 I$$

where, I is the net current threading the surface bounded by a closed path C and μ_0 is the permeability constant.

Ampere's circuital law for conduction current during charging of a capacitor was found inconsistent.

Maxwell argued that the above inconsistency of Ampere's circuital law is because of some missing term.

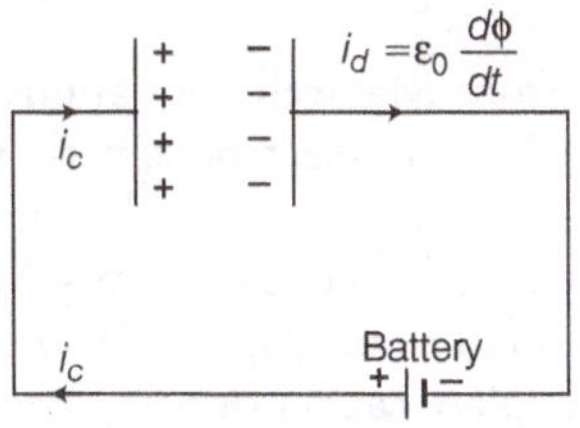

Displacement current

That term must be related to a changing electric field which passes through surface S between the plates of capacitor during charging. So, Maxwell introduced this missing term, i.e. displacement current, in order to make Ampere's circuital law logically consistent.

Ampere's circuital law $\left(\oint \mathbf{B} \cdot d\mathbf{l} = \mu_0 I\right)$ was modified to

$$\oint \mathbf{B} \cdot d\mathbf{l} = \mu_0 (I_c + I_d)$$

where, I_c = conduction current and I_d = displacement current.

It is called **modified Ampere's circuital law** or **Ampere Maxwell's-circuital law.**

Therefore, modified Ampere's circuital law may also be expressed as

$$\oint \mathbf{B} \cdot d\mathbf{l} = \mu_0 \left(I_c + \varepsilon_0 \frac{d\phi_E}{dt}\right)$$

The inferences can be drawn from the above discussion as given below

(i) The conduction and displacement currents are individually discontinuous, but the currents together possess the property of continuity through any closed electric circuit.

(ii) The displacement current is precisely equal to the conduction current, when the two present in different parts of the circuit.

(iii) The displacement current arises due to the rate of change of electric flux (or electric field) between the two plates of the capacitor.

(iv) Just as the conduction current, the displacement current is also the source of varying magnetic field.

Example 1 In an electric circuit, there is a capacitor of reactance 100 Ω connected across the source of 220 V. Find the displacement current.

Sol. Since, displacement current = conduction current.

Therefore, $$I_d = \frac{V}{X_C} = \frac{220}{100} = 2.2\text{ A}$$

Example 2 In which way you can establish an instantaneous displacement current of 1.0 A in the space between the parallel plates of 1 μF capacitor?

Sol. ∴ Displacement current,

$$I_d = \varepsilon_0 \frac{d\phi_E}{dt} = \varepsilon_0 \frac{d}{dt}(EA) \qquad [\because \phi_E = EA]$$

where, E is electric field and A is the area of cross-section.

$$I_d = \varepsilon_0 A \frac{d}{dt}\left(\frac{V}{d}\right)$$

$$\Rightarrow \quad I_d = \frac{\varepsilon_0 A}{d} \times \frac{dV}{dt} = \frac{CdV}{dt} \qquad \left[\because C = \frac{\varepsilon_0 A}{d}\right]$$

$$\Rightarrow \quad \frac{dV}{dt} = \frac{I_d}{C} = \frac{1.0}{10^{-6}} = 10^6 \text{ Vs}^{-1}$$

Thus, an instantaneous displacement current of 1 A can be set up by changing the potential difference across the parallel plates of capacitor at the rate of 10^6 Vs^{-1}.

Maxwell's Equations

Maxwell's equations are the basic laws of electricity and magnetism. These equations give complete description of all electromagnetic interactions. Maxwell on the basis of his equations, predicted the existence of electromagnetic waves.

There are four Maxwell's equations which are explained as given below

Gauss's Law in Electrostatics

This law states that, the total electric flux through any closed surface is always equal to $\frac{1}{\varepsilon_0}$ times the net charge enclosed by that surface. It is given by

$$\oint \mathbf{E} \cdot d\mathbf{S} = \frac{q}{\varepsilon_0}$$

This equation is called **Maxwell's first equation.**

Gauss's Law in Magnetostatics

This law states that, the net magnetic flux through any closed surface is always zero. It is given by

$$\oint \mathbf{B} \cdot d\mathbf{S} = 0$$

This equation is called **Maxwell's second equation.**

Faraday's Law of Electromagnetic Induction

This law states that, the induced emf produced in a circuit is numerically equal to rate of change of magnetic flux through it. It is given by

$$\oint \mathbf{E} \cdot d\mathbf{l} = -\frac{d\phi_B}{dt}$$

This equation is called **Maxwell's third equation.**

Ampere-Maxwell's Circuital Law

This law states that, the line integral of the magnetic field along a closed path is equal to μ_0 times the total current (i.e. sum of conduction current and displacement current) threading the surface bounded by that closed path. It is given by

$$\oint \mathbf{B} \cdot d\mathbf{l} = \mu_0 \left(I_c + \varepsilon_0 \frac{d\phi_E}{dt} \right)$$

This equation is called **Maxwell's fourth equation.**

Electromagnetic Waves

These waves are produced due to the change in electric field **E** and magnetic field **B** sinusoidally and propagating through space such that, the two fields are perpendicular to each other and perpendicular to the direction of wave propagation.

Such waves which can actually propagate in space without any material medium are called electromagnetic waves.

Source of Electromagnetic Waves

An oscillating charge is an example of accelerating charge. It produces an oscillating electric field in space, which produces an oscillating magnetic field, which in turn produces an oscillating electric fields and so on. The oscillating electric and magnetic fields regenerate each other as a wave which propagates through space.

The frequency of EM wave is equal to the frequency of oscillation of charge, i.e.

$$\nu = \frac{1}{2\pi\sqrt{LC}}$$

Electromagnetic waves are also produced when fast moving electrons are suddenly stopped by metal target of high atomic number. These electromagnetic waves are called **X-rays.**

Transverse Nature of Electromagnetic Waves

It can be shown from Maxwell's equations that electric and magnetic fields in an electromagnetic wave are perpendicular to each other and to the direction of wave propagation. If we would consider a parallel plate capacitor [refer to figure on page 312], the electric field **E** inside the parallel plate capacitor was directed perpendicular to the plates. Also, the magnetic field **B** which gives rise to the displacement current was parallel to the capacitor.

Thus, **E** and **B** were perpendicular in that case. But, this observation is a general feature.

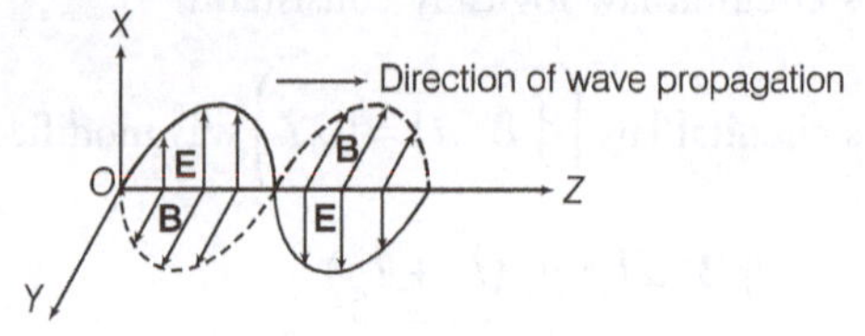

A plane EM wave travelling along Z-axis

In the above figure, we see that permanent curve shows electric field **E** which is along *x*-direction and dotted curve shows magnetic field **B** which is along *y*-direction and the wave propagates along *z*-direction. Both **E** and **B** vary sinusodially and become maximum at same position and time.

Consider a parallelopiped area along *Z*-axis showing variation of electric field. The electric field is varying along *X*-axis, so according to Gauss law, the electric field along *Z*-axis is

$$\oint \mathbf{E} \cdot dS = 0$$

Similarly, it is can be shown that for magnetic field

$$\oint \mathbf{B} \cdot dS = 0 \qquad \text{(along } Z\text{-axis)}$$

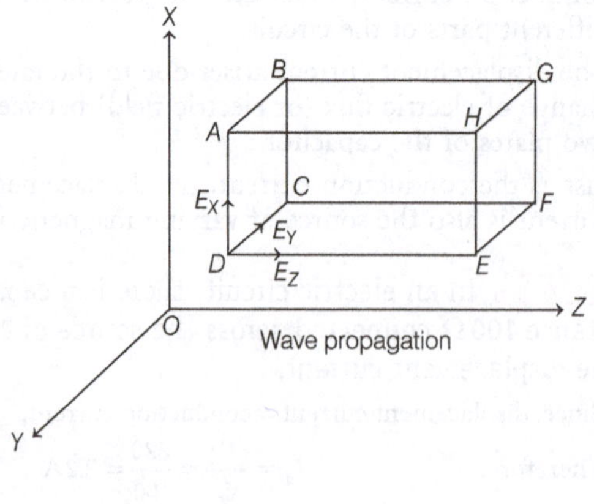

Thus, in electromagnetic wave, **E** and **B** are mutually perpendicular to each other, so they are transverse in nature.

The EM wave propagating in the positive z-direction may be represented by the following equations

Here, $E = E_x = E_0 \sin(kx - \omega t)$

$B = B_y = B_0 \sin(kz - \omega t)$

where, $k = 2\pi / \lambda$, [λ = wavelength]

$\omega = 2\pi\nu$, [ν = frequency]

E_0 = amplitude of varying electric field

and B_0 = amplitude of varying magnetic field.

Important Characteristics of Electromagnetic Waves

Important characteristics of EM waves are listed below

(i) The electromagnetic waves are produced by accelerated charge.

(ii) These waves do not require any material medium for propagation.

(iii) These waves travel in free space with the speed of light ($3 \times 10^8 \text{ ms}^{-1}$), given by the relation $c = 1/\sqrt{\mu_0 \varepsilon_0}$. It means that light waves are electromagnetic in nature.

(iv) Speed of electromagnetic wave in a medium is given by, $v = 1/\sqrt{\mu\varepsilon}$, where ε and μ are the permittivity and magnetic permeability of a material medium, respectively. This means, the speed of EM wave in a medium depends on electric and magnetic properties of a medium.

(v) The direction of variations of electric and magnetic fields are perpendicular to each other and also perpendicular to the direction of wave propagation. Thus, electromagnetic waves are transverse in nature.

(vi) In free space, the magnitudes of electric and magnetic fields in electromagnetic waves are related by $E_0/B_0 = c$ (where, c = speed of light in free space).

(vii) The energy in electromagnetic waves is divided, on an average, equally between electric and magnetic fields.

$$U_e = U_m$$

where, U_e = energy of electric field

and U_m = energy of magnetic field.

(viii) The energy density (energy per unit volume) in an electric field **E** in vacuum is $\frac{1}{2}\varepsilon_0 E^2$ and that in magnetic field **B** is $\frac{B^2}{2\mu_0}$.

$\therefore$ Energy associated with an electromagnetic wave is given by

$$U = \frac{1}{2}\varepsilon_0 E^2 + \frac{1}{2}\cdot\frac{B^2}{\mu_0}$$

Also, average energy density,

$$u_{av} = \frac{1}{4}\varepsilon_0 E_0^2 + \frac{1}{4}\frac{B_0^2}{\mu_0}$$

also $$u_{av} = \frac{1}{2}\varepsilon_0 E_0^2 = \frac{B_0^2}{2\mu_0} \qquad [\because U_e = U_m]$$

(ix) Electromagnetic waves, being uncharged, are not deflected by electric and magnetic fields.

(x) The electromagnetic wave like other waves carries energy and momentum. Since, it has momentum, an electromagnetic wave also exerts pressure called **radiation pressure**.

If wave is incident on a completely absorbing surface, then momentum delivered is given by

Momentum, $p = \frac{U}{c}$

Note Light carries energy from the sun to the earth, thus making life possible on the earth.

(xi) Electromagnetic waves are polarised and can be easily seen in the response of a portable AM radio to a broadcasting station. If an AM radio has a telescopic antenna, it responds to the electric part of the signal. When the antenna is turned horizontal, the signal will be greatly diminished.

Example 3 **An electromagnetic wave is travelling in vacuum with a speed of 3×10^8 m/s. Find its velocity in a medium having relative electric and magnetic permeability 2 and 1, respectively.**

Sol. Given, velocity of electromagnetic wave in vacuum,

$$c = 3 \times 10^8 \text{ m/s}$$

Relative electric permeability, $\varepsilon_r = 2$

and magnetic permeability, $\mu_r = 1$

Since, velocity of electromagnetic wave in a medium can be calculated by

$$v = \frac{1}{\sqrt{\varepsilon_0 \varepsilon_r \mu_0 \mu_r}} = \frac{1}{\sqrt{\varepsilon_0 \mu_0} \times \sqrt{\mu_r \varepsilon_r}}$$

where, $\frac{1}{\sqrt{\varepsilon_0 \mu_0}} = c \Rightarrow v = \frac{c}{\sqrt{\mu_r \varepsilon_r}}$ ...(i)

Therefore, $v = \frac{3 \times 10^8}{\sqrt{2 \times 1}}$

$\Rightarrow$ $v = \frac{3}{\sqrt{2}} \times 10^8$ m/s

Electromagnetic Spectrum

The orderly arrangement of EM waves in increasing or decreasing order of wavelength λ or frequency ν is called electromagnetic spectrum. The range varies from 10^{-12} m to 10^{4} m, i.e. from γ-rays to radio waves.

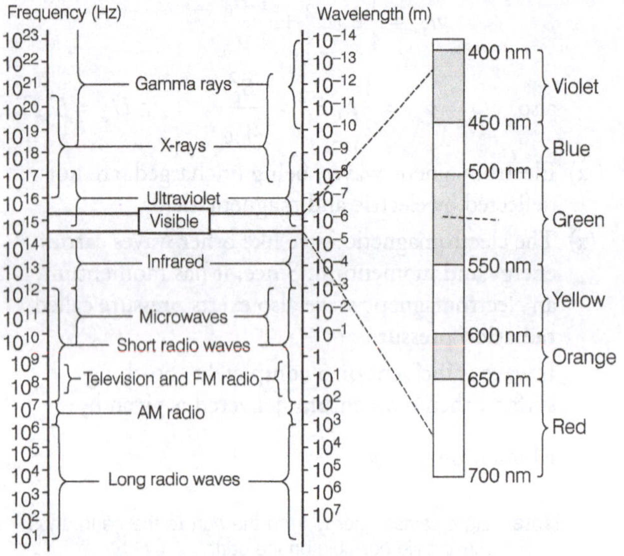

Electromagnetic spectrum with common names for various parts of it

The wavelength ranges, frequency ranges and use of various regions of electromagnetic spectrum are summarised below

Radio waves

These are produced due to oscillating charged particles. The frequency varies from 500 kHz to 1000 MHz.

Uses of radio waves are given below

(i) These are used in AM (Amplitude Modulation) from 530 kHz to 1710 kHz. These are also used in ground wave propagation.

(ii) These are used as TV waves, ranging from 54 MHz to 890 MHz.

(iii) These are used in FM (Frequency Modulation) ranging from 88 MHz to 108 MHz.

(iv) UHF (Ultra High Frequency) waves are used in cellular phones.

Microwaves

These waves are also called **short wavelength radio waves** which are produced by vacuum tubes. Their frequency lies in the range of 1 GHz to 300 GHz (gigahertz).

Uses of microwaves are given below

(i) These are used in RADAR systems for aircraft navigation.

(ii) These are used in microwave oven for cooking purpose.

(iii) These are used in the study of atomic and molecular structures.

(iv) These are used to measure the speed of vehicle, speed of cricket ball, in long-distance wireless communication, etc.

Infrared Waves

These waves were discovered by Herschell. These waves are also called **heat waves.** These waves are produced from the heat radiating bodies and by rotational and vibrational transitions in molecules.

They have high penetration power. Its frequency range is from 3×10^{11} Hz to 4×10^{14} Hz.

Uses of infrared waves are given below

(i) These are used in physical therapy.

(ii) These are used in satellite for army purpose.

(iii) These are used in weather forecasting.

(iv) These are used for producing dehydrated fruits, in green houses to keep the plants warm.

(v) These are used in solar water heater, solar cells and cooker.

Visible Rays

It is that part of spectrum which is visible by human eye and its frequency range is from 4×10^{14} Hz to 7×10^{14} Hz.

Uses of visible rays are given below

Visible rays are used by the optical organs of humans and animals for three primary purposes given below:

(i) To see things and escape danger.

(ii) The visible light emitted or reflected from objects provides us information about the world.

(iii) Helps to do all activities required for life.

(iv) To find other living things with which to consort so as to prolong the species.

Ultraviolet Rays

These rays were discovered by Ritter in 1801. These rays are produced by special lamps and very hot bodies. The sun is an important source of UV-rays but fortunately absorbed by ozone layer at an altitude of about 40-50km and protect us from its harmful effects. Its frequency range is from 10^{14} Hz to 10^{16} Hz.

Uses of ultraviolet rays are given below

(i) These are used in burglar alarm.
(ii) These are used in checking mineral sample.
(iii) These are used to study molecular structure.
(iv) To kill germs in minerals.
(v) To sterilise surgical instruments.
(vi) These rays can be focussed into very narrow beams for high precision applications such as LASIK eye surgery.

X-Rays

These rays were discovered by German professor Roentgen. Its frequency range is from 3×10^{16} Hz to 3×10^{21} Hz.

Uses of X-rays are given below

(i) These are used in surgery to detect the fracture, diseased organs, stones in the body, etc.
(ii) These are used in engineering to detect fault, crack in bridges, testing of welds.
(iii) These are used at metro station to detect metal or explosive material.
(iv) These are used in scientific research.

Gamma (γ) Rays

These rays were discovered by Rutherford. They travel with the speed of light and having high penetration power. The frequency ranges from 3×10^{18} Hz to 5×10^{22} Hz.

Uses of gamma (γ) rays are given below

(i) These are used to produce nuclear reaction.
(ii) These are used in radio therapy for the treatment of tumour and cancer.
(iii) These are used in food industry to kill pathogenic micro-organism.
(iv) These are used to provide valuable information about the structure of atomic nucleus.

Different Types of Electromagnetic Waves

Type	Wavelength range	Production	Detection
Radio wave	> 0.1 m	Rapid acceleration and decelerations of electrons in aerials	Receiver's aerials
Microwave	0.1 m to 1 mm	Klystron valve or magnetron valve	Point contact diodes
Infrared wave	1 mm to 700 nm	Vibration of atoms and molecules	Thermopiles bolometer, Infrared photographic film
Light	700 nm to 400 nm	Electrons in atoms emit light when they move from higher energy level to a lower energy level	The eye, Photocells, Photographic film
Ultraviolet rays	400 nm to 1 nm	Inner shell electrons in atoms moving from higher energy level to a lower energy level	Photocells, Photographic film
X-rays	1 nm to 10^{-3} nm	X-ray tubes or inner shell electrons	Photographic film, Geiger tubes, Ionisation chamber
Gamma rays	$< 10^{-3}$nm	Radioactive decay of the nucleus	Photographic film, ionisation chamber

Topic Practice 1

Multiple Choice Questions

(1 Mark)

1. The charge on a parallel plate capacitor varies as $q = q_0 \cos 2\pi\nu t$. The plates are very large and close together (area = A, separation = d). Neglecting the edge effects, find the displacement current through the capacitor. **NCERT Exemplar**
   (a) $-\sin 2\pi\nu t\ (2\pi\nu)$
   (b) $q_0 \cos 2\pi\nu t$
   (c) $2\pi\ q_0 \nu \sin(2\pi\nu t)$
   (d) $-2\pi\ q_0 \nu \sin(2\pi\nu t)$

2. The speed of electromagnetic wave in vacuum depends upon the source of radiation. It
   (a) increases as we move from γ-rays to radio waves
   (b) decreases as we move from γ-rays to radio waves
   (c) is same for all of them
   (d) None of the above

3. A plane electromagnetic wave of frequency 30 MHz travels in free space along x-direction. The electric field component of the wave at a particular point of space and time $E = 6\ \text{Vm}^{-1}$ along y-direction. Its magnetic field component B at this point would be
   (a) 2×10^{-8} T along z-direction
   (b) 6×10^{-8} T along x-direction
   (c) 2×10^{-8} T along y-direction
   (d) 6×10^{-8} T along z-direction

4. If ε_0 and μ_0 are the electric permittivity and magnetic permeability of free space and ε and μ are the corresponding quantities in the medium, the index of refraction of the medium in terms of above parameter is

(a) $\dfrac{\varepsilon\mu}{\varepsilon_0\mu_0}$ (b) $\left(\dfrac{\varepsilon\mu}{\varepsilon_0\mu_0}\right)^{1/2}$

(c) $\left(\dfrac{\varepsilon_0\mu_0}{\varepsilon\mu}\right)$ (d) $\left(\dfrac{\varepsilon_0\mu_0}{\varepsilon\mu}\right)^{1/2}$

5. Light wave is travelling along y-direction. If the corresponding E vector at any time is along the X-axis, the direction of B vector at that time is along

(a) Y-axis (b) X-axis

(c) $+Z$-axis (d) $-Z$-axis

6. X-rays are not used for radar purposes, because they are not

(a) reflected by target

(b) partly absorbed by target

(c) electromagnetic waves

(d) completely absorbed by target

Very Short Answer Type Questions

(1 Mark)

7. A capacitor has been charged by a DC source. What are the magnitude of conduction and displacement current when it is fully charged?

8. A variable frequency AC source is connected to a capacitor. How will the displacement current change with decrease in frequency? **NCERT Exemplar**

9. The charging current for a capacitor is 0.25 A. What is the displacement current across its plates?

10. How are electric vector (E), magnetic vector (B) and velocity vector (v) oriented in an electromagnetic waves? **ISC 2015, 2008**

11. A charged particle oscillates about its mean position with frequency 10^9 Hz. What is the frequency of electromagnetic wave produced by the oscillators? **NCERT**

12. In which directions do the electric and magnetic field vectors oscillate in an electromagnetic wave propagating along the X-axis?

13. How is the speed of electromagnetic waves in vacuum determined by the electric and magnetic fields?

14. Do electromagnetic waves carry energy and momentum?

15. An electromagnetic wave exerts pressure on the surface on which it is incident. Justify.

16. To which part of the electromagnetic spectrum does a wave of frequency 5×10^{19} Hz belong?

17. One requires 11 eV of energy to dissociate a carbon monoxide molecule into carbon and oxygen atoms. In which region of spectrum, the minimum frequency of the appropriate electromagnetic radiation lies?

18. What physical quantity is the same for X-rays of wavelength 10^{-10} m, red light of wavelength 6800 Å and radio waves of wavelength 500 m? **NCERT**

19. Name the electromagnetic wave/radiation which is used to study crystal structure. **ISC 2023**

20. Name the electromagnetic waves which
    (i) maintain the earth's warmth and
    (ii) are used in aircraft navigation.

21. Name the electromagnetic waves used in LASIK eye surgery and why?

22. To which regions of the electromagnetic spectrum do the following wavelength belong:
    (i) 250 nm (ii) 1500 nm **ISC 2016**

23. Which electromagnetic radiation has wavelength greater than that of X-rays and smaller than that of visible light? **ISC 2012, 10**

24. In which part of electromagnetic spectrum, do the following radiations lie
    (i) having wavelength of 20 nm?
    (ii) having frequency of 10 MHz? **ISC 2009**

Short Answer Type I Questions

(2 Marks)

25. When an ideal capacitor is charged by a DC battery, no current flows. However, when an AC source is used, the current flows continuously. How does one explain this, based on the concept of displacement current?

26. A capacitor made of two parallel plates each of the area A and separation d, is being charged by an external AC source. Show that the displacement current inside the capacitor is the same as the current charging the capacitor.

27. (i) An electromagnetic wave is travelling in a medium with a velocity $\mathbf{v} = v\,\hat{\mathbf{i}}$. Draw a sketch showing the propagation of the electromagnetic wave indicating the direction of the oscillating electric and magnetic fields.
(ii) How are the magnitudes of the electric and magnetic fields related to velocity of the electromagnetic wave?

28. (i) State any one use of infrared radiations.
(ii) State any one source of ultraviolet radiations. **ISC 2020**

29. Mention two applications of Infrared radiation. **ISC 2015**

30. (i) Name the electromagnetic radiation whose frequency is 10^{11} Hz.
(ii) What is the speed of radio waves in vacuum? **ISC 2024**

31. (i) State any one property which is common to all electromagnetic waves.
(ii) Arrange the following electromagnetic waves in increasing order of their frequencies (i.e. begin with the lowest frequency):
Visible light, γ-rays, X-rays, microwaves, radio waves, infrared radiations and ultraviolet radiations. **ISC 2017**

32. Name the part of the electromagnetic spectrum which is
(i) suitable for radar systems used in aircraft navigation.
(ii) produced by bombarding a metal target with high speed electrons. **ISC 2014**

33. (i) In an electromagnetic wave, how are electric vector (**E**), magnetic vector (**B**) and velocity of propagation of the wave (**c**) oriented?
(ii) How long would gamma radiation take to travel from the Sun to the Earth, a distance of 1.5×10^{11} m? **ISC 2013**

34. Microwaves, X-rays, UV-rays, infrared rays. Which of the above electromagnetic waves has
(i) the shortest wavelength?
(ii) the lowest frequency? **ISC 2005**

35. (i) What is the ratio of the speed of gamma rays to that of radio waves in vacuum?
(ii) Name an electromagnetic wave which is used in the radar system used in aircraft navigation. **ISC 2018**

Short Answer Type II Questions

3 Marks

36. How are electromagnetic waves produced by oscillating charges?
Draw a sketch of linearly polarised electromagnetic waves propagating in the z-direction. Indicate the directions of the oscillating electric and magnetic fields.

37. (i) Describe briefly how electromagnetic waves are produced by oscillating charges?
(ii) Give one use of each of the following
(a) Microwaves (b) X-rays
(c) Infrared rays (d) Gamma rays

38. Name the electromagnetic waves, in the wavelength range 10 nm to 10^{-3} nm. How are these waves generated? Write their two uses.

39. Answer the following questions.
(i) Name the electromagnetic waves which are used for the treatment of certain forms of cancer. Write their frequency range.
(ii) Thin ozone layer on top of stratosphere is crucial for human survival. Why?
(iii) Why is the amount of the momentum transferred by the electromagnetic waves incident on the surface so small?

40. Answer the following questions.
(i) Name the electromagnetic waves which are produced during radioactive decay of a nucleus.Write their frequency range.
(ii) Welders wear special glass goggles while working. Why?
(iii) Why are infrared waves often called as heat waves? Give their one application.

41. Name the parts of the electromagnetic spectrum which is
(i) suitable for RADAR systems in aircraft navigations.

(ii) used to treat muscular strain.
(iii) used as a diagnostic tool in medicine.
Write in brief, how these waves can be produced?

42. Name the following constituent radiations of electromagnetic spectrum which
(i) produce intense heating effect.
(ii) is absorbed by the ozone layer in the atmosphere.
(iii) is used for studying crystal structure. Write one more application for each of these radiations.

43. Identify the part of the electromagnetic spectrum which is
(i) suitable for radar system used in aircraft navigation.
(ii) produced by bombarding a metal target by high speed electrons. Write their frequency range.

44. (i) Which segment of electromagnetic waves has highest frequency? How are these waves produced? Give one use of these waves.
(ii) Which EM wave lies near the high frequency end of visible part of EM spectrum? Give its one use. In what way, this component of light has harmful effects on humans?

45. (i) Arrange all the seven types of electromagnetic radiations in increasing order of their frequencies. You must begin with a radiation with lowest frequency and end with the one having the highest frequency. **ISC 2014, 11**
(ii) State how electric vector E, magnetic vector B and velocity vector c are oriented in an electromagnetic wave. **ISC 2015, 08**

46. Name any two electromagnetic waves. State any one similarity and one difference between them. **ISC 2007, 03**

Long Answer Type Question

5 Marks

47. Describe very briefly four regions of electromagnetic spectrum mentioning their special properties/features. **ISC 2002**

Numerical Problems

48. The current in a circuit containing a capacitor is 0.15 A. What is the displacement current and where does it exist? **(1 M)**

49. You are given a 2 μF parallel plate capacitor. How would you establish an instantaneous displacement current of 1 mA in the space between its plates? **NCERT Exemplar (2 M)**

50. Calculate the displacement current between the square plates of side 1 cm of a capacitor, if electric field between the plates is changing at the rate of 3×10^6 V m^{-1} s^{-1}. **(2M)**

51. An electron beam passes through crossed electric and magnetic fields of 3.4×10^4 Vm^{-1} and 2×10^{-3} Wbm^{-2}, respectively. If the path of the beam remains undeviated, calculate the speed of the electrons.
If the electric field is removed. What will be the radius of the circular path described by the electrons? **ISC 2008**

52. A parallel plate capacitor (shown in the figure) made of circular plates each of radius $R = 6.0$ cm has a capacitance $C = 100$ pF. The capacitor is connected to a 230 V AC supply with angular frequency of 300 rad/s.

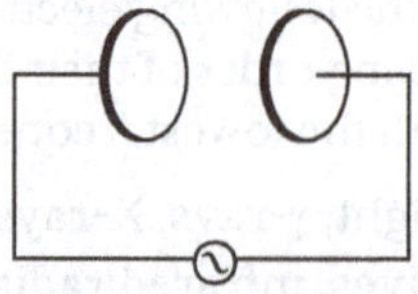

(i) What is the rms value of the conduction current?
(ii) Is the conduction current equal to the displacement current?
(iii) Determine the amplitude of B at a point 3.0 cm from the axis between the plates. **NCERT, (3 M)**

53. A plane electromagnetic wave travels in vacuum along z-direction. What can you say about the directions of electric and magnetic field vectors? If the frequency of the wave is 30 MHz. What is its wavelength? **NCERT (1 M)**

54. A radio can tune into any station in the 7.5 MHz to 12 MHz band. What is its corresponding wavelength? **NCERT (2 M)**

55. The magnetic field of a beam emerging from a fitter facing a floodlight is given by $B = 12 \times 10^{-8} \sin(1.20 \times 10^7\, z - 3.60 \times 10^{15} t)$T. What is the average intensity of the beam? **NCERT Exemplar (2 M)**

56. About 5% of the power of a 100 W light bulb is connected to visible radiation. What is the average intensity of visible radiation at
(i) distance of 1 m from the bulb
(ii) distance of 10 m? Assume that the radiation is emitted isotropically and neglect reflection. **NCERT (2 M)**

57. The amplitude of the magnetic field part of a harmonic electromagnetic wave in vacuum is $B_0 = 510$ nT. What is the amplitude of the electric field part of the wave? **NCERT (2 M)**

58. In a plane, electric field oscillates sinusoidally at a frequency of 2×10^{10} Hz and amplitude 48 V/m.
(i) What is the wavelength of the wave?
(ii) What is the amplitude of the oscillating magnetic field?
(iii) Show that the average energy density of the **E** field equals the average energy density of the **B** field. **NCERT (3 M)**

59. Suppose that the electric field amplitude of an electromagnetic wave is $E_0 = 120$ N/C and that its frequency is $\nu = 50.0$ MHz. (i) Determine B_0, ω, k and λ. (ii) Find expressions for **E** and **B**. **NCERT (3 M)**

60. Suppose that the electric field part of an electromagnetic wave in vacuum is
$$E = [3.1 \cos\{1.8\,y + (5.4 \times 10^6 t)\}]\,\hat{\mathbf{i}}$$
(i) What is the direction of propagation?
(ii) What is the wavelength λ?
(iii) What is the frequency ν?
(iv) What is the amplitude of the magnetic field part of the wave?
(v) Write an expression for the magnetic field part of the wave. **NCERT (3 M)**

61. The terminology of different parts of the electromagnetic spectrum is given in the text. Use the formula $E = h\nu$ (for energy of a quantum of radiation: photon) and obtain the photon energy in units of eV for different parts of the electromagnetic spectrum. In what way are the different scales of photon energies that you obtain related to the sources of electromagnetic radiation? **NCERT (3 M)**

Hints & Solutions

1. (*d*) Displacement current (I_d) is equal to charging current $(I_d = dq/dt)$. Thus,
$$I_d = \frac{dq}{dt} = \frac{d}{dt}(q) = \frac{d}{dt}(q_0 \cos 2\pi\nu t)$$
$$I_d = q_0(-\sin 2\pi\nu t)(2\pi\nu) = -2\pi q_0 \nu \sin(2\pi\nu t)$$

2. (*c*) Speed of electromagnetic wave in vacuum
$$= \frac{1}{\sqrt{\mu_0 \varepsilon_0}} = \text{constant}$$
It shown that speed of electromagnetic wave depends on a absolute permittivity in free space or vacuum (E_0) and absolute permeability in free space or vacuum (μ_0).

3. (*a*) The frequency of electromagnetic wave along x-direction, i.e. $\nu = 30$ MHz

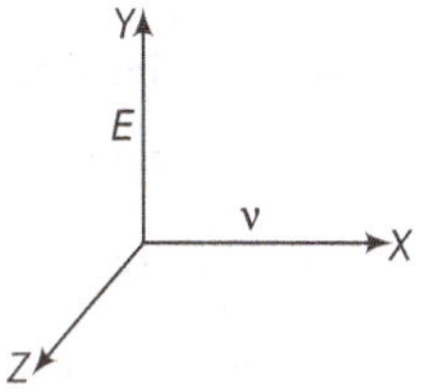

The electric field component of the wave along y-direction, i.e. $E = 6\ \text{Vm}^{-1}$

In electromagnetic, the ratio of the amplitude of electric and magnetic field is always constant and it is equal to velocity of the electromagnetic waves.

i.e. $$\frac{E}{B} = c$$

$$\Rightarrow \quad B = \frac{E}{c} = \frac{6}{3 \times 10^8} = 2 \times 10^{-8}\ \text{T}$$

Magnetic field of component B is 2×10^{-8} T along z-direction.

4. (*b*) Velocity of light in vacuum, $c = \dfrac{1}{\sqrt{\mu_0 \varepsilon_0}}$

Velocity of light in medium, $v = \dfrac{1}{\sqrt{\mu\varepsilon}}$

So, $$n = \frac{c}{v} = \left(\frac{\mu\varepsilon}{\mu_0 \varepsilon_0}\right)^{1/2}$$

5. (*c*) Electromagnetic radiation is a self propagating wave in space with electric and magnetic components. These components oscillate at right angles to each other and to the direction of propagation.

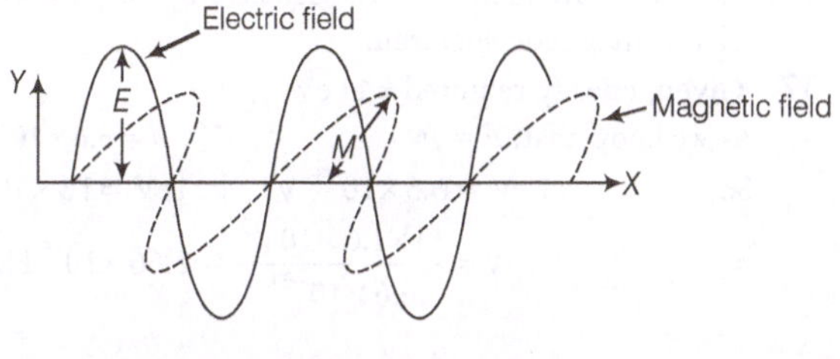

Hence, B is along the Z-axis at that time.

6. (a) X-rays has wavelength about 1 nm to 10^{-3} nm. Which carries minimum wavelength and maximum energy, i.e. $E \propto 1/\lambda$. So, it penetrates the target and hence are not reflected back by target.

7. Electric flux through plates of capacitor, $\phi_E = \frac{q}{\varepsilon_0}$.

where, charge, q = constant (as the capacitor is fully charged)

Displacement current, $I_d = \varepsilon_0 \frac{d\phi_E}{dt} = \varepsilon_0 \frac{d\left(\frac{q}{\varepsilon_0}\right)}{dt} = 0$ (1/2)

Conduction current, $I_c = C\frac{dV}{dt} = 0$ (as voltage becomes constant when the capacitor becomes fully charged). (1/2)

8. Capacitive reactance, $X_C = \frac{1}{\omega C} = \frac{1}{2\pi\nu C}$

$\therefore \quad X_C \propto \frac{1}{\nu}$ (1/2)

As frequency decreases, X_C increases. As the conduction current is inversely proportional to X_C $\left[\because I \propto \frac{1}{X_C}\right]$.

So, displacement current also decreases because the conduction current is equal to the displacement current. (1/2)

9. The displacement current is equal to 0.25 A, as the charging current is 0.25 A.

10. Direction of electric field **E**, direction of magnetic field **B** and direction of propagation of wave are mutually perpendicular to one another.

11. The frequency of electromagnetic wave produced by the oscillators is same as that of oscillating charged particle about its equilibrium position, i.e. 10^9 Hz.

12. **E** and **B** are perpendicular to direction of propagation of light. Also, direction of propagation is parallel to $\mathbf{E} \times \mathbf{B}$. Hence, **E** is along $\hat{\mathbf{j}}$ or $+Y$-axis and **B** is along $\hat{\mathbf{k}}$ or $+Z$-axis.

13. To determine speed of light in vacuum, we use the formula, $c = \frac{E_0}{B_0} = \frac{E_{rms}}{B_{rms}}$

where, E_0 and B_0 are maximum electric field and magnetic field component respectively, of electromagnetic waves.

14. Yes, electromagnetic waves carry energy and momentum.

Momentum, $p = \frac{U}{c}$ and energy density $= \frac{1}{2}\varepsilon_0 E^2$.

15. Electromagnetic wave carries energy and momentum. Since, it has momentum due to this reason it exert pressure, called radiation pressure.

16. A wave of frequency 5×10^{19} Hz belongs to γ-rays of electromagnetic spectrum.

17. Given, energy required = 11 eV

As we know that, $E = h\nu$ $\quad [\because h = 6.6 \times 10^{-34}$ J-s]

So, $\quad 11 \text{ eV} = 6.6 \times 10^{-34} \nu \quad [\because 1 \text{ eV} = 1.6 \times 10^{-19}$ J]

$\Rightarrow \quad \nu = \frac{11 \times 1.6 \times 10^{-19}}{6.6 \times 10^{-34}} = 2.66 \times 10^{15}$ Hz

This frequency of radiation belongs to ultraviolet region.

18. Speed remains same but wavelength changes.

19. To study the structure of crystals, we use X-rays as the distance between 2 atoms in a crystal is very similar to wavelength of X-rays. (1)

20. (i) Infrared rays (ii) Microwaves (½+½)

21. In LASIK eye surgery, ultraviolet rays are used because of their short wavelength they can be focused into very narrow beam.

22. (i) Wavelength 250 nm corresponds to the ultraviolet region of electromagnetic spectrum. (1/2)

(ii) Wavelength 1500 nm corresponds to the infrared region of electromagnetic spectrum. (1/2)

23. Wavelength of ultraviolet radiation (1×10^{-8} m to 4×10^{-7} m) lies in between X-ray and visible light. It is shorter than light wave (4×10^{-7} m to 8×10^{-7} m) and longer than X-ray (1×10^{-11} m to 3×10^{-8} m).

24. Electromagnetic waves lies in the region of

(i) Ultraviolet rays [wavelength, $\lambda = 20$ nm] (1/2)

(ii) radio waves [frequency, $\nu = 10$ MHz] (1/2)

25. If an ideal capacitor is charged by DC battery, current flows momentarily till capacitor gets fully charged after that no current flow. However, when an AC source is connected, then conduction current, $I_c = \frac{dq}{dt}$ starts flowing in the connecting wire. As charging polarity of AC current changes, the capacitor is alternatively charged and discharged with time. This causes change in electric field between plates of the capacitor which causes electric flux to change and gives rise to displacement current in the region between plates of capacitor, as displacement current, $I_d = E_0 \frac{d\phi_E}{dt}$ and $I_d = I_c$ at all instants. (2)

26. Let the alternating emf charging the plates of capacitor be $V = V_0 \sin \omega t$ ...(i)

Charge on the capacitor,

$q = CV = CV_0 \sin \omega t$ [from Eq.(i)]

and instantaneous current, $I = \frac{dq}{dt} = \frac{d}{dt}(CV_0 \sin\omega t)$

$= \omega CV_0 \cos \omega t = I_0 \cos \omega t$ (1)

where, $\quad I_0 = \omega CV_0$

Displacement current, $\quad I_d = \varepsilon_0 \frac{d\phi_E}{dt}$

$\Rightarrow \quad \varepsilon_0 A \frac{d(E)}{dt} = \varepsilon_0 A \frac{d}{dt}\left(\frac{q}{\varepsilon_0 A}\right) = \varepsilon_0 A \frac{d}{dt}\left(\frac{CV_0 \sin\omega t}{\varepsilon_0 A}\right)$

$= \frac{d}{dt}(CV_0 \sin\omega t)$

$= \omega CV_0 \cos\omega t = I_0 \cos\omega t$

Thus, the displacement current inside the capacitor is the same as the current charging the capacitor. (1)

27. (i) Given that velocity $\mathbf{v} = v\,\hat{\mathbf{i}}$, i.e. the wave is propagating along X-axis, so electric field **E** is along Y-axis and magnetic field **B** is along Z-axis. The propagation of electromagnetic wave is shown in the figure.

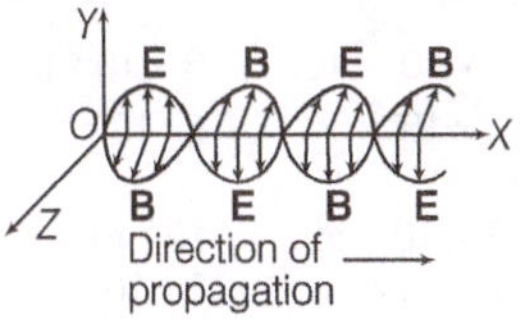

(1)

(ii) Speed of electromagnetic wave can be given as

$$c = \frac{E_0}{B_0} = \frac{E}{B}$$

where, E_0 and B_0 are peak values of E and B or instantaneous values of E and B. (1)

28. (i) Refer to text on page 312 (Infrared Waves).

(ii) Refer to text given on pages 312 and 313 (Ultraviolet Waves). (2)

29. Two applications of infrared radiations are

(i) used to treat sprains and muscular pains,

(ii) used in long distance photography.

30. (i) Infrared radiation has frequency range 3×10^{11} Hz to 4×10^{14} Hz. (1)

(ii) Radio wave is an electromagnetic wave. These waves do not require any material medium for propagation and travel in vacuum with the speed of light, i.e. 3×10^8 m/s. (1)

31. (i) One property which is common to all electromagnetic waves is as follows:

The energy associated with the EM waves is equally divided between electric and magnetic field. (1)

(ii) Electromagnetic waves in increasing order of their frequencies are as follows:

(3×10^3 to 3×10^8 Hz)

Radio waves < Microwaves < Infrared
(4×10^{14} Hz $\rightarrow 8 \times 10^{14}$ Hz)

Radiations < Visible light < Ultraviolet

Radiations < X-rays < Gamma rays
(5×10^{18}- 5×10^{22} Hz) (1)

32. (i) Microwaves are suitable for radar systems used in aircraft navigation. (1)

(ii) When a metal target is bombarded with high speed electrons, X-rays are produced.

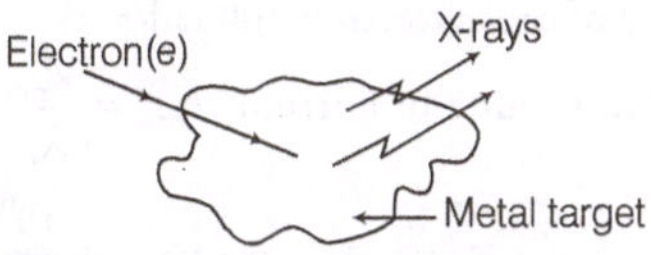

(1)

33. (i) In an electromagnetic waves, electric vector **E** and magnetic vector **B** are perpendicular to each other and **c** (i.e. propagation of electromagnetic wave) is perpendicular to both **E** and **B**.

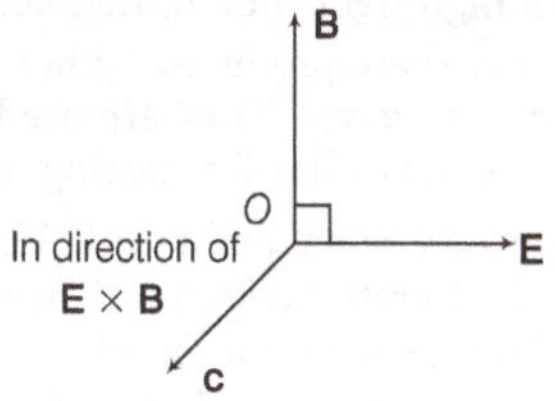

(1)

(ii) Speed of γ-radiation is $c = 3 \times 10^8$ m/s.

Given, distance $= 1.5 \times 10^{11}$ m

Time taken by γ-radiation to travel from the Sun to the Earth is given by

$$\therefore \quad \text{Time} = \frac{\text{Distance}}{\text{Velocity}} = \frac{1.5 \times 10^{11}}{3 \times 10^8} = 5 \times 10^2 \text{ s}$$ (1)

34. (i) The X-rays has the shortest wavelength [$\lambda = 1$ nm]. (1)

(ii) Microwaves has the lowest frequency [$\nu = 10^9$ Hz]. (1)

35. (i) The speed of gamma rays and radio waves in vacuum are same. So, the ratio of speed of gamma rays to that of radio waves will be 1:1. (1)

(ii) Microwave is used in radar system for aircraft navigation. (1)

36. Refer to text on page 310 (Electromagnetic waves).

37. (i) Refer to text on page 310 (Source of electromagnetic waves).

(ii) Refer to text on pages 312 and 313 (Electromagnetic spectrum).

38. Refer to text on pages 312 and 313 (Electromagnetic spectrum).

X-rays are generated, when high speed electrons are bombarded with a metal target.

39. (i) γ-rays. Its frequency range is from 3×10^{18} Hz to 5×10^{22} Hz. (1)

(ii) The thin ozone layer on top of stratosphere absorbs most of the harmful ultraviolet rays coming from the sun towards the earth. They include UVA, UVB and UVC radiations which can destroy the life system on the earth. Hence, this layer is crucial for human survival. (1)

(iii) Momentum transferred = Energy/Speed of light

$$= \frac{E}{c}$$

$$\boxed{= \frac{h\nu}{c} \approx 10^{-22}}$$

Thus, the amount of the momentum transferred by the electromagnetic waves incident on the surface is very small. (1)

40. (i) γ-rays. Its frequency range is from 3×10^{18} Hz to 5×10^{22} Hz. (1)

(ii) Welders wear special glass goggles to protect the eyes from high frequency ultraviolet rays. (1)

(iii) Infrared waves are produced by hot bodies, so they are called heat waves. They are used in physiotherapy,weather forecasting, etc. (1)

41. (i) Microwaves are suitable for RADAR systems that are used in aircraft navigation. These rays are produced by special vacuum tubes, namely klystrons, magnetrons and gunn diodes. (1)

(ii) Infrared rays are used to treat muscular strain. These rays are produced by hot bodies and molecules. (1)

(iii) X-rays are used as a diagnostic tool in medicine. These rays are produced when high energy electrons are stopped suddenly on a metal of high atomic number. (1)

42. Refer to text on pages 312 and 313 (Electromagnetic spectrum).

43. Refer to text on pages 312 and 313 (Electromagnetic spectrum).

44. (i) Gamma rays has the highest-frequency in the electromagnetic waves. These rays are of the nuclear origin and are produced in the disintegration of radioactive atomic nuclei and in the decay of certain subatomic particles. They are used in the treatment of cancer and tumours. (1)

(ii) Ultraviolet rays lie near the high frequency end of visible part of EM spectrum. These rays are used to preserve food stuff. The harmful effect from exposure to ultraviolet (UV) radiation can be life threatening and include premature aging of the skin, suppression of the immune systems, damage to the eyes and skin cancer. (2)

45. (i) Electromagnetic radiations in increasing order of their frequencies are

radio waves < microwaves < infrared radiation < visible light < ultraviolet radiation < X-rays < gamma rays. (1½)

(ii) Refer to text on page 310 (Transverse nature of electromagnetic waves) (1½)

46. Example of two electromagnetic waves are microwaves and radio waves. (1)

Similarity Both the waves travel with the same speed in vacuum as the speed of light (3×10^8 m/s). (1)

Difference Radio waves are having frequency range 3×10^9 to 3×10^4 Hz

while microwaves are having frequency range 3×10^{11} to 1×10^9 Hz. (1)

47. The distribution of electromagnetic radiations according to their wavelength or frequency is called the electromagnetic spectrum. (1)

Four regions of electromagnetic spectrum are as follows:

(i) X-rays (ii) Infrared rays

(iii) Ultraviolet rays (iv) γ-rays (2)

Name	Wavelength (in m)	Frequency (in Hz)	Source
γ-rays	6×10^{-14} to 1×10^{-10}	5×10^{20} to 3×10^{19}	Radioactive decay of the nucleus
X-rays	1×10^{-10} to 3×10^{-8}	3×10^{19} to 1×10^{16}	X-ray tubes or inner shell electrons
Ultraviolet rays	3×10^{-8} to 4×10^{-7}	10^{16} to 8×10^{14}	Excitation of atom, spark and arc lamp
Infrared rays	8×10^{-7} to 3×10^{-5}	4×10^{14} to 1×10^{13}	Excitation of atoms and molecules

(2)

48. We know that, conduction current I_c is equal to the displacement current I_d.

i.e. $I_c = I_d = 0.15$ A [given]

It exists across the capacitor plates.

49. Refer to example 2 on page 309. (1)

So, by applying a varying potential difference of 500V/s, we would produce a displacement current of desired value. (1)

50. We know that, $I_d = \varepsilon_0 A \dfrac{dE}{dt}$

where, $\varepsilon_0 = 8.85\times10^{-12}\ C^2N^{-1}m^{-2}$

Area, $A = 1\ cm^2 = 10^{-4}\ m^2$

$\because \quad \dfrac{dE}{dt} = 3\times10^6\ Vm^{-1}\ s^{-1}$ (1)

$\therefore \quad I_d = 8.85\times10^{-12}\times10^{-4}\times3\times10^6 = 2.7\times10^{-9}$ A (1)

51. Given, $E = 3.4\times10^4$ V/m

$B = 2\times10^{-3}\ Wb/m^2$

$\therefore$ Speed $(v) = \dfrac{E}{B} = \dfrac{3.4\times10^4}{2\times10^{-3}} = 1.70\times10^7$ m/s

Radius of the circular path described by the electrons when electric field is removed is

$$r = \frac{mv}{qB}$$

$$= \frac{9.1\times10^{-31}\times1.70\times10^7}{1.6\times10^{-19}\times2\times10^{-3}}$$

or $r = 4.83\times10^{-2}$ m.

52. Given, radius of plates, $R = 6\ cm = 6\times10^{-2}$ m

Capacitance of capacitor,

$C = 100\ pF = 100\times10^{-12}\ F = 10^{-10}$ F

Voltage of capacitor, $V = 230$ V

Frequency of capacitor, $\omega = 300$ rad/s

(i) The rms value of current, $I_{rms} = \dfrac{V_{rms}}{X_C}$

$\therefore \quad X_C = \dfrac{1}{\omega C} = \dfrac{1}{300\times10^{-10}} = \dfrac{10^{10}}{300}\ \Omega$

$\therefore \quad I_{rms} = \dfrac{230 \times 300}{10^{10}} = 3 \times 23 \times 1000 \times 10^{-10}$

$= 69 \times 10^{-7} = 6.9 \times 10^{-6} A = 6.9 \mu A$ (1)

(ii) Yes, the conduction current is equal to displacement current. (1)

(iii) Given, the distance of point from the axis between the plates, $r = 3 \text{ cm} = 3 \times 10^{-2}$ m

Radius of plates, $R = 6 \text{ cm} = 6 \times 10^{-2}$ m

The magnetic field at a point between the plates,

$$B = \frac{\mu_0}{2\pi R^2} \cdot r \cdot I_d \Rightarrow B = \frac{\mu_0 r}{2\pi R^2} I \quad [\because I_d = I]$$

If $I = I_0$ is maximum value of current, then

$$I = \sqrt{2} I_{rms}$$

$$\therefore \quad B = \frac{\mu_0 r}{2\pi R^2} \sqrt{2} I_{rms}$$

$$= \frac{4\pi \times 10^{-7} \times 0.03 \times \sqrt{2} \times 6.9 \times 10^{-6}}{2\pi \times 0.06 \times 0.06}$$

$= 1.63 \times 10^{-11}$ T (2)

53. **E** and **B** vectors must be in x and y-directions.

As we know, $\lambda = \dfrac{c}{\nu} = \dfrac{3 \times 10^8}{30 \times 10^6} = 10$ m

$(30 \text{MHz} = 30 \times 10^6 \text{Hz})$

54. For 7.5 MHz band,

Wavelength, $\lambda_1 = \dfrac{c}{\nu} = \dfrac{3 \times 10^8}{7.5 \times 10^6} = 40$ m (1)

For 12 MHz band,

Wavelength, $\lambda_2 = \dfrac{c}{\nu} = \dfrac{3 \times 10^8}{12 \times 10^6} = 25$ m

So, wavelength range is from 25 m to 40 m. (1)

55. Magnetic field, $\mathbf{B} = B_0 \sin\omega t$

Given equation,

$$B = 12 \times 10^{-8} \sin (1.20 \times 10^7 z - 3.60 \times 10^{15} t) \text{T}$$

On comparing this equation with standard equation, we get

$B_0 = 12 \times 10^{-8}$ T (1/2)

The average intensity of the beam,

$$I_{av} = \frac{B_0^2}{2\mu_0} \cdot c = \frac{1}{2} \times \frac{(12 \times 10^{-8})^2 \times 3 \times 10^8}{4\pi \times 10^{-7}}$$

$\Rightarrow I_{av} = 1.71 \text{ W/m}^2$ (1½)

56. (i) $\therefore$ Intensity, $I = \dfrac{\text{Power of visible light}}{\text{Area}}$

$= \dfrac{100 \times (5/100)}{4\pi(1)^2} = 0.4 \text{ W/m}^2$ (1)

(ii) $I = \dfrac{100 \times \left(\dfrac{5}{100}\right)}{4\pi(10)^2} = 4 \times 10^{-3} \text{ W/m}^2$ (1)

57. Given, amplitude of the magnetic field part of harmonic electromagnetic wave,

$B_0 = 510 \text{ nT} = 510 \times 10^{-9}$ T (1/2)

Speed of light in vacuum, $c = \dfrac{E_0}{B_0}$ (1/2)

where, E_0 is the amplitude of electric field part of the wave.

$\Rightarrow \quad 3 \times 10^8 = \dfrac{E_0}{510 \times 10^{-9}}$

$\Rightarrow \quad E_0 = 153$ N/C

Thus, the amplitude of the electric field part of wave is 153 N/C. (1)

58. Given, frequency of oscillation, $\nu = 2 \times 10^{10}$ Hz

Speed of wave, $c = 3 \times 10^8$ m/s

Electric field amplitude, $E_0 = 48$ V/m

(i) Wavelength of wave,

$\lambda = \dfrac{c}{\nu} = \dfrac{3 \times 10^8}{2 \times 10^{10}} = 1.5 \times 10^{-2}$ m (1/2)

(ii) The amplitude of the oscillating magnetic field,

$B_0 = \dfrac{E_0}{c} = \dfrac{48}{3 \times 10^8} = 1.6 \times 10^{-7}$ T (1/2)

(iii) The average energy density of electric field,

$$u_e = \frac{1}{4} \varepsilon_0 E_0^2 \quad \ldots(i)$$

As, $E_0 = cB_0$

Putting the value of E_0 in Eq. (i), we get

$$u_e = \frac{1}{4} \varepsilon_0 \cdot c^2 B_0^2 \quad \ldots(ii)$$

Speed of electromagnetic waves, $c = \dfrac{1}{\sqrt{\mu_0 \varepsilon_0}}$ (1)

Putting the value of c in Eq. (ii), we get

$$u_e = \frac{1}{4} \varepsilon_0 B_0^2 \cdot \frac{1}{\mu_0 \varepsilon_0} = \frac{1}{4} \cdot \frac{B_0^2}{\mu_0} = u_b$$

(u_b is average energy density of magnetic field)

Thus, the average energy density of the **E** field equals the average energy density of **B** field. (1)

59. Given, amplitude of an electromagnetic wave, $E_0 = 120$ N/C

Frequency of wave, $\nu = 50 \text{ MHz} = 50 \times 10^6$ Hz

(i) Speed of light in vacuum,

$$c = \frac{E_0}{B_0}$$

$B_0 = \dfrac{E_0}{c} = \dfrac{120}{3 \times 10^8} = 40 \times 10^{-8}$

$= 400 \times 10^{-9}$ T

$= 400$ nT (1/2)

Angular frequency of electromagnetic wave,

$\omega = 2\pi\nu = 2 \times 3.14 \times 50 \times 10^6$

$\omega = 3.14 \times 10^8$ rad/s (1/2)

Wave number of electromagnetic wave,

$$k = \frac{\omega}{c} = \frac{3.14\times 10^8}{3\times 10^8} = 1.05\ \text{rad/m}$$ (1/2)

Wavelength of electromagnetic wave,

$$\lambda = \frac{c}{\nu} = \frac{3\times 10^8}{50\times 10^6} = 6.00\ \text{m}$$ (1/2)

(ii) Expression of electric field, $E = E_0 \sin(kx - \omega t)$

$$E = 120 \sin(1.05x - 3.14\times 10^8 t)$$

Expression of magnetic field B,

$$B = B_0 \sin(kx - \omega t)$$
$$B = 4\times 10^{-7} \sin(1.05x - 3.14\times 10^8 t)$$ (1)

60. (i) The given equation signifies that the electromagnetic wave is moving along Y-axis and also in negative direction, so it moves in $-\hat{j}$-direction. (1/2)

(ii) The electric part of electromagnetic wave in vacuum,

$$E = [3.1 \cos\{1.8\,y + (5.4\times 10^6 t)\}]\,\hat{i}$$

Comparing with standard equation,

$$E = E_0 \cos(ky + \omega t),$$ we get

Angular frequency, $\omega = 5.4\times 10^6$ rad/s

Wave number, $k = 1.8$ rad/m

The amplitude of the electric field part of the wave,

$$E_0 = 3.1\ \text{N/C}$$
$$\lambda = \frac{2\pi}{k} = \frac{2\pi}{1.8} = 3.491\ \text{m}$$
$$\Rightarrow \quad \lambda = 3.5\ \text{m}$$ (1)

(iii) Angular frequency, $\omega = 2\pi\nu$

$$\nu = \frac{\omega}{2\pi} = \frac{5.4\times 10^6 \times 7}{2\times 22} = 0.86\times 10^6\ \text{Hz}$$ (1/2)

(iv) As, $c = \dfrac{E_0}{B_0}$

Amplitude of magnetic field,

$$B_0 = \frac{E_0}{c} = \frac{3.1}{3\times 10^8}$$
$$= 1.03\times 10^{-8}\ \text{T}$$ (1/2)

(v) Expression for the magnetic field part of wave,

$$B = B_0 \cos(ky + \omega t)\hat{k}$$
$$B = 1.03\times 10^{-8} \cos(1.8\,y + 5.4\times 10^6\, t)\,\hat{k}$$ (1/2)

61. Given, energy of photon, $E = h\nu$

For γ-rays

Frequency of γ-rays, $\nu = 3\times 10^{20}$ Hz

Energy of γ-rays, $E = h\nu = 6.6\times 10^{-34} \times 3\times 10^{20}$

$$= 19.8\times 10^{-14}\ \text{J}$$
$$\Rightarrow \quad E = \frac{19.8\times 10^{-14}}{1.6\times 10^{-19}} = 1.24\times 10^6\ \text{eV}$$

The source of γ-rays is nuclear origin. (1)

For X-rays

Frequency of X-rays, $\nu = 3\times 10^{18}$ Hz

Energy of X-rays, $E = h\nu = 6.6\times 10^{-34} \times 3\times 10^{18}$

$$= 19.8\times 10^{-16}\ \text{J}$$
$$\Rightarrow \quad E = \frac{19.8\times 10^{-16}}{1.6\times 10^{-19}} = 1.24\times 10^4\ \text{eV}$$

The retardation of high energy electron produces X-rays. Similarly, we can find for ultraviolet rays, visible rays, infrared rays, microwaves and radio waves. They originate by oscillating current. (1)

Types of radiation	Photon energy
γ-rays	1.24×10^6 eV
X-rays	1.24×10^4 eV
Ultraviolet rays	4.12 eV
Visible rays	2.475 eV
Infrared waves	4.125×10^{-2} eV
Microwaves	4.125×10^{-5} eV
Radio waves	1.24×10^{-6} eV

(1)

Summary

- **Displacement Current** When a capacitor is charged, then electric field is produced due to flow of current inside it. This current is called displacement current. It is given by
$$I_d = \frac{\varepsilon_0 \, d\phi_E}{dt}$$
- **Basic Idea of Displacement Current** Ampere's circuital law for conduction current during a charging of capacitor was found to be inconsistent. Therefore, Maxwell modified Ampere's circuital by introducing displacement current.
- **Maxwell's Equations** Maxwell's equations are the basic laws of electricity and magnetism.
- **Gauss's Law in Electrostatics** The total electric flux through any closed surface is always equal to $\frac{1}{\varepsilon_0}$ times the net charge enclosed by the surface,
i.e. $$\oint_S \mathbf{E} \cdot d\mathbf{S} = \frac{q}{\varepsilon_0}.$$
- **Gauss's Law in Magnetostatics** The net magnetic flux through any closed surface is always zero.
- **Faraday's Law of EMI** The induced emf produced in a circuit is numerically equal to the rate of change of magnetic flux through it.
i.e. $$\oint \mathbf{E} \cdot d\mathbf{l} = \frac{-d\phi_B}{dt}$$
- **Ampere's-Maxwell Circuital Law** The line integral of the magnetic field along a closed path is equal to μ_0 times the total current threading the surface bounded by that closed path,
i.e. $$\oint \mathbf{B} \cdot d\mathbf{l} = \mu(I_c + I_d)$$
- **Electromagnetic Waves** These waves produced due to change in electric field and magnetic field sinusoidally and propagates through space such that the two fields are perpendicular to each other and also perpendicular to the direction of wave propagation.
- **Source of EM Waves** Accelerating charge produces EM waves.
- **Transverse Nature of EM Waves** Since, the electric and magnetic fields in an electromagnetic wave are perpendicular to each other and also to the direction of wave propagation. Hence, electromagnetic waves are transverse in nature.
- **Electromagnetic Spectrum** The orderly arrangement of EM wave in increasing or decreasing order of wavelength or frequency is called electromagnetic spectrum. The range varies from 10^{-12} m to 10^4 m, i.e. from γ-rays to radiowaves.

For Mind Map

Visit : https://goo.gl/iMSztE OR **Scan the Code**

Chapter Practice

Multiple Choice Questions

1 Mark

1 Which of the following relation is correct?

(a) $\sqrt{\varepsilon_0 E_0} = \sqrt{\mu_0 B_0}$ (b) $\sqrt{\mu_0 \varepsilon_0}\ E_0 = B_0$

(c) $E_0 = \sqrt{\mu_0 \varepsilon_0}\ B$ (d) $\sqrt{\mu_0}\ E_0 = \sqrt{\varepsilon_0 B_0}$

2 A cube of edge a has its edges parallel to X, Y and Z-axes of rectangular coordinate system. A uniform electric field **E** is parallel to Y-axis and a uniform magnetic field is **B** parallel to X-axis. The rate at which energy flows through each face of the cube is

(a) $\frac{a^2 EB}{2\mu_0}$ parallel to XY-plane and zero in others

(b) $\frac{a^2 EB}{\mu_0}$ parallel to XY-plane and zero in others

(c) $\frac{a^2 EB}{2\mu_0}$ from all faces

(d) $\frac{a^2 EB}{2\mu_0}$ parallel to YZ- faces and zero in others

3 The ratio of amplitude of magnetic field to the amplitude of electric field for an electromagnetic wave propagating in vacuum is equal to

(a) the speed light in vacuum
(b) reciprocal of speed of light in vacuum
(c) the ratio of magnetic permeability to the electric susceptibility of vacuum
(d) unity

4 An electromagnetic wave of frequency 3 MHz passes from vacuum into a dielectric medium with permittivity $\varepsilon_r = 4$. Then,

(a) the wavelength and frequency both remain unchanged
(b) the wavelength is doubled and the frequency remains unchanged
(c) the wavelength is doubled and the frequency becomes half
(d) the wavelength is halved and the frequency remains unchanged

5 The speed of electromagnetic wave in a medium of dielectric constant 2.25 and relative permeability 4 is

(a) 1×10^{18} m/s
(b) 2.5×10^{8} m/s
(c) 2×10^{8} m/s
(d) 3×10^{8} m/s

6 The dielectric constant of air is 1.006. The speed of electromagnetic wave travelling in air is $a \times 10^8$ m/s. Where, a is about?

(a) 3 (b) 3.88
(c) 2.3 (d) 2.8

Assertion and Reason

Directions (Q. Nos. 7-9) *In the following questions, two statements are given- one labelled Assertion (A) and the other labelled Reason (R). Select the correct answer to these questions from the codes (a), (b), (c) and (d) as given below.*

(a) B-oth Assertion and Reason are true and Reason is the correct explanation of Assertion.
(b) Both Assertion and Reason are true but Reason is not the correct explanation of Assertion.
(c) Assertion is true but Reason is false.
(d) Assertion is false but Reason is true.

7 **Assertion (A)** While applying Ampere's circuital law to given surfaces with same perimeter, the left hand side $\oint B \cdot dl = \mu_0 i(t)$ has not changed but the right hand side is zero.

Reason (R) No current passes through the surface.

8 **Assertion (A)** We needed to do was to set up an AC circuit in which the current oscillate at the frequency of visible light *i.e.*, yellow.

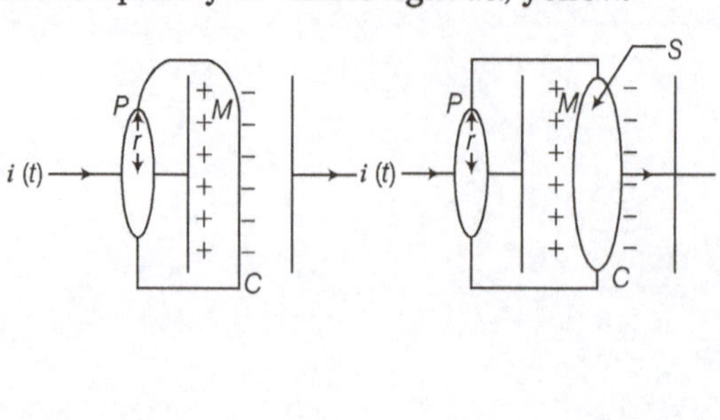

Reason (R) No current passes through the surface.

8 **Assertion (A)** We needed to do was to set up an AC circuit in which the current oscillate at the frequency of visible light *i.e.*, yellow.

Reason (R) The above experiment demonstrates electromagnetic wave.

9 **Assertion (A)** Microwaves are better carriers of signals than optical waves.

Reason (R) Microwaves move faster than optical waves.

Very Short Answer Type Questions

(1 Mark)

10 A capacitor is attached to a variable frequency of an AC source. What will happen to the displacement current with the increase in frequency?

11 What is common between different types of electromagnetic radiations?

12 A laser beam has an intensity of $4\times10^{14}\ \text{W/m}^2$. What will the amplitude of electric field in the beam?

13 To which part of electromagnetic spectrum do the waves emitted by radioactive nuclei belong? What is its frequency range?

14 Write two uses of infrared rays.

Short Answer Type I Questions

(2 Marks)

15 When a plane electromagnetic wave travels in vacuum along y-direction. Write the

(i) ratio of the magnitudes and

(ii) the direction of its electric and magnetic field vectors.

16 Green light of mercury has a wavelength 5×10^{-5} cm.

(i) What is the frequency in Hz and period in second in vacuum?

(ii) What is the wavelength in glass, if refractive index of glass is 1.5?

17 Name the electromagnetic radiation to which waves of wavelength in the range of 10^{-2}m belong. Give one use of this part of electromagnetic spectrum.

18 Find the wavelength of electromagnetic wave of frequency 5×10^{10}Hz in free space. Give its two applications.

Short Answer Type II Questions

(3 Marks)

19. Name the constituent radiation of electromagnetic spectrum which

(i) is used in satellite communication.

(ii) is used for studying crystal structure.

(iii) is emitted during decay of radioactive nuclei.

Write two more uses of each.

20. How are X-rays different from γ-rays? Give a detailed description.

Case Based Question

Directions (Q.No. 21) *This question is case study based question. Read the following paragraph and answer the questions.*

21. Electromagnetic waves are transverse in nature, i.e., electric and magnetic fields are perpendicular to each other and to the direction of wave propagation. Electromagnetic waves are not deflected by electric and magnetic fields.

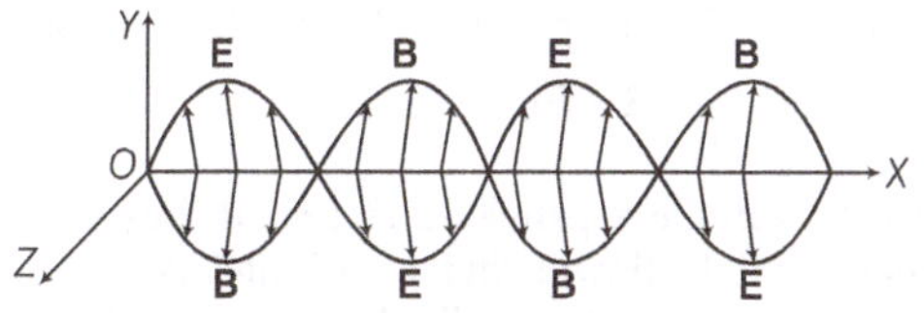

The magnetic field in a plane electromagnetic wave is given by
$B_y = 2\times10^{-7}\sin(0.5\times10^3 x + 1.5\times10^{11} t)$T.

(i) What is the angular frequency of wave?
(a) 0.5×10^3 rad s^{-1}
(b) 1.5×10^{11} rad s^{-1}
(c) 3×10^8 rad s^{-1}
(d) 2×10^{-7} rad s^{-1}

(ii) What is the wavelength of the wave?
(a) 12.6 cm (b) 1.26 cm
(c) 1.26 m (d) 6.12 m

(iii) What is the frequency of the wave?
(a) 2.39 GHz (b) 23.9 MHz
(c) 23.9 GHz (d) 20.3 MHz

(iv) The maximum value of electric field is
(a) $6\times10^2\ \text{Vm}^{-1}$ (b) $6\times10^3\ \text{Vm}^{-1}$
(c) $6\times10^1\ \text{Vm}^{-1}$ (d) $6\ \text{Vm}^{-1}$

(v) Write an expression for the electric field?
(a) $E_y = 60\sin(0.5\times10^3x + 1.5\times10^{11}t)\ \text{Vm}^{-1}$
(b) $E_x = 60\sin(0.5\times10^3x + 1.5\times10^{11}t)\ \text{Vm}^{-1}$
(c) $E_z = 60\sin(0.5\times10^3x + 1.5\times10^{11}t)\ \text{Vm}^{-1}$
(d) $E_y = 60\cos(0.5\times10^3x + 1.5\times10^{11}t)\ \text{Vm}^{-1}$

Answers

1 (*b*) Electric field intensity,

$$E_0 = cB_0$$

or $$c = \frac{E_0}{B_0} \quad \text{...(i)}$$

where, c is speed of light and B_0 is magnetic field.
Also, speed of light,

i.e. $$c = \frac{1}{\sqrt{\mu_0\varepsilon_0}} \quad \text{...(ii)}$$

where, μ_0 and ε_0 are absolute permeability and permittivity in free space in vacuum.
On comparing Eqs. (i) and (ii), we get

$$\frac{E_0}{B_0} = \frac{1}{\sqrt{\mu_0\varepsilon_0}} \Rightarrow \sqrt{\mu_0\varepsilon_0}\times E_0 = B_0$$

2 (*b*) Energy flowing per second per unit area from a face of cube is $\frac{1}{\mu_0}[\mathbf{E}\times\mathbf{B}]$.

It will be in the negative z-direction. It shows that the energy will be flowing in faces of cube parallel to XY-plane and is zero in all other faces. Total energy flowing per second from a face in XY-plane

$$= \frac{1}{\mu_0}(EB\sin 90^\circ)\,a^2 = \frac{EBa^2}{\mu_0}$$

3 (*b*) As energy density,

i.e. $$U = \frac{1}{2}\varepsilon_0 E^2 = \frac{B^2}{2\mu_0} \Rightarrow \varepsilon_0\mu_0 = \frac{B^2}{E^2}$$

or $$\frac{B}{E} = \sqrt{\varepsilon_0\mu_0} = \frac{1}{c}$$

where, c is the speed of light in vacuum.

4 (*d*) Frequency remains unchanged with change of medium.

i.e. $$n\ (\text{refractive index}) = \frac{c}{v} = \frac{1/\sqrt{\varepsilon_0\mu_0}}{1/\sqrt{\varepsilon\mu}} = \sqrt{\varepsilon_r\mu_r}$$

Since, μ_r is very close to 1, $n = \sqrt{\varepsilon_r} = \sqrt{4} = 2$

Thus, λ in a dielectric medium $= \lambda/n = \lambda/2$

5 (*a*) Refractive index, i.e. $n = \sqrt{\varepsilon_r\mu_r} = \sqrt{4\times 2.25} = 3$

So, speed of electromagnetic wave,

i.e. $$v = \frac{c}{n} = \frac{3\times10^8}{3} = 1\times10^8\ \text{m/s}$$

6 (*a*) As, refractive index,

$$n = \sqrt{\varepsilon_r} = \sqrt{1.006},$$

$$v_{\text{air}} = \frac{c}{n} = \frac{3\times10^8\ \text{m/s}}{\sqrt{1.006}} \approx 3\times10^8\ \text{m/s}$$

whereas, $a = 3$

7 (*a*) On applying Ampere's circuital law to such surfaces with the same perimeter, we find that the left hand side of equation $\oint B\cdot dl = \mu_0 i(t)$ has not changed but the right hand side is zero and not $\mu_0 i$. Since, no current passes through the surface.

8 (*c*) We needed to set up an AC circuit in which the current oscillates at the frequency of visible light, *i.e.*, yellow. The frequency of yellow light is about 6×10^{14} Hz, while the frequency that we get even with modern electronic circuits is hardly about 10^{11} Hz. This is why the experimental demonstration of electromagnetic wave had to come in the low frequency region (the radio wave region), as in the Hertz's experiment (1887).

9 (*c*)

10 When frequency of AC source increases, then displacement current also increases.

11 Speed, in vacuum all types of electromagnetic wave travels with same speed, i.e. 3×10^8 m/s.

12 We know that, $E_0 = \sqrt{\dfrac{2I}{\varepsilon_0 c}}$

$$= \sqrt{\frac{2\times4\times10^{14}}{8.85\times10^{-12}\times3\times10^8}}$$

$$= 5.489\times10^8\ \text{N/C}$$

13 Gamma rays, its frequency range is 3×10^{18} Hz to 5×10^{22} Hz.

14 Two uses of infrared rays are
(i) in weather forecasting.
(ii) in production of dehydrated fruits, physiotherapy.

15 Refer to the text on page 311 (Important characteristics of electromagnetic waves).

16 (i) Frequency of the wave, $\nu = \frac{c}{\lambda} = \frac{3 \times 10^8 \text{ m/s}}{5 \times 10^{-5} \text{ cm}}$

$$= \frac{3 \times 10^8 \text{ m/s}}{5 \times 10^{-7} \text{ m/s}} = 6 \times 10^{14} \text{ Hz}$$

Time period, $T = \frac{1}{\nu} = \frac{1}{6 \times 10^{14} \text{ Hz}}$

$$= 0.16 \times 10^{-14} \text{ s}$$

(ii) Refractive index,

$$n = \frac{c}{v}$$

$$\Rightarrow \quad v = \frac{c}{n} = \frac{3 \times 10^8}{1.5}$$

$$= 2 \times 10^8 \text{ m/s}$$

Also, $\nu = \frac{v}{\lambda}$

$$\Rightarrow \quad \lambda = \frac{v}{\nu} = \frac{2 \times 10^8}{6 \times 10^{14}}$$

$$= 0.33 \times 10^{-6} \text{ m}$$

$$= 3.3 \times 10^{-3} \text{ m}$$

17 Refer to text on page 312 (Electromagnetic spectrum).

18 For first part

Given, $c = 3 \times 10^8$, $\nu = 5 \times 10^{10}$ Hz

$$\lambda = \frac{c}{\nu} = \frac{3 \times 10^8}{5 \times 10^{10}} = 0.6 \times 10^{-2} \text{ m}$$

$$= 6 \times 10^{-3} \text{ m}$$

It lies in microwave range.

19 Refer to text on pages 312 and 313 (Electromagnetic spectrum).

20 Refer to text on page 313 (Different types of electromagnetic waves).

21 (i) (*b*) Comparing with given equation, we get

$$\omega = 1.5 \times 10^{11} \text{ rad s}^{-1}$$

(ii) (*b*) Comparing the given equation with magnetic field in a plane

i.e., $$B_y = B_0 \sin \left[2\pi \left(\frac{x}{\lambda} + \frac{t}{T} \right) \right]$$

we get $$\lambda = \frac{2\pi}{0.5 \times 10^3} \text{ m} = 1.26 \text{ cm}$$

(iii) (*c*) As we know, frequency *i.e.,* $\nu = \frac{1}{\text{time taken}}$

$$\nu = \frac{1}{T} = \frac{\omega}{2\pi} = (1.5 \times 10^{11}) / 2\pi$$

$$= 23.9 \text{ GHz}$$

(iv) (*c*) According to Maxwell equation, electric field

i.e., $$E_0 = B_0 c = 2 \times 10^{-7} \times 3 \times 10^8 \text{ ms}^{-1}$$

$$= 6 \times 10^1 \text{ Vm}^{-1}$$

(v) (*c*) The electric field component is perpendicular to the direction of propagation and the direction of magnetic field. Therefore, the electric field component along the *Z*-axis is obtained as

$E_z = 60 \sin (0.5 \times 10^3 x + 1.5 \times 10^{11} t) \text{ Vm}^{-1}$

RELATED ONLINE VIDEOS

Visit : https://www.youtube.com/watch?v=fZnYE3kvhhA

OR **Scan the Code**

Visit : https://www.youtube.com/watch?v=QZhXzgw-Qf0

OR **Scan the Code**

CHAPTER
09

Ray Optics and Optical Instruments

Light is an electromagnetic wave that travels in vacuum with a speed nearly of $3 \times 10^8 \, ms^{-1}$. The reflection and refraction of wave at a medium interface can be analysed geometrically using the concept of 'ray tracing' which is called 'geometrical optics'.

In geometrical optics, path of light is traced by straight lines or rays. This concept is adequate as long as discontinuities and obstacles encountered by light wave are very large compared to wavelength of light.

- Reflection of Light
- Refraction
- Refraction through a Prism and Dispersion
- Refraction at Spherical Surfaces and by Lenses
- Optical Instruments

TOPIC 01 Reflecton of Light

The phenomenon of bouncing back of light rays in the same medium on striking the smooth surface is called **reflection of light**.

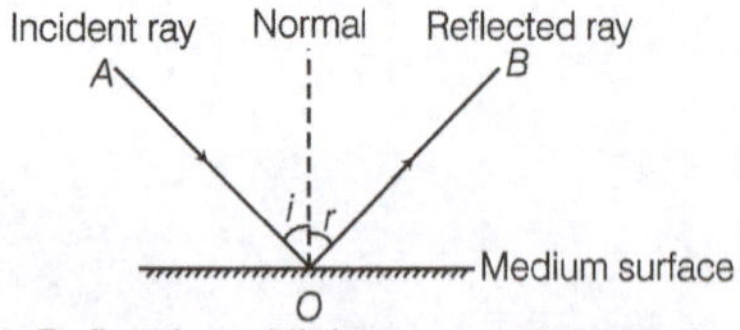

Reflection of light ray at plane surface

Laws of Reflection

The laws of reflection are as given below

(i) The incident ray, the reflected ray and the normal to the reflecting surface at the point of incidence, all lie in the same plane.

(ii) The angle of reflection (r) is equal to the angle of incidence (i), i.e. $i = r$. For normal incidence, $\angle i = 0°$, therefore $\angle r = 0°$. Hence, a ray of light falling normally on a mirror, retraces its path on reflection.

Reflection at a Spherical Mirror

Spherical mirror is a mirror whose reflecting surface is a part of a hollow sphere or the mirror whose reflecting surface is curved 'inward or outward' is called spherical mirror. Spherical mirrors are of two types

Concave Spherical Mirror

A spherical mirror whose reflecting surface is towards the centre of the sphere is called **concave spherical mirror.**

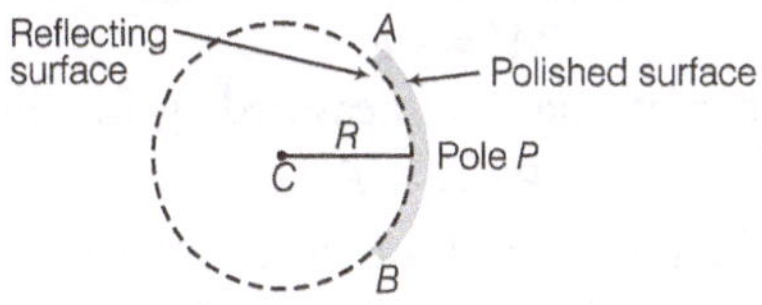

Concave mirror

Convex Spherical Mirror

A spherical mirror whose reflecting surface is away from the centre of the sphere is called **convex spherical mirror.**

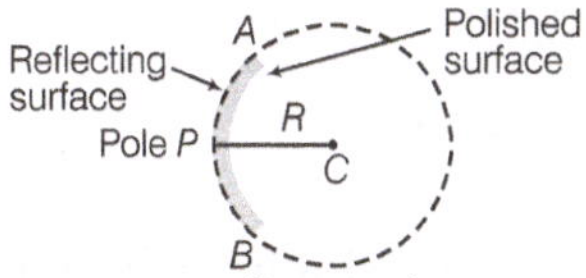

Convex mirror

Sign Convention

In reflection, we adopt following sign convention for measuring distances.

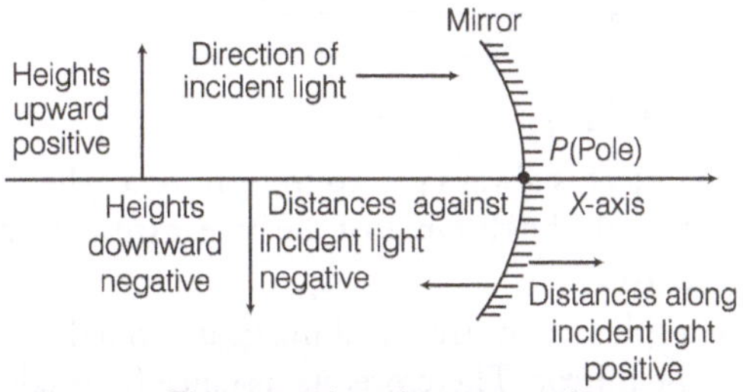

The cartesian sign convention

According to the cartesian sign convention,

(i) All the distances are measured from pole (P) of the mirror or the optical centre(O) of the lens.

(ii) The principal axis of the mirror or lens is taken as X-axis and the pole or optical centre as origin.

(iii) Distances measured in the direction of the incident light are taken as positive and opposite to the direction of incident light as negative.

(iv) The heights measured upwards with respect to X-axis and normal to the principal axis of the mirror or lens are taken as positive and the heights measured downwards are taken as negative.

Focal Length of Spherical Mirrors

When a parallel beam of light is incident on a concave or convex mirror, the reflected rays converge or appear to diverge from a point F on principal axis called **principal focus** of the mirror.

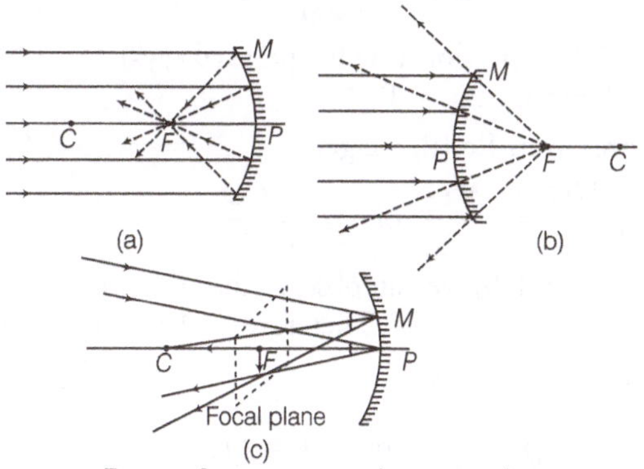

Focus of a concave and convex mirrors

If the paraxial beam of light were incident, making some angle with principal axis, the reflected rays would converge or appear to diverge from a point in a plane through F normal to the principal axis. This is called the **focal plane** of the mirror.

The Relation between Focal Length (f) and Radius of Curvature (R)

The relation between focal length (f) and radius of curvature (R) is given as

$$f = \frac{R}{2}$$

Proof Consider a ray parallel to the principal axis striking the mirror at point M. Then CM will be perpendicular to the mirror at point M. Let θ be the angle of incidence and MD be perpendicular to the principal axis.

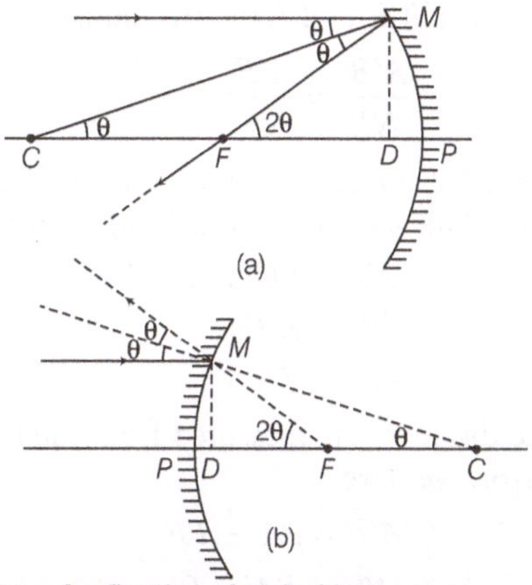

Geometry of reflection of an incident ray on
(a) concave spherical mirror and
(b) convex spherical mirror

Then, $\angle MCP = \theta$

and $\angle MFP = 2\theta$

Now, $\tan\theta = \dfrac{MD}{CD}$

and $\tan 2\theta = \dfrac{MD}{FD}$ ...(i)

For small θ (condition true for paraxial rays), $\tan\theta \approx \theta$ and $\tan 2\theta \approx 2\theta$

Therefore, from Eq.(i), we get

$$\frac{MD}{FD} = 2\frac{MD}{CD} \text{ or } FD = \frac{CD}{2} \quad \text{...(ii)}$$

Again, for small θ, we can observe that the point D is very close to the point P. Therefore, $FD = f$ and $CD = R$.

From Eq.(ii), we have

$$\boxed{f = \frac{R}{2}} \text{ or } \boxed{R = 2f}$$

Mirror Formula

Mirror formula (or equation) is a relation between focal length of the mirror and distances of object and image from the mirror.

Consider an object AB whose image $A'B'$ is formed when light is reflected from mirrors.

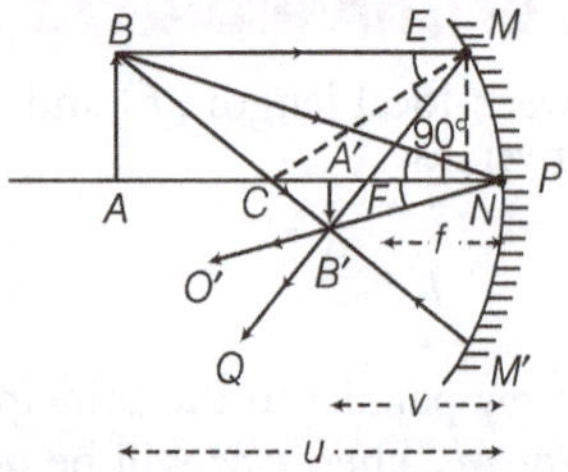

In the above figure, the ray diagram is considering three rays for image formation by a concave mirror. In the figure, triangles $A'B'F$ and NEF are similar.

Then, $\dfrac{A'B'}{NE} = \dfrac{A'F}{NF}$

As, the aperture of the concave mirror is small and the points N and P lie very close to each other, then

$$NF \approx PF \text{ and } NE = AB.$$

$$\Rightarrow \frac{A'B'}{AB} = \frac{A'F}{PF}$$

Since, all the distances are measured from the pole of the concave mirror, we have

$$A'F = PA' - PF$$

$$\therefore \frac{A'B'}{AB} = \frac{PA' - PF}{PF} \quad \text{...(i)}$$

Also, triangles ABP and $A'B'P$ are similar, then

$$\frac{A'B'}{AB} = \frac{PA'}{PA} \quad \text{...(ii)}$$

From Eqs. (i) and (ii), we get

$$\frac{PA' - PF}{PF} = \frac{PA'}{PA} \quad \text{...(iii)}$$

Applying new Cartesian sign convention, we have

$$PA = -u$$

[∵ distance of object is measured against incident ray]

$$PA' = -v$$

[∵ distance of image is measured against incident ray]

$$PF = -f$$

[∵ focal length of concave mirror is measured against incident ray]

Substituting these values in Eq. (iii), we have

$$\frac{-v-(-f)}{-f} = \frac{-v}{-u} \Rightarrow \frac{v-f}{f} = \frac{v}{u} \Rightarrow \frac{v}{f} - 1 = \frac{v}{u}$$

Dividing both sides by v, we get

$$\therefore \boxed{\frac{1}{f} = \frac{1}{u} + \frac{1}{v}}$$

The above relation is called **mirror formula.**

Relation between u, v and R

∵ Focal length of the mirror, $f = \dfrac{R}{2}$

$$\therefore \frac{1}{u} + \frac{1}{v} = \frac{1}{R/2} \Rightarrow \boxed{\frac{1}{u} + \frac{1}{v} = \frac{2}{R}}$$

Important Points

(i) An object is always placed in front of a spherical mirror, so the distance of the object (u) is always negative.

(ii) In a spherical mirror, real image is formed in front of the mirror. Therefore, its distance (v) is taken as negative. However, virtual image is formed at the back of the mirror. So, its distance (v) is taken as positive, as per the new Cartesian sign convention.

(iii) Similarly, focal length of a concave mirror is taken as negative, while that of convex mirror is taken as positive.

Linear Magnification

The ratio of the height of the image (h') formed by a spherical mirror to the height of the object (h) is called the linear magnification produced by the spherical mirror. It is denoted by m.

$\therefore$ Linear magnification, $m = \dfrac{h'}{h} = -\dfrac{v}{u} = \dfrac{f-v}{f} = \dfrac{f}{f-u}$

Here, u, v and f are substituted with proper sign in accordance with sign convention.

The expression for magnification is same for both the concave and convex mirrors.

(i) When $m > 1$, image formed is enlarged.
(ii) When $m < 1$, image formed is diminished.
(iii) When m is positive, image must be erect, i.e. virtual.
(iv) When m is negative, image must be inverted, i.e. real.
(v) In case of concave mirror, m can be either positive or negative but in case of convex mirror, m is positive only.

Example 1 A candle flame is held 3 cm away from a concave mirror of radius of curvature 24 cm. Where is the image formed? What is the nature of the image?

Sol. Given, object distance, $u = -3$ cm

Radius of curvature, $R = -24$ cm

$$\therefore \quad f = \frac{R}{2} = \frac{-24}{2} = -12 \text{ cm}$$

According to mirror formula,

$$\frac{1}{f} = \frac{1}{v} + \frac{1}{u}$$

$$\Rightarrow \quad \frac{1}{v} = \frac{1}{f} - \frac{1}{u} = \frac{1}{(-12)} - \frac{1}{-3}$$

$$\Rightarrow \quad \frac{1}{v} = \frac{1}{-12} + \frac{1}{3} = \frac{-1+4}{12}$$

$$\Rightarrow \quad v = 4 \text{ cm}$$

$$\because \quad \text{Magnification, } m = -\frac{v}{u} = \frac{-4}{-3} = +1.33$$

i.e. The image formed is virtual, erect and magnified.

Example 2 An object is placed in front of a convex mirror of focal length 30 cm. If the image is a quarter of the size of the object, find the position of the image.

Sol. Given, focal length, $f = +30$ cm

Magnification, $m = \frac{1}{4}$, $v = ?$

From mirror's formula,

$$\frac{1}{f} = \frac{1}{u} + \frac{1}{v} \qquad \left[\because m = -\frac{v}{u} \Rightarrow u = -\frac{v}{m}\right]$$

$$\Rightarrow \quad \frac{1}{f} = -\frac{m}{v} + \frac{1}{v}$$

$$\Rightarrow \quad m = \frac{f-v}{f} \quad \Rightarrow \quad \frac{1}{4} = \frac{30-v}{30}$$

$$\Rightarrow \quad 30 = 120 - 4v$$

$$\Rightarrow \quad v = \frac{90}{4} = +22.5 \text{ cm}$$

As, v is positive, therefore a virtual and erect image will be formed on other side of the object.

Uses of Spherical Mirrors

(i) Convex mirror is used as a reflector in street lamps to diverge the light over a large area.
(ii) Convex mirror is used as rear view mirror (or driver's mirror) in vehicles, because it has a wider field of view.
(iii) Concave mirror is used as a reflector in search light, head lights of vehicles, etc.
(iv) Concave mirror is also used as face looking mirror because it forms erect and magnified image.
(v) Spherical mirrors are also used as trick mirrors.

Topic Practice 1

Multiple Choice Questions

1 Mark

1. A ray passing through or directed towards centre of curvature of a spherical mirror is reflected such that it trace back of its path, because
(a) it does not follow law of reflection
(b) angle of incidence is 0°
(c) centre of curvature is midway between object and pole
(d) distance of centre of curvature from focus is equal to its distance from pole

2. If lower half of a concave mirror is blackened, then
(a) image distance increases
(b) image distance decreases
(c) image intensity increases
(d) image intensity decreases

3. An object is placed at 10 cm from a concave mirror of radius of curvature 15 cm, then
(a) it forms an erect image
(b) it forms a small and inverted image
(c) it forms a point image
(d) it forms a magnified, real and inverted image

4. Rear view mirror of a car is of radius of curvature $R = 2$ m. A jogger approaches car (from behind) at a speed of 5 ms^{-1}. The speed of image when jogger is 39 m from the mirror, is
(a) 0.3 cms^{-1} (b) 0.1 $cm\ s^{-1}$
(c) 0.5 $cm\ s^{-1}$ (d) 0.5 $cm\ s^{-1}$

5. A short linear object of length b lies along the axis of a concave mirror of focal length f at a distance u from the pole of the mirror. The size of the image is approximate equal to

(a) $b\left(\frac{u-f}{f}\right)^{1/2}$ (b) $b\left(\frac{f}{u-f}\right)^{1/2}$

(c) $b\left(\frac{u-f}{f}\right)$ (d) $b\left(\frac{f}{u-f}\right)^{2}$

6. If an object is placed at a distance of 10cm in front of a concave mirror of focal length 20cm, the image formed will be **ISC 2023**

(a) real and 20cm in front of the mirror
(b) real and 6.67cm in front of the mirror
(c) virtual and 20cm behind the mirror
(d) virtual and 6.67cm behind the mirror

7. A rod of length 30 cm lies along the principal axis of a concave mirror of focal length 10 cm in such a way that its end closer to the pole is 20 cm away from the mirror. The length of the image is

(a) 10 cm (b) 15 cm
(c) 2.5 cm (d) 5 cm

Very Short Answer Type Questions

1 Mark

8. How can the real image of an object be obtained with a convex mirror?

9. The direction of ray of light incident on a concave mirror is shown by PQ while directions in which the ray would travel after reflection is shown by four rays marked as 1, 2, 3 and 4 in the figure? Which of the four rays correctly shows the direction of reflected rays?

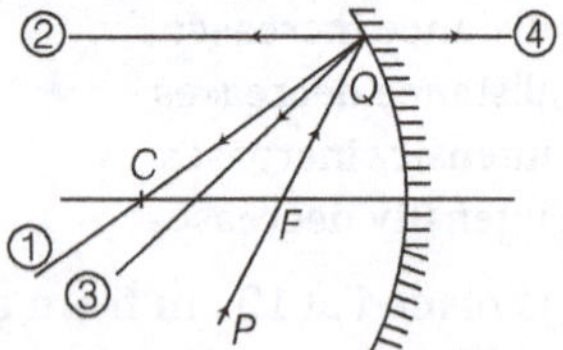

Short Answer Type I Questions

2 Marks

10. Write any one use for each of the following mirrors.
(i) Convex (ii) Concave **ISC 2019**

11. Choose the statement as wrong or right and justify.
(i) Linear magnification of a spherical mirror is given by $\frac{v}{u}$.
(ii) $\frac{1}{v}+\frac{1}{u}=\frac{1}{f}$ can be applied to all types of mirror.

12. Use the mirror equation to show that an object placed between f and $2f$ of a concave mirror produces a real image beyond $2f$.

Short Answer Type II Questions

3 Marks

13. (i) A mobile phone lies along the principal axis of a concave mirror. Show with the help of a suitable diagram the formation of its image. Explain, why magnification is not uniform?
(ii) Suppose the lower half of the concave mirror's reflecting surface is covered with an opaque material. What effect this will have on the image of the object? Explain.

14. An object AB is kept in front of a concave mirror as shown in the figure.

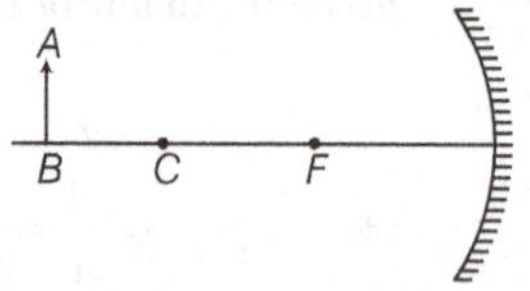

(i) Complete the ray diagram showing the image formation of the object.
(ii) How will the position and intensity of the image be affected, if the lower half of the mirror's reflecting surface is painted black?

15. An infinitely long rod lies along the axis of concave mirror of focal length f. The near end of the rod is at a distance $x > f$ from the mirror f. Then, what will be the length of the image of the rod?

Long Answer Type Questions

5 Marks

16. State and derive mirror formula for a concave mirror.

17. Use the mirror equation to deduce that,
(i) an object placed between f and $2f$ of a concave mirror produces a real image beyond $2f$.

(ii) a convex mirror always produces a virtual image independent of the location of the object.

(iii) the virtual image produced by a convex mirror is always diminished in size and is located between the focus and the pole.

(iv) an object placed between the pole and focus of a concave mirror produces a virtual and enlarged image. **NCERT**

Numerical Problems

18. A square wire of side 3 cm is placed 25 cm away from a concave mirror of focal length 10 cm. What is the area enclosed by the image of the wire? Given, the centre of the wire is on the axis of the mirror, with its two sides normal to the axis. **(2M)**

19. An erect image 3 times the size of the object is obtained with a concave mirror of radius of curvature 36 cm. What is the position of the object? **(2M)**

Hints & Solutions

1. (*b*) As we know, when angle, $i = 0^\circ$ then angle, $r = 0^\circ$ so, when light ray is passes through centre of curvature of a spherical mirror is reflected such that it trace back its path.

2. (*d*) If lower half of a concave mirror is blackened, then image will now only half of the object, but taking the laws of reflection to be true for all points of the remaining part of the mirror, the image will be that of the whole object. However, as the area of the reflecting surface has been reduced, the intensity of the image will be low, i.e. half.

3. (*d*) The focal length, $f = \frac{-15}{2} = -7.5$ cm

The object distance, i.e. $u = -10$ cm, $v = ?$

According to mirror formula, we get $\frac{1}{v} + \frac{1}{u} = \frac{1}{f}$

$$\Rightarrow \quad \frac{1}{v} + \frac{1}{(-10)} = \frac{1}{(-7.5)} \Rightarrow v = \frac{10 \times 7.5}{-2.5} = -30 \text{ cm}$$

The image is 30 cm from the mirror on the same side as the object. Also, magnification, $m = \frac{-v}{u} = -\frac{(-30)}{(-10)} = -3$

Thus, the image is magnified, real and inverted.

4. (*a*) From the mirror equation, we get $v = \frac{fu}{u-f}$

For convex mirror, since $R = 2$ m, $f = 1$ m.

Then, $u = -39$m, $v = \frac{(-39) \times 1}{-39-1} = \frac{39}{40}$ m

Since, the jogger moves at a constant speed of 5 ms^{-1}, after 1s the position of the image v (for $u = -39 + 5 = -34$) is (34/35) m.

The shift in the position of image in 1s is

$$\frac{39}{40} - \frac{34}{35} = \frac{1365-1360}{1400} = \frac{5}{1400} = \frac{1}{280} \text{ m}$$

Therefore, the average speed of the image when the jogger is between 39 m and 34 m from the mirror, is (1/280) ms^{-1} or 0.3 cms^{-1}.

5. (*d*) We know, from the mirror formula, $v = \left(\frac{uf}{u-f}\right)$ ...(i)

On differentiating Eq. (i) both sides w.r.t. u, we get

$$\frac{dv}{du} = \frac{(u-f)f - (uf)}{(u-f)^2} \Rightarrow \frac{dv}{du} = \frac{uf - f^2 - uf}{(u-f)^2}$$

$$\Rightarrow \frac{dv}{du} = -\frac{f^2}{(u-f)^2} \Rightarrow dv = -\left(\frac{f}{u-f}\right)^2 du$$

$$|dv| = \left(\frac{f}{u-f}\right)^2 |du| \quad ...(ii)$$

Here, image size $= |dv|$

Object size $= |du| = b$

On substituting values in Eq. (ii), we get

Image size $= b(f/u-f)^2$.

6. (*c*) $f = -20$ cm

v = image distance

$u = -10$ cm

From mirror formula, $\frac{1}{f} = \frac{1}{u} + \frac{1}{v}$

$$\frac{1}{-20} = \frac{1}{v} + \frac{1}{-10}$$

$$\frac{1}{v} = \frac{1}{-20} + \frac{1}{10}$$

$$\frac{1}{v} = \frac{-1+2}{20}$$

$$v = 20 \text{ cm}$$

The image formed is erect, magnified and virtual.

7. (*d*) By mirror formula, image distance of A,

$$\frac{1}{v} + \frac{1}{u} = \frac{1}{f} \Rightarrow f = -10 \text{ cm}$$

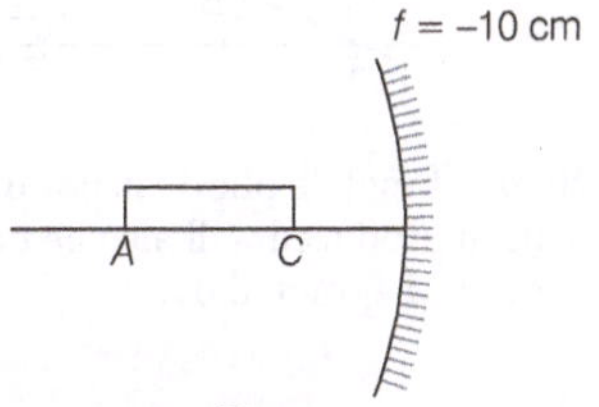

$u = -30$ cm

$\Rightarrow \frac{1}{v_A} = \frac{1}{f} - \frac{1}{u} = \frac{1}{-10} - \frac{1}{(-30)} = \frac{-1}{15}$

$\Rightarrow v_A = -15$ cm

Also, image distance of $C \Rightarrow v_C = -20$ cm $[\because v_C = 2F]$

The length of image $= |v_A - v_C| = |-15-(-20)| = 5$ cm

8. A convex mirror produces a real image of a virtual object. Therefore, if a beam of light from a virtual object converges to a point behind the convex mirror, then its real image will be formed in front of the mirror.

9. The incident ray PQ passes through the focus, so the reflected ray is parallel to the principal axis. So, the answer is ray 2.

10. (i) A convex mirror is used as a reflector in street lamps.

(ii) Concave mirrors are used by ENT doctors to examine ear, nose and throat. (1+1)

11. (i) Wrong, linear magnification of spherical mirror is $-\frac{v}{u}$ (using sign conventions). (1)

(ii) Right, but for plane mirror using this formula, focal length becomes infinite. (1)

12. From the mirror equation, we have

$$v = \frac{uf}{u-f} \quad \text{...(i)}$$

Applying new cartesian sign convention, we get

$f = -$ ve and $u = -$ ve

Given, $f < u < 2f$

$\Rightarrow v = -$ ve [from Eq. (i)]

Magnification is given by $m = -\left(\frac{-v}{-u}\right) = -$ ve

Hence, the image formed is real. (1)

From the mirror formula, when $u = -2f$.

$\Rightarrow \frac{1}{-2f} + \frac{1}{v} = \frac{1}{-f} \Rightarrow \frac{1}{v} = \frac{1}{2f} - \frac{1}{f} = \frac{-1}{2f}$

When the object is at f, then image is formed at infinity. This shows that when $f < u < 2f$, then $\infty > v > 2f$. (1)

13. (i) The ray diagram for the formation of the image of the mobile phone is shown below. The image of the part which is on the plane perpendicular to principal axis will be on the same plane. It will be of the same size, i.e. $B'C = BC$

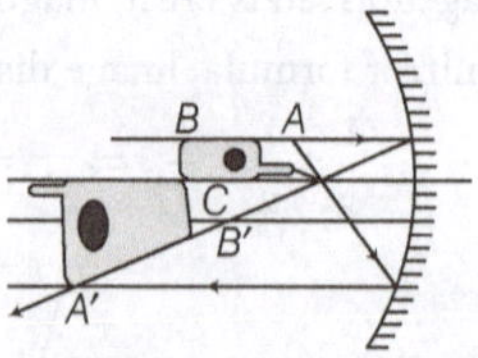

As the shape of mobile phone is not uniform, thus the magnification produced will also be not uniform. This can be seen in diagram above. (1½)

(ii) We may think that the image will now show only half of the object, but considering the laws of reflection to be true for all points of the remaining part of the mirror, the image will be that of the whole object.

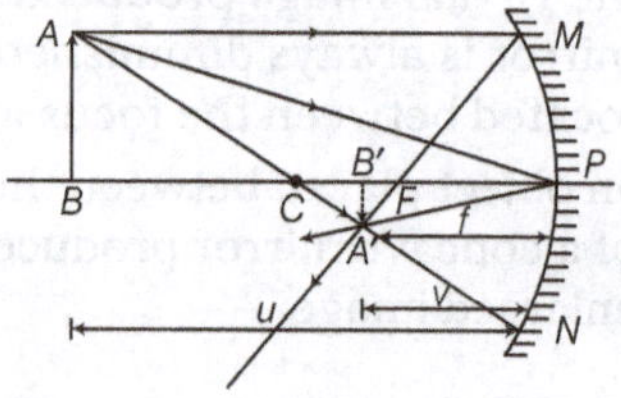

However, as the area of the reflecting surface has been reduced, the intensity of the image will be low, i.e. half. (1½)

14. (i) The ray diagram showing the image formation of the object.

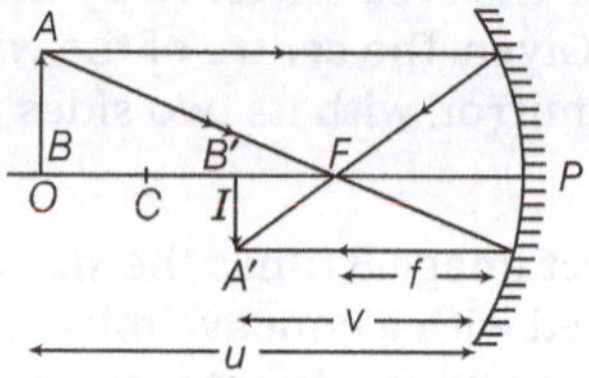

(1½)

(ii) The position of image is unaffected but the intensity of image is reduced as number of rays reduced. (1½)

15. Using mirror formula,

$$\frac{1}{f} = \frac{1}{v} + \frac{1}{u}$$

Here, $u = -u, v = ?, f = -f$

$\therefore \frac{1}{f} = \frac{1}{v} - \frac{1}{u}$

or $\frac{1}{v} = \frac{1}{-f} + \frac{1}{u} \Rightarrow v = \frac{-fu}{-f+u}$ (2)

$\therefore$ Length of the image $= \frac{-fu}{-f+u} - f$

$= \frac{-fu + f^2 - fu}{-f+u} = \frac{f^2}{u-f}$ (1)

16. Refer to the text on page 330 (Mirror formula).

17. (i) Refer to solution of Q. 12 on page 334. (1)

(ii) For convex mirror, $f > 0$

Also, $u < 0$

But from mirror equation,

$\frac{1}{f} = \frac{1}{v} + \frac{1}{u} = \frac{1}{v} + \frac{1}{|-u|}$ [taking u with sign]

$\frac{1}{v} = \frac{1}{f} + \frac{1}{u}$

If f and u to be positive, then

$\frac{1}{v} > 0 \Rightarrow v > 0$

Hence, virtual image is formed. (1)

(iii) For convex mirror, $f > 0, u < 0$

From mirror formula, $\frac{1}{v} = \frac{1}{f} - \frac{1}{u}$

So, $\frac{1}{v} > \frac{1}{f}$ or $v < f$

Also, $\frac{1}{v} > \frac{-1}{u}$ or $\frac{-v}{u} < 1$, i.e. $m < 1$

Thus, image is always located between pole and focus of the mirror and is always diminished in size. (1)

(iv) For concave mirror,

$$f < 0, u < 0, \ |f| > |u| > 0$$

But from mirror equation,

$$\frac{1}{f} = \frac{1}{v} + \frac{1}{u} \Rightarrow \frac{-1}{|f|} = \frac{1}{v} - \frac{1}{|u|}$$

$$\frac{1}{v} = \frac{1}{|u|} - \frac{1}{|f|}$$

$\because$ $|u| < |f| \Rightarrow \frac{1}{|u|} > \frac{1}{|f|}$

$\Rightarrow$ $\frac{1}{v} > 0 \Rightarrow v > 0$

Image is formed on RHS of mirror, i.e. virtual image.

Also, $\frac{1}{f} = \frac{1}{|v|} - \frac{1}{|u|}$

For concave mirror, f is negative.

$\Rightarrow$ $\frac{1}{|v|} < \frac{1}{|u|} \Rightarrow \frac{|v|}{|u|} > 1 \Rightarrow m > 1$

Enlarged virtual image formed on the other side of mirror. (2)

18. Here, $u = -25$ cm, $f = -10$ cm

Using mirror formula, $\frac{1}{f} = \frac{1}{u} + \frac{1}{v}$

$$-\frac{1}{10} = -\frac{1}{25} + \frac{1}{v} \Rightarrow v = \frac{-50}{3}$$

Now, magnification, $m = \frac{-v}{u} = -\left[\frac{\left(-\frac{50}{3}\right)}{(-25)}\right] = -\frac{2}{3}$ (1)

Length and breadth both change in the same proportion.

Area of the object, $A_o = 3 \times 3 = 9\ \text{cm}^2$

$\therefore$ $\frac{A_i}{A_o} = \left(-\frac{2}{3}\right)^2 \Rightarrow A_i = \left(\frac{4}{9}\right) \times 9 = 4\ \text{cm}^2$ (1)

19. Given, magnification, $m = +3$, $R = -36$ cm

Object distance, $u = ?$

Let $u = -x$

$$m = \frac{h_2}{h_1} = \frac{+v}{-u} = 3$$

$\Rightarrow$ $v = -3u \Rightarrow v = 3x$

Applying mirror formula, we have

$$\frac{1}{u} + \frac{1}{v} = \frac{1}{f} = \frac{2}{R} \Rightarrow \frac{1}{-x} + \frac{1}{3x} = \frac{2}{-36}$$ (1)

$\Rightarrow$ $\frac{-3+1}{3x} = \frac{-1}{18} \Rightarrow 3x = 36$

$\Rightarrow$ $x = 12$ cm

or $u = -12$ cm (1)

TOPIC 02 Refraction

Reflection involves change in path of light without any change in the medium, whereas refraction involves change in the path of light due to change in the medium.

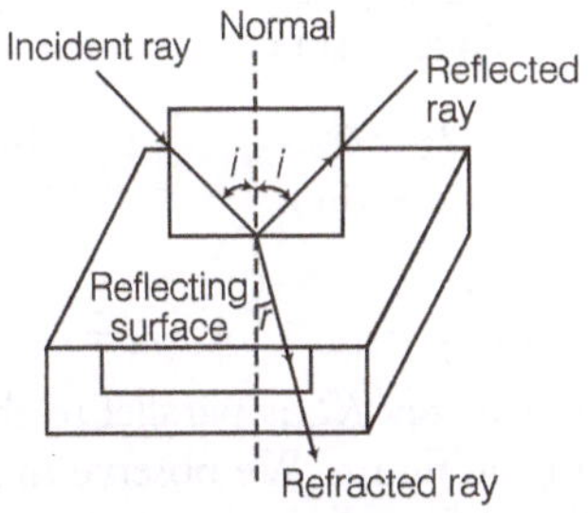

When a beam of light encounters another transparent medium, a part of light gets reflected back into the first medium while the rest enters the other. The direction of propagation of an obliquely incident ray of light, that enters the other medium, changes at the interface of two media. This phenomenon is called **refraction** of light.

Laws of Refraction

(i) The incident ray, the refracted ray and the normal to the refracting surface (or interface) at the point of incidence, all lie in the same plane.

(ii) The ratio of the sine angle of incidence to the sine angle of refraction is constant for the two given media. This constant is denoted by ${}^a\mu_b$ and is called the **relative refractive index** of medium b with respect to medium a.

$\therefore$ $$\frac{\sin i}{\sin r} = {}^a\mu_b$$

This law is also called **Snell's law** of refraction.

Refractive Index

The refractive index or index of refraction μ of a material is the ratio of the speed of light (c) in vacuum to the speed of light in the medium (v).
Mathematically, refractive index is given by the relation

$$\mu = \frac{\text{Speed of light in the vacuum}}{\text{Speed of light in the material}} = \frac{c}{v}$$

It is also referred as absolute refractive index of the substance. Refractive index of medium is inversely proportional to wavelength of light.

$\therefore \quad \mu_{red} < \mu_{violet}$

Relative refractive index is a measure of how much light bends, when it travels from one medium to another medium.
If light travels from optical rarer medium to optical denser medium, then it bends towards the normal, i.e. $i > r$. On the other hand, if light travels from optical denser medium to optical rarer medium, then light bends away from the normal, i.e. $i < r$.

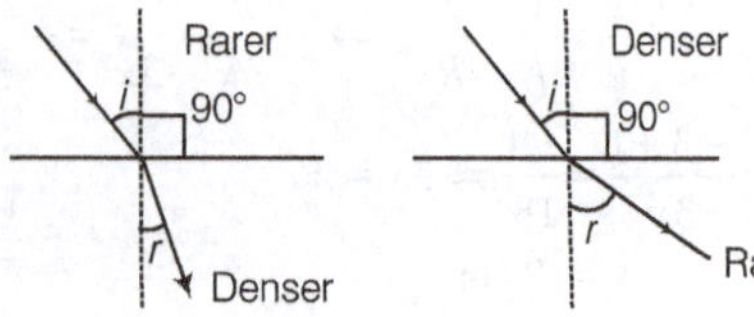

The medium in which the speed of light is higher with respect to other medium, is said to be optically **denser medium.**

Relative refractive index of a pair of media is given by

μ_{21} = refractive index of medium 2 with respect to medium 1 $= \frac{v_1}{v_2}$.

Principle of Reversibility of Light

When a light ray, after suffering any number of reflections and refractions, has its final path reversed, i.e. travels back along its entire initial path, then this is called **principle of reversibility of light.**

Refraction of Light Through a Rectangular Glass Slab

Let $ABCD$ be a rectangular glass slab. A ray of light is incident along MN on the face AB of the rectangular slab at $\angle i_1$. It is refracted along NK with $\angle r_1$.

The refracted ray NK falls on face CD with $\angle i_2$ and emerges out along KL with $\angle r_2$.

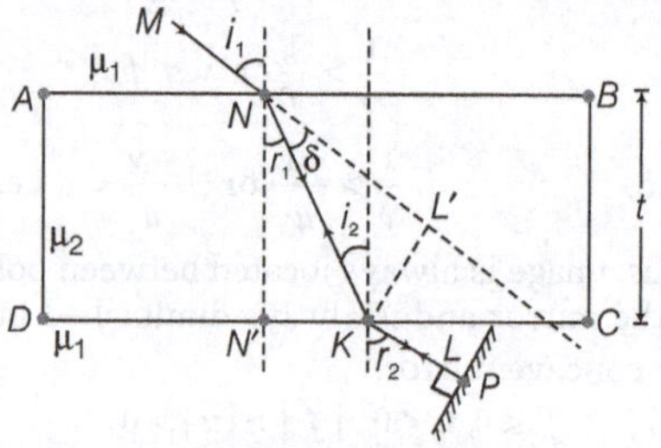

Applying Snell's law at N,

$$\mu_1 \times \sin i_1 = \mu_2 \times \sin r_1$$

or
$$\frac{\sin i_1}{\sin r_1} = \frac{\mu_2}{\mu_1} = {}^1\mu_2 \quad \text{...(i)}$$

Again, applying Snell's law at K,

$$\mu_2 \times \sin i_2 = \mu_1 \times \sin r_2$$

$$\Rightarrow \quad \frac{\mu_1}{\mu_2} = \frac{\sin i_2}{\sin r_2} = {}^2\mu_1 \quad \text{...(ii)}$$

Now, imagine a plane mirror P held normal to KL so that on reflection from mirror, path KL is reversed. The ray would retrace its entire path. For the reversed ray, the application of Snell's law at K gives

$$\mu_1 \times \sin r_2 = \mu_2 \times \sin i_2$$

$$\frac{\mu_2}{\mu_1} = \frac{\sin r_2}{\sin i_2} = {}^1\mu_2 \quad \text{...(iii)}$$

Multiplying Eqs. (ii) and (iii), we get

$$\frac{\sin i_2}{\sin r_2} \times \frac{\sin r_2}{\sin i_2} = {}^2\mu_1 \times {}^1\mu_2$$

$$1 = {}^2\mu_1 \times {}^1\mu_2, \quad \boxed{{}^1\mu_2 = \frac{1}{{}^2\mu_1}}$$

From Eqs. (i) and (iii), we get

$$\frac{\sin i_1}{\sin r_1} = \frac{\sin r_2}{\sin i_2} \quad \text{...(iv)}$$

As, $\quad i_2 = r_1 \quad$ [alternate angles]

$\therefore \quad \sin i_2 = \sin r_1$

From Eq. (iv), we get

$$\sin r_2 = \sin i_1 \quad \text{or} \quad r_2 = i_1$$

Hence, the emergent ray KL is parallel to the incident ray MN as shown in the figure. We observe that the incident ray MN is displaced laterally, on suffering two refractions through a glass slab.

Refraction Through Parallel Multiple Slab

Let a light ray OA travelling in a medium 1 is first refracted along AB in medium 2, then along BC in a parallel medium 3 and finally emerges along CD in its initial medium 1.

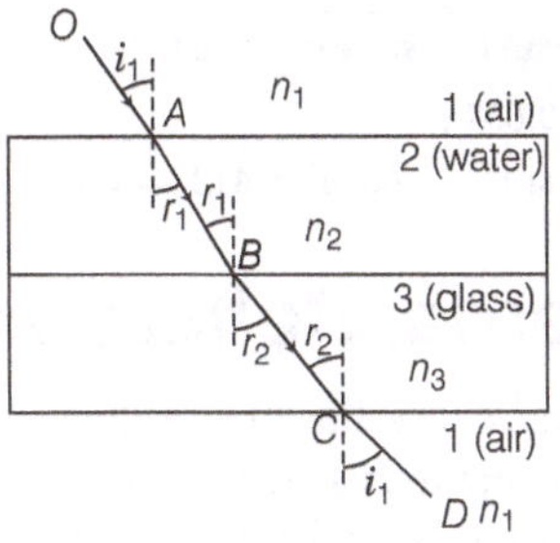

At A, i_1 an r_1 are angles of incidence and refraction at media 1 and 2, then

$$ {}_1n_2 = \frac{\sin i_1}{\sin r_1} \qquad \ldots(\text{i})$$

At B, r_1 is the angle of incidence and r_2 be the angle of refraction at media 2 and 3, then

$$ {}_2n_3 = \frac{\sin r_1}{\sin r_2} \qquad \ldots(\text{ii})$$

At C, r_2 is the angle of incidence and i_1 be the angle of emergent at media 3 and 1. So,

$$ {}_3n_1 = \frac{\sin r_2}{\sin i_1} \qquad \ldots(\text{iii})$$

On multiplying Eqs. (i), (ii) and (iii), we get

$$ {}_1n_2 \times {}_2n_3 \times {}_3n_1 = \frac{\sin i_1}{\sin r_1} \times \frac{\sin r_1}{\sin r_2} \times \frac{\sin r_2}{\sin i_1}$$

$$\boxed{{}_1n_2 \times {}_2n_3 \times {}_3n_1 = 1}$$

or

$$ {}_1n_2 \times {}_2n_3 = \frac{1}{{}_3n_1}$$

$$\Rightarrow \qquad \boxed{{}_1n_3 = {}_1n_2 \times {}_2n_3}$$

Lateral Displacement

When a ray of light passes from one medium to other medium, the shift in the path of light on emerging from a refracting medium with parallel faces is called lateral displacement. It is actually the perpendicular distance between the incident and emergent rays.

It is given by, $d = t\sin(i - r) / \cos r$

Apparent Depth and Normal Shift

The depth of an object immersed in water appears to be lesser than its actual depth. Hence, they are related by the following relation:

$$\text{Refractive index} = \frac{\text{Real depth}}{\text{Apparent depth}}$$

From above discussion, we conclude apparent shift as follows:

When light ray travels from denser to rarer medium

$$H_{\text{apparent}} = \frac{H_{\text{real}}}{\mu_w}$$

Apparent shift, $x = H_{\text{real}} - H_{\text{apparent}}$

$$= H_{\text{real}} - \frac{H_{\text{real}}}{\mu_w} = H_{\text{real}}\left(1 - \frac{1}{\mu_w}\right)$$

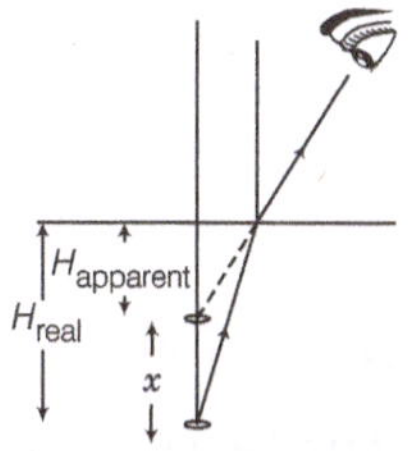

e.g. The depth of an bucket full of water appears to be lesser.

When light ray travels from rarer to denser medium

$$H_{\text{apparent}} = H_{\text{real}} \times \mu$$

Apparent shift, $x = H_{\text{apparent}} - H_{\text{real}}$

$$= H_{\text{real}} \times \mu - H_{\text{real}} = H_{\text{real}}(\mu - 1)$$

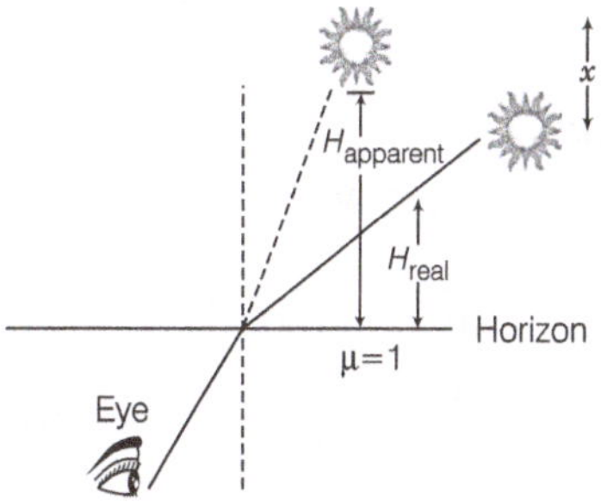

e. g. The Stars look above than they actually are the sun is visible before actual sunrise and after actual sunset due to apparent shift.

Normal shift due to a medium slab

Due to a medium slab, shift observed in position of object

(OO') is $x = t\left(1 - \frac{1}{\mu}\right)$.

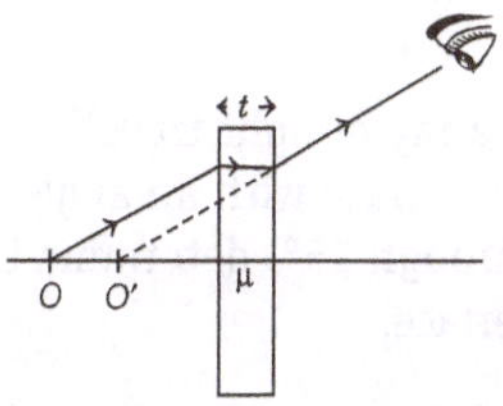

Example 1 Velocity of light in glass is 2×10^8 m/s and that in air is 3×10^8 m/s. By how much would an ink dot appear to be raised, when covered by a glass plate 6 cm thick?

Sol. Given, velocity of light in glass, $v = 2\times10^8$ m/s

Velocity of light in air, $c = 3\times10^8$ m/s

∴ Refractive index of glass with respect to air,

$$^a\mu_g = \frac{c}{v} = \frac{3\times10^8}{2\times10^8} = 1.5$$

∴ Normal shift in the position of ink dot,

$$d = t\left(1-\frac{1}{^a\mu_g}\right) \qquad [\because t = 6\text{ cm}]$$

$$= 6\left(1-\frac{1}{1.5}\right) = \frac{6\times0.5}{1.5} = 2\text{ cm}$$

Critical Angle

Critical angle for a pair of given media in contact can be defined as, "the angle of incidence in denser medium for which angle of refraction in rarer medium is 90°". The value of critical angle depends on the nature of two media in contact.

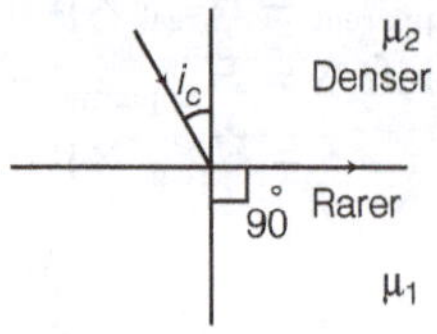

From Snell's law,

$$\mu_2 \times \sin i_c = \mu_1 \times \sin 90°$$

$$\therefore \quad \frac{\mu_1}{\mu_2} = \frac{\sin i_c}{\sin 90°}$$

$$\Rightarrow \quad \frac{\mu_1}{\mu_2} = \sin i_c \qquad [\because \sin 90° = 1]$$

$$\text{or} \quad \frac{\mu_2}{\mu_1} = \frac{1}{\sin i_c} \Rightarrow {}^1\mu_2 = \frac{1}{\sin i_c}$$

Critical Angle of Some Transparent Media

Substance medium	Refractive index	Critical angle
Water	1.33	48.75°
Crown glass	1.52	41.14°
Dense flint glass	1.62	37.31°
Diamond	2.42	24.41°

Example 2 If a ray of light travelling in air is incident on a glass surface with an angle of incidence 40°, it deviates through 15°, determine the critical angle for a glass-air interface.

Sol. Given, angle of incidence, $i = 40°$

Angle of deviation, $\delta = 15°$

Since, ray deviates towards the normal, therefore

$$r = i - \delta = 40° - 15° = 25°$$

As we know that,

$$\mu = \frac{\sin i}{\sin r} = \frac{1}{\sin i_c}$$

$$\Rightarrow \sin i_c = \frac{\sin r}{\sin i} = \frac{\sin 25°}{\sin 40°} = \frac{0.4226}{0.6428}$$

$$\Rightarrow \sin i_c = 0.6574$$

$$\therefore \quad i_c = \sin^{-1}(0.6574) = 41.1° \Rightarrow i_c = 41.1°$$

Total Internal Reflection (TIR)

When a ray of light travelling from denser medium to rarer medium, is incident at the interface of two media at an angle greater than the critical angle for the two media, the ray is totally reflected back to denser medium, this phenomena is called **Total Internal Reflection** (TIR).

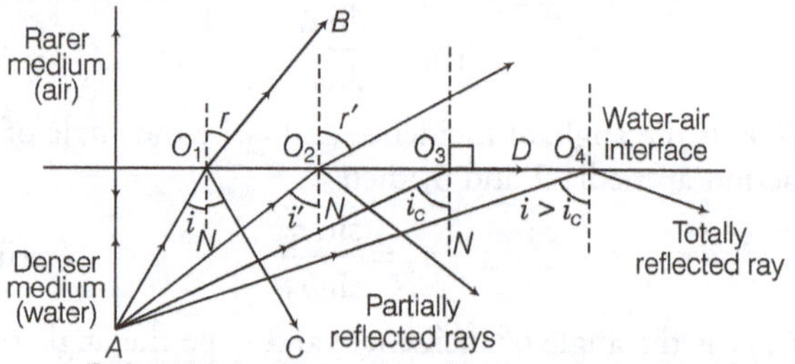

Refraction and internal reflection of rays from a point A in the denser medium (water) incident at different angles at the interface with a rarer medium (air)

Necessary conditions for total internal reflection to take place are as follows

(i) The ray incident on the interface of two media should travel in the denser medium.

(ii) The angle of incidence should be greater than critical angle for the two media.

TIR in Nature and Its Technological Applications

Optical Fibres

An optical fibre is a thin tube of transparent material that allows light to pass through, without being refracted into the air or another external medium. Optical fibres make use of total internal reflection.

Optical fibres are fabricated with high quality composite glass/quartz fibres. The refractive index of core is higher than that of the cladding. When a signal in the form of light is directed at one end of the fibre at a suitable angle, it undergoes repeated total internal reflection along the length of the fibre and finally, comes out from other end.

Optical fibres are fabricated in such a way that light reflected at one side of the inner surface strikes the other at an angle larger than critical angle. Even, if fibre is bent, light can easily travel along the length.

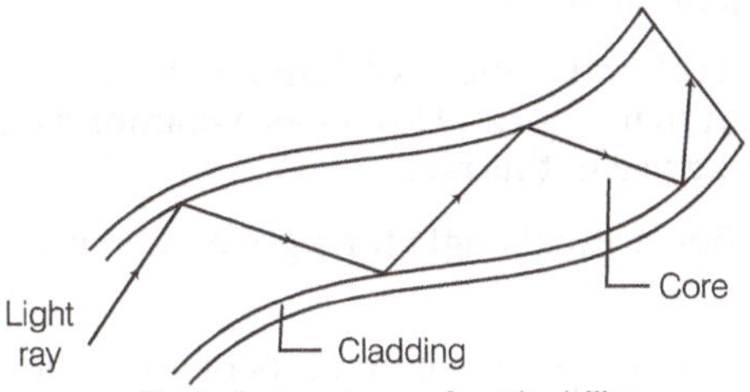

Typical structure of optical fibre

Uses of Optical Fibres

(i) In transmitting electrical and optical signals.
(ii) In visual examination of internal organs like esophagus, stomach and intestine.
(iii) In decorative lamps.

Totally Reflecting Prisms

The refractive index, μ for glass is 1.5, so that critical angle for glass-air interface is 42°. In totally reflecting glass prisms, angle of incidence is made $45°(> i_c)$.

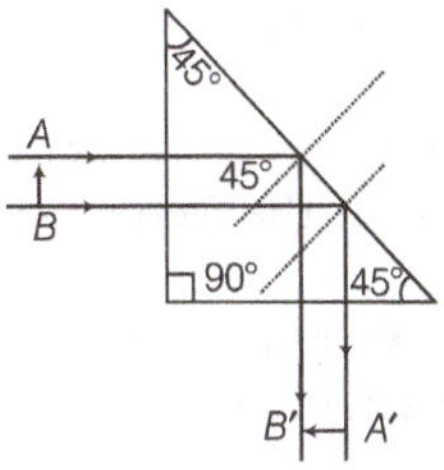

Bending by 90°

Prisms are designed to bend ray by 90° and 180° or to invert image without changing its size by total internal reflection.

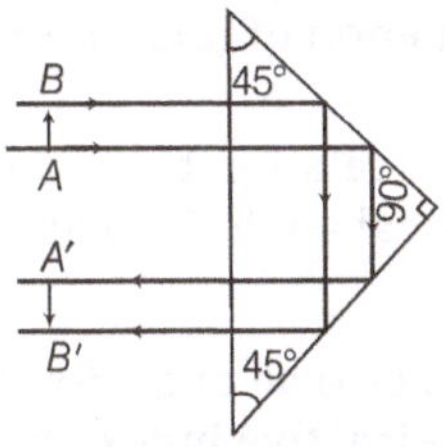

Bending by 180°

Inversion of image

Topic Practice 2

Multiple Choice Questions

1 Mark

1. When a light wave travels from air to glass, **ISC 2017**
   (a) its wavelength decreases
   (b) its wavelength increases
   (c) there is no change in wavelength
   (d) its frequency decreases

2. For the same angle of incidence, the angles of refraction in media P, Q and R are 35°, 25° and 15°, respectively. Which of the following relation hold true for the velocity of light in medium P, Q and R?
   (a) $v_P < v_Q < v_R$ (b) $v_P < v_R < v_Q$
   (c) $v_P > v_Q > v_R$ (d) $v_P > v_R > v_Q$

3. A divergent beam of light from a point source S having divergence angle α falls symmetrically on a glass slab as shown in the figure. The angles of incidence of the two extreme rays are equal. If the thickness of the glass slab is t and its refractive index is n, then the divergence angle of the emergent beam is

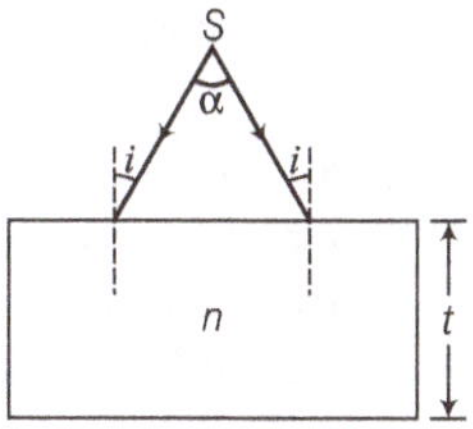

   (a) zero (b) α
   (c) $\sin^{-1}(1/n)$ (d) $2\sin^{-1}(1/n)$

4. A ray of light strikes a transparent rectangular slab of refractive index $\sqrt{2}$ at an angle of incidence of 45°. The angle between the reflected and refracted ray is
   (a) 75° (b) 90°
   (c) 105° (d) 120°

5. As you can seen from Figs. (i) and (ii) shows refraction of light from air to glass and from air to water. Find out the value of the angle θ in the case of refraction as shown in Fig. (iii) will be

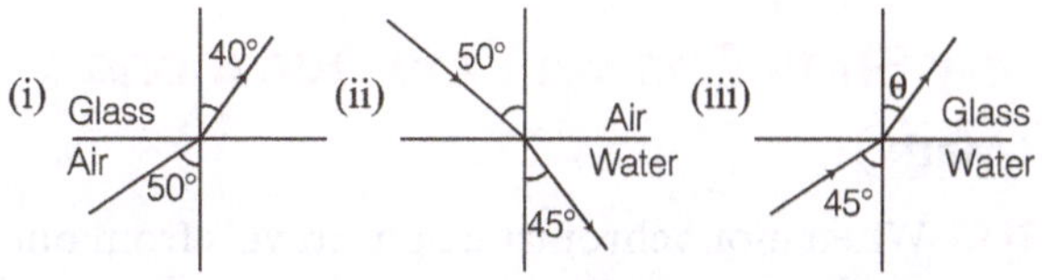

   (a) 30° (b) 50°
   (c) 40° (d) 45°

6. A fish which is at a depth of 12 cm in water ($\mu = 4/3$) is viewed by an observer on the bank of a lake. Its apparent depth as observed by the observer is **ISC 2015**
(a) 3 cm (b) 9 cm
(c) 12 cm (d) 16 cm

7. A green light is incident from the water to the air-water interface at the critical angle (θ). Select the correct statement.
(a) The entire spectrum of visible light will come out of the water at an angle of 90° to the normal.
(b) The spectrum of visible light whose frequency is less than that of green light will come out of the air medium.
(c) The spectrum of visible light whose frequency is more than that of green light will come out to the air medium.
(d) The entire spectrum of visible light will come out of the water at various angles to the normal.

8. Two transparent media *A* and *B* are separated by a plane boundary. The speed of light in medium *A* is 2×10^8 ms^{-1} and in medium *B* is 2.5×10^8 ms^{-1}. The critical angle for which a ray of light going from *A* to *B* is totally internally reflected is
(a) $\sin^{-1}\left(\frac{1}{2}\right)$ (b) $\sin^{-1}\left(\frac{2}{5}\right)$
(c) $\sin^{-1}\left(\frac{4}{5}\right)$ (d) $\sin^{-1}\left(\frac{3}{4}\right)$

9. A ray of light is incident at the glass-water interface at an angle *i*, it emerges finally parallel to the surface of water, then the value of μ_g would be

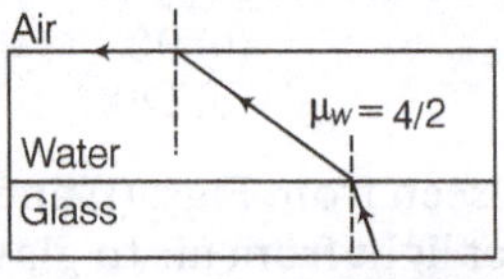

(a) $(4/3)\sin i$ (b) $1/\sin i$
(c) 4/3 (d) 1

Very Short Answer Type Questions

1 Mark

10. When monochromatic light travels from one medium to another, its wavelength changes, but frequency remains same. Explain.

11. A ray of light strikes on air-glass interface at an angle of incidence ($< i = 60°$) and gets refracted at an angle of refraction ($< r$). What will happen to the angle of refraction on increasing the angle of incidence?

12. Why does a crack in a glass window pane appear silvery?

13. The refractive index of diamond is much higher than that of glass. How does a diamond cutter make use of this fact?

14. Define critical angle for a given medium. **ISC 2019**

15. Which of the two main parts of an optical fibre has a higher value of refractive index?

16. Name the physical principle on which the working of optical fibre is based. **ISC 2020, 16, 14**

17. Name the physical principle and one advantage in the use of optical fibres. **ISC 2000**

Short Answer Type I Questions

2 Marks

18. When monochromatic light travels from a rarer to a denser medium, explain the following, giving reasons.
(i) Is the frequency of reflected and refracted light same as the frequency of incident light?
(ii) Does the decrease in speed imply a reduction in the energy carried by light wave?

19. Mention any two situations in which Snell's law of refraction fails.

20. (i) Write the necessary conditions for the phenomenon of total internal reflection to occur.
(ii) Write the relation between refractive index and critical angle for a given pair of optical media.

21. Calculate the critical angle for glass and water pair. (Take, refractive index for glass is 1.50 and the refractive index for water is 1.33.) **ISC 2010**

22. Find critical angle for glass and water pair, given refractive index of glass is 1.62 and that of water is 1.33. **ISC 2016**

23. Draw a diagram to show how an image is produced by a pair of total reflecting prism arranged as in a periscope. **ISC 2001**

24. A ray of light is normally incident on one face of an equilateral prism. Trace the course of the ray through the prism and emerging from it. **ISC 2003**

Short Answer Type II Questions

3 Marks

25. Define the following with required formula.
   (i) Apparent depth
   (ii) Lateral displacement (or shift)
   (iii) Critical angle

26. A beaker contains water upto height h_1 and kerosene of height h_2 above water surface, so that the total height of (water + kerosene) is $h_1 + h_2$. Refractive index of water is μ_1 and that of kerosene is μ_2. What will be the apparent shift in position of the bottom of the beaker as viewed from above?

27. A fish is located at a distance of 10 cm from the wall of fish pond. The thickness of the glass wall is 2 cm. Find the apparent position of the fish. (Take, ${}_a\mu_g = 3/2$ and ${}_a\mu_w = 4/3$) **ISC 2004**

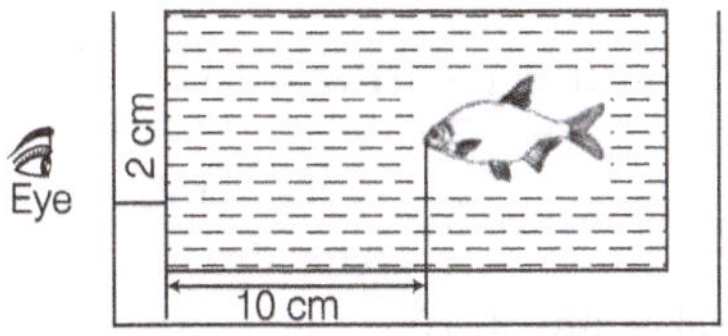

28. Three light rays, red (R), green (G) and blue (B) are incident on a right angled prism ABC at face AB. The refractive indices of the material of the prism for red, green and blue wavelengths are 1.39, 1.44 and 1.47, respectively. Out of the three, which colour of ray will emerge out of face AC?

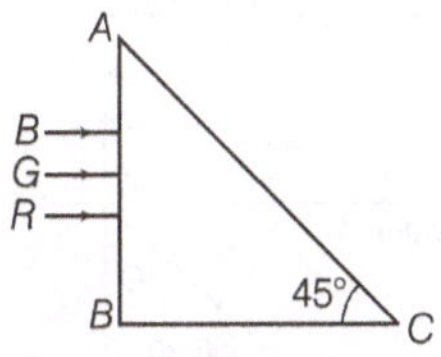

Justify your answer. Trace the path of these rays after passing through face AB.

Long Answer Type Questions

5 Marks

29. A point source of monochromatic light S is kept at the centre C of the bottom of a cylinder. The radius of the circular base of the cylinder is 15.0 cm. The cylinder contains water $\left(\text{refractive index } = \frac{4}{3}\right)$ to a height of 7.0 cm as shown in the figure. Find the area through which light emerges in air.
(Take, $\pi = 22/7$)

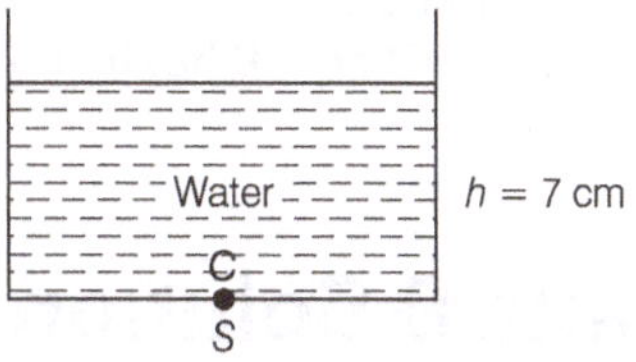

ISC 2009

30. Explain the phenomenon of total internal reflection. Describe how TIR takes place in optical fibre. State any two uses of it.

Numerical Problems

31. What is the ratio of the velocities of two light waves travelling in vacuum and having wavelengths 4000 Å and 8000 Å? **(1 M)**

32. What is the critical angle for a material of refractive index $\sqrt{2}$? **(1 M)**

33. A ray of light is incident at an angle of 45° on one face of a rectangular glass slab of thickness 10 cm and refractive index 1.5. Calculate the lateral shift produced. **(2M)**

34. What is the apparent position of an object below a rectangular block of glass 6 cm thick, if a layer of water 4 cm thick is on the top of the glass? Given, $n_{ga} = 1.5$ and $n_{wa} = 1.33$. **(2M)**

35. A ray PQ incident normally on the refracting face BA is refracted in the prism BAC made of material of refractive index 1.5. Complete the path of ray through the prism. From which face will the ray emerge? Justify your answer.

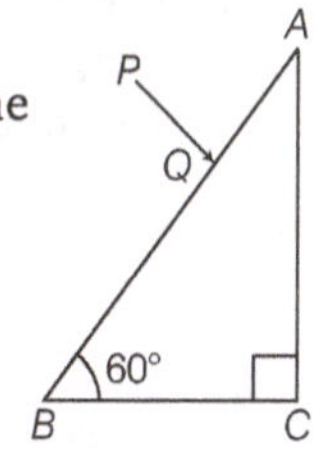

36. A tank is filled with water to a height of 12.5 cm. The apparent depth of a needle lying at the bottom of the tank is measured by a microscope to be 9.4 cm. What is the refractive

index of water? If water is replaced by a liquid of refractive index 1.63 upto the same height, by what distance would the microscope have to be moved to focus on the needle again?

NCERT (3 M)

37. A container is filled with water ($\mu = 1.33$) upto a height of 33.25 cm. A concave mirror is placed 15 cm above the water level and the image of an object placed at the bottom is formed 25 cm below the water level. What will be the focal length?

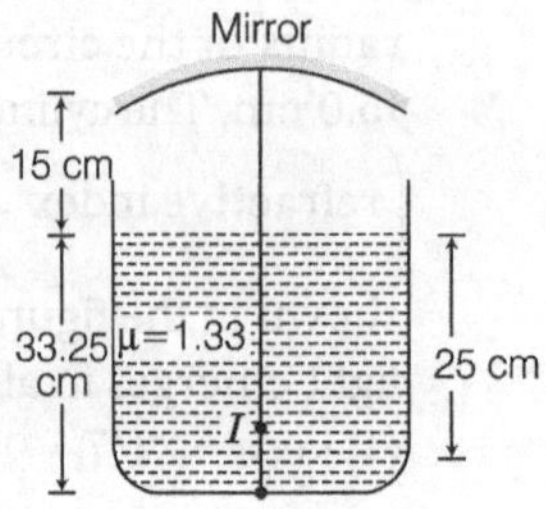

(3 M)

Hints & Solutions

1. (*a*) Its wavelength decreases, because they are related by the formula, $\mu = \dfrac{\lambda_{air}}{\lambda_{glass}}$

Here, $\mu = \dfrac{v}{v}$ as velocity in medium decreases, hence its wavelength decreases.

$\therefore \quad v = v\lambda$

2. (*c*) For same angle of incidence, the angle of refraction is minimum in medium *R*.

As, $\quad \mu = \dfrac{\sin i}{\sin r} \quad$ ...(i)

or $\quad \mu \propto \dfrac{1}{\sin r}$

$\Rightarrow \mu$ is maximum for *R*, since *r* is minimum and hence $\sin r$ is minimum.

Also, $\quad \mu = \dfrac{c}{v} \quad$ ...(ii)

Therefore, if μ is maximum, *v* is minimum, i.e. velocity of light is minimum in medium *R* and order of velocity will be $\quad v_P > v_Q > v_R$

3. (*b*) When a ray of light passes through the glass slab, the emergent rays are parallel to the incident rays.

Here, from figure, $i = e$.

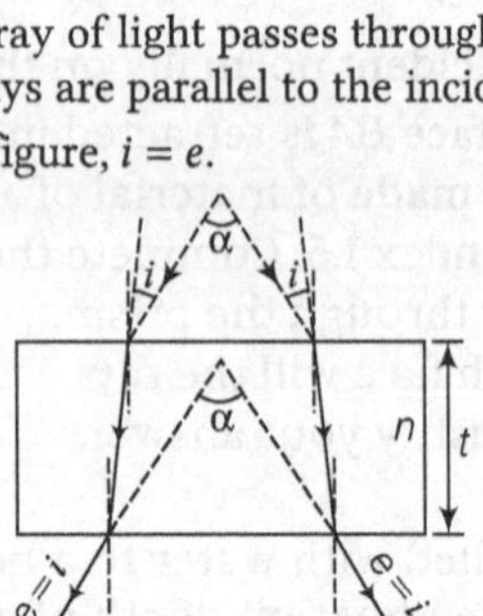

So, divergent angle of the emergent beam is also same, i.e. α.

4. (*c*) Given, $i = 45°$

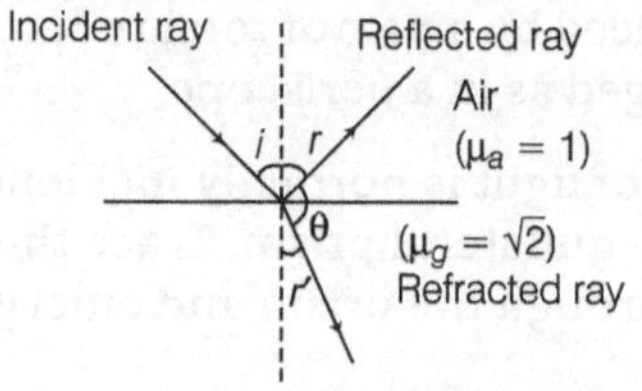

From Snell's law, $\dfrac{\sin i}{\sin r'} = \dfrac{\mu_g}{\mu_a} \Rightarrow \dfrac{\sin 45°}{\sin r'} = \dfrac{\sqrt{2}}{1}$

$\Rightarrow \quad \sin r' = \dfrac{1}{2} \Rightarrow r' = \sin^{-1}\left(\dfrac{1}{2}\right) = 30°$

From diagram, $\quad r + \theta + r' = 180°$

$i + \theta + 30° = 180° \quad (\because i = r)$

$45° + \theta + 30° = 180°$

$\theta = 180° - 75° = 105°$

Hence, the angle between reflected and refracted ray is 105°.

5. (*c*) $\quad {}^a\mu_g = \dfrac{\sin 50°}{\sin 40°} \quad$ ...(i)

${}^a\mu_w = \dfrac{\sin 50°}{\sin 45°} \quad$ ...(ii)

${}^w\mu_g = \dfrac{\sin 45°}{\sin \theta} \quad$ ...(iii)

$\therefore \quad {}^a\mu_w \times {}^w\mu_g = {}^a\mu_g$

$\dfrac{\sin 50°}{\sin 45°} \times \dfrac{\sin 45°}{\sin \theta} = \dfrac{\sin 50°}{\sin 40°}$ [using Eqs. (i), (ii) and (iii)]

$\sin \theta = \sin 40° \quad \Rightarrow \quad \theta = 40°$

6. (*b*) We know that, refractive index $= \dfrac{\text{real depth}}{\text{apparent depth}}$

Now, apparent depth $= \dfrac{\text{real depth}}{\text{refractive index}}$

Here, real depth = 12 cm,

refractive index = 4 / 3

$\therefore$ Apparent depth $= 12 \times \dfrac{3}{4} = 9$ cm

7. (*d*) For total internal reflection of light take place, following conditions must be obeyed.

(i) The ray must travel from denser to rarer medium.

(ii) Angle of incidence (θ) must be greater than or equal to critical angle (*C*), i.e.

$$C = \sin^{-1}\left(\frac{\mu_{rarer}}{\mu_{denser}}\right)$$

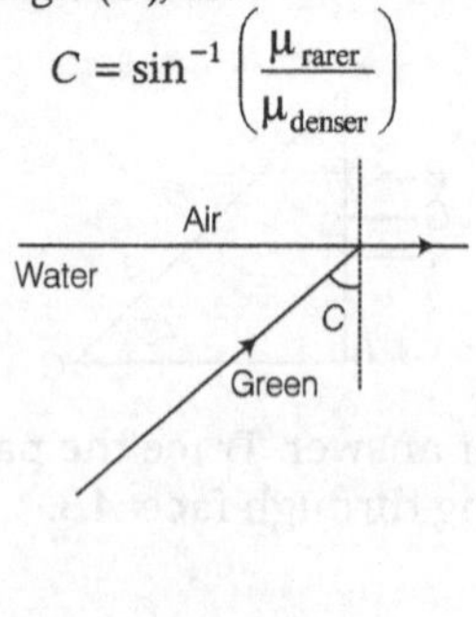

Here, $\sin C = \frac{1}{n_{water}}$ and $n_{water} = a + \frac{b}{\lambda^2}$

If frequency is less $\Rightarrow \lambda$ is greater and hence refractive index, $n_{(water)}$ is less and therefore critical angle increases. So, they do not suffer reflection and come out at angle less than 90°.

8. (c) Given, velocity of light in medium A,

$$v_A = 2 \times 10^8 \text{ ms}^{-1}$$

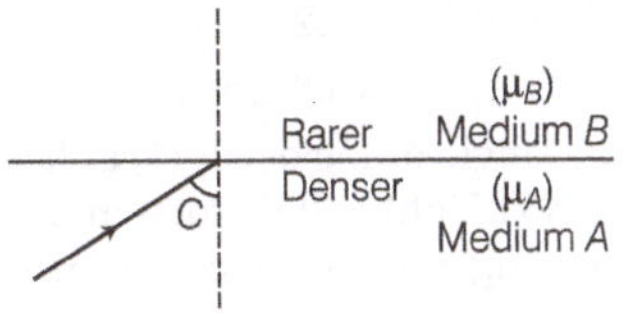

Velocity of light in medium B,

$$v_B = 2.5 \times 10^8 \text{ ms}^{-1}$$

$$\because \quad \frac{v_A}{v_B} = \frac{\mu_B}{\mu_A} = \frac{2}{2.5} = \frac{4}{5}$$

$\Rightarrow$ B is rarer and A is denser medium.

Since, critical angle for pair of media, $C = \sin^{-1}\left(\frac{\mu_r}{\mu_d}\right)$

(where, μ_r = refractive index for rarer medium and μ_d = refractive index for denser medium)

$$\therefore \quad C = \sin^{-1}\left(\frac{4}{5}\right)$$

9. (b) For glass-water interface, applying Snell's law,

$$\frac{\sin i}{\sin r} = \frac{\mu_w}{\mu_g}$$

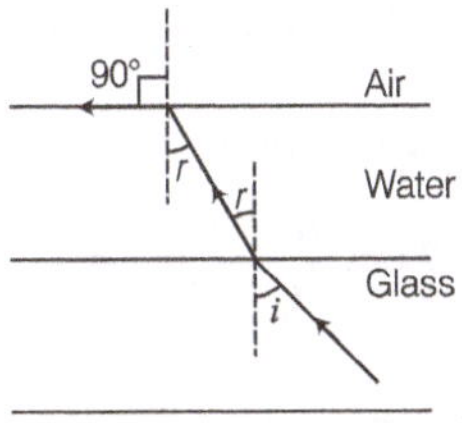

$$\Rightarrow \quad \mu_g = \left(\frac{\mu_w \sin r}{\sin i}\right) \quad \text{...(i)}$$

For water air interface, angle of incidence in water = r

Again, $\frac{\sin r}{\sin 90°} = \frac{1}{\mu_w} \Rightarrow \sin r = \frac{1}{\mu_w}$ ...(ii)

From Eqs. (i) and (ii), we get

$$\mu_g = \frac{(\mu_w) \times \left(\frac{1}{\mu_w}\right)}{\sin i} \Rightarrow \mu_g = \frac{1}{\sin i}$$

10. Because refractive index for a given pair of media depends on the ratio of wavelengths and velocity of light in two media but not on frequency. So, frequency remains constant during refraction of light.

11. From Snell's law, $\mu = \frac{\sin i}{\sin r}$ = constant

Since, angle of incidence increases, the angle of refraction has to increase, so that the ratio remains constant.

12. Whenever rays of light travels through glass, they strike the glass-air interface at an angle greater than critical angle of glass. They are totally reflected, hence crack appears silvery.

13. The refractive index of diamond is much higher than that of glass. Due to high refractive index, the critical angle for diamond-air interface is low. The diamond is cut suitably, so that the light entering the diamond from any face suffers multiple total internal reflections at the various surfaces. This gives sparkling effect to the diamonds.

14. The critical angle for two given media is the angle of incidence in the denser medium for which the angle of refraction in the rarer medium is 90°.

15. There are two main parts of the optical fibre

(i) Core (ii) Cladding

The refractive index of core is greater than that of cladding such that TIR can occurs.

16. Optical fibre works on the principle of total internal reflection. Total internal reflection of light (TIR) is the phenomena, when a ray of light travelling from denser medium to rarer medium is incident at the interface of two media at angle greater than the critical angle for the two media, the ray is totally reflected back to denser medium.

17. The working of optical fibres is based on the principle of total internal reflection of light i.e. when a ray of light travels from a denser medium to a rarer medium such that the angle of incidence is greater than the critical angle for two pairs of media, then the light is reflected back in the same denser medium.

Refer to text on page 339 (Uses of optical fibres).

18. (i) The frequency of reflected and refracted light remains same as that of incident light because frequency only depends on the source of light. (1)

(ii) Since, the frequency remains same, hence there is no reduction in energy. (1)

19. Snell's law of refraction fails in two situations

(i) When TIR (total internal reflection) takes place at angle greater than the critical angle. (1)

(ii) When light is incident normally on a surface, as $i = 0$, $r = 0$. (1)

20. (i) Refer to text on page 338 (Total internal reflection).

(ii) Refer to text on page 338 (Critical angle).

21. Given, refractive index of glass $\mu_g = 1.50$

Refractive index of water $\mu_w = 1.33$

Let C be critical angle, then from Snell's law

$$\sin C = \frac{1}{{}_w\mu_g} = \frac{\mu_w}{\mu_g} = \frac{1.33}{1.50} \quad (1)$$

$$\Rightarrow \quad C = \sin^{-1}\left(\frac{1.33}{1.50}\right) = 62.5° \quad (1)$$

22. Given, refractive index of glass is $\mu_g = 1.62$

refractive index of water is, $\mu_w = 1.33$

From Snell's law of refraction,

$${}^w\mu_g = \frac{\sin i}{\sin r} = \frac{\mu_w}{\mu_g} \quad (1)$$

$\Rightarrow$ For the critical for glass-water pair, $r = 90°$

$$\Rightarrow \frac{\sin i_C}{\sin 90°} = \frac{1.33}{1.62} \Rightarrow \sin i_C = 0.820$$

$$\Rightarrow i_C = \sin^{-1}(0.820) = 55.08° \quad (1)$$

23. The ray diagram of the periscope is shown as below (it uses right angled isosceles prism).

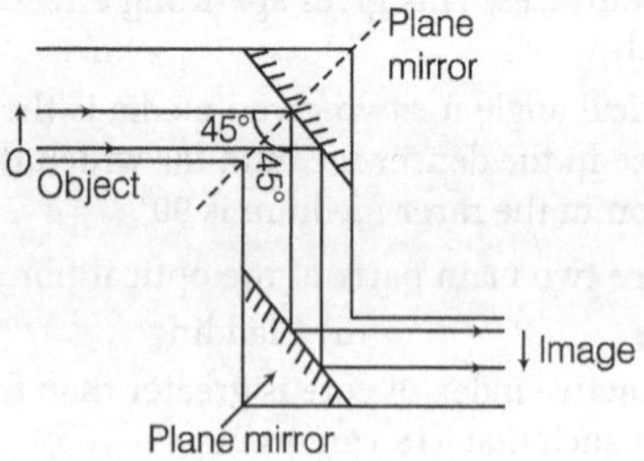

(2)

24. For glass prism, critical angle is

$$i_c = \sin^{-1}\left(\frac{1}{\mu}\right) = \sin^{-1}\left(\frac{1}{3/2}\right)$$

$$= \sin^{-1}\left(\frac{2}{3}\right) = 42°$$

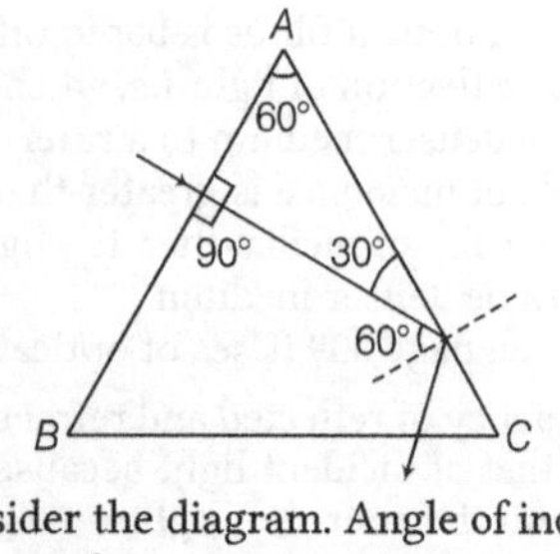

(1)

Now, consider the diagram. Angle of incidence on the face AC, $i = 60° > i_C$.

Hence, the ray is totally internally reflected. (1)

25. (i) Refer to text on page 337 (Apparent depth and normal shift).

(ii) Refer to text on page 337 (Lateral displacement).

(iii) Refer to text on page 338 (Critical angle). (1)

26. $\therefore$ Apparent depth, $d = d_1 + d_2$

$$= \left(1 - \frac{1}{\mu_1}\right)h_1 + \left(1 - \frac{1}{\mu_2}\right)h_2 \quad (1)$$

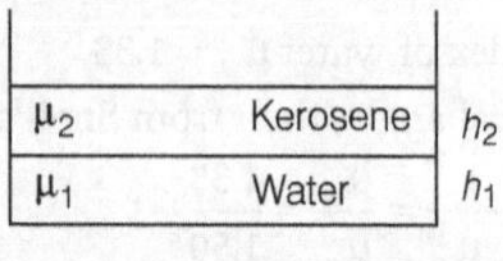

(1)

27. Apparent position can be calculated by adding apparent positions due to glass and water both. (1)

Now,

$$\because \text{ Apparent position} = 2 \times \frac{\mu_g}{\mu_a} + 10 \times \frac{\mu_w}{\mu_a}$$

$$= 2 \times \frac{2}{3} + 10 \times \frac{3}{4} \quad (1)$$

$$= \frac{4}{3} + \frac{30}{4} = \frac{16 + 90}{12}$$

$$= \frac{106}{12} = \frac{53}{6}$$

$$= 8.8 \text{ cm} \quad (1)$$

28. By geometry, angle of incidence (i) at face AC for all three rays is 45°. Light suffers total internal reflection for which the angle of incidence is greater than critical angle.

$$i > i_c \Rightarrow \sin i > \sin i_c \quad (1)$$

or $\sin 45° > \sin i_c$

$$\Rightarrow \frac{1}{\sin 45°} < \frac{1}{\sin i_c} \Rightarrow \sqrt{2} < \mu$$

Total internal reflection takes place on AC for rays with $\mu > \sqrt{2} = 1.414$, i.e. green and blue colour suffer total internal reflection, whereas red undergoes refraction. (1)

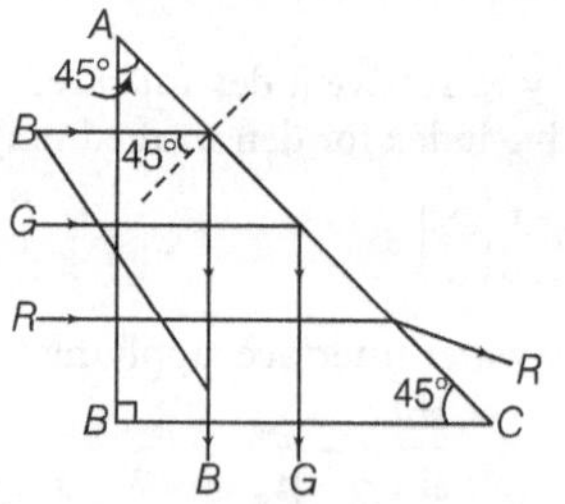

(1)

29. We have to use the concept of critical angle and the area of the circle will be confined within the two totally reflecting points. (1)

According to the question,

Given, $h = 7$ cm, $\frac{\mu_w}{\mu_a} = {}_a\mu_w = \frac{4}{3}$

We can write

$$\sin \theta_c = \frac{1}{{}_a\mu_w} = \frac{3}{4} = 0.75$$

$$\theta_c = \sin^{-1} 0.75 = 48.6° \quad (1)$$

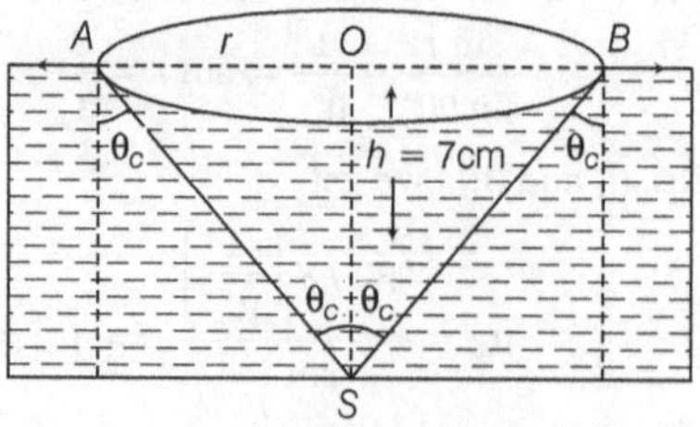

Now, $\tan \theta_c = \frac{\text{Perpendicular}}{\text{Base}} = \frac{r}{h}$

$$\Rightarrow r = h \tan \theta_c = 7 \times \tan 48.6°$$

$\therefore \quad r = 7.94$ cm (approx)

$$\text{Area} = \pi r^2 = \frac{22}{7} \times (7.94)^2 = 198 \text{ cm}^2$$ (1)

30. Refer to text on pages 338 and 339 (Total internal reflection, optical fibres and uses of optical fibres).

31. Since, light travels in vacuum with a constant velocity, i.e. 3×10^8 m/s, hence ratio of velocities of all wavelengths remains same.

32. We know that,

$$\mu = \frac{1}{\sin C} \Rightarrow \sin C = \frac{1}{\mu} = \frac{1}{\sqrt{2}}$$

$$\therefore \quad C = 45°$$

33. Given, $i_1 = 45°$, $t = 10$ cm $= 0.1$ m, $\mu = 1.5$

Lateral shift = ?

By Snell's law, $\mu = \dfrac{\sin i_1}{\sin r_1}$

$$\Rightarrow \quad \sin r_1 = \frac{\sin i_1}{\mu} = \frac{\sin 45°}{1.5}$$

$$\Rightarrow \quad \sin r_1 = \frac{0.707}{1.5} \quad \left[\because \sin 45° = 1/\sqrt{2}, \sqrt{2} = 1.414\right]$$

$$\Rightarrow \quad \sin r_1 = 0.4713$$

$$\Rightarrow \quad r_1 = \sin^{-1}(0.4713) \Rightarrow r_1 = 28.12°$$ (1)

$$\text{Lateral shift} = \frac{t \sin(i_1 - r_1)}{\cos r_1}$$

$$= \frac{0.1 \sin(45° - 28.12°)}{\cos 28.12°}$$

$$= \frac{0.1 \sin 16.88°}{\cos 28.12°}$$

$$= \frac{0.1 \times 0.2904}{0.8819} = 0.033 \text{ m}$$ (1)

34. Here, $\mu = \dfrac{\text{real depth / thickness of object}}{\text{apparent depth}}$ (1/2)

Now, due to refraction at two different boundaries, the apparent depth of object is

$$\text{apparent depth} = \frac{\text{thickness of glass}}{\mu_{glass}} + \frac{\text{thickness of water}}{\mu_{water}}$$ (1/2)

$$= \frac{6}{1.5} + \frac{4}{1.33} = 4 + 3 = 7 \text{ cm}$$ (1)

35. Given, refractive index of the material of the prism, $\mu = 1.5$

$\therefore$ Critical angle for the material,

$$\sin C = \frac{1}{\mu} = \frac{1}{1.5} = 2/3 \Rightarrow C = \sin^{-1}\left(\frac{2}{3}\right) \simeq 42°.$$

From the ray diagram, it is clear that angle of incidence $i = 30° < C$.

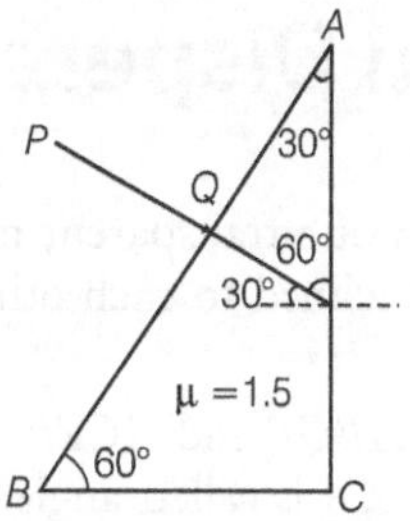

(1)

Therefore, the ray incident at the face AC will not suffer total internal reflection and merges out through this face. (1)

36. ***Case* I** When tank is filled with the water.

Given, the apparent depth = 9.4 cm

Height of water, $t = 12.5$ cm

So, real depth = 12.5 cm

Refractive index of water,

$$\mu_w = \frac{\text{Real depth}}{\text{Apparent depth}}$$

$$= \frac{12.5}{9.4} = 1.33$$ (1½)

***Case* II** When tank is filled with the liquid.

Refractive index of liquid, $\mu_l = 1.63$

Again, $\mu_l = \dfrac{\text{Real depth}}{\text{Apparent depth}}$

$$\Rightarrow \quad 1.63 = \frac{12.5}{\text{Apparent depth}}$$

$$\text{Apparent depth} = \frac{12.5}{1.63} = 7.67 \text{ cm}$$

$\therefore$ The microscope is shifted by $9.4 - 7.67 = 1.73$ cm. (1½)

37. Distance of object from mirror

$$= 15 + \frac{33.25}{4} \times 3 = 39.93 \text{ cm}$$

Distance of image from the mirror

$$= 15 + \frac{25}{4} \times 3$$

$$= 33.75 \text{ cm}$$ (2)

Using mirror formula,

$$\frac{1}{v} + \frac{1}{u} = \frac{1}{f}$$

$$\Rightarrow \quad \frac{1}{-33.75} - \frac{1}{39.93} = \frac{1}{f}$$

$$\therefore \quad f = -18.3 \text{ cm}$$ (1)

TOPIC 03 Refraction Through a Prism and Dispersion

A **prism** is a portion of a transparent medium bounded by two plane faces inclined to each other at a suitable angle.

In the given figure, $ABQP$ and $ACRP$ are the two refracting faces and $\angle A$ is called angle of prism.

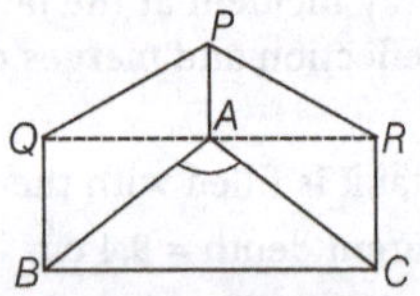

Deviation Produced by a prism

The figure below shows the passage of light through a triangular prism ABC.

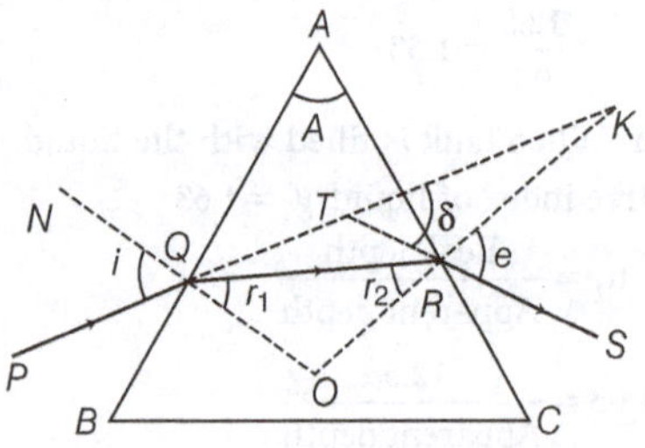

The angles of incidence and refraction at first face AB are i and r_1.

The angle of incidence at the second face AC is r_2 and the angle of emergence is e.

The angle between the emergent ray RS and incident ray PQ is called **angle of deviation** (δ).

Here, $\angle PQN = i$, $\angle SRK = e$

$\angle RQO = r_1$, $\angle QRO = r_2$

$\angle KTS = \delta$, $\angle TQO = i$

and $\angle TQR = i - r_1$ or $\angle TRQ = e - r_2$

In ΔTQR, the side QT has been produced outwards. Therefore, the exterior angle δ should be equal to the sum of the interior opposite angles.

i.e. $\delta = \angle TQR + \angle TRQ = (i - r_1) + (e - r_2)$

$\Rightarrow$ $\delta = (i + e) - (r_1 + r_2)$ ...(i)

In ΔQRO,

$r_1 + r_2 + \angle ROQ = 180°$ ...(ii)

From quadrilateral $AROQ$, we have the sum of angles

$\angle AQO + \angle ARO = 180°$.

This means that the sum of the remaining two angles should be 180°.

i.e. $\angle A + \angle ROQ = 180°$ ...(iii)

[$\angle A$ is called the angle of prism]

From Eqs. (ii) and (iii), we get

$r_1 + r_2 = A$ ...(iv)

Substituting the value from Eq. (iv) in Eq. (i), we obtain

$$\boxed{\delta = (i + e) - A}$$

Deviation Produced by a Small Angled Prism

When angles are small, $\sin i_1 \approx i_1$ and $\sin r_1 \approx r_1$

$\therefore$ $\mu = \dfrac{i_1}{r_1}$

$\Rightarrow$ $i = \mu r_1$ [here, $i_1 = i$]

Similarly, $\mu = \dfrac{i_2}{r_2}$ or $\mu = \dfrac{e}{r_2}$ [$\because i_2 = e$]

$\Rightarrow$ $e = \mu r_2$

$\therefore$ $\delta = i + e - A$

$= \mu r_1 + \mu r_2 - A = \mu(r_1 + r_2) - A$

But $r_1 + r_2 = A$

$\therefore$ $\delta = \mu A - A$

or $\boxed{\delta = (\mu - 1)A}$

This is the angle through which a ray deviates on passing through a thin prism of small refracting angle A.

Example 1 A thin prism of 5° angle gives a deviation of 3.2°. What is the value of refractive index of the material of the prism?

Sol. Given, $A = 5°$, $\delta = 3.2°$, $\mu = ?$

We know that,

$\delta = A(\mu - 1)$

$\therefore$ $\mu = 1 + \dfrac{\delta}{A} = 1 + \dfrac{3.2°}{5°}$

$= 1 + 0.64 = 1.64$

Prism Formula

If the angle of incidence is increased gradually, then the angle of deviation first decreases, attains a minimum value (δ_m) and then again starts increasing.

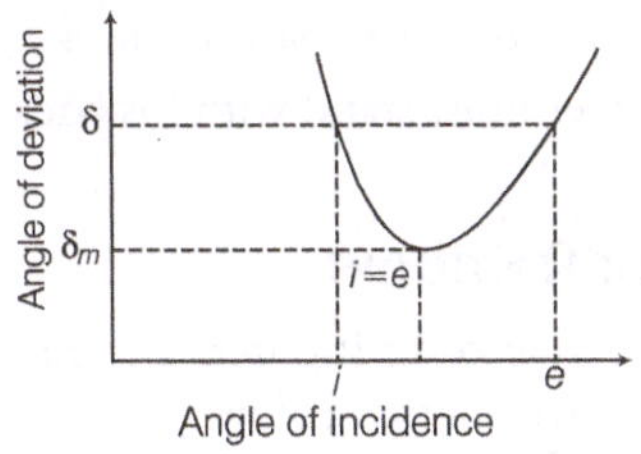

When angle of deviation is minimum, the prism is said to be placed in the minimum deviation position. There is only one angle of incidence for which the angle of deviation is minimum.

When $\delta = \delta_m$ [prism in minimum deviation position]

$$e = i \text{ and } r_2 = r_1 \quad \ldots(i)$$

$\because \quad r_1 + r_2 = A$

$\Rightarrow \quad r + r = A$ or $r = \dfrac{A}{2}$

Also, we have

$$A + \delta = i + e \quad \ldots(ii)$$

Putting $\delta = \delta_m$ and $e = i$ in Eq. (ii), we get

$$A + \delta_m = i + i$$

$$\Rightarrow \quad i = \left(\frac{A + \delta_m}{2}\right)$$

From Snell's law,

$$\mu = \frac{\sin i}{\sin r}$$

$$\therefore \quad \mu = \frac{\sin\left(\dfrac{A + \delta_m}{2}\right)}{\sin \dfrac{A}{2}}$$

This relation is called a **prism formula.**

The refracted ray inside the prism is parallel to the base of prism for equilateral and isosceles prisms.

Example 2 A ray of light suffers minimum deviation, while passing through a prism of refractive index 1.5 and refracting angle 60°. Calculate the angle of deviation and angle of incidence.
(Given, $\sin^{-1}(0.75) = 48.6°$)

Sol. Given, refractive index, $\mu = 1.5$

Angle of prism, $A = 60°$, angle of deviation, $\delta_m = ?$

Angle of incidence, $i = ?$

We know that, $\mu = \dfrac{\sin\left(\dfrac{A + \delta_m}{2}\right)}{\sin\left(\dfrac{A}{2}\right)} \Rightarrow 1.5 = \dfrac{\sin\left(\dfrac{60° + \delta_m}{2}\right)}{\sin\left(\dfrac{60°}{2}\right)}$

$$\Rightarrow \quad 1.5 \sin 30° = \sin\left(\frac{60° + \delta_m}{2}\right)$$

$$\Rightarrow \quad 1.5 \times 0.5 = \sin\left(\frac{60° + \delta_m}{2}\right)$$

$$\Rightarrow \quad \frac{60° + \delta_m}{2} = \sin^{-1}(0.75)$$

$$\Rightarrow \quad \frac{60° + \delta_m}{2} = 48.6°$$

$$\delta_m = 48.6° \times 2 - 60° = 37.2°$$

Also, the angle of incidence,

$$i = \frac{(A + \delta_m)}{2} = \frac{60° + 37.2°}{2} = 48.6°$$

Dispersion by a Prism

The phenomenon of splitting of light into its component colours is known as **dispersion**. The pattern of colour components of light is called the **spectrum** of the sunlight.

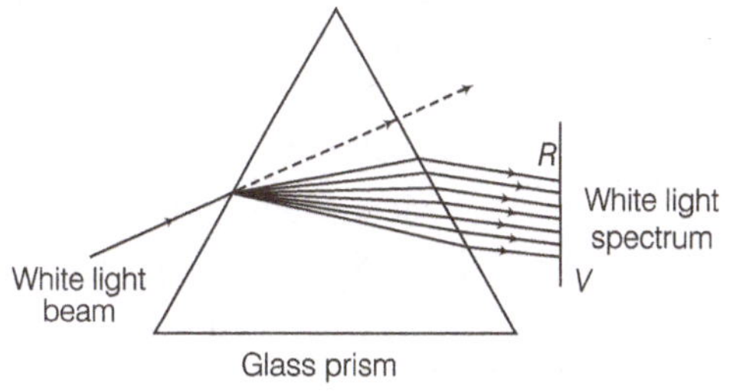

When a narrow beam of sunlight is incident on a glass prism, the emergent light is seen to be consist of seven colours namely violet (V), indigo (I), blue (B), green (G), yellow (Y), orange (O), red (R). The red light bends the least while the violet light bends the most.

Cause of Dispersion

The different colours of the white light have different wavelengths. The wavelength of violet light is smaller than that of red light.

Refractive index of material of prism is maximum for violet colour (minimum wavelength) and minimum for red colour (maximum wavelength). i.e. $\mu_V > \mu_R$

For a small angled prism, we have $\delta = A(\mu - 1)$

Since $\mu_V > \mu_R$, the violet light will suffer greater deviation than red light, i.e. $\delta_V > \delta_R$.

Angular Dispersion

The angular dispersion produced by a prism for white light is the difference in the angle of deviation for two extreme colours, violet and red.

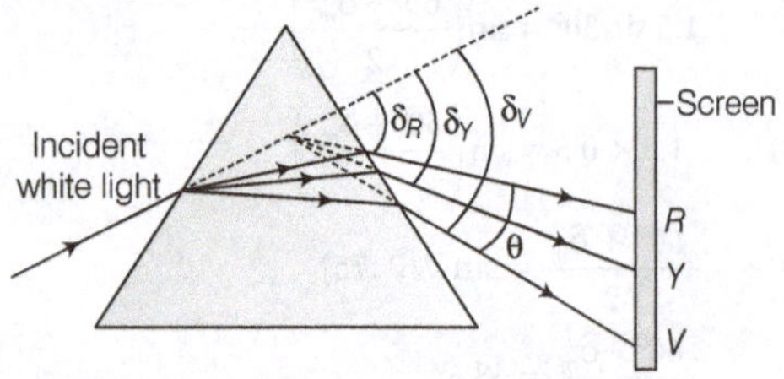

According to given figure, angular dispersion

$$\theta = \delta_v - \delta_r = (\mu_v - \mu_r)A$$

where, δ_μ = deviation angle of violet light,

δ_r = deviation angle of red light,

μ_v = refractive index for violet light,

μ_r = refractive index for red light,

A = angle of prism.

Dispersive Power (ω)

Dispersive power of a medium or prism is defined as the ratio of angular dispersion to the mean deviation produced by the medium or prism. It is represented by ω.

$$\text{Dispersive power, } \omega = \frac{\text{Angular dispersion}}{\text{Mean deviation}}$$

$$= \frac{\delta_V - \delta_R}{\delta} = \frac{(\mu_V - \mu_R)A}{(\mu - 1)A}$$

$$\omega = \frac{\mu_V - \mu_R}{(\mu - 1)}$$

The dispersive power of a medium or prism depends on the nature of material and it does not depend upon angle of prism.

Natural Phenomena Due to Sunlight

The spectrum of colours that we see around us all the time is possible only due to sunlight. The rainbow, blue colour of the sky, white clouds, the red hue at sunrise and sunset, etc., are some of the natural phenomena.

The Rainbow

Rainbow is an example of the dispersion of sunlight by the water drops in the atmosphere. It is a spectrum of sun's light in nature. It occurs in the form of concentric coloured circular arcs in the sky, when the sun shines on rain drops during or after the shower.

This phenomenon occurs due to combined effect of dispersion, refraction and total internal reflection of sunlight by spherical drop of water.

Necessary conditions for the rainbow to take place.

(i) Sun should be shining in part of the sky while it is raining in the opposite part of the sky.

(ii) The observer must stand with his back towards the sun.

Formation of Rainbow

Sunlight is first refracted as it enters a raindrop, due to which different wavelengths (colours) of white light separate into its different colours. Longer wavelength of light (red) bends the least while the shorter wavelength (violet) bends the most.

The component rays of white light strike the inner surface of the water drop and get internally reflected, if the angle between the refracted ray and normal to the drop surface is greater than the critical angle (here 48°). The reflected light is refracted again as it comes out of the drop.

It is found that the violet light emerges at an angle of 40° related to the incoming sunlight and red light emerges at an angle 42°. The sun rays incident on a water drop get refracted twice and reflected internally one time by a drop.

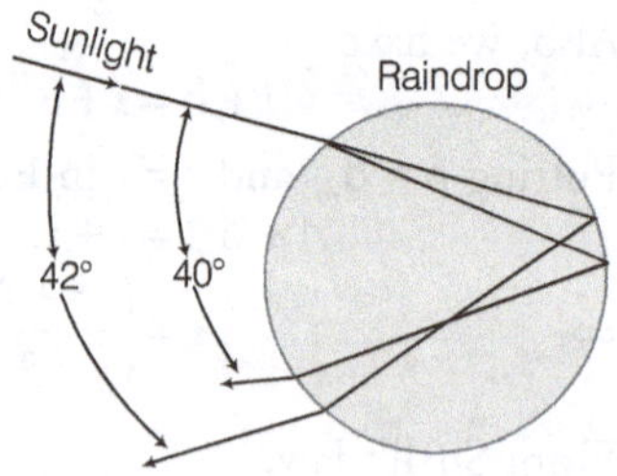

Generally, there are two kinds of rainbows

(i) Primary rainbow

(ii) Secondary rainbow

Primary Rainbow The primary rainbow is a result of three steps process. It is formed by the rays which undergo one internal reflection and two refractions before emerging finally from the water droplets.

In primary rainbow, red colour is on the top and violet on the bottom.

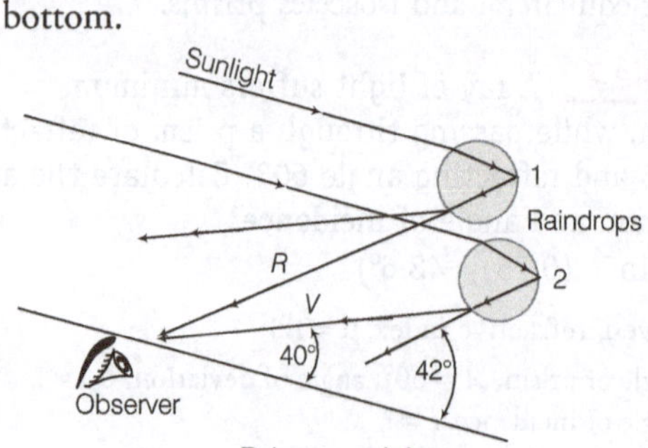

Primary rainbow

Secondary Rainbow The secondary rainbow is a result of four steps process. It is formed by the rays which undergo two internal reflections and two refractions before emerging finally from the water droplets.

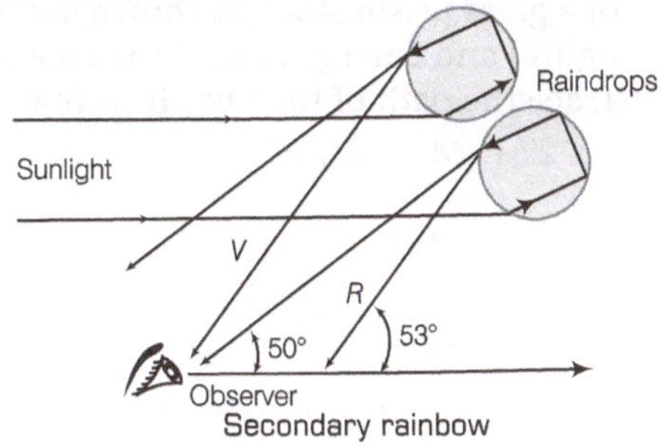

Secondary rainbow

Topic Practice 3

Multiple Choice Questions

1 Mark

1. A ray of light incident at an angle θ on a refracting face of a prism emerges from the other face normally. If the angle of the prism is 5° and the prism is made of a material of refractive index 1.5, the angle of incidence is **NCERT Exemplar**

   (a) 7.5° (b) 5° (c) 15° (d) 2.5°

2. Two beams of red and violet colours are made to pass separately through a prism (angle of prism is 60°). When light travels parallel to the base of the prism, the angle of refraction is *r*. Which of the given statements about *r* is/are correct?
   (a) *r* is 30° for both the colours
   (b) *r* is greater for violet colour
   (c) *r* is greater for the red colour
   (d) *r* is equal but not 30° for both the colours

3. The refractive index of glass is 1.520 for red light and 1.525 for blue light. Let D_1 and D_2 be the angles of minimum deviation for red and blue light respectively, in the prism of this glass, then
   (a) $D_1 < D_2$
   (b) $D_1 = D_2$
   (c) $D_1 > D_2$
   (d) D_1 can be less than or greater than D_2 depending upon the angles of the prism

4. A plot of angle of deviation *D versus* angle of incidence. For a triangular prism is shown below.

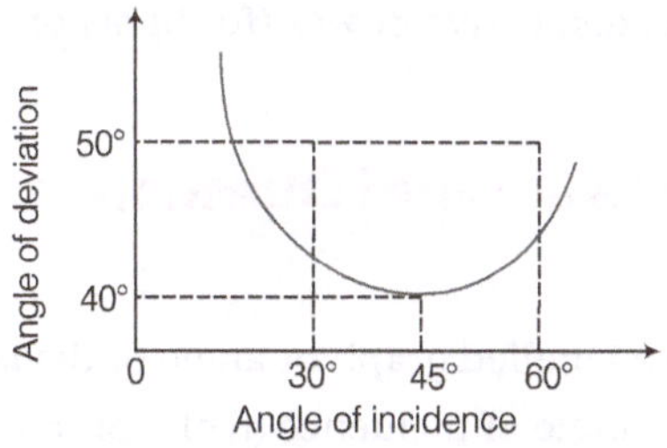

   The angle for incidence for which the light ray travels parallel to the base is
   (a) 30° (b) 60°
   (c) 45° (d) data insufficient

5. A thin prism P_1, with angle 4° made from a glass of refractive index 1.54 is combined with another thin prism P_2 made from glass of refractive index 1.72 to produce dispersion without deviation. The angle of the prism P_2 is
   (a) 5.33° (b) 4°
   (c) 3° (d) 2.6°

Very Short Answer Type Questions

1 Mark

6. Write the relationship between angle of incidence *i*, angle of prism *A* and angle of minimum deviation δ_m for a triangular prism.

7. In a regular prism, what is the relation between angle of incidence and angle of emergence when it is in the minimum deviation position? **ISC 2017**

8. How does the angle of minimum deviation of a glass prism vary, if the incident violet light is replaced by red light? Give reason.

9. A ray of light falls on a right angled prism *ABC* (*AB* = *BC*) and travels as shown in the figure. What is the refractive index of the material of the prism?

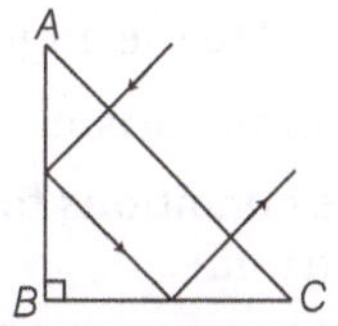

   ISC 2006

10. Draw a labelled ray diagram for the production of pure spectrum. **ISC 2002**

11. Name an optical device, which when used with a spectrometer, can determine the wavelength of the given monochromatic light. **ISC 2010**

12. Define dispersive power (for light) of a medium. **ISC 2003**

Short Answer Type I Question

(2 Marks)

13. Draw a labelled graph of angle of deviation (δ) *versus* angle of incidence (i) of a prism. **ISC 2020**

14. Draw ray diagram to illustrate the formation of primary rainbow by refraction and total internal reflection of sunlight in water drops. **ISC 2005, 03**

15. Name any two phenomena which take place in the formation of a rainbow. **ISC 2023**

Short Answer Type II Questions

(3 Marks)

16. For any prism, show that refractive index of its material is given by

$$n \text{ or } \mu = \sin\left(\frac{A+\delta_{\min}}{2}\right) \Big/ \sin\left(\frac{A}{2}\right)$$

where, the terms have their usual meanings. **ISC 2018, 10**

17. (i) A ray of light incident of face AB of an equilateral glass prism, shows minimum deviation of 30°. Calculate the speed of light through the prism.

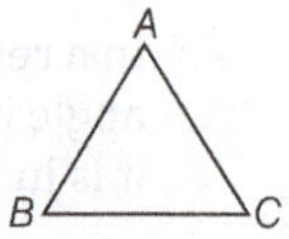

(ii) Find the angle of incidence at face AB, so that the emergent ray grazes along the face AC.

18. For a glass prism($\mu = \sqrt{3}$), the angle of minimum deviation is equal to the angle of the prism. Find the angle of the prism. **NCERT Exemplar**

19. (i) State three conditions for formation of pure spectrum.
(ii) Draw a ray diagram illustrating the measurement of the angle of a prism using a spectrometer. **ISC 2007**

Long Answer Type Questions

(5 Marks)

20. (i) A ray PQ of light is incident on the face AB of a glass prism ABC (as shown in the figure) and emerges out of the face AC. Trace the path of the ray. Show that

$$\angle i + \angle e = \angle A + \angle \delta$$

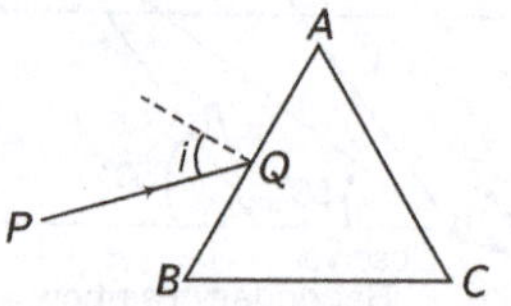

where, δ and e denote the angle of deviation and angle of emergence, respectively. Plot a graph showing the variation of the angle of deviation as a function of angle of incidence. State the condition under which $\angle\delta$ is minimum.

(ii) Find out the relation between the refractive index (μ) of the glass prism and $\angle A$ for the case, when the angle of prism (A) is equal to the angle of minimum deviation (δ_m). Hence, obtain the value of the refractive index for angle of prism $A = 60°$.

21. What is meant by pure and impure spectrum? Explain briefly how you will set up a spectrometer to obtain pure spectrum? Draw a diagram of a spectrometer and describe its parts. **ISC 2000**

Numerical Problems

22. A ray of light incident on an equilateral glass prism ($\mu_g = \sqrt{3}$) moves parallel to the base line of the prism inside it. Find the angle of incidence for this ray. **(2 M)**

23. Calculate angle of minimum deviation (δ_m) for a regular glass prism. (Take, refractive index of glass = 1.6). **ISC 2011 (1 M)**

24. What is the angle of refraction made by a ray of light inside a regular, i.e. an equilateral glass prism in the minimum deviation? **ISC 2011 (1 M)**

25. The angle of an equilateral glass prism is 59.5°. The angle of minimum deviation is 38.5°. Without using the value of refractive index of

the glass. Calculate the angle of incidence for a ray of light suffering minimum deviation.
ISC 2007 (1 M)

26. A ray EF of monochromatic light is incident on the refracting surface AB of a regular glass prism (refractive index = 1.5) at an angle of incidence of $i = 55°$. If it emerges through the adjacent face AC, calculate the angle of emergence 'e'.

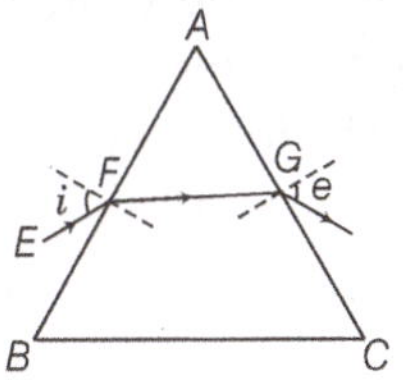

ISC 2010 (1 M)

27. In the figure, ABC is the cross-section of a right angled prism with angle $B = 60°$ and angle $A = 30°$. PQ is a ray incident normally at Q. Copy the diagram and complete the passage of the ray through the prism.

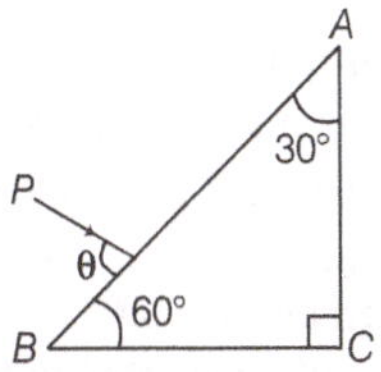

Explain briefly what happens at the interfaces between glass and air?

Calculate sin i_2, where i_2 is the angle of emergence in air. Take, critical angle for glass as 42° and refractive index of glass is 1.5.
ISC 2007 (1 M)

28. A ray of light which is incident in air on the surface of a glass block is deviated through 15°. The angle of incidence in air is 60°. What is the angle of refraction in glass? Also, calculate the critical angle for a glass-air interface.
ISC 2005 (1 M)

29. Figure given below shows a ray of monochromatic light LM incident on the first surface AB of a regular (equilateral) glass prism ABC. The emergent ray grazes the adjacent surface AC. Calculate the angle of incidence. (Refractive index of glass = 1.5) **ISC 2024**

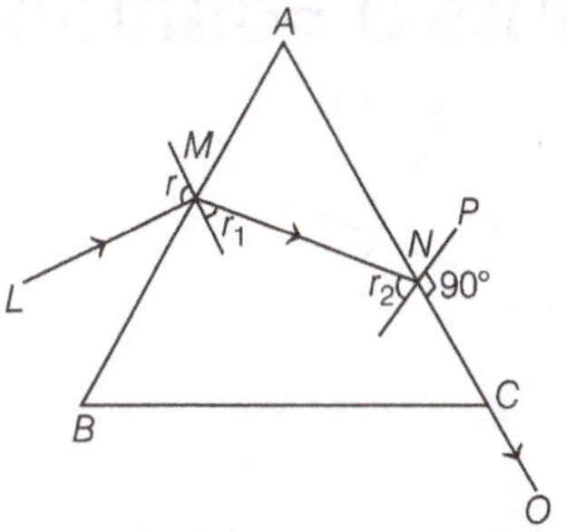

30. Find the angle of incidence at which a ray of monochromatic light should be incident on the first surface AB of a regular glass prism ABC, so that the emergent ray grazes the adjacent surface AC. (Take, refractive index of glass = 1.56). **ISC 2016 (3 M)**

31. Define dispersive power of the material of prism. The refractive indices of a prism for prism for violet, yellow and red colours are 1.632, 1.620 and 1.613 respectively. Calculate the dispersive power of the material of the prism.
ISC 2005 (3 M)

32. Calculate dispersive power of a transparent material given: $n_v = 1.56, n_r = 1.54, n_y = 1.55$. **(1 M)**

33. Calculate dispersive power of glass, accurately upto three decimal places from following data.
   (i) Refractive index of glass for red colour = 1.60
   (ii) Refractive index of glass for yellow colour = 1.61
   (iii) Refractive index of glass for violet colour = 1.62 **ISC 2010 (1 M)**

34. Find the angular dispersion produced by a thin prism of 5° having refractive index for red light 1.50 and for violet 1.60. **(2 M)**

35. White light is incident on one of the refracting surface of a prism of angle 5°. If the refractive indices for red and blue colours are 1.641 and 1.659 respectively, then what will be the angular separation between these two colours when they emerge out? **(1 M)**

36. The refractive indices of a material for red, violet and yellow colour lights are 1.52, 1.62 and 1.59, respectively. Calculate the dispersive power of the material. If the mean deviation is 40°, what will be the angular dispersion produced by a prism of this material? **ISC 2006 (2 M)**

Hints & Solutions

1. (a)

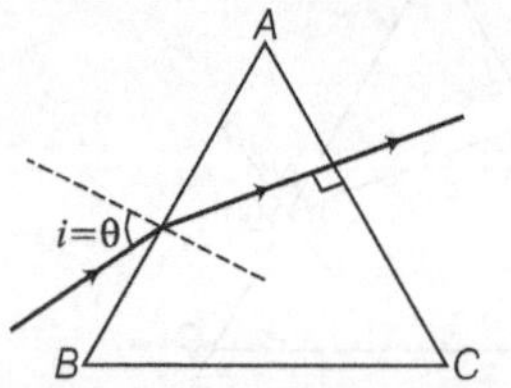

Given, $i = \theta$, $A = 5°$, $\mu = 1.5$

For ray emerging normally from AC,

$$e = 0$$

From relation, $A + D = i + e$, we have

$\Rightarrow 5° + D = \theta + 0 \Rightarrow i = \theta = 5° + D$

Also, for small angles, $D = (\mu - 1)A = 0.5 \times 5° = 2.5°$

So, $i = \theta = 5° + 2.5° = 7.5°$

2. (a) For minimum deviation, the light of the colours must travel symmetrically inside the prism, i.e. parallel to the base,

$\Rightarrow \quad r_1 = r_2 = r \Rightarrow r_1 + r_2 = A \Rightarrow 2r = A$

$\therefore \quad r = \dfrac{A}{2} = \dfrac{60°}{2} = 30°$

3. (a) As, refractive index, $\mu = \dfrac{\sin(A + D_{min})}{\sin A/2}$

Angle of prism is constant, $D_{min} \propto \mu$

$\because \quad \mu_b > \mu_r \Rightarrow D_2 > D_1$

4. (c) When light ray travels parallel to the base, the light suffers minimum deviations.

So, for minimum deviation, $D_{min} = 40°$

$i = e = 45°$ (from graph)

5. (c) For no deviation, the mean deviate.

Hence, both the prims must be same.

$$D_{m1} = D_{m2}$$

$\Rightarrow \quad (\mu_1 - 1)A_1 = (\mu_2 - 1)A_2$

$\Rightarrow \quad A_2 = \dfrac{(\mu_1 - 1)}{(\mu_2 - 1)} A_1 = \dfrac{(1.54 - 1) \times 4°}{(1.72 - 1)} = 3°$

6. The relation between the angle of incidence i, angle of prism A and the angle of minimum deviation δ_m, for a triangular prism is given as $i = \dfrac{A + \delta_m}{2}$.

7. For minimum deviation position, $\delta = i_1 + i_2 - A$

where, i_1 = angle of incidence, i_2 = angle of emergence

A = angle of the prism.

8. Wavelength of violet light is smaller than that of red light. Also, angle of minimum deviation,

$$\delta_m = (\mu - 1)A$$

$\Rightarrow \quad \delta_m \propto \mu$

As, $\quad \mu_R < \mu_V$

$\Rightarrow \quad (\delta_m)_R < (\delta_m)_V$

As deviation is less for red light, hence angle of deviation decreases.

9. For the ray incident on the face,

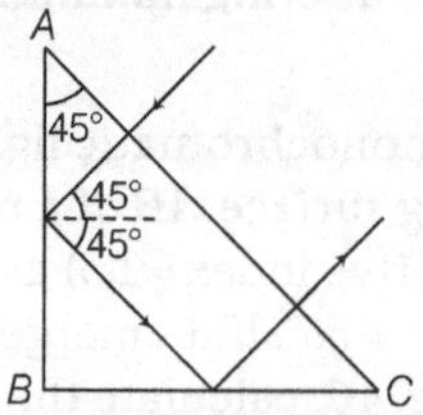

As there is total internal reflection takes place at AB.

Angle of incidence $i >$ Critical angle i_c

In this case $i > i_c$, $\mu = \text{cosec } i_c$

where, μ = refractive index of prism

$\therefore \quad \mu > \text{cos ec } 45° \Rightarrow \mu > \sqrt{2}$

10. Refer to text on page 347 (Dispersion by a prism).

11. Prism.

12. Refer to text on page 348 {Dispersive power (ω)}.

13. Refer to graph on page 347 (Prism formula).

14. Refer to text on page 348 (Primary rainbow).

15. There are three phenomena for the formation of rainbow are following

(i) Refraction

(ii) Dispersion

(iii) Total internal reflection.

The Sun shines on a water droplets.

16. Refer to text on page 347 (Prism formula).

17. (i) Given, angle of minimum deviation, $\delta_m = 30°$

$\therefore$ Angle of prism, $A = 60°$

By prism formula, reflected index,

$$\mu = \frac{\sin \frac{\delta_m + A}{2}}{\sin A/2} = \frac{\sin \frac{30° + 60°}{2}}{\sin 30°}$$

$$= \frac{\sin 45°}{\sin 30°} = \frac{1}{\sqrt{2}} \times 2 = \sqrt{2}$$

Also, $\mu = \dfrac{\text{speed of light in vacuum } (c)}{\text{speed of light in prism } (v)}$

$\Rightarrow \quad v = c/\mu$

$= (3 \times 10^8/\sqrt{2})$ m/s

Hence, speed of light through prism is $(3 \times 10^8/\sqrt{2})$ m/s (1½)

(ii) Critical angle i_c is given as,

$\sin i_c = \dfrac{1}{\sqrt{2}} \quad [\because \sin i_c = \dfrac{1}{\mu}]$

$\Rightarrow \quad i_c = 45°$

$A = r + i_c = 60° \Rightarrow r = 60° - 45° = 15°$

Using Snell's law, $\dfrac{\sin i}{\sin r} = \sqrt{2}$

$\Rightarrow \quad \sin i = \sqrt{2} \sin r = \sqrt{2} \times \sin 15°$

$\therefore \quad i = \sin^{-1}(\sqrt{2} \sin 15°)$ (1½)

18. The relationship between refractive index, prism angle A and angle of minimum deviation δ_m is given by

$$\mu = \frac{\sin[(A+\delta_m)/2]}{\sin(A/2)}$$

Given, $\delta_m = A$

Substituting the value of δ_m, we have

$$\therefore \quad \mu = \frac{\sin A}{\sin(A/2)} \quad (1)$$

On solving, we have

$$\mu = \frac{2\sin\frac{A}{2}\cos\frac{A}{2}}{\sin\frac{A}{2}} = 2\cos\frac{A}{2}$$

For the given value of refractive index, $\mu = \sqrt{3}$, we have

$$\cos\frac{A}{2} = \frac{\sqrt{3}}{2} \text{ or } \frac{A}{2} = 30^\circ \text{ or } A = 60^\circ$$

This is the required value of prism angle. (2)

19. (i) Three conditions for the formation of pure spectrum are as follows:

(a) The slit should be narrow.

(b) The rays falling on the prism should be parallel.

(c) The prism should be placed in minimum deviation position. (1½)

(ii) **Measuring the angle of a prism** The spectrum can be used to measure angle of a prism. The spectrometer is levelled and adjusted for parallel rays. The telescope is rotated for different positions T_1 and T_2. The images of the slit is coincided with vertical cross wire.

The difference of angular position for two positions T_1 and T_2 is calculated as $2A$, where A is the angle of prism.

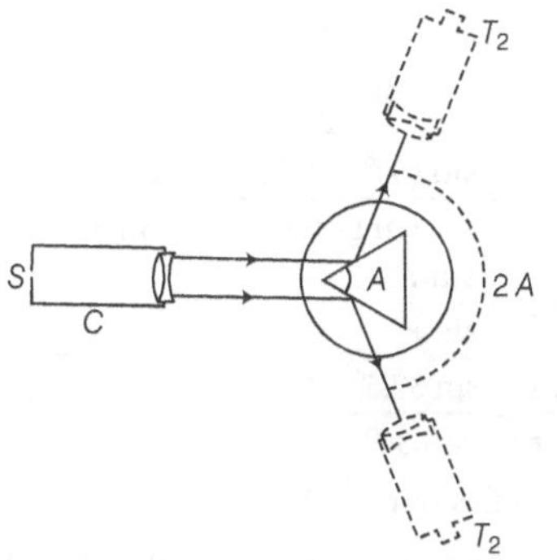

(1½)

20. (i) Refer to text on pages 346 and 347 (Deviation produced by a small angled prism, prism formula). (2)

(ii) Refer to solution of Q.18 on page 353. (1)

Since, $\angle A = 60^\circ$ [given]

$$\therefore \quad \mu = 2\cos\left(\frac{60^\circ}{2}\right) = 2\cos 30^\circ$$

$$= 2\times\frac{\sqrt{3}}{2} = \sqrt{3} = 1.732 \quad (2)$$

21. **Impure spectrum** Spectrum is said to be impure in which there is a over lapping of different colours.

Pure spectrum Pure spectrum is one in which there is no over lapping of different colours take place.

Spectrometer It is an instrument used to study the spectra of luminous objects and also to find out the refractive index of any refracting material say, glass in the form of a prism.

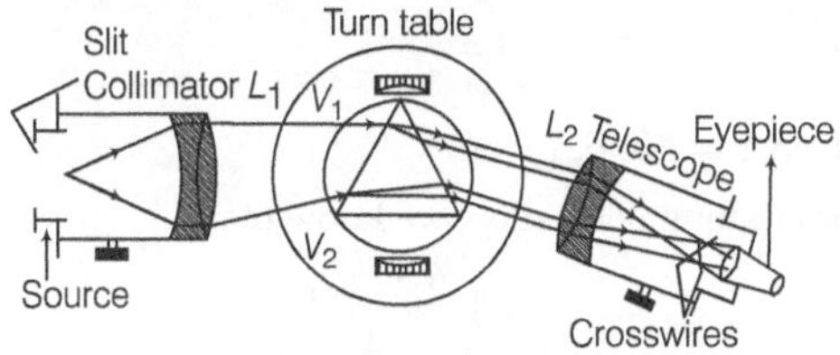

(2)

The main parts of a spectrometer are as follows:

(i) **Collimator** It is a tube provided with a narrow slit S at one end and a converging lens at the other end. The narrow slit S is located at the focus of the lens. When a source of light is placed in front of S a parallel beam of light emerges from the collimator. These rays are incident on the refractive surface of a prism. (1)

(ii) **Prism table** It has a flat circular top, capable of rotating about its vertical axis. The prism is placed on the table with its refracting edge parallel to the slit. (1)

(iii) **Telescope** It is an astronomical telescope filled with an eyepiece and crosswires. The spectrum is formed on the focal plane of the telescope and is viewed with an eyepiece having both of its lenses achromatic.

For the production of a pure spectrum, it is necessary that the slit should be very narrow and the incident beam of light should be parallel. Before using, the length of the telescopic tube is so adjusted that the image of the spectrum is well focussed.

In this position, rays of different wavelengths (or colours) will be focussed at different points, thus producing a pure spectrum. (1)

22. To draw the ray diagram for the refraction from the prism. Following things should be kept in mind.

(i) Draw normal to the point of incidence. (1/2)

(ii) Consider each boundary of the prism as separate interface and draw the ray diagram for the refraction taking place.

The reflection of light through prism is shown below.

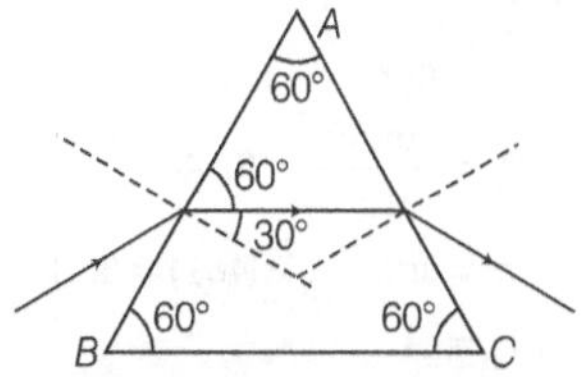

(1/2)

By geometry, angle of refraction,

$$r = 30^\circ$$

Refractive index, $\mu = \sqrt{3}$ $\left[\text{from Snell's law, } \mu = \frac{\sin i}{\sin r}\right]$

$\Rightarrow \quad \sin i = \mu \sin r = (\sqrt{3})\sin(30^\circ) = \frac{\sqrt{3}}{2}$

Angle of incidence, $i = 60^\circ = \frac{\pi}{3}$

$\Rightarrow \quad i = \frac{\pi}{3}$ (1)

23. Given, $\mu = 1.6$, $\delta_{min} = ?$

For minimum deviation, we know that,

$$\mu = \frac{\sin\left(\frac{A + \delta_{min}}{2}\right)}{\sin\left(\frac{A}{2}\right)}$$

Symbols have their usual meaning.

$$1.6 = \frac{\sin\left(\frac{60^\circ + \delta_{min}}{2}\right)}{\sin\left(\frac{60^\circ}{2}\right)}$$

$$\Rightarrow \quad 0.8 = \sin\left(\frac{60^\circ + \delta_{min}}{2}\right)$$

$$\Rightarrow \quad \frac{60^\circ + \delta_{min}}{2} = 53.13^\circ$$

$$\therefore \quad \delta_{min} = 46.26^\circ$$

24. When refraction takes place through a prism

$\angle A = r_1 + r_2$

$\angle A$ = Angle of prism $\angle r_1$ and $\angle r_2$ are refracting angle.

For minimum deviation,

$$r_1 = r_2 = r \Rightarrow \angle A = 2r$$

$$\Rightarrow \quad 60^\circ = 2r \Rightarrow r = 30^\circ$$

25. As, we know for the case of minimum deviation,

$$i = \frac{A + \delta_{min}}{2}$$

where, δ_{min} = minimum deviation angle,

i = angle of incidence.

Given, $\angle A = 59.5^\circ$, $\delta_{min} = 38.5^\circ$

$$i = \frac{59.5 + 38.5}{2} \Rightarrow i = 49^\circ$$

26. At F, applying Snell's law

$$\frac{\sin i}{\sin r_1} = \mu = 1.5$$

$i = 55^\circ$ [given]

$$\sin r_1 = \frac{\sin 55^\circ}{1.5} = 0.5461$$

Now, $r_1 = \sin^{-1}(0.5461) = 33.1^\circ$

$r_1 + r_2 = A$

$\therefore \quad r_2 = 60^\circ - 33.1^\circ = 26.9^\circ$

At G, $\frac{\sin e}{\sin r_2} = \mu = 1.5$

$\Rightarrow \quad \sin e = 1.5 \times \sin 26.9^\circ = 1.5 \times 0.453 = 0.68$

$\therefore \quad e = 42.7^\circ$

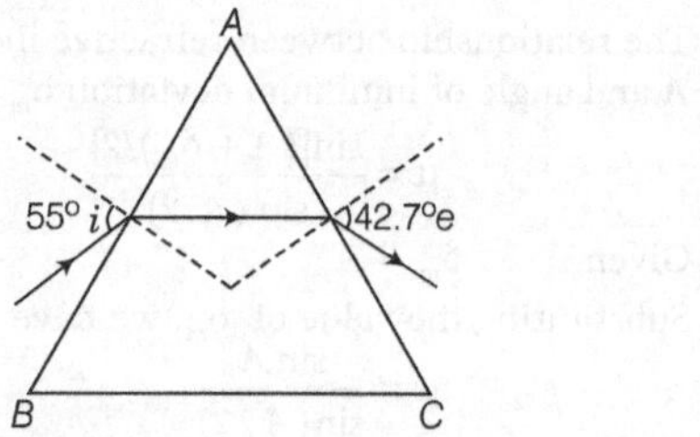

27. Consider the diagram in which ray of light P, strikes at 90°, it goes undeviated and then it strikes on the face BC at an angle of incidence 60°, which is greater than the critical angle for the glass-air surface.

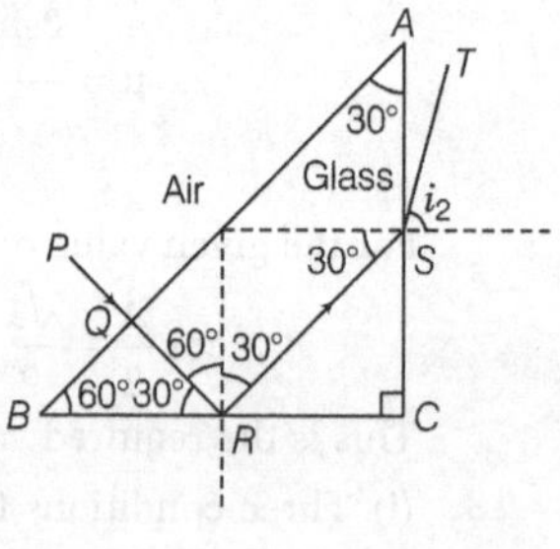

Hence, on the surface BC, total internal reflection of light will take place.

Totally, internally reflected ray, then strikes on the face AC at S, at the angle of incidence 30°, where the refraction of light will take place such that i_2 will be final angle of emergence.

Using Snell's law, $\frac{\sin 30^\circ}{\sin i_2} = {}_g\mu_a = \frac{1}{{}_a\mu_g}$

Hence, $\sin i_2 = \sin 30^\circ \times {}_a\mu_g$

$\Rightarrow \quad \sin i_2 = \frac{1}{2} \times 1.5 = 0.75 = \frac{3}{4}$

28. We will apply Snell's law at each face.

As, $${}_a\mu_g = \frac{\sin\left(\frac{\delta_m + A}{2}\right)}{\sin\frac{A}{2}}$$

$${}_a\mu_g = \frac{\sin(60^\circ + 15^\circ)/2}{\sin 60^\circ/2} = \frac{\sin 37.5^\circ}{\sin 30^\circ}$$

$${}_a\mu_g = \frac{\sin i}{\sin r}$$

So, $\frac{\sin i}{\sin r} = \frac{\sin 37.5^\circ}{\sin 30^\circ}$

Angle of refraction = 30°

For refractive index, $${}_a\mu_g = \sin\frac{\left(\frac{\delta_{min} + A}{2}\right)}{\sin\left(\frac{A}{2}\right)}$$

$\delta_{min} = 15^\circ$, $\angle i = 60^\circ$

$${}_a\mu_g = \frac{\sin(60^\circ + 15^\circ)/2}{\sin 60/2^\circ} = \frac{\sin 37.5^\circ}{\sin 30^\circ} = 1.217$$

$\sin i_c = \frac{1}{{}_a\mu_g}$ [$\because$ i_c = critical angle]

$\Rightarrow \quad \sin i_c = \frac{1}{1.217} = \sin^{-1} 0.821^\circ = 55.2$

29.

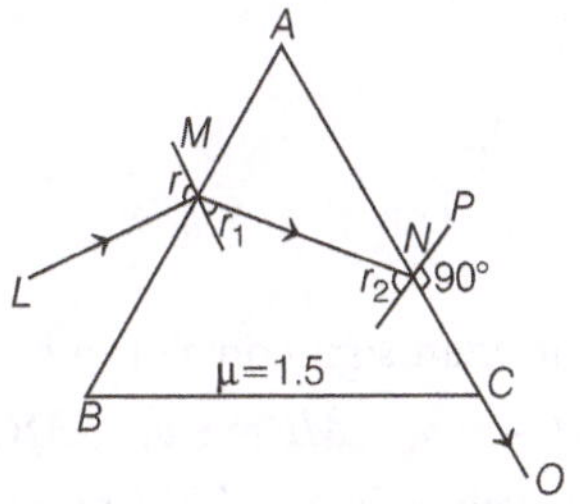

The refracted ray *NO* will just suffer total internal reflection or grazes the surface *AC*, if it is incident at the critical angle i_c. i.e. $r_2 = i_c$

Now, for face *AC*,

$$\sin i_c = \frac{1}{\mu} = \frac{1}{1.50} = 0.66$$

$$i_c = r_2 = 41.29°$$

But $r_2 + r_1 = A =$ Angle of prism

$\Rightarrow \quad r_1 = A - r_2 = A - i_c = 60° - 41.29° = 18.70°$

From Snell's law, $\mu = \dfrac{\sin i}{\sin r_1}$

$\Rightarrow \quad \sin i = \mu \sin (18.70°) = 1.5 \times 0.320 = 0.480$

$\Rightarrow \quad i = \sin^{-1} (0.480) = 28.68°$

Thus, angle of incidence, $i \approx 29°$

30. According to the question,

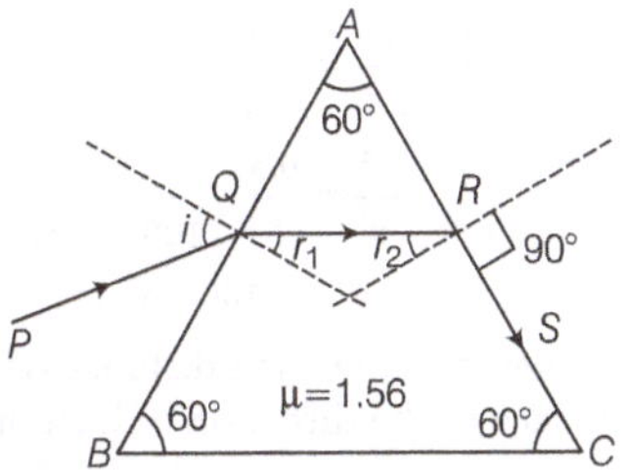

The refracted ray *RS* will just suffer total internal reflection or grazes the surface *AC*. If it is incident at the critical angle i_c. i.e. $r_2 = i_c$ (1)

Now, for face *AC*

$$\sin i_c = \frac{1}{\mu} = \frac{1}{1.56}$$

$\Rightarrow \quad i_c = r_2 = 41°$

But $\quad r_2 + r_1 = A$

$\Rightarrow \quad r_1 = A - r_2 = A - i_c = 60° - 41° = 19°$ (1)

From Snell's law,

$$\mu = \frac{\sin i}{\sin r_1} \Rightarrow \sin i = \mu \sin 19°$$

$$= 1.56 \times 0.325 = 0.507$$

$\Rightarrow \quad i = \sin^{-1} 0.507 \approx 30°$

Thus, angle of incidence, $i \approx 30°$. (1)

31. Refer to text on page 348 (Dispersive power, ω).

Dispersive power,

$$\omega = \frac{\delta}{\delta_Y}$$

$$= \frac{\delta_V - \delta_R}{\delta_Y} = \frac{\mu_r - \mu_R}{\mu_Y - 1} \qquad [\because \delta = \mu - 1]$$

Given, $\mu_V = 1.632$ (refractive index for violet)

$\mu_Y = 1.620$ (refractive index for yellow)

$\mu_R = 1.613$ (refractive index for red)

Thus, $\quad \omega = \dfrac{1.632 - 1.613}{1.620 - 1}$

$$= \frac{0.019}{0.62} = 0.03$$ (2)

32. Given, refractive index of violet colour, $n_v = 1.56$

Refractive index of red colour, $n_r = 1.54$

Refractive index of yellow colour, $n_y = 1.55$

∴ Dispersive power can be calculated as

$$\omega = \frac{n_v - n_r}{n_y - 1} = \frac{1.56 - 1.54}{1.55 - 1}$$

$$\omega = \frac{0.02}{0.55} = 0.036$$

33. Given, refractive index for violet, $\mu_V = 1.62$

Refractive index for yellow, $\mu_Y = 1.61$

Refractive index for red, $\mu_R = 1.60$

Dispersive power, $\omega = \dfrac{\mu_V - \mu_R}{\mu_Y - 1}$

$$= \frac{1.62 - 1.60}{1.61 - 1.00} = \frac{0.02}{0.61} = 0.032$$

34. ∴ Angular dispersion

$= \delta_V - \delta_R = (\mu_V - 1)A - (\mu_R - 1)A$ (1)

$= (1.6 - 1)5 - (1.5 - 1)5$

$= 0.5$ (1)

35. Angle of prism, $\quad A = 5°, \mu_R = 1.641, \mu_B = 1.659$

As we know that, $\delta = (\mu - 1)A$ (1/2)

So, $\quad \delta_B = (\mu_B - 1)A$ and $\delta_R = (\mu_R - 1)A$

∴ $\quad \delta_B - \delta_R = (\mu_B - \mu_R)A = (1.659 - 1.641) \times 5$

$= 0.09°$ (1/2)

36. Given, refractive index of red light, $n_R = 1.52$,

Refractive index of violet light, $n_V = 1.62$,

Refractive index of yellow light, $n_Y = 1.59$

So, dispersive power,

$$\omega = \frac{n_V - n_R}{n_Y - 1} = \frac{1.62 - 1.52}{1.59 - 1}$$

$$= \frac{0.1}{0.59} = 0.17$$ (1)

∴ Angular dispersion, $\delta_V - \delta_R = \omega \times \delta_Y$

$= 0.17 \times 40°$

$= 6.78°$ (1)

TOPIC 04 Refraction at Spherical Surfaces and by Lenses

Refraction at a Spherical Surface

Consider refraction at a spherical surface that separates media of refractive indices n_1 and n_2.

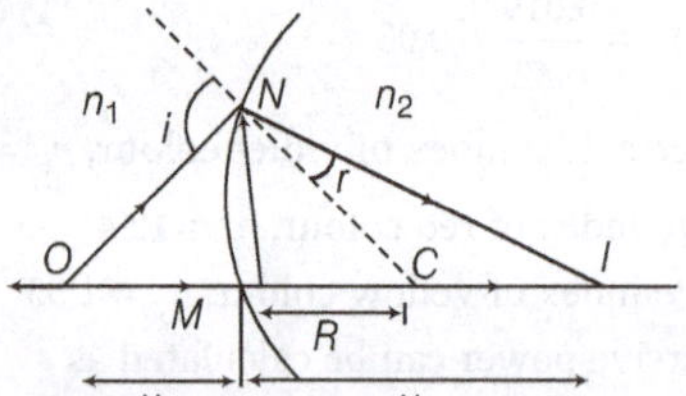

Refraction at a spherical surface

In the figure, the geometry of formation of image I of an object O and the principal axis of a spherical surface with centre of curvature C and radius of curvature R is shown. Sign convention is same as that used for curved mirrors.

For small angles, $\tan\theta \approx \sin\theta \approx \theta$

So, from figure, we have

$$\angle NOM = \frac{MN}{OM}$$

$$\angle NCM = \frac{MN}{MC}$$

$$\angle NIM = \frac{MN}{MI}$$

For ΔNOC, i is the exterior angle.

$$\therefore \quad i = \angle NOM + \angle NCM = \frac{MN}{OM} + \frac{MN}{MC} \qquad \ldots\text{(i)}$$

For ΔNIC, $\angle NCM$ is the exterior angle.

$$\therefore \quad \angle NCM = r + \angle NIM \text{ or } r = \angle NCM - \angle NIM$$

i.e.
$$r = \frac{MN}{MC} - \frac{MN}{MI} \qquad \ldots\text{(ii)}$$

By Snell's law, $n_1 \sin i = n_2 \sin r$

For small angles, $n_1 i = n_2 r$

Substituting the values of i and r from Eqs. (i) and (ii), we get

$$n_1\left(\frac{MN}{OM} + \frac{MN}{MC}\right) = n_2\left(\frac{MN}{MC} - \frac{MN}{MI}\right)$$

or
$$\frac{n_1}{OM} + \frac{n_2}{MI} = \frac{n_2 - n_1}{MC} \qquad \ldots\text{(iii)}$$

Applying new Cartesian sign conventions,

$$OM = -u, \quad MI = +v, \quad MC = +R$$

Substituting these values in Eq. (iii), we get

$$\boxed{\frac{n_2}{v} - \frac{n_1}{u} = \frac{n_2 - n_1}{R}}$$

This equation holds for any curved spherical surface.

Magnification produced by a spherical surface is

$$m = \frac{h'}{h} = \frac{n_1 v}{n_2 u}$$

Example 1 Light from a point source in air falls on a spherical glass surface ($n = 1.5$ and radius of curvature $= 20$ cm). The distance of the light source from the glass surface is 100 cm. At what position the image is formed?

Sol. Given, object distance, $u = -100$ cm,

$R = +20$ cm, $n_1 = 1$, $n_2 = 1.5$, image distance, $v = ?$

We know that, $\frac{n_2}{v} - \frac{n_1}{u} = \frac{n_2 - n_1}{R}$

$$\Rightarrow \quad \frac{1.5}{v} + \frac{1}{100} = \frac{1.5 - 1}{20}$$

$$\Rightarrow \quad \frac{1.5}{v} = \frac{0.5}{20} - \frac{1}{100} = \frac{2.5 - 1}{100} = \frac{1.5}{100}$$

$$v = +100 \text{ cm}$$

Thus, the image is formed at a distance of 100 cm from the glass surface in the direction of incident light.

Lens

Lens is a transparent medium bounded by two surfaces of which one or both surfaces are spherical.

Convex or Converging Lens

A lens which is thicker at the centre and thinner at its ends is called convex lens. Convex lenses are of three types as shown below.

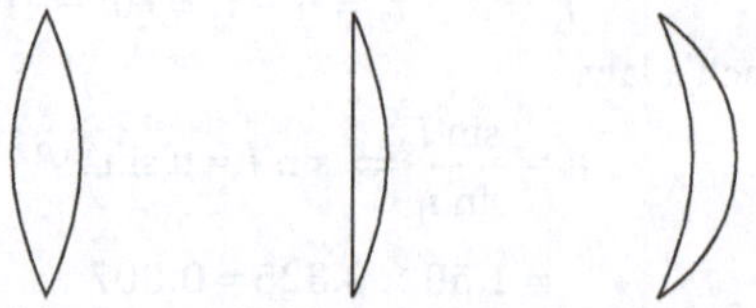

(a) Double convex lens (b) Plano-convex lens (c) Concavo-convex lens

Note A convex lens is also known as converging lens because it converges a parallel beam of light rays passing through it. A double convex lens is simply called convex lens.

Concave or Diverging Lens

A lens which is thinner at the centre and thicker at its ends is called a concave lens. Concave lenses are of three types as shown below.

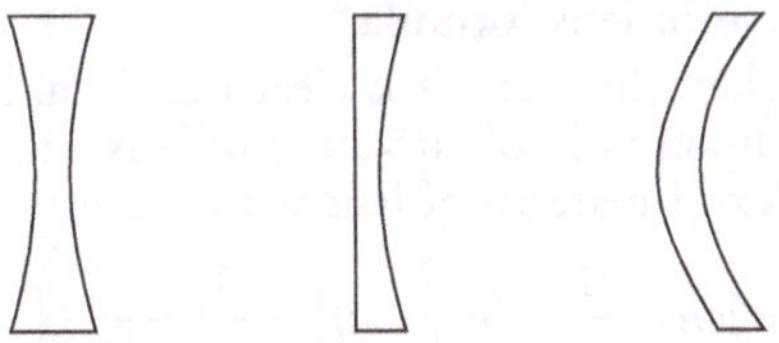

(a) Double concave lens (b) Plano-concave lens (c) Convexo-concave lens

Note A concave lens is also known as diverging lens because it diverges a parallel beam of light rays passing through it. A double concave lens is simply called concave lens.

Some Definitions Related to Lenses

(i) **Optical centre** The optical centre is a point lying on the principal axis of the lens, directed to which incident rays pass without any deviation in the path, i.e. the centre point of a lens is known as its optical centre.

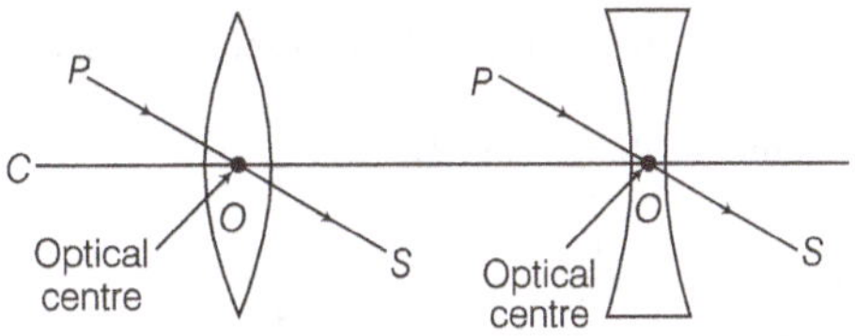

(ii) **Centre of curvature** The centres of the two imaginary spheres of which the lens is a part, are called centres of curvature of the lens. A lens has two centres of curvature with respect to its two curved surfaces.

(iii) **Radii of curvature** The radii of the two imaginary spheres of which the lens is a part are called radii of curvature of the lens. A lens has two radii of curvature. These may or may not be equal.

(iv) **Principal axis** The imaginary line joining the two centres of curvature is called principal axis of lens. Principal axis also passes through the optical centre.

(v) **Principal focus** Lens has two principal foci.

(a) **First principal focus** It is a point on the principal axis of lens, the rays starting from this point in convex lens or rays directed to this point in concave lens become parallel to principal axis after refraction.

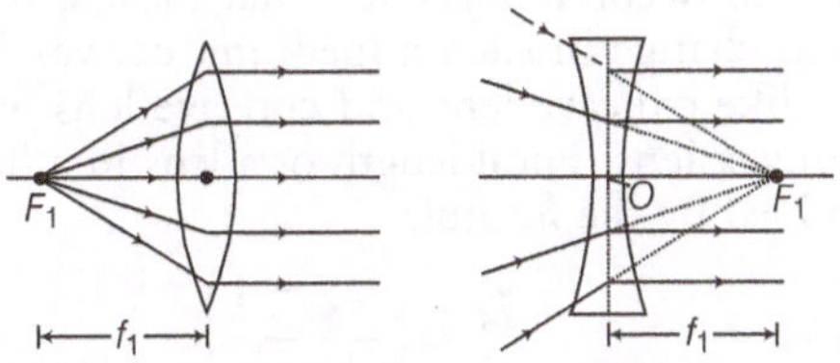

(b) **Second principal focus** It is a point on the principal axis at which the rays coming parallel to the principal axis converge (convex lens) or passing through it appear to diverge (concave lens) at this point after refraction from the lens.

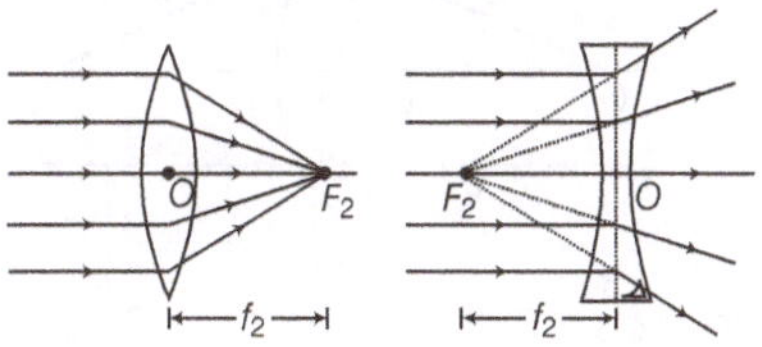

Both the foci of convex lens are real, while that of concave lens are virtual. When medium on two side of lens are not same, then ratio of two focal lengths $f_1 : f_2 = n_1 : n_2$.

(vi) **Aperture** The effective diameter of the circular outline of a spherical lens is called its aperture.

Image Formation in Lenses

For drawing ray diagrams in lenses like spherical mirrors, we consider any two of the following rays.

(i) Rays which are parallel to the principal axis after refraction, will pass through principal focus in case of convex lens and will appear to be coming from principal focus in case of concave lens.

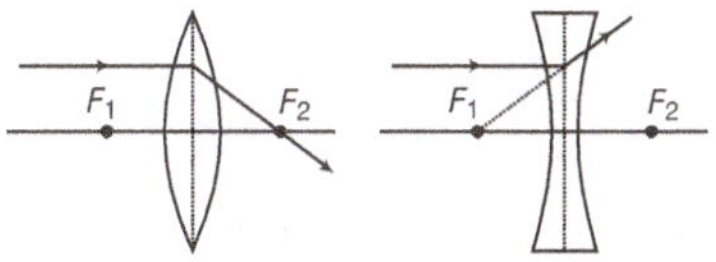

(ii) Rays passing through or directed to the focus will emerge parallel to the principal axis.

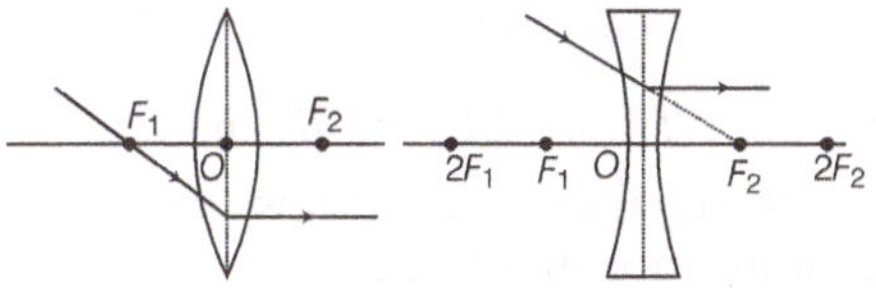

(iii) Rays directed to optical centre will emerge out undeviated.

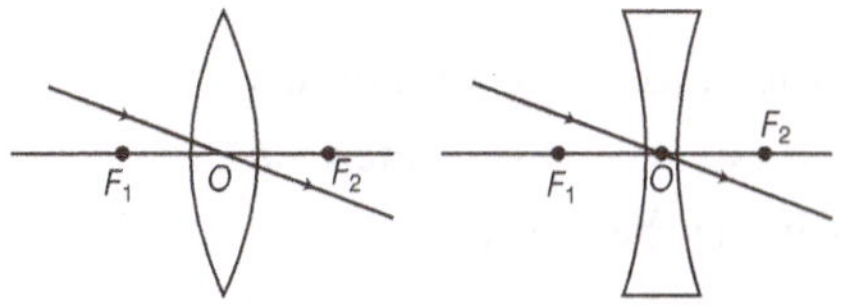

Refraction by a Lens : Lens Maker's Formula

Two main assumptions made for the derivation are

(i) The lens is thin, so that distances measured from the poles of its surfaces can be taken as equal to the distance from the optical centre of the lens.

(ii) The aperture of the lens is small, so the incident ray and refracted ray make small angles with the principal axis of the lens.

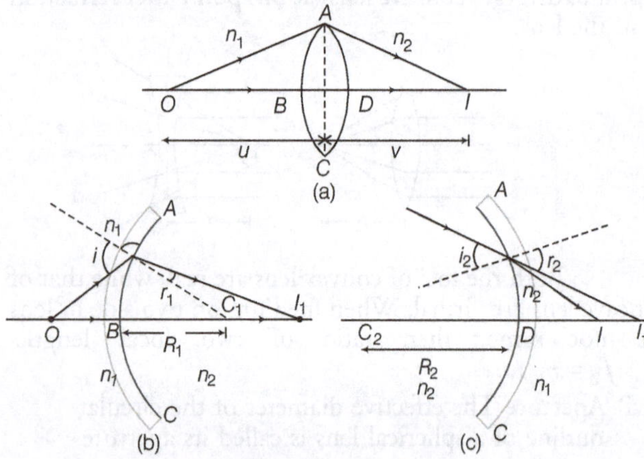

The above figures show the image formation by a convex lens.

Applying the equation for spherical refracting surface to the first interface ABC, we get

$$\frac{n_1}{OB}+\frac{n_2}{BI_1}=\frac{n_2-n_1}{BC_1} \quad \ldots\text{(i)}$$

A similar procedure applied to the second interface ADC, we get

$$-\frac{n_2}{DI_1}+\frac{n_1}{DI}=\frac{n_2-n_1}{DC_2} \quad \ldots\text{(ii)}$$

For a thin lens, $BI_1 = DI_1$

Adding Eqs. (i) and (ii), we get

$$\frac{n_1}{OB}+\frac{n_1}{DI}=(n_2-n_1)\left(\frac{1}{BC_1}+\frac{1}{DC_2}\right)$$

Now, $OB=-u$, $DI=+v$, $BC_1=+R_1$ and $DC_2=-R_2$

Substituting these values in Eq. (ii), we get refraction formula for thin lens as

$$\frac{1}{v}-\frac{1}{u}=(n_{21}-1)\left(\frac{1}{R_1}-\frac{1}{R_2}\right) \quad \ldots\text{(iii)}$$

Suppose the object is at infinity, i.e.

$$u\to\infty, \quad \text{then} \quad v\to f$$

So, Eq. (iii) can be written as

$$\frac{n_1}{f}=(n_2-n_1)\left(\frac{1}{R_1}-\frac{1}{R_2}\right) \quad \ldots\text{(iv)}$$

or $$\boxed{\frac{1}{f}=(n_{21}-1)\left(\frac{1}{R_1}-\frac{1}{R_2}\right)} \quad \left[\because n_{21}=\frac{n_2}{n_1}\right] \ldots\text{(v)}$$

Eq. (v) is known as the **lens Maker's formula.**

From Eqs. (iii) and (iv), we get

$$\boxed{\frac{1}{v}-\frac{1}{u}=\frac{1}{f}} \quad \ldots\text{(vi)}$$

Eq. (vi) is the **thin lens formula.**

From lens maker's formula, it is clear that focal length of lens depends upon radii of curvature of lens and refractive index of material of lens w.r.t. its surroundings.

For biconcave lens, $\frac{1}{f}=(n_{21}-1)\left(-\frac{1}{R_1}-\frac{1}{R_2}\right)$

For plano-convex lens, $\frac{1}{f}=(n_{21}-1)\left(\frac{1}{R}-\frac{1}{\infty}\right)$

$$\Rightarrow \quad \frac{1}{f}=\frac{(n_{21}-1)}{R}$$

Example 2 **The radii of curvature of the surfaces of a double convex lens are 20 cm and 40 cm, respectively and its focal length is 20 cm. What is refractive index of the material of the lens?**

Sol. Given, $R_1 = 20$ cm, $R_2 = -40$ cm, $f = 20$cm, $n = ?$

We know that, $\frac{1}{f}=(n-1)\left(\frac{1}{R_1}-\frac{1}{R_2}\right)$

$$\Rightarrow \quad \frac{1}{20}=(n-1)\left(\frac{1}{20}+\frac{1}{40}\right)$$

$$\Rightarrow \quad \frac{1}{n-1}=20\left(\frac{2+1}{40}\right)=\frac{3}{2}$$

$$\Rightarrow \quad n-1=\frac{2}{3} \Rightarrow 3n=5 \Rightarrow n=\frac{5}{3}$$

Hence, the refractive index of the material of the lens is 5/3.

Dependence of Focal Length on Refractive Index

Refractive index of material of lens depends upon the medium in which it is kept. If lens is immersed in a liquid whose refractive index with respect to air is less than the refractive index of material of lens with respect to air, then focal length of the lens increases.

If lens is immersed in a liquid whose refractive index with respect to air is more than the refractive index of material of the lens with respect to air, then focal length will become negative. That means, the nature of lens will change in such a medium, convex lens will behave like concave lens and concave lens will behave like convex lens. Focal length of a lens in a liquid can be determined by the formula,

$$\frac{f_l}{f_a}=\left(\frac{n_{ga}-1}{n_{gl}-1}\right)$$

Dependence of Focal Length on the Radii of Curvature

From lens maker's formula, it is clear that the focal length of a lens of large radii of curvature is large and that of a lens of small radii of curvature is small. In simple words, the focal length of thin lens is large and that of thick lens is small.

Linear Magnification Produced by a Lens (m)

Linear magnification of a lens is defined as, the ratio of the height of the image formed by the lens to height of the object.

$$\text{Linear magnification } (m) = \frac{\text{Height of image } (I)}{\text{Height of object } (O)} = \frac{v}{u}$$

Other formulae for linear magnification are

$$m = \frac{v}{u} = \frac{f-v}{f} = \frac{f}{f+u}$$

Example 3 The focal length of a thin biconvex lens is 20 cm. When an object is moved from a distance of 25 cm in front of it to 50 cm, the magnification of its image changes from m_{25} to m_{50}.

Find the ratio of $\frac{m_{25}}{m_{50}}$.

Sol. Since, magnification, $m = \frac{f}{f+u} \Rightarrow m_{25} = \frac{20}{20-25} = -4$

Similarly, $m_{50} = \frac{20}{20-50} = \frac{-2}{3}$

Therefore, $\frac{m_{25}}{m_{50}} = (-4)\left(\frac{-3}{2}\right) = 6$

Power of a Lens

The ability of a lens to converge or diverge the rays of light incident on it is called the **power of the lens.**

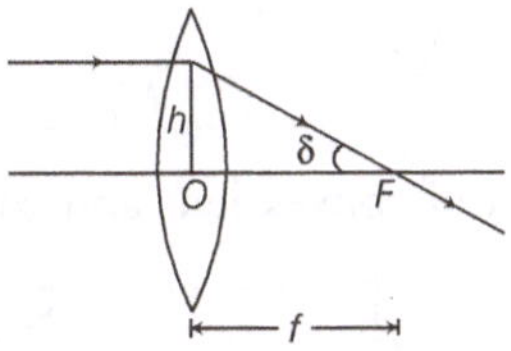

A lens of more power bends a parallel ray by larger amount, so its focal length is small and *vice-versa.*

Thus, power of a lens, $P = \frac{1}{f}$.

The SI unit of power of lens is dioptre (D). The power of a lens is measured as the reciprocal of its focal length (in metre).

$$P = \frac{1}{f\ (\text{in m})}$$

If $f = 1\,\text{m}$, then $P = 1\,\text{m}^{-1} = 1\,\text{dioptre (D)}$

According to the lens Maker's formula for a lens,

$$\frac{1}{f} = (\mu - 1)\left(\frac{1}{R_1} - \frac{1}{R_2}\right) \qquad \left[\because P = \frac{1}{f}\right]$$

We have,

$$\boxed{P = (\mu - 1)\left(\frac{1}{R_1} - \frac{1}{R_2}\right)}$$

Here, R_1 and R_2 are to be measured in metre.

For converging (convex) lens, power is positive and for diverging (concave) lens, power is negative.

Example 4 If the radii of curvature of the faces of a double convex lens are 9 cm and 15 cm, respectively and the refractive index of glass is 1.5, then determine the focal length and the power of the lens.

Sol. Given, radii of curvature, $R_1 = 9$ cm, $R_2 = -15$ cm, refractive index, $\mu = 1.5$, $f = ?$, $P = ?$

According to lens Maker's formula,

$$\frac{1}{f} = (\mu - 1)\left(\frac{1}{R_1} - \frac{1}{R_2}\right)$$

$$\Rightarrow \quad \frac{1}{f} = (1.5 - 1)\left[\frac{1}{9} - \left(\frac{-1}{15}\right)\right]$$

$$\Rightarrow \quad \frac{1}{f} = (0.5)\left(\frac{1}{9} + \frac{1}{15}\right) = (0.5)\left(\frac{5+3}{45}\right)$$

$$\Rightarrow \quad \frac{1}{f} = 0.5 \times \frac{8}{45} \Rightarrow f = \frac{45}{4} = 11.25\text{ cm}$$

$$\therefore \text{Power,} \quad P = \frac{1}{f} = \frac{1}{11.25 \times 10^{-2}} = \frac{10000}{1125} = 8.88\text{ D}$$

Combination of Thin Lenses in Contact

Consider two lenses A and B of focal lengths f_1 and f_2 placed in contact with each other. An object is placed at a point O beyond the focus of the first lens A.

The first lens produces an image at I_1 (virtual image), which serves as a virtual object for the second lens B, producing the final image at I.

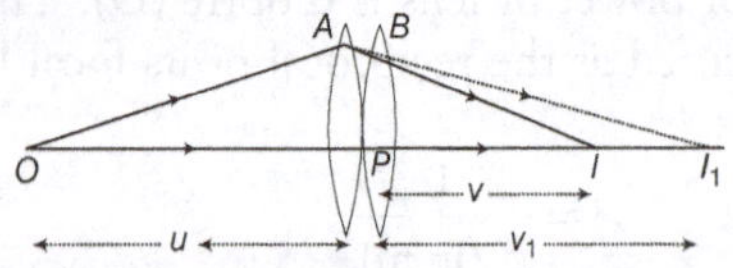

Since, the lenses are thin, we assume the optical centres (P) of the lenses to be co-incident.

For the image formed by the first lens A, we obtain

$$\frac{1}{v_1} - \frac{1}{u} = \frac{1}{f_1} \quad \ldots(i)$$

For the image formed by the second lens B, we get

$$\frac{1}{v} - \frac{1}{v_1} = \frac{1}{f_2} \quad \ldots(ii)$$

Adding Eqs. (i) and (ii), we get

$$\frac{1}{v} - \frac{1}{u} = \frac{1}{f_1} + \frac{1}{f_2} \quad \ldots(iii)$$

If the two lens system is regarded as equivalent to a single lens of focal length f. We have,

$$\frac{1}{v} - \frac{1}{u} = \frac{1}{f} \quad \ldots(iv)$$

From Eqs. (iii) and (iv), we get

$$\boxed{\frac{1}{f} = \frac{1}{f_1} + \frac{1}{f_2}} \quad \ldots(v)$$

For several thin lenses of focal lengths $f_1, f_2, f_3, \ldots$, the effective focal length is

$$\boxed{\frac{1}{f} = \frac{1}{f_1} + \frac{1}{f_2} + \frac{1}{f_3} + \ldots} \quad \ldots(vi)$$

In terms of power, Eq. (vi) can be written as

$$\boxed{P = P_1 + P_2 + P_3 + \ldots}$$

Example 5 Two thin lenses are in contact and the focal length of the combination is 80 cm. If the focal length of one lens is 20 cm, then what would be the power of the another lens?

Sol. Given, combined focal length, $F = 80$ cm, $f_1 = 20$ cm, $P_2 = ?$

$$\therefore \quad P = \frac{100}{F\text{ (cm)}} = \frac{100}{80} = 1.25\text{ D}$$

$$\Rightarrow \quad P_1 = \frac{100}{f_1} = \frac{100}{20} = 5\text{ D}$$

We know that, $P_1 + P_2 = P$

$$\therefore \quad P_2 = P - P_1 = 1.25 - 5 = -3.75\text{ D}$$

Magnification by Combination of Lenses

When lenses are used in combination, each lens magnifies the image formed by the preceding lens. Thus, the magnification m of the final image is given by

$$\boxed{m = m_1 \times m_2}$$

Combination of Lens and Mirror

Let an object be placed in front of a co-axial arrangement of a lens and a mirror held at a suitable distance apart and object is placed in front of the lens.

The following cases arises in the combination of lens and mirror.

(i) **Combination of concave lens and concave mirror**

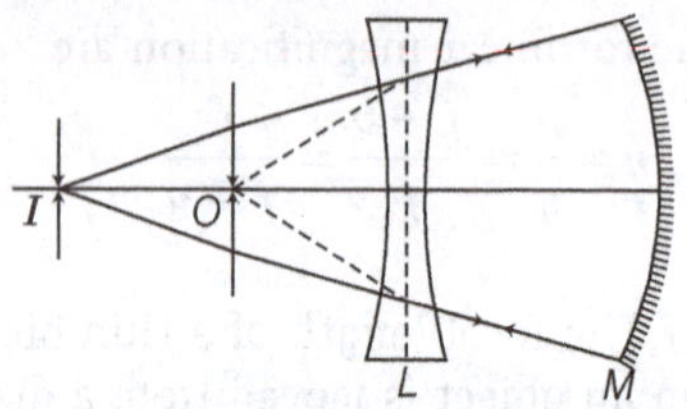

(ii) **Combination of concave lens and plane mirror**

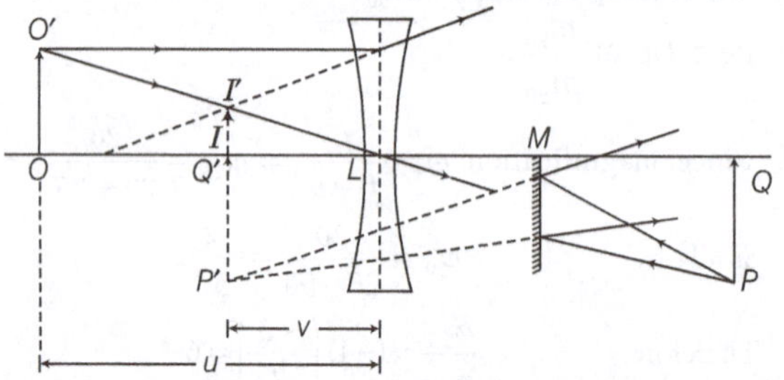

(iii) **Combination of convex lens and convex mirror**

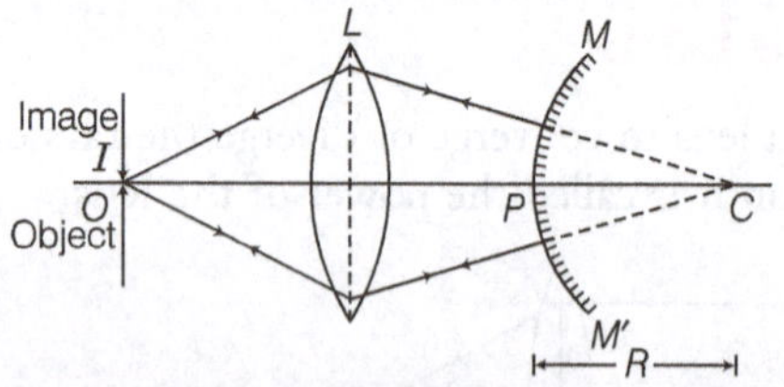

(iv) **Combination of convex lens and concave mirror**

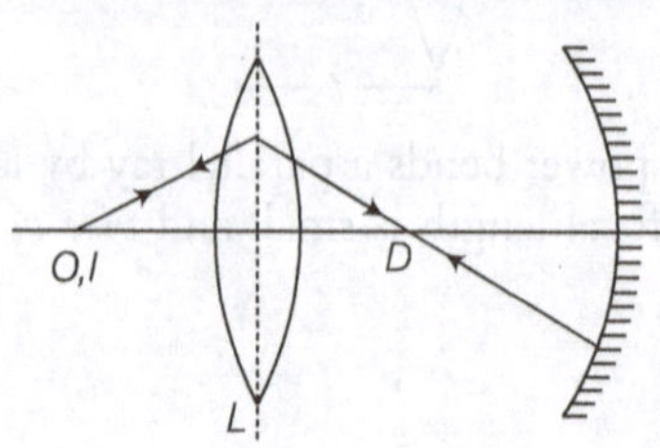

The nature and size of the image will be studied as follow.

- First calculate the position, size and nature of image formed by the lens alone considering that mirror is not there.
- The image formed by the lens acts as real or virtual object for mirror. Using mirror formula, we can calculate the position, size and nature of image formed by mirror.

This calculation will give us the final position, size and nature of image of the given object formed by the combination of lens and mirror.

Topic Practice 4

Multiple Choice Questions

1 Mark

1. A point source of light at the surface of a sphere comes a parallel beam of light of emerge from the opposite surface of the sphere. The refractive index of the material of the sphere is
(a) 1.5 (b) 5/3 (c) 2 (d) 2.5

2. Which of the following is not the case with the image formed by concave lens?
(a) It may be erect or inverted
(b) It may be magnified or diminished
(c) It may be real or virtual
(d) Real image may be between the pole and focus or beyond focus

3. A student measures the focal length of a convex lens by putting an object pin at a distance u from the lens and measuring the distance v of the image pin. The graph between u and v plotted by the student should look like

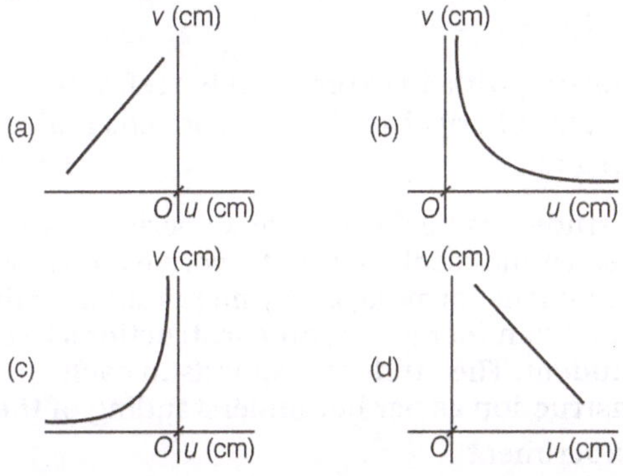

4. The radius of curvature of the curved surface of a plano-convex lens is 20 cm. If the refractive index of the material of the lens be 1.5, it will **NCERT Exemplar**
(a) act as a convex lens only for the objects that lie on its curved side
(b) act as a concave lens for the objects that lie on its curved side
(c) act as a convex lens irrespective of the side on which the object lies
(d) act as a concave lens irrespective of side on which the object lies

5. For a given lens, the magnification was found to be twice as large as when the object was 0.15 m distant from it as when the distance was 0.2 m. The focal length of the lens is
(a) 1.5 m (b) 0.20m
(c) 0.10 m (d) 0.05 m

6. A concave mirror of focal length f_1 is placed at a distance of d from a convex lens of focal length f_2. A beam of light coming from infinity and falling on this convex lens-concave mirror combination returns to infinity. The distance d must be equal
(a) $f_1 + f_2$ (b) $-f_1 + f_2$
(c) $2f_1 + f_2$ (d) $-2f_1 + f_2$

Very Short Answer Type Questions

1 Mark

7. State one assumption made in deriving the formula $\frac{n_2}{v} - \frac{n_1}{u} = \frac{n_2 - n_1}{R}$ for refraction at a spherical interface. **ISC 2003**

8. How does focal length of a convex lens change with increase in wavelength of incident light? **ISC 2014**

9. Refractive index of the material of a concave lens is μ. The lens is immersed in a medium of refractive index μ_1 ($\mu_1 > \mu$). A parallel beam of light is incident on the lens. Draw a diagram to show the path of emergent rays. **ISC 2005**

10. Write down the lens maker's formula using standard symbols. **ISC 2002**

11. The lens shown in figure is made of two different materials of refractive indices μ_1 and μ_2, respectively. A point object is placed on the principal axis. How many images of the object will be formed by the lens?

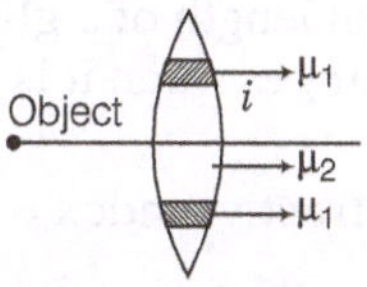

ISC 2001

12. What is the relation between the refractive indices n_1 and n_2, if the behaviour of light rays is as shown in the given figure?

Here, n_1 and n_2 are the refractive indices of the surrounding medium and the lens, respectively.

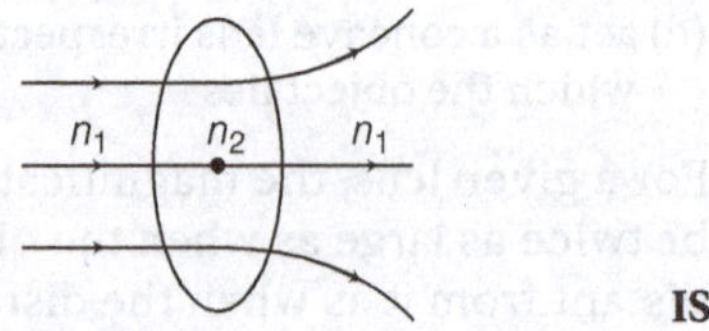

ISC 2000

13. What type of lens is an air bubble inside water?

14. A concave lens of refractive index 1.5 is immersed in a medium of refractive index 1.65. What is the nature of the lens?

15. A biconvex lens made of a transparent material of refractive index 1.25 is immersed in water of refractive index 1.33. Will the lens behave as a converging or a diverging lens? Give reason.

16. Under what condition, does a biconvex lens of glass having a certain refractive index act as a plane glass sheet when immersed in a liquid?

17. A glass lens is immersed in water. How is power of the lens affected?

Short Answer Type I Questions

2 Marks

18. Obtain an expression for refraction at a single convex spherical surface, i.e. the relation between μ_1 (rarer medium), μ_2 (denser medium), the object distance u, image distance v and radius of curvature R. ISC 2011

19. Where will you keep an object in front of a
   (i) convex lens in order to get a virtual and magnified image?
   (ii) concave mirror to get a real and diminished image? ISC 2020

20. When two thin lenses of focal lengths f_1 and f_2 are kept co-axially and in contact, prove that their combined focal length f is given by

$$\frac{1}{f}=\frac{1}{f_1}+\frac{1}{f_2}$$ ISC 2020, 14, 08

21. State how focal length of a glass lens (refractive index 1.56) changes when it is completely immersed in
   (i) water (refractive index = 1.33)
   (ii) a liquid (refractive index = 1.65). ISC 2016

22. A convex lens L and a plane mirror M are arranged as shown below.

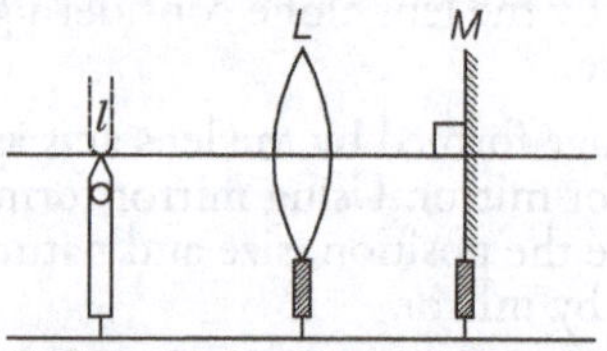

Position of object pin O is adjusted in such a way that the inverted image I formed by the lens mirror combination coincides with the object pin O. Explain how and when this happens. ISC 2013

23. The sunglasses have curved surfaces, but their power zero. Why? ISC 2005

24. A convex lens and a plane mirror are kept at a distance of 10 cm as shown in the diagram below. Parallel rays incident on the convex lens after reflection from the mirror form an image at the optical centre. Complete the ray diagram and find out the focal length of the lens.

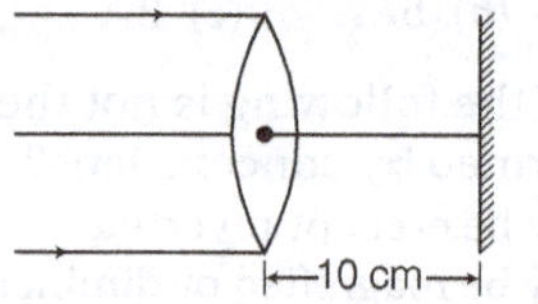

ISC 2005

25. A student measures the focal length of a convex lens by putting an object pin at a distance u from the lens and measuring the distance v of the image pin. What will be the graph drawn between u and v?

Short Answer Type II Questions

3 Marks

26. Starting with an expression for refraction at a single spherical surface, obtain lens maker's formula. ISC 2023, 17

27. A student is performing an experiment to determine focal length of a convex lens by using lens formula, i.e. by no parallax method. The Examiner gives some instructions to the Student. The Student responds to each instruction as per her understanding of the experiment.

State whether the student's response is correct or incorrect. Give a reason for your answer.

   (i) **Examiner** Image formed by the lens is magnified. Reduce the size of the image.

Student moves the lens towards the object pin.

(ii) **Examiner** Plot a graph of $(1/v)$ against $(1/u)$.

Student takes $(1/v)$ on Y-axis and $(1/u)$ on X-axis.

(iii) **Examiner** Write the relation between the optical power (P) and the focal length (f) of the convex lens.

Student writes $P = 2f$. **ISC 2024**

28. Define power of a lens. Write its units. Deduce the relation $\frac{1}{f} = \frac{1}{f_1} + \frac{1}{f_2}$ for two thin lenses kept in contact coaxially.

29. An equiconvex lens of focal length f is cut into two equal halves in thickness. What is the focal length of each half ?

Long Answer Type Questions

5 Marks

30. (i) A point object O is kept in a medium of refractive index n_1 in front of a convex spherical surface of radius of curvature R which separates the second medium of refractive index n_2 from the first one, as shown in the figure.

Draw the ray diagram showing the image formation and deduce the relationship between the object distance and the image distance in terms of n_1, n_2 and R.

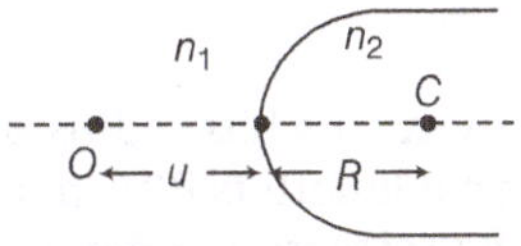

(ii) When the image formed above acts as a virtual object for a concave spherical surface separating the medium n_2 from $n_1 (n_2 > n_1)$, draw this ray diagram and write the similar [similar to (i)] relation. Hence obtain the expression for the lens Maker's formula.

31. A Student is performing an experiment to determine image formation by lenses.

The Examiner gives some instructions to the Student. The Student responds to each instruction as per his/her understanding of the experiment.

State whether the students' response is correct or incorrect. Give a reason for your answer.

(i) **Examiner** Ray goes straight without any deviation through lens.

Student Ray passes through the focus of the lens.

(ii) **Examiner** Object is between optical centre and focus.

Student Image is real, erect and diminished.

(iii) **Examiner** Image is always on the same side of the lens as the object.

Student Image formed by concave lens.

Numerical Problems

32. A converging lens of focal length 40 cm is kept in contact with a diverging lens of focal length 30 cm. Find the focal length of the combination. **ISC 2017 (1 M)**

33. Two thin lenses having optical power of − 10 D and + 6D are placed in contact with each other. Find the focal length of the combination. **(1 M)**

34. Find the focal length and nature of a lens whose optical power is − 5 D. **ISC 2013 (1 M)**

35. A thin convex lens (L_1) of focal length 80 cm and a thin concave lens (L_2) of focal length f are kept co-axially, 20 cm apart as shown in figure below. When a narrow and parallel beam of light is incident on the convex lens, beam emerging from the concave lens is also a parallel beam. Find the value of f.

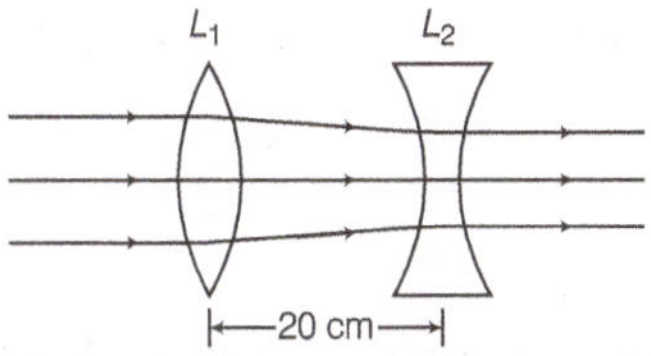

ISC 2012 (1 M)

36. A thin converging lens of focal length 15 cm is kept in contact with a thin diverging lens of focal length 20 cm. Find the focal length of this combination. **ISC 2018, 09 (1 M)**

37. A biconvex spherical lens has focal length 20 cm. If it is split into two halves to form two plano-convex lenses, what is the focal length of each plano-convex lens? **ISC 2007 (1 M)**

38. The figure below shows the positions of a point object O, two lenses, a plane mirror and the final image I which coincides with the object. The focal length of the convex lens is 20 cm. Calculate the focal length of the concave lens.

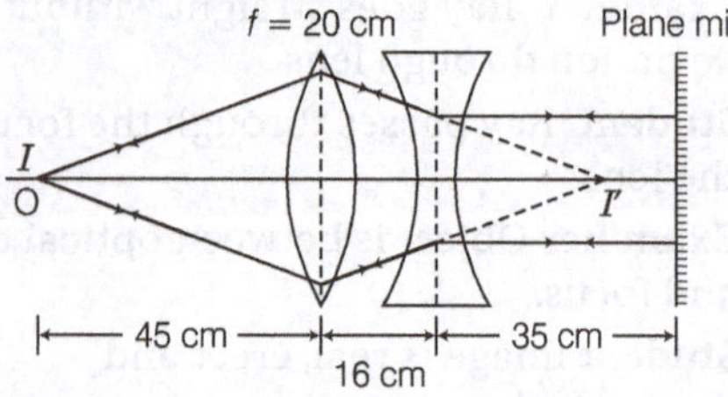

ISC 2014 (2 M)

39. Figure below shows a parallel beam of monochromatic light incident on a convex spherical surface, radius of curvature $R = 30$ cm, which separates glass (refractive index = 1.6) from air. Find the position of the image formed due to refraction of light at this single spherical surface.

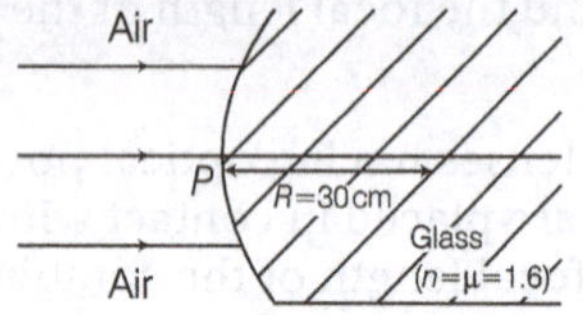

ISC 2012 (2 M)

40. Where should an object be kept on the principal axis of a convex lens of focal length 20 cm in order to get an image, which is double of the size of the object? **ISC 2011 (2 M)**

41. An equi-convex lens of glass having focal length of 10 cm is split into two identical plano-convex lenses each having focal length f_1 as shown below. Find the value of f_1.

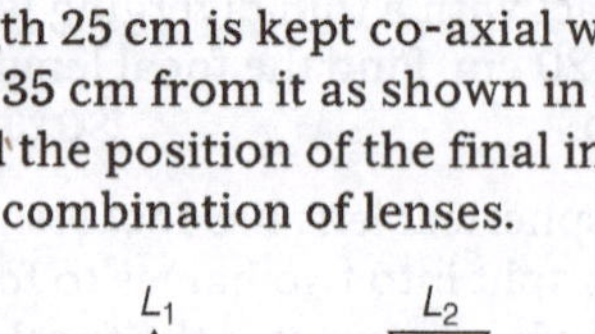

ISC 2010 (2 M)

42. An illuminated point object O is kept 20 cm from a thin convex lens L_1 of focal length 15 cm as shown below. A thin diverging lens L_2 of focal length 25 cm is kept co-axial with the first lens and 35 cm from it as shown in the figure. Find the position of the final image formed by this combination of lenses.

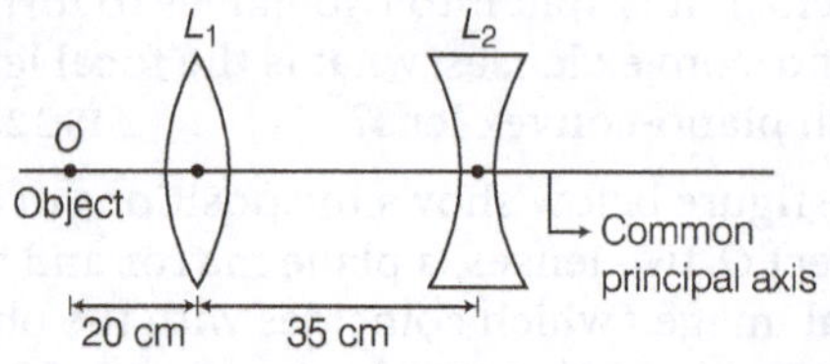

ISC 2010 (2 M)

43. A thin convex lens which is made of glass (refractive index 1.5) has a focal length of 20 cm. It is now completely immersed in a transparent liquid having refractive index 1.75. Find the new focal length of the lens.

ISC 2009 (2 M)

44. A plano-convex lens made of glass ($n = 1.5$) has a focal length 10 cm.

(i) Calculate the radius of curvature of its curved surface.

(ii) If an identical plano-convex lens is placed in contact with the first (plane surfaces facing each other), what will be the power (in dioptres) of the combination?

ISC 2007 (2 M)

45. See below the diagram.

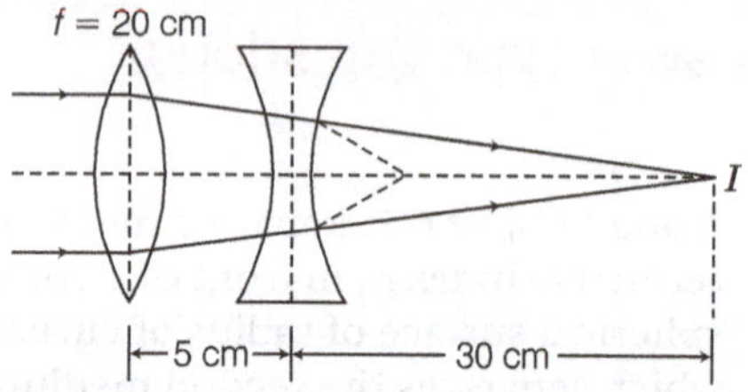

Calculate the focal length of concave lens with the help of above ray diagram. The focal length of convex lens is 20 cm. **ISC 2004 (2 M)**

46. A convex lens of focal length $f = 20$ cm is combined with a diverging lens of power 6.5 D. What are the power and focal length of the combination? **ISC 2003 (2 M)**

47. A plano-convex lens has radius of curvature 10 cm. Its focal length is 80 cm under water. Calculate the refractive index of the material of the lens, given refractive index of water is 4/3. **ISC 2002 (2 M)**

48. A point object O is placed at a distance of 15 cm from a convex lens L of focal length 10 cm as shown in the figure below. On the other side of the lens, a convex mirror M is placed such that its distance from the lens is equal to the focal length of the lens. The final image formed by this combination is observed to coincide with the object O. Find the focal length of the convex mirror.

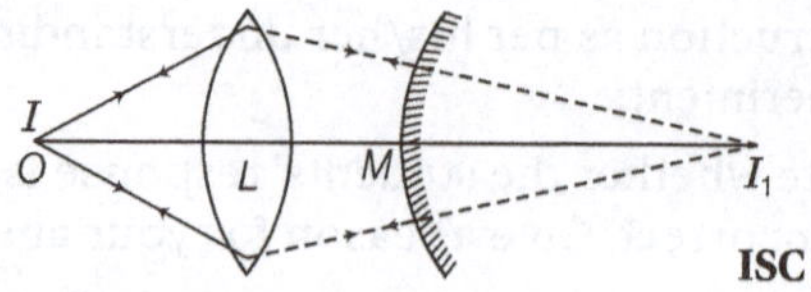

ISC 2015 (3 M)

Hints & Solutions

1. (c) For refraction at surface A x B,

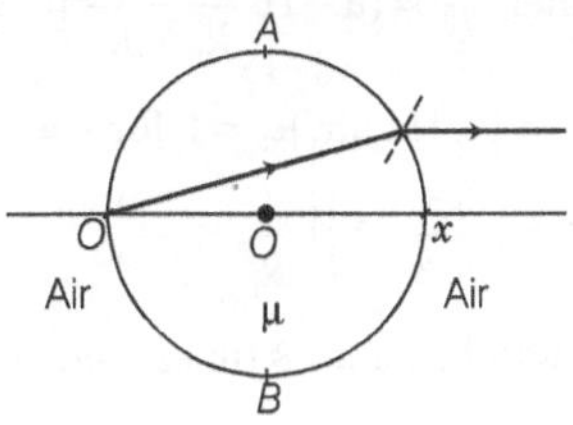

$$u = -2R$$
$$v = +\infty$$

So, applying $\frac{\mu_2}{v} - \frac{\mu_1}{u} = \frac{\mu_2 - \mu_1}{R}$

$\Rightarrow \quad \frac{1}{\infty} - \frac{\mu}{(-2R)} = \frac{1-\mu}{-R}$

$\Rightarrow \quad \frac{\mu}{2R} = \frac{(\mu - 1)}{R}$

$\Rightarrow \quad \mu = 2\mu - 2$

$\therefore \quad \mu = 2$

2. (a) For a real object in concave lens, the image is always virtual, erect, diminished and on the same side of the lens as object.

3. (c) From lens formula,

$$\frac{1}{v} - \frac{1}{u} = \frac{1}{f} = \text{constant}$$

This represents a hyperbola.

Both (b) and (c) is hyperbolic curve, but (c) represents correctly.

4. (c) Here, given $\mu = 1.5$

If object lies on plane side

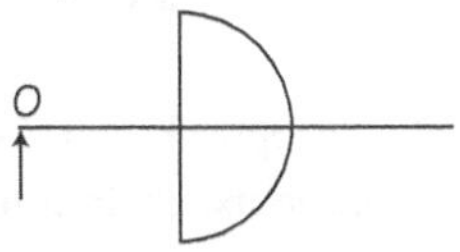

(a)

$R_1 = \infty, R_2 = -20\,\text{cm}$

$$\frac{1}{f} = (\mu - 1)\left(\frac{1}{R_1} - \frac{1}{R_2}\right) = (1.5 - 1)\left(\frac{1}{\infty} + \frac{1}{20}\right) = \frac{1}{40}$$

$\Rightarrow \quad f = +40$ cm

The lens behaves as convex. If object lies on its convex side $R_1 = 20\,\text{cm}, R_2 = \infty$

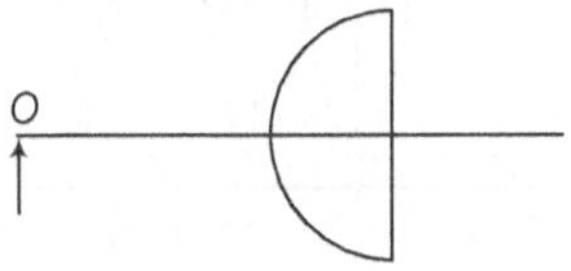

(b)

$$\frac{1}{f'} = (\mu - 1)\left(\frac{1}{R_1} - \frac{1}{R_2}\right) = (1.5 - 1)\left(\frac{1}{20} - \frac{1}{\infty}\right) = \frac{1}{40}$$

$\Rightarrow \quad f' = 40\,\text{cm}$

Thus, lens behaves as convex.

5. (c) Magnification, $|m| = \frac{|v|}{|u|}$

***Case* I** $\quad \mu_1 = -0.15\text{ m} = -15$ cm

$v_1 = ?$

$m_1 = ?$

***Case* II** $\quad \mu_2 = -0.2\text{ m} = -20$ cm

$v_2 = ?$

$m_2 = ?$

Given, $\quad |m_1| = 2|m_2|$

$\Rightarrow \quad \frac{|v_1|}{|u_1|} = 2\frac{|v_2|}{|u_2|} \Rightarrow \frac{|v_1|}{|v_2|} = \frac{2 \times 15}{20} = \frac{3}{2}$

$\Rightarrow \quad |v_1| = \frac{3}{2}|v_2|$

or $\quad v_1 = \frac{3}{2}v_2$

Applying lens equation,

$$\frac{1}{v} - \frac{1}{u} = \frac{1}{f} \text{ or } \frac{1}{f} = \frac{1}{v_1} - \frac{1}{u_1} \quad \text{...(i)}$$

and

$$\frac{1}{f} = \frac{1}{v_2} - \frac{1}{u_2} \quad \text{...(ii)}$$

From Eqs. (i) and (ii), we get

$$\frac{1}{v_1} - \frac{1}{u_1} = \frac{1}{v_2} - \frac{1}{u_2}$$

$\Rightarrow \quad \left(\frac{v_2 - v_1}{v_1 v_2}\right) = \left(\frac{u_2 - u_1}{u_1 u_2}\right) \Rightarrow \frac{v_2 - \frac{3}{2}v_2}{\frac{3}{2}v_2 \cdot v_2} = \left(\frac{-5}{300}\right)$

$\Rightarrow \quad \frac{-v_2}{3v_2^2} = \frac{-5}{300}$ or $v_2 = \frac{-300}{15}$

or $\quad v_2 = +20$ cm

Similarly, $\quad v_1 = +30$ cm

From Eq. (i), we get

$$\frac{1}{f} = \frac{1}{+30} - \frac{1}{(-15)} = \frac{3}{30}$$

$\therefore \quad f = 10\text{ cm} = 0.10\text{ m}$

6. (c) According to question, the ray diagram will be

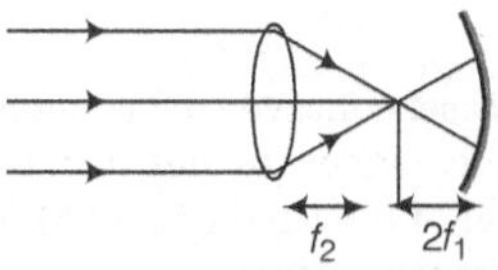

So, distance d between convex lens and concave mirror is given by $\quad d = 2f_1 + f_2$

7. The assumption is that we concerned the rays to be paraxial (rays close to principal axis) only.

8. Refractive index (μ) varies inversely with the wavelength (λ) of light used and for convex lens focal length (f) is given by

$$\frac{1}{f} = (\mu - 1)\left(\frac{1}{R_1} - \frac{1}{R_2}\right)$$

where, R_1 and R_2 are radius of curvature of two surfaces. So, on increasing wavelength, refractive index decreases and focal length increases.

9. The behaviour is reversed in accordance with lens maker's formula.

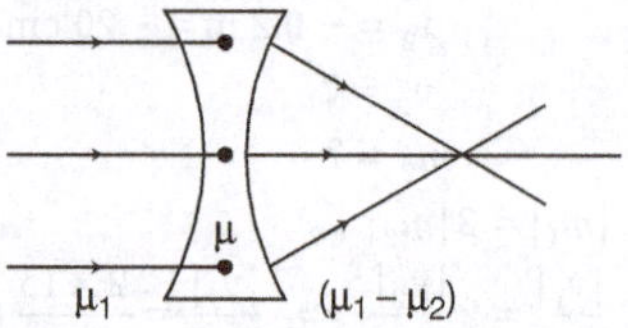

$$\frac{1}{f} = \left(\frac{\mu_2}{\mu_1} - 1\right)\left(\frac{1}{R_1} - \frac{1}{R_2}\right)$$

where, symbols have their usual meaning.

$$\frac{1}{f} = \left(\frac{\mu}{\mu_1} - 1\right)\left(\frac{1}{R_1} - \frac{1}{R_2}\right) = +\text{ve}$$

$\Rightarrow$ f = focal length is positive, hence it will behave as convex lens.

10. Lens maker's formula is

$$\frac{1}{f} = (\mu - 1)\left(\frac{1}{R_1} - \frac{1}{R_2}\right)$$

where, f is focal length of lens,

μ is refractive index of material of lens,

R_1 is radius of curvature of first surface

and R_2 is radius of curvature of second surface.

11. Two images of the point object will formed by lens, because lens is formed from two different materials of different refractive indices μ_1 and μ_2.

12. From figure, it is clear that the convex lens is behaving as a concave lens. It happens only when the refractive index of the lens material is less than the medium in which lens is placed. Therefore, $n_1 > n_2$.

13. It is clearly visible that air bubble acts as a diverging lens (concave lens) in water.

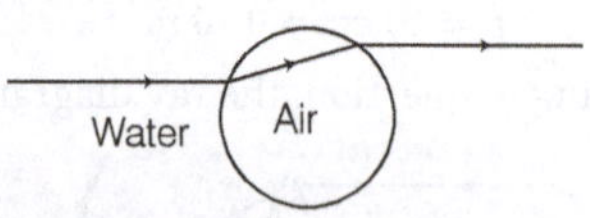

14. In the given case, concave lens is immersed in a medium having refractive index greater than the refractive index of the material of the lens ($1.65 > 1.5$). Therefore, it will behave as a converging lens.

15. When a lens is placed in a liquid, where refractive index is more than that of the material of lens, then the nature of the lens changes. So, when a biconvex lens of refractive index 1.25 is immersed in water (refractive index 1.33), i.e. in the liquid of higher refractive index, its nature will change. So, biconvex lens will act as diverging lens.

16. When refractive index of lens is equal to the refractive index of liquid, it will behave like plane glass sheet.

17. We know that, $\frac{1}{f} = (\mu - 1)\left(\frac{1}{R_1} - \frac{1}{R_2}\right)$

For glass $\mu_2 = 1.5$, for air, $\mu_1 = 1$, for water $\mu = 1.33$

$$\therefore \quad \frac{1}{f} = \left(\frac{1.5}{1.33} - 1\right)\left(\frac{1}{R_1} - \frac{1}{R_2}\right)$$

So, focal length becomes 8 times, hence power becomes $\frac{1}{8}$th of the initial value.

18. Refer to text on page 356 (Refraction at a spherical surface).

19. (i) To get a virtual, magnified image of an object from convex lens, we have to keep the object between optical centre and focus of the lens.

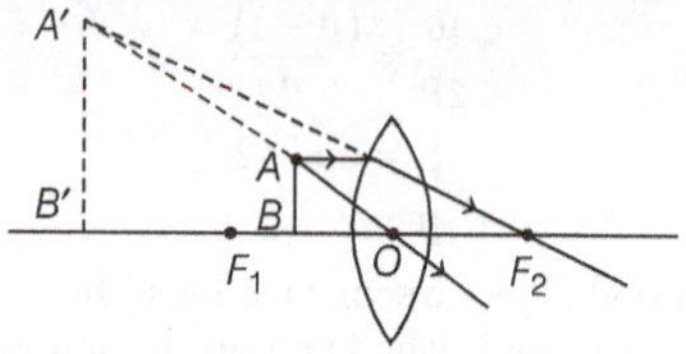

(ii) To get a real, diminished image of an object from a concave mirror, the object has to be kept beyond centre of curvature C.

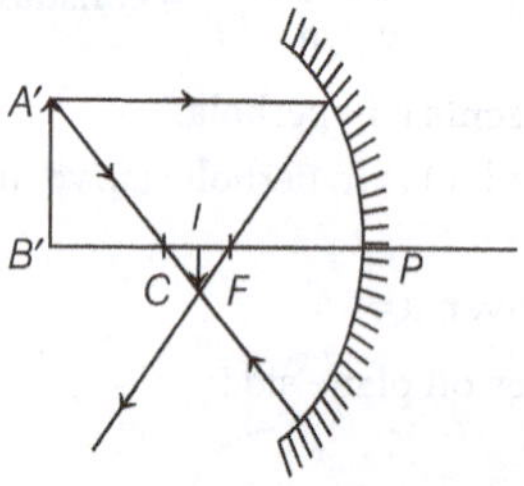

20. Suppose C_1, C_2 be the optical centres of two thin convex lenses L_1 and L_2 held co-axially in contact with each other in air.

Suppose f_1 and f_2 are their respective focal lengths as shown in the figure.

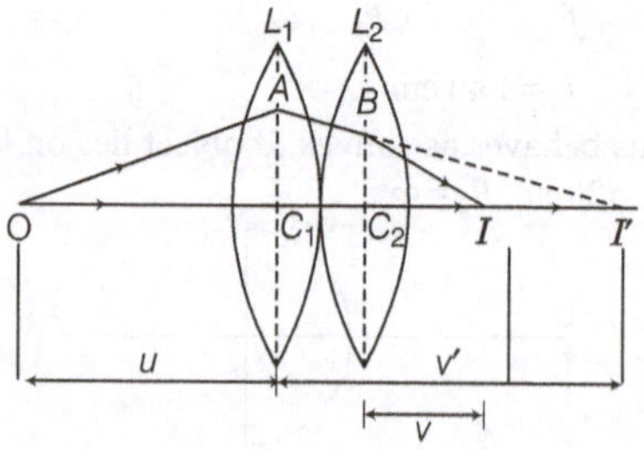

Let a point object O be placed on the common principal axis at a distance $OC_1 = u$. The lens L_1 alone would form its image at I, where $C_1I' = v'$. From the lens formula,

$$\frac{1}{v'} - \frac{1}{u} = \frac{1}{f_1} \quad ...(i)$$

I' would serve as a virtual object for lens L_2, which forms a final image I at distance $C_2I = v$.

Since, the lenses are thin, therefore for the lens, L_2, $u = C_2I' \approx C_1I' = v'$

From the lens formula for L_2, $\frac{1}{v} - \frac{1}{v'} = \frac{1}{f_2} \quad ...(ii)$

On adding Eqs. (i) and (ii), we get

$$\frac{1}{v} - \frac{1}{u} = \frac{1}{f_1} + \frac{1}{f_2} \quad ...(iii)$$

Let the two lenses be replaced by a single lens of focal length f, which forms image I at distance v, of an object at distance u from the lens. For this lens,

$$\frac{1}{v} - \frac{1}{u} = \frac{1}{f} \quad ...(iv)$$

From Eqs. (iii) and (iv), we get

$$\frac{1}{f} = \frac{1}{f_1} + \frac{1}{f_2}$$ (2)

21. According to the question,

$\mu_{glass} = 1.56$, $\mu_{water} = 1.33$, $\mu_{liquid} = 1.65$

From lens maker formula, $\frac{1}{f} = \left(\frac{\mu_2}{\mu_1} - 1\right)\left(\frac{1}{R_1} - \frac{1}{R_2}\right)$

For air, $\frac{1}{f} = (\mu_2 - 1)\left(\frac{1}{R_1} - \frac{1}{R_2}\right) \quad ...(i)$

(i) For water,

$$\frac{1}{f_w} = \left(\frac{\mu_2}{1.33} - 1\right)\left(\frac{1}{R_1} - \frac{1}{R_2}\right) \quad ...(ii)$$

On dividing Eq. (i) by Eq. (ii), we get

$$\frac{f_w}{f} = \frac{(\mu_2 - 1)}{\left(\frac{\mu_2}{1.33} - 1\right)},$$

$$f_w = f\left(\frac{(\mu_2 - 1)}{\frac{\mu_2}{1.33} - 1}\right) = \frac{f(1.56 - 1)}{\frac{1.5}{1.3} - 1} = 3.33f$$

Focal length is positive and it becomes 3.33 times, so the nature of lens remains same. (1)

(ii) For liquid, $\frac{1}{f_l} = \left(\frac{\mu_2}{1.65} - 1\right)\left(\frac{1}{R_1} - \frac{1}{R_2}\right) \quad ...(iii)$

On dividing of Eq. (i) by Eq. (iii), we get

$$\frac{f_l}{f} = \frac{(\mu_2 - 1)}{\left(\frac{\mu_2}{1.65} - 1\right)} = f\left(\frac{1.5 - 1}{\frac{1.5}{1.65} - 1}\right)$$

$$= -\frac{0.5f}{0.09} = 5.55f \text{ (approx.)}$$

Focal length becomes 5.55 times and is negative, i.e. nature of lens get reversed. (1)

22. Consider the ray diagram shown in the figure. It is clear from the figure that, when the object pin O lies in the focal plane of the lens L, the rays of light starting from O after refraction from the lens become parallel to the principal axis of the lens and therefore they strike normally on the plane mirror M kept behind the lens at a small distance. (1)

Due to normal incidence ($i = 0$), angle of reflection $r = 0°$, i.e. the rays are reflected back by the plane mirror on the same path and then they enter the lens as a parallel beam. The lens converges these rays in its focal plane, hence image I is formed just above the object pin O. The image I is inverted, real and of same size as that of the object O as shown in figure.

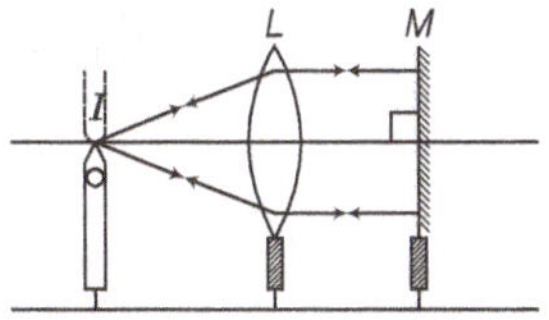

(1)

23. The sunglasses have curved surfaces, the curved surface have the radii of curvature equal. (1/2)

Since, $R_1 = R_2 = R$

$$P = \frac{1}{f} = (n-1)\left(\frac{1}{R_1} - \frac{1}{R_2}\right)$$

where, P = power of lens. (1/2)

$$\Rightarrow \quad P = \frac{1}{f} = (n-1)\left(\frac{1}{R} - \frac{1}{R}\right) = 0$$

$\therefore \quad P = 0$ (1)

24. Consider the ray diagram shown, parallel rays after refraction through the lens converge towards the point F, which is the focus of the lens.

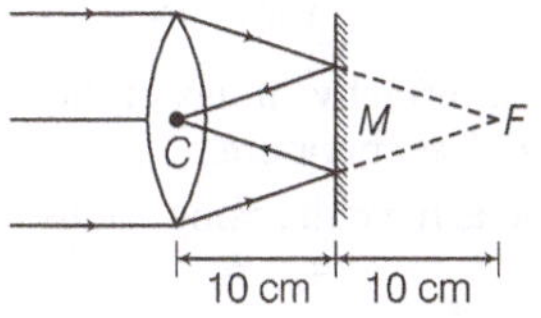

The refracted rays after reflection from the plane mirror placed in the path meet at the optical centre C of lens. Thus, C is the image of the virtual point object F formed by the plane mirror. (1)

Hence, $MF = MC = 10$ cm

The focal length of the lens is given by

$f = CF = MC + MF = 10 + 10 = 20$ cm (1)

25. As we know that, $\frac{1}{v} - \frac{1}{u} = \frac{1}{f}$

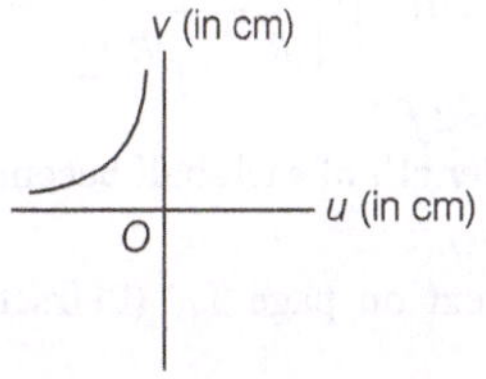

(1+1)

26. Refer to text on page 357 and 358 (Refraction by a lens : lens Maker's formula).

27. (i) Student's response is incorrect.
On decreasing the distance between lens and object, image formed by lens is magnified but increasing the distance between lens and object, forms a small size image.

(ii) Student's response is correct.
The graph between $\frac{1}{u}$ and $\frac{1}{v}$ for a thin convex lens in order to determine its focal length is plotted as shown in the figure.

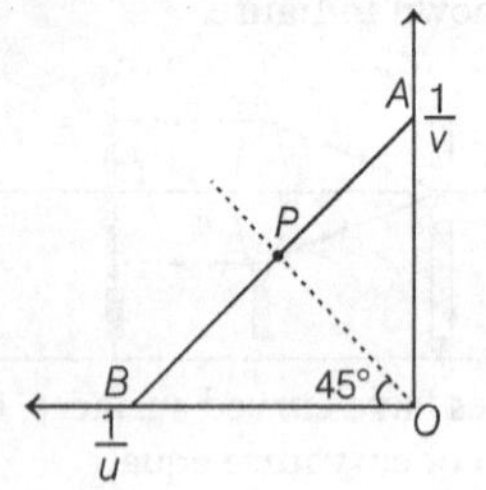

(iii) Student's response is incorrect.
The correct relation between the optical power and focal length is

$$\text{Power, } P = \frac{1}{f\ (\text{in m})}$$

Thus, the power of lens or mirror is inversely proportional to the focal length.

28. Refer to text on page 359 and 360 (Power of a lens, combination of thin lenses in contact).

29. Focal length can be given as

$$\frac{1}{f} = (\mu - 1)\left(\frac{1}{R_1} - \frac{1}{R_2}\right)$$

where, μ is the refractive index of the lens medium. R_1 and R_2 are radii of curvature.
Equiconvex lens have the same radius of curvature, i.e. $R_1 = -R_2$

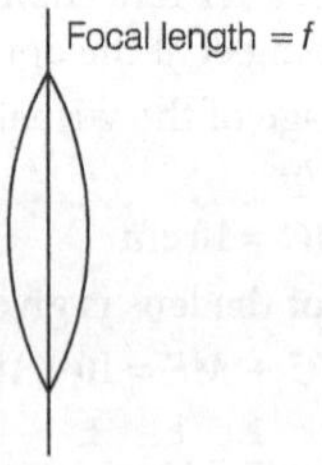

(1½)

$$\therefore \quad \frac{1}{f'} = (\mu - 1)\left[\frac{1}{R} - \left(-\frac{1}{R}\right)\right] \Rightarrow \frac{1}{f'} = \frac{2(\mu - 1)}{R}$$

$$\therefore \quad f' = 2f$$

Hence, focal length of each half becomes twice of the original value. (1½)

30. (i) Refer to text on page 356 (Refraction at a spherical surface).

(ii) Now, the image I' acts as a virtual object for the second surface that will form a real at I. As, refraction takes place from denser to rarer medium,

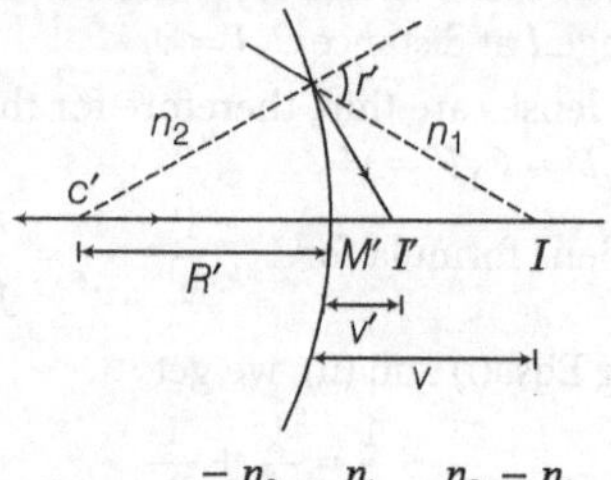

$$\therefore \quad -\frac{n_2}{v} + \frac{n_1}{v'} = \frac{n_2 - n_1}{R'} \quad \text{...(v)}$$

On adding Eqs. (iv) and (v), we get

$$\frac{1}{f} = (n_{21} - 1)\left(\frac{1}{R} - \frac{1}{R'}\right) \left[\because n_{21} = \frac{n_2}{n_1}, \frac{1}{f} = \frac{1}{v} - \frac{1}{u}\right] \quad (2)$$

31. (i) Incorrect response by Student.
A ray passing through the optical centre of the lens goes straight without any deviation.

(ii) Incorrect response by Student.
When the object is between the optical centre C and the focus of the lens, then a virtual and erect image, larger than the object is formed on the same side of the lens as the object.

(iii) Correct response by Student.
The image formed by a concave lens is always erect, virtual, smaller than the object and is formed between the lens and the focus on the same side of the lens as the object.

32. The focal length of the combination will be

$$\frac{1}{f} = \frac{1}{f_1} + \frac{1}{f_2} = \frac{1}{40} + \frac{1}{(-30)}$$

$$= \frac{1}{40} - \frac{1}{30} = \frac{3-4}{120} = -\frac{1}{120}$$

$$\Rightarrow f = -120\text{ cm} = -\frac{120}{100} = -1.2\text{ m}$$

33. According to the question,

$$P_1 = -10\text{ D}, \ P_2 = +6\text{ D}$$

Let power $P_3 = P_1 + P_2$

$$P_3 = -10 + 6 = -4\text{ D}$$

As we know, power $= \frac{1}{f(\text{m})}$

$$\Rightarrow -4 = \frac{1}{f} \Rightarrow f = -\frac{1}{4} = -0.25\text{ m}$$

34. According to the question,
Power of a lens = − 5 D

$$\text{Focal length (metre)} = \frac{1}{\text{Power of lens}} = \frac{1}{-5/100}$$

$$= -20\text{ cm}$$

Since, focal length of lens is negative, so it is concave lens.

35. In lens L_2, $v = \infty$, $u = 80 - 20 = 60$ cm

As, $\frac{1}{v} - \frac{1}{u} = \frac{1}{f_2} \Rightarrow \frac{1}{\infty} - \frac{1}{60} = \frac{1}{f_2}$

$\Rightarrow \quad f_2 = -60$ cm

Hence, focal length of L_2 is -60 cm.

36. Given,

Focal length of converging lens, $f_1 = 15$ cm

Focal length of diverging lens, $f_2 = -20$ cm

Since, $\frac{1}{f_{\text{equivalent}}} = \frac{1}{f_1} + \frac{1}{f_2}$

$\Rightarrow \quad \frac{1}{f_{\text{equivalent}}} = \frac{1}{15} + \left(-\frac{1}{20}\right) = \frac{4-3}{60} = \frac{1}{60}$

$\therefore \quad f_{\text{equivalent}} = 60$ cm

37. We know that, $\frac{1}{f} = (\mu - 1)\left(\frac{2}{R}\right)$

$\Rightarrow \quad R = 2f(\mu - 1)$

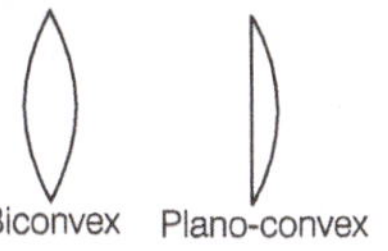

When lens splits $\frac{1}{f_1} = (\mu - 1)\left(\frac{1}{R}\right)$

$\Rightarrow \quad f_1 = \frac{R}{(\mu - 1)} = 2f = 2 \times 20 = 40$ cm

Hence, focal length gets doubled.

38. The image formed by the lens will act as object and by applying lens formula for the different lens, we will get the focal length of concave lens.

For convex lens,

$f = 20$ cm, $u = -45$ cm and $v = ?$

By lens formula, $\frac{1}{v} - \frac{1}{u} = \frac{1}{f}$

Symbols have their usual meaning.

$\Rightarrow \quad \frac{1}{v} - \frac{1}{(-45)} = \frac{1}{20} \Rightarrow v = 36$ cm (1)

For concave lens,

$u = 36 - 16 = 20$ cm, $v = \infty$ and $f = ?$

$\frac{1}{v} - \frac{1}{u} = \frac{1}{f} \Rightarrow \frac{1}{\infty} - \frac{1}{20} = \frac{1}{f}$

$\Rightarrow \quad f = -20$ cm

Negative sign shows that lens is concave. (1)

39. According to the question,

$R = 30$ cm, $n_2 = 1.6$, $n_1 = 1$ [for air]

We know that, $\frac{n_2}{v} - \frac{n_1}{u} = \frac{n_2 - n_1}{R}$ (1/2)

Now, by putting the values,

(where, symbols have their usual meaning)

$\frac{1.6}{v} + \frac{1}{\infty} = \frac{1.6 - 1}{30}$

$\Rightarrow \quad \frac{1.6}{v} = \frac{0.6}{30} \Rightarrow \frac{1}{v} = \frac{1}{5 \times 16}$

$\Rightarrow \quad \frac{1}{v} = \frac{1}{80} \Rightarrow v = 80$ cm

This position of image is 80 cm from the point P. (1½)

40. Given, focal length, $f = 20$ cm

Magnification, $m = 2$

We know that, magnification, $m = v/u$ (1/2)

So, $\quad 2 = \frac{v}{u}$ [by question, $m = 2$]

or $\quad v = 2u$ (1/2)

We know that, $\frac{1}{v} + \frac{1}{u} = \frac{1}{f}$ [for convex lens]

where, symbols have their usual meaning. (1/2)

$\frac{1}{2u} + \frac{1}{u} = \frac{1}{20} \Rightarrow u = 30$ cm

Hence, object should be placed at 30 cm. (1/2)

41. As, we know from lens maker's formula that,

$\frac{1}{f} = (\mu - 1)\left(\frac{1}{R_1} - \frac{1}{R_2}\right)$ (1/2)

Now, for biconvex lens,

$\frac{1}{10} = (\mu - 1)\left(\frac{1}{R} + \frac{1}{R}\right) = \frac{2(\mu - 1)}{R} \Rightarrow R = 20(\mu - 1)$ (1/2)

For plano-convex lens,

$\frac{1}{f_1} = (\mu - 1)\left(\frac{1}{R} - \frac{1}{\infty}\right)$

$\Rightarrow f_1 = \frac{1}{\mu - 1} \times R = \frac{1}{\mu - 1} \times 20(\mu - 1) \Rightarrow f_1 = 20$ cm (1)

42. For convex lens, $\frac{1}{f_1} = \frac{1}{v_1} - \frac{1}{u_1}$

Now, by putting the values given in question (symbols have their usual meaning.)

$\Rightarrow \frac{1}{15} = \frac{1}{v_1} - \left(-\frac{1}{20}\right) = \frac{1}{v_1} + \frac{1}{20}$

$\Rightarrow \frac{1}{v_1} = \frac{1}{15} - \frac{1}{20} = \frac{4-3}{60} = \frac{1}{60}$

$\Rightarrow v_1 = 60$ cm

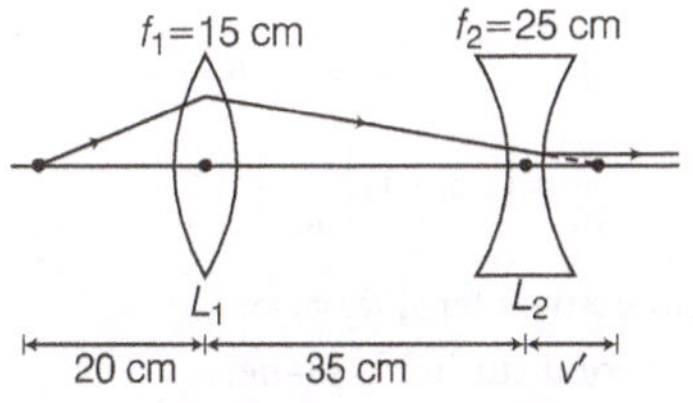

(1)

For concave lens, $v_1 = u_2 = 25$ cm $= (60$ cm $- 35$ cm$)$

$\frac{1}{f_2} = \frac{1}{v_2} - \frac{1}{u_2}$

$$\frac{1}{-25} = \frac{1}{v_2} - \frac{1}{25} \Rightarrow \frac{1}{v_2} = 0$$

$\therefore$ $v_2 = \infty$

The final image is at infinity. (1)

43. We have to apply lens maker's formula separately for each case.

According to the question,

Given, refractive index of glass w.r.t. air,

$${}_a\mu_g = 1.5,$$

Focal length for initial case, $f = 20$ cm

Refractive index of liquid w.r.t. air, ${}_a\mu_l = 1.75$

So, from lens marker's formula,

$$\frac{1}{f} = (\mu - 1)\left(\frac{1}{R_1} - \frac{1}{R_2}\right)$$

$$\Rightarrow \frac{1}{R_1} - \frac{1}{R_2} = C \quad \text{[say]}$$

where, μ = relative refractive index, R_1 and R_2 are radii of curvatures.

$$\frac{1}{f} = (\mu - 1) C$$

In air, $\frac{1}{f} = ({}_a\mu_g - 1) C$ ...(i)

In liquid, $\frac{1}{f_1} = ({}_l\mu_g - 1) C$

$$\frac{1}{f_1} = \left(\frac{{}_a\mu_g}{{}_a\mu_l} - 1\right) C \quad \text{...(ii)}$$ (1)

On dividing Eq. (i) by Eq. (ii), we get

$$\frac{1/f}{1/f_1} = \frac{{}_a\mu_g - 1}{\frac{{}_a\mu_g}{{}_a\mu_l} - 1} = \frac{1.5 - 1}{\frac{1.5}{1.75} - 1}$$

$$\frac{f_l}{f} = \frac{0.5 \times 1.75}{1.5 - 1.75}$$

$$f_l = \frac{0.5 \times 1.75}{-0.25} \times 20$$

$$f_l = -70 \text{ cm}$$ [concave] (1)

44. Given, refractive index, $n = 1.5$

Focal length, $f = 10$ cm

Applying lens maker's formula,

$$\frac{1}{f} = (n - 1)\left(\frac{1}{R_1} - \frac{1}{R_2}\right)$$

$$\Rightarrow \frac{1}{10} = (1.5 - 1)\left(\frac{1}{R_1}\right)$$

[for plano-convex lens, $R_2 = \infty$]

Because second surface is plane.

$$\Rightarrow \frac{1}{10} = \frac{0.5}{R_1}$$

$$\Rightarrow R_1 = 5 \text{ cm}$$ (1)

When two plano-convex lenses are placed side by side, this combination acts as biconvex lens. Now, by lens maker's formula,

$$\frac{1}{f} = (n - 1)\left(\frac{1}{R_1} - \frac{1}{R_2}\right)$$

$$\Rightarrow \frac{1}{f} = (n - 1)\frac{2}{R_1} = \frac{0.5 \times 2}{5} = \frac{1}{5}$$

$[\because R_1 = R = R_2 = 5 \text{ cm}]$

$$\Rightarrow f = 5 \text{ cm} = 0.05 \text{ m}$$

$\therefore$ Power, $P = \frac{1}{f(\text{m})} = \frac{100}{5}$

$$= +20 \text{ D}$$ (1)

45. From the ray diagram, it is clear that

object distance, $u = +15$ cm

Image distance, $v = 30$ cm

Now, by lens formula, $\frac{1}{f} = \frac{1}{v} - \frac{1}{u}$

[where, f = focal length] (1)

$$\Rightarrow \frac{1}{f} = \frac{1}{30} - \frac{1}{15} \Rightarrow \frac{1}{f} = \frac{1-2}{30}$$

$$f = -30 \text{ cm}$$ (1)

46. Given, focal length, $f = 20 \text{ cm} = 20 \times 10^{-2}$ m

and power, $P_2 = 6.5$ D

We know, power, $P_1 = \frac{1}{f_1} = \frac{1}{20 \times 10^{-2}} = 5$ D (1/2)

Power of the combination,

$$P_{\text{equivalent}} = P_1 + P_2 = 5 + 6.5 = 11.5 \text{ D}$$ (1/2)

Focal length of the combination,

$$f_{\text{eq}} = \frac{1}{P} = \frac{1}{11.5} \text{ m} = 8.7 \text{ cm}$$ (1)

47. According to lens maker's formula,

$$\frac{1}{f} = (\mu - 1)\left(\frac{1}{R_1} - \frac{1}{R_2}\right)$$

But for plano-convex lens, $R_2 = \infty$ and thus

$$\frac{1}{f} = (\mu - 1)\left(\frac{1}{R_1}\right)$$

When the lens is placed in water, then

$$\frac{1}{f_\omega} = (\mu_0 - 1)\left(\frac{1}{R_1}\right) = \left(\frac{{}_a\mu_l}{{}_a\mu_w} - 1\right)\left(\frac{1}{R_1}\right)$$ (1)

On substituting the values, we get

$$\frac{1}{80} = \left(\frac{{}_a\mu_l}{4/3} - 1\right)\left(\frac{1}{10}\right)$$

$$\Rightarrow \left(\frac{{}_a\mu_l}{4/3} - 1\right) = \frac{10}{80} = \frac{1}{8}$$

$$\Rightarrow \frac{{}_a\mu_l}{4/3} = 1 + \frac{1}{8} = \frac{9}{8}$$

$$\Rightarrow \quad {}_a\mu_l = \frac{9}{8} \times \frac{4}{3}$$

$$\Rightarrow \quad {}_a\mu_l = \frac{3}{2} \quad \text{(1)}$$

48. Given, $u = -15$ cm, $f = 10$ cm, $d = f = 10$ cm (convex lens)

For lens, $\frac{1}{v} - \frac{1}{u} = \frac{1}{f}$ (1/2)

Substituting the all values,

$$\frac{1}{v} - \frac{1}{(-15)} = \frac{1}{10} \quad (\because u = -15 \text{ cm})$$

$$\frac{1}{v} = \frac{1}{10} - \frac{1}{15} = \frac{3-2}{30} = \frac{1}{30} \quad \text{(1)}$$

$$\Rightarrow \quad v = 30 \text{ cm}$$

$\therefore$ $MI = LI - LM = 30 - 10 = 20$ cm (1/2)

Now, the focal length,

$$f = \frac{20}{2} = 10 \text{ cm} \quad \text{(1)}$$

TOPIC 05 Optical Instruments

Using the reflecting and refracting properties of mirrors, lenses and prisms, many optical instruments have been designed like microscopes and telescopes.

Simple Microscope

Microscope is an optical instrument which forms large image of close and minute objects. A simple microscope is a converging lens of small focal length.

Case I **When the image is formed at the near point**

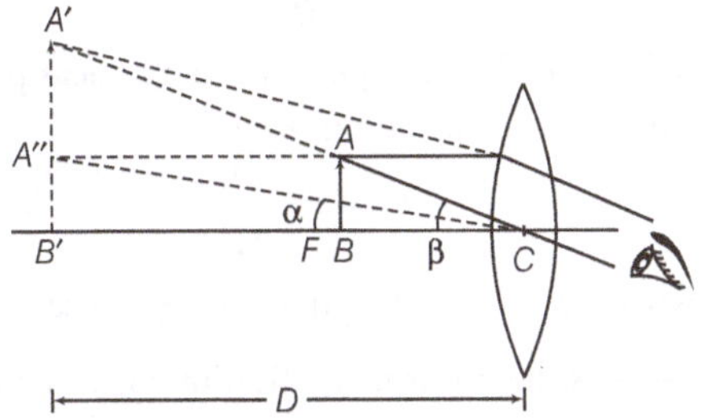

The **angular magnification** or **magnifying power** of a simple microscope is defined as the ratio of the angle β subtended at the eye by image at the near point and the angle α subtended at the unaided eye by the object at the near point.

$\therefore$ Magnifying power, $m = \frac{\beta}{\alpha}$ ...(i)

In $\Delta A'B'C$, $\tan\beta = \frac{A'B'}{D}$

In $\Delta A''B''C$, $\tan\alpha = \frac{A''B'}{D} = \frac{AB}{D}$

Since, the angles are small, then

$\tan\alpha \approx \alpha$ and $\tan\beta \approx \beta$

$$\therefore \quad \beta = \frac{A'B'}{D} \quad \text{and} \quad \alpha = \frac{AB}{D}$$

From Eq. (i), we have

$$m = \frac{A'B'}{D} \times \frac{D}{AB} = \frac{A'B'}{AB}$$

This gives the linear magnification produced by the lens.

It can be proved that, $\frac{A'B'}{AB} = \frac{v}{u}$

We know that, $\frac{1}{v} - \frac{1}{u} = \frac{1}{f}$

Multiplying both sides by v, we have

$$\frac{v}{v} - \frac{v}{u} = \frac{v}{f}$$

$$\Rightarrow \quad 1 - m = \frac{v}{f} \Rightarrow m = 1 - \frac{v}{f}$$

$$\therefore \quad \boxed{m = 1 + \frac{D}{f}}$$

[$\because v = -D$ because image is formed at near point]

In this case, the eye is placed behind the lens at a distance a, then

$$\boxed{m = 1 + \frac{D-a}{f}}$$

Case II **When the image is formed at infinity**

i.e. $v = \infty$

In this case, $\beta = \frac{AB}{f}$ and $\alpha = \frac{AB}{D}$

$$\therefore \quad m = \frac{AB}{f} \times \frac{D}{AB} = \frac{D}{f}$$

$$\boxed{m = \frac{D}{f}}$$

Example 1 A convex lens of focal length 5 cm is used as a simple microscope. What will be the magnifying power when the image is formed at the least distance of distinct vision?

Sol. Given, focal length, $f = 5$ cm

Least distance of distinct vision, $D = 25$ cm

$\therefore$ Magnification, $m = \left(1 + \frac{D}{f}\right) = \left(1 + \frac{25}{5}\right) = 6$

Compound Microscope

A compound microscope consists of two convex lenses coaxially separated by some distance. The lens nearer to the object is called the **objective.** The lens through which the final image is viewed is called the **eyepiece.**

Working

The objective of compound microscope forms the real, inverted and magnified image of the object. This image serves as the object for the second lens, i.e. eyepiece which produces the final image, which is enlarged and virtual. The first inverted image is thus near the focal plane of the eyepiece, at a distance appropriate for final image formation at infinity or a little closer for image formation at the near point. The final image is inverted with respect to the original object.

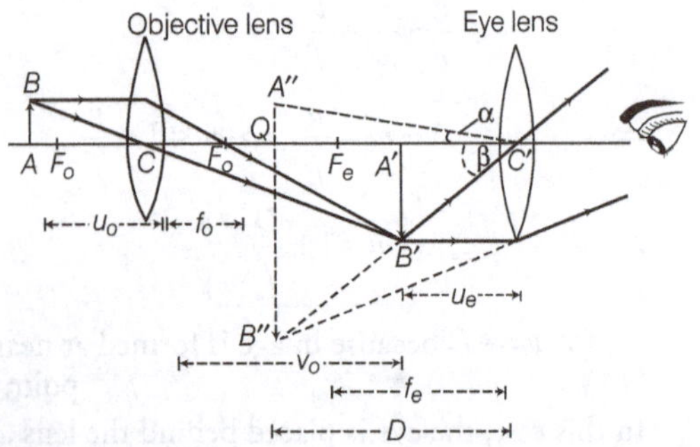

Angular magnification or **magnifying power** of a compound microscope is defined as the ratio of the angle β subtended by the final image at the eye to the angle α subtended by the object seen directly, when both are placed at least distance of distinct vision.

$\therefore$ Angular magnification, $m = \frac{\beta}{\alpha}$

Since, the angles are small, then

$$\alpha \approx \tan\alpha \text{ or } \beta \approx \tan\beta$$

$$\therefore \quad m = \frac{\tan\beta}{\tan\alpha} \quad \text{...(i)}$$

From right angled $\Delta C'QB''$, we have

$$\tan\beta = \frac{B''Q}{C'Q} = \frac{B''Q}{D} = \frac{A''B''}{D}$$

Also, from right angled $\Delta C'A''Q$, we have

$$\tan\alpha = \frac{A''Q}{C'Q} = \frac{AB}{D} \quad [\because A''Q = AB]$$

Substituting the values of $\tan\alpha$ and $\tan\beta$ in Eq. (i), we have

$$m = \frac{B''Q}{D} \times \frac{D}{AB} = \frac{B''Q}{AB}$$

$$\Rightarrow \quad m = \frac{B''Q}{A'B'} \times \frac{A'B'}{AB}$$

Thus, the magnification produced by the compound microscope is the product of the magnification produced by the eyepiece and objective.

$$\therefore \quad \boxed{m = m_e \times m_o} \quad \text{...(ii)}$$

where, m_e and m_o are the magnifying powers of the eyepiece and objective, respectively.

The linear magnification of the real inverted image produced by the eyepiece is $\frac{A''B''}{A'B'}$.

Case I **When the final image is formed at near point**

Linear magnification is given by

$$m_e = 1 + \frac{D}{f_e} \quad \text{...(iii)}$$

where, f_e is focal length of the eyepiece

$\frac{A'B'}{AB}$ is the linear magnification of the object produced by the objective.

$$m_o = \frac{v_o}{u_o} \quad \text{...(iv)}$$

From Eqs. (ii), (iii) and (iv), we have

$$m = \frac{v_o}{u_o}\left(1 + \frac{D}{f_e}\right) \quad \text{...(v)}$$

We know that, $\frac{1}{v_o} - \frac{1}{u_o} = \frac{1}{f_o}$

Multiplying both sides by v_o, we have

$$\frac{v_o}{v_o} - \frac{v_o}{u_o} = \frac{v_o}{f_o}$$

$$\Rightarrow \quad -\frac{v_o}{u_o} = -1 + \frac{v_o}{f_o}$$

$$\Rightarrow \quad \frac{v_o}{u_o} = 1 - \frac{v_o}{f_o}$$

Substituting the value of $\frac{v_o}{u_o}$ in Eq. (v), we have

$$m = \left(1 - \frac{v_o}{f_o}\right)\left(1 + \frac{D}{f_e}\right)$$

Case II **When the final image is at infinity**

If u_o is the distance of the object from the objective and v_o is the distance of the image from the objective, then the magnifying power of the objective is

$$m_o = \frac{v_o}{u_o}$$

When the final image is at infinity, then angular magnification is given by

$$m_e = \frac{D}{f_e}$$

The total magnification when image is at infinity is given by

$$m = m_o \times m_e = \left(\frac{v_o}{u_o} \times \frac{D}{f_e}\right)$$

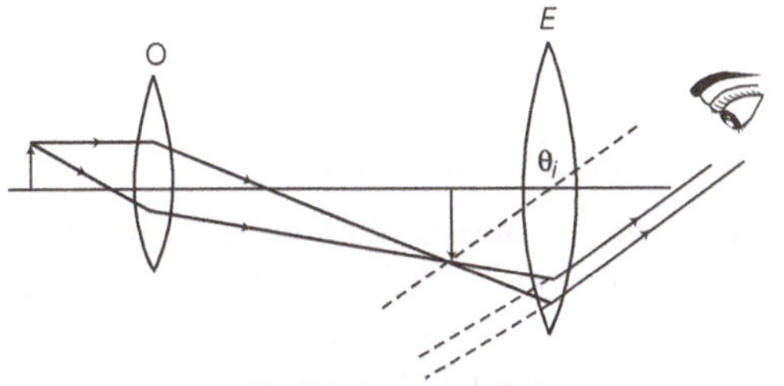

Final image at infinity

If the object is very close to the principal focus of the objective and the image formed by the objective is very close to the eyepiece, then

$$m = \frac{-L}{f_o} \cdot \frac{D}{f_e}$$

where, L = length of the tube of microscope

In this case, the microscope is said to be in normal adjustment.

Example 2 A compound microscope has an objective of focal length 1 cm and an eyepiece of focal length 2.5cm. An object has to be placed at a distance of 1.2 cm away from the objective for the normal adjustment. Determine the angular magnification and length of microscope tube.

Sol. Given, focal length of objective, $f_o = 1$ cm

Focal length of eyepiece, f_e = 2.5 cm

Object distance, $u_o = -1.2$ cm

$$\because \quad \frac{1}{v_o} - \frac{1}{u_o} = \frac{1}{f_o}$$

$$\Rightarrow \quad \frac{1}{v_o} = \frac{1}{u_o} + \frac{1}{f_o}$$

$$\Rightarrow \quad \frac{1}{v_o} = 1 - \frac{1}{1.2} = \frac{0.2}{1.2}$$

$$\Rightarrow \quad v_o = \frac{1.2}{0.2} \Rightarrow v_o = 6 \text{ cm}$$

$\because$ Angular magnification, $m = \frac{v_o}{|u_o|}\left(1 + \frac{D}{f_e}\right)$

$$\Rightarrow \quad m = \frac{6}{|-1.2|}\left(1 + \frac{25}{2.5}\right) = 55$$

$\therefore$ Length of microscope tube,

$$L = v_o + f_e = (6 + 2.5) = 8.5 \text{ cm}$$

Astronomical (Refracting) Telescope

An astronomical telescope is an optical instrument which is used for observing distinct images of heavenly bodies like stars, planets, etc., when the final image is formed at infinity.

Astronomical telescope has two convex lenses coaxially separated by some distance. The lens towards the object is called **objective** and has much larger aperture than the eyepiece of the lens towards the eye.

Working

Light from the distant object enters the objective and real image is formed at second focal point of objective. The eyepiece magnifies this image producing a final inverted image.

Case I **When the final image is formed at infinity**

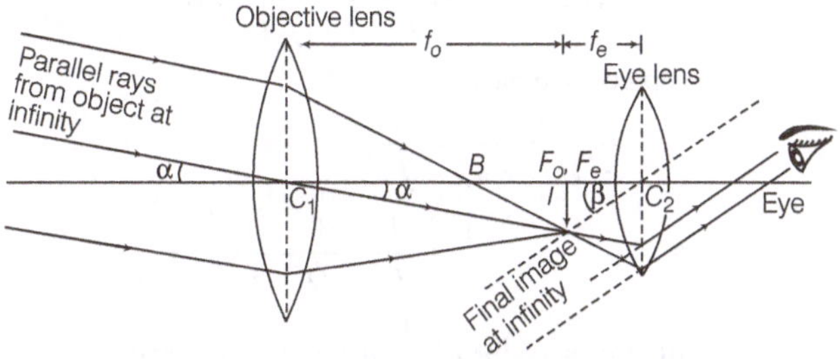

Angular magnification is given by

$$m = \frac{\beta}{\alpha}$$

Since, β and α are very small.

$$\therefore \quad \beta \approx \tan\beta$$

$$\text{or} \quad \alpha \approx \tan\alpha$$

$$\Rightarrow \quad m = \frac{\tan\beta}{\tan\alpha} \quad \ldots\text{(i)}$$

Now, $\tan\alpha = \frac{I}{f_o}$ and $\tan\beta = \frac{I}{-f_e}$

where, I is the image formed by the objective, f_o and f_e are the focal lengths of objective and eyepiece, respectively.

Substituting the values of $\tan\alpha$ and $\tan\beta$ in Eq. (i), we get

$$m = \frac{-\frac{I}{f_e}}{\frac{I}{f_o}} \quad \text{or} \quad \boxed{m = -\frac{f_o}{f_e}}$$

Case II **When final image is formed at near point**

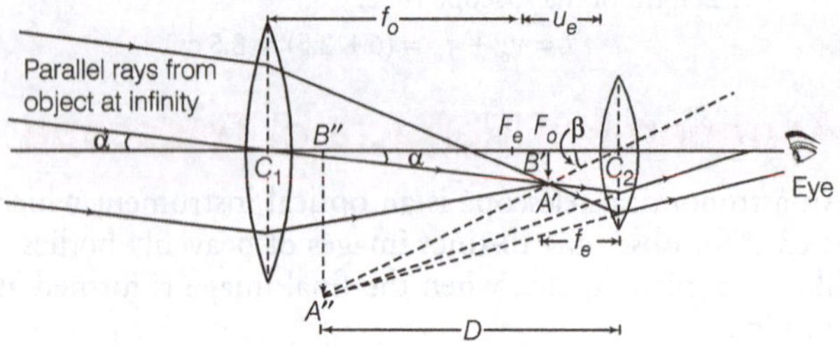

Angular magnification, $m = \frac{\beta}{\alpha}$

$$\Rightarrow \quad m = \frac{\tan\beta}{\tan\alpha} \quad [\because \beta \text{ and } \alpha \text{ are small}]$$

$$\Rightarrow \quad m = \frac{\frac{A'B'}{C_2B'}}{\frac{A'B'}{C_1B'}} = \frac{C_1B'}{C_2B'} \Rightarrow m = \frac{f_o}{-u_e} \quad \ldots\text{(i)}$$

Using lens formula $\left(\frac{1}{v} - \frac{1}{u} = \frac{1}{f}\right)$ for the eyepiece, we have

$$\frac{1}{-D} - \frac{1}{-u_e} = \frac{1}{f_e}$$

$$\Rightarrow \quad \frac{1}{u_e} = \frac{1}{f_e} + \frac{1}{D} = \frac{1}{f_e}\left(1 + \frac{f_e}{D}\right)$$

Putting the value of $\frac{1}{u_e}$ in Eq. (i), we have

$$\boxed{m = -\frac{f_o}{f_e}\left(1 + \frac{f_e}{D}\right)}$$

Example 3 A telescope consists of two lenses of focal lengths 20 cm and 5 cm. Obtain its magnifying power when the final image is (i) at infinity (ii) at 25 cm from the eye.

Sol. (i) When the final image is at infinity,

$$m = -\frac{f_o}{f_e} = \frac{-20}{5}$$

$$\Rightarrow \quad m = -4$$

(ii) When the final image is at 25 cm from the eye, i.e. $D = 25$ cm,

$$m = \frac{-f_o}{f_e}\left(1 + \frac{f_e}{D}\right) = \frac{-20}{5}\left(1 + \frac{5}{25}\right)$$

$$\Rightarrow \quad m = -4.8$$

Reflecting Telescope

Reflecting telescope is also known as **Cassegrain Telescope**, which was designed by Guillaume Cassegrain, shown in figure below. Reflecting telescope is an improvement over refracting or astronomical telescope. To obtain a bright image of a distant star by refracting telescope, it is essential to have an objective of large aperture, so that it may collect more light coming from the object. But to deal with such a big lens is problem in terms of using and making and it is too costly. The same bright image of a distant object can be obtained by using a concave mirror of large aperture in place of objective.

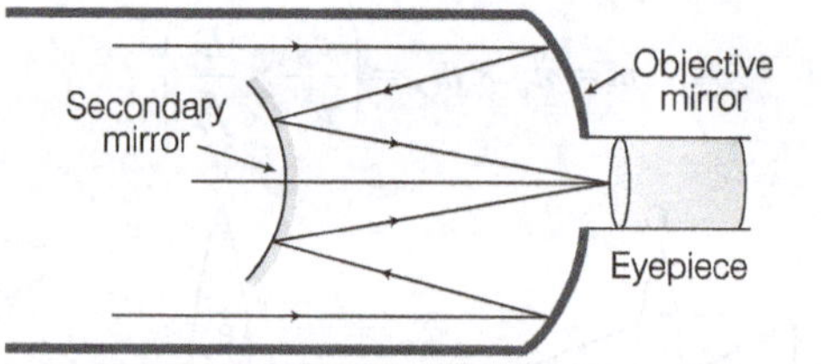

Reflecting telescope consists of concave mirror of large aperture and large focal length (objective). A convex mirror is placed between the concave mirror and its focus. A small convex lens works as eyepiece.In the reflecting telescope, parallel rays from a distant object are intercepted and focused by a reflecting concave mirror rather than a refracting lens. One popular configuration of mirror and eyepiece is called the Newtonian reflecting type telescope, named after its designer Newton.

The parallel beam of light coming from the distant object (star) is reflected by concave parabolic mirror M_1, on the plane mirror M_2. The plane mirror M_2 is inclined at an angle of 45° to axis of the mirror M_1.

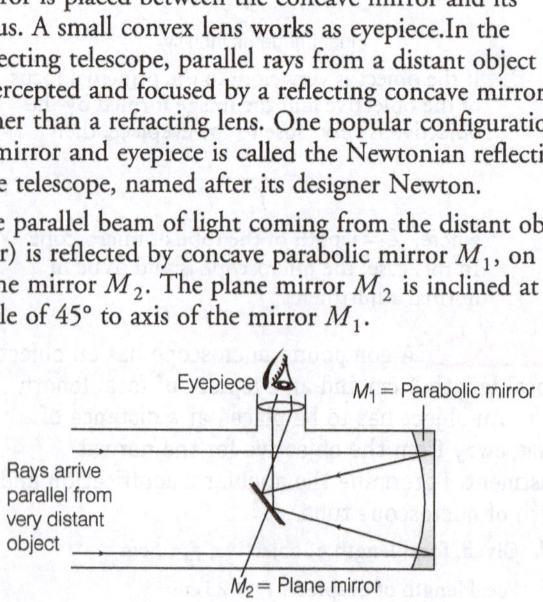

The plane mirror reflects the beam and a real image is formed in front of eyepiece. The eyepiece acts as a magnifier and the final magnified image of the distant object can be observed by the eye.

If f_0 is focal length of the concave spherical mirror and f_e be the focal length of eye-piece, the magnifying power of the reflecting telescope is $m = \frac{f_0}{f_e}$.

Advantages of Reflecting Telescope over Refracting Telescope

For astronomical telescope, the mirror affords several advantages over the objective lens. A mirror is easier to produce with a larger diameter, so that it can intercept rays crossing a larger area and direct them to the eyepiece. The mirror can be made parabolic to reduce spherical aberration. Aberration is further reduced because passage through one layer of glass (the objective lens) is eliminated.

Resolving Power of Optical Instrument

The ability of an instrument to produce distinctly separate images of two close objects is called resolving power of an optical instrument.

Resolving Power of a Microscope

It is defined as the reciprocal of the distance between two objects which can be just resolved when seen through the microscope.

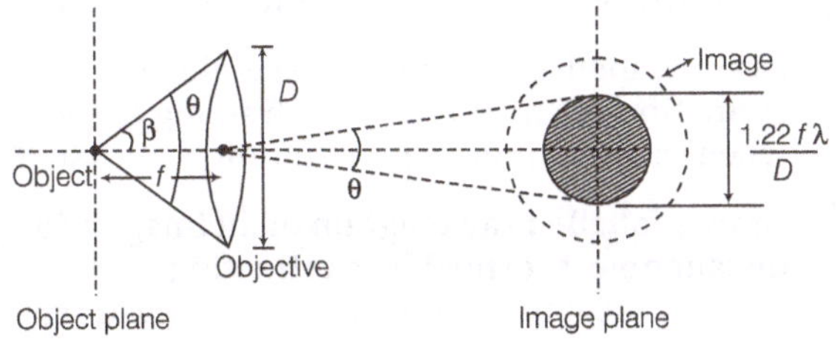

$$\text{Resolving power} = \frac{1}{\Delta d} = \frac{2\mu \sin \beta}{1.22\,\lambda}$$

where, $\mu \sin \beta$ = numerical aperture

Therefore, resolving power of a microscope depends on

(i) wavelength λ.

(ii) refractive index of the medium between the object and the objective.

(iii) half angle θ of the cone of light from one of the objects, i.e. β.

Example 4 Assume that light of wavelength 6000 Å is coming from a star. What is the limit of resolution of a telescope whose objective has a diameter of 100 inch?

Sol. The diameter of the objective, $D = 100$ inch = 254 cm

Wavelength of light, $\lambda = 6000\text{ Å} = 6 \times 10^{-5}$ cm

∴ Limit of resolution,

$$\Delta\theta \approx \frac{1.22\,\lambda}{D} = \frac{(1.22)(6 \times 10^{-5})}{254}$$

$$\approx 2.9 \times 10^{-7} \text{ rad}$$

Topic Practice 5

Multiple Choice Questions

1 Mark

1. If the focal length of objective lens is increased, then magnifying power of
   (a) microscope will increase but that of telescope decrease
   (b) microscope and telescope both will increase
   (c) microscope and telescope both will decrease
   (d) microscope will decrease but that of telescope will increase

2. A telescope consists of two thin lenses of focal lengths 0.3 m and 3 cm, respectively. It is focused on Moon which subtends an angle of 0.5° at the objective. Then, the angle subtended at the eye by the final image will be
   (a) 5° (b) 0.25°
   (c) 0.5° (d) 0.35°

3. An astronomical telescope has an angular magnification of magnitude 5 for distant objects. The separation between the objective and the eyepiece is 36 cm and the final image is formed at infinity. The focal length f_o of the objective and the focal length f_e of the eyepiece are
   (a) $f_o = 45$ cm and $f_e = -9$ cm
   (b) $f_o = -7.2$ cm and $f_e = 5$ cm
   (c) $f_o = 50$ cm and $f_e = 10$ cm
   (d) $f_o = 30$ cm and $f_e = 6$ cm

4. Advantage of reflecting telescopes are
   (a) no chromatic aberration
   (b) parabolic reflecting surfaces are used
   (c) weighs of mirror are much less than a lens of equivalent optical quality
   (d) All of the above

5. Choose the correct option. In an astronomical telescope of refracting type
(a) eyepiece has greater focal length
(b) objective has greater focal length
(c) objective and eyepiece have equal focal length
(d) eyepiece has greater aperture than the objective
ISC 2013

Very Short Answer Type Questions

1 Mark

6. What is meant by a microscope in normal use ? **ISC 2023**

7. Define the angular magnification of an optical instrument. **ISC 2004**

8. Why should the objective lens of a compound microscope have a small focal length?

9. How will you distinguish between a compound microscope and a telescope simply by seeing it?

10. State any one advantage of using a reflecting telescope in place of a refracting telescope. **ISC 2015**

11. Why all over the world, giant telescopes are of reflecting type? State any one reason. **ISC 2009**

12. Draw ray diagram to illustrate the formation of image at infinity in a refracting telescope. **ISC 2003**

Short Answer Type I Questions

2 Marks

13. What should be the position of the object relative to the biconvex lens, so that this lens behaves like a magnifying glass?

14. How does the magnification of a magnifying glass differ from its magnifying power?

15. Explain the statement: 'Angular magnification of a compound microscope in normal use is 30'. **ISC 2010**

16. (i) Define the magnifying power of a microscope in terms of visual angles.
(ii) What is the advantage of a compound microscope over a simple microscope? **ISC 2004**

17. Draw a schematic ray diagram of a compound microscope with the final image formed at infinity. **ISC 2000**

18. Draw a schematic arrangement of a reflecting telescope (Cassegrain) showing how rays coming from a distant object are received at the eyepiece. Write its two important advantages over a refracting telescope.

19. Draw a labelled ray diagram of an image formed by a compound microscope, when the final image lies at the least distance of distinct vision (D). **ISC 2015, 13, 11**

Short Answer Type II Questions

3 Marks

20. (i) Draw a neat labelled ray diagram of a compound microscope. Explain briefly its working.
(ii) Why must both the objective and the eyepiece of a compound microscope have short focal lengths?

21. Draw a ray diagram showing the image formation by a compound microscope. Hence, obtain the expression for total magnification, when the image is formed at infinity.

22. With the help of a ray diagram, obtain an expression for the magnifying power of a simple microscope, when the image is formed at the least distance of distinct vision. **ISC 2019, 07**

23. Derive the formula for angular magnification of a compound microscope, when the final image is formed at the least distance of distinct vision. Draw the required ray diagram. **ISC 2015**

24. Draw a labelled ray diagram showing the formation of an image by a refracting telescope when the final image lies at infinity. **ISC 2015**

25. Draw a labelled ray diagram of an image of a distant object formed by a refracting astronomical telescope in normal adjustment. Write (do not derive) an expression for its magnifying power. **ISC 2008**

26. (i) Draw a ray diagram to show how the image of a distant object is formed by a refracting astronomical telescope, when in normal use.
(ii) State one advantage of a reflecting astronomical telescope over a refracting astronomical telescope. **ISC 2006**

Long Answer Type Question

5 Marks

27. (i) Draw the ray diagram for the formation of image by a refracting telescope having the final image formed at infinity.
(ii) For refracting telescope, define the angular magnification and derive the formula for the same for image formed at infinity.
ISC 2002

28. *Read the passage given below and answer the question that follow.*
There are two types of lenses : Converging lenses and Diverging lenses, depending on whether they converge or diverge an incident beam of light. They are also called convex or concave lenses. Lenses are usually made of glass. Convex lenses are more popular as they form a real image of an object. They are widely used in our daily life, for instance, in microscopes, telescopes, projectors, cameras, spectacles, etc. Microscopes are used to view small and nearby objects whereas telescopes are used to see distant objects.
(i) State any one factor on which focal length of a lens depends.
(ii) Give an example where a convex lens behaves like a diverging lens.
(iii) What type of lens is used in a camera ?
(iv) Write an expression for magnifying power of a compound microscope when its final image lies at the least distance of distinct vision (D).
(v) State any one difference between reflecting telescope and a refracting telescope.
ISC 2023

Numerical Problems

29. The near vision of an average person is 25 cm. To view an object with an angular magnification of 10, what should be the power of the microscope? **NCERT Exemplar (2 M)**

30. You are given two converging lenses of focal length 1.25 cm and 5 cm to design a compound microscope. If it is desired to have a magnification of 30, then find out the separation between the objective and eyepiece. **(2 M)**

31. A compound microscope consists of two convex lenses having focal length of 1.5 cm and 5 cm. When an object is kept at a distance of 1.6 cm from the objective, the final image is virtual and lies at a distance of 25 cm from the eyepiece. Calculate magnifying power of the compound microscope in this set-up. **ISC 2020**

32. A convex lens of a focal length 5 cm is used as a simple microscope. Where should an object be placed, so that the image formed by it lies at the least distance of distinct vision ($D = 25$ cm)?
ISC 2015 (2 M)

33. A compound microscope consists of two convex lenses of focal lengths 2 cm and 5 cm. When an object is kept at a distance of 2.1 cm from the objective, a virtual and magnified image is formed 25 cm from the eyepiece. Calculate the magnifying power of the microscope. **ISC 2016 (3 M)**

34. A compound microscope consists of an objective of focal length 2 cm and an eyepiece of focal length 5 cm. When an object is kept 2.4 cm from the objective, final image formed is virtual and 25 cm from the eyepiece. Determine magnifying power of this compound microscope in this setup, i.e. in normal use.
ISC 2012 (3 M)

35. A convex lens of focal length 5 cm is to be used as a simple microscope. Where should an object be kept, so that image formed by the lens lies at least distance D of distinct vision ($D = 25$ cm)? Also, calculate the magnifying power of this instrument in this setup.
ISC 2009 (3 M)

36. In a compound microscope, it consists of two convex lenses of focal length 1.5 cm and 10 cm, the object is 2 cm from the objective and the final image is formed at the least distance of distinct vision ($D = 25$ cm). Find the distance of separation of the two lenses. **ISC 2008 (3 M)**

37. An astronomical telescope uses two lenses of powers 10 D and 1 D. If the final image of a distant object is formed at infinity, calculate the length of the telescope. **ISC 2014 (2 M)**

38. An astronomical telescope consists of two thin convex lenses having focal lengths of 140 cm and 5 cm. The telescope is adjusted to be in normal adjustment.
(i) What is the angular magnification, i.e. magnifying power of the telescope in this setup?
(ii) What is the distance between the two lenses equal to? **ISC 2011 (2 M)**

39. An astronomical telescope consists of two convex lenses having focal lengths 80 cm and 4 cm. When it is in normal adjustment, what is its

(i) length?

(ii) magnifying power? **ISC 2009 (2 M)**

40. An astronomical telescope is adjusted to form the final image at infinity. The separation between the lenses is 80 cm. The angular magnification is 15. Calculate the focal lengths of the objective lens and the eyepiece. **ISC 2007 (3 M)**

41. Define magnifying power of an optical instrument. An astronomical refracting telescope consists of two lenses of focal lengths 75 cm and 5 cm. Calculate the magnifying power of the telescope, when the final image is formed at a distance of 25 cm from the eye. **ISC 2005 (3 M)**

42. Consider a telescope whose objective lens has a focal length of 100 cm and the eyepiece has focal length 1 cm. What will be the magnification of the given telescope? **(1 M)**

43. Two lenses of focal lengths 6 cm and 50 cm are to be used for making a telescope. Which will you see for the objective? **(1 M)**

Hints & Solutions

1. (*d*) For microscope, $m = \frac{L}{f_0}\frac{D}{f_e}$

$\Rightarrow \quad m \propto \frac{1}{f_0}$

For telescope, $\quad m = \frac{f_0}{f_e},\ m \propto f_0$

The magnifying power of microscope will decrease but the magnifying power telescope will increase.

2. (*a*) For a telescope,

Angular magnification $= \frac{\beta}{\alpha} = \frac{f_o}{f_e}$

$\therefore \quad \frac{\beta}{0.5^\circ} = \frac{0.3}{0.03} \Rightarrow \beta = 5^\circ$

3. (*d*) For a telescope, $|m| = \frac{|f_o|}{|f_e|} = 5 \quad$ ...(i)

and length of the telescope,

$$L = |f_o| + |f_e| = 36 \quad \text{...(ii)}$$

From Eqs. (i) and (ii), we get

$$f_e = 6\,\text{cm} \quad \text{and} \quad f_o = 30\,\text{cm}$$

4. (*d*) Reflecting telescopes are used because of following advantages

(i) no chromatic aberration.

(ii) parabolic reflecting surfaces are used.

(iii) Weighs of mirror are much less than a lens of equivalent optical quality.

5. (*b*) In an astronomical telescope of refracting type, objective has greater focal length than eyepiece. Thus, option (b) is correct.

6. A microscope is an instrument that can be used to observe small objects, even cells.

7. Angular magnification of an optical instrument is defined as the ratio of the visual angle subtended by the image formed by the instrument at the eye to the visual angle subtended by the object at an unaided eye, i.e.

$$M = \frac{\beta}{\alpha}$$

8. The angular magnification of eyepiece is $\left(1 + \frac{d}{f_e}\right)$.

Hence, as f_e decreases angular magnification increases.

Also, the magnification of the object lens is $\frac{v}{u}$.

The object lies close the focus of the objective lens $u = f_o$. Therefore, to increase the magnification f_o should be small.

9. In compound microscope objective lens has smaller aperture and smaller focal length than the eyepiece, while in telescope, the objective has a larger aperture and larger focal length than the eyepiece.

10. Reflecting telescope removes chromatic and spherical aberration, high resolving power.

11. It has a large aperture due to which it gathers more light and brighter image is obtained.

12. Refer to text on page 373 (Astronomical (refracting) telescope case I diagram).

13. Whenever object is placed within the focus of the biconvex lens, we will obtain enlarged image, hence the biconvex lens behaves like a magnifying lens. (2)

14. The **magnification** of a magnifying glass depends upon, where it is placed between the user's eye and the object being viewed and the total distance between them, while the **magnifying power** is equivalent to angular magnification. (2)

15. The statement can be explained as the visual angle subtended on eye with telescope is 30 times more than the angle without telescope, when the object is at the least distance of distinct vision. (2)

16. (i) Refer to answer 7 on page 378. (1)

(ii) In a simple microscope, there is only one lens, whereas in a compound microscope, there are two lenses. Therefore, the magnifying power of a compound microscope is more than that of a simple microscope. (1)

17. Refer to text on page 373 (Case I : when the final image is formed at infinity).

18. Refer to text on pages 374 and 375 (Reflecting telescope and Advantages of reflecting telescope over refracting telescope).

19. Refer to text on pages 372 and 373 (Compound microscope, case I).

20. (i) Refer to text on pages 372 and 373 (Compound microscope). (1½)

(ii) f_o and f_e of compound microscope must be small, so as to have large magnifying power as

$$m = \frac{-1}{f_o}\left(1 + \frac{D}{f_e}\right)$$ (1½)

21. Refer to text on page 373 (Compound microscope, Case II).

22. Refer to text on page 371 (Simple microscope, Case I).

23. Refer to text on pages 372 and 373 (Compound microscope, case I).

24.

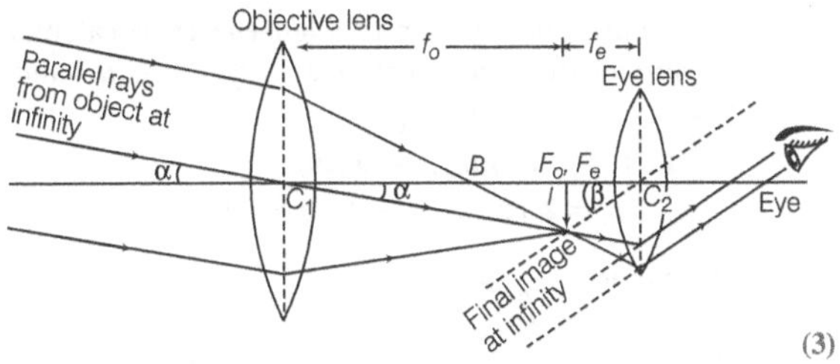

(3)

25. Refer to the text on pages 373 and 374 (Astronomical (refracting) telescope).

26. (i) Refer to the text on pages 373 and 374 (Astronomical (refracting) telescope). (1½)

(ii) In reflecting telescope, image formed is brighter, whereas in refracting telescope, due to absorption and refraction by objective lens some loss of light (intensity of light is lost) occurs, so image is not so bright. (1½)

27. (i) Refer to the text on pages 373 and 374 (Astronomical (refracting) telescope, case I). (3)

(ii) Refer to the text on pages 373 and 374 (Case I, when the final image is formed at infinity). (2)

28. (i) Focal length of a lens depends on the refractive index of the glass from which it is made and on the curvature of its surfaces.

(ii) A convex lens behaves like a diverging lens when it is kept in a transparent medium with greater refractive index than that of the lens. An air bubble in water behaves like a diverging lens.

(iii) Convex lens are widely used in cameras.

(iv) Refer to text on pages 372 and 373 (Compound microscope).

(v) Reflecting telescopes uses mirrors while refracting telescopes use lenses.

29. The least distance of distinct vision of an average person, (i.e. D) is 25 cm, in order to view an object with magnification of 10.

Here, $v = D = 25$ cm and $u = f$

But the magnification, $m = v/u = D/f$

$$\therefore \quad m = \frac{D}{f}$$

$$\Rightarrow \quad f = \frac{D}{m} = \frac{25}{10} = 2.5 = 0.025 \text{ m}$$ (1)

and $$P = \frac{1}{0.025} = 40 \text{ D} \qquad \left[\because P = \frac{1}{f}\right]$$

This is the required power of lens . (1)

30. Given, $f_o = 1.25$ cm, $f_e = -5$ cm

Magnification, $m = 30$, $D = 25$ cm

If the object is very close to the principal focus of the objective and the image formed by the objective is very close to eyepiece, then magnifying power of a microscope is given by

$$m = -\frac{L}{f_o}\cdot\frac{D}{f_e}$$

$$\Rightarrow \quad 30 = \frac{L}{1.25}\cdot\frac{25}{5}$$ (1)

$$\Rightarrow \quad L = \frac{125 \times 30 \times 5}{25 \times 100}$$

$$\Rightarrow \quad L = \frac{25 \times 30}{100} \Rightarrow L = \frac{30}{4}$$

$$\Rightarrow \quad L = 7.5 \text{ cm}$$

This is a required separation between the objective and the eyepiece. (1)

31. Given, $f_o = 1.5$ cm, $f_e = 5$ cm

$u_o = -1.6$ cm and $v_e = 25$ cm

For the objective lens, $\frac{1}{f_o} = \frac{1}{v_o} - \frac{1}{u_o}$

$$\frac{1}{v_o} = \frac{1}{f_o} + \frac{1}{u_o} = \frac{1}{1.5} - \frac{1}{1.6}$$

$$\frac{1}{v_o} = \frac{10}{16 \times 15}$$

$$v_o = \frac{16 \times 15}{10} = \frac{240}{10} = 24 \text{ cm}$$

Now, magnification, i.e. magnifying power of the microscope,

$$m = -\frac{v_o}{u_o}\left(1 + \frac{D}{f_e}\right) = -\frac{24}{1.6}\left(1 + \frac{25}{5}\right) = -90$$

32. According to the question, focal length of convex lens $(f) = 5$ cm

i.e. $\quad f = +5$ cm

Image distance $(v) = -D = -25$ cm

Now, from thin lens formula,

$$\frac{1}{v} - \frac{1}{u} = \frac{1}{f}$$

So, $\frac{1}{u} = \frac{1}{v} - \frac{1}{f}$ (1)

$$\Rightarrow \quad u = \frac{vf}{f - v} = \frac{-25 \times 5}{5 - (-25)}$$

$$= \frac{-25 \times 5}{30} = -4.2 \text{ cm}$$ (1)

33. Here, $f_0 = 2$ cm, $f_e = 5$ cm, $u_0 = 2.1$ cm, $v_e = 25$ cm, $v_0 = ?$

For the objective lens, $\frac{1}{f_0} = \frac{1}{v_0} - \frac{1}{u_0}$

$$\Rightarrow \quad \frac{1}{v_0} = \frac{1}{f_0} + \frac{1}{u_0} = \frac{1}{2} + \left(\frac{1}{-2.1}\right)$$

$$\Rightarrow \quad \frac{1}{v_0} = \frac{0.1}{4.2}$$

$$\Rightarrow \quad v_0 = 42 \text{ cm}$$ (1½)

Now, magnification, i.e. magnifying power of the microscope,

$$M = \frac{v_0}{u_0}\left(1 + \frac{D}{f_e}\right)$$

$$= \frac{42}{2.1}\left(1 + \frac{25}{5}\right) = 20(6) = 120$$ (1½)

34. According to the question,

Given, object distance of objective lens,

$u_0 = 2.4$ cm, $D = 25$ cm

Focal length of eyepiece, $f_e = 5$ cm

Focal length of objective, $f_0 = 2$ cm

Image distance of objective lens, $v_0 = ?$

Applying lens formula, for objective,

$$\frac{1}{v_0} - \frac{1}{u_0} = \frac{1}{f_0}$$

$$\Rightarrow \quad \frac{1}{v_0} = \frac{1}{f_0} + \frac{1}{u_0} = \frac{1}{2} - \frac{1}{2.4} = \frac{1.2 - 1}{2.4}$$

$$\Rightarrow \quad \frac{1}{v_0} = \frac{0.2}{2.4} = \frac{2}{24} = \frac{1}{12}$$

$$\Rightarrow \quad v_0 = 12 \text{ cm}$$ (1½)

Magnifying power, $M = \frac{-v_0}{u_0}\left(1 + \frac{D}{f_e}\right) = \frac{-12}{-2.4}\left(1 + \frac{25}{5}\right)$

$$= 5 \times (6) = 30$$

$$\Rightarrow \quad M = 30$$

The final image in each case is virtual and erect. (1½)

35. When final image formed by a simple microscope, is at the least distance of distinct vision (D), the magnifying power is $M = 1 + \frac{D}{f}$.

Given, $f = 5$ cm, $D = -25$ cm

By lens formula, $\frac{1}{f} = \frac{1}{v} - \frac{1}{u}$ (1)

$$\Rightarrow \quad \frac{1}{u} = \frac{1}{v} - \frac{1}{f} = -\frac{1}{25} - \frac{1}{5}$$

$$= \frac{-1 - 5}{25} = \frac{-6}{25}$$

$$\therefore \quad u = \frac{-25}{6} = -4.166 \text{ cm}$$

$$= -4.17 \text{ cm}$$ (1)

Magnifying power of a simple microscope,

$$M = 1 + \frac{D}{f} = 1 + \frac{25}{5} = 6$$ (1)

36. The separation between two lenses can be calculated by the sum of the object distance of eyepiece (u_e) and image distance of objective (v_0).

Given, $f_0 = 1.5$ cm, $f_e = 10$ cm,

$u_0 = 2$ cm, $v_e = -25$ cm $= D$

For eyepiece, $\frac{1}{f_e} = \frac{1}{v_e} - \frac{1}{u_e}$

$$\Rightarrow \quad \frac{1}{u_e} = \frac{1}{v_e} - \frac{1}{f_e} = -\frac{1}{25} - \frac{1}{10} = -\frac{7}{50}$$

$$\Rightarrow \quad u_e = -7.14 \text{ cm}$$ (1)

For objective,

$$\frac{1}{v_0} = \frac{1}{u_0} + \frac{1}{f_0} = -\frac{1}{2} + \frac{1}{1.5} = \frac{-3 + 4}{6} = \frac{1}{6}$$

$$\Rightarrow \quad v_0 = 6 \text{ cm}$$ (1)

Distance of separation

$$= v_0 + u_e = (6 + 7.14) = 13.14 \text{ cm}$$ (1)

37. We can write power,

$$P = \frac{100}{f \text{ (in cm)}} \Rightarrow f = \frac{100}{P}$$

$$\therefore \quad f_1 = \frac{100}{10} = 10 \text{ cm} \Rightarrow f_2 = \frac{100}{1} = 100 \text{ cm}$$ (1)

Length of telescope $= f_1 + f_2 = 110$ cm (1)

38. According to the question,

Given, $f_o = 140$ cm, $f_e = 5$ cm

(i) Angular magnification,

$$M = \frac{-f_o}{f_e} = \frac{-140}{5} = -28$$ (1)

(ii) Distance between the lenses,

$$L = f_o + f_e = 140 + 5 = 145 \text{ cm}$$ (1)

39. Given, $f_o = 80$ cm, $f_e = 4$ cm

(i) Length of the telescope = $f_o + f_e = 84$ cm (1)

(ii) Magnifying power,

$$M = \frac{-f_o}{f_e} = \frac{-80}{4} = -20$$ (1)

40. Let f_o and f_e are the focal lengths of the objective and the eyepiece, respectively. When final image is at infinity,

Given, $L = f_o + f_e = 80\text{ cm}$, $M = 15$, $M = \frac{f_o}{f_e}$

$\Rightarrow \quad f_o = 15 f_e, L = f_o + f_e$ ...(i) (1½)

Putting the values of f_o and L in Eq. (i), we get

$$80 = 15 f_e + f_e, \quad f_e = 5 \text{ cm}$$

So, $f_o = 15 f_e = 15 \times 5, \quad f_o = 75$ cm (1½)

41. Magnifying power of the optical instrument The magnifying power or the angular magnification of an optical instrument is defined as the ratio of the angle subtended by the image at the eye to the angle subtended by the object at the unaided eye. (2)

Magnifying power of the telescope,

$$M = \frac{f_o}{f_e}\left(1 + \frac{f_e}{D}\right) = \frac{75}{5}\left(1 + \frac{5}{25}\right) = 18$$ (1)

42. Magnification of telescope is given by

$$m = \frac{f_o}{f_e} = \frac{100}{1} = 100$$

43. Yes, these lenses can be used for making a telescope. Since, the objective lens has large aperture and focal length, hence the lens having focal length will be used as objective lens.

SUMMARY

- **Reflection of Light** It is the phenomenon of change in the path of light without any change in medium.
- **Laws of Reflection** Incident ray, reflected ray and the normal to the reflecting surface at the point of incidence, all lies in the same plane. Angle of incidence is always equal to the angle of reflection.
- **Mirror formula** is given by, $\frac{1}{v}+\frac{1}{u}=\frac{1}{f}$.
- **Linear Magnification** The ratio of size of the image formed by the spherical mirror to the size of the object is called linear magnification, i.e. $m=\frac{I}{O}=\frac{-v}{u}$
- **Refraction** It is the phenomenon of change in the path of light as it goes from one medium to another medium.
- **Laws of Refraction** Incident ray, refracted ray and the normal to the refracting surface at the point of incidence, all lies in the same plane.

  According to second law, $(\sin i / \sin r) = {}_1\mu_2$. This is called Snell's law of refraction.
- **Refractive Index** It is equal to the ratio of speed of light in vacuum to the speed of light in the material.
- **Principle of Reversibility of Light** When a light rays, after suffering any number of reflections and refractions, its final path is reversed and it travels back along its entire initial path.
- **Expression for Lateral Displacement**

$$D=\frac{t \sin(i_i - r_i)}{\cos r_1}$$

- **Apparent Depth and Real Depth**

$${}^{a}\mu_{w}=\frac{\text{Real depth}}{\text{Apparent depth}}$$

- **Critical Angle** The angle of incidence in denser medium corresponding to which angle of refraction in rarer medium is 90°.
- **Total Internal Reflection** (TIR) The ray on the interface of two media should travel in the denser medium. The angle of incidence should be greater than the critical angle for the two media.
- **Refraction at Spherical Surfaces** The equation which holds the good for any curved spherical surface is given by $\frac{n_2}{v}-\frac{n_1}{u}=\frac{n_2-n_1}{R}$
- **Lens** It is a transparent medium bounded by two surfaces of which one or both surfaces are spherical. It is of two types.

  Convex lens is thicker at the centre and thinner at its end.

  Concave lens is thinner at the centre and thicker at its end.
- **Lens formula** $\frac{1}{v}-\frac{1}{u}=\frac{1}{f}$
- **Lens Maker's formula** $\frac{1}{f}=(\mu-1)\left(\frac{1}{R_1}-\frac{1}{R_2}\right)$
- **Power of a Lens** It is the ability to converge or diverge the rays of incident light.

$$P=\frac{1}{f}$$

Also, $$P=(\mu-1)\left(\frac{1}{R_1}-\frac{1}{R_2}\right)$$

- **Prism** A prism is a portion of transparent medium bounded by two plane faces inclined to each other at a suitable angle.
- **Refraction of Light through a Prism** The relation between angle of deviation and angle of prism is $\delta=(\mu-1)A$.
- **Prism Formula** It is given by, $\mu=\frac{\sin\left[\frac{A+\delta_m}{2}\right]}{\sin\left[\frac{A}{2}\right]}$
- **Angle of minimum deviation** $\delta_m=(\mu-1)A$
- **Simple Microscope** It forms the large image of close and minute objects. It is a converging lens of small focal length.
- **Compound Microscope** It consists of two convex lenses coaxially separated by some distance. One is objective and another is eyepiece.
- **Astronomical Telescope** It has two convex lenses coaxially separated by some distance, which is used for observing distinct images of heavenly by bodies like stars, planet, etc.
- **Refracting and Reflecting Telescope** Refracting telescope is used for observing the distinct images of heavenly bodies like stars, planets, etc.

  Reflecting telescope is an improvement over refracting telescope.
- **Resolving power of a microscope** $=\frac{2\mu\sin\beta}{1.22\,\lambda}$

For Mind Map

Visit : https://goo.gl/XruCAg OR **Scan the Code**

Chapter Practice

Multiple Choice Questions

1 Mark

1 The plano-convex lens of focal length 20 cm and 30 cm are placed together to from a double convex lens. The final focal length will be

(a) 12 cm
(b) 60 cm
(c) 20 cm
(d) 30 cm

2 At what angle should a ray of light be incident on the face of a prism of refracting angle 60°, so that it just suffers total internal reflection at the other face? The refractive index of the material of the prism is 1.524.

(a) 30°75′
(b) 29°75′
(c) 28°75′
(d) 27°75′

3 The image of a small electric bulb fixed on the wall to a room is to be obtained on the opposite wall 3 m away by means of a large convex lens. What is the maximum possible focal length of the lens required for the purpose?

(a) 3 m
(b) 0.75 m
(c) 0.45 m
(d) 0.25 m

4 A small pin fixed on a table top is viewed from above from a distance of 50 cm. By what distance would the pin appear to be raised, if it is viewed from the same point through a 15 cm thick glass slab held parallel to the table? Refractive index of glass = 1.5. Does the answer depend on the location of the slab?

(a) 5 cm, yes
(b) 5 cm, no
(c) 10 cm, data insufficient
(d) None of the above

5 A screen is placed 90 cm from an object, the image of the object on the screen is formed by a convex lens at two different locations separated by 20 cm. Determine the focal length of the lens.

(a) 20.5 cm
(b) 19.5 cm
(c) 23.2 cm
(d) 21.4 cm

6 For a normal eye, the far point is at infinity and the near point of distinct vision is about 25 cm infront of the eye. The cornea of the eye provides a converging power of about 40 D and the least converging power of the eyelens behind the cornea is about 20 D. From this rough data estimate the range of accommodation (i.e. range of converging power of its eyelens) of a normal eye.

(a) 20-24 D
(b) 18-22 D
(c) 64-68 D
(d) 35-40 D

7 A person with a normal near point 25 cm using a compound microscope with an objective of focal length 8.0 mm and eyepiece of focal length 2.5 cm can bring an object placed at
9.0 mm from the objective in sharp focus. What is the separation between the two lenses? How much is the magnifying power of the microscope?

(a) 7.2, 89
(b) 9.4, 88
(c) 8.6, 90
(d) 9.4, 75

8 A man with normal near point (25 cm) reads a book with small print using a magnifying glass: a thin convex lens of focal length 5 cm. What is the closest and the farthest distance at which he can read the book when viewing through the magnifying glass?

(a) – 4.2 cm, – 5 cm
(b) 4.2 cm, 5 cm
(c) – 4.2 cm, 5 cm
(b) 4.2 cm, – 5 cm

9 A giant refracting telescope at an observatory has an objective lens of focal length 15 m. If an eyepiece of focal length 1.0 cm is used, what is angular magnification of the telescope?

(a) 1200
(b) 1000
(c) 1300
(d) 1500

10 A small telescope has an objective lens of focal length 144 cm and an eyepiece of focal length 6.0 cm. What is the magnifying power of the telescope? What is the separation between the objective and the eyepiece?

(a) – 24, 150 cm
(b) – 25, 150 cm
(c) – 24, 160 cm
(d) – 25, 160 cm

Assertion and Reason

Directions (Q. Nos. 11-15) *In the following questions, two statements are given- one labelled Assertion (A) and the other labelled Reason (R). Select the correct answer to these questions from the codes (a), (b), (c) and (d) as given below*

(a) Both Assertion and Reason are true and Reason is the correct explanation of Assertion.
(b) Both Assertion and Reason are true but Reason is not the correct explanation of Assertion.
(c) Assertion is true but Reason is false.
(d) Assertion is false but Reason is true.

11 **Assertion** For a simple microscope, the angular size of the object equals the angular size of the image.

Reason Magnification is achieved as the small object can be kept much closer to the eye than 25 cm and hence, it subtends a large angle.

12 **Assertion** A convex mirror is preferred over a plane mirror in vehicles to observe traffic coming from behind.

Reason Images formed by convex mirrors are erect and diminished in size.

13 **Assertion** The radius of curvature of a mirror is double of the focal length.

Reason A concave mirror of focal length f in air is used in a medium of refractive index 2, then the focal length of mirror in medium becomes $2f$.

14 **Assertion** Optical fibres make use of total internal reflection.

Reason Light undergoes sucessive total internal reflections as it moves through an optical fibre.

15 **Assertion** Angle of deviation depends on the angle of prism.

Reason For thin prism, $\delta = (\mu - 1)A$.

Very Short Answer Type Questions

1 Mark

16 At what angle, is a ray of light falling normally on a mirror reflected?

17 Does size of mirror affect the nature of the image?

18 Why does a convex lens of glass $\mu = 1.5$ behave as a diverging lens when immersed in carbon disulphide of $\mu = 1.65$?

Short Answer Type I Questions

2 Marks

19 Where should an object be placed from a convex lens to form an image of the same size? Can it happen in case of a concave lens?

20 A 4 cm tall light bulb is placed at a distance of 8.30 cm from a double convex lens having a focal length of 15.2 cm. Calculate the position and size of the image of the bulb.

Short Answer Type II Questions

3 Marks

21 Minimum deviation suffered by violet, yellow and red beams passing through an equilateral transparent prism are 39.2°, 38.7° and 38.4°, respectively. Calculate the dispersive power in the medium.

22 A beam of light strikes a glass sphere of diameter 15 cm converging towards a point 30 cm behind the pole of the spherical surface. Find the position of the image, if μ of glass is 1.5.

Long Answer Type Questions

5 Marks

23 (i) Explain with reason, how the power of a diverging lens changes when (a) it is kept in a medium of refractive index greater than that of the lens. (b) incident red light is replaced by violet light.

(ii) Three lenses L_1, L_2 and L_3 each of focal length 30 cm are placed coaxially as shown in the figure. An object is held at 60 cm from the optic centre of lens L_1. The final real image is formed at the focus of L_3. Calculate the separation between (a) (L_1 and L_2) and (b) (L_2 and L_3).

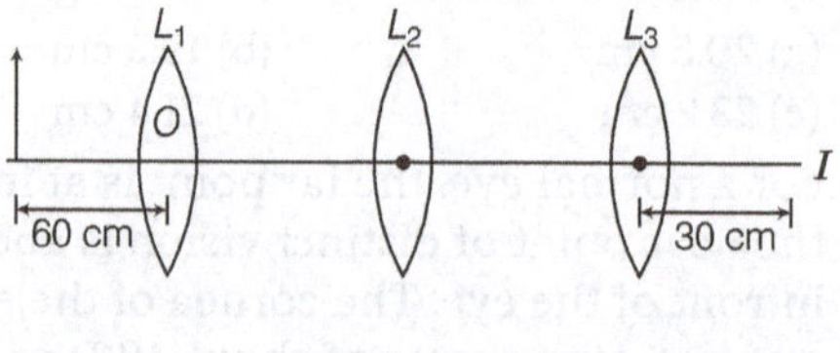

24 (i) Deduce the expression by drawing a suitable ray diagram for the refractive index of a triangular glass prism in terms of the angle of minimum deviation (D) and the angle of prism (A).

Draw a plot showing the variation of the angle of deviation with the angle of incidence.

(ii) Calculate the value of the angle of incidence when a ray of light incident on one face of an equilateral glass prism produces the emergent ray, which just grazes along the adjacent face. Refractive index of the prism is $\sqrt{2}$.

Case Based Questions

Directions (Q. No. 25) *These questions are case study based questions. Read the following paragraph and answer the questions.*

25. Refractive Index

The refractive index or index of refraction μ of a material is the ratio of the speed of light (c) in vacuum to the speed of light in the medium (v).

Mathematically, refractive index is given by the relation

$$\mu = \frac{\text{Speed of light in the vacuum / air}}{\text{Speed of light in the material}} = \frac{c}{v} = \frac{\sin i}{\sin r}$$

It is also referred as absolute refractive index of the substance.

Relative refractive index is a measure of how much light bends, when it travels from one medium to another medium.

If light travels from optical rarer medium to optical denser medium, then it bends towards the normal, i.e. $i > r$. On the other hand, if light travels from optical denser medium to optical rarer medium, then light bends away from the normal, i.e. $i < r$.

(i) When monochromatic light travels from one medium to another, its wavelength changes but frequency remains same. Explain.

(ii) For the same value of angle of incidence, the angles of refraction in three media A, B and C are 15°, 25° and 35°, respectively. In which medium, would the velocity of light be minimum?

(iii) A ray of light strikes on air-glass interface at an angle of incidence ($\angle i = 60°$) and gets refracted at an angle of refraction ($\angle r$). What will happen to the angle of refraction on increasing the angle of incidence?

(iv) What is the speed of light in the glass of refractive index 1.5? (Given, speed of light in air is 3×10^8 m/s).

Answers

1 (*a*) Given, $f_1 = +20$ cm, $f_2 = +30$ cm

So, for equivalent focal length,

$$\frac{1}{f} = \frac{1}{f_1} + \frac{1}{f_2} \Rightarrow \frac{1}{f} = \frac{1}{20} + \frac{1}{30}$$

$$\therefore \quad f = \frac{20 \times 30}{20 + 30} = \frac{600}{50} = 12 \text{ cm}$$

2 (*b*) Angle of prism, $A = 60°$

Refractive index of prism, $\mu = 1.524$

Let i be the angle of incidence. The critical angle is i_c, because it just suffers total internal refraction, so we use critical angle,

$$\sin i_C = \frac{1}{\mu} = \frac{1}{1.524} = 0.6561 \Rightarrow i_C = 41°$$

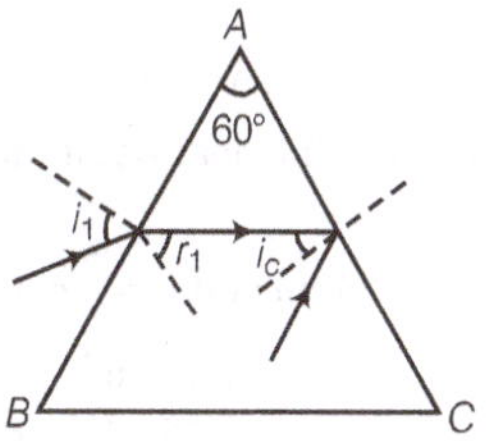

For a prism $r_1 + r_2 = A$, here $r_2 = i_c$

$\therefore \quad r_1 + i_C = A \Rightarrow r_1 + 41° = 60° \Rightarrow r_1 = 19°$

Using the formula, $\mu = \dfrac{\sin i_1}{\sin r_1}$

or $\sin i_1 = 1.524 \sin 19° = 1.524 \times 0.3256$

or $\quad i_1 = \sin^{-1}(0.4962)$

$\Rightarrow \quad i_1 = 29°75'$

Thus, the angle should be 29°75′.

3 (*b*) The minimum distance between an object and its real image is $4f$.

$$\therefore \quad 4f_{\max} = D \text{ or } f_{\max} = \frac{D}{4} = \frac{3\text{ m}}{4} = 0.75 \text{ m}$$

4 (*b*) Given, thickness of glass slab (real depth) = 15 cm

Refractive index of glass ${}^a\mu_g$ with respect to air = 1.5

Using the formula ${}^a\mu_g = \dfrac{\text{Real depth}}{\text{Apparent depth}} = \dfrac{15}{{}^a\mu_g}$

Apparent depth of pin $y = \frac{15}{1.5} = 10$ cm

Distance by which the pin appears to be raised

$= \text{Real depth} - \text{Apparent depth} = 15 - 10 = 5$ cm

The answer does not depend on the location of the slab.

5 (*d*) As shown in figure, let O and I be the positions of object and image respectively and L_1 and L_2 be the two conjugate positions of the lens.

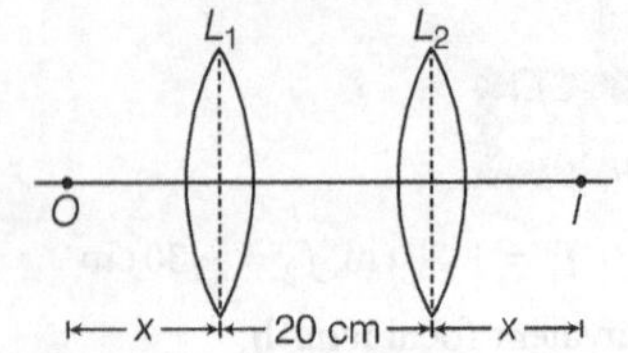

Obviously, $x + 20 + x = 90$ cm or $x = 35$ cm

When the lens is in position L_1, we have

$$u = -x = -35 \text{ cm}, \; v = 20 + x = 20 + 35 = 55 \text{ cm}$$

$$\therefore \quad \frac{1}{f} = \frac{1}{v} - \frac{1}{u} = \frac{1}{55} + \frac{1}{35} = \frac{7+11}{385} = \frac{18}{385}$$

or $\quad f = \frac{385}{18} = 21.4$ cm

6 (*a*) To see objects at infinity, the eye uses its least converging power $= 40 + 20 = 60$ D

$\therefore$ Approximate distance between the retina and the cornea eyelens = focal length of the eyelens

$$= \frac{100}{P} = \frac{100}{60} = \frac{5}{3} \text{ cm}$$

To focus an object at the near point on the retina, we have

$$u = -25 \text{ cm and } v = \frac{5}{3} \text{ cm}$$

$\therefore$ Focal length f should be given by

$$\frac{1}{f} = \frac{1}{v} - \frac{1}{u} = \frac{3}{5} + \frac{1}{25} = \frac{15+1}{25} = \frac{16}{25} \Rightarrow f = \frac{25}{16} \text{ cm}$$

Corresponding converging power = 64 D.

Power of the eyelens = 64 − 40 = 24 D

Thus, the range of accommodation of the eyelens is roughly 20 to 24 D.

7 (*b*) Here, $f_0 = 0.8$ cm, $u_0 = -0.9$ cm, $v_0 = ?$

As, $\frac{1}{v_0} - \frac{1}{u_0} = \frac{1}{f_0}$

$$\therefore \quad \frac{1}{v_0} = \frac{1}{f_0} + \frac{1}{u_0} = \frac{1}{0.8} - \frac{1}{0.9} = \frac{0.9 - 0.8}{0.9 \times 0.8} = \frac{0.1}{0.8 \times 0.9}$$

or $\quad v_0 = \frac{0.8 \times 0.9}{0.1} = 7.2$ cm

Now, for the eyepiece, we have

$$f_e = 2.5 \text{ cm}, \; v_e = -D = -25 \text{ cm}, \; u_e = ?$$

$$\therefore \quad \frac{1}{u_e} = \frac{1}{v_e} - \frac{1}{f_e} = -\frac{1}{25} - \frac{1}{2.5} = \frac{-1-10}{25} = \frac{-11}{25}$$

or $\quad u_e = -\frac{25}{11} = -2.27$ cm

Hence the separation between the to lenses

$= v_0 + |u_e| = 7.2 + 2.27 = 9.47$ cm

Magnifying power,

$$m = m_0 \times m_e = \frac{v_0}{|v_0|}\left(1 + \frac{D}{f_e}\right) = \frac{7.2}{0.9}\left(1 + \frac{25}{2.5}\right) = 88$$

8 (*a*) For the closest distance, $v = -25$ cm, $f = 5$ cm, $u = ?$

As $\quad \frac{1}{v} - \frac{1}{u} = \frac{1}{f}$

$$\therefore \quad \frac{1}{u} = \frac{1}{v} - \frac{1}{f} = \frac{1}{-25} - \frac{1}{5} = \frac{-1-5}{25} = \frac{-6}{25}$$

or $\quad u = -\frac{25}{6}$ cm $= -4.2$ cm

This is the closest distance at which the man can read the book.

For the farthest image

$$v = \infty, \; f = 5 \text{ cm}, \; u = ?$$

$$\therefore \quad \frac{1}{u} = \frac{1}{v} - \frac{1}{f} = \frac{1}{\infty} - \frac{1}{5} = 0 - \frac{1}{5} = -\frac{1}{5}$$

$$u = -5 \text{ cm}$$

This is the farthest distance at which the man can read the book.

9 (*d*) Here, $f_0 = 15$ cm, $f_e = 1.0$ cm $= 0.01$ m

Angular magnification, $m = \frac{f_0}{f_e} = \frac{15}{0.01} = 1500$

10 (*a*) Given, focal length of objective lens, $f_o = 144$ cm

Focal length of eyepiece, $f_e = 6$ cm

Magnifying power of the telescope in normal adjustment (i.e. when the final image is formed at ∞),

$$m = -\frac{f_o}{f_e} = -\frac{144}{6} = -24$$

$\therefore$ Separation between lenses, $L = f_o + f_e = 144 + 6 = 150$ cm

11 (*c*) The formation of image with simple microscope is shown below.

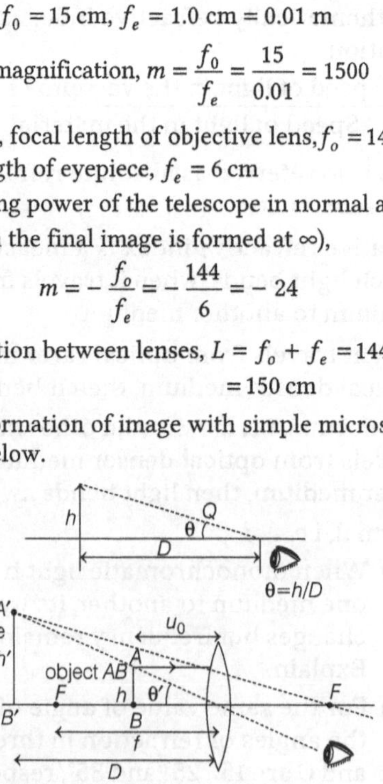

Here, $\theta' = \frac{h}{u_0} = \frac{h'}{D} = \frac{h'}{25}$

where, $D = 25$ cm (least distance of distinct vision)

Here, θ' is same for both object and image, hence Assertion is true.

Magnification, $m = \frac{\theta'}{\theta} = \frac{D}{u_0}$

Hence, if $u_0 < D$ (25 cm), hence the value of θ' will obtain large.

So, option (c) is the correct.

12 (*a*) A convex mirror produces smaller images which increases the field of view as compared to a plane mirror of the same size. Also in case of convex mirror, the image is erect like in plane mirror.

13 (*c*) Focal length of a mirror does not depend on the medium in which mirror is held. It depends on the radius of the sphere from which it is made. However, focal length of a lens depends on medium.

14 (*b*) Optical fibres are fabricated with high quality composite glass or quartz fibers. Each fibre consists of a core and cladding. The refractive index of the material of the core is higher than that of the cladding.

When a signal in the form of light is directed at one end of the fibre at a suitable angle, it undergoes repeated total internal reflections along the length of the fibre and finally comes out at the other end.

15 For a thin prism, the relation between angle of deviation δ, angle of prism A and refractive index μ is $\delta = (\mu - 1)A$.

16 A ray of light which is incident normally on a mirror, is reflected along the same path, i.e. the angle of incidence as well as the angle of reflection is zero.

17 Nature of the image is independent of the size of image. Image can be real or virtual depending upon the position of object.

18 Here, $\mu = \frac{\mu_g}{\mu_c} = \frac{1.5}{1.65} < 1$

$\therefore \quad \frac{1}{f} = (\mu - 1)\left(\frac{1}{R_1} - \frac{1}{R_2}\right)$ Hence, it becomes negative.

So, it behaves like a diverging lens.

19 The image of an object situated at $2f$ is also obtained at the same distance l of same size on other side of the convex lens. No, it cannot be possible in case of concave lens as it forms only diminished and enlarged images.

20
$$\frac{1}{f} = \frac{1}{d_o} + \frac{1}{d_i}$$

$$\Rightarrow \quad \frac{1}{15.2} = \frac{1}{8.30} + \frac{1}{d_i}$$

$$0.0658 = 0.120 + \frac{1}{d_i}$$

$$\Rightarrow \quad -0.0547 = \frac{1}{d_i} \Rightarrow -18.3 \text{ cm} = d_i$$

Also here, $\quad d_i = -18.3$ cm

$$\therefore \quad \frac{h_i}{h_o} = \frac{-d_i}{d_o}$$

$$\Rightarrow \quad \frac{h_i}{(4.00)} = -\frac{(-18.3)}{8.30}$$

$$h_i = \frac{-(4.00)\cdot(-18.3)}{8.30}$$

$$h_i = 8.81 \text{ cm}$$

21 $\therefore$ Dispersive power $= \frac{\mu_v - \mu_r}{\mu_y - 1} = \frac{\left(\frac{\delta_v}{A}\right) - \left(\frac{\delta_r}{A}\right)}{\left(\frac{\delta_y}{A}\right)}$ $\quad [\because \delta = (\mu - 1)A]$

$$= \frac{39.2 - 38.4}{38.7} = 0.0204$$

22 Here, $\mu_1 = 1, \mu_2 = 1.5, u = -\infty, R = \frac{15}{2} = 7.5$ cm

$\therefore$ Using $\frac{\mu_2}{v} - \frac{\mu_1}{u} = \frac{\mu_2 - \mu_1}{R}$

$$\Rightarrow \quad \frac{1.5}{v} - \frac{1}{(-\infty)} = \frac{1.5 - 1}{7.5} \Rightarrow v = 22.5 \text{ cm}$$

23 (i) The power of a lens is given by

$$P = \frac{1}{f} = (\mu - 1)\left(\frac{1}{R_1} - \frac{1}{R_2}\right)$$

For a diverging lens, f = –ve, therefore power is also negative

$$P = -(\mu - 1)\left(\frac{1}{R_1} - \frac{1}{R_2}\right)$$

(a) When lens is kept in a medium of refractive index greater than that of lens, then $(\mu - 1)$ becomes negative, thus, power of lens becomes positive and a diverging lens will behaves like a converging lens.

(b) The refractive index of the material of a lens increases with the decrease in wavelength of the incident light. So, the focal length will decrease with decrease in wavelength and thus, the power will increase, when a ray of red light is replaced by violet light.

(ii) For lens L_1, $\frac{1}{f} = \frac{1}{v} - \frac{1}{u}$

where, $f = \pm 30$ cm,

$u = -60$ cm

and $\quad v = 60$ cm

For lens L_3, $\frac{1}{f''} = \frac{1}{v''} - \frac{1}{u''}$,

where, $f'' = +30$ cm, $u'' = \infty$ and $v'' = +30$ cm

Thus, the refracted ray from lens L_2 becomes parallel to principal axis. So, the image formed by L_1 lies at first focus of L_2, i.e. 30 cm from L_2.

(a) Distance between L_1 and $L_2 = 60 + 30 = 90$ cm

(b) Distance between L_2 and L_3 may take any value.

24 (i) Refer to text on pages 346 and 347 (Deviation produced by a prism and prism formula)

(ii) Given, the emergent ray grazes along the face AC,

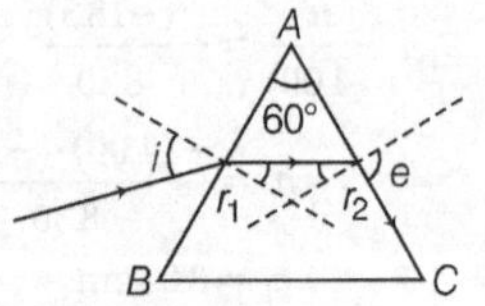

$e = 90°$

$\mu = \sqrt{2}$

$$\frac{\sin i}{\sin r_1} = \mu = \frac{\sin e}{\sin r_2}$$

$$\Rightarrow \quad \frac{\sin 90°}{\sin r_2} = \sqrt{2}$$

i.e. $\sin r_2 = \frac{1}{\sqrt{2}}$ or $r_2 = 45°$

$$\Rightarrow \quad r_1 + r_2 = \angle A = 60°$$

$$r_1 = 60 - r_2 = 15°$$

$$\Rightarrow \quad \frac{\sin i}{\sin 15°} = \sqrt{2}$$

$$\Rightarrow \quad i = 21.47°$$

25 (i) Because refractive index for a given pair of media depends on the ratio of wavelengths and velocity of light in two media but not on frequency. So, frequency remains constant during refraction of light.

(ii) From Snell's law, $\mu = \frac{\sin i}{\sin r} = \frac{c}{v}$

$\Rightarrow v \propto \sin r$, for given value of i.

Smaller the angle of refraction, smaller the velocity of light in medium.

Velocity of light is minimum in medium A as the angle of refraction is minimum, i.e. 15°.

(iii) From Snell's law, $\mu = \frac{\sin i}{\sin r}$ = constant

Since, angle of incidence increases, the angle of refraction has to increase, so that the ratio remains constant.

(iv) $\mu = \frac{\text{Speed of light in air}}{\text{Speed of light in the glass}} = \frac{c}{v}$

$$\Rightarrow v = \frac{c}{\mu} = \frac{3 \times 10^8}{1.5} = 2 \times 10^8 \text{ m/s}$$

CHAPTER

10

Wave Optics

The connection between waves and rays of light is described by wave optics. The wave theory of light was put forward by Huygens' in 1678 and later on modified by Fresnel. According to this theory, light is a form of energy which travels in the form of transverse wave. The speed of light in a medium depends upon the nature of medium.

In this chapter, we will study about the various phenomena (i.e. interference of light, diffraction of light) related to the wave nature of light.

- Huygens' Principle
- Interference of Light
- Diffraction of Light

TOPIC 01 Huygens' Principle

Wavefront

It is the locus of points (wavelets) having the same phase (a surface of constant phase) of oscillations. A wavelet is the point of disturbance due to propagation of light. A line perpendicular to a wavefront is called a **ray**.

Depending on the shape of source of light, wavefronts can be of three types, which are given below

(i) **Spherical wavefront** When the source of light is a point source, the wavefront is a sphere with centre as the source.

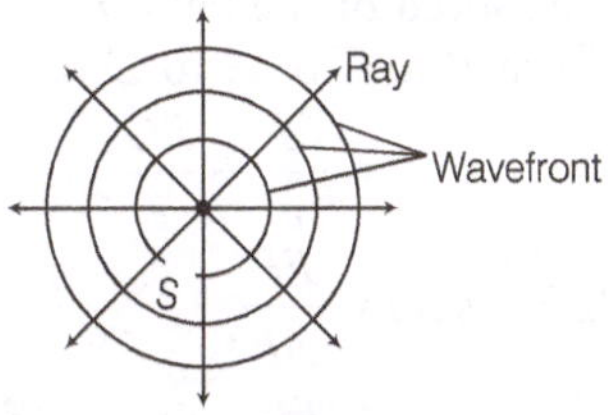

Spherical wavefront

(ii) **Cylindrical wavefront** When the source of light is linear, e.g. a straight line source, slit etc. as shown in the figure. All the points equidistant from the source lie on a cylinder. Therefore, the wavefront is cylindrical in shape.

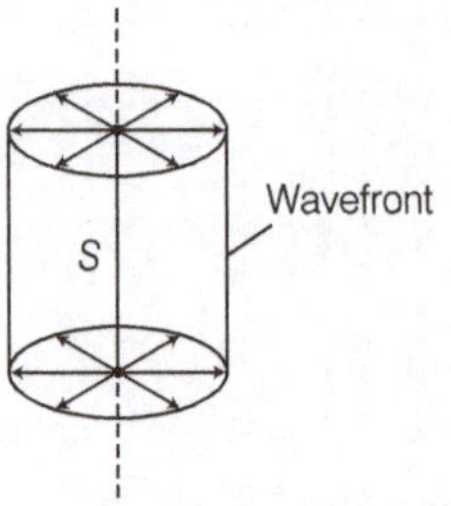

Cylindrical wavefront

(iii) **Plane wavefront** When the point source or linear source of light is at very large distance, a small portion of spherical or cylindrical wavefront appears to be plane. Such a wavefront is called a plane wavefront.

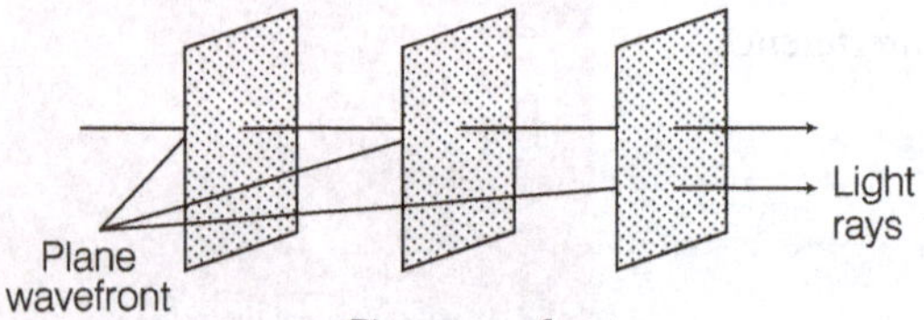

Plane wavefront

Hence, the wavefront is a surface of constant phase. The speed with which the wavefront moves outwards from the source is called the **speed of the wave.** The energy of the wave travels in a direction perpendicular to the wavefront.

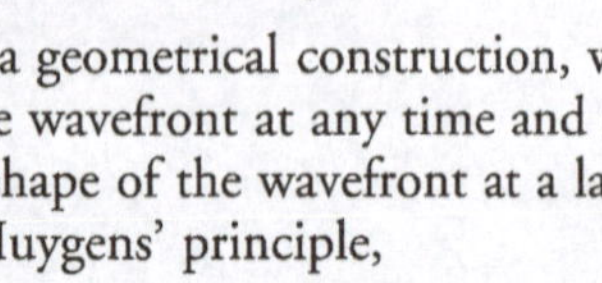

Plane wavefront

Huygens' Principle

It is essentially a geometrical construction, which gives the shape of the wavefront at any time and allows us to determine the shape of the wavefront at a later time. According to Huygens' principle,

(i) Each point on the given wavefront (called primary wavefront) is the source of a secondary disturbance (called secondary wavelets) and the wavelets emanating from these points spread out in all directions with the speed of the wave.

(ii) A surface touching these secondary wavelets, tangentially in the forward direction at any instant gives the new wavefront at that instant. This is called secondary wavefront.

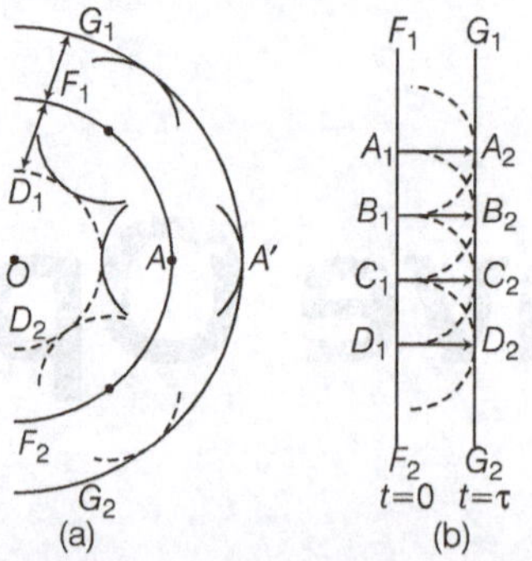

In Fig. (a), F_1F_2 is the section of the given spherical wavefront and G_1G_2 is the new wavefront in the forward direction. In Fig. (b), F_1F_2 is the section of the given plane wavefront and G_1G_2 is the new wavefront in the forward direction.

Refraction and Reflection of Plane Waves Using Huygens' Principle

Huygens' principle can be used to explain the phenomena of reflection and refraction of light on the basis of wave theory of light.

Laws of Reflection at a Plane Surface

Let 1, 2, 3 be the incident rays and 1′, 2′, 3′ be the corresponding reflected rays.

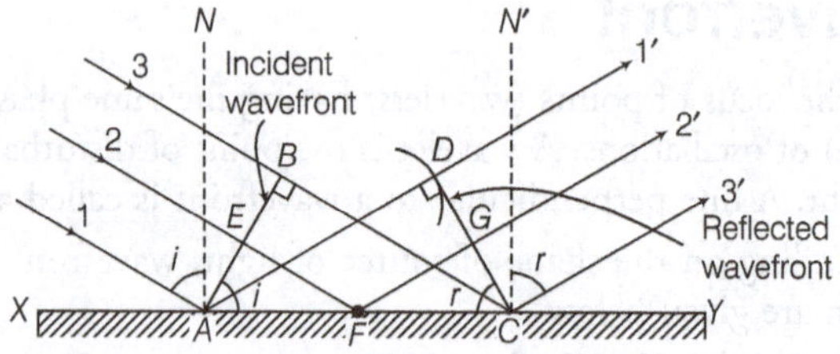

Laws of reflection by Huygens' principle

If c is the speed of the light, t is the time taken by light to go from B to C or A to D or E to G through F, then

$$t = \frac{EF}{c} + \frac{FG}{c} \quad \ldots(i)$$

In ΔAEF, $\sin i = \dfrac{EF}{AF}$

In ΔFGC, $\sin r = \dfrac{FG}{FC}$ or $t = \dfrac{AF \sin i}{c} + \dfrac{FC \sin r}{c}$

$$\Rightarrow \quad t = \frac{AC \sin r + AF (\sin i - \sin r)}{c}$$

$[\because FC = AC - AF]$

For rays of light from different parts on the incident wavefront, the values of AF are different. But light from different points of the incident wavefront should take the same time to reach the corresponding points on the reflected wavefront.

So, t should not depend upon AF. This is possible only, if

$$\sin i - \sin r = 0$$

i.e. $\sin i = \sin r$ or $\angle i = \angle r$ ...(ii)

which is the **first law of reflection.**

Further, the incident wavefront AB, the reflecting surface XY and the reflected wavefront CD are all perpendicular to the plane of the paper. Therefore, incident ray, normal to the mirror XY and reflected ray all lie in the plane of the paper. This proves the **second law of reflection.**

Laws of Refraction (Snell's Law) at a Plane Surface

Let 1, 2, 3 be the incident rays and $1', 2', 3'$ be the corresponding refracted rays.

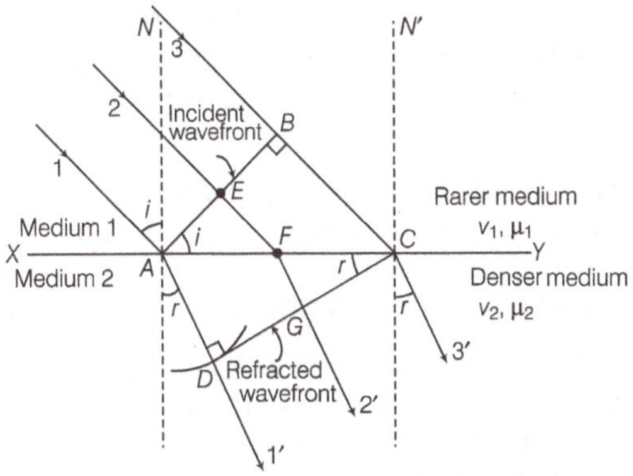

Laws of refraction by Huygens' principle

If v_1, v_2 are the speeds of light in the two media and t is the time taken by light to go from B to C or A to D or E to G through F, then $t = \dfrac{EF}{v_1} + \dfrac{FG}{v_2}$

In ΔAFE, $\sin i = \dfrac{EF}{AF}$

In ΔFGC, $\sin r = \dfrac{FG}{FC}$

$$\Rightarrow \quad t = \frac{AF \sin i}{v_1} + \frac{FC \sin r}{v_2} \quad \text{...(iii)}$$

$$\Rightarrow \quad t = \frac{AC \sin r}{v_2} + AF\left(\frac{\sin i}{v_1} - \frac{\sin r}{v_2}\right)$$

For rays of light from different parts on the incident wavefront, the values of AF are different. But light from different points of the incident wavefront should take the same time to reach the corresponding points on the refracted wavefront. So, t should not depend upon AF. This is possible only, if

$$\frac{\sin i}{v_1} - \frac{\sin r}{v_2} = 0$$

$$\Rightarrow \quad \frac{\sin i}{\sin r} = \frac{v_1}{v_2} \quad \text{...(iv)}$$

Now, if c represents the speed of light in vacuum, then $\mu_1 = \dfrac{c}{v_1}$ and $\mu_2 = \dfrac{c}{v_2}$ are known as the **refractive indices** of medium 1 and medium 2, respectively.

In terms of refractive indices, Eq. (iv) can be written as

$$\mu_1 \sin i = \mu_2 \sin r$$

$$\Rightarrow \quad \boxed{\mu = \frac{\sin i}{\sin r}}$$

This is known as **Snell's law of refraction.**

Further, if λ_1 and λ_2 denote the wavelengths of light in medium 1 and medium 2, respectively and if the distance BC is equal to λ_1, then the distance AD will be equal to λ_2, thus

$$\frac{\lambda_1}{\lambda_2} = \frac{BC}{AD} = \frac{v_1}{v_2}$$

or $$\frac{v_1}{\lambda_1} = \frac{v_2}{\lambda_2}$$

$$\Rightarrow \quad \nu_1 = \nu_2 \quad \left[\because \frac{v}{\lambda} = \nu\right]$$

Hence, the frequency does not change on refraction. Thus, **frequency** ν being a characteristic of the source, remains the same as light travels from one medium to another.

Also, **wavelength** is directly proportional to the (phase) speed and inversely proportional to refractive index.

$$\therefore \quad \lambda' = \frac{\lambda}{\mu}, \ \mu = \frac{\lambda}{\lambda'} = \frac{c\lambda}{v\lambda} = \frac{c}{v}$$

Example 1

(i) When monochromatic light is incident on a surface separating two media, the reflected and refracted lights both have the same frequency as the incident frequency. Explain, why?

(ii) When light travels from a rarer to a denser medium, the speed decreases. Does the reduction in speed imply a reduction in the energy carried by the light wave?

Sol. (i) Reflection and refraction arises through interaction of incident light with the atomic constituents of matter. Atoms may be viewed as oscillators, which take up the frequency of the external agency (light) causing forced oscillations.

The frequency of light emitted by a charged oscillator equals its frequency of oscillation. Thus, the frequency of scattered light equals the frequency of incident light.

(ii) No, the energy carried by a wave depends on the amplitude of the wave, not on the speed of wave propagation.

Topic Practice 1

Multiple Choice Questions

1 Mark

1. What type of wavefronts are associated with a source at infinity ? **ISC 2023**
(a) Cylindrical wavefronts
(b) Plane wavefronts
(c) Spherical wavefronts
(d) All types of wavefronts

2. Ray diverging from a point source on a wavefront are
(a) cylindrical (b) spherical
(c) plane (d) cubical

3. If a source is at infinity, then wavefronts reaching to observer are
(a) cylindrical (b) spherical
(c) plane (d) conical

4. Huygens' principle of secondary wavelets may be used to
(a) find the velocity of light in vacuum
(b) explain the particle's behaviour of light
(c) find the new position of a wavefront
(d) explain photoelectric effect

Very Short Answer Type Questions

1 Mark

5. What is the phase difference between any two points lying on the same wavefront? **ISC 2020**

6. In the given figure, there are two points P and Q, what is the phase difference between them?

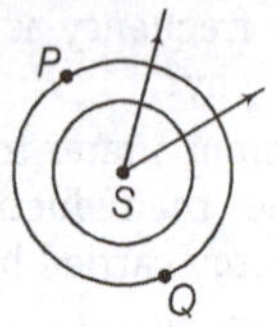

7. What type of wavefront is generated from a line source of light? **ISC 2017, 08, 04**

8. What is the shape of the wavefront diverging from a point source of light? **ISC 2020, 04**

9. State anyone postulate of Huygens' wave theory. **ISC 2011, 03, 01**

Short Answer Type Questions

2 Marks

10. (i) Differentiate between a ray and a wavefront.
(ii) What is the phase difference between any two points on a wavefront?

11. What is the shape of the wavefront on earth for sunlight? **NCERT Exemplar**

12. Construct a diagram to show the wave characteristics of light.

13. What is the shape of the wavefront in each of the following cases?
(i) Light diverging from point source.
(ii) The portion of the wavefront of light from a distant star intercepted by the earth. **NCERT**

14. If d is the distance covered by a light wave in the air in t seconds and D is the distance covered in a medium of refractive index μ in the same time, then prove that $d = \mu D$. **ISC 2006**

15. Light of wavelength 5000 Å propagating in air gets partly reflected from the surface of water. How will the wavelengths and frequencies of the reflected and refracted light be affected?

Short Answer Type Questions

3 Marks

16. Using Huygens' wave theory, show that (for refraction of light)
$$\frac{\sin i}{\sin r} = \text{constant}$$
where, terms have their usual meanings. You must draw a neat and labelled diagram. **ISC 2024**

17. On the basis of Huygens' wave theory, show that when light is incident on a plane mirror obliquely, angle of reflection is equal to the angle of incidence. **ISC 2010, 06**

18. Derive Snell's law of refraction using Huygens' wave theory. **ISC 2016**

19. You have learnt in the text how Huygens' principle leads to the laws of reflection and refraction.Use the Huygens' principle to deduce directly that a point object placed in front of a plane mirror produces a virtual image whose distance from the mirror is equal to the distance of the object from the mirror. NCERT

Long Answer Type Questions

5 Marks

20. On the basis of Huygens' wave theory of light, show that the angle of reflection is equal to angle of incidence. You must draw a labelled diagram for this derivation. ISC 2023

21. On the basis of Huygens' wave theory, prove Snell's law of refraction of light. Draw a neat and labelled diagram. [Postulates of Huygens' wave theory not required. ISC 2012, 05, 02, 00

22. (i) State Huygens' principle. Using this principle, draw a diagram to show how a plane wavefront incident at the interference of the two media gets refracted when it propagates from a rarer to a denser medium.
Hence, verify Snell's law of refraction.
(ii) Is the frequency of reflected and refracted light same as the frequency of incident light?

23. (i) Use Huygens' geometrical construction to show how a plane wavefront at $t = 0$ propagates and produces a wavefront at a later time.
(ii) Verify, using Huygens' principle, Snell's law of refraction of a plane wave propagating from a denser to a rarer medium.
(iii) When monochromatic light is incident on a surface separating two media, the reflected and refracted light both have the same frequency. Explain, why ?

24. (i) A plane wavefront approaches a plane surface separating two media. If medium 1 is optically denser and medium 2 is optically rarer, using Huygens' principle, explain and show how a refracted wavefront is constructed?
(ii) Verify Snell's law.
(iii) When a light wave travels from a rarer to a denser medium, the speed decreases. Does it imply reduction in its energy? Explain.

Numerical Problems

25. Light of wavelength 5000 Å falls on a plane reflecting surface. What are the wavelength and frequency of the reflected light? For what angle of incidence is the reflected ray normal to the incident ray? NCERT (1 M)

26. (i) The refractive index of glass is 1.5. What is the speed of light in glass? (Speed of light in vacuum is 3×10^8 ms^{-1})
(ii) Is the speed of light in glass independent of the colour of light? If not, which of the two colours red and violet travels slower in a glass prism? NCERT (2 M)

Hints & Solutions

1. (*b*) The plane wavefront is obtained when the small part of the spherical or cylindrical wavefront originates from a distant source, like infinity .

2. (*b*) Wavefronts emitting from a point source are spherical wavefronts.

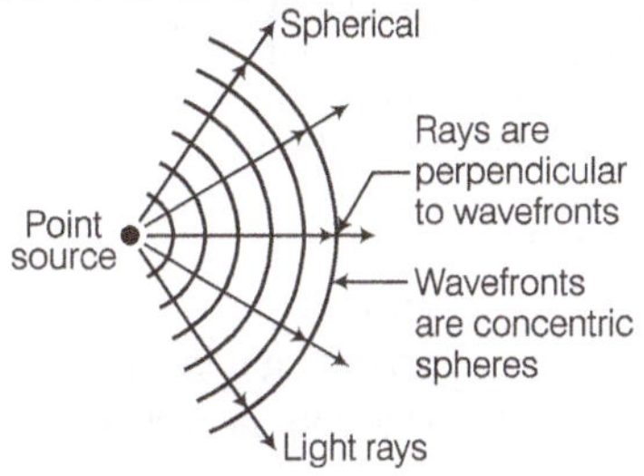

3. (*c*) Rays reaching from a source at infinity are parallel and when we draw a surface perpendicular to each ray, we get a plane wavefront.

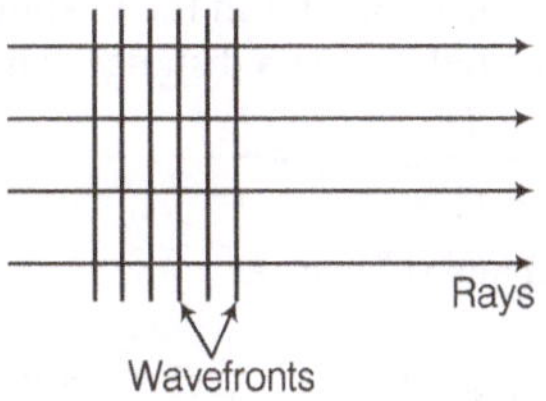

4. (*c*) Every point on a given wavefront act as a secondary source of light and emits secondary wavelets which travels in all directions with the speed of light in the medium. A surface touching all these secondary wavelets tangentially in the forward direction, gives new wavefront at that instant of time.

5. The phase difference between any two points lying on the same wavefront is zero.

6. Since, the two points P and Q are at the same locus of the source S, so the phase difference between them equals to zero.

7. A line source of light produces cylindrical wavelength.
8. Refer to the text on page 389 (Spherical wavefront).
9. According to Huygens' principle, each point on the given wavefront (called primary wavefront) is the source of a secondary disturbance (called secondary wavelets) and the wavelets emanating from these points spread out in all directions with the speed of the wave.
10. Refer to the text on page 389 (Wavefront).
11. We know that, the sun is at very large distance from the earth. Assuming sun as spherical, it can be considered as point source situated at infinity.

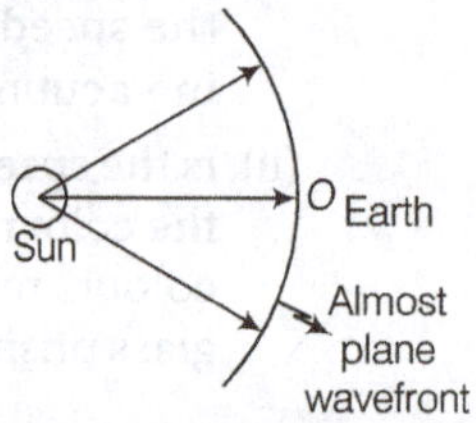

Due to the large distance the radius of wavefront can be considered as large (infinity) and hence, wavefront is almost plane. (2)
12. Refer to the text on pages 389 and 390 (Wavefront).
13. (i) Refer to the text on page 389 (Spherical wavefront). (1)

(ii) As, the star (i.e. source of light) is very far off, i.e. at infinity, the wavefront intercepted by the earth must be a plane wavefront.

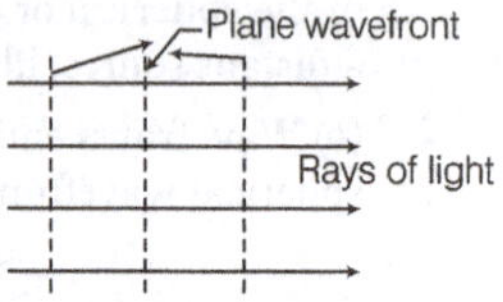

(1)

14. We know that,

Refractive index of medium (μ)

$$= \frac{\text{Speed of light in air } (c)}{\text{Speed of light in medium } (v)}$$

Let c_1 be the velocity of light in the air, then time t taken by it to cover a distance d is $t = \frac{d}{c_1}$ or $c_1 = \frac{d}{t}$ ...(i)

If c_2 is the velocity of light in the medium and during the same time t, a light cover a distance D is

$$t = \frac{D}{c_2} \text{ or } c_2 = \frac{D}{t} \quad \text{...(ii)}$$

(1)

From Eqs. (i) and (ii), we get

$$\frac{c_1}{c_2} = \frac{d/t}{D/t} \therefore \mu = \frac{d}{t} \times \frac{t}{D} = \frac{d}{D} \Rightarrow d = \mu D \left[\because \frac{c_1}{c_2} = \mu\right]$$

(1)

15. The frequency and wavelength of reflected wave will not change. The refracted wave will have same frequency. The velocity of light in water is given by

$$v = f\lambda$$

where, v = velocity of light, f = frequency of light and λ = wavelength of light.

If velocity will decrease, then wavelength (λ) will also decrease. (2)

16. Refer to the text on page 391 [Laws of reflection (snell's law) at a plane surface].
17. Refer to the text on pages 390 and 391 [Laws of reflection (snell's law) at a plane surface].
18. Refer to the text on page 391 [Laws of refraction (Snell's law) at a plane surface].
19. In the figure, P is a point object placed at a distance r from a plane mirror M_1M_2. With P as centre and $PO = r$ as radius, draw a spherical arc AB. This is the spherical wavefront from the object, incident on M_1M_2.

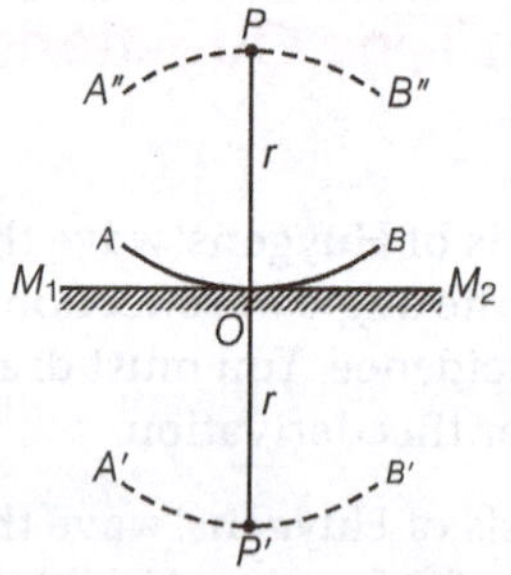

(3)

20. Refer to the text on pages 390 and 391 (Laws of reflection at a plane surface).
21. Refer to the text on page 390 [Laws of refraction (snell's law) at a plane surface].
22. (i) Refer to the text on pages 390 and 391 (Huygens' principle and Laws of refraction at a plane surface). (4)

(ii) The frequency of reflected and refracted light remains same as the frequency of incident light because frequency only depends on the source of light. (1)

23. (i) Refer to the text on page 390 (Huygens' principle).

(ii) Refer to the text on page 391 [Laws of refraction (snell's law) at a plane surface].

(iii) Refer to the sol. of Example 1(i) on pages 391 and 392.

24. (i) and (ii) refer to the text on pages 390 and 391 (Refraction and reflection of plane waves using Huygens' principle).

(iii) Refer to the sol. of Example 1 (ii) on page 392.

25. On the reflection, there is no change in wavelength and frequency. So, wavelength of reflected light will be 5000Å. Frequency of the reflected light,

$$\nu = \frac{c}{\lambda} = \frac{3 \times 10^8}{5 \times 10^{-7}} = 6 \times 10^{14}\,\text{Hz}$$

(1/2)

For $i = 45°$, reflected ray becomes normal to the incident ray. (1/2)

26. (i) Here, refractive index, $\mu = 1.5$

$$c = 3 \times 10^8\,\text{m s}^{-1}, v = ?$$

As, $\mu = \frac{c}{v} \Rightarrow v = \frac{c}{\mu} = \frac{3 \times 10^8}{1.5} = 2 \times 10^8\,\text{ms}^{-1}$ (1)

(ii) No, the refractive index and the speed of light in a medium depend on wavelength, i.e. colour of light. We know that, $\mu_v > \mu_r$. Therefore, $v_{\text{violet}} < v_{\text{red}}$. Hence, violet component of white light travels slower than the red component. (1)

TOPIC 02 | Interference of Light

Phase of Wave Motion

During the propagation of wave each particle copies the motion of another particle at its left with a time delay of x/v, where x is the separation between the two particles and v is velocity of wave. For the particles P and W, shown in figure, the separation is $\Delta x = vT$ and the particle W copies the motion of P after a time delay of $\Delta x/v = T$.

The motion of any particle at any instant is identical in all respect to its motion of a time period T later. So, a delay of one time period is equivalent to no delay and hence the particles P and W are in phase or can be said as vibrating in the same phase. They reach their extreme positions together, they cross their mean position together.

Their displacements and velocities are identical at any instant. Same point is true for any pair of particles separated by a distance vT. This separation is called the **wavelength** of the wave and is denoted by the Greek letter λ. Thus, $\lambda = vT$.

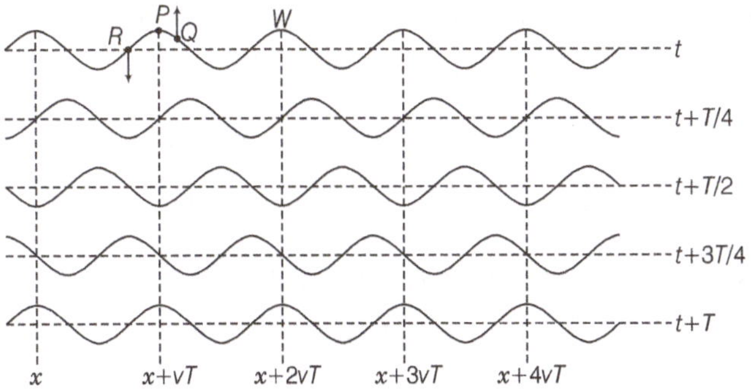

Superposition Principle

According to this principle, at a particular point in the medium, the resultant displacement (y) produced by a number of waves is the vector sum of the displacements produced by each of the waves ($y_1, y_2, \ldots$).

i.e. $$y = y_1 + y_2 + y_3 + y_4 + \ldots$$

Clearly, each wave contributes as if the other wave is not present.The superposition principle which was stated first for mechanical waves is equally applicable to the electromagnetic (light) waves.

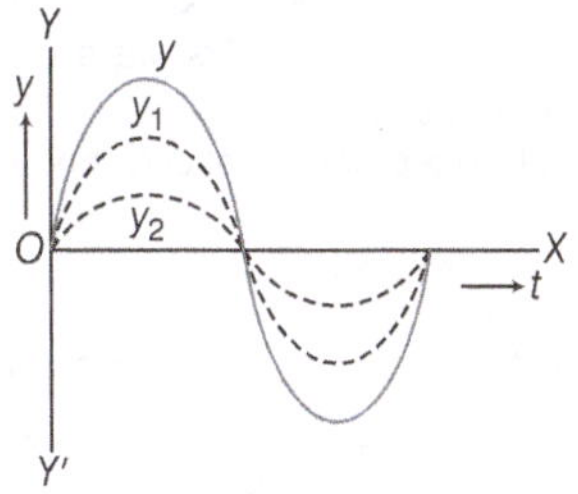

Superposition of waves

Interference of Light Waves

When two light waves of exactly equal frequency having constant phase difference w.r.t. time travelled on same direction and superimpose (overlap) with each other, then intensity of resultant wave does not remain uniform in space.

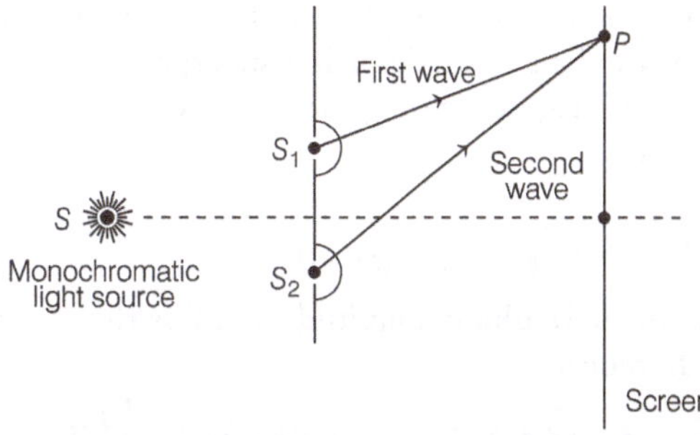

Interference of Monochromatic light by double slit

This phenomenon of formation of maximum intensity at some points and minimum intensity at some other points by two identical light waves travelling in same direction is called the **interference of light**.

At the points, where the resultant intensity of light is maximum, interference is said to be **constructive**. At the points, where the resultant intensity of light is minimum, the interference is said to be **destructive**.

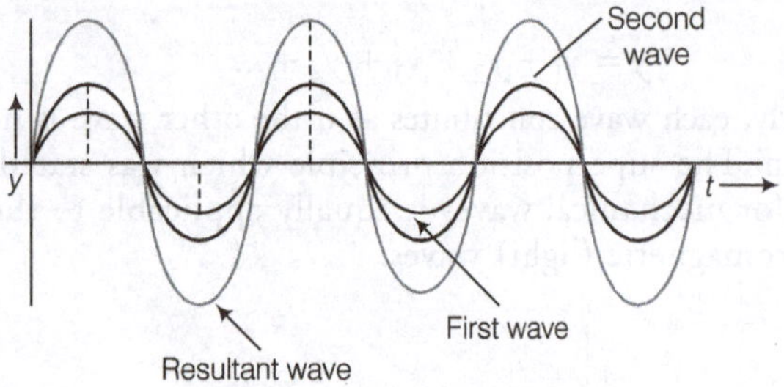

(a) Constructive interference

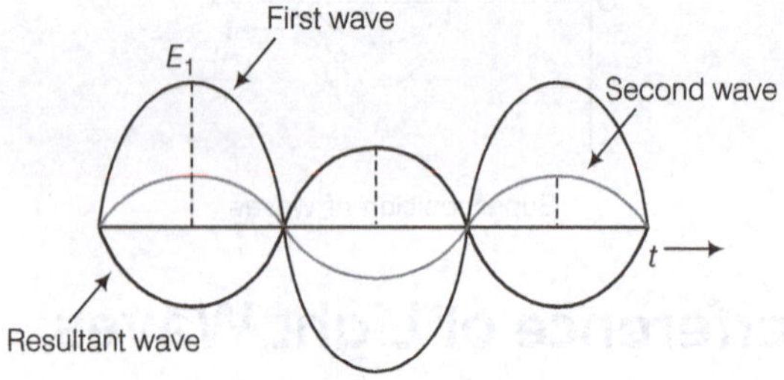

(b) Destructive interference

Let the waves from two sources of light be represented as

$$y_1 = a \sin \omega t \quad \text{and} \quad y_2 = b \sin(\omega t + \phi)$$

where, a and b are the respective amplitudes of the two waves and ϕ is the constant phase angle by which second wave leads the first wave. Applying superposition principle, the magnitude of the resultant displacement of the waves is

$$y = y_1 + y_2$$

or $$y = A \sin(\omega t + \theta)$$

where, A is the resultant amplitude and θ is the resultant **phase difference.**

$$\therefore \quad A = \sqrt{a^2 + b^2 + 2ab \cos \phi} \text{ and } \tan \theta = \frac{b \sin \phi}{a + b \cos \phi}$$

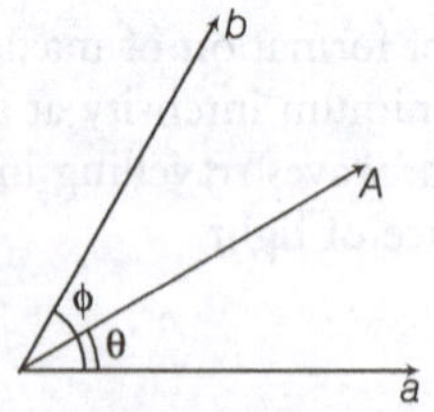

Resultant of amplitudes *a* and *b*

As, intensity is directly proportional to the square of the amplitude of the wave, i.e. $I \propto a^2$

So, $$I_1 = ka^2, I_2 = kb^2$$

$\therefore$ Resultant intensity, $I_R = kA^2$

$$= k(a^2 + b^2 + 2ab \cos \phi)$$

$$\therefore \quad \boxed{I_R = I_1 + I_2 + 2\sqrt{I_1 I_2} \cos \phi}$$

Conditions for Constructive Interference

The condition for constructive interference at a point is the **phase difference** between the two waves reaching the point should be zero or an even integral multiple of 2π or **path difference** should be integral multiple of full wavelength,

i.e. Phase difference $= 2n\pi$, where $n = 0, 1, 2, 3, \ldots$

Path difference $= n\lambda$, where $n = 0, 1, 2, 3, \ldots$

Resultant intensity, $I_R = I_1 + I_2 + 2\sqrt{I_1 I_2}$

$$= (\sqrt{I_1} + \sqrt{I_2})^2$$

Conditions for Destructive Interference

The condition for destructive interference at a point is the phase difference between the two waves reaching the point should be an odd integral multiple of π or path difference between the two waves reaching the point should be an odd integral multiple of half of the wavelength,

i.e. Phase difference $= (2n - 1)\pi$, where $n = 1, 2, 3, \ldots$

Path difference $= (2n - 1)\dfrac{\lambda}{2}$, where $n = 1, 2, 3, \ldots$

Resultant intensity, $I_R = I_1 + I_2 - 2\sqrt{I_1 I_2}$

$$= (\sqrt{I_1} - \sqrt{I_2})^2$$

Comparison of Intensities of Maxima and Minima

As, $I_{max} \propto (a + b)^2$ and $I_{min} \propto (a - b)^2$

$$\therefore \quad \frac{I_{max}}{I_{min}} = \frac{(a + b)^2}{(a - b)^2} = \frac{\left(\frac{a}{b} + 1\right)^2}{\left(\frac{a}{b} - 1\right)^2}$$

$$\Rightarrow \quad \boxed{\frac{I_{max}}{I_{min}} = \frac{(r + 1)^2}{(r - 1)^2}}$$

where, $r = \dfrac{a}{b}$ (ratio of amplitudes)

Example 1 Light waves from two coherent sources having intensities I and $2I$ cross each other at a point with a phase difference of 60°. What is the resultant intensity at that point?

Sol. Here, $I_1 = I$ and $I_2 = 2I$, $\phi = 60°$

∴ Resultant intensity,

$$I_R = I_1 + I_2 + 2\sqrt{I_1 I_2}\cos\phi$$
$$= I + 2I + 2\sqrt{I \times 2I}\cos 60°$$
$$= 3I + I\sqrt{2} = I(3+\sqrt{2}) = 4.414\,I$$

Example 2 Light wave from two coherent sources of intensities in ratio 64:1 produces interference. Calculate the ratio of maxima and minima of the interference pattern.

Sol. Ratio of intensities of coherent sources,

i.e. $$\frac{I_1}{I_2} = \frac{64}{1} = \frac{8^2}{1^2};\ \frac{I_{max}}{I_{min}} = ?$$

We have, $I_1 \propto a^2$, $I_{max} \propto (a+b)^2$

and $I_2 \propto b^2$, $I_{min} \propto (a-b)^2$

$$\Rightarrow \quad \frac{I_1}{I_2} = \frac{a^2}{b^2} = \frac{64}{1} \Rightarrow \frac{a}{b} = \frac{8}{1};\ a = 8b$$

So, $$\frac{I_{max}}{I_{min}} = \frac{(a+b)^2}{(a-b)^2} = \frac{(8b+b)^2}{(8b-b)^2} = \frac{81b^2}{49b^2} = 81:49$$

Coherent and Incoherent Sources

Light sources are of two types, i.e. coherent and non-coherent light sources. The sources of light which emit light waves of same wavelength, same frequency and are in same phase or having constant phase difference are known as **coherent sources.**

Two such sources of light, which do not emit light waves with constant phase difference are called **incoherent sources.**

Need of Coherent Sources for the Production of Interference Pattern

As discussed earlier, when two monochromatic waves of intensity I_1, I_2 and phase difference ϕ meet at a point, then the resultant intensity is given by

$$I = I_1 + I_2 + 2\sqrt{I_1 I_2}\cos\phi$$

Here, the term $2\sqrt{I_1 I_2}\cos\phi$ is called interference term.

There are two possibilities.

(i) If $\cos\phi$ remains constant with time, then the total intensity at any point will be constant. The intensity will be maximum $(\sqrt{I_1} + \sqrt{I_2})^2$ at points, where $\cos\phi$ is 1 and minimum $(\sqrt{I_1} - \sqrt{I_2})^2$ at points, where $\cos\phi$ is −1. The sources in this case are coherent.

(ii) If $\cos\phi$ varies continuously with time assuming both positive and negative value, then the average value of $\cos\phi$ will be zero over time interval of measurement. The interference term averages to zero. There will be same intensity $I = I_1 + I_2$ at every point. The two sources in this case are incoherent.

Requirements for Obtaining Two Coherent Sources of Light

Following are the requirements (conditions) for obtaining two coherent sources of light

(i) Coherent sources of light should be obtained from a single source by some device.
Two coherent sources can be obtained either by
  (a) the source and its virtual image (Lloyd's mirror).
  (b) the two virtual images of the same source (Fresnel's biprism)
  (c) two real images of the same source (Young's double slit).

(ii) The two sources should give monochromatic light.

(iii) The path difference between light waves from two sources should be small.

(iv) Coherent sources can be produced by two methods:
  (a) By division of wavefront (Young's double slit experiment).
  (b) By division of amplitude (partial reflection or refraction in thin films).

Young's Double Slit Experiment

Suppose S_1 and S_2 are two fine slits, a small distance d apart. They are illuminated by a strong source S of monochromatic light of wavelength λ. MN is a screen at a distance D from the slits.

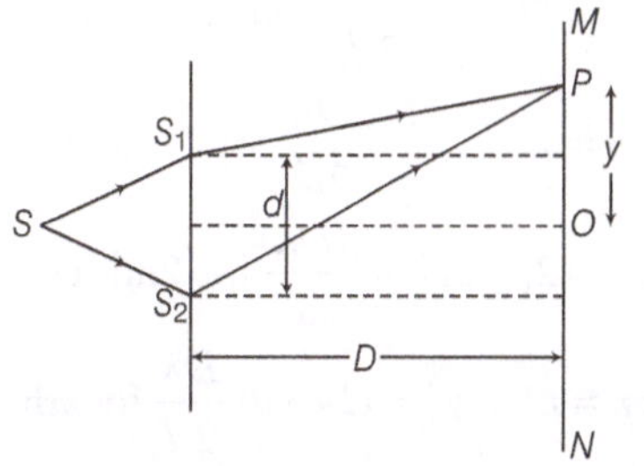

Young's double slit arrangement to produce interference pattern

Consider a point P at a distance y from O, the centre of screen.

The path difference between two waves arriving at point P is equal to $S_2P - S_1P$.

Now,

$$(S_2P)^2 - (S_1P)^2 = \left[D^2 + \left(y + \frac{d}{2}\right)^2\right] - \left[D^2 + \left(y - \frac{d}{2}\right)^2\right]$$

$$= 2yd$$

Thus, $S_2P - S_1P = \dfrac{2yd}{S_2P + S_1P}$

But $S_2P + S_1P \approx 2D$

$\therefore \quad S_2P - S_1P \approx \dfrac{dy}{D}$

For Constructive Interference (Bright Fringes)

Path difference $= \dfrac{dy}{D} = n\lambda$, where, $n = 0, 1, 2, 3, \ldots$

$\therefore \quad y = \dfrac{nD\lambda}{d} \qquad [\because n = 0, 1, 2, 3, \ldots]$

Hence, for $n = 0$, $y_0 = 0$ at O central bright fringe

for $n = 1$, $\quad y_1 = \dfrac{D\lambda}{d}$ for 1st bright fringe

for $n = 2$, $\quad y_2 = \dfrac{2D\lambda}{d}$ for 2nd bright fringe

for $n = n$, $\quad y_n = \dfrac{nD\lambda}{d}$ for nth bright fringe

The separation between two consecutive bright fringes is $\quad \beta = \dfrac{nD\lambda}{d} - \dfrac{(n-1)D\lambda}{d} = \dfrac{D\lambda}{d}$

For Destructive Interference (Dark Fringes)

Path difference $= \dfrac{dy}{D} = (2n-1)\dfrac{\lambda}{2}$

or $\quad y = (2n-1)\dfrac{D\lambda}{2d}$, where, $n = 1, 2, 3, \ldots$

Hence, for $n = 1$, $\quad y_1' = \dfrac{D\lambda}{2d}$ for 1st dark fringe

for $n = 2$, $\quad y_2' = \dfrac{3D\lambda}{2d}$ for 2nd dark fringe

for $n = n$, $\quad y_n' = (2n-1)\dfrac{D\lambda}{2d}$ for nth dark fringe

The separation between two consecutive dark fringes is

$$\beta' = (2n-1)\frac{D\lambda}{2d} - \{2(n-1)-1\}\frac{D\lambda}{2d} = \frac{D\lambda}{d}$$

Fringe Width

The distance between two consecutive bright or dark fringes is called fringe width W.

$\therefore$ Fringe width, $\boxed{W = \dfrac{D\lambda}{d}}$

The above formula is free from n that means the width of all fringes is same.

Fringe width is directly proportional to λ. Hence, the fringes of red light (longer wavelength) are broader than the fringes of blue light (shorter wavelength).

Angular Fringe Width

The angular position of the nth bright fringe is

$$\theta_n = \frac{x_n}{D} = \frac{nD\lambda / d}{D} = \frac{n\lambda}{d}$$

Angular distance between consecutive fringe width is given by

$$\theta = \theta_{n+1} - \theta_n = \frac{\lambda}{d}$$

Intensity of the Fringes

For a bright fringe, $\phi = 2n\pi$

and $\quad \cos\phi = \cos 2n\pi = 1$

So, $\quad I_R = I_{max} = I_1 + I_2 + 2\sqrt{I_1 I_2} = 4I$

[as, $I_1 = I_2 = I$ in YDSE]

$\therefore$ Intensity of a bright fringe $= 4I$

For a dark fringe, $\phi = (2n-1)\pi$

$\Rightarrow \quad \cos\phi = -1$

So, $\quad I_R = I_{min} = I_1 + I_2 - 2\sqrt{I_1 I_2} = 0$

$\therefore$ Intensity of a dark fringe $= 0$

Note If YDSE apparatus is immersed in a liquid of refractive index μ, then wavelength of light and hence fringe width decreases μ times.

Distribution of Intensity

The distribution of intensity in Young's double slit experiment is shown below

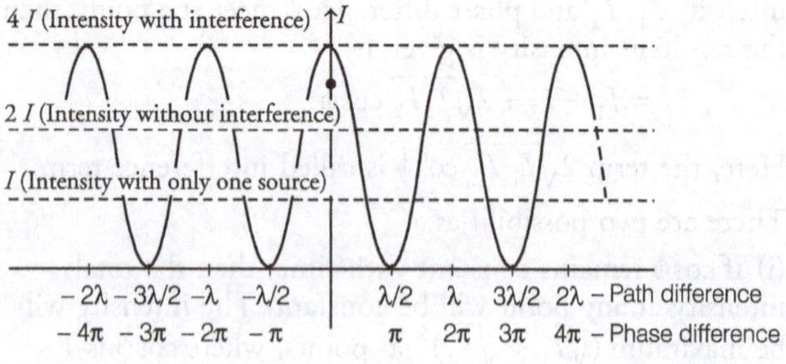

Relation among Intensity, Amplitude of the Wave and Width of the Slit

If W_1 and W_2 are widths of two slits from which intensities of light I_1 and I_2 emanate, then

$$\boxed{\frac{I_1}{I_2} = \frac{a^2}{b^2} = \frac{W_1}{W_2}}$$

where, a and b are the respective amplitudes of two waves.

Example 3 Two slits are made one millimetre apart and the screen is placed one metre away. What is the fringe separation when blue-green light of wavelength 500 nm is used? **NCERT**

Sol. Here, $d = 1\text{mm} = 1\times10^{-3}\text{ m}, \ D = 1\text{m}$,

$$\lambda = 500\text{nm} = 500\times10^{-9}\text{ m} = 5\times10^{-7}\text{ m}$$

As, fringe width, $\beta = \frac{D\lambda}{d}$

$$\therefore \qquad \beta = \frac{1\times5\times10^{-7}}{1\times10^{-3}} = 5\times10^{-4}\text{ m} = 0.5\text{ mm}$$

Example 4 In Young's experiment, the width of the fringes obtained with light of wavelength 6000 Å is 2 mm. What will be the fringe width, if the entire apparatus is immersed in a liquid of refractive index 1.33?

Sol. As, $\beta = \frac{D\lambda}{d}$ and $\beta_1 = \frac{D\lambda_1}{d}$

$$\therefore \quad \frac{\beta_1}{\beta} = \frac{\frac{D\lambda_1}{d}}{\frac{D\lambda}{d}} = \frac{\lambda_1}{\lambda} = \frac{1}{\mu} \quad \text{or} \quad \beta_1 = \frac{\beta}{\mu} = \frac{2}{1.33} = 1.5\text{ mm}$$

Example 5 Distance between the slits, in YDSE, shown in figure is $d = 20\,\lambda$, where λ is the wavelength of light used.

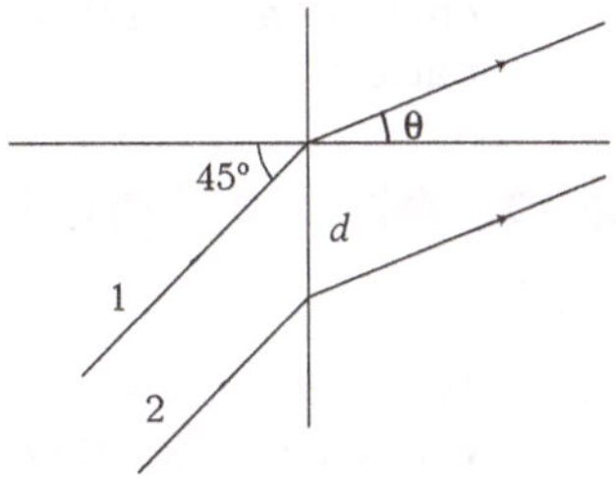

Find the angle θ, where

(i) central maxima (where path difference is zero) is obtained.

(ii) third order maxima is obtained.

Sol. Ray 1 has a longer path than that of ray 2 by a distance $d\sin45°$, before reaching the slits. Afterwards ray 2 has a path longer than ray 1 by a distance $d\sin\theta$. The net path difference is therefore, $d\sin\theta - d\sin45°$.

(i) Central maximum is obtained, where net path difference is zero,

$$d\sin\theta - d\sin45° = 0 \Rightarrow \theta = 45°$$

(ii) Third order maxima is obtained, where net path difference is $3\,\lambda$, i.e.

$$d\sin\theta - d\sin45° = 3\lambda$$

$$\Rightarrow \qquad \sin\theta = \sin45° + \frac{3\lambda}{d}$$

Putting $d = 20\,\lambda$, we have

$$\sin\theta = \sin45° + \frac{3\lambda}{20\lambda}$$

$$\therefore \qquad \theta \approx 59°$$

Conditions for Sustained Interference

In order to obtain a well-defined observable interference pattern, the intensity at points of constructive and destructive interference must be maintained maximum and almost zero, respectively.

For this, following conditions must be satisfied

(i) The two sources producing interference must be coherent.

(ii) The two interfering waves must have the same plane of polarisation.

(iii) The two sources must be very close to each other and the pattern must be observed at a larger distance to have sufficient width of the fringe $\left(\frac{D\lambda}{d}\right)$.

(iv) The sources must be monochromatic, otherwise the fringes of different colours will overlap.

(v) The two waves must be having same amplitude for better contrast between bright and dark fringes.

Topic Practice 2

Multiple Choice Questions

1 Mark

1. The figure shows a Young's double slit experiment, where P and Q are the slits. The path lengths PX and QX are $n\lambda$ and $(n+2)\lambda$ respectively, where n is a whole number and λ is the wavelength. Taking, path difference at the central fringe as zero, what is formed at X?

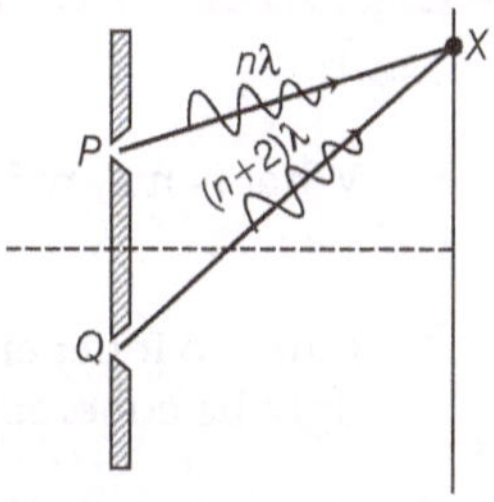

(a) First bright (b) First dark
(c) Second bright (d) Second dark

2. In Young's double slit experiment, intensity at a point is $\left(\frac{1}{4}\right)$ of the maximum intensity.

Angular position of this point is

(a) $\sin^{-1}(\lambda/d)$ (b) $\sin^{-1}(\lambda/2d)$
(c) $\sin^{-1}(\lambda/3d)$ (d) $\sin^{-1}(\lambda/4d)$

3. The Young's double slit experiment is done in a medium of refractive index 4/3. A light of 600 nm wavelength is falling on the slits having 0.45 mm separation. The lower slit S_2 is covered by a thin glass sheet of thickness 10.4 μm and refractive index 1.5. The interference pattern is observed on a screen placed 1.5 m from the slits as shown in the figure.

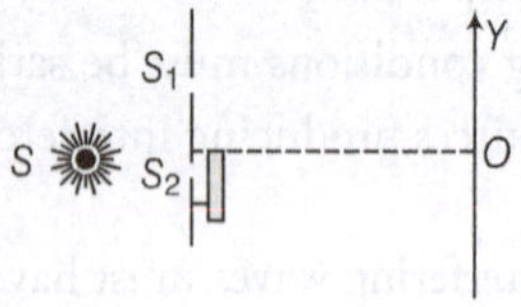

The location of the central bright fringes on the Y-axis is

(a) 4.0 mm (b) 4.33 mm
(c) 5 mm (d) 4.5 mm

4. In Young's double slit experiment, two disturbance arriving at a point P have phase difference of $\pi/2$. The intensity of this point expressed as a fraction of maximum intensity I_0 is

(a) $\frac{3}{2}I_0$ (b) $\frac{1}{2}I_0$ (c) $\frac{4}{3}I_0$ (d) $\frac{3}{4}I_0$

5. Two monochromatic light wave of same amplitudes of $2A$ interferring at a point have a phase difference of 60°. The intensity at that point will be proportional to

(a) $5A^2$ (b) $12A^2$ (c) $7A^2$ (d) $19A^2$

Very Short Answer Type Questions

1 Mark

6. What is meant by coherent sources of light? **ISC 2014**

7. Can two independent monochromatic sources of light be coherent? Explain very briefly. **ISC 2000**

8. State one condition for obtaining sustained interference of light. **ISC 2011, 04**

9. How did Fresnel constructed a biprism in order to study interference of light? **ISC 2012**

10. Can two sodium vapour lamps act as coherent sources? Explain in brief. **ISC 2009**

11. How will the fringe pattern change, if the screen is moved away from the slits?

12. How does the fringe width in Young's double slit experiment change when the distance of separation between the slits and screen is doubled?

13. If the source of light used in Young's double slit experiment is changed from red to violet, what will happen to the fringe?

14. How does the angular separation of interference fringes change in Young's experiment, if the distance between the slits is increased?

15. What should be the path difference between two waves reaching a point for obtaining constructive interference in Young's double slit experiment? **ISC 2019**

16. Young's double slit experiment was performed with monochromatic light of blue colour. The experiment was then repeated, first with light of red colour and then with light of yellow colour. Which colour pattern will have maximum separation (i.e. fringe width)? **ISC 2010, 08, 06**

17. How is fringe width of an interference pattern in Young's double slit experiment affected, if the two slits are brought closer to each other? **ISC 2017**

18. In Young's double slit experiment, if white light is used in place of monochromatic light, what changes are observed in the interference pattern? **ISC 2004**

Short Answer Type I Questions

2 Marks

19. Two light waves of amplitudes a and b interfere with each other. Calculate the ratio of intensities of a maxima to that of a minima.

20. What are the conditions for obtaining two coherent sources of light?

21. How will the interference pattern in Young's double slit experiment get affected, when

(i) distance between the slits S_1 and S_2 reduced.

(ii) the entire set up is immersed in water? Justify your answer in each case.

22. In Young's double slit experiment, two coherent sources S_1 and S_2 are placed at a distance D from screen, such that a bright fringe is obtained at a distance y from the centre line of screen. Give the value of y for which there is a bright fringe.

23. In Young's double slit experiment, what is meant by 'fringe width' or 'fringe separation'? State two ways of increasing the fringe width without changing the source of light. **ISC 2009, 01**

24. Give four conditions for obtaining sustained interference.

Short Answer Type II Questions

3 Marks

25. In Young's double slit experiment, show that

$$\beta = \frac{\lambda D}{d}$$

where the terms have their usual meaning.

ISC 2024

26. Consider a two slit interference arrangement (shown in figure) such that the distance of the screen from the slits is half the distance between the slits. Obtain the value of D in terms of λ such that the first minima on the screen falls at a distance D from the centre O.

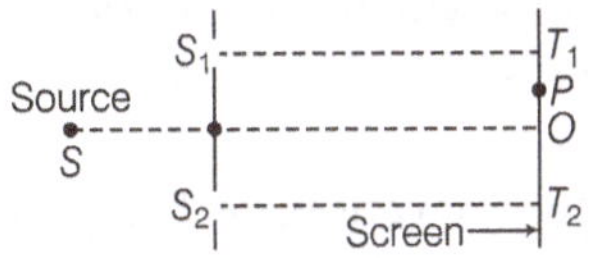

NCERT Exemplar

27. (i) What is the essential condition for obtaining a sustained interference?
(ii) In Young's double slit experiment, the distance of the 4th bright fringe from the centre of the interference pattern is 1.5 mm. The distance between the slits and the screen is 1.5 m and the wavelength of light used is 500nm. Calculate the distance between the two slits. **ISC 2023**

28. Choose the statement as right or wrong and justify.
(i) For a coherent source, initial phase difference between two sources must have same finite value.
(ii) Resultant intensity of interference is given by $I_R = I_1 + I_2 + 2\sqrt{I_1 I_2}\cos\phi$.
(iii) Two independent light bulbs fail to produce interference.

29. In Young's double slit experiment, the screen is kept at a distance of 1.2 m from the plane of the slits. The two slits are separated by 5 mm and illuminated with monochromatic light having wavelength 600 nm. Calculate
(i) fringe width, i.e. fringe separation of the interference pattern.
(ii) distance of 10th bright fringe from the centre of the pattern. **ISC 2020**

30. The intensity at the central maxima (O) in a Young's double slit experiment is I_0. If the distance OP equals one-third of fringe width of the pattern, show that the intensity at point P would be $I_0/4$.

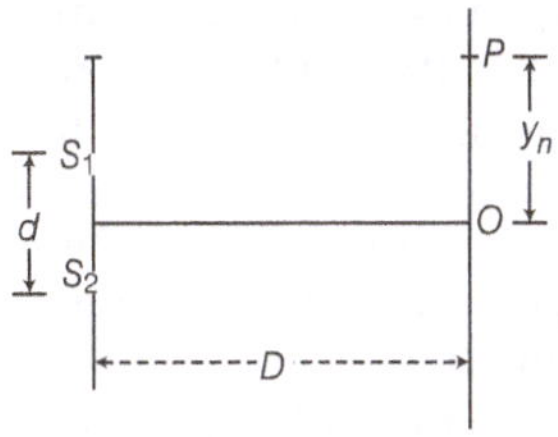

Long Answer Type Questions

5 Marks

31. With the help of a labelled diagram, show that fringe separation β in Young's double slit experiment is given by $\beta = \frac{\lambda D}{d}$, where the terms have their usual meaning. **ISC 2015, 13, 06**

32. (i) What is the effect on the interference fringes to a Young's double slit experiment when **ISC 2019**
(a) the width of the source slit is increased?
(b) the monochromatic source is replaced by a source of white light? Justify your answer in each case.
(ii) The intensity at the central maxima in Young's double slit experiment set up is I_0. Show that the intensity at a point, where the path difference is $\lambda/3$, is $I_0/4$.

33. (i) Consider two coherent sources S_1 and S_2 producing monochromatic waves to produce interference pattern.
Let the displacement of the wave produced by S_1 be given by $Y_1 = a\cos\omega t$ and the displacement by S_2 be $Y_2 = a\cos(\omega t + \phi)$.

Find out the expression for the amplitude of the resultant displacement at a point and show that the intensity at that point will be $I = 4a^2\cos^2\frac{\phi}{2}$

Hence, establish the conditions for constructive and destructive interference.

(ii) What is the effect on the interference fringes in Young's double slit experiment when

(a) the width of the source slit is increased;

(b) the monochromatic source is replaced by a source of white light?

34. (i) (a) Two independent monochromatic sources of light cannot produce a sustained interference pattern. Give reason.

(b) Light waves each of amplitude a and frequency ω, emanating from two coherent light sources superpose at a point.

If the displacements due to these waves is given by $y_1 = a\cos\omega t$ and $y_2 = a\cos(\omega t + \phi)$, where, ϕ is the phase difference between the two, obtain the expression for the resultant intensity at the point.

(ii) In Young's double slit experiment, using monochromatic light of wavelength λ, the intensity of light at a point on the screen, where path difference is λ, is K units. Find out the intensity of light at a point where path difference is $\lambda/3$.

35. A student is performing an experiment to determine interference of light using Young's doube slit experiment.

The Examiner gives some instructions to the Student. The Student responds to each instruction as per his/her understanding of the experiment.

State whether the students response is correct or incorrect. Give a reason for your answer.

(i) **Examiner** Interference pattern by two independent light sources obtained such as two bulbs.

Student cannot be obtained because phase difference varies with time continuously.

(ii) **Examiner** Write the resultant intensity of light at any point in space in mathematical form.

Student $I = I_1 + I_2 + 2I_1I_2\cos\phi$

(iii) **Examiner** The width of all bright fringes is same.

Student The separation between the slits is much larger than the distance D of the screen.

Numerical Problems

36. Obtain the ratio of the interference fringe widths β_1 and β_2 obtained with monochromatic red light of $\lambda_1 = 660$ nm and ultraviolet light of $\lambda_2 = 330$ nm. **ISC 2003 (1 M)**

37. In Young's double slit experiment, using monochromatic light of wavelength 600 nm, the interference pattern was obtained on a screen kept 1.5 m away from the plane of the two slits. Calculate the distance between the two slits, if fringe separation/fringe width was found to be 1.0 mm. **ISC 2012 (2 M)**

38. In Young's double slit experiment using monochromatic light of wavelength 600nm, 5th bright fringe is at a distance of 0.48 mm from the centre of the pattern. If the screen is at a distance of 80 cm from the plane of the two slits, calculate

(i) distance between the two slits.

(ii) fringe width, i.e. fringe separation.

ISC 2017 (3 M)

39. Laser light of wavelength 630 nm is incident on a pair of slits which are separated by 1.8 mm. If the screen is kept 80 cm away from the two slits, calculate

(i) fringe separation, i.e. fringe width.

(ii) distance of 10th bright fringe from the centre of interference pattern. **ISC 2015 (3 M)**

40. In Young's double slit experiment, using monochromatic light, the fringes are obtained on a screen placed at some distance from the slits. If the screen is moved by 5×10^{-2} m towards the slits, the change in the fringe width is 3×10^{-5} m. If the distance between the two slits is 10^{-3} m. Calculate the wavelength of the light used. **ISC 2014, 05, 04 (3 M)**

41. In Young's double slit experiment using monochromatic light L_1 of wavelength 700 nm, 10th bright fringe was obtained at a certain point P on a screen.

Which bright fringe will be obtained at the same point P, if monochromatic light of wavelength 500 nm is used in place of L_1. (No other alterations were made in the experimental set up.) **ISC 2011 (3 M)**

42. The distance between the first and the sixth bright fringes formed in Young's double slit experiment (measured by a spectrometer) is found to be 12.5 mm. The separation between the slits 0.12 mm and the distance of the screen from the slits is 60 cm. Calculate
(i) the fringe width.
(ii) the wavelength of the light used (in nm). **ISC 2007, 00 (3 M)**

43. Light waves from coherent sources arrive at two points on a screen with path difference of 0 and $\lambda/2$. Find the ratio of intensities at the points. **(1 M)**

44. In a double slit experiment using light of wavelength 600 nm, the angular width of the fringe formed on a distant screen is 0.1°. Find the spacing between the two slits. **NCERT (1 M)**

45. In Young's double slit experiment using light of wavelength 630 nm, angular width of a fringe formed on a distant screen is 0.2°. What is the spacing between the two slits? **(1 M)**

46. In Young's double slit experiment, the slits are separated by 0.28 mm and the screen is placed 1.4 m away. The distance between the central bright fringe and the fourth bright fringe is measured to be 1.2 cm, determine the wavelength of light used in the experiment. **NCERT (1 M)**

47. The amplitudes of light waves from two slits in Young's experiment are in ratio $\sqrt{2}:1$, what is the ratio of slit widths? **(1 M)**

48. Widths of two slits in Young's experiment are in the ratio 4 : 1. What is the ratio of the amplitudes of light waves from them? **(1 M)**

49. A beam of light, consisting of two wavelengths 560 nm and 420 nm, is used to obtain interference fringes in a Young's double slit experiment. Find the least distance from the central maxima, where the bright fringes due to both the wavelengths coincide. The distance between the two slits is 4 mm and the screen is at a distance of 1m from the slits. **(3 M)**

50. A beam of light consisting of two wavelengths 650 nm and 520 nm, is used to obtain interference fringes in a Young's double slit experiment.
(i) Find the distance of the third bright fringe on the screen from the central maximum for wavelength 650 nm.
(ii) What is the least distance from the central maximum, where the bright fringes due to both the wavelengths coincide? **NCERT (3 M)**

51. Laser light of wavelength 630 nm incident on a pair of slits produces an interference pattern in which the bright fringes are separated by 7.2 mm. Calculate the wavelength of another source of laser light which produce interference fringes separated by 8.1 mm using same pair of slits. **(2 M)**

52. In a Young's double slit experiment, the angular width of the fringe is found to be 0.2° on a screen placed 1 m away. The wavelength of light used is 600 nm. What will be the angular width of the fringe, if the entire experimental apparatus is immersed in water? Take, refractive index of water to be 4/3. **NCERT, (2 M)**

53. The ratio of the intensities at minima to the maxima in the Young's double slit experiment is 9 : 25. Find the ratio of the widths of the two slits. **(1 M)**

54. In Young's double slit experiment, the two slits 0.15 mm apart are illuminated by monochromatic light of wavelength 450 nm. The screen is 1 m away from the slits.
Find the distance of the second
(i) bright fringe.
(ii) dark fringe from the central maxima. **(2 M)**

Hints & Solutions

1. (c) Path difference $= QX - PX = (n+2)\lambda - n\lambda = 2\lambda$ ...(i)

For constructive interference or bright band,
Path difference $= \Delta x = n\lambda$ (where, $n = 1, 2, \ldots$)
From Eq. (i), it is obvious that second bright band is formed as $n = 2$.

2. (c) Using relation, $I = I_{max}\cos^2\left(\frac{\Delta\phi}{2}\right)$,

where, $\Delta\phi$ = total phase difference

Given, $I = \frac{I_{max}}{4}$ at certain point

$$\Rightarrow \frac{I_{max}}{4} = I_{max}\cos^2\left(\frac{\Delta\phi}{2}\right) \text{ or } \frac{1}{4} = \cos^2\left(\frac{\Delta\phi}{2}\right)$$

$$\Rightarrow \quad \cos\left(\frac{\Delta\phi}{2}\right) = \cos\left(\frac{\pi}{3}\right) \quad \text{or} \quad \Delta\phi = \left(\frac{2\pi}{3}\right)$$

Path difference, $\Delta x = \frac{\lambda}{2\pi} \times \Delta\phi = \frac{\lambda}{2\pi} \times \frac{2\pi}{3} = \frac{\lambda}{3}$ ...(i)

For Young's double slit experiment, we know, path difference $= d\sin\theta$ ...(ii)

where, θ = angular separation of the point.

Using Eqs. (i) and (ii), we get

$$\frac{\lambda}{3} = d\sin\theta \Rightarrow \sin\theta = \frac{\lambda}{3d} \Rightarrow \theta = \sin^{-1}\left(\frac{\lambda}{3d}\right)$$

3. (*b*) Shift produced due to insertion of slab,

$$\Delta x = t\left(\frac{\mu_g}{\mu_m} - 1\right)\frac{D}{d}$$

$$= 10.4 \times 10^{-6}\left(\frac{1.5}{4/3} - 1\right)\frac{1.5}{0.45 \times 10^{-3}} = 4.33 \text{ mm}$$

Thus, the central maximum is obtained at a distance 4.33 mm below point O on the screen as the slab is placed in the path of lower slit.

4. (*b*) The resultant intensity, $I = I_0 \cos^2\frac{\phi}{2}$

Here, I_0 is the maximum intensity and $\phi = \frac{\pi}{2}$

$$I = I_0 \cos^2\left(\frac{\pi}{2 \times 2}\right) = I_0 \cos^2\frac{\pi}{4}$$

$$I = \frac{I_0}{2}$$

5. (*b*) Here, $A_1 = 2A, A_2 = 2A, \phi = 60°$

$$R = \sqrt{A_1^2 + A_2^2 + 2A_1A_2\cos\phi}$$

$$= \sqrt{(2A)^2 + (2A)^2 + 2 \times 2A \times 2A \times \cos 60°} = A\sqrt{12}$$

As, intensity $\propto$ (amplitude)^2

Therefore, $I \propto 12A^2$

6. Two sources of light having same frequency and constant phase difference with time are known as coherent sources of light.

7. As phase difference between two independent monochromatic sources of light keeps on changing with time, hence the sources cannot be coherent.

8. The sources must be coherent for obtaining sustained interference of light.

9. Consider the diagram. Fresnel constructed the biprism by joining two thin biprisms A_1BC and A_2BC.

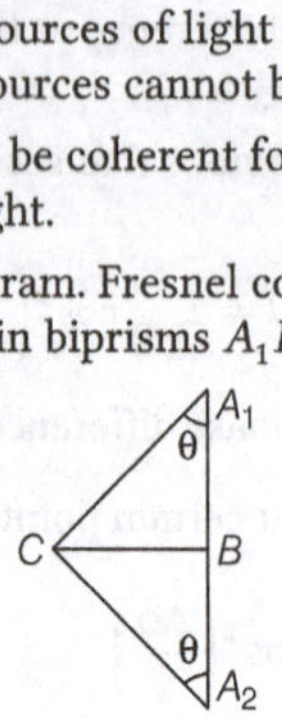

$$A_1 = A_2 \approx \frac{1}{2}°$$

10. The light waves emitted by two sodium vapour lamps cannot be coherent.

The conditions of maxima and minima will change rapidly on the screen producing a uniform illumination.

11. With increase of D, fringe width also increases as

$$\beta = \frac{D\lambda}{d}$$

or $\beta \propto D$

12. As we know that, fringe width,

$$\beta = \frac{\lambda D}{d}$$

Here, $D' = 2D$

So, $\beta' = \frac{2\lambda D}{d}$

$\Rightarrow \beta' = 2\beta$

13. If the source of light used in Young's double slit experiment is changed from red to violet, then their consecutive fringes will come closer (β decrease).

$\because \lambda_{violet} < \lambda_{red}$

14. Angular separation decreases with the increase of separation between the slits as, $\theta = \frac{\lambda}{d}$

15. Path difference between the interfering waves,

$$x = \frac{\lambda}{2\pi}\phi$$

For maximum intensity, $\phi = 2m\pi$

$$x = \frac{\lambda}{2\pi}(2m\pi)$$

$$x = m\lambda$$

16. In YDSE, we know the fringe width, $\beta = \frac{D\lambda}{d}$.

where, D distance between source and screen and d is distance between sources (i.e. slits). As D and d are fixed, i.e. $\beta \propto \lambda$

And we know that λ for red is more than λ for blue. So, β is more for red colour.

17. According to Young's double slit experiment, fringe width, $\beta = \frac{D\lambda}{d}$

where, D = distance between slit and screen

and d = distance between two slits.

If d decreases, i.e. distance between two slits decreases, β will increase.

18. The interference pattern due to different component colours of white light overlap (incoherently). The central bright fringes for different colours are at the same position and therefore the central bright fringe is white. And offer few fringe no clear fringe pattern is seen.

19. Refer to the text on page 396 (Comparison of intensities of maxima and minima).

20. Refer to the text on page 397 (Requirements for obtaining two coherent sources of light).

21. (i) The fringe width of interference pattern increases with the decrease in separation between S_1 and S_2 as

$$\beta \propto \frac{1}{d}$$ (1)

(ii) The fringe width decreases as wavelength gets reduced, when interference set up is taken from air to water as, $\beta \propto \lambda$ (1)

22. Refer to text on page 398 (For constructive interference).

23. **Fringe width** is the separation between two consecutive bright or dark fringes.

The fringe width, $\beta = \frac{\lambda D}{d}$ (1)

To increase fringe width (β) without changing source of light, we should

(i) increase D (distance between slit and screen)

(ii) decrease d (distance between two slits) (2)

24. Refer to the text on page 399 (Conditions for sustained interference).

25. Refer to text on pages 397 and 398 (Young's double slit experiment).

26. From the given figure, of two slit interference arrangement, we can write

$$T_2P = T_2O + OP = D + x$$

and $T_1P = T_1O - OP = D - x$

$$S_1P = \sqrt{(S_1T_1)^2 + (PT_1)^2} = \sqrt{D^2 + (D - x)^2}$$

and $S_2P = \sqrt{(S_2T_2)^2 + (T_2P)^2} = \sqrt{D^2 + (D + x)^2}$

The minima will occur when $S_2P - S_1P = (2n - 1)\frac{\lambda}{2}$

i.e. $[D^2 + (D + x)^2]^{1/2} - [D^2 + (D - x)^2]^{1/2} = \frac{\lambda}{2}$

[for first minima, $n = 1$] (1)

If $x = D$, we can write, $[D^2 + 4D^2]^{1/2} - [D^2 + 0]^{1/2} = \frac{\lambda}{2}$

$\Rightarrow \quad [5D^2]^{1/2} - [D^2]^{1/2} = \frac{\lambda}{2} \Rightarrow \sqrt{5}D - D = \frac{\lambda}{2}$

$\Rightarrow \quad D(\sqrt{5} - 1) = \lambda/2$ or $D = \frac{\lambda}{2(\sqrt{5} - 1)}$

Putting $\sqrt{5} = 2.236 \Rightarrow \sqrt{5} - 1 = 2.236 - 1 = 1.236$

$$D = \frac{\lambda}{2(1.236)} = 0.404\,\lambda$$ (1)

27. (i) Refer to text on page 399 (Conditions for sustained interference) (1)

(ii) $d = ?$

$D = 1.5\,\text{m}$

$y_4 = 1.5\,\text{mm} = 0.0015\ \text{m}$

$\lambda = 500\ \text{m} = 5 \times 10^{-7}\,\text{m}$

Distance between the slits,

$$d = \frac{n \times \lambda \times d}{y_n} = \frac{4 \times 5 \times 10^{-7} \times 1.5}{0.0015} = 2 \times 10^{-3}\,\text{m}$$ (1)

28. (i) Refer to text on page 397 (Need of coherent sources for the production of interference pattern).

(ii) Refer to text on pages 395 and 396 (Interference of light waves).

(iii) Two independent light bulbs are an example of incoherent sources of light and hence fail to produce interference.

29. (i) Given, wavelength of light = 600 nm,

D = distance between slits and screen = 1.2 m

and d = distance between two slits = 5 mm $= 5 \times 10^{-3}$ m

According to YDSE,

Fringe width, $w = \frac{D\lambda}{d} = \frac{1.2 \times 600 \times 10^{-9}}{5 \times 10^{-3}}$

$= 1.44 \times 10^{-4} = 0.144$ mm (1)

(ii) Position of 10th bright fringe, $x_{10\text{th}} = n\frac{\lambda D}{d}$

$= nw = 10 \times 0.144 = 1.44$ mm (1)

30. Given, $OP = y_n$

The distance OP equals one-third of fringe width of the pattern.

i.e $\quad y_n = \frac{\beta}{3} = \frac{1}{3}\left(\frac{D\lambda}{d}\right) = \frac{D\lambda}{3d} \quad \Rightarrow \quad \frac{dy_n}{D} = \frac{\lambda}{3}$ (1)

Path difference $= S_2P - S_1P = \frac{dy_n}{D} = \frac{\lambda}{3}$

$\therefore$ Phase difference, $\phi = \frac{2\pi}{\lambda} \times$ path difference

$= \frac{2\pi}{\lambda} \times \frac{\lambda}{3} = \frac{2\pi}{3}$ (1)

If intensity at central fringe is I_0, then intensity at a point P, where phase difference ϕ, is given by $I = I_0 \cos^2 \phi$

$\Rightarrow \quad I = I_0\left(\cos\frac{2\pi}{3}\right)^2 = I_0\left(-\cos\frac{\pi}{3}\right)^2$

$= I_0\left(-\frac{1}{2}\right)^2 = \frac{I_0}{4}$

Hence, the intensity at point P would be $\frac{I_0}{4}$. (1)

31. Refer to text on pages 397 and 398 (Young's double slit experiment).

32. (i) (a) For interference fringes to be seen, $\frac{s}{S} \leq \frac{\lambda}{d}$ condition should be satisfied where, s = size of the source and d = distance of the source from the plane of two slits. As, the source slit width increases, fringe pattern gets less and less sharp. When the source slit is so wide, the above condition does not get satisfied and the interference pattern disappears. (1)

(b) The interference pattern due to the different colour components of white light overlap. The central bright fringes for different colours are at the same position. Therefore, central fringes are white. And on the either side of the central fringe (i.e. central maxima), coloured bands will appear.The fringe closed on either side of central white fringe is red and the farthest will be blue. After a few fringes, no clear fringe pattern is seen. (1)

(ii) Refer to Q.30 (ii) on page 401. (3)

33. (i) Given, the displacements of two coherent sources $y_1 = a\cos\omega t$ and $y_2 = a\cos(\omega t + \phi)$

By principle of superposition,

$$y = y_1 + y_2 = a\cos\omega t + a\cos(\omega t + \phi)$$

$$y = a\cos\omega t + a\cos\omega t\cos\phi - a\sin\omega t\sin\phi$$

$$y = a(1+\cos\phi)\cos\omega t + (-a\sin\phi)\sin\omega t$$

Let $a(1+\cos\phi) = A\cos\theta$ ...(i)

and $a\sin\phi = A\sin\theta$ ...(ii)

$\therefore\ y = A\cos\theta\cos\omega t - A\sin\theta\sin\omega t$

$\Rightarrow y = A\cos(\omega t + \theta)$ ...(iii)

Squaring and adding Eqs. (i) and (ii), we get

$$(A\cos\theta)^2 + (A\sin\theta)^2$$

$$= a^2(1+\cos\phi)^2 + (a\sin\phi)^2\ A^2(\cos^2\theta + \sin^2\theta)$$

$$= a^2(1+\cos^2\phi + 2\cos\phi) + a^2\sin^2\phi$$

$$\Rightarrow\ A^2\times 1 = a^2 + a^2 + 2a^2\cos\phi = 2a^2(1+\cos\phi)$$

$$\Rightarrow\ A^2 = 2a^2\left(2\cos^2\frac{\phi}{2}\right) = 4a^2\cos^2\left(\frac{\phi}{2}\right)$$

If I is the resultant intensity, then

$$I = 4a^2\cos^2\frac{\phi}{2}$$ (1½)

Refer to text on page 398 {For constructive interference (bright fringes) and for destructive interference (dark fringes)}. (1½)

(ii) (a) Refer to Q. 32 (i) (a) on page 401.

(b) Refer to Q. 320 (i) (b) on page 401. (2)

34. (i) (a) Two independent monochromatic sources of light cannot produce a sustained interference pattern because their relative phases are changing randomly. When d is negligibly small, fringe width β which is proportional to $1/d$ may become too large. Even a single fringe may occupy the screen. Hence, the pattern cannot be detected. (1)

(b) Refer to Q. 33 (i) on pages 401 and 402. (2)

(ii) Refer to Q. 30 on page 401. (2)

35. (i) Correct response by Student.

Interference pattern by two independent light sources cannot be obtained because phase difference varies with time continuously.

(ii) Incorrect response by Student.

The correct mathematical formula is

$$I = I_1 + I_2 + 2\sqrt{I_1 I_2}\cos\phi$$

where, ϕ is the phase difference.

(iii) Incorrect response by Student.

The width of all bright fringes is same provided the distance D of the screen from the slits is much larger than the separation d between the slits.

36. We know that, fringe width, $\beta = \dfrac{\lambda D}{d}$ (1/2)

According to question, by taking the ratio of two different situation,

$$\frac{\beta_1}{\beta_2} = \frac{\lambda_1 D/d}{\lambda_2 D/d} = \frac{\lambda_1}{\lambda_2} = \frac{660}{330} = 2:1$$ (1/2)

37. Given, fringe width, $\beta = 1\text{ mm} = 10^{-3}$ m

Wavelength, $\lambda = 600$ nm, $D = 1.5$ m, $d = ?$

We know that, $\beta = \dfrac{D}{d}\lambda$ [from YDSE] (1)

Distance between two slits,

$$d = \frac{D\lambda}{\beta} = \frac{(1.5)(600\times 10^{-9})}{10^{-3}} = 9\times 10^{-4}\text{ m}$$ (1)

38. Given, wavelength, $\lambda = 600\text{ nm} = 600\times 10^{-9}$ m

5th bright fringe observed at distance, $x = 0.48$ mm $= 0.48\times 10^{-3}$ m

Distance between screen and slits,

$$D = 80\text{ cm} = 80\times 10^{-2}\text{m}$$

(i) Distance between two slits, nth bright fringe is observed at, $X_n = \dfrac{nD\lambda}{d}$

$$\Rightarrow\ 0.48\times 10^{-3} = \frac{5\times 80\times 10^{-2}\times 6000\times 10^{-9}}{d}$$

$$\Rightarrow\ d = \frac{5\times 80\times 10^{-2}\times 600\times 10^{-9}}{0.48\times 10^{-3}}$$

$$= 5\times 10^{-3}\text{m}$$ (2)

(ii) Fringe width, i.e. fringe separation

It is given by

$$\beta = \frac{D\lambda}{d} = \frac{80\times 10^{-2}\times 600\times 10^{-9}}{5\times 10^{-3}} = 9.6\times 10^{-5}\text{m}$$ (1)

39. Given, $\lambda = 630\text{ nm} = 630\times 10^{-9}$ m,

$d = 1.8\text{ mm} = 1.8\times 10^{-3}$ m and $D = 80$ cm $= 0.80$m

(i) Fringe width is given by $\beta = \dfrac{\lambda D}{d}$

$$= \frac{630\times 10^{-9}\times 0.80}{1.8\times 10^{-3}}$$

$$= 2.8\times 10^{-4}\text{ m}$$ (1)

(ii) Distance of 10th bright fringe from the centre, $x = \dfrac{n\lambda D}{d}$

Here, $n = 10$

$$\therefore\ x = \frac{10\times 630\times 10^{-9}\times 0.80}{1.8\times 10^{-3}}$$

$$= 10\times 2.8\times 10^{-4}$$

$$= 2.8\times 10^{-3}\text{ m}$$ (2)

40. In YDSE, the fringe width depends upon the distance of the screen (D) and slit width (d).

In Young's double slit experiment, the fringe width is given by

$$\beta = \frac{D}{d}\lambda \qquad \text{... (i)}$$

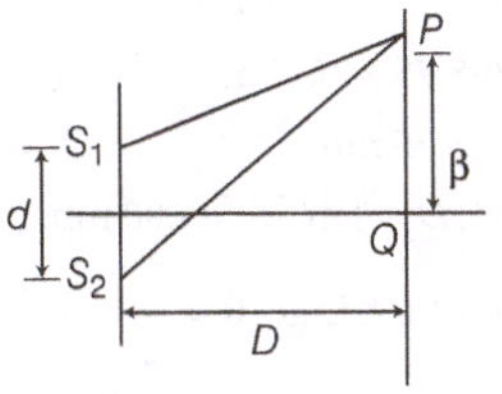

(1)

Let the new fringe width be β'.

We can write, $\beta' = \frac{D'}{d}\lambda$ ... (ii)

From Eqs. (i) and (ii), we get

$$\beta - \beta' = \Delta\beta = \frac{\lambda}{d}[D - D'] = \frac{\lambda}{d}\Delta D$$

Given, $\Delta\beta = 3 \times 10^{-5}$ m, $\Delta D = 5 \times 10^{-2}$ m

$d = 10^{-3}$ m, $\lambda = ?$

where, λ = wavelength of light. (1)

Now, $3 \times 10^{-5}\text{ m} = \frac{\lambda}{10^{-3}\text{ m}} \times 5 \times 10^{-2}\text{ m}$

$$\lambda = \frac{3 \times 10^{-5} \times 10^{-3}}{5 \times 10^{-2}} = 0.6 \times 10^{-6}$$

$$= 6 \times 10^{-7}\text{ m}$$

$\Rightarrow \quad \lambda = 6000$ Å (1)

41. According to the question, for the same arrangement of YDSE, the ratio of d/D remains constant.

$$y_n = n\frac{D}{d}\lambda \qquad (1/2)$$

Given, $\lambda_1 = 700$ nm, $n_1 = 10$th bright fringe,

$\lambda_2 = 500$ nm, $n_2 = ?$

We know that, $y = n\frac{D\lambda}{d}$ (1/2)

For the same point, x is constant and for same arrangement, then $\frac{d}{D}$ is constant. (1)

$\Rightarrow \quad n_1\lambda_1 = n_2\lambda_2$

$\Rightarrow \quad 10 \times 700 = n_2 \times 500$

or $\quad n_2 = \frac{10 \times 700}{500} = 14$ (1)

42. (i) We know that, $y_n = n\frac{D\lambda}{d}$

where, $n = 0, 1, 2, \ldots$

Here, $y_6 - y_1 = 12.5$ mm (1½)

$$y_6 - y_1 = \frac{D\lambda}{d}(6-1) = 5\beta \qquad \left[\because \beta = \frac{D\lambda}{d}\right]$$

So, fringe width $(\beta) = \frac{12.5}{5} = 2.5$ mm (1½)

(ii) Since, $\beta = \frac{D\lambda}{d}$

Given, $D = 60\text{cm} = 0.6$ m,

$d = 0.12\text{ mm} = 0.12 \times 10^{-3}$ m

$\Rightarrow \quad 2.5 \times 10^{-3} = \frac{0.6 \times \lambda}{0.12 \times 10^{-3}}$

$\lambda = 5 \times 10^{-7}\text{ m} = 5000$ Å (1½)

43. As, $I = I_0\cos^2\phi$

$\because$ Phase difference, $\phi = \frac{2\pi x}{\lambda}$ path difference.

So, $\quad I_1 = I_0\cos^2\left(\frac{2\pi \times 0}{\lambda}\right) = I_0$ (1/2)

and $\quad I_2 = I_0\cos^2\left(\frac{2\pi}{\lambda} \times \lambda/2\right)$

$= I_0\cos^2(\pi) = I_0$

$\therefore \quad \frac{I_1}{I_2} = \frac{1}{1}$ (1/2)

44. Here, $\lambda = 600\text{ nm} = 600 \times 10^{-9}\text{ m} = 6 \times 10^{-7}$ m

$\Rightarrow \quad 0.1° = \frac{0.1\pi}{180}$ rad

From angular width, $\theta = \frac{\lambda}{d}$ (1/2)

$\Rightarrow \quad d = \frac{\lambda}{\theta} = \frac{6 \times 10^{-7}}{\frac{\pi}{180} \times 0.1} = 3.44 \times 10^{-4}$ m (1/2)

45. Angular width, $\theta = \frac{\lambda}{d}$

Here, $\theta = 0.2°$ $\lambda = 630\text{ nm} = 630 \times 10^{-9}$ m (1/2)

$\Rightarrow \quad d = \frac{630 \times 10^{-9} \times 180}{0.2 \times \pi}$

$= 1.80 \times 10^{-4}$ m (1/2)

46. Here, slit width, $d = 0.28\text{ mm} = 0.28 \times 10^{-3}$ m

Distance between slit and screen, $D = 1.4$ m

$y = 1.2\text{ cm} = 1.2 \times 10^{-2}$ m, $n = 4$, $\lambda = ?$

For constructive interference, $y = n\lambda\frac{D}{d}$ or $\lambda = \frac{yd}{nD}$ (1/2)

$$= \frac{1.2 \times 10^{-2} \times 0.28 \times 10^{-3}}{4 \times 1.4} = 6 \times 10^{-7}\text{ m} \qquad (1/2)$$

47. We know that, $\frac{I_1}{I_2} = \frac{a^2}{b^2} = \frac{W_1}{W_2}$ (1/2)

$\Rightarrow \quad \frac{W_1}{W_2} = \frac{(\sqrt{2})^2}{(1)^2} = \frac{2}{1}$ (1/2)

48. We know that, $\frac{W_1}{W_2} = \frac{I_1}{I_2} = \frac{a^2}{b^2} = \frac{4}{1}$

$\Rightarrow \quad \frac{a}{b} = 2:1$

49. Given, distance between the screen and slit, $D = 1$ m

Slit width, $d = 4 \times 10^{-3}$ m

$\lambda_1 = 560$ nm, $\lambda_2 = 420$ nm

Let nth order bright fringe of λ_1 coincides with $(n+1)$th order bright fringe of λ_2.

$\therefore \quad \frac{Dn\lambda_1}{d} = \frac{D(n+1)\lambda_2}{d} \quad (\lambda_1 > \lambda_2)$ (1)

$\Rightarrow \quad n\lambda_1 = (n+1)\lambda_2$

$\Rightarrow \quad \frac{n+1}{n} = \frac{\lambda_1}{\lambda_2}$

$\therefore \quad 1 + \frac{1}{n} = \frac{560 \times 10^{-9}}{420 \times 10^{-9}} \Rightarrow 1 + \frac{1}{n} = \frac{4}{3}$

$\therefore \quad n = 3$ (1)

$\therefore$ Least distance from the central fringe where bright fringe of two wavelengths coincides

= distance of 3rd order bright fringe of λ_1

$\therefore \quad y_n = \frac{3D\lambda_1}{d}$

$= \frac{3 \times 1 \times 560 \times 10^{-9}}{4 \times 10^{-3}} = 0.42 \times 10^{-3}$ m

$\therefore \quad y_n = 0.42$ mm

3rd bright fringe of λ_1 and 4th bright fringe of λ_2 coincide at 0.42 mm from central fringe. (1)

50. Here, $\lambda_1 = 650$ nm $= 650 \times 10^{-9}$ m,

$\lambda_2 = 520$ nm $= 520 \times 10^{-9}$ m

Suppose, d = distance between two slits

D = distance of screen from the slits

(i) For third bright fringe, $n = 3$

$\therefore \quad y = n\lambda_1 \frac{D}{d} = 3 \times 650 \frac{D}{d}$ nm

$= 1950 \frac{D}{d}$ nm (1)

(ii) $\therefore n\lambda_2 = (n-1)\lambda_1$ (for bright fringes)

$\Rightarrow \quad 520n = 650n - 650$

$\Rightarrow \quad 650 = 130n$

$\Rightarrow \quad n = 5$

$\therefore$ Least distance form the central maximum,

$x = n\lambda_2 \frac{D}{d}$

$= 5 \times 520 \times \frac{D}{6}$

$= 2600 \frac{D}{d}$ nm (2)

51. According to the question, $\frac{\beta_1}{\beta_2} = \frac{\lambda_1}{\lambda_2}$

[$\because$ D and d are same]

Here, $\beta_1 = 7.2 \times 10^{-3}$ m,

$\beta_2 = 8.1 \times 10^{-3}$ m

and $\lambda_1 = 630 \times 10^{-9}$ m (1)

Wavelength of another source of laser light,

$\lambda_2 = \frac{\beta_2}{\beta_1} \times \lambda_1 = \frac{8.1 \times 10^{-3}}{7.2 \times 10^{-3}} \times 630 \times 10^{-9}$ m

$\therefore \quad \lambda_2 = 708.75 \times 10^{-9}$ m

$= 708.75$ nm (1)

52. Here, $\theta_1 = 0.2°, D = 1 \text{m}, \lambda_1 = 600 \text{ nm}, \mu = 4/3$

Angular width of a fringe, $\theta = \frac{\lambda}{d}$

$\frac{\theta_2}{\theta_1} = \frac{\lambda_2}{\lambda_1} = \frac{1}{\mu} = \frac{3}{4}$

$\Rightarrow \quad \theta_2 = \frac{3}{4} \times \theta_1 = \frac{3}{4} \times 0.2° = 0.15°$ (2)

53. $\frac{I_{min}}{I_{max}} = \frac{9}{25} = \frac{(a-b)^2}{(a+b)^2}$

$\Rightarrow \quad \frac{a-b}{a+b} = \frac{3}{5}$

$\Rightarrow \quad a = 4b$

As, $\quad \frac{W_1}{W_2} = \frac{a^2}{b^2}$

$= \frac{(4b)^2}{b^2} = \frac{16}{1}$

54. (i) The distance of nth order bright fringe from central fringe is given by

$y_n = \frac{nD\lambda}{d}$ (1/2)

For second bright fringe,

$y_2 = \frac{2D\lambda}{d}$

$= \frac{2 \times 1 \times 4.5 \times 10^{-7}}{1.5 \times 10^{-4}}$

$y_2 = 6 \times 10^{-3}$ m

The distance of the second bright fringe

$y_2 = 6$ mm (1/2)

(ii) The distance of nth order dark fringe from central fringe is given by

$y'_n = (2n-1)\frac{D\lambda}{2d}$ (1/2)

For second dark fringe, $n = 2$

$y'_n = (2 \times 2 - 1)\frac{D\lambda}{2d} = \frac{3D\lambda}{2d}$

$\Rightarrow \quad y'_n = \frac{3}{2} \times \frac{1 \times 4.5 \times 10^{-7}}{1.5 \times 10^{-4}}$

$= 4.5 \times 10^{-3}$ m

$\therefore$ The distance of the second dark fringe

$y'_n = 4.5$ mm (1/2)

TOPIC 03 Diffraction of Light

Diffraction of Light

The phenomenon of bending of light around the sharp corners and the spreading of light within the geometrical shadow of the opaque obstacles is called diffraction of light.

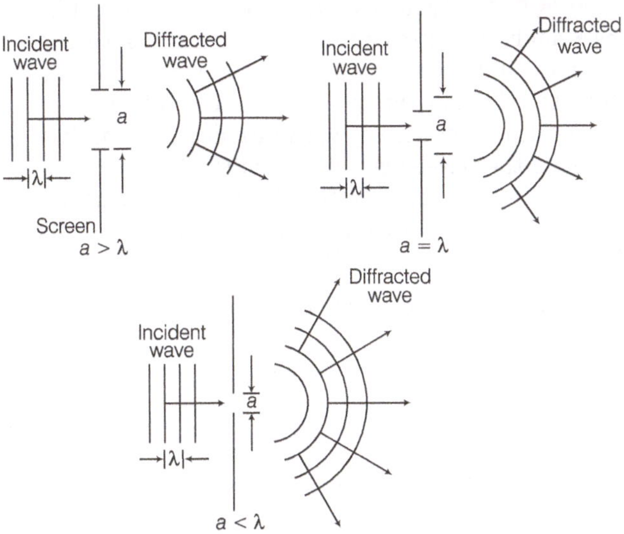

Diffraction of waves for slits of different width

The light thus deviates from its linear path. The deviation becomes much more pronounced, when the dimensions of the aperture or the obstacle are comparable to the wavelength of light.

Note Diffraction is a general characteristic exhibited by all types of waves. For visible light, λ is very small ($\approx 10^{-6}$ m). Therefore, diffraction of visible light is not so common as obstacles/apertures of this size are hardly available.

Fraunhofer Diffraction Due to a Single Slit

A parallel beam of light with a plane wavefront is made to fall on a single slit LN. As width of the slit $LN = a$ is of the order of wavelength of light, therefore diffraction occurs when beam of light passes through the slit.

The wavelets from the single wavefront reach the centre C on the screen in same phase. Hence, interfere constructively to give central maximum (bright fringe).

The diffraction pattern obtained on the screen consists of a central bright band, having alternate dark and weak bright bands of decreasing intensity on both sides.

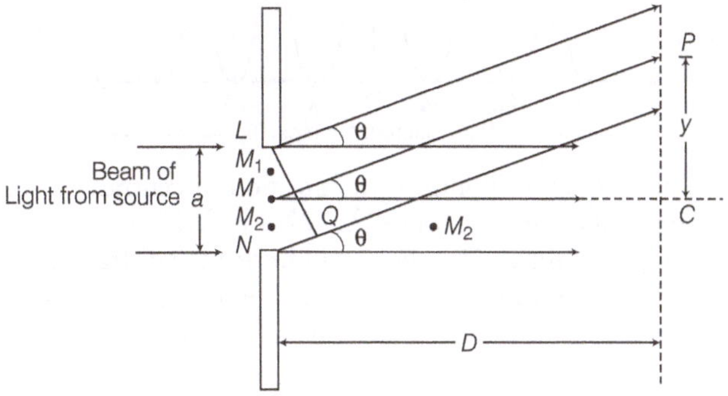

Geometry of single slit diffraction

Consider a point P on the screen at which wavelets travelling in a direction, make an angle θ with MC. The wavelets from points L and N will have a path difference equal to NQ.

From the right angled ΔLNQ, we have

$$NQ = LN \sin\theta$$

or $$NQ = a \sin\theta$$

To establish the condition for secondary minima, the slit is divided into 2, 4, 6,... equal parts such that corresponding wavelets from successive regions interfere with path difference of $\lambda/2$.

Or for ***n*th secondary minima**, the slit can be divided into $2n$ equal parts.

Hence, for nth secondary minima,

$$\text{Path difference} = \frac{a}{2}\sin\theta = \frac{\lambda}{2}$$

or $$\boxed{\sin\theta_n = \frac{n\lambda}{a},\ (n = 1, 2, 3, \ldots)}$$

To establish the condition for secondary maxima, the slit is divided into 3, 5, 7, ... equal parts such that corresponding wavelets from alternate regions interfere with path difference of $\lambda/2$.

Or for ***n*th secondary maxima**, the slit can be divided into $(2n+1)$ equal parts.

Hence, for nth secondary maxima,

$$a\sin\theta_n = (2n+1)\frac{\lambda}{2} \qquad [n = 1, 2, 3, \ldots]$$

or $$\boxed{\sin\theta_n = (2n+1)\frac{\lambda}{2a}}$$

Hence, the diffraction pattern can be graphically shown as below

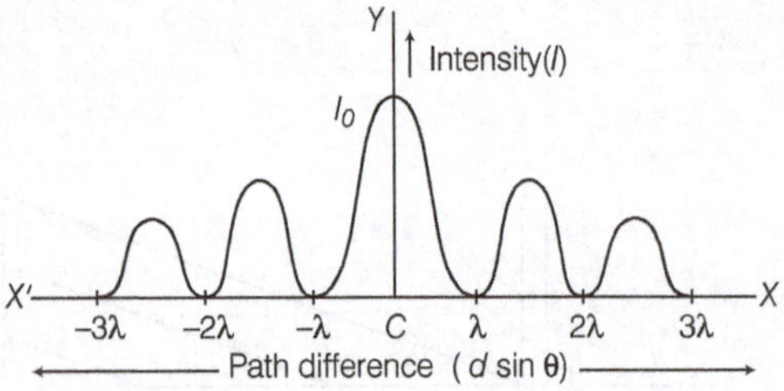

The point C corresponds to the position of central maxima. And the position $-3\lambda, -2\lambda, -\lambda, \lambda, 2\lambda, 3\lambda \ldots$ are secondary minima. The above conditions for diffraction maxima and minima are exactly reverse of mathematical conditions for interference maxima and minima.

Width of Central Maximum

It is the distance between first secondary minimum on either side of the central bright fringe C.

For first secondary minimum,

$$a \sin\theta = \lambda \quad \text{or} \quad \sin\theta = \frac{\lambda}{a} \quad \ldots\text{(i)}$$

If θ is small, $\sin\theta \approx \theta = \dfrac{y}{D}$ ...(ii)

From Eqs. (i) and (ii), we get

$$\frac{y}{D} = \frac{\lambda}{a} \quad \text{or} \quad y = \frac{D\lambda}{a}$$

$$\boxed{\text{Width of central maximum} = 2y = \frac{2D\lambda}{a}}$$

As, the slit width a increases, width of central maximum decreases.

$$\therefore \quad \boxed{\text{Angular width of central maxima, } 2\theta = \frac{2\lambda}{a}}$$

Example 1 A beam of light whose wavelength 4000 Å is diffracted by a single slit of width 0.2 mm. Give the angular position of the second minima.

Sol. Given, wavelength, $\lambda = 4000$ Å

Slit width, $a = 0.2 \text{ mm} = 0.2 \times 10^{-3}$ m

Width of second minima = ?

For nth minima, $a\sin\theta = n\lambda$

$$\therefore \quad 0.2 \times 10^{-3} \sin\theta = 2 \times 4000 \times 10^{-10}$$

For θ to be very small; $\sin\theta \approx \theta$

$$\therefore \quad \theta = \frac{2 \times 4000 \times 10^{-10}}{0.2 \times 10^{-3}} = 4 \times 10^{-3} \text{ rad}$$

Example 2 A slit 4 cm wide is irradiated with microwaves of wavelength 2 cm. Find the angular spread of central maximum, assuming incidence normal to the plane of the slit.

Sol. Here, $a = 4 \text{ cm} = 4 \times 10^{-2}$ m,

$\lambda = 2 \text{ cm} = 2 \times 10^{-2}$ m

$\therefore$ Angular spread of central maximum (2θ) is

$$2\theta = \frac{2\lambda}{a} = \frac{2 \times 2 \times 10^{-2}}{4 \times 10^{-2}} = 1 \text{ rad}$$

Example 3 Angular width of central maximum in the Fraunhoffer diffraction pattern of a slit is measured. The slit is illuminated by light of wavelength 6000 Å. When the slit is illuminated by light of another wavelength, then the angular width decreases by 30%. Calculate the wavelength of this light. The same decrease in the angular width of central maximum is obtained when the original apparatus is immersed in a liquid. Find the refractive index of the liquid.

Sol. Angular width of central maximum $= \dfrac{2\lambda}{a}$

$$\lambda_1 = 600 \text{ nm}, \theta_1 = \frac{2\lambda_1}{a} \quad \ldots\text{(i)}$$

$$\theta_2 = \theta_1 \times 0.7 = \frac{2\lambda_2}{a} \quad \ldots\text{(ii)}$$

On dividing Eq. (i) by Eq. (ii), we get

$$\frac{1}{0.7} = \frac{\lambda_1}{\lambda_2} = \frac{600}{\lambda_2}$$

Wavelength, $\lambda_2 = 420$ nm

When immersed in liquid, $\lambda_2 = \lambda_1/\mu$

$$\theta_2 = \theta_1 \times 0.7 \quad \ldots\text{(iii)}$$

$$\Rightarrow \quad \frac{2\lambda_1/\mu}{a} = \frac{2\lambda_1}{a} \times 0.7 \Rightarrow \frac{1}{0.7} = \mu$$

$\therefore$ Refractive index of the liquid,

$$\mu = \frac{10}{7} = 1.42$$

Example 4 Intensity curve for a single slit diffraction pattern is shown below. Find the ratio of the intensities of the secondary maxima to the intensity of the central maximum for the single-slit Fraunhofer diffraction pattern.

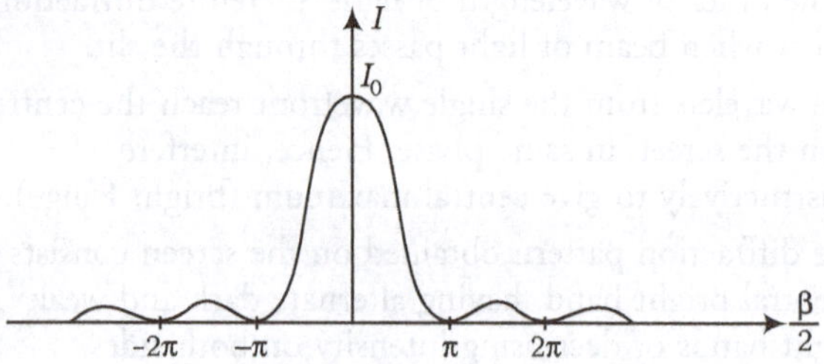

Sol. To a good approximation, the secondary maxima lie midway between the zero points. From figure, we see that this corresponds to $\beta/2$ values of $3\pi/2$, $5\pi/2$, $7\pi/2$,

$$\therefore \quad \frac{I_1}{I_0} = \left[\frac{\sin(3\pi/2)}{(3\pi/2)}\right]^2 = \frac{1}{9\pi^2/4} = 0.045$$

and
$$\frac{I_2}{I_0} = \left[\frac{\sin(5\pi/2)}{5\pi/2}\right]^2 = \frac{1}{25\pi^2/4} = 0.016$$

i.e. the first secondary maxima (the ones adjacent to the central maximum) have an intensity of 4.5% that of the central maximum and the next secondary maxima have an intensity of 1.6% that of the central maximum.

Difference in Diffraction Pattern at a Single Slit due to Monochromatic Light and White Light

For monochromatic light, the diffraction is of alternate bright and dark bands of unequal widths. The central bright fringe has maximum intensity and the intensity of successive secondary maxima decreases rapidly.

If the source is of white light, the diffraction pattern is coloured. The central maximum is white but other bands are coloured . As bandwidth $\propto \lambda$, therefore red band width is wider than the violet band width.

Difference between Interference and Diffraction

(i) The interference pattern has a number of equally spaced bright and dark bands. Where as the diffraction pattern has a central bright maximum, which is twice as wide as the other maxima. The intensity falls as we go to successive maxima away from the centre on either side.

(ii) We calculate the interference pattern by superposing two waves originating from the two narrow slits. Whereas the diffraction pattern is a superposition of a continuous family of waves originating from each point on a single slit.

(iii) For a single slit of width a, the first null of the interference pattern occurs at an angle of λ/a. At the same angle of λ/a, we get a maxima (not a null) for two narrow slits separated by a distance a.
One must understand that both distances between two slits in Young's double slit experiment, d and a width of each slit have to be quite small, to be able to observe good interference and diffraction patterns respectively. e.g. d must be of the order of a millimeter or so and must be even smaller of the order of 0.1 of 0.2 mm.

Topic Practice 3

Multiple Choice Questions

(1 Mark)

1. Which of the given phenomenon is based on the fact that light waves are transverse electromagnetic waves?
(a) Diffraction
(b) Interference
(c) Polarisation
(d) All of these

2. If we observe the single slit diffraction with wavelength λ and slit width e, the width of the central maxima is 2θ. On decreasing the slit width for the same λ.
(a) θ increases
(b) θ remains unchanged
(c) θ decreases
(d) θ increases or decreases depending on the intensity of light

3. In diffraction from a single slit, the angular width of the central maxima does not depend on
(a) λ of light used
(b) width of slit
(c) distance of slits from the screen
(d) ratio of λ and slit width

Very Short Answer Type Questions

(1 Mark)

4. What is the condition for first minima in case of diffraction due to a single slit?

5. How does the angular separation between fringes in single slit diffraction experiment change when the distance of separation between the slit and screen doubled?

6. In Fraunhofer diffraction, how is the angular width of the central bright fringe affected when slit separation is increased? **ISC 2018**

7. Explain how the intensity of diffraction pattern changes as the order(n) of the diffraction band varies?

8. State any one difference between interference of light and diffraction of light. **ISC 2015**

Short Answer Type Questions

2 Marks

9. (i) What is meant by diffraction of light?
(ii) In Fraunhofer diffraction, what kind of source of light is used and where is it situated? **ISC 2017**

10. Show graphically, the intensity distribution in Fraunhofer's single slit diffraction experiment. Label the axes. **ISC 2015**

11. What will be the effect on the width of the central bright fringe in the diffraction pattern of a single slit, if
(i) the monochromatic light of smaller wavelength is used.
(ii) slit is made narrower. **ISC 2013**

12. Draw a labelled graph showing the variation in intensity of diffracted light with diffracting angle in a single slit Fraunhofer diffraction experiment. **ISC 2024**

13. Draw a labelled graph to show the variation in intensity of diffracted light with angular position, in a single slit diffraction experiment. **ISC 2012, 09, 07**

14. For a single slit of width a, the first minimum of the interference pattern of a monochromatic light of wavelength λ occurs at an angle of $\frac{\lambda}{a}$. At the same angle of $\frac{\lambda}{a}$, we get a maximum for two narrow slits separated by a distance a. Explain.

15. State briefly two features which can distinguish the characteristic features of an interference pattern from those observed in the diffraction pattern due to a single slit.

Long Answer Type Question

5 Marks

16. (i) Obtain the conditions for the bright and dark fringes in diffraction pattern due to a single narrow slit illuminated by a monochromatic source. Explain clearly, why the secondary maxima go on becoming weaker with increasing of their order?
(ii) When the width of the slit is made double, how would this affect the size and intensity of the central diffraction band? Justify your answer.

Numerical Problems

17. A parallel beam of light of wavelength 500 nm falls on a narrow slit and the resulting diffraction pattern is observed on a screen 1 m away. It is observed that the first minimum is at a distance of 2.5 mm from the centre of the screen. Find the width of the slit. **NCERT (1 M)**

18. Yellow light ($\lambda = 6000$ Å) illuminates a single slit of 1×10^{-4} m. Calculate the distance between two dark lines on either side to the central maximum, when the diffraction pattern is viewed on a screen kept 1.5 m away from the slit. **(1 M)**

19. A parallel beam of light of 500 nm falls on a narrow slit and the resulting diffraction pattern is observed on a screen 1 m away. It is observed that the first minima is at a distance of 2.5 mm from the centre of the screen. Calculate the width of the slit. **(2 M)**

20. Two wavelength of sodium light of 590 nm and 596 nm are used in turn to study the diffraction taking place at a single slit of aperture 2×10^{-6} m. The distance between the slit and the screen is 1.5 m.Calculate the separation between the position of first maxima of the diffraction pattern obtained in the two cases. **(2 M)**

21. Two wavelengths of sodium light 590nm and 596 nm are used in turn to study the diffraction at a single slit 4mm. The distance between the slit and the screen is 2m. Calculate the separation between the positions of the first maximum of diffraction pattern in two cases. **(1 M)**

22. Fraunhofer diffraction from a single slit of width 1.24×10^{-6} m is observed with the light of wavelength 6200 Å. Calculate the angular width of the central maximum. **ISC 2005 (1 M)**

23. Monochromatic light of wavelength 650 nm falls normally on a slit of width 1.3×10^{-4} cm and the resulting Fraunhofer diffraction is obtained on a screen. Find the angular width of the central maxima. **ISC 2016 (2 M)**

24. Determine the angular separation between the central maxima and the first order maxima of the diffraction pattern due to a single slit of width 0.25 mm when light of wavelength 5890 Å is incident on its normally.

ISC 2006, 00 (3 M)

Hints & Solutions

1. (c) The phenomenon of polarisation is based on the fact that the light waves are transverse electromagnetic waves. Diffraction and interference can be explained by wave theory of light.

2. (a) Angular width of central maxima $(2\theta) = \frac{2\lambda}{d} = \frac{2\lambda}{e}$

$\Rightarrow \quad 2\theta \propto \frac{\lambda}{e}$

$\Rightarrow \quad \theta \propto \frac{1}{e}$ (for λ = constant)

Thus, on decreasing slit width (e), then θ will increase.

3. (c) Angular width of central maxima $= 2\theta = \frac{2\lambda}{d}$.

Thus, θ does not depend on D, i.e. distance between the slits and the screen.

4. For first minima, $\sin\theta_1 = 1 \times \lambda / a = \lambda / a$

5. Angular width, $2\theta = \frac{2\lambda}{a}$

i.e. it is independent of the distance of separation between the slit and screen.

6. The angular width θ of the central bright fringe in Fraunhofer single slit diffraction experiment is given by $\theta = \frac{\lambda}{e}$.

When the slit width or separation e is increased, the angular width θ will decrease.

7. In diffraction pattern, intensity of alternate dark and weak bright bands decreases as compare to central bright band.

8. The interference pattern has a number of equally spaced bright and dark bands. The diffraction pattern has a central bright maxima, which is twice as wide as the other maxima. The intensity falls, as we go to successive maxima away from the centre on either side.

9. (i) The phenomenon of bending of light around the edges or the sharp corners and then spreading of light within the geometrical shadow of opaque obstacles is called diffraction of light. (1)

(ii) **Fraunhofer diffraction** In this type of diffraction, the source of light is not necessary to be monochromatic or white light, but the expression calculated for the central maxima and minima, we considered it to be monochromatic. And the source of light is being placed at large distance from the screen, i.e. effectively at infinity. (1)

10. The graph of variation in the intensity of diffracted light in a single slit experiment is shown in the figure. Here, intensity of the central maxima will be maximum and that of other will gradually decreases.

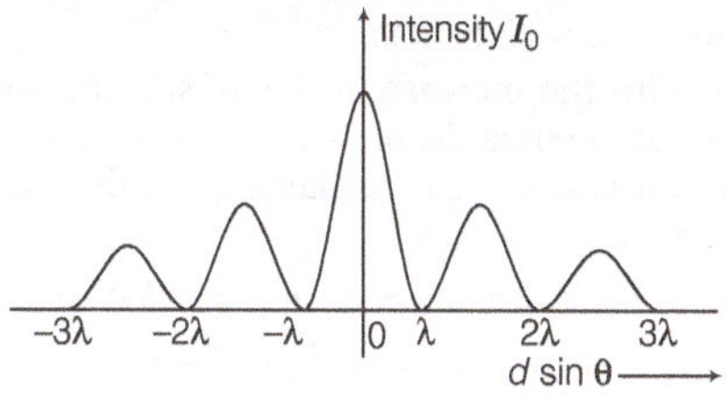

(1)

For central bright fringe, $\theta = 0°$

For first dark fringe,

$$d \sin\theta = \pm\lambda \Rightarrow \sin\theta = \pm\frac{\lambda}{d}$$ (1)

11. We know that, width of the central bright fringe in the diffraction pattern of a single slit is $\beta = \frac{2D\lambda}{d}$. (1)

where, D = distance of the screen, d = width of the slit and λ = wavelength of light.

(i) As $\beta \propto \lambda$, when λ is smaller, then β decreases. (1/2)

(ii) As $\beta \propto \frac{1}{d}$, when slit is made narrower, β increases. (1/2)

12. Refer to text on page 410.

13. Refer to Q. 10 on page 412.

14. In diffraction, angular position, $\theta = \frac{\Delta x}{a}$

For first minima, $\Delta x = \lambda$

$\therefore \quad \theta = \frac{\lambda}{a}$ (1)

In interference, $d = a$ (given) and angular position,

$$\theta = \frac{\Delta x}{a}$$

$\therefore$ Angular position of first maxima $(\Delta x = \lambda)$ (1)

15. Refer to the text on page 411 (Difference between interference and diffraction).

16. (i) Refer to text on pages 409 and 410. (2)

(ii) As, the number of point sources increases, their contribution towards intensity also increases. intensity varies as square of the slit width. Thus, when the width of the slit is made double the original width, intensity will get four times of its original value. (1)

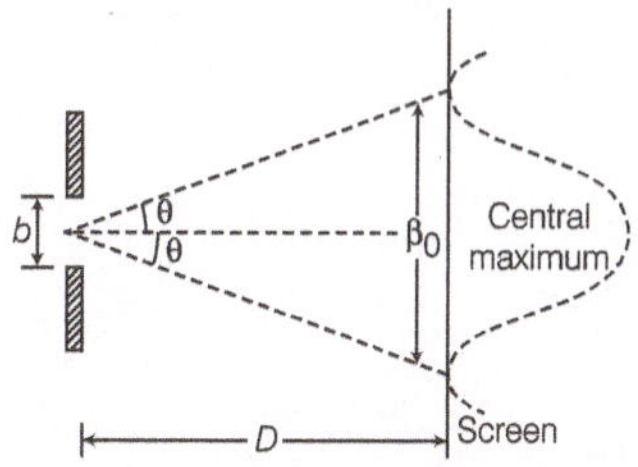

Width of central maximum is given by $\beta = \frac{2D\lambda}{b}$

where, D = distance between screen and slit,

λ = wavelength of the light

and b = size of slit. (1)

So, with the increase in size of slit, the width of central maxima decreases. Hence, double the size of the slit would result as half the width of the central maxima. (1)

17. Given, $D = 1$ m, $n = 1$, $y = 2.5$ mm $= 2.5 \times 10^{-3}$ m

$\lambda = 500$ nm $= 5 \times 10^{-7}$ m, $d = ?$

The condition for minima is $d\frac{y}{D} = n\lambda$ (1/2)

$$\Rightarrow \quad d = \frac{n\lambda D}{y} = \frac{1 \times 5 \times 10^{-7} \times 1}{2.5 \times 10^{-3}}$$

$= 2 \times 10^{-4}$ m $= 0.2$ mm (1/2)

18. Given, $\lambda = 6000\ \text{Å} = 6 \times 10^{-7}$ m and $d = 1 \times 10^{-4}$ m

Separation between slit and screen, $D = 1.5$ m

$\therefore$ The separation between two dark lines on either side of the central maximum

= fringe width of central maximum (1/2)

$$= \frac{2D\lambda}{d} = \frac{2 \times 1.5 \times 6 \times 10^{-7}}{1 \times 10^{-4}}$$

$= 18 \times 10^{-3}$ m $= 18$ mm (1/2)

19. The distance of the nth minima from the centre of the screen is given by $x_n = \frac{nD\lambda}{a}$ ...(i)

where, D = distance of slit from screen = 1 m

λ = wavelength of the light = 500 nm

$= 500 \times 10^{-9}$ m, $n = 1$,

$x_n = 2.5$ mm $= 2.5 \times 10^{-3}$ m,

and a = width of the slit for first minima = ? (1)

Putting these values in Eq. (i), we get

$$2.5 \times 10^{-3} = \frac{(500 \times 10^{-9})}{a}$$

$\Rightarrow \quad a = 2 \times 10^{-4}$ m $= 0.2$ m (1)

20. For $\lambda_1 = 590$ nm

Location of 1st maxima, $y_1 = (2n+1)\frac{D\lambda_1}{2a}$

If $n = 1 \Rightarrow y_1 = \frac{3D\lambda_1}{2a}$

For $\lambda_2 = 596$ nm

Location of 2nd maxima, $y_2 = (2n+1)\frac{D\lambda_2}{2a}$ (1)

If $n = 1 \Rightarrow y_2 = \frac{3D\lambda_2}{2a}$

$\therefore$ Path difference $= y_2 - y_1 = \frac{3D}{2a}(\lambda_2 - \lambda_1)$

$$= \frac{3 \times 1.5}{2 \times 2 \times 10^{-6}}(596 - 590) \times 10^{-9} = 6.75 \times 10^{-3} \text{ m}$$ (1)

21. Given, $\lambda_1 = 590$ nm, $\lambda_2 = 596$ nm,

$D = 2$ m, $d = 4$ mm

Refer to sol. 20 on page 414.

Path difference, $y_2 - y_1 = 4.5 \times 10^{-6}$ m (2)

22. In Fraunhofer diffraction from a single slit, central maxima is given by $a \sin\theta = n\lambda$

where, a = width of a slit

and λ = wavelength of the light.

$$\Rightarrow \sin\theta = \frac{n\lambda}{a} = \frac{6200 \times 10^{-10} \times 1}{1.24 \times 10^{-6}} = 0.5$$

$\Rightarrow \quad \theta = 30°$ (1/2)

$\therefore$ Angular width of the central maxima,

$2\theta = 2 \times 30° = 60°$ (1/2)

23. In single slit diffraction, first minimum occurs at

$$d\sin\theta = \lambda \text{ or } \sin\theta = \frac{\lambda}{d}$$

As, $\lambda << d$, so $\theta = \frac{\lambda}{d}$ ($\because \sin\theta = \theta$) (1)

Now, angular width of central maxima,

$$\phi = 2\theta = \frac{2\lambda}{d} = \frac{2 \times 650 \times 10^{-9}}{1.3 \times 10^{-4} \times 10^{-2}} = \frac{13000}{13} \times 10^{-3} = 1 \text{ rad}$$ (1)

Thus, the angular width of the central maxima is 1 rad.

24. To find the angular separation we have to apply condition of maxima for diffraction from a single slit. (1)

The angular separation between the central maxima,

$$d\sin\theta = (2n+1)\frac{\lambda}{2}$$

where, symbols have their usual meaning. (1)

For first order maxima, $n = 1$

$$\sin\theta = \frac{3 \times 5890 \times 10^{-10}}{2 \times 0.25 \times 10^{-3}} \Rightarrow \theta = 0.0035 \text{ rad}$$ (1)

SUMMARY

- **Wave optics** describes the connection between the waves and rays of light.
- **Wavefront** is the locus of points (wavelets) having the same phases of oscillations.
- Wavefronts can be of three types
  - (i) Spherical wavefront
  - (ii) Cylindrical wavefront
  - (iii) Plane wavefront
- **Huygens' Principle** is essentially a geometrical construction, which gives the shape of a wavefront at any time allows us to determine the shape of the wavefront at a later time.
- **Superposition Principle of Waves** states that at a particular point in the medium, the resultant displacement produced by the number of the displacements produced by each of the waves.
- **Interference of Light Waves** is the phenomenon of redistribution of light energy in a medium on the account of superposition of light waves from two coherent sources.
- **Coherent Sources** of light emit the light waves with constants phase difference.
- **Incoherent Sources** of light emit the light do not waves with a constants phase difference.
- **Young's Double Slit Experiment**

  (i) For constructive interference (bright fringes),

  $$\text{Path difference} = \frac{dy}{D} = n\lambda$$

  $$\Rightarrow \quad y = \frac{nD\lambda}{d}$$

  (ii) For destructive interference (dark fringes), path difference

  $$\frac{dy}{D} = (2n-1)\frac{\lambda}{2}$$

  $$\Rightarrow \quad y = (2n-1)\frac{D\lambda}{2d}$$

- **Intensity of Fringes**
  - (i) For bright fringe, $I_R = I_1 + I_2 + 2\sqrt{I_1 I_2}$
  - (ii) For dark fringe, $I_R = I_1 - I_2 - 2\sqrt{I_1 I_2}$
- **Fringe Width** is given as, $W = \frac{D\lambda}{d}$
- **Relation Between Intensity, Amplitude of the Wave and Width of Slit**

  It is given by, $\frac{I_1}{I_2} = \frac{a^2}{b^2} = \frac{W_1}{W_2}$
- **Conditions for Interference** The intensity at the points of constructive and destructive interference must be maintained maximum and zero, respectively.
- **Diffraction of Light** Bending of light around the sharp corners an spreading of light with in the geometrical shadow of opaque obstacles is called diffraction of light.
- In diffraction pattern, angular width of the central maxima is

  $$2\theta = \frac{2\lambda}{a}$$
- **Difference between Interference and Diffraction** The interference pattern has number of equally spaced dark and bright bands while the diffraction pattern has central bright maximum.

For Mind Map

Visit : https://goo.gl/jQHSFu OR **Scan the Code**

Chapter Practice

Multiple Choice Questions

(1 Mark)

1 In Young's double slit experiment, a glass plate is placed before a slit which absorbs half the intensity of light. Under this case,
(a) the brightness of fringes decreases
(b) the fringe width decreases
(c) no fringes will be observed
(d) the bright fringes become fainter and the dark fringes have finite light intensity

2 The maximum intensity of fringes in Young's experiment is I. If one of the slit is closed, then the intensity at that place becomes I_0. Which of the following relation is correct?
(a) $I = I_0$
(b) $I = 2I_0$
(c) $I = 4I_0$
(d) There is no relation between I and I_0

3 In a single slit diffraction experiment, a converging lens of focal length f is placed after the slits and the screen is placed at its focus. The size of the central maxima on the screen will
(a) $f\,a/\lambda$ (b) $f\,\lambda/a$
(c) $2f\,\lambda/a$ (d) $2f\,a/\lambda$

Assertion and Reason

Directions (Q. Nos. 4-8) *In the following questions, two statements are given- one labelled Assertion (A) and the other labelled Reason (R). Select the correct answer to these questions from the codes (a), (b), (c) and (d) as given below*
(a) Both Assertion and Reason are true and Reason is the correct explanation of Assertion.
(b) Both Assertion and Reason are true but Reason is not the correct explanation of Assertion.
(c) Assertion is true but Reason is false.
(d) Assertion is false but Reason is true.

4 **Assertion** In interference and diffraction, light energy is redistributed.

Reason There is no gain or loss of energy, which is consistent with the principle of conservation of energy.

5 **Assertion** Wavefronts obtained from light emitted by a point source in an isotropic medium are always spherical.

Reason Speed of light in isotropic medium is constant.

6 **Assertion** When a plane wave passes through a thin prism, the emerging wavefront gets tilted.

Reason Speed of light is less in glass than in air.

7 **Assertion** The fringe closest on either side of the central white fringe in case of interference pattern due to white light is red and the farthest appears blue.

Reason The interference patterns due to different component colours of white light overlap.

8 **Assertion** All bright interference bands have same intensity.

Reason All bands receive same light from two sources.

Very Short Answer Type Questions

(1 Mark)

9 State the conditions that must be satisfied for two light sources to be coherent.

10 In Young's double slit experiment, if the distance between the slits is halved, what changes in the fringe width will take place?

11 Suppose while performing double slit experiment, the space between the slits and the screen is filled with water. How does the interference pattern change?

Short Answer Type I Questions

(2 Marks)

12 Derive fringe separation formula for YDSE.

13 Obtain the expression for the maximum slit width for diffraction.

Long Answer Type Question

(5 Marks)

14 What do you understand by coherent sources? Obtain expression for fringe width of a bright fringe. Write expression for the angular width of fringe.

Case Based Questions

Directions (Q. No. 15) *These questions are case study based questions. Read the following paragraph and answer the questions.*

15 The phenomenon of bending of light around the sharp corners and the spreading of light within the geometrical shadow of the opaque obstacles is called diffraction of light. The light thus deviates from its linear path. The deviation becomes much more pronounced, when the dimensions of the aperture or the obstacle are comparable to the wavelength of light. According to Fresnel, diffraction occurs on the account of mutual interference of secondary wavelets starting from portions of the wavefront which are not blocked by the obstacle or from portions of the wavefront which are allowed to pass through the aperture.

(i) What should be the order of the size of obstacle/aperture for observing diffraction of light?

(ii) Who discovered diffraction of light?

(iii) Does the diffraction of light give any information about the nature of light waves?

(iv) State whether diffraction of light takes place at the two slits in the Young's interference experiment.

(v) In what way is diffraction from each slit releated to the interference pattern in Young's double slit experiment?

Answers

1. (*d*) As intensity of one of source is reduced. So, bright fringe become faint and dark fringe is less dark, i.e. finite light intensity.

2. (*c*) Suppose slit width's are equal, so they produces waves of equal intensity say I'. Resultant intensity at any point $I_R = 4I' \cos^2 \phi$, where ϕ is the phase difference between the waves at the point of observation. For maximum intensity,

$$\phi = 0° \Rightarrow I_{max} = 4I' = I \quad \text{...(i)}$$

Also, when one slit is closed,

$$I' = I_0 \quad \text{...(ii)}$$

From Eqs. (i) and (ii), we get

$$4I_0 = I$$

3. (*b*) In Young's experiment and the single slit diffraction, we have assumed that the screen on which the fringes are formed is at a large distance.

The two or more paths from the slits to the screen were treated as parallel. This situation also occurs when we place a converging lens after the slits and place the screen at the focus. Parallel paths from the slit are combined at a single point on the screen.

Note that the lens does not introduce any extra path differences in a parallel beam. This arrangement is often used, since it gives more intensity than placing the screen far away. If f is the focal length of the lens, then we can easily work out the size of the central bright maximum. In terms of angles, the separation of the central maximum from the first null of the diffraction pattern is λ/a. Hence, the size on the screen will be $f\lambda/a$.

4. (*a*) In interference and diffraction, light energy is redistributed. If it reduces in one region, producing a dark fringe and it increases in another region, producing a bright fringe. There is no gain or loss of energy, which is consistent with the principle of conservation of energy.

5. (*a*) When the speed of light is independent of direction, the secondary waves are spherical.

6. (*a*)

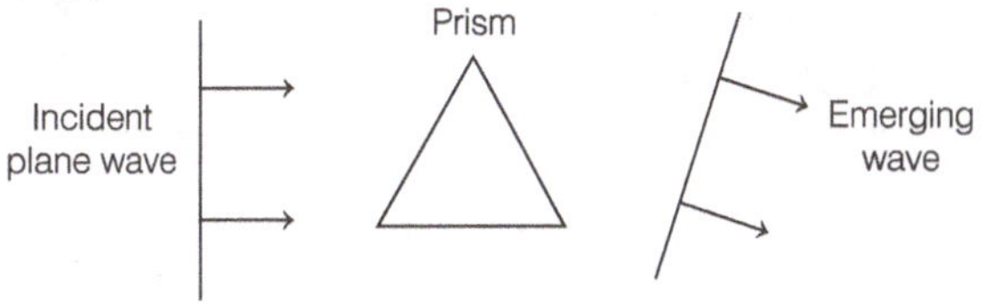

7. (*b*) The interference patterns due to different colours of white light overlap incoherently.

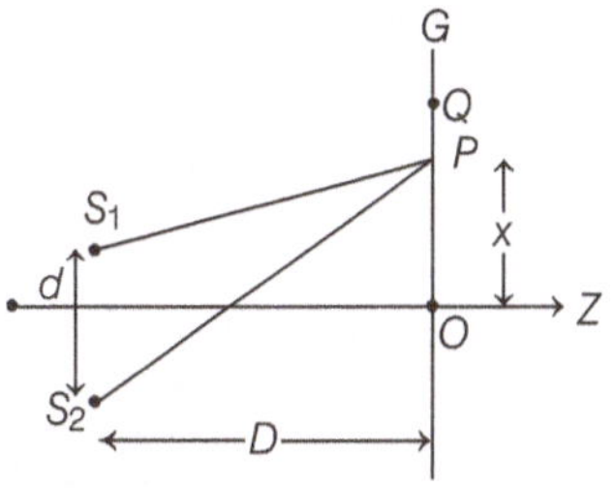

The central bright fringes for different colours are at the same position, therefore the central fringe is white. For a point P at which $S_2P - S_1P = \frac{\lambda_b}{2}$ where $\lambda_b = 4000$ represents the wavelength for the blue colour, the blue component will be absent and the fringe will appear red in colour. Slightly farther away, where

$S_2Q - S_1Q = \lambda_b = \frac{\lambda_r}{2}$, where $\lambda_r = 8000$ is the wavelength for the red colour, the fringe will be predominantly blue. Thus, the fringe closest on either side of the central white fringe is red and the farthest will appear blue.

8. (c) All bright interference bands have same intensity but all bands do not receive same light from two sources.

9. (i) The two sources should give monochromatic light.
   (ii) The path difference between light waves from two sources should be small.

10. Fringe width, $W \propto \frac{1}{d}$, hence W is doubled.

11. The pattern will remain same, but slightly shifted.

12. Refer to text on page 398 (Fringe width).

13. Refer to the text on page 410 (Width of central maximum).

14. Refer to text on pages 397 and 398 (Coherent and incoherent sources and Young's double slit experiment for constructive interference (bright fringe), angular fringe width).

15. (i) It should be the order of wavelength of light used.
   (ii) Grimaldi
   (iii) No light does not give any information about the nature of light.
   (iv) Yes, the light waves arriving at each slit are diffracted. The diffracted waves emerging from the shits then interfere.
   (v) The intensity of interference fringes is modified by the diffraction pattern of each slit.

RELATED ONLINE VIDEOS

Visit : https://www.youtube.com/watch?v=gliLaaeZHwg
OR **Scan the Code**

Visit : https://www.youtube.com/watch?v=CAe3lkYNKt8
OR **Scan the Code**

Visit : https://www.youtube.com/watch?v=Z6TQSVLMKE4
OR **Scan the Code**

Visit : https://www.youtube.com/watch?v=-mNQW5OShMA
OR **Scan the Code**

Visit : https://www.youtube.com/watch?v=9UkkKM1IkKg
OR **Scan the Code**

CHAPTER 11

Dual Nature of Radiation and Matter

The Maxwell's equations of electromagnetism and Hertz experiments on generation and detection of electromagnetic waves established the wave nature of light in 1887. But the discoveries of photoelectric effect by Hertz, Compton effect by Compton, established the particle nature of light. Hence, it was concluded that light has **dual nature**.

- Photoelectric Effect
- Matter Waves

TOPIC 01 Photoelectric Effect

The phenomenon of emission of electrons from the surface of metal, when radiations of suitable frequency fall on it, is called photoelectric effect. The emitted electrons are called **photoelectrons** and the current, so produced is called **photoelectric current.**

Note Non-metals also show photoelectric effect. Liquids and gases can also show this effect but to limited extent.

Hertz's Observations

In 1887, Heinrich Hertz discovered the phenomenon of photoelectric emission while working with his electromagnetic wave experiment, by means of spark discharge. He observed that high voltage sparks across the detector loop were enhanced when the emitter plate was illuminated by ultraviolet light from an arc lamp. It was accounted as follows:

When suitable radiations fall on a metal surface, some electrons near the surface absorb enough energy from the incident radiations, to overcome the attraction of the positive ions in the material of the surface. This helps them to escape from the surface of the material to the surrounding space.

Hallwachs' and Lenard's Observations

During 1886 -1902, Wilhelm Hallwachs and Philipp Lenard made a detailed study of photoelectric effect. Lenard observed that, if a potential difference is applied across the two metal plates enclosed in an evacuated tube, then there is no flow of current in the circuit. However, when one plate (called emitter plate) enclosed in the evacuated tube, kept at negative potential is exposed with ultraviolet radiations, current begins to flow in the circuit.

As soon as ultraviolet radiations falling on the emitter plate are stopped, the current flowing is also stopped. Thus, light falling on the surface of emitter causes current in the external circuit. From his observation, Hallwachs concluded that negatively charged particles were ejected out from the zinc plate under the action of ultraviolet radiations. After the discovery of electron in 1897, it became evident that the exposure of emitter plate with the incident light causes the electrons to emit also. Due to negative charge, the emitted electrons are pushed towards the collector plate by the applied electric field.

Hallwachs and Lenard also observed that when ultraviolet light fell on the emitter plate, no electrons were emitted, until the frequency of the incident light was smaller than a certain minimum value, called the threshold frequency. This minimum frequency depends on the nature of the material of the emitter plate.

Note

- The photoelectric emission is independent of temperature of cathode.
- Lenard's found that the time lag between the incidence of photon and the emission of electron is less than 10^{-8} s.

Experimental Study of Photoelectric Effect

The figure given below shows the experimental setup for the study of photoelectric effect.

The setup consists of an evacuated glass or quartz tube which encloses a photosensitive plate C (called **emitter**) and a metal plate A (called **collector**). A transparent quartz window is sealed onto the glass tube which permits ultraviolet radiation to pass through it and irradiate the photosensitive plate C.

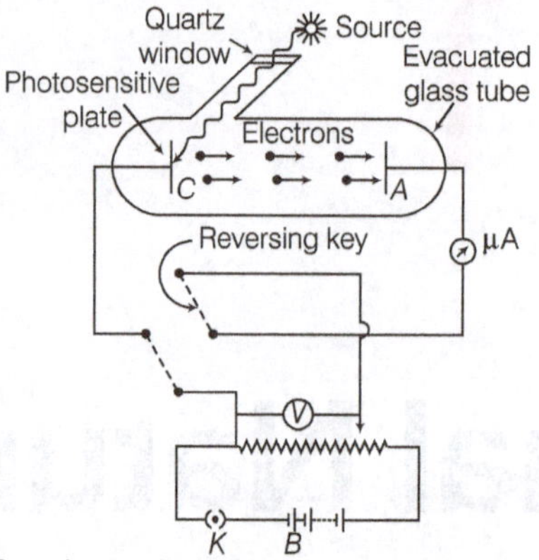

Experimental arrangement for the study of photoelectric effect

The electrons are emitted by the plate C and are collected by the plate A. When the collector plate A is positive with respect to the emitter plate C, then the electrons are attracted to it. Hence, photoelectric current is constituted. This emission of electrons causes flow of electric current in the circuit.

The potential difference between the emitter and collector plates is measured by a voltmeter (V), whereas the resulting photocurrent flowing in the circuit is measured by a microammeter (μA).

The experimental arrangement given above is used to study the variations of photocurrent with intensity of radiation, frequency of radiation and the potential difference between the plates A and C.

Effect of Intensity of Light on Photoelectric Current

For a fixed frequency of incident radiation and accelerating potential, the photoelectric current increases linearly with increase in intensity of incident light.

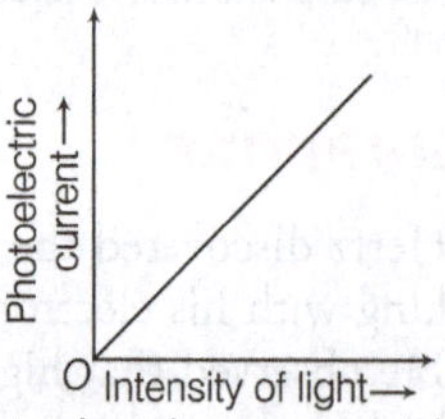

Variation of photoelectric current with intensity of light

As, the photoelectric current is directly proportional to the number of photoelectrons emitted per second. So, the number of photoelectrons emitted per second is directly proportional to the intensity of the incident radiation.

Effect of Potential on Photoelectric Current

For a fixed frequency and intensity of incident light, photoelectric current increases with increase in potential applied to the collector as shown in the graph.

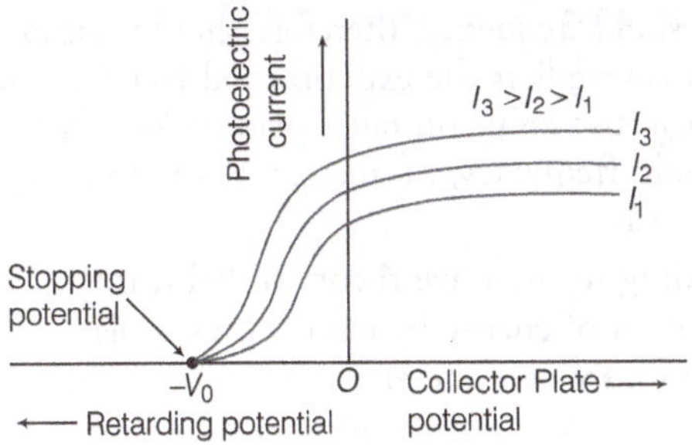

From the above graph, we can observe that,

(i) After a certain value of accelerating potential, when all photo electrons reach the plate A, the photocurrent ceases. On increasing the value of accelerating potential, this maximum value of photoelectric current is called **Saturation current.**

(ii) When the potential is decreased, the current decreases but does not become zero at zero potential. This shows that even in the absence of accelerating potential, few photoelectrons manages to reach the plate A on their own due to their kinetic energy.

(iii) For a particular frequency of incident radiation, when minimum negative potential V_0 is applied to the plate A w.r.t. C, photoelectric current becomes zero at a particular value of negative potential V_0 called **stopping potential** or **cut-off potential.**

Stopping potential is independent of the illumination power of the source and the distance between the source and emitter surface.

In this condition, the stopping potential is sufficient to repel even the most energetic photoelectron with maximum kinetic energy K_{max}. Photoelectric current becomes zero whenever no electron even the fastest photoelectrons cannot reach the plate A. Hence, maximum kinetic energy is given as,

$$K_{max} = eV_0 = \frac{1}{2} m v_{max}^2$$

where, m is the mass of photoelectron and v_{max} is the maximum velocity of emitted photoelectron.

Note For the radiation of a given frequency and material of plate C, the value of stopping potential V_0 is independent of the intensity of the incident radiation. It means, the maximum kinetic energy of emitted photoelectron depends on the light source and the emitter plate material but is independent of intensity of incident radiation.

Effect of Frequency of Incident Radiation on Stopping Potential

If we take radiations of different frequencies but of same intensity. For each radiation, we study the variation of photoelectric current against the potential difference between the plates as shown in the graph below.

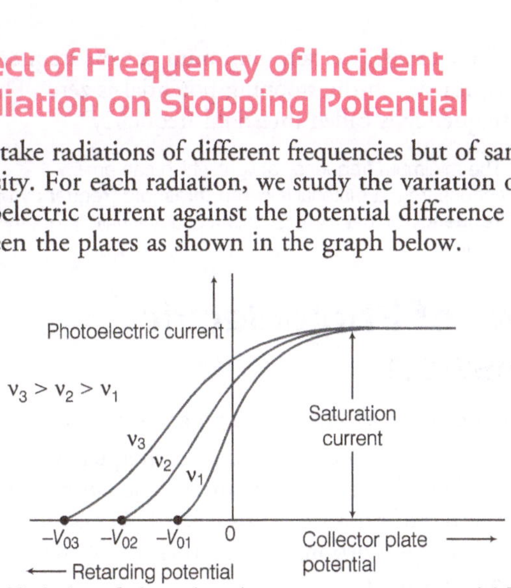

Variation of photoelectric current *versus* potential for different frequencies but constant intensity of incident

From the above graph, we can observe that,

(i) The value of stopping potential is different for radiation of different frequencies but the value of saturation current (for given intensity) remains constant.

(ii) The value of stopping potential is more negative for incident radiation of higher frequency. This means that the energy of the emitted electrons depends on the frequency of incident radiations. Greater the frequency of incident radiation, greater is the maximum kinetic energy of photoelectrons, consequently greater retarding potential or stopping potential is required to stop them completely.

(iii) The value of saturation current depends upon the intensity of incident radiation but is independent of the frequency of the incident radiation.

If we plot a graph between stopping potential and the frequency of the incident radiation for two different metals A and B, we get the graph as shown below.

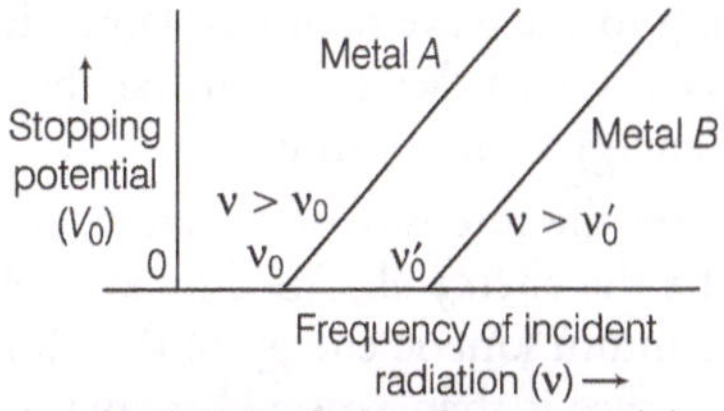

Variation of stopping potential *versus* frequency of incident

From the graph, we can observe that,

(i) The stopping potential V_0 varies linearly with the frequency of incident radiation for a given photosensitive material.

(ii) There exists a certain minimum cut-off frequency ν_0 for which the stopping potential is zero. This frequency is called threshold frequency.

Note The minimum frequency of light which can emit photoelectrons from a material is called **threshold frequency** or **cut-off frequency** of that material. It is a characteristic property of that material.

Laws of Photoelectric Emission

The laws of photoelectric emission are as follows

(i) For a given material and a given frequency of incident radiation, the photoelectric current or number of photoelectrons ejected per second is directly proportional to the intensity of the incident light.

(ii) For a given material and frequency of incident radiation, saturation current is found to be proportional to the intensity of incident radiation, whereas the stopping potential is independent of its intensity.

(iii) For a given material, there exists a certain minimum frequency of the incident radiation below which no emission of photoelectrons takes place. This frequency is called **threshold frequency**.

(iv) The photoelectric emission is an instantaneous process. The time lag between the incidence of radiations and emission of photoelectrons is very small, less than even 10^{-9} s.

Photoelectric Effect and Wave Theory of Light

Huygens' wave theory of light could not explain the photoelectric emission due to the following main reasons:

(i) According to the wave nature of light, the free electrons at the surface of the metal absorb the radiant energy continuously.

The greater the intensity of radiation, the greater should be the energy absorbed by each electron. The maximum kinetic energy of the photoelectrons on the surface is then expected to increase with increase in intensity.

But according to experimental facts, the maximum kinetic energy of ejected photoelectrons is independent of intensity of incident radiation.

(ii) According to wave theory of light, no matter what the frequency of radiation is, a sufficiently intense beam of radiation should be able to impart enough energy to the electrons, so that they exceed the minimum energy needed to escape from metal surface.

A threshold frequency, therefore should not exist which contradicts the experimental fact that, no photoelectric emission takes place below that threshold frequency, no matter whatsoever may be its intensity.

(iii) According to the wave theory of light, the absorption of energy by electron takes place continuously over the entire wavefront of the radiation. Since, a large number of electrons absorb energy, the energy absorbed per electron per unit time turns out to be small. Hence, it will take hours or more for a single electron to come out of the metal which contradicts the experimental fact that photoelectric emission is instantaneous.

Einstein's Photoelectric Equation

Quantisation of Radiation

In 1905, Albert Einstein explained the various laws of photoelectric emission on the basis of Planck's quantum theory. According to that theory, the energy of an electromagnetic wave is not continuously distributed over the wavefront of waves. Instead of this, these waves travel in the form of discrete packets or bundles of energy called **quanta** of energy of radiation

Each quantum of energy photon radiates an energy, which is given by

$$E = h\nu$$

where, h is Planck's constant and ν is the frequency of light radiation.

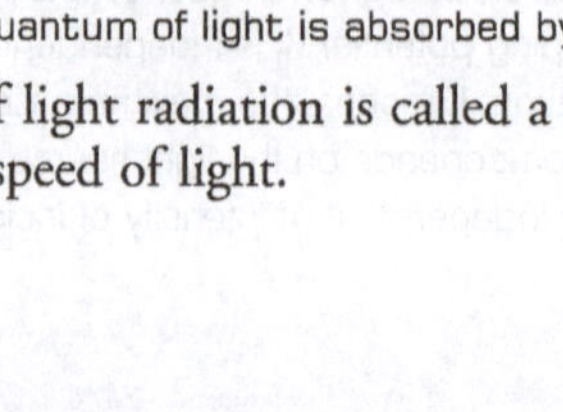

Emission of photoelectron by a metal surface when a quantum of light is absorbed by it

One quantum of light radiation is called a photon, which travels with the speed of light.

When a quantum of light radiation of energy $h\nu$ falls on a metal surface, then this energy is absorbed by the electron and is used in following two ways

(i) A part of energy is used to overcome the surface barrier and come out of the metal surface. This part of energy is called **work function.** It is expressed as $\phi_0 = h\nu_0$.

(ii) The remaining part of the energy is used in giving a velocity v to the emitted photoelectron. This is equal to the maximum kinetic energy of the photoelectrons $\left(\frac{1}{2}mv_{max}^2\right)$, where m is the mass of the photoelectron.

According to the law of conservation of energy,

$$h\nu = \phi_0 + \frac{1}{2}mv_{max}^2 = h\nu_0 + \frac{1}{2}mv_{max}^2$$

$$\therefore \quad \frac{1}{2}mv_{max}^2 = K_{max} = h(\nu - \nu_0) = h\nu - \phi_0$$

$$\therefore \quad \boxed{K_{max} = h\nu - \phi_0}$$

This equation is called **Einstein's photoelectric equation.**

Some more important informations regarding to photoelectric effect.

(i) Photoelectric emission takes place only when the electron is loosly bound to the metal. It can never take place with completely free electron, because it is impossible for a photon to give up all its energy and momentum to a electron.

(ii) The kinetic energy of electrons emitted from the surface layer of metal is maximum.

(iii) Photons are electrically neutral. So, they are not deflected by electric and magnetic fields.

Example 1 The electric field associated with a monochromatic beam of light becomes zero, with frequency 2.4×10^{15} times per second. Find the maximum kinetic energy of the photoelectrons when this light falls on a metal surface whose work function is 2.0 eV.

Sol. Given, $\phi_0 = 2.0$ eV, $h = 6.63 \times 10^{-34}$ J-s, $KE_{max} = ?$

In one complete vibration twice the electric field becomes zero, so the frequency of incident light is given by

$$\nu = \frac{1}{2} \times 2.4 \times 10^{15} = 1.2 \times 10^{15} \text{ Hz}$$

Hence, maximum kinetic energy,

$$KE_{max} = h\nu - \phi_0 = \frac{6.63 \times 10^{-34} \times 1.2 \times 10^{15}}{1.6 \times 10^{-19}} - 2$$

$$= 2.97 \text{ eV}$$

Relation between Stopping Potential (V_0) and Threshold Frequency (ν_0)

Maximum kinetic energy is given by

$$K_{max} = h(\nu - \nu_0)$$

Also, $$K_{max} = eV_0$$

$$\therefore \quad \boxed{eV_0 = h(\nu - \nu_0)} \quad \text{...(i)}$$

If λ = wavelength of the incident radiation,

λ_0 = threshold wavelength of the metal surface and

c = velocity of light.

Then, $\nu = \frac{c}{\lambda}$ and $\nu_0 = \frac{c}{\lambda_0}$

Putting these values in Eq. (i), we get

$$eV_0 = h\left(\frac{c}{\lambda} - \frac{c}{\lambda_0}\right)$$

$$\therefore \quad \boxed{eV_0 = hc\left(\frac{1}{\lambda} - \frac{1}{\lambda_0}\right)} \quad \text{...(ii)}$$

Example 2 The work function of caesium is 2.14 eV. Calculate

(i) the threshold frequency for caesium and

(ii) the wavelength of the incident light, if the photocurrent is brought to zero by a stopping potential of 0.60 V.

Given, $h = 6.63 \times 10^{-34}$ J-s.

Sol. Here, $V_0 = 0.60$ V, $\phi_0 = 2.14$ eV $= 2.14 \times 1.6 \times 10^{-19}$ J

(i) Threshold frequency, $\nu_0 = \frac{\phi_0}{h}$ $\quad [\because \phi_0 = h\nu_0]$

$$= \frac{2.14 \times 1.6 \times 10^{-19}}{6.63 \times 10^{-34}}$$

$$= 5.16 \times 10^{14} \text{ Hz}$$

(ii) We have, $eV_0 = \frac{hc}{\lambda} - \phi_0 \Rightarrow \lambda = \frac{hc}{(eV_0 + \phi_0)}$

$$= \frac{6.63 \times 10^{-34} \times 3 \times 10^8}{(1.6 \times 10^{-19} \times 0.60 + 2.14 \times 1.6 \times 10^{-19})}$$

$$\approx 454 \times 10^{-9} \text{ m}$$

$$= 454 \text{ nm}$$

Verification of Laws of Photoelectric Emission Based on Einstein's Photoelectric Equation

Einstein's photoelectric equations is

$$K_{max} = \frac{1}{2} mv^2_{max} = h(\nu - \nu_0)$$

This equation successfully explains the laws of photoelectric emission. These are as follows

(i) If $\nu < \nu_0$, then $\frac{1}{2} mv^2_{max}$ is negative which is not possible therefore, for photoelectric emission to take place, $\nu > \nu_0$.

(ii) Since, one photon emits one electron, so the number of photoelectrons emitted per second is directly proportional to the intensity of incident light.

(iii) It is clear that $\frac{1}{2} mv^2_{max} \propto \nu$, as h and ν_0 are constants. This shows that kinetic energy of the photoelectrons is directly proportional to the frequency of the incident light.

(iv) Photoelectric emission is due to elastic collisions between a photon and an electron. As such there cannot be any significant time lag between the incidence of photon and emission of photoelectron.

Graphs Related to Photoelectric Effect From Einstein Photoelectric Equation

The important graphs related to photoelectric effect are as follows

(i) **Frequency ν and stopping potential V_0 graph**

It is used to determine Planck's constant.

We know that,

$$eV_0 = h\nu - \phi_0 \Rightarrow V_0 = \frac{h\nu}{e} - \frac{\phi_0}{e}$$

So, $V_0 \propto \nu$

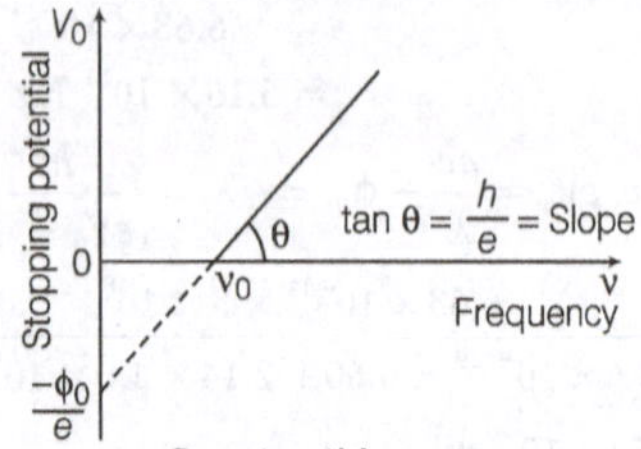

Graph of V_0 *versus* ν

It could be seen that, V_0 *versus* ν curve is a straight line with slope = (h/e) and is independent of the nature of material.

(ii) **Frequency ν and maximum kinetic energy graph**

As, $K_{max} = h\nu - \phi_0$

$\Rightarrow K_{max} \propto \nu$

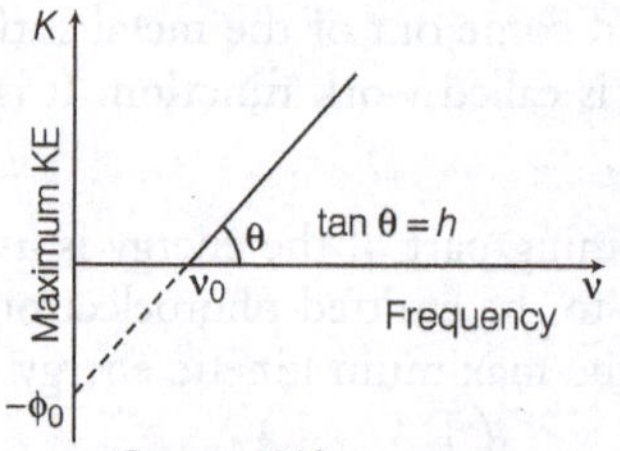

Graph of K_{max} *versus* ν

(iii) **Frequency ν and photoelectric current I graph**

The graph given below shows that, the photoelectric current I is independent of frequency of the incident light, till intensity remains constant.

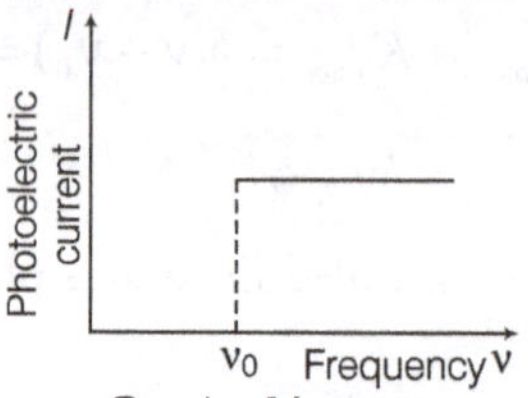

Graph of I *versus* ν

(iv) **Intensity and stopping potential V_0 graph**

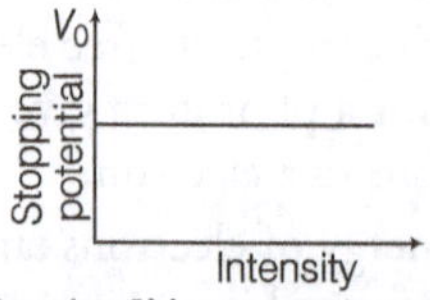

Graph of V_0 *versus* intensity

(v) **Photoelectric current I and time lag t graph**

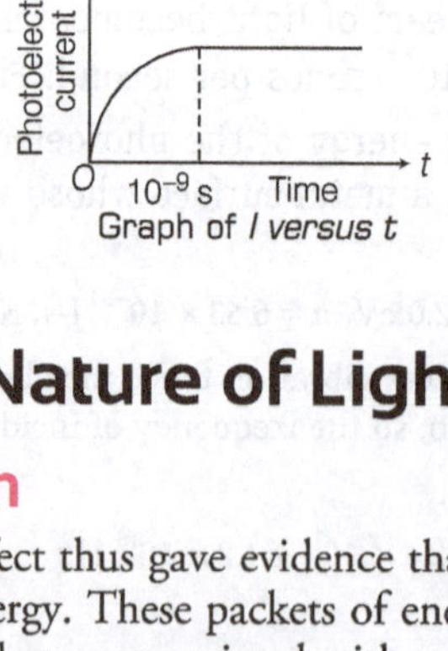

Graph of I *versus* t

Particle Nature of Light :

The Photon

Photoelectric effect thus gave evidence that light consists of packets of energy. These packets of energy were called **light quantum** that are associated with particles named as **photons.** So, photons confirm the particle nature of light.

Energy of a photon is given by

$$E = h\nu = \frac{hc}{\lambda}$$

where, h is the Planck's constant, ν is the frequency of radiation or photon, c is the speed of light and λ is the wavelength of photon.

The **momentum of photon** is given by

$$p = \frac{E}{c} = \frac{h\nu}{c} = \frac{h}{\lambda} \text{ kg ms}^{-1}$$

Example 3 The momentum of photon of electromagnetic radiation is 3.3×10^{-29} kg ms^{-1}. Find out the frequency and wavelength of the wave associated with it.

Sol. Given, $p = 3.3 \times 10^{-29}$ kg ms^{-1},

$h = 6.63 \times 10^{-34}$ J-s

$c = 3 \times 10^8$ m/s, $\nu = ?$ and $\lambda = ?$

Since, $E = h\nu = mc^2 = mc \times c = p \times c$

$$\therefore \quad \nu = \frac{pc}{h} = \frac{3.3 \times 10^{-29} \times 3 \times 10^8}{6.63 \times 10^{-34}}$$

$$= 1.5 \times 10^{13} \text{ Hz}$$

and $$\lambda = \frac{c}{\nu} = \frac{3 \times 10^8}{1.5 \times 10^{13}}$$

$$= 2 \times 10^{-5} \text{ m}$$

Characteristic Properties of Photons

Different characteristic properties of photons are given below

(i) In interaction of radiation with matter, radiation behaves as if it is made up of particles called **photons.**

(ii) A photon travels at a speed of light c in vacuum (i.e. 3×10^8 m/s).

(iii) It has zero rest mass, i.e. the photon cannot exist at rest. According to the theory of relativity, the mass m of a particle moving with velocity v, comparable with the velocity of light c is given by

$$m = \frac{m_0}{\sqrt{1 - \frac{v^2}{c^2}}} \Rightarrow m_0 = m\sqrt{1 - \frac{v^2}{c^2}}$$

where, m_0 is the mass of the particle at rest.

(iv) The inertial mass of a photon is given by

$$m = \frac{E}{c^2} = \frac{h}{c\lambda} = \frac{hv}{c^2}$$

(v) Photons travel in a straight line.

(vi) Irrespective of the intensity of radiation, all the photons of a particular frequency ν or wavelength λ have the same energy $E\left(= h\nu = \frac{hc}{\lambda}\right)$ and momentum, $p\left(= \frac{h\nu}{c} = \frac{h}{\lambda}\right)$.

(vii) Energy of a photon depends upon frequency of the photon, so the energy of the photon does not change when photon travels from one medium to another.

(viii) Wavelength of the photon changes in different media, so velocity of a photon is different in different media.

(ix) Photons are not deflected by electric and magnetic fields. This shows that photons are electrically neutral.

(x) In a photon-particle collision (such as photoelectron collision), the energy and momentum are conserved. However, the number of photons may not be conserved in a collision.

(xi) Photons may show diffraction under given conditions.

(x) Brighter light means more photons, not more energetic photons.

Example 4 Monochromatic light of wavelength 632.8 nm is produced by a helium-neon laser. The power emitted is 9.42 mW.

(i) Find the energy and momentum of each photon in the light beam.

(ii) How many photons per second, on the average, arrive at a target irradiated by this beam? (Assume the beam to have uniform cross-section, which is less than the target area.)

(iii) How fast does a hydrogen atom have to travel in order to have the same momentum as that of the photon?

NCERT

Sol. Given, wavelength of monochromatic light,

$$\lambda = 632.8 \text{ nm} = 632.8 \times 10^{-9} \text{ m}$$

$$\text{Power} = 9.42 \text{ mW} = 9.42 \times 10^{-3} \text{ W}$$

(i) Energy of each photon, $E = \frac{hc}{\lambda}$

$$= \frac{6.63 \times 10^{-34} \times 3 \times 10^8}{632.8 \times 10^{-9}} = 3.14 \times 10^{-19} \text{ J}$$

We know that momentum of each photon, $p = \frac{h}{\lambda}$

$$p = \frac{6.63 \times 10^{-34}}{632.8 \times 10^{-9}} = 1.05 \times 10^{-27} \text{ kg-m/s}$$

(ii) Let n be the number of photons per second.

So, $n = \dfrac{\text{Power}}{\text{Energy of each photon}}$

$= \dfrac{9.42 \times 10^{-3}}{3.14 \times 10^{-19}}$

$= 3 \times 10^{16}$ photons /s

(iii) Momentum, $p = mv$

$\therefore$ Velocity of hydrogen atom, $v = \dfrac{p}{m} = \dfrac{1.05 \times 10^{-27}}{1.66 \times 10^{-27}}$

$= 0.63$ m / s

[$\because m = 1.66 \times 10^{-27}$ kg (mass of electron)]

Topic Practice 1

Multiple Choice Questions

1 Mark

1. Photoelectric effect involves

(a) conversion of nuclear energy into electrical energy

(b) conversion of atomic energy into electrical energy

(c) conversion of electronic energy into electrical energy

(d) conversion of light energy into electrical energy

2. Photoemission with visible light is possible in

(a) alkali metals

(b) alkaline Earth metals

(c) metalloids

(d) semiconductors

3. Variation of photoelectric current with intensity of light is

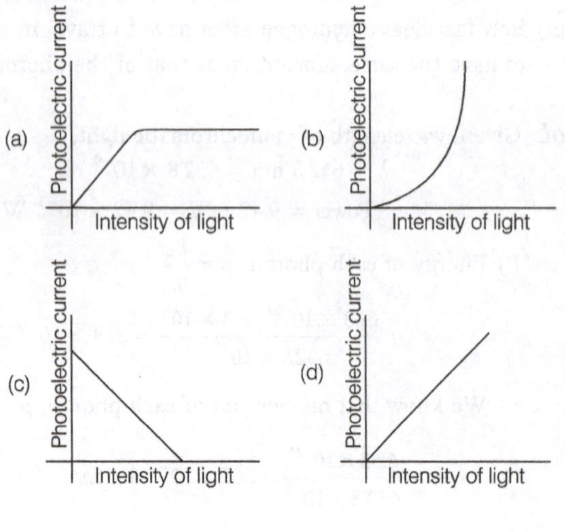

4. For the graph shown,

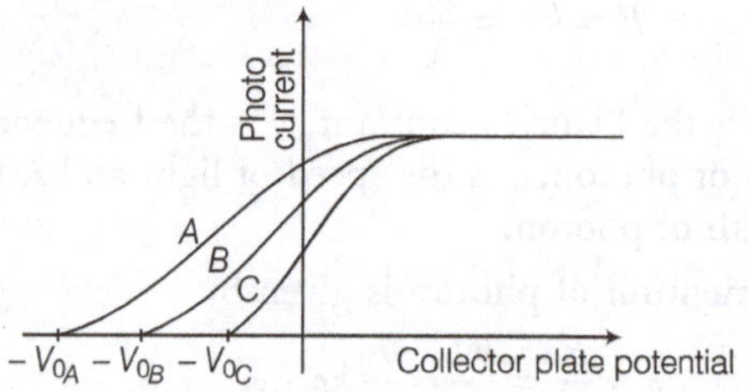

If f denotes frequency of incident light

(a) $f_A > f_B > f_C$ (b) $f_A < f_B < f_C$

(c) $f_A = f_B = f_C$ (d) $f_B > f_C$ and $f_B > f_A$

5. Einstein's photoelectric equation is

(a) $E_{max} = h\lambda - \phi_0$ (b) $E_{max} = \dfrac{hc}{\lambda} - \phi_0$

(c) $E_{max} = h\nu + \phi_0$ (d) $E_{max} = \dfrac{hc}{\lambda} + \phi_0$

6. The energy associated with light of which of the following colours is minimum? **ISC 2019**

(a) Violet (b) Red

(c) Green (d) Yellow

7. Greater the frequency of incident light

(a) lesser is the maximum kinetic energy of emitted electrons

(b) lesser is the minimum kinetic energy of emitted electrons

(c) greater is the maximum kinetic energy of emitted electrons

(d) greater is the minimum kinetic energy of emitted electrons

8. In photoelectric effect experiment, the slope of the graph of the stopping potential *versus* frequency gives the value of **ISC 2020**

(a) $\dfrac{h}{e}$ (b) h (c) $\dfrac{e}{h}$ (d) $\dfrac{hc}{e}$

Very Short Answer Type Questions

1 Mark

9. With reference to photoelectric effect, define threshold wavelength. **ISC 2018, 14**

10. Describe in brief what is observed when moving electrons are allowed to fall on a thin graphite film and the emergent beam falls on a fluorescent screen. **ISC 2017**

11. Name the phenomena or experiment which proves particle nature of electromagnetic radiations. **ISC 2013**

12. In photoelectric effect, what is meant by the term threshold frequency? **ISC 2011, 01**

13. How can the work function of tungsten be increased? **ISC 2007**

14. Do all the electrons that absorb a photon come out as photoelectrons? **NCERT Exemplar**

15. Two metals X and Y, when illuminated with appropriate radiation, emit photoelectrons. The work function of X is higher than of Y. Which metal will have higher value of threshold frequency?

16. Two metals A and B have work functions 2 eV and 4 eV respectively. Which metal has lower threshold wavelength for photoelectric effect?

17. For a given photosensitive material and with a source of constant frequency of incident radiation, how does the photoelectric current vary with the intensity of incident light?

18. The given graph shows the variation of photoelectric current I *versus* applied voltage V for two different photosensitive materials and for two different intensities of the incident radiations. Identify the pairs of curves that correspond to different materials but same intensity of incident radiation.

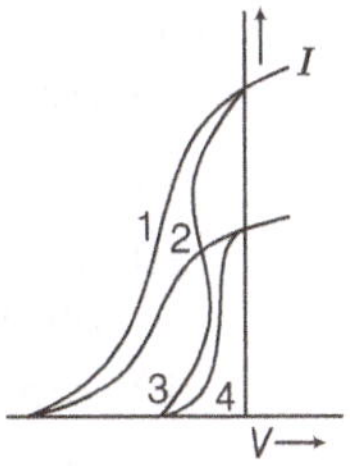

19. The graph shows the variation of stopping potential with frequency of incident radiation for two photosensitive metals A and B.

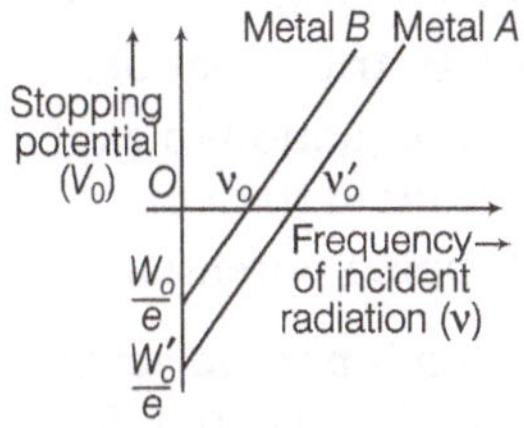

Which one of the two has higher value of work function? Justify your answer.

20. Ultraviolet radiations of different frequencies ν_1 and ν_2 are incident on two photosensitive materials having work functions W_{01} and W_{02} ($W_{01} > W_{02}$) respectively. The kinetic energy of the emitted electrons is same in both the cases. Which one of the two radiations will be of higher frequency?

21. If the frequency of incident radiation is equal to the threshold frequency, what will be the value of stopping potential?

22. Write down the relation between the wavelength and momentum of a photon.

23. Write down the relation between the energy and momentum of the photon.

24. How does photoelectric emission differ from thermionic emission?

25. Why is cut-off potential of a photometal negative?

26. How does photoelectric effect reject the wave nature of light?

Short Answer Type I Questions

2 Marks

27. Define the following with reference to photoelectric effect. **ISC 2019**
    (i) Threshold frequency f_0
    (ii) Stopping potential V_S

28. In photoelectric effect, what is meant by the terms
    (i) work function?
    (ii) stopping potential? **ISC 2008, 01**

29. There are materials which absorb photons of shorter wavelength and emit photons of longer wavelength. Can there be stable substances which absorb photons of larger wavelength and emit light of shorter wavelength. **NCERT Exemplar**

30. Write Einstein's photoelectric equation. **ISC 2014**

31. Two monochromatic radiations, blue and violet, of the same intensity are incident on a photosensitive surface and cause photoelectric emission. Would
    (i) the number of electrons emitted per second?
    (ii) the maximum kinetic energy of the electrons be equal in the two cases? Justify your answer.

32. (i) In the explanation of photoelectric effect, we assume one photon of frequency ν collides with an electron and transfers its energy. This leads to the equation for the maximum energy E_{max} of the emitted

electron as, $E_{max} = h\nu - \phi_0$, where ϕ_0 is the work function of the metal. If an electron absorbs 2 photons (each of frequency ν), what will be the maximum energy for the emitted electron?

(ii) Why is this fact (two photon absorption) not taken into consideration in our discussion of the stopping potential? **NCERT Exemplar**

Short Answer Type II Questions

3 Marks

33. (i) In an experiment on photoelectric effect, how does stopping potential change, if at all, when intensity of incident monochromatic UV-radiation is increased?

(ii) Ultraviolet light is incident metals *P*, *Q* and *R*, having work functions 8eV, 2eV and 4eV respectively.

(a) Which metal has lowest threshold frequency for photoelectric effect?

(b) For which metal is the value of E_{max} minimum?

(**Note** E_{max} is maximum kinetic energy of the emitted photoelectrons). **ISC 2024**

34. Plot a labelled graph of (V_s), where V_s is stopping potential of photoelectrons *versus* frequency ν of incident radiation. How will you use this graph to determine the value of Planck's constant? Explain. **ISC 2017, 09**

35. Predict and Explain:
Light of a particular wavelength does not eject electrons from the surface of a given metal.

(i) Should the wavelength of the light be increased or decreased in order to make ejection of electrons possible?

(ii) Choose the best explanation from among the following:

(a) The energy of a photon is proportional to its frequency, i.e. inversely proportional to its wavelength. To increase the energy of the photons, so they can eject electrons, one must decrease their wavelength.

(b) The photons have too little energy to eject electrons. To increase their energy, their wavelength should be increased.

36. Sketch the graphs showing variation of stopping potential with frequencies of incident radiations for two photosensitive materials *A* and *B* having threshold frequencies $\nu_A > \nu_B$.

(i) In which case is the stopping potential more and why?

(ii) Does the slope of the graph depend on the nature of the material used? Explain.

37. Define the term "cut-off frequency" in photoelectric emission. The threshold frequency of a metal is f. When the light of frequency $2f$ is incident on the metal plate, the maximum velocity of photo-electron is v_1. When the frequency of the incident radiation is increased to $5f$, the maximum velocity of photoelectron is v_2. Find the ratio $v_1 : v_2$.

38. Plot a graph showing the variation of stopping potential with frequency of incident radiation for two different photosensitive materials having work functions W_{01} and W_{02} ($W_{01} > W_{02}$). On what factors does the

(i) slope?

(ii) intercept of the lines depend?

39. (i) State two important features of Einstein's photoelectric equation.

(ii) Radiation of frequency 10^{15} Hz is incident on two photosensitive surfaces *P* and *Q*. There is no photoemission from surface *P*. Photoemission occurs from surface *Q* but photoelectrons have zero kinetic energy. Explain these observations and find the value of work function for surface *Q*.

40. (i) Write the important properties of photons which are used to establish Einstein's photoelectric equation.

(ii) Use this equation to explain the concept of

(a) threshold frequency.

(b) stopping potential.

41. Write Einstein's photoelectric equation and mention which important features in photoelectric effect can be explained with the help of this equation.The maximum kinetic energy of the photoelectrons gets doubled when the wavelength of light incident on the surface changes from λ_1 to λ_2. Derive the expressions for the threshold wavelength λ_0 and work function for the metal surface.

Numerical Problems

42. The photoelectric cut-off voltage in a certain experiment is 1.5 V. What is the maximum kinetic energy of photoelectrons emitted? **NCERT (1 M)**

43. Monochromatic light of wavelength 396 nm is incident on the surface of a metal whose work function is 1.125 eV. Calculate
 (i) the energy of an incident photon (in eV).
 (ii) the maximum kinetic energy of photoelectrons (in eV). **ISC 2023 (3 M)**

44. In an experiment on photoelectric effect, the slope of the cut-off voltage *versus* frequency of incident light is found to be 4.12×10^{-15} V-s. Calculate the value of Planck's constant. **NCERT (2 M)**

45. Find the
 (i) maximum frequency.
 (ii) minimum wavelength of X-rays produced by 30 kV electrons. **NCERT (2 M)**

46. The threshold frequency for a certain metal is 3.3×10^{14} Hz. If light of frequency 8.2×10^{14} Hz is incident on the metal, predict the cut-off voltage for the photoelectric emission. **NCERT (2 M)**

47. If radiation of wavelength 5000 Å is incident on a surface of work function 1.2 eV, find the value of stopping potential. Given, $h = 6.62 \times 10^{-34}$ J-s. **(2 M)**

48. Light of frequency 7.21×10^{14} Hz is incident on a metal surface. Electrons with a maximum speed of 6×10^5 m/s are ejected from the surface. What is the threshold frequency for photoemission of electrons? **NCERT (2 M)**

49. Consider a metal exposed to light of wavelength 600 nm. The maximum energy of the electron doubles when light of wavelength 400 nm is used. Find the work function in eV. **NCERT Exemplar (2 M)**

50. Aluminium and calcium have photoelectric work functions of $\phi_{Al} = 4.28$ eV and $\phi_{Ca} = 2.87$ eV, respectively.
 (i) Which metal requires higher frequency light to produce photoelectrons? Explain.
 (ii) Find out the minimum frequency that will produce photoelectrons from each surface. **(2 M)**

51. The work function of caesium metal is 2.14 eV. When light of frequency 6×10^{14} Hz is incident on the metal surface, photoemission of electrons occurs. What is the
 (i) maximum kinetic energy of the emitted electrons?
 (ii) stopping potential?
 (iii) maximum speed of the emitted photoelectrons? **NCERT (3 M)**

52. Monochromatic radiation of wavelength 640.2 nm (1 nm = 10^{-9} m) from a neon lamp irradiates a photosensitive material made of calcium or tungsten. The stopping voltage is measured to be 0.54 V. The source is replaced by an iron source and its 427.2 nm line irradiates the same photocell. Predict the new stopping voltage. **NCERT (3 M)**

53. A mercury lamp is a convenient source for studying frequency dependence of photoelectric emission, since it gives a number of spectral lines ranging from the UV to the red end of the visible spectrum. In our experiment with rubidium photocell, the following lines from a mercury source were used

$$\lambda_1 = 3650 \text{ Å}, \ \lambda_2 = 4047 \text{ Å}, \ \lambda_3 = 4358 \text{ Å},$$
$$\lambda_4 = 5461 \text{ Å}, \ \lambda_5 = 6907 \text{ Å}$$

The stopping voltages respectively were measured to be

$$V_{01} = 1.28 \text{ V}, \quad V_{02} = 0.95 \text{ V},$$
$$V_{03} = 0.74 \text{ V}, \quad V_{04} = 0.16 \text{ V}, \quad V_{05} = 0$$

Determine the value of Planck's constant *h*, the threshold frequency and work function for the material. **NCERT (3 M)**

54. What is the energy of a photon in eV corresponding to the visible light of maximum wavelength? **(1 M)**

55. The energy flux of sunlight reaching the surface of the earth is 1.388×10^3 W/m^2. How many photons (nearly) per square metre are incident on the earth per second? Assume that the photons in the sunlight have an average wavelength of 550 nm. **NCERT (2 M)**

56. How many photons per second does a 100 W bulb emit if its efficiency is 10% and wavelength of light emitted is 500 nm? **(2M)**

57. Calculate the momentum of a photon of energy 6×10^{-19} J. **ISC 2017 (1 M)**

58. Two metals *A* and *B* have work functions 4 eV and 6 eV, respectively. Which metal has lower threshold wavelength for photoelectric effect? **ISC 2016 (1 M)**

59. Threshold frequency of a certain metal for photoelectric emission is 5×10^{14} Hz. Calculate its work function. **ISC 2012, 09 (1 M)**

60. If the frequency of the incident radiation is increased from 4×10^{15} Hz to 8×10^{15} Hz, by how much will the stopping potential for a given photosensitive surface go up? **ISC 2014 (3 M)**

61. Threshold wavelength of certain metal is 792 nm. What is the maximum kinetic energy of photoelectrons emitted by this metal, if it is exposed to ultraviolet light of wavelength 396 nm? **ISC 2010 (3 M)**

62. The work function of sodium is 2.28 eV.
(i) What is the minimum energy for a quantum of radiation to cause photoelectric emission from sodium surface?
(ii) Calculate the wavelength of this radiation. **ISC 2009 (3 M)**

63. The threshold wavelength of tungsten is 2400 Å when tungsten is illuminated with light of wavelength 1600 Å. Find
(i) the work function.
(ii) the maximum KE of emitted electron.
(iii) the stopping potential. **ISC 2005 (3 M)**

64. Photoelectrons are emitted from a metal surface when UV-light of wavelength λ = 300 nm is incident on it. The minimum negative potential required to stop the emission of electrons is 0.54 V. Calculate
(i) the energy of the incident photons.
(ii) the maximum kinetic energy of the photoelectrons emitted.
(iii) the work function of the metal. **ISC 2003, 2000 (4 M)**

65. A monochromatic source emits light of frequency 5×10^{14} Hz. Calculate the energy and the momentum of photons emitted by the source. **(2 M)**

66. An electric bulb of 60 W emits 15% of the total radiation as visible light of wavelength 6000 Å. How many light ray photons is it radiating per second? **(2 M)**

67. An electron is accelerated from rest to 1000 V potential. Calculate the wavelength associated with moving electron.
(Take, mass of electron = 9×10^{-31} kg) **(3 M)**

68. A metal has work function 2 eV and is illuminated by monochromatic light of wavelength 500 nm.
Calculate
(i) the threshold wavelength.
(ii) the maximum energy of photons.
(iii) the stopping potential. **(3 M)**

69. Calculate the momentum of a photon of green light of λ = 500 nm in SI unit. **(1 M)**

70. A radio transmitter of 300 W emits radio waves of wavelength 30 m. How many photons are emitted from the transmitter per second? **(2 M)**

71. Work function of a metal is 2 eV. Calculate the threshold wavelength for this metal. **(1 M)**

72. In an experiment of photoelectric effect, the graph of maximum kinetic energy E_k of the emitted photoelectrons *versus* the frequency ν of the incident light is a straight line *AB* as shown in figure below.

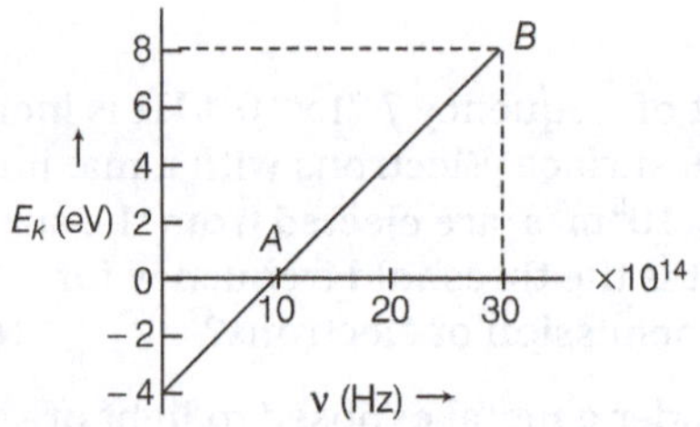

Find
(i) the threshold frequency of the metal.
(ii) the work function of the metal.
(iii) the stopping potential for the photoelectrons emitted by the light of frequency $\nu = 30\times10^{14}$ Hz. **ISC 2015 (3 M)**

73. Photoelectric threshold frequency of an alkali metal is 5.0×10^{14} Hz. Calculate the work function of this metal. **ISC 2008 (1 M)**

74. In a photoelectric cell, retarding potential of 0.5 V is required to block the movement of electrons from the cathode when monochromatic light of wavelength 400 nm is incident on its surface. Find the work function of the material of the cathode. **ISC 2013 (3 M)**

75. Ultraviolet light of wavelengths 800 Å and 700 Å, when allowed to fall on hydrogen atoms in their ground state, is found to liberate electrons with kinetic energy 1.8 eV and 4.0 eV, respectively. Find the value of Planck's constant. **(3 M)**

Hints & Solutions

1. (*d*) Photoemission involves conversion of light energy into electrical energy.It is observed that many metals emit electrons when light shines upon them.
2. (*a*) Some alkali metals such as, lithium, sodium, potassium, caesium and rubidium are sensitive even to visible light. All these photosensitive substances emit electrons when they are illuminated by light.
3. (*d*) Photocurrent varies linearly with intensity. The photocurrent is directly proportional to the number of photoelectrons emitted per second. This implies that the number of photoelectrons emitted per second is directly proportional to the intensity of incident radiation.
4. (*a*) Stopping potential is more negative for higher frequency of incident radiation and *vice-versa*. Thus, form graph.

$$\nu_{0A} > \nu_{0B} > \nu_{0C} \Rightarrow f_A > f_B > f_c$$

5. (*b*) Einstein's photoelectric equation is given by

$$E_{max} = h\nu - \phi_0 \text{ or } E_{max} = \frac{hc}{\lambda} - \phi_0 \quad \left[\because \nu = \frac{c}{\lambda}\right]$$

where, ϕ_0 = work function.

6. (*b*) The energy of light,

$$E = \frac{hc}{\lambda} \text{ or } E \propto \frac{1}{\lambda}$$

Since, red colour has maximum wavelength. So, the energy of light for red colour will be minimum.

7. (*c*) When frequency of incident radiation increases, the maximum kinetic energy of emitted electrons also increases.
8. (*a*) From Einstein's photoelectric equation,

$$h\nu = V_0 e + W_0$$

$$\Rightarrow \quad V_0 = \frac{h\nu}{e} - \frac{W_0}{e} \quad \text{... (i)}$$

Equation of line, $y = mx + c$ ...(ii)

By comparing Eqs. (i) and (ii), we get slope $(m) = \frac{h}{e}$.

9. The maximum wavelength of light which is capable of ejecting photoelectrons from a metal is called the threshold wavelength for that metal.
10. When moving electrons are allowed to fall on a thin graphite film, then the electrons from the graphite film will be knocked out, after gaining sufficient energy from the collision with the moving electrons and then this beam of emergent electrons fall on the fluorescent screen, due to which visible radiation will be produced from the screen (i.e. fluorescence), helping in identifying that emission of electrons had been started from the thin film.
11. Photoelectric effect is the phenomena which proves particle nature of electromagnetic radiation.
12. Refer to text on page 422 (Laws of photoelectric emission).
13. Work function of tungsten can be increased by coating it with thorium whose work function is lower than tungsten.
14. In photoelectric effect, we can observe that most electrons get scattered into the metal by absorbing a photon.

Thus, all the electrons that absorb a photon does not come out as photoelectron. Only a few comes out of metal whose energy becomes greater than the work function of metal.

15. Since, work function is given as,

$$W_0 = h\nu_0 \Rightarrow W_0 \propto \nu_0$$

As work function of metal X is higher than metal Y, so metal X has higher threshold frequency than metal Y.

16. We know that,

$$\lambda_0 = \frac{hc}{\phi_0} \quad \left[\because \phi_0 = \frac{hc}{\lambda_0}\right]$$

$$\therefore \quad \lambda_0 \propto \frac{1}{\phi_0}$$

Hence, Metal B has lower threshold wavelength.

17. The photoelectric current increases linearly with the intensity of incident radiation. Refer to figure on page 420 (Effect of intensity of light on photoelectric current).
18. Curves 1 and 2 correspond to similar materials, while curves 3 and 4 represent different materials, since the value of stopping potential for the pair of curves (1 and 2) and (3 and 4) are the same. For given frequency of the incident radiation, the stopping potential is independent of its intensity. So, the pairs of curves (1 and 3) and (2 and 4) correspond to different materials but same intensity of incident radiation.

19. Metal A has higher value of work function because the slopes of both materials are constant and the intercept of the line depends on work function.

20. As, $K_{max} = h\nu - W_0$

$$\therefore \quad \nu = \frac{K_{max} + W_0}{h}$$

$\because W_{01} > W_{02}$ and K_{max} is same, hence $\nu_1 > \nu_2$.

21. We know that,

$$K_{max} = eV_0 = h(\nu - \nu_0)$$

Here, $\nu = \nu_0$

$\therefore \quad eV_0 = h(\nu_0 - \nu_0)$

$\Rightarrow \quad eV_0 = 0$

$\therefore \quad V_0 = 0$

Hence, stopping potential becomes zero when frequency of incident radiation is equal to threshold frequency.

22. Wavelength, $\lambda = \frac{h}{p}$, where h = Planck's constant

and p = momentum of particle.

23. Energy of the photon, $E = p \times c$, where p is the momentum of the photon and c is the velocity of the light.

24. In photoelectric emission, light energy ejects free electrons from a metal, while in thermionic emission heat energy does the same.

25. Free electrons of higher kinetic energy reach anode even at zero plate potential. These electrons can be stopped to reach the anode at negative potential.

26. According to wave theory, increase in the intensity of light means more light energy. In photoelectric effect, emission is not possible till the frequency of the light is more than threshold frequency whatever be the intensity of light.

27. (i) The lowest frequency of light which can emit photoelectrons from a material is called the threshold frequency f_0. (1)

(ii) The negative potential at which the photoelectric current becomes zero is called stopping potential V_s.

28. (i) The minimum amount of energy of incident radiation required to just eject an electron from the outermost surface of metal is known as work function (ϕ) of the metal. It is given as

$$\phi_0 = h\nu_0 = \frac{hc}{\lambda_0}$$

where, ν_0 and λ_0 are the threshold frequency and threshold wavelength, respectively. (1)

(ii) **Cut-off potential/Stopping potential** For a particular frequency of the incident radiation, the minimum negative (retarding) potential V_0 given to the metallic plate so, that the emission of electrons stops or photocurrent becomes zero, is called cut-off or stopping potential. It gives the maximum kinetic energy of an ejected electrons.

i.e. $KE_{max} = eV_0$

$$\Rightarrow \frac{1}{2} mv_{max}^2 = eV_0$$

where v_{max} = velocity of electron

and V_0 = cut-off potential (1)

29. According to first statement, when the materials which absorb photons of shorter wavelength has high energy of the incident photon on the material and low energy of emitted photon of longer wavelength. (1)

But in second statement, the energy of the incident photon is low for the substances which has to absorb photons of larger wavelength and energy of emitted photon is high to emit light of shorter wavelength. This means in this statement material has to supply the energy for the emission of photons. But this is not possible for a stable substances. (1)

30. Refer to text on pages 422 and 423 (Einstein's photoelectric equation).

31. The intensities for both the monochromatic radiations are same but their frequencies are different. It represents

(i) the number of electrons ejected in two cases are same because it depends on the number of incident photons. (1)

(ii) No, as $KE_{max} = h\nu - \phi_0 = hc/\lambda - \phi_0$

[Einstein's photoelectric equation]

$\therefore$ The KE_{max} of violet radiation will be more. (1)

32. (i) Here, given, $E_{max} = h\nu - \phi_0$

It is given that, an electron absorbs 2 photons each of frequency ν.

Now, maximum energy for emitted electrons,

$$E'_{max} = 2 \times h\nu - \phi_0$$
$$= 2h\nu - \phi_0$$ (1)

(ii) The probability of absorbing 2 photons by the same electron is very low.

Hence, such emission will be negligible. (1)

33. (i) Stopping potential does not change at all, only photoelectric current increases linearly with intensity of incident monochromatic UV-radiation. (1)

(ii) (a) Threshold frequency is given by $\nu_0 = \frac{\phi_0}{h}$

So, $\phi_0 \propto \nu_0$

Thus, metal having less work function will have lowest threshold frequency.

Thus, metal Q has lowest threshold frequency.

(b) According to photoelectric equation,

E_{max} = (Energy of photon) − (Work function of metal)

$$= h\nu - h\nu_0 \Rightarrow h(\nu - \nu_0)$$

For a particular incident radiation frequency ν, the metal with maximum the value of work function, minimum will be the energy.

Hence, metal P will have E_{max} minimum. (2)

34. Graph for V_s and ν is as follows

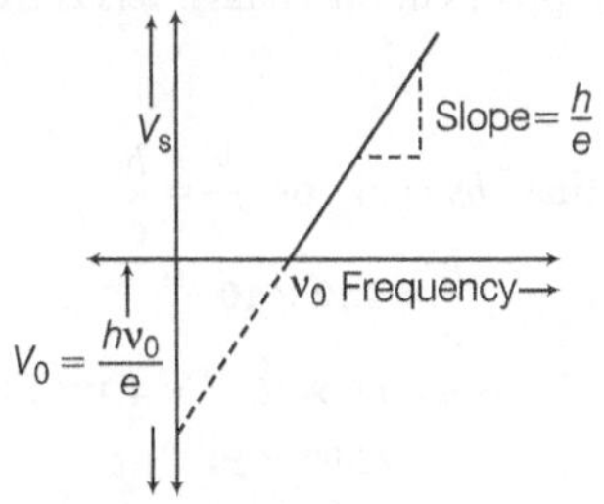

(1/2)

Determination of Planck's constant

As from the graph it is clear that slope of the graph is given by

$$\text{Slope} = \frac{h}{e}$$

where, h = Planck's constant
and e = charge on an electron (1/2)

Now, from Einstein's photoelectric equation,

$$K_{max} = h\nu - \phi$$

$$\Rightarrow \quad eV_0 = h\nu - \phi$$

$$\Rightarrow \quad V_0 = \left(\frac{h}{e}\right)\nu - \frac{\phi}{e}$$ (1)

Comparing this equation with

$$y = mx + c,$$

Slope of (V_0, ν) graph $= \frac{h}{e}$.

So, Planck's constant h = slope (V_0, ν) graph. (1)

35. (i) Since, we know that, to eject an electron, a photon must have energy at least as great as work function (W_0) and thus the minimum or cut-off frequency to eject an electron is $f_0 = \frac{W_0}{n}$.

If the incident light has the frequency below this cut off frequency, electrons are not ejected from the metal surface, so we have to increase the value of frequency, i.e. decrease the value of wavelength $\left(\text{as } \nu = \frac{c}{\lambda}\right)$. (1½)

(ii) (a) is the best explanation. (1½)

36. For the graph, refer to text on page 424 (Graph related to photoelectric effect from Einstein photoelectric equation). (1)

(i) From the graph for the same value of ν , stopping potential is more for material B.

$$\text{As, } V = \frac{h}{e}(\nu - \nu_0)$$

$\therefore$ V is higher for lower value of ν_0.

Here $\nu_B < \nu_A$, so $V_B > V_A$. (1½)

(ii) Slope of the graph is given by $\frac{h}{e}$, which is constant for all the materials. Hence, slope of the graph does not depend on the nature of the material used. (1½)

37. **Cut-off frequency** The frequency of incident radiation below threshold frequency is called cut-off frequency.

Given that threshold frequency of metal is f and frequency of light is $2f$. Using Einstein's equation for photoelectric effect, we can write (1½)

$$h(2f - f) = \frac{1}{2}mv_1^2 \quad \ldots \text{(i)}$$

Similarly, for light having frequency $5f$, we have

$$h(5f - f) = \frac{1}{2}mv_2^2 \quad \ldots \text{(ii)}$$

Using Eqs. (i) and (ii), we find

$$\frac{f}{4f} = \frac{v_1^2}{v_2^2}$$

$$\Rightarrow \quad \frac{v_1}{v_2} = \sqrt{\frac{1}{4}} \Rightarrow \frac{v_1}{v_2} = \frac{1}{2}$$ (1½)

38. Refer to the text and graph on page 424 (Graphs related to photoelectric effect from Einstein photoelectric equation (i)).

39. (i) Refer to text on pages 422 and 421 (Einstein's photoelectric equations). (1½)

(ii) Energy of incident photon is less than work function of P but just equal to that of Q.

For Q, Work function,

$$\phi_0 = \frac{h\nu}{e}(\text{eV})$$

$$= \frac{6.6 \times 10^{-34} \times 10^{15}}{1.6 \times 10^{-19}}$$

$$= 4.1 \text{ eV}$$ (1½)

40. (i) Refer to text on page 425 (Characteristics properties of photons). (1)

(ii) Since, Einstein's photoelectric equation is given by

$$\text{KE}_{max} = \frac{1}{2}mv_{max}^2$$

$$= h\nu - h\nu_0 = eV_0$$

(a) For a given material, there exist a certain minimum frequency of the incident radiation, below which no emission of photoelectron takes place. This frequency is called threshold frequency (ν_0). Above threshold frequency, the maximum kinetic energy of the emitted photoelectron or equivalent stopping potential is independent of the intensity of the incident light but depends only upon the frequency of the incident light. (1)

(b) If the collecting plate in the photoelectric apparatus is made at high negative potential, then most of the high energetic electrons get repelled back along the same path and the photoelectric current in the circuit becomes zero. So, for a particular frequency of incident radiation, the minimum negative potential for which the electric current becomes zero is called cut-off or stopping potential (V_0). (1)

41. Einstein's photoelectric equation and its features

Refer to text on pages 422 and 423. (2)

According to the photoelectric equation,

$$K_{max} = \frac{1}{2}mv_{max}^2 = h\nu - \phi_0$$

$$K_{max} = \frac{hc}{\lambda_1} - \phi_0 \quad ...(i)$$

Let the maximum kinetic energy for the incident radiation (of wavelength λ_2) be K'_{max}.

$$\Rightarrow \quad K'_{max} = \frac{hc}{\lambda_2} - \phi_0 \quad ...(ii)$$

From Eqs. (i) and (ii), we get

$$\frac{hc}{\lambda_2} - \phi_0 = 2\left(\frac{hc}{\lambda_1} - \phi_0\right) \quad [\because K'_{max} = 2K_{max}]$$

$$\Rightarrow \quad \phi_0 = hc\left(\frac{2}{\lambda_1} - \frac{1}{\lambda_2}\right)$$

$$\Rightarrow \quad h\nu_0 = hc\left(\frac{2}{\lambda_1} - \frac{1}{\lambda_2}\right)$$

$$\frac{c}{\lambda_0} = c\left(\frac{2}{\lambda_1} - \frac{1}{\lambda_2}\right)$$

$$\Rightarrow \quad \frac{1}{\lambda_0} = \left(\frac{2}{\lambda_1} - \frac{1}{\lambda_2}\right)$$

$$\Rightarrow \quad \lambda_0 = \left(\frac{\lambda_1\lambda_2}{2\lambda_2 - \lambda_1}\right) \quad (1)$$

42. Given, cut-off voltage, $V_0 = 1.5\text{V}$

Maximum kinetic energy is given by

$$KE_{max} = eV_0 = 1.5 \text{ eV} = 1.5 \times 1.6 \times 10^{-19}$$

$$= 2.4 \times 10^{-19} \text{ J}$$

43. $\lambda = 396 \text{ nm} = 396 \times 10^{-9} \text{ m}$

$$W = 1.125 \text{ eV} = 1.125 \times 1.6 \times 10^{-19} \text{ J}$$

(i) $KE = \frac{hc}{\lambda} = \frac{6.6 \times 10^{-34} \times 3 \times 10^8}{396 \times 10^{-19}} = 5 \times 10^{19}$ eV (1)

(ii) $KE = \frac{hc}{\lambda} - W = \frac{6.6 \times 10^{-34} \times 3 \times 10^8}{396 \times 10^{-19}} - 1.125 \times 1.6 \times 10^{-19}$

$$KE = 5 \times 10^{-9} \text{ J}$$

$$KE = \frac{5 \times 10^{-9}}{1.6 \times 10^{-19}} = 3.125 \times 10^{10} \text{ eV} \quad (2)$$

44. Given, slope of graph,

$$\tan\theta = 4.12 \times 10^{-15} \text{ V-s}$$

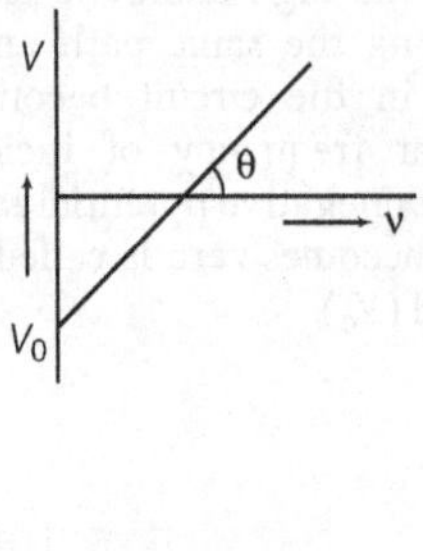

Charge on electron, $e = 1.6 \times 10^{-19}$ C

Slope of graph of cut off voltage *versus* frequency is

$$\tan\theta = \frac{V}{\nu} \quad (1/2)$$

We know that, $h\nu = eV$ or $\frac{V}{\nu} = \frac{h}{e}$ (1/2)

$$\therefore \quad \frac{h}{e} = 4.12 \times 10^{-15}$$

$$\Rightarrow \quad h = 1.6 \times 10^{-19} \times 4.12 \times 10^{-15}$$

$$= 6.592 \times 10^{-34} \text{J-s} \quad (1)$$

45. (i) Energy $= eV = h\nu$

or $\nu = \frac{eV}{h} = \frac{1.6 \times 10^{-19} \times 30 \times 10^3}{6.63 \times 10^{-34}} = 7.24 \times 10^{18}$ Hz (1)

(ii) As, $c = \nu\lambda$

$\therefore$ Wavelength, $\lambda = \frac{c}{\nu} = \frac{3 \times 10^8}{7.24 \times 10^{18}} = 0.0414$ nm (1)

46. Using the formula for kinetic energy,

Cut-off voltage, $V_0 = \frac{h(\nu - \nu_0)}{e}$ (1/2)

$$= \frac{6.63 \times 10^{-34}\ (8.2 \times 10^{14} - 3.3 \times 10^{14})}{1.6 \times 10^{-19}} = 2.03 \text{ V} \quad (1½)$$

47. Given, $\lambda = 5000\text{Å} = 5 \times 10^{-7}$ m

and $\phi_0 = 1.2\text{eV} = 1.2 \times 1.6 \times 10^{-19}\text{J}$

$$= 1.92 \times 10^{-19}\text{J}$$

We know that, $eV_0 = h\nu - h\nu_0 = \frac{hc}{\lambda} - \frac{hc}{\lambda_0}$

$$= hc/\lambda - \phi_0 \quad \left[\because \phi_0 = \frac{hc}{\lambda_0}\right] \quad (1)$$

$$\therefore V_0 = \frac{hc}{e\lambda} - \frac{\phi_0}{e} = \frac{6.62 \times 10^{-34} \times 3 \times 10^8}{1.6 \times 10^{-19} \times 5 \times 10^{-7}} - \frac{1.92 \times 10^{-19}}{1.6 \times 10^{-19}}$$

$$= 2.4825 - 1.2 = 1.28 \text{ V} \quad (1)$$

48. Given, $\nu = 7.21 \times 10^{14}$ Hz, $m = 9.1 \times 10^{-31}$ kg

$$v_{max} = 6 \times 10^5 \text{ m/s}$$

Let ν_0 be the threshold frequency.

Use the formula for kinetic energy,

$$KE = \frac{1}{2}mv_{max}^2 = h\nu - h\nu_0 \quad (1)$$

$$= \frac{1}{2} \times 9.1 \times 10^{-31} \times (6 \times 10^5)^2 = 6.63 \times 10^{-34}(\nu - \nu_0)$$

or $\nu - \nu_0 = \frac{36 \times 9.1 \times 10^{-21}}{2 \times 6.63 \times 10^{-34}} = 2.47 \times 10^{14}$ Hz

$$\therefore \quad \nu_0 = 4.74 \times 10^{14} \text{ Hz} \quad (1)$$

49. Given, for the first condition, $\lambda = 600$ nm

For the second condition, $\lambda' = 400$ nm

$$K'_{max} = 2K_{max} \quad (1)$$

Here, $K'_{max} = \frac{hc}{\lambda} - \phi \Rightarrow 2K_{max} = \frac{hc}{\lambda'} - \phi_0$

$$\Rightarrow 2\left(\frac{1240}{600}-\phi\right)\approx\left(\frac{1240}{400}-\phi\right) \quad [\because hc \approx 1240 \text{ eV-nm}]$$

$$\Rightarrow \phi=\frac{1240}{1200}=1.03 \text{ eV}$$ (1)

50. Given, $\phi_{Al}=4.28\text{eV}, \phi_{Ca}=2.87\text{eV}$

Also, $\phi = h\nu_0$

$\therefore$ $\phi_{Al}=4.28\text{eV}=h\nu_{0Al}$

$$\Rightarrow \nu_{0Al}=\frac{4.28\times1.6\times10^{-19}}{6.62\times10^{-34}}=1.03\times10^{15}\text{Hz}$$ (1)

Similarly, $\nu_{0Ca}=\frac{2.87\times1.6\times10^{-19}}{6.62\times10^{-34}}=6.93\times10^{14}\text{Hz}$

(i) Aluminium requires higher frequency of light to produce photoelectrons, i.e. 1.03×10^{15} Hz (1/2)

(ii) Ca has minimum frequency, i.e. 6.93×10^{14} Hz that will produce photoelectrons from each surface. (1/2)

51. (i) Given, work function, $\phi_0 = 2.14$ eV, $\nu=6\times10^{14}$ Hz

$\therefore K_{max}=h\nu-\phi_0$

$=6.63\times10^{-34}\times6\times10^{14}-2.14$

$=\frac{6.63\times6\times10^{-20}}{1.6\times10^{-19}}\text{ eV}-2.14$

$=2.48-2.14=0.34$ eV (1)

(ii) Let stopping potential be V_0.

We know that,

$\text{KE}_{max}=eV_0$

$\Rightarrow$ $0.35\text{ eV}=eV_0$

$\therefore$ $V_0=0.35$ V (1)

(iii) Maximum kinetic energy, $\text{KE}_{max}=\frac{1}{2}mv_{max}^2$

$0.35\text{ eV}=\frac{1}{2}mv_{max}^2$

where, v_{max} is the maximum speed and m is the mass of electron.

$$\frac{0.35\times2\times1.6\times10^{-19}}{9.1\times10^{-31}}=v_{max}^2 \quad [\because e=1.6\times10^{-19}]$$

$\Rightarrow$ $v_{max}^2=0.123\times10^{12}$

$\Rightarrow$ $v_{max}=350713.55$ m/s

$=350.7$ km/s (1)

52. Here, for neon lamp, $\lambda=640.2\text{ nm}=640.2\times10^{-9}\text{ m}$

$V_0=0.54$ V

We know that, $eV_0=\frac{hc}{\lambda}-\phi_0$

$\therefore$ Work function, $\phi_0=\frac{hc}{\lambda}-eV_0$

$$=\frac{6.63\times10^{-34}\times3\times10^8}{640.2\times10^{-9}}-1.6\times10^{-19}\times0.54$$

$=(3.1\times10^{-19}-0.864\times10^{-19})$ J

$=2.236\times10^{-19}$ J (1)

For iron source, $\lambda=427.2\text{ nm}=427.2\times10^{-9}\text{ m}$

$$\therefore eV_0=\frac{hc}{\lambda}-\phi_0=\frac{6.63\times10^{-34}\times3\times10^8}{427.2\times10^{-9}}-2.236\times10^{-19}$$

$=(4.656\times10^{-19}-2.236\times10^{-19})$ J

$=2.42\times10^{-19}$ J (1)

$\therefore$ Stopping potential, $V_0=\frac{2.42\times10^{-19}}{e}$

$=\frac{2.42\times10^{-19}}{1.6\times10^{-19}}=1.51$ V (1)

53. Given, the following wavelengths from a mercury source were used

$\lambda_1=3650$ Å

$\lambda_2=4047$ Å

$\lambda_3=4358$ Å

$\lambda_4=5461$ Å

$\lambda_5=6907$ Å

The stopping voltages are as follows:

$V_{01}=1.28$ V, $V_{02}=0.95$ V, $V_{03}=0.74$ V

$V_{04}=0.16$ V and $V_{05}=0$

Frequencies corresponding to wavelengths,

$$\nu_1=\frac{c}{\lambda_1}=\frac{3\times10^8}{3650\times10^{-10}}=8.219\times10^{14}\text{ Hz}$$

Similarly,

$\nu_2=7.412\times10^{14}$ Hz, $\nu_3=6.884\times10^{14}$ Hz

$\nu_4=5.493\times10^{14}$ Hz, $\nu_5=4.343\times10^{14}$ Hz (1)

As we know that, $eV_0=h\nu-\phi_0$

$$V_0=\frac{h\nu}{e}-\frac{\phi_0}{e}$$

As the graph between V_0 and frequency ν is a straight line.

The slope of this graph gives the values of $\frac{h}{e}$. (1/2)

$$\therefore \frac{h}{e}=\frac{V_{01}-V_{04}}{\nu_1-\nu_4}$$

$$=\frac{1.28-0.16}{(8.219-5.493)\times10^{14}}$$

$$=\frac{1.12}{2.726\times10^{14}}$$

$$h=\frac{1.12\times1.6\times10^{-19}}{2.726\times10^{14}}=6.573\times10^{-34}\text{ J-s}$$ (1/2)

As, $\nu_{average}=5\times10^{14}$ Hz [given]

$\therefore$ Work function, $\phi_0=h\nu_0$

$=6.573\times10^{-34}\times5\times10^{14}$

$=32.865\times10^{-20}$ J

$=2.05$ eV (1)

54. Maximum wavelength of visible light (i.e. of red light) is 7800 Å.

∴ Energy of red light,

$$E = \frac{hc}{\lambda} \cong \frac{12400 \text{ (eV - Å)}}{7800 \text{ (Å)}} = 1.6 \text{ eV}$$

55. Energy of a photon, $E = \frac{hc}{\lambda}$ (1/2)

∴ Number of photons incident per square metre per second,

$$n = \frac{P}{E} = \frac{P}{\frac{hc}{\lambda}} = \frac{P\lambda}{hc}$$

$$= \frac{(1.388 \times 10^3) \times 550 \times 10^{-9}}{(6.63 \times 10^{-34}) \times (3 \times 10^8)}$$

$$= 3.84 \times 10^{21} \text{ photons/m}^2\text{-s}$$ (1/2)

56. Here, $\lambda = 500 \text{ nm} = 5 \times 10^{-7}$ m

Energy of one photon

$$= \frac{hc}{\lambda} = \frac{6.63 \times 10^{-34} \times 3 \times 10^8}{5 \times 10^{-7}} = 3.98 \times 10^{-19} \text{ J}$$

A bulb of 100 W supplied 100 J of energy per second. (1)

∴ Energy released per second as visible photons

$$= \frac{100 \times 10}{100} = 10 \text{ J}$$ (1/2)

∴ Number of photons emitted per second as visible light

$$= \frac{10}{3.98 \times 10^{-19}} = 2.5 \times 10^{19}$$ (1/2)

57. Given, $E = 6 \times 10^{-19}$ J

Momentum, $p = \frac{E}{c}$

where, c is speed of light $= \frac{6 \times 10^{-19}}{3 \times 10^8}$

$$= 2 \times 10^{-27} \text{ J ms}^{-1}$$

58. Given, work function of metal A, $\phi_{0A} = 4$ eV

Work function of metal B, $\phi_{0B} = 6$ eV

Therefore, threshold wavelength of metal A,

$$\lambda_{0A} = \frac{hc}{\phi_{0A}} = \frac{hc}{4} \quad \text{... (i)}$$

Similarly, threshold wavelength of metal B,

$$\lambda_{0B} = \frac{hc}{\phi_{0B}} = \frac{hc}{6} \quad \text{... (ii)}$$

On comparing Eqs. (i) and (ii), we can say that

$$\lambda_{0A} > \lambda_{0B}$$

i.e. Threshold wavelength of metal A is greater than that of metal B.

59. Given, threshold frequency, $\nu_0 = 5 \times 10^{14}$ Hz

So, work function is given by

$$\phi = h\nu_0$$

$$\Rightarrow \quad \phi = 6.64 \times 10^{-34} \times 5 \times 10^{14}$$

$$\phi = 3.3 \times 10^{-19} \text{ J}$$

$$\therefore \quad \phi = \frac{3.3 \times 10^{-19}}{1.6 \times 10^{-19}} = 2.06 \text{ eV}$$

60. According to Einstein's photoelectric equation,

$$KE_{max} = h\nu - \phi$$

where, $h\nu$ = Energy of incident photon,

ϕ = work function.

Now for 1st case,

$$KE_1 = h \times 4 \times 10^{15} - h\nu_0 \quad [\because \phi = h\nu_0]$$

For 2nd case,

$$KE_2 = h \times 8 \times 10^{15} - h\nu_0$$ (1)

Change in KE = $KE_2 - KE_1$

$$= h(8 \times 10^{15} - 4 \times 10^{15})$$

$$= h \times 4 \times 10^{15}$$

As, $KE_1 = eV_1$ and $KE_2 = eV_2$ (1)

So, $eV_2 - eV_1 = h \times 4 \times 10^5$

$$\Rightarrow \quad (V_2 - V_1) = \frac{h}{e} \times 4 \times 10^{15}$$

$$\Rightarrow \quad (V_2 - V_1) = \frac{6.64 \times 10^{-34} \times 4 \times 10^{15}}{1.6 \times 10^{-19}}$$

$$= 16.5 \text{ V}$$ (1)

61. Given, threshold wavelength,

$$\lambda_0 = 792 \text{ nm} = 792 \times 10^{-9} \text{ m},$$

Incident wavelength, $\lambda = 396$nm

$$= 396 \times 10^{-9} \text{ m}$$

So, by Einstein's photoelectric equation,

Maximum kinetic energy

$$KE_{max} = h\nu - \phi$$ (1)

So, $$KE_{Max} = \frac{hc}{\lambda} - \frac{hc}{\lambda_0}$$

[ϕ = work function, $h\nu$ = energy]

$$= hc\left[\frac{1}{\lambda} - \frac{1}{\lambda_0}\right] \quad [\text{as } \nu = c/\lambda]$$ (1)

$$= 6.6 \times 10^{-34} \times 3 \times 10^8 \left[\frac{1}{396 \times 10^{-9}} - \frac{1}{792 \times 10^{-9}}\right]$$

$$= 24.98 \times 10^{-20} \text{ J}$$

$$= 25 \times 10^{-20} \text{ J}$$ (1)

62. (i) Given, work function,

$$\phi_0 = 2.28 \text{ eV}$$

So, minimum energy for photocurrent

$$\phi = 2.28 \times 1.6 \times 10^{-19}$$

$$= 3.648 \times 10^{-19} \text{ J}$$ (1½)

(ii) As we know that, $E = \frac{hc}{\lambda}$

So, $\lambda = \frac{hc}{E} = \frac{6.6\times 10^{-34} \times 3\times 10^{8}}{3.648\times 10^{-19}\ J}$

$= 5.428\times 10^{-7}$ m

$= 5428$ Å (1½)

63. Given, threshold wavelength,

$\lambda_0 = 2400$ Å $= 2400\times 10^{-10}$ m

Wavelength of incident light,

$\lambda = 1600$ Å $= 1600\times 10^{-10}$ m

(i) So, work function $\phi = \frac{hc}{\lambda_0}$

$= \frac{6.6\times 10^{-34} \times 3\times 10^{8}}{2400\times 10^{-10}}$

$= 8.256\times 10^{-19}$ J $= 5.16$ eV (1)

(ii) Maximum kinetic energy

$KE_{max} = \frac{hc}{\lambda} - \frac{hc}{\lambda_0}$

[from Einstein photoelectric equation]

$\Rightarrow KE_{max} = hc\left[\frac{1}{1600\times 10^{-10}} - \frac{1}{2400\times 10^{-10}}\right]$

$= \frac{hc}{10^{-10}}\left[\frac{2400-1600}{1600\times 2400}\right]$

$= \frac{6.6\times 10^{-34}\times 3\times 10^{8}\times 800}{10^{-10}\times 1600\times 2400}$

$= 4.125\times 10^{-19}$ J $= 2.578$ eV (1)

(iii) Stopping potential, $KE_{max} = eV_0$

$\Rightarrow V_0 = \frac{KE_{max}}{e}$

$V_0 = \frac{2.57e}{e} = 2.57$ V (1)

64. In this type of questions, from the given values of h, c and λ, we can calculate the energy incident on metal and then after from the given stopping potential we will calculate maximum kinetic energy of ejected electrons.

(i) Given, Planck's constant

$h = 6.6\times 10^{-34}$ J/s,

$c = 3\times 10^{8}$ m/s

Incident wavelength,

$\lambda = 300$ nm $= 300\times 10^{-9}$ m,

Stopping potential, $V_0 = 0.54$ V

$e = 1.6\times 10^{-19}$ C

Now, $E = \frac{hc}{\lambda} = \frac{6.6\times 10^{-34}\times 3\times 10^{8}}{300\times 10^{-9}}$

$= 6.63\times 10^{-19}$ J

$= \frac{6.63\times 10^{-19}}{1.6\times 10^{-19}} = 4.14$ eV (2)

(ii) Maximum kinetic energy $= eV_0$

$= 1.6\times 10^{-19}\times 0.54$

$= \frac{1.6\times 10^{-19}\times 0.54}{1.6\times 10^{-19}} = 0.54$ eV (1)

(iii) Now, work function (ϕ) of metal

= Energy incident − Maximum kinetic energy

$= 4.14$ eV $- 0.54$ eV

$= 3.6$ eV (1)

65. Energy of photon, $E = h\times$ (Frequency of photon)

$= 6.6\times 10^{-34}\times 5\times 10^{14}$

$= 3.3\times 10^{-19}$ J

Momentum of photon, $p = \frac{E}{c} = \frac{3.3\times 10^{-19}}{3\times 10^{8}}$

$= 1.1\times 10^{-11}$ N-s

66. Visible radiation $= \frac{60\times 15}{100} = 9$ W or 9 J/s

Energy of one photon $= \frac{hc}{\lambda}$

$= \frac{6.6\times 10^{-34}\times 3\times 10^{8}}{6\times 10^{-7}}$

$= 3.3\times 10^{-19}$ J (1)

Hence, number of photons released per second

$= \frac{9}{3.3}\times 10^{19} = 2.73\times 10^{19}$ /second (1)

67. Momentum of photon, $p = \sqrt{2meV}$

$= \sqrt{2\times 9\times 10^{-31}\times 1.6\times 10^{-19}\times 1000}$

$= 16.9\times 10^{-24}$ N-m (1½)

Now, wavelength, $\lambda = \frac{h}{p} = \frac{6.6\times 10^{-34}}{16.9\times 10^{-24}}$

$= 3.9\times 10^{-11}$ m

$= 0.39$ Å (1½)

68. (i) The wavelength, $\lambda_0 = \frac{hc}{W}$

$= \frac{6.6\times 10^{-34}\times 3\times 10^{8}}{2\times 1.6\times 10^{-19}}$

$= 6187\times 10^{-10}$

$= 6187$ Å (1)

(ii) Energy of photon $= \frac{hc}{\lambda} = \frac{6.6\times 10^{-34}\times 3\times 10^{8}}{500\times 10^{-9}}$

$= 3.96\times 10^{-19} = 2.48$ eV (1)

(iii) Kinetic energy of photoelectron

= Energy of photon − Work function

$= 2.48 - 2 = 0.48$ eV

Therefore, stopping potential, $V_c = 0.48$ V (1)

69. Momentum of photon, $p = \frac{h}{\lambda} = \frac{6.6 \times 10^{-34}}{5 \times 10^{-7}}$

$= 1.32 \times 10^{-27}$ kg-m/s

70. Energy of one radio wave photon,

$E = \frac{hc}{\lambda} = \frac{6.6 \times 10^{-34} \times 3 \times 10^8}{30}$

$= 6.6 \times 10^{-27}$ J (1)

Number of photons emitted per second

$= \frac{300}{6.6 \times 10^{-27}}$

$= 4.5 \times 10^{28}$/second (1)

71. Work function, $W = \frac{hc}{\lambda_0}$

or $\lambda_0 = \frac{hc}{W} = \frac{6.6 \times 10^{-34} \times 3 \times 10^8}{2 \times 1.6 \times 10^{-19}}$

$= 6.1875 \times 10^{-7}$ m $= 6187.5$ Å

72. (i) Threshold frequency $(\nu_0) = 10 \times 10^{11}$ Hz (1)

(ii) $W = (h\nu_0) = 6.6 \times 10^{-34} \times 10 \times 10^{14}$

$= 6.6 \times 10^{-19}$ J $= 4.125$ eV (1)

(iii) $E_k = 8 \times 1.6 \times 10^{-19}$ J $= 8$ eV

$V_s = \frac{8 \times 1.6 \times 10^{-19}}{1.6 \times 10^{-19}}$

$V_s = 8.0$ V (1)

73. Given, $\nu_0 = 5 \times 10^{14}$ Hz

Work function, $W = h\nu_0$

$= 6.6 \times 10^{-34} \times 5 \times 10^{14}$

$= 3.3 \times 10^{-19}$ J

$= \frac{33 \times 10^{-19}}{16 \times 10^{-19}}$ eV

$W = 2.062$ eV

74. Given, $V = 0.5$ V

So, stopping potential = 0.5 V

$\lambda = 400$ nm

$W = ?$

We know, $E_n = eV_0$ (1)

We also know, photoelectric equation,

$h\nu = W + E_n$

$\frac{hc}{\lambda} = W + E_n$ (1)

$\frac{6.6 \times 10^{-34} \times 3 \times 10^8}{400 \times 10^{-9}} = W + 0.5 \times 1.6 \times 10^{-19}$

$\Rightarrow \quad W = 4.95 \times 10^{-19} - 8 \times 10^{-20}$

$= 4.15 \times 10^{-19}$ J

$W = 2.59$ eV (1)

75. Energy of a light ray photon = Work function + Kinetic energy

or $\frac{hc}{\lambda} = \frac{hc}{\lambda_0} + E_k$

In first case, $\frac{hc}{800 \times 10^{-10}} = \frac{hc}{\lambda_0} + 1.8$ eV

In second case, $\frac{hc}{700 \times 10^{-10}} = \frac{hc}{\lambda_0} + 4.0$ eV (1)

Subtracting the two equations, we get

$\frac{hc}{10^{-10}}\left[\frac{1}{700} - \frac{1}{800}\right] = (4.0 - 1.8)$ eV

or $\frac{hc}{10^{-10}} \times \frac{100}{700 \times 800} = 2.2 \times 1.6 \times 10^{-19}$

or $h = \frac{2.2 \times 1.6 \times 10^{-19} \times 700 \times 800 \times 10^{-10}}{100 \times 3 \times 10^8}$

$= 6.57 \times 10^{-34}$ J-s (2)

TOPIC 02 Matter Waves

Wave theory of electromagnetic radiations explained the phenomenon of interference, diffraction and polarisation of light.

On the other hand, quantum theory of electromagnetic radiations successfully explained the photoelectric effect, Compton effect, black body radiation, X-rays spectra, etc.

From photoelectric and Compton effects, it is clear that a particle (photon of radiation) is colliding against another particle (electron). It is due to this reason it was concluded that, in photoelectric effect and Compton effect, the radiation possesses particle nature.

It means radiation sometimes behaves as a wave and sometimes as a particle. Therefore, Louis Victor de-Broglie suggested that the particles like electrons, protons, neutrons, etc., have dual nature, i.e. they can have particle as well as wave nature.

Note Matter cannot exist both as a particle and as a wave simultaneously. At a particular instant of time, it is either the one or the other aspect, i.e. the two aspects are complementary to each other.

Wave Nature of Particles: (de-Broglie Hypothesis)

According to de-Broglie, a wave is associated with moving material particle which controls the particle in every respect. The wave associated with moving material particle is called **matter wave** or **de-Broglie wave** whose wavelength is called **de-Broglie wavelength** which is given by

$$\lambda = \frac{h}{mv}$$

where, m and v are the mass and velocity of the particle and h is Planck's constant.

According to Planck's quantum theory, the energy of the photon is given by

$$E = h\nu = \frac{hc}{\lambda} \quad \text{...(i)}$$

According to Einstein's theory, the energy of the photon is given by

$$E = mc^2 \quad \text{...(ii)}$$

Therefore, from Eqs. (i) and (ii), we get

$$\lambda = \frac{h}{mc} \text{ or } \boxed{\lambda = \frac{h}{p}}$$

where, $p = mc$ is momentum of a photon.

If a material particle of mass m is moving with velocity v, then momentum of the particle,

$$p = mv.$$

According to de-Broglie hypothesis, the wavelength of wave associated with moving material particle becomes

$$\boxed{\lambda = \frac{h}{p} = \frac{h}{mv}}$$

which is the expression for de-Broglie wavelength.

From the above expression following observations we made

(i) The de-Broglie wavelength $\lambda \propto \frac{1}{v}$. If the particle moves faster, then the wavelength will be smaller and *vice-versa*.

(ii) If the particle is at rest $(v = 0)$, then the de-Broglie wavelength is infinite $(\lambda = \infty)$. Such a wave cannot be visualised.

(iii) The de-Broglie waves cannot be electromagnetic in nature because electromagnetic waves are produced by motion of charged particles.

(iv) The wavelength of a wave associated with moving particle defines a region of uncertainty, within which the whereabouts of the particle are unknown.

These facts lead to Heisenberg's uncertainty principle. According to this principle, it is not possible to measure both the position and momentum of a particle at the same time exactly. There is always some uncertainty (Δx) in the specification of position and some uncertainty (Δp) in the specification of momentum. The product of Δx and Δp is of the order of $\hbar$, (with $\hbar = \frac{h}{2\pi}$),

i.e. $\Delta x \, \Delta p \approx \hbar = \frac{h}{2\pi}$.

Common Features of Matter Waves

Some common features of matter waves are as given below

(i) Matter waves can travel in vacuum and hence they are not mechanical waves.

(ii) Matter waves are probability waves, amplitude of which gives the probability of existence of the particle at the point. If at a point, the amplitude of the wave is A, then probability of the particle being found in a small volume dV around that point is $|A|^2 \, dV$.

Relation between de-Broglie Wavelength (λ) and Temperature (T)

From kinetic theory of gases, the average kinetic energy of a particle at a given temperature T kelvin is given by

$$K = \frac{3}{2} kT$$

where, k = Boltzmann constant.

If a particle of mass m is moving with velocity v, then its kinetic energy is, $K = \frac{1}{2} mv^2$

Momentum of particle is

$$p = mv = \sqrt{2mK}$$

$$= \sqrt{2m \times \frac{3}{2} kT} = \sqrt{3mkT}$$

$$\Rightarrow \quad \boxed{\text{de-Broglie wavelength, } \lambda = \frac{h}{p} = \frac{h}{\sqrt{3mkT}}}$$

Example 1 An electron and a photon each have a wavelength 1.00 nm. Calculate

(i) their momentum.

(ii) the energy of the photon.

(iii) the kinetic energy of electron. **NCERT**

Sol. Given, $\lambda = 1$ nm $= 1 \times 10^{-9}$ m, $h = 6.63 \times 10^{-34}$ J-s, $c = 3 \times 10^8$ m/s, $p = ?, E = ?, K = ?$

(i) Momentum of the photon, $p_p = \frac{h}{\lambda}$

$$= \frac{6.63 \times 10^{-34}}{1 \times 10^{-9}} = 6.63 \times 10^{-25} \text{ kg-m/s}$$

Momentum of the electron, $p_e = \frac{h}{\lambda}$

$$= \frac{6.63 \times 10^{-34}}{1 \times 10^{-9}} = 6.63 \times 10^{-25} \text{ kg-m/s}$$

(ii) Energy of the photon,

$$E = \frac{hc}{\lambda} = \frac{6.63 \times 10^{-34} \times 3 \times 10^8}{1 \times 10^{-9}} = 1.99 \times 10^{-16} \text{ J}$$

(iii) Kinetic energy of the electron,

$$K = \frac{p^2}{2m_e}$$

$$= \frac{(6.63 \times 10^{-25})^2}{2 \times 9.1 \times 10^{-31}} = 2.41 \times 10^{-19} \text{ J}$$

Example 2 **A proton and an electron have same de-Broglie wavelength. Which of them moves fast and which possesses more kinetic energy? Justify your answer.**

Sol. Kinetic energy of particle of mass m having momentum p is given by

$$K = \frac{p^2}{2m} \Rightarrow p = \sqrt{2mK}$$

The de-Broglie wavelength, $\lambda = \frac{h}{p} = \frac{h}{\sqrt{2mK}}$

$$\therefore \quad p = \frac{h}{\lambda} \quad \text{...(i)}$$

$$\text{and} \quad K = \frac{h^2}{2m\lambda^2} \quad \text{...(ii)}$$

If λ is constant, then from Eq. (i), we get

$$p = \text{constant, i.e. } m_p v_p = m_e v_e$$

$$\text{or} \quad \frac{v_p}{v_e} = \frac{m_e}{m_p} < 1 \text{ or } v_p < v_e$$

If λ is constant, then from Eq. (ii),

$$K \propto \frac{1}{m}$$

$$\therefore \quad \frac{K_p}{K_e} = \frac{m_e}{m_p} < 1 \text{ or } K_p < K_e.$$

It means that the velocity of electron is greater than that of proton. Kinetic energy of electron is greater than that of proton.

Example 3 **Find de-Broglie wavelength of neutron at 127° C. Given, mass of neutron $= 1.66 \times 10^{-27}$ kg, Boltzmann constant, $k = 1.38 \times 10^{-23}$ J mol^{-1} K^{-1}, and Planck's constant, $h = 6.63 \times 10^{-34}$ J-s.**

Sol. Here, $T = 127°\text{C} = 127 + 273 = 400$ K

Energy of neutron at 127° C,

$$E = \frac{3}{2} kT = \frac{3}{2} \times 1.38 \times 10^{-23} \times 400$$

$$= 8.28 \times 10^{-21} \text{ J}$$

$$\therefore \quad \lambda = \frac{h}{\sqrt{2mE}}$$

$$= \frac{6.63 \times 10^{-34}}{\sqrt{2 \times 1.66 \times 10^{-27} \times 8.28 \times 10^{-21}}}$$

$$= 1.264 \times 10^{-10} \text{ m}$$

$$= 1.264 \text{ Å}$$

de-Broglie Wavelength of an Electron

Let an electron of charge e having mass m be accelerated from rest through a potential difference V, then

Gain in kinetic energy of an electron $= \frac{1}{2}mv^2$

Work done on the electron $= eV$

$$\therefore \quad \frac{1}{2}mv^2 = eV$$

$$\Rightarrow \quad v = \sqrt{\frac{2eV}{m}}$$

Momentum is given by $p = mv = \sqrt{2eVm}$

The wavelength associated with moving charge is given by

$$\lambda = \frac{h}{p} = \frac{h}{\sqrt{2meV}} \qquad \dots (i)$$

If accelerated charge is electron, then $\lambda = \frac{h}{\sqrt{2eVm_e}}$

where, m_e = mass of electron.

Substituting the numerical values of h, m_e and e in Eq. (i) we get

$$\lambda = \frac{6.63 \times 10^{-34}}{\sqrt{2 \times 9 \times 10^{-31} \times 1.6 \times 10^{-19} \times V}}$$

$$= \frac{12.27}{\sqrt{V}} \times 10^{-10} \text{m}$$

$$= \frac{12.27}{\sqrt{V}} \text{Å} = \frac{1.227}{\sqrt{V}} \text{nm}$$

Example 4 Determine the de-Broglie wavelength associated with an electron, accelerated through a potential difference of 100 V.

Sol. Given, potential difference $(V) = 100$ V

$\therefore$ de-Broglie wavelength $(\lambda) = \frac{12.27}{\sqrt{V}} = \frac{12.27}{\sqrt{100}}$

$= 1.227$ Å

In this case, the wavelength associated with an electron is of the order of wavelength of X-rays.

Davisson and Germer Experiment

The wave nature of electron was verified by Davisson and Germer experiment in 1927. The experimental arrangement is shown in the figure given below. It consists of an electron gun which comprises of a tungsten filament F, coated with barium oxide and heated by a low voltage power supply. Electrons emitted by the filament are accelerated to a desired velocity by applying suitable potential from a high voltage power supply.

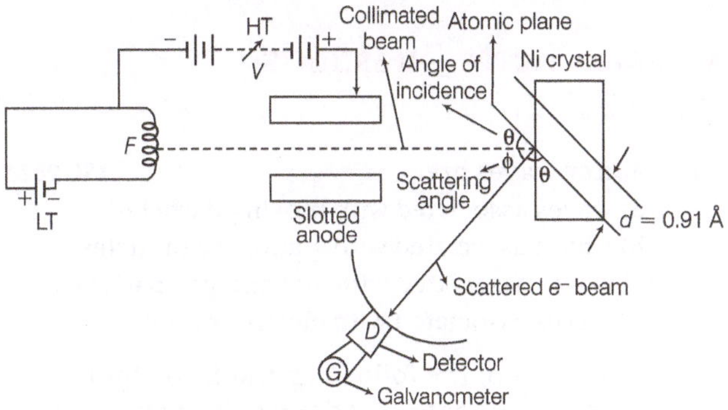

Experimental arrangement to demonstrate the wave nature of electron

They are made to pass through a cylinder with free holes along its axis, producing a fine collimated beam. This collimated beam is then made to fall on the surface of a nickel crystal. The electrons in the beam are scattered in all directions by the atoms of the crystal.

The scattered beam of electrons is received by the detector which can be rotated at any angle.

The energy of the incident beam of electrons can be varied by changing the applied voltage to the electron gun.

After performing the experiment, many times for different values of applied voltage, it was observed that the intensity of scattered beam of electrons was found to be maximum when angle of scattering is 50° and the accelerating potential is 54 V.

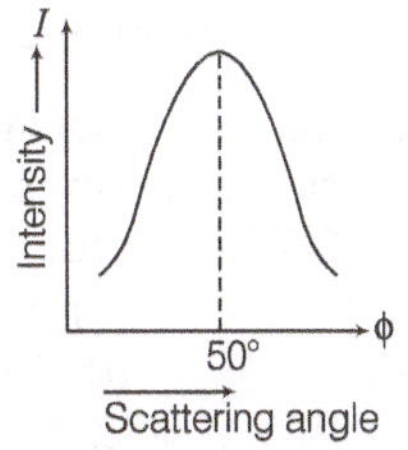

Graph obtained between incident beam and intensity of scattered beam at 54 V for Davisson and Germer experiment

According to de-Broglie's hypothesis,

$$\lambda = \frac{12.27}{\sqrt{V}} \text{Å} = \frac{12.27}{\sqrt{54}} = 0.167 \text{nm}$$

$\therefore$ de-Broglie wavelength of moving electron at $V = 54$ V is 1.67Å

which is in close agreement with 1.65 Å.

This proves the existence of de-Broglie waves for the slow moving electrons.

Topic Practice 2

Multiple Choice Questions

1 Mark

1. Matter waves are **ISC 2023**
(a) waves associated with moving particles.
(b) waves associated with stationary particles.
(c) waves associated with any charged particles.
(d) waves associated with electrons only.

2. Which one of the following graphs in figure represents variation of de-Broglie wavelength (λ) of a particle having linear momentum (p)? **ISC 2011**

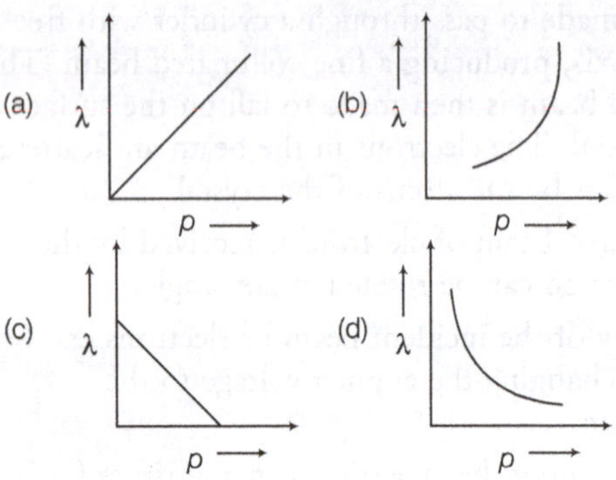

3. The de-Broglie wavelength λ
(a) is proportional to mass
(b) is proportional to momentum
(c) inversely proportional to momentum
(d) does not depends on momentum

4. de-Broglie wavelength associated with an electron, accelerating through a potential difference of 100 V lies in the region of
(a) Gamma rays (b) X-rays
(c) Ultravoilet (d) Visible region

5. The de-Broglie wavelength associated with a molecule at $T(K)$ is
(a) $\dfrac{h}{\sqrt{3mKT}}$ (b) $\dfrac{h}{\sqrt{\frac{3}{2}mKT}}$
(c) $\dfrac{h}{\sqrt{\frac{1}{3}mKT}}$ (d) 0

6. The de-Broglie wavelength (λ) associated with a moving electron having kinetic energy (E) is given by **ISC 2024**
(a) $\dfrac{2h}{\sqrt{2mE}}$ (b) $\dfrac{2\sqrt{2mE}}{h}$ (c) $\dfrac{h}{\sqrt{2mE}}$ (d) $\sqrt{2mhE}$

7. In Davisson experiment, if applied accelerating voltage is increased. Then, diffracted electron beam will have the maximum at a value of θ that **NCERT Exemplar**
(a) will be larger than the earlier value
(b) will be the same or earlier value
(c) will be less than the earlier value
(d) will depend on target

Very Short Answer Type Questions

1 Mark

8. What consideration led de-Broglie to suggest that material particles can also show wave property?

9. Show graphically the variation of de-Broglie wavelength λ with the potential V through which an electron is accelerated from rest.

10. Write the expression for the de-Broglie wavelength associated with a charged particle having charge q and mass m, when it is accelerated by a potential V.

11. A photon and an electron have the same de-Broglie wavelength, which one has higher total energy?

12. A proton and an electron have same kinetic energy. Which one has greater de-Broglie wavelength and why?

13. Why is the wave nature of matter, so insignificant in our daily life?

14. An electron and a proton have the same de-Broglie wavelength. Which one of these has higher kinetic energy?

15. An electron and a proton possess the same kinetic energy. Which of the two has greater de-Broglie wavelength? Write down the formula used.

16. What is the relation between wavelength and momentum of moving electrons? **ISC 2013**

17. Name the phenomena or an experiment which proves wave nature of particle. **ISC 2013**

18. de-Broglie wavelength of electrons of kinetic energy E is λ. What will be its value, if kinetic energy of electrons made $4E$? **ISC 2010**

19. (i) What is de-Broglie hypothesis?
(ii) What conclusion can be drawn from Davisson and Germer's experiment? **ISC 2020**

Short Answer Type I Questions

2 Marks

20. Why is the wave nature of matter not more apparent to our daily observations?

21. Show that the wavelength of electromagnetic radiation is equal to the de-Broglie wavelength of its quantum (photon). **NCERT**

22. (i) What are matter waves?
(ii) Show with the help of a labelled graph how their wavelength (λ) varies with their linear momentum (p). **ISC 2014**

23. A proton and an α-particle are accelerated through the same potential. Which one of the two has
(i) greater value of de-Broglie wavelength associated with it?
(ii) less kinetic energy? Give reasons to justify your answer.

24. The two lines marked A and B in the given figure, show a plot of de-Broglie wavelength λ *versus* $\frac{1}{\sqrt{V}}$, where V is the accelerating potential for two nuclei ${}^2_1\text{H}$ and ${}^3_1\text{H}$.

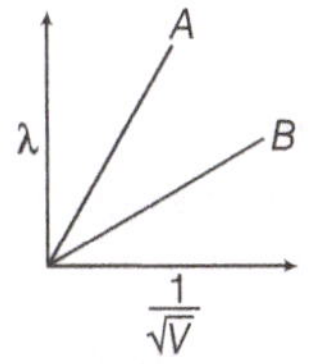

(i) What does the slope of the lines represent?
(ii) Identify, which of the lines corresponded to these nuclei.

25. (i) State de-Broglie hypothesis.
(ii) With reference to photoelectric effect, define threshold wavelength.

26. (i) State how de-Broglie wavelength (λ) of moving particles varies with their linear momentum (p).
(ii) State any one phenomenon in which moving particles exhibit wave nature. **ISC 2015**

27. (i) What are matter waves?
(ii) Show with the help of a labelled graph how their wavelength (λ) varies with their linear momentum (p).

Short Answer Type II Questions

3 Marks

28. An electron, α-particle and a proton have the same de-Broglie wavelengths. Which of these particle has
(i) minimum kinetic energy?
(ii) maximum kinetic energy and why?
In what way has the wave nature of electron beam exploited in electron microscope?

29. Electrons are emitted from the cathode of a photocell of negligible work function, when photons of wavelength λ are incident on it. Derive the expression for the de-Broglie wavelength of the electrons emitted on terms of the wavelength of the incident light.

Numerical Problems

30. (i) Find the Broglie wavelength of electrons moving with a speed of 7×10^6 ms^{-1}.
(ii) Describe in brief what is observed when moving electrons are allowed to fall on a thin graphite film and the emergent beam fall on a fluorecent screen. **ISC 2017 (3 M)**

31. de-Broglie postulated that the relationship, $\lambda = \frac{h}{p}$ is valid for relativistic particles. Find out the de-Broglie wavelength for an (relativistic) electron whose kinetic energy is 3 MeV. **(1 M)**

32. Find the momentum of a photon of energy 3.0 eV. **ISC 2009 (1 M)**

33. Calculate the momentum of photon of green light of λ = 500 nm in SI unit. **ISC 2007 (1 M)**

34. What is the momentum (p) of photon from ultraviolet light of wavelength λ = 332 nm. **ISC 2005 (1 M)**

35. An electron is accelerated under a potential difference of 150 V. What is de-Broglie's wavelength? **(1 M)**

36. A monochromatic source emits light of frequency 5×10^{14} Hz. Calculate the energy and the momentum of photons emitted by the source. **(1 M)**

37. Calculate the wavelength of an electron of energy 400 eV. **(1 M)**

38. In Davisson-Germer experiment, if the angle of diffraction is 52°, then find the glancing angle. (1 M)

39. A particle is moving three times as fast as an electron. The ratio of the de-Broglie wavelength of the particle to that of the electron is 1.813×10^{-4}. Calculate the particle's mass and identify the particle. (2M)

40. The wavelength of light from the spectral emission line of sodium is 589 nm. Find the kinetic energy at which
(i) an electron and
(ii) a neutron would have the same de-Broglie wavelength? NCERT (2 M)

41. (i) For what kinetic energy of a neutron will associated de-Broglie wavelength be 1.40×10^{-10} m?
(ii) Also, find the de-Broglie wavelength of a neutron, in thermal equilibrium with matter, having an average kinetic energy of $(3/2)\ kT$ and temperature is 300 K. NCERT (2 M)

42. Calculate the
(i) momentum.
(ii) de-Broglie wavelength of the electrons accelerated through a potential difference of 56 V. NCERT (2 M)

43. Find the ratio of the de-Broglie wavelength, associated with protons, accelerated through a potential of 128 V and α-particles, accelerated through a potential of 64 V. (2 M)

44. A proton and an α-particle have the same de-Broglie wavelength. Determine the ratio of
(i) their accelerating potentials.
(ii) their speeds. (2 M)

45. An electron is accelerated through a potential difference of 64 V. What is the de-Broglie wavelength associated with it? To which part of the electromagnetic spectrum does this value of wavelength correspond? (2 M)

46. An electron gun with its collector at a potential of 100 V fires out electrons in a spherical bulb containing hydrogen gas at low pressure ($\sim 10^{-2}$ mm of Hg). A magnetic field of 2.83×10^{-4} T curves the path of the electrons in a circular orbit of radius 12.0 cm. (The path can be viewed

because the gas ions in the path focus, the beam by attracting electrons and emitting light by electron capture, this method is known as the fine beam tube method.) Determine e/m from the data. NCERT (2 M)

47. (i) Estimate the speed with which electrons emitted from a heated emitter of an evacuated tube impinge on the collector maintained at a potential difference of 500 V with respect to the emitter. Ignore the small initial speeds of the electrons. The specific charge of the electron, i.e. its e/m is given to be 1.76×10^{11} C/kg.
(ii) Use the same formula you employ in (i) to obtain electron speed for a collector potential of 10 MV. Do you see what is wrong? In what way is the formula to be modified? NCERT (2 M)

48. An electron microscope uses electrons of energy 48.4 keV. What is the wavelength of the electron wave? How many times resolving power of this microscope is more than that of an ordinary microscope that uses visible light of wavelength 5500 Å? (2 M)

49. What is the
(i) momentum? (ii) speed?
(iii) de-Broglie wavelength of an electron with kinetic energy of 120 eV? NCERT (3 M)

50. What is the de-Broglie wavelength of
(i) a bullet of mass 0.040 kg travelling at the speed of 1.0 km/s?
(ii) a ball of mass 0.060 kg moving at a speed of 1.0 m/s?
(iii) a dust particle of mass 1.0×10^{-9} kg drifting with a speed of 2.2 m/s? NCERT (3 M)

51. Compute the typical de-Broglie wavelength of an electron in a metal at 27 °C and compare it with the mean separation between two electrons in a metal which is given to be about 2×10^{-10} m. NCERT (3 M)

52. Find the typical de-Broglie wavelength associated with a He atom in helium gas at room temperature (27° C) and 1 atm pressure and compare it with the mean separation between two atoms under these conditions. NCERT (3 M)

53. A monochromatic source of light emits light of wavelength 198 nm. Calculate
(i) the energy of each photon.
(ii) the momentum of photons. **ISC 2011 (3 M)**

54. Electrons initially at rest, are passed through a potential difference of 2 kV. Calculate their
(i) final velocity.
(ii) de-Broglie wavelength. **ISC 2009 (3 M)**

Hints & Solutions

1. (*a*) The wave associated with each moving particle is called matter waves.

2. (*d*) As, $\lambda \propto \frac{1}{p}$. The correct graph is

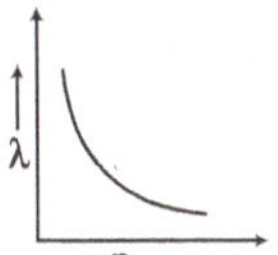

3. (*c*) $\because \lambda = \frac{h}{p}$

$\Rightarrow \lambda \propto \frac{1}{p}$ or λ is inversely proportional to momentum.

4. (*b*) $\lambda = \frac{1.227}{\sqrt{V}}\text{nm} = \frac{1.227}{\sqrt{100}} = 0.123$ nm

which is in X-ray region.

5. (*a*) We know that for molecule,

$K_0 = 3/2\,kT = KE$

$$\lambda = \frac{\lambda}{\sqrt{2K_0}} = \frac{\lambda}{\sqrt{2\times 3/2\,kTm}} = \frac{\lambda}{\sqrt{3mkT}}$$

where, k = Boltzmann's constant

$= 1.38\times 10^{-23}$ J/K

6. (*c*) The de-Broglie wavelength (λ) associated with a moving electron,

$$\lambda = \frac{h}{p} \quad \text{...(i)}$$

and kinetic energy, $E = \frac{1}{2}mv^2 = \frac{p^2}{2m}$

$$p = \sqrt{2mE} \quad \text{...(ii)}$$

[From Eqs. (i) and (ii)]

So, $\lambda = \frac{h}{\sqrt{2mE}}$

Hence, option (c) is correct.

7. (*c*) When accelerating voltage is increased, wavelength will reduce as $\lambda = \frac{1.227}{\sqrt{V}}$ nm.

Also, $\lambda \propto \theta$ for diffraction minima. Hence, θ will be lesser than earlier value.

8. The following considerations led de-Broglie to suggest that material particles can also show wave property
(i) The Einstein's mass-energy relationship $E = mc^2$, i.e. matter can be converted into energy and *vice-versa*. (1/2)
(ii) Wave nature loves symmetry, hence from symmetry, consideration particles like electrons, protons should exhibit wave nature when in motion. (1/2)

9. We know that, $\lambda \propto \frac{1}{\sqrt{V}}$

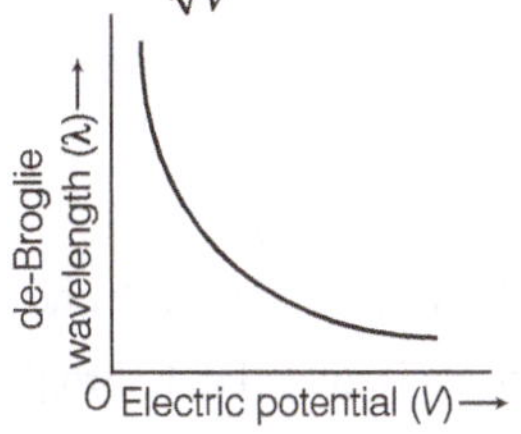

$\Rightarrow \lambda^2 V = \text{constant}$ $\left[\because \text{constant} = \frac{1}{\sqrt{2me}}\right]$

10. de-Broglie wavelength,

$$\lambda = \frac{h}{p} = \frac{h}{\sqrt{2mqV}}$$

11. Total energy of an electron, $E_e = mc^2$

Total energy of a photon, $E_p = \frac{hc}{\lambda}$

de-Broglie wavelength of electron of mass m moving with velocity v,

$$\lambda = \frac{h}{mv}$$

$$\Rightarrow \quad m = \frac{h}{\lambda v}$$

$\therefore$ Energy of an electron,

$$E_e = mc^2 = \frac{hc^2}{\lambda v}$$

$$\therefore \quad \frac{E_e}{E_p} = \frac{\frac{hc^2}{\lambda v}}{\frac{hc}{\lambda}} = \frac{c}{v}$$

As $c >> v$, therefore the total energy of electron is more than the total energy of photon.

12. de-Broglie wavelength,

$\lambda = \frac{h}{p} = \frac{h}{\sqrt{2mK}}$, where K = kinetic energy

For given KE, $\lambda \propto \frac{1}{\sqrt{m}}$

Since, electrons have smaller mass, i.e. $\lambda_e > \lambda_p$.
For given kinetic energy, electrons have greater de-Broglie wavelength as these have smaller mass.

13. In our daily life, we deal with bigger (macroscopic) particles and their wavelength is of the order of 10^{-35} m or less. Hence, wave effect is insignificant.

14. Wavelength, $\lambda = \dfrac{h}{\sqrt{2mE}}$.

Since, the wavelength is same,

$$E \propto \frac{1}{m}$$

Mass of proton is more than the mass of electron. Hence, the energy of electron would be more than the energy of proton.

15. $\therefore \lambda = \dfrac{h}{p} = \dfrac{h}{\sqrt{2mE}}$

As, E = constant, $\lambda \propto \dfrac{1}{\sqrt{m}}$.

16. The relation between wavelength and momentum of moving electrons is given by de-Broglie relation, $\lambda = \dfrac{h}{p}$

where, λ = wavelength,
h = Planck's constant and
$p = mv$ = momentum of electrons.

17. The experiment which proves wave nature of particle is Davisson and Germer experiment.

18. As from de-Broglie relation, $\lambda = h/p$

and we know that, $KE = \dfrac{p^2}{2m}$

$$\therefore \quad p = \sqrt{2m\, KE}$$

Now, $\lambda = \dfrac{h}{\sqrt{2m\, KE}}$ ...(i)

According to the question,
New kinetic energy = 4KE

$\therefore$ New wavelength, $\lambda' = \dfrac{h}{\sqrt{2m \times 4\, KE}}$

$\lambda' = \dfrac{h}{2\sqrt{2m\, KE}}$ ...(ii)

From Eqs. (i) and (ii), we get

$$\lambda' = \frac{1}{2} \times \lambda \Rightarrow \lambda' = \frac{\lambda}{2}$$

So, new wavelength is the half of the first wavelength when kinetic energy of electrons made $4E$.

19. (i) According to de-Broglie, a wave is associated with every moving particle.

Wavelength of this wave is $\lambda = \dfrac{h}{p}$.

where, h is Planck's constant
and p is the momentum of the moving particle. (1/2)

(ii) Davisson and Germer's experiment proves the wave nature of the electron. (1/2)

20. The de-Broglie wavelength associated with a body of mass m, moving with velocity v is given by $\lambda = \dfrac{h}{mv}$.

Since, the mass of the objects used in our daily life is very large, hence the de-Broglie wavelength associated with them is quite small and is not visible. Hence, the wave nature of matter is not more apparent to our daily observations. (1+1)

21. The momentum of an electromagnetic wave of frequency ν, wavelength λ is given by

$$p = \frac{h\nu}{c} = \frac{h}{\lambda} \text{ or } \lambda = \frac{h}{p}$$ (1)

de-Broglie wavelength of photon, $\lambda = \dfrac{h}{p}$

Thus, wavelength of electromagnetic radiation is equal to the de-Broglie wavelength. (1)

22. (i) Waves associated with moving particles or with the wave nature of particles are called matter waves or equivalent. (1)

(ii)

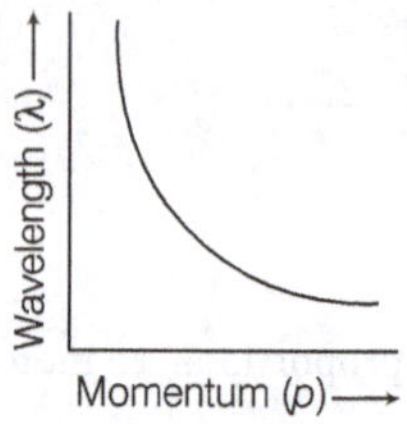

(1)

23. (i) The de-Broglie wavelength of a particle is given

$$\lambda = \frac{h}{\sqrt{2mV_0 q}}$$

So, potential V_0 is same.
Since, α-particle and proton both are accelerated through the same.

$$\therefore \quad \lambda \propto \frac{1}{\sqrt{mq}} \text{ or } \frac{\lambda_\alpha}{\lambda_p} = \sqrt{\frac{m_p q_p}{m_\alpha q_\alpha}}$$

As, charge on α-particle = 2 × charge on proton

$$q_\alpha = 2q_p \Rightarrow \frac{q_p}{q_\alpha} = \frac{1}{2}$$

Mass of α-particle = 4 × mass of proton

$$m_\alpha = 4 \times m_p \Rightarrow \frac{m_p}{m_\alpha} = \frac{1}{4}$$

$$\therefore \quad \frac{\lambda_\alpha}{\lambda_p} = \sqrt{\frac{1}{4} \cdot \frac{1}{2}} = \frac{1}{2\sqrt{2}}$$

$$\Rightarrow \quad \lambda_p = 2\sqrt{2}\lambda_\alpha$$

i.e. proton has greater de-Broglie wavelength than that of α-particle. (1)

(ii) KE $\propto q$ (for same accelerating potential)
The charge of an α-particle is more as compared to a proton. So, it will have a greater value of KE. Hence, proton will have lesser KE. (1)

24. de-Broglie wavelength of accelerating charged particle is given by

$$\lambda = \frac{h}{\sqrt{2mqV}}$$

$$\Rightarrow \quad \lambda\sqrt{V} = \frac{h}{\sqrt{2mq}} = \text{constant}$$

(i) The slope of the lines represents $\frac{h}{\sqrt{2mq}}$

where, h = Planck's constant, q = charge and m = mass of charged particle. (1)

(ii) $_1H^2$ and $_1H^3$ carry same charge (as they have same atomic number).

$$\therefore \quad \lambda\sqrt{V} \propto \frac{1}{\sqrt{m}}$$

The lighter mass, i.e. $_1H^2$ is represented by line of greater slope, i.e. A and similarly, $_1H^3$ by line B. (1)

25. (i) Every moving particle is associated with a wave whose wavelength is given by $\lambda = \frac{h}{p}$,

where, h = Planck's constant and p = momentum of the particle. (1)

(ii) It is the minimum wavelength of light, i.e. sufficient to eject an electron from just upto the surface of the metal. (1)

26. (i) According to Planck's quantum theory, the energy of the photon is

$$E = h\nu = \frac{hc}{\lambda} \quad \text{...(i)}$$

According to Einstein's theory, the energy of the photon is

$$E = mc^2 \quad \text{...(ii)}$$

From Eqs. (i) and (ii), we get

$$\lambda = \frac{h}{mc} \text{ or } \lambda = \frac{h}{p} \Rightarrow \lambda \propto \frac{1}{p}$$

where, p is momentum of a photon. (1)

(ii) The phenomenon in which moving particles exhibit wave nature is diffraction effect with beams of electrons scattered by crystals and it is verified by Davisson and Germer experiment. (1)

27. (i) A wave associated with the motion of a particle of atomic or subatomic size that describes effects such as the diffraction of beams of particles by crystals. (1)

(ii) The de-Broglie wavelength, $\lambda = \frac{h}{p}$

$\Rightarrow \lambda p$ = constant

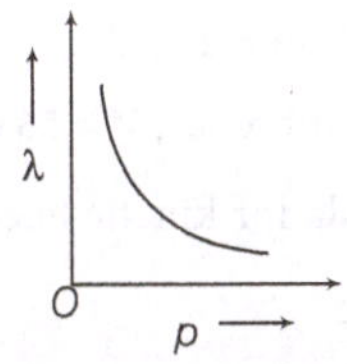

So, graph between λ and p is rectangular hyperbola, shown in adjacent figure. (1)

28. de-Broglie matter wave equation,

$$\lambda = \frac{h}{p} = \frac{h}{\sqrt{2mK}} \quad \left[\because K = \frac{p^2}{2m}\right]$$

where, K is kinetic energy and m is mass of particle.

$$K = \frac{h^2}{2m\lambda^2} \quad \text{[for same wavelength } \lambda\text{]}$$

$$\Rightarrow \quad K \propto \frac{1}{m}$$

$$\Rightarrow \quad K_e : K_\alpha : K_p = \frac{1}{m_e} : \frac{1}{m_\alpha} : \frac{1}{m_p} \quad (1)$$

where, m_e, m_p and m_α are masses of electron, proton and α-particle, respectively.

Also, K_e, K_α and K_p are their respective kinetic energies.

$$\because \quad m_\alpha > m_p > m_e$$

$$\Rightarrow \quad K_e > K_p > K_\alpha \quad (1/2)$$

(i) α-particle possesses minimum kinetic energy. (1/2)

(ii) Electron has maximum kinetic energy.

The magnifying power of an electron microscope is inversely related to wavelength of radiation used. Smaller wavelength of electron beam in comparison to visible light increases the magnifying power of microscope. (1)

29. We know that, $\frac{hc}{\lambda} = \frac{hc}{\lambda_0} + \frac{1}{2}mv^2$ (1)

Neglecting the work function, we get

$$\frac{hc}{\lambda} = \frac{1}{2}mv^2$$

$$\Rightarrow \quad v = \sqrt{\frac{2mhc}{\lambda}} \quad (1)$$

de-Broglie wavelength is given by,

$$\lambda_e = \frac{h}{mv}$$

$$\therefore \quad \lambda_e = \frac{h\sqrt{\lambda}}{\sqrt{2mhc}} = \sqrt{\frac{h\lambda}{2mc}} \quad (1)$$

30. (i) We know that, $\lambda = \frac{h}{p}$ and $p = mv$

$$\Rightarrow \lambda = \frac{h}{mv} = \frac{6.6 \times 10^{-34}}{91 \times 10^{-31} \times 7 \times 10^6}$$

$$\lambda = 1.03 \text{Å or } 0.103 \text{ nm} \quad (1)$$

(ii) A beam of electrons is accelerated in an electron gun to a potential of between 3500 V and 5000 V and then allowed to fall on a very thin sheet of graphite (see diagram below). The electron diffract from the carbon atoms and the resulting circular pattern on the screen (see diagram below) is very good evidence for the wave nature of the electrons.

The diffraction pattern observed on the screen is a series of concentric rings. This is due to the regular spacing of the carbon atoms in different layers in the graphite. However, since the graphite layers overlay each other in an irregular way the resulting diffraction pattern is circular.

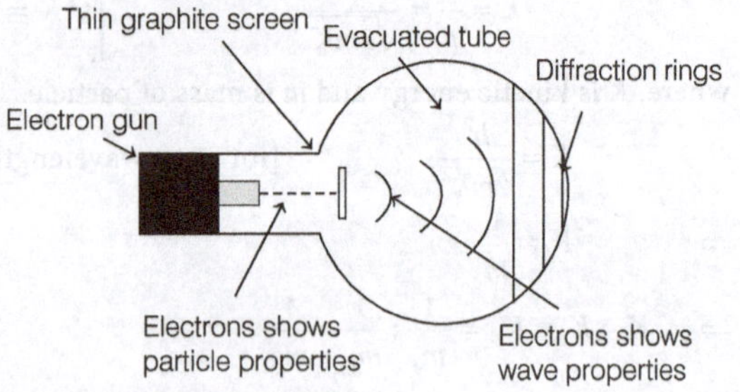

(2)

31. de-Broglie wavelength, $\lambda = \dfrac{h}{\sqrt{2mK}}$

Substituting the given values, we get

$$\lambda = 3.58 \times 10^{-3} \text{ m}$$

32. Given, photon of energy $= 3.0 \text{ eV} = 3 \times 1.6 \times 10^{-19}$ J

As we know that,

$$\text{Momentum, } p = \frac{\text{Energy}}{c \text{ (Velocity of light)}} = \frac{3 \times 1.6 \times 10^{-19} \text{ J}}{3 \times 10^{8} \text{ m/s}}$$

$$= 1.6 \times 10^{-27} \text{ kg-m/s}$$

33. Given, wavelength,

$$\lambda = 500 \text{ nm} = 500 \times 10^{-9} \text{ m}$$

According to de-Broglie relation,

$$\lambda = \frac{h}{p} \quad \text{[where, } p = \text{momentum]}$$ (1/2)

$$\therefore \quad p = \frac{h}{\lambda} = \frac{6.6 \times 10^{-34} \text{ J-s}}{500 \times 10^{-9} \text{ m}}$$

$$= 1.32 \times 10^{-27} \text{ kg-m/s}$$ (1/2)

34. Given, wavelength, $\lambda = 332 \text{ nm} = 332 \times 10^{-9}$ m

So, from de-Broglie relation,

$$\lambda = \frac{h}{p}$$

$$\Rightarrow \quad p = \frac{h}{\lambda} = \frac{6.6 \times 10^{-34} \text{ J-s}}{332 \times 10^{-9} \text{ m}}$$

$$= 2 \times 10^{-27} \text{ kg-m/s}$$

35. We know that, $\lambda = \dfrac{12.2}{\sqrt{V}} \text{ Å} = \dfrac{12.2}{\sqrt{150}} = 1 \text{ Å}$

36. Energy of photon,

$$E = h \times \text{(Frequency of photon)}$$

$$= 6.6 \times 10^{-34} \times 5 \times 10^{14} = 3.3 \times 10^{-19} \text{ J}$$

Momentum of photon,

$$p = \frac{E}{c} = \frac{3.3 \times 10^{-19}}{3 \times 10^{8}} = 1.1 \times 10^{-11} \text{ N-s}$$

37. The wavelength of electron,

$$\lambda = \frac{h}{\sqrt{2mK}} = \frac{6.6 \times 10^{-34}}{\sqrt{2 \times 9 \times 10^{-31} \times 400 \times 1.6 \times 10^{-19}}} = 0.62 \text{ Å}$$

38. Glancing angle,

$$\theta = 90^\circ - \frac{\phi}{2} = 90^\circ - \frac{52^\circ}{2} = 64^\circ$$

39. Given, $v_{\text{particle}} = 3\, v_{\text{electron}}$

and $\lambda_{\text{particle}} = 1.813 \times 10^{-4}\, \lambda_{\text{electron}}$

As, $\lambda = \dfrac{h}{mv}$ [de-Broglie equation]

$$\Rightarrow \quad \frac{m_{\text{particle}}}{m_{\text{electron}}} = \frac{\lambda_{\text{electron}} \times v_{\text{electron}}}{\lambda_{\text{particle}} \times v_{\text{particle}}}$$

$$= \frac{\lambda_{\text{electron}} \times v_{\text{electron}}}{1.813 \times 10^{-4} \times \lambda_{\text{electron}} \times 3v_{\text{electron}}}$$ (1)

$$\therefore \quad m_{\text{particle}} = 1839\, m_{\text{electron}}$$

$$= 1839 \times 9.1 \times 10^{-31} = 1.673 \times 10^{-27} \text{ kg}$$ (1)

$\therefore$ Particle is either a proton or a neutron.

40. Given, wavelength of light, $\lambda = 589 \text{ nm} = 589 \times 10^{-9}$ m

Mass of electron, $m_e = 9.1 \times 10^{-31}$ kg

Mass of neutron, $m_n = 1.675 \times 10^{-27}$ kg

Planck's constant, $h = 6.63 \times 10^{-34}$ J-s

(i) Using formula, $\lambda = \dfrac{h}{\sqrt{2mK}}$

Kinetic energy of electron,

$$K_e = \frac{h^2}{2\lambda^2 m_e} = \frac{(6.63 \times 10^{-34})^2}{2 \times (589 \times 10^{-9})^2 \times 9.1 \times 10^{-31}}$$

$$= 6.96 \times 10^{-25} \text{ J}$$ (1)

(ii) Kinetic energy of neutron,

$$K_n = \frac{h^2}{2\lambda^2 m_n} = \frac{(6.63 \times 10^{-34})^2}{2 \times (589 \times 10^{-9})^2 \times 1.675 \times 10^{-27}}$$

$$= 3.81 \times 10^{-28} \text{ J}$$ (1)

41. (i) Refer to Example 1 (iii) on page 440.

$\text{KE} = 6.714 \times 10^{-21}$ J, using $K = \dfrac{h^2}{2m\lambda^2}$ (1)

(ii) Kinetic energy associated with temperature,

$$\text{KE} = \frac{3}{2}kT = \frac{3}{2}(1.38 \times 10^{-23}) \times 300 = 6.21 \times 10^{-21} \text{ J}$$

[$\because$ absolute temperature, $T = 300$ K and Boltzmann's constant, $k = 1.38 \times 10^{-23}$ J/K]

$$\text{KE} = 6.21 \times 10^{-21} \text{ J}$$ (1/2)

de-Broglie wavelength associated with kinetic energy,

$$\lambda = \frac{h}{\sqrt{2m_n \text{KE}}} = \frac{6.63 \times 10^{-34}}{\sqrt{2 \times 1.675 \times 10^{-27} \times 6.21 \times 10^{-21}}}$$

$$= 1.45 \times 10^{-10} \text{ m} = 1.45 \text{ Å}$$ (1/2)

42. Given, potential difference, $V = 56$ V

(i) Use the formula for kinetic energy, $eV = \dfrac{1}{2}mv^2$

$$\Rightarrow \quad \frac{2\,eV}{m} = v^2$$

$$\Rightarrow \quad v = \sqrt{\frac{2eV}{m}}$$ (1/2)

where, m is mass and v is velocity of electron.

Momentum associated with accelerated electron,

$$p = mv = m\sqrt{\frac{2eV}{m}} = \sqrt{2\,eVm}$$

$$= \sqrt{2 \times 1.6 \times 10^{-19} \times 56 \times 9 \times 10^{-31}}$$

$$= 4.02 \times 10^{-24} \text{ kg-m/s}$$ (1/2)

(ii) $\lambda = 0.164$ nm; refer to Example 4 on page 441. (1)

43. de-Broglie wavelength is given by

$$\lambda = \frac{h}{\sqrt{2mK}} = \frac{h}{\sqrt{2mqV}} \qquad [\because K = qV]$$

$$\Rightarrow \quad \lambda \propto \frac{1}{\sqrt{mqV}}$$

Ratio of de-Broglie wavelengths of proton and α-particle is given by

$$\frac{\lambda_p}{\lambda_\alpha} = \sqrt{\frac{m_\alpha q_\alpha V_\alpha}{m_p q_p V_p}} = \sqrt{\left(\frac{m_\alpha}{m_p}\right)\left(\frac{q_\alpha}{q_p}\right)\left(\frac{V_\alpha}{V_p}\right)}$$ (1)

Here, $\frac{m_\alpha}{m_p} = 4, \frac{q_\alpha}{q_p} = 2 \Rightarrow \frac{V_\alpha}{V_p} = \frac{64}{128} = \frac{1}{2}$

[$\because$ α-particle is 4 times heavier than proton and it has double the charge than that of proton]

$$\Rightarrow \quad \frac{\lambda_p}{\lambda_\alpha} = \sqrt{4 \times 2 \times \frac{1}{2}} = 2 \Rightarrow \lambda_p : \lambda_\alpha = 2:1$$ (1)

44. (i) The de-Broglie wavelength of a particle is given by

$$\lambda = \frac{12.27}{\sqrt{V}} \text{Å}$$

[where, V is the accelerating potential of the particle]

$$\because \quad \lambda_p = \lambda_\alpha \qquad \text{[given]}$$

$$\Rightarrow \quad \frac{12.27}{\sqrt{V_p}} = \frac{12.27}{\sqrt{V_\alpha}} \Rightarrow \frac{V_p}{V_\alpha} = 1$$ (1)

(ii) The de-Broglie wavelength of a particle is given by

$$\lambda = \frac{h}{mv}$$

$$\therefore \quad \lambda_p = \frac{h}{m_p \cdot v_p} \text{ and } \lambda_\alpha = \frac{h}{m_\alpha v_\alpha}$$

We know that, $m_\alpha = 4\, m_p$

$$\because \quad \lambda_p = \lambda_\alpha \qquad \text{[given]}$$

$$\therefore \quad \frac{h}{m_p \cdot v_p} = \frac{h}{4m_p \cdot v_\alpha} \Rightarrow \frac{v_p}{v_\alpha} = 4$$ (1)

45. Given that, $V = 64$V

Now, from the de-Broglie equation,

$$\lambda = \frac{12.27}{\sqrt{V}}\text{Å} = \frac{12.27\text{Å}}{\sqrt{64}} \qquad [\therefore V = 64\text{V}]$$

$$= \frac{12.27}{8}\text{Å} = 0.153 \text{ nm}$$ (1)

This wavelength belongs to the X-ray part of the electromagnetic radiation. (1)

46. Given, potential at anode, $V = 100$ V

Magnetic field, $B = 2.83 \times 10^{-4}$ T

Radius of circular path, $r = 12$ cm $= 0.12$ m

Kinetic energy, KE $= \frac{1}{2}mv^2$ $\left[\because m_e = 9.1 \times 10^{-31} \text{ kg and } e = 1.6 \times 10^{-19} \text{C}\right]$

So, $$eV = \frac{1}{2}mv^2$$

$$\Rightarrow 1.6 \times 10^{-19} \times 100 = \frac{1}{2} \times 9.1 \times 10^{-31} \times v^2$$

$$\Rightarrow \quad v^2 = \frac{2 \times 1.6 \times 10^{-17}}{9.1 \times 10^{-31}} = 5.93 \times 10^6 \text{ m/s}$$

As, the angle between **v** and **B** is 90°. (1)

The magnetic force ($F_m = evB$) is balanced by the centripetal force.

i.e. $$evB = \frac{mv^2}{r} \text{ or } \frac{e}{m} = \frac{v}{Br} = \frac{5.93 \times 10^6}{2.83 \times 10^{-4} \times 0.12}$$

$\therefore$ Specific charge of an electron,

$$\frac{e}{m} = 1.74 \times 10^{11} \text{ C/kg}$$ (1)

47. (i) Given, potential difference, $V = 500$ V

Specific charge of the electron,

$$e/m = 1.76 \times 10^{11} \text{ C/kg}$$

Kinetic energy of an electron,

$$\text{KE} = \frac{1}{2}mv^2 = eV \Rightarrow v = \sqrt{\frac{e}{m} \times 2V} \quad \text{...(i)}$$

$$= \sqrt{1.76 \times 10^{11} \times 2 \times 500}$$

$$= 1.326 \times 10^7 \text{ m/s}$$ (1)

(ii) Potential, $V = 10 \text{ MV} = 10^7$ V

Again from Eq. (i), $v = \sqrt{\frac{2e}{m}V}$

$$= \sqrt{2 \times 1.76 \times 10^{11} \times 10^7}$$

$$= 1.8762 \times 10^9 \text{ m/s}$$

This speed is greater than the speed of light, which is not possible. As v approaches to c, then mass

$$m = \frac{m_0}{\sqrt{1 - \frac{v^2}{c^2}}}$$ (1)

48. Accelerating potential of electron,

$$V = 48.4 \times 10^3 = 48400 \text{ V}$$

Wavelength of electron wave,

$$\lambda = \frac{12.27}{\sqrt{V}}\text{Å} = \frac{12.27}{\sqrt{48400}} = 0.055\text{Å}$$

Wavelength of the visible light $= 5500$ Å (1)

Since, resolving power of any instrument is inversely proportional to wavelength.

Resolving power of electron microscope $= \frac{5500Å}{0.055Å}$

$= 10^5$ times the resolving power of optical microscope. (1)

49. Given, kinetic energy = KE = 120 eV

(i) Momentum, $p = \sqrt{2\,eVm} = \sqrt{2\,\text{KE}\cdot m}$ $[\because \text{KE} = eV]$

$= \sqrt{2 \times 120 \times 1.6 \times 10^{-19} \times 9.1 \times 10^{-31}}$

$= 5.91 \times 10^{-24}$ g-m/s (1)

(ii) We know that momentum, $p = mv$

or $v = \frac{p}{m} = \frac{5.91 \times 10^{-24}}{9.1 \times 10^{-31}} = 6.5 \times 10^6$ m/s (1)

(iii) de-Broglie wavelength associated with electron,

$1 = \frac{12.27}{\sqrt{V}}$ Å $= \frac{12.27}{\sqrt{120}}$ Å $= 0.112 \times 10^{-9}$ m $= 0.112$ nm (1)

50. (i) Given, mass of bullet, $m = 0.040$ kg

Speed of bullet, $v = 1000$ m/s

de-Broglie wavelength, $\lambda = \frac{h}{mv} = \frac{6.63 \times 10^{-34}}{0.040 \times 1 \times 10^3}$

$= 1.66 \times 10^{-35}$ m (1)

(ii) Mass of the ball, $m = 0.060$ kg and speed of the ball, $v = 1$ m/s

$$\lambda = \frac{h}{mv} = \frac{6.63 \times 10^{-34}}{0.060 \times 1} = 1.1 \times 10^{-32} \text{ m}$$ (1)

(iii) Mass of a dust particle, $m = 1 \times 10^{-9}$ kg and speed of the dust particle, $v = 2.2$ m/s

$$\lambda = \frac{h}{mv} = \frac{6.63 \times 10^{-34}}{1 \times 10^{-9} \times 2.2}$$

$= 3.0 \times 10^{-25}$ m (1)

51. Given, temperature,

$T = 27\,°\text{C} = 27 + 273 = 300$ K

Separation, between two electrons, $r = 2 \times 10^{-10}$ m

Momentum $p = \sqrt{3m\,kT}$

$= \sqrt{3 \times 9.11 \times 10^{-31} \times 1.38 \times 10^{-23} \times 300}$

$[\because k = 1.38 \times 10^{-23}$ J/K$]$

$= 1.06 \times 10^{-25}$ kg-m/s (1)

de-Broglie wavelength, $\lambda = \frac{h}{p} = \frac{6.63 \times 10^{-34}}{1.06 \times 10^{-25}}$

$= 62.6 \times 10^{-10}$ m (1)

Mean separation, $r = 2 \times 10^{-10}$ m

$\therefore \quad \frac{\lambda}{r} = \frac{62.6 \times 10^{-10}}{2 \times 10^{-10}} = 31.3$

We can see that de-Broglie wavelength is much greater than the electron separation. (1)

52. Mass of helium atom,

$$m = \frac{\text{Atomic weight}}{\text{Avogadro's number}} = \frac{4 \times 10^3}{6 \times 10^{23}} \text{ g}$$

Boltzmann constant, $k = 1.38 \times 10^{-23}$ J mol^{-1} K^{-1}

de-Broglie wavelength, $\lambda = \frac{h}{\sqrt{3\,mkT}}$ (1/2)

$= \frac{6.63 \times 10^{-34}}{\sqrt{3 \times \frac{4 \times 10^3}{6 \times 10^{23}} \times 1.38 \times 10^{-23} \times 300}}$ $\left[\because T = 27°\text{ C} = (27 + 273)\text{K} = 300\text{ K}\right]$

$= 0.73 \times 10^{-10}$ m (1)

Now, $pV = RT = kNT$ or $\frac{V}{N} = \frac{kT}{p}$

Mean separation, $r = \left(\frac{V}{N}\right)^{1/3} = \left(\frac{kT}{p}\right)^{1/3}$ (1)

$= \left[\frac{1.38 \times 10^{-23} \times 300}{1.01 \times 10^5}\right]^{1/3} = 3.4 \times 10^{-9}$ m

$\therefore \quad \frac{\lambda}{r} = \frac{0.73 \times 10^{-10}}{3.4 \times 10^{-9}} = 0.021$ (1/2)

53. (i) Given, wavelength

$\lambda = 198$ nm $= 198 \times 10^{-9}$ m

As we know that, energy of photon,

$E = \frac{hc}{\lambda} = \frac{6.6 \times 10^{-34} \times 3 \times 10^8}{198 \times 10^{-9}}$ (1½)

$= 10^{-18}$ J

(ii) As wavelength of photon is given by

$\lambda = \frac{h}{p}$

$\Rightarrow \quad p = \frac{h}{\lambda} = \frac{6.6 \times 10^{-34}\text{ J-s}}{198 \times 10^{-9}\text{ m}}$

$= 3.33 \times 10^{-27}$ kg-m/s (1½)

54. (i) Given, potential difference, $V = 2$ kV $= 2000$ V

and we know that, $eV = \frac{1}{2}mv^2$

So, $v^2 = \frac{2eV}{m} \Rightarrow v = \sqrt{\frac{2eV}{m}}$

$= \sqrt{\frac{2 \times 1.6 \times 10^{-19} \times 2000}{9.1 \times 10^{-31}}}$

$= \sqrt{\frac{6.4}{9.1} \times 10^{15}} = 2.65 \times 10^7$ m/s (2)

(ii) Now, de-Broglie wavelength for electrons is given by

$\lambda = \frac{12.27}{\sqrt{V}}$ Å $= \frac{12.27}{\sqrt{2 \times 10^3}} = 0.274$ Å (1)

SUMMARY

- **Photoelectric Effect** It is the phenomenon of emission of electrons from the metal surface, when the radiations of suitable frequency falls on it.
- **Hertz's Observation** He observed that high voltage sparks across the detector loop were enhanced when the emitter plate was illuminated by UV light from an arc lamp.
- **Hallwachs and Lenard's Observations** They also observed that UV light falls on the emitter plate, no electrons were emitted at all when the frequency of incident light was smaller than a certain minimum value is called threshold frequency.
- **Effect of Intensity of Light on Photoelectric Current** For a fixed frequency of incident radiation photoelectric current increases linearly with increase in intensity of incident light.
- **Effect of Potential on Photoelectric Current** For a fixed frequency and intensity of incident light, photoelectric current increases with increase in potential applied to the collector.
- **Einstein's Photoelectric Equation**

  $$K_{max} = \frac{1}{2} m{v^2}_{max} = (h\nu - \phi_0)$$

  where, m is the mass of photoelectron, v_{max} is the maximum velocity of emitted electron and h is Planck constant.

  This equation is called Einstein's photoelectric equation.
- **Relation between Stopping Potential and Threshold Wavelength** The relation between stopping potential and threshold wavelength is $eV_0 = hc\left[\frac{1}{\lambda} - \frac{1}{\lambda_0}\right]$
- **Particle Nature of Light Photon** Photoelectric effect gave the evidence that light consists of packets of energy and these packets of energy are called light quanta, that are associated with photons.
- **Characteristic Properties of Photon**

  Photons has zero rest mass.

  Photons travel in a straight line.

  Photons may show diffraction under given conditions

  The inertial mass of a photon is $m = \frac{hc}{\lambda}$.
- **Dual Nature of Radiation** Wave theory of electromagnetic radiations explained the phenomenon of interference, diffraction, etc, whereas quantum theory successfully explained the photoelectric effect, Compton effect, etc. So, Louis de-Broglie suggested that the particles like electrons, protons, etc. have dual nature of radiation.
- **Wave Nature of Particles (de-Broglie Hypothesis)** According to de-Broglie, a wave is associated with moving material particle which control the particle in every respect. The wave associated with moving material particle is called matter wave. It is given by,

  $$\lambda = \frac{h}{p} = \frac{h}{mv}$$

  where, $p = mv$ is momentum of electron.
- **Relation between de-Broglie Wavelength and Temperature** It is given by $\lambda = \frac{h}{\sqrt{3mkT}}$
- **de-Broglie Wavelength of an Electron** It is given by $\lambda = \frac{h}{\sqrt{2eVm}}$.
- **Davisson and Germer Experiment** The objective of this experiment was to establish the wave nature of electron.

For Mind Map

Visit : https://goo.gl/tx4iWL OR **Scan the Code**

Chapter Practice

Multiple Choice Questions

(1 Mark)

1 Photoelectric effect involves
(a) conversion of nuclear energy into electrical energy
(b) conversion of atomic energy into electrical energy
(c) conversion of electronic energy into electrical energy
(d) conversion of light energy into electrical energy

2 The cathode of a photoelectric cell is changed such that the work function changes from W_1 to W_2 $(W_2 > W_1)$. If the current before and after change are I_1 and I_2, all other conditions remaining unchanged and assuming $(E_1 > W_2)$, then
(a) $I_1 = I_2$
(b) $I_1 < I_2$
(c) $I_1 > I_2$
(d) $\frac{W_1}{W_2} = \frac{I_1}{I_2}$

3 An electron is emitted from a metal surface, when
(a) $h\nu > \phi_0$
(b) $h\nu < \phi_0$
(c) $h\nu = \phi_0$
(d) $0 < h\nu < \phi_0$

4 In Davisson experiment, if applied accelerating voltage is increased, then diffracted electron beam will have the maximum at a value of θ that

NCERT Exemplar

(a) will be larger than the earlier value
(b) will be the same or earlier value
(c) will be less than the earlier value
(d) will depend on target

Very Short Answer Type Questions

(1 Mark)

5 Define the term stopping potential in relation to photoelectric effect.

6 Show graphically the variation of photoelectric current with frequency of the incident photons.

7 Two metals M_1 and M_2 have work functions 2 eV and 4 eV, respectively. Which of the two has a higher threshold wavelength for photoelectric emission?

8 The frequency ν of incident radiation is greater than threshold frequency ν_0 in a photocell. How will the stopping potential vary, if frequency ν is increased, keeping other factors constant.

9 The de-Broglie wavelength associated with an electron accelerated through a potential difference V is λ. What will be its wavelength when the accelerating potential is increased to 5 V?

10 With what purpose Davisson-Germer experiment for electrons was performed?

Short Answer Type I Questions

(2 Marks)

11 When a photon of energy 3 eV incident on a metal surface of work function 3 eV, emits one electron from metal surface. If energy of photon is increased to 9 eV, then how many electrons are emitted from metal surface? Give reason.

12 An electron is accelerated through a potential difference of 250 V. What is the de-Broglie wavelength associated with it? To which part of electromagnetic spectrum does this wavelength correspond?

13 The de-Broglie wavelength of a body moving with speed v is λ. On its way, it losses some of its mass and gains twice the speed. Kinetic energy also increases to twice of its initial value. What will be the new value of de-Broglie wavelength?

14 For what kinetic energy of a neutron, will the associated de-Broglie wavelength be 2.64×10^{-10} m?

15 The de-Broglie wavelength of a particle of kinetic energy K is λ. What would be the wavelength of the particle, if its kinetic energy were $\frac{K}{4}$?

16 Ultraviolet light of wavelength 200 nm is incident on polished surface of iron. Work function of the surface is 4.71 eV. Calculate its stopping potential.

Short Answer Type II Questions

(3 Marks)

17 Write Einstein's photoelectric equation relating the maximum kinetic energy of the emitted electron to the frequency of the radiation incident on a photosensitive surface. State clearly, the basic elementary process involved in photoelectric effect.

18 Define the terms threshold frequency and stopping potential in the study of photoelectric emission. Explain briefly the reasons, why wave theory of light is not able to explain the observed features in photoelectric effect?

19 Light of wavelength 2500 Å falls on a metal surface of work function 3.5 eV. What is the kinetic energy (in eV) of

(i) the fastest and

(ii) the slowest electrons emitted from the surface? If the same light falls on another surface of work function 5.5 eV, what will be the energy of emitted electrons?

20 What are the energies of photons at the (i) violet and (ii) red ends of the visible spectrum? The wavelength of light is about 390 nm for violet and about 760 nm for red.

Answers

1 (*d*) Photoemission involves conversion of light energy into electrical energy.It is observed that many metals emit electrons when light shines upon them.

2 (*a*) Photocurrent depends only on intensity of light. As in given problem, only work function is changed, so current values are same.

3 (*a*) Einstein's photoelectric equation is $K_{max} = h\nu - \phi_0$

where, K_{max} = maximum kinetic energy of emitted electrons,

h = Planck's constant,

ν = frequency of incident radiation

and ϕ_0 = work function of metal.

Since, K_{max} must be non-negative.

So, photoelectric emission is possible only, if

$$h\nu > \phi_0 \quad \text{or} \quad \nu > \nu_0$$

where, $$\nu_0 = \frac{\phi_0}{h}$$

4 (*c*) When accelerating voltage is increased, wavelength will reduce as $\lambda = \frac{1.227}{\sqrt{V}}$ nm

Also, $\lambda \propto \theta$ for diffraction minima. Hence, θ will be lesser than earlier value.

5 For a particular frequency of incident radiation, the minimum negative (retarding) potential V_0 given to collecting plate A for which the photoelectric current becomes zero, is called cut-off or stopping potential.

6 Variation of photoelectric current (i) with frequency (ν) of the incident photons is given as

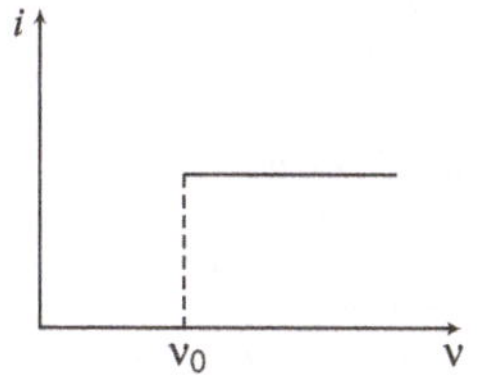

[$\nu_0 \rightarrow$ threshold frequency]

7 We know that, $E_0 = h\nu_0 = \frac{hc}{\lambda_0}$

Thus, λ_0 or threshold wavelength is inversely proportional to the energy or work-function. So, metal M_1 has higher threshold wavelength for photoelectric emission.

8 We know that, $\frac{1}{2}mv^2{}_{max} = eV_0 = h(\nu - \nu_0)$

Here, the frequency of the incident radiation is greater than the threshold frequency. Therefore, the value of stopping potential (V_0) increases with increase in frequency (ν) of the incident radiation and KE will also increases.

9 Given, $V_1 = 1\text{V},\ V_2 = 5\text{V},\ \lambda_1 = \lambda,\ \lambda_2 = ?$

Since, $\lambda \propto \frac{1}{\sqrt{V}}$

$$\Rightarrow \frac{\lambda_2}{\lambda_1} = \sqrt{\frac{V_1}{V_2}} = \sqrt{\frac{\text{V}}{5\text{V}}}$$

$$\lambda_2 = \frac{\lambda_1}{\sqrt{5}} = \frac{\lambda}{\sqrt{5}}$$

10 The purpose of Davisson-Germer experiment was to demonstrate the wave nature of the electron.

11 Only one electron is emitted from the metal surface when energy of photon is increased to 9 eV, because increased energy of photon provide kinetic energy to the emitted electron. Number of emitted electrons increase only on increasing intensity of incident radiation.

12 Refer to Q. 45 on page 444.

13 **Hint** $\lambda = \frac{h}{\sqrt{2mK}}$

de-Broglie wavelength remains same.

14 Refer to the Q. 41 (i) on page 444.

15 As we know, de-Broglie wavelength,

$$\lambda = \frac{h}{p} = \frac{h}{\sqrt{2mK}}$$

Hence, $K_1 = \dfrac{h^2}{2m\,\lambda_1^2}$ ...(i)

If according to the question,

$$K_2 = \frac{K_1}{4}$$

$$K_2 = \frac{h^2}{2\lambda_2^2}$$

$$\frac{K_1}{4} = \frac{h^2}{2m\lambda_2^2} \quad \text{..(ii)}$$

From Eqs. (i) and (ii), we get

$$\frac{\frac{K_1}{4}}{K_1} = \frac{h^2}{2m\lambda_2^2} \times \frac{2m\lambda_1^2}{h^2}$$

$$\frac{1}{4} = \frac{\lambda_1^2}{\lambda_2^2} \Rightarrow \frac{\lambda_1}{\lambda_2} = \frac{1}{2}$$

Hence, wavelength of the particle double the wavelength when kinetic energy is $\frac{1}{4}$ th.

16 Given, $\lambda = 200\text{ nm} = 200 \times 10^{-9}\text{m}$

$$KE_{max} = h\nu - \phi$$

$$KE_{max} = eV_0$$

$$eV_0 = h\nu - \phi$$

$$eV_0 = \frac{hc}{\lambda} - \phi$$

$$\therefore 1.6 \times 10^{-19} V_0 = \frac{6.6 \times 10^{-34} \times 3 \times 10^8}{200 \times 10^{-9}} - 4.71 \times 1.6 \times 10^{-19}$$

$$V_0 = 6.19 - 4.17 = 1.48 = 1.50\text{V}$$

17 Refer to the text on pages 422 and 423 (Einstein's photoelectric equation).

18 Refer to the text on page 422 (Law of photoelectric emission, photoelectric effect and wave theory of light)

19 (i) We know that, $\dfrac{hc}{\lambda} = W_0 + KE_{max}$

$$KE_{max} = \frac{hc}{\lambda} - W_0$$

$$= \left[\frac{(6.63 \times 10^{-34} \times 3 \times 10^8)}{2500 \times 10^{-10}} \times \frac{1}{(1.6 \times 10^{-19})} - 3.5\right]$$

$$= (4.97\text{ eV} - 3.5\text{ eV}) = 1.47\text{ eV}$$

So, the KE of the fastest = 1.47 eV

(ii) The KE of slowest particle = eV

No photoelectrons will be emitted from another surface of work function 5.5 eV.

20 We know that, $E = \dfrac{hc}{\lambda}$ joule

or $$E = \frac{hc}{\lambda \times 1.6 \times 10^{-19}}\text{eV}$$

$$\therefore \quad \lambda_V = \frac{6.63 \times 10^{-34} \times 3 \times 10^8}{390 \times 10^{-9} \times 1.6 \times 10^{-19}} = 3.17\text{eV}$$

$$\therefore \quad \lambda_R = \frac{6.63 \times 10^{-34} \times 3 \times 10^8}{760 \times 10^{-9} \times 1.6 \times 10^{-19}} = 1.63\text{eV}$$

RELATED ONLINE VIDEOS

Visit : https://www.youtube.com/watch?v=-s21XdkEF80
OR **Scan the Code**

Visit : https://www.youtube.com/watch?v=24iEQXWlr68
OR **Scan the Code**

Visit : https://www.youtube.com/watch?v=Ho7K27B_Uu8
OR **Scan the Code**

CHAPTER

12

Atoms

All elements consist of very small invisible particles called **atoms.** Atoms of same element are same and atoms of different elements are different.

Every atom is a sphere of radius of the order 10^{-10}m, in which entire mass is uniformly distributed and negative charged electrons revolve around the nucleus.

The first model of atom was proposed by JJ Thomson in 1898 called **plum pudding model** of the atom. Later, Rutherford worked on it and named this model as Rutherford's planetary model of atom in 1911. In 1913, Niels Bohr worked on the model named as Bohr model of H-atom.

- α-Particles Scattering Experiment
- Rutherford's Atomic Model
- Electron Orbits
- Bohr's Atomic Model
- Hydrogen Spectrum or Line Spectra of Hydrogen Atom

α-Particles Scattering Experiment

This experiment was suggested by Rutherford in 1911 as given in the figure below

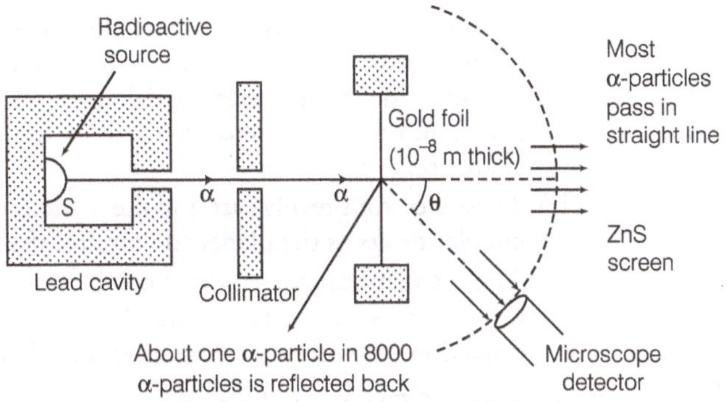

Experimental arrangement for Rutherford's theory

In this experiment, H Geiger and E Marsden took $^{214}_{83}Bi$ as a source for α-particles. A collimated beam of α-particles of energy 5.5 MeV was allowed to fall on 2.1×10^{-7} m thick gold foil. The α-particles were observed through a rotatable detector consisting of a zinc sulphide screen and microscope and it was found that α-particles got scattered. These scattered α-particles produced scintillations on the zinc sulphide screen. Now, these scintillations were counted at different angles from the direction of incident beam.

Observations

Rutherford made the following observations from his experiment that are given below

(i) Most of the α-particles passed through the gold foil without any appreciable deflection.

(ii) Only about 0.14% of the incident α-particles scattered by more than 1°.

(iii) About one α-particle in every 8000 α-particles deflected by more than 90°.

The total number of α-particles (N) scattered through an angle (θ) is shown in the figure given below

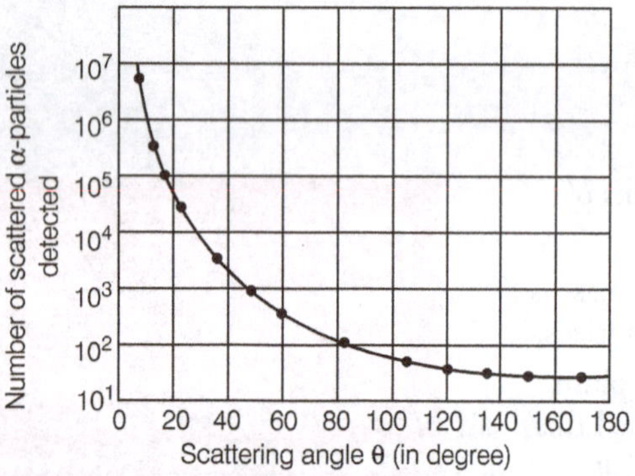

Experimental data points (shown by dots) on scattering of α-particles by a thin foil at different angles

(iv) The number of α-particles scattered per unit area $N(\theta)$ at scattering angle θ varies inversely as $\sin^4\theta/2$.

$$N(\theta) \propto \frac{1}{\sin^4 \theta/2}$$

(v) The force between α-particles and nucleus is given by

$$F = \frac{1}{4\pi\varepsilon_0} \cdot \frac{(2e)(Ze)}{r^2}$$

where, r is the distance between the α-particles and the nucleus. This force is directed along the line joining the α-particle and the nucleus. The magnitude and direction of this force on α-particle continuously changes as it approaches the nucleus and recedes away from it.

Conclusions

On the basis of his experiment, Rutherford concluded that

(i) Atom has a lot of empty space and practically the entire mass of the atom is confined to an extremely small central core called **nucleus**, whose size is of the order from 10^{-15} m (1 fermi) to 10^{-14} m.

(ii) Scattering of α-particles (positively charged) is due to the Coulomb's law for electrostatic force of repulsion between the positive charge of nucleus and α-particles.

(iii) Distance between electron and nucleus is from 10^4 to 10^5 times the size of the nucleus itself.

(iv) More is the distance of the velocity vector of an α-particle from the central line of the nucleus, lesser is the angle of scattering.

Example 1 The number of α-particles scattered at an angle of 90° is 100 per minute. What will be the number of α-particles, when it is scattered at an angle of 60°?

Sol. Number of α-particles scattered at an angle of θ is given by

$$N \propto \frac{1}{\sin^4\theta/2} \Rightarrow \frac{N_1}{N_2} = \left(\frac{\sin\frac{\theta_2}{2}}{\sin\frac{\theta_1}{2}}\right)^4$$

$$\Rightarrow \frac{100}{N_2} = \left(\frac{\sin 30^\circ}{\sin 45^\circ}\right)^4 \Rightarrow \frac{100}{N_2} = \frac{4}{16} \Rightarrow N_2 = 400$$

Rutherford's Atomic Model

The essential features of Rutherford's nuclear model of the atom or planetary model of the atom are as follows

(i) Every atom consists of a central core, called the **atomic nucleus**, in which the entire positive charge and almost entire mass of the atom is concentrated.

(ii) The size of nucleus is of the order of 10^{-15} m, which is very small as compared to the size of the atom which is of the order of 10^{-10} m.

(iii) The atomic nucleus is surrounded by certain number of electrons. As atom on the whole is electrically neutral, the total negative charge of electrons surrounding the nucleus is equal to total positive charge on the nucleus.

(iv) These electrons revolve around the nucleus in various circular orbits as the planets do around the sun.

The centripetal force required by electrons for revolution is provided by the electrostatic force of attraction between the electrons and nucleus.

Distance of Closest Approach

As the α-particle approaches the nucleus, the electrostatic force of repulsion due to nucleus increases and the kinetic energy of α-particle goes on converting into the electrostatic potential energy.

At a certain distance r_0 from the nucleus, whole of the KE of α-particle gets converted into electrostatic potential energy and α-particles cannot go further close to nucleus, this distance (r_0) is called **distance of closest approach.**

At distance of closest approach,

KE of α-particle (K) = Electrostatic potential energy (U)

$$K = \frac{1}{4\pi\varepsilon_0} \cdot \frac{(Ze)(2e)}{r_0}$$

$$= \frac{1}{4\pi\varepsilon_0} \cdot \frac{2Ze^2}{r_0}$$

[∵ charge on α-particle is $+2e$ and charge on nucleus is Ze, where Z is atomic number]

$$\therefore \quad r_0 = \frac{1}{4\pi\varepsilon_0} \cdot \frac{2Ze^2}{K} \text{ or } \boxed{r_0 = \frac{1}{4\pi\varepsilon_0} \cdot \frac{2Ze^2}{\left(\frac{1}{2}mv^2\right)}}$$

where, m = mass of α-particle and v = initial velocity of α-particle.

From the formula, it is clear that distance of closest approach of α-particle to the nucleus depends on the kinetic energy of α-particle.

Example 2 In a head on collision between an α-particle and gold nucleus, the closest distance of approach is 4×10^{-14} m. Calculate the initial kinetic energy of α-particle.

Sol. Here, closest distance of approach, $r_0 = 4 \times 10^{-14}$ m,

Gold's atomic number, $Z = 79$, $KE_i = ?$

$$\therefore KE_i \text{ of } \alpha\text{-particle} = \frac{Ze(2e)}{4\pi\varepsilon_0 r_0} = \frac{2Ze^2}{4\pi\varepsilon_0 r_0}$$

$$= \frac{2 \times 79 \times (1.6 \times 10^{-19})^2 \times 9 \times 10^9}{4 \times 10^{-14}}$$

$$= 9.1 \times 10^{-13} \text{ J}$$

Angle of Scattering (θ)

Angle by which α-particle gets deviated from its original path around the nucleus is called **angle of scattering**.

In case of head on collision, the α-particle rebounds back ($\theta = \pi$).

The α-particle goes nearly undeviated for a small deflection ($\theta = 0°$).

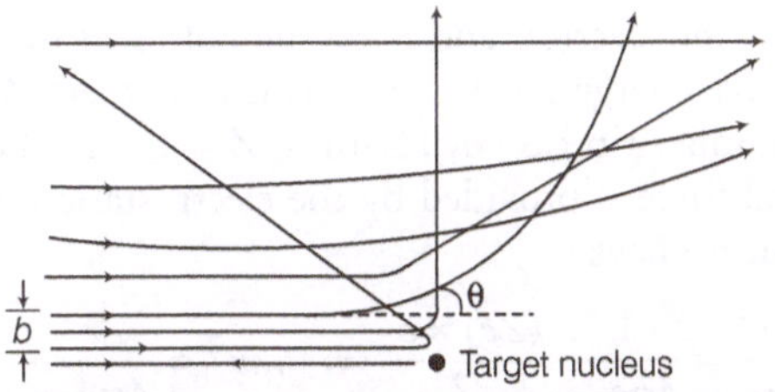

Trajectory of α-particles in the Coulombic field of a target nucleus. Scattering angle θ is depicted

Electron Orbits

The Rutherford nuclear model of the atom pictures the atom as an electrically neutral sphere consisting of a very small, massive and positively charged nucleus at the centre surrounded by the revolving electrons in their respective dynamically stable orbits.

The electrostatic force of attraction F_e between the revolving electrons and the nucleus provides the requisite centripetal force (F_c) to keep them in their orbits. Thus, for a dynamically stable orbit in a H-atom,

$$F_c = F_e$$

$$\Rightarrow \quad \frac{mv^2}{r} = \frac{1}{4\pi\varepsilon_0} \cdot \frac{e^2}{r^2} \quad [\because Z = 1]$$

Thus, the relation between the orbit radius and the electron velocity is

$$r = \frac{e^2}{4\pi\varepsilon_0 mv^2}$$

The kinetic energy (K) and electrostatic potential energy (U) of the electron in H-atom are

$$K = \frac{1}{2}mv^2 = \frac{e^2}{8\pi\varepsilon_0 r} \quad \left[\because mv^2 = \frac{e^2}{4\pi\varepsilon_0 r}\right]$$

and

$$U = -\frac{e^2}{4\pi\varepsilon_0 r}$$

(the negative sign in U signifies that the electrostatic force is in the $-r$ direction or attractive in nature.)

Thus, the total mechanical energy E of the electron in a H-atom is

$$E = K + U = \frac{e^2}{8\pi\varepsilon_0 r} - \frac{e^2}{4\pi\varepsilon_0 r}$$

$$\boxed{E = -\frac{e^2}{8\pi\varepsilon_0 r}}$$

The total energy of the electron is negative. This implies the fact that the electron is bound to the nucleus. If E is positive, then an electron will not follow a closed orbit around the nucleus and it would leave the atom.

Example 3 It is found experimentally that 13.6 eV energy is required to separate a H-atom into a proton and an electron. Compute the orbital radius and velocity of the electron in a H-atom.

Sol. Total energy of the electron in H-atom,

$$TE = -13.6 \text{ eV} = -13.6 \times 1.6 \times 10^{-19} \text{ J}$$

$$= -2.2 \times 10^{-18} \text{ J}$$

Total energy is

$$TE = \frac{-e^2}{8\pi\varepsilon_0 r} \Rightarrow r = \frac{-e^2}{8\pi\varepsilon_0 TE}$$

$$= \frac{-9\times 10^9 \times (1.6\times 10^{-19})^2}{2\times(-2.2\times 10^{-18})}$$

$$= 5.3\times 10^{-11}\ \text{m}$$

$\therefore$ Velocity of the revolving electron, $v = \frac{e}{\sqrt{4\pi\varepsilon_0 mr}}$

$$= \frac{1.6\times 10^{-19}}{\sqrt{4\times 3.14\times 8.85\times 10^{-12}\times 9.1\times 10^{-31}\times 5.3\times 10^{-11}}}$$

$$= 2.2\times 10^6\ \text{m/s}$$

Drawbacks of Rutherford's Model

Rutherford's model encountered (faced) two major drawbacks

Regarding Stability of Atom

Electrons revolving around the nucleus have centripetal acceleration. According to classical electromagnetic theory, the electrons must radiate energy in the form of electromagnetic wave.

Due to this continuous loss of energy of the electrons, the radii of their orbits should be continuously decreasing and ultimately the electrons should fall in the nucleus. Thus, atom cannot remain stable.

Regarding Explanation of Line Spectrum

Due to continuous decrease in radii of electron's orbit, the frequency of revolution of electron will also change. According to classical theory of electromagnetism, frequency of EM wave emitted by electron is equal to the frequency of revolution of electron.

So, due to continuous change in frequency of revolution of electron, it will radiate EM waves of all frequencies, i.e. the spectrum of these waves will be continuous in nature. But, this is not the case. Experimentally we get discrete line spectrum. Rutherford's model was unable to explain line spectrum.

Bohr's Atomic Model

Bohr combined classical and early quantum concepts and gave his theory in the form of three postulates

These three postulates are as follows

(i) **Bohr's first postulate** was that an electron in an atom could revolve in certain stable orbits without the emission of radiant energy, contrary to the predictions of electromagnetic theory. According to this postulate, each atom has certain definite stable states in which it can exist and each possible state has definite total energy. These are called the **stationary states** of the atom.

(ii) **Bohr's second postulate** states that the electron revolves around the nucleus only in those orbits for which the angular momentum is some integral multiple of $h/2\pi$, where h is the Planck's constant $(= 6.63\times 10^{-34}\ \text{J-s})$.

Thus, the angular momentum (L) of the orbiting electron is quantised, i.e. $L = \frac{nh}{2\pi}$

As, angular momentum of electron $= mvr$

$\therefore$ For any permitted (stationary) orbit

$$\boxed{mvr = \frac{nh}{2\pi}}$$

where, n = any positive integer 1, 2, 3, ...

It is also called **principal quantum number.**

(iii) **Bohr's third postulate** states that an electron might make a transition from one of its specified non-radiating orbits to another of lower energy. When it does so, a photon is emitted having energy equal to the energy difference between the initial and final states.

The frequency of the emitted photon is given by

$$h\nu = E_i - E_f$$

where, E_i and E_f are the energies of the initial and final states and $E_i > E_f$.

Bohr's Theory

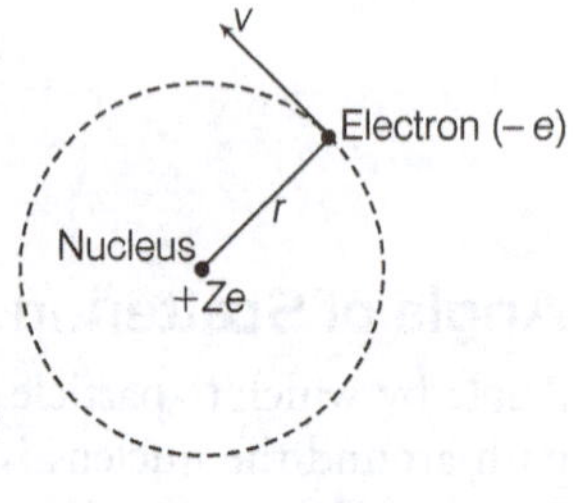

Bohr's model is valid for all one-electron atoms or ions which consists of a tiny positively charged nucleus and an electron revolving in a stable circular orbit around the nucleus. These one-electron atoms or ions can be called hydrogen like atoms. For example, singly ionised helium (He^+) and doubly ionised lithium (Li^{2+}).

Let e, m and v be respectively the charge, mass and velocity of the electron and r be the radius of the orbit. The positive charge on the nucleus is Ze, where Z is the atomic number (in case of H-atom, $Z = 1$). As, the centripetal force is provided by the electrostatic force of attraction, we have

$$\frac{mv^2}{r} = \frac{1}{4\pi\varepsilon_0}\cdot\frac{(Ze)\times e}{r^2} \Rightarrow mv^2 = \frac{Ze^2}{4\pi\varepsilon_0 r} \quad \text{...(i)}$$

From the second postulate, the angular momentum of the electron is

$$mvr = n\frac{h}{2\pi} \quad ...(ii)$$

where, n (= 1, 2, 3, ...) is **principal quantum number.**

From Eqs. (i) and (ii), we get

$$\boxed{r = n^2 \frac{h^2\varepsilon_0}{\pi m Z e^2}} \quad ...(iii)$$

This is the equation for the radii of the permitted orbits. According to this equation,

$$r_n \propto n^2$$

Since, $n = 1, 2, 3, ...$ it follows that the radii of the permitted orbits increase in the ratio $1 : 4 : 9 : 16 : ...$, from the first orbit. Clearly, the stationary orbits are not equally spaced.

Bohr Radius

The radius of the first orbit ($n = 1$) of H-atom ($Z = 1$) will be

$$\boxed{r_1 = \frac{h^2\varepsilon_0}{\pi m e^2}}$$

This is called **Bohr radius** and its value is 0.53 Å. Since, $r \propto n^2$, the radius of the second orbit of H-atom will be (4×0.53) Å and that of the third orbit (9×0.53) Å.

Velocity of Electron in Stationary Orbits

We can obtain formula for the velocity of electron in permitted orbits. From Eq. (ii), we have

$$v = n\frac{h}{2\pi m r}$$

Putting the value of r from Eq. (iii), we get

$$v = \frac{Ze^2}{2h\varepsilon_0} \cdot \frac{1}{n}$$

where, principal quantum number, $n = 1, 2, 3, ...$

Thus, $v \propto \frac{1}{n}$

This shows that the velocity of electron is maximum in the lowest orbit ($n = 1$) and goes on decreasing in higher orbits. The velocity of electron in the first orbit ($n = 1$) of H-atom ($Z = 1$) is

$$v_1 = \frac{e^2}{2h\varepsilon_0} = 2.19 \times 10^6 \text{ ms}^{-1}$$

$$\frac{v_1}{c} = \frac{2.19 \times 10^6 \text{ ms}^{-1}}{3 \times 10^8 \text{ ms}^{-1}} = \frac{1}{137}$$

Hence, $\boxed{v_1 = \frac{c}{137}}$ $\quad [\because c = 3 \times 10^8 \text{ m/s}]$

Frequency of Electron in a Stationary Orbit

It is the number of revolutions completed per second by the electron in a stationary orbit around the nucleus.

It is represented by ν.

From $\quad v = r\omega = r(2\pi\nu) \quad [\because \omega = 2\pi\nu]$

$\therefore \quad \nu = \frac{v}{2\pi r}$

Putting the values of v and r in above equation, we get

$$\nu = \frac{1}{2\pi r} \cdot \frac{Ze^2}{2h\varepsilon_0} \cdot \frac{1}{n} \Rightarrow \nu = \frac{1}{4\pi\varepsilon_0} \cdot \frac{Ze^2}{nhr}$$

$$\boxed{\nu = \frac{kZe^2}{nhr}} \quad \left[\because k = \frac{1}{4\pi\varepsilon_0}\right]$$

Energy of Electron in Stationary Orbit

The energy E of an electron in an orbit is the sum of kinetic and potential energies.

Using Eq. (i) in Bohr's theory $mv^2 = \frac{Ze^2}{4\pi\varepsilon_0 r}$

The kinetic energy of the electron is

$$\text{KE} = \frac{1}{2}mv^2 = \frac{Ze^2}{8\pi\varepsilon_0 r}$$

Substituting the value of r from Eq. (iii), we get kinetic energy of the electron in the nth orbit

$$\boxed{\text{KE} = \frac{mZ^2e^4}{8\varepsilon_0^2 h^2} \cdot \left(\frac{1}{n^2}\right)}$$

In terms of Rydberg constant R, its simplified form is

$$\text{KE} = \frac{Rhc}{n^2} \quad \left[\because R = \frac{me^4}{8\varepsilon_0^2 ch^3}\right]$$

The potential energy of the electron in an orbit of radius r due to the electrostatic attraction by the nucleus is given by

$$\text{PE} = \frac{1}{4\pi\varepsilon_0} \cdot \frac{(Ze)(-e)}{r} = -\frac{1}{4\pi\varepsilon_0} \cdot \frac{Ze^2}{r}$$

In terms of Rydberg constant R, its simplified form is

$$PE = -\frac{2Rhc}{n^2}$$

The total energy of the electron is

$$E = KE + PE = \frac{Ze^2}{8\pi\varepsilon_0 r} - \frac{Ze^2}{4\pi\varepsilon_0 r}$$

$$= -\frac{Ze^2}{8\pi\varepsilon_0 r} = -\frac{Rhc}{n^2}$$

Substituting the value of r from Eq. (iii), we get

$$E = -\frac{mZ^2e^4}{8\varepsilon_0^2 h^2}\left(\frac{1}{n^2}\right)$$

where, $n = 1, 2, 3, \ldots$. This is the expression for the energy of the electron in the nth orbit.

For hydrogen atom $Z = 1$, substituting the standard values, we get $E_n = \frac{-13.6}{n^2}$ eV.

Negative energy of the electron shows that the electron is bound to the nucleus and is not free to leave it.

Energy Levels

The energy of an atom is the least, when its electron is revolving in an orbit closest to the nucleus, i.e. for which $n = 1$. For $n = 2, 3, \ldots$ the absolute value of energy E is smaller, so the energy is progressively larger in outer orbits.

The lowest state of the atom is called the **ground state**, this state has lowest energy. The energy of this state is -13.6 eV. Therefore, the minimum energy required to free the electron from the ground state of the H-atom is -13.6 eV. It is called **ionisation energy** of the H-atom.

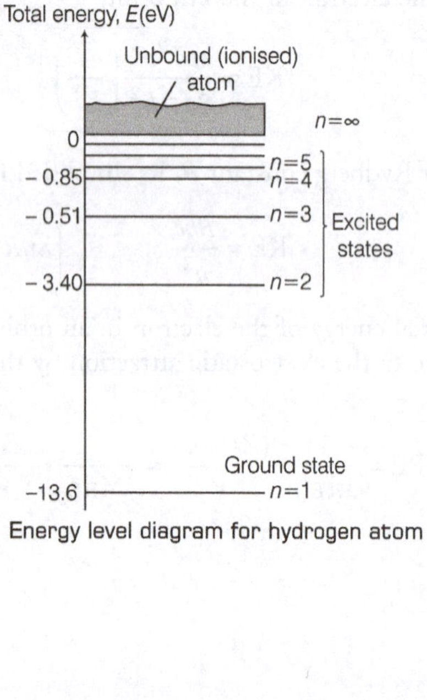

Energy level diagram for hydrogen atom

At room temperature, most of the H-atoms are in ground state. When an atom receives some energy (i.e. by electron collisions), the atom may acquire sufficient energy to raise electron to higher energy state. In this condition, the atom is said to be in **excited state**. From the excited state, the electron can fall back to a state of lower energy, emitting a photon equal to the energy difference of the orbit.

Suppose in the excited atom, an electron jumps from some higher energy state n_2 to a lower energy state n_1. The energy difference between these states is

$$E_2 - E_1 = \frac{mZ^2e^4}{8\varepsilon_0^2 h^2}\left(\frac{1}{n_1^2} - \frac{1}{n_2^2}\right)$$

According to Bohr's third postulate, the frequency ν of the emitted electromagnetic wave (photon) is

$$\nu = \frac{E_2 - E_1}{h}$$

$$= \frac{mZ^2e^4}{8\varepsilon_0^2 h^3}\left(\frac{1}{n_1^2} - \frac{1}{n_2^2}\right)$$

The corresponding wavelength λ of the emitted radiation is given by

$$\frac{1}{\lambda} = \frac{\nu}{c} = \frac{mZ^2e^4}{8\varepsilon_0^2 ch^3}\left(\frac{1}{n_1^2} - \frac{1}{n_2^2}\right)$$

$\frac{1}{\lambda}$ is called **wave number** (number of waves per unit length).

In the last equation, the quantity $\frac{me^4}{8\varepsilon_0^2 ch^3}$ is a constant known as **Rydberg constant** R and its value is $1.097 \times 10^7 \text{ m}^{-1}$.

i.e. $$\frac{me^4}{8\varepsilon_0^2 ch^3} = R$$

Thus, $$\frac{1}{\lambda} = Z^2R\left(\frac{1}{n_1^2} - \frac{1}{n_2^2}\right)$$

This is Bohr's formula for hydrogen and hydrogen like atoms ($He^+, Li^{2+}, \ldots$).

For hydrogen atom ($Z = 1$), we have

$$\frac{1}{\lambda} = R\left(\frac{1}{n_1^2} - \frac{1}{n_2^2}\right)$$

Example 4 What is the ratio of radii of the orbits corresponding to second excited state and ground state in a H-atom?

Sol. For second excited state, $n = 3$

Ground state occurs for $n = 1$

Since, $r_n = r_0 n^2$ and $r_n \propto n^2$

$$\Rightarrow \quad \frac{r_2}{r_1} = \left(\frac{n_2}{n_1}\right)^2 = \left(\frac{3}{1}\right)^2$$

$$r_2 : r_1 = 9 : 1$$

where, r_2 and r_1 are radii corresponding to second excited state and ground state of the atom.

Example 5

(i) The radius of the innermost electron orbit of a hydrogen atom is 5.3×10^{-11} m. Calculate its radius in $n = 2$ orbit.

(ii) The total energy of an electron in the second excited state of the hydrogen atom is -1.51 eV. Find out its

(a) kinetic energy and

(b) potential energy in this state.

Sol. (i) Given, Bohr radius, $r_1 = 5.3 \times 10^{-11}$ m

We know that, $r_n = n^2 r_1$

Let r_2 be radius of the orbit for $n = 2$.

$\therefore \; r_2 = (2)^2 \times 5.3 \times 10^{-11} = 2.12 \times 10^{-10}$ m

(ii) Given, total energy of an electron in second excited state, $E = -1.51$ eV

(a) Kinetic energy of electron is equal to negative of the total energy,

$\therefore \quad K = -E = -(-1.51) = 1.51$ eV

(b) Potential energy of electron is equal to negative of twice of its kinetic energy.

$$U = -2K = -2 \times 1.51 = -3.02 \text{ eV}$$

Hydrogen Spectrum or Line Spectra of Hydrogen Atom

Hydrogen spectrum consists of discrete bright lines in a dark background and it is specifically known as **hydrogen emission spectrum.** There is one more type of hydrogen spectrum that exists where we get dark lines on the bright background, it is known as **absorption spectrum.**

Balmer found an empirical formula by the observation of a small part of this spectrum and it is represented by

$$\frac{1}{\lambda} = R\left(\frac{1}{2^2} - \frac{1}{n^2}\right), \text{ where } n = 3, 4, 5, \ldots$$

where, R is a constant called **Rydberg constant** and its value is $1.097 \times 10^7 \text{ m}^{-1}$.

So, $\quad \frac{1}{\lambda} = 1.522 \times 10^6 \text{ m}^{-1} = 656.3 \text{ nm for } n = 3$

Other series of spectra for hydrogen were subsequently discovered and known by the name of their discoverers. The lines of Balmer series are found in the visible part of the spectrum. Other series were found in the invisible parts of the spectrum.

e.g. **Lyman series** in the **ultraviolet region** and **Paschen, Brackett** and **Pfund** in the **infrared region.**

The wavelengths of line in these series can be expressed by the following formulae

(i) **For Lyman series**

$$\frac{1}{\lambda} = R\left(\frac{1}{1^2} - \frac{1}{n^2}\right), \text{ where } n = 2, 3, 4, \ldots$$

(ii) **For Balmer series**

$$\frac{1}{\lambda} = R\left(\frac{1}{2^2} - \frac{1}{n^2}\right), \text{ where } n = 3, 4, 5, \ldots$$

(iii) **For Paschen series**

$$\frac{1}{\lambda} = R\left(\frac{1}{3^2} - \frac{1}{n^2}\right), \text{ where } n = 4, 5, 6, \ldots$$

(iv) **For Brackett series**

$$\frac{1}{\lambda} = R\left(\frac{1}{4^2} - \frac{1}{n^2}\right), \text{ where } n = 5, 6, 7, \ldots$$

(v) **For Pfund series**

$$\frac{1}{\lambda} = R\left(\frac{1}{5^2} - \frac{1}{n^2}\right), \text{ where } n = 6, 7, 8, \ldots$$

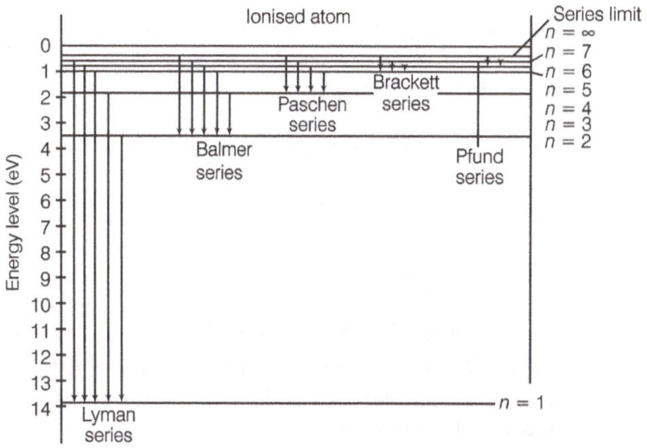

Line spectra of the H-atom

Explanation

The different series of hydrogen spectrum can be explained by Bohr's theory. According to Bohr's theory, if the ionised state of hydrogen atom be taken as zero energy level, then the energies of the different energy levels of the atom can be expressed by the following formula.

$$E_n = -\frac{Rhc}{n^2}, \text{ where } n = 1, 2, 3, \ldots$$

where, R is Rydberg constant and h is Planck constant. The integer n is called principal quantum number.

When the atom gets energy from outside, its electron goes from the lowest energy level to some higher energy level. But it returns from there, within 10^{-8} s, to the lowest energy level directly or through other lower energy levels. While returning back, the atom emits photons.

Example 6 The energy of the electron in the ground state of hydrogen is – 13.6 eV. Calculate the energy of the photon that would be emitted, if electron was to make a transition corresponding to the emission of the first line of the Lyman series of the H-atom.

Sol. Here, energy of e^- in ground state of H-atom = −13.6 eV

i.e. $E_1 = -13.6$ eV

For $n = 2, E_2 = -3.4$ eV $\left[\because E_n = -\frac{13.6}{n^2} \text{ eV}\right]$

The energy of photon corresponding to the first line is given by $E = E_2 - E_1$

$\therefore \quad E = [-3.4 - (-13.6)]$ eV $= 10.2$ eV

Example 7 In H-atom, a transition takes place from $n = 3$ to $n = 2$ orbit. Calculate the wavelength of the emitted photon, will the photon be visible? To which spectral series will this photon belong?

(Take, $R = 1.097 \times 10^7 \text{ m}^{-1}$)

Sol. The wavelength of the emitted photon is given by

$$\frac{1}{\lambda} = R\left(\frac{1}{n_1^2} - \frac{1}{n_2^2}\right)$$

When the transition takes place from $n = 3$ to $n = 2$, then

$$\frac{1}{\lambda} = (1.097 \times 10^7)\left(\frac{1}{2^2} - \frac{1}{3^2}\right) = 1.097 \times 10^7 \times \frac{5}{36}$$

$$\therefore \quad \lambda = \frac{36}{1.097 \times 10^7 \times 5}$$

$$= 6.563 \times 10^{-7} \text{ m} = 656.3 \text{ Å}$$

Since, λ falls in the visible (red) part of the spectrum, hence the photon will be visible. This photon is the first member of the Balmer series.

Limitations of Bohr's Model

The limitations of Bohr's model are as follows

(i) This model is applicable only to a simple atom like hydrogen having $Z = 1$. This theory fails, if $Z > 1$.

(ii) It does not explain the fine structure of spectral lines in H-atom.

(iii) This model does not explain why orbits of electrons are taken as circular whereas elliptical orbits are also possible.

Topic Practice

Multiple Choice Questions

1 Mark

1. In Geiger-Marsden experiment, collimation of α-particles into a narrow beam is done by passing

(a) α-particles through a narrow gap between lead bricks
(b) α-particles through gold foil
(c) α-particles through an electric field
(d) α-particles through a magnetic field

2. In Rutherford's model, kinetic energy of revolving electron into hydrogen atom is given by

(a) $K = \frac{e^2}{4\pi\varepsilon_0 r}$ (b) $K = \frac{e^2}{8\pi\varepsilon_0 r^2}$
(c) $K = \frac{-e^2}{8\pi\varepsilon_0 r}$ (d) $K = \frac{e^2}{8\pi\varepsilon_0 r}$

3. If E_P and E_K represent potential energy and kinetic energy respectively of an orbital electron, then according to Bohr's theory, **ISC 2015**

(a) $E_K = -E_P/2$ (b) $E_K = E_P$
(c) $E_K = 2E_P$ (d) $E_K = 2E_P$

4. Total energy of an electron in the ground state of hydrogen atom is –13.6 eV. Its total energy when hydrogen atom is in the first excited state, is **ISC 2016**

(a) + 13.6 eV (b) + 3.4 eV
(c) – 3.4 eV (d) – 54.4 eV

5. White light is passed through sodium vapours contained in a thin walled glass flask and the transmitted light is examined with the help of spectrometer. The spectrum, so obtained is **ISC 2012**

(a) absorption spectrum (b) solar spectrum
(c) band spectrum (d) continuous spectrum

Very Short Answer Type Questions

1 Mark

6. Draw the graph between total number of α-particles scattered at different angles.

7. Why is the classical (Rutherford) model for an atom of electron orbiting around the nucleus is not able to explain the atomic structure?

8. Mention any one postulate of Bohr's theory of hydrogen atom. **ISC 2007**

9. If a hydrogen atom goes from III excited state to II excited state, what kind of radiation is emitted? **ISC 2009**

10. According to Bohr, 'angular momentum of an orbiting electron is quantised'. What is meant by this statement? **ISC 2017**

11. Find the angular momentum of an electron when it is the second Bohr's orbit of hydrogen atom. **ISC 2023, 11**

12. What is the ratio of radii of the orbits corresponding to first excited state and ground state in a H-atom?

13. Consider two different H-atoms. The electron in each atom is in an excited state.

    Is it possible for the electrons to have different energies, but the same orbital angular momentum according to the Bohr's model? **NCERT Exemplar**

14. Describe absorption spectrum of sodium. **ISC 2009**

15. Name the series of lines in the hydrogen spectrum which lies in the ultraviolet region. **ISC 2019, 13**

16. Wavelengths of the first lines of the Lyman series, Paschen series and Balmer series, in hydrogen spectrum are denoted by λ_L, λ_P and λ_B, respectively. Arrange these wavelengths in increasing order. **ISC 2015**

17. When H_α-line of the Balmer series in the emission spectrum of H-atom is obtained?

18. How are various lines of Lyman series formed? Explain on the basis of Bohr's theory. **ISC 2015**

Short Answer Type I Questions

2 Marks

19. Define the distance of closest approach. An α-particle of kinetic energy K is bombarded on a thin gold foil. The distance of the closest approach is r. What will be the distance of closest approach for an α-particle of double the kinetic energy?

20. An α-particle moving with initial kinetic energy K towards a nucleus of atomic number Z approaches a distance d at which it reverses its direction. Obtain the expression for the distance of closest approach d in terms of the kinetic energy of α-particle K.

21. Using Rutherford's model of the atom, derive the expression for the total energy of the electron in H-atom. What is the significance of total negative energy possessed by the electron?

22. Explain in brief, why Rutherford's model cannot account for the stability of an atom?

23. State Bohr's postulate of hydrogen atom that gives the relationship for the frequency of emitted photon in a transition.

24. Figure given below is the energy level diagram for hydrogen atom. Study the transitions shown and answer the following questions. **ISC 2024**
    (i) State the type of spectrum obtained.
    (ii) Name the series of spectrum obtained.

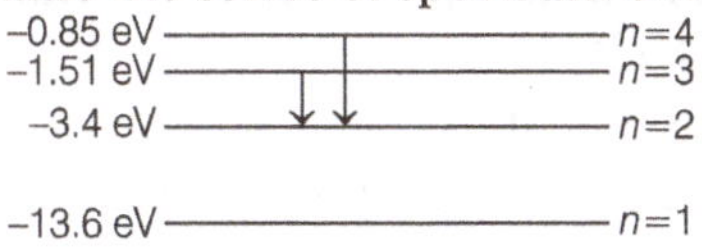

Short Answer Type II Questions

3 Marks

25. What conclusion was drawn by Rutherford based on Geiger-Marsden's experiment on scattering of α-particles? **ISC 2012**

26. Why is the classical (Rutherford) model for an atom of electron orbiting around the nucleus not able to explain the atomic structure? **ISC 2007**

27. In the Rutherford scattering experiment, the distance of closest approach for an α-particle is d_0. If α-particle is replaced by a proton, how much kinetic energy in comparison to α-particle will be required to have the same distance of closest approach d_0. **ISC 2005**

28. Draw energy level diagram for hydrogen atom, showing first four energy levels corresponding to $n = 1, 2, 3$ and 4. Show transitions responsible for
    (i) absorption spectrum of Lyman series.
    (ii) emission spectrum of Balmer series. **ISC 2016**

29. On the basis of Bohr's theory, derive an expression for the radius of the nth orbit of an electron of hydrogen atom. **ISC 2014**

30. State the postulate of Bohr's regarding
(i) angular momentum of an electron.
(ii) emission of photon.
(iii) total energy of an electron orbiting around the nucleus of an atom is always negative. What is the significance of this? **ISC 2013**

31. (i) Name a series of lines of hydrogen spectrum which lies in
(a) visible region, (b) UV region.
(ii) Write Bohr's formula to calculate wavelength (λ) of visible light emitted by hydrogen and explain the meaning of each and every symbol used. **ISC 2023, 11**

32. (i) What is a continuous emission spectrum? Name one source of light which produces such a spectrum.
(ii) Explain in brief why dark lines are observed in the solar spectrum. **ISC 2010**

33. Draw a level diagram of hydrogen, shown by a downward or an upward arrow, a transition which results in
(i) emission line of Balmer series.
(ii) emission line of Lyman series.
(iii) absorption line of Lyman series. **ISC 2010**

34. Draw the energy level diagram of a hydrogen atom and draw arrows to show transitions responsible for
(i) absorption lines by Lyman series.
(ii) emission lines by Balmer series.
ISC 2020, 2008

35. Differentiate between line, band and continuous spectra. What type of substances give rise to these spectra? **ISC 2007**

36. Using the relevant Bohr's postulates, derive the expression for the
(i) velocity of the electron in the nth orbit
(ii) radius of the nth orbit of the electron in H-atom.

37. State any two Bohr's postulates and write the energy value of the ground state of the hydrogen atom. **ISC 2019**

38. Using Bohr's postulates for H-atom, show that the total energy (E) of the electron in the stationary states can be expressed as the sum of kinetic energy (K) and potential energy (U), where $K = -2U$. Hence, deduce the expression for the total energy in the nth energy level of hydrogen atom.

39. State the Bohr's postulate of angular momentum of an electron.
(i) What is the velocity of an electron is the 3rd orbit of hydrogen atom, if its velocity in the 1st orbit is v_0?
(ii) Radius of the 1st orbit of hydrogen atom is r_0. What will be the radius of the 4th orbit?
ISC 2024

40. Using Bohr's postulates, obtain an expression for the total energy of the electron in the stationary states of the H-atom. Hence, draw the energy level diagram showing how the line spectral corresponding to Balmer series occur due to transition between energy levels.

41. (i) Lyman series of hydrogen is available both in emission and absorption, but Balmer series is available only in emission, not in absorption. Give reason.
(ii) The electron in H-atom is initially in the third excited state. What is the maximum number of spectral lines which can be emitted when it finally moves to the ground state?

Long Answer Type Questions

5 Marks

42. Draw a schematic arrangement of the Geiger-Marsden's experiment for studying α-particles scattering by a thin foil of gold. Describe briefly by drawing trajectories of the scattered α-particles. How this study can be used to estimate the size of the nucleus? **ISC 2010**

43. Obtain an expression for the frequency of radiation emitted when a hydrogen atom de-excites from level n to level $(n-1)$. For large n, show that this frequency equals to the classical frequency of revolution of the electron in the orbit. **NCERT**

44. Using Bohr's postulates, derive an expression for the frequency of radiation emitted when electron in H-atom undergoes transition from higher energy state quantum number (n_i) to the lower energy state (n_f).
When electron in H-atom jumps from energy state $n_i = 4$ to $n_f = 3, 2, 1$. Identify the spectral series to which the emission lines belong.

Numerical Problems

45. Calculate angular momentum of an electron in the third Bohr orbit of hydrogen atom. **ISC 2016 (1 M)**

46. The energy on the first Bohr's orbit is – 27.2 eV. What will be the energy in the third orbit? **ISC 2005 (1 M)**

47. Calculate the shortest wavelength of electromagnetic radiation present in Balmer series of hydrogen spectrum. **ISC 2015 (2 M)**

48. Energy levels of H-atom are given by

$$E_n = \frac{-13.6}{n^2}\,\text{eV}$$

where, n = principal quantum number to calculate the wavelength of electromagnetic radiation emitted by hydrogen atom resulting from the transition $n = 2$ to $n = 1$. **ISC 2012 (3 M)**

49. For Bohr's model of the hydrogen atom, the energy of the electron in ground state is found to be – 13.6 eV.

(i) Draw energy level diagram for the hydrogen atom and mark the values of energy (in eV at $n = 2$ and $n = \infty$).

(ii) Obtain the maximum energy of photon emitted by the hydrogen atom in eV. **ISC 2005 (2 M)**

50. An electron revolves around the nucleus of hydrogen atom in a circular orbit of radius 5×10^{-11} m. Calculate

(i) intensity of electric field of the nucleus of the position of the electron.

(ii) electrostatic potential energy of the hydrogen nucleus and electron system. **ISC 2010 (3 M)**

51. Wavelength of 1st line (H_α) of Balmer series of hydrogen is 656.3 nm. Find the wavelength of its 2nd line (H_β). **ISC 2009 (3 M)**

52. From Bohr's energy quantisation formula, determine the target wavelength in the Balmer series of hydrogen atom spectrum. **ISC 2006 (3 M)**

53. In a hydrogen atom, a transition of electrons takes place from 3rd orbit to 2nd orbit. Calculate the wavelength of the emitted photon. To which spectral series will this photon belong? **ISC 2005 (3 M)**

54. α-particles having kinetic energy of 1.8 MeV each are incident on a thin gold foil from a large distance. Applying the principle of conservation of energy, find the distance of closes approach of the α-particle from the gold nucleus. (Take, atomic number of gold = 79) **ISC 2009 (3 M)**

Hints & Solutions

1. (*a*) α-particles emitted by $^{214}_{83}\text{Bi}$ radioactive source were collimated into a narrow beam by their passage through lead bricks.

2. (*d*) The kinetic energy (K) of the electron in hydrogen atom is

$$K = \frac{1}{2} mv^2 = \frac{e^2}{8\pi\varepsilon_0 r}$$

3. (*a*) Since, according to Bohr's theory, kinetic energy (E_K) is equal to half of potential energy with negative sign.

i.e. $$E_K = -\frac{E_P}{2}$$

4. (*c*) The energy of electron in any state is given by

$$E_n = -\frac{13.6}{n^2}$$

For $n = 2$ (first excited state), $E_n = -\frac{13.6}{(2)^2} = -3.4$ eV

5. (*a*) Absorption spectrum will be observed.

6.

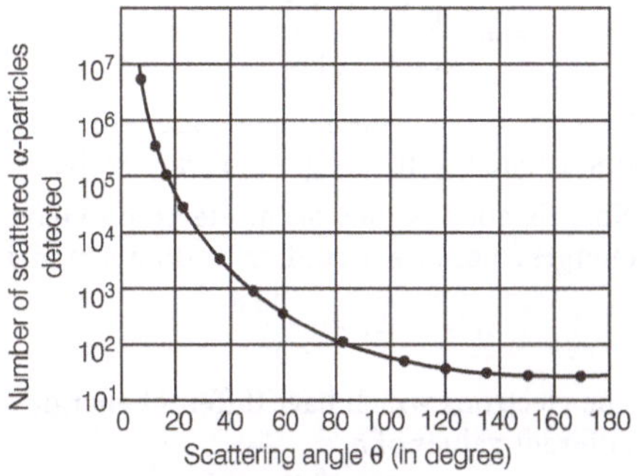

Experimental data points (shown by dots) on scattering of α-particles by a thin foil at different angles

7. (i) Rutherford model could not justify the stability of nucleus.

(ii) It does not explain the line spectrum of hydrogen atom.

8. One of the Bohr's postulate is electron can revolve only in those orbits in which its angular momentum is an integral multiple of $h/2\pi$

[where, h = Planck's constant].

9. Because the wavelength falls in the visible part of the spectrum,

i.e. $\frac{1}{\lambda} = 1.097 \times 10^7 \left(\frac{1}{2^2} - \frac{1}{3^2}\right) = 656.3 \text{ nm}$

10. According to Bohr, 'angular momentum of an orbiting electron is quantised' – it means of all the possible circular orbits, the electrons are permitted to circulate only in those orbits in which the angular momentum of an electron is an integral multiple of $\frac{h}{2\pi}$, h being Planck's constant. Therefore, for any permitted orbit,

$$L = mvr = \frac{nh}{2\pi}, n = 1, 2, 3, ...$$

where, L, m and v are the angular momentum, mass and the speed of the electrons, r is the radius of the permitted orbit and n is positive integer called principal quantum number.

Thus, the angular momentum of the orbiting electron is quantised, has certain value $\frac{nh}{2\pi}$.

11. Angular momentum $= \frac{nh}{2\pi}$

where, $n = 2$ [for 2nd Bohr's orbit]

So, $L = \frac{2h}{2\pi} = \frac{h}{\pi} = \frac{6.6 \times 10^{-34}}{3.14} = 2.1 \times 10^{-34} \text{ kg-m}^2/\text{s}$

12. For first excited state, $n = 2$ Ground state occurs for $n = 1$

Since, $r_n = r_0 n^2$ and $r_n \propto n^2$

$$\Rightarrow \frac{r_2}{r_1} = \left(\frac{n_2}{n_1}\right)^2 = \left(\frac{2}{1}\right)^2$$

So, $r_2 : r_1 = 4 : 1$, where r_2 and r_1 are radii corresponding to first excited state and ground state of the atom.

13. No, it is not possible for the electron to have different energies, because according to Bohr's model,

$$E_n = \frac{-13.6}{n^2}$$

The electrons which have different energies, have different values of n.

Angular momentum, $mvr = \frac{nh}{2\pi}$, so as n changes angular momentum changes.

14. When sodium atoms absorb energy. The energy absorbed by sodium atom is equivalent to the corresponding wavelength. Thus, it shows absorption spectrum and it emits a line spectrum of 589.6 nm of wavelength.

15. Lyman series lies in ultraviolet region in hydrogen spectrum.

16. The arrangement of different series of wavelength in increasing order is that

$$\lambda_P > \lambda_B > \lambda_L$$

17. H_α-line of the Balmer series in the emission spectrum of H-atom is obtained in visible region, because

$$\frac{1}{\lambda} = R\left(\frac{1}{2^2} - \frac{1}{n^2}\right)$$

where, $n = 3, 4, 5, ...$

18. Bohr postulated that Lyman series is obtained when an electron jumps to first orbit ($n_1 = 1$) from any outer orbit ($n_2 = 2, 3, 4, ...$).

Wave numbers of spectral lines of Lyman series can be calculated as

$$\bar{\nu} = R\left[\frac{1}{1^2} - \frac{1}{n_2^2}\right]$$

where, $n_2 = 2, 3, 4, ...$

19. Refer to the text on pages 456 and 457 (Distance of closest approach).

The distance of closest approach is given by

$$\frac{1}{4\pi\varepsilon_0} \cdot \frac{2e \times Ze}{r} = K \;(K = \text{KE of } \alpha\text{-particle}) \quad ...(i)$$

i.e. $r \propto \frac{1}{K}$ (1)

Let r_0 be the new distance of closest approach for a twice energetic α-particle.

$$\frac{r_0}{r} = \frac{K}{2K} = \frac{1}{2}$$

$\Rightarrow r_0 = \frac{r}{2}$ (1)

20. Refer to the text on pages 456 and 457 (Distance of closest approach).

21. Refer to the text on pages 459 and 460 (Energy of electron in stationary orbit).

22. Refer to the text on page 458 (Regarding stability of atom).

23. An atom can emit or absorb radiation in the form of discrete energy photons only when an electron jumps from a higher to a lower orbit or from a lower to a higher orbit, respectively. (1)

Frequency condition $h\nu = E_i - E_f$

where, ν is frequency of radiation emitted, E_i and E_f are the energies associated with stationary orbits of principal quantum numbers n_i and n_f, respectively (where $n_i > n_f$). (1)

24. Refer to text on Page no 461 (Hydrogen spectrum or Line spectra of hydrogen atom). (1 + 1)

25. On the basis of Geiger-Marsden's experiment, Rutherford concluded that

(i) most of space inside the atom is empty. (1)

(ii) at the centre of atom, there is a small space, where the whole of positive charges is concentrated. (1)

(iii) the atomic nucleus is surrounded by negatively charged electrons equal to total positive charge on the nucleus. (1)

26. The classical model could not explain the stability of atom as the negatively charged electrons are revolving around the nucleus are accelerated and emits energy as the result, the radius of the electrons on circular paths goes on decreasing. Ultimately, electrons fall into the nucleus, which is not true for an atom. (3)

27. When α-particle is replaced by proton, then there will be a change in atomic number and mass of the particle.

$\because$ For a given distance of closest approach,
Kinetic energy $\propto Z$ (charge on particle)

$$\Rightarrow \quad \frac{K_{\text{proton}}}{K_\alpha} = \frac{e}{2e} = \frac{1}{2} \text{ [where, } e \text{ is charge on proton]}$$

$$\therefore \quad K_{\text{proton}} : K_\alpha = 1:2 \qquad (3)$$

28. The energy level diagram of hydrogen atom is shown below. It consists of discrete bright lines in a dark background, known as emission spectrum.

(i) The transitions responsible for absorption spectrum of Lyman series can be written from outer orbit to first orbit, hence it is in ultraviolet. Its shown below

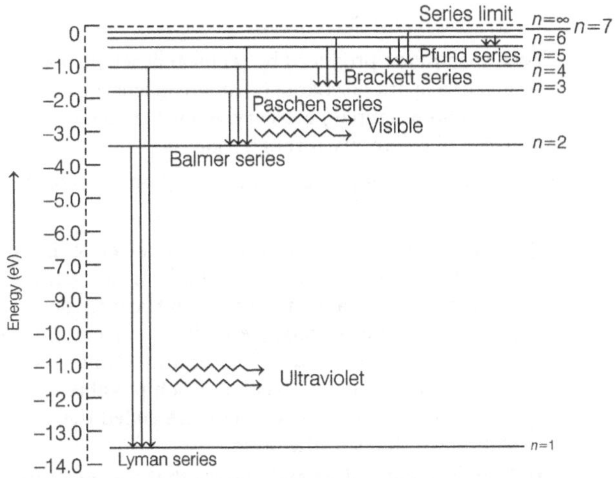

Here, we get dark lines on the bright background.

or **Absorption spectrum of Lyman series** In Lyman series, the electrons jumps from outer orbit to first orbit. So, its absorption spectrum will be

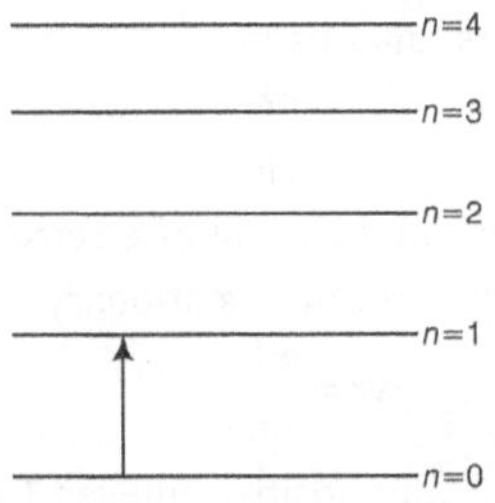

(2)

(ii) **Emission spectrum of Balmer series** In Balmer series, the electrons jumps from any outer orbit to the second orbit.

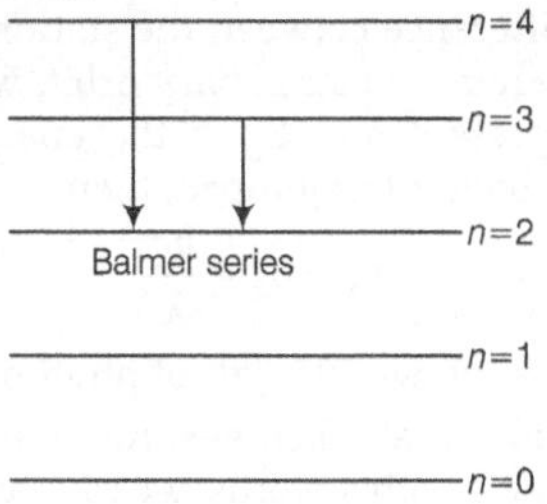

(1)

29. A hydrogen-like atom consists of a tiny positively charged nucleus and an electron revolving in a stable circular orbit around the nucleus.

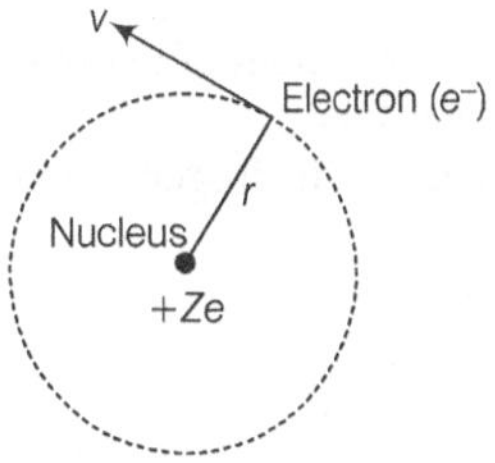

(1)

Let e, m and v be respectively the charge, mass and velocity of the electron and r be the radius of the orbit. The positive charge on the nucleus is Ze, where Z is the atomic number. As, the centripetal force is provided by the electrostatic force of attraction, we have

$$\frac{mv^2}{r} = \frac{1}{4\pi\varepsilon_0} = \frac{(Ze)\times e}{r^2} \text{ or } mv^2 = \frac{Ze^2}{4\pi\varepsilon_0 r} \qquad \text{...(i)}$$

From the second postulate, the angular momentum of the electron is

$$mvr = \frac{nh}{2\pi} \qquad \text{...(ii)}$$

where, $n = (1, 2, 3, \ldots..)$ is the principal quantum number. (1)

From Eqs. (i) and (ii), we get

$$r = \frac{n^2 h^2 \varepsilon_0}{\pi m Z e^2}$$

This is the equation for the radii of the permitted orbit.

According to this equation, $r_n = n^2$

Since, $n = 1, 2, 3, \ldots.$

For Bohr radius, $n = 1$ and $Z = 1$

$$\text{So,} \quad r_1 = \frac{h^2 \varepsilon_0}{\pi m e^2} \qquad (1)$$

30. (i) The orbit in which electron revolves has fixed angular momentum or it is integral multiple of

$$\frac{h}{2\pi}, \text{ i.e. } L = mvr = \frac{nh}{2\pi} \text{ [where, } n = 0, 1, 2, 3, 4] \qquad (1)$$

(ii) The electron can jump from one stationary orbit to other. If it jumps from an orbit from higher energy to lower energy, it emits photons and when it jumps from lower energy to higher energy, it absorbs photon.

The photon emitted or absorbed is in contrast with the energy difference between the stationary orbits, i.e.if E_1 is the energy of stationary orbit, where electron is initially present and E_2 is the energy of stationary orbit to which it has jumped, then

$$E_1 - E_2 = \frac{hc}{\lambda}$$

where, λ is the wavelength of photon. (1)

(iii) This signifies that when electron is in free state it has zero energy. In other words, we can say that there exists mutual attractive force between electron and nucleus which bind them together. Negative energy signifies that the electron is bound to the nucleus and not free to leave it. (1)

31. (i) (a) Balmer series of lines of hydrogen spectrum lies in visible spectrum.

(b) Lyman series of hydrogen spectrum lies in UV region. (1½)

(ii) For hydrogen atom,

$$\frac{1}{\lambda} = Z^2 R_H \left(\frac{1}{n_1} - \frac{1}{n_2^2} \right)$$

where, λ = wavelength,

R_H = Rydberg constant,

n_1 = lower energy state

and n_2 = higher energy state. (1½)

32. (i) Continuous spectra contains all the wavelengths from one end to other without any gap. It is due to light from incandescent solid luminous gas flame. The spectrum is unbroken in this case. The colour of band changes from point to point. (1½)

(ii) Dark lines are observed in solar spectrum due to the absorption of certain wavelength of emitted radiation by the atmospheric particle. (1½)

33. The diagram is given as below.

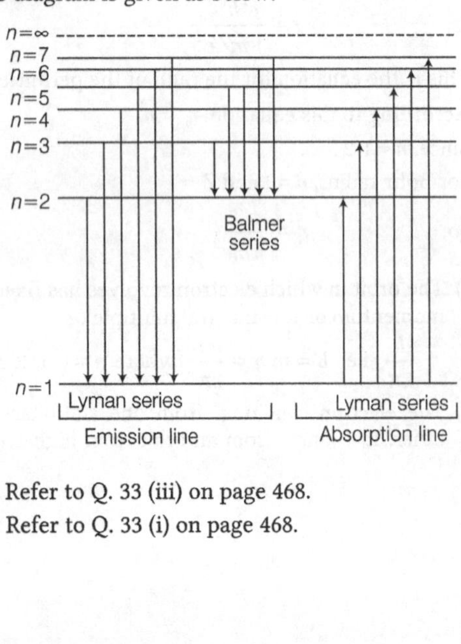

(3)

34. (i) Refer to Q. 33 (iii) on page 468.

(ii) Refer to Q. 33 (i) on page 468.

35. Difference between line, band and continuous spectra are

Continuous Spectra	Band Spectra	Line Spectra
It contains all the wavelengths from one end to other end of spectra without any gap.	It is given by chemical compounds (e.g. by CO_2 or ammonia gas in discharge tube).	It is formed by light emitted by atoms of elements in vapour phase.
It is due to light from incandescent solid dense luminous gas. The flame spectrum is unbroken.	The large number of luminous band is present. Bands are sharply defined.	It consists of bright lines in different regions. All the lines do not have same intensity.
The colour of band changes from point to point.	Each band consists of a large number of lines being more crowded at the sharp edge and gradually fade away.	It is discontinuous spectrum. Each line corresponds to particular wavelength.

These spectra are produced by (a) incandescent solid or vapour (b) a spark discharge (c) an arc discharge (d) sodium vapour lamp (e) mercury vapour lamp (f) discharge of electricity through a gas, etc. (3)

36. Refer to the text on pages 458 and 459 (Bohr's theory).

37. The two postulates are as follows

(i) **Bohr's first postulate** was that an electron in an atom could revolve in certain stable orbits without the emission of radiant energy, contrary to the predictions of electromagnetic theory. According to this postulate, each atom has certain definite stable states in which it can exist and each possible state has definite total energy. These are called the stationary states of the atom.

(ii) **Bohr's second postulate** states that the electron revolves around the nucleus only in those orbits for which the angular momentum is some integral multiple of $h/2\pi$, where h is the Planck's constant ($= 6.63 \times 10^{-34}$ J-s)

Thus, the angular momentum (L) of the orbiting electron is quantised,

i.e. $$L = \frac{nh}{2\pi}$$

As, angular momentum of electron = mvr

∴ For any permitted (stationary) orbit

$$mvr = \frac{nh}{2\pi}$$

where, n = any positive integer 1, 2, 3, ...

It is also called principal quantum number.

The energy value of the ground state of the hydrogen atom, $E = -13.6$ eV

38. Refer to the text on pages 459 and 460 (Energy of electron in stationary orbits).

39. Bohr's second postulate states that the electron revolves around the nucleus only in those orbits for which the angular momentum is some integral multiple of $h/2\pi$.

Thus, angular momentum of the orbiting electron is quantised, i.e. $L = \frac{nh}{2\pi}$ (1)

for any permitted (stationary) orbit, $mvr = \frac{nh}{2\pi}$

(i) Velocity of 1st orbit, $v_0 = (1)\frac{h}{2\pi mr}$

Velocity in 3rd orbit will be

$$v' = (3)\frac{h}{2\pi mr} = 3(v_0)$$ (1)

(ii) Radius of 1st orbit of hydorgen atom,

$$r_0 = (1)^2 \frac{h^2\varepsilon_0}{\pi mZe^2}$$

Radius of 4th orbit of hydorgen atom will be

$$r' = (4)^2 \frac{h^2\varepsilon_0}{\pi mZe^2} = (4)^2 r_0 = 16r_0$$ (1)

40. Refer to the text on pages 459 and 460 (Energy of electron in stationary orbit). (1½)

In H-atom when an electron jumps from the orbit n_i to orbit n_f, the wavelength of the emitted radiation is given by

$$\frac{1}{\lambda} = R\left(\frac{1}{n_f^2} - \frac{1}{n_i^2}\right)$$

where, R = Rydberg constant $= 1.097\times 10^7\ \text{m}^{-1}$ (1/2)

For Balmer series, $n_f = 2$ and $n_i = 3, 4, 5, \ldots$

$$\frac{1}{\lambda} = R\left(\frac{1}{2^2} - \frac{1}{n_i^2}\right)$$

where, $n_i = 3, 4, 5, \ldots$

These spectral lines lie in the visible region. (1/2)

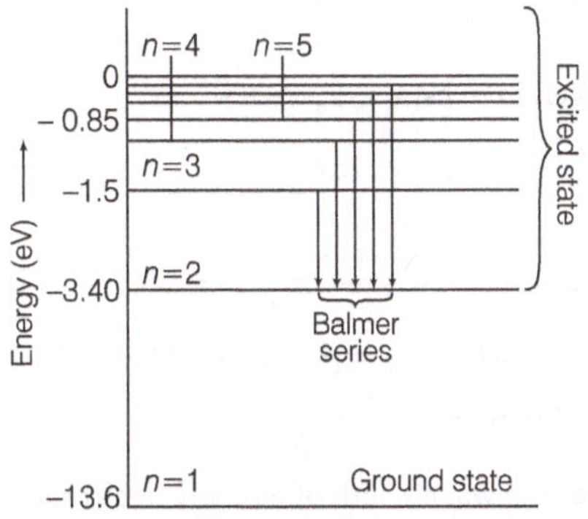

(1/2)

41. (i) For Balmer series absorption transitions are those which will start from the second energy level ($n = 2$). But at ordinary temperatures, almost all the atoms remain in their lowest energy level, i.e. $n = 1$. But, absorption transitions can start only from $n = 1$ level, not from $n = 2, 3, 4, \ldots$ levels.

Hence, at ordinary temperatures, only Lyman series is found in absorption spectrum of hydrogen atom. (1)

(ii) Given, the electron in H-atom is initially in third excited state.

$\therefore\ n = 4$

And the total number of spectral lines of an atom that can exist is given by the relation

$$= \frac{n(n-1)}{2}$$ (1/2)

Here, $n = 4$

So, number of spectral lines $= \frac{4(4-1)}{2} = \frac{4\times 3}{2} = 6$

Hence, when a H-atom moves from third excited state to ground state, it emits six spectral lines. (1/2)

42. Given figure shows a schematic diagram of Geiger-Marsden's experiment.

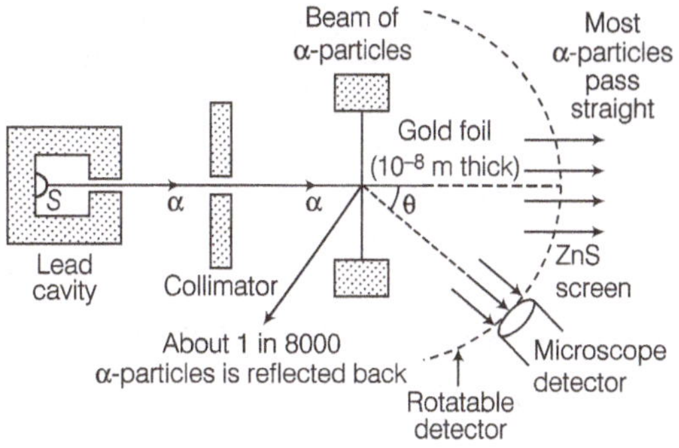

(2)

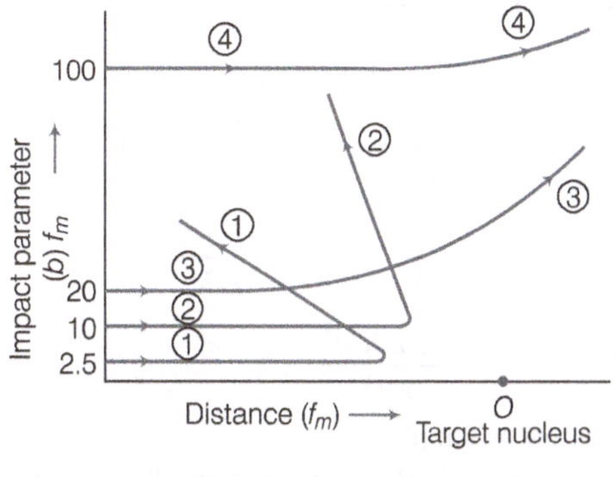

(1)

The size of nucleus can be obtained by finding the distance of closest approach, which is given by

$$r_0 = \frac{1}{4\pi\varepsilon_0}\cdot\frac{2Ze^2}{(\text{KE})}$$

where, $+Ze$ = charge in nucleus

$+2e$ = charge on α-particle

and $\frac{1}{4\pi\varepsilon_0} = K$ = Coulomb constant. (2)

43. Let ν be the frequency when a hydrogen atom jumps from level n to $(n-1)$.

i.e. $n_1 = (n-1)$

$n_2 = n$

Energy, $E = h\nu = E_2 - E_1$

$$\Rightarrow \nu = \frac{1}{2} \cdot \frac{mc^2\alpha^2}{h} \times \left[\frac{1}{(n-1)^2} - \frac{1}{n^2}\right]$$

$$= \frac{mc^2\alpha^2}{2h}\left[\frac{n^2-(n-1)^2}{n^2(n-1)^2}\right]$$

$$= \frac{mc^2\alpha^2[(n+n-1)(n-n+1)]}{2hn^2(n-1)^2}$$

$$= \frac{mc^2\alpha^2(2n-1)}{2hn^2(n-1)^2} \quad (1)$$

For large values of n, $(2n-1 \approx 2n)$, $(n-1 \approx n)$, we have

$$\nu = \frac{mc^2\alpha^2 2n}{2hn^2n^2} = \frac{mc^2\alpha^2}{hn^3} \qquad \left[\because \alpha = \frac{2\pi Ke^2}{cn}\right]$$

$$= \frac{mc^2}{hn^3} \cdot \frac{4\pi^2K^2e^4}{c^2n^2}$$

$$= \frac{4\pi^2K^2me^4}{hn^5} \quad \text{...(i)} \quad (1)$$

In Bohr's atomic model, velocity of nth orbit,

$$v = \frac{hn}{2\pi mr}$$

and radius, $r = \dfrac{n^2h^2}{4\pi^2mKe^2}$

Thus, frequency of oscillation

$$\nu = \frac{v}{2\pi r} = \frac{nh}{2\pi mr}\left(\frac{4\pi^2mKe^2}{2\pi n^2h^2}\right)$$

$$= \frac{Ke^2}{nhr} = \frac{Ke^2}{nh}\left(\frac{4\pi^2 mKe^2}{n^2h^2}\right)$$

$$= \frac{4\pi^2mK^2e^4}{n^3h^3}$$

It is same as Eq. (i).

So, we can say that for large values of n, the classical frequency of revolution of electron in nth orbit is same as the frequency of radiation emitted when hydrogen atom de-excites from level n to level $(n-1)$. (3)

44. Refer to the text on pages 458 and 459. (Bohr's atomic model and frequency of electron). (3)

As, $\nu = Rc \times \left(\dfrac{1}{n_f^2} - \dfrac{1}{n_i^2}\right)$

Here, higher state is $n_i = 4$ and lower state is

$n_f = 3, 2, 1$

For the transition,

$n_i = 4$ to $n_f = 3 : \rightarrow$ Paschen series

$n_i = 4$ to $n_f = 2 : \rightarrow$ Balmer series

$n_i = 4$ to $n_f = 1 : \rightarrow$ Lyman series (2)

45. According to postulate of Bohr's model of hydrogen atom,

Angular momentum of electron, $mvr = \dfrac{nh}{2\pi}$ (1/2)

$$= \frac{(3)\times(6.6\times 10^{-34})}{2\times 3.14} \quad (\because n = 3)$$

$$= 3.15 \times 10^{-34} \text{ m} \quad (1/2)$$

46. According to Bohr's postulate,

Energy of nth orbit, $E \propto \dfrac{1}{n^2}$

So, $E_1 \propto \dfrac{1}{n_1^2}$ and $E_2 \propto \dfrac{1}{n_2^2} \Rightarrow \dfrac{E_1}{E_2} = \dfrac{n_2^2}{n_1^2}$

As, $n_1 = 1$, $n_2 = 3$, $E_1 = -27.2$ eV (1/2)

So, $E_2 = E_1 \dfrac{n_1^2}{n_2^2} = -27.2 \text{ eV} \times \dfrac{1^2}{3^2}$

$$= \frac{-27.2}{9} = -3.02 \text{ eV} \quad (1/2)$$

47. The wavelength (λ) of different spectral lines of Balmer series is given by

$$\frac{1}{\lambda} = R\left[\frac{1}{2^2} - \frac{1}{n_2^2}\right] \quad (1)$$

$\because$ For shortest wavelength, $n_2 = \infty$.

$$\therefore \frac{1}{\lambda} = 1.097 \times 10^7 \left[\frac{1}{2^2} - \frac{1}{\infty}\right]$$

$$\frac{1}{\lambda} = \frac{1.097 \times 10^7}{4}$$

$$\Rightarrow \lambda = \frac{4}{1.097 \times 10^7} = 3.646 \times 10^{-7} \text{m} \Rightarrow \lambda = 364.6 \text{ nm} \quad (1)$$

48. As given in question, $E_n = \dfrac{-13.6}{2^2}$ eV

So, for $n = 2$, $E_n = \dfrac{-13.6}{2^2} = -3.4$ eV

and for $n = 1$, $E_n = \dfrac{-13.6}{1^2} = -13.6$ eV (1)

So, $E = E_2 - E_1 = [-3.4 - (-13.6)]$ eV

As we know that, $\Delta E = \dfrac{hc}{\lambda} = 10.2$ eV (1)

where, λ = wavelength of emitted electromagnetic radiation

$$\Rightarrow \lambda = \frac{hc}{10.2} = \frac{6.6 \times 10^{-34} \times 3 \times 10^8}{10.2 \times 1.6 \times 10^{-19}}$$

$$= 1.213 \times 10^{-7} \text{ m} = 121.3 \text{ nm} \quad (1)$$

49. (i) Energy diagram is given as follows

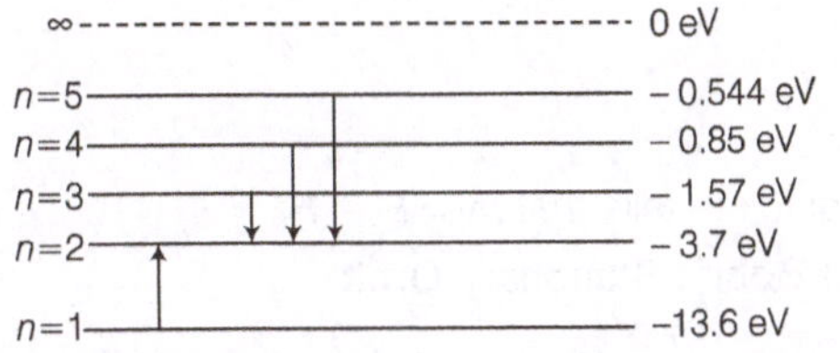

(1)

(ii) Maximum energy of photon is given by

$$\Delta E = E_{\infty} - E_1 \Rightarrow 0-(-13.6) = 13.6 \text{ eV}$$ (1)

50. As given in question,

(i) Radius, $r = 5\times10^{-11}$ m, charge, $q = +e$

So, electric field, $E = \dfrac{q}{4\pi\varepsilon_0 r^2} = 9\times10^9 \times \dfrac{1.6\times10^{-9}}{(5\times10^{-11})^2}$

$\left[\because \dfrac{1}{4\pi\varepsilon_0} = 9\times10^9\right]$

$= 5.76\times10^{11}$ NC^{-1} (1½)

(ii) As potential energy of system is given by

$$U = \frac{1}{4\pi\varepsilon_0}\frac{q_1q_2}{r}$$

$$= \frac{9\times10^9\times(1.6\times10^{-19})\times(-1.6\times10^{-19})}{5\times10^{-11}}$$

$= -4.608\times10^{-18}$ J (1½)

51. As we know that,

$$\frac{1}{\lambda} = Z^2 R_H\left(\frac{1}{n_1^2}-\frac{1}{n_2^2}\right)$$

For Balmer series, first line $(1+\alpha)$

$n_1 = 2$, $n_2 = 3$, $\lambda = 656.3$ nm

$$\Rightarrow \frac{1}{656.3\times10^{-9}\text{ m}} = R_H\left(\frac{1}{2^2}-\frac{1}{3^2}\right) = R_H\left(\frac{1}{4}-\frac{1}{9}\right)$$

$\Rightarrow R_H = 1.09\times10^7$ m^{-1} (1½)

For Balmer series 2nd line (H_β)

$n = 2$, $n_2 = 4$ [given]

$$\frac{1}{\lambda} = R_H\left(\frac{1}{n_1^2}-\frac{1}{n_2^2}\right)$$

$$\Rightarrow \frac{1}{\lambda} = 1.09\times10^7\left(\frac{1}{4}-\frac{1}{16}\right)$$

$\therefore \lambda = 4.89\times10^{-7}$ m [approx] (1½)

52. As we know that, energy is inversely proportional to the wavelength, so for largest wavelength in Balmer series, electron should fall from $n=3$ to $n=2$. (1)

Now, according to the formula to calculate wavelength.

So, $\dfrac{1}{\lambda} = R_H\left(\dfrac{1}{n_1^2}-\dfrac{1}{n_2^2}\right)$ [where, R_H = Rydberg constant]

$\Rightarrow \dfrac{1}{\lambda} = 1.097\times10^7\left(\dfrac{1}{4}-\dfrac{1}{9}\right)$ $[\because n_1 = 2, n_2 = 3]$

$$\therefore \lambda = \frac{36\times10^{-7}}{1.097\times5}$$

$= 6563\times10^{-10}$ m $= 656.3$ nm (2)

53. Refer to example 7 on page 462.

54. Let the distance of closest approach of the α-particle be r_0.

So, by principle of conservation of energy,

Kinetic energy KE = Potential energy PE (1)

$$\Rightarrow \text{KE} = U = \frac{1}{4\pi\varepsilon_0}\cdot\frac{Ze(2e)}{r_0}$$

$$\Rightarrow r_0 = \frac{1}{4\pi\varepsilon_0}\cdot\frac{2Ze^2}{\text{KE}}$$ (1/2)

$$= \frac{9\times10^9\times2\times79\times(1.6\times10^{-19})}{1.8\times1.6\times10^{-13}}$$

$= 1.264\times10^{-13}$ m

where, $+Ze$ = charge in nucleus,

$+2e$ = charge on α-particle

and $\dfrac{1}{4\pi\varepsilon_0} = K$ = Coulomb constant. (1½)

SUMMARY

- **α-Particle Scattering Experiment by Rutherford** In this experiment, a collimated beam of α-particles of energy 5.5 MeV was allowed to fall on 2.1×10^{-7}m thick gold foil. The α-particles were observed through a rotatable detector consisting of zinc sulphide screen and microscope and it was found that α-particles got scattered, which produce scintillations on zinc sulphide screen.
- **Rutherford's Model of Atom** According to this model, every atom consists of a central core called the nucleus of an atom and the size of the nucleus is of the order of 10^{-15} m. The atomic nucleus is surrounded by certain number of electrons and they revolve around the nucleus in various circular orbits.
- **Drawbacks of Rutherford's Model** It could not explain
  (i) stability of atom.
  (ii) line spectrum.
- **Distance of Closest Approach** At a certain distance r_0 from the nucleus, whole of the kinetic energy of α-particles cannot go further closed to the nucleus.
- **Scattering Angle** Angle by which α-particles get deviated from its original path around the nucleus is called angle of scattering.
- **Electron Orbits** The total mechanical energy E of electron in a hydrogen atom is $E = \frac{-e^2}{8\pi\varepsilon_0 r}$.
- **Bohr's Atomic Model** Bohr's combined classical and early quantum concepts and gave his theory in the form of three postulates.
  First postulate state that an electron could revolve in a certain stable orbits without the emission of radiant energy.
  Second postulate tells that $mvr = \frac{nh}{2\pi}$.
  [angular moment of an electron, $L = mvr$]
  Third postulate tells that $h\nu = E_2 - E_1$.
- **Radii of Bohr's Stationary Orbits**
$$r = \frac{n^2h^2\varepsilon_0}{\pi mZe^2} \Rightarrow r \propto n^2$$
- **Velocity of Electrons in Bohr's Stationary Orbits**
$$v = \frac{Ze^2}{2n4\varepsilon_0} \Rightarrow v \propto \frac{1}{n}$$
- **Frequency of Electrons in Bohr's Stationary Orbits**
$$\nu = \frac{kZe^2}{nhr} \Rightarrow \nu \propto \frac{1}{n}$$
- **Total Energy of Electrons in Bohr's Stationary Orbits**
$$E = \frac{-me^4Z^2}{8n^2\varepsilon_0^2h^2} \Rightarrow E_n = \frac{-13.6}{n^2}\text{eV}$$
- **Energy Levels** The energy of an atom is the least when its electron is revolving in an orbit closest to the nucleus.
- **Hydrogen Spectrum** It consists of discrete bright lines a dark background and is known as hydrogen emission spectrum.
  There is one more type of hydrogen spectrum exists, where we get dark lines on the bright background, it is known as absorption spectrum.
- **Formulae for the Spectral Series of Hydrogen**

  Lyman series $\frac{1}{\lambda} = R\left(\frac{1}{1^2} - \frac{1}{n^2}\right)$, where $n = 2, 3, 4, \ldots$

  Balmer series $\frac{1}{\lambda} = R\left(\frac{1}{2^2} - \frac{1}{n^2}\right)$, where $n = 3,4,5, \ldots$

  Paschen series $\frac{1}{\lambda} = R\left(\frac{1}{3^2} - \frac{1}{n^2}\right)$, where $n = 4,5,6, \ldots$

  Brackett series $\frac{1}{\lambda} = R\left(\frac{1}{4^2} - \frac{1}{n^2}\right)$ where $n = 5, 6, 7, \ldots$

  Pfund series $\frac{1}{\lambda} = R\left(\frac{1}{5^2} - \frac{1}{n^2}\right)$, where $n = 6, 7, 8, \ldots$

For Mind Map

Visit : https://goo.gl/MWvV5x OR **Scan the Code**

Chapter Practice

Multiple Choice Questions

1 Mark

1 From Rutherford's experiment, estimated sizes of nucleus and atom are
(a) 10^{-15} m, 10^{-10} m (b) 10^{-15} m, 10^{-14} m
(c) 10^{-15} m, 10^{-20} m (d) 10^{-15} m, 10^{-15} m

2 α-particles are scattered due to
(a) attraction of electrons
(b) repulsion of nucleus
(c) both (a) and (b)
(d) gravitational pull of neutrons

3 As the electron in Bohr orbit of hydrogen atom passes from state $n = 2$ to $n = 1$, the kinetic energy (K) and potential energy (U) changes as
(a) K becomes twice, U becomes four times
(b) K becomes four times, U becomes twice
(c) K becomes four times, U also four times
(d) K becomes twice, U also two times

4 The ground state energy of hydrogen atom is – 13.6 eV. What is potential energy of electrons in this state?
(a) Zero (b) – 27.2 eV (c) 1 eV (d) 2 eV

5 Highest energy level of an electron corresponds to $n = \infty$ and it has an energy of
(a) zero (b) ∞ (c) 13.6 eV (d) – 13.6 eV

Assertion and Reason

Directions (Q. Nos. 6-7) *In the following questions, two statements are given- one labeled Assertion (A) and the other labelled Reason (R). Select the correct answer to these questions from the codes (a), (b), (c) and (d) as given below*
(a) Both Assertion and Reason are true and Reason is the correct explanation of Assertion.
(b) Both Assertion and Reason are true but Reason is not the correct explanation of Assertion.
(c) Assertion is true but Reason is false.
(d) Assertion is false but Reason is true.

6. **Assertion (A)** Large angle of scattering of alpha particles led to the discovery of atomic nucleus.
Reason (R) Entire positive charge of atom is concentrated in the central core.

7. **Assertion (A)** Atom as a whole is electrically neutral.
Reason (R) Atom contains equal amount of positive and negative charges.

Very Short Answer Type Questions

1 Mark

8 In α-particle experiment, most of the α-particles passed through the gold foil without any observable deflection. Why?

9 Why was gold foil used in α-particle scattering?

10 What is the ratio of mass of an α-particle to that of an electron?

11 Calculate the radius of the first orbit of H-atom. Show that the velocity of electron in the first orbit is 1/137 times the velocity of light.

12 Name the spectral series of H-atom lying in the infrared region.

Short Answer Type I Questions

2 Marks

13 Explain, why scattering of α-particles in Rutherford's experiment is not affected by the mass of the nucleons?

14 Derive the expression for the wavelength of the H-atom for different spectral series.

15 How can elements be identified by the study of the line spectrum?

Short Answer Type II Questions

3 Marks

16 Derive and explain the significance of negative energy of an electron in an orbit. What is the energy possessed by an electron for $n = \infty$?

17 Draw energy levels for the hydrogen atom.

18 What does an emperical formula mean? Hence, explain that how Balmer proposed this formula?

19 Using Bohr's postulates, derive the expression for the total energy of the electron revolving in n th orbit of hydrogen atom. Find the wavelength of H_α line, given the value of Rydberg constant, $R = 1.1 \times 10^7 \text{ m}^{-1}$.

20 What is the difference between emission spectra and absorption spectra?

21 Explain the origin of spectral lines of hydrogen using Bohr's theory.

22 (i) If hydrogen atoms are excited to the 4th energy level, how many different wavelengths are possible for the emitted radiation?
(ii) What do you mean by excitation potential?

Long Answer Type Questions

5 Marks

23 (i) State the basic assumption of the Rutherford model of an atom. Explain in brief, why this model cannot account for the stability of an atom?
(ii) Using Bohr's postulates, derive the expression for radius of electron in nth orbit of electron in hydrogen atom.

24 (i) Using postulates of Bohr's theory of hydrogen atom, show that
(a) the radii of orbits increase as n^2 and
(b) the total energy of the electron increases as $1/n^2$, where n is the principal quantum number of the atom.
(ii) Calculate the wavelength of H_α-line in Balmer series of hydrogen atom.
Given, Rydberg constant, $R = 1.097 \times 10^7 \text{ m}^{-1}$.

Case Based Question

Directions (Q.No. 25) *The question is case study based question. Read the following paragraph and answer the questions.*

25. At room temperature, most of the H-atoms are in ground state. When an atom receives some energy (i.e. by electron collisions), the atom may acquire sufficient energy to raise electron to higher energy state. In this condition, the atom is said to be in excited state.

From the excited state, the electron can fall back to a state of lower energy, emitting a photon equal to the energy difference of the orbit.

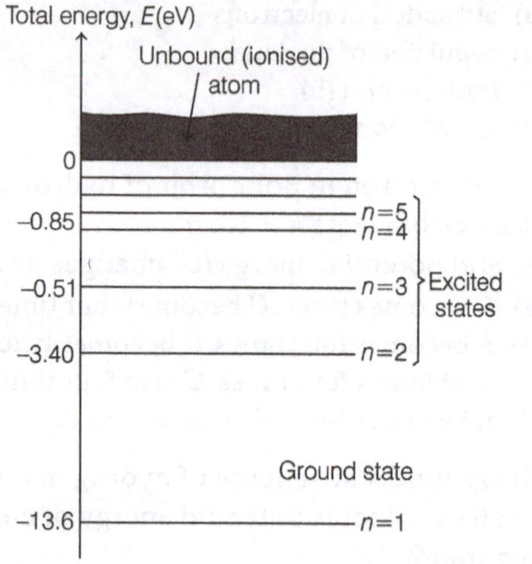

In a mixture of H–He$^+$ gas (He$^+$ is single ionised He atom), H-atoms and He$^+$ ions are excited to their respective first excited states. Subsequently, H atoms transfer their total excitation energy to He$^+$ ions (by collisions).

(i) The quantum number n of the state finally populated in He$^+$ ions is
(a) 2 (b) 3 (c) 4 (d) 5

(ii) The wavelength of light emitted in the visible region by He$^+$ ions after collisions with H-atoms is
(a) 6.5×10^{-7} m (b) 5.6×10^{-7} m
(c) 4.8×10^{-7} m (d) 4.0×10^{-7} m

(iii) The radius of the ground state orbit of H- atom is
(a) $\dfrac{\varepsilon_0}{h\pi me^2}$ (b) $\dfrac{h^2\varepsilon_0}{\pi me^2}$
(c) $\dfrac{\pi me^2}{h}$ (d) $\dfrac{2\pi h\varepsilon_0}{me^2}$

Answers

1 (*a*) Rutherford's experiments suggested the size of the nucleus to be about 10^{-15} m to 10^{-14} m and size of atom is about 10^{-10} m.

2 (*b*) When α-particle comes near a nucleus, then due to the intense electric field there α-particle scatters through a large angle. The atomic electrons, being so light, do not appreciably affect the α-particles.

3 (*c*) As we know, potential energy $U = 2E, K = -E$

and $$E = -\frac{13.6}{n^2}$$

For state $n = 1$, $E_1 = \frac{-13.6}{(1)^2} = -13.6$

For state $n = 2$, $E_2 = \frac{-13.6}{(2)^2} = \frac{E_1}{4}$

$\Rightarrow$ $E_1 = 4E_2$

But, $K = -E$, so $K_1 = 4K_2$

Similarly, for state $n = 1$, potential energy

$$(U_1) = 2E = 2\times\frac{-136}{(1)^2} = -2\times 13.6$$

For state $n = 2$, potential energy

$$(U_2) = 2E = 2\times\frac{-13.6}{(2)^2} = \frac{-2\times 13.6}{4}$$

$$U_2 = \frac{U_1}{4}$$

$\Rightarrow$ $U_1 = 4U_2$

4 (*b*) If E_n = Total energy of Bohr's atom, then $U_n = 2E_n$

and $K = 1\,E_n$

So, $U_1 = 2\times(-13.6 \text{ eV}) = -27.2$ eV

5 (*a*) For $n = \infty$, energy of an electron at nth level, i.e.

$$E_n = -\frac{13.6}{n^2}$$

$\Rightarrow$ $E_\infty = 0$

6 (*a*) α-particle is positively charged, so is the nucleus, the large angle of scattering of α-particle shows that the nucleus is positively charged and concentrated in the central core.

7 (*a*)

8 Most of the α-particles passed through the gold foil without any appreciable (observable) deflection, it means atom has a lot of empty space whose entire mass and positive charge is confined to an extremely small central core called nucleus.

9 Gold was used in α-particle scattering due to following reasons

(i) Gold can be beaten into extremely thin foil.

(ii) As gold nucleus is heavy, it can produce a large deflection in the path of α-particle.

10 We have, mass of α-particle

$$({}_2He^4) = 4\times 1.67\times 10^{-27} \text{ kg}$$

Mass of electron $= 9.1\times 10^{-31}$ kg

$$\therefore \quad \frac{m_\alpha}{m_e} = \frac{4\times 1.67\times 10^{-27}}{9.1\times 10^{-31}} = 7341$$

Hence, α-particle is 7341 times heavier than electron.

11 We have, radius of n th orbit,

$$r_n = \frac{n^2h^2\varepsilon_0}{\pi mZe^2} \quad \text{...(i)}$$

For $n = 1$,

$$r_1 = \frac{h^2\varepsilon_0}{\pi me^2} = \frac{(6.63\times 10^{-34})^2\times(8.85\times 10^{-12})}{(3.14)\,(9.1\times 10^{-31})\,(1.6\times 10^{-19})^2} = 0.53\,\text{Å}$$

By Bohr's postulate, we can also write as $v = \frac{nh}{2\pi mr}$ ...(ii)

Putting Eq. (ii) in Eq. (i), we get $v = \frac{Ze^2}{2h\varepsilon_0}\cdot\frac{1}{n}$

For $n = 1$, we get

$$v_1 = \frac{e^2}{2h\varepsilon_0} = 2.19\times 10^6$$

or we can write it as $= \frac{c}{137}$

12 Brackett and Pfund series of H-atom lying in the infrared region.

13 The electrostatic force of attraction between α-particles and nucleus is $\approx 10^{36}$ stronger than the gravitational force, i.e.

$$\frac{F_g}{F_e} = \frac{\frac{Gm_\alpha M_{\text{nucleus}}}{r^2}}{\frac{Kq_\alpha q_{\text{nucleus}}}{r^2}} \approx 10^{-36}$$

Hence, scattering of α-particles is not affected by the mass of nucleus significantly.

14 Refer to the text on page 461 (Hydrogen spectrum or line spectra of hydrogen atom).

15 Each elements have atoms having definite energy levels and they are different from the energy levels of other elements. The atoms of an element emit spectrum of radiation which has certain definite lines of frequencies, different from those of all other elements.

16 Refer to the text on pages 459 and 460. (Energy of electron in stationary orbit) at $x = \infty$, $E = 0$

17 Refer to the text on page 460 (Energy levels).

18 An empirical formula is based solely on observation and experiments but not necessarily supported by theory.

The spacing between the spectral lines within certain sets of the hydrogen spectrum decreases in a regular way. As the wavelength decreases, the lines appear close together and weaker in intensity. Balmer found a simple empirical formula for the observed wavelengths.

$$\frac{1}{\lambda} = R\left(\frac{1}{2^2} - \frac{1}{n^2}\right)$$

19 Refer to the text on pages 459 and 460 (Energy of electron in stationary orbits).

20 Refer to the text on page 461 (Hydrogen spectrum or line spectra of hydrogen atom).

21 Refer to the text on pages 461 and 462 (Hydrogen spectrum or line spectra of hydrogen atom).

22 (i) Number of wavelength for the emitted radiation will be 6, corresponding to transitions

$$n = 4 \to 3,\ 4 \to 2,\ 4 \to 1$$

as well as $3 \to 2,\ 3 \to 1$ and $2 \to 1$.

(ii) The minimum accelerating potential required to energise an electron which on collision can excite an atom is called the 'excitation potential' of that atom.

23 (i) Refer to the text on page 456 (Rutherford' atomic model).

(ii) Refer to the text on pages 458 and 459 (Bohr's atomic model and Bohr's theory).

24 (i) (a) Refer to the text on pages 458 and 459 (Bohr's theory).

(b) Refer to the text on pages 459 and 460 (Energy of electron in stationary orbit). **(2½)**

(ii) We know that, $\frac{1}{\lambda} = R\left[\frac{1}{n_1^2} - \frac{1}{n_2^2}\right]$

For H_α-line in Balmer series.

$$n_1 = 2,\ n_2 = 3$$

$$\therefore \quad \frac{1}{\lambda} = R\left[\frac{1}{2^2} - \frac{1}{3^2}\right]$$

$$= 1.097 \times 10^7 \left[\frac{1}{4} - \frac{1}{9}\right]$$

$$= 1.097 \times 10^7 \left[\frac{9-4}{36}\right]$$

$$\frac{1}{\lambda} = 1.097 \times 10^7 \left[\frac{5}{36}\right]$$

or $$\lambda = \frac{36}{5 \times 1.097} \times 10^{-7}$$

$$\lambda = 6.56 \times 10^{-7}\ \text{m}$$ **(2½)**

25 (i) (c) $E_n = \frac{-13.6}{n^2}(Z^2)$

In first excited state, $E_{H_2} = 3.4$ eV

and $E_{He} = -13.6$ eV

So, H_2 atom gives excitation energy (13.6 − 3.4 = 10.2 eV) to helium atom.

Now energy of He ion = − 13.6 + 10.2

= − 3.4 eV

Again, $E = \frac{-13.6}{n^2} \times Z^2$

$$\Rightarrow \quad -3.4 = \frac{-13.6}{n^2} \times (2)^2 \Rightarrow n = 4$$

(ii) (c) $\frac{1}{\lambda} = \frac{13.6\, Z^2}{hc}\left[\frac{1}{n_1^2} - \frac{1}{n_2^2}\right]$

Here $n_1 = 3$ and $n_2 = 4$

$$\Rightarrow \quad \lambda = 4.8 \times 10^{-7}\ \text{m}$$

(iii) (b) Radius of the permitted orbit,

$$r = \frac{n^2 h^2 \varepsilon_0}{\pi\, m Z e^2}$$

For hydrogen atom in ground state, i.e.

$$n = 1,\ Z = 1$$

$$= \frac{h^2 \varepsilon_0}{\pi m\, e^2}$$

RELATED ONLINE VIDEOS

Visit : https://www.youtube.com/watch?v=wilNTUZoAiw
OR **Scan the Code**

Visit : https://www.youtube.com/watch?v=WgJbBcVFI2I
OR **Scan the Code**

Visit : https://www.youtube.com/watch?v=wOmYCiv3Ebo
OR **Scan the Code**

CHAPTER

13

Nuclei

Rutherford established that a central core exists in every atom which contains entire positive charge and more than 99% mass of the atom, this central core was named as **Nucleus**. In this chapter, we will study the constituents of nucleus and how they are held together. Further, we will proceed with the topics, size, mass, density and stability of **Nuclei**. And finally, we will have a look at the associated nuclear phenomena such as radioactivity, nuclear fission and nuclear fusion.

- Nucleus and Its Composition
- Radioactivity and Nuclear Energy

TOPIC 01 Nucleus and Its Composition

In every atom, the positive charge and mass are densely concentrated at the centre of the atom forming its nucleus. The overall dimensions of a nucleus are much smaller than those of an atom. The radius of the nucleus is smaller than the radius of an atom by a factor of 10^4. This means the volume of a nucleus is about 10^{-12} times the volume of the atom.

Atomic Mass Unit

The unit to express atomic mass is **atomic mass unit (u)**.

Atomic mass unit is defined as $\frac{1}{12}$th of the mass of carbon $^{12}C_6$ atom.

$$\text{Unified atomic mass unit, } 1\text{u} = \frac{\text{mass of one } ^{12}C_6 \text{ atom}}{12}$$

$$= \frac{1.992647 \times 10^{26}\ \text{kg}}{12} = 1.660539 \times 10^{-27}\ \text{kg}$$

Atomic masses are measured by an instrument called **mass spectrometer**.

The bigger unit is called 1 MeV.

$$1\ \text{MeV} = 10^6\ \text{eV} = 1.602 \times 10^{-13}\ \text{J}$$

According to Einstein's mass-energy relation, $E = mc^2$

The energy equivalence of 1 amu = 931 MeV

Composition of Nucleus

The nucleus was first discovered in 1911 by Lord Rutherford and his associates by experiments on scattering of α-particles on atoms. He found that the scattering results could be explained, if atoms consist of a small, central, massive and positive core surrounded by orbiting negative charge electrons.

The experimental results indicated that the size of the nucleus is of the order of 10^{-14} m and is thus 10000 times smaller than the size of atom. The study of radioactivity revealed that nucleus is not a composite body, but it is made of nucleons. The composition of a nucleus can be described using following terms and symbols.

Atomic Number (Z)

Atomic number of an element is the number of protons present inside the nucleus of an atom of the element. It is also equal to the number of electrons revolving in various orbits around the nucleus of the neutral atom.

Atomic number, Z = Number of protons
= Number of electrons (in a neutral atom)

Mass Number (A)

Mass number of an element is the total number of protons and neutrons inside the atomic nucleus of the element.

Mass number, A = Number of protons + Number of neutrons

= Number of electrons (in a neutral atom) + Number of neutrons

= Atomic number + Number of neutrons = $Z + N$

The term **nucleon** is also used for neutron and proton. Thus, the number of nucleons in an atom is its mass number A.

Nuclear species or nuclides are shown by the notation $^{A}_{Z}X$, where X is the chemical symbol of the species.

Example 1 In a nucleus of $_{92}U^{238}$, find the number of protons and the number of neutrons.

Sol. Number of protons, $Z = 92$

$\therefore$ Number of neutrons, $N = A - Z = 238 - 92 = 146$

Size of Nucleus

The size of the nucleus has been measured with the help of a variety of experiments involving the scattering of particles such as neutrons, protons, electrons, etc.

From all these experiments, it is found that the volume of the nucleus is directly proportional to the number of nucleons (mass number) constituting nucleus.

If R is the radius of the nucleus having mass number A,

then $\frac{4}{3}\pi R^3 \propto A \Rightarrow R \propto A^{1/3} \Rightarrow \boxed{R = R_0 A^{1/3}}$

where, $R_0 = 1.2 \times 10^{-15}$ m is the range of nuclear size.

It is also known as **nuclear unit radius.** Owing to the small size of the nucleus, fermi (fm) is found to be a convenient unit of length in nuclear physics.

It is given as, 1 fermi (fm) = 10^{-15} m

Example 2 Obtain the approximate value of the radius of a nucleus $_{92}U^{238}$. Take, R_0 is 1.2×10^{-15} m.

Sol. Given, $A = 238$, $R_0 = 1.2 \times 10^{-15}$ m

As, $R = R_0 A^{1/3} = 1.2 \times 10^{-15} (238)^{1/3}$

$\therefore$ $R = 7.437 \times 10^{-15}$ m

Nuclear Density

Density of nuclear matter is the ratio of mass of nucleus and its volume. If m is the average mass of a nucleon and A is the mass number of element, then the mass of nucleus = mA.

If R is the nuclear radius, then

$$\text{volume of nucleus} = \frac{4}{3}\pi R^3 = \frac{4}{3}\pi (R_0 A^{1/3})^3 = \frac{4}{3}\pi R_0^3 A$$

As, density of nuclear matter = $\frac{\text{Mass of nucleus}}{\text{Volume of nucleus}}$

$$\therefore \quad \boxed{\rho = \frac{mA}{\frac{4}{3}\pi R_0^3 A}} \quad \text{or} \quad \boxed{\rho = \frac{3m}{4\pi R_0^3}}$$

Thus, the density of nucleus is a constant, **independent of A**, for all nuclei. Different nuclei are like drops of liquid of constant density. The density of nuclear matter is approximately 2.3×10^{17} kg/m^3. This density is very large as compared to an ordinary matter.

Example 3 Given the mass of iron nucleus as 55.85u and $A = 56$. Find the nuclear density. **NCERT**

Sol. Given, mass, $m = 55.85\,u = 55.85 \times 1.67 \times 10^{-27}$ kg

Volume, $V = \frac{4}{3}\pi R^3 = \frac{4}{3}\pi (R_0 A^{1/3})^3 = \frac{4}{3}\pi R_0^3 \times A$

$\therefore$ Nuclear density, $\rho = \frac{m}{V} = \frac{3 \times 55.85 \times 1.67 \times 10^{-27}}{4 \times \frac{22}{7} \times (1.2 \times 10^{-15})^3 \times 56}$

$= 2.29 \times 10^{17}$ kg/m^3

Example 4 Supposing that protons and neutrons have equal masses. Calculate how many times nuclear matter is denser than water? Take, mass of a nucleon $= 1.67 \times 10^{-27}$ kg and $R_0 = 1.2 \times 10^{-15}$ m.

Sol. Density of nucleus (of water),

$$\rho = \frac{3m}{4\pi R_0^3} = \frac{3 \times 1.67 \times 10^{-27}}{4 \times \frac{22}{7} \times (1.2 \times 10^{-15})^3}$$

$$= \frac{7 \times 3 \times 1.67 \times 10^{18}}{88 \times 1.2 \times 1.2 \times 1.2} = 2.307 \times 10^{17} \text{ kg/m}^3$$

Density of water, $\rho' = 10^3$ kg/m^3

$$\therefore \quad \frac{\rho}{\rho'} = \frac{2.307 \times 10^{17}}{10^3} = 2.307 \times 10^{14}$$

Classification of Nuclei :
Isotopes, Isobars and Isotones

The nuclei has been classified on the basis of the number of protons (atomic number) or the total number of nucleons (mass number) in them.

(i) **Isotopes** or **Isoprotons**
The atoms of element whose nuclei have the same number of protons, but different number of neutrons or we can say that they have same atomic number, but different mass number are called the 'isotopes' of that element.
The isotopes of some elements are as

Hydrogen : ${}_1H^1$(proton), ${}_1H^2$(deuterium), ${}_1H^3$(tritium)

Oxygen : ${}_8O^{16}$, ${}_8O^{17}$, ${}_8O^{17}$

Neon : ${}_{10}Ne^{20}$, ${}_{10}Ne^{21}$, ${}_{10}Ne^{22}$

Chlorine : ${}_{17}Cl^{35}$, ${}_{17}Cl^{31}$

Uranium : ${}_{92}U^{235}$, ${}_{92}U^{238}$

(ii) **Isobars** The nuclei which have the same number of nucleons (i.e. mass number), but different number of protons and different number of neutrons are called 'isobars'. Their atomic numbers (Z) are different, but mass number (A) is same. Therefore, they have different places in the periodic table and differ in chemical properties also. Since, in isobars, the numbers of fundamental particles are different, they differ in physical properties also. The nuclei of isobars belong to the different elements. Some examples of isobars are as

$${}_1H^3 \text{ and } {}_2H^3, \; {}_{11}Na^{23} \text{ and } {}_{12}Mg^{23}$$

(iii) **Isotones** The nuclei having equal number of neutrons are called 'isotones'. For them, both the atomic number (Z) and the mass number (A) are different, but the value of $(A - Z)$ is same. Some examples of isotones are as

${}_3Li^7$ and ${}_4Be^8$, ${}_{17}Cl^{37}$ and ${}_{19}K^{39}$, ${}_{11}Na^{23}$ and ${}_{12}Mg^{24}$

Mass-Energy and Nuclear Binding Energy

Mass-Energy Relation

Einstein showed that mass is another form of energy and anything having mass has an equivalent amount of energy and *vice-versa*. Einstein's mass-energy equivalence equation is $E = mc^2$

where, E is the energy, m is the mass and c is the velocity of light in vacuum (approximately equal to 3×10^8 m/s).

Mass Defect

The sum of the masses of neutrons and protons forming a nucleus is more than the actual mass of the nucleus. This difference of masses is known as **mass defect**.

Mass defect (Δm) = (Mass of protons + Mass of neutrons) − Mass of nucleus

Binding Energy of Nucleus

If a certain number of neutrons and protons are brought together to form a nucleus of a certain charge and mass, an energy E_b will be released in the process. The energy E_b is called the binding energy of the nucleus.

Thus, the binding energy of a nucleus may be defined as the energy equivalent to the mass defect of the nucleus.

If we separate a nucleus into its nucleons, we would have to supply a total energy equal to E_b, to those particles from Einstein equation,

$$E_b = \Delta mc^2 \quad \text{[where, } \Delta m = \text{mass defect]}$$

$$E_b = [Zm_p + (A - Z)m_n - M]c^2$$

where, M is mass of nucleus, m_p is the mass of proton and m_n is the mass of neutron.

The mass defect reappears as equivalent energy $(\Delta m)c^2$, which is liberated during the formation of nucleus. Conversely, an amount Δmc^2 of external energy is required to break the nucleus into protons and neutrons. This energy is called **binding energy**.

The binding energy of a nucleus is defined as **the minimum energy required to separate its nucleons and place them at rest and infinite distance apart.**

Average Binding Energy Per Nucleon of a Nucleus

It is the average energy spend to remove a nucleon from the nucleus to infinite distance. It is given by total binding energy divided by the mass number of the nucleus.

$$\text{Binding energy per nucleon} = \frac{\text{Total binding energy}\,(BE)}{\text{Number of nucleons}\,(A)}$$

or

$$E_{\text{bn}} = \frac{E_b}{A}$$

Example 5 A given coin has a mass of 3.0 g. Calculate the nuclear energy that would be required to separate all the neutrons and protons from each other. For simplicity assume that the coin is entirely made of ${}^{63}_{29}\text{Cu}$ atoms (of mass 62.92960 u). **NCERT**

Sol. Given, mass of coin = 3g

Atomic mass of Cu = 63

Mass of ${}^{63}_{29}\text{Cu}$, $m = 62.92960$ u

Avogadro's number = 6.023×10^{23}

Mass of proton, $m_p = 1.007825$ u

Mass of neutron, $m_n = 1.008665$ u

Nuclear energy required to separate neutrons and protons, $E_b = ?$

Since, each atom of copper contains 29 protons and 34 neutrons. Therefore, mass defect of each atom using the relation,

$$\Delta m = [Z m_p + (A - Z) m_n] - M$$

$$\Delta m = [29 \times 1.007825 + 34 \times 1.008665] - 62.92960$$

$$= 0.591935 \text{ u}$$

$$\text{Number of atoms in 3 g coin} = \frac{6.023 \times 10^{23} \times 3}{63}$$

$$= 2.868 \times 10^{22}$$

Total mass defect of all atoms,

$$(\Delta m)_{\text{total}} = 0.591935 \times 2.868 \times 10^{22} = 1.6977 \times 10^{22}$$

The nuclear energy required (E_b) to separate all the neutrons and protons from each other and can be calculated by using the relation,

$$E_b = (\Delta m) \times c^2 = (\Delta m)\, c^2 \times 931 \text{MeV}/c^2$$

$$[\because 1 \text{ u} = 931 \text{MeV}]$$

$$= 1.6977 \times 10^{22} \times 931 \text{ MeV}$$

$$= 1.58 \times 10^{25} \text{ MeV}$$

Example 6 Find the binding energy per nucleon of ${}_{20}\text{Ca}^{40}$ nucleus. Given, $m({}_{20}\text{Ca}^{40}) = 39.962589$ u, $m_n = 1.008665$ u and $m_p = 1.007825$ u. Take, 1 amu = 931 MeV/c^2.

Sol. In a nucleus of ${}_{20}\text{Ca}^{40}$,

Number of protons = 20

Number of neutrons = 40 − 20 = 20

Total mass of 20 protons and 20 neutrons

$$= 20 m_p + 20\, m_n = 20(m_p + m_n)$$

$$= 20\,(1.007825 + 1.008665)$$

$$= 40.3298 \text{ u}$$

Mass defect, $\Delta m = 40.3298 - 39.962589 = 0.367211$ u

Total binding energy = $0.367211 \times 931 = 341.873441$ MeV

$$E_b \text{ per nucleon}, E_{\text{bn}} = \frac{341.873441}{40}$$

$$= 8.547 \text{ MeV/nucleon}$$

Binding Energy Curve

It is a plot of the binding energy per nucleon E_{bn} *versus* the mass number A for a large number of nuclei.

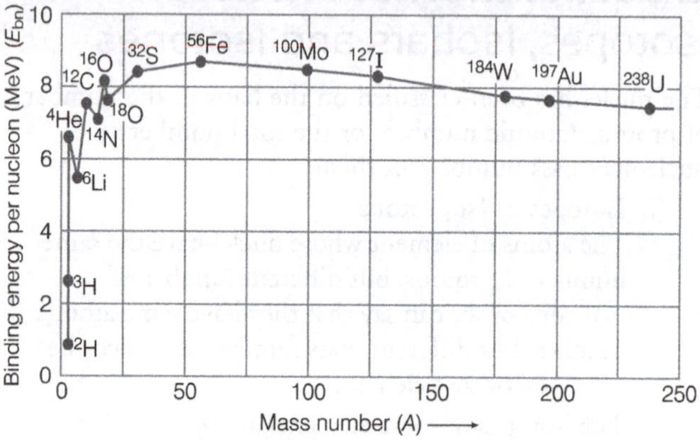

Binding energy per nucleon as a function of mass number

The following are the features of the plot

(i) Average BE/nucleon for lighter nuclei; like ${}_1\text{H}^1$, ${}_1\text{H}^2$, ${}_1\text{H}^3$ is small.

(ii) For mass numbers ranging from 2 to 20, there are sharply defined peaks corresponding to ${}_2\text{He}^4$, ${}_6\text{C}^{12}$, ${}_8\text{O}^{16}$, etc. The peaks indicate that these nuclei are relatively more stable than the other nuclei in their neighbourhood.

(iii) The BE curve has a broad maximum peak in the range $A = 30$ to $A = 120$, which is practically constant corresponding to average binding energy per nucleon is 8.8 MeV per nucleon for ${}_{26}\text{Fe}^{56}$.

(iv) As, the mass number increases, the BE/nucleon decreases gradually falling to about 7.6 MeV per nucleon for ${}_{92}\text{U}^{238}$. The decrease may be due to Coulomb repulsion between the protons. The heavy nuclei are therefore, relatively less stable.

Conclusions

Following conclusions are obtained from the graph

(i) A very heavy nucleus $A = 240$ has lower E_{bn} compared to that of a nucleus with $A = 120$. Thus, if a nucleus $A = 240$ breaks into two $A = 120$ nuclei, nucleons get more tightly bound. Energy would be released in this process (nuclear fission).

(ii) When two light nuclei ($A \le 10$) join to form a heavier nucleus, E_{bn} of fused heavier nuclei is more than the E_{bn} of lighter nuclei. Energy would be released in this process (nuclear fusion).

Pair Production

When an energetic γ-ray photon falls on a heavy substance, it is absorbed by some nucleus of the substance and an electron and a positron are produced.

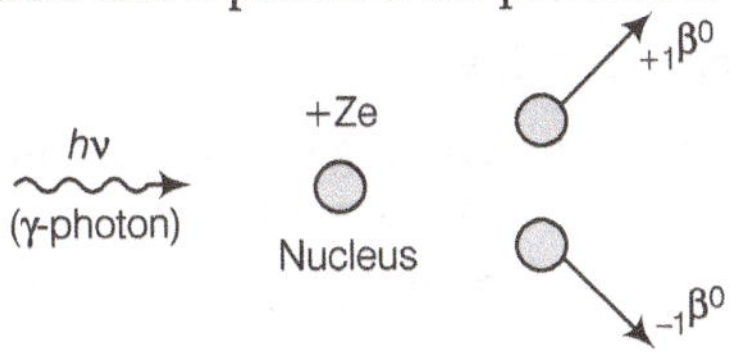

This phenomenon is called 'pair production' and may be represented by the equation

$$h\nu \longrightarrow {}_{+1}\beta^0 + {}_{-1}\beta^0$$

From the equation $E = mc^2$, the least energy (of photon) required for pair production will be

$$E = 2\,(9.1\times 10^{-31}\text{ kg})\,(3.0\times 10^{8}\text{ m/s})^2$$

$$= 1.64\times 10^{-13}\text{ J}$$

$$= \frac{1.64\times 10^{-13}}{1.6\times 10^{-13}}\text{ MeV}$$

$$= 1.02\text{ MeV}$$

Hence, for pair production, it is essential that the energy of γ-photon must be at least 1.02 MeV.

Pair Annihilation

The converse phenomenon of pair production is called pair annihilation. When an electron and a positron come very close to each other, they annihilate each other by combining together and two γ-photons are produced. This phenomenon can be represented by the following equation:

$$_{+1}\beta^0 + {}_{-1}\beta^0 \longrightarrow h\nu + h\nu$$

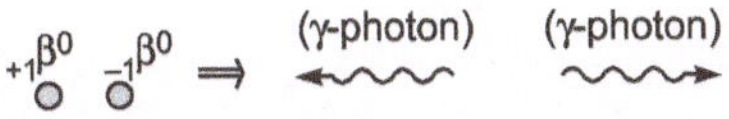

Nuclear Stability

The stability of a nucleus is determined by the value of its binding energy per nucleon. Higher the binding energy of nucleon, more stable is the nucleus. The stability of nucleus is also determined by its neutron to proton ratio.

Nuclear Force

From binding energy curve, we have seen that for average mass of nuclei, the binding energy per nucleon is approximately 8 MeV, which is much larger than the binding energy in atoms. Thus, for binding a nucleus together, there must be a strong attractive force of a totally different kind.

The force must be strong enough to overcome the repulsion between protons and to bind both protons and neutrons into tiny nuclear volume. The constancy of binding energy per nucleon is a consequence of the fact that nuclear force is short-ranged.

Topic Practice 1

Multiple Choice Questions

1 Mark

1. Nuclides with same mass numbers are called
   (a) isotopes (b) isotones
   (c) isobars (d) isomers

2. As compared to ^{12}C atom, ^{14}C atom has
   (a) two extra protons and two extra electrons
   (b) two extra protons, but no extra electrons
   (c) two extra neutrons and no extra electrons
   (d) two extra neutrons and two extra electrons

3. If A = mass number of a nucleus, Z = atomic number and N = neutron number, then
   (a) $A = \frac{N}{Z}$ (b) $A + N = Z$
   (c) $A = Z - N$ (d) $A = Z + N$

4. Ratio of mass of nucleus with mass of atom is nearing to
   (a) 1 (b) 10 (c) 10^3 (d) 10^{10}

5. Energy equivalent to 1 kg of substance is
   (a) 931 MeV (b) 9×10^{12} J
   (c) 9×10^{16} J (d) 932 MeV

Very Short Answer Type Questions

1 Mark

6. Select the pairs of isotopes and isotones from the following nuclei.
$^{22}_{11}Na$, $^{24}_{12}Mg$, $^{24}_{11}Na$, $^{23}_{10}Na$.

7. Define 'unified atomic mass unit'. **ISC 2009**

8. Two nuclei have different number of protons and different number of neutrons. Can they have the same radii and same nuclear density?

9. The isotope $^{16}_{8}O$ has 8 protons, 8 neutrons and 8 electrons, while $^{8}_{4}Be$ has 4 protons, 4 neutrons and 4 electrons. Yet the ratio of their atomic masses is not exactly 2. Why?

10. $^{3}_{2}He$ and $^{3}_{1}He$ nuclei have the same mass number. Do they have same binding energy? **NCERT Exemplar**

11. Why do stable nuclei never have more protons than neutrons? **NCERT Exemplar**

12. What is pair production? **ISC 2024**

Short Answer Type I Questions

2 Marks

13. From the relation $R = R_0A^{1/3}$, where R_0 is a constant and A is the mass number of a nucleus, show that the nuclear matter density is nearly constant (i.e. independent of A). **NCERT**

14. Check whether the given statement is correct or incorrect, if incorrect then correct it with proper explanation.
Statement : The order of magnitude of density of nuclear matter is $10^4 kg/m^3$.

15. The mass of a nucleus is less than the sum of the masses of constituent neutrons and protons. Comment.

16. If both the numbers of protons and neutrons are conserved in a nuclear reaction like

$$_6C^{12} + _6C^{12} \longrightarrow _{10}Ne^{20} + _2He^4$$

In what way is the mass converted into energy? Explain.

17. Sketch a graph showing the variation of binding energy per nucleon of a nucleus with its mass number. **ISC 2017**

18. With the help of a suitable example and an equation, explain the term pair production. **ISC 2015**

19. What is meant by pair annihilation? Write a balanced equation for the same. **ISC 2018**

20. Draw a plot of potential energy between a pair of nucleons as a function of their separation. Mark the regions where potential energy is
(i) positive and (ii) negative.

Short Answer Type II Questions

3 Marks

21. Answer the following.
(i) Why is the binding energy per nucleon found to be constant for nuclei in the range of mass number (A) lying between 30 and 170?
(ii) When a heavy nucleus with mass number $A = 240$ breaks into two nuclei, $A = 120$, energy is released in the process.

Numerical Problems

22. Obtain approximately the ratio of the nuclear radii of the gold isotope $^{197}_{79}Au$ and the silver isotope $^{107}_{47}Ag$. **NCERT (1M)**

23. Calculate the energy in fusion reaction $^{2}_{1}H + ^{2}_{1}H \longrightarrow ^{3}_{2}He + n$, where BE of $^{2}_{1}H$ = 2.23 MeV and of $^{3}_{2}He$ = 7.73 MeV. **(1M)**

24. Determine the nuclear radii of
(i) $^{60}_{27}Co$ (ii) $^{197}_{79}Au$. **(2 M)**

25. How much energy will be created, if 1 g of matter is destroyed completely? **ISC 2010 (1 M)**

26. A heavy nucleus X of mass number 240 and binding energy per nucleon 7.6 MeV is splitted, into two fragments Y and Z of mass numbers 110 and 130. The binding energy of nucleons in Y and Z is 8.5 MeV per nucleon. Calculate the energy released per fission in MeV. **(2M)**

27. Obtain the binding energy (in MeV) of a nitrogen nucleus ($^{14}_{7}N$), given $m\,(^{14}_{7}N) = 14.00307\,u$. **NCERT (2 M)**

28. The neutron separation energy is defined as the energy required to remove a neutron from the nucleus. Obtain the neutron separation energies of the nuclei $^{41}_{20}Ca$ and $^{27}_{13}Al$ from the following data :

$m(^{40}_{20}Ca) = 39.962591\,u$

$m(^{41}_{20}Ca) = 40.962278\,u$

$m(^{26}_{13}Al) = 25.986895\,u$

$m(^{27}_{13}Al) = 26.981541\,u$ **NCERT (2 M)**

29. A nuclide 1 is said to be the mirror isobar of nuclide 2, if $Z_1 = N_2$ and $Z_2 = N_1$.
   (i) What nuclide is a mirror isobar of $^{23}_{11}Na$?
   (ii) Which nuclide out of the two mirror isobars have greater binding energy and why? **NCERT (2 M)**

30. (i) Two stable isotopes of lithium $^{6}_{3}Li$ and $^{7}_{3}Li$ have respective abundances of 7.5% and 92.5%. These isotopes have masses 6.01512 u and 7.01600 u, respectively. Find the atomic mass of lithium.
   (ii) Boron has two stable isotopes $^{10}_{5}B$ and $^{11}_{5}B$. Their respective masses are 10.01294 u and 11.00931 u, and the atomic mass of boron is 10.811 u. Find the abundances of $^{10}_{5}B$ and $^{11}_{5}B$. **NCERT (3 M)**

31. In a periodic table, the average atomic mass of magnesium is given as 24.312 u. The average value is based on their relative natural abundance on the earth.

The three isotopes and their masses are $^{24}_{12}Mg$ (23.98504 u), $^{25}_{12}Mg$ (24.98584 u) and $^{26}_{12}Mg$(25.98259 u). The natural abundance of $^{24}_{12}Mg$ is 78.99% by mass. Calculate the abundances of other two isotopes. **NCERT (3 M)**

32. The three stable isotopes of neon $^{20}_{10}Ne$, $^{21}_{10}Ne$ and $^{22}_{10}Ne$ have respective abundances of 90.51%, 0.27% and 9.22%. The atomic masses of three isotopes are 19.99 u, 20.99 u and 21.99 u, respectively. Obtain the average atomic mass of neon. **NCERT (3 M)**

33. (i) What is the nuclear density of $^{228}_{90}Th$?
   (ii) Is the nuclear density of an α-particle ($^{4}_{2}He$) to be greater than, less than or equal to $^{228}_{90}Th$? Explain.
   (iii) Determine the nuclear density of an α-particle. **NCERT (3 M)**

34. Obtain the binding energy of the nuclei $^{56}_{26}Fe$ and $^{209}_{83}Bi$ in units of MeV from the following data:

$m\,(^{56}_{26}Fe) = 55.934939\,u$

$m\,(^{209}_{83}Bi) = 208.980388\,u$ **NCERT (3 M)**

35. Calculate binding energy of oxygen nucleus ($^{16}_{8}O$) from the data given below **ISC 2020 (2 M)**

Mass of a proton = 1.007825u

Mass of a neutron = 1.008665u

Mass of $^{16}_{8}O$ = 15.994915u

36. Calculate mass defect and binding energy per nucleon of $^{20}_{10}Ne$, given

Mass of $^{20}_{10}Ne$ = 19.992397 u

Mass of $^{1}_{1}H$ = 1.007825 u

Mass of $^{1}_{0}n$ = 1.008665 u **ISC 2024, 17 (3 M)**

Hints & Solutions

1. (c) All nuclides with same mass number A are called isobars. e.g. The nuclides, $^{3}_{1}H$ and $^{3}_{2}He$ are isobars.

2. (c) For $^{12}_{6}C$, $A = 12 = N + Z$, $Z = 6 \Rightarrow N = 6$

For $^{14}_{6}C$; $A = 14 = N + Z$, $Z = 6 \Rightarrow N = 8$

Also, number of electrons in both atoms = number of protons = $Z = 6$.

3. (d) The composition of a nucleus can be described using the following terms and symbols

Z = atomic number = number of protons

N = neutron number = number of neutrons

A = mass number = $Z + N$

= total number of protons and neutrons.

4. (a) As nearly 99.9% mass of atom is in nucleus.

$$\therefore \quad \frac{\text{Mass of nucleus}}{\text{Mass of atom}} = \frac{99.9}{100} = 0.99 \approx 1$$

5. (c) Using $E = mc^2$

$$\text{Energy, } E = 1 \times (3 \times 10^8)^2\,J = 1 \times 9 \times 10^{16}$$
$$= 9 \times 10^{16}\,J$$

Thus, if one kilogram of matter is converted to energy, there is a release of enormous amount of energy.

6. Isotopes = $^{22}_{11}Na$, $^{24}_{11}Na$
(both have same atomic number, i.e. 11)
Isotones = $^{24}_{11}Na$, $^{23}_{10}Na$
(both have same number of neutrons, i.e. 13)

7. Atomic mass unit is defined as one-twelfth of the mass of one carbon atom ($_6C^{12}$) isotope.

i.e. $1 \text{ amu} = \frac{1}{12}$ (mass of a carbon atom)

8. Since, radius of nucleus (i.e. $R = R_0A^{1/3}$) is proportional to the cube root of its mass number, hence nuclei will have same radii, if their mass numbers are same. But nuclear density is independent on mass number. It remains constant for all nuclei, i.e. 2.3×10^{17} kg/m^3.

9. It is because of the fact that the mass of a nucleus is slightly less than the mass of it's constituent nucleons. This decrease in mass is called mass defect. Since, the mass defect in case of $^{16}_{8}O$ is not exactly twice the mass defect in case of $^{8}_{4}Be$, so the ratio of the atomic masses is not exactly same.

10. Since, the repulsive force between protons is missing in ^3_1He, so the binding energy of ^3_1He is greater than that of ^3_2He, because in ^3_1He, only one proton whereas in ^3_2He there exists repulsive force between two protons.

11. Because the protons are positively charged, so they repel each other. Since, this repulsion force is more, so that an excess of neutrons are required to reduce this repulsion.

12. Refer to text on page 481 (Pair production).

13. Refer to text on page 478 (Size of nucleus).

14. Given statement is incorrect because the order of magnitude of density of nuclear matter is the order of 10^{17} kg/m^3. **(2)**

15. When nucleons approach each other to form a nucleus, they strongly attract each other. Their potential energy decreases and becomes negative. It is the potential energy which holds the nucleons together in the nucleus. The decrease in PE results in the mass of nucleons inside the nucleons. **(2)**

16. The sum of masses of nuclei of product element is less than sum of masses of reactants and hence, loss of mass takes place during the reaction. This difference of mass of product element and reactant converts into energy and liberated in the form of heat. **(1)**
Here, sum of masses of $_{10}Ne^{20}$ and $_2He^4$ is less than the sum of masses of two $_6C^{12}$ and conversion of this mass defect is used to produce energy. **(1)**

17. Refer to text on page 480 (Binding energy curve). **(2)**

18. Refer to text on page 481 (Pair production). **(2)**

19. Refer to text on page 481 (Pair annihilation). **(2)**

20. The graph between the potential energy of a pair of nucleons as a function of their separation is given below

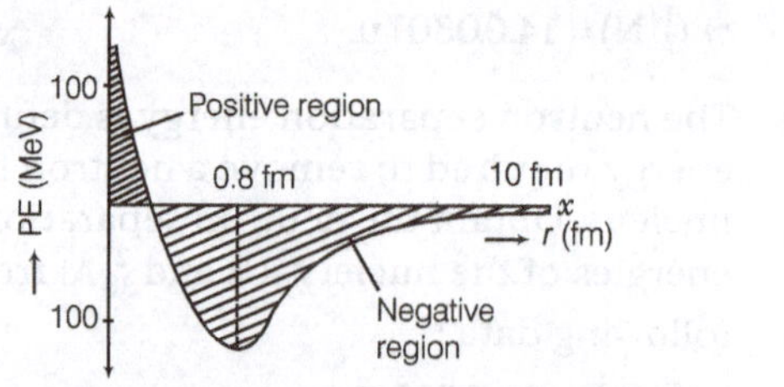

Graphical representation of potential energy of nucleons *versus* distance (separation) **(1)**

(i) For distance less than 0.8 fm, negative PE decreases to zero and then becomes positive. **(1/2)**

(ii) For distances larger than 0.8 fm, negative PE goes on decreasing. **(1/2)**

21. (i) The binding energy per nucleon for nucleus of range, $30 < A < 170$ is close to its maximum value. So, the nucleus belongs to this region is highly stable and does not show radioactivity. **(1)**

(ii) Binding energy per nucleon is smaller for heavier nuclei than the middle ones, i.e. heavier nuclei are less stable. When a heavier nucleus such as nucleus of mass number 240 splits into lighter nuclei (mass number 120), the BE/nucleon changes from about 7.6 MeV to 8.4 MeV. Greater BE of the product nuclei result in the liberation of energy. **(2)**

22. Radius of nuclei, $R = R_0A^{1/3}$

where, A is the mass number of nucleus and R_0 is an empirical constant. **(1/2)**

$\therefore \quad R \propto A^{1/3}$

$$\Rightarrow \quad \frac{R_{gold}}{R_{silver}} = \left(\frac{A_{gold}}{A_{silver}}\right)^{1/3} = \left(\frac{197}{107}\right)^{1/3}$$

$= 1.225 = 1.23$ **(1/2)**

23. According to question,

$$^2_1H + ^2_1H \rightarrow ^3_2He + {}_0n^1$$

$\therefore$ Energy of fusion = Binding energy of ^3_2He
$- 2 \times$ Binding energy of ^2_1H
$= 7.73 - 2 \times 2.23 = 3.27$ MeV

24. Refer to the Example 2 on page 478.

25. From energy-mass relation,
Given, mass, $m = 1 \text{ g} = 10^{-3}$ kg
As we know that, $E = mc^2 = 10^{-3} \times (3 \times 10^8)^2 = 9 \times 10^{13}$ J
where, m = mass of the body and c = velocity of light.

26. In these type of questions, we have to keep in mind about the difference of mass involved between output and input. Energy will be involved accordingly. **(1)**
Energy released per fission
$= (110 + 130) \times 8.5 \text{ MeV} - 240 \times 7.6 \text{ MeV}$
$= 240 \times (8.5 - 7.6) \text{ MeV} = 240 \times 0.9 = 216 \text{ MeV}$ **(1)**

27. Mass of proton, $m_p = 1.00783$ u

Mass of neutron, $m_n = 1.00867$ u

In $^{14}_{7}N$, there are 7 protons and 7 neutrons.

$\therefore$ Mass defect, $\Delta m = (7m_p + 7m_n) - m$

$= 7 \times 1.00783 + 7 \times 1.00867 - 14.00307 = 0.11243$ u **(1)**

Binding energy of nitrogen nucleus $= \Delta m \times 931$MeV

$= 0.11243 \times 931$MeV $= 104.67$ MeV **(1)**

28. (i) When a neutron is separated from $^{41}_{20}Ca$, we are left with $^{40}_{20}Ca$ and the reaction becomes

$$^{41}_{20}Ca \longrightarrow {}^{40}_{20}Ca + {}_0n^1$$

Mass defect,

$$\Delta m = m(^{40}_{20}Ca) + m(_0n^1) - m(^{41}_{20}Ca)$$

$$= 39.962591 + 1.008665 - 40.962278$$

$$= 0.008978 \text{ u}$$

Energy for separation of neutron $= \Delta m \times 931$

$= 0.008978 \times 931$

$= 8.358$ MeV **(1)**

(ii) When a neutron is separated from $^{27}_{13}Al$, we are left with $^{26}_{13}Al$. Thus, the reaction becomes

$$^{27}_{13}Al \longrightarrow {}^{26}_{13}Al + {}^{1}_{0}n$$

Mass defect, $\Delta m = m(^{26}_{13}Al) + m(_0n^1) - m(^{27}_{13}Al)$

$= 25.986895 + 1.008665 - 26.981541$

$= 0.014019.$ Energy for separation of neutron

$= \Delta m \times 931 = 0.014019 \times 931$

$= 13.06$ MeV **(1)**

29. (i) According to the question, a nuclide 1 is said to be mirror isobar of nuclide 2, if $Z_1 = N_2$ and $Z_2 = N_1$. Now, in $^{23}_{11}Na$, $Z_1 = 11$, $N_1 = 23 - 11 = 12$

$\therefore$ Mirror isobar of $^{23}_{11}Na$ is $^{23}_{12}Mg$, for which

$Z_2 = 12 = N_1$ and $N_2 = 23 - 12 = 11 = Z_1$ **(1)**

(ii) As, $^{23}_{12}Mg$ contains even number of protons (12) against $^{23}_{11}Na$ which has odd number of protons (11), therefore $^{23}_{11}Mg$ has greater binding energy than $^{23}_{11}Na$. **(1)**

30. (i) Atomic mass of Li = Weighted average of the isotopes

$$= \frac{7.5 \times 6.01512 + 92.5 \times 7.01600}{7.5 + 92.5}$$

$$= \frac{45.1134 + 648.98}{100} = 6.94 \text{ u}$$ **(1)**

(ii) Suppose x and y are the abundances of $^{10}_{5}B$ and $^{11}_{5}B$, respectively.

Atomic mass of boron

= Weighted average of the isotopes

$$= \frac{x \times 10.01294 + y \times 11.00931}{100}$$

$$\Rightarrow \quad 10.811 = \frac{x \times 10.01294 + (100 - x) \times 11.00931}{100}$$

$[\because y = (100 - x)]$

$\Rightarrow \quad 1081.1 = 10.01294x + 1100.931 - 11.00931x$

$\Rightarrow \quad 0.99637x = 19.831$

$\Rightarrow \quad x = 19.90$

$y = (100 - x) = 80.1$

So, abundance percent $^{10}_{5}B = 19.90\%$

Abundance percent of $^{11}_{5}B = 80.1\%$ **(2)**

31. Given, atomic mass of Mg = 24.312 u

Mass of $^{24}_{12}Mg = 23.98504$ u

Mass of $^{25}_{12}Mg = 24.98584$ u

Mass of $^{26}_{12}Mg = 25.98259$ u

Abundance of $^{24}_{12}Mg = 78.99\%$

Let the abundance of $^{25}_{12}Mg$ be x %.

The abundance of $^{26}_{12}Mg = 100 - 78.99 - x$

$= (21.01 - x)\%$

Atomic mass = Weight average of masses

$$= \frac{\text{Abundance of the isotopes}}{\text{Total abundance}}$$ **(1)**

$\Rightarrow$ 24.312

$$= \frac{78.99 \times 23.98504 + x \times 24.98548 + (21.01 - x) \times 25.98259}{100}$$

$\Rightarrow \quad x = 9.303\%$

So, the abundance of $_{12}Mg^{25}$ is 9.303% and the abundance of $_{12}Mg^{26}$ is 11.71%. **(2)**

32. Given, abundance per cent of $Ne^{20} = 90.51\%$

Abundance per cent of $Ne^{21} = 0.27\%$

Abundance per cent of $Ne^{22} = 9.22\%$

Mass of $Ne^{20} = 19.99$ u

Mass of $Ne^{21} = 20.99$ u

Mass of $Ne^{22} = 21.99$ u **(1)**

Average atomic mass, m = Weighted average of all isotopes

$$= \frac{90.51 \times 19.99 + 0.27 \times 20.99 + 9.22 \times 21.99}{90.51 + 0.27 + 9.22}$$

$$= \frac{1809.29 + 5.67 + 202.75}{100}$$

$$= \frac{2017.71}{100} = 20.18$$ **(2)**

33. (i) We know that,

$$\rho = \frac{3m}{4\pi R_0^3}$$

$$\therefore \quad \rho = \frac{3 \times 1.6 \times 10^{-17} \text{ kg}}{4 \times 3.14 \times (1.2 \times 10^{-15})^3}$$

$$= 2.3 \times 10^{17} \text{ kg/m}^3$$ **(1)**

(ii) Nuclear density (ρ) is independent of mass number, hence nuclear density of α-particle ($^{4}_{2}He$) and thorium ($^{228}_{90}Th$) is equal to each other. **(1)**

(iii) For α-particle, also nuclear density is equal to 2.3×10^{17} kg/m^3, as nuclear density is independent of mass number. **(1)**

34. Given, $m_p = 1.00783$ u, $m_n = 1.00867$ u

(i) For $^{56}_{26}$Fe, there are 26 protons and $(56-26)=30$ neutrons.

Δm = mass of nucleons − mass of nucleus

$= 26m_p + 30m_n - m$

$= 26\times 1.00783 + 30\times 1.00867 - 55.934939$

$= 0.528741$ u

Total binding energy $= \Delta m \times 931$ MeV

$= 0.528741 \times 931$

$= 492.26$ MeV

Binding energy per nucleon

$$= \frac{\text{Binding energy}}{\text{Number of nucleons}} = \frac{492.26}{56}$$

$= 8.790$ MeV **(1½)**

(ii) For $^{209}_{83}$Bi, there are 83 protons and $(209-83)=126$ neutrons.

Δm = mass of nucleons − mass of nucleus

$= 83\,m_p + 126\,m_n - m$

$\Delta m = 83\times 1.00783 + 126\times 1.00867 - 208.980388$

$= 1.761922$ u

Binding energy $= \Delta m \times 931$ MeV

$= 1.761922\times 931 = 1640.35$ MeV

Binding energy per nucleon

$$= \frac{\text{Binding energy}}{\text{Number of nucleons}} = \frac{1640.35}{209}$$

$= 7.848$ MeV

Thus, binding energy per nucleon of Fe is more than Bi. **(1½)**

35. In the nucleus of $^{16}_{8}$O,

Number of protons = 8

Number of neutron = 16 − 8 = 8

Total mass of 8 protons and 8 neutrons

$= 8m_p + 8m_n$

$= 8(1.007825) + 8\times(1.008665)$

$= 8(1.007825 + 1.008665)$

$= 8\times 2.01649$

$= 16.13192$ u

Mass defect, $\Delta m = 16.13192 - 15.994915$

$= 0.137005$ u

Total binding energy $= 0.137005 \times 931$

$= 127.551655$ MeV

$= 127.55$ MeV **(2)**

36. In a nucleus of $^{20}_{10}$Ne

Number of protons = 10

Number of neutrons = 20 − 10 = 10

Total mass of 10 protons and 10 neutrons

$= 10m_p + 10m_n = 10(m_p + m_n)$

$= 10\times(1.007825 + 1.008665)$

$= 10\times 2.01649$ u $= 20.1649$ u **(1)**

Mass defect, $\Delta m = 20.1649 - 19.992397$

$= 0.172503$ u

Total binding energy $= 0.172503 \times 931$

$= 160.600293$ MeV **(1)**

$$E_b \text{ per nucleon} = \frac{160.600293}{20}$$

$= 8.03001465$ MeV/nucleon **(1)**

TOPIC 02 Nuclear Energy

Nuclear Energy

Nuclear energy is the energy released during the transformation of nuclei with less total binding energy to nuclei with greater binding energy.

Two distinct ways of obtaining energy from nucleus are as follows:

1. Nuclear fission   2. Nuclear fusion

Nuclear Fission

Nuclear fission is the phenomenon of splitting of a heavy nucleus (usually $A > 230$) into two or more lighter nuclei by the bombardment of proton, neutron, α-particle, etc.

Energies associated with nuclear processes are about a million times larger than chemical process.

In fission, a heavy nucleus like $^{235}_{92}$U breaks into two smaller fragments by the bombardment of thermal neutron (low energy or slow moving).

e.g. $^{235}_{92}\text{U} + {}^{1}_{0}n \longrightarrow {}^{141}_{56}\text{Ba} + {}^{92}_{36}\text{Kr} + 3\,{}_{0}n^{1} + Q$

(Energy released)

Q-value here refer to the energy released in the nuclear process, which can be determined using Einstein's mass - energy relation, $E = mc^2$. The *Q*-value is equal to the difference of mass of products and reactants multiplied by square of velocity of light. Energy released per fission of

$^{235}_{92}U$ is 200.4 MeV. The fragment nuclei produced in fission are highly unstable. They are highly radioactive and emit β-particles in succession until each reaches to a stable end product.

Example 1 The atomic mass of uranium $^{238}_{92}U$ is 238.0508 u while that of thorium $^{234}_{90}Th$ is 234.0436 u and that of helium $^{4}_{2}He$ is 4.0026 u, alpha decay converts $^{238}_{92}U$ into $^{234}_{90}Th$ as shown

$$^{238}_{92}U \longrightarrow ^{234}_{90}Th + ^{4}_{2}He + \text{energy}$$

Determine the energy released in this reaction.

Sol. The fission reaction is, $^{238}_{92}U \longrightarrow ^{234}_{90}Th + ^{4}_{2}He + Q$

So, $\Delta m = m_U - m_{Th} - m_{He}$

Mass defect, $\Delta m = 238.0508 - (234.0436 + 4.0026)$

$= 0.00464$ u $\quad [\because 1\text{u} = 931 \text{MeV}]$

As, $E = \Delta m \times c^2 = 0.0046 \times 931 = 4.28$ MeV

where, c = velocity of light.

Nuclear Chain Reaction

In the nuclear fission reaction, there is a release of extra neutrons.

The extra neutrons in turn initiate fission process, producing still more neutrons and so on.

Thus, a chain of nuclear fission is set up called **nuclear chain reaction.** The chain reactions may be of two types:

Uncontrolled Chain Reaction

During fission reaction, neutrons released are again absorbed by the fissile isotopes, the cycle repeats to give a chain reaction, i.e. self-sustaining and gives off energy at a rate that increases rapidly with time leading to large amount of radiation. This is called **uncontrolled chain reaction.**

Controlled Chain Reaction

If by some means, the reaction is controlled in such a way that only one of the neutrons emitted in a fission causes another fission, then the fission rate remains constant and the energy is released steadily. Such a chain reaction is called a controlled chain reaction. It is used in a nuclear reactor.

Criticality Whether the mass of a fissionable material can continue a chain reaction depends on the size of the fissionable material. The minimum mass of a fissile material required to produce a self sustained chain reaction without any supply of neutrons from outside is known as critical mass. The condition of the reaction is known as criticality.

The sustained fissibility of nuclear chain reaction depends on the multiplication factor or reproduction factor K.

$$K = \frac{\text{Rate of production of neutrons}}{\text{Rate of loss of neutrons}}$$

(i) If $K = 1$, the operation of reactor is said to be **critical.** It is what we wish to be for steady power operation.

(ii) If $K > 1$, the reaction rate and reactor power increases exponentially. In this case, reaction is **super-critical** and can even explode.

(iii) If $K < 1$, the reaction gradually stops. And the condition is called **sub-critical.**

Nuclear Fusion

Nuclear fusion is the phenomenon of fusing two or more lighter nuclei forming a single heavy nucleus.For fusion to take place, the two nuclei must come close enough so that, attractive short range nuclear force is able to affect them. Since both the nuclei are positively charged particles, so they experience Coulomb's repulsion. Therefore, they must have enough energy to overcome this Coulomb barrier.

e.g. $\quad {}_1H^1 + {}_1H^1 \longrightarrow {}_1H^2 + {}_1e^+ + \nu + 0.42 \text{ MeV}$

$${}_1H^2 + {}_1H^2 \longrightarrow {}_2He^3 + {}_0n^1 + 3.27 \text{ MeV}$$

$${}_1H^2 + {}_1H^2 \longrightarrow {}_1H^3 + {}_1H^1 + 4.03 \text{ MeV}$$

Fusion of hydrogen nuclei into helium nuclei is the source of energy of most of the stars including the sun.

Energy Generation in Sun and Stars

Thermonuclear fusion is the source of energy output in the interior of stars. The interior of the sun has a temperature of 1.5×10^7 K, which is considerably less than the estimated temperature required for fusion of particles of average energy.

Fusion in the sun involves protons whose energies are much above the average energy, i.e. protons which are in the high velocity come under Maxwell-Boltzmann distribution. The fusion reaction in the sun is a multi-step process in which the hydrogen is fused into helium. The **proton-proton** (p, p) **cycle** by which this occurs is represented by the following sets of reactions:

$$ {}_1^1\text{H} + {}_1^1\text{H} \rightarrow {}_1^2\text{H} + e^+ + \nu + 0.42 \text{ MeV} \quad \text{...(i)}$$

$$ e^+ + e^- \rightarrow \gamma + \gamma + 1.02 \text{ MeV} \quad \text{...(ii)}$$

$$ {}_1^2\text{H} + {}_1^1\text{H} \rightarrow {}_2^3\text{He} + \gamma + 5.49 \text{ MeV} \quad \text{...(iii)}$$

$$ {}_2^3\text{He} + {}_2^3\text{He} \rightarrow {}_2^4\text{He} + {}_1^1\text{H} + {}_1^1\text{H} + 12.86 \text{ MeV} \quad \text{...(iv)}$$

For the fourth reaction to occur, the first three reactions must occur twice, in case two light helium nuclei unite to form ordinary helium nucleus. If we consider the combination 2(i) + 2(ii) + 2(iii) + (iv), the net effect is

$$ 4{}_1^1\text{H} + 2e^- \rightarrow {}_2^4\text{He} + 2\nu + 6\gamma + 26.7 \text{ MeV}$$

or $(4{}_1^1\text{H} + 4e^-) \rightarrow ({}_2^4\text{He} + 2e^-) + 2\nu + 6\gamma + 26.7 \text{ MeV}$

Thus, four hydrogen atoms combine to form ${}_2^4\text{He}$ atom with a release of 26.7 MeV of energy. As the hydrogen in the core gets depleted and becomes helium, the core starts to cool. The star begins to collapse under its own gravity, which increases the temperature of the core.

The age of the sun is about 5×10^9 yr and it is estimated that there is enough hydrogen in the sun to keep it going for another 5 billion years.

Example 2 In a certain star, three α-particles undergo fusion in a single reaction to form ${}_6^{12}\text{C}$ nucleus. Calculate the energy released in this reaction in MeV.

(Take, $m({}_2^4\text{He}) = 4.002604$ u and $m({}_6^{12}\text{C}) = 12.000000$ u)

Sol. Fusion reaction is

$$ 3{}_2^4\text{He} \longrightarrow {}_6^{12}\text{C} + Q$$

Mass of three helium nucleus

$$ {}_2\text{He}^4 = 3 \times 4.002604 \text{ u} = 12.007812 \text{ u}$$

Mass of ${}_6\text{C}^{12} = 12.000000$ u

Mass defect, $\Delta m = 12.007812 - 12.000000 = 0.007812$ u

Energy released, $E = \Delta m \times 931 = 0.007812 \times 931$

$= 7.272972$ MeV

Nuclear Reactor

It is a device that can initiate a self-sustaining controlled chain reaction of a fissionable material. They are used at nuclear power plants for generating electricity and in propulsion of ships.

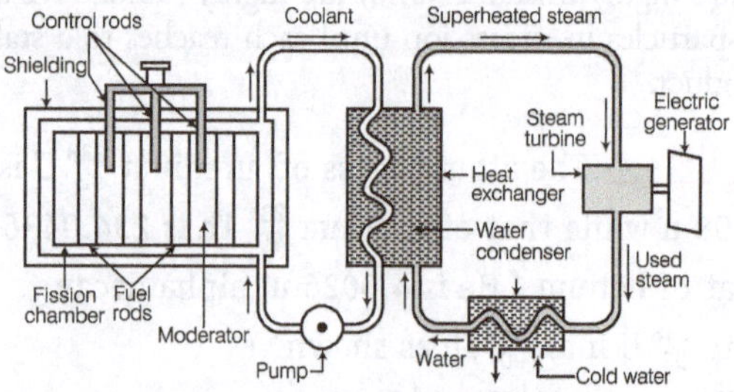

Nuclear reactor

Construction

The key components of nuclear reactor are as follows:

(i) **Nuclear fuel** It is a material that can be **burned** by **nuclear fission** or **fusion** to derive nuclear energy. The common fuels used in nuclear reactor are ${}^{233}\text{U}$, ${}^{235}\text{U}$, ${}^{239}\text{Pu}$, etc.

(ii) **Nuclear reactor core** It is the portion of a nuclear reactor containing the nuclear fuel components where the nuclear reaction takes place.

(iii) **Moderator** It is a medium to slow down the fast moving secondary neutrons produced during the fission. Heavy water, graphite, deuterium, paraffins, etc., acts as moderator.

(iv) **Control rods** It is used in nuclear reactors to control the rate of fission of uranium and plutonium. These are made of chemical elements capable of absorbing many neutrons without fissioning themselves such as silver, indium, boron and cadmium.

(v) **Coolant** It is a liquid used to remove heat from nuclear reactor core and transfer it to electrical generator and environment. Ordinary water under high pressure is used as coolant.

(vi) **Shielding** (Casing) It is the protective covering made of concrete wall to protect from harmful radiations.

Atom Bomb

In the atomic bomb an increasing uncontrolled chain reaction occurs in a very short time when two pieces of Uranium-235 are rapidly brought to form a mass greater than the critical size, by fast neutrons. Atom bomb may consists of P^{239} also. After explosion a temperature of $10^7\,^\circ\text{C}$ and a pressure of several million atmosphere is produced. Nuclear holocaust or nuclear apocalypse is a theoretical scenario involving widespread destruction and radioactive fallout through the use of nuclear weapons.